THE
NEW BOOK
OF
KNOWLEDGE

THE
NEW BOOK
OF
KNOWLEDGE

Grolier Incorporated, Danbury, Connecticut

VOLUME 3

C

C, the third letter of the English alphabet, was also the third letter in the Phoenician, Hebrew, and Greek alphabets. The Phoenicians and Hebrews called it *gimel*. The Greeks called it *gamma*. These early versions of C had one thing in common. They were pronounced G as in *game*. But another ancient people, called the Etruscans, gave the letter the K sound as in *cat*.

The Etruscans ruled in Rome during the 6th century B.C. The Romans adapted the Greek alphabet during a time when they were very much influenced by the Etruscans. So at first the Roman C had two sounds: the G sound and the K sound. Since this was very confusing, the Romans later introduced the letter G for words beginning with the G sound and kept the C for words that began with the K sound.

In English, C generally has the "hard" (as in *cat*) sound before A, O, and U, as in *candy, cow,* and *cup*. The hard C is also used before all consonants except H. The "soft" C, as in *circle,* is used before E, I, and Y *(cent, cinnamon, cypress)*.

The combination CH is pronounced so many different ways (as in *chilly, chemistry,* and *chaperone*) that it might almost be a separate letter. In the alphabets of some languages, such as Welsh and Spanish, CH has a place of its own.

C is "silent," or unspoken, before the letter T in some words, such as *indict*. In other words, such as *trick,* the C and K give exactly the same sound. The C is merely extra.

In a series, C is the third member. In chemistry C stands for the element carbon. As a grade, C indicates average on a report card.

C is also an abbreviation: C for 100 (from the Latin *centum*), C for Celsius (in many thermometers), c. for chapter, and c. for *circa,* a Latin word meaning "about." A C with a circle around it (©) stands for copyright.

Reviewed by MARIO PEI
Author, *The Story of Language*

See also ALPHABET.

President George Washington (far right) met with his cabinet officers for the first time in 1791. From left to right are Henry Knox (War), Thomas Jefferson (Foreign Affairs), Edmund Randolph (Attorney General), and Alexander Hamilton (Treasury).

CABINET OF THE UNITED STATES

No American president can possibly be an expert in all of the administrative areas for which the executive head of government is responsible. Consequently, a president must rely on a group of advisers, carefully selected for their knowledge and experience in various fields, to provide advice and information on the issues and developments affecting each of the executive departments of government. This group of advisers is called the cabinet.

Each president, with the consent of the Senate, appoints a group of cabinet officers called **secretaries** (with the exception of the Department of Justice head who is called the attorney general) to head each of the 14 executive departments.

The United States Constitution makes no specific provision for a presidential cabinet. It says only that the president ". . . may require the opinion, in writing, of the principal officer in each of the executive departments, upon any subject relating to the duties of their respective offices. . . ." The first recorded cabinet meeting took place between President George Washington and his department heads in 1791.

The term "cabinet" comes from the Italian word *cabinetto*, meaning "a small room" (hence, a private meeting place). Cabinet meetings are held in the Cabinet Room at the White House. Although there is no official schedule, some presidents have met with their cabinets on a weekly basis. These meetings commonly are attended by the vice president, the U.S. ambassador to the United Nations, and any other executive branch officials that the president might designate. Together, these men and women bring a wealth of experience and expertise to the discussions of solutions to the problems that face the country.

In the United Kingdom and several other Western European countries, the term "cabinet" is used to refer to a form of government known as the parliamentary form of government. In these countries, cabinet officers are elected officials who serve and are responsible to the legislative body.

The United States cabinet system has little in common with the European systems. American cabinet officers may not be members of Congress. Because they are not elected officials, they are responsible only to the president, who may dismiss them at any time. Cabinet officers are expected to resign when a president leaves office, since it is customary for incoming presidents to choose their own staff.

JAMES ADAMS EICHNER
Author, *The First Book of the Cabinet of the President of the United States*

THE UNITED STATES CABINET

Year Created	Department
1789	*State (Foreign Affairs)
1789	*Treasury
1789	War
1798	Navy
1849	*Interior
1862	*Agriculture
1870	*Justice
1872	Post Office
1903	Commerce and Labor
1913	*Commerce
1913	*Labor
1947	*Defense
1953	Health, Education, and Welfare (HEW)
1965	*Housing and Urban Development (HUD)
1966	*Transportation
1977	*Energy
1979	*Health and Human Services
1979	*Education
1988	*Veterans Affairs

* departments now in existence

The Departments of War and Navy were absorbed into the Department of Defense in 1947. The Department of Agriculture became a cabinet-level office in 1889. The postmaster general had been a cabinet officer since 1829; however, the Post Office Department lost its cabinet status in 1971. The head of the Department of Justice (the attorney general) has been a cabinet officer since 1789. The Department of Health, Education, and Welfare was reorganized as the Department of Health and Human Services in 1979.

CABOT, JOHN (1451?–1498) AND SEBASTIAN (1480?–1557?)

In 1497 an Italian sea captain sailing under the English flag touched the coast of North America. John Cabot may have been the first European to set foot on the North American continent after the Viking explorer Leif Ericson, who had landed there five centuries before. Cabot's discovery became the basis for the English claim to North America.

John Cabot

John Cabot's Italian name was Giovanni Caboto. He was born in Genoa, probably in 1451. Later his family moved to Venice, where Cabot became a merchant. On one of his trading voyages, he visited Mecca, in what is now Saudi Arabia. Mecca was a great trade center where products from Europe and Asia were bought and sold. But the overland journey to obtain spices and other goods from the East was long and slow. Like Columbus, Cabot believed that the earth was a globe and that Asia could be more easily reached by sailing west across the Atlantic Ocean.

After nearly a month at sea, John Cabot and his crew sight land. They think they have reached Asia, but they are actually looking at what is now Canada.

Cabot tried to get Spain or Portugal to back an ocean voyage to Cathay (China). But Spain had already sent Columbus, and Portugal had plans for a voyage to Asia around the southern tip of Africa. Cabot then went to England. There he obtained the backing of a group of merchants and of the English king, Henry VII.

Cabot sailed from Bristol late in May, 1497, with a crew of 18, on a small ship named the *Matthew*. On June 24 he landed somewhere on the coast of North America—probably Newfoundland or Cape Breton Island, in what is now Canada. Cabot was sure he had reached the northeast coast of Asia, and he sailed back to England to report to the King.

Encouraged by the news, Henry VII gave Cabot a small fleet and sent him on another voyage in 1498. This voyage is shrouded in mystery. It is believed that Cabot first sailed back to Newfoundland and then went south as far as Chesapeake Bay before storms wrecked most of his ships. One ship may have reached the Caribbean Sea. For many years it was believed that Cabot survived this voyage and died in England the following year. But because of more recent evidence, historians now believe that Cabot perished when his ship went down in a storm.

Sebastian Cabot

Sebastian Cabot, son of John Cabot, was born in Venice around 1480 and may have sailed with his father on the first voyage to North America. At any rate, Sebastian later falsely claimed credit for both of his father's voyages. The record was finally set straight in the 1800's, when historians found documents that proved the voyages were made by John Cabot.

But Sebastian did have a worthy career as an explorer, navigator, and business promoter. In the early 1550's, he helped found the Company of Merchant Adventurers (later the Muscovy Company) in England. The company sent ships in search of a northeast passage to Asia. One ship reached Russia and helped to open trade between England and that country. Sebastian Cabot died about 1557.

HENRY I. KURTZ
Author, *John and Sebastian Cabot*

See also EXPLORATION AND DISCOVERY.

CACTUS

A cactus (plural, cacti) is a remarkable example of the way plants have adapted to extreme conditions. Cacti have the basic structures and processes of plants. But the work done by leaves in most other plants goes on in the stems and branches of cacti. And in the hot, dry regions where cacti are among the few green plants, their spine-covered branches and stems and their absence of leaves have allowed them to survive.

The distant ancestors of the cactus had leaves and grew like the more familiar plants of today. But during millions of years, the earth's climate changed. Those parts of the Americas where the cactus ancestors grew became hotter and drier. Gradually these regions turned into desert or near desert. All this time the cactus ancestors were adapting to the changing conditions.

For example, as the climate became drier, the roots of cacti gradually spread out, closer to the surface of the ground. That is how cacti quickly absorb water from the earth after a rainfall.

The water taken in through the roots of a cactus is stored in its spongy or hollow stem. The outer layer of the plant is thick and waxy, preventing the escape of water. The outer skin is also ribbed. Some cacti have ribs that fold and expand like an accordion, depending on how much water is contained within the stem.

Although most cacti are leafless, they carry on the normal food-making activities of plants. The leaves of other plants are thin structures that contain many breathing pores; in the course of the food-making process, water is given off to the air through these pores. But in cacti the stems and branches have taken over the work of the leaves. The thick skins have few pores, and the water is retained.

There are still some members of the cactus family that have leaves and stems like more familiar plants—the lemon vine of the West Indies is one. In most cacti the leaves have developed into spines, needles, or hairs. These growths now serve to protect the cacti—which are often the only green plants in an area—from animals.

The true cacti are native only to the Western Hemisphere. They grow mainly in the dry lands of South America, Central America, and

Saguaro, prickly pear, jumping cholla, ocotillo, and other cacti co-exist in deserts of the American Southwest. Cacti can survive for months or even years without rain.

SAGUARO CACTUS

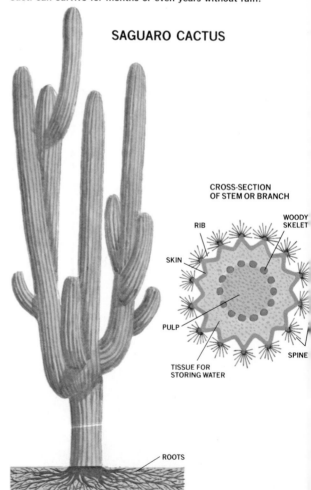

CROSS-SECTION
OF STEM OR BRANCH

RIB

WOODY
SKELET

SKIN

PULP

TISSUE FOR
STORING WATER

SPINE

ROOTS

the southwestern United States. Mexico has the greatest number and variety of cacti. A few cacti have extended their ranges as far north as Canada.

In South Africa, Madagascar, and Sri Lanka, there is the mistletoe cactus, a small plant that grows on trees. Probably the seeds of these plants were carried from the Americas by birds. Cacti have been introduced to many parts of the world by people. (The African deserts have native plants that resemble cacti, but these are actually daisies and milkweeds that have adapted to desert life.)

▶KINDS OF CACTI

Today there are perhaps 1,500 species of cacti. They are divided into several groups, depending on their shape. As a family the cacti belong to the succulents (from the Latin *succulentus,* meaning "juicy"). The succulents include the many kinds of plants that store large amounts of water.

The Prickly Pears. The prickly pears are probably the best known of all the cacti. There are about 250 species. They grow mainly in the United States and Mexico, but they have been introduced into many other countries.

The prickly pear bears a sweet, juicy fruit that looks like a pear. This fruit is what gives these plants their name. Their flowers are often large and colorful, varying from bright red to yellow.

The hedgehog cactus lives in the deserts of the American Southwest. Spring rains provide the proper conditions for these dramatic colorful flowers to bloom.

Barrel Cacti. These thick, heavy cacti are from an inch to almost 12 feet (3.6 meters) tall and can be more than 3 feet (1 meter) in diameter. Their trunklike bodies have ribs with hooked spines. In spring they have yellow flowers. One kind, the bisnaga, may grow about 9 feet (2.7 meters) tall and have a diameter of more than 3 feet (1 meter). Bisnagas this large are probably over 1,000 years old.

All barrel cacti store in their trunks the water collected by their roots. By cutting off the top of a barrel cactus and pounding the pulp inside, one can obtain liquid. In emergencies this can be used as drinking water.

The Saguaro. The saguaro, the largest of the cacti, may grow as high as 40 feet (12 meters). Large ones may be over 200 years old. Saguaros grow in the southwestern United States. The blossom is the state flower of Arizona.

Most large saguaros contain one or more holes in which woodpeckers make their homes. Tiny desert owls also live in these holes, where they are safe from most enemies.

At certain times the saguaro sprouts side branches. A relative of the saguaro is known as the organ-pipe cactus because its many branches make it look like a church organ.

Peyote Cactus. This cactus grows in the southwestern United States and Mexico. A narcotic drug, mescaline, is obtained from the plant.

Night-blooming Cereus. Closely related to the saguaro and the organ-pipe cactus is the night-blooming cereus. This cactus looks like a tangle of dead sticks. But one night in early summer, it bursts into a mass of white blooms.

Hedgehog Cacti. These cacti are also known as strawberry cacti because their red fruits resemble strawberries. Indians once considered this fruit a delicacy. The fruits are covered with spines that give the plants their common name, hedgehog cacti.

These cacti are small, at most about 6 inches (15 centimeters) tall. Often grown in rock gardens, they bloom in various colors.

Pincushion Cacti. These are among the most widely grown of all household plants. Their natural range is from Mexico to Canada. They have spiral rows of "warts" tipped with clusters of spines, which are often as colorful as their large flowers.

ROSS E. HUTCHINS
Author, *This Is a Flower*

CAECILIANS. See AMPHIBIANS.

CAESAR, GAIUS JULIUS (100?–44 B.C.)

Julius Caesar was a remarkable man who rose to supreme power in the Roman Republic. He was witty, charming, generous, keenly intelligent, and a talented orator and writer. He was also a cunning politician and a brilliant but ruthless military leader. Although he never wore a crown, he laid the foundation for the Roman Empire. His very name, Caesar, became the title of Roman emperors.

Early Years and Career. Caesar was probably born on July 13, 100 B.C. He belonged to a noble Roman family whose declining fortunes were improved by successful marriages. His aunt Julia married the popular general Marius, and Caesar's first wife, Cornelia, was a daughter of Marius' ally Cinna. After the deaths of Marius and Cinna, however, their supporters were defeated by the Roman general Sulla, forcing Caesar into virtual exile in 81 B.C.

Returning to Rome after Sulla's death in 78 B.C., he began his climb to power by winning election to political office. He won additional elections by emphasizing his connections with the dead hero Marius and by sponsoring public games.

Consul, Governor, and General. When Sulla's old friends tried to block Caesar's career, he outwitted them by getting another popular general, Pompey, and the wealthy noble Crassus to back his election as consul in 59 B.C. The three men then forged an alliance, known as the First Triumvirate, to further their political ambitions.

For his part, Caesar obtained the governorship of three Roman provinces—Illyricum (on the coast of the Adriatic Sea), Cisalpine Gaul (northern Italy), and Transalpine Gaul (southeastern France). During this period he won great glory and wealth, conquering the Gauls and twice invading Britain (55 and 54 B.C.). Although not a professional soldier, Caesar combined speed and daring to achieve his victories, earning him the fierce loyalty of his troops. His *Commentaries on the Gallic War* is considered a model of clear, precise Latin prose.

Crossing the Rubicon. Meanwhile, Pompey, jealous of Caesar's successes, joined his enemies in the Roman Senate in an attempt to deprive Caesar of his armies and to prevent his election to a second consulship. In 49 B.C., Caesar took the momentous step of leading his troops across the Rubicon, the river separating Cisalpine Gaul from Italy proper. This was illegal under Roman law, and it began a civil war that soon engulfed most of the empire.

Caesar quickly captured Rome. Pompey fled to Greece, where Caesar finally defeated him at the Battle of Pharsalus (48 B.C.). Pompey again escaped, this time to Egypt, but he was murdered before Caesar could reach him. In Egypt, politics and personal attraction allied Caesar with the young princess Cleopatra. He made her queen of Egypt before he left for a swift campaign against rebels in Asia Minor. See the article on Cleopatra in Volume C.

Dictator of Rome. Caesar returned in triumph to Rome in 45 B.C. and was named dictator. Hoping that kindness and generosity would gain him friendship and loyalty, he gave Roman citizenship to many Gauls and appointed old political enemies to important posts. His numerous reforms included a revised calendar (the Julian calendar). He also improved governmental efficiency, promoted education, increased employment, and gave land to poor farmers.

Caesar went too far, however, when he accepted appointment as dictator for life in 44 B.C., for it meant the end of the Roman Republic. Old friends and enemies alike conspired to kill him. On March 15 (the Ides of March), 44 B.C., while at a meeting of the Senate, he was attacked and stabbed to death.

ALLEN M. WARD
University of Connecticut
Coauthor, *A History of the Roman People*

CAGNEY, JAMES. See MOTION PICTURES (Profiles: Movie Stars).

CAIRO

Cairo is the capital and largest city of Egypt. With a population of about 6,000,000, it is also by far the largest city in Africa. The number of people in its metropolitan area is estimated to be as high as 14,000,000.

Cairo is situated on the banks of the Nile River. The main part of the city lies on the east bank of the river and on two islands. Suburbs line the west bank.

Some of the people in the crowded streets of the city wear traditional, long, flowing Arab robes. Others wear modern, European-style clothing. Ninety percent of the people are Muslims. Beautiful mosques with domed roofs and slender, graceful minarets reach up to the sky. When the Muslim call to prayer is heard, five times a day, many people stop what they are doing to kneel and touch their foreheads to the ground in prayer, even on the sidewalks.

In Cairo the past and the present live together. On a summer's day the sun blazes down on a huge statue of Ramses II. This ancient statue recalls the time over 3,000 years ago when Ramses II was the king of Egypt. It stands in the middle of a busy, traffic-filled square and looms over the main railway station. Against it the station looks very much part of the world today, alive with the noise and bustle of modern times.

In the crowded bazaars of the old section of the city, brass workers hammer and fashion plates of elaborate design. Weavers work with the same sure skill as their ancestors did before them. In the twisting, narrow streets of this quarter—scarcely wider than alleys—are donkey carts, mules, and, occasionally, a camel. Thousands of shops, large and small, sell almost every item imaginable.

The modern sections of Cairo have broad, sparkling streets, ultramodern department stores, theaters, movie houses, and even movie studios. The many movies made in this Hollywood on the Nile are distributed all over the world.

▶ CAIRO TODAY

Cairo is a center of government, trade, commerce, and culture. Bridges link the islands of Zamalik and Roda, in the Nile River, and the suburbs of Giza and Imbaba, on the west bank of the Nile, with the rest of the city. Most of Cairo's government offices, hotels, and museums are located in the western part of the city, along the Nile or on the islands. Western Cairo is the most modern part of the

Cairo, the capital of Egypt and the largest city in Africa, is situated on the banks of the Nile River. The city includes two islands, Zamalik (Gezira) and Roda.

7

A Cairo merchant sells carrots from a donkey cart. In the distance are the great pyramids of Giza and part of the campus of the University of Cairo.

city. To the east, away from the Nile, many of the buildings are hundreds of years old. This part of Cairo is famous for its crowded bazaars, its mosques, and its historic landmarks. Textiles, iron and steel, chemicals, paper, and refined sugar are among the products manufactured in or near the city, for Cairo is also a major industrial center.

Many famous landmarks have helped to make Cairo a popular tourist attraction. The Citadel, a huge fortress built by the Arab hero Saladin in the 1170's, dominates the city skyline. Within its walls are mosques, palaces, and government buildings. A massive project to restore the Citadel and other Islamic landmarks was begun in the 1980's. At the western edge of the city stands one of the Seven Wonders of the Ancient World—the pyramids of Giza. These great tombs of stone were built for kings of the fourth dynasty nearly 5,000 years ago. Nearby is the Great Sphinx, a huge statue with the body of a lion and the head of King Chephren (Khafre), the pharaoh who built the second great pyramid at Giza.

▶A CULTURED, CROWDED CITY

Cairo is a city of culture—of art, of libraries, and of many fine museums, including the Museum of Modern Art, the Museum of Islamic Art, and the Coptic Museum. The Egyptian (National) Museum is considered to be the greatest museum of its kind in the world. It contains priceless Egyptian relics, such as a statue of Chephren dating back to about 2520 B.C. This statue is considered one of the finest pieces of Egyptian sculpture in existence. In the history-filled halls of the museum are the treasures from the tomb of King Tutankhamen. Al-Azhar University, the best known of Cairo's institutions of higher learning, was founded in the A.D. 900's. It has been called the oldest university in the world.

In recent years, the population has expanded so rapidly that severe strains have been placed on city services such as transportation, sewage, and housing. Building construction is one of the city's major economic activities. One reason Cairo is so crowded is that there is little room for the city to spread out without encroaching on much needed farmland.

The Cairo subway—the first subway in Africa—was opened in 1987. It is hoped that it will help to relieve some of the traffic congestion in one of the world's busiest cities.

▶HISTORY

Cairo's site is an ancient one, dating back some 3,000 years or more. Egyptian, Greek, Roman, and Arab settlements existed here before the Fatimid dynasty from Tunisia conquered Egypt in A.D. 969 and established the present city as their capital. The city's name comes from the Arabic *Al Qahirah*, meaning "the victorious."

Cairo prospered until the 1400's, when it slowly began to decline. The city was captured by the Ottoman Turks in 1517. It remained under Turkish rule until 1798, when the French led by Napoleon I defeated the Turks. Turkish and British forces recaptured the city from the French in 1801. In 1863, Cairo replaced Alexandria as the national capital. In 1882 the British defeated the Egyptians at the battle of Tel el Kebir, solidifying their control of Egypt and its capital.

Cairo regained its importance in the years after World War I (1914–18). During World War II (1939–45), it was the scene of several important conferences held by the victorious Allied leaders. Britain's influence ended in 1956, when its troops evacuated Cairo and departed from Egypt. In the years since, the city has continued to grow while remaining a cultural center of the Arab world.

Reviewed by JOHN A. WILLIAMS
American University in Cairo

CALAMITY JANE. See MONTANA (Famous People).
CALCULATORS. See ARITHMETIC.
CALCULUS. See MATHEMATICS; MATHEMATICS, HISTORY OF.

CALCUTTA (KOLKATA)

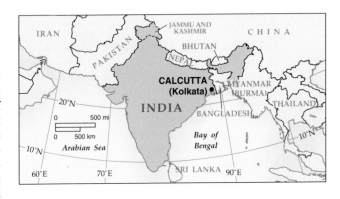

Calcutta (Kolkata), a great port city and the capital of the state of West Bengal, is the industrial, commercial, and cultural center of eastern India. The city sprawls along the east bank of the Hooghly River in the delta of the Ganges River, about 80 miles (129 kilometers) north of the Bay of Bengal. With a population of more than 4 million, Calcutta is the third largest city in India. Approximately 12 million people live in its greater metropolitan area, which is the second largest metropolitan area in India, after Bombay (Mumbai).

The City. Calcutta is an intellectual and cultural center. The National Library has the nation's largest collection of books and documents. The University of Calcutta, founded in 1857, is one of the world's largest universities.

The port city of Calcutta is the capital of the Indian state of West Bengal. It is one of the world's most densely populated cities.

Calcutta is a city of contrasts. There are wide streets with large white houses and green lawns. There are also narrow, winding streets where the people live huddled together in slums. The city has such a desperate housing shortage that at least 1 million people sleep in the streets. Many of the city's ill and destitute take refuge at the Missionaries of Charity, founded by Mother Teresa (Agnes Gonxha Bojaxhiu) (1910–97), a Roman Catholic nun who was a resident of Calcutta and one of the world's great humanitarians.

Economic Activity. Chowringhee Road is Calcutta's main thoroughfare. The wide avenue is lined with fashionable shops, banks, modern restaurants, movie theaters, clubs, and office buildings. Dalhousie Square is the heart of Calcutta's business district. Calcutta is also known for its many paper, steel, and jute mills, iron foundries, tanneries, and printing presses.

History. Calcutta was founded in 1690 as a trading base of the British East India Company. Because of its excellent location for trade, its nearness to mineral deposits, and its importance as headquarters for the British administration, Calcutta grew in size and importance. When the British government took control of India in 1858, Calcutta became the formal capital of British India. The national capital was transferred to Delhi in 1912. Calcutta served as the capital of Bengal Province until 1947, when India and Pakistan gained their independence. The eastern two-thirds of the province was then separated to form what is now Bangladesh. Calcutta's rapid population growth has placed enormous strain on its ability to provide employment and transportation, as well as housing, for its people.

DAVID FIRMAN
Towson State University

CALDECOTT, RANDOLPH (1846–1886)

Randolph Caldecott was an artist whose spirited illustrations for children's stories have become so well known and so loved that the award presented annually in the United States to "the most distinguished picture book" is named the Caldecott Medal.

Randolph Caldecott was born on March 22, 1846, in Chester, England. Even as a small boy, his talent for drawing and carving animals in wood was obvious. His father, however, discouraged Randolph's fondness for art. At 15, the young man left home to work in a bank in Shropshire. He often suffered from ill health, and he was limited in his activities. So he became an eager observer of town and country life. He watched farmers and animals at work and at markets and fairs. He observed people doing their daily chores or riding and hunting or enjoying country dances. He stored these lively scenes in his memory and in his sketchbook.

At 21, Caldecott moved to Manchester and worked five more years as a bank clerk. He kept on with his sketching, and his comic drawings soon began to appear in *London Society* and other newspapers. In 1872 he moved to London and began a career as an artist. His reputation was solidly established when he illustrated Washington Irving's *Old Christmas* and *Bracebridge Hall*.

With the publication in 1878 of *The Diverting History of John Gilpin* and *The House that Jack Built*, Caldecott created true picture books in which story and illustrations became inseparable. He produced 16 picture books, including *The Babes in the Wood*, *The Frog He Would A-Wooing Go*, and *Three Jovial Huntsmen*. These books show his talent for bringing to life, in just a few lines drawn with his pen, the vigor of a galloping horse or a romping child. His characters have readable expressions and make lively gestures. His babes in the woods really are little lost children, and his jolly huntsmen really are hardriding and carefree. Some of Caldecott's illustrations were in color, printed from engraved wooden blocks.

In 1880, Caldecott married Marion Brind. Six years later, while visiting the United States, he suddenly died in St. Augustine, Florida, on February 12, 1886.

Randolph Caldecott's work is memorable because he never forgot the importance of the story, and he knew just how to create pictures that made the story come alive.

LEE KINGMAN
Editor, *The Illustrator's Notebook*

See also CALDECOTT AND NEWBERY MEDALS.

This illustration from *The Diverting History of John Gilpin* shows Randolph Caldecott's talent for bringing a story to life through his sketches of the characters.

CALDECOTT AND NEWBERY MEDALS

Two of the major awards for excellence given to writers of children's books are the Caldecott Medal and the John Newbery Medal.

The Caldecott Medal has been given annually since 1938 by the American Library Association (ALA) to the artist of the most distinguished American picture book for children. It was named for the famous English illustrator Randolph Caldecott. A biography of Caldecott precedes this article.

The John Newbery Medal is awarded annually by the ALA to the author of the most distinguished American children's book. The author must be a citizen or permanent resident of the United States. The award was established in 1922 and named for John Newbery, an English bookseller who was a pioneer of children's book publishing. A biography of Newbery can be found in Volume N of this encyclopedia.

Striking illustrations for *Smoky Night*, Eve Bunting's book about a boy witnessing the 1992 Los Angeles riots, earned artist David Diaz the 1995 Caldecott Medal.

CALDECOTT MEDAL WINNERS

1938 Dorothy P. Lathrop, *Animals of the Bible* (Bible selections by Helen Dean Fish).
1939 Thomas Handforth, *Mei Li*.
1940 Ingri and Edgar P. d'Aulaire, *Abraham Lincoln*.
1941 Robert Lawson, *They Were Strong and Good*.
1942 Robert McCloskey, *Make Way for Ducklings*.
1943 Virginia Lee Burton, *The Little House*.
1944 Louis Slobodkin, *Many Moons* (James Thurber).
1945 Elizabeth Orton Jones, *Prayer for a Child* (Rachel Field).
1946 Maud and Miska Petersham, *The Rooster Crows*.
1947 Leonard Weisgard, *The Little Island* (Golden MacDonald).
1948 Roger Duvoisin, *White Snow, Bright Snow* (Alvin Tresselt).
1949 Berta and Elmer Hader, *The Big Snow*.
1950 Leo Politi, *Song of the Swallows*.
1951 Katherine Milhous, *The Egg Tree*.
1952 Nicolas Mordvinoff, *Finders Keepers* (Mordvinoff and Will Lipkind).
1953 Lynd Ward, *The Biggest Bear*.
1954 Ludwig Bemelmans, *Madeline's Rescue*.
1955 Marcia Brown, *Cinderella* (Charles Perrault).
1956 Feodor Rojankovsky, *Frog Went A-Courtin'* (John Langstaff).
1957 Marc Simont, *A Tree Is Nice* (Janice May Udry).
1958 Robert McCloskey, *Time of Wonder*.

1959 Barbara Cooney, *Chanticleer and the Fox*.
1960 Marie Hall Ets, *Nine Days to Christmas* (Ets and Aurora Labastida).
1961 Nicolas Sidjakov, *Baboushka and the Three Kings* (Ruth Robbins).
1962 Marcia Brown, *Once a Mouse*.
1963 Ezra Jack Keats, *The Snowy Day*.
1964 Maurice Sendak, *Where the Wild Things Are*.
1965 Beni Montresor, *May I Bring a Friend?* (Beatrice Schenk de Regniers).
1966 Nonny Hogrogian, *Always Room for One More* (Sorche Nic Leodhas).
1967 Evaline Ness, *Sam, Bangs & Moonshine*.
1968 Ed Emberley, *Drummer Hoff*.
1969 Uri Shulevitz, *The Fool of the World and the Flying Ship* (Arthur Ransome).
1970 William Steig, *Sylvester and the Magic Pebble*.
1971 Gail E. Haley, *A Story, A Story*.
1972 Nonny Hogrogian, *One Fine Day*.
1973 Blair Lent, *The Funny Little Woman* (Arlene Mosel).
1974 Margo and Harve Zemach, *Duffy and the Devil*.
1975 Gerald McDermott, *Arrow to the Sun*.
1976 Leo and Diane Dillon, *Why Mosquitoes Buzz in People's Ears: A West African Tale* (Verna Aardema).
1977 Leo and Diane Dillon, *Ashanti to Zulu: African Traditions* (Margaret Musgrove).
1978 Peter Spier, *Noah's Ark*.
1979 Paul Goble, *The Girl Who Loved Wild Horses*.
1980 Barbara Cooney, *Ox-Cart Man* (Donald Hall).
1981 Arnold Lobel, *Fables*.
1982 Chris Van Allsburg, *Jumanji*.
1983 Marcia Brown, *Shadow* (Blaise Cendrars).
1984 Alice and Martin Provensen, *The Glorious Flight*.
1985 Trina Schart Hyman, *Saint George and the Dragon*.

1986	Chris Van Allsburg, *The Polar Express*.
1987	Richard Egielski, *Hey, Al*.
1988	John Schoenherr, *Owl Moon* (Jane Yolen).
1989	Stephen Gammell, *Song and Dance Man* (Karen Ackerman).
1990	Ed Young, *Lon Po Po: A Red-Riding Hood Story from China*.
1991	David Macaulay, *Black and White*.
1992	David Weisner, *Tuesday*.
1993	Emily Arnold McCully, *Mirette on the High Wire*.
1994	Allen Say, *Grandfather's Journey*.
1995	David Diaz, *Smoky Night* (Eve Bunting).
1996	Peggy Rathmann, *Officer Buckle and Gloria*.
1997	David Wisniewski, *Golem*.
1998	Paul O. Zelinsky, *Rapunzel*.
1999	Mary Azarian, *Snowflake Bentley*.
2000	Simms Taback, *Joseph Had a Little Overcoat*.

A facsimile of the Newbery Medal is embossed on the cover of every book that has won the award. The original gold medal is presented to the author.

JOHN NEWBERY MEDAL WINNERS

1922	Hendrik van Loon, *The Story of Mankind*.
1923	Hugh Lofting, *The Voyages of Doctor Dolittle*.
1924	Charles Boardman Hawes, *The Dark Frigate*.
1925	Charles J. Finger, *Tales from Silver Lands*.
1926	Arthur Bowie Chrisman, *Shen of the Sea*.
1927	Will James, *Smoky, the Cowhorse*.
1928	Dhan Gopal Mukerji, *Gay-Neck*.
1929	Eric P. Kelly, *Trumpeter of Krakow*.
1930	Rachel Field, *Hitty, Her First Hundred Years*.
1931	Elizabeth Coatsworth, *The Cat Who Went to Heaven*.
1932	Laura Adams Armer, *Waterless Mountain*.
1933	Elizabeth Foreman Lewis, *Young Fu of the Upper Yangtze*.
1934	Cornelia Meigs, *Invincible Louisa*.
1935	Monica Shannon, *Dobry*.
1936	Carol Ryrie Brink, *Caddie Woodlawn*.
1937	Ruth Sawyer, *Roller Skates*.
1938	Kate Seredy, *The White Stag*.
1939	Elizabeth Enright, *Thimble Summer*.
1940	James H. Daugherty, *Daniel Boone*.
1941	Armstrong Sperry, *Call It Courage*.
1942	Walter D. Edmonds, *The Matchlock Gun*.
1943	Elizabeth Janet Gray, *Adam of the Road*.
1944	Esther Forbes, *Johnny Tremain*.
1945	Robert Lawson, *Rabbit Hill*.
1946	Lois Lenski, *Strawberry Girl*.
1947	Carolyn Sherwin Bailey, *Miss Hickory*.
1948	William Pène du Bois, *The Twenty-One Balloons*.
1949	Marguerite Henry, *King of the Wind*.
1950	Marguerite de Angeli, *The Door in the Wall*.
1951	Elizabeth Yates, *Amos Fortune, Free Man*.
1952	Eleanor Estes, *Ginger Pye*.
1953	Ann Nolan Clark, *Secret of the Andes*.
1954	Joseph Krumgold, *. . . and now Miguel*.
1955	Meindert DeJong, *The Wheel on the School*.
1956	Jean L. Latham, *Carry On, Mr. Bowditch*.
1957	Virginia Sorensen, *Miracles on Maple Hill*.
1958	Harold Keith, *Rifles for Watie*.

1959	Elizabeth G. Speare, *The Witch of Blackbird Pond*.
1960	Joseph Krumgold, *Onion John*.
1961	Scott O'Dell, *Island of the Blue Dolphins*.
1962	Elizabeth G. Speare, *The Bronze Bow*.
1963	Madeleine L'Engle, *A Wrinkle in Time*.
1964	Emily Neville, *It's Like This, Cat*.
1965	Maia Wojciechowska, *Shadow of a Bull*.
1966	Elizabeth Borten de Treviño, *I, Juan de Pareja*.
1967	Irene Hunt, *Up a Road Slowly*.
1968	E. L. Konigsburg, *From the Mixed-Up Files of Mrs. Basil E. Frankweiler*.
1969	Lloyd Alexander, *The High King*.
1970	William Armstrong, *Sounder*.
1971	Betsy Byars, *The Summer of the Swans*.
1972	Robert C. O'Brien, *Mrs. Frisby and the Rats of NIMH*.
1973	Jean C. George, *Julie of the Wolves*.
1974	Paula Fox, *The Slave Dancer*.
1975	Virginia Hamilton, *M. C. Higgins the Great*.
1976	Susan Cooper, *The Grey King*.
1977	Mildred D. Taylor, *Roll of Thunder, Hear My Cry*.
1978	Katherine Paterson, *Bridge to Terabithia*.
1979	Ellen Raskin, *The Westing Game*.
1980	Joan W. Blos, *A Gathering of Days*.
1981	Katherine Paterson, *Jacob Have I Loved*.
1982	Nancy Willard, *A Visit to William Blake's Inn: Poems for Innocent and Experienced Travelers*.
1983	Cynthia Voigt, *Dicey's Song*.
1984	Beverly Cleary, *Dear Mr. Henshaw*.
1985	Robin McKinley, *The Hero and the Crown*.
1986	Patricia MacLachlan, *Sarah, Plain and Tall*.
1987	Sid Fleischman, *The Whipping Boy*.
1988	Russell Freedman, *Lincoln: A Photobiography*.
1989	Paul Fleischman, *Joyful Noise: Poems for Two Voices*.
1990	Lois Lowry, *Number the Stars*.
1991	Jerry Spinelli, *Maniac Magee*.
1992	Phyllis Reynolds Naylor, *Shiloh*.
1993	Cynthia Rylant, *Missing May*.
1994	Lois Lowry, *The Giver*.
1995	Sharon Creech, *Walk Two Moons*.
1996	Karen Cushman, *The Midwife's Apprentice*.
1997	E. L. Konigsburg, *The View from Saturday*.
1998	Karen Hesse, *Out of the Dust*.
1999	Louis Sachar, *Holes*.
2000	Christopher Paul Curtis, *Bud, Not Buddy*.

This part of a Victorian children's calendar illustrates the months: January cold, a February valentine, March winds, April showers, May festivals, and June roses.

CALENDAR

A calendar is a system for keeping track of time. It is a kind of clock for the entire year. While a clock measures seconds, minutes, and hours, a calendar measures days, weeks, and months.

Calendars are very useful in our daily lives. They remind us what day of the week it is, what date it is, and what month it is. Calendars also let a person look ahead to dates throughout the year. For example, if you want to know what day of the week your birthday falls on, you can look it up in advance on a calendar. Wall calendars, desk calendars, pocket calendars, and date books are useful in planning our schedules and remembering our appointments and other planned events. For example, if you are told that you will have a school test or a doctor's appointment on March 15, you can write a note in the calendar box for that day. That way you will be reminded of it whenever you look at your calendar. Finally, calendars often provide such information as the dates of holidays. Some calendars even indicate what time the sun will rise and set, what time the tide will come in and go out, and what day the moon will be full.

▶HOW THE MODERN WESTERN CALENDAR MEASURES TIME

The basic units of the calendar are the day, week, month, and year. Our modern calendar year has 365 days, divided into 12 months as well as 52 weeks (with one extra day); each week has 7 days. These divisions of time are based on the movements of the earth, the moon, and the sun.

A **day** is the amount of time it takes for the sun to rise, set, and rise again. Each day includes a period of sunlight and darkness. This is determined by the rotation of the earth on its axis and the position of the sun (see the article on TIME). In our calendar today, we group sequences of 7 days—Sunday, Monday, Tuesday, Wednesday, Thursday, Friday, and Saturday—into units of **weeks.** (How each day got its name is a fascinating story, which is told in the article DAYS OF THE WEEK.) Each week makes up a row of seven boxes on the calendar.

In early calendars a **month** was the amount of time it took for the moon to complete its cycle of phases—from new moon to full moon and back to new moon. In fact, the word "month" comes from the word "moon." As we now know, however, each cycle of the moon takes about 29½ days. If we were to have 12 months of 29½ days each, that would give us only 354 days in a year instead of 365 —not enough! And if we were to have 13 months of 29½ days each, that would give us 383½ days in a year—too many! In the modern Western calendar, therefore, all 12 months have 28–31 days—adding up to 365 for the whole year. A simple rhyme can help you remember how many days there are in each month:

Thirty days hath September,
April, June, and November.
All the rest have thirty-one,
except February—
which hath 28 and in leap year 29.

To find out more about the months of the year, see articles under the name of each individual month.

Finally, a **year** is the amount of time it takes the earth to revolve around the sun. Astronomers have determined that the journey actually takes 365 days, 5 hours, 48 minutes, and 46 seconds. But how can a calendar be accurate if it has only 365 days? How can the extra time be taken into account? The answer is **leap year.** To make up the extra time, one day is added to the calendar every 4 years. That day becomes February 29. A leap year thus has 366 days. Leap year comes in years whose number can be divided by four (such as 1984, 1988, and 1992). The exceptions to this rule are "century" years (1800, 1900, and so on). A century year is a leap year only if it can be divided by 400.

The addition of an extra day in leap year can raise some funny questions. What if you were born in a leap year on February 29? Would you have a birthday only once every 4 years? Of course not. You would still be getting older every year. People born on February 29 usually celebrate their non–leap-year birthday on the closest date—February 28 or March 1.

▶ EARLY CALENDARS

There are many ways in which people become aware of the passing of time. They have always seen the changing of the seasons. They notice changes in climate, vegetation, and the number of hours of sunlight in a day. Most important, people throughout history have observed the daily movement of the sun and the monthly cycle of the moon. Most early calendars were based on the moon (lunar calendar), the sun (solar calendar), or a combination of the moon and sun (lunisolar calendar).

More than 10,000 years ago, the ancient Egyptians had a calendar in which there were 12 months, or lunar cycles, to the year. Each month had 30 days, so there were 360 days to the year. Because it takes the earth nearly 365¼ days to circle the sun, however, this calendar lost a few days each year. Eventually the differences got out of hand, so people tried to invent a more accurate calendar. Around 4000 B.C., 5 extra days were added at the end of each year. This calendar still lost a day every few years, but it was an improvement.

The Babylonian, Chaldean, and Assyrian calendars all had 12 months of 29 or 30 days each. These ancient Mesopotamian peoples added an extra month about every 3 years to keep their calendars in time with the sun. The ancient Chinese also had 12 lunar months with an extra month added occasionally.

In the Americas the Maya and other peoples also used calendars. In the Maya system the days were placed in groups of 20 to form a kind of month, or *unial*. Eighteen *unials* formed a year, or *tun*, of 360 days. Five extra days were added to make the year 365 days long. A period of 20 years was called a *katun*, and *katuns* were also grouped by 20's.

The 7-day week of the present Western calendar is taken from the ancient Hebrew calendar. This division of time is mentioned in the Bible. The Hebrews probably got the idea of the 7-day week from the Babylonians.

▶ THE ROMAN CALENDAR

The calendar used today by most people in North America and Europe had its beginnings in the ancient Roman calendar. In fact, the word "calendar" comes from the Latin word *Kalendae*, which was what the Romans called the first day of every month. How the Roman calendar developed and changed tells us a great deal about how the Western calendar system works today.

Each Roman month had 3 fixed points—the Kalends, the Nones, and the Ides. The Ides generally fell at the full moon of the lunar month. In March, May, July, and October, the Nones were the 7th day, and the Ides the 15th. In the other months the Nones were the 5th day, and the Ides the 13th. All other days were counted as so many days before the Kalends, Nones, or Ides.

At one time the ancient Roman calendar had only 10 months. The year began in March, when farmers began their work for the coming growing season. At some point, perhaps as early as 153 B.C., the Romans changed to a 12-month system and moved the beginning of the year to January.

The 12-month Roman year originally consisted of 355 days. March, May, July, and October had 31 days. February had 28, and the other months had 29. Because this year did not fit with the actual solar year, extra days were added each year to make the calendar more correct. The extra period, called the Intercalaris, was usually 22 or 23 days long.

Over the years this calendar became wildly out of sequence with the natural cycle. In 46 B.C. the Roman leader Julius Caesar decided that it had to be revised. He introduced a calendar that had 365 days, and he established the leap year system by adding an extra day every 4 years. This new calendar became known as the **Julian calendar,** named for its inventor.

All in all, the calendar used today in North America and Europe owes much to the old Roman system. Starting the new year on January 1 and adding leap years are just two examples of Roman influence. From the Romans, too, come the names of the months and the system of starting the day at midnight.

▶ MODERN CALENDAR SYSTEMS

The Julian calendar was an important breakthrough, but it was not perfect. By the Middle Ages it was out of step with the seasons and needed reform. In 1582, Pope Gregory XIII proposed certain changes. For one year he dropped 10 days from the calendar to make it correspond more closely with the seasons. He also dropped leap years in century years, unless those years could be divided by 400.

Pope Gregory's calendar became known as the **Gregorian** or **New Style calendar.** It was more precise than the Julian or **Old Style calendar,** but it was not accepted immediately. The Gregorian calendar was adopted in England and North America in 1752, in Rumania and Greece in 1824, in Russia in 1918, and in Turkey in 1927. Today the Gregorian calendar is used throughout most of the Western world, especially for public affairs and business.

Because Pope Gregory dropped several days from the calendar, the changeover from the Julian (Old Style) to the Gregorian (New Style) meant that the dates for certain events would be altered. The birth date of George Washington is a good example. Washington was actually born on February 11, 1731, when Old Style dating was still being used. But when colonial Virginia adopted the New Style

This 5th-century Roman calendar shows the system devised by Julius Caesar. The Julian calendar introduced the leap year and was used over 1,500 years.

in 1752, the date of Washington's birth became February 22. Also, because the first day of the year was switched from March 25 to January 1, Washington was now said to have been born in 1732! Such changes can be a source of confusion in history books if Old Style or New Style dating is not taken into account. THE NEW BOOK OF KNOWLEDGE generally translates all Old Style dates into New Style. Thus, Washington's birthday is cited as February 22, 1732 (New Style), although his birth date on the Old Style calendar is February 11, 1731.

There has been no major attempt to revise the Gregorian calendar, but people have tried to develop a calendar in which each date falls on the same day of the week each year. One such calendar is called the **fixed calendar,** or world calendar. It has 13 months of 28 days. The months are identical, and each contains 4 weeks. This calendar has been considered by the United Nations, but it has never been adopted. Another kind of calendar, the **perpetual calendar,** makes it possible to determine the day of the week for any given date in any year. A perpetual calendar can be useful for finding out what day of the week you were born or what day of the week a historical event occurred.

Even as new kinds of calendars have been developed, some people continue to follow ancient, traditional systems. The Jewish religion, for example, maintains the ancient Hebrew calendar. The Chinese follow their traditional calendar. And Muslims also have their own calendar. It is interesting to compare these different systems.

The Hebrew Calendar. In the Hebrew calendar, the new year starts in the fall. There are 12 months, with a 13th month added in certain years. This extra month is added seven times over every period of 19 years, called the Metonic cycle. Each month in the Hebrew calendar is either 29 or 30 days, depending on changes in the moon. The names of the months are Tishri, Heshvan, Kislev, Tebet, Shebat, Adar, Nisan, Iyar, Sivan, Tammuz, Ab, and Elul. The extra month, Veadar, follows Adar. An important feature of the Hebrew calendar is the weekly sabbath, or day of rest. This corresponds to Saturday on the modern calendar.

The Chinese Calendar. The Chinese calendar also has 12 lunar months, with a 13th added in leap year. The Chinese new year, however, never falls on the same day. The year begins during the month in which the sun enters a certain star constellation (or zodiac sign) in the sky. This can occur any time between January 20 and February 19. Another interesting feature of the Chinese system is that years are grouped in 12's. Each year is named for one of 12 animals.

The Islamic Calendar. The Islamic, or Muslim, calendar has 12 months (29 or 30 days each), but extra days or months are not added to keep time with the sun. Thus, 33 Muslim years are equal to 32 solar years. Also, the seasons do not keep in steady line with the calendar.

An important difference between the modern Gregorian calendar and the older calendars still in use is the numbering of years. The modern calendar began counting with the birth of Christ. That was year 1. However, the Hebrew calendar began 3,760 years before the birth of Christ. And the Muslim calendar numbers years from the flight of Mohammed from Mecca to Medina, which took place 622 years after Christ was born. Thus, what many people call the year 2000 is the year 5760 for the Jewish religion and the year 1378 for

AUGUST

Many children use their own calendars to plan their busy schedules. This calendar is designed as a date book for children. It allows space for notes, and stickers are supplied to mark special days.

the Islamic faith. However, most people who still follow ancient calendars also keep track of the modern Gregorian calendar.

▶ MANY CALENDARS, MANY USES

The passing of days, months, and years is determined by cycles of the sun and moon. The sun "disappears" and returns again; the moon regularly repeats its phases. Because of this, people have often regarded time as cyclical—repeating the same pattern again and again. To reflect this, some ancient calendars were circular in form.

Today many calendars are arranged to present time as linear—following a straight line—rather than cyclical. Days are arranged in rows of boxes, one after another. Weeks are stacked in columns. Months progress from page to page. This arrangement helps us plan and keep track of important dates.

In addition to calendars for day-to-day scheduling, there are also calendars deeply rooted in the symbols and holidays of the year. The **church calendar**, for example, assigns special significance to every day of the year and has periods of time devoted to the approach of important days. For example, Advent leads up to the 12 days of Christmas week.

We also have different calendars that reflect who we are and what we do. Probably the most important calendar for children is the school calendar, which shows when school begins and ends and when vacations fall. Each calendar—desk calendar, school calendar, religious calendar, or some other special calendar—keeps time for one aspect of our lives. Together they show the many different aspects of our lives and the different ways in which we measure time.

JOHN F. SANTINO
Director, *Living Celebrations* series

See also DAYS OF THE WEEK; TIME; and articles on individual months.

CALHOUN, JOHN C. (1782–1850)

John Caldwell Calhoun, the South's leading statesman in the years before the U.S. Civil War, was born on March 18, 1782, near Abbeville, South Carolina. He graduated from Yale College and then studied law. In 1810 he was elected to Congress. At that time the United States and Great Britain were quarreling over the rights of American ships. Calhoun became a leader of the War Hawks, a group of young nationalists who believed the matter could be settled only by war. The War of 1812 followed.

In 1817, President Monroe made Calhoun secretary of war. In 1824 he was elected vice president under John Quincy Adams. When Andrew Jackson became president in 1829, Calhoun again became vice president.

Calhoun was stern-looking, with icy blue eyes. A brilliant and intense man, his consuming interest was politics. Early in his political career, he had fought for a strong federal government. But loyalty to his state changed Calhoun's views. He became a defender of states' rights against the federal government.

In 1828, Congress passed a tariff (a tax on imported goods) that hurt Southern planters. To protest this tariff, Calhoun wrote the *South Carolina Exposition*. In it he said that if the federal government overstepped its power in passing a law, the people could refuse to obey it.

Calhoun's theory became known as nullification. And when Congress passed a new tariff in 1832, South Carolina nullified it. President Jackson threatened to send soldiers to make the state obey. But the crisis was avoided by a compromise.

In 1832, Calhoun resigned the vice presidency to enter the Senate, where he could better serve the interests of his state and the South. Except for one year (1844) as President Tyler's secretary of state, he spent the rest of his life as a senator.

Calhoun made his last appearance in the Senate in 1850. The senate was debating the Compromise of 1850, which dealt with the problem of slavery in the western states. Though very ill, Calhoun insisted on protesting the compromise. A month later, on March 31, 1850, Calhoun died. Among his last words were, "The South, the poor South."

STUART ROCHESTER
Historian, U.S. Department of Defense

See also COMPROMISE OF 1850.

CALIFORNIA

In the 1500's, the Spanish author Garcí Or-dóñez de Montalvo wrote a popular romance novel in which the heroine, Queen Calafía, ruled over California, a fabled and distant island inhabited by Amazons. In 1542, when the European mariner Juan Rodríguez Cabrillo first explored the California coast, he claimed the land for Spain and named it after the mythical island paradise.

State flag

California, the largest of the Pacific Coast states, occupies the southwest corner of mainland United States. The third largest state after Alaska and Texas, California contains both the lowest point in the Western Hemisphere (Death Valley) and the highest point in the "Lower 48" states (Mount Whitney). Its climate and topography are characterized by great variety and contrast. The 840-mile (1,352-kilometer) Pacific coastline rises from the sandy beaches of the south to the up-lifted, rocky headlands of Monterey Peninsula and Cape Mendocino in the north. Northern California experiences rainfall similar to that in Oregon and Washington, while relatively little moisture falls in the southern deserts near the Mexican border. The coastal plains and valleys, settled by the early Spanish explorers and Christian missionaries in the 1700's, contain the state's most densely populated areas and chief industrial centers.

California has by far the largest population of the fifty states. About 75 percent of its nearly 30 million residents live in the south, where the days are sunnier, warmer, and drier than in the north. Two great cities, Los Angeles and San Francisco, dominate the state's cultural and economic life.

If California were its own country, it would be one of the ten richest nations in the world. An astounding variety of goods are produced there, from aerospace and computer equipment and industrial machinery to motion pictures and women's swimwear.

Although increasingly industrialized, California remains the number one agricultural state in the nation. A vast farming region is located in the Central Valley, which extends from the Cascade Range in the north to the Tehachapi Pass near Los Angeles. Peaches, pears, and plums ripen in hundreds of orchards, while grapes, almonds, walnuts, and fields of wheat and barley stretch out in every direction.

Originally a Spanish colony, California passed under the control of Mexico in 1822 and was ceded to the United States in 1848 after the Mexican War. About that time, gold was discovered at John Sutter's mill in the foothills of the Sierra Nevada. By 1849 a great gold rush had brought thousands of fortune hunters to California. Now known as the Golden State, California's promise of opportunity has yet to diminish.

▶ LAND

California's long shorelines, towering mountains, fertile valleys, northern forests, and arid deserts provide spectacular scenery.

Land Regions

In the middle of the state is the Central Valley, a great alluvial plain that is walled on all sides by numerous mountain ranges. The two largest deserts of the United States, the Mojave and Colorado, lie within the Basin and Range in the southeast.

The Cascade Range, a volcanic range in northern California, includes the snow-covered cone of Mount Shasta and Lassen Peak, which is occasionally active.

Opposite page, clockwise from left: **Flowers grown for commercial sale decorate fields near San Diego. Cypress Point juts into the Pacific Ocean near Carmel-by-the-Sea. San Francisco, California's fourth largest city, rises beyond the Golden Gate Bridge.**

State flower:
Golden poppy

State tree:
California redwood

FACTS AND FIGURES

Location: Western United States; bordered on the north by Oregon, on the east by Nevada and Arizona, on the south by Arizona and Mexico, and on the west by the Pacific Ocean.
Area: 158,706 sq mi (411,049 km^2); rank, 3rd.
Population: 31,408,000 (1994 estimate); rank, 1st.
Elevation: *Highest*—14,495 ft (4,418 m) at Mount Whitney in the Sierra Nevada; *lowest*—282 ft (86 m) below sea level in Death Valley.

Capital: Sacramento.
Statehood: September 9, 1850; 31st state.
State Motto: *Eureka* ("I have found it").
State Song: "I Love You, California."
Nickname: Golden State.
Abbreviations: CA; Cal.; Calif.

State bird:
California valley quail

The **Coast Ranges** parallel the seashore from the Oregon boundary to southern California and include the Santa Cruz, Diablo, and Santa Lucia ranges. Within these mountains lie some of the state's most picturesque and fertile valleys, such as the Napa, Santa Clara, and Salinas. They also contain two of California's most active earthquake fault lines, the San Andreas and the Hayward.

The **Klamath Mountains**, extending southward from Oregon, include the forested Siskiyou and Salmon mountains.

Los Angeles lowlands, the group of Channel Islands south of Los Angeles, and the Laguna Mountains.

The **Basin and Range**, a region that covers much of the western United States, enters both northeastern and southeastern California. The northeastern part contains a high lava plateau known as the Modoc Plateau. The southeastern part is made up of desert basins separated by bare mountain ranges. Death Valley, the Salton Sea, and the Mojave and Colorado deserts are located there. Two

Left: The fertile Napa Valley, known for its vineyards and wine industry, lies within the Coast Ranges. *Right:* Big Sur is a tranquil vacation retreat on the Pacific Ocean.

The **Sierra Nevada**, the Spanish name for "snowy mountains," run from the Cascade Range in the north to the Mojave Desert in the south and contain Lake Tahoe, Mount Whitney, and Yosemite, Kings Canyon, and Sequoia national parks.

The **Central Valley**, nestled between the Coast Ranges to the west and the Sierra Nevada to the east, contains California's two most productive agricultural regions, the Sacramento and San Joaquin valleys.

The **Los Angeles Ranges**, also known as the Transverse Ranges, link the Coast Ranges and the Sierra Nevada and mark the southern boundary of California's great Central Valley. They include the San Gabriel and San Bernardino mountains.

The **Peninsular Ranges** are also called the San Diego Ranges. They include most of the

fertile valleys, the Coachella and Imperial, are irrigated by waters transported from the Colorado River.

Rivers, Lakes, and Coastal Waters

California's major river systems are the Sacramento and the San Joaquin, both in the Central Valley. They carry runoff water from the mountains to San Francisco Bay. Among the major tributaries of these two systems are the Pit, Feather, Yuba, American, Mokelumne, Stanislaus, Merced, and Kings rivers. Northern California is also watered by streams that flow into the Pacific Ocean, including the Klamath, Mad, Eel, and Russian rivers. The only major river in southern California is the Colorado, which forms the border between California and Arizona. It flows into the Gulf of California.

California's largest freshwater lakes are Lake Tahoe, which it shares with Nevada, and Clear Lake, in the Coast Ranges north of San Francisco. Salt lakes are found in desert areas. These include the Salton Sea, in the Colorado Desert, and Mono Lake, east of Yosemite National Park. Shasta Lake, an artificial lake on the Sacramento River, is California's largest reservoir.

The Pacific Ocean, the largest body of water in the world, forms California's western border. The state's total shoreline, including

Winter temperatures are mild in California, particularly in the deserts and the Central Valley. The coastal sections from San Francisco to San Diego are protected in winter by mild air from the ocean and by the mountains. At high elevations there are heavy snowfalls.

In summer the coastline is usually cool and cloudy, and the Pacific Ocean can be chilly, even in August. The desert areas of the southeast, however, are extremely hot for much of the year.

Left: Elephant seals are protected at Point Año Nuevo, north of Monterey Bay.
Right: Sand dunes typify the desert lands of Death Valley National Monument.

sounds, bays, and offshore islands, is more than 3,400 miles (5,470 kilometers) long.

Climate

California's summers are almost without rain, except for occasional thunderstorms in the mountains and deserts. During the winter, storms from the Pacific Ocean pass over the state. They are strongest in northern California, where practically all the rainfall occurs from October through April. The Klamath Mountains and the northern Coast Ranges are the state's wettest areas, receiving as much as 100 inches (2,540 millimeters) of rain a year. In southern California, almost all the rain falls between November and March and averages 17 inches (432 millimeters). The desert regions of the southeast experience little measurable rainfall.

Plant and Animal Life

California is renowned for its redwood trees. Forests of giant redwoods extend down the coastline below San Francisco, while the famed giant sequoia is found in the Sierra Nevada. The Sierra also sustains large forests of ponderosa, bristlecone, sugar, and Jeffrey pines; red, white, and Douglas firs; spruces; and other evergreen trees. Monterey and Torrey pines grow along the seashore. Ornamental and fruit trees have also adapted to California's climate and soil. Among these are the date, palm, pepper, acacia, Monterey cypress, and Australian eucalyptus. Cacti and yucca, such as the Joshua tree, bloom in the deserts.

At least 400 species of mammals and reptiles and 600 types of birds make their homes in California. In arid regions are found desert tortoises, horned toads, kangaroo rats,

Yosemite National Park is located in central California at the edge of the Sierra Nevada. High granite cliffs surround the Yosemite Valley, carved out by glaciers that once moved down the Merced River. Established in 1890, the park is visited by more than 3 million people each year.

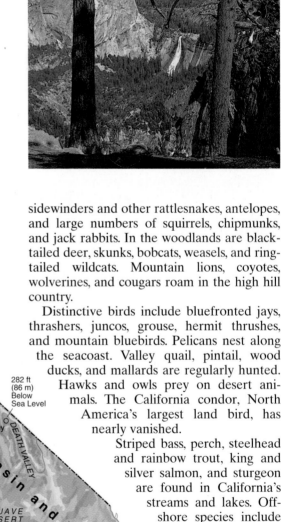

CALIFORNIA
Landforms

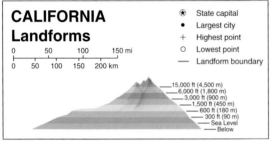

✪	State capital
•	Largest city
+	Highest point
○	Lowest point
—	Landform boundary

0   50   100   150 mi
0   50 100 150 200 km

15,000 ft (4,500 m)
6,000 ft (1,800 m)
3,000 ft (900 m)
1,500 ft (450 m)
600 ft (180 m)
300 ft (90 m)
Sea Level
Below

sidewinders and other rattlesnakes, antelopes, and large numbers of squirrels, chipmunks, and jack rabbits. In the woodlands are black-tailed deer, skunks, bobcats, weasels, and ring-tailed wildcats. Mountain lions, coyotes, wolverines, and cougars roam in the high hill country.

Distinctive birds include bluefronted jays, thrashers, juncos, grouse, hermit thrushes, and mountain bluebirds. Pelicans nest along the seacoast. Valley quail, pintail, wood ducks, and mallards are regularly hunted. Hawks and owls prey on desert animals. The California condor, North America's largest land bird, has nearly vanished.

Striped bass, perch, steelhead and rainbow trout, king and silver salmon, and sturgeon are found in California's streams and lakes. Offshore species include red snapper, squid, abalone, skip jack, tuna, clams, and mackerel.

Natural Resources

Despite rapid urbanization, approximately 40 percent of California's land is still covered by forests, mostly located in the north. In recent years the logging industry has become more conservation-minded, planting new trees to replace ones that are cut down.

California has great mineral wealth. Its tungsten deposits are the largest in the United States. The state's chief gold and silver finds are in the foothills of the Sierra. Nonmetallic deposits include boron, sand and gravel, asbestos, barite, clays, coal, and diatomite. Petroleum and natural gas deposits can be found in the southern Central Valley and along the southern seacoast. Gemstones, such as agate, jade, and jasper, are commercially mined.

One of the state's greatest challenges has been to transport water from the north—the areas of heavy rain and melted snow—to the south, where the majority of Californians live. Aqueducts (channels and large pipelines) and canals transport huge quantities of this precious resource. A state water project carries it from the northern rivers via the Oroville Dam on the Feather River, northeast of Sacramento. Other important water storage facilities include the Shasta and Friant dams, which process water southward from the Sacramento-San Joaquin river system. A major portion of California's water supply, however, comes from surrounding states. Hoover Dam on the Colorado River diverts huge quantities of water from Arizona and Nevada into the Los Angeles basin.

▶ PEOPLE

California is a state of great ethnic diversity. The majority of people claim European descent, but few came directly from Europe; most came from other U.S. states. Spanish is the most common language after English. More than 25 percent of California's population is of Hispanic origin, mostly from Mexico, the Caribbean, and Latin America. Nearly 10 percent of the population is of Asian descent. The African American population grew rapidly after World War II, when there was a heavy migration from rural areas of the South. Today African Americans make up about 7 percent of the population. Less than 250,000 Native Americans remain in California. About 15 percent live on the state's numerous reservations.

Education

American settlers founded California's first school in what had once been the stable at the Spanish mission in Santa Clara. The state's first constitution, drafted in 1849, provided for free elementary schools, but the taxes needed to support them were not collected until 1866. State funds for high schools were not raised until 1903. A few years later, funds were made available for two-year colleges. These junior, or community, colleges now number more than 100.

The state-supported University of California, founded in 1868, has nine campuses. They are located in Berkeley, Davis, Irvine, Los Angeles, Riverside, San Diego, San Francisco, Santa Barbara, and Santa Cruz.

California State University, made up of 20 separate institutions, is the nation's largest state-supported college system. Campuses are located in Arcata, Bakersfield, Carson, Chico, Fresno, Fullerton, Hayward, Long Beach, Los Angeles, Northridge, Pomona, Rohnert Park, Sacramento, San Bernardino, San Diego, San Francisco, San Jose, San Luis Obispo, San Marcos, and Turlock.

California also has many private colleges and universities, as well as a large number of

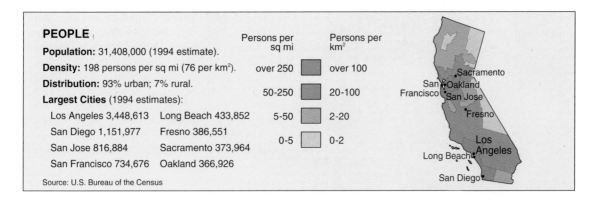

PEOPLE

Population: 31,408,000 (1994 estimate).

Density: 198 persons per sq mi (76 per km²).

Distribution: 93% urban; 7% rural.

Largest Cities (1994 estimates):

Los Angeles 3,448,613	Long Beach 433,852
San Diego 1,151,977	Fresno 386,551
San Jose 816,884	Sacramento 373,964
San Francisco 734,676	Oakland 366,926

Persons per sq mi	Persons per km²
over 250	over 100
50-250	20-100
5-50	2-20
0-5	0-2

Source: U.S. Bureau of the Census

Left: Sand castles crown Pacific Beach.
Right: Flamenco dancers enliven Old Town, San Diego. *Below:* Berkeley is the main campus of the University of California.

professional, technical, and business colleges. Among the best-known private institutions of higher learning are Stanford University, near Palo Alto; the University of Southern California (USC), in Los Angeles; Pepperdine University, in Malibu; Pomona College, in Claremont; and the California Institute of Technology (Cal Tech), in Pasadena.

Libraries, Museums, and the Arts

In 1899 a workable public library system was set up, featuring a loan service among libraries. Today more than 200 public libraries with nearly 4,000 branches serve Californians. Rural areas are reached by bookmobiles.

The state has several noted research libraries. The Bancroft Library at the University of California in Berkeley is renowned for its holdings in the history of the American West. The Huntington Library, Art Gallery, and Botanical Gardens in San Marino collects rare books and manuscripts in the fields of English and American history and literature. The Hoover Institution on War, Revolution, and Peace at Stanford University houses important documents and books on world affairs, especially since 1900.

The State Museum in Sacramento exhibits Native American tools and crafts. The Oakland Museum focuses on California's art and cultural heritage. Among the museums featuring Western European art are the J. Paul Getty Museum in Malibu and the Norton Simon Museum in Pasadena. For more information on the state's leading museums and performing arts institutions, see the articles on Los Angeles, San Diego, and San Francisco in the appropriate volumes.

Sports

California has a wide range of professional sports teams. Football teams include the San Francisco 49ers, the Oakland Raiders, and the San Diego Chargers. Baseball teams include the Anaheim Angels, the Oakland Athletics, the Los Angeles Dodgers, the San Diego Padres, and the San Francisco Giants. Basketball is represented by the Golden State Warriors, the Los Angeles Clippers, the Los Angeles Lakers, and the Sacramento Kings. Hockey is played by the Anaheim Mighty

Ducks, the Los Angeles Kings, and the San Jose Sharks.

▶ ECONOMY

In nearly every economic category, California leads all other states in gross state product, the total value of its goods and services. It is first in agriculture, manufacturing, construction, transportation and utilities, wholesale and retail trade, government, finance, insurance, real estate, and business and personal services. The state employs about 11 percent of the entire nation's working population.

Services

With more than 29 million permanent residents and about 100 million tourists visiting each year, California has an enormous need for personal and business services. Half of all California workers are employed in offices and stores. Most of the banking, transportation, construction, insurance, oil, and publishing companies serving the western United States maintain their home offices in California. Perhaps California's best-known service is the production of motion pictures and television programs, filmed in and near Hollywood.

Manufacturing

California's three leading manufacturing industries are food processing, transportation equipment, and electrical and electronic equipment. California's farms supply raw materials for the many factories that prepare canned and frozen fruits and vegetables. The engineering and scientific research necessary to produce sophisticated aircraft, such as the stealth bomber and missiles, and television and communication equipment originated in California. Computers were developed in "Silicon Valley" in the San Jose area. Other important industries include automobile assembly as well as paper, fiber, cement, and clothing manufacturing.

Agriculture

California also leads the nation in agricultural production and income. Farm output each year exceeds the value of all the gold that was ever mined in the state. Agriculture stimulates other industries with its use of fuel, fertilizer, farm machinery, and packing containers. Most of California's 7 million acres (2.8 million hectares) of farmland is located in the Central Valley.

Because of its temperate climate, California grows as many as 59 principal crops all year long. Grapes and oranges are the leading fruits; tomatoes and lettuce are the leading vegetables. California accounts for nearly all of the nation's output of almonds, apricots, avocados, artichokes, broccoli, brussels sprouts, dates, figs, garlic, nectarines, olives, peaches, plums, melons, persimmons, pomegranates, and walnuts.

The state ranks second only to Oregon in the production of softwoods, mostly from the Cascade and northern Sierra ranges. It is a major supplier of lumber and paper for Japan and other Pacific Rim countries.

Top: Hollywood is the motion picture capital of the world. *Left:* A technician inspects a computer chip. *Below:* Computer production is one of the state's most profitable enterprises.

Manufacturing: Food processing, transportation equipment, electric and electronic equipment, industrial machinery and equipment.

Agriculture: Dairy products, greenhouse products, grapes, cattle and calves.

Minerals: Petroleum, natural gas, borax, tungsten.

Services: Wholesale and retail trade; finance, insurance, and real estate; business, social, and personal services; transportation, communication, and utilities; government.

*Gross state product is the total value of goods and services produced in a year.

Percentage of Gross State Product* by Industry

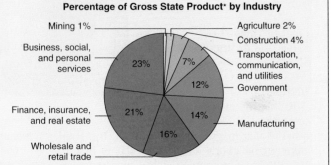

Mining 1%
Business, social, and personal services 23%
Agriculture 2%
Construction 4%
Transportation, communication, and utilities 7%
Government 12%
Manufacturing 14%
Wholesale and retail trade 16%
Finance, insurance, and real estate 21%

Source: U.S. Bureau of Economic Analysis

Clockwise from above: Artichokes, lettuce, and grapes are among the dozens of crops grown in California, the most productive agricultural state in the nation.

Mining and Construction

California has no coal and few iron deposits. Overuse of its once-rich oil and natural gas fields has made the state dependent on imports from Alaska, Texas, and elsewhere. The state's gold deposits have also been heavily mined, although it still ranks second among the states in production. California is the leading producer of tungsten ore, and much of the world's supply of boron, used in the making of glassware and cleansing products, comes from the deserts near Death Valley.

California's immense construction industry requires sand, gravel, and limestone for cement and concrete. Gypsum goes into making wallboard for homes and offices. Bridge and road construction and repair is ongoing, particularly in areas damaged by floods, earthquakes, and other natural disasters.

Transportation

A 175,000-mile (281,635-kilometer) network of roads crisscrosses California, joining remote rural and mountain areas to the major metropolitan centers. Many historic trails are now highways. Highway 101 parallels most of El Camino Real (The Royal Highway), which once connected Spanish missions from San Francisco to San Diego. Interstate 15 follows the Old Spanish Trail. Interstate 5, sometimes called California's Main Street, runs the length of the state. Several dozen railroads still provide passenger and freight service. Trucks are used widely to transport goods and produce.

California has some 450 airfields and more than 200 public airports. It is the southern terminus for the polar air route to Europe as well as a major gateway to Asia. Major international airports are located in Los Angeles and San Francisco. Others are located in San Diego, San Jose, and Oakland.

California also relies on water transportation. Lumber, petroleum, and other heavy cargoes are moved by ship between Eureka, San Francisco, Los Angeles, and San Diego. Inland river ports are also located in Sacramento and Stockton.

Communication

Computer technology has greatly transformed California's communications industries. Research and Development (R&D) centers are maintained by such private firms as the International Telephone and Telegraph Company as well as by the California Institute of Technology in Pasadena.

The best known of California's 600 weekly and 130 daily newspapers are the *Los Angeles Times*, the *Los Angeles Herald Examiner*, the *San Francisco Chronicle*, the *Sacramento Bee*, and the *San Jose Mercury-News*. California also has approximately 235 AM and 240 FM radio stations. It also has a growing number of commercial and public television stations and leads the nation in its number of cable-television subscriptions. Radar and television relay stations operate from various mountain peaks. Large astronomical observatories also are located on Mounts Hamilton, Wilson, and Palomar.

▶ CITIES

Ninety-three percent of all Californians live in urban areas. The state has more than a dozen cities and metropolitan areas with populations exceeding 200,000. Los Angeles has more than 3 million residents, and San Diego has well over 1 million.

Sacramento, the state capital since 1854, is located at the northern end of California's Central Valley at the junction of the Sacramento and American rivers. The city was once a major commercial crossroad and was the western terminus for the Pony Express and California's first railroad, the Sacramento Valley.

Today, however, it has evolved into a legislative and commercial metropolis that is rather remote from the state's major cities. Government is the main employer.

Los Angeles, settled in 1781 by 11 couples with 22 children, has become the largest and most populous city in the western United States. It is known for the production of motion pictures and television programs and as a center of the space program, the garment and furniture trades, fishing, and automobile assembly. In addition, the Port of Los Angeles handles much of the shipping between Japan and other Asian countries. For more information, see the article on Los Angeles in Volume L.

San Diego, with its excellent harbor, was the site of the first Spanish settlement in California (1769). The San Diego-La Jolla area has become a significant educational and scientific research center, renowned for the design of aerospace, oceanographic, and communications equipment. For more information, see the article on San Diego in Volume S.

San Jose, also once a Spanish settlement, has become California's third largest city. It is located in "Silicon Valley," so called for its thriving computer and electronics industries. For more information, see the article on San Jose in Volume S.

Los Angeles, California's largest city, is the second largest city in the nation. More than 14.5 million people live in its greater metropolitan area.

Places of Interest

Disneyland, in Anaheim

San Carlos de Borromeo Mission, in Carmel-by-the-Sea

Hearst Castle, near San Luis Obispo

Lake Tahoe

Alcatraz Island, located in San Francisco Bay, was once a high security penitentiary for some of America's most hardened criminals, including Chicago gangster Al Capone. It was said that no one ever escaped from "the Rock," although several died in the attempt. It is now a popular tourist attraction.

Carmel, Pacific Grove, and Monterey are some of the most scenic coastal towns in North America. A few features include Point Lobos, Pebble Beach Golf Course on 17-Mile Drive, and the Monterey Bay Aquarium.

Death Valley National Park, known as the hottest and driest spot in the United States, commemorates a number of early pioneers who died trying to cross the desert. On July 10, 1913, the temperature reached a record high of 134°F (57°C).

Disneyland, in Anaheim, founded by Walt Disney in 1955, is one of the world's most famous amusement parks, visited by millions every year. It is divided into five sections: Adventureland, Fantasyland, Frontierland, Tomorrowland, and Main Street, U.S.A.

Hearst Castle, formally known as San Simeon, is located near San Luis Obispo. Built as a pleasure palace by newspaperman William Randolph Hearst, it became a playground for Hollywood's most noted celebrities. Today it is a tourist attraction, owned and operated by the state. The castle contains imported artworks, a Roman temple, and a swimming pool inlaid with gold.

Lake Tahoe, on the border between California and Nevada, is one of the state's most popular ski resorts.

Sea World, at San Diego's Mission Bay, offers displays of sea life and live shows featuring whales, porpoises, sharks, and sea turtles.

Sequoia National Park contains the oldest and tallest specimens of giant sequoias, notably the General Sherman Tree, estimated to be at least 2,500 years old. It stands 275 feet (83.8 meters) high and measures 103 feet (31.4 meters) around the base.

Spanish Missions, California's oldest buildings, serve as reminders of colonial days when Franciscan missionaries sought to convert the Native Americans to Christianity. The first of California's 21 missions was San Diego de Alcalá, built in 1769. La Purísima Concepcíon, founded in 1787 near Lompoc, is a state historical monument. Also of note are San Carlos de Borromeo Mission in Carmel-by-the-Sea, Mission Santa Bárbara in Santa Barbara, and the ruins of the mission at San Juan Capistrano, famous for the sparrows that return to it every year on or near March 19th.

Yosemite National Park is the best known and the largest of California's national parks. Its spectacular waterfalls, sheer cliffs, and giant sequoia groves attract millions of visitors every year.

Recreation Areas. California has a wide variety of state and national parks and monuments. For more information, contact the Department of Parks and Recreation, P.O. Box 942896, Sacramento, California 94296-0001.

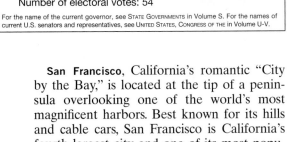

Between 1850 and 1854, California's capital moved from Monterey to San Jose to Vallejo to San Francisco. In 1854, Sacramento became the permanent site.

San Francisco, California's romantic "City by the Bay," is located at the tip of a peninsula overlooking one of the world's most magnificent harbors. Best known for its hills and cable cars, San Francisco is California's fourth largest city and one of its most popular tourist attractions. Founded in 1776 as a mission dedicated to St. Francis of Assisi, today's city is an important Pacific port and a major center of finance. For more information, see the article on San Francisco in Volume S.

▶ **GOVERNMENT**

From 1846 to 1849, California's governors were military officers. After 1850, the first state constitution authorized the election of public officials. The current state constitution, heavily revised in 1879, provides for three branches of government—executive, legislative, and judicial.

The executive branch is headed by a governor, lieutenant governor, secretary of state, attorney general, treasurer, and superintendent of public education. All are elected to 4-year terms.

The legislature consists of a senate and assembly, which meet each year after January 1. A speaker presides over the 80-member assembly and exercises considerable influence over its operations. The senate consists of 40 members who serve 4-year terms; half of the senators are up for election every two years.

California citizens can propose legislation if 5 percent sign a petition to the government. If approved by a majority of the voters during the next election, the proposal becomes law. No action is required by the legislature.

California's judicial branch is headed by a supreme court, which oversees all the lower courts in the state. It is made up of a chief justice and six associate justices. Supreme court justices and district court judges are appointed by the governor but are subject to voter approval. Lower court judges are elected directly by the people.

▶ **HISTORY**

Native Americans settled in California about 12,000 years ago. They lived off the waters and land, fishing, hunting game, and gathering fruits and nuts. By the time Spanish explorers first came into contact with them in the mid-1500's, there were more than a dozen major tribal groups, including the Hupa, Maidu, Yuma, Pomo, and Mojave. For more information, see INDIANS, AMERICAN (In the Far West: California) in Volume I.

Exploration and Colonization

The first Europeans to explore California were Juan Rodríguez Cabrillo in 1542 and Sir Francis Drake in 1579. Two centuries passed before the Spanish colonized the region. In 1769, Gaspar de Portolá led a Spanish expedition to establish California's first pueblos (towns) and presidios (forts). He was accompanied by Father Junípero Serra, who founded a chain of Catholic missions, from San Diego to Sonoma, to introduce Christianity to the natives.

California remained a remote and sparsely settled province until the late 1700's, when the threat of Russian occupation from Alaska prompted the Spanish to increase the size of their military forces. Spain's authority, however, remained weak, and in 1822, Mexico took control of California, having declared its independence from Spain the previous year. In this new era, American traders, trappers, and whalers also began to arrive in California. Some came overland, across the deserts and mountains. Others, especially Yankee traders, came by ship.

The Bear Flag Revolt and American Conquest

The Republic of Mexico held only a loose control over California, and gradually American settlers began pressuring the United States government to acquire the territory. In June 1846, not knowing that the United States was already at war with Mexico over Texas, a few of these newcomers captured the Mexican presidio in Sonoma. They raised a flag—displaying one star and the image of a grizzly bear—and declared California an independent republic. California was annexed to the United States at the end of the Mexican War with the signing of the Treaty of Guadalupe Hidalgo on February 2, 1848.

The Gold Rush

On January 24, 1848, nine days before the United States acquired California, gold was discovered on land owned by John Sutter on the south fork of the American River, near Sacramento. Within the next two years, tens of thousands of gold seekers, nicknamed forty-niners in 1849, came from all over the world to seek their fortunes. As a result of this population explosion, California was admitted to the Union as the 31st state on September 9, 1850.

INDEX TO CALIFORNIA MAP

• County Seat   Counties in parentheses   ★ State Capital

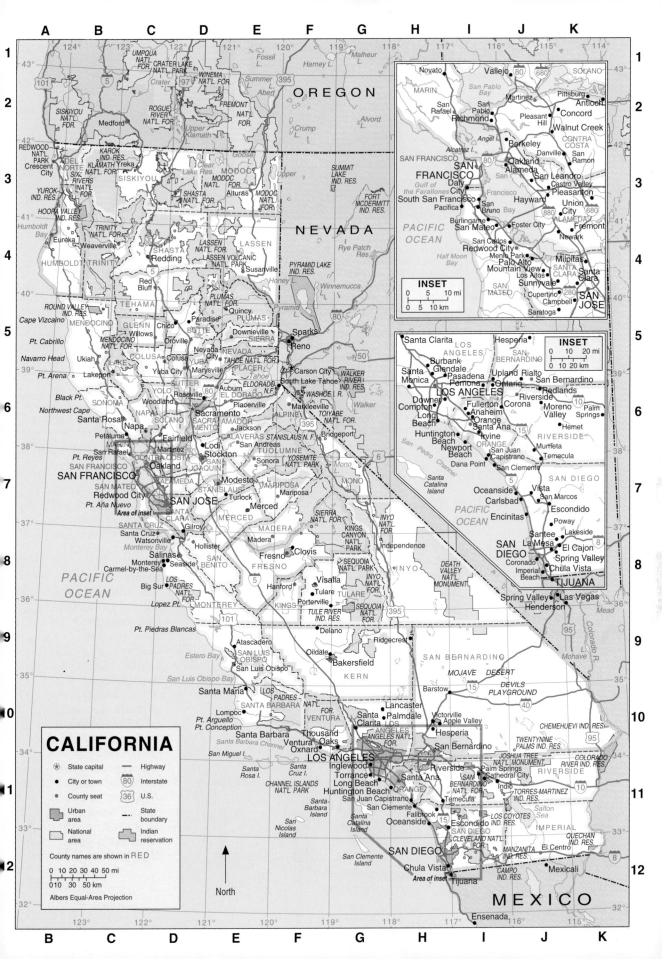

Famous People

Consult the Index to find more information in *The New Book of Knowledge* about the following people who were born in California or are otherwise associated with the state: conservationist John Muir (1838–1914); botanist Luther Burbank (1849–1926); newspaper tycoon William Randolph Hearst (1863–1951); writers Robert Frost (1874–1963), Jack London (1876–1916), and John Steinbeck (1902–68); World War II general George S. Patton (1885–1945); children's entertainment pioneer Walt Disney (1901–66); physicist Luis Walter Alvarez (1911–88); baseball great Joe DiMaggio (1911–); Presidents Richard M. Nixon (1913–94) and Ronald Reagan (1911–); film actors Marilyn Monroe (1926–62), Shirley Temple (1928–), and Clint Eastwood (1930–); and tennis legend Billie Jean King (1943–).

Cesar Estrada Chavez (1927–93), born in Yuma, Arizona, formed the United Farm Workers, an affiliate of the AFL-CIO. The son of a migrant farmworker,

John Steinbeck

Ronald Reagan

Chavez devoted himself to bettering the working conditions of Mexican-American farm laborers. From 1966 until 1978, he organized nationwide boycotts of California produce, including grapes, lettuce, and citrus fruits, forcing growers to sign contracts with the union members.

Isadora (Dora Angela) Duncan (1877–1927), born in San Francisco, was a pioneer of modern dance. Rejecting the formality of ballet training, Duncan developed her own style that more freely. expressed human emotion. Barefooted and wearing flowing, classical Greek robes, Duncan caused a sensation in America and Europe.

Bret Harte (1836–1902), born Francis Brett Harte in Albany, New York, is best known for his stories of mining-camp life during the California gold rush. "The Luck of Roaring Camp" (1868) and the enormously popular "The Outcasts of Poker Flat" (1869) were published in the *Overland Monthly*, a magazine that Harte edited from 1868 to 1870. He later became a diplomat, serving as a U.S. counsel in Prussia (1878–80) and Scotland (1880–85).

George Lucas (1944–), born in Modesto, is one of Hollywood's most successful film directors and producers. He co-wrote and directed *American Graf-*

Economic Growth

When the supply of gold declined, some miners turned to farming. At first wheat and barley were the leading crops, as they did not need irrigation and could be shipped long distances without spoiling. After the Civil War (1861–65), the building of new dams and irrigation systems brought water from the north, vastly increasing agricultural production.

Railroad construction in the late 1860's ended California's geographical isolation from the eastern states. After 1887, a rate

On April 18, 1906, a devastating earthquake hit San Francisco. Earth tremors and the resulting fires destroyed some 28,000 buildings. More than 500 people were killed or missing.

war between the Southern Pacific and Santa Fe railroads made travel affordable, and thousands of people migrated to southern California, accelerating the growth of Los Angeles.

Social and Political Developments

By 1900, California's government was dominated by the interests of wealthy bankers and railroad barons. Average working men and women, seeking to clean up widespread corruption at the state and local levels, pledged to "kick the Southern Pacific [railroad] out of politics forever." Political housecleaning began in 1911 under the governorship of Hiram W.

fiti (1973) as well as his first blockbuster hit *Star Wars* (1977), an intergalactic science fiction fantasy. He later produced two sequels, *The Empire Strikes Back* (1980) and *Return of the Jedi* (1983), in addition to the megahits *Raiders of the Lost Ark* (1981), *Indiana Jones and the Temple of Doom* (1984), and *Indiana Jones and the Last Crusade* (1989), directed by Steven Spielberg. His company, Lucasfilm, Ltd., operates the world-renowned special-effects studio Industrial Light & Magic.

Leland Stanford

Sally Kirsten Ride (1951–), born in Encino, became the first American woman to travel in space. After earning a physics degree from Stanford University in 1977, she was selected to become an astronaut. She flew on the 7th and 13th space shuttle missions in 1983 and 1984. Ride served on the commission that investigated the 1986 *Challenger* disaster. In 1989 she became head of the Space Institute of the University of California at San Diego.

Jonas Edward Salk (1914–95), born in New York City, was an acclaimed microbiologist who developed the first vaccine against polio, a crippling and often deadly disease. In 1960 he founded the Salk Institute for Biological Studies in La Jolla, a nonprofit research organization. Salk was working on an AIDS vaccine at the time of his death.

Father Junípero Serra (1713–84), born on the Spanish island of Majorca, was a Franciscan priest and one of the famous missionaries in America. He founded the first mission, at San Diego, in 1769. For 15 years he built other missions and baptized more than 6,000 Native Ameri-

Shirley Temple

cans. He is buried at San Carlos de Borromeo Mission in Carmel-by-the-Sea.

Leland Stanford (1824–93), born in Watervliet, New York, was one of the most famous railroad builders of the late 1800's. A successful merchant in Sacramento, he served as governor of California (1861–63). In 1861, Stanford cofounded the transcontinental Central Pacific Railroad and served as its president until his death. He founded the Southern Pacific Railroad Company in 1870. In 1885, Stanford established Stanford University near Palo Alto as a memorial to his son.

Johnson (1866–1945). The legislature passed a series of notable reforms that established a new railroad commission, gave women the vote, and increased the overall power of the voters.

Depression Years and World War II

In the 1930's, Californians were strongly affected by the national economic collapse known as the Great Depression. The state was suddenly besieged by thousands of migrants from the Midwest who had been forced by drought to abandon their homes and farms. Overwhelmed by the unemployed, the state tried to close its borders.

From 1941 to 1945, during World War II, accelerated production of war materials helped absorb the glut of unemployed workers. Californians met the enormous wartime demand for airplanes and ships, and the state became a major embarkation center for Pacific combat areas.

Industrial Expansion and Population Growth

Between 1945 and 1955, California's population increased by more than 4 million. The era was characterized by the building of freeways, airports, factories, and schools, and a continuing shift away from an agricultural society toward an industrial one.

Following the Vietnam War in the 1970's, thousands of Asians immigrated to California. More recently, the state has absorbed a burdensome number of legal, as well as illegal, aliens from Mexico, the Caribbean, Latin America, and throughout the world.

Additional stresses in recent years have included overcrowding, rising crime rates, racial tensions, financial setbacks, and a string of natural disasters. These have ranged from floods, mudslides, and forest fires to two earthquakes, one in the San Francisco-Oakland area in 1989 and another in Northridge, near Los Angeles, in 1994. Despite the challenges of living in an unpredictable environment, most Californians agree that there is no place else on earth they would rather live.

ANDREW ROLLE
Author, *California: A History*

See also LOS ANGELES; SAN DIEGO; SAN FRANCISCO; SAN JOSE.

CALORIES. See NUTRITION.

CALVIN, JOHN (1509–1564)

John Calvin was a leader of the Protestant Reformation, a religious movement that swept through Europe in the 1500's. It divided the Christian world into the Catholic Church and numerous new Protestant churches, many of which were strongly influenced by Calvin's ideas.

Calvin was born in Noyon, France, on July 10, 1509. His father, who worked for a local bishop, sent John to the University of Paris at the age of 14 to prepare him for the priesthood. There he devoted himself to the study of Latin, philosophy, and logic—the science of reasoning. In 1528 he went to the city of Orléans to study law. The logic of law appealed to Calvin and influenced his religious thinking in later years.

In 1531, Calvin returned to Paris. It was about this time that he became interested in the new Protestant faith. Because the government did not tolerate these new religious ideas, Calvin was forced to flee from Paris and, finally, from France altogether. For several years he wandered from city to city. He began to write his great work, *Institutes of the Christian Religion*, in which he described his interpretation of Christianity. It eventually became one of the most important documents of Protestant beliefs.

By 1536, Calvin was becoming known to Protestant leaders outside of France. During a visit to Geneva, Switzerland, he was persuaded to stay to help spread Protestant ideas. Except for one short period in Strasbourg, where he married and served as a church pastor, Calvin lived in Geneva for the rest of his life. He and his wife, Idelette, had several children, but unfortunately, none lived beyond infancy.

Under Calvin's leadership, Geneva became the center of Protestantism. The church essentially wrote the city's laws and governed every part of daily life. The laws were strict. Genevans received religious education and were expected to be serious and hardworking. Peforming plays, dancing, and singing—except of church psalms—were forbidden. So were gambling and swearing. The punishment for disobedience was severe.

Calvin also worked to strengthen the Protestant movement throughout Europe. He corresponded with political and religious

John Calvin, a leader of the Protestant Reformation, believed that people cannot influence their spiritual destiny through their actions, as it has already been determined, or predestined, who will receive salvation.

leaders and published commentaries on the Bible. He established the Genevan Academy to train students for work in the church. Yet he continued to preach and perform other duties of a church pastor. Calvin died on May 27, 1564, after suffering from health problems for many years.

Calvin's views on Christianity were stern. He believed that people, by nature, were sinful and could receive salvation only through God's grace. According to Calvin, God had decided long ago which people, whom Calvin called "the elect," would receive grace. This was Calvin's doctrine of **predestination**, meaning "determined in advance."

Calvin also believed that people could never truly know or understand God. Because of this, they had to rely strictly on the Bible for direction in their lives. Their lifelong task was to struggle against sin and try to make the world obedient to God's laws.

Calvin's ideas had spread through much of Europe by the time of his death. In various places his ideas were interpreted differently, which gave rise to different sects, or groups, of the Protestant religion. The Puritans, who left England to settle in the American colonies, were followers of Calvin. They called their churches Congregationalist, Presbyterian, Evangelical, and Reformed. Baptists and Unitarians also adopted some of Calvin's ideas, attesting to his continuing influence.

Reviewed by HUGH T. KERR
Princeton Theological Seminary

See also PROTESTANTISM; REFORMATION.

CAMBODIA

Cambodia (also known for a time as Kampuchea) is a nation of Southeast Asia. In the northwestern part of the country lie the ruins of the abandoned city of Angkor, a reminder of Cambodia's great past—and of its uncertain future. Angkor was the capital of the Khmer Empire, which centuries ago ruled a large area in Southeast Asia. Wars and foreign conquest eventually drove the Khmer kings from Angkor. In 1863, what was then the kingdom of Cambodia fell under the rule of France. Cambodia regained its independence in 1953, but in the years that followed, it was caught up in the struggles of stronger powers and devastated by civil war.

▶ THE PEOPLE

Cambodia is mainly a land of rural people, who cultivate the fertile rice-growing regions of the country. Life traditionally has revolved around the family, the village, the rice fields, and the local Buddhist temple.

Most of the people are of Khmer stock. Minority groups include Vietnamese, Chinese, and Chams. The official language is Khmer, although French, which dates from the colonial period, is still spoken by some Cambodians. Buddhism is the country's dominant faith. Special efforts are being made to preserve the traditional songs and dances of the old Khmer court, ancient arts that have been admired throughout the world.

▶ THE LAND

Cambodia is a part of mainland Southeast Asia, sharing borders with Thailand, Laos, and Vietnam. Most of the country consists of a saucer-shaped basin surrounded on three sides by hills and mountains. The Elephant Range lies on the southwest and the Cardamom Range on the west. In the north the Dangrek Range forms part of the boundary with Thailand. In the east, along the Vietnamese border, are a series of hills that make up part

Cambodia's ancient grandeur is reflected in the ruins of Angkor, capital of the Khmer Empire, which once ruled much of Southeast Asia. Here, two Buddhist monks stroll before the temple complex of Angkor Wat, which dates from the 1100's.

Rice is the chief crop grown in the area between the Mekong River and the Tonle Sap (Great Lake), the country's most fertile and densely populated region.

of the Annamese Cordillera. Cutting through the hills north of the Cardamom Range is a lowland area that stretches from Thailand to the Mekong River.

The Mekong and Tonle Sap. The Mekong, Southeast Asia's longest river, is one of Cambodia's most important geographical features. Flowing through the country for more than 400 miles (640 kilometers) before entering Vietnam, it is Cambodia's main avenue of transportation and its chief source of water for irrigation. The river is connected to a large, shallow lake, the Tonle Sap (Great Lake). This region is Cambodia's heartland. It traditionally has had the country's largest population, the most productive rice fields, and much of its commercial fishing. It is also the site of Cambodia's past and present capitals and major cities.

Climate and Natural Resources. Cambodia has a tropical climate, marked by wet and dry seasons. During the rainy season the central basin receives moderately heavy rainfall. For the rest of the year, there is very little rainfall, and the Mekong River supplies the additional water needed for irrigation. The average

yearly temperature varies between 70 and 95°F (21 and 35°C).

In addition to its fertile soil, Cambodia has large areas of forests, which are a source of timber, a principal export. Wild animal life includes elephants, tigers, bears, and a variety of birds and reptiles.

▶ **THE ECONOMY**

Cambodia's economy was shattered by years of war and political upheaval. Restoration of the country's economic well-being is a major task of its present government.

Agriculture. The economy is based largely on agriculture. Most of the people practice subsistence farming, growing rice, vegetables, and fruits and raising poultry for their own use on small plots of land. The main food crop is rice. At one time Cambodia produced a surplus of rice for export, chiefly from the rich farming areas of the Mekong River valley and the basin of the Tonle Sap. Rubber, grown on large plantations, is a leading commercial crop and, along with timber, a major export.

Fishing, Manufacturing, and Mining. Fishing is an important economic activity on the Tonle Sap and in coastal waters. Manufacturing consists mainly of textile production, the processing of agricultural products, and other light industry. Some phosphates and gemstones (particularly sapphires and rubies) are

FACTS and figures

KINGDOM OF CAMBODIA is the official name of the country.

LOCATION: Southeast Asia.

AREA: 69,898 sq mi (181,035 km²).

POPULATION: 9,000,000 (estimate).

CAPITAL: Phnom Penh.

MAJOR LANGUAGE: Khmer (official).

MAJOR RELIGION: Buddhist.

GOVERNMENT: Constitutional monarchy. **Head of state**—king. **Head of government**—prime minister. **Legislature**—National Assembly.

CHIEF PRODUCTS: Agricultural—rice, rubber, corn and other vegetables, sugarcane, bananas and other fruits, livestock. **Manufactured**—agricultural and forestry products, textiles. **Mineral**—phosphates, gemstones (sapphires, rubies).

MONETARY UNIT: New riel (1 riel = 100 sen).

mined, but the country's other mineral resources, mainly deposits of iron ore, bauxite (aluminum ore), and manganese, still remain to be developed.

▶CITIES

Phnom Penh (also spelled Pnompenh) is Cambodia's capital and largest city and the center of its transportation and commerce. It is located in the southern part of the country, at the junction of the Mekong and Tonle Sap rivers. Dating from the 1400's, the city replaced Angkor as the capital of the old Khmer Empire. It became the capital of the kingdom of Cambodia in the 1860's. The city's population has shifted dramatically over the years. It is now estimated at about 700,000.

The second largest city is Battambang, located in western Cambodia. Kompong Som is the country's port on the Gulf of Thailand.

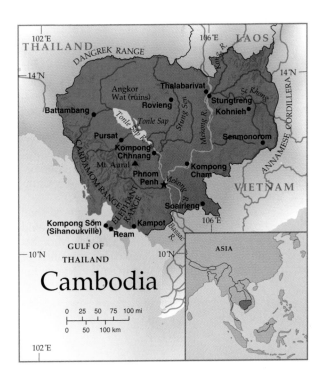

Daily life in Phnom Penh, Cambodia's capital and largest city, returned to normal after years of war and political upheaval.

▶GOVERNMENT

Cambodia has had a number of different governments in its recent history. (See History section.) It is now a constitutional monarchy. Under the Constitution of 1993, the king is head of state and commander of the armed forces. Legislative power is vested in an elected National Assembly. The government, consisting of the cabinet of ministers, is headed by a prime minister. The prime minister is appointed by the king, from representatives of the political party with the largest number of seats in the legislature. All laws passed by the National Assembly are subject to review by the Constitutional Council.

▶HISTORY

The Khmer Empire. The kingdom of Funan ruled in what is now Cambodia from about A.D. 100 to the 400's. The Khmer people established their own kingdom between the A.D. 500's and 600's, and over the next 800 years, they extended their domination over neighboring states. By the 1300's the Khmer Empire was the most powerful in mainland Southeast Asia. During this period, Khmer culture and art flourished, centered in the capital at Angkor. (A representation of its great temple complex of Angkor Wat appears on the present-day Cambodian flag.)

Decline and French Colonization. The empire declined between the 1300's and 1800's as the Khmers lost much of their territory in wars with the Thais and Vietnamese. In 1863, France established a protectorate over the kingdom of Cambodia and made it part of French Indochina, which also included Vietnam and Laos. In 1941 the 18-year-old Norodom Sihanouk was made king of Cambodia. He became a leader in the movement for Cambodian independence, achieved in 1953.

The Sihanouk Era. Sihanouk relinquished the throne to his father in 1955 so that he could play a more active role in politics. After his father died in 1960, Sihanouk became chief of state but declined the title of king. Despite his

King Norodom Sihanouk, Cambodia's constitutional monarch, was a dominant political figure during most of his country's recent history.

efforts to maintain Cambodia's neutrality, the country was drawn into the struggle between the Communist and non-Communist forces in neighboring Vietnam. (An article on the Vietnam War appears in Volume U-V.)

The Khmer Republic. In 1970, Sihanouk was overthrown in a coup led by General Lon Nol, the prime minister and head of the army. Lon Nol, who later became president, renamed the country the Khmer Republic, abolishing the monarchy. The new government followed an anti-Communist policy supported by the United States. South Vietnamese and U.S. troops entered Cambodia to attack the North Vietnamese and Vietcong strongholds. The Lon Nol government was also engaged in a civil war against troops of the Communist Khmer Rouge (Red Khmer).

The Khmer Rouge. The government of the Khmer Republic fell in 1975 to the Khmer Rouge forces, which set up a government called Democratic Kampuchea, led by Pol Pot (1925?–98). The Khmer Rouge attempted to create a revolutionary society that would not be dependent on foreign trade or aid. Its methods were harsh and frequently brutal. The teeming populations of Phnom Penh and other cities, swelled by refugees from the fighting, were forcibly evacuated to the countryside to toil in the fields. Private property was abolished and individually owned plots of land were re-organized into state-run collective farms. The policies of the Khmer Rouge government further disrupted an economy devastated by war. Under its rule, as many as 2 million Cambodians died of starvation, disease, and exhaustion. Others fled the country.

The People's Republic. In 1978, Vietnamese troops invaded Cambodia. They drove the Khmer Rouge forces out of Phnom Penh in 1979 and established a Vietnamese-supported government, the People's Republic of Kampuchea. The new government gained control of most of the country, although Khmer Rouge guerrilla forces continued to operate in rural areas until 1999. The last Vietnamese troops eventually departed from Cambodia in 1989.

Return of Sihanouk. Under a United Nations peace plan, a transitional government was established in 1990, and multiparty elections were held in 1993. Sihanouk returned as king and head of state. The new government was an uneasy coalition headed by Sihanouk's son, Prince Ranariddh, and by Hun Sen, a leader of the former Vietnamese-backed regime.

In 1997 Hun Sen seized power from the prince, who went into exile. In a controversial election in 1998, Hun Sen's party won the most seats in the legislature but not a majority. Hun Sen agreed to form a coalition government, with himself as premier and Prince Ranariddh as president. In 1999, Cambodia became the last Southeast Asian country admitted to the Association of Southeast Asian Nations (ASEAN).

L. A. PETER GOSLING
Center for South and Southeast Asian Studies
University of Michigan

CAMDEN. See NEW JERSEY (Cities).

CAMELS

Camels are easy to recognize because they have humps on their backs. They are large, strong animals that are especially suited to living in the desert.

If necessary, camels can go without food and water for days at a time. Fat is stored in a camel's hump and serves as energy, or food. As the animal is nourished by the fat, the hump begins to shrink. When the camel begins to eat and drink again, the hump returns to its former size.

Scientists are still trying to understand how camels can go without water for long periods of time. They do know that camels obtain a certain amount of water from the green plants they graze on. Scientists also know that camels do not begin to perspire, or give off water from their bodies, until their body temperatures are very high. Contrary to popular belief, camels do not store water in their humps.

The camel is suited to desert life in other ways, as well. Its broad, padded feet stay on top of the sand as it walks. When sand blows, the camel can shut its nostrils into narrow slits. And its long, silky lashes and thick eyebrows help protect the camel's eyes from the hot sun. The camel also has thick, calloused pads on its knees and chest which allow it to kneel comfortably on the sand.

Camels are often used as a source of food and other supplies in the desert. The meat tastes similar to beef, and the milk can be used to make cheese. The fat from the camel's hump can be melted and used to make butter. The hair of the camel is woven to make cloth, tents, and carpets, and the camel's skin is used to make shoes and other leather goods.

There are two main types of camels—Arabian and Bactrian. Arabian camels, often called dromedaries, have one hump. Bactrian camels have two humps on their backs. The Arabian camel lives mainly in the deserts of North Africa and the Arabian Peninsula.

The Arabian camel is often used as a beast of burden. It can carry about 600 pounds (270 kilograms) of weight. Thus it is often referred to as the ship of the desert.

Bactrian camels are found on the plains and deserts of central Asia, where the winters are cold. Their fur is longer than that of the Arabian camel. The Bactrian camel can carry a pack over deep snow in weather that is below 0°F (−18°C). It can stay alive on scrub plants that few other animals would eat.

Camels belong to a large group of animals called hoofed mammals. The camel family includes four animals of South America: the guanaco, vicuña, llama, and alpaca.

Reviewed by MICHAEL E. CARLETON
Smithsonian Institution

See also HOOFED MAMMALS.
CAMERAS. See PHOTOGRAPHY.

The Arabian camel (*left*) is identified by its single hump and relatively short hair. Bactrian camels (*right*) have double humps and long fur that helps them survive cold winters.

CAMEROON

In 1471 a Portuguese sailor and explorer named Fernão do Po anchored his fleet at the mouth of the Wouri River on the west coast of Africa near what is today the port of Douala. Attracted by the masses of shrimp in the water, the sailors named the river *Rio dos Camarões* (Portuguese for "river of the shrimps"). Soon after, the Spanish arrived. They changed the name to *Camarones* (the Spanish word for "shrimps"). Eventually the name was applied not only to the river but also to the land surrounding it. In English the country became known as Cameroon.

▶THE PEOPLE

People of nearly 200 ethnic groups live in modern Cameroon. In the south are people of mostly Bantu and semi-Bantu origin. Thousands of Pygmies live in the deep forests of the south and southwest. Most of the groups of the north are Muslims of Sudanese origin. Christians live mainly in the south. Many people follow traditional African religions.

Because many different groups have settled in Cameroon over the centuries, more than 100 languages and dialects are spoken. People must sometimes learn three or more languages in order to understand their neighbors in adjoining villages.

The Europeans who colonized Africa brought their languages, too. In the first half of the 1900's, Cameroon had three colonial governments and three different languages. Grandparents had to learn German. Their children learned some French and some English. And now all must learn French and English as well as their local languages.

Education is required and free through the primary grades. The country's only university, the University of Yaoundé, has campuses in several cities.

▶THE LAND

Cameroon is situated on the western coast of Africa. Its Atlantic coastline is a dense mangrove swamp, with Douala its main port. Southern Cameroon is mountainous, with lush tropical rain forests. The hilly Adamawa plateau occupies most of central Cameroon. Farther north the plateau flattens out into semi-arid grasslands.

Rainfall is heavy in the south except for two short dry seasons, from December to February and from July to September. The village of Debundscha, on the coast, is one of the wettest places in the world. The north has a long, rainy, tropical summer, and a dry season lasting from November to April. Many different animals live in Cameroon's dense forests and on its rugged plateaus.

Left: One of the main streets in Yaoundé, the capital of Cameroon, is Avenue du 21 Août 1940 (Avenue of August 21, 1940). The date celebrates the arrival of Free French forces in World War II. Right: A village chief is welcomed home with drums and raised spears.

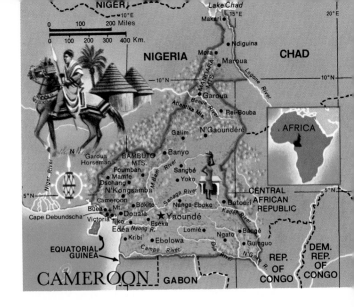

THE ECONOMY

Cameroon is one of the more prosperous countries in tropical Africa. Its economy is based mainly on agriculture and the production of petroleum.

Cameroon is one of the world's leading producers of cacao (cocoa beans). Food crops include corn, millet, and sorghum. Cattle provide meat, hides, and other livestock products.

In addition to petroleum, Cameroon produces natural gas and has major deposits of bauxite (aluminum ore). Important industries include aluminum smelting, the processing of agricultural products, and the manufacture of lumber and other forestry products.

HISTORY AND GOVERNMENT

Following the first Portuguese explorations in the late 1400's, Cameroon became a source of slaves for the Americas. Britain became involved in the area in the early 1800's, while engaged in efforts to suppress the slave trade.

The first Cameroon colony was established by Germany in 1884 after it signed treaties with local chiefs. German Cameroon (Kam-

erun) included not only present-day Cameroon but some of the surrounding region as well. The Germans created vast plantations for growing cash crops such as bananas, palm kernels, and peanuts. After Germany's defeat in World War I (1914–18), it lost all of its African colonies. Britain and France divided Cameroon between them.

On January 1, 1960, after a decade of unrest, the eastern (French) region received its independence and became the Republic of Cameroon. The following year, British Cameroons (made up of the Northern and Southern Cameroons) held a referendum under the guidance of the United Nations. Northern Cameroon became part of Nigeria on June 1, 1961. Southern Cameroon joined the Republic of Cameroon to form the Federal Republic of Cameroon on October 1, 1961. The name Republic of Cameroon was restored in 1984.

In 1986, Cameroon experienced a rare and horrific natural disaster when carbon dioxide gas discharged from Lake Nyos in the north. Approximately 1,700 people were killed.

The government of Cameroon is headed by a president. The legislative body is called the National Assembly. The president and the legislators are elected to 5-year terms.

Cameroon has had only two presidents since independence—Ahmadou Ahidjo, who held office until his resignation in 1982, and Paul Biya. Although Biya has since been re-elected three times, most recently in 1997, Cameroon's democratic process has been called into question by his political opponents.

SANFORD GRIFFITH
New York University

FACTS and figures

REPUBLIC OF CAMEROON (République du Cameroun) is the official name of the country.

LOCATION: West Africa.

AREA: 183,569 sq mi (475,442 km²).

POPULATION: 15,000,000 (estimate).

CAPITAL: Yaoundé.

LARGEST CITY: Douala.

MAJOR LANGUAGES: French, English (both official), various African languages.

MAJOR RELIGIOUS GROUPS: Traditional African religions, Christian, Muslim.

GOVERNMENT: Republic. **Head of state**—president. **Head of government**—prime minister. **Legislature**—National Assembly.

CHIEF PRODUCTS: Agricultural—corn, millet, sorghum, cacao (cocoa beans), coffee, bananas, oil palm kernels, cotton, livestock. **Manufactured**—petroleum products, processed agricultural products, lumber and other forestry products, textiles. **Mineral**—petroleum, natural gas, bauxite (local deposits under development).

MONETARY UNIT: African Financial Community (CFA) franc (1 CFA franc = 100 centimes).

CAMPBELL, KIM (1947–   )

Kim Campbell became Canada's first woman prime minister on June 25, 1993. She came to power on the retirement of Prime Minister Brian Mulroney, whom Campbell succeeded as leader of the Progressive Conservative Party.

Campbell was born Avril Phaedra Campbell on March 10, 1947, in Port Alberni on Vancouver Island. She later changed her name to Kim. She grew up in Vancouver, where she received a B.A. in political science from the University of British Columbia (UBC). After pursuing graduate studies at the London School of Economics, she returned to Vancouver to lecture in political science at UBC and at Vancouver Community College (Langara). In 1980 she returned to UBC, graduating with a law degree in 1983.

After gaining admission to the bar, Campbell served as executive director of the office of Bill Vander Zalm, the premier of British Columbia. After Premier Vander Zalm resigned in 1986, Campbell ran for the leadership of the Social Credit Party of British Columbia. Although unsuccessful, she later won election to the provincial legislature. By 1988, Campbell had set her sights on the national political scene and switched to the Progressive Conservative Party, which then was in power. In the general elections of 1988, she won a seat in the House of Commons, marking her first victory in what was to become a meteoric rise to national prominence.

Campbell was first appointed to the cabinet in 1989 as minister of state for Indian and northern affairs and within a few months had been named minister of justice. She held this position until 1993, when she was appointed minister of defense.

Campbell's election to succeed the retiring Brian Mulroney as leader of the Progressive Conservative Party in June 1993 ensured that she would serve as Canada's 19th prime minister for as long as her party continued to hold a majority of seats in Parliament. Although Campbell was popular in her own right, in the general elections of October 1993 she and her party were soundly defeated by the Liberal Party, led by Jean Chrétien. Two months later, Campbell resigned as party leader.

ANDREW HEARD
Simon Fraser University

CAMP FIRE BOYS AND GIRLS

Camp Fire Boys and Girls is a nonprofit youth development organization that teaches young people the skills of companionship, leadership, and individualism through participation in group activities. Each year, Camp Fire serves 700,000 people with the help of more than 65,000 volunteers throughout the United States.

Through a wide variety of programs, Camp Fire helps boys and girls develop new skills, learn the importance of good citizenship, and make new friends. It also teaches the value of differences among people and respect for individual beliefs.

▶SYMBOLS

The name Camp Fire was chosen originally because the hearth, with its fire, has symbolized the home from early times. "Camp" was added to suggest the outdoors. Camp Fire's watchword is "Wohelo" (from the words *wo*rk, *he*alth, and *lo*ve), and its slogan is

Camp Fire activities include Starflight programs, for the youngest members (wearing red vests), and Discovery programs, for pre-teens (in blue vests).

National Projects Badges

Save the Bluebirds	Salute to Hospitalized Veterans	National Art Competition	Project Good Earth	Project Involvement	Celebrate Camp Fire	Many Cultures
A Gift of Peace	In Pursuit of Peace	Imagine No Hunger	Friendship Across the Ages	Weather Ready	Project Handclasp	Project Contact

"Give Service." All Camp Fire programs are based on the idea of helping others and giving service in the spirit of Wohelo.

Camp Fire members wear uniforms that reflect the agency's colors—red, white, and blue. Wearing uniforms is an important part of being a Camp Fire member. At special times, members wear ceremonial clothing trimmed with the beads and emblems they have earned for their accomplishments throughout their years with Camp Fire.

▶ PROGRAMS

One of Camp Fire's main goals is to help young people feel good about themselves. Self-esteem, self-reliance, and leadership skills are developed through five types of programs: clubs, camping opportunities, before- and after-school child care, youth leadership programs, and specific self-reliance courses that teach individual skills.

Boys and girls can participate in Camp Fire programs from birth (through day care programs) through age 21. These programs are funded by membership dues, fees, contributions, grants, and fund-raising activities. Many groups are formed in neighborhoods and meet in homes. Each group has at least one adult leader and sometimes as many as five.

Many communities offer day and resident camp opportunities, which are supplemented by short-term outdoor experiences, including overnight camping trips. Churches, synagogues, schools, and community centers may offer use of their facilities.

Clubs

There are four Camp Fire club programs for specific age groups. They are Starflight, Adventure, Discovery, and Horizon.

Starflight. Starflight activities are for children in kindergarten through the second grade. Starflight club members are encouraged to play together, to learn about themselves, and to be creative. They also go on supervised field trips to zoos, museums, and other interesting places.

Adventure. Young people in the third, fourth, and fifth grades participate in Adventure Club activities. At this level, members explore five "trails": The Great Outdoors; Creative Living; Helping People; Me, My Family, and Community; and New Knowledge and Skills. Adventurers are allowed to plan many of their own activities and projects according to their particular interests. Once they have completed the activities in any of the five categories, they are rewarded with beads, badges, and emblems for their participation and accomplishments.

Discovery. Students in the sixth, seventh, and eighth grades participate in a variety of programs, including outdoor sports, camping, cooking, and creative arts. They may also work as volunteers for community services. During these adolescent years, Discovery Club members are encouraged to reflect on themselves and on their relationships with members of their family and with their friends. Program activities help them define their social values and develop positive self-images.

Horizon. Students in ninth through twelfth grades take part in activities that will prepare them for adult responsibilities, such as group discussions about parenting and making career choices. They also spend four to six months completing a series of "Reflection" projects that include the "Celebrate Me Reflection," "Choices and Decisions Reflection," "Mapping My Way," and "Making it on My Own." They have a great deal of freedom in developing these projects that are intended to help them develop self-worth, give service, and learn the qualities of leadership.

Camp Fire's highest honor is the Wohelo Medallion. It is given to those Horizon Club members who have successfully completed the four reflection projects, demonstrated a commitment to Camp Fire's ideals, and have given service to their community.

Other Programs. In addition to national projects and programs, local Camp Fire councils also develop programs that help meet the specific needs of their particular communities. Such programs include a camp that helps children cope with the death of a family member; a camp for children with life-threatening illnesses; and a program that teaches young people how to baby-sit for children with disabilities.

▶ HISTORY

Camp Fire Girls was founded in 1909 by Luther Halsey Gulick, M.D., and Charlotte Vetter Gulick at Camp Sebago-Wohelo in Maine. Their goals were to teach young women responsibility and help them develop useful skills.

In 1979 the name Camp Fire Girls was changed to Camp Fire to reflect the inclusion of boys in Camp Fire programs. In 1993 the name was changed to Camp Fire Boys and Girls to emphasize the coeducational aspect of the organization. Today all family members can participate in Camp Fire activities. For more information about Camp Fire, consult your local phone directory or write to Camp Fire Boys and Girls, 4601 Madison Avenue, Kansas City, Missouri, 64112-1278.

Reviewed by KEVIN WORLEY
Camp Fire Boys and Girls

CAMPING

Camping, in a variety of forms, is an important recreational activity. Each year, millions of people turn to the great outdoors for relaxation. Many beautiful places—fine lakes and streams, lush mountain trails, and vast wilderness areas—can be enjoyed only by those who camp.

There are several reasons why camping is so popular. It allows people to explore new surroundings and be close to nature. Camping trips that include hiking, cycling, canoeing, or cross-country skiing provide many opportunities for physical activity. And camping is far less expensive than staying in a hotel or motel.

▶ KINDS OF CAMPING

For many people, camping means sleeping in a tent. Some choose to spend the night in a tent in their own backyards. But for most, camping means packing a tent and some food and belongings in a car and driving to a desired camping destination. Tent campers may pitch their tents at state, provincial, or national parks or at privately run campgrounds.

Other people choose to camp using a recreational vehicle (RV). RV's range in size from small trailers to large mobile homes. These vehicles provide living quarters for campers and carry modern conveniences such as sinks, refrigerators, and toilets.

▶ CAMPING EQUIPMENT

If you plan to camp in a tent, you will need basic equipment such as a tent, bedding, proper clothing, camping tools, food and cooking supplies, and a first aid kit. You should make a list of things you will need and check them off as you include them.

Tents. Tents range from those made of lightweight material to larger, heavier types. Lighter ones are preferred because they are inexpensive and easy to carry. They can be folded to a small size and packed comfortably in a backpack. They are also easy to set up. Heavier ones are generally used when camping in one place for long periods of time. The tent to use is the one that serves best for the kind of camping you plan.

Camping is an enjoyable way to explore new surroundings. *Left:* Experiencing the beauty of nature in an unspoiled, secluded setting is one of the advantages of camping with a tent. *Below:* Recreational vehicles equipped with modern conveniences can be driven directly to a site, allowing campers to enjoy many of the comforts of home.

Bedding. Sleeping in a tent is wonderful if you are warm and comfortable. A good sleeping bag provides insulation from the cold. Many different colors and styles are available to choose from. But you will not be comfortable with just a sleeping bag between your body and the ground. Some campers gather dry leaves, grass, or pine needles and shape them to make the ground more comfortable. A waterproof ground cloth of plastic or rubber is placed over the bedding material to keep the sleeping bag dry. Other campers prefer to use lightweight foam pads or air mattresses for insulation and comfort.

Clothing and Personal Gear. Since your first camping trip will probably be during summer, take clothing that will protect you from the sun, rain, insects, and brush. This means a waterproof, hooded poncho, a sweater or jacket, shorts and long trousers, plus underwear and extra socks. Sturdy shoes worn over wool socks make a good combination.

You will also need toilet articles such as a toothbrush, toothpaste, shampoo, and soap. Other essential items include a hat, sunglasses, sunscreen, compass, maps, and a flashlight. Some campers like to bring a camera and a pair of binoculars. Some like a good book to read on their camping trip.

Campers should always bring waterproof matches, extra batteries, a knife, a small ax, and a lantern. A tool kit is also handy to have.

Cooking Tools and Food. Camp meals can be prepared over an open fire, but many campers prefer to bring along portable propane-fueled cookstoves. Cooking utensils include a frying pan, cooking pots in several sizes, and knives, forks, and spoons. Covered plastic storage containers and a roll of heavy-duty aluminum foil will also come in handy.

Camp meals should be simple but nourishing. Perishable items such as milk and eggs can be kept in a cooler, but if you are spending several days camping, you will need a supply of packaged and canned foods as well. Good food choices include breakfast cereals, pancake mix, peanut butter, canned tuna, rice and pasta, dried fruits, and nuts. Fresh fruits and vegetables will keep for several days. Packaged meals such as macaroni and cheese are convenient and easy to prepare.

First Aid. Good campers know enough about first aid to take care of such things as cuts, blisters, scratches, burns, sunburn, and insect bites. A few simple first aid supplies in your kit are very important. Put the following in a small plastic box: two or three sterile compresses, six adhesive bandages, a small bottle of antiseptic, a small tube of burn ointment, insect repellant, a roll of sterile gauze, adhesive tape, and a needle for removing splinters.

▶ AT THE CAMPSITE

Selecting a Site. Selecting the right campsite is important wherever and however you camp. The RV camper should check park facilities and reserve the necessary parking space in advance. Campsites with showers, toilets, recreational areas, shopping places, and electrical outlets are available. For the large mobile homes, plumbing hookups are possible.

You can find out about campsites from state, provincial, and federal park departments and from Scout and camping organizations. Road maps from gasoline companies and pamphlets from automobile associations list public and privately owned campsites. The reference section in your library is also a good source.

For those who plan to camp by tent, your campsite should be a flat, dry area. The best campsite has open areas with some trees for shade and level ground. The open side of the tent should face away from the direction of possible storms and wind. Remove all stones and sticks from the ground area. Never sweep or rake up the leaves on your campsite except on the spot where your cooking fire is made. The natural ground cover keeps the campsite from getting muddy and also keeps the soil from washing away when rain falls.

It is best to have the openings of the tent covered by mosquito netting so that mosquitoes cannot get through. There should be no gap between the bottom of the tent and the ground. The best protection is to have a floor made of a waterproof fabric that is sewn to the walls of the tent.

Once in a while it rains so hard that water may run under your tent. Usually this happens because the ground slopes into the tent. It may be necessary to stop the water by making a ditch at the uphill edge of your tent and directing the water around the tent to drain downhill. Remember, do not ditch unless necessary; then replace the soil and stamp it down well.

There are times when campers must find emergency shelter. Protection may be found

The irresistible combination of water, sunshine, and picturesque mountain scenery makes this area in the German Alps a popular camping site.

Did you know that . . .

the longest camping journey took just under two years? Most people take a couple of weeks to go camping. Not Harry Coleman and Peggy Larson! This enterprising couple took a Volkswagen Camper and traveled a distance of 143,716 miles. Their trip started on August 20, 1976, and ended on April 20, 1978. The trip, listed as the longest camping journey ever, took the two of them through 113 countries.

under an overhanging rock ledge or a large fallen tree. The leeward side (the side opposite the wind) of a cliff or a large boulder will give protection.

Campfires. A campfire is an enjoyable part of the camping experience. To build a fire, first collect materials to use for tinder, such as dry weeds, bark, or pine needles. You will also need small twigs, larger sticks, and an armful of wood.

With all this material ready, you can lay your fire. The fireplace should be out in the open. Pick the spot and scrape away all leaves and ground cover right down to bare dirt. In rocky country, several flat rocks in a circle can serve as a fireplace.

When the fireplace is ready, lay a small finger-sized stick across a few stones. Put some tinder under the stick and lay a handful of twigs on top. Now add a few larger twigs and light the tinder. Your wood should start to burn quickly. Add larger sticks of wood as the fire burns brighter.

Cooking fires should be kept small. The high flames of a newly started fire may be used to bring liquids to a boil. When the fire burns lower, leaving a bed of hot coals, meat can be broiled and stews can simmer slowly.

Never leave your fire unattended. Have a pail of water nearby in case a sudden gust of wind takes it out of control. Always put out your fire when you leave it or break camp. Put it **dead out** with water, as follows: Spread out the burning sticks. Sprinkle the sticks and hot coals with water. Turn over the burning sticks and sprinkle again. Repeat stirring and sprinkling until there is no heat in the coals. The wet, cool ashes can be scattered when breaking camp. Cover the bare ground around the fire spot with leaves and humus (organic ground material) that were removed before making up your fireplace.

Sanitation. Every campsite becomes a tiny new home or community. You must have the same protection for your health as you do at home—simple sanitary facilities for the disposal of waste food (garbage) and waste water as well as body waste. Public camping areas have these facilities. When making camp in other places, you must be sure to plan for disposal of waste.

Burn all waste such as paper and plastic wrappings. Glass jars and empty tin cans that have been flattened should be put in a plastic

Although portable stoves are often used for cooking, relaxing around a campfire remains a favorite camp activity. Toasting marshmallows adds to the fun.

bag and carried to a trash can. Never bury garbage or other kitchen waste, because animals will dig it up.

Body waste should be disposed in a **latrine**, or toilet. Generally campgrounds have public rest rooms. In backwoods and wilderness areas, you will have to dig your own latrine. Locate it in a secluded area away from your campsite and its water supply. A latrine for overnight camping with several friends may be a hole about 18 inches (46 centimeters) deep and 12 inches (30 centimeters) across. Pile the dirt nearby. Drive a stake in the ground to hold the paper roll. Make a paddle to cover the latrine after each use. Fill the hole with dirt before leaving the campsite. Mound the dirt and stamp it down.

Safety and Camp Etiquette. Safe drinking water is important. Public and private campgrounds typically provide good water supplies. If you are camping in an area that does not have an authorized water source, bring bottled water if possible. If you must take water from a lake or stream, boil it for at least five minutes before using it for cooking or drinking.

Water purification tablets may be purchased from drugstores or camp-equipment suppliers. Two kinds are available: Halazone tablets and tablets containing iodine. Make sure they are fresh.

If you plan to hike on your camping trip, be aware of poisonous plants such as poison sumac, poison oak, and poison ivy. Before you start your hike, tell someone who will not be with you that you are leaving and what your estimated return time will be.

Good campers always leave a clean campsite. In fact, it is hard to tell where a good camper has set up camp. All the holes have been filled and the fireplace is cleaned. Leaves have been scattered back over the ground so that the soil will not wash away in the rain.

▶OTHER KINDS OF CAMPING

Campers do not only travel by car or RV. Today's camper may be a backpacker—a camper whose equipment is carried on the back. Bicyclists and canoeists may be campers as well. In the winter, properly trained campers can enjoy their surroundings.

Backpacking. Backpackers can go to areas in the wilderness that a vehicle cannot reach.

Packing your things for a trip is really quite simple. Be sure your pack is waterproof so that none of your equipment gets wet. A pack is a bag filled with bags. Put extra clothing in one or more plastic bags. Force the air out after putting items in, then seal the bag with a rubber band or wire twist. Toilet articles go into another bag. Food should be packed in plastic bags or containers.

When packing, be sure to place soft, flat items so that they form a cushion against your back. Put items you will need last at the bottom. Heavier items should be near the top. A flashlight and first aid kit should also be included.

For more information on backpacking, see the article HIKING AND BACKPACKING in Volume H.

Bicycle Camping. Bicycle camping allows the camper to travel through wilderness areas over paved roads. Cyclists do not experience the seclusion of the out-of-the-way campsites of the backpacker, but they are immersed in the wilderness for much of their travels.

Bicycle campers cannot wear heavy backpacks while cycling, so they cannot carry as much equipment as other campers. Some equipment and food are stored in handlebar and seat packs, but most equipment is stored in side bags called **panniers**. Since bicycle campers travel on paved roads, they pass through towns and villages and can purchase

Campers do not only travel by car or RV. *Below left:* Backpackers carry their camping gear on their backs. *Below right:* Other campers explore new areas on bicycles.

on a regular basis any food or supplies that may be needed.

Canoeing. Canoeing through the wilderness allows campers to enjoy the stillness of lake paddling as well as the excitement of crashing through high waves in wild white-water rapids. Canoe campers go to areas rich in lakes and rivers so they may paddle for days or weeks, camping nightly on the water's edge.

White-water canoeing requires considerable skill and training. Canoeists must have knowledge of several paddling strokes. Rapids should be well scouted before the canoeist decides to navigate through them. Often rapids are too dangerous, and campers must carry canoes, food, and gear over land until the river can be safely paddled again. Carrying canoes and gear over land is often called **portaging**. Portage trails are found around dangerous rapids and waterfalls, and between lakes unconnected by water routes.

Winter Camping. Safe winter camping requires experience, knowledge, and special skills as well as proper equipment and clothing. Camping during winter is for the experienced camper only.

▶ORGANIZED CAMPING

Another type of camping is known as organized camping. You may have heard these spoken of as summer camps, the majority of which are attended by children. Children's camps are designed to suit children of different needs, tastes, and ages, so there are many different kinds. There are organized camps for boys, for girls, and for boys and girls together. Many are resident camps, where the campers spend from a week to the entire summer. There are some organized camps, known as day camps, in which the campers spend the day and go home each night.

There are also family camps which have facilities and programs for the entire family. Some camps provide dining room services, but in others, families prepare their own meals. Housing may range from cabins to campsites for RV's and tents.

Some organized camps are located in the mountains; some are on rivers, lakes, or seashores. Others are in farm or ranch country. Each of these offers different activities such as hiking and backpacking, sailing, or horseback riding.

Assisted by a counselor, youngsters at a summer camp set out on a canoe trip. Organized camps offer participants a wide variety of activities.

There are camps for children with special physical needs, such as those who are disabled or overweight. But there are also regular camps that accommodate disabled campers, if their disabilities do not prevent them from participating in the camp program.

When looking for a camp, it is important to learn about the purposes of the camp as well as the philosophy of the camp director. Some camps emphasize learning skills, while others focus on group participation in activities.

The American Camping Association publishes *The Parents' Guide to Accredited Camps*. For more information, write to the American Camping Association, Bradford Woods, Martinsville, Indiana 46151.

RUSSELL A. TURNER
National Director of Camping
Boy Scouts of America

Reviewed by BRUCE KAUFSTEIN
Pack and Paddle, Inc., Wilderness Tours

See also BICYCLING; BOATS AND BOATING; BOY SCOUTS; CAMP FIRE BOYS AND GIRLS; CANOEING; FIRST AID; GIRL SCOUTS; HIKING AND BACKPACKING.

CANADA

Canada is the largest country in the Western Hemisphere and the second largest country in the world, after Russia. However, because much of its rugged and barren northland is uninhabitable, Canada is also one of the world's most sparsely settled countries. Approximately 85 percent of its population of 31 million people lives within 180 miles (300 kilometers) of the United States border.

Canada is a self-governing confederation within the British Commonwealth of Nations. Ottawa, Ontario, is the capital city and the seat of the federal government. The country is made up of ten provinces and three territories. The provinces, from east to west, are Newfoundland and Labrador; the three Maritime Provinces—Nova Scotia, New Brunswick, and Prince Edward Island; Quebec; Ontario; the three Prairie Provinces—Manitoba, Saskatchewan, and Alberta; and British Columbia. The

Canada, the second largest country in the world, is a democratic and multicultural society. *Clockwise from top:* Royal Canadian Mounted Police wear ceremonial outfits. The Houses of Parliament, seat of the federal government, are located in Ottawa, Ontario. Caribou furs protect these Inuit children from the cold temperatures of the Northwest Territories. Native peoples make up about 4 percent of Canada's population.

territories, from east to west, are Nunavut, the Northwest Territories, and the Yukon Territory. Nunavut, the newest territory, was established in 1999 for the self-government of Canada's Inuit (formerly known as Eskimo) population.

In 1534, the French, led by Jacques Cartier, became the first Europeans to colonize Canada. The name *kanata*—the Huron-Iroquois word for "village"—appeared in Cartier's diaries at this time. However, the settlers chose to call their home New France.

Soon after the French arrived, British colonists followed, lured by the wealth of the fur trade, forests, and teeming fishing grounds. For the next 200 years, the British and French, each with their own Native Indian allies, fought for dominance of the territory. The dispute was finally settled in favor of the British with their victory in the French and Indian War (1754–63). Nevertheless, many French settlers remained in Canada, where they maintained their own society.

▶ **PEOPLE**

Like the United States, Canada is largely a nation of immigrants. More than 100 different ethnic groups are represented, in addition to various Native populations.

In the distant past, the largest numbers of immigrants came from France and the British Isles, followed later by Germany, Hungary, Italy, the Netherlands, and the United States. Many settled in Ontario, while others were drawn to rich farmlands in the West. Today's immigrants come mainly from Hong Kong, China, India, and the Philippines. Most of the 200,000 newcomers who arrive each year settle in British Columbia, Quebec, and Ontario (particularly in Toronto).

Canada has several distinct societies, each with its own language, religion, culture, and traditions. English Canadians—by far the majority—are found throughout most of inhabited Canada. French Canadians, the second largest group, are mostly concentrated in the province of Quebec, where they are called *Québécois*. Large communities also reside in northern and eastern Ontario; Manitoba; and the Maritime provinces, where they are known as Acadians.

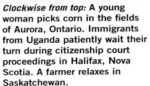

Clockwise from top: A young woman picks corn in the fields of Aurora, Ontario. Immigrants from Uganda patiently wait their turn during citizenship court proceedings in Halifax, Nova Scotia. A farmer relaxes in Saskatchewan.

This article describes the general characteristics of Canada—its people, land, climate, natural resources, economy, major cities, and cultural heritage. For more information on Canada, consult the following articles in this volume:
CANADA, ARMED FORCES OF
CANADA, ART AND ARCHITECTURE OF
CANADA, GOVERNMENT OF
CANADA, HISTORY OF
CANADA, LITERATURE OF
Also consult the individual articles on the provinces and territories in the appropriate volumes.

Eastern Orthodox Christians, Muslims, Buddhists, Hindus, and Sikhs are also represented.

Education

Each province and territory is responsible for the elementary and secondary education of its children. School attendance is compulsory until the age of 16 or 18, depending on the particular province or territory. Schools for Native peoples and for the children of armed forces members serving overseas are funded by the federal government.

Until 1998, Quebec's school system was divided according to religious denomination, and most of the schools were Roman Catholic. Today Quebec's schools are organized by language. About 87 percent of the schools are French speaking and 13 percent are English speaking. The children of most immigrants entering Quebec are required to attend French-language schools, reflecting Quebec's trend toward French Canadian nationalism.

Colleges and Universities. Canada has more than 80 public colleges and universities and 145 community colleges. The larger universities offer a wide range of subjects and grant doctorates as well as master's and bachelor's degrees. Institutions are funded by provincial and federal governments, religious orders, or private sources.

The largest university in Canada is the University of Toronto, which is noted for its medical school. McGill University, in Montreal, is also known for its medical school. The University of New Brunswick, in Fredericton, is known for its forestry and engineering programs. The Université de Montréal is the largest university in French Canada.

Canada's Native peoples, who occupied the land long before history was recorded, make up about 4 percent of today's total population. They are divided into four groups—First Nations peoples (also known as status Indians, which means they are registered with the federal government); Inuit; métis (people of mixed Indian and European ancestry); and non-status (or non-registered) Indians. About 50 percent of the First Nations peoples live on the 2,370 reserves (reservations) in Canada that are set aside for their use only.

Inuit make up about 4 percent of the total Native population. Most live in Nunavut, northern Labrador, northern Quebec, and the Northwest Territories.

Language

In 1969, the Official Languages Act was passed, making both English and French official languages. All government and legal business is conducted in both languages. But approximately 17 percent of all Canadians list neither English nor French as their mother tongue. Among these people, the most commonly spoken languages are Chinese, Italian, and Punjabi.

Religion

Forty-five percent of the Canadian population is Roman Catholic, especially within the French-speaking communities. About 36 percent is of Protestant faith. Many other religions are practiced, particularly in urban areas. Montreal has a large Jewish community.

Canadians enjoy all types of sports, particularly professional ice hockey, which draws fans from around the country.

CANADA is the official name of the country.

LOCATION: Northern North America. **Northernmost land point**—Cape Columbia, on Ellesmere Island. **Southernmost land point**—Middle Island, off Pelee Island in Lake Erie. **Easternmost land point**—Cape Spear, on the island of Newfoundland. **Westernmost land point**—Mount St. Elias, in the Yukon Territory.

AREA: 3,851,809 sq mi (9,976,185 km²).

PHYSICAL FEATURES: Highest point—19,524 ft (5,951 m), Mount Logan, in the Yukon Territory. **Lowest point**—sea level. **Chief rivers**—Mackenzie, Yukon, St. Lawrence, Nelson, North and South Saskatchewan, Peace, Churchill, Fraser, Ottawa, Athabasca, St. John. **Chief lakes**—Superior, Huron, Great Bear, Great Slave, Erie, Winnipeg, Ontario, Athabasca, Reindeer, Winnepegosis, Nipigon, Manitoba, Lake of the Woods. **Chief mountain peaks**—Logan, St. Elias, Lucania, King, Steele, Wood, Vancouver.

POPULATION: 28,846,761 (1996 census).

CAPITAL: Ottawa.

LARGEST CITY: Toronto.

MAJOR LANGUAGES: English, French (both official).

MAJOR RELIGIOUS GROUPS: Christian (Roman Catholic and Protestant), Jewish, Muslim.

GOVERNMENT: Constitutional monarchy. **Head of state**—queen. **Head of government**—prime minister. **Legislature**—Parliament (Senate and House of Commons).

CHIEF PRODUCTS: Agricultural—livestock, dairy products, wheat, tobacco, barley, vegetables, flaxseed, potatoes. **Manufactured**—paper and other wood products, motor vehicles, petroleum refining, slaughtering and meat processing, iron and steel, metal smelting and refining, machinery and equipment. **Mineral**—petroleum and natural gas, nickel, zinc, uranium, platinum, aluminum, lead, asbestos. **Chief exports**—newsprint, wheat, lumber, metals, chemicals, motor vehicles. **Chief imports**—motor vehicle parts, automobiles, machinery, chemicals, crude petroleum.

MONETARY UNIT: Canadian dollar (1 dollar = 100 cents).

NATIONAL HOLIDAY: Canada Day, July 1 (commemorates passing of the British North America Act in 1867).

NATIONAL ANTHEM: "O Canada."

NATIONAL SYMBOL: Maple leaf.

MOTTO: *A Mari usque ad Mare* ("From sea to sea").

Laval University, founded as a religious seminary in Quebec City in 1663, is the oldest French-language university in North America. Other highly notable institutions include York University in Toronto; the University of Waterloo in Ontario; the University of Western Ontario in London; the University of Alberta in Edmonton; and the University of British Columbia in Vancouver.

Libraries and Museums

Canada's many public libraries are organized under provincial law and administered by municipal and regional boards. Also available to the public are numerous school and university libraries as well as special libraries—such as the Library of Parliament and the Canada Institute for Scientific and Technical Information. The National Library of Canada, founded in Ottawa in 1953, specializes in Canadiana—writings by, about, or of interest to Canadians.

Canada has more than 20 public museums. Important collections are held in the National Gallery of Canada, the Canadian Museum of Nature, and the National Museum of Science and Technology, in Ottawa, and in the Canadian Museum of Civilization in Hull,

Quebec. Notable regional museums include Royal Tyrrell Museum in Drumheller, Alberta, which contains the largest collection of dinosaur skeletons in North America, and the Maritime Museum of the Atlantic in Halifax, Nova Scotia, noted for its collections of small boats and ship models.

Sports, Parks, and Recreation

Canadians are enthusiastic sports fans. Ice hockey, which probably began in Kingston, Ontario, in 1855, draws the largest crowds. There are six Canadian teams in the National Hockey League (NHL)—the Vancouver Canucks, Calgary Flames, Edmonton Oilers, Toronto Maple Leafs, Montreal Canadiens, and Ottawa Senators. Furthermore, some half a million amateur players are enrolled in the Canadian Hockey Association. Some of history's most famous hockey players have come from Canada, including Bobby Orr, Gordie Howe, and Wayne Gretzky.

Canada has two professional major league baseball teams, the Toronto Blue Jays and the Montreal Expos. The National Professional Soccer League (an indoor league) has teams in Edmonton and Montreal. The professional Canadian Football League (CFL) is composed of eight teams, divided into Eastern and Western conferences.

Canada's system of national and provincial parks has successfully preserved the country's best recreational land for the benefit of the general public. Some parks, such as Quetico Provincial Park in Ontario, are set aside as wilderness areas, where no development is allowed. Others, developed under government supervision, provide camping and boating facilities. Wildlife is protected throughout the parks system.

Many Canadians enjoy the rugged outdoors. Every summer thousands camp in the country's magnificent forests and swim, sail, and fish in the numerous lakes and rivers and the long stretches of coastal beaches. In the winter many people flock to ski slopes and curling and skating rinks. Cross-country skiing and snowshoeing are becoming increasingly popular.

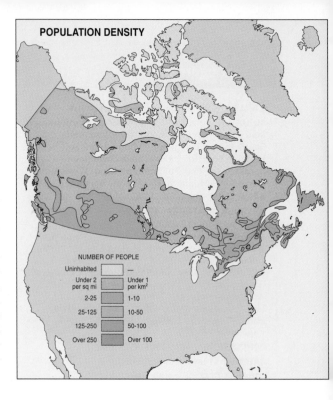

POPULATION DENSITY

NUMBER OF PEOPLE		
Uninhabited	—	
Under 2 per sq mi		Under 1 per km²
2-25		1-10
25-125		10-50
125-250		50-100
Over 250		Over 100

▶ LAND

Canada, which occupies the northern third of the North American continent, covers an area of approximately 3.6 million square miles (9.3 million square kilometers). It is bordered on the south by the United States and four of the Great Lakes, on the east by the Atlantic Ocean, on the west by the Pacific Ocean, and on the north by the Arctic Ocean.

Land Regions

Canada contains eight major landforms. These are the Appalachian Highlands, the Great Lakes–St. Lawrence Lowlands, the Hudson Bay Lowlands, the Canadian Shield, the Interior Plains, the Rocky Mountains, the Pacific Ranges and Lowlands, and the Arctic Islands.

The Appalachian Highlands cover the island of Newfoundland, the Maritime Provinces, and the Gaspé Peninsula of Quebec. Most of the island of Newfoundland consists of low, rugged plateaus. The Avalon Peninsula, in southeastern Newfoundland, has gently rolling land, some of which is suitable for farming.

Large parts of Nova Scotia and New Brunswick have a rough land surface with many hills and valleys. Prince Edward Island has a nearly level land surface covered with fertile farmland. Other good farming areas in the Maritime Provinces lie along the southern shores of Northumberland Strait and in the valley of the St. John River, which flows into the Bay of Fundy.

The coastlines of Newfoundland and the Maritime Provinces are deeply indented with bays and in-

Dairy cows graze in the hills of the Gaspé Peninsula, Quebec. This rolling region is part of the Appalachian Highlands.

lets that provide splendid harbors for fishing fleets. The historic fishing ground known as the Grand Banks lies off the southeastern coast of Newfoundland.

The Great Lakes–St. Lawrence Lowlands, which make up Canada's smallest land region, lie in southern Quebec and Ontario. They are divided by countless small islands called the Thousand Islands. The broad, level plains in the western part of the region, known as the Great Lakes Lowland, is excellent farm country. The valley of the St. Lawrence River in the eastern part is equally good for farming. This region is the most heavily populated and industrialized.

The Hudson Bay Lowlands follow the southern shoreline of Hudson Bay and James Bay. Most of the land is flat and consists of poorly drained bog and swampland.

The Canadian Shield, Canada's largest region, covers about half the country. Its vast expanse of rocks, forests, lakes, and swamps, dating back nearly 4 billion years, is one of the oldest regions on Earth. The Shield extends over most of northern and eastern Canada and encircles Hudson Bay like a jagged horseshoe. Enormous deposits of nickel, zinc, copper, iron, and other minerals are located here. Little of this region is suitable for farming.

The Interior Plains, Canada's major agricultural lands, extend across large parts of the Prairie Provinces and a segment of northeast British Columbia. They are part of the Great Plains of North America. The Interior Plains lie on three different levels, rising like steps toward the west. The eastern plains consist chiefly of broad, sweeping prairies and fertile farmlands. In the southern prairies, where the land is dry, rivers have been dammed to provide irrigation for farms and cattle ranches. In the western prairies the land becomes gently rolling, rising gradually until it merges with the foothills of the Rocky Mountains. Rivers cut through these plains, exposing seams of coal. Rich deposits of crude oil, natural gas, and phosphates also lie beneath the surface.

The Rocky Mountains, which make up a major portion of the North American Cordillera, extend 3,000 miles (4,800 kilometers) from Alaska to Mexico. In Canada they pass through Alberta, British Columbia, and the Yukon and Northwest territories. For more information, see the article ROCKY MOUNTAINS in Volume Q-R.

The Pacific Ranges and Lowlands, the westernmost of Canada's land regions, consist of towering mountain ranges separated by deep valleys and high plateaus. The Coast Mountains, along the Pacific coast of British Co-

FACTS ABOUT CANADA'S PROVINCES AND TERRITORIES

PROVINCE	CAPITAL	AREA			POPULATION		JOINED CANADIAN CONFEDERACY
		sq mi	(km²)	Rank	1996 census	Rank	
Alberta	Edmonton	255,285	(661,188)	4th	2,696,826	4th	Sept. 1, 1905 (with Saskatchewan, as the 8th and 9th provinces)
British Columbia	Victoria	366,255	(948,600)	3rd	3,724,500	3rd	July 20, 1871 (6th province)
Manitoba	Winnipeg	251,000	(650,090)	6th	1,113,898	5th	July 15, 1870 (5th province)
New Brunswick	Fredericton	28,354	(73,436)	8th	738,133	8th	July 1, 1867 (one of the four original provinces)
Newfoundland	St. John's	156,185	(404,517)	7th	551,792	9th	March 31, 1949 (10th province)
Nova Scotia	Halifax	21,425	(55,491)	9th	909,282	7th	July 1, 1867 (one of the four original provinces)
Ontario	Toronto	412,582	(1,068,587)	2nd	10,753,573	1st	July 1, 1867 (one of the four original provinces)
Prince Edward Island	Charlottetown	2,184	(5,657)	10th	134,557	10th	July 1, 1873 (7th province)
Quebec	Quebec City	594,860	(1,540,700)	1st	7,138,795	2nd	July 1, 1867 (one of the four original provinces)
Saskatchewan	Regina	251,700	(651,900)	5th	990,237	6th	Sept. 1, 1905 (with Alberta, as the 8th and 9th provinces)

TERRITORY	SEAT OF TERRITORIAL GOVERNMENT	AREA		POPULATION	JOINED CANADIAN CONFEDERACY
		sq mi	(km²)		
Northwest Territories	Yellowknife	1,304,896	(3,379,684)	64,402	July 15, 1870
Nunavut	Iqaluit	770,000	(2,000,000)	25,000	April 1, 1999
Yukon Territory	Whitehorse	186,299	(482,515)	30,766	June 13, 1898

Above: Wheat grows in vast fields in southwestern Saskatchewan. This area is part of the Interior Plains, Canada's main agricultural region. *Right:* Snowcapped mountains are reflected in the waters of Moraine Lake, located in Banff National Park, Alberta. *Opposite page:* Colorful boats brighten the harbor of Peggy's Cove, in Nova Scotia.

lumbia and the Yukon Territory, contain the highest peaks. Eastward lie the Columbia, Purcell, Selkirk, and Cariboo ranges, as well as the St. Elias, which contains Mount Logan, Canada's highest point.

The western rim of this region is composed of a submerged mountain chain, sometimes referred to as the Insular Mountains. These mountains cover almost all of Vancouver Island and the Queen Charlotte Islands, off the mainland of British Columbia.

The Arctic Islands, or Arctic Archipelago, lie mostly north of the Arctic Circle. The islands cover more than 500,000 square miles (1.3 million square kilometers), or approximately one-seventh of Canada's total land area. The largest islands are Baffin, Ellesmere, Victoria, and Banks. Cape Columbia, on Ellesmere Island, is Canada's northernmost point. It lies about 500 miles (800 kilometers) from the North Pole. Many peaks on Baffin and Ellesmere islands rise above 6,000 feet (1,800 meters). Massive glaciers move slowly down the sides of these mountains to the sea.

Rivers and Lakes

Canada contains one-third of all the fresh water on Earth. Many of its rivers and lakes are linked together in large river systems that drain different areas of the country. Geographers call these areas drainage basins. The most important are the Atlantic, Hudson Bay, Pacific, and Arctic basins.

The Atlantic Basin contains the St. Lawrence River, its tributaries, and the Great Lakes. These waters drain most of southeastern Canada through the Gulf of St. Lawrence into the Atlantic Ocean. Tributaries of the St. Lawrence include the Ottawa, St. Maurice, and Saguenay rivers. Other important rivers in this basin are the Niagara, the Detroit, and the St. Marys. The Niagara River, which connects Lake Erie with Lake Ontario, is the site of the spectacular Niagara Falls. The St. Lawrence Seaway, the world's longest navigable inland waterway, connects the Atlantic Ocean with the Great Lakes. Other important rivers in eastern Canada are the Churchill, which flows across Labrador into the Atlantic Ocean, and the St. John, which flows through New Brunswick into the Bay of Fundy.

The Hudson Bay Basin is drained by the rivers flowing into Hudson Bay and by the lakes that connect the rivers. The basin covers the southern half of the Interior Plains and a large part of the Canadian Shield. The main rivers are the North and South Saskatchewan and the Nelson. Their chief tributaries are the Bow, Oldman, and Red Deer rivers. The Severn and the Churchill flow directly into Hudson Bay. The largest lakes in the system are Winnipeg, Manitoba, and Winnipegosis.

The Pacific Basin is drained by the rivers that begin in the Rockies and the Coast Mountains of British Columbia and flow into the Pacific Ocean. The principal river here is the Fraser. Its chief tributaries are the Nechako, Chilcotin, and Thompson rivers. The Stikine, Skeena, and Nass rivers, as well as many lesser streams, rise in the northern interior of British Columbia.

The Yukon, Canada's second longest river, originates in the Yukon Territory and flows northwestward through Alaska into the Bering Sea. Nevertheless, it is usually considered part of the Pacific Basin.

The Arctic Basin is the most extensive of the four major drainage basins. It contains Canada's longest river, the Mackenzie, which flows for 2,634 miles (4,240 kilometers). The Athabasca, Peace, and Liard rivers—as well as the Great Bear, Great Slave, and Athabasca lakes—are part of the Mackenzie

system. Together these waters drain an area of about 900,000 square miles (2,330,000 square kilometers).

Coastal Waters

Many waters penetrate the coasts of Canada and surround the offshore islands. In addition to these major coastal waters are countless bays, channels, sounds, and other inlets, which give Canada one of the most irregular coastlines in the world. Laid out in a straight line, it would measure nearly 60,000 miles (97,000 kilometers), or more than twice the distance around the world at the equator.

Hudson Bay, the largest of these waters, cuts an enormous part out of the northeastern mainland. Together with James Bay, its southern extension, Hudson Bay covers an area about twice the size of California. The bay is connected with the Atlantic Ocean and the Arctic Ocean.

The Gulf of St. Lawrence is a large inlet of the Atlantic Ocean. It lies at the mouth of the St. Lawrence River and is almost encircled by the Maritime Provinces, the island of Newfoundland, and southeastern Quebec. Northumberland Strait separates Prince Edward Island from Nova Scotia and New Brunswick.

The Bay of Fundy, another large inlet of the Atlantic Ocean, lies between Nova Scotia and New Brunswick. Its tides, probably the highest in the world, sometimes rise to a height of 50 feet (15 meters).

The Inside Passage, in the west, is a natural waterway that runs from Seattle, Washington, along Canada's western coast, to Skagway, Alaska—a distance of about 1,000 miles (1,600 kilometers). The mountainous coastline of British Columbia is indented by hundreds of fiords leading off from the Inside Passage. Juan de Fuca Strait lies between the state of Washington and Vancouver Island.

Climate

Canada, for the most part, is a land of cold winters and moderately warm summers.

In the extreme northern regions, the spring and fall seasons are short and summers are cool. Winters are long and cold, and for five months or more, temperatures drop below

Rain forests flourish in the mild, wet climate of Canada's western coast, including the Queen Charlotte Islands in British Columbia.

0°F (–18°C). Annual snowfall, which covers this land for up to ten months of the year, can range anywhere between 39 to 118 inches (100 to 300 centimeters). North of the Arctic Circle, the sun does not rise for several months during winter, and for several months in the summer, the sun never sets.

In the Maritime Provinces, onshore winds, common only in spring and summer, reach the coast laden with moisture, producing coastal fog and low clouds. In winter, an occasional flow of southeasterly air provides a spell of milder temperatures. In Newfoundland, spring and summer can be quite cool.

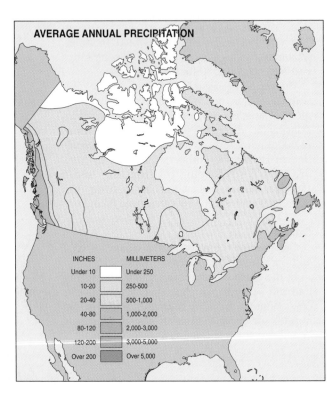

AVERAGE ANNUAL PRECIPITATION

INCHES	MILLIMETERS
Under 10	Under 250
10-20	250-500
20-40	500-1,000
40-80	1,000-2,000
80-120	2,000-3,000
120-200	3,000-5,000
Over 200	Over 5,000

The waters of the Labrador current can hold July temperatures in coastal areas at about 60°F (15°C).

The climate of southern Quebec and Ontario is like that of the northeastern United States. Summers are warm and humid. Winters are relatively cold, with annual snowfall ranging from about 50 to 90 inches (125 to 230 centimeters). The heaviest annual snowfall in eastern Canada—which usually exceeds 150 inches (380 centimeters)—occurs north of the Gulf of St. Lawrence in Quebec and Labrador.

In the deep Interior Plains, winters are much colder and the summers are much hotter than they are on either coast. Snow arrives in the Interior Plains in early November and remains until April. However, some of the heaviest snowfall can occur in early fall and spring. Winter temperatures average about 14°F (–10°C) but can drop as low as –22°F (–30°C); when combined with strong winds, dangerously low windchills can result. Frequently, in southern Alberta, a severe cold wave is broken by a warm wind called a chinook that descends from the Rocky Mountains. As a result, the temperature may rise sharply within the span of one hour. The Prairie Provinces are relatively dry, and southern sections of Alberta and Saskatchewan are partly arid.

The climate on the west coasts of Vancouver Island and British Columbia is the mildest—and the wettest. Rainfall on western Vancouver Island averages more than 100 inches (2,500 millimeters) a year. Henderson Lake on Vancouver Island, which receives an average annual precipitation of 265 inches (6,700 millimeters), is the wettest location in Canada. Along the coast of British Columbia, the average yearly precipitation ranges between 50 and 100 inches (1,200 and 2,500 millimeters). More rain falls in this area in a single winter month than the Prairie Provinces receive during an entire year. Rainfall on the mainland averages more than 60 inches (1,500 millimeters). Very little snow falls along the coast.

Plant Life

Forestlands, which include some 150 native species of trees, dominate Canada's plant life. Along the Pacific coast, ancient coniferous trees are found, such as western red cedar,

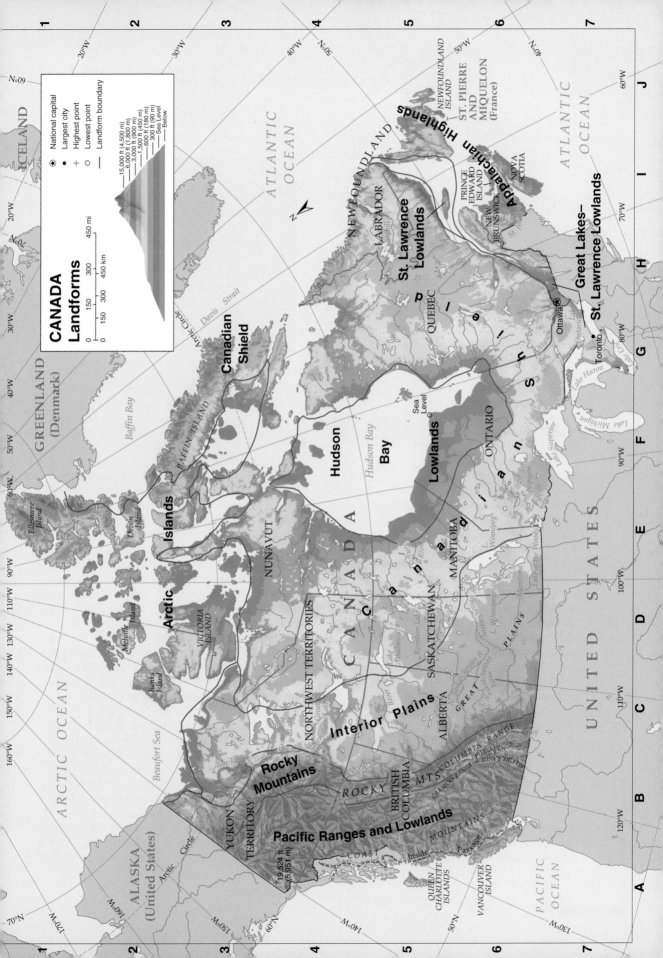

CANADA
Landforms

Legend:
- ⊛ National capital
- • Largest city
- + Highest point
- ○ Lowest point
- — Landform boundary

Elevation scale:
- 15,000 ft (4,500 m)
- 6,000 ft (1,800 m)
- 3,000 ft (900 m)
- 1,500 ft (450 m)
- 600 ft (180 m)
- 300 ft (90 m)
- Sea Level
- Below

Scale:
0 150 300 450 km
0 150 300 450 mi

ARCTIC OCEAN

ALASKA (United States)

YUKON TERRITORY

Pacific Ranges and Lowlands

COAST MOUNTAINS

QUEEN CHARLOTTE ISLANDS

VANCOUVER ISLAND

Inside Passage

Rocky Mountains

ROCKY MTS.

COLUMBIA RANGE

SELKIRK RANGE
PURCELL RANGE
CARIBOO RANGE

BRITISH COLUMBIA

PACIFIC OCEAN

Beaufort Sea

NORTHWEST TERRITORIES

Great Bear Lake

Great Slave Lake

Mackenzie R.

Peace River

Interior Plains

ALBERTA

SASKATCHEWAN

Lake Athabasca

Reindeer Lake

Athabasca R.

N. Saskatchewan R.

S. Saskatchewan R.

GREAT PLAINS

Nelson R.

MANITOBA

L. Winnipeg

L. Winnipegosis
L. Manitoba

Lake of the Woods

Banks Island

Melville Island

VICTORIA ISLAND

Arctic Islands

Canadian Shield

BAFFIN ISLAND

Devon Island

Ellesmere Island

NUNAVUT

Baffin Bay

Davis Strait

Arctic Circle

Hudson Bay

Hudson Bay Lowlands

ONTARIO

Lake Superior

Lake Huron

Lake Nipigon

Lake Michigan

Great Lakes–St. Lawrence Lowlands

Lake Ontario

Lake Erie

Toronto

Ottawa ⊛

Ottawa R.

QUEBEC

LABRADOR

Churchill R.

NEWFOUNDLAND

St. Lawrence Lowlands

St. Lawrence R.

Appalachian Highlands

NEW BRUNSWICK

PRINCE EDWARD ISLAND

NOVA SCOTIA

NEWFOUNDLAND ISLAND

ST. PIERRE AND MIQUELON (France)

ATLANTIC OCEAN

GREENLAND (Denmark)

ICELAND

UNITED STATES

C A N A D A

Sea Level ○

19,524 ft (5,951 m) +

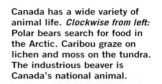

Canada has a wide variety of animal life. *Clockwise from left:* Polar bears search for food in the Arctic. Caribou graze on lichen and moss on the tundra. The industrious beaver is Canada's national animal.

western hemlock, Sitka spruce, and Douglas fir. Inland these forests give way to open grasslands and stands of ponderosa pine. The higher elevations of the Rocky Mountains feature fir and aspen.

The Interior Plains contain the parkland belt, which consists of both trees (mostly aspen) and grasslands. The southern region is covered with short and mixed grasses, whose level of growth depends on available moisture. Elsewhere in the plains region is the Boreal Forest, a major forest zone, containing mainly white and black spruce.

Alpine fir and lodgepole pine are the most abundant trees in the far west. Balsam fir and jack pine are more evident in the eastern interior. Deciduous trees, pine, and spruce are the most common in the Great Lakes–St. Lawrence Lowlands and the eastern coastal regions.

Arctic tundra in the vast northern regions covers approximately one-quarter of the country. The dry climate and frozen ground, called permafrost, prevents tree growth. Vegetation, therefore, consists of mosses, lichen, dwarf bushes, and heather. Some shrubs and lichen grow so slowly that their progress is measured in inches per century.

Some 15 percent of Canada is covered by wetlands—areas of bogs, swamps, and marshes. They are important as a habitat for migrating waterfowl. One of the world's largest wetlands lies south of Hudson Bay.

Animal Life

From the frozen tundra of the Arctic regions to the warm, moist rain forests of coastal British Columbia, Canada is home to an extensive array of mammals, birds, reptiles, and amphibians.

The abundance of Canada's fur-bearing animals provided the incentive for early exploration and settlement by Europeans. Beavers, wolves, lynxes, polar bears, and mink are prized for the warmth and quality of their fur. Seals and walruses are prized for their skins.

The remote, unsettled areas of Canada, as well as the parks and wildlife sanctuaries, abound with wildlife. Deer, moose, black bears, and coyotes can also be found close to towns and cities. Grizzly bears, cougars, and bighorn sheep are found in scattered locations. Herds of caribou and reindeer graze on the lichen and moss that blanket the tundra of the northlands. Buffalo, which once roamed the prairies by the hundreds of thousands, are now protected in Wood Buffalo National Park, in parts of northern Alberta and the Northwest Territories.

Notable fish include walleye, salmon, lake trout, pike, bass, and sturgeon. The most common waterfowl are the mallard, American black duck, and Canada goose. Birds of note include the osprey, bald eagle, and red-winged blackbird.

As in other industrialized nations, Canada's animal population has suffered as a result of urban developments encroaching on their natural habitats.

Natural Resources

Few countries in the world can match the abundance of Canada's natural resources. The most important of these are forests, minerals, soils, fresh water, waterpower, fish, and fur-bearing animals.

Forests. Canada's forests cover about 1.6 million square miles (4.1 million square kilometers)—nearly 50 percent of Canada's land surface and 10 percent of all the world's forestlands.

Although trees are harvested in all provinces and territories, British Columbia supplies half the wood used for wood products. The most valuable tree in these forests is the towering Douglas fir. Softwood trees (such as spruce, pine, fir, and white birch), which supply timber for lumber and pulpwood, grow in a wide belt that stretches across Canada from the Atlantic to the Pacific. Ontario accounts for 25 percent of the country's pulpwood production, followed by Quebec and Alberta.

The forests are valuable in many other ways. They help prevent soil erosion, sustain fish habitats, provide homes for wild animals, and absorb carbon dioxide from the air.

Soils. Only 7 percent of Canada's total land area has soils rich enough for cultiva-

tion. They are found in the fertile river valleys in southern and northeastern British Columbia and the grasslands that stretch from the Great Lakes to the Rocky Mountains. Good soils also exist in the Maritime Provinces along the St. John River valley of New Brunswick, the Annapolis Valley of Nova Scotia, and throughout Prince Edward Island.

Minerals. The largest concentration of Canada's vast mineral wealth lies in the Canadian Shield, where copper, iron ore, gold, zinc, lead, silver, cobalt, titanium, and uranium are mined in quantity. Diamonds are found in the Northwest Territories. Manitoba and Ontario have the world's largest nickel deposits. Saskatchewan and New Brunswick are among the world's leading producers of potash. Quebec's Eastern Townships produce a significant portion of the world's supply of asbestos. The mines of Alberta and British Columbia yield an abundance of coal. Labrador and Quebec are rich in iron ore.

Canada is the world's third largest producer of natural gas, and it is self-sufficient in petroleum. Some 75 percent of the crude petroleum output comes from the Alberta oil wells and the Athabasca tar sands, located along the Athabasca River in northeastern Alberta. Geologists estimate that Alberta's tar sands contain twice the known reserves of

Dams, such as this one on the Kootenay River in British Columbia, have been built on each of Canada's major rivers to harness waterpower. Hydroelectric power provides more than 60 percent of Canada's electrical energy.

Saudi Arabia. However, the process of extracting these oils is expensive.

Waterpower. Many of Canada's rivers and lakes are abundant sources of hydroelectric power, which provides more than 60 percent of the country's electrical energy. Nearly half the total amount is generated in Quebec.

The two largest hydroelectric plants are located in eastern Canada, one on the Churchill River in Labrador and the other on La Grande River in northwestern Quebec near James Bay. Each plant has a capacity exceeding 5,000 megawatts. Other major plants are located on the Manicougan, upper Columbia, Peace, Nelson, St. Lawrence, and Niagara rivers.

▶ **ECONOMY**

In colonial times, fur trapping, fishing, and logging were Canada's primary industries. Today, the service industries make up the largest segment of the economy, followed by manufacturing, construction, and mining.

Services

Service industries account for some 70 percent of the country's gross domestic product, or GDP (the total value of goods and services produced in a year).

Community, business, and personal services, which include tourism, make up the largest and fastest-growing segment of the economy. They account for just over 25 percent of the GDP. Other services contributing to the GDP are finance, insurance, and real estate; wholesale and retail trade; transportation, communication, and utilities; and government, which includes education and health care. Government services once accounted for a significant percentage of total employment, but in recent years the number of jobs in this segment has declined due to cuts in federal and provincial spending.

Manufacturing

Canada's vast natural resources provide the raw materials used to manufacture count-

INDEX TO CANADA POLITICAL MAP

less products. The leading manufactures are transportation equipment—including automobiles, trucks, railroad locomotives, and aircraft—and processed foods, particularly meat and fish products. Other important industries produce chemicals, electrical and electronic equipment, fabricated metal products, wood and paper products, printed materials, and petroleum refining. Approximately 75 percent of Canada's manufactured goods are produced in Ontario and Quebec.

Agriculture and Fisheries

Ninety percent of Canada's produce comes from the Great Lakes–St. Lawrence Lowlands and the Prairie Provinces. Other fertile areas are located in the lowlands of the Maritime Provinces and in the river valleys of British Columbia.

Important grain crops, especially wheat and canola, are grown on the prairies. The wheat belt extends from northeastern British Columbia, through Alberta and southern Saskatchewan and into southwestern Manitoba. Saskatchewan is the leading wheat-producing province. Many grain crops are grown to provide feed for livestock. Irrigated crops, such as alfalfa, sugar beets, potatoes, peas, beans,

and lentils, are produced on the dry fringes of the wheat belt.

Livestock—dairy and beef cattle, sheep, hogs, and poultry—earn more income for the individual Canadian farmer than the sale of grain. The most important dairy-farming areas are in the Great Lakes–St. Lawrence Lowlands and in the lower Fraser River valley of British Columbia. The southern parts of Manitoba, Quebec, Alberta, and Ontario are important hog-producing areas.

The Great Lakes–St. Lawrence Lowlands and the southern interior of British Columbia are the chief fruit- and vegetable-growing centers. Prince Edward Island—known as Canada's garden province—is the country's major potato-growing area.

Two of the world's most productive fishing grounds lie off Canada's East and West coasts. One of these—off the southeastern shores of Newfoundland—is the famous Grand Banks, which has been an important fishing area since the early 1600's. However, overfishing has caused a virtual elimination of cod and a tremendous decline of haddock, pollock, and halibut. The coastal waters off British Columbia and the inlets of the Inside Passage are famous for salmon, halibut, and shellfish. Salmon is the most valuable fish in the Pacific fisheries, but their numbers are also declining due to overfishing as well as the development of hydroelectric power projects along the Columbia River. The decline of the salmon and lobster populations in the Atlantic are also reaching crisis levels. Consequently, aquaculture (fish farming) has become a growing industry.

Canada's inland lakes yield great numbers of freshwater fish—trout, whitefish, walleye, perch, sturgeon, pike, and many others. All together, about 3 billion pounds (1.35 billion kilograms) of fish and shellfish are taken from Canadian coastal and inland waters every year.

Canada has taken steps to protect its fishing industry from foreign competition. In 1976, it established a limit of 200 nautical miles (370 kilometers) off its coasts. Other protective measures are being considered as Canada works toward rebuilding its depleted fish stocks.

Mining

Canada is the world's largest producer of potash and uranium and a major producer of

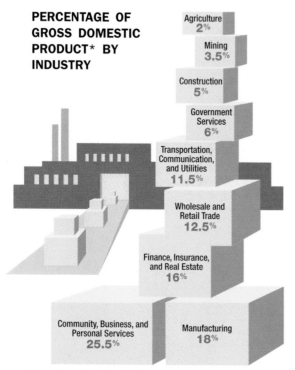

PERCENTAGE OF GROSS DOMESTIC PRODUCT* BY INDUSTRY

Agriculture 2%
Mining 3.5%
Construction 5%
Government Services 6%
Transportation, Communication, and Utilities 11.5%
Wholesale and Retail Trade 12.5%
Finance, Insurance, and Real Estate 16%
Community, Business, and Personal Services 25.5%
Manufacturing 18%

*Gross domestic product is the total value of goods and services produced in a year.

Source: Statistics Canada

Left: Canada controls some of the world's most productive fishing grounds. *Below:* The manufacture of transportation equipment contributes to the strength of the country's economy.

nickel, zinc, sulfur, asbestos, and cadmium. It also ranks as a producer of platinum, cobalt, gold, and lead. Nova Scotia is the leading source of North America's gypsum, used in wallboard manufacture. Coal, mined principally in western Canada, is burned to produce electricity and steel.

Uranium is produced chiefly in northern Saskatchewan. Nearly 25 percent of the world's nickel comes from Ontario and Manitoba. Copper is mined mostly in Ontario, British Columbia, and Quebec. All the asbestos mined in Canada comes from the Eastern Townships of Quebec. There are more than 30 active gold mines, most of them in Ontario and Quebec.

Construction

Construction accounts for approximately 5 percent of the GDP. Large projects, such as the building of roads and highways and the development of oil and gas reserves, have maintained a steady growth. The continuing growth of major cities has also increased the demand for the construction of new housing.

Energy

Canada has a great wealth of energy resources. More than 70 percent of the country's total energy production comes from petroleum and natural gas. Historically, coal was the primary source of energy in Canada. However, its importance has diminished due to developments in nuclear and hydroelectric power.

Foreign Trade

Because Canada has a relatively small population, many of its mineral resources and manufactured products cannot be sold at home but must be exported. And because its primary trading partner is the United States, the strength of the Canadian economy is largely dependent on a strong American economy. In 1994, Canada, the United States, and Mexico officially adopted the North American Free Trade Agreement (NAFTA). This measure has helped strengthen the economies of all three countries by eliminating trade barriers between them, such as taxes on imported goods.

Exports. Exports account for about 28 percent of the GDP. Canada exports mostly raw materials, crops and livestock, and semiprocessed products. Of these exports, some 70 percent goes to the United States and more than 10 percent goes to countries in the Far East. Canada is one of the world's leading exporters of fish and nuclear technology.

Imports. Imports also account for about 28 percent of the GDP. More than 80 percent of the imports come from the United States, primarily in the form of finished, industrial goods.

Transportation

Considering Canada's enormous size and relatively small population, the country's transportation systems are remarkable.

Railways. Canada has two transcontinental railway systems, the Canadian Pacific Railway and the Canadian National Railways. Their chief function is to move freight, particularly manufactured goods and coal, grain, and potash. Passenger service is provided by VIA Rail, which provides service to some 450 communities from coast to coast. There are, in addition, some 50 regional, or short-line, rails that branch out from the main lines. In total, Canada's rail systems form a network covering more than 50,000 miles (80,000 kilometers).

Roadways. Although many places in northern Canada cannot be reached by automobile, there is a wide-ranging network of motor routes in the more settled areas. More than 540,000 miles (870,000 kilometers) of roads stretch from the Atlantic to the Pacific and from southern Ontario to Alaska. The most notable is the Trans-Canada Highway, which extends from St. John's, Newfoundland, to Victoria, British Columbia—a distance of approximately 4,800 miles (7,700 kilometers).

Canada's vast network of roadways continues to be improved and expanded, in part to accommodate the rapid expansion of the trucking industry. Trucks now haul more than half of Canada's transported goods.

Ferries and bridges connect inhabited islands with the Canadian mainland. The Confederation Bridge, opened in 1997, is the longest marine bridge in the world. It extends over 7 miles (11 kilometers) and joins Prince Edward Island to mainland New Brunswick.

Airways. Canada's two major commercial airlines are Air Canada and Canadian Airlines International (CAI). Air Canada provides service between major Canadian cities, the United States, Asia, the Caribbean, and Europe. CAI flies to Japan, China, and other parts of Asia as well as Latin America. Each airline operates regional airlines across the country, providing links to and from smaller communities.

In the far north, bush pilots still carry mail and supplies to fur trappers, geologists, and

A large cargo ship in Vancouver is loaded with wood and wood products for export to other countries. Vancouver is Canada's busiest port.

other isolated workers. Helicopters are used for exploring and mapping.

Ports and Waterways. Every year, more than 100,000 vessels sail in and out of Canada's 300 commercial ports and harbors. Montreal, Halifax, St. John, and Quebec City are the main Atlantic ports. Vancouver, situated on an inlet of the Pacific Ocean, is Canada's busiest port. Another major Pacific port is Prince Rupert.

The St. Lawrence Seaway, connecting the Great Lakes and the Atlantic Ocean, allows oceangoing vessels to enter ports in Toronto, Hamilton, Sault Ste. Marie, and Thunder Bay on the Great Lakes. From April through December when it is ice-free, the seaway makes it possible for these inland ports to engage in direct overseas trade. For more information, see the article SAINT LAWRENCE RIVER AND SEAWAY in Volume S.

Communication

Despite long distances between settled areas, Canadians are closely linked by telephone, computer networks, radio, television, and newspapers.

The Canadian Broadcasting Corporation (CBC) operates two radio networks and two television networks, one of each in English and French. The CBC is a publicly owned national service, responsible to the federal government. There are about 20 CBC TV stations and over 60 CBC radio stations in the country. Approximately 100 commercial television stations and 500 commercial radio stations operate throughout the country. The National Film Board produces documentary films for Canadian television. In the early 1970's, federal legislation was passed requiring that a certain amount of all the material shown on Canadian television and broadcast over the radio should be from Canadian sources exclusively. This ruling about Canadian content has increased opportunities for Canadian writers, producers, and performers.

Some 20 major daily newspapers are published in all the major cities, serving both the English- and French-speaking communities. A number of newspapers also appear in other languages. Toronto alone publishes more than 100 newspapers for various ethnic communities.

▶ **MAJOR CITIES**

Until the beginning of the 1900's, most Canadians lived on farms or in small villages. Today more than 75 percent of the population lives in large towns and cities, mostly located in the fertile and heavily industrialized Great Lakes–St. Lawrence Lowlands.

About half the entire population lives in the country's nine largest metropolitan areas—Toronto, Montreal, Vancouver, Ottawa/Hull, Edmonton, Calgary, Quebec City, Winnipeg, and Hamilton. These cities also attract the largest numbers of immigrants and young people.

Ottawa, the national capital, is located in eastern Ontario. The metropolitan area, which includes the city of Hull across the Ottawa River, is home to more than 1 million people. For more information, see the article on Ottawa in Volume O.

Toronto, with more than 4 million people in its metropolitan area, is Canada's largest city. Situated in southern Ontario, on the northern shore of Lake Ontario, Toronto is Canada's primary center of business and finance. For more information, see the article on Toronto in Volume T.

Montreal, located in Quebec on the St. Lawrence Seaway, was founded by Roman Catholic missionaries in 1642. It is one of the world's largest inland seaports and a major industrial center. More than 3.3 million people reside in the metropolitan area of this predominantly French-speaking city. For more information, see the article on Montreal in Volume M.

Vancouver, on the coast of British Columbia, has a metropolitan population of about 2 million. Its magnificent harbor is the second largest in Canada and one of the busiest on the Pacific coast of North America. For more information, see the article on Vancouver in Volume U-V.

Quebec City, the capital of Quebec, is the unofficial capital of French Canada and a

City lights sparkle in Toronto, Canada's largest metropolitan center. The capital of Ontario, Toronto also serves as a center of commerce and culture.

center of French Canadian culture. For more information, see the article on Quebec City in Volume Q-R.

Also see the articles EDMONTON and WINNIPEG in the appropriate volumes.

▶ CULTURAL HERITAGE

For hundreds of years, Canadian culture was slow to develop, due primarily to an ex-

Above: Dancers from the Royal Winnipeg Ballet rehearse for a production of *Swan Lake*. **Below:** Skillfully carved and painted totem poles are representative of the distinctive art created by Canada's Northwest Coast Indians.

tremely small and scattered population. Furthermore, until the Canadian federation was established in 1867, there existed little sense of a national identity. A distinctly Canadian culture began to emerge in the early 1900's, as more and more immigrants entered the country and advances in telecommunications connected distant populations. Culture was reinforced in 1957 when the federal government established the Canada Council, which provided funds to aid the arts, humanities, and social sciences. In 1978 the council was divided into the Arts Council and the Humanities and Social Sciences Council.

Music

Canada has many organizations dedicated to the musical

arts. Among the nation's major opera companies are the Canadian Opera Company in Toronto, the Vancouver Opera Association, the Edmonton Opera Company, l'Opéra de Montréal, and the Manitoba Opera Association in Winnipeg. There are also several symphony orchestras, including the National Arts Centre in Ottawa and the Toronto Symphony. The Roy Thomson Hall in Toronto is a major center for musical performances. Montreal's cultural center, the Place des Arts, presents concerts, operas, and symphonies.

Some of the most prominent Canadians in the world of music include the conductors Mario Bernardi, Victor Feldbrill, and Nicholas Goldschmidt; bandleader Guy Lombardo; and singers Mary Lou Fallis, Maureen Forrester, and Jon Vickers. Other well-known musicians and composers are Gabrielle Charpentier, Andre Gagnon, Glenn Gould, and Oscar Peterson.

Annual music festivals are held in Winnipeg, Stratford, Vancouver, and Montreal. A group called Les Jeunesses Musicales du Canada presents music to young audiences in Quebec, as does the Festival Concert Society in western Canada. The most prominent choral society is the Toronto Mendelssohn Choir, which tours Canada and overseas.

Canada has a rich collection of traditional British, French, and Native folk songs. Many of Canada's most popular singers have incorporated the Canadian folk tradition into their music. Notable Canadian popular and folk musicians have included Bryan Adams, Leonard Cohen, Celine Dion, k.d. lang, Gordon Lightfoot, Sarah McLachlan, Joni Mitchell, Alanis Morissette, Buffy Sainte-Marie, Shania Twain, and Neil Young.

Art and Architecture

Many significant contributions have been made in the world of Canadian art and architecture. For more information, see the article CANADA, ART AND ARCHITECTURE OF in this volume.

Literature

Canada has a flourishing literary culture. It is home to many fine writers whose names and works are respected worldwide. For more information, see the article CANADA, LITERATURE OF in this volume.

Theater

The National Theatre School, founded in Montreal in 1960, conducts classes in both French and English. Students receive professional training in acting, directing, stage production, and stage design.

Montreal is the major center of French-Canadian theater, including such troupes as Le Théâtre du Nouveau Monde and Le Patriote. The largest centers of English-speaking theater are Montreal, Toronto, and Vancouver. In Toronto, major theatrical groups play in centers such as the Tarragon Theater, the Saint Lawrence Center, the Royal Alexandra Theater, the Hummingbird Center (formerly the O'Keefe Center), and the Young People's Theatre.

In 1953 the now famous Stratford Shakespearean Festival opened in Stratford, Ontario. In 1962 the Shaw Festival opened at Niagara-on-the-Lake, near Niagara Falls, Ontario. It features the plays of the dramatist George Bernard Shaw. Leading Canadian stage actors have included Colleen Dewhurst, Martha Henry, William Hutt, Kate Nelligan, Christopher Plummer, and Kate Reid.

Dance

Canada has seven ballet companies and a national ballet school. The National Ballet of Canada, Canada's largest dance company, makes its home in Toronto but performs throughout the world. Les Grands Ballets Canadiens of Montreal performs both on the stage and on television. The Royal Winnipeg Ballet, founded in 1939, is Canada's oldest dance company.

Film

The National Film Board of Canada, founded in 1939, has an outstanding reputation for both documentary and animated films. Canada has also produced some of the world's most famous actors and filmmakers. Among them are screen stars Hume Cronyn, Michael J. Fox, Anna Paquin, Mary Pickford, Keanu Reeves, William Shatner, and Donald and Kiefer Sutherland; comedians Dan Aykroyd, John Candy, Jim Carrey, Phil Hart-

Demonstrators gathered at the Museum of Civilization, across the Ottawa River from Parliament Hill, to show their support for national unity.

man, Mike Myers, and Martin Short; and directors Denys Accand, James Cameron, David Cronenberg, Atom Egoyan, François Girard, and Norman Jewison.

▶ THE FUTURE

Canada's future world position and economic strength depend in part on the question of national unity. In recent decades, a French Canadian movement in Quebec toward independence has gained momentum, and various Native groups have achieved self-rule. So far, however, the majority of Canadians have rejected the possibility of Quebec becoming its own country.

In the meantime, as new immigrants and Native peoples increase their voices in society, Canada will continue to build upon its diverse cultural mosaic and historic traditions. Natural resources such as forests, gas, oil, and fresh water will continue to nurture a strong economy. Cities will expand to support the growing population. And the increasing demand for computer-based technologies will allow people to live in and interact from smaller towns and rural areas. The growth of technology, communication, and other service industries will undoubtedly help Canada maintain a prominent world position in the 21st century.

GARY T. WHITEFORD
University of New Brunswick

See also articles on individual cities, provinces, and territories in Canada.

CANADA, ARMED FORCES OF

The Canadian Forces (CF) provide a modern, multipurpose military force that can be called to combat anywhere in the world. Their three key roles are to defend Canada; to contribute to the defense of North America; and to promote international peace and stability. At home they help Canadians during times of domestic crisis and assist in handling civil emergencies when requested by the government. International commitments are conducted under the authority of the United Nations, the North Atlantic Treaty Organization (NATO), or other alliances.

Organization. After the confederation of the Canadian provinces in 1867, Canada's central government formally organized the Canadian Army (1871), the Royal Canadian Navy (1910), and the Royal Canadian Air Force (1924). In 1967, these three military branches were combined into one unit called the Canadian Armed Forces. This was done to eliminate costly duplication of effort; to achieve an organization better suited to assisting the United Nations operations; and to simplify the command structure.

Today the Canadian Forces are made up of approximately 60,000 regular and 30,000 reserve personnel. These men and women serve in five operational commands—the Maritime Command (navy), Land Force Command (army), Air Command (air force), Canadian Forces Recruiting/Education/Training, and Canadian Forces Northern Area.

Enlistment and Training. Canadian citizens age 17 and over with at least a tenth grade education may enlist in the regular force as noncommissioned members. Candidates must successfully complete ten weeks of basic training. Officer applicants must have a university degree or be selected for a training plan that allows them to com-

Members of the three branches of the Canadian Forces are pictured in their dress uniforms. *Clockwise from left:* air force, navy, and army.

plete a degree in their first period of service. Under the Regular Officer Training Plan, students receive a university degree from the Royal Military College or another approved Canadian university in exchange for five years of active service.

History. After the British took control of Canada in 1763, the main objective of Canada's military was to assist Great Britain in its wars. Canadians have fought in the American Revolutionary War, the War of 1812, the Northwest Rebellion, the Boer War, World War I, World War II, and the Persian Gulf War.

As a member of the United Nations, Canada sent troops to Korea in 1950. Canadian troops were later committed to peacekeeping operations in many other parts of the world, including Egypt, Israel, Indochina, Kashmir, Zaire (now the Democratic Republic of Congo), and Cyprus.

In the 1950's, in response to the rise of the Soviet Union, Canada and the United States built three radar lines across Canada, including the Distant Early Warning (DEW) line, which crosses the northern mainland of Canada. When these lines were completed, Canada became part of the North American Air Defense Organization (NORAD).

Canada has been a member of the North Atlantic Treaty Organization (NATO) since its establishment in 1950. Canadian vessels have been assigned to NATO. Canada is also responsible for anti-submarine defense of the North West Atlantic Zone.

GEORGE F. G. STANLEY
Formerly, Royal Military College of Canada
Reviewed by Office of Public Affairs
Department of National Defense, Canada

See also NORTH ATLANTIC TREATY ORGANIZATION (NATO).

The oldest artistic traditions in Canada are those of native peoples. *Above:* An Inuit soapstone carving depicts a camp scene with an attacking polar bear. *Left:* The colorful embroidery on this bag is characteristic of the decorative art of native Indian tribes.

CANADA, ART AND ARCHITECTURE OF

The art and architecture of Canada consists of two separate traditions: the art of native peoples, who have lived in the country for thousands of years; and the art of descendants of Europeans, who began arriving about 400 years ago.

▶ NATIVE ART AND ARCHITECTURE

Canada's native peoples—both Indian and Inuit (formerly called Eskimos)—divide into several tribal groups, which differ greatly in language, customs, and environment. As a result, there are many native artistic traditions.

Native American Art. Prehistoric rock carvings and paintings are the earliest surviving examples of native American art. The exact meaning of these simple images is unknown. Later Indian art showed great variety in design and materials. Colorful geometric and floral patterns embroidered on clothing were common to native tribes across Canada. Drums, masks, and other objects used in religious ceremonies or to mark special events also were richly decorated. Among the most dramatic of all Indian art forms were the carved totem poles of the Northwest Coast Indians.

In the 1800's, native Indian art was produced mainly for tourists, but the last half of the 1900's saw a revival of traditional forms such as carving. In addition, new forms emerged among the eastern woodland tribes, such as the Ojibwa and Cree, who began to illustrate their legends in striking paintings. Other Indian artists who do not work in the traditions of native art seek acceptance in the wider artistic world.

Inuit Art. The earliest examples of Inuit art are delicate carvings made from bone, ivory, or antler in the shapes of faces, figures, and birds. Later, traditional art forms were neglected during centuries of producing objects for trade with Europeans. Today, carving in soapstone and ivory as well as newer art forms such as drawing and printmaking show the delicacy, simplicity, and reverence for nature that characterize Inuit art.

Architecture. Traditional native cultures also produced notable buildings. The longhouse of the Iroquois, the tipi (teepee) of the Plains Indians, and the Arctic Inuit's igloo were all well suited to each tribe's particular lifestyle and environment. Today, however, most traditional native dwellings have been replaced by conventional modern houses.

▶ FRENCH COLONIAL PERIOD

Permanent French settlements were founded in Canada in the early 1600's, and Canada

Château Richer, near Quebec City, was built in the late 1600's, during the French colonial period. Its design is based on building traditions imported from Europe.

became a colony of France in 1663. For the next century the art and architecture of the colony was dependent on styles imported from France.

Almost all early artists were French-born clergymen who specialized in religious works. They decorated local churches with paintings and wooden sculpture in the baroque style. By the mid-1700's, merchants in Montreal and Quebec City had grown wealthy enough to purchase works of art, creating a small market for portraits and landscape paintings.

The two most common building types in French Canada were the homestead and the parish church. They were built in the French medieval and baroque styles.

▶ BRITISH COLONIAL PERIOD

After 1760, when Canada became a British colony, the main source for styles in art and architecture shifted from France to England.

While sculpture continued to be mainly decorative works carved in wood, painting underwent several new developments. British officers stationed at forts throughout eastern Canada sought to accurately depict the Canadian landscape in detailed watercolor paintings. More imaginative paintings of nature were produced by immigrant British watercolor artists.

The works of two artists from the mid-1800's are landmarks of Canadian art. Paul Kane traveled across the country recording the lifestyle of Canada's Indians in sketches and paintings. Cornelius Krieghoff is best known for his scenes of life in rural Quebec.

Architecture of the period, especially for public buildings, was greatly influenced by the Georgian style then popular in England. The early 1800's also saw a revival of the medieval Gothic style for both churches and public buildings.

▶ THE NEW NATION

The modern Canadian nation was founded in 1867, and artists were inspired by a new sense of national pride. Landscape artists such as Lucius O'Brien and John Fraser, painting in the romantic style, celebrated the country's dramatic natural features.

A close connection with Europe persisted at the turn of the century. Many of the best painters of the time, including Paul Peel, Robert Harris, and William Brymner, trained in Paris and returned to introduce Canadians to various current styles, such as impressionism and post-impressionism. James Wilson Morrice and Horatio Walker gained wide international reputations.

New sculptural techniques and use of materials such as plaster and bronze allowed artists to portray subjects with greater expression and realism. Quebecois sculptors, including Marc-Aurèle Suzor-Coté and Philippe Hébert, ex-

The Man That Always Rides (1849–55) is one of many Native American portraits by Paul Kane. The artist worked from the sketches he made on journeys through Canada's Native American country, and his paintings form a record of a vanishing culture.

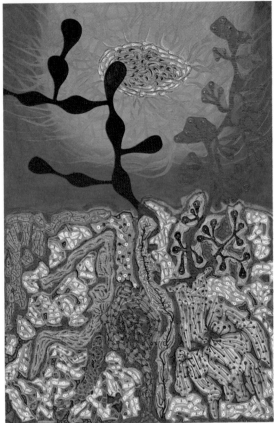

The detailed and brightly colored *Végétaux Marins* (1964), by Alfred Pellan, is a surrealistic rendering of sea vegetation.

The Solemn Land (1921), by J. E. H. MacDonald, conveys the majesty of Canada's rugged northland. Like the other members of the Group of Seven, MacDonald portrayed his country's natural beauty in an effort to create a uniquely Canadian art.

pressed their pride in French Canàdian history by producing public monuments.

In architecture the Gothic revival continued its popularity, along with revivals of other styles of the past.

▶ **THE MODERN ERA**

Painting in the 1920's was dominated by the Toronto-based artists known as the Group of Seven. Dedicated to producing a truly nationalist art, they concentrated on portraying Canada's rugged northern wilderness. Important contributions were also made by Tom Thomson, whose landscapes inspired the Group of Seven; Emily Carr; and David Milne.

In 1939, John Lyman founded the Contemporary Arts Society, which encouraged the development of a modern art. The principles of surrealism were brought to Canada in the 1940's by a group of artists—notably Paul-Emile Borduas and Jean-Paul Riopelle—who came to be called the Automatistes. In the 1950's, Toronto was introduced to abstract expressionism and other modernist styles with the works of Painters Eleven. After 1960, Canadian painters continued to work in a variety of styles. But painting ceased to be as dominant in Canadian art as it was in the past.

Notable sculptors working after 1920 included Albert Laliberté, Suzor-Coté, and Elizabeth Wyn Wood. In the early 1950's the modernist styles of cubism and constructivism appeared in the sculptures of Anne Kahane and Louis Archambault. Great diversity in style, material, and subject marks contemporary Canadian sculpture. Sculptors work in plastic, neon, and fiberglass as well as traditional materials.

Canada's earliest skyscrapers, built in Toronto and Montreal in the 1920's and 1930's, were among the first buildings to display the curved lines and reduced details of art deco, a style that remained popular until World War II. After 1945, many factories, schools, and offices were built in the international style, which uses simple shapes and modern materials such as steel, glass, and concrete. Later, postmodernist designs, which combine elements of past architectural styles, began to appear in major cities.

KEN DEWAR
Education Services, Art Gallery of Ontario

CANADA, GOVERNMENT OF

The government of Canada is a federation, or union, of provinces and territories that were once British and French colonies. Established on July 1, 1867, the federation in some ways is similar to the federal union of the United States. The federal, or central, government of Canada takes care of national business, such as defense, the regulation of trade and commerce, and international relations.

Canada has ten provinces, each with its own popularly elected provincial government. The provinces administer local matters, such as health care, education, roads and highways, and lands and forests. Canada also has three sparsely populated territories—the Yukon Territory, the Northwest Territories, and Nunavut—that are governed by councils whose members are elected by the people. Nunavut, carved from the eastern section of

In 1982, Prime Minister Pierre Trudeau (seated) looked on as Queen Elizabeth II of the United Kingdom signed the Constitution Act. This law gave Canadians the power to amend their own constitution.

the Northwest Territories, was proclaimed Canada's newest territory on April 1, 1999.

▶ THE FEDERAL GOVERNMENT

Canada is a constitutional monarchy with a parliamentary system of government patterned after that of the United Kingdom. It has three separate branches—the executive, the legislative, and the judicial. The seat of the federal government is Parliament Hill in Ottawa, Ontario.

The official head of state is the ruling monarch of the United Kingdom (currently Queen Elizabeth II, who is also Queen of Canada). She is represented by a governor-general, who is the official head of Parliament, Canada's legislative body. The governor-general serves a 5-year term and has very limited powers beyond signing bills into law.

In the parliamentary system of government, the executive branch (the prime minister and the cabinet) and the legislative branch (the parliament, or assembly) are really combined into one body, because members of the cabinet are also members of Parliament. The actual head of the government is the prime minister, who chooses the cabinet ministers from his own political party.

Canada is governed by the political party that wins a majority of parlia-

PRIME MINISTERS OF CANADA SINCE CONFEDERATION (1867)

Date	Name	Political Party
1867–73	Sir John Alexander Macdonald	Conservative
1873–78	Alexander Mackenzie	Liberal
1878–91	Sir John Alexander Macdonald	Conservative
1891–92	Sir John Joseph Caldwell Abbott	Conservative
1892–94	Sir John Sparrow David Thompson	Conservative
1894–96	Sir Mackenzie Bowell	Conservative
1896	Sir Charles Tupper	Conservative
1896–1911	Sir Wilfrid Laurier	Liberal
1911–17	Sir Robert Laird Borden	Conservative
1917–20	Sir Robert Laird Borden	Unionist
1920–21	Arthur Meighen	Unionist
1921–26	William Lyon Mackenzie King	Liberal
1926	Arthur Meighen	Conservative
1926–30	William Lyon Mackenzie King	Liberal
1930–35	Richard Bedford Bennett	Conservative
1935–48	William Lyon Mackenzie King	Liberal
1948–57	Louis Stephen St. Laurent	Liberal
1957–63	John George Diefenbaker	Progressive Conservative*
1963–68	Lester Bowles Pearson	Liberal
1968–79	Pierre Elliott Trudeau	Liberal
1979–80	Charles Joseph Clark	Progressive Conservative
1980–84	Pierre Elliott Trudeau	Liberal
1984	John Napier Turner	Liberal
1984–93	Martin Brian Mulroney	Progressive Conservative
1993	Kim Campbell	Progressive Conservative
1993–	Jean Chrétien	Liberal

*The Conservatives officially became the Progressive Conservatives in 1942.

mentary seats in an election. The leader of the majority party becomes the prime minister. The party with the second largest number of elected seats is called Her Majesty's Loyal Opposition. Canada's two major political parties are the Liberal and the Progressive Conservative parties. Others include the Reform Party, the Bloc Québécois, and the New Democratic Party.

The Cabinet and Parliament

The cabinet system is not written into the Canadian constitution but is part of British parliamentary custom. The cabinet ministers advise the prime minister and run the various governmental departments. The system of government in Canada is often called responsible government, because the cabinet sits in Parliament and is responsible to it. The cabinet holds power only as long as the majority of the House of Commons has confidence in it (that is, votes the same way).

The federal Parliament of Canada is made up of two houses, the Senate (the upper chamber) and the House of Commons (the lower chamber). The Senate has 104 members, who represent entire provinces. The exceptions are those from Quebec, who represent specific districts of that province. Each province has a fixed number of senators, who are appointed by Canada's governor-general on the recommendation of the prime minister. Senators may serve until the age of 75. The senators' powers are limited: They do little more than give advice and make minor changes in bills.

The lower chamber of Parliament is called the House of Commons. Its 301 representatives, called Members of Parliament, or MP's, are directly elected by the voters. Therefore, the House of Commons has much more power than the Senate.

Canada's Constitution

The British North America Act of 1867 provided the framework for the federation. This document, now called the Constitution Act of 1867, could be amended only in the United Kingdom. The Canada Act of 1982, passed by the British Parliament, gave Canada full authority over its constitution.

Revisions to the constitution were laid out in a section called the Constitution Act of 1982. Among them is the Charter of Rights and Freedoms, which guarantees broad rights, such as freedom of speech, freedom of worship, and the right to due process of law. It also lists specific rights, such as the right to an education in either the French or English language. The revised constitution also recognizes the rights of Canada's native population and strengthens the provinces' ownership of their natural resources.

GOVERNORS-GENERAL OF CANADA SINCE CONFEDERATION (1867)

Term Began	Name
1867	Charles Stanley Monck, Viscount Monck
1869	John Young, Baron Lisgar
1872	Frederick Temple Blackwood, Marquess of Dufferin and Ava
1878	John Douglas Sutherland Campbell, Marquess of Lorne
1883	Henry Charles Keith Petty-Fitzmaurice, Marquess of Lansdowne
1888	Frederick Arthur Stanley, Baron Stanley of Preston
1893	John Campbell Hamilton Gordon, Earl of Aberdeen
1898	Gilbert John Elliot, Earl of Minto
1904	Albert Henry George Grey, Earl Grey
1911	H. R. H. Arthur William Patrick Albert, Duke of Connaught
1916	Victor Christian William Cavendish, Duke of Devonshire
1921	Julian Hedworth George Byng, Viscount Byng of Vimy
1926	Freeman Freeman-Thomas, Viscount Willingdon of Ratton
1931	Vere Brabazon Ponsonby, Earl of Bessborough
1935	John Buchan, Baron Tweedsmuir
1940	Alexander Augustus Frederick William Alfred George Cambridge, Earl of Athlone
1946	Harold Rupert Leofric George Alexander, Viscount Alexander of Tunis
1952	Vincent Massey
1959	Georges Philias Vanier
1967	(Daniel) Roland Michener
1974	Jules Léger
1979	Edward Richard Schreyer
1984	Jeanne Mathilde Sauvé
1990	Ramon Hnatyshyn
1994	Roméo LeBlanc
1999	Adrienne Clarkson

Sir John A. Macdonald

Alexander Mackenzie

Sir Wilfrid Laurier

Sir John Alexander Macdonald (1815–91), a Conservative (served 1867–73), was the first prime minister of Canada. See the biography MACDONALD, SIR JOHN A. in Volume M.

Alexander Mackenzie (1822–92), a Liberal (served 1873–78), was born in Logierait, Scotland. Mackenzie immigrated to Upper Canada in 1842. He edited a Liberal newspaper, the *Lambton Shield* (1852–54), and served in the provincial legislature. In 1867, Mackenzie won a seat in the House of Commons and soon became leader of the Liberal Party. In 1873, following a scandal in Sir John A. Macdonald's administration, Mackenzie was chosen prime minister. He also named himself minister of public works. Mackenzie's popularity suffered, partly due to the economic depression of 1874–78 and his failure to negotiate an acceptable trade policy with the United States. The Liberals were defeated in the 1878 elections. Mackenzie remained as party leader until 1880 and kept his seat in Parliament until his death.

Sir John Joseph Caldwell Abbott (1821–93), a Conservative (served 1891–92), was born in St. Andrews, Quebec. Abbott served as dean of the Faculty of Law at McGill University for 25 years (1855–80). His political career began in 1857 with his election to the legislature of the province of Canada, where he served until the Dominion of Canada was formed in 1867. After confederation, Abbott served in the Canadian House of Commons (1867–74; 1880–87) and was appointed to the Senate in 1887. Four years later, in the summer of 1891, he was chosen prime minister, following the death of Sir John Macdonald. Because of ill health, Abbott was forced to resign his position in November 1892.

Sir John Sparrow David Thompson (1844–94), a Conservative (served 1892–94), was born in Halifax, Nova Scotia. Thompson served as attorney general and premier (1882) of Nova Scotia and sat on the provincial supreme court (1882–85). In 1885 he was elected to the Canadian House of Commons, serving as minister of justice (1885–91) under Prime Ministers John A. Macdonald and John J. C. Abbott. Thompson succeeded Abbott as prime minister in 1892. A skilled diplomat, he successfully negotiated fishing rights for Great Britain in the Bering Sea. He died suddenly at Windsor Castle on a visit to meet Queen Victoria.

Sir Mackenzie Bowell (1823–1917), a Conservative (served 1894–96), was born in Rickinghall, England. He immigrated to Upper Canada at the age of 10, became a printer's apprentice, and rose to owner and editor of the Belleville *Intelligencer*. Elected to the House of Commons in 1867, Bowell became a senator in 1892 and served as minister of customs and trade. In 1894 he was chosen prime minister, following the death of John S. D. Thompson, but he proved unable to provide strong party leadership. The resignations of several of his cabinet ministers persuaded him to give up his office in 1896. Bowell continued to serve in the Senate until 1906. He was one of only two Canadians to serve as a senator and prime minister at the same time.

Sir Charles Tupper (1821–1915), a Conservative (served 1896), was born in Amherst, Nova Scotia. He was active in provincial politics, serving in the legislature and as premier. In 1867 he became one of the "Fathers of Confederation," who helped establish the Dominion of Canada. Tupper was elected to the House of Commons and served in several cabinet posts under Prime Minister John A. Macdonald. As minister of railways and canals, he helped bring about the completion of the Canadian Pacific Railway. He was chosen to replace Bowell as prime minister, but he held the office less than two months, having failed to unite the Conservative Party.

Sir Wilfrid Laurier (1841–1919), a Liberal (served 1896–1911), was Canada's first French-speaking prime minister. See the biography LAURIER, SIR WILFRID in Volume L.

Sir Robert Laird Borden (1854–1937), a Conservative (served 1911–20), was born in Grand Pré, Nova Scotia. Borden achieved early success as a lawyer. In 1896 he ran for election to Parliament and won, and in 1901 he became the leader of the Conservative Party. He became prime minister in 1911. Borden led Canada through World War I (1914–18). He insisted that Canadian soldiers fight in their own units and that Canada participate in war decisions with Britain. He formed the Union Party in 1917.

Amendments to the constitution must be approved by the federal Parliament and by any seven of the provinces that together contain at least half of Canada's total population.

Election Procedures

General elections, in which all eligible Canadians over 18 years of age can vote, are held every five years. A change of government occurs in one of two ways. The first is when a government loses its majority support in a general election. The second is when a government is defeated by a vote of "no confidence" in the House of Commons, meaning that the majority of elected representatives no longer supports the govern-

Sir Robert Borden

William Lyon Mackenzie King

Louis Saint Laurent

Brian Mulroney

Arthur Meighen (1874–1960), a Conservative (served 1920–21; 1926), was born in Anderson, Ontario. First elected to the House of Commons from Manitoba in 1911, he was named secretary of state, minister of mines, and minister of the interior in 1917. Meighen succeeded Robert Borden as prime minister in 1920, serving little more than one year before his Unionist party was defeated in a general election. Meighen returned to power briefly in 1926 as a Conservative, until a new election brought his defeat. In 1932, Prime Minister Bennett appointed Meighen to the Senate, where he served as Conservative leader until 1935, and again briefly in 1941. He retired from politics in 1942.

William Lyon Mackenzie King (1874–1950), a Liberal (served 1921–25; 1925–26; 1926–30; 1935–48), served the most terms as prime minister. See the biography KING, WILLIAM LYON MACKENZIE in Volume J-K.

Richard Bedford Bennett (1870–1947), a Conservative (served 1930–35), was born near Hopewell Cape, New Brunswick. In 1898 he entered politics and served in the provincial legislature. In 1911 he was elected to the House of Commons from Calgary East. He served as minister of justice and attorney general (1921), minister of finance (1926), and leader of the Conservative Party (1927–38). When the Conservatives won the general election of 1930, Bennett became prime minister. The Conservatives lost support due to the hardships of the Great Depression and were defeated in the 1935 elections. Bennett retired from Parliament three years later and moved to England.

Louis Stephen Saint Laurent (1882–1973), a Liberal (served 1948–57), was born in Compton, Quebec. A constitutional lawyer, he served as president of the Canadian Bar Association (1930–32) and was appointed minister of justice in 1941. In 1946 he was named minister of external affairs. He became prime minister in 1948, following the resignation of William Lyon Mackenzie King. Saint Laurent negotiated the entry of Newfoundland into Canada as the tenth province.

John George Diefenbaker (1895–1979), a Progressive Conservative (served 1957–63), was the first member of the Progressive Conservative Party to become prime minister. See the biography DIEFENBAKER, JOHN GEORGE in Volume D.

Lester Bowles Pearson (1897–1972), a Liberal (served 1963–68), was a former chairman of the council of NATO (North Atlantic Treaty Organization) and president of the General Assembly of the United Nations. He won the Nobel Peace Prize in 1957 for his help negotiating the Suez Crisis. See the biography PEARSON, LESTER B. in Volume P.

Pierre Elliott Trudeau (1919–2000), a Liberal (served 1968–79; 1980–84), is best remembered for negotiating the Constitution Act of 1982. See the biography TRUDEAU, PIERRE ELLIOTT in Volume T.

Charles Joseph Clark (1939–), a Progressive Conservative (served 1979–80), was the youngest prime minister in Canadian history. See the biography CLARK, CHARLES JOSEPH in this volume.

John Napier Turner (1929–), a Liberal (served 1984), briefly stepped in as prime minister after the resignation of Prime Minister Trudeau. See the biography TURNER, JOHN NAPIER in Volume T.

(Martin) Brian Mulroney (1939–), a Progressive Conservative (served 1984–93), became prime minister after his party won the largest landslide victory in Canadian history. See the biography MULRONEY, MARTIN BRIAN in Volume M.

Kim Campbell (1947–), a Progressive Conservative (served 1993), was the first woman to serve as prime minister of Canada. See the article CAMPBELL, KIM in this volume.

Jean Chrétien (1934–), a Liberal (served 1993–), became prime minister when the Liberal Party was returned to power. See the biography CHRÉTIEN, JEAN in this volume.

ment's policies. After a vote of no confidence, an election may be held before the five-year period has expired to allow the voters to choose a new government.

▶ **PROVINCIAL GOVERNMENTS**

Canada's provincial legislatures (parliaments) work much like the federal Parliament, but each province has only one legislative body (unicameral legislature), which is similar to the House of Commons. Provincial legislatures are elected at least every five years.

Each province has a legislative assembly, headed by a premier. (In Quebec the legislative assembly is called the National Assembly and is headed by a prime minister. In Newfoundland the legislative assembly is called the House of Assembly.) Legislative assemblies make the laws concerning health care, education, property rights, direct taxation, civil rights, administration of justice and civil laws, and municipal affairs. Every province also has a lieutenant governor, who is appointed by the federal government to serve as the Queen's representative.

An enthusiastic crowd greets Jean Chrétien, the head of the Liberal Party and prime minister of Canada since 1993.

▶ MUNICIPAL GOVERNMENTS

Each municipality (county, township, parish, or district) is usually governed by an elected municipal council and a mayor (or reeve). Municipalities control their own civil services, such as fire and police departments.

▶ THE COURTS

The judicial branch of government is separate from the executive and legislative branches. All judges in Canada are appointed, either by the federal government or by the provincial governments.

Criminal laws, or laws concerning crimes that affect people, can be made only by the federal Parliament. These laws apply to all Canadians. Civil laws, or laws concerning such

matters as debts and land ownership, are made by the provincial legislatures. Therefore, different provinces may have different civil laws. The province of Quebec, for example, follows French civil law, while other provinces follow British civil law, which is quite different.

The most important court in Canada is the federal Supreme Court, established in 1875. It is the final court of appeals in both civil and criminal cases. It also decides disputes between the federal and provincial governments. One chief justice and eight associate justices preside over the Supreme Court.

Each province has its own supreme court, which hears important cases or appeals from lower courts. Below these supreme courts are the division courts, which try only civil cases, and the circuit (or district) courts, which can try less important criminal or civil cases within their district.

At the bottom of this court system are the magistrates, or justices of the peace, who hear minor cases.

▶ LAW ENFORCEMENT

Most cities and larger towns have their own police force to keep law and order within the boundaries of their municipality. Small villages may have only one police officer (or constable). However, the police departments in cities such as Montreal and Toronto employ thousands of men and women, including experts in special fields, such as crime detection.

The famous Mounties—the Royal Canadian Mounted Police—are employed by the federal government. They work in all parts of Canada. The Mounties also enforce provincial laws, except in Ontario and Quebec, which have their own provincial police. The Mounties even enforce municipal laws in towns that are too small to have their own police force.

JOHN S. MOIR
University of Toronto
Reviewed by RODNEY H. COOPER
University of New Brunswick

See also PARLIAMENTS; PRIME MINISTER; SUPREME COURT OF CANADA.

While searching for a northwest sea passage to Asia in 1534, Jacques Cartier discovered Canada's Gulf of St. Lawrence and claimed all of the surrounding territory for France.

CANADA, HISTORY OF

When the glaciers retreated at the end of the last Ice Age, about 25,000 B.C., Indians and Eskimos (Inuit) gradually made their way across the land bridge that once connected Asia and North America (where the Bering Strait now separates the Russian Federation from Alaska).

Europeans did not voyage to the North American continent until the 1000's A.D. About the year 1000 the Viking Leif Ericson came across the Atlantic Ocean and probably landed at L'Anse aux Meadows in what is now northern Newfoundland. Another 500 years passed before any permanent European settlements were made in Canada.

In 1497, Giovanni Caboto (John Cabot), an Italian explorer, set out in an English ship, the *Matthew*, to find a western route to Asia. Instead he discovered a "New Found Land," teeming with fish. Cabot had stumbled on the great cod fisheries of the Grand Banks off Newfoundland.

Throughout the 1500's, fishermen from England, France, Spain, and Portugal ventured in ever-growing numbers to fish in Newfoundland's waters. The French and English set up permanent bases on shore. They salted and dried the cod so it would not spoil on the voyage to Europe. French fishing stations spread out toward the Gulf of St. Lawrence. The English tended to remain in eastern Newfoundland. Sir Humphrey Gilbert, an English explorer, formally claimed that territory for England in 1583.

Trading with the local native peoples developed at the fishing stations. In exchange for pots, axes, knives, and other implements, the natives offered various furs, particularly beaver pelts. Soon shiploads of beaver skins were bound for Europe. As the fur trade developed in the New World, it spread westward, eventually reaching both the Arctic and the Pacific coasts.

▶ NEW FRANCE

On his first trip to the New World in 1534, the French explorer Jacques Cartier reached the Gulf of St. Lawrence and claimed the surrounding territory for France. The name Canada first appeared in a narrative Cartier wrote to record his discoveries. The word came from a Huron-Iroquois Indian word, *kanata*, meaning village or community.

On his second trip to Canada, in 1535, Cartier sailed up the St. Lawrence River in what is thought to be the first interior exploration of the river. He was stopped by rapids just west of the present city of Montreal. The mighty St. Lawrence led to the Great Lakes and the heartland of America. Cartier's achievement claimed for France one of the main gateways to the North American continent.

Before 1600 the fur trade was already flourishing at Tadoussac, a trading post on the lower St. Lawrence. The king of France offered generous fur trading privileges to anyone who would settle a permanent colony.

Samuel de Champlain made his first voyage to "New France" in 1603. His explorations led to the settlement of Port Royal in Acadia (now Annapolis Royal, Nova Scotia) off the Bay of Fundy. Champlain soon realized that Port Royal was poorly situated for controlling the rich fur trade along the St. Lawrence. In 1608 he founded Quebec on that river. It soon became the hub of the fur trade and the heart of New France. By 1615, Champlain had pushed westward and explored the Ottawa River, Lake Ontario, and Georgian Bay in Lake Huron. He sent men into the wilderness to live and trade among the native peoples. These adventurers helped build friendly relationships with the Huron and Algonkin, two Native American tribes.

The Iroquois Almost Destroy New France

The Quebec settlement grew slowly, and when Champlain died in 1635, it had fewer than 200 inhabitants. Catholic missionaries saw the colony as a center for spreading Christianity among the native peoples, and in 1642, Montreal was established as an Indian mission. Jesuits braved the wilds as far as the Great Lakes to convert the natives to their religion.

At that time the Five (later Six) Nations of the Iroquois were the most powerful tribes in the territory. The Iroquois were involved in the fur trade, dealing with the Dutch in the Hudson Valley (now in New York State). This pitted the Iroquois and the Dutch against the Hurons and the French in the race to gain control of the best furs. In 1648 the Iroquois began to attack their rivals, and for two years the frontier was aflame as Iroquois slaughtered Hurons, destroyed mission villages, and murdered Jesuits.

Once they had crushed the Hurons, the Iroquois turned on the French, raiding Montreal and farms near Quebec. The colonists sent desperate pleas for help to France.

New France Builds an Inland Empire

By 1660, France was the most powerful nation in Europe. After winning a series of wars on the European continent, King Louis XIV was able to turn his attention to the problems of his colonies and rebuild his overseas empire. In 1663 he made New France a province of France and appointed a royal governor and an *intendant* (business manager) to oversee provincial affairs. Troops were sent to subdue the Iroquois. Settlers then flocked to farms in *seigneuries.* These were large tracts of land along the St. Lawrence granted by the king to *seigneurs* (landlords), who rented portions out to *habitants* (settlers). By 1672 more than 6,000 people lived in the St. Lawrence colony. An era of peace, plenty, and expansion had begun.

The fishing industry boomed. The fur trade, nearly wiped out during the Iroquois War, enjoyed a healthy revival and again expanded westward. French explorers and traders pushed beyond the Great Lakes. To the southwest Father Jacques Marquette and Louis Jolliet explored the Mississippi River, traveling as far south as the Arkansas River. Robert Cavelier, the Sieur de la Salle, opened the Ohio and Illinois country and then went on to find the mouth of the Mississippi River in 1682. New western posts arose, such as Fort Frontenac (now called Kingston) and Niagara. By 1700 the French had built a mighty inland empire, stretching from Quebec to the Gulf of Mexico.

In the 1600's the French and British competed for Canada's fish and furs. The French built inland trading posts along the rivers and Great Lakes, whereas the British tended to settle along the seacoasts where they could use their navy to protect their interests.

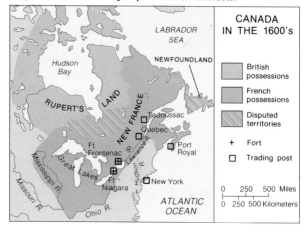

On September 13, 1759, Quebec fell to the British after an attack led by General James Wolfe. Both Wolfe and his French rival, General Montcalm, were fatally wounded.

Struggle with the English for Supremacy

The expansion of New France brought further conflict. The Iroquois again unleashed their anger toward the French settlers and in 1689 destroyed the little village of Lachine, near Montreal. (This began a series of French and Indian wars that were to continue occasionally for nearly 100 years.) But more important, the Iroquois made an alliance with the English, who had taken New York and the Hudson Valley from the Dutch.

Across North America, English and French interests were locked in a grim rivalry for the future of the continent. In the far north the English followed the route to Hudson Bay, which Henry Hudson had sailed in 1609. By 1670 the Hudson's Bay Company was established, and the French fur traders began to feel the competition of this active rival. English and French fishermen clashed in the Newfoundland and Acadian fishing grounds, regions claimed by the English. To the south, British colonists traded in the vast territories west of the Appalachian Mountains, which the French considered their own.

Early in 1689 the rivalry between the English and the French broke into open warfare both in Europe and in North America. In North America the French and their Indian allies made war on the English and their allies, the Iroquois. The war extended from Hudson Bay, where the French and English fur traders fought for control, down to the frontiers of New England and New York.

In 1701 the War of the Spanish Succession erupted in Europe. Called Queen Anne's War in the colonies, it dragged on for a dozen years until France reached a compromise with England in 1713 and Austria in 1714. The French were allowed to place Philip of Anjou, the grandson of King Louis XIV, on the Spanish throne in exchange for colonial territory. France gave to England the mainland of Acadia (renamed Nova Scotia, or "New Scotland"), most of Newfoundland, and the Hudson Bay territory (Rupert's Land).

In the years following the war, New France's growth was dangerously slow compared to that of the English colonies in North America. In spite of all the bloodshed in the past, France and Britain still had not yet settled their rivalry for supremacy in the New World. The final struggle took place in the 1750's with the French and Indian War, which was connected to the Seven Years' War in Europe (1756–63). The French fought bravely and skillfully, but the British had far greater resources. In 1758 several French forts fell to the British. In 1759 the British Army under General James Wolfe attacked the main French stronghold of Quebec. In September the British won the Battle of Quebec; the next year the remaining French forces surrendered at Montreal. By the Treaty of Paris (1763), New France was handed over to the British. British dominance was now assured in that vast region.

▶ BRITISH CANADA

In 1763 the French colony on the St. Lawrence was reorganized as the British province of Quebec, but life for its 60,000 French inhabitants stayed much the same on their seigneurial farms. Most English settlers never went north to Quebec. They preferred to go west rather than live among their recent enemies. Eventually, a British-appointed governor, Sir Guy Carleton, recognized the French character of Quebec and persuaded the British Parliament to grant the French people of Quebec certain rights to pursue their own legal and religious customs. The Quebec Act of 1774 made these rights official.

Canada and the American Revolutionary War

The Quebec Act angered the British merchants in Montreal even though it added to Quebec the lands westward to the Ohio and Mississippi rivers, where they did much of their fur trading. Resentment also spread to the 13 original British colonies. The American colonists now saw the west, land that they planned to settle, as part of a French-speaking Catholic province under the French law and land systems. American colonists listed the Quebec Act among the Intolerable Acts, which ignited the Revolutionary War in America. Early in that war, Americans tried to take the city of Quebec, but Carleton successfully defended the city in the winter of 1775. British sea power prevented further American attacks.

Factors other than the presence of the British Royal Navy kept Canadians out of the Revolutionary War. Canadians in Newfoundland and Hudson Bay were too far away from the fighting to get involved in it. French Canadians in Quebec stayed quiet largely because of the Quebec Act, which the Americans had loudly criticized for favoring the French and the Catholics. Catholic French Canadians were not attracted to the possibility of being absorbed into a large Protestant, English-speaking republic. By the time the war ended in 1781, the Canadian colonists were firmly on the side of the British.

Britain finally recognized the independence of the United States in 1783. Some 40,000 loyalists—American colonists who had remained loyal to the king of England during the Revolution—fled to Canada. About 30,000 of them took the sea route to Nova Scotia. So many of them moved to the open lands across the Bay of Fundy, near St. John, that a separate province, New Brunswick, was set up in 1784. The remaining 10,000 fleeing loyalists marched overland to Quebec province. They settled around Lake Ontario, near Niagara, and on the upper St. Lawrence, beyond the French-occupied areas. In 1791 this influx brought on the division of the St. Lawrence Valley into two separate provinces (accomplished by the Constitution Act of 1791). To the west was English-speaking Upper Canada, later to become Ontario, with the English law and land system its settlers desired. In the east was Lower Canada, mainly French in language and tradition, with its French laws and the rights granted by the Quebec Act.

Age of Prosperity

By 1800 the British colonies in North America consisted of Upper and Lower Canada, the three coastal, or Maritime, provinces (Nova Scotia, New Brunswick, and Prince Edward Island), and Newfoundland. To the west stretched a vast, untamed territory known simply as the Northwest.

The colonies were thriving, especially Upper Canada, where most of its 90,000 inhabitants were engaged in wheat farming. Lumbering prospered in the Ottawa Valley, New Brunswick, and Nova Scotia; farming flourished on Prince Edward Island; and fishing was the mainstay of Newfoundland and Nova Scotia. Schooners built in Nova Scotia sailed the seas to trade in foreign ports. They carried dried codfish, tanned hides, and other products to exchange for rum, molasses, and sugar.

In the broad land northwest of the Great Lakes, the fur trade ruled supreme. Since the 1780's the leading Montreal fur merchants had pooled their interests in the North West Company to carry on an inland trade. The members of this St. Lawrence company—Nor'Westers, as they were called—competed for western furs with the older Hudson's Bay Company.

In 1789, Nor'Wester Alexander Mackenzie went down the river that bears his name to the Arctic. Four years later he traveled by way of the Peace and Fraser rivers to the Pacific. Mackenzie, Simon Fraser, and David Thompson explored much of the western half of British North America in the service of the North West Company. The Hudson's Bay Company also began an aggressive westward advance.

There was fierce competition between the two fur companies until 1821, when they merged under the name Hudson's Bay Company.

When the War of 1812 broke out between the United States and Britain, American forces tried to invade Canada. They were stopped by a few regiments of British regulars, helped by a combination of loyalists, French-Canadian soldiers, fur traders, and Indians. Many Americans who had settled in Upper Canada fought against their former country. They felt that their own lands and properties were in danger. They were Americans no longer—they were Canadians.

▶ SELF-GOVERNMENT AND CONFEDERATION

From 1815 to 1850, almost 1 million immigrants arrived from Britain to settle in the Canadian colonies. Together with the great migration came an upsurge in wheat production and in the lumber industry. Steamships regularly traveled the rivers and lakes. Canals were dug to improve the St. Lawrence waterways. On the Atlantic coast the Maritime provinces enjoyed tremendous prosperity as the days of the sailing ships reached their highest point. Some of the world's finest clipper ships were launched from the New Brunswick shipyards.

However, the rapid growth of the country brought with it many problems. Now that the colonies were doing well, the people demanded more say in the government. These demands became so insistent that two brief rebellions erupted during 1837 in Upper and Lower Canada.

Fearing another revolutionary war, the British sent John George Lambton, the first earl of Durham, with orders to investigate the causes of the discontent. In 1839, Lord Durham's report recommended that the colonists be given control over their own affairs. He also recommended that Upper and Lower Canada be reunited into one province, which was accomplished by the Act of Union of 1840. It took nearly ten years until responsible self-government was fully established. This was achieved largely through the work of political leaders of the Reform and Liberal parties such as Robert Baldwin and Louis Lafontaine in the new province of Canada and Joseph Howe in Nova Scotia.

The 1850's were marked by another era of prosperity. New avenues of trade were opened by the Reciprocity Treaty of 1854 with the United States. At the same time a railroad-building boom exploded throughout Canada. By 1860 the Grand Trunk Railway ran across the province of Canada, and there was constant talk of an Intercolonial Railway, serving as a link to the Maritime provinces and their Atlantic ports.

Confederation. This helped raise the question of a general union of all of the colonies, which together might be able to afford great railways. Quarrels between French and English in Canada also called for a better form of union. Thus at Charlottetown in September 1864, Canadian and Maritime representatives discussed a plan for a broad federal union called a confederation. They agreed, and the plan was fully worked out at a large conference in Quebec in October. But it ran into strong opposition in the Maritimes, where local provincial loyalties were strong. Prince Edward Island and Newfoundland pulled out completely. Then, in 1866, the United States ended its twelve-year-old Reciprocity Treaty. The provinces had to draw together to find new trade among themselves. The Maritimes then decided they wanted the Intercolonial Railway that was promised with Confederation. The plan went through at last. In 1867 the British North America Act was passed. Upper and Lower Canada became Ontario and Quebec. These two provinces were united with Nova Scotia and New Brunswick to found the modern Canadian nation.

From 1791 until 1840 the old province of Quebec was divided into two separate colonies, each with its own legislature. Upper Canada followed British traditions; Lower Canada followed French traditions.

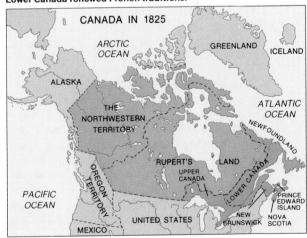

In 1864, the "Fathers of the Confederation" met in Quebec to discuss the union of Britain's North American colonies. Three years later the Dominion of Canada was founded.

▶ THE CANADIAN NATION

After Confederation the federal government for years was in the hands of John A. Macdonald, one of Canada's greatest prime ministers and nation builders. His first task was to complete the Confederation. In the east he brought in Prince Edward Island in 1873.

In the north and west, Macdonald's government carried through the transfer to Canada of the lands owned by the Hudson's Bay Company. This was accomplished by 1870, and the next year British Columbia was added to the union. But in the Red River colony in present-day Manitoba, many inhabitants objected to being handed over to Canada in this transfer of land. They wanted a choice in the matter.

For that reason they backed Louis Riel, leader of the métis (people who had both French and Indian ancestors), in a movement to block the transfer. It was scarcely a rebellion. All Riel and his supporters wanted was a chance to arrange terms for the colony's entry into Canada. Unfortunately, during this Red River uprising, Riel had executed a Canadian, Thomas Scott, who had resisted his authority. That act had in it the seeds of future troubles.

The Northwest Rebellion of 1885

The Indians and métis of the Saskatchewan Valley worried as settlement moved westward. Many of these people were hunters, and they feared for their way of life. Once again they turned to Louis Riel. This time he led them in a bloody uprising known as the Northwest Rebellion. Troops were rushed out to put down the rebellion and restore order. Riel was sentenced to death for his acts, and Canadian opinion was divided over the sentence.

In Quebec the people saw Riel as a French-Canadian hero. In Ontario, Riel was looked on as a traitor and the murderer of Thomas Scott. The execution of Riel late in 1885 left a deep scar in French-Canadian feelings.

The Golden Age of Wilfrid Laurier

Wilfrid Laurier, a brilliant French Canadian and leader of the Liberal Party became prime minister in 1896. At that time, Montreal and Toronto factories boomed; settlers flowed to the plains by way of the Canadian Pacific Railway, which was completed in 1885; and huge grain crops poured east to market. In 1905, two new western provinces—Alberta and Saskatchewan—were created. Large-scale mining developed in northern Ontario, Quebec, and British Columbia. Between 1896 and 1914, hydroelectric plants and paper mills arose in central Canada. The city of Vancouver grew rapidly on the Pacific coast. So did Winnipeg, Edmonton, and Regina on the prairies. Some 2.5 million immigrants entered Canada from Europe and the United States.

A change also took place in Canada's foreign relations as Laurier tried to increase Canada's control over its foreign affairs. Laurier's party lost power in 1911. But Robert Borden, his Conservative successor, did not change the push for Canada to assume more responsibility for its own foreign affairs. Under Borden's leadership, Canada entered World War I (1914–18) to help Britain and her allies. When the war ended, Borden won for Canada the right to sign the Treaty of Versailles (1919) and to join the League of Nations. Canada had finally found its place among the nations of the world.

Depression, War, and Peace

Borden's policies in Canada itself were less successful. The French Canadians had opposed the military draft, and this opposition left another deep split between the English and the French. Borden retired in 1920, and the Liberals returned to power the next year. It was the task of the new Liberal prime minister, Mackenzie King, to re-establish national unity. King was an unusually skillful politician. He accomplished this task over a career that lasted until 1948.

King also advanced Canada's status with the British Empire. In 1926 the dominions of the empire (including Canada) were recognized as free and equal partners in what is now the Commonwealth of Nations. The British Parliament passed the Statute of Westminster in 1931, making Canadian independence a practical reality.

When World War II broke out in September 1939, Canada rallied to Britain's side. The Canadian war effort was a great one. Canadian troops participated in the Sicilian and Italian campaigns and in the Normandy invasion. The Navy patrolled the North Atlantic convoy routes and fought desperate battles with lurking Nazi U-boats. In the air, Canadian pilots flew missions from the Battle of Britain in 1940 until the last bombs fell on Berlin in May 1945.

Following the war, Canada enjoyed prosperity. Rich deposits of oil, natural gas, uranium, and iron ore were discovered and developed; industry flourished; and more than 1 million immigrants arrived. In 1949, Newfoundland became Canada's tenth province, and Canada joined the North Atlantic Treaty Organization (NATO), thereby making a permanent commitment to defend Western Europe. In 1959, the completion of the St. Lawrence Seaway connected the St. Lawrence River to the Great Lakes.

The Quebec Separatist Movement

There was growing unrest in the French-Canadian province of Quebec, where a separatist movement developed. The separatists demanded that Quebec break away from Canada and form an independent French-speaking nation. The Liberals gained power under Lester B. Pearson in 1963. Pearson tried to satisfy Quebec by strengthening Quebec's representation in his own cabinet and party.

One of Pearson's French-speaking ministers, Pierre Elliott Trudeau, succeeded him as prime minister in 1968. Trudeau's aim was to prove that French-Canadian culture could flourish in a united Canada.

In 1976 the separatist Parti Québécois (Quebec Party) won control of the provincial government, promising to hold a referendum on Quebec's future. However, in referendums held in 1980 and 1995, Quebecers rejected independence for their province.

A New Constitution

Although Trudeau was unable to resolve the issue of how to share power between the provinces and the federal government, he did achieve a major goal—a truly Canadian constitution. Since 1867, all amendments to the Canadian Constitution had to be approved by the British Parliament. But the Constitution Act of 1982 gave Canada the power to amend its own constitution.

Trudeau resigned in 1984 and was succeeded by John N. Turner, who served briefly until the Progressive Conservatives won election in 1984. The new prime minister, Brian Mulroney, continued to try to reach a constitutional agreement with Quebec that would recognize Quebec as a "distinct society" within the Canadian federation. Known as the Meech Lake Accord, it failed to win approval.

In 1991, Mulroney unveiled a new reform program. It included a provision to create a self-governing territory, called Nunavut, for Canada's Eskimo (Inuit) population in the Northwest Territories. A plebiscite approved the measure in 1992. But Mulroney's plans for constitutional reform were defeated in a later referendum.

In 1993, Mulroney won approval for the North American Free Trade Agreement (NAFTA) with the United States and Mexico (ratified in 1994). He resigned soon after and was succeeded by Kim Campbell, Canada's first woman prime minister. Later that year, the Progressive Conservatives were defeated by the Liberals, and Jean Chrétien became prime minister. The Liberals were returned to power in 1997. In April 1999, the new territory of Nunavut, carved out of the Northwest Territories, came into being.

J. M. S. CARELESS
University of Toronto
Reviewed by ROBERT BOTHWELL
University of Toronto

CANADA, LITERATURE OF

Canadian literature is written in English and French, the country's two official languages. This reflects the fact that Canada was a colony first of France (from 1663 to 1760) and then of England (from 1760 to 1867). After 1760, when France surrendered Canada to English control, the French people living in Canada preserved their heritage despite English dominance. Thus, a literature in the French language, centered in Quebec, thrived along with the literature of the English majority.

After Confederation in 1867, the new nation slowly began to develop its own literature, distinct from that of Europe and of Canada's neighbor, the United States. Canadian literature found its own voice in the early 1900's. Today, Canadian writers have a world audience.

Roger Lemelin's critically acclaimed novel *Au pied de la pente douce* (*The Town Below*) pioneered a trend toward social realism in modern French Canadian literature.

Margaret Atwood's numerous works of fiction, poetry, and criticism have established her as one of Canada's major contemporary authors writing in English.

▶ EARLY WRITING

The earliest examples of Canadian literature were written by explorers, traders, and others who opened up the Canadian wilderness. Their writings are mainly journals that describe the natural wealth of the newfound land and the hardships and rewards of pioneer life.

The works of writers in the early 1800's were mainly descriptive, focusing on the land itself and on life in the pioneer settlements and growing towns. An interesting writer of this period is Susanna Moodie (1803–85), who moved to Canada from England in 1832. Her autobiographical book *Roughing It in the Bush* (1852) offers a revealing account of the pioneer experience.

Many poets and novelists of this period responded to the Canadian scene using the literary styles and techniques of Europe. For example, early Canadian poets writing in English were influenced by the romantic and Victorian poetry then popular in England. Similarly, novelists writing in French imitated the novels of Victor Hugo and other French romantics. Often, these styles were not well suited to describing the new world. In general, both young cultures needed more time to find their distinctive voices.

▶ 1867 TO WORLD WAR I

The modern Canadian nation was founded in 1867. Gradually, as more provinces joined the confederacy, that nation stretched across the continent from sea to sea. These events created a sense of national pride and encouraged the development of a Canadian literature.

Four writers have come to be known as the "Poets of the Confederation": Charles G. D. Roberts (1860–1943), Bliss Carman (1861–1929), Archibald Lampman (1861–99), and Duncan Campbell Scott (1862–1947). Their poetry captured the beauty and variety of the Canadian landscape.

Among the most important fictional works of the period were the animal stories of Charles G. D. Roberts and Ernest Thompson Seton (1860–1946). These stories, with their close observation of nature, marked the beginning of a realistic Canadian fiction.

Many writers of this period used Canada's small villages and towns as the settings for their books. This technique, called **regionalism**, was to become an important element in later Canadian literature. The country's huge size forced writers to focus on small regions that were familiar to them. And, in the course of writing about life in these local settings, writers could often express ideas and themes of universal importance.

Two early regional writers were Ralph Connor (1860–1937), whose real name was Charles William Gordon, and Lucy Maud Montgomery (1874–1942). Connor, a minister, used his fiction to present moral lessons. In his stories and novels, set in small towns of the frontier, good is always rewarded and evil punished. Montgomery's popular first novel, *Anne of*

Top left: An illustration from the 1908 edition of L. M. Montgomery's *Anne of Green Gables*, showing Anne's arrival at her new home. *Above:* "Sugar Making," a scene from *Roughing It in the Bush*, Susanna Moodie's firsthand account of pioneer life. *Left:* The title character of *Red Fox*, written by Charles G. D. Roberts.

Green Gables (1908), tells the story of an imaginative young orphan growing up on Prince Edward Island. This book and its many sequels vividly portray the dreams of youth.

French Canadian fiction continued the traditions of the romantic rural novel, which had begun in 1846 with *La Terre paternelle* (*The Homestead*) by Patrice Lacombe (1807–63). This form of regional novel usually depicted the peaceful life of the small Quebec village.

▶ **MODERN TIMES**

While earlier Canadian literature depicted the immense landscape of the country, later writers focused on the individual human being within that landscape.

Modern Quebec literature began with two novels that portrayed life in the city rather than in small villages. *Au pied de la pente douce* (1944; *The Town Below*) by Roger Lemelin (1919–92) was set in one of Quebec City's poor sections. *Bonheur d'occasion* (1945; *The Tin Flute*) by Gabrielle Roy (1909–83) took place in a poor neighborhood of Montreal. These works were among the first to examine the lives of the urban working class.

English Canadian fiction entered the modern period with the publication of *The Double Hook* (1959) by Sheila Watson (1909–98), an openly anti-regional novel set in rural British Columbia.

The 1960's saw an explosion of fiction, poetry, and drama in both English and French. The major figure of the decade was Margaret Laurence (1926–87), a novelist, short-story writer, and essayist. In the fictional prairie town of Manawaka, the setting for five of her books, she created a regional world that was universal in its depiction of human life.

The playwright, fiction writer, and translator Michel Tremblay (1942–) focused on the alienated working class of urban Quebec. His plays have brought international attention to a growing Quebec theater. Contemporary Quebec literature has also been enlivened by the haunting short stories of Roch Carrier (1937–), the bleak prose and poetry of Marie-Claire Blais (1939–), and the feminist writings of Nicole Brossard (1943–).

Modern English Canadian literature is dominated by Margaret Atwood (1939–), whose numerous works present the Canadian individual confronting the modern world. Atwood's many contemporaries include Robert Kroetsch (1927–), whose fiction and poetry explore the Canadian west; Alice Munro (1931–), noted for her short stories of rural life; and Michael Ondaatje (1943–), whose works portray the disorder of contemporary life.

DAVID STAINES
University of Ottawa

CANALS

Canals are channels or ditches filled with water. Sometimes they are natural channels, but most often they have been made by people. The earliest canals were probably dug to bring water from rivers or lakes to irrigate dry land. Other canals were used to drain water away from swampy cities and towns.

Early in history, people found another important use for canals—transportation. A canal can join two cities. It can give an inland city access to the sea. It can provide an inland waterway in a country that has few rivers.

Natural bodies of water, such as rivers, lakes, or seas, can be connected by canals to provide shorter or safer water routes. Canals are also sometimes built in rivers that are too swift or too shallow for boats to use.

Two main types of canals are used for transportation: ship canals and barge canals. Ship canals are used by large seagoing vessels. Barge canals are used by cargo-carrying barges and small ships.

Canals may be built all on one level, or they may go from one level to another by means of **locks.** Locks are sections of a canal with watertight gates at each end. The gates can be

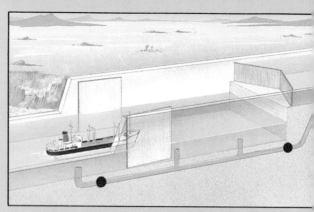

1 How a Lock Works: To go from a lower to a higher level in a canal, a ship first sails into a lock through its open lower gates, which then close behind the ship.

opened and closed to let water in or out and let boats through.

A ship going from a lower to a higher level in a canal first sails into a lock through its open lower gates. The gates are shut behind it. Water is allowed to flow into the lock until the level of water in the lock is as high as the water in the upper level of the canal. Then the upper gates are opened, and the ship proceeds on its way. If ships must be lifted a great distance, more than one lock is used. If a ship

The Corinth Canal in Greece is a deep-ditch ship canal, connecting the Ionian and Aegean seas. Built between 1882 and 1893, the canal is only 4 miles (6.3 kilometers) long. But for most ships, it saves a 202-mile (325-kilometer) voyage around southern Greece. The canal has no locks because its entire length is at sea level.

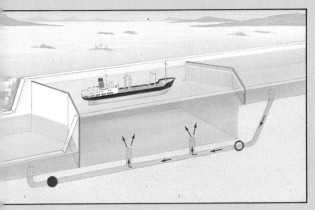

2 Water is let into the closed lock, raising the water level until both the water and the ship have reached the same level as the upper part of the canal.

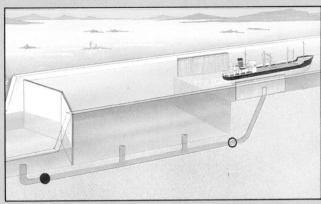

3 When the ship reaches the upper level, the upper gates are opened and the ship sails on its way. To lower a ship in a canal, this process is reversed.

is descending to a lower level, the process is simply reversed.

Except in very small locks, the lock is always filled or emptied through small openings in the gates or through pipes in the bottom of the lock. If the gates themselves were opened to let water in or out, the water would rush in or out with terrific force, damaging the ship or washing away the canal banks.

▶CANAL DESIGN

Canals are planned to follow the easiest and least expensive route. They are built to use as little water as possible. Water supply is always a problem for canals. To reduce the amount of water needed and to cut down construction costs, canals are made as narrow as possible. But this also limits the size of ships or barges that can use the canals. Most canals cannot accommodate oil-carrying "supertankers," for example. Sometimes canals are so narrow that ships cannot pass each other. Such narrow canals have special wide basins where ships can pass.

After a canal has been built, it must be maintained. Silting up, or becoming filled with soil, is one of the main problems in canal maintenance. Caving in of banks is another serious problem. The banks are often lined with concrete or masonry to prevent cave-ins. Soil is removed from canal bottoms by dredges.

Water leaking out through the soil beneath the canal is also a problem. To prevent this, the bottom of the canal is usually lined with clay. Rock, earth, or concrete is packed on top of the clay to form a tight seal.

▶HISTORY OF CANALS

Nearly 4,000 years ago the Egyptians built one of the earliest known canals for transportation. It connected the Nile River with the Red Sea. Ships could travel from the Mediterranean to the Red Sea by sailing along the Nile and through the canal.

One of the greatest canal systems in the world is the Grand Canal of China. Including its side branches, it covers more than 1,200 miles (1,900 kilometers). It links China's most important rivers. In Europe the Romans were the first great canal builders. Roman canals were mostly built for irrigation and drainage, but some were used for transportation.

Until the development of locks, canals could only be built on one level. This limited the number of places where canals could be built. The first step in the development of locks was to build dams along rapidly falling streams to create a series of deep, quiet ponds on different levels. Boats were hauled over the sloping faces of the dams.

The next improvement in locks was the invention of sluice gates. These gates in the dams were raised and lowered vertically, like windows. The first gates of this type were used on China's Grand Canal in A.D. 984. At first sluice gates were not built in pairs, as they were later. Because there was no second gate to hold back the water in a part of the canal, each time the one gate was opened, water rushed out and was wasted.

The modern type of lock gate, known as the miter gate, was invented by Leonardo da Vinci in the 15th century. It has two halves and swings open like a double door.

SOME WELL-KNOWN CANALS OF THE WORLD

CANAL	COUNTRY	YEAR COMPLETED	APPROX. LENGTH	OTHER FACTS
Canal du Midi	France	1681	150 mi (241 km)	Connects Atlantic and Mediterranean Sea; has three aqueducts and one tunnel.
Corinth	Greece	1893	4 mi (6.3 km)	Cut through solid rock; 261 ft (80 m) deep at one point. Swift tidal currents limit its usefulness.
Erie (now New York State Barge)	U.S.A. (N.Y. State)	1825 (remodeled 1903–18)	525 mi (845 km)	Links Lake Erie and Atlantic Ocean by way of the Hudson River; extension to Lake Champlain.
Grand	China	Around A.D. 620	More than 1,200 mi (1,900 km)	Links China's major river systems; one of the earliest known canals.
Kiel	Germany	1895	61 mi (98 km)	Connects Baltic and North seas. Strategically important in World Wars I and II.
Manchester Ship	United Kingdom	1894	35 mi (56 km)	Connects the inland city of Manchester with the Irish Sea.
Panama	Panama	1914	51 mi (82 km)	Connects Atlantic and Pacific oceans.
Welland	Canada	1932	26 mi (42 km)	Links Lake Erie to Lake Ontario and St. Lawrence Seaway; has 8 locks.
Sault Ste. Marie ("Soo Canals")	U.S.A. and Canada	1855 1895	1.6 mi (2.6 km) 1.4 mi (2.3 km)	Two separate, parallel canals, one in each country. Link Lake Superior with Lake Huron. Considered part of the St. Lawrence Seaway.
Suez	Egypt	1869	107 mi (172 km)	Links Mediterranean and Red seas.

The first sizable American canal was the Erie Canal, begun in 1817 and completed in 1825. Completion of the Erie Canal allowed the products of the Great Lakes region to flow to Europe through New York City. The success of the Erie Canal led to a great spurt of canal building. "Canal fever" was particularly strong in Ohio and Indiana. Unfortunately for the canal promoters, railroads were being perfected at the same time. Railroads could carry freight nearly as cheaply as canal barges—and much faster.

In their heyday the old canals presented a colorful picture. The passenger and freight barges were pulled by sturdy teams of mules or horses that walked along a path on the canal bank. Boats lined up at the locks waiting their turn to pass through. The canal barges were slow and often crowded. But they were much more pleasant to ride than the bone-rattling, dusty stagecoaches of that period.

The 19th century saw some bold ventures in the building of ship canals. Probably the most famous of these canals is the Suez Canal, built by a French company between 1859 and 1869. The Suez Canal enabled ships to go from Europe to the Far East without making the long voyage around Africa.

The Panama Canal is considered one of the engineering marvels of the 20th century. Completed in 1914, it links the Atlantic and Pacific oceans, eliminating the long trip around the southern tip of South America.

The longest ship canal system in North America is the St. Lawrence Seaway. It is a combination of canals, lakes, and rivers that have been deepened by dredging. Opened in 1959, the seaway permits large oceangoing ships to reach the Great Lakes.

Many advances have been made in air and ground transportation, but water is still the cheapest means of transportation for heavy products like automobiles, machinery, and oil.

GEORGE N. BEAUMARIAGE, JR.
California State University—Sacramento

See also ERIE CANAL; PANAMA CANAL; SAINT LAWRENCE RIVER AND SEAWAY; SUEZ CANAL.

CANARIES. See BIRDS AS PETS

PAPUA
NEW GUINEA

INDIAN

OCEAN

AUSTRALIA

PACIFIC

OCEAN

★CANBERRA

NEW
ZEALAND

CANBERRA

Canberra is the capital of the nation of Australia. Situated in the southeastern part of the country, it forms a part of the Australian Capital Territory. Canberra has an area of 12 square miles (31 square kilometers) and a population of about 255,000.

A Planned City. Canberra was planned and designed as Australia's national capital, much as Washington, D.C., was planned as the national capital of the United States.

An artificial lake, Lake Burley Griffin, divides the center of Canberra into northern and southern sections, which are connected by two bridges. In the southern section are located Capital Hill, Parliament House and other main government buildings, the National Gallery, and the National Library. The northern section is the site of the Civic Center (the city's main commercial and shopping area), the Australian National University, the Australian Academy of Science, the Royal Military College, the Australian War Memorial, and the Australian-American Memorial. The Australian-American Memorial is a tall shaft of gleaming metal with the figure of an eagle at its top. It expresses the appreciation of the Australian people for United States assistance during World War II.

Canberra's planners included numerous parks, trees, shrubs, and flowers in the city's design. It is a family-oriented city as well as the seat of government. In the nearby suburbs are spacious residential neighborhoods with many well-equipped schools.

Economy. Canberra's economy is based largely on the activities of the federal government, which employs the majority of the city's workers.

History. Canberra is a relatively young city. Until the end of the 19th century it was still a cluster of scattered houses situated on a treeless plain, which was used for grazing sheep. In 1909 the area was selected as the site of Australia's national capital. A worldwide competition was held in 1911 to choose a plan for the new city. The design of an American architect, Walter Burley Griffin, of Chicago, Illinois, was adopted, and construction began two years later.

The city grew slowly at first, delayed by two world wars and the Great Depression of the 1930's. Although Parliament was transferred from the city of Melbourne in 1927, the real expansion of Canberra began in 1945, following the end of World War II. The name Canberra is believed to come from the language of the Australian aborigines, the country's first inhabitants, and to mean "meeting place." It is an appropriate name for a national capital.

Reviewed by SHARYN KALNINS
Australian Capital Territory
Schools Authority

The Australian National Gallery in Canberra houses a notable collection of Australian art as well as art from around the world. The building's design is typical of the modern appearance of Canberra, which was carefully planned as Australia's national capital.

CANCER

Cancer is a disease of uncontrolled cell growth. It is one of our society's most serious health problems, second only to heart disease as a cause of death in the United States. In a single year, more than 1 million Americans will develop cancer.

Cancer's unregulated growth can be seen as cancer cells (colored green) invade the bronchial tract, crowding out healthy cilia-producing cells.

▶ HOW CANCER DEVELOPS

Normal cell growth is controlled by signals that tell cells to divide when there is a need for new cells and then to stop dividing when that need is met. When these signals do not function normally, a neoplasm (meaning "new growth"), or tumor, forms.

The reason this happens is not completely understood. Changes in cell behavior may be related to a tiny piece of genetic material in the cell called a **proto-oncogene**. When the proto-oncogene is activated, or started up, it can lead to changes that cause the cell to lose control of what happens during cell division. Another gene, called a **tumor suppressor gene**, is able to stop abnormal cell division. But if this gene is lost or becomes damaged, a tumor can develop.

Tumors can be benign or malignant. Both kinds of tumors are abnormal. However, malignant tumors are usually much more harmful than benign tumors.

A tumor is **benign** when the cells of the tumor are enclosed in a membrane that keeps them from escaping into other bodily tissues. Healthy tissues can be damaged by benign tumors when the cell mass grows large enough to compress them. Benign tumors are not considered cancerous.

Malignant tumors are cancerous. Their cells, which are not enclosed in a membrane, can easily invade and destroy nearby tissues even when the primary tumor is still very small. In addition, the cells of a malignant tumor can enter the circulatory system or lymphatic system. This enables the cancerous cells to travel throughout the body and establish secondary cancers in distant organs. When this happens, the cancer is said to **metastasize**. These secondary cancers are known as **metastases**. Uncontrolled growth, disruption of healthy tissues, and the ability to metastasize are the characteristics of a cancerous tumor.

▶ TYPES OF CANCER

Because the human body is made up of many kinds of cells—and cancer can develop in any cell type—cancer is not a single disease. It is a family of more than one hundred related diseases, all of which are characterized by uncontrolled cell growth.

Similarities between human cancers exist, and many different systems have been developed to classify them. One method separates cancers into four types: carcinoma, sarcoma, leukemia, and lymphoma.

A **carcinoma** is a cancer that develops in the skin, the linings of body parts or organs (such as the mouth, stomach, or bowel), or in glandular tissue (such as the breast or prostate gland). A **sarcoma** is a cancer originating in bone, muscles, or connective tissues, such as tendons.

The terms "carcinoma" and "sarcoma" are often combined with words that specify a cell type or organ to identify the site where the cancer originated. For example, a hepatocellular carcinoma is a cancer that began in the cells of the liver. An osteosarcoma is cancer of the bone.

A **leukemia** is a cancer of the bone marrow. Bone marrow is the source of red blood cells, white cells (which fight infection), and platelets (cells that prevent uncontrolled bleeding). **Lymphomas** are cancers that originate in the lymph nodes.

▶ CAUSES OF CANCER

Nutritional disorders, hormonal imbalances, certain viral infections, and disorders of the immune system all have been identified as factors that can contribute to the development of cancer. For example, the acquired immune deficiency syndrome (AIDS), caused by the human immuno-deficiency virus, leads to an increased risk of lymphoma and sarcoma. Genetic abnormalities also can cause cancer. If these abnormalities are inherited, an entire family may have a high risk for a particular kind of cancer.

Certain substances, called **carcinogens**, can transform a healthy cell into a cancerous one. They do this by activating the proto-oncogene or by interacting with genetic abnormalities in the cell. Examples of carcinogens are chemicals such as benzene, fibers such as asbestos, and radiation from a variety of sources, such as ultraviolet (UV) sunlight, X rays, and radioactive elements. Some substances, such as tobacco and tobacco smoke, contain many different carcinogens. Researchers have found that carcinogens can interact with each other to greatly increase the cancer risk. For example, the highest known risk of lung cancer is in a smoker who also works as a uranium miner. (Uranium is a radioactive element.)

▶ **CANCER DIAGNOSIS AND STAGING**

Special tests to detect some kinds of cancers can be performed even before any noticeable symptoms appear. Examples include a mammogram, which is an X ray that can detect breast tumors too small to be felt, and a laboratory test for blood in the stools, which may indicate colon cancer. When performed regularly, procedures such as these help with early diagnosis. They have reduced the incidences of certain cancers and increased the chances that people with cancer will be cured.

If a tumor is thought to be cancerous, a piece of tumor tissue is removed—in a procedure called a **biopsy**—and examined under a microscope. The appearance of the tumor cells reveals whether the tumor is benign or malignant and also helps in predicting the course, or **prognosis**, of the disease.

An evaluation, called **staging**, is used to determine the extent to which the cancer has spread. This information is necessary in order to plan an effective course of treatment.

▶ **CANCER TREATMENT**

Although cancer was described as early as 1600 B.C., the ability to cure cancer is a relatively recent achievement. Before the 1900's, few people with cancer survived. Today more than half of those Americans who develop cancer will also be cured of it. An individual is considered cured of cancer when he or she has been treated and is free of cancer for five years or more. In many cases such a person has the same life expectancy as someone who never had cancer.

Kinds of Cancer Treatment

There are three standard methods that are used to treat cancer: surgery, radiotherapy (radiation therapy), and chemotherapy (drug therapy). Treatment can consist of just one kind of therapy or a combination of two or all three therapies.

Surgery. Around 1900, ether became available to produce anesthesia (a condition in which the patient is unconscious and feels no pain). This made operations to remove tumors possible. Medical advances such as antibiotics, blood transfusions, and improved surgical procedures helped to make surgical treatment of cancer more successful.

Radiotherapy. The discovery that radiation, in the form of X rays, is deadly to cancer cells led to **radiotherapy**, the treatment of cancer with radiation. For some forms of cancer that are restricted to a limited area, such as those that occur in the skin or larynx (voice box), radiotherapy can replace surgery as the primary treatment. For cancers that are not treatable with surgery, radiotherapy provides an alternative.

Radiation also has been put to use in detecting cancer. Low-level radiation allows doctors to see very small tumors deep within the body using sound waves and computer-

---

CANCER'S WARNING SIGNS

Early detection helps provide the best chance for successful treatment of this serious disease. The American Cancer Society has developed a list of seven danger signals that can be early signs of cancer. You should consult a physician if you develop any one of these symptoms:
- Unusual bleeding or discharge
- A lump or thickening in the breast or other tissues
- A sore that does not heal
- Change in bowel or bladder habits
- Persistent cough or hoarseness
- Difficulty with swallowing or persistent indigestion
- Change in the appearance of a mole or wart

enhanced X rays, called CT (computerized tomography) scans.

Chemotherapy. In 1947, research scientists discovered that folic acid, a vitamin, increased the number of abnormal white blood cells in children with leukemia. When these children were given a drug that reduced the effects of folic acid, the number of leukemia cells decreased. This observation that drugs could kill cancer cells led to the development of **chemotherapy**, the use of drugs to treat cancer.

Drugs that are used in chemotherapy work by interfering with the genetic material in cancer cells and with the cells' ability to divide. Because drugs are carried in the bloodstream, they are especially useful for treating cancers that have metastasized through the bloodstream.

A wide variety of anticancer drugs are now in use. When used alone, most can reduce the size of a tumor only temporarily. However, when several drugs are combined, the treatment can be much more effective. Several cancers once considered fatal, including childhood leukemia and Hodgkin's disease, are now successfully treated using this technique.

In the 1980's and 1990's, researchers found that large doses of some chemotherapy drugs can improve the chance for a cure in diseases like lymphoma and breast cancer. But extremely high doses of chemotherapy also increase the chances that stem cells, which are found in the bone marrow, will be destroyed. Red blood cells, white cells, and platelets all develop from stem cells. If the stem cells cannot be restored, it is likely that death will occur from anemia, bleeding, or infection.

Fortunately, stem cells can often be collected before treatment begins, either from the person with cancer or from that person's relative, and then frozen. When the chemotherapy is finished, the stem cells are returned by injection to the individual undergoing treatment, and blood-cell production can continue. This procedure is known as a **bone marrow transplant** (also called a **stem cell transplant**).

Side Effects of Cancer Treatments

Most forms of cancer treatment cause some undesirable side effects. The side effects of surgery can include the loss of an organ or a body part, the formation of scars, or the development of complications such as bleeding or infections.

The toxic (harmful) effects of radiotherapy are related to the damaging effects of X rays on healthy tissues that lie within the treatment area. When bone marrow is in the treatment area, problems such as anemia, bleeding, and infection can develop. During treatment, individuals may have to deal with hair loss, skin irritation, fatigue, nausea, or diarrhea. Years after radiotherapy, second cancers can develop in the radiated area.

Side effects of chemotherapy may include anemia, bleeding, infection, hair loss, nausea, vomiting, diarrhea, and fatigue. Fortunately, new antinausea medications and drugs to help bone marrow recover its normal function have been developed. These aids have made it much easier for people to tolerate chemotherapy and radiotherapy. Most side effects disappear once the treatment is completed. Occasionally some long-term side effects occur in people who have been cured of cancer. One of these is infertility (the inability to have children).

▶ CURRENT RESEARCH

Cancer researchers are constantly seeking new ways to detect

During radiotherapy, cells are bombarded with X rays. A delicate balance must be reached where as many cancer cells as possible are destroyed with as little damage as possible to healthy tissues.

and treat cancer. One promising method is **immunotherapy**, the use of techniques to strengthen the body's own immune system. One technique uses **antibodies**, substances made by the immune system to attack foreign organisms. Monoclonal, or purified, antibodies that target certain kinds of cancer can be produced in the laboratory. These antibodies are used to detect the presence of cancer and even to treat it.

Researchers have also developed experimental techniques for restoring normal cell division in cancerous cells. This can be done with drugs that interfere with regulatory signals in the cell. It also can be done by introducing genes directly into tumor cells in a procedure known as **gene therapy**.

Recently, scientists have discovered drugs that fight certain cancerous tumors by blocking **angiogenesis**—the formation of blood vessels. Without a supply of blood, the tumors stop growing and eventually die.

▶ PREVENTING CANCER

Scientists and other health professionals are not the only people that can alter the future course of cancer. Individuals can also take an active part in the fight against cancer. Researchers estimate that approximately 80 percent of human cancers are caused, at least in part, by environmental factors and lifestyle. Some of these factors are easier to control than others.

The most striking example of an avoidable carcinogen is cigarette smoke, which is associated with a high risk for lung cancer. Rare just a century ago, lung cancer is the leading cause of cancer death among both men and women, claiming the lives of more than 160,000 Americans each year. Cigarette smoking also increases the likelihood of developing cancer of the mouth, throat, esophagus, stomach, bladder, and pancreas and of developing leukemia.

Avoiding prolonged exposure to sunlight and wearing a hat and sunscreen can reduce the risk of skin cancer in white- or light-skinned people. The risk of breast and bowel cancers can be reduced by improving dietary habits. The National Cancer Institute recommends that Americans should reduce the amount of fat they eat (especially animal fat) and increase their intake of fruits, vegetables, and whole-grain cereals.

An active campaign is being waged to keep young people from becoming part of a grim statistic: One of every four adult Americans smokes cigarettes daily.

It's Just Not Cool.

Smoking is an addiction that kills

More than 400,000 people die every year from smoking-related diseases. That's more than from alcohol, cocaine, crack, heroin, murders, suicide, car accidents, and AIDS *combined*.

Great American SMOKEOUT®
AMERICAN CANCER SOCIETY

Third Thursday in November

The U.S. Occupational Safety and Health Administration passes and enforces regulations to decrease workers' exposure to carcinogens in the workplace. For people with a high cancer risk due to inherited factors, genetic tests and early detection programs may reduce the risk of dying from cancer. For people struggling against cancer, the American Cancer Society provides support through its local chapters. In addition, it supports a cancer information service that supplies information on cancer prevention, diagnosis, and treatment.

VINCENT T. DEVITA, JR., M.D.
Director, National Cancer Institute
SUSAN MOLLOY HUBBARD
International Cancer Information Center
National Cancer Institute
Revised and updated by
BARBARA BURTNESS, M.D.
Yale University School of Medicine

CANDLES

Candles are made out of wax or tallow (cattle or sheep fat) that is shaped around loosely braided strands of twisted cotton fibers, called wicks. When a wick is lighted, heat begins to melt the wax. The wick then absorbs the melted wax, drawing it up toward the flame, where the wick and wax are gradually burned off.

Candle Manufacturing

The candlemaker begins by preparing the wicks. First, they are braided to help them bend toward the flame and burn away completely. Then they are pickled (treated in a chemical solution) so that they will not absorb too much wax and drown the flame.

Candles are made by covering wicks with wax in any of three different ways—dipping, molding, or rolling.

Dipping. In colonial times, a candle was made by dipping a wick over and over again into a vat of melted wax. Today, candles are machine-dipped. Many candles can be made in the exact same smooth, tapered shape at the same time. To make a standard-size ¾-inch-diameter candle, the wick must be dipped into the wax 24 to 30 times.

Molding. To make molded candles, wax is poured into molds that have wicks already strung through them. When the wax has set, pistons push the candles out and the process is repeated. Birthday candles and novelty shapes, such as Christmas trees and Halloween pumpkins, can all be fashioned in molds.

Rolling. The third method of candle manufacturing is similar to wrapping dough around a filling. The wax is kneaded and rolled into a sheet. Then it is wound around a wick until the candle is the right size.

Decoration. The delicate colors of candles come from mixing aniline, or oil, dyes with the wax. Candles can also be painted, sculpted, carved, and scented to produce an endless variety of interesting colors, shapes, designs, and aromas.

History

How the first candle came about is not known. Perhaps when primitive people were roasting animals, they poked the carcasses with sticks to test for tenderness. The sticks, covered with animal fat, would have burned brightly. Thus, the torch was created. An improvement was made by dipping twigs in resin, pitch, or oil to make the light last longer. Later, bundles of fat-dipped reeds took the place of twigs and were called rushlights.

The early Egyptians made candles. Their funeral services were lighted and possibly perfumed by cone-shaped lumps of wax or tallow.

By the 1200's candles were in general use. In Paris and other cities chandlers traveled from door to door restocking each household's supply of candles and soaps.

The tallow used to make early candles gave off a disagreeable odor. Beeswax and spermaceti wax from the sperm whale had no smell and lasted well, but most people could not afford these expensive waxes.

In the 1800's chemists discovered how to use animal fats to make stearic acid. This hard, waxlike substance became a leading candle making material because it was inexpensive and abundant.

Today, most candles are made with petroleum or refining paraffin waxes. These waxes are treated to make them stay hard. A few candlemakers still use other types of waxes such as carnauba from palm trees or bayberry wax.

Candles today are used mainly for decoration. They are put to their most practical use when we experience an electrical power failure. Candles are an important part of many religious ceremonies, and they are often burned as memorials to the dead. Candles have many uses, but perhaps their greatest appeal is the warmth and beauty of their flames.

RALPH A. AJELLO
President, The Candle Craftsman

CANDY AND CANDY MAKING

Candy is the American word for a variety of sweet-tasting foods. In other English-speaking countries, candy is called ''sweets'' or ''sugar confectionary.''

Everyone knows that children love candy, but statistics indicate that adults indulge with equal enthusiasm. In the United States, each person consumes an average of about 9 pounds (4.1 kilograms) of candy each year. In addition, each person also eats an average of nearly 10 pounds (4.5 kilograms) of chocolate a year—making a grand total of 19 pounds of candy. Candy is even more popular in Europe. The United Kingdom holds the record with a combined average consumption of candy and chocolate of about 28 pounds (12.9 kilograms) per person per year!

Because of its high sugar content, candy is known as a high-energy food. Although candy is rich in sugar and occasionally contains high amounts of fats, it contains few vitamins and minerals and usually very little protein. Thus candy should be consumed as a delicious treat rather than as a substitute for more nutritious foods.

▶CANDY INGREDIENTS

Candy is so popular because it tastes so good. Sugar is the main ingredient. Candy was once sweetened with honey, but it was found that boiling the juices of sugarcane created ''invert sugar,'' a sweetener similar to honey but less likely to crystallize, or become grainy, when used in candy. In modern candymaking, corn syrup is the other basic ingredient. The addition of corn syrup, manufactured from corn flour, allows the candymaker to obtain better control of the texture of the finished product. Of the more than 2,000 kinds of candy, the vast majority of them are made from this basic boiled mixture of sugar and corn syrup. The proportion of the ingredients, the length of time the mixture is boiled, the temperature to which it is cooked, and the way in which the mixture is handled after it is cooled determine the texture of the finished candy.

Chocolate, of course, is one of the most popular candy ingredients. The chocolate coating of various forms of candy, fruits, and nuts is a common practice, and the chocolate bar is one of the most popular forms of candy. For more information on chocolate and how it is processed for use as candy, see the article CHOCOLATE in this volume.

Other ingredients commonly used in candymaking are vegetable fats and butter; milk —usually concentrated and sweetened; aerating agents such as egg whites; gelling substances such as gelatin, agar, and pectin; fruits, including jam; and nuts—whole or ground. Various natural flavors such as peppermint, vanilla, coconut, or cocoa may be blended with these ingredients for flavor or coloring. Some candies contain artificial flavors or colors.

Highly specialized machines have been developed to make almost any kind of candy. Above, an ''enrobing'' machine is applying a chocolate coating to hard candy centers, while at left a machine ''pulls'' toffee.

▶ TYPES OF CANDY

Hard Candies. Hard candies are the kind that you can suck on for a long time. Lollipops, fruit drops, candy canes, and mints are hard candies. They are among the simplest of candies to produce. A solution of sugar and corn syrup is boiled to a specific temperature and then cooled, flavored, and colored. As the mixture cools, it gradually hardens. While it is still soft enough to mold, it is pressed into shapes by machines.

Fondant and Fondant Centers. Fondant is the sweet, creamy kind of candy that seems to melt in your mouth. Fondant candies are often chocolate-covered. Fondant, like hard candy, is made by boiling a solution of sugar and corn syrup. For fondants, however, the two ingredients are in different proportions and the temperature is held lower. The mixture is cooled and then vigorously beaten until it forms a smooth white paste. To make shaped centers for chocolate candies, the fondant is remelted, flavored, and colored and then poured into molds of the desired decorative shape. The liquid fondant will harden as it cools, after which it can be removed from the mold and covered with chocolate—either by hand or by machine.

Caramels and Fudge. Caramels and fudge are made by boiling a sugar and corn-syrup solution with condensed milk. It is the temperature to which the mixture is allowed to climb and the addition of the milk that give the unique caramel flavor. In making caramel candies, the proportion of sugar to corn syrup is such that the caramel does not form crystals on cooling. In making fudge, crystals are encouraged to form by the higher proportion of sugar, rapid mixing, or by the addition of some fondant. Caramel and fudge both "set" as they cool and can be cut into sections.

Marshmallows and Nougat. If a boiled sugar and corn-syrup solution is mechanically beaten with an aerating agent such as egg white or gelatin, a candy "foam" is produced that may be cast into shapes like fondant. Marshmallow has a light airy texture, while nougat is more dense because fat has been added to it. Soft nougats are popular fillings for candy bars.

Jellies and Gums. To make jellies or gumdrops, gelatin is dissolved into the basic sugar and corn-syrup solution. Flavoring and coloring are added, and the warm solution is left to set in molds. Gumdrops are similar in composition to jellies but have a lower moisture content because they are dried in a warm oven after they are cast.

Marzipan and Nut Pastes. To make marzipan, ground almonds are added to a sugar and corn-syrup solution. Other kinds of nut candies are made by grinding roasted nuts into hard candy or chocolate.

Panned Candies. Jellybeans and malted milk balls are two of the many candies made by the unique process of panning. In this technique, nuts, raisins, or other candy pieces are coated with sugar by rotating in a "Volvo" pan in which the pieces roll over one another. Sugar syrup is applied during rotation and then dried off by means of a stream of air, leaving a layer of sugar glaze on the surface of each piece. Chocolate may be applied by a similar process.

Other Candies. There are many varieties of candy using special processes of manufacture.

Hard candies	
Fondants and fondant centers	
Caramels and fudge	
Marshmallow and nougats	
Jellies and gums	
Marzipan and nut pastes	
Panned candies	

Licorice strips, for example, are made by forcing the plastic paste through orifices (openings). This is called "extrusion."

HISTORY

Historically the art of candy making has extended over some 3,500 years and is described in ancient Egyptian writings. Later, in the Roman era, it was well established. During the excavation of the town of Herculaneum, a candy kitchen was discovered with pans and other implements similar to those used today.

Candy making is now an almost completely automated process. Where once candies had to be manufactured one batch at a time, each batch being cooked individually in a pan, now modern industry is fully mechanized for both production and packaging, thereby providing a variety of good quality candies at minimum cost.

Modern methods include the use of a continuous process in which the syrup is boiled in a thin film by high pressure or under vacuum. Candy bars are now formed in multiple extrusion machines. Mechanical depositing is used for hard candies, fondant, and marshmallows. Raw materials are automatically dispensed in required proportions, and temperatures are controlled by electronic methods.

BERNARD W. MINIFIE
Author, *Chocolate, Cocoa and Confectionary: Science and Technology,* 2nd edition

---

CANNADY, BEATRICE. See OREGON (Famous People).

CANNING. See FOOD PRESERVATION.

CANNON, ANNIE JUMP. See ASTRONOMY (Profiles); DELAWARE (Famous People).

CANNON, CLARENCE A. See UNITED STATES, CONGRESS OF THE (Profiles: House Representatives).

CANNON, JOSEPH GURNEY. See UNITED STATES, CONGRESS OF THE (Profiles: Speakers of the House).

CANOEING

A canoe is a type of boat enjoyed by both beginners and experts. A properly trained and equipped canoeist can navigate almost any body of water. Canoeists can slip silently across a lake or paddle down a river. Experienced experts can even challenge white water, rapids named for the white foam created when water moves swiftly over rough, rocky riverbeds. Canoeing provides pleasure, excitement, and the thrill of competition all the way to the level of the Olympic Games.

EQUIPMENT

A canoe is a simple-looking boat, flat on the bottom and pointed at each end. Some are built with square **sterns** (the rear of the boat) to hold a small motor. Canoes range from about 32 to 40 inches (81 to 102 centimeters) wide. Wider canoes do not tip over as easily as narrow ones.

Most canoes today look very much like those crafted by early North American Indians. But the size and shape of modern canoes do vary according to the use and the number of paddlers normally carried.

A canoe designed for large bodies of water might be 17 to 20 feet (about 5 to 6 meters) long. It will have a **keel,** a ridge down the center bottom that helps keep the canoe on

Most modern canoes are made of strong, lightweight space-age materials—but they still look very much like those built by North American Indians centuries ago.

course. It can have high sides if it is meant to carry cargo or camping equipment, or low sides if easy entry and lighter weight are desired. Light weight is very important when the canoeist has to **portage,** which means to carry the canoe around shallow or rough water or to another body of water.

Canoes used on rivers may be 12 to 17 feet (3.6 to 5 meters) long. They have no keel because they must be able to turn quickly. A canoe used in white water is shaped for the quick turns required to avoid rocks and other hazards. It is short and narrow and has a bottom curved like a banana. To keep out water, it may have removable covers or a deck.

Canoes are made of one of any number of materials that are strong and lightweight. In recent years the wood frame covered by painted canvas has been replaced by man-made materials such as fiberglass and strong plastics that have been developed to combine light weight, strength, and durability. Aluminum canoes are also common.

Paddles can be made of wood, fiberglass, aluminum, or plastic. To find the correct length for you, stand with the blade by your foot. The grip should reach your eyes if you are the stern paddler, or your chin if you are in the bow. Paddles for white water have wider blades and T-shaped grips for better control.

Knee pads are necessary when paddlers use the kneeling position. Kneeling is preferred over sitting for added stability and safety.

Federal law requires all boats to be equipped with a life jacket for each passenger.

A wise boater will also have a bailer, or scoop to remove water, and a painter, an 8- to 20-foot (about 2.5- to 6-meter) rope attached to the bow (front of the boat) for tying up the boat when not in use.

White-water slalom competitions challenge the expert. The canoe must pass through gates—pairs of poles suspended over the swiftly moving, foaming water.

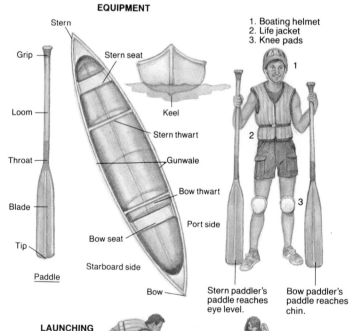

EQUIPMENT

Stern
Grip
Loom
Throat
Blade
Tip
Paddle

Stern seat
Keel
Stern thwart
Gunwale
Bow thwart
Port side
Bow seat
Starboard side
Bow

1. Boating helmet
2. Life jacket
3. Knee pads

Stern paddler's paddle reaches eye level.

Bow paddler's paddle reaches chin.

LAUNCHING A CANOE

When entering a canoe, balance it by putting one hand on each gunwale, taking care not to pinch your fingers if the canoe lies against a dock. Step into the center of the canoe and kneel. The first paddler in steadies the canoe while others enter.

SAFE CANOEING

Everyone in the canoe should be a good swimmer. It is always a good idea to wear your life jacket — it is the mark of an experienced canoeist.

Skilled paddlers:
— are able to get in and out of the canoe correctly.
— know the basic paddle strokes.
— are able to control the canoe alone.
— can launch and dock the canoe correctly.
— can right an overturned canoe.
— can enter a floating or swamped canoe from the water.
— know the warning signs of dangerous water and weather.
— know how to load passengers properly and maintain stability.

White-water canoeists:
— are properly trained by a qualified instructor.
— never canoe alone.
— wear a life jacket and boating helmet on the river. (Do not substitute other sports helmets. They do not drain and thus can hold the swimmer's head under water.)

To find out how you can learn to canoe, contact your local canoeing club or Red Cross chapter.

PADDLING POSITIONS

One paddler kneels in the bow and one in the stern, keeping knees spread for better balance. Passengers sit on the bottom. Paddling alone is done from the center. Paddler positions are chosen to keep the canoe level from side to side and the bow slightly higher than the stern, which improves steering.

COMPETITION

Member organizations of the American Canoe Association organize races according to established rules. Olympic-style events are held on lakes. Single paddlers or crews of two or four paddlers compete in 500-, 1,000-, and 10,000-meter races in canoes and kayaks with highly specialized racing designs.

Canoe marathon races take place on rivers. Men, women, and children can compete in separate events. A marathon course may be as long as 20 miles (32 kilometers).

White-water slalom competitions are over courses marked with **gates,** pairs of poles suspended from wires strung over the course. Penalties are assessed for touching or missing the gates. The winner is the competitor with the lowest score of time plus penalty points.

There are also races for sailing canoes and propelling a canoe with a 12- to 14-foot (3.4- to 4.3-meter)-long pole.

HISTORY

From the time a human first rode on a floating log, people have tried to find ways to travel on water. When they hollowed out a log, they and their belongings could ride inside. These **dugouts** were the first canoes.

Several kinds of canoes developed from the dugout. In the South Pacific the Polynesians built oceangoing **catamarans** by adding sails and **outriggers,** floating framework extending out to the sides to prevent tipping. North American Indians built canoes with light wood frames. The Eskimos (Inuit) covered the frame, including the top, with animal skins. They put a hole in the top for the paddler. This canoe, called a **kayak,** was so watertight that it could be taken into icy Arctic waters in pursuit of seal and whale. The paddler stayed dry even if the kayak rolled over. Indians in less frigid climates covered the wood frame with tree bark sealed with pine pitch.

Reviewed by DONALD JARRELL
Editor, *American Canoe Association Instructor's Manual*

CANTON. See GUANGZHOU.
CANTOR, GEORG. See MATHEMATICS, HISTORY OF (Profiles).
CAPE TOWN. See SOUTH AFRICA (Major Cities).

BASIC STROKES
Straight or bow stroke — Reach forward with the paddle, dip the blade into the water, and pull back along the side of the canoe. End the stroke at your position.

PADDLING
When paddling on the starboard side of the canoe, the paddler's right hand is near the paddle blade and the left hand is on the grip. When paddling on the port side, reverse the hands. Bow and stern paddlers paddle on opposite sides in unison. The stern paddler is usually responsible for steering.

"J" or stern stroke — Reach forward, dip the blade into the water, and pull back parallel to the keel. At the end of the stroke, give the paddle a little outward twist. This stroke helps keep the canoe on a straight course.

STROKES TO MOVE SIDEWAYS
Pushaway — Place paddle vertically into the water right next to you, with the blade parallel to the keel. Push the blade outward, away from you.

Draw stroke — Reach straight out to the side with the blade parallel to the keel. Dip the blade into the water, and pull the blade in toward you.

ENTERING A SWAMPED CANOE FROM THE WATER
With the canoe full of water and upright, press down on the gunwale nearest you and reach across to the far side. Pull yourself across, rolling into a sitting position. When your hips are inside, carefully swing your legs into the canoe. Proceed slowly. It is easy for the canoe to roll over when swamped.

CAPE VERDE

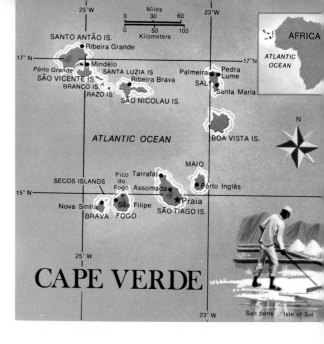

Salt pens   Isle of Sal

The nation of Cape Verde consists of an archipelago, or chain of islands, located in the Atlantic Ocean off the west coast of Africa. Formerly a territory of Portugal, the islands gained their independence in 1975.

The People. About 70 percent of Cape Verde's population is of mixed Portuguese and black African ancestry. The remainder are Africans and Europeans. Almost half the people live on the island of São Tiago, where the capital and largest city, Praia, is located.

Portuguese is the official language. But a variety of local dialects are spoken, some of which combine Portuguese with African languages. The majority of the people are Roman Catholics.

The Land. The Cape Verde archipelago consists of ten islands and five smaller islets. The ten main islands are São Tiago, Santo Antão, São Vicente, São Nicolau, Sal, Boa Vista, Fogo, Maio, Brava, and Santa Luzia.

The islands are volcanic in origin and for the most part arid and mountainous. The climate is generally hot and dry. Rainfall is sparse and drought is frequent. There are few minerals other than salt and limestone.

FACTS and figures

REPUBLIC OF CAPE VERDE (República do Cabo Verde) is the official name of the country.

LOCATION: Atlantic Ocean west of Africa.

AREA: 1,557 sq mi (4,033 km²).

POPULATION: 400,000 (estimate).

CAPITAL AND LARGEST CITY: Praia.

MAJOR LANGUAGES: Portuguese (official), Crioulo.

MAJOR RELIGION: Christian (chiefly Roman Catholic).

GOVERNMENT: Republic. **Head of state**—president. **Head of government**—prime minister. **Legislature**—National People's Assembly.

CHIEF PRODUCTS: Corn, potatoes, sugarcane, bananas, cassava, salt, livestock, fish.

MONETARY UNIT: Cape Verde escudo (1 escudo = 100 centavos).

Economy. Most Cape Verdeans earn their living from agriculture or fishing. However, the limited rainfall, frequent drought, and soil erosion often make farming difficult. On many of the islands the land is suitable only for grazing goats, sheep, and some cattle. The country's chief exports are fish, salt, and bananas.

Many Cape Verdeans have emigrated to other countries to find work. The money they send home to their families plays an important part in Cape Verde's economy.

History and Government. Cape Verde was uninhabited when the Portuguese first arrived there in 1462. For many years the islands prospered from the slave trade, especially in the transshipment of slaves between West Africa and America. After the abolition of slavery, the islands became an important refueling stop for ships crossing the Atlantic Ocean.

Cape Verdeans began an armed struggle for independence from Portugal in the 1960's. They won their independence in 1975.

The government consists of a legislature, the National People's Assembly; a prime minister who heads the Council of Ministers and is responsible to the Assembly; and a president who is the chief executive. A single political party, the African Party for the Independence of Cape Verde (PAICV), led the country from independence until 1991, when Cape Verde's first multi-party elections brought the Movement for Democracy (MPD) to power.

RICHARD J. HOUK
De Paul University

CAPILLARY ACTION.   See LIQUIDS.

CAPITALISM

Capitalism is an economic system in which most of the industries and businesses in a country are privately owned by individuals, rather than by the government. Capitalists are people who use their own wealth (or other people's money) to make more wealth.

No matter what their business, capitalists aim to make a profit. But this does not mean that they can charge very high prices or sell bad goods. If they do, they will probably lose business to others with better goods or lower prices. Competition forces capitalists to sell the best goods at the lowest possible price.

Competition is an important feature of capitalism. The profits made by individual capitalists in free competition benefit the economy of a whole country. As capitalists make profits, they can expand their businesses and put more people to work.

Early Capitalism

Before the 1700's, the ruling classes of most countries practiced an economic policy known as mercantilism, designed to ensure their military and economic strength. They regulated production, controlled trading companies, and placed restrictions on imported goods. But the Industrial Revolution, which began in the mid-1700's, created a new middle class of wealthy merchants and industrialists with large amounts of money (known as capital) to invest in business activities.

The Need for Reform

In the early stages of the Industrial Revolution, many people believed that capitalism would work best if governments followed a hands-off policy toward business. This idea was best expressed by the English economist Adam Smith in his landmark book *An Inquiry into the Nature and Causes of the Wealth of Nations* (1776), which criticized the mercantile system and its limit of free trade.

But without regulations, factory owners often abused their power, and workers suffered. People commonly worked ten to twelve hours a day. Women and children, in particular, worked under dangerous conditions for very low pay.

Reformers cried out against these conditions. One of the most outspoken was the German revolutionary Karl Marx, a founder of communism. In 1867 he published *Das Kapital*, claiming that capitalism must die of its own cruelty and greed.

Changing Capitalism

Even before Marx attacked the capitalist system, labor unions had begun to develop. The early founders of unions criticized the brutal side of capitalism. But most believed that bad working conditions could be improved without destroying the system. Although at one time unions were illegal, they slowly grew stronger and gained acceptance.

Laws have also modified the capitalist system. In the late 1800's some capitalists built companies so huge and powerful that they did away with almost all competition. (One powerful company acting alone is known as a monopoly. A group of such companies is called a trust.) The Sherman Antitrust Act (1890) outlawed monopolies in the United States, and President Theodore Roosevelt, while in office (1901–09), enforced the law so strongly that he became known as the Trust Buster. Later, during the Great Depression of the 1930's, President Franklin D. Roosevelt introduced a broad social welfare program to help the needy as part of his New Deal legislation. Today, the federal social security and unemployment insurance programs give Americans protections they did not have before the 1930's. Government-funded welfare programs also provide aid for people in need.

Government plays an important role in the modern capitalist, or free enterprise, system. Many nations now combine capitalism with some government control of the economy. A government may own and operate such vital industries as steel, petroleum, banking, railroads, and airlines, while allowing private ownership of most other industries. It may also regulate companies that supply services needed for public health or convenience, such as the utilities that provide water, electricity, and natural gas.

Most people in democratic capitalist countries today feel that the free enterprise system should be maintained. But they also look to government to protect them from the excesses that marked capitalism in the past.

Reviewed by MARCUS NADLER
New York University

See also COMMUNISM; ECONOMICS; SOCIALISM; TRADE AND COMMERCE.

CAPITAL PUNISHMENT

Capital punishment, also known as the death penalty, is the execution (or killing) of a criminal as punishment for a crime. The practice has long been the subject of great debate. Many countries have abolished it, and most of those that have not, including the United States, usually sentence a person to death only for the most serious crime, murder.

Supporters of capital punishment argue that death is the only penalty severe enough for a crime such as murder. They believe it is the only way to protect society from criminals who may kill again and that it is the most effective way to discourage others from committing similar crimes. Opponents of capital punishment argue that society can be protected by sentencing the most dangerous criminals to life in prison. They also point to studies indicating that societies that allow capital punishment actually have more serious crime problems than those that do not.

Worldwide, the trend has been against capital punishment. In the United States, opposition grew in the mid-1900's as many Americans began to believe that the death penalty was being imposed unfairly against poor people and racial minorities, and that wealthy white defendants who committed similar crimes were given lesser sentences. In 1972, the U.S. Supreme Court ruled in *Furman* v. *Georgia* that capital punishment violated the Constitution's ban against "cruel and unusual punishment." But in time, states began enacting laws that would impose the death penalty more fairly. In 1976, the Supreme Court found these laws constitutional, and executions resumed. Today, 37 states and the federal government impose the death penalty. The most common form of execution is lethal injection (the introduction of a deadly drug into the bloodstream).

MICHAEL KRONENWETTER
Author, *Capital Punishment:
A Reference Handbook*

CAPITOL, UNITED STATES

The United States Capitol in Washington, D.C., is where the U.S. Congress meets to make the nation's laws. One of the nation's most treasured landmarks, the Capitol stands on Capitol Hill, surrounded by congressional office buildings, the Library of Congress, and the Supreme Court. To the west, the broad, grassy Mall stretches to the Washington Monument and the Lincoln Memorial. Millions of people visit the Capitol every year.

The building's interior contains more than 500 rooms. Among the most important are the legislative chamber of the Senate in the north wing; that of the House of Representatives in the south wing; and the rotunda, the building's large, circular central room. The fresco painted on the rotunda's domed ceiling, *The Apotheosis of George Washington* by Constantino Brumidi, is among the best known of the Capitol's many works of art.

▶ HISTORY

In 1792 a competition to design the Capitol was held by the federal government. William Thornton, a self-taught architect, won the contest with a design inspired by classical

Greek and Roman architecture. On September 18, 1793, President George Washington laid the cornerstone of the building. Congress first met in the completed north wing in November 1800. Construction was taken over by Benjamin Latrobe in 1803, and the south wing was completed in 1807. But British troops set fire to the Capitol in 1814 during the War of 1812, and much of the interior had to be rebuilt.

After the war, noted Boston architect Charles Bulfinch completed the Capitol as Thornton and Latrobe had planned it. Between 1818 and 1829 he rebuilt the two wings and the west terraces. He also built the

Capitol's first dome, made of wood covered with copper plating.

As the nation expanded, it outgrew the Capitol. More space was needed for Congress. In the 1850's, architect Thomas U. Walter oversaw the additions to the north and south wings—one for the Senate and one for the House of Representatives. He also supervised the construction of the present, higher dome. The Capitol was completed when the dome was finished on December 2, 1863.

Since 1863 the Capitol has been maintained and updated. Central heating, electricity, elevators, and air conditioning have been added. The only major structural change came in 1959–60, when workers removed the crumbling sandstone of the east front and added a 32-foot (10-meter) marble extension. In 1983, Congress voted to restore the sandstone of the original west front wings.

FRED SCHWENGEL
President, U.S. Capitol Historical Society

CAPONE, ALPHONSE (AL). See CHICAGO (Famous People).
CAPOTE, TRUMAN. See LOUISIANA (Famous People).
CAPRA, FRANK. See MOTION PICTURES (Profiles: Directors).

CARAVAGGIO, MICHELANGELO MERISI DA (1571–1610)

The stormy life of the painter Michelangelo Merisi began in northern Italy near Milan. At 13 he was apprenticed to a local artist, but his career began in Rome when he was about 21. He became known as Caravaggio, after the town where he was born.

Caravaggio at first painted small still-life pictures—fruits and flowers—and simple pictures of ordinary boys who were sometimes dressed to look like figures from ancient myths. Caravaggio's talent soon attracted the attention of a wealthy patron, Cardinal del Monte, who became his protector.

In 1599, Caravaggio began painting large religious pictures for churches in Rome. These paintings depicted religious figures as ordinary people of his own day. This concept was so shocking at that time that some of Caravaggio's paintings were rejected by the priests. But other people thought that he was the greatest painter of his time—an opinion shared by art historians today.

Caravaggio had a violent temper. In 1606 he killed a man and fled Rome. He went to Naples and continued to paint, then went to Malta to join the Knights of Saint John of Jerusalem, a military and religious order. But he got into trouble and again had to escape. After painting in Sicily and Naples, Caravaggio heard that he was to be pardoned by the pope. He set out for Rome, only to die on the way, on July 18, 1610.

HOWARD HIBBARD
Author, *Caravaggio*

CARAWAY, HATTIE. See ARKANSAS (Famous People).

The *Entombment* (1602-04), by the Italian painter Caravaggio, shows the body of Christ being lowered into the tomb. Brilliantly highlighted areas contrast with the dark background, creating a dramatic effect.

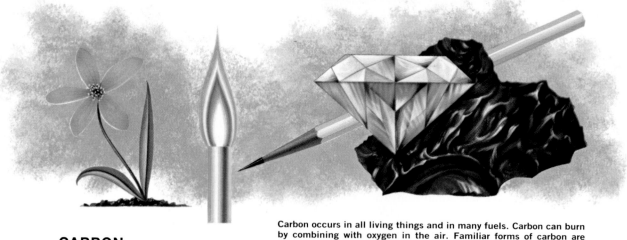

Carbon occurs in all living things and in many fuels. Carbon can burn by combining with oxygen in the air. Familiar forms of carbon are coal, graphite, and diamonds.

CARBON

Carbon is a common element (chemical symbol, C) that all of us have seen. It occurs in several forms, and the best known is probably coal. That immediately tells you something about this form of carbon: It can burn. When coal burns, it combines with the oxygen in the air and forms a gas called carbon dioxide.

Most of the common substances that burn also contain carbon; that is, they have carbon atoms in their structure. When such materials as wood, gasoline, or paper burn, carbon dioxide is produced. The food we eat also contains carbon atoms in its structure. Within our bodies this food undergoes a process somewhat like slow burning—and the air we breathe out contains carbon dioxide.

It is possible to heat wood while keeping oxygen away from it. Without oxygen the wood cannot burn. But the part of the wood that is not carbon is driven off as gases. What remains is called charcoal. It is almost pure carbon. When charcoal is used to make a fire, it burns without a flame. It lasts longer and burns hotter than wood.

Ordinary coal can be similarly treated, for it is not wholly made of carbon. If coal is heated to drive off other materials, the remains are chiefly carbon. This form is called coke.

When coke or charcoal is heated with iron ore, the carbon takes part in a process that removes oxygen from the ore. As a result the metal (iron) is left. Pure iron is not very hard. But if a small amount of carbon is added, the mixture is steel. Steel is much harder than pure iron. The manufacture of iron and steel uses more carbon than any other industry.

Carbon has many varied uses. Powdered charcoal can be formed in such a way as to be full of tiny holes. The charcoal then serves as a filter. As air is drawn through the holes, the charcoal traps gases and chemicals. Such charcoal is put in the gasmasks used by soldiers and fire fighters.

There is a soft kind of carbon that flakes off if scraped across paper. It leaves a black mark behind. This form of carbon is called graphite. What most people call the "lead" in a pencil is really graphite.

Another form of carbon is not black but is as transparent as glass. This is diamond. Diamond forms when carbon is heated to a high temperature and squeezed under great pressure. Scientists now know how to make tiny diamonds in the laboratory, but all big diamonds occur naturally. They form deep in the earth, over millions of years, and are brought near the surface by shifting in the rock. Diamond is the hardest substance known. Diamond powder will cut the hardest steel.

Like all other substances, carbon is made up of atoms. But carbon atoms are unusual in that they can combine with one another and form long, complicated molecules. These chainlike and ringlike molecules become the core of compounds formed when other kinds of atoms are attached to the carbon atoms. That is why carbon exists in many forms and compounds.

Complicated carbon compounds occur in all living bodies. All the important substances that make up the human body contain carbon atoms. Life as we know it would be impossible without carbon.

ISAAC ASIMOV
Boston University School of Medicine

See also ELEMENTS, CHEMICAL.

CARBON MONOXIDE POISONING. See POISONS AND ANTIDOTES.

CARD GAMES

Card games are a good way to learn new skills and to have inexpensive fun at the same time. Card games help us learn mathematics and logic and provide mental exercise that stimulates our attention to detail and improves memory.

▶ CARD GAME TERMS

The Deck. A ''regular'' **deck** of cards has 52 cards. The deck is divided into four **suits** of 13 cards each. The suits, pictured in the diagram below, are spades, hearts, diamonds, and clubs. There are ten **number cards** and three **face cards.** The ace (A) is number one, and the other cards are numbered from 2 to 10. The three cards with faces on them, sometimes called **picture cards,** are known as the king (K), queen (Q), and jack (J).

In many games, the cards have a value or rank, with 2 being the lowest value and the other cards having higher value in order, that is, 2, 3, 4, 5, 6, 7, 8, 9, 10, jack, queen, king, and ace. In some card games, the rank or value of the cards is different, and in other games the suit or value does not matter.

Regular decks come with one or two extra cards called **jokers.** The jokers belong to no suit, but in some games they have special uses.

Shuffle, Cut, Deal, and Hand. To **shuffle** the deck means to mix the deck of cards so that the same suits and same numbers are not together. After the deck is shuffled, it is usually cut. To **cut** the deck of cards, the deck is placed face down on the table. A player lifts about half the cards, puts them next to the rest of the pack or deck, and then places the bottom half on top.

To **deal** means to hand out cards from the deck to the players. The person who hands out the cards for a game is called the **dealer.** In almost all games, the dealer hands out the cards to the players in a clockwise direction. The dealer starts by giving a card or cards to the player on his or her left and continues around to the other players. Play often proceeds from left to right.

A **hand** is the term for the cards a player holds in his or her hand before they are played.

Tricks, Trumps, Lead, and Follow Suit. Many games require players to win **tricks.** A trick is one card played, in turn, by each player at the table. The trick is won by the player playing the card with the highest rank or value.

In some games, one suit is chosen as **trumps.** The other suits are ''plain suits.'' Any card of a trump suit is more powerful than any card of a plain suit.

The **lead** is the first card played toward a trick. Often the player sitting to the left of the dealer is the player to lead or play first. To **follow suit** is to play a card of the same suit as the card that was led.

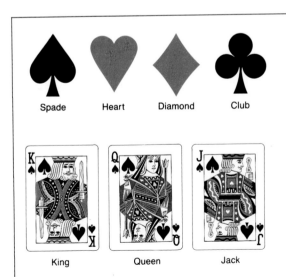

Spade   Heart   Diamond   Club

King   Queen   Jack

What is the origin of the suits in a deck of playing cards? Why are there three face cards in each suit?

It was in Europe, where playing cards have been used for at least 800 years, that the cards were divided into groups or suits. Each of the suits represented one of the four social classes of life in the Middle Ages. The nobility were represented by swords, which later became spades. The clergy were represented by cups, which later became hearts. Merchants were represented by coins, which turned into diamonds, and peasants were represented by staves, which later became clubs.

In each suit there are three picture, or face, cards: a king (K), a queen (Q), and a jack (J), sometimes called the knave. Early decks of cards contained portraits honoring actual kings, queens, and princes. Many decks in use today include picture cards with costumes worn by the kings of England in the 15th and 16th centuries.

Many games call for counting the number of cards won to decide the winning player or winning team. Sometimes the number of tricks won determines the winner. Other times the cards are assigned point values, and the player with the highest number of points at the end of play is the winner.

▶TYPES OF CARD GAMES

Nearly all card games belong to one of three groups: (1) games in which the object is to get rid of all cards held in the hand; (2) games in which high cards win tricks; or (3) games in which the object of the game is to put the cards together in order and/or in sets. Card games played by one person alone are called **solitaire.** In other games two or more players compete individually, or games can be played that require players to play with one or more partners as a team.

▶RULES

Before playing any game, it is important for all players to know the rules or at least to agree on how the game should be played, how to keep score, and how to win the game. Books are available that include the rules for many games.

The more games you know how to play, the more fun you can have with cards. The following section gives you the rules for a number of popular games you can play with cards.

GAMES FOR ONE—SOLITAIRE GAMES

When you are ill or on a trip or if you are just alone and want to entertain yourself, there are many solitaire games that you can play for relaxation or to challenge yourself. The following games are fun for one. Always shuffle the cards thoroughly before you begin any game.

Idiot's Delight

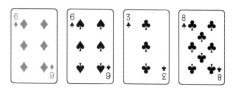

Object:	To discard all of the cards in the deck except the four aces.
Deck:	Shuffle a 52-card deck and hold it in your hand.
Play:	Ace is the highest card, followed by king, queen, jack, and then the number cards from high to low.

Begin the game by dealing four cards face up in a row.

Discard any card that is lower in number or value than another card of the same suit. For example, if a three of clubs and an eight of clubs are showing, you may discard the three. Fill the empty space where the three of clubs was with the top card from your hand. Continue to discard the lowest card of each suit showing and to fill empty spaces until all cards are a different suit and thus you can no longer discard.

Deal four cards from your hand face up on top of the four cards showing. Begin discarding as before.

Whenever a space occurs because you have discarded all cards in one of the four piles, fill the space with the top card from any other pile. Spaces should be filled before a new row of four cards is dealt. Continue play until all the cards in your hand are gone. You deal all the cards only once. You win the game if you go through the deck once and discard all the cards except the four aces.

Up and Down

Object:	To turn all of the cards face up without matching any card with the number you call.
Deck:	Shuffle a 52-card deck and hold it in your hand.
Play:	Pay no attention to the suits; only the value of the cards matters. Out loud or to yourself say "ace" (or "one"), and turn the top card over. If it is not an ace, place it face up on the bottom of the deck. Say or think "two," and turn the next card face up. If it is not a two, put it face up on the bottom of the deck. Continue counting three through ten, then jack, queen, and king while turning over the cards.

If you happen to turn up any card as you call it, the game is over and you lose. For example, if you call "five" and a five turns up, you lose. If you can count through the deck from ace to king three times without turning up a "called card," you win the game.

Pairing Off

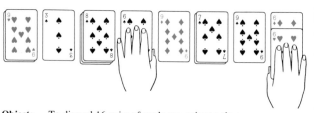

Object:	To discard 16 pairs of cards one pair at a time.
Deck:	Remove all of the picture cards, aces, and tens.
Play:	Shuffle the 32 cards. Deal out eight cards in a row face up. Cover these with another eight cards also face up. Continue dealing until you have four cards in each of the eight piles.

Now pick up and discard any two cards that match, for example, two sixes. You may discard only two cards (one pair) at a time. You win if you can pair off and discard all of the cards.

Even Up

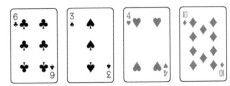

Object: To discard pairs of cards that add up to an even number.

Deck: Remove all of the picture cards from the pack.

Play: Shuffle the 40 cards. Hold the deck and deal one card face up. Deal a second card face up next to the first. If the two cards add up to an odd number, such as the six and three above, lay down another card. Keep laying down cards until two add to an even number, such as the ten and four above. Pick up the two cards adding to an even number and put them on a discard pile. Any two cards lying next to each other that add to an even number can be discarded. Go through the deck once. If all the cards end up in the discard pile, you win.

Round the Clock

Object: To arrange the cards in sets of four, face up in a circle.

Deck: All 52 cards.

Play: Deal the cards into 13 piles of four cards each, face down, in the shape of a clock as shown.

Each pile is given a value the same as numbers on a clock, with twelve at the top, three on the right, six on the bottom, and so on. The extra pile in the center (No. 13) is the pile where kings will be placed as they are turned over.

Begin by taking the top card from the 13 pile; look at it, and slip it face up under the pile of its own number or value. For example, if the first card taken from the 13 pile is a three, slip it face up under the four cards in the three o'clock position. Then take the top card from the number three pile and look at it. If, for example, it is a queen, put it under the pile in the twelve o'clock position. If a card is turned up with the same number as the pile where it belongs, just put it under and take the next card. If there is no next card face down, take instead the top card of the next higher pile. When a king is turned over, it is placed in the center of the clock. You win the game if you are able to turn up all the cards and place them in the proper piles (four all alike) before you turn up four kings. You lose and the game is over if you turn up four kings.

War

Players: 2 to 4

Object: To win all the cards.

Deck: A regular 52-card deck. Pay no attention to the suits. Ace is the highest ranking card, followed by king, queen, jack, and then the number cards in descending order.

Play: Deal out all the cards. Some players may get an extra card. All players keep their cards face down in a pile in front of them.

Play begins when each player turns over the top card from his or her pile. The player with the highest card wins all the other cards turned over and puts them face down under his or her pile. If two or more players turn up highest cards that match, a "War" begins. Each player who has a matching card now takes the next card from his or her pile and puts it face down on the matching card. Then these players put a third card face up. The highest card wins all the cards. If the cards are alike again, the war goes on, with each player who has a matching card placing a card face down and another face up until a player with the highest card wins all. When you have no more cards, you are out of the game. Other players continue until one player wins all the cards.

Old Maid

Players: 2 to 8

Object: To match cards in pairs and not get stuck with the "Old Maid."

Deck: Remove three queens, but leave the queen of spades. The queen of spades is the "Old Maid."

Play: Deal out all the cards one at a time. It does not matter if some players get one more. The players look at their hands for pairs (such as two sixes, two kings, and so on) and discard every pair they find face up. After all pairs have been discarded, the player to the left of the dealer holds his or her cards as a fan with the backs facing the dealer. The dealer takes one of the cards. If it forms a pair with a card he or she already has, the pair is discarded. If not, the dealer adds the card to his or her hand. The player to the dealer's left now takes a card from the hand of the player to his or her left. Play continues around the table. Players who are able to discard all of their cards drop out of the game. When 24 pairs of cards have been discarded, one card will remain—the "Old Maid." The player stuck with the "Old Maid" is the loser.

Go Fish

Players: 2 to 8

Object: To be the player to collect the most sets of four of a kind.

Deck: All cards in a regular 52-card deck.

Play: If there are two players, deal seven cards to each. If there are more than two players, deal five cards to each player. Any cards not dealt to players are placed in a pile face down.

The dealer starts. The dealer asks any other player for a card to match one of the cards he or she has in hand. For example, if the dealer has a two, three, eight, ten, and a jack in hand, the dealer may ask Player 2, "Do you have any eights?" If Player 2 has any eights, then Player 2 must give them all to the dealer.

The dealer may ask the same player or some other player for another card needed. If the player has the card, it must be given over to the dealer. If the player does not have the card, he or she tells the dealer to "Go Fish" a card from the pile of extra cards. If the dealer fishes and catches the card asked for, he or she shows it to the other players and gets to fish again. If not, the dealer's turn is over and the player to the left asks someone for a card. When any player gets four of a kind, he or she shows them to the other players and puts them face down at his or her place.

If a player runs out of cards before the fish pile is gone, he or she picks five cards from the fish pile and continues to play. The game ends when all the players are out of cards and the fish pile is gone. The winner is the player who has the most sets of four of a kind.

Crazy Eights

Players: 2 to 6
Object: To be the first to get rid of all your cards or, failing that, to have the fewest points.
Deck: A regular 52-card deck.
Play: If there are two players, deal seven cards to each. If there are three or more players, deal five cards to each. All cards not dealt are placed face down in the middle of the table. These cards make up the draw pile. Turn over the top card of the draw pile and place it next to the draw pile to start a discard pile. If the top card is an eight, however, it is shuffled back into the draw pile and a new card is turned.

In Crazy Eights, each player in turn plays a card from his or her hand to match the top card on the discard pile. Cards match if they are the same suit or the same rank or any eight, because eights are wild cards. If a player is unable to match the top card on the discard pile by playing a card from his or her hand, the player takes cards one at a time from the draw pile until one that can be played is drawn. If all cards are taken from the draw pile and the player is unable to play, the player passes his turn.

All eights are wild, and an eight can be played regardless of the last card on the discard pile. The player playing the eight names any suit, and the next card played must be of that suit or another eight. Play continues until one player has no more cards.

Sometimes no one can play and all the cards in the draw pile are gone. This situation is called a block, and the game ends. When the game ends by a block, the player holding the least number of points wins.
Scoring: The winner of each game receives the total amount of points left in the other players' hands as follows: 50 points for each eight, 10 points for each picture card, and 1 point for each ace, while all other cards equal their value. Scores can be recorded. The first player to get 300 points or more wins.

Hearts

Players: 3 to 7
Object: To avoid taking hearts in tricks.
Deck: From a regular 52-card deck, eliminate the following cards depending on how many are playing:

Players	Discarded cards
3	1
4	0
5	2
6	4
7	3

Play: The cards rank in regular order with ace high. The entire deck is dealt out one card at a time. Each player should receive an equal number of cards.

The player to the left of the dealer leads with any card.

Players must follow suit if they are able. If not, any card may be played. The trick is won by the player playing the highest card of the suit led. The winner of each trick leads next. When all cards have been played, each player counts the number of heart cards he or she has collected.

A score card may be kept, and play may continue with a certain time limit or for a certain number of hands.

The winner is the player with the lowest total score.

I Doubt It

Players: 3 to 6
Object: To be the first player out of cards.
Deck: A regular 52-card deck; ace is low.
Play: Shuffle and deal all the cards. It does not matter if some players get an extra card. The player on the dealer's left starts by taking one card and placing it face down on the table, calling out "ace." The next player to the left plays a card face down and calls out "two." As the third player adds a card to the discard pile, the player says "three." Play continues through ten, jack, queen, and king, then starts again with ace. A card does not have to be what the player says it is. Another player may question the claim by saying, "I doubt it." If the card played is not what it is supposed to be, the player who "pretended" must take up all the cards in the discard pile and add them to his or her hand. If the card is the right one, the player who doubted must pick up the whole discard pile and play continues. Instead of playing one card, any player may in turn put down two or more cards at a time by saying, for example, "I am playing two sixes."

The winner is the first player safely out of cards.

Concentration

Players: 2 to 8
Object: To collect the most pairs of cards.
Deck: A regular 52-card deck.
Play: Shuffle the cards.

Deal all the cards face down on a large table or on the floor. The cards may be spread out in any pattern, but a little space should be left between cards. The player to the left of the dealer starts the game by turning any two cards face up and leaving them where they are. All the players look at the two cards as they are turned over. If the two cards match, the player picks them up, keeps them, and turns up two more cards. If the two cards chosen are not a pair, the player must turn both face down again leaving them exactly where they were. Then the next player tries to find a pair and play continues in order until all the cards have been picked up in pairs. The player who collects the greatest number of pairs is the winner.

Rummy

Players: 2 to 6

Object: To be the first player out of cards after obtaining or playing on sets of three of a kind, four of a kind, or a run of three or more cards of the same suit in sequence.

Deck: A regular 52-card deck.

Play: Each player receives ten cards when two play, seven cards when three or four play, and six cards when five or six play. After dealing, the rest of the deck is placed face down in the center of the table and becomes the draw pile. The top card of the draw pile is turned face up and placed beside it to start the discard pile. The player to the left of the dealer starts, and thereafter the play continues to the left or clockwise. Each player begins a turn with a draw and ends it by discarding one card. When drawing, the player has a choice of taking either the top card from the draw pile or the top card of the discard pile.

Players may discard any card but may not draw from the discard pile and return the same card in the same turn. The discard pile must be kept neat so previous discards do not stick out from underneath the pile.

Players try to get rid of cards in their hands by collecting sets of three or four matched cards of equal rank (for example, three fours or four aces) or by collecting three or more cards of the same suit in sequence, such as six, seven, and eight of clubs. Players may lay down face up in front of them one or more matched sets (at least three cards in each set) or they may build on (add to) sets already on the table, either their own or their opponents'.

The player who goes out first by getting rid of all cards in hand wins. If no one goes out before the last card from the draw pile is taken, the discard pile is turned over to form a new draw pile and play continues. The next player in turn after the last card is drawn has a choice between the discard and the top of the new draw pile. The winner scores points for the total value of the cards remaining in other players' hands when the game ends whether the remaining cards form matched sets or not. Picture cards count ten points each. Aces count one, and all numbered cards count their value. When a player goes out, every player shows his full hand.

If a player ''goes rummy'' by laying down his entire hand in one turn, having not previously laid down any cards, the player gets double the number of points from every other player. Score can be kept until one player obtains 500 points.

▶ **HISTORY OF CARD GAMES**

The very first playing cards were probably made in China or India many hundreds of years ago. From these countries card games spread throughout the Far East and across the Indian Ocean to Arabia and Egypt. In earlier times, cards were used for telling fortunes as well as for playing games.

The first playing cards were painted by hand. Later cards were printed from woodcuts. The design was carved on a block of wood that was covered with ink and pressed against paper. Color was added later. Some of the early playing cards were round in shape, and some were square. It was many years before cards became rectangular in shape and easy to handle. Originally cards had no numbers in the corners. A player had to look carefully at the front of each card and count the number of pips, or spots, on the card to know its value. In the late 1800's index numbers were placed in the corners. Then it was easier to hold many cards in a fan shape and see every card at a glance.

Modern cards are printed on pasteboard and coated with plastic to make them last longer. The advantage of cards made of pasteboard is that it is impossible to see through them even when they are held under a strong light.

Playing cards were first brought to America by the sailors on Columbus' first voyage in 1492. Almost all of the founding fathers of our country, including George Washington, Thomas Jefferson, and John Q. Adams, found time to play cards. Benjamin Franklin not only played cards but also printed and sold them.

Card games are played in just about every country in the world today, and games that are similar are played in many different countries. Most of the games that are played today are based on old ones that have been played for hundreds of years.

More than 200 years ago, the rules for many card games were written down by Edmond Hoyle, an English lawyer, in a publication entitled *Hoyle's Games*. Hoyle saw 16 editions of his book printed and distributed on several continents before he died at the age of 90. The phrase ''according to Hoyle,'' which means playing according to the rules, became part of our language.

JOHN BELTON
Author, *Let's Play Cards*

CAREERS. See VOCATIONS.

Map labels:
GULF OF MEXICO · U.S.A. FLORIDA · Miami · BAHAMAS · CARIBBEAN SEA AND ISLANDS · ATLANTIC OCEAN · TROPIC OF CANCER · STRAITS OF FLORIDA · Havana · CUBA · MEXICO · ISLE OF PINES · Camaguey · Guantánamo · TORTUGA IS · GRAND CAYMAN · HAITI · DOMINICAN REPUBLIC · Port-au-Prince · Santo Domingo · San Juan · VIRGIN IS. (U.K.) · ANGUILLA · ST. MARTIN · JAMAICA · Port Royal · Kingston · Ponce · (U.S.A.) · PUERTO RICO · ISLANDS · Leeward · ST. KITTS-NEVIS · ANTIGUA AND BARBUD · BELIZE · CARIBBEAN · ANTILLES · Islands · MONTSERRAT · GUADELOUPE · DOMINICA · MARTINIQUE · HONDURAS · SEA · ST. LUCIA · BARBAD · LESSER ANTILLES · Windward · ST. VINCENT AND THE GRENADINES · NICARAGUA · GRENADA · TOBAGO · ARUBA · CURAÇAO · BONAIRE · MARGARITA ISLAND · Port of Spain · TRINIDAD · TORTUGA ISLAND · TRINIDAD AND TOBAGO · COSTA RICA · PANAMA · VENEZUELA · COLOMBIA · GUYANA · GEO BUCTEL · Miles 100 200 300 400 500 · Kilometers 100 200 300 400 500 600 700

CARIBBEAN SEA AND ISLANDS

The Caribbean Sea is a part of the Atlantic Ocean, situated between the mainlands of Mexico, Central and South America, and the islands of the Antilles. The Antilles are the main island group of the West Indies. They stretch for more than 2,000 miles (3,220 kilometers) and form the boundary between the Caribbean Sea and the Atlantic.

Named for the Carib Indians, who once inhabited some of the islands, the Caribbean Sea covers an area of about 750,000 square miles (1,942,500 square kilometers). The Panama Canal links the Caribbean with the Pacific Ocean, making the sea one of the world's major waterways.

Island Groups. The islands of the Caribbean consist of two main groups: the Greater An-

The Iron Market is a famous landmark as well as a busy marketplace in Port-au-Prince, the capital of Haiti. Haiti shares the island of Hispaniola with the Dominican Republic.

Two harbors illustrate the contrast in terrain found on Caribbean islands. *Left:* Willemstad is the capital of Curaçao, which is low and flat. *Below:* St. George's is the capital of hilly Grenada. *Bottom:* The Caribbean's mild climate has helped make tourism one of its main industries.

tilles and the Lesser Antilles. The Greater Antilles include the four largest islands—Cuba, Hispaniola (shared by the nations of Haiti and the Dominican Republic), Jamaica, and Puerto Rico. The Lesser Antilles include the Leeward and Windward Islands. The Virgin Islands and the Netherlands Antilles are usually included in the Lesser Antilles. Barbados and Trinidad and Tobago are generally considered to be a part of this group as well.

Land and Climate. The islands are part of two mountain chains, which reach their highest point in Hispaniola. The mountains have been worn away on many of the islands of the Lesser Antilles, but others still have active volcanoes. A few of the larger islands have wide, fertile valleys.

The Caribbean region has a moderate climate, cooled by the breezes of the trade winds. Temperatures range from about 70 to 85°F (21 to 29°C). Rainfall is heaviest in the summer months. Hurricanes often develop in the late summer or early fall and may cause widespread damage.

Sugar and its by-products are among the chief exports of the Caribbean islands. *Left:* The sugarcane crop is harvested mechanically in Cuba, one of the world's leading sugar producers. *Below:* Rum, made from molasses produced in the manufacturing of sugar, is bottled in a plant in Puerto Rico.

People. The Indian inhabitants of the islands died out soon after the arrival of the first European settlers. The majority of the Caribbean peoples today are blacks, descendants of Africans brought to the region as slaves in past centuries. Others include whites, Chinese, and people whose ancestors came from what is now India and Pakistan. The varied languages of the islands include English, Spanish, French, and Dutch.

Economy. For centuries the chief products of the Caribbean have been sugar, coffee, tropical fruits, and spices. While these are still important exports, the economic emphasis in recent years has been on industrial development. Puerto Rico has a considerable manufacturing base. Curaçao and Trinidad have petroleum refineries. Cuba has one of the world's largest deposits of nickel, and Jamaica produces bauxite, a chief source of aluminum. Because of the islands' pleasant climate, clear blue waters, and sparkling beaches, tourism has long been an important industry.

Early History. In 1492 Christopher Columbus reached the Caribbean on his first voyage of discovery for Spain. The Spanish established early settlements on the islands of the Greater Antilles. When their colonies flourished, other European nations began to take an interest in the Caribbean, and for 300 years there was a struggle for power in the region.

In the 1600's, France acquired western Hispaniola (now Haiti), Martinique, and Guadeloupe. The British established themselves in Barbados and later gained control of Jamai-

---

PRINCIPAL ISLANDS IN THE CARIBBEAN

Greater Antilles

Cuba, Hispaniola (Haiti and the Dominican Republic), Jamaica, Puerto Rico **(U.S.)**.

Lesser Antilles

Anguilla **(Br.)**, Antigua and Barbuda, Aruba **(Neth.)**, Barbados, Bonaire **(Neth.)**, Curaçao **(Neth.)**, Dominica, Grenada, Guadeloupe **(Fr.)**, Martinique **(Fr.)**, Montserrat **(Br.)**, Saba **(Neth.)**, St. Eustatius **(Neth.)**, St. Kitts and Nevis, St. Lucia, St. Martin **(Fr.-Neth.)**, St. Vincent and the Grenadines, Trinidad and Tobago, British Virgin Islands, U.S. Virgin Islands (St. Croix, St. John, St. Thomas).

Other Islands

Cayman Islands **(Br.)**, Margarita **(Venez.)**, Tortuga **(Venez.)**

Islands are independent except where noted: **Br.** = Britain; **Fr.** = France; **Neth.** = Netherlands; **U.S.** = United States; **Venez.** = Venezuela.

---

ca, Trinidad, Tobago, and other islands, eventually becoming the dominant power in the Caribbean. The Dutch colonized several islands, including Curaçao and Aruba. Denmark acquired the Virgin Islands. The Caribbean was also a profitable hunting ground for pirates, who plundered Spanish treasure ships and settlements.

U.S. Influence. As a result of the Spanish-American War (1898), Cuba won its independence and Puerto Rico became a territory (now a commonwealth) of the United States. In 1917 the United States purchased the islands of St. Croix, St. John, and St. Thomas (the U.S. Virgin Islands) from Denmark.

Independence. Haiti was the first Caribbean state to gain its independence, following a slave revolt against the French near the end of the 1700's. The Dominican Republic, on the eastern part of Hispaniola, gained independence from Spain in the mid-1800's, and Cuba became a republic in 1902.

Most of the rest of the British-governed Caribbean islands won independence between the 1960's and 1980's: Jamaica and Trinidad and Tobago (1962); Barbados (1966); Grenada (1974); Dominica (1978); St. Lucia and St. Vincent and the Grenadines (1979); Antigua and Barbuda (1981); and St. Kitts and Nevis (1983).

The Caribbean today is a product of both its geography and history. Its geography created a distinct Caribbean region. Its history has given it a culture combining European, African, American, and Asian influences.

Reviewed by A. CURTIS WILGUS
Former Director
School of Inter-American Studies
University of Florida
Author, *Historical Atlas of Latin America*

See also ANTIGUA AND BARBUDA; BARBADOS; CUBA; DOMINICA; DOMINICAN REPUBLIC; GRENADA; HAITI; JAMAICA; PUERTO RICO; SAINT KITTS AND NEVIS; SAINT LUCIA; SAINT VINCENT AND THE GRENADINES; TRINIDAD AND TOBAGO.

CARILLONS. See BELLS AND CARILLONS.

CARNEGIE, ANDREW (1835–1919)

Andrew Carnegie built the steel industry in the United States and became rich. But he believed a wealthy person's money belonged to the community in which it was earned. In the last 18 years of his life, he shared much of his fortune with other people.

Carnegie was born in Dunfermline, Scotland, on November 25, 1835. When he was 13, the family moved to the United States and settled in Pittsburgh, Pennsylvania.

In 1850, Carnegie went to work for the Pittsburgh telegraph office, first as a messenger and later as an operator. Thomas Scott, the superintendent of the Pennsylvania Railroad's western division, hired him as his personal clerk in 1853. Six years later, Carnegie himself became superintendent. During the Civil War (1861–65), Scott served as assistant secretary of war, and Carnegie helped him set up railroads and a telegraph system for the Union Army.

Meanwhile, Carnegie began to invest in different businesses—oil fields, ironworks, and companies that made railroad locomotives and sleeping cars. In 1865 he resigned from the railroad to concentrate on iron and steel manufacturing. He foresaw that the United States would need more and more steel, and he consequently became known as the Steel King. In 1901 he sold his steel empire. It became part of the United States Steel Corporation.

Carnegie once declared, "He who dies rich, dies disgraced." He used his fortune to help other people. He founded the Carnegie Institute of Pittsburgh, which has a library, a museum of fine arts, and a museum of natural history. He also founded a school of technology (now part of Carnegie-Mellon University, in Pittsburgh). Through the Carnegie Corporation of New York, he gave large sums to establish free libraries and to further education. Much of Carnegie's wealth went to promote world peace, through the Carnegie Endowment for International Peace. And he set up the Carnegie Institute of Washington to fund scientific research.

Carnegie died on August 11, 1919, shortly after the end of World War I.

Reviewed by GERALD KURLAND
Author, *Andrew Carnegie*

CARNEGIE, DALE. See MISSOURI (Famous People).

One of the most elaborate carnivals in the United States takes place in New Orleans during Mardi Gras. This two-week celebration precedes the 40-day Christian season of Lent.

CARNIVALS

What do you think of when you hear the word "carnival"? Do you think of a traveling show that comes to town with exciting rides and games of chance? An entertainment put on by the local volunteer fire department or some other community organization to raise money? Or a yearly celebration like the Mardi Gras in New Orleans or the winter carnival in Quebec City? All of these are carnivals, and they aim to provide fun for people.

The word "carnival" comes from the Latin words *carnem levare*, "to put aside flesh [meat]." It seems closely related to the Latin expression *carne vale!* ("flesh, farewell!"). The carnival had its origin hundreds of years ago in the feasting and merrymaking just before the beginning of Lent. (Lent is the long period of penance before Easter during which Christians may fast and eat no meat.)

▶MARDI GRAS AND SIMILAR CARNIVALS

Pre-Lenten carnivals are still held each year in many towns and cities of Europe and the Americas where the people are mostly Catholic. Among the most famous carnivals are those of Nice, France; Munich, Germany; and Rio de Janeiro, Brazil. Carnivals generally include parades of costumed merrymakers and colorful floats, street dancing, and fancy dress balls. There may also be fireworks and "battles" with flowers or confetti.

The carnival season begins officially on Twelfth Night (January 6). But most of the celebrating occurs just before the beginning of Lent on Ash Wednesday. The French call the last of the carnival "Mardi Gras," which means "Fat Tuesday" (from the custom of using up all fats on the day before Lent).

Mardi Gras is celebrated with a carnival in several cities of the United States that were founded by French or Spanish settlers. The most famous is the festival in New Orleans, Louisiana. There the term "Mardi Gras" stands for the two-week carnival period before Lent.

Special organizations, called krewes, prepare the festivities of Mardi Gras in New Orleans. The first, the Mystic Krewe of Comus, was formed in 1857. Its purpose was to celebrate Mardi Gras with good taste. Invitation to membership in a krewe is considered an honor.

The most famous events of Mardi Gras are the parades (with floats and marchers in colorful costumes) and the balls. Each procession and ball has a different theme. An important part of the Mardi Gras is the appearance of Rex, king of the carnival. He is chosen for his outstanding leadership in the community. But his identity is supposed to be kept secret.

TRAVELING CARNIVALS

Carnivals that move from town to town originated in the United States in the late 1890's. Today they sometimes operate in connection with fairs or in amusement parks. To raise money, fire departments, churches, and schools often sponsor the visit of a traveling carnival. Groups that are similar to American carnivals now tour in many other countries. In Britain, traveling carnivals are known as fun fairs.

Early carnivals in the United States all traveled by railroad. Since good highways are plentiful today, most carnivals now travel in trucks. Traveling carnivals always play outdoors, and their season runs from early spring to late fall. In the southern United States, a few carnivals play winter dates.

The "front end" of the show lot is the main entrance. It is lined with concessions. Here are refreshment stands, with everything from cotton candy to frankfurters, and games of skill and chance, with prizes for the winners.

At the "back end" of the lot are the rides and often a huge fun house. Children's rides may include small fire engines, a merry-go-round, carts, and boats. Major carnivals, which are attended by many people, may have up to 75 rides for adults. The Giant Wheel, Sky Fighter, and Octopus are just a few. Many rides are manufactured in the United States. Others are imported from Europe.

When a carnival is not on the road, it is in winter quarters, usually in the same part of the country where it plays. Here equipment is repaired and repainted and made ready for the spring opening. The canvas tents are mended, and the concession booths are repainted and repaired.

Carnival life is not easy. The lots are often muddy and washed out by summer rains. If the weather is dry, dust may cover the concession stands and rides. The usual routine consists of unpacking and setting up, working the stands, repacking and loading up, and moving to the next town. A carnival usually moves once a week. The people of these traveling shows take great pride in what they do. People of a carnival are a closely knit group. Often entire families work for the same show. The ownership and management of almost all large carnivals has been passed on from one generation to the next.

Carnivals are very popular because they offer a wide variety of entertainment. More individual tickets are sold each year to carnivals and carnival attractions than to any other live entertainment in the United States. Totals of ticket sales are close to those of movie ticket sales. Very few of the hundreds of smaller fairs could exist without the attraction of a carnival. Even large state fairs depend on carnivals to increase the number of visitors.

Traveling carnivals continue to thrive because they furnish a type of entertainment in which people can take part directly.

JOSEPH W. McKENNON
Curatorial Consultant
Ringling Museum of the Circus

See also CIRCUS.

Brilliant colors and lively music set the stage for the fun and games of traveling carnivals. Merry-go-rounds and Ferris wheels add to the festive atmosphere.

An age-old Christmas custom continues to this day: During the holiday season, people gather together to sing carols, Christmas songs of joy and good cheer.

CAROLS

Carols are songs associated with the Christmas season. Since Christmas is a season of joy and good cheer, most carols are joyous and cheerful in character. They have lilting rhythms and pleasing melodies. They are easy to sing and easy to remember. The words may be religious or nonreligious. Some of the oldest songs we know are Christmas carols.

Carols began as dance songs. In the Middle Ages the word "carol" meant to dance in a ring while singing. This explains the lively character of so many of the old carols. Not all carols have been about Christmas. The earliest were songs celebrating May Day and the seasons of the year. Carols dating from the 1400's in England dealt with a variety of subjects—even politics. Many of the old French carols consisted of religious words sung to popular tunes of the day. (In France a Christmas carol is called a *noël*.)

The oldest English carol that is still sung regularly today is "The Boar's Head." It was first published in England in 1521. Two other English carols, "Wassail Song" and "Down in Yon Forest," are among the oldest songs of any kind that we know. The first is a drinking song; the second was sung by wandering troubadours in the Middle Ages. The most popular of the old English carols today is probably "God Rest Ye Merry, Gentlemen." "The First Noel," one of the oldest of all carols, may have come from France, or it may be of English origin. We do not know the names of the composers of any of these old carols.

The composers of carols that were written in more recent times are known. One of the most beautiful of all religious melodies is *Adeste Fideles* ("O Come, All Ye Faithful"). Both the words and music probably were written by an English music teacher named John Francis Wade and published in 1751. The words to the stirring "Hark! The Herald Angels Sing!" were written in 1739 by the English hymn writer Charles Wesley. They were later adapted to a melody by Felix Mendelssohn. Another English hymn writer, Isaac Watts, wrote the popular carol "Joy to the World" in 1719. It was later arranged to the music of George Frederick Handel by the American composer Lowell Mason. A minister in Philadelphia named Phillips Brooks wrote the words to "O, Little Town of Bethlehem" in 1868 after a visit to Christ's birthplace. His church organist, Lewis Redner, composed the melody.

In Germany and Austria a carol is called a *Weihnachtslied* ("Christmas song"). The beautiful German carol, "Lo, How a Rose E'er Blooming" (1609) by Michael Praetorius, is a well-known favorite outside Germany. The most popular of all Christmas carols is perhaps "Silent Night, Holy Night!" *(Stille Nacht, Heilige Nacht!)*. Joseph Mohr, pastor of a little church in Oberdorf, Austria, wrote the words on Christmas Eve, 1818. The organist of his church, Franz Gruber, composed the music the same evening and the carol was sung at midnight Mass. Today it is sung throughout the world.

Popular modern carols include "Jingle Bells" (1857), by J. Pierpont, and Irving Berlin's "White Christmas" (1942).

DAVID EWEN
Music Historian

CARPENTRY. See WOODWORKING.
CARPETBAGGERS. See RECONSTRUCTION PERIOD.
CARPETS. See RUGS AND CARPETS.
CARROLL, CHARLES. See MARYLAND (Famous People).

CARROLL, LEWIS (1832–1898)

Lewis Carroll was the pen name of Charles Lutwidge Dodgson, a shy professor of mathematics whose delightful books *Alice's Adventures in Wonderland* and *Through the Looking-Glass* are read and loved by children and adults throughout the world.

Charles Lutwidge Dodgson was born on January 27, 1832, in the tiny village of Daresbury in Cheshire, England. His father was a country parson, and Charles was the eldest son in a family of eleven children.

As a boy, Charles enjoyed entertaining his brothers and sisters with games and tricks. He wrote stories and drew pictures for a series of homemade family magazines. These activities laid the foundations for his later work as a writer of children's books.

At the age of 14, Charles was sent to Rugby School. There, his stammer made him a target for bullying, and he was deeply unhappy. In 1851 he entered Christ Church College, Oxford University. After graduating, he remained at Oxford as a mathematics teacher and later was ordained a church deacon.

In his spare time he wrote humorous poems and articles for publication in magazines. In 1856 he began to sign these works with the pen name Lewis Carroll, derived from a Latin version of his first and middle names. He also took up the new art of photography, and over the next 25 years he produced outstanding portraits of prominent people of the Victorian time. But his loveliest photographs were of little girls.

One of his favorite photography subjects was Alice Liddell, daughter of the dean of Christ Church. Alice was not quite 4 years old when Carroll first saw her at play with her sisters Lorina and Edith. He became the children's friend and photographed them often.

On July 4, 1862, when Alice was 10, Carroll and his friend Robinson Duckworth took the sisters boating on the River Isis. As they rowed, Carroll made up a story about "Alice's adventures underground." Alice begged him to write it down, and so he produced a written version with drawings, which he gave her as a Christmas present.

In 1865, Carroll published Alice's story under the title *Alice's Adventures in Wonderland*, with illustrations by John Tenniel. Full of humor and fantasy, and featuring strange

Lewis Carroll, an English clergyman, mathematics professor, and author, wrote *Alice in Wonderland* as a gift for a child friend. The book has become a classic of children's literature.

creatures like the White Rabbit and the Cheshire Cat, the book was an immediate success.

Carroll's work on a sequel was interrupted by the death of his father in 1868. Carroll became head of the family and leased a large house in Guildford for his brothers and sisters. He continued to live in Oxford during the school year.

Through the Looking-Glass, the sequel to *Alice's Adventures in Wonderland*, was published in 1872 and was another success. It contains some of Carroll's best-loved work, including the nonsense poem "Jabberwocky." By this time the real Alice was grown up. After she married and left Oxford, Carroll rarely saw her. But he sent her copies of all his books.

Carroll gave up his teaching post to concentrate on writing. *The Hunting of the Snark* (1876) is his greatest full-length nonsense poem. Its mysterious last line, "For the Snark *was* a Boojum you see," came into his head when he was out walking, and the rest of the poem followed later. His novels *Sylvie and Bruno* (1889) and *Sylvie and Bruno Concluded* (1893), which combine an adult love story with a fairy tale, took 20 years to write. They contain much of Carroll's personal views of life. He also published mathematical writings under his real name. These include *Euclid and His Modern Rivals* (1879) and *The Game of Logic* (1886).

Carroll remained a bachelor all his life. He continued to enjoy friendships with many young children, but none were as great an inspiration to him as Alice. He died in Guildford on January 14, 1898.

ANNE CLARK AMOR
Author, *Lewis Carroll: A Biography*

ALICE'S ADVENTURES IN WONDERLAND

In this story, a little girl named Alice follows a white rabbit down a rabbit-hole and finds herself in Wonderland, where all sorts of unusual things occur. In the following excerpt, Alice meets three of Wonderland's strange inhabitants at "A Mad Tea-Party."

There was a table set out under a tree in front of the house, and the March Hare and the Hatter were having tea at it: a Dormouse was sitting between them, fast asleep, and the other two were using it as a cushion, resting their elbows on it, and talking over its head. "Very uncomfortable for the Dormouse," thought Alice; "only, as it's asleep, I suppose it doesn't mind."

The table was a large one, but the three were all crowded together at one corner of it. "No room! No room!" they cried out when they saw Alice coming. "There's *plenty* of room!" said Alice indignantly, and she sat down in a large arm-chair at one end of the table.

"Have some wine," the March Hare said in an encouraging tone.

Alice looked all round the table, but there was nothing on it but tea. "I don't see any wine," she remarked.

"There isn't any," said the March Hare.

"Then it wasn't very civil of you to offer it," said Alice angrily.

"It wasn't very civil of you to sit down without being invited," said the March Hare.

"I didn't know it was *your* table," said Alice: "it's laid for a great many more than three."

"Your hair wants cutting," said the Hatter. He had been looking at Alice for some time

with great curiosity, and this was his first speech.

"You should learn not to make personal remarks," Alice said with some severity: "It's very rude."

The Hatter opened his eyes very wide on hearing this; but all he *said* was, "Why is a raven like a writing-desk?"

"Come, we shall have some fun now!" thought Alice. "I'm glad they've begun asking riddles—I believe I can guess that," she added aloud.

"Do you mean you think you can find out the answer to it?" said the March Hare.

"Exactly so," said Alice.

"Then you should say what you mean," the March Hare went on.

"I do," Alice hastily replied; "at least—at least I mean what I say—that's the same thing, you know."

"Not the same thing a bit!" said the Hatter. "Why, you might as well say that 'I see what I eat' is the same thing as 'I eat what I see' "!

"You might just as well say," added the Dormouse, which seemed to be talking in its sleep, "that 'I breathe when I sleep' is the same thing as 'I sleep when I breathe'!"

"It *is* the same thing with you," said the Hatter, and here the conversation dropped, and the party sat silent for a minute, while Alice thought over all she could remember about ravens and writing-desks, which wasn't much.

The Hatter was the first to break the silence. "What day of the month is it?" he said, turning to Alice: he had taken his watch out of his pocket, and was looking at it uneasily, shaking it every now and then, and holding it to his ear.

Alice considered a little, and then said, "The fourth."

"Two days wrong!" sighed the Hatter. "I told you butter wouldn't suit the works!" he added, looking angrily at the March Hare.

"It was the *best* butter," the March Hare meekly replied.

"Yes, but some crumbs must have got in as well," the Hatter grumbled: "you shouldn't have put it in with the breadknife."

The March Hare took the watch and looked at it gloomily; then he dipped it into his cup of tea, and looked at it again: but he could think of nothing better to say than his first remark, "It was the *best* butter, you know."

CARSON, KIT (1809–1868)

Fur trapper, scout, soldier, and Indian fighter, Kit Carson was one of the first to explore the American West. He opened up the overland trails that contributed greatly to westward settlement.

Born Christopher Carson in Kentucky on December 24, 1809, Kit's parents moved to Missouri while he was still a baby. At 15, Kit was apprenticed to a saddle maker. A year later he ran away to join a wagon train heading west, and he settled in Taos, New Mexico. He soon earned a reputation as a daring trapper and hunter, and he gained an extensive knowledge of the frontier trails. Kit was well known to the Indians, and they called him the Little Chief.

In 1842, Carson met Lieutenant John C. Frémont, whom Congress had sent west to explore the Rocky Mountains. Frémont hired Carson to guide him over the rugged, un-

Kit Carson played an important role in the westward expansion of the United States. In the 1840's this famous frontiersman and fur trapper guided John C. Frémont's expeditions across the Rocky Mountains to California.

mapped Rockies. Between 1842 and 1845, Carson piloted three expeditions across the mountains to California.

When the Mexican War broke out in 1846, Carson acted as an army scout. He once saved a unit that had been surrounded by Mexicans. During the Civil War, in the 1860's, he fought on the Union side and commanded the 1st New Mexico Volunteers. In addition to fighting the Confederates, he also was ordered to fight Apache, Navajo, and Kiowa, but he did so reluctantly, for he was sympathetic to the Indians. By the end of the Civil War, Carson had risen to the rank of brigadier general. He died on May 23, 1868.

Reviewed by MARY LEE SPENCE
University of Illinois

See also FRÉMONT, JOHN CHARLES.

CARSON, RACHEL (1907–1964)

Rachel Louise Carson was an American writer and marine biologist. Her writings helped focus attention on ecology—the relationship between living things and their environment.

Carson was born in Springdale, Pennsylvania, on May 27, 1907. Her interest in nature began in childhood as she observed the living things around her in the fields and woods near her home. She claimed to be happiest "with wild birds and creatures as companions."

Her fascination with the sea and its creatures led to several books about marine life. One of her books, *The Sea Around Us* (1951), became a bestseller and won the National Book Award for nonfiction. *Silent Spring* (1962) was to become her most famous book. In it, Carson warned that pesticides were poisoning the environment. She painted a nightmarish picture of the future: "It was a spring without voices. . . . there was now no sound; only silence lay over the fields and woods and marsh." It was a silent spring, Carson

explained, because pesticides had killed the birds and other living things.

At the time, Carson's book created a huge uproar. But further research supported many of her findings and led to restrictions on pesticide use.

Carson graduated from the Pennsylvania College for Women in 1929 and received a masters degree from Johns Hopkins University in 1932. For many years after graduation, she worked for the U.S. Fish and Wildlife Service. Carson died on April 14, 1964. Six years later, the U.S. government honored her by naming a coastal area in Maine the Rachel Carson National Wildlife Refuge.

KARYN L. BERTSCHI
Science writer

JAMES EARL CARTER, JR. (1924–   )
39th President of the United States

FACTS ABOUT CARTER

Known As: Jimmy
Birthplace: Plains, Georgia
Religion: Baptist
College Attended: U.S. Naval Academy, Annapolis, Maryland
Occupation: Naval officer, farmer, businessman
Married: Rosalynn Smith
Children: John, James Earl 3rd, Jeffrey, Amy
Political Party: Democratic

Office Held Before Becoming President: Governor of Georgia
President Who Preceded Him: Gerald R. Ford
Age on Becoming President: 52
Years in the Presidency: 1977–1981
Vice President: Walter F. Mondale
President Who Succeeded Him: Ronald W. Reagan

DURING CARTER'S PRESIDENCY

The Department of Energy was established by Congress (1977). The Senate approved treaties (1978) giving Panama eventual control of the Panama Canal. The Department of Education was established by Congress (1979). *Below:* President Carter helped negotiate a peace treaty signed by Israel and Egypt (1979). *Left:* The United States and the People's Republic of China officially established diplomatic relations (1979). Iranians seized the U.S. Embassy in Tehran (1979) and held Americans hostage for more than 14 months. *Above:* The 1980 Olympics in Moscow were boycotted by the United States to protest the Soviet invasion of Afghanistan (1979).

CARTER, JAMES EARL, JR. When we think of Abraham Lincoln, we see him as a poor boy of the frontier, studying by candlelight, working in a country store, splitting logs, striving to make something of himself. We may wonder at his ability to travel from a log cabin to the White House. His story has helped form the American dream—that a person coming from a modest background can attain spectacular success.

James Earl (Jimmy) Carter, Jr., achieved that dream. His roots were in the southwestern part of Georgia, where members of his family had struggled to make a living for 150 years. He was the first Carter to finish high school. From such beginnings he went on to become president of the United States.

EARLY YEARS

Carter was born in the little town of Plains, Georgia (population about 650), on October 1, 1924. He was the first child of James Earl Carter and Lillian Gordy Carter. Later two daughters, Gloria and Ruth, and another son,

William, were born to the Carters. The elder Carter was the manager of a grocery store. In time he was able to acquire some farmland of his own in Archery, just outside Plains.

When Jimmy was not going to school, he was working on the farm. He sold peanuts as a sideline and saved the money he earned. Of his childhood, Carter later said: "In general, the early years of my life on the farm were full and enjoyable, isolated but not lonely. We always had enough to eat . . . but no money to waste."

NAVAL OFFICER AND BUSINESSMAN

Jimmy graduated from high school with very high marks. From his first days at school, he had wanted to attend the United States Naval Academy at Annapolis. An uncle whom he idolized had been in the Navy. At the same time, it meant a chance for an education, for there was little money in the family to pay for college.

Carter received an appointment to the Naval Academy in 1942. But first he spent a year at the Georgia Institute of Technology in Atlanta, taking courses that would help him to pass the entrance examinations to Annapolis. He entered the academy in 1943. There he adapted to the strict discipline, did well in his studies, ran track and cross-country, and played on the lightweight football team. He graduated in 1946 in the upper 10 percent of his class. Soon after, he married Rosalynn Smith, whose family lived near Plains. He had met her in his last year at the Naval Academy. The Carters had four children: John, James Earl 3rd (Chip), Jeffrey, and Amy.

Carter spent seven years in the Navy, attaining the rank of lieutenant (senior grade). During part of that time he worked with Admiral Hyman G. Rickover in the nuclear submarine program. Carter's ambition then was to become an admiral. But when his father died in 1953, Carter felt that it was necessary to return to the family farm.

But he was not content to be just a peanut farmer. He bought a peanut sheller and began to supply large peanut processors. Then he expanded his operation into peanut warehousing. Eventually, with some hard work, the Carters became relatively prosperous.

▶STATE SENATOR AND GOVERNOR

Carter's interest in politics can be traced at least in part to his father, who had served a year in the Georgia state legislature. In 1962, Carter ran for the state Senate. He lost by a few votes. But when violations of voting rules were discovered, he challenged the results and was declared the winner.

In 1966, Carter first declared himself a candidate for the U.S. House of Representatives but then decided to try for the Democratic nomination for governor of Georgia. He lost in the primary election, but he made a good showing. Carter devoted himself to his business and to civic affairs until 1970. Then he tried again for the governorship. He defeated a former governor of the state in the primary and won the election easily.

Perhaps Carter's most important contribution as governor was in increasing efficiency in the state government. Hating waste, he reduced the number of state agencies from 300 to 22. He appointed a considerable number of blacks to state jobs. He also ordered that a portrait of Martin Luther King, Jr., be placed alongside portraits of other famous Georgians in the state capitol building. It was the first portrait of a black to hang in the capitol, a gesture Carter felt was long overdue.

▶CAMPAIGN FOR THE PRESIDENCY

Carter announced his candidacy for the presidency late in 1974. He campaigned tirelessly, sought the support of Democratic leaders, and built an efficient political staff. His soft southern drawl and wide smile became familiar across the country. By the time of the Democratic National Convention in New York in the summer of 1976, he had already won enough delegates to assure his nomination. The only question that remained was whom he would pick as the vice presidential candidate. He chose Walter F. Mondale, a liberal senator from Minnesota. In the election, Carter defeated the Republican candidate, President Gerald R. Ford. Carter received 297 electoral votes to Ford's 240.

Born in the small town of Plains in Georgia, Jimmy Carter led a typical country life as a boy. At the age of 16 (*right*), he attended a camp sponsored by the Future Farmers of America. *Below:* On graduation day from the U.S. Naval Academy in 1946, Carter had his new ensign's stripes pinned on by his mother, Lillian (*right*), and his future wife, Rosalynn (*left*).

Left: Carter's vice president was Walter Mondale (*rear*), who ran unsuccessfully for president in 1984. *Right:* The First Couple relax with their daughter, Amy.

▶ THE WHITE HOUSE YEARS

The new President adopted a casual style. Carter chose to walk instead of ride down Pennsylvania Avenue after his inauguration. He also requested that the presidential theme, "Hail to the Chief," not be played every time he entered a public place. Many people welcomed this simplicity. But others were critical of Carter's style, which sometimes seemed less than forceful. They wondered how he would deal with the country's problems.

Domestic Issues. At home, Carter's administration faced major problems in the areas of energy supply and the economy. Soon after taking office, Carter asked Congress to create a new Department of Energy. He proposed legislation to reduce oil consumption, increase U.S. oil production, and encourage the use of other energy sources. Congress approved the new department and, after much debate, some of the legislation.

Inflation soon became the leading economic problem. In 1978, Carter called for voluntary limits on wage and price increases. The limits had little effect. Later, controls were imposed on credit. The government hoped that by discouraging borrowing, it would lessen the rate of inflation.

However, a new gasoline shortage and continuing economic problems brought Carter's popularity at home to an all-time low by July, 1979. In a televised speech, Carter said that the United States was facing a "crisis of confidence." He promised to provide strong leadership, and he outlined a new energy program.

Carter's Foreign Policy. In foreign policy, Carter often stressed moral principles. His goals, he said, were peace, arms control, economic co-operation, and the advancement of human rights. His efforts toward peace in the Middle East were widely acclaimed. In the fall of 1978, the leaders of Egypt and Israel met with him at Camp David, Maryland, and agreed on basic principles for a peace treaty. A treaty was signed in 1979. But negotiations on details of the peace made slow progress.

Carter concluded new treaties with Panama, giving the country control of the Panama Canal by the year 2000. These treaties were controversial, but they were ratified by the U.S. Senate in 1978. Diplomatic relations with the People's Republic of China were established in 1979. In June, 1979, Carter signed a new strategic arms limitation treaty with the Soviet Union. But this treaty met with strong opposition in Congress.

The Iran Crisis and Afghanistan. At the end of 1979 two issues arose that severely tested Carter's leadership. In November, Iranian militants seized the U.S. Embassy in Tehran and

held the Americans there hostage. In December, the Soviet Union sent troops into Afghanistan to put down a rebellion against that country's Communist government.

To free the hostages, the United States attempted to negotiate with Iranian leaders. Carter also halted trade with Iran. He appealed to the United Nations and the World Court. When these measures were not successful, Carter ordered military action to try to free the hostages, but the rescue mission failed.

As a result of the Soviet action in Afghanistan, Carter asked Congress to delay consideration of the new arms treaty. He limited trade with the Soviet Union and called for a boycott of the 1980 Summer Olympic Games, which were held in Moscow.

Defeat in 1980, and Later Years. In the 1980 election, Carter was badly beaten by his Republican challenger, Ronald W. Reagan, a former governor of California, who won 489 electoral votes to Carter's 149. Ironically, on January 21, 1981, the day after Carter left office, the U.S. hostages were freed.

In later years, Carter wrote several books, established the Carter Center at Emory University, and worked for Habitat for Humanity building housing for the poor. He helped monitor elections in Panama and other developing nations and fostered peace talks in Somalia in 1989. His most ambitious peace efforts came in 1994, under President William (Bill) Clinton. He met with North Korea's leaders over the issue of international inspection of their nuclear sites and led a U.S. delegation to Haiti to persuade its military rulers to return power peacefully to an elected president whom they had overthrown.

GODFREY SPERLING, JR.
Chief, Washington News Bureau
The Christian Science Monitor

Above: Iranians seized the U.S. Embassy in Tehran in 1979, holding Americans hostage for over 14 months. *Below:* President Ronald Reagan attended the opening of the Jimmy Carter Library in Atlanta, Georgia, in 1986.

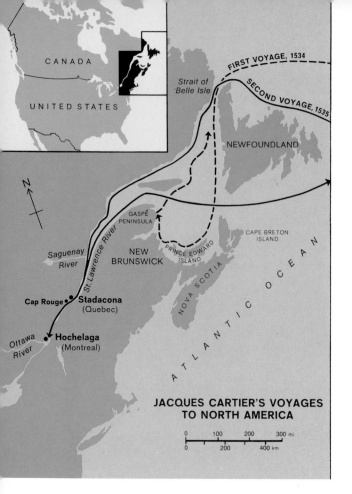

JACQUES CARTIER'S VOYAGES TO NORTH AMERICA

CARTIER, JACQUES (1491–1557)

Like many explorers who sailed to America, Jacques Cartier hoped to find a short route to Asia. Though he never found a route to the riches of Asia, Cartier discovered the St. Lawrence River and established the first French settlement in North America, in what is now Canada.

Cartier was born in the French seaport of St. Malo in 1491—a year before Columbus sailed for America. Little is known about his early life except that he became a skillful sailor and navigator and may have made a voyage to North America as early as 1524.

The Northwest Passage. A few years earlier, the Portuguese explorer Ferdinand Magellan had reached the Pacific Ocean by sailing around the southern tip of South America. But many geographers believed that a shorter passage to Asia could be found by sailing northwest—around North America. (No one then knew how vast North America was.) In 1534, King Francis I of France sent Cartier to find this Northwest Passage.

Cartier sailed into the Gulf of St. Lawrence through the Strait of Belle Isle, north of Newfoundland. After exploring the coasts of western Newfoundland, Prince Edward Island, and New Brunswick, he stopped at the Gaspé Peninsula. There Cartier erected a cross and claimed all the land for King Francis. He met friendly Indians and took two of them back to France with him. The Indians told of a land rich in gold and silver, called the kingdom of the Saguenay. They said this land could be reached by way of the Ottawa River.

Mont Réal. Cartier believed that this river might be the Northwest Passage. So in 1535 he returned to North America with three ships. He sailed up the mighty St. Lawrence River past the Indian village of Stadacona, the site of modern Quebec city. He reached the Indian village of Hochelaga. There he climbed a steep hill hoping to see the mythical kingdom of the Saguenay. Cartier called the hill Mont Réal (Mount Royal). Today the city of Montreal stands on the site.

Cartier's interest was kept alive by more tales of gold and silver mines to the west. But bad weather forced him to return to Stadacona, where he spent the winter. The men had no fresh fruits and vegetables, and many of them died of scurvy (a disease caused by lack of vitamin C). When Cartier returned to France the next spring, he had to leave one ship behind because he had lost so many men.

His Last Voyage. Though Cartier had failed to find the Northwest Passage, the French Government was excited by his reports of gold and silver. They decided to establish a colony in North America. In 1541 an expedition of ten ships set out under the Sieur de Roberval, with Cartier as pilot. Roberval turned back, but Cartier continued. A few miles above Stadacona, Cartier built a fort and named it Cap Rouge. He spent the winter collecting what he thought were gold and diamonds. When spring came he hurried back to France. But the "gold" and "diamonds" proved to be worthless, and the government refused to spend any more money on New France. Cartier returned to sailing and trading. On September 1, 1557, he died at St. Malo.

Cartier's settlement lasted only a year, but it was the beginning of New France—the French empire in North America.

JOHN S. MOIR
University of Toronto

CARTOONS

A cartoon is a drawing or a series of drawings that tells a story with a message—either funny or serious. Because they exaggerate people's weaknesses and poke fun at current customs, cartoons may make us laugh, but they can also make us think about important matters.

The term cartoon originally described an artist's first rough sketch for a painting or other work of art. Today it refers to any one of several kinds of drawings. The **editorial cartoon** (or political cartoon) is a drawing intended to dramatize the news or sway public opinion. The **comic strip** is a series of drawings that appears as a regular feature in newspapers or magazines. Some comic strips have a story that continues from one day to the next, while others have a humorous new situation each day, but all feature a set of established characters. A **panel cartoon** is similar to a comic strip, using established characters, but consists of a single drawing rather than a series. A **gag cartoon** is a single panel, or perhaps a series of panels, in which the characters appear only once, not as a continuing feature. Still another type of cartoon is the **animated cartoon**, which you can read about in the article ANIMATION.

▶ **THE FIRST CARTOONS**

The art of cartooning began with the English artist William Hogarth (1697–1764), who drew pictures that poked fun at the social customs of his times. Another English artist, Thomas Rowlandson (1756–1827), mastered the art of caricature, which is the exaggeration of human features to make people look ridiculous. Another important step in the development of the cartoon was provided by the work of the French artist Honoré Daumier (1808–79), known for his funny but bitter attacks on powerful people. His cartoons once landed him in jail for six months. But Daumier had made his mark on journalism. The editorial cartoon soon became a regular feature of journals and magazines throughout Europe.

The first important American cartoonist was Thomas Nast (1840–1902). His work was a regular feature of the American magazine *Harper's Weekly*. Nast's cartoons attacking Tammany Hall, a corrupt political organization in New York City, and its leader, William

Left: Editorial cartooning was established in America by Thomas Nast, whose work is credited with the downfall of "Boss" Tweed, a corrupt political leader. *Below:* Today's editorial cartoons, such as those of Mike Peters, continue to call attention to problems by poking fun at them.

THERE'S ANOTHER GROUP HERE COMPLAINING ABOUT OUR NEUTRON BOMB TESTING...

Reprinted by permission UFS, Inc.

"Boss" Tweed, led to Tweed's arrest, trial, and imprisonment. Nast is credited with the popularization of many symbols still in use today, including the character of Uncle Sam, the Republican Party's elephant, and the Democrats' donkey.

▶ **EDITORIAL CARTOONS**

Early in the 1900's the political cartoon began to disappear from the humor magazines. The political cartoonists went to work for the newspapers instead because their work could appear every day and be more up to date. Editorial cartoons, so called because they are usually run on a newspaper's editorial page, have changed since the days of Nast. They have become less political and more humorous. In the 1960's, John Fischetti began to combine gag cartoons with editorial cartoons. He set a trend that made the editorial cartoon even more popular. Some current masters of this political humor are Pat Oliphant, Jeff MacNelly, and Mike Peters.

In 1896, *The Yellow Kid* (*upper left*) became America's first color comic. *The Katzenjammer Kids* (*left*), begun in 1897, is the longest continuously running comic strip still in publication. In 1907, Mutt and Jeff (*above*) starred in the first comic strip to appear in a daily newspaper.

▶ COMIC STRIPS

Comic strips as we know them are one of the few art forms created in America (two others are jazz and musical comedy). It is estimated that comic strips are read by more than 200,000,000 people every day, making them the world's most popular art form.

Comic strips began when Joseph Pulitzer, publisher of the New York *World*, asked cartoonist Richard Outcault to create a continuous character dressed in yellow so that the newspaper could experiment with yellow color printing. The result was *The Yellow Kid*, a depiction of Irish slum life in 1895.

William Randolph Hearst, publisher of the New York *Journal*, sensed a real circulation builder in these "funny papers." He commissioned a whole staff of cartoonists to create the first color comic section, which appeared in the *Journal*'s Sunday edition. *The Katzenjammer Kids*, *Alphonse and Gaston*, *Happy Hooligan*, and *Little Nemo in Slumberland* were among the most popular. Soon daily comics in black and white were added. The first one, introduced in 1907, was the forerunner of Bud Fisher's *Mutt and Jeff*.

Syndication. Other smaller newspapers around the country wanted to carry comic strips but could not afford to hire their own cartoonists. As a result, the system of syndication was born. The syndicate (an agency) hires cartoonists, helps develop their features, and then sells their work to many individual newspapers. A small paper might pay $5.00 a week for a comic, while a larger one might pay more than $100.00. The largest syndicates today are King Features, United Features, Tribune Media Services, and Universal Press.

Comics Reach Middle Age. More and more publishers and syndicates began to carry comics, and, at one time, there were over a hundred syndicates selling comics. The second wave of comic strips took over as the industry grew. *Bringing up Father* (also known as *Maggie and Jiggs*), *Moon Mullins*, *Mutt and Jeff*, *Toonerville Trolley*, *Barney Google*, *Skippy*, *Harold Teen*, *Smitty*, *Mr. and Mrs.*, *The Timid Soul*, and *Blondie* were among the favorite strips in the early 1930's.

Story Strips. In the mid-1930's a new form of comic began to appear—the story strip. Using more attractive, realistic artwork rather than humorous artwork to tell exciting stories that continued from day to day, these strips quickly built up a great following. *Dick Tracy*, *Little Orphan Annie*, *Gasoline Alley*, *Terry and the Pirates*, *Buck Rogers*, *Tarzan*, *Prince Valiant*, *Wash Tubbs and Captain Easy*, *Buz Sawyer*, and *Flash Gordon* are a few examples. Some of these new strips, such as *Popeye*, *Li'l Abner*, and *Alley Oop*, combined a continuous story with humor.

Comic Strips Today. After World War II the third wave of comics took over. Most of the comics emerging in the early 1950's are still published today. Among the most widely syndicated comics are *Peanuts, Blondie, Beetle Bailey, Garfield, Hagar the Horrible, Family Circus, Hi and Lois, B. C., The Wizard of Id, Dennis the Menace,* and *Andy Capp.* Other strips with enthusiastic but smaller readerships include *Doonesbury* and such story strips as *Mary Worth, Rex Morgan,* and *Brenda Starr.*

Licensing. The syndicates make full use of the comic characters by licensing them to publishers and manufacturers. Licensing has become an even larger business than syndication. *Snoopy, Garfield,* and *Popeye,* the leaders in the field, earn many millions of dollars a year for their use on hundreds of products, such as toys and clothing, that are distributed throughout the world.

▶ GAG CARTOONS

Even though fewer magazines use fewer cartoons, gag cartooning is still a thriving art. The one-panel gag cartoon was at its height when magazines like *The Saturday Evening Post* and *Collier's* bought as many as 50 a week. The only weekly magazine that still features large numbers of cartoons is *The New Yorker,* which has published such great talents over the years as James Thurber, Charles Addams, Peter Arno, Whitney Darrow, William Steig, Charles Saxon, Roz Chast, and George Booth.

▶ PANEL CARTOONS

Newspaper panel cartoons are making a comeback, with way-out humor leading the way. Others have social-political content, such as in *Berry's World,* or comment on domestic life, as do *The Lockhorns* and *Hazel.*

Opposite page: Continuous stories such as *Li'l Abner* and *Dick Tracy* characterized the strips of the 1930's.

Today's leading comic strips appear in more than 1,500 papers. From upper left, they are *Blondie* by Dean Young and Denis Lebrun, *Hagar the Horrible* by Chris Browne, *Peanuts* by Charles Shultz, *Garfield* by Jim Davis, and *Beetle Bailey* by Mort Walker.

▶ HOW A CARTOONIST WORKS

Most cartoonists work at home. When they get an idea, or a "gag," they draw it in pencil on a sheet of heavy bristol board, about twice the size it will be printed. When the pencil drawing is perfected, they rule the borders and ink in the lettering. Then they go over their pencil lines, usually in black India ink. Then they erase the pencil lines. A week's worth of strips are sent to the syndicate at a time.

A Career as a Cartoonist. Cartooning is a very competitive business. King Features alone receives more than 2,000 submissions from would-be cartoonists each year. If you feel that you would like to have your work considered, send about three weeks' worth of cartoon strips to the syndicate of your choice. To be considered by a magazine, send ten drawings at a time to the magazine cartoon editor. Always include a stamped, self-addressed envelope for the return of the work.

MORT WALKER
Creator, *Beetle Bailey*

See also ANIMATION; COMIC BOOKS.

CARVER, GEORGE WASHINGTON (1864–1943)

George Washington Carver was one of America's greatest agricultural scientists. He was born near Diamond Grove, Missouri. The exact birthdate is not known. His parents were slaves of Moses Carver. While George was still a baby, his mother was kidnapped and his father died. He remained with the Carvers and took their name.

As a young boy, he showed his love of growing things by caring for sick plants. The neighbors called him the plant doctor.

In 1894, Carver became the first black student to graduate from the Iowa State Agricultural College in Ames. Two years later he earned his master's degree in agricultural science there. He taught at the college, becoming its first black teacher.

In 1896, Carver was invited by Booker T. Washington to become head of the agricultural department at Tuskegee Institute, then a new black college in Alabama. With the help of his students, Carver built a laboratory.

For nearly 50 years, Carver taught at Tuskegee and worked in his laboratory, seeking ways to help Southern farmers. He showed the cotton farmers how such crops as peanuts and sweet potatoes would enrich soil worn out by years of cotton planting.

Carver also discovered new uses for these plants. From peanuts he made butter, coffee, ink, and soap. From sweet potatoes he made flour, cereals, glue, dyes, and rubber. Carver gave his discoveries to the world, asking no profit for himself. In recognition, he received many awards and honors.

Carver died on January 5, 1943. His birthplace is a national monument. At Tuskegee are the Carver Research Foundation, which he founded in 1940, and the Carver Museum, which contains exhibits of his work.

DANIEL S. DAVIS
Author, *Struggle for Freedom: The History of Black Americans*

CARVING. See SCULPTURE; WOOD CARVING.

CASSATT, MARY (1844–1926)

Mary Cassatt was the foremost American woman painter of the 19th century. She was also the only American to exhibit paintings with the French impressionists—artists who revolutionized painting by using bright colors, small brushstrokes, and informal subjects.

Cassatt was born on May 22, 1844, in Allegheny City (now a part of Pittsburgh), Pennsylvania. She knew early that she wanted to be a painter. In 1861 she enrolled at the Pennsylvania Academy of the Fine Arts. Several years later, she went to Europe to study the old masters in churches and museums.

In 1872, Cassatt had a painting accepted for the Paris Salon, the official exhibition sponsored by the French Academy of Fine Arts. A year later, she settled permanently in Paris. She soon became aware of the impressionists, especially of Edgar Degas, who became her teacher and lifelong friend. The work of the impressionists was not approved by the Academy. But it appealed to Cassatt. She stopped entering works for the Salon and exhibited with the impressionists.

Cassatt made women her main subject. In her work, we see women in their everyday

Breakfast in Bed, painted by Mary Cassatt in 1897.

lives. Often they are seen enjoying and caring for their children, especially babies.

The taste of Cassatt's time was for highly idealized mothers and children. In contrast, Cassatt painted people as she saw them, often plain and awkward. But her truth reveals a beauty that has endured. Cassatt's work became popular in Paris, and she was the first impressionist to support herself by her art.

Cassatt never married. She died in her country house outside Paris on June 14, 1926.

FRANK GETLEIN
Author, *Mary Cassatt*

Left: The ruins of Urquart Castle, in Scotland, overlook Loch Ness. *Right:* The Alcazar, a hilltop castle in Segovia, Spain, was once a residence of the kings of Castile.

CASTLES

Castles were homes that also were fortresses. Many were built in Europe during the Middle Ages, when wars were fought and lands defended by powerful individuals rather than by central governments.

During the Middle Ages, a king often granted land to wealthy noblemen. In return, these men pledged their loyalty to the king and promised to supply him with armed fighting men called knights. The noblemen built fortified homes—castles—from which their knights could control and defend the surrounding countryside. In addition to providing safety, the castle was also a sign of the nobleman's power and position in society.

▶CONSTRUCTION

Although some early castles were built of earth and timber, most castles were made almost entirely of stone. A large stone castle was very expensive and time-consuming to build. Stone had to be quarried. Trees had to be felled to make beams, doors, and temporary platforms. Lead had to be produced for the roofs, glass for the windows, and plaster for the walls. Often these materials had to be transported over long distances. Construction

might take 20 years and employ more than 2,000 workers.

▶DESIGN

The heart of the castle was the residence of its lord—the hall where he held court, the chamber where he and his family lived, and the chapel where they prayed. These rooms might be in separate areas or grouped within a single building, sometimes in a tall stone structure called a **keep.** Thick-walled and fire-proof, the keep was one of the safest places in the castle.

These buildings and an inner courtyard, or **bailey,** were enclosed by a high stone wall called a **curtain wall.** The curtain wall was topped by a **battlement**—a narrow wall that had alternating high and low segments. Guards standing on a walkway behind the battlement could look out over the low parts but could take cover behind the high segments, which were called **merlons.** Each merlon contained a loophole through which arrows could be shot. Towers built along the curtain wall provided both secure places from which to defend the castle and extra living space.

The entrance through the castle walls was protected by a **gatehouse,** which had several sets of doors and a sliding gate called a **port-**

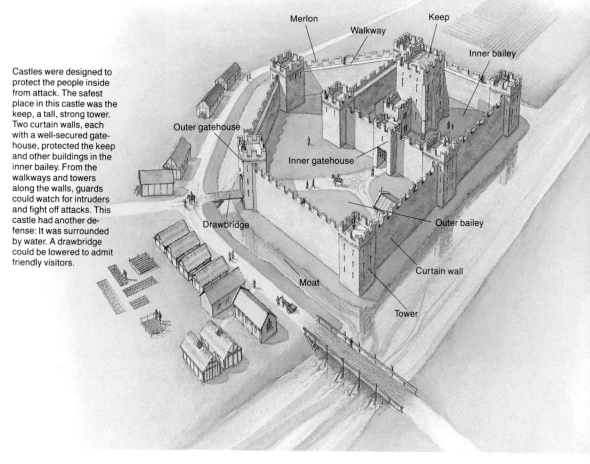

Castles were designed to protect the people inside from attack. The safest place in this castle was the keep, a tall, strong tower. Two curtain walls, each with a well-secured gatehouse, protected the keep and other buildings in the inner bailey. From the walkways and towers along the walls, guards could watch for intruders and fight off attacks. This castle had another defense: It was surrounded by water. A drawbridge could be lowered to admit friendly visitors.

Labels in illustration: Merlon · Walkway · Keep · Inner bailey · Outer gatehouse · Inner gatehouse · Outer bailey · Drawbridge · Curtain wall · Moat · Tower

cullis. A second curtain wall might be built outside the first, enclosing an outer bailey. A **moat** (a deep trench filled with water) around the castle provided yet another barrier.

▶ATTACKS ON A CASTLE

A castle could be attacked in several ways. The attackers could attempt to climb over the walls or try to knock them down with special war machines such as battering rams and stone-throwing catapults. They could prevent supplies from reaching the castle and starve the occupants into surrender. The most feared method of attack was by mining—attackers tunneled under the castle walls, causing them to collapse. A well-manned castle that had plenty of food and water rarely fell to direct assault. Still, the most effective castles were those whose strong and forbidding appearance discouraged any attack at all.

▶LIFE IN A CASTLE

A castle was like a small town filled with stable hands, cooks, and other servants, administrators, soldiers, huntsmen, horses, and hounds. Very few women lived or worked in castles. Almost all the jobs were done by men who hoped to advance their careers by serving the lord of the castle, who expected to live in the greatest comfort and style. When he ate or held court, he was surrounded by as much ceremony as a bishop in a cathedral.

▶CASTLES TODAY

Gradually, as times changed, people no longer needed to live in fortified homes, constantly preparing for attack. They made their castles more livable or moved away into more comfortable houses. Today, very few castles are still used as homes. Some have been turned into museums, but most have fallen into ruin. Ruined or inhabited, thousands of castles in Europe are open to the public. They provide a glimpse of life in an earlier time.

BRIAN K. DAVISON
Author, *Explore a Castle*

See also FEUDALISM; KNIGHTS, KNIGHTHOOD, AND CHIVALRY.

CASTOR AND POLLUX. See GREEK MYTHOLOGY (Profiles).

CASTRO, FIDEL (1926–   )

Fidel Castro Ruz, a fiery speaker and firm believer in the idea of revolution, took power in Cuba in 1959. Under him, Cuba became the first Communist nation in the Americas.

Castro was born on August 13, 1926, at Mayarí, in eastern Cuba. His parents were well-to-do farmers. At 19, he entered the University of Havana to study law. While there, he became involved in politics.

Castro became a lawyer in 1950, and he ran for parliament in 1952. But on March 10, before the election, Fulgencio Batista seized power in a military coup. Castro began to organize opposition to Batista. On July 26, 1953, Castro and his supporters stormed the Moncada army post, on the outskirts of Santiago, in an attempt to launch a revolution.

The attack failed, and Castro was tried and jailed. But his defense speech was so eloquent that he became the symbol of the opposition. He was set free in 1955 and went to Mexico. There he formed a group called the 26th of July Movement and planned his return to Cuba —as head of an army of liberation.

That "army," made up of only about 80 soldiers, invaded Cuba on December 2, 1956. Most were killed or captured by Batista's forces, but the revolution gradually gained more fighters. After two years of fighting, the rebels won. Batista fled Cuba on January 1, 1959.

Castro became prime minister in February. Most Cubans supported him, but many, especially the wealthy, fled. Castro came to power as a nationalist, but he soon began to move toward Communism. The United States had extensive business interests in Cuba, and Castro opposed this. He nationalized foreign companies and signed a trade agreement with the Soviet Union. In 1961 the United States ended relations with Cuba and also backed a group of Cuban exiles in an unsuccessful attempt to overthrow Castro, at the Bay of Pigs.

Castro transformed Cuba into first a socialist and then a Communist state. Health services and education are free, and illiteracy has been almost wiped out. But Cuba has serious economic problems and has depended heavily on Soviet aid. This aid ended in 1991, with the dissolution of the Soviet Union. However, Castro declared that Cuba would remain Communist.

JOHN GERASSI
City University of New York, Queens College

See also CUBA.

CATARACTS. See BLINDNESS.
CATERPILLARS. See BUTTERFLIES AND MOTHS.

CATHEDRALS

Cathedrals are Christianity's most glorious contribution to the art of building. Those who planned and built the world's great cathedrals spared no effort to make the structures worthy expressions of their faith and sources of pride to the community.

During the Middle Ages all of Western Europe was Roman Catholic, and each community had its own church. These churches were grouped into districts called dioceses. Each diocese was under the authority of a bishop. This system still exists. The main church of the diocese contained the throne of the bishop. In Latin the name of this church was *ecclesia cathedralis*, or "cathedral church." In English it has been shortened to cathedral.

St. Basil's Cathedral, in Moscow, was begun in 1555. The design, with its colorful domed towers, combines native Russian architecture with the Byzantine style.

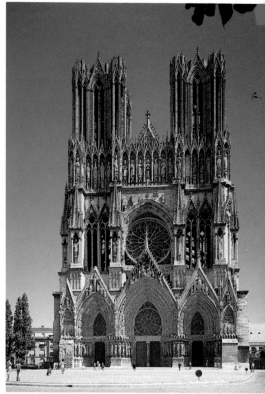

Left: The Cathedral of Pisa, Italy, begun in 1063, is an example of early Romanesque architecture. *Right:* Reims Cathedral, begun in 1211, is built in the French Gothic style.

▶CONSTRUCTION AND STYLES OF CATHEDRALS

Most European cathedrals were constructed with the floor plan in the general shape of a cross. The long part of the cross is the **nave** and serves as the assembly room for the congregation. The two arms of the cross are the **transepts,** and the fourth part, containing the altar and choir, is the **apse.** The section where the four parts meet is the **crossing.** Towers or domes were often built over the crossings.

Cathedrals have been built in nearly every architectural style. But most of the very famous European cathedrals were either Byzantine, Romanesque, Gothic, or Renaissance.

Byzantine. In the first centuries A.D., the center of Christianity was Asia, not Europe, and the first great Christian empire was centered in the city of Byzantium (later Constantinople; now Istanbul, Turkey). Architecture in the Byzantine Empire was a combination of styles that came from the Middle East and from ancient Rome. Hagia Sophia, one of the first Byzantine cathedrals, is a masterpiece of styles combined from East and West.

Romanesque. Gradually the Christian center moved to Europe. Rome had become entirely Christian, and the barbarians from European countries north of Italy were slowly being converted. Northern art began to influence traditional Roman art, and a new style, called Romanesque, was born. An early Romanesque cathedral (11th century) in Pisa, Italy, contains many decorative features that are clearly Byzantine. But St. Ambrogio's Cathedral, begun only 25 years later, is purely Romanesque and contains little Eastern influence.

Gothic. By the 12th century the Germanic peoples from the North—Germans, Goths, Franks, Lombards—dominated European Christianity. Their cathedrals had an upward thrust, as though reaching toward heaven. Architecture was the main artistic tool for religious expression in the period.

Most of Europe's very famous cathedrals are in the Gothic style. Because there are so many Gothic cathedrals throughout Europe— every country had its own kind of Gothic style

—this type of building has become associated with cathedrals. In fact, St. John the Divine, the world's largest Gothic cathedral, was built not during the Middle Ages but in the 19th and 20th centuries, not in Europe but in New York City, and it is not Roman Catholic but Episcopal.

Renaissance. In the 14th century a new spirit began to grow in Italy. People were encouraged to investigate ideas and to experiment with new discoveries. This period was called the Renaissance, which means rebirth, because there was a reawakening of interest in the learning and arts of classical Greece and Rome.

Renaissance architects looked back to the pre-Christian architecture of Greece and Rome. They combined qualities of old and new architecture. St. Peter's in Rome (which is not officially a cathedral because it is not the seat of the bishop) is an outstanding example of a Renaissance building. Its interior reflects the attention paid to fine structural detail, and the dome, designed by the great sculptor, painter, and architect Michelangelo, is a masterpiece in itself.

▶**MODERN CATHEDRALS**

Most 20th-century cathedrals are modern versions of the Gothic style. However, when the Gothic cathedral in Coventry, England, was destroyed by bombs in World War II, the Episcopal church leaders decided to replace it with a modern structure. The new Coventry Cathedral, completed in 1962, is for the most part purely modern—one of the few cathedrals in the world that belong only to our time.

Reviewed by AARON H. JACOBSEN
Author, *The Medieval Sketchbook*

See also ARCHITECTURE; GOTHIC ART AND ARCHITECTURE; ROMANESQUE ART AND ARCHITECTURE; STAINED-GLASS WINDOWS.

CATHER, WILLA. See AMERICAN LITERATURE (The Early 1900's); NEBRASKA (Famous People).

Left: The dome of St. Peter's Basilica, Rome, was designed by the great Renaissance architect Michelangelo. *Right:* St. Mary's Cathedral, in San Francisco, was built in 1971.

CATHERINE

Catherine was the name of two empresses of Russia, who ruled during the 1700's. The second, known as Catherine the Great, was the more important, for she put a distinctive and lasting stamp on Russian history.

Catherine I (1684–1727) reigned as empress from 1725 to 1727. The daughter of a Lithuanian peasant, she was born Marfa Skavronskaya and worked as a household servant until taken prisoner in 1702 by the Russians. She attracted the interest of Emperor Peter I, the Great (ruled 1682–1725), became his close companion, and married him in 1712. Catherine became empress in 1725, after Peter I's death. Protests that she, as a woman and a commoner, had only a weak claim to the throne were brushed aside by regiments of the palace guard loyal to her. Her brief reign left no historical mark.

Catherine II (1729–96), the Great, was empress from 1762 to 1796. Born a German princess, Sophia Augusta Frederika of Anhalt-Zerbst, in 1745 she married the heir to the Russian throne, the future Peter III (ruled 1762–63). Catherine was intelligent and energetic. Wanting to be accepted in Russia, she learned the language and studied its history. Soon after her husband, who was widely unpopular, came to the throne, Catherine took part in a plot by the palace guard to remove him. Peter III was killed by the plotters and Catherine succeeded him.

During her long reign, Catherine shaped both domestic and foreign policy. She was moved in all she did to win power and glory for herself and for Russia. Her extensive correspondence with leading French writers of the Enlightenment, an intellectual movement in the West, was part of her effort to have Russia accepted as a great European power.

In 1767, Catherine issued her famous *Instruction*, which called for enlightened social, economic, and administrative reforms. However, she pointed out that Russia's vast territory required a strong central government and insisted that her own absolute power remain untouched. She also turned thousands of peasants into serfs, bound by law to the land, to be given as gifts to her favorites and to satisfy noble landowners. In 1773 there was a massive peasant uprising, which required the efforts of Catherine's best generals to put

Empress Catherine II (reigned 1762–96), called the Great, expanded Russia's territory, promoted Western culture, and built schools and sumptuous palaces.

down. On her orders, the captured rebel leader Emelian Pugachev was cruelly executed. Her final gesture of solidarity with the Russian nobility was the Charter of the Gentry (1785), which guaranteed their privileges, including the right to own serfs.

Catherine's assertive foreign policy led to wars with Turkey (1768–74; 1787–92) and Sweden (1788–90), and to the three partitions of Poland, which erased that country from the map of Europe. As a result, Russia acquired the Crimea and the north shore of the Black Sea, as well as territory in what is today Lithuania, Poland, Belarus, and Ukraine.

At home, Catherine promoted Western culture in all its forms. Schools were built, mainly for children of the nobility, and sumptuous palaces, most of them designed by foreign architects. Russian literature, music, and art imitated Western models. This policy, however, led to the widening of the already deep cultural gap separating the Westernized privileged classes of Russia and the oppressed peasants.

PETER CZAP, JR.
Amherst College

CATHOLIC CHURCH. See ROMAN CATHOLIC CHURCH.

CATS

When many people think of their favorite pet, the image they have is of a purring cat curled up on a comfortable chair, sunbathing on a windowsill, or nestled in someone's lap. The domestic cat has been around for thousands of years, wherever there have been human beings. The ancient Egyptians were among the first people to domesticate the wildcats that lived near their settlements. By 1500 B.C., cats were not only adored as pets, they were also considered sacred animals in Egypt. Evidence suggests that cats had been domesticated in India and China by about this time too.

Ancient Egypt's domestic cat probably descended from a species, or kind, of North African wildcat called *Felis silvestris lybica*. It is this wildcat that is also the most likely ancestor of all domestic cats. Wildcats, along with domestic cats, lions, tigers, bobcats, and many other species, belong to the cat family. You can read more about the different species of cats in the article CATS, WILD in this volume. This article focuses on the domestic cat and tells how to select and take care of a feline pet.

The affectionate companionship that a pet cat provides to its loving owner is evident in a contented purr, a playful swipe of a paw, or the warmth of its furry body nestled close.

▶ SELECTING A CAT

Cats make wonderful pets. They are independent, active, and interesting to watch. They also can be very affectionate and playful. Many cats live for ten to twenty years, some even longer, so they often become honored members of a household and long-time companions to people of all ages.

Domestic cats depend almost completely on their owners for their health, safety, comfort, and well-being. Before deciding to get a kitten or cat, prospective cat owners need to make sure they can comfortably take care of their new pet. They should have a clean, quiet, draft-free place to put the cat's bed. They should have enough money to feed the cat, maintain its litter box, and provide routine and emergency veterinary care. They should have time to play with the cat daily and groom it daily or weekly.

Once the decision has been made to adopt a cat, prospective owners need to decide on the type of cat they want. Cats can be classified as **purebreds**, meaning that their parents belong to the same breed, or as **mixed breeds**, meaning that their parents belong to two or more different breeds. Purebred cats generally cost more than mixed-breed cats do, with some rare breeds of purebreds costing thousands of dollars. Often mixed-breed cats cost very little or nothing at all: They can be adopted from humane society pet shelters or from families whose cat had a litter of kittens. Mixed-breed cats tend to live longer than purebred cats, making them a good choice for many people.

BREEDS OF CATS

Although the common cat has been a domestic animal for thousands of years, it was not until the mid-1800's that people made serious attempts to produce new breeds of cats. Numerous breeds have been developed since that time, with distinctive characteristics such as different colored coats or fluffy fur.

Abyssinians Regal. These shorthaired cats resemble sculptures of the sacred cats of ancient Egypt. Each hair has two or three bands of color, giving the cat's coat its ticked appearance.

American and British Shorthairs. The American shorthair can trace its ancestors back to the British shorthairs brought to America by early settlers. In fact, the first American shorthair may have come to this continent on the Mayflower. These breeds incorporate a variety of coat colors and patterns, including calico, tabby, and tortoiseshell.

Japanese Bobtail. Although it has been bred for hundreds of years in Japan, the Japanese bobtail was not seen outside of Japan until the late 1960's. It is a friendly cat with a short, stubby tail. Those with patches of three colors are considered to be symbols of good luck.

Maine Coon Cat. According to fable, the Maine coon, with its longhaired coat and fluffy tail, resulted from a cross between a domestic cat and a wild raccoon. No one knows its true origins, although some people believe the Maine coon was brought to North America by the Vikings.

Persian

Russian Blue

Manx. This tailless shorthaired cat has been bred on the Isle of Man, off the west coast of England. Only the purebred Manx has no tail at all; other varieties have a tiny bump, a movable tail, or a small tail.

Persian. A longhaired breed with a small, appealing face, Persians require daily grooming by their owners to keep their coats healthy and free of tangles.

Russian Blue. The contrast of its shimmering dark coat and its glistening green eyes gives this breed its stunning beauty. Russian blues probably originated on an island off the Arctic coast of Russia, where their thick, dense coats would have been important to their survival.

Siamese. Bred more than 400 years ago as pets for the royal family of Thailand (formerly called Siam), Siamese are now very popular in England, America, and Europe. The Siamese's colored points—ear tips, nose, paws, and tail—darken over the years.

Sphynx. This rare, almost hairless breed of cats was first bred in Canada in 1966. Their skin is pink in places where white or gray hair would have appeared and gray where black hair would have grown. Kittens have very wrinkly skin, but adults have smooth skin over their bodies and are wrinkled only around the face.

Siamese

Siamese

Sphynx

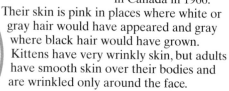
Japanese Bobtail

Manx

Both purebred and mixed-breed cats can have either long hair or short hair. Longhaired cats require daily brushing to keep their coats healthy, shiny, and free of tangles. Shorthaired cats need to be brushed less frequently and so are easier for busy people to care for. Different types of cats have different personalities: Some types of cats tend to be very independent, while others like more attention; some tend to be quiet, and others make a variety of mews and calls; some are especially friendly with children and other pets, and others tend to be much shyer. Before going out to look for a pet, decide whether you have the time to groom a longhaired cat. Also consider the type of personality you would enjoy most in a pet. Considering these factors will help you pick the best cat for your household.

A veterinarian can help you select a healthy cat and, when visited regularly, help you to keep your cat free of disease.

You can look for a pet by going to a pet store or an animal shelter or by looking at magazine, newspaper, or on-line advertisements run by people who breed cats or have them for sale. If you are looking for a purebred cat, local cat clubs may have helpful information. If you are buying a cat, buy from a breeder with a good reputation or a pet store where the animals are given personal attention and are well cared for. When you go to adopt or buy a cat, take a close look at the animals' surroundings. Check to see that they are clean and neat and they smell fresh. They should also provide the animals with ample room to move around. If they meet all these requirements, you can probably get a good pet there.

When choosing a cat, make sure your cat is clean and appears healthy. Watch how the cat moves, to make sure it has no injuries or birth defects. Pick up the cat and note how it responds to gentle stroking and handling. A cat that either cringes at your touch or hisses or spits at you may not make a good pet. If you are adopting a kitten that will be left alone for long periods of time each day, you might consider bringing home one of its littermates as well. Kittens of the opposite sex usually make the best companions for each other.

Whether it is a cozy chair, a pet bed, or a soft pillow on the floor, a cat's bed needs to be someplace that is quiet and warm.

CAT ASSOCIATIONS

If you want to learn more about cats, there are a number of different organizations you can join. Each organization sponsors a number of clubs. Some of the clubs focus on a particular breed of cats; other clubs do not focus on a breed but bring together cat lovers from a particular region. Most of these clubs put out newsletters that give information about cats and their care. Many clubs also sponsor cat shows in which both purebred and mixed-breed cats can win prizes for their appearance and beauty. Several of the most prominent organizations include the Cat Fanciers' Federation, the American Cat Fanciers' Association, and the Canadian Cat Association.

▶ CARING FOR YOUR CAT

Once you have decided on a specific cat, ask staff members at the store or pet shelter for advice on feeding, grooming, and providing veterinary care for the animal. Get the cat's health records and take the cat to a veterinarian for an examination as soon as possible. A checkup is essential before you introduce your new cat to any other pets in your household.

When you bring your cat home, ask your family to give it a gentle reception and place its bed in a warm, quiet, out-of-the-way place

To grow and develop properly, a cat must have a balanced diet that includes proteins, fats, vitamins, and minerals.

where your cat can go if it wants to be alone. Feed your cat regularly, two or three times a day, using the foods and amounts specified by your vet. Give your cat a full bowl of fresh, cold water every day.

Set up your cat's litter box in a secluded spot away from the cat's feeding area and its bed. Show the cat the litter box and move its front paws in the litter a few times. For most kittens and cats, this is all you need to do to train them to use their box. If your cat has an accident, clean it up as soon as possible. Then patiently show your cat the litter box and praise the cat after it uses it the next few times. Keep the litter box clean by scooping out the feces every day and rinsing out the litter box and replacing the litter weekly. Cats with clean, dry litter boxes rarely have accidents.

Groom your cat by brushing its coat with a cat brush or comb daily or weekly and clipping its claws every few weeks. Your veterinarian can show you how to do this safely. Cats often mark their territory by sharpening their claws on furniture. Providing your cat with a scratching post and training the cat to use it can help prevent the furniture from being damaged.

Help keep your cat safe by preventing problems before they occur. Keep poisons, including cleaning fluids, fertilizers, insecticides, and automotive fluids, in sealed, cat-proof

The irresistible appeal of a litter of kittens keeps many cat owners from having their cats neutered. But all too often, these kittens end up in animal shelters and are destroyed if not adopted.

containers or locked up in a cabinet. Make sure that poisonous plants, including azaleas, birds of paradise, ivies, philodendrons, and poinsettias, are out of the cat's reach. You might grow a pot of nontoxic grass or parsley for your cat to munch on to keep the cat from chewing up houseplants. Secure the screens on all windows, so that if the cat sits on the inside window ledge, it cannot fall outside. Most important, keep your pet indoors. Cats that go outside are at very great risk for a variety of diseases and for injuries due to car accidents and fights with other animals.

Take your cat to the veterinarian once a year for a routine checkup. During the examination, the cat will be vaccinated against some of the more common feline diseases and have its general health checked. If you notice changes in your cat's weight, disposition, eating habits, coat, or use of the litter box, you should consult your veterinarian. Such changes could be a sign of illness.

Cats are very active breeders, sometimes producing two litters of kittens a year. On the average, most litters are made up of three to five kittens. A responsible pet owner can prevent the birth of unwanted cats by having their pet undergo a surgical procedure, called neutering, that removes some of a cat's reproductive organs. A male kitten should be neutered (or castrated) between 4 and 9 months of age, while a female kitten should be neutered (or spayed) between 4 and 6 months of age.

Providing a safe place to live and a good diet and being attentive to health are all important aspects of caring for a cat. However, more important than any other things an owner can provide are loving attention and opportunities for play. Forming a caring bond with your cat will enrich your life and help make your home a warm and rewarding place to be.

ELIZABETH KAPLAN
Series Coauthor, *Ask Isaac Asimov*

CATS, WILD

Cats are mammals that have long, powerful bodies and rounded heads with pointed ears and large eyes. Their sleek, four-legged bodies are covered with fine fur that may be marked with spots or stripes. Their well-developed senses, speedy reactions, and sharp teeth and claws make cats skillful hunters. All of them, whether large or small, feed on other animals. In fact, it is this characteristic that places them in the group of mammals called **carnivores**, or meat eaters.

There are about 36 different species, or kinds, of cats that make up the cat family.

The sleek, graceful creatures called cats are found in a wide variety of environments. Deep within a tropical forest, a tiger (*left*) surveys his surroundings; a lioness (*below*) guards her position on the shore of a savanna watering hole; these cougars (*right*) make their home on craggy, snow-swept peaks.

There are several ways of classifying them. One of the most common methods separates cats into four groups. The largest group consists of the most species—about 28. These include domestic cats, wildcats, pumas, and lynxes. Another group consists of the big cats, including lions, tigers, jaguars, leopards, and snow leopards. The other two groups contain one species each—the cheetah and the clouded leopard. This article will focus on cats that are found in the wild. For a detailed discussion of domestic cats, see the article CATS.

▶ DISTRIBUTION OF CATS

Cats are native to all the continents except Australia and Antarctica. In addition, one species, the domestic cat, has been introduced by people to many places, including islands, where no cats had lived before. In such places, domestic cats running wild often kill large numbers of small native animals, such as birds and rodents. Some of these creatures have been entirely wiped out by the free-roaming cats.

The large, powerfully built saber-toothed cat known as *Smilodon* was an ancient relative of today's wild cats. Its curved, fanglike teeth—this cat's distinguishing feature—were about 8 inches (20 centimeters) long.

Cats are adaptable creatures that can be found in a wide variety of habitats. Open plains, wooded grasslands, forests, and tropical jungles and swamps are all home to various members of the cat family. Cats are even found in cold areas where blizzards sweep the land.

The cat with the greatest geographical range is the cougar, or puma. It can be found from northern Canada almost to the southern tip of South America. The cat with the smallest range is the little Iriomote cat, which inhabits only the island of Iriomote near Okinawa, in southern Japan. Rare and secretive, it was a species scientists did not even know existed until 1967. Some researchers believe that this scarce creature resembles some prehistoric ancestors of modern cats.

▶ **THE FIRST CATS**

The first catlike creatures are thought to have appeared about 55 million years ago. Scientists believe that these early cats were small animals resembling mongooses or weasels. As millions of years passed, the early cats grew and evolved, producing many different kinds of catlike creatures.

Some of the ancient catlike creatures grew exceptionally large and fierce. Perhaps the best known of these extraordinary prehistoric animals are the sabertoothed cats. The sabertooths had muscular bodies, with powerful weapons built into their upper jaws—dagger-sharp teeth as long as butcher knives. Scientists believe that the sabertooths preyed on very large animals, even young mammoths. The cats probably killed by jumping on the backs of their prey, holding on with their claws, and then stabbing them to death with their huge teeth.

By about 35 million years ago, the types of cats that existed looked very much like modern cats. It is this group of cats that developed into the many different cats, large and small, that are living today.

▶ **CHARACTERISTICS OF CATS**

Cats vary widely in size. They range in weight from about 6 pounds (2.7 kilograms) to 600 pounds (272 kilograms) and in length from 20 inches (51 centimeters) to 9 feet (2.7 meters). But whatever their size, appearance, and habitat, modern cats share many characteristics. They are muscular, with deep chests, rounded heads, and short muzzles, or snouts. Their forward-looking eyes are set well apart. This gives them a wide field of vision, which helps as they scan the countryside for prey. In the rear of each eye, there is a layer of cells that reflects light, like a mirror. With this feature, cats are able to get the most out of the dim light available at night. This is a valuable trait since cats spend much

The difference in size and the ability to purr rather than roar set the group of small cats, which includes the cougar (*below*) and the serval (*below right*), apart from the big cats.

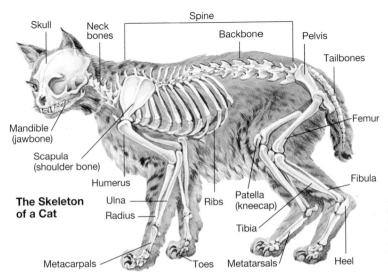

The Skeleton of a Cat

Skull
Neck bones
Spine
Backbone
Pelvis
Tailbones
Mandible (jawbone)
Scapula (shoulder bone)
Humerus
Ulna
Radius
Ribs
Patella (kneecap)
Femur
Fibula
Tibia
Metacarpals
Toes
Metatarsals
Heel

About 250 bones make up the cat's skeleton (*left*). This rigid framework supports and protects the soft body tissues. Special muscles, tendons, and ligaments work together to extend (*above*) and retract (*top*) the sharp, hooked claws of a cat.

of the day sleeping and hunt mainly after the sun goes down.

Cats also have very good hearing and a keen sense of smell. The whiskers on their snouts are very sensitive to touch, which is an important feature to have when moving about in the dark. A cat's teeth are used for holding prey and cutting up meat. Toward the front of its mouth are long fanglike canine teeth—two in the upper jaw, and two in the lower jaw. These are used to bite and seize prey and tear flesh. Farther back in a cat's jaws are large teeth with sharp surfaces that are used for cutting.

Cats have pads on their feet and travel on their toes, silencing their footsteps when tracking and creeping up on prey. Their clawed toes help them to grip the ground as they run, to scramble up trees, and to cling to prey. All cats but the cheetah can retract their claws into bony coverings, called sheaths, when they are not in use.

All cats, except for lions, are solitary animals. For most of their lives they live alone, coming together only when it is time to mate. After mating, most male cats immediately go off on their own. Female cats stay with their offspring and care for them until they are able to live on their own. A young cat learns basic tasks

from its mother, but it also learns from other offspring through its play. When young cats tussle with and chase one another about, they are exercising their muscles and building endurance. They are learning how to defend themselves. Equally important, moreover, they are learning how to interact with their own kind.

Even though the majority of cats are loners, they do communicate with members of their own species. Sometimes one cat will leave a message for other cats. A leopard that leaves deep scratches on a tree and sprays them with urine is telling other leopards of its presence. Its purpose may be to keep others out of its hunting territory or perhaps to at-

Cats share some traits that are not readily seen. With mouth agape (*left*), a lion reveals papillae on the surface of its tongue. These hard, spiny projections are used to scrape meat off bones. The reflective lining of the eye shines in the dark when a light is beamed at a cat's eyes (*above*).

tract a mate. Not all cats deliver messages in the same way. While some spray urine and deposit other body secretions, others use sounds to produce their messages. Cats roar, yowl, and meow. Small cats also purr as a method of communication.

The size of a cat's territory is not always the same; it can get bigger or smaller depending on the situation. In Siberia, animals live such great distances from each other that tigers must roam over territories of 50 square miles (129 square kilometers) to find prey. Sometimes the territories of differ-

ent tigers overlap. But the areas involved are so vast, the cats seldom meet. In southern Asia, animals live much closer together, and tigers do not have to travel as far to find food. Their territories are about 23 to 40 square miles (60 to 104 square kilometers), much smaller than the territories of tigers in Siberia.

Scientists have closely studied the social life of lions. Because they live in wide-open country, lions are probably the easiest cats to observe. The lion lives in a family group called a **pride**. A typical lion pride has about 15 members. It is a stable group that consists of a male leader, one or two other adult males, and several females and their young.

The females are generally all related—they are mothers, daughters, sisters, and aunts. They never leave the pride. When male offspring are 2 or 3 years of age, they are usually driven out of the pride by the adult males. The young males may wander together or split up. Either way, they search for a new pride, which they will try to take over by driving off or killing its males.

Roaring seems to help members of a pride keep in touch when they are spread out across the countryside. Pride males must constantly be alert for invaders, and they will defend their hunting grounds fiercely against other groups of lions. Prides sometimes go to war with one another. The conflict may not stop until one pride has been totally defeated and chased away or even wiped out.

▶ **THE LIFE CYCLE OF CATS**

Cats are relatively long-lived animals. Many species have been known to live for more than twenty years. While the basic life cycle of all cats is similar, it can differ

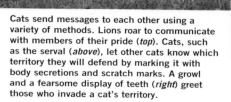

Cats send messages to each other using a variety of methods. Lions roar to communicate with members of their pride (*top*). Cats, such as the serval (*above*), let other cats know which territory they will defend by marking it with body secretions and scratch marks. A growl and a fearsome display of teeth (*right*) greet those who invade a cat's territory.

depending on factors such as the species of cat and where a cat lives.

Courtship and Mating

Male cats can mate at almost any time, but females cannot. Depending on the species, female cats mate from only once a year to every few years. Chemical changes in a female's body prepare her for mating. When these changes occur depends largely on climate. In warm climates, they can take place in almost any month. Tigers in the tropics, for example, are known to mate throughout the

to attract a mate. Female cats may also leave a urine trail for the male to follow. Female lions, or lionesses, do not have to attract males from a distance, because unlike other cats, both sexes live together in groups. Even so, a lioness lets the males know she is ready to mate by becoming very playful.

Reproduction

Like other mammals, cats reproduce by the process of sexual reproduction. During sexual reproduction, an egg (the female sex cell) is fertilized when it is united with sperm (the

Sprawled out under a tree, a lion pride slumbers. Free from the fear of most predators, big cats are able to spend about two-thirds of their day sleeping.

year. Tigers in Siberia, on the other hand, mate only in midwinter. The reason for the difference is linked to when the cubs, or offspring, are born. Tiger cubs are born a little more than three months after their parents mate. This means that in Siberia, the mother gives birth in the spring. If the cubs were born in the frigid winter, the chances of their survival would be much lower than when the weather was warming. In the tropics, where the winters are warm, the season in which the cubs are born makes little difference.

Female cats that are ready to mate let the males know through special behaviors. The female cougar emits ear-shattering screams, while the female tiger, or tigress, roars loudly

male sex cell). Fertilization takes place in the female's body. For this to occur, the male uses a special organ, the penis, to release sperm into the female.

An offspring gestates, or develops, within the female's body from the fertilized egg. The time it takes for gestation depends on the species of cat. Big cats, such as the jaguar and leopard, give birth about three and a half months after mating. Most smaller species, such as the serval and ocelot, give birth about two and a half months after mating. The size of a litter also varies; depending on the cat,

A cheetah and her young survey their surroundings (*below*). They represent the typical cat family unit. Most males do not stay after mating to participate in the care of the young. One exception is the lion. Males not only live with the females and their offspring, but they take part in caring for the cubs and are tolerant of their playful attentions (*right*).

leopards, and tigers can see; and lion cubs sometimes remain blind for up to two weeks.

The young of all wild cats are born with some kinds of markings on their fur, whether or not they will have spots and stripes when adults. A cougar cub, for example, has black spots until it is about 6 months old. Scientists believe that the markings on young cats serve as a form of camouflage to protect them from enemies—and the helpless young do have many enemies.

Packs of spotted hyenas often attack young caracals, leopards, and even lions, especially when their mother is not nearby. Pythons will climb into the trees and hunt clouded leopard cubs. Young bobcats are occasionally killed by great horned owls. Among the enemies of young cats are other cats. Leopards will eat cheetah cubs, and lions will attack young leopards, cheetahs, and even other lion cubs.

Like other mammals, newborn cats feed on milk produced by their mother. They grow very rapidly. A lion cub weighing several pounds at birth can double its weight in two weeks. In two and a half months, it can weigh almost 20 pounds (9 kilograms). A male tiger cub can grow to 150 pounds (68 kilograms) in nine months. By the time it is 2 years old, it can weigh more than 400 pounds (181 kilograms). As a rule, smaller cats depend on

from one to six young can be produced. Many cats give birth in sheltered, hidden places. The bobcat will often use a hollow log or a space under the roots of a tree. The lynx has her young in thick brush, the clouded leopard in a hollow tree, and the snow leopard in a cave or under a ledge.

Care of the Young

Newborn cats vary in size. Asian golden cats weigh about 8 ounces (227 grams), and sand cat kittens only about 2 ounces (57 grams), while the cubs of the big cats are between 1 and 3 pounds (0.5 kilogram and 1.4 kilograms). All cats are born blind and helpless. They depend completely upon their mother's care. Young such as the lynx, caracal, snow leopard, and cougar open their eyes in about 7 to 10 days. It takes about a week to two weeks before young jaguars, clouded

mother's milk for a shorter period of time than larger species do. For instance, the small bobcat nurses for two months, while the large lion offspring nurses for four months. However, the young begin eating scraps of meat while still drinking milk. Clouded leopard and cougar cubs, for instance, first try meat at about 6 weeks of age. In most species of cats, the male has nothing to do with the care of the young.

Once they are able to move about with ease, young cats begin following their mother about. As their mother looks for prey, they troop behind her. Once she starts the hunt itself, they hide in the brush until she brings them food. As they become stronger, the mother stops carrying prey to them. Instead, she makes a chirping sound that means "come and get it." The cubs move to the place where their mother has made her kill, and they begin to feed. Soon the mother cat begins to teach her young offspring to hunt. Often she will catch prey but not kill it. Instead, she carries it to the cubs and then releases it for them to chase. Their instinct tells them to go after the prey, but at first they do not know how to kill it, even if they manage to knock it down. The mother does the job for them. Eventually, after long weeks of practice, they learn how to make a kill.

Young lions learn to hunt differently because, unlike other cats, they hunt in a group. From a distance, the cubs watch the elders creep up on game and attack it. Soon afterward they follow the older lions and observe the hunt close up. When they are about 6 months of age, they begin learning to stalk prey, and by the age of a year, they have learned to kill the prey with the help of the adults. It may take a few months more before they can handle the task on their own.

Tiger cubs go through a similar type of education. At a few months of age, they actually can kill small creatures such as ground birds. However, it takes much longer before they can bring down large animals such as deer and gaur, which are large wild oxen. As they become larger and stronger, the tigress begins to capture large prey for them. She will catch a gaur, then knock it down. While she pins it to the ground, the cubs attack it. She repeats this lesson over and over, until the cubs learn how to kill their victim. When young cats learn to hunt, they begin to stray farther

away from their mother for longer and longer periods of time. Eventually, they set out on their own.

▶ HOW CATS LIVE

Just as cats share a basic life cycle, they also share a common lifestyle. All cats must accomplish certain tasks, such as finding food, to survive. Each species displays its own special traits, or behaviors, in the distinctive way it carries out these tasks.

Hunting

Cats all have the same diet: the flesh of other animals. They also share many of the same features that make them able hunters. Along with keen senses of sight, hearing, and smell, they have thin and powerful bodies. Cats are agile animals that can move quietly and leap with great power.

While they share similar characteristics, the different species of cats have their own distinctive ways of finding, pursuing, and bringing down prey. Lions feed mostly on antelopes, zebras, and other large animals. Most of the pride's hunting is done by the lionesses. They usually hunt together, using several types of tactics, such as ambushing their prey: A few lionesses will hide in the small shrubs or tall grass while the rest drive prey toward them. Then they charge in for the kill. Sometimes they pick out a single animal and encircle it. Then they rush in at their victim from all directions. Often they hunt by stalking. If you have ever watched a house cat try to sneak up on a bird, you know how a lion stalks. It creeps slowly with its belly to the ground. It freezes. Then it creeps again. When it is close enough, usually within about 100 yards (91 meters), it charges. If a lion does not bring down its target with its first rush, it may chase it for about another hundred yards or so. If it still fails to make a kill, the lion gives up and begins looking for another victim.

The cougar is a superb stalker. When it creeps up on a deer, the cougar hides behind brush and boulders as much as it can. When it is close to the deer, it stops and its muscles tense. Then it explodes into motion and rushes at its victim. If the rush is successful, the cougar seizes the deer with its claws and bites it in the back of the neck. If the bite alone does not kill the deer, the cougar twists its head and breaks the neck of its victim.

The jaguar prefers to lie in wait for prey, often on a tree branch close to the ground. Jaguars feed on animals such as deer and peccaries, which are piglike animals. The jaguar waits for its prey to approach and then leaps upon it. The name "jaguar," in fact, is a South American Indian word for a creature that "kills prey with one bound."

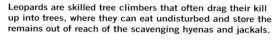

Leopards are skilled tree climbers that often drag their kill up into trees, where they can eat undisturbed and store the remains out of reach of the scavenging hyenas and jackals.

What is a cat's best defense?

Staying out of sight is the method that cats use most often to protect themselves when an enemy is near. The colors and patterns of their coats, such as the lion's muted brown fur (*top*), the tiger's striped fur (*middle*), and the leopard's spotted fur (*bottom*), help them blend into their environment. Sometimes they become almost invisible—like the lioness who so closely matches her surroundings that she is almost totally concealed as she quietly peers out between the stalks of dried grass (*left*).

This protective camouflage helps cats avoid enemies, as well as catch prey. Unseen, they are able to stalk and then pounce upon their victims before an escape can be made.

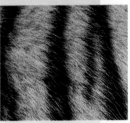

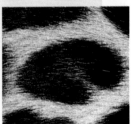

reach speeds of almost 70 miles (113 kilometers) an hour. Cheetahs usually hunt gazelles, which run at speeds of about 45 miles (72 kilometers) an hour and twist and turn easily. Still, the cheetah catches its prey quickly—the average chase covers about 550 feet (168 meters) and lasts only 20 seconds.

Defense

The number of natural enemies a cat has depends on its size. Small cats are preyed on by a variety of animals, including large snakes and large birds such as eagles. Adult lions and tigers have virtually no natural enemies, except for human beings, roving packs of hyenas, and rival members of their own species. Other big cats, such as the leopard, have few enemies as well.

Whatever their size, cats rely largely on staying out of sight to protect themselves. The colors and patterns of their coats help camouflage them. But cats are fierce fighters when cornered or seriously threatened. With their powerful muscles, sharp teeth and claws, and agility, cats are well equipped to fight for their lives.

The caracal, a medium-size cat with long legs, is a fierce hunter with dazzling speed. It has many different methods of catching its prey, which include ground birds, rodents, and even small antelopes. Often it creeps up and then springs on its catch. However, its most spectacular method is a feat of acrobatics: It can rocket several feet off the ground into a flock of birds and snatch a bird out of the air with its claws.

No other cat catches prey like the cheetah. It is capable of explosive bursts of speed. Indeed, the cheetah is the fastest of all land animals. In a matter of three seconds, it can

Migration

Although cats do not migrate over long distances like some other animals, they will enlarge their territories to follow their food supply. For example, when the antelope herds leave the Serengeti Plain during the dry season, lion prides may move from the center of their territories into areas they seldom visit at

The cheetah is built for speed. Its slender build and highly flexible spine allow it to make astonishingly long and rapid strides, and its unsheathed claws supply additional traction during rapid acceleration.

Many cats, such as the endangered tiger (*left*) and the rare snow leopard (*below*), are clinging to survival. It is the continued destruction of their habitats that poses the biggest threat to their existence.

other times of year. Lone lions often follow the herds over distances of hundreds of miles.

The snow leopard makes seasonal migrations as it treks up and down the mountains of its home range. Although it may travel only a short distance, the climate changes greatly. During the summer, the snow leopard ranges high into the mountains, sometimes to an altitude of almost 20,000 feet (6,096 meters) above sea level. When winter comes, the storms, cold, and snow at that altitude are too much even for the snow leopard, as well as for the wild goat and sheep on which it preys. The snow leopard follows these animals to lower altitudes, often to less than 5,000 feet (1,524 meters) above sea level. There, although weather may be cold, it is much less severe than at higher altitudes.

▶ THE FUTURE OF CATS

Over time, the populations of many species of cats have decreased significantly. Some are now so few in number that they are threatened with extinction. For instance, there are probably fewer than 9,000 snow leopards remaining in the wild. There are two main reasons why cat populations have declined, and both are due to human activities. Some activities lead directly to the death of cats. The

great demand for fur and medicinal products has led to the killing of vast numbers of cats for their beautiful coats and their body parts. Cats, especially large cats such as lions and tigers, have also been killed because they attack livestock and, sometimes, people.

Most often human activities lead indirectly to the death of cats. As more land is developed for human use, there is less range for cats and their prey. Even when people are not living on range occupied by cats, activities such as logging destroy their habitat.

In recent years, conservationists from nations around the world have taken steps to protect cats. In India, large preserves have been established where tigers may roam freely. Not many years ago, the first preserve for jaguars was created in the Central American country of Belize. Laws now protect endangered cats from being hunted. Even with these laws established, some furs are still marketed illegally to feed the demand for fur products. Citizen organizations have also worked to save cat populations. While some groups lobby for more laws to protect cats, others try to decrease the demand for fur by making the wearing of fur unpopular.

Ultimately, cats are no different from the other living things, including people, that are affected by human activities. The needs of cats and of human beings must be balanced by sound conservation practices so there will continue to be a place for all on this planet.

EDWARD R. RICCIUTI
Coauthor, *The Audubon Society Book of Wild Animals*
Reviewed by JAMES G. DOHERTY
Curator of Mammals, The Bronx Zoo

See also CATS; ENDANGERED SPECIES; LEOPARDS; LIONS; TIGERS.

CATT, CARRIE LANE CHAPMAN. See IOWA (Famous People); WOMEN'S RIGHTS MOVEMENT (Profiles).

CATTLE

Cattle are mammals that belong to a large family of animals called Bovidae, which includes sheep, goats, water buffaloes, American bisons, and antelopes. They are four-legged animals with large muscular bodies, long tails, and hooves that are cloven, or divided. Cattle are bred and raised throughout the world for the meat and milk they provide. They also supply materials for the manufacture of various other products, such as leather, soap, oil, fuel, fertilizer, glue, brushes, gelatin, and pharmaceutical drugs.

These animals are often referred to as ruminants, or cud chewers, because of the way they digest their food. When cattle feed, food is taken in, chewed, and swallowed. The food is partially digested in the rumen (a compartment of the stomach). The partially digested food, or cud, is then brought back up from the rumen into the mouth and chewed again before it is swallowed for the final time.

The way in which cattle feed allows the animals to digest tough, fibrous plants, which many other animals cannot digest. Cattle convert these plants into milk and meat for human consumption. This is especially important because more than half of the world's agricultural land cannot produce food crops. However, the land can produce grasses and other vegetation used by cattle.

People around the world, from the grassy ranges of Kenya in East Africa (*above*) to the plains of Iowa (*left*), value cattle as one of the most important livestock animals.

▶ **TYPES OF CATTLE**

Cattle have been selected over time to have specialized traits. **Beef cattle** produce high-quality meat, **dairy cattle** are used for milk production, and **dual-purpose cattle** produce both milk and meat. Adult female cattle of any type are called cows, while young females are heifers. All males are called bulls, unless they have been altered so that they cannot reproduce. Then they are called steers. A newborn, either male or female, is called a calf. A group of cattle is called a herd.

Approximately 1.3 billion cattle are found throughout the world. In most countries, cattle are raised to provide meat and milk. However, in India, which has the most cattle of any country in the world, the cow is considered sacred by the Hindus who live there. Hindus neither kill cattle nor eat their meat. The cattle are raised for draft and milk rather than for beef. The countries of the former Soviet Union rank second in the number of existing cattle, followed by the United States, Brazil, and China.

Beef Cattle and the Beef Cattle Industry

Beef is an important agricultural product, especially in the United States. There are several different breeds that are raised as a meat source in the United States. Their characteristics vary depending on the breed. To produce a high-quality beef that is flavorful and nutritious, cattle producers often breed different varieties together to combine each breed's special traits. The varieties that are most common in the United States include the Brahman, Angus, Hereford, Polled Hereford, Charolais, and Simmental.

Among the chief breeds of beef cattle in the United States are the Hereford (*left*) and Angus (*above*), which produce lean meat well mixed with fat; the thick, well-muscled Charolais (*right*), which grows quickly; and the sturdy Brahman (*below left*), which has a strong ability to resist diseases and parasites.

Not all beef comes from mature, grain-fed beef cattle. Dairy cows and breeding cows are also used for meat when they are no longer productive. Called cow beef, the meat from these animals is used mostly as ground beef or for canned beef and sausages.

Veal is another kind of beef that comes chiefly from milk-fed male dairy calves weighing between 100 and 200 pounds (45 to 90 kilograms). Female dairy calves are usually kept for milk production instead of being slaughtered for meat.

A highly specialized industry has developed to produce beef, especially in the United States. Each phase in the production—breeding, raising, and finishing (fattening up) the cattle—usually takes place on a different farm or ranch. The phases, or units, of production generally consist of cow-calf, stocker/grower, and feedlot operations. Other agribusinesses, including the packing companies that slaughter, process, and distribute beef to wholesalers and retailers, are also an important part of the beef industry.

Cow-Calf Operations. Producing calves is the first step in beef cattle production. This typically takes place on family-run farms and ranches in regions where the land is not suitable for other farming enterprises, such as growing crops.

Calves are born nine months after the mating of mature cows and bulls. They begin nursing milk and later eating forage, such as grasses and other plants. The calves live by their mother's side for six to eight months, by which time they weigh from 400 to 600 pounds (180 to 270 kilograms).

Before they are weaned (meaning they no longer nurse from their mothers), calves are usually worked, or processed, in a number of ways. They receive individual identification in the form of an eartag, brand, or tattoo; they are vaccinated against certain diseases, such as pneumonia; and the males usually undergo castration (an operation in which their reproductive organs are removed) so that they cannot produce offspring.

Some female calves are kept and raised to maturity as replacements for the cows who become old or sick. At about 15 months of age, a cow is old enough to be bred. If it remains healthy, it can produce calves for the next eight to twelve years.

A typical cow-calf producer in the United States owns 35 to 40 cows, although a few ranchers own 25,000 to 40,000 cows. These herds are considered small to ranchers in South America, who may own up to 200,000 cows on a single ranch. Some cow-calf ranchers, called purebreeders or seedstock producers, specialize in raising cattle that are used to help other ranchers with breeding tasks.

Stocker/Grower Operations. After the calves are weaned, they may be sold to growers (also called stocker operators). The growers help the calves gain weight. Often these calves, called stockers, weigh only 350 to 450 pounds (160 to 200 kilograms) and have not been worked. When the stocker cattle reach 600 to 700 pounds (270 to 320 kilograms), they are sold to feedlots for the final growth phase.

Feedlot Operations. The final segment of beef production is called finishing. In specially designed feed yards that may contain 20,000 to 100,000 cattle, the animals are fed high-energy grain diets, which help them gain weight rapidly. Finished cattle are typically 18 to 30 months old and range in weight from 1,000 to 1,300 pounds (455 to 590 kilograms).

Dairy Cattle

Cheese and yogurt are just two of the nutritious foods that originate with milk from dairy cows. Dairy cattle have been selected over time for their ability to efficiently convert grasses and grains into milk, rather than into the large amounts of muscle and fat that are found in beef cattle. In fact, among all types of domestic livestock, dairy cattle are the most efficient at producing protein and energy from their food. In the United States dairy industry, one cow's average yearly production is 16,000 pounds (7,260 kilograms) of milk, which contains 528 pounds (240 kilograms) of high-quality protein.

The most popular breed of dairy cattle is the Holstein, which is the top-volume milk producer. It is followed by the Jersey, which is prized for the high percentage of butterfat in its milk rather than for the amount produced.

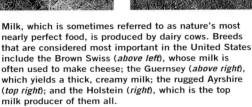

Milk, which is sometimes referred to as nature's most nearly perfect food, is produced by dairy cows. Breeds that are considered most important in the United States include the Brown Swiss (*above left*), whose milk is often used to make cheese; the Guernsey (*above right*), which yields a thick, creamy milk; the rugged Ayrshire (*top right*); and the Holstein (*right*), which is the top milk producer of them all.

Other common dairy breeds include the Guernsey, Ayrshire, and Brown Swiss.

Dairy cattle often live in barns where elaborate machinery is used to collect and process the milk. The cows must be milked twice a day, which before modern machinery was a long, difficult task for the dairy farmer. Today, however, automatic milking machines, collection containers, and processing equipment limit the amount of human labor that is required.

Herds of dairy cattle vary in size from 30 to 50 cows on small farms to 2,000 cows or more on large commercial dairy farms. In the United States, the leading states in milk production are California, Wisconsin, New York, Pennsylvania, Minnesota, and Texas. Dairy production sites are often located near population centers, which in recent years has caused concern from city dwellers about environmental problems.

To read more about dairy cattle and the dairy industry, consult the article DAIRYING AND DAIRY PRODUCTS in Volume D.

Dual-Purpose Cattle

Several breeds of cattle have been selected to produce both milk and meat. They are not as specialized as their beef or dairy counterparts but still can produce good-quality beef and satisfactory volumes of milk. Examples of dual-purpose breeds include the Milking Shorthorn, South Devon, and Red Poll, all of which were originally found in Britain.

▶ KEEPING CATTLE HEALTHY

Veterinarians work closely with farmers and ranchers to prevent disease and infestation by such parasites as liver flukes, grubs, lice, and ticks. Some diseases, such as leptospirosis and brucellosis, are special threats to a mother cow or young calf. Others, such as blackleg, malignant edema, and redwater, commonly harm calves and cattle under 2 years of age. Respiratory diseases, such as

Many young people acquire the knowledge and skills needed to raise and care for cattle through educational programs sponsored by 4-H and FFA.

pneumonia, typically affect mature cattle, especially when they are brought into contact with other cattle in feedlots or during shipping. Such diseases are especially costly to the cattle industry, because many animals can become sick in a short time. Most of these diseases and infestations are preventable with vaccinations and other health management programs.

A few diseases that harm cattle also can harm people. These include tuberculosis, brucellosis (known as undulate fever in humans), intestinal vibriosis, skin anthrax, foot-and-mouth disease, and bovine spongiform encephalopathy, or mad-cow disease (a brain disorder linked to Creutzfeldt-Jakob disease in humans). Because almost all cattle farmers and ranchers use modern disease-prevention programs, very few cases of cattle-caused diseases occur in humans. In addition, cooking and pasteurization help kill most disease-causing organisms.

▶ CATTLE SHOWS AND AUCTIONS

Livestock exhibitions are where cattle are shown to buyers, breeders, and other members of the cattle industry. Some exhibitions are competitions, where the animals are evaluated by expert judges. Most states also have state, county, and regional fairs where farmers and young people belonging to 4-H and FFA groups can exhibit their cattle. Many other nations also have cattle shows.

Auctions are where much of the buying and selling of cattle take place. Breed associations often promote purebred cattle at auctions, which are held on ranches or at livestock shows. Sometimes private sales are held on ranches without the help of agents.

LARRY BOLEMAN
Texas A & M University

See also COWBOYS; DAIRYING AND DAIRY PRODUCTS; HOOFED MAMMALS; MEAT AND MEAT PACKING; MILK.

CATTON, BRUCE. See MICHIGAN (Famous People).

CAVES AND CAVERNS

It had its beginnings some 60 million years ago, long before two-legged creatures walked on earth. As rains poured down on the bed of limestone and rivers flowed over it, the soft rock was nibbled away by the acid rainwater until hair-thin cracks began to appear. More acid rain fell. The water trickled down, enlarging the cracks. It found new paths between the layers of stone. The paths widened into tunnels. The tunnels crisscrossed and grew into rooms. Over millions of years the rooms grew bigger and bigger. By the time the mazelike network of passageways and rooms was discovered in 1901, the most spectacular system of caverns found in North America—the Carlsbad Caverns—had formed.

It is hard to imagine just how big a cave can be. Some of the rooms in this natural wonder are about 1,000 feet (300 meters) under the ground. The cave's largest room could hold ten football fields. In one place its ceiling is as high as a 30-story building. In 1930, this underground wonderland in the foothills of the Guadalupe Mountains, New Mexico, was established as Carlsbad Caverns National Park.

▶ INSIDE THE CAVE

With nothing to stop the flow of acid rainwater through the tunnels and rock-walled rooms, huge areas of limestone were devoured. But then the work of the acid rainwater was brought to a halt. The earth's crust

An elaborate landscape of stalactites and stalagmites decorate the Big Room in Carlsbad Caverns (*top*). This cave room, covering an area of 14 acres (5.7 hectares), is so enormous that the U.S. Capitol building could fit inside. The slow dripping of water over thousands of years (*above*) forms the fantastic structures found in caves such as Carlsbad Caverns.

wrinkled and folded. The bed of limestone tilted up and became part of a mountain range. The water that etched its way through the limestone rock slowly drained away.

Still, Carlsbad Caverns did not look as it does today. As raindrops trickled down to the empty cave rooms over the centuries, something new began to happen. Water started to decorate the cave.

About 1 million years ago a single drop of rainwater clung to the ceiling of Carlsbad's Big Room. As the water dripped, a tiny ring of lime crystallized on the ceiling. A second

The large tunnels of this lava cave (*left*) formed as lava flowed and cooled. The constant action of waves against rock lining the shore formed this sea cave (*right*).

drop—and a third, a fourth, a fifth—left lime in the same place. As time passed, the rings of lime formed a little stone "icicle."

Another drop of water dripped to the floor of the cave. Again the lime was left behind. As time passed, thousands of drops fell on the same spot. The specks of lime formed what looked like a stubby stone candle.

The icicle of stone on the ceiling is called a **stalactite**. The stubby candle on the floor is a **stalagmite**. (Think of the *c* in stalactite as standing for *c*eiling and the *g* in stalagmite as standing for *g*round. This will help you to remember which is which.) Sometimes the icicle-like stalactites and the stubby stalagmites meet in the middle to form columns.

Stalactites, stalagmites, and columns are not the only cave formations. Lime-laden water covers cave walls with rippling **flowstone**. It forms curtains of **dripstone** when it oozes from cracks in the ceiling. It builds a border of **rimstone** when it evaporates from a pool on the floor. It coats sand grains with layer after layer of lime until each grain is transformed into a **cave pearl**.

The ceilings of some caves are covered with short, hollow stalactites that look like soda straws. Others have glittering stone needles on their walls or stone pincushions bristling from the floor. There are delicate cave feathers, graceful cave flowers, and a strange stalactite (called a **helictite**) that grows sideways and up

as well as down. The color of cave formations varies also. They can be white, red, brown, or a combination of colors, depending on the minerals that form them.

In Carlsbad these weird and beautiful stone shapes stopped growing when the climate changed. Rains fell less often. Rivers grew shallow. Water seldom reached the rooms deep under the ground. Today scientists speak of the great caves as "dead."

▶ **KINDS OF CAVES**

Although no two caves look alike, all of the really big caves in the world were formed in the same way. They were hollowed out of limestone (or related rocks like gypsum and marble) by acid water. They are called **solution caves**. A more familiar word for them is **caverns**.

Caverns are not the only kind of cave. For example, **sea caves** are formed by the steady pounding of waves on the rocky cliffs along the shore. The waves do not dissolve the rock. They dig it out, grinding away at it year after year with pebbles and fine sand. The best-known sea caves are the Blue Grotto in Italy's island of Capri (grotto is still another word for cave) and Fingal's Cave in the Scottish Hebrides.

North America's largest sea cave is Sea Lion Cave in Oregon. Herds of sea lions raise their families in the cave's big room. Other sea caves are scattered along the Atlantic and Pacific coasts, as well as the shores of the Great Lakes and the Bay of Fundy.

In the western part of the United States and on the volcanic islands of Hawaii there are hundreds of **lava caves**. These formed after hot, melted rock welled up from deep inside the earth. Rivers of the liquid rock, called lava, flowed above ground. Even when the surfaces of the lava rivers cooled, forming a hard crust, their fiery interiors traveled on. The hollow, hardened tubes they left behind are lava caves. Lava caves are usually tunnels only a yard or so under the ground. Lava stalactites hang from their ceilings, and their floors are covered with ripple marks made by the fiery rivers that formed them.

Some lava caves contain huge beds of ice. Ages ago cold air from the surface entered the cave. The tube-shaped cave became a trap for the cold air. When rain or snow carried water to the cave, the water froze, making the porous lava rock still colder. The thicker the ice became, the less likelihood there was of its melting. Even in the desert, there are caves with perpetual ice.

In Canada and the northwestern United States there are also **glacial ice caves**. Hollowed out of glaciers, these caves have roofs and walls of ice. They grow bigger when warm air reaches them and smaller when it is cold. As they grow, blocks of ice often tumble from ceilings and walls. Glacial caves are usually too dangerous to explore.

During the Ice Age, when great glaciers covered large parts of North America, still another kind of cave was born. In the path of a glacier, boulders were split off from rocky hillsides. After the ice sheet melted, streams tumbled the boulders about and enlarged the openings in the hills. These openings, which never became very big, are **splitrock** or **boulder caves**. They are found chiefly in New England.

▶ **LIFE IN CAVES**

Almost every cave is inhabited, but most caves are not suitable places for humans to make their homes. Caves are usually too dark, cold, and wet to live in. In the past, some people, such as Cro-Magnons and Neanderthals, did live in caves. The traces they have left indicate that when they lived in caves, they stayed close to the entrances. If they ventured to the inner parts of caves, it was for special ceremonies. It is possible that in some remote areas of the world, there are people who still live in caves much as the earliest cave dwellers did. However, most caves are populated by animals and plants.

Some animals found in caves do not live there permanently. Birds build nests near the entrance. Skunks use caves as a nursery in which to rear babies. During the winter, caves get new residents as bears, snakes, and many insects settle down to sleep. But these creatures are not true cave dwellers. They take shelter in the cave only when they cannot find any place better.

The real cave dwellers live deep inside the cave. Some, like rats and bats, leave the cave to find food. But there are insects, fishes, and

True cave dwellers live deep inside the cave. The salamander (*far right*) may venture out into the daylight, but the cave cricket (*right*) has adapted to life in the dark. It has no color and uses its extra-long feelers to find food. Many cave animals are blind, for there is nothing to see in the darkness of the cave.

Careful observers may be able to locate a cave by the comings and goings of animals, such as bats, that must leave the cave to find food.

salamanders that spend their whole lives in black cave rooms. A long line of their ancestors lived in the same place. During centuries of darkness these creatures have lost their coloring, becoming white or pale pink or transparent. Many are now blind, making up for eyesight with better hearing or a sharper sense of touch or smell.

The blind and wingless cave beetle is covered with fine hairs. The ghostly blindfish that swim in underground streams are unusually sensitive to vibrations. Blind cave salamanders are rarer than the blindfish. Some kinds can see when they are born, although their eyelids grow together later on.

While these animals are able to adapt to cave life, few plants can. Molds and mushrooms flourish in the damp, dark underground rooms, but green plants cannot live without light. Only in caves that have been wired for electricity will you see green moss and feathery ferns on the rocky ledges.

▶ USES OF CAVES

Today, caves in the United States are used mostly for recreation by sightseers and **spelunkers**, people who explore caves as a hobby (from the Latin word *spelunca*, which means "cave"). Spelunkers must be specially trained and equipped.

From the early 1800's through the Civil War, caves in the southern United States were important sources of nitrates, an essential ingredient in gunpowder. Caves in the southern United States and Mexico have also been a source of bat guano (manure), which is used as a phosphate fertilizer.

Since the late 1980's, however, the U.S. government has passed laws aimed at protecting caves from human activities, such as mining in areas near caves. Authorities hope to preserve the fragile habitats, valuable artifacts, and water resources of many caves.

▶ FINDING A CAVE

Out riding one summer afternoon, a New Mexican cowboy named Jim White spotted a dark, funnel-shaped cloud of bats rising from a sandy hillside. He searched the hillside to find where the thousands of bats had come from. His explorations led him from a yawning hole in the ground through tunnels slippery with bat droppings to an enormous room. He had never seen anything like it before—great stone formations hung from the ceiling and rose from the floor. Searching for the bats' home, White had discovered Carlsbad Caverns!

Most caves are found by accident. However, **speleologists**, the scientists who study caves, are learning to locate them by examining rock formations and following the paths of underground streams.

There are about 30,000 known caves in North America, 17,000 of which are in the United States. They occur in every state except Rhode Island and Louisiana. More than 130 caves have been opened to the public for study and enjoyment. Of these, 15 are in the national parks or monuments, and 30 are in state parks. The remainder are privately owned and operated.

The best part of a cave tour can come when the guide turns out the lights. The jet blackness is darker than anything you have experienced before. It is a world where the sun never shines. For a few seconds time rolls backward, and you can picture the ancient beginnings of caves and caverns.

DOROTHY STERLING
Author, *The Story of Caves*

See also BATS; GLACIERS; ICE AGES; PREHISTORIC ART; PREHISTORIC PEOPLE; SPELUNKING.

CEDAR RAPIDS. See IOWA (Cities).
CELLOPHANE. See PLASTICS.

CELLS

Almost all living things are made of cells. Some tiny forms of life consist of only one cell. Larger forms of life are built of many cells. That is why cells are called the basic units of life.

The human body is made of billions upon billions of cells. That tells you something about cells—they are tiny. Most cells are so small that they can be seen only with a microscope. In fact, the existence of cells became known only after the microscope was invented. They were first noticed in plant tissues. This is not surprising, because most plant cells are larger than animal cells.

An animal cell of average size is about 1/1,000 of an inch long. The smallest cells are probably the bacteria. These one-celled forms of life can barely be seen even with a microscope. Nerve cells are probably the largest cells. Some of them are more than 3 feet (1 meter) long.

There are a great many kinds of cells. Each kind, as a rule, specializes in one particular activity. For example, in animals some cells expand and contract; these are muscle cells. Other cells are sensitive to light; these cells form the retina of the eye.

Modern microscopes show that cells are far from simple. They contain many complicated structures, and they are constantly active. Cells convert food substances into energy that in turn is used to do various kinds of work. The cell also makes new cell material—more living matter.

With few exceptions, a single cell does not live very long. But if it divides, the two new cells start life afresh. That is, instead of aging and dying, the old cell becomes two new cells in a process called cell division.

Because of its constant activity, the cell is much more than a structural unit in a living organism. It is itself the unit of life. Life is an activity, or a process, forever changing, even though the appearance may remain the same. This is one of the most important ideas in biology.

Cells exist in a variety of sizes and shapes. Some cells are independent organisms, such as these paramecia (*top*). Other cells, such as those in an onion skin (*center*), form the tissue of plants and animals. Still others carry out special functions, such as a nerve cell in the human brain (*bottom*).

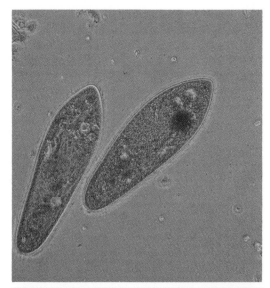

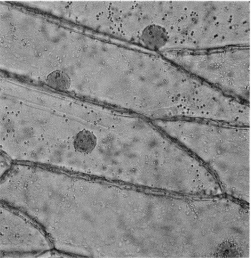

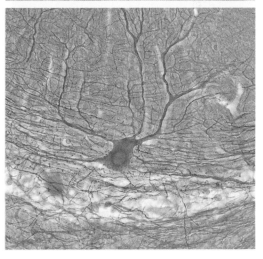

All cells have three main parts: the cell membrane, the cytoplasm, and the nucleus. The **cell membrane** is the outside surface of the cell. Inside the membrane is the **cytoplasm.** This is a mass of colorless material that holds many other tiny cell parts. The **nucleus** is usually near the center of the cell. It is round or oval in shape and has an outer membrane of its own.

The cell membrane, cytoplasm, and nucleus work together. All three are necessary to the life of the cell. Together, they constitute what is called **protoplasm.**

The Cell Membrane

The cell membrane is the boundary separating the interior of the cell from the outside. Everything that enters or leaves the cell must pass through it. Water, salts, oxygen, and food substances pass steadily into the cell through the membrane. Carbon dioxide, waste substances, and also water and salts pass out of the cell. There is a continual traffic through the cell membrane in both directions.

The Cytoplasm

The cytoplasm is the region where most of the chemical work of the cell is conducted. New cell materials are manufactured here, and old materials are broken down and eliminated. Organic (carbon-containing) compounds from food substances are used to build new cell structures or to supply energy for cell activities. Oxygen is needed to keep these processes going. Carbon dioxide, water, and excess heat are produced as unwanted products.

The Cell Nucleus

The cell nucleus is responsible for determining the nature of the cell and for directing its activities, especially cell division. When a cell is about to divide in two, threadlike material in the nucleus, called **chromatin,** groups together into a number of slender, bent rods called **chromosomes.** Chromosomes contain all the information a cell needs to carry on its life processes. They are made up of a complex chemical (a **nucleic acid**) called deoxyribonucleic acid, or DNA for short. In the nucleus, DNA occurs as fine, spirally coiled threads that in turn coil around one another, like a twisted ladder. All the chromosome material is confined within the nucleus, except when a cell is in the process of division. (You can read more about cell division later in this article or in the GENETICS article in Volume G.)

Small, round bodies called **nucleoli** are also found in the nucleus. They contain another kind of nucleic acid—ribonucleic acid, or RNA, which is important in making proteins.

Structures in the Cytoplasm

In the cytoplasm are a variety of specialized structures important for cell activities. One of these is a sausage-shaped body called a **mitochondrion** (plural, mitochondria). These complex bodies have been called the powerhouse of the cell. They are responsible for converting simple organic substances, such as sugar, into energy that the cell needs to carry out its activities.

Another structure, the **endoplasmic reticulum** (or ER), is made up of many membranes. In some cells these membranes extend, layer after layer, all the way from the nucleus to the cell surface. Along the reticulum are enormous numbers of minute granules called **ribosomes.** These structures are especially important, for it is here that proteins are made.

The cytoplasm also contains structures called **Golgi bodies.** They are involved in the secretion of cell products and may also help in protein manufacture.

The structures discussed so far are present in both animal and plant cells. However, in several important ways animal and plant cells differ from one another.

▶ANIMAL CELLS AND PLANT CELLS

Both animal cells and plant cells require organic substances, such as sugar, to provide the energy they need for growth and other activities. However, animal cells cannot manufacture these organic substances themselves—they must obtain them from outside sources. Animal cells also require atmospheric oxygen, whereas plant cells usually do not.

Most plant cells can manufacture their own sugars and other basic substances.They do this by using the energy obtained from light, together with water, carbon dioxide, and certain other raw materials. This manufacturing process is called **photosynthesis,** a process you can read more about in the PHOTOSYNTHESIS article in Volume P. In photosynthesis, water is split into hydrogen and oxygen by means of light energy. The oxygen is passed into the

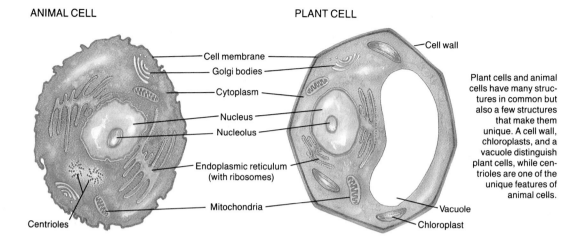

ANIMAL CELL

PLANT CELL

- Cell membrane
- Golgi bodies
- Cytoplasm
- Nucleus
- Nucleolus
- Endoplasmic reticulum (with ribosomes)
- Mitochondria
- Centrioles
- Cell wall
- Vacuole
- Chloroplast

Plant cells and animal cells have many structures in common but also a few structures that make them unique. A cell wall, chloroplasts, and a vacuole distinguish plant cells, while centrioles are one of the unique features of animal cells.

atmosphere, where it is available for use by animal cells. The hydrogen combines with carbon dioxide, in a series of complicated steps, to produce the sugar glucose.

Light is absorbed by the green pigment **chlorophyll.** Chlorophyll is confined in small, round, green discs called **chloroplasts** distributed around the plant cell cytoplasm. Each chloroplast represents a small factory for photosynthesis.

Most plant cells are also distinguished by having a large internal sac of fluid called the **vacuole.** This contains a salt solution important to the life of the cell. In addition, a plant cell possesses a strengthening **cell wall** made up of a material called **cellulose.** This wall is found outside the living cell membrane. Plant cells tend to become boxed in by their rigid external walls. Much of the strength and toughness of a plant comes from that.

Animal cells are more exposed to their environment than plant cells, and their surface membrane is generally more active. Animal cells take in water, dissolved salts, and other substances by a process of **diffusion** through the tiny pores of the cell membrane. In addition, many kinds of animal cells can take in these substances and even particles by a process of cell drinking called **pinocytosis.** In this process the membrane pushes out or folds in here and there. It does so in such a way that small droplets of water or particles of food substances are captured and passed into the cell interior.

The cell membrane of some animal cells produces intricately constructed hairlike structures extending from the cell surface. These show a regularly beating, whiplike movement. They either move the cell through the external fluid or move the fluid past the cell. Also part of this outer region are the very fine fibrils (little fibers) that cause a cell to contract and expand, as in muscle cells. The long, drawn-out extensions of certain cells, which we call nerve fibers, are also part of the same region. Altogether, the outer region of animal cells is strikingly sensitive and responsive to influences from outside.

▶ CELL DIVISION

One of the most remarkable things a cell can do is become two cells. Most kinds of cells—both plant and animal—can divide into two cells exactly like the original. In doing so they go through a complicated process called **mitosis.** During mitosis, chromosomes in the cell nucleus divide and separate. In most animal cells the process is set in motion by a pair of small bodies called **centrioles,** which lie close to the nucleus. In the cells of many plants, the process begins without the help of any such structures. (Strictly speaking, "mitosis" refers only to the division of the nucleus of a cell. However, it is sometimes used to mean division of the entire cell.)

Each centriole becomes a center from which fibers grow in all directions, forming a radiating or star-shaped pattern known as an **aster.** Between the two centers the fibers run together, forming a bridgelike structure called the **spindle.** The spindle assists in the division process of the chromosomes in the nucleus.

AN ANIMAL CELL DIVIDING BY MITOSIS

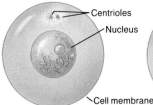

Centrioles
Nucleus
Cell membrane

1. An animal cell before cell division by mitosis begins.

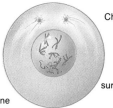

2. Chromosomes pair up in the nucleus; centrioles divide.

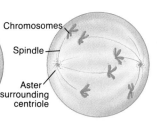

Chromosomes
Spindle
Aster surrounding centriole

3. Spindle fibers begin to form; nuclear membrane breaks down.

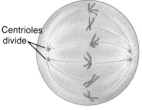

Centrioles divide

4. Chromosomes move midway between the asters.

5. Pairs of chromosomes are pulled apart toward the asters.

6. Spindles lengthen as chromosomes move closer to asters.

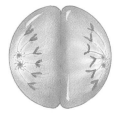

7. Cell membrane starts to pinch in two at cell's center.

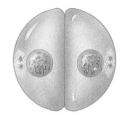

8. Nuclear membrane forms around chromosomes. Mitosis is complete.

During division of the nucleus, the long, threadlike chromosomes become shorter and wider. At the same time the nuclear membrane disappears. Each chromosome, already duplicated, separates lengthwise so that each chromosome has now formed a pair. The duplicated chromosomes move to the equator (center) of the spindle. From there the two sets of chromosomes are pulled apart by special spindle fibers. In this way each of the two cells about to be formed receives a complete set of chromosomes. From this set a new nucleus is reconstructed, exactly like the original nucleus.

Cell division continues as the two asters and their spindle become steadily larger. In effect the two centers push each other apart. Finally, a furrow appears at the cell surface around the middle of the cell. The furrow deepens and divides the whole cell in two. Then each centriole, if it has not already done so, divides into two. Each new pair is ready to bring about division of the new cell when needed. And when a cell's division finally ends, each new cell resulting from the division is a complete, exact copy of the old cell.

One special type of cell is formed by a kind of cell division called **meiosis.** Meiosis is the process by which male and female reproductive cells are formed. During this process, a cell divides twice, creating four new cells. The unique feature of meiosis is that it produces cells with only half the usual number of chromosomes. This is so that when a male cell and a female cell combine during sexual reproduction, the new cell that is formed will have the normal number of chromosomes. This cell then divides again and again—by mitosis—until a complete, new individual is formed. (You can read more about this in the article EGGS AND EMBRYOS in Volume E and the article REPRODUCTION in Volume R.)

The importance of cell division is very great indeed. The life of an individual cell is generally short. The cell ages and dies. If it undergoes division, however, each new cell starts life afresh. So, as long as divisions continue, aging and death are postponed. Also, as cells multiply in this way, the body they compose continues to grow. Anything that stops cell multiplication stops growth. Even when the body is fully grown, many kinds of cells are continually dying and have to be replaced by new cells. As the body grows older, cell replacement becomes slower, and the body ages.

N. J. BERRILL
McGill University

See also AGING; BODY, HUMAN; EGGS AND EMBRYOS; GENETICS; PLANTS; REPRODUCTION.

CELTS

Evidence of the Celts (or Kelts) in Europe dates from long before the days of the Roman Empire. We owe to them many stirring tales of gods and goddesses and of heroes such as King Arthur and the Knights of the Round Table. To the Celts, calendar festivals were of great importance. We still celebrate their Samain, the eve of November 1, a time when humans could go into the otherworld and the divine inhabitants of that world could come into ours. Today we call it Halloween.

The classical writers tell us that the people we call Celts knew themselves by this name. The different groups of Celts were closely linked by language, religion, and culture. At the height of their power, about 300 B.C., they occupied all the land between the Baltic and Mediterranean seas and between the Black Sea and the Atlantic coast. Most of them were brought under Roman rule by the 1st century B.C.

The ancient Celts left few written records. They never formed a great empire, as the Romans did. Yet they created an important civilization in Europe north of the Alps, where they introduced the use of iron. With their superb skill in fashioning weapons and tools of this metal, they created one of Europe's major revolutions in technology. They carried on trade far beyond their own settlements.

The Celts produced works of art—beautifully decorated weapons, personal ornaments, ceramics, glass, and coins—quite different from anything else in the ancient world.

How We Have Learned About the Celts. The Celts built dwellings and other buildings such as shops and stables. The defenses of their forts—in both wood and stone, according to the material available—and many of their stone buildings survive today. But the Celts preferred to pass on their culture by word of mouth rather than by written records.

We know about the Celts partly through archaeology and partly through the writings of their Greek and Roman conquerors, especially Julius Caesar. We have also learned about the ancient Celts from peoples who are their descendants and who still speak Celtic languages. There are small and diminishing numbers of Celtic speakers among the Welsh, the Bretons of northwestern France, the Scots, and the Irish.

One of Ireland's great treasures is the Ardagh chalice, or cup—an example of late (8th century) Celtic art.

Celtic groups lived in present-day Great Britain and Ireland long before the Romans began their conquest of Britain in 55 B.C. The Romans remained there for 400 years. But they never entered Ireland or conquered the mountainous northern and western parts of Britain. The Celts in those areas kept their way of life and their pagan Celtic religion until they were converted to Christianity about A.D. 450. Later, monks, poets, and scribes carefully wrote down the great heroic tales and preserved the poetry and mythology that their ancestors, the pagan Celts, had passed down through the ages by word of mouth.

Where the Celts Lived. The Celts had a highly developed civilization by about 800 or 700 B.C. Their heartland was probably the small area in present-day Switzerland and Germany where three great rivers—the Rhine, the Rhone, and the Danube—begin. Along these and other rivers, Celtic groups expanded until they reached their height between 500 and 50 B.C. The Gauls were one of the best-known Celtic groups. They lived in present-day France and parts of adjoining countries. Other Celts spread as far east as Slovakia or beyond and as far south as Italy and Spain.

Way of Life and Culture. Archaeologists call the earlier Iron Age in Celtic civilization (about 800 to 500 B.C.) the Hallstatt culture. It is named for a Celtic settlement discovered at Hallstatt, Austria. The culture of the later Iron Age (500 to 50 B.C.) is named

La Tène, for a site called La Tène (The Shallows) at the Lake of Neuchâtel, in Switzerland.

Finds made at the Hallstatt site in the mid-1800's show that the Celts had a large settlement there. They mined salt and traded with other peoples. There are hundreds of graves where noble Celts were buried in wooden chambers under mounds of earth. In the chambers were many objects made by Celtic artisans—swords and shields, metal drinking vessels, four-wheeled wagons and horse bridles. The Celts believed in a life after death. Warriors would need all this equipment, along with joints of wild boar (a favorite food), on their long journey to the otherworld.

La Tène was one of the Celts' many holy places, for they worshiped water whether in the form of lake, river, or spring. To such places they brought gifts for their deities and threw these offerings into the water. This was the origin of the wishing well. Many objects made by the Celts have been found at La Tène since excavations began there in the 1880's. These objects are richly decorated with fanciful birds and animals and elaborate designs composed of circles, swirls, and curves. The designs are often imitated by modern artists.

We know that many of the Celts were farmers. They grew wheat and other grains and raised cattle, sheep, and hogs. Sometimes they lived in large hilltop villages defended by huge walls of timber and stone. Inside, everything was well planned. There were small dwellings for the people and a large building where the chief, or king, lived and held feasts for the noble warriors. The smiths had their metalworking shops in one place, and huge quantities of grain were stored in another part of the village.

Other persons besides kings and warriors held a high place in Celtic society. These were the bards, who composed and recited verses about gods and heroes and their deeds; the smiths, who were thought to have magic powers; and the druids, who performed religious ceremonies and administered Celtic law.

Celtic women dressed in long tunics or loose trousers and wore hair ornaments, bracelets, rings, and pins. The men washed their hair with lime to stiffen and lighten it. They wore tunics, trousers, and great blanketlike cloaks. Their jewelry included torques (neck rings), armlets, and ornamental belt buckles. For war, the Celts carried spears, wore swords, and dodged enemy blows behind tall, oblong shields. When they killed an enemy, they cut off the head and carried it proudly home to keep as proof of their courage and skill.

The Celts worshiped many gods and goddesses. They enjoyed festivals, feasting and drinking, hunting, fighting, and cattle raiding. They admired courage, fine appearance, good speaking, generosity, and hospitality. Archaeological research is constantly turning up new information about the Celts and their contributions to the world.

ANNE ROSS
Author, *Everyday Life of the Pagan Celts*

See also ARTHUR, KING; ENGLISH ART AND ARCHITECTURE; FRANCE; IRELAND; LANGUAGES; SCOTLAND; WALES.

The Celts carved this gigantic horse on a chalk hill near Uffington, England.

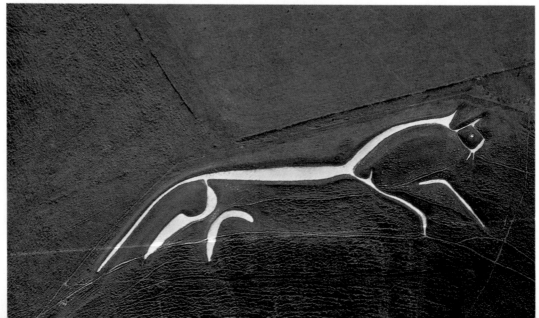

CEMENT AND CONCRETE

Cement is one of the most useful materials in modern building. By itself it is a soft powder. But when it is mixed with water and allowed to harden, cement can bind sand or gravel into a hard, solid mass.

Cement is used chiefly as an ingredient of mortar and concrete. Mortar is a mixture of lime, cement, sand, and water. Concrete is a mixture of cement, water, sand and gravel or broken stone.

Mortar is too weak to be used by itself as a material for building. It can, however, be used to bind together bricks or stones into masonry. Mortar is also used to make a protective coating called stucco.

Concrete is very strong because of the gravel and stone mixed in it. When concrete is poured into molds, or forms, and allowed to harden, it will stand by itself. Because it is poured while still soft, concrete can be molded into odd shapes that would be impossible to make with other materials. For this reason modern architects often use concrete in the buildings they design.

▶ HOW IS CEMENT MADE?

Modern cement is made by heating a crushed mixture of limestone and clay or slag (a by-product of metal refining) to a very high temperature. This mixture is heated in a huge furnace until large, glassy cinders called clinkers are formed. The clinkers are then ground into a powder. When water is added to the powder, a complicated chemical reaction takes place. The result is a durable artificial stone that will not dissolve in water. In fact, this type of cement will actually harden under water. For this reason it is called hydraulic cement, from the Greek word *hydor,* meaning "water."

Before hydraulic cement was discovered, a kind of cement was made from lime and water. Lime is a white, powdery substance that is made by heating limestone. Plain lime cement hardened very slowly in the air. It would not harden at all under water. It was not as strong as hydraulic cement.

The Romans discovered how to make a type of hydraulic cement in the 2nd or 3rd century B.C. by mixing volcanic ash with their lime. This discovery is still ranked as one of Rome's greatest achievements.

Soon after the Romans had learned how to make their cement, they used it to make concrete. Many of their most impressive structures were built of concrete. Some of these are still standing today.

It was not always possible to get volcanic ash or cement rock (a kind of limestone) to make hydraulic cement; so people began to try to make it artificially. By the early 19th century several French and English builders had succeeded in this task. The best of these cements was made by an English bricklayer named Joseph Aspdin. In 1824, Aspdin invented a cement that he called portland cement. He gave it this name because it looked like a kind of stone found on the Isle of Portland.

Since the end of the 19th century all building cement has been made artificially. Cement manufacturers no longer have to depend on supplies of natural cement rock or volcanic ash. By preparing their own mixtures, the manufacturers can make cements that are specially suited to almost any use.

▶ BUILDING WITH CEMENT

The knowledge of how to make concrete had been lost at the end of the Roman Empire. Until the late 18th century, there is no record of building with concrete. Aspdin's invention of portland cement sparked a revival of building with concrete. During much of the 19th century, builders used concrete in the same way as stone. It was poured into solid masses for walls, arches, and vaults. It was also cast into blocks and laid like stone or brick masonry. Concrete block is still used in some small buildings.

One difficulty with concrete is that it is porous; that is, it is easily penetrated by water. Water can get into small holes or cracks in the concrete and then freeze, expand, and crack the concrete. When concrete is used where there might be a problem with water (for instance, in underground foundations or in structures that are exposed to seawater), the concrete is often coated with tar or waterproofing paint.

Reinforced Concrete

Like brick and stone, concrete has high compressive strength. That is, it can stand forces that press directly on it. But it has little tensile strength, which is the ability to resist

Concrete is often used to make floors. In this picture, the concrete had been poured over a reinforcing steel grid; then it is spread to make an even surface.

being pulled apart. To overcome this weakness, engineers have developed ways to reinforce concrete with steel bars. The bars are put into the concrete at places where it might pull apart under normal loads.

For example, a concrete beam or floor slab tends to be pulled apart on the bottom and pushed together at the top. The steel bars are located near the bottom of the beam or slab, where the extra strength is needed.

Columns that have to support shifting loads, such as columns that hold up a bridge, may be subjected to bending in any direction. To counteract this bending, steel bars are set in the concrete column. The bars are linked by steel hoops so that a sort of cage is formed inside the concrete. This steel cage gives the column added strength.

Concrete can be made even stronger by prestressing. Steel cables are stretched by powerful machinery while the concrete is being poured around them. When the concrete has hardened, the steel cables are released. The cables contract like a stretched spring that has been released. The contraction helps pull the concrete together and prevents it from being stretched by tension. This makes it more able to stand heavy loads. Prestressed concrete is used where very heavy loads must be carried, as in the beams of highway bridges.

The invention of reinforced concrete in the late 19th century and the later invention of prestressed concrete have allowed engineers to use concrete in many more ways than they could in the past. Concrete is now used in building everything from the thin, curving walls of modern buildings to huge, massive dams or bridge piers. Because it can be used in so many ways and costs relatively little, concrete has become a very popular building material.

Besides its usefulness as a structural material, concrete serves well as a decoration for buildings. Crushed glass or colored stone can be mixed into concrete to create beautiful floors and walls. Bits of crushed marble or granite are set in concrete to form a type of flooring called terrazzo. Terrazzo floors are often used in large public buildings such as museums.

CARL W. CONDIT
Co-editor, *Technology and Culture*

See also BRICKS AND MASONRY; BUILDING CONSTRUCTION.

CENSUS

Usually, people think of a census as an official count of the population of a country. This kind of census, called a population census, has been taken since ancient times. "Census" comes from the Latin word *censere*, meaning "to assess, or tax." The Romans took the most complete censuses in the ancient world, beginning in the 500's B.C. Government officials, called censors, made a register of people and their property. One purpose was to identify persons for military service. The other was to place a value on property so that taxes could be collected.

▶ **MODERN CENSUSES AROUND THE WORLD**

Today almost every country takes an official population census, usually once every five or ten years. And most countries take other kinds of censuses, such as censuses of agriculture, industry, trade, and government. These censuses are scientifically designed to provide the statistics (facts and figures) that the people of a country need to understand economic and social conditions. Such statistics provide the basis for good government, economic progress, conservation of natural re-

sources, and the welfare of all the people. This kind of census taking began to be developed in the United States and in European countries in the 1700's.

After World War II (1939–45), the United Nations and other international organizations set up programs to coordinate the timing of censuses in countries around the world, as well as the kinds of information that the various countries gathered. As a result, census reports have become more uniform. And the number of countries gathering statistics about agriculture, business and industry, trade, education, housing, and the like has risen steadily. This information has become increasingly valuable for economic and social planning, especially in the developing countries of the world.

Many countries have special agencies that are responsible for their censuses. In Canada, for example, censuses are taken by Statistics Canada, an agency of the Department of Industry, Trade, and Commerce. The Bureau of the Census of the Department of Commerce takes United States censuses.

▶ **UNITED STATES CENSUSES**

The U.S. Constitution requires a population census every ten years, and such a census has been taken regularly since 1790. The main reason for conducting the census was for apportioning (distributing) the membership of the U.S. House of Representatives among the states. Later, Congress authorized the gathering of a great deal of information about each person. These statistics are used in many ways. For example, the amount of government aid given to a school district is based partly on the number of school-age children the census shows to be living there.

During the years, Congress has requested that many other kinds of censuses be taken at regular times. These include censuses of manufacturing, mining, agriculture, fisheries, employment, construction, foreign trade, and energy sources. Census information is available to the public in a wide variety of publications, such as *The Statistical Abstract of the United States*, as well as through the Census Bureau Web site.

ROBERT E. KENNEDY, JR.
University of Minnesota
Reviewed by KENNETH PREWITT
Director, United States Census Bureau

WONDER QUESTION

How is the U.S. population census taken?

The 2000 population census was taken chiefly by mail. Every household received a census form to be filled out and mailed back. This form asked six questions about every person in the household (including age, sex, ethnicity, race) and whether the residence was rented or owned. Every sixth household received a longer, more detailed questionnaire about the individuals and their housing arrangements. If the form was not returned or was not filled out properly, an employee of the Bureau of the Census, called a census enumerator, visited the household to gather the needed information.

Questionnaires from the census offices all over the nation were optically scanned, using a technology called "intelligent character recognition." The resulting data was fed into computers, which then produced the statistical information desired, without revealing the identity of any of the respondents.

CENTIPEDES AND MILLIPEDES

Centipedes and millipedes are small animals with wormlike bodies and many legs. Although they are often confused with each other, it is easy to tell them apart. A centipede's body is slightly flattened, and each segment (joint) has only one pair of legs. A millipede's body is more rounded, and each segment has two pairs of legs.

These many-legged animals look as if they might be spiders or insects, but they are not. They are close relatives of spiders and insects,

but they are classified separately. The many kinds of centipedes form a class by themselves; the many kinds of millipedes form another class.

▶ **HOW THEY ARE ALIKE**

However, centipedes and millipedes share several features. Both have a great many legs, as their names indicate. (Centipede means "hundred feet or legs" and millipede means "thousand feet or legs.") The number ranges from 15 pairs to about 200 pairs, depending on the kind. In both classes the animals have long, slender bodies, made up of many segments. A few are born with their full number of segments and legs, but most grow new segments as they age. The last segment divides in two, and then the new last segment divides again. Such division continues until the animal has its adult number of segments.

The heads of centipedes and millipedes have antennae—long feelers like those of insects. Some kinds have simple eyes, but others are blind. They have tiny insectlike mouths.

Centipedes and millipedes have hard outer shells enclosing their muscles and body organs. These shells serve as skeletons. The shell's outer layer is shed from time to time, thus allowing an increase in size. Many of the body segments have air pores, which connect to an internal system of tiny tubes. These tubes allow air to reach parts of the body.

Centipedes and millipedes have a nerve center in the head—a kind of simple brain. A nerve cord runs along the lower part of the body, with smaller nerve centers in each body segment.

The digestive system consists of a tube that goes from the mouth through the body. Wastes are given off through an opening at the end of the body.

The blood-circulation system is simple. It consists of a tubelike heart, which pumps the blood from one end of the body to the other.

▶ **CENTIPEDES**

Most of the common centipedes have 15 pairs of legs. The two front legs are fangs. They are connected to glands that secrete (give off) a poisonous fluid.

Centipedes use the poison to kill their

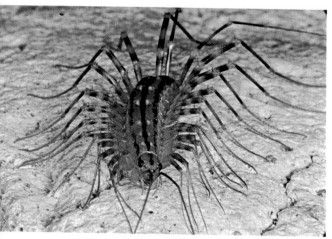

Above: Centipedes are nocturnal creatures. They hunt for food only at night and hide from light during the day. Below: This millipede can roll its slender body into a ball to protect itself from danger.

prey—usually slugs, earthworms, and insects. Sometimes centipedes kill and eat each other. (Only a few species are plant eaters.) The poison also helps them to digest their prey by dissolving its body tissues. Although the poison can cause intense pain and swelling, a centipede's bite is not fatal to human beings.

Centipedes live in damp places almost everywhere, but they are most common in warm, tropical regions. They hide during the day and become active at night. Their flattened bodies enable them to lie protected in cracks, under boards or stones, or in rotten logs.

Probably the most common variety is the house centipede, *Scutigera forceps,* often found in human dwellings. About 5 centimeters (2 inches) long, these creatures have 15 pairs of long, bent legs, which make them look like many-legged spiders. They feed on small insects and rarely bother human beings. But their bites can cause some pain.

The largest centipede, *Scolopendra gigas,* lives on an island in the West Indies. It may grow to a length of 30 centimeters (12 inches). It feeds mostly on insects but sometimes captures and eats mice and lizards.

There are a few centipedes that light up in the dark. One of these, the *Geophilus electricus,* is blind. The function of its light may be to attract prey.

Some centipedes bear their young alive. Most of the others lay eggs that hatch without help from the female. In a few species, the female guards her eggs until they hatch.

▶ **MILLIPEDES**

Millipedes vary in length from about 1.5 to 300 millimeters (1/16 inch to 12 inches). The larger kinds are found in warm countries. Most have about 35 segments. Millipedes feed on decaying vegetation. In damp weather they may eat living plants, especially the roots. A few of the tropical millipedes feed on dead animal matter.

Millipedes have no poison fangs. When disturbed, they defend themselves by coiling up like watchsprings or rolling into balls. Many kinds have poison or stink glands along the sides of their bodies. The substance given off by these glands repels insects and other enemies. Some millipedes give off a poison that can kill insects.

Centipedes lay their eggs in soil or decayed wood. In a few species, the female guards the eggs from predators by coiling her body around them.

Millipedes are slow-moving animals. Their numerous legs (some species, or kinds, have up to 115 pairs of legs) move one after the other in wavelike motions along each side of the body. They can usually be found in damp places under logs or leaves.

Most millipedes become active at night. And for a long time it was believed that they responded to the changes in temperature and light. Then scientists experimented by keeping millipedes in unchanging conditions. In theory, this should have confused the animals, but it did not. The millipedes kept up their regular daily cycle of activities. It seems that millipedes are governed by built-in "clocks," which cause them to leave their hiding places at certain times and crawl about.

A common millipede found in the eastern United States is *Spirobolus marginatus.* It is 10 centimeters (about 4 inches) long and about as thick as a pencil. Its color ranges from reddish brown to black. A variety of millipede found in California—the *Luminodesmus sequoiae*—lights up.

Millipedes lay their eggs in groups of 25 to 50. Among some kinds, the females cement bits of earth together with saliva to form dome-shaped nests within which the eggs are laid.

ROSS E. HUTCHINS
Author, *Insects*

See also BIOLUMINESCENCE; INSECTS.

CENTRAL AFRICAN REPUBLIC

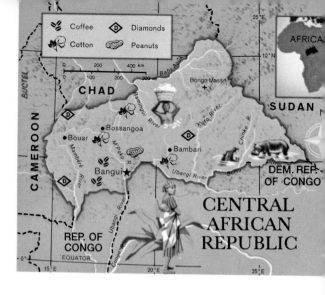

The Central African Republic is an appropriately named nation, for it is located in the heart of Africa close to the center of the continent. In area it is slightly smaller than the state of Texas, but it has a population less than one-fifth that of Texas. At one time a colony of France, the Central African Republic gained its independence in 1960.

▶ THE PEOPLE

The people of the Central African Republic belong to many different ethnic groups. The largest groups are the Banda, the Baya, and the Mandjia.

The majority of the people are farmers who live in small villages governed by traditional chiefs. The main food crops are cassava (a starchy root) and millet (a grain), which are dried and pounded into flour. This is cooked into a porridge and is eaten with meat, chicken, or fish sauce and very hot pepper.

FACTS and figures

CENTRAL AFRICAN REPUBLIC (République Centrafricaine) is the official name of the country.

LOCATION: Central Africa.

AREA: 240,535 sq mi (622,984 km²).

POPULATION: 3,400,000 (estimate).

CAPITAL AND LARGEST CITY: Bangui.

MAJOR LANGUAGES: French (official), Sango (national).

MAJOR RELIGIOUS GROUPS: Christian, traditional African religions, Muslim.

GOVERNMENT: Republic. **Head of state**—president. **Head of government**—prime minister. **Legislature**—National Assembly and Economic and Regional Council.

CHIEF PRODUCTS: Cotton, coffee, cassava, millet, sorghum, peanuts, lumber and wood products, processed agricultural products, diamonds, gold.

MONETARY UNIT: African Financial Community (CFA) franc (1 CFA franc = 100 centimes).

Language and Religion. French is the official language, but it is spoken by only a relatively few Central Africans. Sango, one of several African languages, is more widely used and serves as the national language.

Followers of traditional African religions and Christians (both Protestants and Roman Catholics) make up the country's largest religious groups. Muslims are found in smaller numbers and live mainly in the north.

▶ THE LAND

The Central African Republic is a vast plateau, largely covered by rolling grassland. In the southwest are tropical rain forests and in the northeast, barren hills. The climate is tropical, with generally high temperatures and humidity and considerable rainfall.

The Ubangi River, a major tributary of the Congo River, is the only river in the country that is navigable for any important distance. The country's southern rivers flow into the Ubangi. The northern rivers, including the Shari, drain northward into Lake Chad.

Plant and Animal Life. Many tropical plants, including oil palms and giant kapok trees, are found in the country. Bananas, mangoes, and papayas are grown near most of the villages.

Elephants, buffalo, lions, leopards, antelope, and monkeys live in the grassy plateau region. In the north are large game preserves, where animals are protected from hunters. Crocodiles and hippopotamuses are found in the rivers. Brightly colored birds, reptiles, and a variety of insects abound, including termites, which build nests of red earth as high as 10 feet (3 meters).

Cities. Once almost an entirely rural country, the Central African Republic now has an urban population of more than 40 percent. The capital and largest city is Bangui, which has more than 500,000 inhabitants. Located on the Ubangi River, it is an important port, handling most of the country's foreign trade. Other major towns include Bambari, Bossangoa, and Boaur.

▶ **THE ECONOMY**

The Central African Republic is one of Africa's least developed nations. In recent years, however, it has been achieving steady, although slow, economic growth.

Agriculture employs more than 60 percent of the working population. The main commercial crops are cotton and coffee, which are important exports. Diamonds and gold are the chief minerals, with diamonds providing the country's largest single source of income. There are also known deposits of uranium, iron ore, and other minerals, but the Central African Republic lacks the facilities, chiefly transportation, to fully develop them.

The country's areas of forest are a source of lumber and other wood products, which also represent important exports. Manufacturing industry is limited, based mainly on the processing of agricultural products and the manufacture of cotton textiles and wood products, mainly paper and furniture.

▶ **HISTORY AND GOVERNMENT**

The French arrived in what is now the Central African Republic in the late 1800's. They gained control over the territory, which they called Ubangi-Shari. In 1910, Ubangi-Shari was joined with the neighboring French colonies (now independent nations) of Chad, Gabon, and Congo to form French Equatorial Africa.

Ubangi-Shari won self-government as the Central African Republic in 1958 and gained complete independence in 1960.

Since Independence. The nation's first president was David Dacko. He was deposed in 1966 in a military coup that brought Colonel Jean-Bedel Bokassa to power. In 1976, Bokassa changed the country's name to the Central African Empire and declared himself Emperor Bokassa I. His rule was marked by violence, cruelty, and financial extravagance that almost ruined the country's economy. In 1979 he was overthrown by Dacko, who resumed the presidency and restored the name Central African Republic.

In 1981, Dacko was again deposed by the army, under General André Kolingba, who established a military government. Civilian government was restored in 1993 with the election of Ange-Felix Patasse as president. Patasse was re-elected in 1999.

JOHN A. BALLARD
University of Ibadan (Nigeria)

Gold is one of the Central African Republic's chief minerals. Once fashioned into jewelry, it serves as a form of wealth as well as adornment.

CENTRAL AMERICA

Central America is an isthmus (a narrow bridge of land) at the southern tip of the North American continent, with coasts on both the Pacific Ocean and the Caribbean Sea (an arm of the Atlantic Ocean).

The term "Central America" generally refers to the countries of Guatemala, Honduras, El Salvador, Nicaragua, Costa Rica, and Panama, republics that share a common history. Geographically, Belize is also included.

▶ PEOPLE

The more than 34 million people of Central America belong to several ethnic groups. Guatemala is a largely Indian nation. Its citizens are heirs of the Maya civilization, which flourished in the region before the coming of the Europeans. Honduras, El Salvador, and Nicaragua also have a strong Indian heritage, although the people today are mainly mestizo—of mixed Indian and European (chiefly Spanish) ancestry. The population of

The people of Central America have many different ancestries. *Clockwise from above:* A Mayan woman from Guatemala; a Hispanic boy from Honduras; a Kuna Indian woman from Panama; and an African Creole man from Belize.

Costa Rica is largely Spanish in origin. Many people in Belize are descended from black African slaves brought there from the West Indies. Panama contains a mixture of all these different groups.

Language. Spanish is the major language in almost all the Central American nations. In Belize, a former British colony, English is the official language, though Spanish is widely spoken. Some of the Indians still speak their ancient languages.

Religion. Traditionally, most Central Americans have been Roman Catholics. In the past few decades, however, many people have turned to a sect of Protestantism that has proved more compatible with native Indian beliefs. For example, by the end of the 1900's, more than 50 percent of the people in Guatemala were Evangelical Protestants.

Most residents of Belize belong to the Church of England.

Rural Life. The populations of most Central American countries have long been divided into wealthy landowners and poor *campesinos* (peasants). Land ownership is the chief form of wealth in Central America and the main source of political power. Most of the people depend on the big landowners for their living. Some *campesinos* can find only

seasonal work. Others toil on the big estates in return for the right to grow food for themselves on a small patch of ground.

City Life. Some landless peasants that move to the cities in search of work frequently find that jobs are scarce, especially for the uneducated and unskilled. Most of them exchange rural poverty for the bleak life of an urban slum. In order to add to their incomes, they often leave the city at harvesttime to work on the large estates. Many fami-

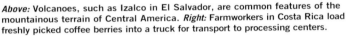

Above: Volcanoes, such as Izalco in El Salvador, are common features of the mountainous terrain of Central America. *Right:* Farmworkers in Costa Rica load freshly picked coffee berries into a truck for transport to processing centers.

lies hope that education—more available in the cities—will lead to a better life for their children.

LAND

Land Regions. Central America covers an area of about 202,000 square miles (523,000 square kilometers). The main geographical feature is steep mountains, which extend almost from ocean to ocean. There are many volcanoes, some of which are still active. Earthquakes are common, and some cities have been destroyed by earthquakes more than once.

There are two main breaks in the mountains—one in Nicaragua and one in Panama. These two countries are mostly low-lying and have areas of dense jungle. Northern Guatemala and much of Belize are also jungle lowland. Most of the people of Guatemala, Costa Rica, Honduras, and El Salvador live in the highlands.

Rivers, Canals, and Coastal Waters. Central America is surrounded by water, with the Pacific Ocean to the south and west and the Atlantic Ocean and Caribbean Sea to the north and east. The Panama Canal, completed in 1914, connected these two great oceans, allowing passenger and freight traffic to pass easily between them. For more information, see the article PANAMA CANAL in Volume P. Few of Central America's numerous rivers are navigable.

Climate. The climate in Central America is tropical, and temperatures generally are high. The highland regions experience wet and dry seasons, whereas the low-lying regions receive heavy rainfall throughout the year.

Natural Resources. Central America's most important resources are its soils, which support agriculture, and its hardwood forests. Small deposits of precious metals, such as gold and silver, are also found there. Production of nickel has become significant in Guatemala, where oil has also been found in the remote northern jungles. Hydroelectric power is the only readily available source of energy.

ECONOMY

Agriculture. Central America is mainly an agricultural region. The chief export crops are grown on large plantations or estates (*latifundia* or *fincas*).

In the highlands the chief export is coffee—the leading export of Guatemala, El Salvador, and Costa Rica. In the coastal tropical areas, bananas and cotton are the main commercial crops. Sugarcane and rice also flourish along the coast. Hemp (used in making rope) and chicle (used in chewing gum) are important products of the jungle regions.

Areas that are too mountainous for farming are used to raise livestock. Forested areas provide valuable hardwoods such as mahogany. Fishing is important along the coast.

Manufacturing and Trade. Panama derives much of its income from fees paid by ships using the Panama Canal. There is some industry, particularly in El Salvador, Guatema-

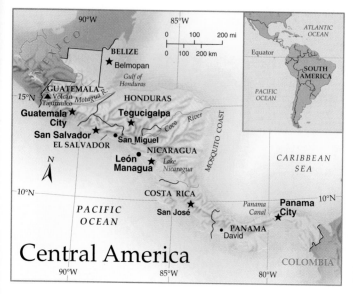

Central America

Copán, in Honduras. Several other Indian groups settled in Central America south of Honduras.

Christopher Columbus sailed along the coast of Central America in 1502. The Spanish explorer Vasco Núñez de Balboa crossed the Isthmus of Panama in 1513. The Spanish conquered the Indians and ruled the region for 300 years.

Independence. In 1821, Guatemala, El Salvador, Honduras, Nicaragua, and Costa Rica declared their independence from Spain and then formed their own federation, the United Provinces of Central America. But the federation did not last because the widely separated settlements had different interests. With the aid of the United States, Panama gained its independence from Colombia in 1903. Belize (formerly British Honduras) remained a British colony until 1981.

Liberals and Conservatives. During the 1800's, much of Central America was torn by political struggles between liberal and conservative groups. Conservatives believed in having an official state religion; social positions determined by birth; and a strong central government dominated by high-ranking church and state representatives. Liberals favored a more open economy (particularly to increase agricultural exports); a decentralized government; and an end to church influence in politics. Neither group represented the social or political interests of the poor.

la, and Costa Rica. But it employs only a relatively small part of the labor force.

While Central American countries export large amounts of certain agricultural products, they must import most of the things they need, including some foods.

▶ **MAJOR CITIES**

All of the major cities in Central America are capital cities. They include Belize City (Belize); Guatemala City (Guatemala); Tegucigalpa (Honduras); San Salvador (El Salvador); Managua (Nicaragua); San José (Costa Rica); and Panama City (Panama). For more information, see the articles on individual countries in the appropriate volumes.

▶ **HISTORY**

The Maya and the Colonial Era. Maya-speaking peoples have lived in the northern part of Central America for about 3,000 years. Maya civilization reached its height from about A.D. 325 to 975. The ruins of huge Maya temples and monuments can still be seen at places such as Piedras Negras and Tikal, in Guatemala, and

With a population of approximately 1.2 million, Guatemala City is the largest of the Central American cities. It is the capital of Guatemala as well as a center of commerce and education.

The disputes between liberals and conservatives often led to civil wars, and sometimes even to invasions of neighboring countries. The liberals, who were mostly landowners, benefited when the cultivation of coffee began in the late 1800's. The value of the land increased rapidly. So did the power and income of the landowners.

The Rise of the Military. By the early 1900's, a pattern of forceful leadership had emerged within the Central American governments. Some leaders became dictators who held office for long periods of time. Armies also grew powerful and usually supported the interests of the wealthy landowners. Yet the dictators and the military did promote agricultural expansion and the building of roads and railroads.

A Period of Revolutions. Since World War II (1939–45), there have been several revolutions in Central America led by people seeking social and economic change. In Costa Rica, a brief civil war in 1948 led to a middle-class reform movement that increased social services, restored a tradition of democracy and free elections, and abolished the army. In Guatemala, leaders who wanted to improve the lives of the poor became increasingly inspired by Communist ideals. But in 1954 the Guatemalan government was overthrown with the help of the United States, whose leaders were determined to suppress the rise of Communism in Latin America. In Nicaragua, widespread discontent with the long-ruling Somoza family erupted into civil war in 1978. The war was won by the Sandinistas, who established a leftist, anti-U.S. government in Nicaragua in 1979. Opposition to the Sandinistas by the U.S.-backed *contras*, a guerrilla group, brought renewed civil war. Leftist guerrillas in El Salvador and Guatemala sought to overthrow the governments of those nations.

Peace Efforts. Efforts by Central American presidents in the 1980's were aimed at

Guerrilla rebel groups in Central America have fought a series of civil wars since World War II to establish governments headed by civilians instead of the military.

ending civil wars in Nicaragua and El Salvador. Agreements based on a 1987 peace plan offered by Costa Rica's president led to elections in Nicaragua in 1990, which the Sandinistas lost, and to the disbanding of the *contra* forces.

New civilian governments also were elected in Guatemala, Honduras, and El Salvador in the mid- and late-1980's. At the same time, Costa Rica maintained its long tradition of democratic government. A peace accord ending El Salvador's civil war was signed in 1992. Guatemala's long civil war ended in 1996. Central Americans also have tried to benefit their region by participating in the Organization of American States (OAS) and the Central American Common Market.

Central America Today. Central America has limited resources and one of the highest population growth rates in the world. Industry at present cannot provide enough jobs for the landless, and falling prices for many exports make it harder for governments to meet the needs of their peoples. The future stability of the region depends on finding solutions to its political, social, and economic problems.

In 1998, disaster struck Central America when Hurricane Mitch killed more than 10,000 people and left nearly 3 million homeless, mostly in Honduras and Nicaragua. The storm also caused billions of dollars in property damages, raising even greater uncertainty about the future of the region's economy.

KENNETH J. GRIEB
University of Wisconsin, Oshkosh

Reviewed by THOMAS M. DAVIES, JR.
Director, Center for Latin American Studies
San Diego State University

See also INDIANS, AMERICAN (Central America); LATIN AMERICA; MAYA; ORGANIZATION OF AMERICAN STATES (OAS); PANAMA CANAL; and articles on individual Central American countries.

CENTRAL INTELLIGENCE AGENCY

The Central Intelligence Agency (CIA) is the United States government agency responsible for conducting foreign intelligence operations. Its purpose is to collect, evaluate, and distribute information on the military, political, economic, scientific, technological, and social conditions of other nations.

The CIA is divided into five divisions called directorates. **Administration** oversees daily operations; **Intelligence** collects and reports on information gathered by all U.S. intelligence services; **Science and Technology** records information on scientific and technological progress; **Planning and Coordination** monitors the development and production of weapons throughout the world; and **Operations** performs secret intelligence gathering and military-type operations.

The CIA is managed by the Director of Central Intelligence (DCI), who is appointed by the president with the approval of the Senate. The DCI also coordinates the intelligence activities of eleven other U.S. government agencies, including the Federal Bureau of Investigation (FBI) and the Drug Enforcement Administration (DEA).

Directors of Central Intelligence		
Name	Took Office	Under President
Roscoe H. Hillenkoetter	1947	Truman
Walter Bedell Smith	1950	Truman
Allen Dulles	1953	Eisenhower
John A. McCone	1961	Kennedy, L. B. Johnson
William Raborn	1965	L. B. Johnson
Richard Helms	1966	L. B. Johnson, Nixon
James Schlesinger	1973	Nixon
William Colby	1973	Nixon, Ford
George Bush	1976	Ford
Stansfield Turner	1977	Carter
William Casey	1981	Reagan
William Webster	1987	Reagan, Bush
Robert M. Gates	1991	Bush
R. James Woolsey, Jr.	1993	Clinton
John M. Deutch	1995	Clinton
George J. Tenet	1997	Clinton

History

The CIA was created in 1947 by President Harry S. Truman in response to the Cold War with the Soviet Union. The agency has always been controversial, and its secret operations—especially those designed to weaken or discredit certain foreign governments—have been the subject of congressional examination and public debate. In 1975 the agency was reorganized after congressional hearings disclosed that it had engaged in illegal activities. Since Cold War tensions ended in the late 1980's, some Americans have questioned the continued need for a CIA.

RAFAELA ELLIS
Author, *The Central Intelligence Agency*

CENTRIFUGAL FORCE.   See EARTH; GRAVITY AND GRAVITATION.

CERAMICS

The word ceramics comes from the Greek word *keramos*, meaning potter's clay or pottery. Pottery is the oldest form of ceramics, and potterymaking is one of the oldest crafts.

Pieces of pottery and other early ceramic products, including bricks and glass, have been found that were made before the beginning of recorded history.

Ceramics today include pottery, whiteware (china and porcelain), construction products such as bricks and pipes, glass, enamels, cement, and abrasives. Engineers and scientists also have developed many new ceramic products for use in industry.

Pottery is the oldest form of ceramics. This Peruvian jug was made before A.D. 600.

▶HOW CERAMICS ARE MADE

Traditional ceramics are made from earthy materials—clay, sand, or ground rock—that have been subjected to high temperatures. Heat binds the materials together and hardens them. Most ceramics share certain qualities. They resist heat, pressure, corrosion, and moisture.

Several kinds of clay are used to make ceramics. Common clays, which contain many impurities, are used chiefly in brickmaking. Kaolin clay is the purest type of clay. It is used to make fine china and porcelain. When fired, it turns a pure white. Fireclays have a slightly different mineral composition. They can withstand high temperatures.

Manufacturers often mix powdered minerals into clay to produce specific qualities in their products. The clay and other materials are then mixed with water. Just the right amount of water must be added—if there is too much, the clay will be too soft to hold its shape. If there is too little, the clay will be stiff and difficult to shape.

Individual pieces of pottery can be shaped by hand on a potter's wheel. But manufacturers use several methods to make many copies of the same object. In **slip casting**, a mixture of clay and water is poured into a plaster mold of the object. The mold absorbs the water and retains a thin coating of clay on the inside. More and more of the mixture is poured in, and the clay coating becomes thicker. When the coating is thick enough, it is allowed to harden. Then it is lifted out of the mold and trimmed, or **fettled**.

Another method of forming ceramics is **jiggering**. In this method a plaster mold is used to shape one surface of the article—for instance, the upper surface of a plate or the outside surface of a cup or bowl. The mold rotates, just as a potter's wheel does. Clay is forced down onto the spinning mold, so that it takes the shape of the mold on one surface. The other surface is shaped by a tool mounted on a lever.

A third method of shaping clay ceramics is to press the clay directly into a mold. Ceramic pipes and bricks are formed by a fourth method, **extrusion**. In this method, the clay is forced through the opening of a die (shaping tool).

After the piece has been formed, it is trimmed and dried. It is then ready for firing. This is done in a **kiln**—a special furnace for heating and hardening ceramics. High temperatures are needed, ranging from about 1200 to 3270°F (650 to 1800°C). The length of firing is just as important as the temperature. The clay is fired for varying periods of time depending on its ingredients and on the product being made.

Glazes are transparent, glassy coatings that are applied to the surfaces of many ceramic products after firing. They do two things— they beautify the object, and they prevent it from absorbing liquids. After the glaze is applied, the article is fired again.

▶CERAMIC PRODUCTS

Ceramic materials are used to make a wide range of products. Descriptions of some of these products follow.

Dinnerware and Decorative Ceramics. Because ceramics can hold liquid and resist extreme temperatures, they make excellent dinnerware. Porcelain, which is very hard and translucent, is the finest dinnerware. It is often called china, after the country that first produced it. Stoneware is another popular kind of dinnerware. It is strong and very resistant to heat and cold. And because clay can be shaped into many forms, ceramics are often used in figurines and decorative objects.

Construction Materials. Porcelain is also used to make sinks, bathtubs, and similar building fixtures. But many other ceramic materials are used in construction. They include brick and cement for walls and foundations; tiles for roofs, floors, and bathroom walls;

Ceramic insulators for electrical lines are rolled into huge kilns to be fired.

Machines are used to apply the decoration to factory-produced ceramic dinnerware.

drainpipes; gypsum for plaster walls and ceilings; glass for windows; and fiberglass for insulation.

Abrasives. Very hard ceramic materials are used in grinding, polishing, and sanding. These materials include sand, aluminum oxide, and silicon carbide.

Electrical Products. Some ceramics, such as porcelain, will not conduct electricity. They are used as insulation in high-voltage power lines and in products that range from automobile spark plugs to sophisticated electrical circuits. Other ceramic materials develop an electrical charge under pressure. They are used in phonographs, sonar, and ultrasonic devices.

Heat-Resistant Ceramics. Ceramics that can hold up under extremely high temperatures are called **refractories**. Refractories have many uses today—as linings in steelmaking furnaces, in nose cones for rockets and protection for other spacecraft, and in tail pipes for rocket and jet engines.

Special Products. Special ceramics are used in many industries. The fuel elements in most nuclear power plants are made of a ceramic material, as are many of the reactors' structural parts. Magnetic ceramics are used in computer memory cores and telecommunications equipment. Ceramics are also used in lasers. In medicine, special porcelains are used to make dentures and artificial joints.

Sometimes ceramics are combined with other materials. For example, glass fibers are used to reinforce plastics. And ceramics are combined with metals to make materials called **cermets**. Cermets combine the qualities of ceramics with the tensile strength of metals.

Reviewed by HANS NOWOTNY
University of Connecticut

See also BRICKS AND MASONRY; CEMENT AND CONCRETE; ENAMELING; GLASS; POTTERY.

CEREALS. See GRAIN AND GRAIN PRODUCTS.
CEREBRAL PALSY. See DISEASES.

CERVANTES SAAVEDRA, MIGUEL DE (1547–1616)

Spain's greatest writer was Miguel de Cervantes—the creator of Don Quixote, one of the best-known characters in world literature. Cervantes was born in 1547, probably on September 29, in Alcalá de Henares, near Madrid. His father was a poor barber-surgeon who moved his family from town to town in search of a practice.

Little is known of Cervantes' early life, but his writings show that he must have acquired a good education in one way or another. In 1569 he went to Italy, where he served briefly in the household of Giulio (later Cardinal) Acquaviva in Rome. He then joined a company of the Spanish army stationed there.

Cervantes fought bravely in the naval battle of Lepanto (off the coast of Greece). In this battle an allied Christian force, under the command of Don Juan of Austria, defeated the Muslim Turkish navy, on October 7, 1571. Cervantes was wounded and lost the use of his left hand. In 1575 he sailed for Spain, but he was kidnapped by pirates and taken to Algiers as a slave. He made several unsuccessful attempts to escape before he was ransomed by his family five years later.

Cervantes returned to Spain and tried to earn his living by writing plays. But his marriage in 1584 and the death of his father in 1585 added to his responsibilities. In 1587 he went to Seville, where preparations for a Spanish attack on England were under way. He was hired to gather all of the military provisions for the Armada, the invading fleet. Later he was given a job collecting taxes, but he was imprisoned twice as a result of his irregular accounts.

After he left government service in 1597, Cervantes wrote short stories and began his masterpiece, *Don Quixote*. The first part of this book was published in 1605. It described the adventures, many based on Cervantes' own, of the mad knight, Don Quixote of La Mancha. The novel presented a brilliant picture of Spanish society and was an immediate success. The second part appeared in 1615. Cervantes' other works include a pastoral novel, *The Galatea* (1585), and a collection of short stories, *Exemplary Novels* (1613). He died on April 23, 1616, in Madrid.

Reviewed by MELVEENA McKENDRICK
Author, *Cervantes*

CÉZANNE, PAUL (1839–1906)

The study of modern painting often begins with the work of the painter Paul Cézanne. His paintings had so great an influence on modern art that the artist Georges Braque said, "We all start from Cézanne."

Cézanne was born in Aix-en-Provence, in southern France, on January 19, 1839. Although he spent much of his adult life in Paris, the town drew him back time and time again. There, as boys, he and his school friend Émile Zola wandered through the hills, reciting poetry. Together they dreamed of fame and success in Paris.

Cézanne's father, a wealthy banker, wanted his son to be a success in business or law. But in 1861 he finally permitted Cézanne to go to Paris. He hoped his son's paintings would be accepted by the Paris Salon, the exhibition sponsored by the French Academy of Fine Arts. Cézanne did not like the kind of paintings shown at the Salon. But he craved recognition, and he submitted a painting. When it was rejected, he was deeply hurt.

Because he was drawn naturally to country life, Cézanne disliked Paris. He neither combed his beard nor cared how much paint covered his coat. He was gloomy, awkward, and hot-tempered, and he had few friends.

In 1886, Zola wrote a book about a painter who was a failure. Everyone thought that Cézanne was the model for the artist in the book. Cézanne was so hurt that he never again spoke to his one close friend.

During the same year his father died and left Cézanne a rich man with enough money for himself, his wife (Hortense Fiquet), and their son, Paul.

Throughout the last 20 years of his life, Cézanne isolated himself from people and devoted himself entirely to his work. He died in Aix on October 22, 1906.

It took years of searching for Cézanne to find the way to express his ideas. In his mature paintings he tried to show the geometric forms—cylinders, cones, spheres—that he saw in nature. By using blocks of color he built up the appearance of solid shapes. To emphasize volume—the roundness of an apple or the thickness of a stone—he changed the actual appearance of objects. This distortion of shapes led directly to the style of painting called cubism.

Only ten years before his death, a small group of painters recognized Cézanne's genius. But even they did not foresee his impact on the painting of the 20th century.

Reviewed by FRANK GETLEIN
Author, *The French Impressionists*

Mount Sainte-Victoire with Tall Pine (1886–88), by Cézanne.

CHAD

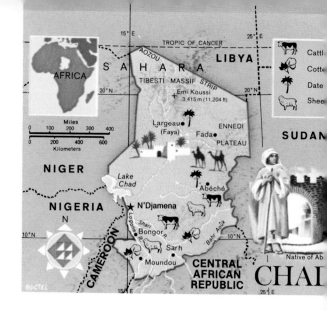

Chad is the fifth largest nation of Africa in area. It is located in the north central part of the continent, extending from the vast Sahara desert in the north to the savanna region of tropical Africa in the south. Chad was at one time a colony of France, before gaining its independence in 1960.

▶THE PEOPLE

Southern Chad. Although large in area, Chad has a relatively small population, which is unevenly distributed. More than half the people live near Lake Chad or in the Logone and Shari (Chari) river valleys of southern Chad. Of the country's many ethnic groups, the largest and most settled is the Sara. They are chiefly farmers, who grow food for their own use, mainly grains, vegetables, and spices for seasoning. The fish that abound in Lake Chad and in the rivers provide an important part of their diet. The Sara are mostly Christians or animists who practice a traditional African religion.

Central and Northern Chad. Most of the people of the central grasslands of Chad are herders of cattle, goats, sheep, and other livestock. They may also do some farming and trading. Northern Chad has only about 2 percent of the population, although it makes up almost half of the country's total land area.

This is a desert region. Its people live in scattered oases, where date palms supply food, shade, and fuel. Most inhabitants of the central and northern regions are Muslims, who have been influenced by their fellow Muslims of North Africa.

Language. French and Arabic are the official languages of Chad. A variety of African languages, including Sara, also are spoken.

Generally, life for most of the people of Chad is hard. Drought, caused by lack of rainfall, frequently threatens crops and livestock. Few people live in towns, and in the countryside all members of a family must labor on the land to feed themselves.

▶THE LAND

Chad is a landlocked country, far from any outlet to the sea. It has three distinctive regions: the savanna of the southern-central river valleys; the central grasslands; and the north-

Most of Chad's population lives in the southern part of the country. The south is mainly a region of small villages, whose people earn their living as farmers.

ern desert. The chief body of water is Lake Chad, into which flow the principal rivers, the Logone and the Shari. The size of Lake Chad varies with the wet and dry seasons.

Climate. Chad's climate is hot and extremely dry. Rain falls in the summer and early autumn. The amount of rainfall is moderate in the southern savanna region but decreases as one travels north. When the rains are delayed, drought may result.

Cities. Most of Chad's few large cities and towns are located in its southern region. The capital and largest city, N'Djamena (formerly Fort-Lamy), has a population of more than 500,000. It is the nation's economic center. Moundou is the second largest city.

▶ ECONOMY

Most Chadians earn their living by farming, fishing, or raising livestock. The main food crops include millet, sorghum, cassava (manioc), yams, sweet potatoes, and rice. The most important commercial crop is cotton, which provides more than half of the country's export income. Livestock and animal products also are exported. Industry is limited chiefly to the manufacture of textiles and the processing of agricultural products.

Chad has known deposits of petroleum and uranium. But a long civil war has delayed the exploration for all minerals and has hurt industrial development in general. Lack of transportation also has hampered economic growth. Chad has no railroads, and its waterways are navigable for only part of each year.

▶ HISTORY AND GOVERNMENT

Early History. Various African kingdoms flourished around Lake Chad in ancient times. Because of its strategic location, linking the Sahara of North Africa with tropical Africa, Chad has attracted conquerors through much of its history. In the 11th century, Arabs from the north brought the Muslim religion to the area, while raiding it for slaves. When the French arrived in the 1890's, the local kingdoms were already in decline. By 1913, France had control of the region.

Independence and Civil War. Chad won complete independence from France in 1960. Five years later civil war broke out, mainly between the Muslims of the north and the Christians and animists of the south who then controlled the government. In 1979 a provisional government representing all of Chad's ethnic and religious groups was formed under Goukouni Oueddei.

Recent Events. Goukouni's chief rival was Hissène Habré, like Goukouni a Muslim and northerner. At one time the two were allies. In 1980, fighting broke out between their forces, with France backing Habré and Libya supporting Goukouni. By 1986, Habré controlled southern Chad and was recognized as the country's president by most other nations.

Libya had long occupied the Aozou area in northern Chad. In 1986 fighting broke out in the north between Chadian government forces and Libyan troops and their Chadian allies. A cease-fire was declared in 1987, after a victory by Chadian government troops, but the Aozou remained in dispute.

Meanwhile, a new rebel movement, led by Idris Deby, had arisen. In 1990, Deby's forces captured N'Djamena. Habré fled and Deby took control of the government as president. He was returned as president in elections held in 1996. In 2000, Habré became the first former head of state to be charged in another country (Senegal) for crimes against humanity, including 40,000 cases of political murder.

ANN E. LARIMORE
Michigan State University

VIRGINIA THOMPSON ADLOFF
Coauthor, *Conflict in Chad*

FACTS and figures

REPUBLIC OF CHAD (République du Tchad) is the official name of the country.

LOCATION: North central Africa.

AREA: 495,754 sq mi (1,284,000 km²).

POPULATION: 7,700,000 (estimate).

CAPITAL AND LARGEST CITY: N'Djamena.

MAJOR LANGUAGES: French, Arabic (both official), Sara.

MAJOR RELIGIOUS GROUPS: Muslim, Christian, animist.

GOVERNMENT: Republic. **Head of state and government**—president. **Legislature**—National Assembly.

CHIEF PRODUCTS: Agricultural—cotton, millet, sorghum, cassava, yams, sweet potatoes, rice. **Manufactured**—textiles, processed foods.

MONETARY UNIT: African Financial Community (CFA) franc (1 CFA franc = 100 centimes).

Marc Chagall's painting *I and the Village* (1911) is based on memories of his childhood. The Museum of Modern Art, New York.

CHAGALL, MARC (1887–1985)

A soldier the size of a teacup and a fish playing a violin make perfect sense in a dream. They also make sense in the paintings of Marc Chagall, where dreams and fantasy are real, past and present are one, and the laws of gravity do not exist.

Marc Chagall was born on July 7, 1887, of a poor family in the Jewish ghetto of Vitebsk, Russia. Memories of early childhood—happy and sad—fill his pictures, as do themes from the Bible and folklore.

At the age of 20, Chagall went to St. Petersburg, where he studied scenery design. He lived in Paris from 1910 to 1914 and then returned to Russia for a visit. When World War I began in 1914, Chagall decided to remain in Vitebsk.

During the Russian Revolution of 1917, he became commissar of fine arts for Vitebsk and set up an art school there. With his wife, Bella, he moved to Berlin in 1922 and to Paris the following year. In 1941 they left France to escape the conquering Nazis. Bella died in the United States in 1944. Chagall later returned to France, and remarried in 1952. He died at St. Paul de Vence on March 28, 1985.

The art of Marc Chagall is expressed in many forms. His oil paintings and watercolors hang in museums all over the world. His panels and ceiling murals decorate opera houses in Paris and New York City. His work in stained glass includes twelve windows in a synagogue in Jerusalem representing the twelve tribes of Israel. Among his other works are stage settings and costumes for operas and book illustrations. In 1973, the French government honored Chagall by opening a museum in the city of Nice devoted exclusively to his work. It is called the National Museum of the Marc Chagall Biblical Message.

Reviewed by HAROLD SPENCER
University of Connecticut

CHAIN REACTION. See NUCLEAR ENERGY.

CHAIN STORES. See RETAIL STORES.

CHAMBERLAIN, JOSHUA. See MAINE (Famous People).

CHAMBERLAIN FAMILY

The Chamberlains were a famous family of British statesmen who greatly influenced British politics for more than seventy years.

Joseph Chamberlain, the founder of the dynasty, was born in London, England, on July 8, 1836. His success as a manufacturer inspired him to enter politics, and he was first elected mayor of Birmingham (1873–76), where he became famous for his sweeping social reforms. He was elected to Parliament as a Liberal in 1876.

In 1880, Chamberlain was appointed president of the Board of Trade in the cabinet of Prime Minister Gladstone, where he proposed radical reforms in commercial law. However, in 1886 he opposed Gladstone's Irish Home Rule Bill and broke with the government. He then became leader of the Liberal-Unionists, who favored preserving union with Ireland.

In 1895 Chamberlain became colonial secretary (1895–1903) under Prime Minister Lord Salisbury. His policies in South Africa resulted in the Boer War (1899–1902). In 1903 he suggested that British imperial nations should be given preferential tax treatment. Chamberlain's tariff proposal split the Conservative Party, which was overwhelmingly defeated in the election of 1906. Three days after his 70th birthday, in 1906, Chamberlain was struck down with paralysis. He took no further part in politics and died on July 2, 1914.

Sir Austen Chamberlain, the eldest son of Joseph Chamberlain, was born Joseph Austen Chamberlain in Birmingham on October 16, 1863. A Unionist-Conservative member of Parliament (1892–1937), he held several high cabinet offices, including chancellor of the exchequer (1903–05 and 1919–21). As foreign secretary (1924–29) under Prime Minister Stanley Baldwin, Chamberlain negotiated the Locarno Pact (1925), a series of treaties that attempted to settle border disputes with Germany following World War I. For his efforts, Chamberlain won one of two Nobel peace prizes awarded in 1925. He died in London on March 16, 1937.

Neville Chamberlain became prime minister of Great Britain on May 28, 1937, just ten weeks after the death of Sir Austen. Born on March 18, 1869 in Birmingham, Arthur Neville was Joseph Chamberlain's second son. Like his father, Neville became mayor of Birmingham (1915–16). He was elected to Parliament as a Conservative in 1918.

Unlike his father and half-brother, Neville Chamberlain's government expertise was entirely in home affairs, having served as minister of health (1923, 1924–29, and 1931) and as chancellor of the exchequer (1923–24 and 1931–37). When he became prime minister, he was forced to focus on world affairs.

At the Munich Conference in September 1938, Chamberlain met with the German and Italian dictators, Adolf Hitler and Benito Mussolini. In an effort to preserve peace among the European powers, Chamberlain agreed to accept Hitler's demand that Czechoslovakia surrender to Germany certain disputed border regions. By signing the Munich Agreement, Chamberlain believed he had achieved "peace for our time." However, Hitler's occupation of further territory in March 1939 convinced Chamberlain to abandon his "policy of appeasement," and on September 3, 1939, just two days after Hitler's forces invaded Poland, Chamberlain's government declared war on Germany.

On May 10, 1940, having failed to check Germany's invasion of Norway, Chamberlain resigned his office. He continued to serve in the cabinet of his successor, Winston Churchill, until cancer claimed his life on November 9, 1940.

ALAN PALMER
Author, *The Penguin Dictionary of Modern History*

CHAMBER MUSIC

Chamber music is music written to be performed by a small number of players. There must be more than one but fewer than a dozen. There should be only one player to each written part. Usually there is no conductor. Chamber music is best heard in an ordinary room or a small hall. It can be performed at home for the players' own pleasure or in a concert.

Any combination of instruments can be used in chamber music. The most popular are the stringed and woodwind instruments and the piano. A piece for two players is called a duo. Three players make a trio, and four make a quartet. There are quintets (five players), sextets (six), septets (seven), and octets (eight). Pieces for more than eight players are rare. A piece for three stringed instruments alone is a string trio; for four, a string quartet, and so on. If a piano or woodwind is used in place of one of the strings, the piece becomes a piano trio, or oboe quartet, or clarinet quartet, and so on. There are also pieces for woodwinds alone and for woodwinds and piano.

How did chamber music come about? From medieval times through the 1700's, musicians in Europe had two employers—the church and the nobility. When they were not performing in church services, musicians were hired to provide musical entertainment in a chamber of a noble's palace. This is how chamber music got its name. Old King Cole's fiddlers three were no doubt chamber musicians.

Early chamber music used early instruments like the recorder, harpsichord, and viol. The

String quartets are the best known of the instrumental groups that perform chamber music. A string quartet is made up of two violins, a cello, and a viola.

viols were an important family of stringed instruments in the 1500's and 1600's. There were treble (high), tenor (middle), and bass (low) viols, just as today we have violins, violas, and cellos.

Many fine composers of chamber music flourished in England during Queen Elizabeth's reign. Two of the best known were William Byrd (1543?–1623) and Orlando Gibbons (1583–1625). A very popular form of vocal chamber music was the madrigal. It was a short piece sung by voices often accompanied by instruments.

During the latter part of the 1600's and first half of the 1700's, the trio sonata was the most important form of chamber music. A typical trio sonata was played by two violins, cello, and a keyboard instrument, which doubled the cello part and added harmonies. Important composers of these pieces include Henry Purcell (1659–95), Arcangelo Corelli (1653–1713), Johann Sebastian Bach (1685–1750), and George Frederick Handel (1685–1759).

Golden Age of Chamber Music. Most of the chamber music we hear today has been written since the middle of the 1700's. By then the viols had given way to the more brilliant-sounding violins, and the piano was replacing the harpsichord. Composers began to write pieces made up of three or four movements, or separate sections.

Among the greatest chamber music composers were Franz Joseph Haydn (1732–1809), Wolfgang Amadeus Mozart (1756–91), Ludwig van Beethoven (1770–1827), and Franz Schubert (1797–1828). Haydn was mainly responsible for the early development of the string quartet (two violins, viola, and cello). He wrote 83 such works. Mozart, who wrote 26 string quartets, claimed he learned how to write them from Haydn. Beethoven further developed the forms of Haydn and Mozart and added elements of drama and expressiveness. Beethoven, with Schubert, led the way that chamber music was to follow for more than 100 years.

All over Europe musicians composed and performed chamber works. Luigi Boccherini (1743–1805) alone wrote more than 100 quartets, 155 quintets, 60 trios, and many other pieces. Chamber music was a part of early colonial life in America. Even Thomas Jefferson played chamber music.

Most of the important composers of the 1800's wrote chamber music: Felix Mendelssohn (1809–47), Robert Schumann (1810–56), Johannes Brahms (1833–97), Antonin Dvořák (1841–1904), and many others.

Something about the sound of two violins, viola, and cello has appealed to nearly all composers of the last 200 years. The largest amount of chamber music has been written for string quartet. As a result, most professional chamber music groups have been string quartets. During the 1800's these ensembles began traveling from city to city giving concerts. Today string quartets from many countries perform everywhere.

Modern Chamber Music. Chamber music composers in the 1900's began to explore ways of making new sounds. Claude Debussy (1862–1918) and Maurice Ravel (1875–1937) created colorful musical impressions. Béla Bartók (1881–1945), Anton Webern (1883–1945), and Alban Berg (1885–1935) invented new sound effects with stringed instruments. Arnold Schoenberg (1874–1951) and Paul Hindemith (1895–1963) wrote pieces for unusual combinations of instruments. New works continue to be written today, and millions of new listeners are discovering the exciting experience of hearing chamber music.

ROBERT MANN
Juilliard String Quartet

CHAMBERS, WHITTAKER. See SPIES (Profiles).

CHAMELEONS. See LIZARDS.

CHAMPLAIN, SAMUEL DE (1567?–1635)

Samuel de Champlain was the founder of Quebec and one of Canada's most famous explorers. His work as colonizer, explorer, and mapmaker earned him the title "Father of New France." His books, especially *Voyages*, give a vivid picture of travel, discovery, and Native American life in the New World.

Champlain was born about 1567 in Brouage, France. Between 1599 and 1601, he traveled to the West Indies on a Spanish expedition. On his return, he was made royal geographer to King Henry IV of France.

Champlain first visited Canada in 1603, sailing up the Saint Lawrence River as far as present-day Montreal. He later mapped the Atlantic coast as far south as Cape Cod. In 1608, Champlain was sent to establish a fur-trading post at Quebec—the Indian name for "the place where the waters narrow." There he made alliances with the Algonkian and Huron Indians against their enemies, the Iroquois.

Traveling westward along the Ottawa River, Champlain crossed Lake Nipissing and continued on to Georgian Bay. He then crossed Lake Ontario into New York, making the first known record of explorations of these regions.

In 1612 the fur companies appointed Champlain governor of Quebec. Many years later, in 1628, England and France went to war.

CHAMPLAIN'S EXPEDITIONS

English ships blockaded Quebec and began to starve out the settlers. Champlain was forced to surrender his fort the following year.

He returned to Quebec in 1633 and found it in ruins. Champlain began to rebuild the colony and started another settlement up the St. Lawrence River, at Trois-Rivières. He died in Quebec on Christmas Day, 1635.

JOHN S. MOIR
University of Toronto

See also CANADA (Canadian History—New France).

CHANDLER, RAYMOND. See MYSTERY AND DETECTIVE STORIES (Profiles).

CHANUKAH. See HANUKKAH.

CHAOS THEORY. See MATHEMATICS, HISTORY OF.

CHAPARRAL. See BIOMES.

CHAPLIN, CHARLIE (1889–1977)

Charlie Chaplin found the secret to making people laugh. With a little derby hat, cane, baggy pants, and tiny mustache, Chaplin created the famed Little Tramp of silent films.

Charles Spencer Chaplin was born on April 16, 1889, in London. His family was very poor. Charlie showed an early gift for performing and longed to be an actor. He went to the United States in 1910 as part of a vaudeville troupe. In 1913 the troupe toured the United States, and Chaplin met film producer Mack Sennett. His first short film, *Making a Living*, was made in 1914 for Sennett. By 1915, Chaplin was internationally famous and was earning $1,250 a week.

His talent was extraordinary. He wrote, directed, and produced most of his films. He even composed the music for those with sound. A short man, he could move with amazing quickness. He invented brilliant comic situations that became classics. For example, in *The Gold Rush* (1925), a starving tramp makes an enjoyable meal of his shoe.

Of the eighty films that Chaplin made, the best known include *The Kid* (1921), *City Lights* (1931), and *The Great Dictator* (1940).

Charlie Chaplin, as the Little Tramp, appeared with child actor Jackie Coogan in *The Kid* (1921). Chaplin was both director and star of this popular movie.

Verdoux (1947), about a man who murders women for their money, and *Limelight* (1952), about an aging vaudeville performer.

Chapin became quite wealthy and successful. But controversy surrounded him. He was criticized for not becoming an American citizen, for his friendships with women, and for his political views, which some people thought leaned toward Communism. In 1952, when Chaplin sailed for England, the U.S. attorney general ordered that he not be allowed back into the United States without an investigation of his political views.

Chaplin, settled in Switzerland with his fourth wife, Oona O'Neill, daughter of playwright Eugene O'Neill. They had been married in 1943. They had a large family—five daughters and three sons. In 1972, Chaplin revisited the United States to accept honors from the film community. He was knighted by Queen Elizabeth II in 1975. When he died in Switzerland on December 25, 1977, the world mourned one of the greatest creative artists of the century.

WILLIAM WOLF
Film Critic, Cue magazine

In *The Great Dictator*, Chaplin used his first speaking role to satirize the political views of Adolf Hitler.

After World War II, Chaplin abandoned the Little Tramp character. He made *Monsieur*

CHARADES

Charades is a team game in which a name or title is acted out in pantomime, usually syllable by syllable, for the actor's teammates to guess. No one really knows the origin of the name "charades," but some experts believe that it comes from the old Spanish word *charrada* meaning "clownishness."

▶ **EARLY CHARADES**

Charades first became popular in continental Europe during the late 1700's. It originated not in the form of a game, however, but as a literary puzzle. In a puzzle charade the answer was a word (referred to as "my whole") that could be broken into word/syllables ("my first," "my second," and so on) and presented part by part in a verse or poem. The object for the solver was to guess "my whole" from the clues. For example, the answer word

PAGEANT might be broken into PAGE and ANT and appear in a verse as follows:

My first's a portion of a book,
  A busy insect is *my second;*
Whenever on *my whole* you look,
  A splendid show it must be reckoned.

During the 1700's and 1800's, puzzle charades were composed by many noted writers, including Jane Austen and Victor Hugo. These charades are still popular in some European countries, and in the United States they are written and solved by the members of the National Puzzlers' League.

▶ **THE GAME OF CHARADES**

The modern game of charades is based on the old literary puzzle. To play, two teams composed of an equal number of players

BOOK (Open book)	TELEVISION SHOW (TV screen)	NUMBER OF WORDS
	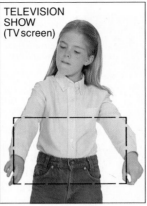	

Charades is a game of pantomime, where players act out the names of popular books, television shows, movies, plays, or songs without speaking. Actors offer clues, using hand gestures, such as the ones pictured here. Their teammates must interpret the clues and try to solve the puzzle as quickly as possible.

FIRST WORD	THIRD SYLLABLE	SOUNDS LIKE	THAT'S IT!

gather in separate groups. Each secretly selects answers for the other team to act. The answers can be names of books, movies, songs, or television shows, familiar proverbs or quotations, or other titles or expressions that most of the players are likely to know. Each answer is written on a slip of paper and put in a hat. There should be one slip for every player on the opposing team.

When both teams are ready, they get together and the first actor draws a slip from the other team's hat. The player's goal is to act out the answer and get the teammates to guess it as quickly as possible. The player may not speak, make sounds, or use any props from the room. Only actions and gestures may be used to convey the answer.

For example, if the answer were "Robin Hood," and you were the actor, you might pretend to rob one of the players; then you might cup your left hand and push your right index finger into it to signal "in," and lastly pretend to be pulling a hood over your head.

Players are timed from the moment they say they are ready to begin. The other members of

the team may ask questions and venture guesses, but the actor may answer only with nods and gestures. When the player's answer is guessed, a person from the other team draws a slip and begins. After every player has had a turn as actor, the team that used less total acting time is the winner.

Certain signals have become standard in charades to simplify and speed up the game. You can learn some of the better-known signals by referring to the descriptive photographs at the top of this page.

Charades do not have to be played competitively to be enjoyed. For a group of fewer than ten players, one person may act out an answer for the whole group. The person who correctly guesses the answer then becomes the next actor, and the person who just acted supplies the next answer to be performed. But competitive or not, charades is a time-tested game that can add fun and laughter to many friendly gatherings.

WILL SHORTZ
Games magazine

CHARCOAL. See FUELS.

CHARLEMAGNE
(742?–814)

Charlemagne, or Charles the Great, was king of the Franks. He conquered much of Europe and is often regarded as the founder of the Holy Roman Empire (800).

In the A.D. 400's, as the Roman Empire in the West was coming to an end, a Germanic tribe known as the Franks began to build a kingdom in what is now France. In the 700's, under the Frankish rulers Charles Martel and his son Pepin the Short, the kingdom grew to include much of western Europe.

About the year 742, Pepin had a son named Charles, who now is better known as Charlemagne, which means Charles the Great. He became one of the greatest kings of the Middle Ages. Much of what we know about Charlemagne comes from the writings of a monk named Einhard. Einhard says that Charlemagne was brave and strong, was very tall, and had blond hair and a moustache. He learned to read Latin, which was a rare accomplishment then—even for kings—but he never learned to write. He would sign his name by making a cross and the letters "KRLS."

Charlemagne's Kingdom

In 768, Charlemagne inherited half of his father's kingdom. The other half went to his brother, Carloman. When Carloman died in 771, Charlemagne became sole ruler of the Franks. Charlemagne devoted most of his 43-year reign to expanding his realm and converting his subjects to Christianity. Among those he conquered were the Lombards of northern Italy, the Saxons of northern Germany, the Slavs of central Europe, the Avars, who lived along the Danube River, and the powerful dukes of Bavaria. By 800, his kingdom covered most of what is today France, Belgium, the Netherlands, Switzerland, Austria, western Germany, northern Italy, and parts of Spain and eastern Europe.

Charlemagne divided his kingdom into districts, and to each he assigned a governor. Bishops were placed in charge of church matters, and ambassadors traveled throughout the huge kingdom to see that the king's orders were obeyed.

Under Charlemagne's influence, farming, commerce, and religion were encouraged, and a rough code of laws was developed. Charlemagne was particularly interested in education, and he brought scholars and monks to his capital at Aachen (in present-day Germany), where he created a palace school. Monastery schools also were built and were open to the sons of serfs as well as nobles.

Charlemagne is Named Emperor

On Christmas Day in the year 800, Pope Leo III placed a crown on Charlemagne's head, declaring him emperor of the Romans. This event is sometimes regarded as the founding of the Holy Roman Empire. Charlemagne ruled as emperor until his death in 814.

Charlemagne left his kingdom to his only surviving son, Louis I (Louis the Pious). After Louis's death, the empire was divided among his sons, Lothair I, Charles II (Charles the Bald), and Louis the German. From these three kingdoms, created by the Treaty of Verdun in 843, came the modern nations of western Europe.

Reviewed by KENNETH S. COOPER
George Peabody College

See also HOLY ROMAN EMPIRE.

CHARLEMAGNE'S EMPIRE IN 814

TREATY OF VERDUN (843)

CHARLES

Dozens of European rulers have reigned (r.) under the name Charles. Discussed in this article are two kings of England, ten kings of France, sixteen kings of Sweden, and seven Holy Roman Emperors.

▶KINGS OF ENGLAND, SCOTLAND, AND IRELAND
Charles I (1600–1649) (r. 1625–49) was the only English monarch ever to be executed. Between 1629 and 1640 he tried to rule the country without a parliament, but he had to call one in 1640 because he needed money to fight the Scots. Further conflicts between the king and Parliament led to the outbreak of the English Civil War in 1642. Oliver Cromwell, the leader of the Parliamentary Army, defeated Charles's forces at the battles of Marston Moor (1644) and Naseby (1645). Charles was taken prisoner in 1647, charged with treason, and publicly executed in London in January 1649.

Charles II (1630–85) (r. 1660–85), the son of Charles I, became king when Parliament restored the monarchy in 1660, two years after Cromwell's death. In 1670 he made the secret Treaty of Dover with King Louis XIV of France and promised to try to convert England to Roman Catholicism.

▶KINGS OF FRANCE
Charles I was known as Charlemagne, or Charles the Great. For more information, see the article CHARLEMAGNE in this volume.

Charles II (the Bald) (823–877) (r. 843–877), Charlemagne's grandson, was the first to rule France as a separate kingdom. He was later recognized as Holy Roman Emperor.

Charles III (the Simple) (879–929) (r. 898–922) gave away Normandy to the Viking leader Rollo in 911. He was accepted as ruler of Lotharingia but was deposed in 922.

Charles IV (the Fair) (1294–1328) (r. 1322–28) was the last king of the Capetian dynasty that had ruled France for more than three hundred years. He warred against England through much of his reign.

Charles V (the Wise) (1338–80) (r. 1364–80) created a new tax system that allowed him to reorganize the army and form a new navy. With assistance from his general, Bertrand du Guesclin, he carried on the Hundred Years' War with England, seeking to regain the terri-

Charles I was captured by Oliver Cromwell during the English Civil War. Parliament found the king guilty of treason and executed him in 1649.

tory that had been lost to the English at the battles of Crécy (1346) and Poitiers (1356). Between 1369 and 1375, Guesclin's forces virtually drove the English out of France.

Charles VI (the Mad or Well-Beloved) (1368–1422) (r. 1380–1422), for much of his life, suffered bouts of insanity. During the Hundred Years' War, his army was defeated by England's Henry V at the Battle of Agincourt (1415). By the Treaty of Troyes (1420), Charles VI allowed Henry V to marry his daughter Catherine, and agreed that the couple's offspring should succeed to the thrones of both England and France.

Charles VII (the Well-Served) (1403–61) (r. 1422–61) had been effectively excluded from succeeding the throne by the Treaty of Troyes (1420); but when his father died in 1422, most of the French south of the Loire region remained loyal and recognized him as king. With the help of Joan of Arc, Charles VII's forces broke the siege of Orléans in 1429 and drove the English out. He was crowned king at Rheims Cathedral in July of that year. Charles VII went on to recapture from the English all of northern France (except Calais), putting an end to the Hundred Years' War.

Charles VIII (1470–98) (r. 1483–98) laid claim to the throne of Naples and invaded Italy in 1494. He was crowned in Naples in 1495, but was quickly driven out of Italy by hostile forces. He was planning a second invasion when he died.

Charles IX (1550–74) (r. 1560–74) left the duties of governing to his mother, Catherine de Medici. In 1572 he agreed to her demand for a massacre of the Protestant Huguenots. This event became known as the St. Bartholomew's Day Massacre.

Charles X (1757–1836) (r. 1824–30) was the last Bourbon king of France. His fondness for the pre-Revolutionary ways of life brought him into conflict with those liberals who had supported the Revolution. He abdicated (gave up the throne) in 1830.

▶ KINGS OF SWEDEN

Charles I through **Charles VII** were early tribal leaders in Sweden.

Charles VIII (1408–70) (r. 1448–70) helped free Sweden from Danish rule. He was the first king of the independent country.

Charles IX (1550–1611) (r. 1604–11), who was a Protestant, deposed Sigismund, the reigning Catholic king, in 1599. He ruled as regent until he became king in 1604. Then he followed an aggressive foreign policy and made war on Denmark and Poland.

Charles X (1622–60) (r. 1654–60) also fought Denmark and Poland in the Great Northern War. He came to the throne upon the abdication of Queen Christina in 1654. He opened up a sea route to the Baltic and brought Sweden to the height of her power.

Charles XI (1655–97) (r. 1660–97) was granted absolute power by Parliament in 1693.

Charles XII (1682–1718) (r. 1697–1718) fought against Poland, Denmark, and Russia. His defeat by the Russian czar, Peter the Great, at Poltava in 1709 made Russia the dominant power in Eastern Europe. He was killed in battle in Norway.

Charles XIII (1748–1818) (r. 1809–18) accepted the crown after the forced abdication of Gustav Adolf. However, he soon relinquished power to his adopted son, former French marshal Bernadotte.

Charles XIV (1763–1844) (r. 1818–44), the adopted son of Charles XIII, was elected Crown Prince in 1810. Born Jean Baptiste Jules Bernadotte in Pau, France, he had a successful army career in France during the Revolution. In 1810 he took control over Swedish affairs. He brought about the union of Sweden and Norway in 1814. He succeeded to the throne as Charles XIV in 1818.

Charles XV (1826–72) (r. 1859–72), king of Sweden and Norway, established friendly relations with Denmark and gave over much of his constitutional authority to Parliament.

Charles XVI (1946–   ) (r. 1973–   ) succeeded his grandfather, King Gustav VI Adolf. According to the country's revised 1971 constitution, the king now participates in ceremonial functions only.

▶ EMPERORS OF THE HOLY ROMAN EMPIRE

Charles I. For more information, see the article CHARLEMAGNE in this volume.

Charles II (the Bald) (823–877) (r. 875–77), king of the western Franks since 843, negotiated the Treaty of Mersen (870), which partitioned Lotharingia.

Charles III (the Fat) (839–888) (r. 881–87), the youngest son of Louis the German, was the last to rule Charlemagne's reunited empire (except for Burgundy).

Charles IV (1316–78) (r. 1355–78) was also king of Germany and Bohemia (1346–78). In 1356 he issued the Golden Bull, arranging for future emperors to be chosen by a fixed group of electors. Under him, Prague became the political and cultural capital of the Holy Roman Empire.

Charles V. For more information, see the article HABSBURGS in Volume H.

Charles VI (1685–1740) (r. 1711–40), the archduke of Austria and king of Hungary, fought for but failed to take the Spanish throne during the War of the Spanish Succession (1701–14). In 1713 he issued the Pragmatic Sanction, to guarantee that his daughter, Maria Theresa, would succeed him to rule all Habsburg lands (as he had no male heir).

Charles VII (1697–1745) (r. 1742–45) was the elector of Bavaria (1726–43; 1745). He was chosen emperor during the War of the Austrian Succession (1740–48). He lost Bavaria to an Austrian occupation in 1743 but recovered it shortly before his death.

W. M. ORMROD
University of York

CHARLES, PRINCE. See ENGLAND, HISTORY OF (The Monarchy in Recent Times).

CHARLESTON. See SOUTH CAROLINA (Cities).

CHARLOTTE. See NORTH CAROLINA (Cities).

CHASE, SALMON P. See OHIO (Famous People).

In the *Canterbury Tales*, medieval pilgrims (*above*) entertain one another with stories on their way to the shrine of Thomas à Becket in Canterbury, England. The collection of 24 tales is the most famous work of English writer Geoffrey Chaucer (*right*).

CHAUCER, GEOFFREY (1340?–1400)

The greatest figure of medieval English literature—and one of the first great humorists of modern Europe—was Geoffrey Chaucer, the son of a London wine merchant. His most famous work, the *Canterbury Tales*, gives a vivid picture of English life in the 1300's.

Little is known about Chaucer's early years. In 1356 he became a page in the household of Prince Lionel, a son of Edward III. Three years later he took part in a military expedition to France and was taken prisoner. King Edward paid part of his ransom, and Chaucer returned to England in 1360. In the years that followed, he married one of the queen's attendants and held a number of government posts, including that of controller of customs in London. He made several trips to France and to Italy, where he may have met the Italian writers Petrarch and Boccaccio.

Chaucer wrote throughout his life. His first long poem was *The Book of the Duchess* (1369), written on the death of Lady Blanche, the first wife of John of Gaunt. It follows the style of the elegant French verse then popular. Italian literature influenced a later work, *Troilus and Criseyde*.

Chaucer began compiling his *Canterbury Tales* about 1386. He wrote about a group of pilgrims traveling to a shrine at Canterbury.

Each is a colorful and unique character, and each tells a story along the way. Chaucer himself was so skillful a storyteller that his account of their pilgrimage is as entertaining as the individual tales. He borrowed the design of the work from Boccaccio's *Decameron*, and he took the plots of the tales from many sources. But he wrote in an entirely original way—with robust humor and deep insight.

Chaucer died on October 25, 1400, in a small house he had rented on the grounds of Westminster Abbey, in London. His burial spot at the abbey is known as Poets' Corner.

Reviewed by GEORGIA DUNBAR
Hofstra University

CHAVEZ, CESAR. See CALIFORNIA (Famous People).
CHAVEZ, DENNIS. See NEW MEXICO (Famous People).

CHECKERS

Checkers (or draughts, as it is called in England) is a board game for two players. The object of checkers is to block or capture all the other player's pieces. The rules of checkers are not hard to learn, and it is a favorite children's game. But it can also be a real test of skill between experts. Many players study it as they would a science and learn hundreds of special moves to begin or end a game.

▶ **HOW OLD IS CHECKERS?**

No one is certain exactly when checkers was invented. Board games somewhat similar to checkers were played in ancient Egypt. But the first game closely resembling modern checkers did not appear until about the year 1200, probably in southern France. Checkers was not well known until the 1400's. Then it spread quickly throughout Europe and, later, to nearly the entire world.

In the 1800's there was great interest in checkers as a tournament game. Today it is played mainly for fun. But tournaments are sometimes held. In the United States, these are sponsored by the American Checker Federation.

Different versions of checkers are played in different countries. The simplest version is American checkers, or British draughts.

▶ **HOW AMERICAN CHECKERS IS PLAYED**

American checkers is played on a board marked off into 64 light and dark squares. Each player is given twelve round checkers, or men. One player's checkers are dark, and the other's are light.

The players sit facing each other, with the board between them. The board is placed so that a dark square is in the corner to each player's left. The players place their men on the dark squares of the three rows nearest to them. The two center rows are empty.

The player who has the dark checkers begins the game by moving a checker one space toward the other player. Because all play must be on dark squares, the checker must move forward diagonally, to the dark square to its left or the dark square to its right. A checker may move only onto an empty square.

The player with the light checkers then moves in the same way. The game continues with each person moving in turn.

Jumping. As players advance toward each other's territory, they may find one or more of their checkers blocked by an opponent's checker. When this happens, the advancing checker may be able to capture the checker that is blocking it by jumping over it. The square beyond the checker that is jumped must be empty, or the jump cannot be made. Players cannot jump over their own checkers.

Checkers that are jumped are removed from play. Players may jump two or more checkers in one turn if there is an empty square beyond each one. The player can make all the jumps in one direction or zigzag left and right, so long as the jumping checker lands on an empty square between each jump and keeps moving forward.

In modern checkers, players must jump whenever possible. If more than one jump is possible, the player may choose between them. Formerly, players did not have to make a jump. But failure to jump resulted in a penalty.

Kings. A checker that reaches the row of squares nearest the other player becomes a king. Unlike an ordinary checker, a king can move and make jumps backward as well as forward. To show that a checker has become a king, another checker of the same color (taken from the pile of captured checkers) is put on top of it as a crown. From then on, the two checkers are played as one.

Ending the Game. A game ends when one player has captured all the other player's

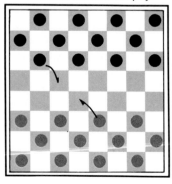

The board at the start of play.

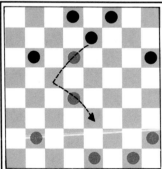

How to make a double jump.

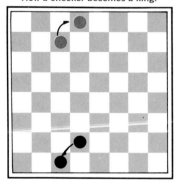

How a checker becomes a king.

checkers or has made it impossible for the other player to move. A player who cannot move loses. If both players agree that neither one can win, the game is a draw. In a draw, no one wins or loses.

If only one player thinks that the game will be a draw, that player can limit the other player to 40 moves. If the other player does not make progress (such as advancing an uncrowned checker) in those 40 moves, the game is a draw.

Other Rules. In the official rules for tournaments, each player is given a five-minute time limit for each move. At the end of five minutes, the player is warned and given one minute more. A player who does not move by the end of the extra minute loses the game.

Under another rule, a player who touches a checker must move it. If the move starts in a certain direction, it must finish in that direction. These rules are often ignored in friendly games played only for fun.

▶ **OTHER VERSIONS OF CHECKERS**

Pool checkers, also played on a 64-square board, is popular in Spain, Portugal, Brazil, Russia, and some parts of the United States. In this game, uncrowned men may jump forward or backward. But they must move forward when they are not jumping. Kings may move any number of squares diagonally, even when jumping.

International checkers and Canadian checkers also use these rules. These games are played on larger boards, with more pieces. International checkers is played on a board with 100 squares. It is popular in France, Russia, Poland, and other European countries, as well as in Indonesia and parts of Africa. Canadian checkers uses a 144-square board. In these games, when more than one jump is possible, a player usually must choose the jump that captures the most pieces.

R. WAYNE SCHMITTBERGER
Games magazine

CHECKING ACCOUNT. See BANKS AND BANKING.

CHEERLEADING

"Let's Go! Let's Fight! Let's Win!"

These spirited words are just one of many yells used by cheerleaders. Working in groups of five to twenty people (known as squads), cheerleaders generate enthusiasm at sporting events. They encourage team spirit while performing showy and entertaining routines that include steps taken from gymnastics and popular dances.

Cheerleaders are also responsible for crowd leadership. Dressed in colorful uniforms and perhaps using props such as pom-poms or megaphones, they must first attract the crowd's attention. Then it is up to the cheerleading squad to direct the spectators' expressions of support as they urge a sports team to victory. They do this by leading cheers such as those on the following page. A successful cheerleading squad can actually mean the difference between good and poor sportsmanship on the part of the fans.

Each year more than 1 million grade school, junior and senior high school, and college students are involved in cheerleading. Its participants work for virtually every kind of team sport, from football and basketball to wrestling and ice hockey.

How Cheerleading Began

Cheerleading originated in the United States. Its roots go back to the honor societies and fraternities formed on U.S. college campuses in the late 1700's. Members of such groups wrote songs and rhymes to express their pride in their clubs and schools.

When college football began in the late 1800's, each college's clubs sat together at games and competed against one another for attention and support. Their songs and rhymes formed the beginnings of traditional "yells," or cheers, some of which are still used today.

The initial movement of cheerleading was almost exclusively an all-male activity among the colleges of the original Big Ten intercollegiate athletic conference in the Midwest. By the early 1900's it had spread to almost all U.S. universities and colleges (and some in Canada) and into some high schools. During World War I, when much of America's male population was fighting overseas, female students began to dominate cheerleading activities. With the exception of college sports, where cheerleading squads usually have equal numbers of male and female cheerleaders, this trend continues today.

Because of their high visibility at sporting events that are aired on national television, adult, professional cheerleaders have brought widespread attention to all forms of this popular activity.

Becoming a Cheerleader

As with other athletic activities, good cheerleading technique requires years of preparation. An aspiring high school cheerleader must develop sufficient athletic skill and learn to perform gymnastics routines, a variety of different jumps, modern dances, partner lifts and mounts, and a wide variety of arm motions.

Once the candidates learn these skills and their own school's style of cheerleading, they usually appear before a panel of judges that may include faculty members, sports team coaches, and student leaders. Such tryouts, held in the spring of each year, result in the selection of the cheerleading squad for the coming school year.

Cheerleading Camps and Competitions

About 65 percent of U.S. junior and senior high schools send their cheerleading squads to summer training camps. These programs are offered by organizations such as the World Cheerleading Association, the National Cheerleaders Association, and the Universal Cheerleaders Association. The purpose of these programs is to help mold a newly selected cheerleading squad into a unified team and also to give interested young people a chance to learn cheerleading skills. While at cheerleading camp, students learn new cheers and stunts, share spirit-raising ideas, and earn awards for their achievements.

Some cheerleading squads also participate in cheerleading competitions. There are numerous regional competitions as well as the annual International Open Cheerleading Championships held in Nashville, Tennessee, for elementary through high school students and the College Cheerleading and Dance Team National Championships in Orlando, Florida, for college cheerleaders. At these competitions, squads from many states show off their techniques and original routines. In addition to competing for awards, the cheerleaders also have the opportunity to watch the different cheerleading styles from around the country.

Cheerleading organizations also try to promote safe cheerleading practices. Flips, leaps, jumps, and other acrobatic steps have become a popular part of many cheerleading routines. As with any physical activity, these movements can be dangerous, however, if done without supervision or careful training. Some schools have banned certain techniques to reduce the risk of injury, while others have increased safety measures.

Randy L. Neil
President, International Cheerleading
Foundation, Inc.
Coauthor, The Official Cheerleader's Handbook

Almost every major university has at least one traditional cheer or yell that has been used for decades. Two examples are listed below.

University of California, Los Angeles (UCLA), from the 1920's:

> U RAH! RAH! RAH!
> C RAH! RAH! RAH!
> L RAH! RAH! RAH!
> A RAH! RAH! RAH!
> U-C-L-A! FIGHT! FIGHT! FIGHT!
> (followed by school fight song)

University of Arkansas, Fayetteville, from the 1930's: The Razorback Hog Call

> (yelled in a high soprano voice)
> SOO-O-O-O-EY. PIG! SOOEY!
> SOO-O-O-O-EY. PIG! SOOEY!
> SOO-O-O-O-EY. PIG! SOOEY!
> GO-O-O-O . . . RAZORBACKS!

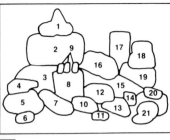

This selection of popular cheeses from Europe includes spiced Pompadour (1); Parmesan (2); Emmental (3); Cheddar (4); Gouda (5); Camembert (6); Chèvre (7); Stilton (8, 10); Sapsago (9); Limburger (11); Doux de Montagnes (12); Brie (13); pressed Ricotta (14); Gruyère (15); Provolone (16); Colby (17); Muenster (18); Leyden (19); Roquefort (20); and Edam (21).

CHEESE

Cheese is one of the foods made from milk. Cheese keeps better than milk, but it has many of the same nutrients as milk. Hundreds of kinds of cheese are enjoyed by people all over the world.

The origin of cheese making is unknown, but references to it date back many centuries. One account claims that an Arab merchant tasted milk that had curdled in a goatskin bag. The cheese curd pleased him, and a new food was discovered.

The Bible mentions cheese as well as milk. In Chapter 17 of I Samuel, David is instructed by his father to ''carry these ten cheeses to the captain of their thousand.'' Homer in Book Nine of the *Odyssey* described Ulysses' discovery of cheese made from goat's milk in the cave of the dreadful one-eyed cyclops. Other Greek and Roman scholars wrote about cheese and how it was manufactured over 2,000 years ago.

From this ancient background, hundreds of different kinds of cheese have been developed throughout the world. The four main kinds of cheese are soft, semisoft, hard, and very hard. Soft cheeses, such as cream cheese or Brie, can be spread like butter. Stilton, Limburger, Monterey Jack, and other semisoft cheeses can be cut easily, even when cold.

Some of the most popular cheeses are hard cheeses. There are several types of Swiss cheese, such as Gruyère—which is commonly made in France—and Emmental. Cheddar cheese is sometimes named after the place where it is made, such as Wisconsin, Vermont, or New Zealand cheddar. Parmesan and Romano are examples of very hard cheeses. These cheeses are often grated and used in cooked dishes.

There are several reasons that so many varieties of cheese can be made. First, milk—the basis of cheese—comes from other animals beside the cow. The milks of camels, goats, sheep, and water buffalo each yield cheese with a different flavor. Krutt is a cheese made in the Asiatic steppes from camel's milk by drying the curd in the sun. Roquefort is a famous French cheese made from sheep's milk. Goat cheese is a standard food in mountainous countries. Surati is a cheese made in India from buffalo's milk. The curd is drained in baskets and can be eaten fresh.

Also, even if only one kind of milk is used, different processes and curing (aging) methods produce different cheeses. Cheeses may be cured for different lengths of time, smoked, processed (blended with other cheeses), or flavored with seeds, spices, or wine. Cheese making is described step-by-step in the article DAIRYING AND DAIRY PRODUCTS in Volume D.

NORMAN F. OLSON
University of Wisconsin—Madison

See also MILK.

CHEKHOV, ANTON (1860–1904)

Anton Pavlovich Chekhov is Russia's best-known modern playwright and a master of the short story. He was born in Taganrog on January 17, 1860. He worked in his father's grocery store as a boy. But in 1876 his father went bankrupt and fled to Moscow. Anton took on his father's responsibilities, and the family came to call him Father Antosha (a nickname for Anton).

After graduating from high school, Chekhov entered the medical school of Moscow University. He received his M.D. degree in 1884 and began practicing medicine. He also wrote short stories to support the family. Between 1880 and 1885, he wrote hundreds of stories for magazines. He became known as a creator of ''mood literature,'' in which the atmosphere is more important than the action.

Chekhov wrote his first play at the age of 18, but all that survives is the title, *Without Fathers*. Chekhov himself considered *Ivanov* (1889) to be his first play. *The Sea Gull* (1896) was poorly received at first, but it was a great success at the Moscow Art Theater two years later. The theater eventually adopted a sea gull as its emblem.

Chekhov rewrote another failed play, *The Wood Demon*, which was produced in 1899 under the title *Uncle Vanya*. Its success gave Chekhov the courage to work on *The Three Sisters*, a play about the vain hope of the sisters to go to Moscow, which represents all that is missing in their dull lives.

Chekhov still practiced medicine occasionally. In 1901 he married an actress, Olga Knipper. The marriage was happy, although Chekhov had to spend winters in Yalta, where the climate was better for his health. From Yalta he wrote to his wife in Moscow, ''The next play I am going to write will be very funny.'' It took him two years to finish this funny play, *The Cherry Orchard*, a seemingly simple story about a family that must sell a beloved orchard. It is not a comedy in the usual sense, and at first it, too, was not a success. But it is now considered a masterpiece.

In 1904, Chekhov's doctor ordered him to go to a tuberculosis specialist in Badenweiler, Germany. On July 2, 1904, he died there. His body was taken back to Russia for burial.

IRENE KIRK
Author, *Anton Chekhov*

CHEMICAL INDUSTRY

Many things people use are made entirely or partly from chemicals. Chemicals are used to manufacture such products as drugs, permanent-press fabrics, fertilizers, pens, film, and dishwashing or laundry detergents. The manufacture of these and many other products depends on the chemical industry.

▶ANCIENT CRAFT TO MODERN INDUSTRY

The chemical industry has ancient roots. People in ancient Egypt and Mesopotamia made such chemical products as pigments for paints, dyes to stain cloth, alkali for glassmaking, and various glazes for pottery. During the Middle Ages, chemistry was used to make such products as saltpeter for gunpowder, alum for tanning hides, potash for soap and glassmaking, and lime for mortar.

Scientists of the 1600's and 1700's helped develop the modern chemical industry. They learned to make purer chemicals than the ones made in the past, and they studied the reactions that took place when one chemical was mixed with another. In the late 1700's, the Industrial Revolution increased the demand for chemical products. Textile mills needed dyes and bleaches to color and whiten cloth. Some manufacturers began to specialize in making chemicals for such industries as dyeing and glassmaking.

▶THE CHEMICAL INDUSTRY TODAY

The modern chemical industry is quite different from the chemical industries of the past. Today's industry depends on the latest advances in science and engineering. Large chemical plants produce huge amounts of chemicals each day. The purity of the chemicals and the quality of final products are carefully checked. Special instruments monitor chemical processes, and every step of the manufacturing process is closely controlled.

Today's chemical industry is highly automated. One technician at a computerized panel can monitor and control all the steps in a complex chemical process.

In addition, today's chemical industry is highly automated.

Chemicals made by the chemical industry may be classified in several ways. **Organic chemicals** contain carbon atoms. They are used to make such products as dyes, medicines, plastics, paints, glues, and synthetic fabrics. **Inorganic chemicals** do not contain carbon. Sulfuric acid, which is used to make fertilizer, is an inorganic chemical. So is hydrogen peroxide, which is used to bleach textiles. **Fine chemicals** are of very high purity and are usually made and used in small quantities. Artificial flavorings, dyes, and drugs are examples of fine chemicals. **Heavy chemicals**, which are not as purified as fine chemicals, are the "workhorses" of the chemical industry. Thousands of tons of heavy chemicals are produced each year. There are about 25 heavy chemicals, including sulfuric acid, nitric acid, ammonia, and chlorine.

Research is the heart of the chemical industry. Chemical companies depend on their researchers to develop new and better ways of making chemicals. There are two kinds of research. **Basic research** tries to find new facts and ideas, regardless of whether or not there are useful purposes for them. **Applied research** is more practical. It starts with the goal of making a certain product and then uses substances and ideas that are already known to produce it.

The chemical industry is controversial at times. Some chemicals have been linked to serious health problems such as cancer. Others pose a threat to the environment. Chemical wastes can seep into waterways and kill fish and plant life. Harmful chemicals can leak into the air and damage people's health. In 1984, for example, more than 2,500 people died in Bhopal, India, when a chemical leaked from a pesticide-manufacturing plant.

Many new projects are currently underway in the chemical industry. Chemicals are being used to develop superstrong, lightweight materials that can be used to make everything from canoes to army helmets. Special chemicals are being developed for the electronics industry, and researchers on U.S. space shuttles are studying chemical production in outer space.

WILLIAM E. CHACE
Chemical Manufacturers Association

See also CHEMISTRY; DRUGS; HAZARDOUS WASTES; NYLON AND OTHER SYNTHETIC FIBERS; PLASTICS.

CHEMICAL POLLUTION   See HAZARDOUS WASTES.

Chemists analyze substances in order to understand their chemical properties and also to learn how chemicals can be put to use in practical and beneficial ways.

CHEMISTRY

Chemistry is the science that deals with the composition, structure, and properties of substances. It also deals with the changes that these substances undergo. Because the study of chemistry involves every possible kind of substance, it is central to the understanding of many other sciences.

The atomic theory is one of the most fundamental parts of the science of chemistry. This theory states that all substances are made up of tiny particles far too small to be seen, even with the strongest microscopes. These tiny particles are called **atoms.** Everything—glass, brick, iron, water, the stars in the sky, and your own body—is made up of atoms.

There are many kinds of atoms. So far we know of at least 115 different kinds. But most of them are quite rare. Only about a dozen kinds of atoms are really common here on Earth.

Then how can there be so many different things on Earth? The answer is that atoms are like the letters of the alphabet—all the words in the English language are built out of only 26 letters. A particular kind of material, or **substance,** is formed when atoms combine. Even just a few kinds of atoms can combine in a large number of different arrangements.

Each different arrangement makes up a different substance.

Sometimes a substance is made up of combinations of only one kind of atom. Such a substance is called an **element.** Iron is made up of one kind of atom, as are sulfur and aluminum. These are examples of elements.

When a substance is made up of combinations of more than one kind of atom, it is a **compound.** The substance ferrous sulfide is a compound because it is made up of pairs of two different kinds of atoms. Each pair consists of one iron atom and one sulfur atom.

A group of two or more atoms tightly bound together is called a **molecule.** The pairs of atoms in ferrous sulfide, for example, are molecules. Atoms in a molecule can also be the same element. An oxygen molecule is made up of two oxygen atoms.

▶ **CHEMICAL AND PHYSICAL CHANGES**

Understanding how substances can be changed is essential to understanding chemistry. But not all changes involve principles of chemistry.

For example, you can break up a bar of iron into tiny pieces. Each tiny piece is still iron, because the atom arrangement has not been changed. This is a **physical change.** You can magnetize a piece of iron. You can let an electric current pass through it. Or you can heat it red hot. These, too, are physical changes.

You can mix iron with something else without changing the atom arrangement. Suppose you mixed powdered iron with powdered sulfur. In this mixture each little grain of iron is still iron. And each little grain of sulfur is still sulfur.

You can easily separate the mixture again, because iron and sulfur have different **properties.** A magnet passed through the mixture will attract the iron and leave the sulfur behind. A liquid called carbon disulfide will dissolve the sulfur and leave the iron behind.

But what if you heated the mixture of powdered iron and sulfur? That would bring about a different kind of change. A blackish material would form, in which you could no longer see separate little bits of grayish iron or yellow sulfur.

The new material would have a new set of properties, unlike those of either iron or sulfur. The new substance would not be attracted by a magnet. It would not dissolve in carbon disulfide.

You would now have a substance called ferrous sulfide. When the iron and sulfur were heated, each sulfur atom combined with an iron atom, forming molecules of ferrous sulfide. That is, a new arrangement of atoms was formed, and it made up a new substance with new properties. This is an example of a **chemical change,** which is also called a **chemical reaction.**

Chemical changes go on all about us. Whenever coal or oil burns, that is a chemical change. The rusting of iron is a chemical change. When food is cooked, it goes through many chemical changes. Chemical changes also go on inside the body at all times. These are the many kinds of changes that interest a chemist.

▶ SYMBOLS, FORMULAS, AND EQUATIONS

Chemists often refer to the different elements and the compounds they form. They do this so often that a special shorthand language has been worked out. Each element is represented by one or two letters taken from its name. This is the **chemical symbol** of the element.

Often the chemical symbol is just the initial or the first two letters of the element. For example, the chemical symbol of sulfur is S and for aluminum is Al. Sometimes the symbol is taken from the Latin name. For example, the Latin name for iron is *ferrum.* The symbol for iron is Fe.

Symbols can be used to show the atomic makeup of a molecule. The ferrous sulfide molecule contains one iron atom and one sulfur atom. So the molecule is written FeS. This is an example of a **chemical formula,** a way of showing the atomic makeup of a molecule by means of symbols.

Whenever a chemical reaction takes place, atoms are rearranged. Therefore the details of the reaction can be shown in chemical symbols. When iron and sulfur are mixed and heated, ferrous sulfide forms. To put this quickly, we can write:

$$Fe + S \xrightarrow{\triangle} FeS$$

That is a **chemical equation.** It says that an atom of iron combines with an atom of sulfur to form a molecule of ferrous sulfide. The little triangle over the arrow stands for heat. It means that the mixture has to be heated before

Chemical changes take place when atoms are rearranged to form new substances. Such a change occurs when iron combines with air to form rust, or iron oxide.

the chemical reaction takes place. (Light, electricity, and even other chemicals can also bring about—or at least speed up—chemical reactions. Any substance that makes a reaction go faster, without itself seeming to be changed, is called a **catalyst.**)

When a symbol is written by itself, it stands for one atom of a particular element. What if a molecule contains more than one atom of that element?

The chemical reaction in which hydrogen and oxygen combine to form water cannot be written $H_2 + O_2 \xrightarrow{\triangle} H_2O$. This would say that 2 hydrogen atoms combine with 2 oxygen atoms to form a molecule of water. But the molecule of water contains 2 hydrogen atoms and only 1 oxygen atom. What happened to the other oxygen atom?

The reaction must be written:

$$2H_2 + O_2 \xrightarrow{\triangle} 2H_2O$$

O_2, you remember, stands for 2 oxygen atoms or 1 oxygen molecule. H_2 stands for 2 hydrogen atoms or 1 hydrogen molecule. So $2H_2$ stands for 2 hydrogen molecules (or 4 atoms). Therefore the equation shows that 2 hydrogen molecules and 1 oxygen molecule combine to form 2 molecules of water. The 2 molecules of water are made up of 4 hydrogen atoms and 2 oxygen atoms all together. All the atoms are accounted for, and the result is a **balanced chemical equation.**

Individual atoms bond in certain combinations to form molecules

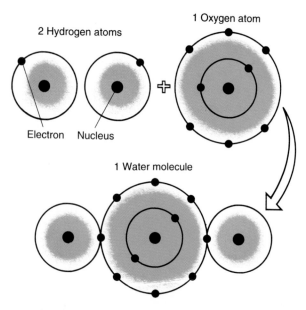

2 Hydrogen atoms

1 Oxygen atom

Electron Nucleus

1 Water molecule

ALPHABETICAL TABLE OF ELEMENTS

ELEMENT	SYMBOL	ELEMENT	SYMBOL
Actinium	Ac	Neodymium	Nd
Aluminum	Al	Neon	Ne
Americium	Am	Neptunium	Np
Antimony	Sb	Nickel	Ni
Argon	Ar	Niobium	Nb
Arsenic	As	Nitrogen	N
Astatine	At	Nobelium	No
Barium	Ba	Osmium	Os
Berkelium	Bk	Oxygen	O
Beryllium	Be	Palladium	Pd
Bismuth	Bi	Phosphorus	P
Bohrium	Bh	Platinum	Pt
Boron	B	Plutonium	Pu
Bromine	Br	Polonium	Po
Cadmium	Cd	Potassium	K
Calcium	Ca	Praseodymium	Pr
Californium	Cf	Promethium	Pm
Carbon	C	Protactinium	Pa
Cerium	Ce	Radium	Ra
Cesium	Cs	Radon	Rn
Chlorine	Cl	Rhenium	Re
Chromium	Cr	Rhodium	Rh
Cobalt	Co	Rubidium	Rb
Copper	Cu	Ruthenium	Ru
Curium	Cm	Rutherfordium	Rf
Dubnium	Db	Samarium	Sm
Dysprosium	Dy	Scandium	Sc
Einsteinium	Es	Seaborgium	Sg
Erbium	Er	Selenium	Se
Europium	Eu	Silicon	Si
Fermium	Fm	Silver	Ag
Fluorine	F	Sodium	Na
Francium	Fr	Strontium	Sr
Gadolinium	Gd	Sulfur	S
Gallium	Ga	Tantalum	Ta
Germanium	Ge	Technetium	Tc
Gold	Au	Tellurium	Te
Hafnium	Hf	Terbium	Tb
Hassium	Ha	Thallium	Tl
Helium	He	Thorium	Th
Holmium	Ho	Thulium	Tm
Hydrogen	H	Tin	Sn
Indium	In	Titanium	Ti
Iodine	I	Tungsten	W
Iridium	Ir	Ununbium *	Uub
Iron	Fe	Ununhexium *	Uuh
Krypton	Kr	Ununnilium *	Uun
Lanthanum	La	Ununoctium *	Uuo
Lawrencium	Lr	Ununquadium *	Uuq
Lead	Pb	Unununium *	Uuu
Lithium	Li	Uranium	U
Lutetium	Lu	Vanadium	V
Magnesium	Mg	Xenon	Xe
Manganese	Mn	Ytterbium	Yb
Meitnerium	Mt	Yttrium	Y
Mendelevium	Md	Zinc	Zn
Mercury	Hg	Zirconium	Zr
Molybdenum	Mo		

* Provisional name

STRUCTURAL FORMULAS

When different atoms combine to form a molecule, they follow certain rules. For instance, a single hydrogen atom can combine with only one other atom. A single oxygen atom, however, can combine with two other atoms. A single nitrogen atom can combine with three other atoms.

This combining power is called **valence.** Hydrogen has a valence of one; oxygen, a valence of two; and nitrogen, a valence of three.

Sometimes formulas are written so as to show the valence. It is shown by little dashes between the atoms. The molecules of hydrogen, oxygen, and nitrogen can be written: H—H, O=O, N≡N. The hydrogen atoms are shown held together by a **single bond;** the oxygen atoms, by a **double bond;** and the nitrogen atoms, by a **triple bond.**

The formula of water (H_2O) can be written H—O—H. Here each bond of the oxygen atom is shown to be holding one of the hydrogen atoms. A molecule of a gas called ammonia (NH_3) can be shown with the three valence bonds of the nitrogen atom each connected to a hydrogen atom:

$$
\begin{array}{c}
H \\
| \\
H-N-H.
\end{array}
$$

Such formulas show the exact way in which the different atoms of the molecule are connected by bonds. They are called **structural formulas.**

Structural formulas are particularly important to chemists dealing with carbon compounds. For it often happens that the atoms within the molecule can be aranged in more than one way. Each different arrangement is a different compound.

As an example, imagine a molecule made up of 2 carbon atoms, 6 hydrogen atoms, and 1 oxygen atom. These can be put together in two different ways:

$$
\begin{array}{cc}
\begin{array}{c}
H \quad H \\
| \quad | \\
H-C-C-O-H \\
| \quad | \\
H \quad H \\
\textbf{ethyl alcohol}
\end{array}
&
\begin{array}{c}
H \qquad H \\
| \qquad | \\
H-C-O-C-H \\
| \qquad | \\
H \qquad H \\
\textbf{dimethyl ether}
\end{array}
\end{array}
$$

In both compounds all the carbon atoms have four valence bonds. The oxygen atom has two, and the hydrogen atoms have one. In each compound the number of each kind of atom is the same. But the arrangement is different.

The compound with the molecule shown on the left is ethyl alcohol. It is the alcohol that is found in beer and wine. The compound with the molecule shown on the right is dimethyl ether. Its properties are completely different from those of ethyl alcohol. Ethyl alcohol is a clear liquid with a rather pleasant, sweetish smell. Dimethyl ether is a gas with a much sharper smell. If a small piece of the metal sodium is added to ethyl alcohol, a chemical reaction takes place. Bubbles of hydrogen gas are given off. If sodium is exposed to dimethyl ether, nothing happens.

So you have two different substances with molecules made up of the same atoms in different arrangements. Such substances are called **isomers.** The larger a molecule, the greater the number of isomers that can be built up out of its atoms.

ATOMIC STRUCTURE

To understand something about how and why atoms combine, let's take a look at the way they are built.

The atom is made up of three types of particles: the **proton,** the **neutron,** and the **electron.** The protons and the neutrons are heavy particles that are located at the very center of the atom. They form the atomic nucleus. The electrons are very light particles. They are spread throughout the outer regions of the atom and orbit the nucleus. (You can read more about atoms in the ATOMS article in Volume A.)

Atomic structures of four different elements

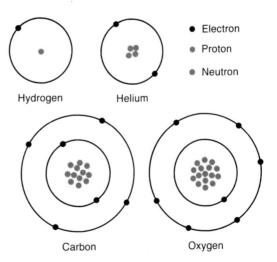

- ● Electron
- ● Proton
- ● Neutron

Hydrogen   Helium

Carbon   Oxygen

The proton and the electron both carry an electric charge. All protons are charged the same way, and this charge is said to be **positive.** All electrons are charged in another way, **negative.** The neutrons have no electric charge at all.

The atomic nucleus contains all the protons of the atom. Therefore the nucleus has a positive charge. Each proton has a charge equal to $+1$. The number of protons in the nucleus is said to be the **atomic number** of that atom. All atoms with the same atomic number behave exactly alike.

The electric charge on the electron is exactly as large as the electric charge on the proton. The electron's charge is negative, however. So we call it -1.

Each atom has exactly enough electrons to balance the protons. The negative electric charges of the electrons balance the positive electric charges of the protons. The atom as a whole is electrically **neutral.**

The Periodic Table

As chemists began to understand atomic structure, they realized that the atoms of some elements were similar in certain ways to the atoms of other elements. They saw, for example, that if the elements were arranged by atomic number, their valences changed in an orderly fashion. Let's look at this list of the first 20 elements:

atomic number	element	valence
1	hydrogen	$+1$
2	helium	0
3	lithium	$+1$
4	beryllium	$+2$
5	boron	$+3$
6	carbon	$+$ or -4
7	nitrogen	-3
8	oxygen	-2
9	fluorine	-1
10	neon	0
11	sodium	$+1$
12	magnesium	$+2$
13	aluminum	$+3$
14	silicon	$+$ or -4
15	phosphorus	-3
16	sulfur	-2
17	chlorine	-1
18	argon	0
19	potassium	$+1$
20	calcium	$+2$

(Elements that lose electrons in a chemical reaction have a $+$ valence. Those that attract electrons have a $-$ valence.)

It is possible to arrange the elements in rows in such a way that elements with the same valences and very similar properties fall into the same column.

VALENCES	+1	+2	+3	±4	−3	−2	−1	0
ROW 1	H 1							He 2
ROW 2	Li 3	Be 4	B 5	C 6	N 7	O 8	F 9	Ne 10
ROW 3	Na 11	Mg 12	Al 13	Si 14	P 15	S 16	Cl 17	A 18
ROW 4	K 19	Ca 20						

By looking at the chart, you can determine that helium, neon, and argon (in the far right-hand column) are similar elements. They are not chemically active and seldom combine with other chemicals. Each has a valence of zero.

Hydrogen, lithium, sodium, and potassium (in the far left-hand column) are all very active. These elements have very similar properties, and each has a valence of $+1$.

If you were to arrange all 115 elements in a chart that grouped together similar elements, you would have created one of the most important tools in chemistry—the periodic table. The periodic table has helped chemists and physicists explain and predict properties of many elements. It is especially important to students learning chemistry. You can see the complete periodic table in the article ELEMENTS, CHEMICAL in Volume E.

Electron Shells and Ions

When any two atoms combine and form a bond, it is their electrons that take part in the bond. The protons and neutrons are not touched. When the bond is formed, the electrons may undergo changes in position or condition. When these changes occur, a chemical reaction has taken place.

An atom's electrons are arranged in groups referred to as **electron shells.** Lithium, with an atomic number of 3, has its 3 electrons arranged in two shells: 2 in the inner shell and 1 in the outer. Its arrangement is 2, 1. Sodium, with an atomic number of 11, has three electron shells; the arrangement is 2, 8, 1. Potassium, with an atomic number of 19, has

4 electron shells, and the arrangement is 2, 8, 8, 1.

An atom tends to rearrange its electrons so that its outermost shell holds 8 electrons. (However, the innermost electron shell can hold only 2 electrons at most.)

Knowing how an atom's electrons are arranged helps chemists predict how an atom will behave when a bond is formed. A sodium atom, with its electrons arranged 2, 8, 1, can easily lose one electron. Its second shell, with 8 electrons, becomes the outermost shell. A chlorine atom, with its electrons arranged 2, 8, 7, can easily gain one electron. Its outermost shell then has 8 electrons.

If a sodium atom collides with a chlorine atom, an electron passes from the former to the latter. The sodium atom, with an electron gone, now has only 10 electrons to balance the 11 protons in the nucleus. There is one positive charge left over. Therefore the sodium atom now has a charge of +1.

An atom with an electric charge is called an **ion.** Instead of a sodium atom we have a sodium ion. The sodium atom has the symbol Na (from its Latin name, *natrium*), and the sodium ion has the symbol Na⁺.

The chlorine atom, with an electron gained, now has 18 electrons but only 17 protons in the nucleus. It has one negative charge too many. So it, too, is an ion. But it is a negatively charged one. Its symbol is Cl⁻.

The properties of ions are different from those of neutral atoms. Sodium is a poisonous metal, and chlorine is a poisonous gas. But their ions are mild and gentle. When sodium and chlorine react together, they form ions. The ions in turn form crystals called sodium chloride. This is ordinary table salt.

When two chlorine atoms collide, something different happens. Each can pick up an electron, but neither is likely to give one up. Instead, each contributes an electron to be shared with the other. The two atoms combine, sharing a pair of electrons. They form the molecule Cl_2. Here a chemical reaction takes place without the forming of ions.

The number of electrons transferred or shared depends on the arrangement of the electrons in the atom. It depends especially on the number of electrons in the outermost shell. Each atom can transfer or share a particular number of electrons. (That is, each element has a valence.)

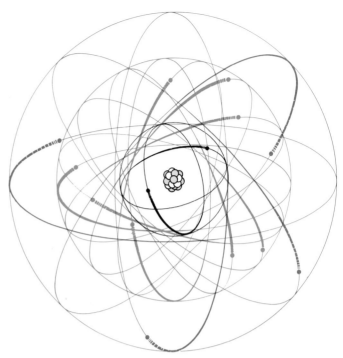

The 14 electrons in a silicon atom are found in three electron shells: 2 in the innermost shell (black), 8 in the next shell (blue), and 4 in the next (pink).

Isotopes and Atomic Weight

All the atoms of a particular element have the same atomic number. But they may not all be completely alike. In addition to the protons in the nucleus, there are neutrons as well, and the neutrons may vary in number.

For instance, all chlorine atoms have 17 protons, and all have the atomic number of 17. Some chlorine atoms, however, have 18 neutrons in the nucleus, while some have 20.

All protons and all neutrons have the same mass. If we consider the mass of each proton and neutron to be 1, we can work out the mass of an entire atom just by adding up the number of protons and neutrons in its nucleus. (The electrons are so light that they can be ignored.)

Chlorine atoms with 17 protons and 18 neutrons in the nucleus have a **mass number** of 35. Those with 17 protons and 20 neutrons in the nucleus have a mass number of 37. These two varieties of chlorine atom can be written as chlorine-35 and chlorine-37. Their symbols are Cl^{35} and Cl^{37}.

Atoms of the same element that differ only in their number of neutrons are called **isotopes.** In other words, Cl^{35} and Cl^{37} are two isotopes of chlorine. Because isotopes have the same atomic number (number of protons), they have the same chemical properties.

IMPORTANT TERMS IN CHEMISTRY

ACID: A substance that releases hydrogen ions when dissolved in water. The more hydrogen ions, the stronger the acid. A strong acid is hydrochloric acid (HCl).

ALCOHOL: An organic substance with a molecule that contains an oxygen and hydrogen atom in combination (–OH). An example is ethyl alcohol (C_2H_5OH), which is found in beer and wine. See ALCOHOL.

ALKALI: A strong base. That is, it has a strong tendency to combine with hydrogen ions. Two examples are sodium hydroxide (NaOH) and potassium hydroxide (KOH).

ALKALI METALS: A family of soft, silvery white metals that react very readily with other substances. Lithium, sodium, and potassium are alkali metals.

ALLOTROPES: Different forms of a particular element. The element carbon, for example, can occur as graphite or diamond. These are allotropes of carbon.

ALLOY: A mixture of metals. Bronze is an alloy of copper and tin. Brass is an alloy of copper and zinc. See ALLOYS.

ANALYSIS: Testing to find out what a substance is made of. When the exact amount of each element present is determined, the testing is called **quantitative analysis.**

ATOM: The smallest particle that can take part in a chemical reaction. All substances are made up of atoms. See ATOMS.

ATOMIC NUMBER: The number of protons in each atom of a particular element. Each element has its own atomic number. The atomic number of hydrogen, for example, is 1; the atomic number of oxygen is 8.

ATOMIC WEIGHT: The average weight of the atoms of a particular element. Such a weight is not absolute. It is relative to the most common type of carbon atom, which is given a weight of exactly 12. The atomic weight of hydrogen is 1.00797; the atomic weight of oxygen is 15.9994.

BASE: A substance that will combine with hydrogen ions. A base is the opposite of an acid, which gives off hydrogen ions. A strong base is also called an alkali. In solution a base will neutralize an acid.

BOND: The force holding two neighboring atoms together; occurs when atoms share electrons or when electrons are transferred from one atom to another.

CATALYST: A substance that increases the speed of a chemical reaction. The catalyst is not used up during the reaction.

COMBUSTION: A chemical reaction that produces heat and usually light as well. The combination of coal with oxygen in the air is a form of combustion.

COMPOUND: A substance made up of molecules containing atoms of two or more elements. Examples are water (H_2O) and sodium bicarbonate ($NaHCO_3$).

COVALENT BOND: The type of linkage between two neighboring atoms when pairs of electrons are shared. The linkage in molecules of carbon dioxide (CO_2) is covalent.

CRYSTAL: A solid body with a definite regular shape and flat sides. This shape results from the orderly arrangement of the atoms or molecules making up the solid. Substances such as salt and sugar form crystals. See CRYSTALS.

DISTILLATION: The process of turning a liquid to vapor by careful boiling and then cooling the vapor so that it becomes liquid again. Salts and impurities that will not turn to vapor can be removed in this way.

ELECTROLYTE: A substance that when dissolved can carry an electric current. An example is sodium chloride.

ELECTRON: An atomic particle that carries a negative electric charge. It is found in the outer regions of the atom.

ELEMENT: A substance made up of atoms all of one type, that is, with the same atomic number. Examples are oxygen, iron, and copper. See ELEMENTS, CHEMICAL.

EQUATION, CHEMICAL: An expression of the way in which a chemical change takes place. Hydrogen and oxygen combining to form water may be shown by the chemical equation $2H_2 + O_2 \rightarrow 2H_2O$.

FLUID: A form of matter in which the atoms or molecules are able to flow freely. This is true for liquids and gases, which are both fluids, but not true of solids.

FORMULA, CHEMICAL: An expression of the makeup of a substance, using the symbols of the elements. The chemical formula of sulfuric acid is H_2SO_4. This means that a sulfuric acid molecule contains 2 atoms of hydrogen, 1 atom of sulfur, and 4 atoms of oxygen.

GAS: A form of matter in which atoms or molecules are so far apart they hardly affect one another. A gas has no definite shape and does not take up a definite amount of space. The most common gas is air. See GASES.

HALOGENS: A family of colored nonmetallic elements that react very readily with other substances. They have a strong tendency to gain electrons in chemical reactions.

INERT: Describes a substance that does not easily combine with other substances. Gold, nitrogen, and glass are all inert substances. A substance such as oxygen that does combine easily is called active.

INORGANIC SUBSTANCE: One that does not contain carbon atoms as part of its main structure. Water, salt, and glass are examples.

ION: Any atom or group of atoms that carries either a positive or negative electric charge. Examples are sodium ion (Na^+), chloride ion (Cl^-), and sulfate ion ($SO_4^=$). A negatively charged ion may be called an **anion**; a positively charged ion, a **cation.** See IONS AND IONIZATION.

IONIC BOND: The type of linkage between two atoms that is produced when electrons are transferred from one atom to another. The atom losing the electrons becomes a positively charged ion. The one gaining the electrons becomes a negatively charged ion. The two ions are held together by the attraction of the opposite charges.

ISOMERS: Substances containing the same types of atoms in the same numbers but in different arrangements. Examples are ethyl alcohol (C_2H_5OH) and dimethyl ether (CH_3OCH_3); each has 2 carbon atoms, 6 hydrogen atoms, and 1 oxygen atom, but they are arranged differently.

ISOTOPES: Two or more types of atoms that have the same number of protons in their nuclei but different numbers of neutrons. (This gives isotopes the same atomic number but different mass numbers.) Chlorine, for example, is made up of two isotopes, Cl^{35} and Cl^{37}.

LIQUID: A form of matter in which the atoms or molecules are closer together than those in a gas. A particular quantity of liquid takes up a definite amount of space but has no definite shape. The most common liquid is water. See LIQUIDS.

MASS: Mass is the quantity of matter in an object. If two objects are weighed under the same conditions, the object with the greater mass weighs more.

MASS NUMBER: The number of neutrons plus the number of protons in the nucleus of an atom. The fluorine atom, for example, has 9 protons and 10 neutrons in its nucleus. It has a mass number of 19.

MATTER: Anything that occupies space and has mass. See MATTER.

MOLECULAR WEIGHT: The weight of a molecule, determined by adding the atomic weights of the various atoms making it up. Since the atomic weight of hydrogen is about 1 and the atomic weight of oxygen is about 16, the molecular weight of water (H_2O) is 1 plus 1 plus 16, to equal 18.

MOLECULE: A group of atoms that remain together and act as a unit. The molecule of oxygen is O_2 and of water is H_2O.

NEUTRAL: (1) Neither acid nor base. Water is neutral. (2) Carrying neither a positive electric charge nor a negative one. An iron atom is neutral.

NEUTRON: An atomic particle found in the nucleus of all atoms (except the common type of hydrogen atom). It carries no electric charge.

NUCLEUS, ATOMIC: The tiny central region of an atom. It contains all the protons and neutrons of the atom. Almost all the mass of the atom is in the nucleus.

ORGANIC SUBSTANCE: One that contains carbon atoms as a main part of its structure. The first substances of this type that were studied had been formed by living organisms. That is how the name arose.

PERIODIC TABLE: An arrangement of the elements in order of atomic number, placed in rows and columns so elements having similar properties are grouped together. See ELEMENTS, CHEMICAL.

POLYMER: A substance composed of large molecules built up of a number of smaller molecules strung together. Most plastics are polymers.

PROTON: An atomic particle found in the nucleus of all atoms. It carries a positive electric charge.

REACTION, CHEMICAL: Any chemical change.

SALT: A compound formed when an acid reacts with a base. When hydrochloric acid (HCl) reacts with the base sodium hydroxide (NaOH), sodium chloride (NaCl), or salt, is formed. See SALT.

SOLID: A form of matter in which the atoms or molecules are held tightly in place. For this reason a solid does not change its shape easily. See SOLIDS.

SOLUTION: A solid, liquid, or gas thoroughly mixed with another solid, liquid, or gas. The part of the solution that is present in the largest amount is called the **solvent.** The less abundant substance is called the **solute** and is dissolved in the solvent.

STRUCTURAL FORMULA: A formula that shows the arrangement of atoms in a molecule.

SYMBOL, CHEMICAL: A sign used to represent an element or its atom. Examples are C for carbon, Cl for chlorine, and Fe for iron (from its Latin name, *ferrum*).

SYNTHESIS: The combining of simple molecules by chemists in a way that produces more complicated molecules.

VALENCE: The number of bonds by which an atom of a particular element usually combines with other atoms. This occurs when atoms either transfer electrons or share them. The valence of carbon, for example, is 4.

Chemistry is put to many practical uses. Helium, an inert gas, keeps metal from burning while being welded (*left*). Copper sulfate is sprayed on grapes (*above*) to keep parasites from destroying the crop.

These isotopes are well mixed throughout nature. In any sample of chlorine gas, there will be a mixture of these two isotopes—approximately three atoms of Cl^{35} for each atom of Cl^{37}. For that reason the average mass of the chlorine atoms in an actual sample of chlorine gas is about 35½, and that is said to be the **atomic weight** of chlorine.

Some elements are made up of only a single variety of atom. Or they may have several varieties, but with one common and the others very rare. In that case the atomic weight of the element is very close to the atomic weight of the common variety.

▶ BRANCHES OF CHEMISTRY

This article lists just a few of the subjects that interest chemists. In fact, chemists' interests are spread so widely that chemistry overlaps many other sciences. For example, some chemists want to know how fast reactions go and what can be done to change their speed. They might want to know how a salt solution can carry an electric current. Questions like these are answered by using methods similar to those used by physicists. This branch of chemistry is called **physical chemistry.**

Chemists also study the many chemical processes that take place inside living organisms. They want to know how foods are broken down and digested, for example, or how oxygen binds with hemoglobin in the blood. Their field of study is called **biochemistry.**

The branch of chemistry that deals with compounds containing carbon is called **organic chemistry.** The study of other compounds takes place in **inorganic chemistry. Analytical chemistry** is concerned with identifying chemical substances, determining their amounts in a mixture, and separating mixtures into their individual components.

Specialized branches of chemistry include **astrochemistry,** the study of the origin and interaction of chemicals in space. **Geochemistry** is related to the science of geology and is applied in areas such as mineral-ore processing. **Nuclear chemistry** deals with the use of nuclear power and the safe disposal of nuclear wastes. **Environmental chemistry** focuses on the impact of the environment.

Chemistry is put to use in the search for new energy sources, in efforts to fight disease, and in efforts to improve agricultural yields and increase the world's food supply. Chemistry in fact touches many parts of our lives and has been put to use since human history began.

ISAAC ASIMOV
Boston University School of Medicine

See also ATOMS; BIOCHEMISTRY; BODY CHEMISTRY; ELEMENTS, CHEMICAL.

For centuries, alchemists tried to turn common metals into gold. They never succeeded, but in their search they found many new chemicals in their unusual laboratories.

CHEMISTRY, HISTORY OF

Long before the beginning of recorded history, people were making use of chemical changes. When primitive people learned to start a fire, they were making a chemical change: the burning of fuel in air. With fire they could make more chemical changes, such as cooking food or baking pottery.

Somewhere in the Middle East, perhaps around 4000 B.C., people discovered another kind of chemical change. They found that when certain types of rock (called ores) were heated in a wood fire, shiny drops of copper were produced. Copper could be beaten into shape and made into ornaments or other objects. When heated together with tin, a metal mixture—or alloy—was formed. The copper-tin alloy was bronze, and it was much harder than copper alone.

Discoveries of chemical changes in metal were extremely useful to prehistoric people. A bronze shield was much better protection than a leather one. And a bronze-tipped spear was a better weapon or tool than a stone-tipped one. Metal tools made it easier to construct buildings and to kill and butcher animals for food. About 1400 B.C., methods for producing iron were developed in Asia. Iron weapons

and tools proved to be even better than bronze ones.

Despite all these discoveries, ancient people did not understand the chemical changes they were bringing about. By following a "recipe," they could achieve a certain result. But they did not know why the recipes worked over and over again.

▶ GREEK SCIENCE

The Greeks were the first people who tried to make sense out of chemical changes and the first to approach chemistry as a science.

What was the earth made of? What were its elements? These questions fascinated Greek scientists. Around 600 B.C. a Greek named Thales put forward his idea. He thought the whole world was made up of different forms of water. Earth, he said, was hardened water. Air was thinned-out water. This was the first chemical theory in history.

Other Greeks did not agree. For many years they argued. Then around 450 B.C., Empedocles suggested a different theory. He thought that there were four elements: earth, water, air, and fire. At the time this seemed to be right, and the argument stopped.

About 100 years later, Aristotle decided that these four elements made up only the earth itself. He said that the heavens were made up of a fifth element. He called it aether. Belief in these elements of the Greeks lasted more than 2,000 years.

But what were elements made of? Around 400 B.C., Democritus had suggested that everything was made up of tiny particles. These particles were so tiny that they could not be divided up into smaller pieces. So he called them atoms, from a Greek word meaning "something that cannot be cut." Each element, he said, had atoms of a particular shape. Substances were made up of combinations of these atoms. How did one substance change to another? It changed when the atoms were pulled apart and put together in another arrangement.

Democritus was on the right track. But most of the ancient Greeks did not believe him. Aristotle thought atoms could not exist, and his arguments won out. However, people never entirely forgot Democritus' ideas. And more than 2,000 years later, the idea of atoms was to appear again.

▶ALCHEMY

Metalworking continued to be important to ancient civilizations. But it took on new importance when Greek theories mixed with knowledge from Egypt and Mesopotamia.

For instance, Egyptian metalworkers knew how to make imitation gold by mixing copper with other metals. The mixture was not gold, of course, but it had the color of gold. However, a Greek theory said that gold and copper were really made of the same matter. They differed only in their "form." So it followed that one could make gold from copper or even from lead.

Naturally metalworkers began to try to make real gold. This was probably the beginning of a study called *chemia*. Exactly where this word comes from no one knows, but it is the root of our word "chemistry."

As time passed, Arabs conquered Mesopotamia and Egypt and took up the study of *chemia*, which they called *al chemia* (*al* is Arabic for "the"). This expression has come down to us as "alchemy."

The most important Arabian alchemist was Jābir ibn-Hayyān. He lived about A.D. 750 and is also known by the Latin form of his name, Geber. He started the search for a certain dry powder that came to be called the philosopher's stone. We now know there is no such thing, but alchemists believed that the philosopher's stone would turn common metals into valuable gold. They searched for it for hundreds of years.

By the 1100's, Arabian books were reaching Europe. Books on alchemy (and other subjects) were translated into Latin. Europeans then began to search for the philosopher's stone. But European alchemy also bogged down in the search for gold. In fact, so many people pretended they could make gold that "alchemist" came to be another word for "faker."

With all their experimenting, alchemists did make important chemical discoveries. They learned to prepare pure alcohol. They prepared strong acids such as sulfuric acid and nitric acid that could be used to bring about chemical changes never known before. New materials like arsenic, zinc, and bismuth were also studied.

▶THE NEW SPIRIT

In the early 1500's a Swiss doctor named Paracelsus practiced alchemy. But he was not an ordinary alchemist. Paracelsus did not think it was very important to find methods for making gold. He thought alchemists should search for medicines to cure sickness.

Paracelsus has a special value to the history of chemistry. He wanted to end the ancient beliefs and start over. He also wanted to test ideas by experiments. During his time the experimental view slowly took hold.

In the 1580's an Italian scientist named Galileo showed that it was very important to make accurate measurements during experiments. More could be learned in this way than in any other. His work in physics and astronomy helped to establish the principles of modern science.

In England a scientist named Robert Boyle greatly admired Galileo and his precise methods. He set up experiments that would measure things scientifically.

Boyle trapped some air and put it under pressure. If he measured the pressure and then doubled it, the air was forced into half its original space (or volume). If he tripled the pressure, the volume was reduced to a third. This discovery is still called Boyle's law, and with it exact measurement entered the world of chemistry.

Robert Boyle (*left*) was one of the first scientists to use precise measurements and to test new ideas with experiments. Antoine Lavoisier (*right*) helped determine the composition of water by igniting a mixture of hydrogen and oxygen with an electric spark.

In 1661, Boyle published a book that upset the old Greek idea of four or five elements. He offered a new idea based on experiment. If a substance could be divided into simpler parts, it was not an element. (The alloy bronze is an example.) If it could not be divided into simpler parts, it was an element. (Copper and tin are two examples.) The only way to find out was to experiment.

Phlogiston

A German chemist named Georg E. Stahl had an idea, which he advanced around 1700. His idea centered on an invisible substance he called phlogiston. Anything, he said, that contained phlogiston could burn. Wood and coal were full of phlogiston, and so they burned. As they burned, the phlogiston passed out into the air. The ashes that were left behind lacked phlogiston and could burn no more.

Stahl also thought that metals were full of phlogiston. When they rusted, they lost phlogiston to the air. So the rust that was produced lacked phlogiston.

The phlogiston theory seemed to explain how metals were obtained from ore. The phlogiston from burning wood or coal passed into the ore, which is a kind of metal rust. As the phlogiston left the coal or wood, that became ash. As the phlogiston entered the ore, that became metal. There were many things the phlogiston theory could not explain, however, and scientists kept seeking to understand the nature of matter.

The Father of Chemistry

It was a French chemist, Antoine L. Lavoisier, who was able to make sense out of the phlogiston mystery in the 1700's. He insisted that one must measure things as Galileo had done and as Boyle had done. For instance, when wood burned and supposedly lost phlogiston, it lost weight. When metal rusted and lost phlogiston, it gained weight. How could phlogiston bring about a loss sometimes and a gain at other times? Something had to be wrong. The only way to straighten things out was to measure.

Lavoisier heated metal in a closed container. Although the metal rusted, the container and metal did not change in weight. If the metal gained weight as it rusted, then something else in the container must have lost just enough weight to balance the gain. The something else had to be the air in the container. In other words, a metal was not losing phlogiston when it rusted. It was gaining something from the air.

Lavoisier decided that phlogiston could not be involved. Instead, air must be made up of two different gases. The gas in which things burned well he called oxygen. The other gas, in which things did not burn at all, was called nitrogen.

Lavoisier argued that matter is never created or destroyed. It only changes its form. This is the law of conservation of matter.

Lavoisier went on to write the first modern textbook of chemistry. He, along with several others, made up a system for naming chemicals that is still used. The system finally made it possible for chemists to understand each other. For all these deeds Lavoisier has been called the father of chemistry.

▶ THE ATOMIC THEORY

During the 1700's more elements were discovered. Some were metals such as cobalt, nickel, molybdenum, and manganese. The gases called oxygen, nitrogen, and hydrogen were also elements. By 1800 some 30 different elements were known. This raised a problem.

Chemists had to explain why elements remained different. Iron and nickel, for instance, were very similar in a number of ways. Yet one could not be changed entirely into the other. They always stayed a little different.

John Dalton advanced the atomic theory—that all substances are made up of atoms. His experiments showed that each kind of atom had its own unique weight.

In 1803 the British chemist John Dalton advanced an atomic theory. The theory was something like the one put forward by Democritus more than 2,000 years before. But Democritus had only guessed. Dalton had carried out experiments and made measurements.

Dalton said that everything was made of atoms. Each element was made up of a different kind of atom. And one kind of atom could not be changed into another. That was why iron could not be changed into nickel, or lead into gold. All four were elements. Each had its own special kind of atom.

The atoms of different elements, Dalton said, had different weights. Dalton tried to work out the different weights of the atoms (atomic weights), starting with hydrogen as 1.

In the 1820's a Swedish chemist, Jöns Jakob Berzelius, analyzed many substances carefully. He measured exactly how much of each element was present in each substance. From such experiments he calculated quite accurate atomic weights.

Berzelius also suggested that each element be given a chemical symbol. This was usually the initial letter of the name of the element; sometimes a second letter was used, too. That is, the symbol of oxygen is O, while the symbol of aluminum is Al. These symbols could be used to write the formulas of substances. A formula told what atoms combined to make up a particular substance.

The Periodic Table

Chemists were sure that certain substances contained atoms of unknown metals. However, these metal atoms could not be pried loose from oxygen atoms. In 1807 the British chemist Humphry Davy melted such substances. Then he passed an electric current through the hot liquid. This separated the atoms. Davy discovered new metallic elements, such as sodium, potassium, calcium, and magnesium.

More elements were discovered by other methods. Aluminum was discovered, as well as bromine, iodine, selenium, and others. By the 1860's about 60 different elements were known, and there was no sign of an end. How could chemists make sense out of all these elements? Some were metals, and some were gases. Some were hard to combine with other elements, while some were easy. Some were heavy, and some were light.

Chemists tried to arrange the elements in the order of their atomic weights. Perhaps then they could make sense out of the list. The most successful arranger was a Russian chemist, Dmitri I. Mendeleev. In 1869 he arranged the elements in rows and columns. In his arrangement all the elements in a group had similar properties. This is called a periodic table. (You can find the periodic table in the ELEMENTS, CHEMICAL article in Volume E.)

To make the elements fit properly, Mendeleev had to leave some empty places. He announced that these empty places contained elements that had not yet been discovered. He picked three such elements and then figured out what their properties would have to be. In the 1870's and 1880's those three elements were discovered. They matched Mendeleev's predictions exactly. At last the elements were beginning to make sense.

▶ORGANIC CHEMISTRY

Meanwhile chemists had come to realize that chemical substances could be divided into two main classes. Some, such as salt and water, could be heated and neither burn nor change their nature. They might melt or boil, but if cooled down, they were their original selves again. However, substances like sugar and olive oil changed. If heated, they either burned or else charred and gave off vapors. In either case, even gentle heating changed their nature.

Substances like sugar and olive oil contain carbon and come from living or once-living organisms. So in 1807, Berzelius suggested that they be called organic. Substances like salt and water came from the nonliving world. They were inorganic.

At first chemists believed that organic chemicals could be formed only within living creatures. However, in 1828 a German chemist named Friedrich Wöhler showed this was not true. He formed an organic substance (urea) from an inorganic substance (ammonium cyanate), and he did it in a test tube. Through the 1830's and 1840's other organic substances were formed in this way.

From 1860 on, organic chemists began to put atoms together in many ways. They learned to manufacture all sorts of new compounds. Some could be used for dyes, others for explosives, medicines, plastics, fibers—indeed, for almost anything.

Organic chemistry no longer concentrated on compounds formed by living organisms. After all, thousands of organic compounds were being formed and studied. And many of these were never found in living creatures. Organic chemists were content to deal with any compound that contained carbon. Inorganic chemists dealt with all other compounds—those that did not contain carbon.

However, life-chemistry did not lose its importance. A new branch of chemistry was developing. Its interest centered mainly on the chemical changes in living creatures. This was called **biochemistry** (life-chemistry).

▶PHYSICAL CHEMISTRY

As chemistry had been developing, so had the science of physics. Physics deals with various forms of energy, such as heat, light, electricity, and magnetism. From about 1850 on, chemists began to apply the findings of physics to chemistry. In this way, physical chemistry was developed.

For instance, physicists knew what happened if sunlight passed through a prism. It broke up into a series of colors, called a spectrum. In 1859 a German chemist, Gustav R. Kirchhoff, made an interesting discovery. He showed that each element, when heated red hot, produced a spectrum made up of separate lines of color. An instrument called the spectroscope allowed the light of a glowing mineral to shine through a narrow slit. The light was passed through a prism, and then the exact location of the different color lines was measured. Each element had its own pattern of lines. This meant that the different elements in the mineral could be detected.

Unknown elements were located by this method—that is, their color lines revealed them. In 1868, for example, the element helium was located in the sun by a study of the lines in the sun's spectrum. It was not located on earth until 1895.

Two important discoveries made in the late 1800's provided clues to the structure of the atom. In 1896 a French scientist, Antoine Henri Becquerel, discovered that the element uranium gave off a constant stream of electrons and other kinds of intense energy. This energy became known as radioactivity. In 1898 the Polish-born French scientist Marie Curie discovered two more radioactive elements, polonium and radium. The work of

Becquerel and Curie seemed to show that atoms might be made of smaller particles, some of which were electrons.

▶ **MODERN CHEMISTRY**

In 1909 the new picture of the structure of the atom fell into place. The British scientist Ernest Rutherford found that each atom had a nucleus, containing positively charged particles called protons. Outside the nucleus were electrons that were negatively charged. Then in 1914 another British scientist, Henry G. J. Moseley, found that the atoms of each element had a special number of protons in the nucleus. In 1913, Danish scientist Niels Bohr had discovered that the electrons of each atom behaved as though they were arranged in layers. These electron layers determined the chemical properties of the atom.

In the 1940's and 1950's, techniques were found to tap the energy within the nucleus of the atom. This intense nuclear energy was found to be useful both for weapons and for producing electricity. In the late 1960's, scientists began looking more carefully at the energy in the atom. They theorized that a particle smaller than the proton, called the quark, might be the atom's energy source.

In the mid-20th century, scientists found ways to make very pure chemical crystals of germanium and silicon. These crystals could conduct electricity, making it possible to build smaller and faster circuits for computers and other electronic devices. Silicon crystals and other forms of silicon were found to be useful for changing the sun's energy into electricity for powering pocket calculators and orbiting satellites.

Biochemistry became more and more important as its vital role in physiology became known. Newer instruments and techniques enabled scientists to determine the structure of large, complicated protein molecules. Once they knew the structure of these molecules, biochemists could make many chemicals that until then were produced only by living organisms. They were able to make chemicals such as insulin, needed by diabetics.

In recent decades, chemists have discovered ways to use extremely long chains of atoms and molecules (called polymers) for many purposes. They have learned to alter molecules in tiny bacteria and other organisms to change their chemical abilities. Several new atomic elements, not found in nature, have even been formed in research laboratories.

ISAAC ASIMOV
Author, *A Short History of Chemistry*

See also ATOMS; BIOCHEMISTRY; ELEMENTS, CHEMICAL; NUCLEAR ENERGY; PHYSICS.

CHENEY, RICHARD BRUCE. See WYOMING (Famous People).

CHERNENKO, KONSTANTIN (1911–1985)

Konstantin Ustinovich Chernenko served as leader of the Soviet Union from 1984 to 1985. He was born in the village of Bolshaya Tes in Siberia on September 24, 1911. As a youth he worked on a farm. In 1931 he joined the Communist Party and began his rapid advance through its ranks. He became friendly with Leonid Brezhnev, who later became the leader of the Soviet Union. As Brezhnev's career flourished, so did Chernenko's.

When Brezhnev became president of the Soviet Union in 1960, Chernenko moved closer to the center of power. In 1964, Brezhnev was named general secretary of the Communist Party. Chernenko became a member of the Central Committee of the party in 1971. In 1978 he was raised to full membership in the Politburo, the small group within the Central Committee that actually ruled the Soviet Union. Brezhnev wanted Chernenko to succeed him as head of the party. But when Brezhnev died in 1982, party leaders chose Yuri Andropov as general secretary. In February 1984, after only 15 months in office, Andropov died. Chernenko was then chosen general secretary of the party, and later, president of the Soviet Union.

Chernenko made several important decisions, including renewing arms control talks with the United States in 1985. But Chernenko was in his 70's and in poor health, and his own term as Soviet leader was to be short. He died on March 10, 1985, and was succeeded by Mikhail Gorbachev, who began the reforms that led to the breakup of the Soviet Union.

RONALD GRIGOR SUNY
University of Michigan

CHERRY. See PEACH, PLUM, AND CHERRY.

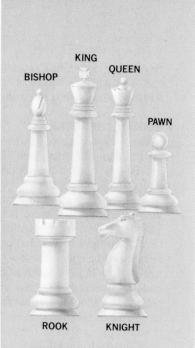

Chess is a game of mental skill enjoyed by people of all ages. The two players move chessmen, or chess pieces, on a checkered board of 64 squares.

CHESS

Chess is the most popular war game ever invented. The kings and queens who lead the two chess armies must face all kinds of dangerous situations. They are attacked and defended by castles, bishops, knights on horseback, and common soldiers. Eventually one of the kings is trapped and he must surrender to the other army. Every new game of chess is a different battle, and the two players are the generals who plan the battle.

Since its origin in India and Persia more than 13 centuries ago, chess, the "royal game," has provided many exciting hours of play for both children and adults.

The word "chess" is derived from the Persian word *shah,* which means "king." The term "checkmate," signifying that the enemy king is threatened and cannot be saved, can be traced to an Arabic phrase, *shah mat,* which means "the king is dead."

Many English words that are used in the game of chess, like "checkmate," "stalemate," "pawn," and "gambit," have become important words in our everyday language.

Chess is popular in Russia and other republics that made up the former Soviet Union. Chess heroes there are as famous as baseball heroes are in the United States. Russian masters have won many world championships since the end of World War II.

Even though many people think that chess is very complicated, its rules are really easier to learn than the rules of many other indoor games. Almost all the world's great players— the international grandmasters of chess— learned the moves and were strong players before they were 16. Bobby Fischer, an international grandmaster and world champion, won his first title as United States champion when he was only 14 years old. Among the youngest grandmasters in chess history is Hungarian Peter Leko, who became a grandmaster at age fourteen.

Chess can be played at a variety of speeds. Youngsters as well as masters often enjoy playing at "lightning" speed, allowing only 1 to 10 seconds for each move. Under these regulations, most games are completed within 15 minutes. Friendly games between amateurs of equal strength, played with no specific time limit, usually last about an hour. In international and world title competition, there are automatic clocks that control the amount of time taken by each player. These serious matches normally last about 4 hours.

The Fédération Internationale des Echecs (FIDE) is the worldwide organization of chess players. It has members from more than 100 countries, as far apart as Australia and Iceland, or the Philippines and Tunisia. The

United States Chess Federation (USCF) controls chess rules and activities in the United States.

There are tournaments in different sections of the United States and Canada almost every weekend. These events are ordinarily open to anyone who wishes to play, regardless of age or playing experience. Most of these tournaments are rated by the USCF according to a numerical system, and everyone who enters receives a national rating that depends on his or her performance in that tournament. Thousands of active chess players hold national USCF ratings, and every year hundreds of newcomers are added to the list. Usually there are about 400 players who hold the rank of either senior master or master. Many more players have lower ratings, which range from expert down to classes A, B, C, etc.

▶ THE RULES OF CHESS

The rules of chess have been a subject for special study by mathematicians, military strategists, psychologists, and even by designers of modern electronic computers.

The Pieces

There are two opposing sides in chess, one consisting of light-colored (white) pieces and the other of dark-colored (black) pieces. Each side has sixteen pieces. The eight more important of these pieces are the king, the queen, two rooks (or castles), two bishops, and two knights. The other eight pieces in each army are the pawns.

The Board

The chessboard is the same as the checkerboard. It has 64 squares, 32 light-colored (white) and 32 dark-colored (black). All 64 squares are used in playing chess.

The board is always placed so that the first row ends with a white square on each player's right. The eight rows that run vertically between the two players are called **files.** The eight horizontal rows that run from left to right are called **ranks.** Straight lines of the same-colored squares running in a slantwise direction are called **diagonals.**

Setting Up the Board

At the start of a game, the two rooks occupy the extreme right and left squares of the first rank; the two knights stand next to the rooks; the two bishops are placed next to the knights; the queen is "on her color" (that is, the white queen on a white square and the black queen on a black square); and the king stands on the one remaining square along the first rank. When you set up the pieces in this way, the white queen will be on the same file as the black queen, and the white king on the same file as the black king. The pawns are then lined up in the rank directly in front of the more important pieces.

The Moves of the Pieces

Much of the variety and excitement of chess is due to the fact that each type of piece moves in a different manner. You should become very familiar with the moves of each piece before you try to play an actual game.

The King. Although the king is the most important piece in chess and must always be protected from capture, he is not the most powerful and active piece on the board. The king may move only to a square that touches the one on which he stands. Thus, in the diagram on the following page, the king on square A can move to any one of eight different squares, whereas the king on square B can move only to one of three different squares.

A chessboard is always placed so that each player has a light square at the nearest right-hand corner. Each player begins with 16 pieces, set up as shown. The queen sits on a square of her own color at the beginning of the game.

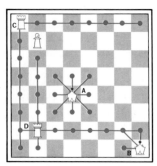

Moves of the king and moves of the rook.

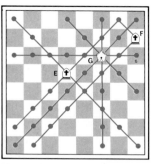

Moves of the bishop and moves of the queen.

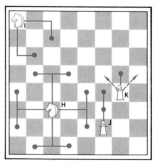

Moves of the knight and pawn. The V-shaped capture.

The Rook. The chess castle can move any number of squares left or right along an unblocked rank or up and down an unblocked file. In the diagram the rook on square C can move to and stop on any one of 14 different squares. The rook on square D, however, has a choice among only 12, since the white pawn blocks its movement farther along the file.

The Bishop. The bishop may move any number of squares along an unblocked diagonal. Therefore, a bishop that starts a game on a black square will remain on the black squares throughout the game. In the diagram the bishop on square E can move to any one of 13 squares, and the bishop on square F to any one of seven.

The Queen. The queen is the most powerful of all the pieces. She can move horizontally, vertically, or diagonally any number of squares along a line that is not blocked. In other words the queen combines the moves of the rook and bishop. In the diagram the queen on square G can move to any one of 25 squares.

The Knight. The horse-shaped knight is the favorite piece of many players because of its very mysterious way of moving. The knight's move will remind you of the letter L: it moves two squares in either a horizontal or vertical direction and then one square in the other direction. The knight on square H in the diagram can move to any one of eight squares; the knight on square I to only one of two. A knight standing on a white square always ends up on a black square after its move, and vice versa. Unlike the other pieces, the knight can jump over pieces between its original square and the square to which it moves. However, it can capture only enemy pieces that are standing on the square it finally lands on.

The Pawn. Because pawns are so weak, you may not pay much attention to them. But they are really very important. A lowly pawn may often rise to higher rank in the chess army.

The pawn may move one or two squares straight ahead on its first move, as illustrated by the pawn on square J in the diagram. Once it has made its first move, however, it can advance only one square at a time. The pawn, unlike the other pieces, can only move forward. Also, unlike the other pieces, which capture enemy pieces in the same way as they regularly move, a pawn may only capture an enemy piece that stands one square in front of it in a diagonal direction (the V-shaped capture), as shown by the pawn on square K.

If two opposing pawns block each other's advance on the same file, neither pawn can move or capture the other. If a pawn manages to reach the other side of the board (the eighth rank), it must be promoted immediately (as part of the same move) to any stronger piece except the king. Since the queen is the most powerful of the pieces, pawns that reach the eighth rank are almost always replaced by queens. It is therefore possible for a player to have nine queens at the same time—the original queen and eight others resulting from pawn promotions—but of course this does not happen very often.

Capturing

A chess piece captures an enemy piece by moving onto the square occupied by that enemy piece. The enemy piece is removed from the board, and the capturing piece replaces it on that square. Two pieces can never occupy the same square. A player is not forced to capture an enemy piece unless there is no other legal move to make.

Play and the Object of the Game

White always starts the game by moving one of his pieces—usually a pawn, in order to open up diagonals and files for the stronger pieces behind the pawns. Then black makes a move. From then on the players continue to alternate moves until the game is over. No player is permitted to let a turn pass. The player must make a move.

The goal of the game is to trap the opponent's king so that he cannot avoid capture. Whenever one of the players threatens to capture an opponent's king, the player calls "Check!" A king that is checked must be guarded from this threat at once in one of three ways: (1) by moving the king to another square where he cannot be captured by any enemy piece, (2) by capturing the piece that threatens the king, or (3) by placing another piece between the king and the enemy piece that is giving check. It is against the rules to ignore a check or to place a king where he can be captured. Therefore, a king is never really captured, and always remains on the board until the game ends. The game ends when a king is in check and there is no way for him to avoid capture. This is called **checkmate,** and it means victory for the other player.

When one player has secured a large advantage—for example, by capturing the opponent's queen without losing an important piece in exchange—it usually will be easy to corner the opponent's king and eventually checkmate him. That is why many players will resign (surrender before checkmate) if they are far behind in pieces or in position.

Drawn Games

A game is called a draw (tie) if any one of the following occurs: (1) Both players agree to a draw during the game (in some competitions, the players must each make at least 30 moves before they may agree to draw). (2) Neither player has enough pieces left for a possible checkmate (for example, only the two kings remain on the board or one player has a king and a bishop or knight against the opponent's king). (3) One player, whose turn it is to play, has no legal move and is not in check. This is called **stalemate** (note the difference between checkmate and stalemate—after checkmate the player also has no legal move, but his or her king is in check). (4) The same position is repeated three times during a game, with the same player about to move. (5) One player can prove that the opponent's king can be checked endlessly (perpetual check); this rule usually reduces to rule "4" above, where the same position is repeated three times or more. (6) Neither side has made a capture or moved a pawn for the last 50 moves.

Special Rules

Castling. There is only one situation in chess when you can move two pieces simultaneously. This is a special move involving only the king and rook. If (1) the king and a rook have not yet moved during the game, and (2) the squares between the king and this rook are unoccupied, and (3) the king is not in check, and (4) the king will not have to move across a square threatened by an enemy piece, then the king may be moved two squares toward the rook, and the rook (as part of the same move) placed on the square directly on the other side of the king. It is possible to castle on the kingside (where only two squares separate the king and rook) or on the queenside (where three squares separate the king and rook). Each player can castle only once during a single game. Castling normally occurs early in the game, and it is usually done to place the king in a safer position.

En Passant. *En passant* (French for "in passing") is a special way of capturing with a pawn. It occurs very rarely. If a pawn has reached its fifth rank, and an enemy pawn

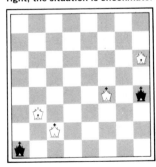

At lower left, a stalemate. At right, the situation is checkmate.

Castling kingside (*right*); castling queenside (*left*).

The rare opportunity to capture *en passant.*

advancing two squares on its first move passes a square on which it could have been captured in the usual V-shaped way by the pawn on the fifth rank, then the pawn on the fifth rank may capture the advancing pawn as if it had moved only one square forward on its first move. This capture must be made on the very next move. If not taken advantage of immediately, the opportunity to capture *en passant* is lost.

▶CHESS NOTATION

Every game of chess can be recorded in the form of a code, so that after the game is over, it can be studied by the players or by other interested people. World-championship games are often published in newspapers in this code, and all chess books use it to record the moves. You will need to know chess notation if you decide to read some of the many books written about chess strategy and chess heroes.

In this code every piece has a letter symbol: K—king, Q—queen, R—rook, N—knight (Kt is sometimes used as the symbol for knight, but since it can be confused with K, N is preferred), B—bishop, and P—pawn. The pieces on the kingside of the board at the start of a game are called the KR (king's rook), KN (king's knight), and KB (king's bishop). Those on the queenside are the QR (queen's rook), QN (queen's knight), and QB (queen's bishop). Each pawn is identified by the piece that stands behind it at the start of the game (KP is the king's pawn, QRP the queen's rook pawn). The files are also given the name of the piece that stands on that file at the beginning of the game (for example, the QR file). The ranks are numbered 1 through 8. Rank 1 for white is rank 8 for black, and vice versa. Each square is identified by its rank and file. For example, the first square on the queen's rook file, from white's side of the board, is called QR1 for white and QR8 for black. The diagram shows the numbering of the squares from white's side of the board.

A move is recorded by identifying the piece moved (K,Q,R,N,B, or P), following it with a hyphen (-), and then naming the square on which it has been placed. Thus, "P-QR4" means "a pawn has moved to the fourth square on the queen's rook file," and "R-Q4" means "a rook has moved to the fourth square on the queen file." A capture is noted by "x"; therefore "RxB" means "rook captures bishop." Castling kingside is written "O-

QR8	QN8	QB8	Q8	K8	KB8	KN8	KR8
QR7	QN7	QB7	Q7	K7	KB7	KN7	KR7
QR6	QN6	QB6	Q6	K6	KB6	KN6	KR6
QR5	QN5	QB5	Q5	K5	KB5	KN5	KR5
QR4	QN4	QB4	Q4	K4	KB4	KN4	KR4
QR3	QN3	QB3	Q3	K3	KB3	KN3	KR3
QR2	QN2	QB2	Q2	K2	KB2	KN2	KR2
QR1	QN1	QB1	Q1	K1	KB1	KN1	KR1

Chess players can study past games of great masters through the use of a code called chess notation. The above notation is from white's side of the board only.

O," and castling queenside, "O-O-O." *En passant* is written "PxP e.p." "Check" is usually abbreviated "ch."

Here are two very short games of chess. See if you can replay these games using the code described above. First set up the pieces in their starting positions and then make the following moves. Don't forget that white always moves first. To determine who plays white, one player hides a white pawn in one fist and a black pawn in the other. The opponent chooses one fist and plays that color. The number of the move is given before each notation of white and black moves.

GAME 1		
Move Number	White	Black
1.	P-KN4	P-K4
2.	P-KB4	Q-R5 chmate

GAME 2		
Move Number	White	Black
1.	P-K4	P-K4
2.	B-QB4	B-QB4
3.	Q-R5	N-KB3
4.	QxKBP chmate	

▶OTHER SUGGESTIONS AND RULES

The queen is the most powerful piece and is about nine times stronger than a pawn. If the queen is given the value of 9, then the next strongest piece (the rook) is worth about 5. The bishops and knights are worth about 3½ each. The pawn is worth only 1. From these figures you can see that two bishops (7 points) are worth more than a rook (5 points), and that two rooks (10 points) are worth more than a queen (9 points). You should always calculate these values before exchanging any of your pieces for one of your opponent's. Incidentally, the king is not given a numerical value because the king can never be captured or exchanged.

If you touch a piece without having stated beforehand that you are only adjusting its position on a square (by saying "I adjust," or the French phrase "*J'adoube*"), then you must move it. If you touch an enemy piece, then you must capture it if you can do so legally. You cannot take back a legal move and make another once you have removed your hand from the piece. It is a good idea to follow these rules strictly because you will learn much faster if you do not take moves back. Also, your opponent will not like it very much if you take back a move after he or she has made the next move and given away a strategy, or plan.

As soon as you have learned the moves and played a few games, it would be a good idea to join a chess club in your town or school. You can improve in chess most quickly by playing with opponents who are equal to or better than you. So do not play only with those whom you always beat.

ELIOT HEARST
Captain, 1962 U.S. Chess Olympiad Team
Reviewed by BOBBY FISCHER
International Grandmaster
and World Chess Champion

CHIANG KAI-SHEK (1887–1975)

Chiang Kai-shek led the Chinese people through eight years of war against Japan and was elected China's first constitutional president in 1948. Although he was forced to retreat to Taiwan when the Chinese Communists gained control of the mainland in 1949, Chiang never abandoned his claim to be the legal ruler of all China. He headed the Nationalist government on Taiwan until his death.

Chiang was born into a merchant family in Chekiang Province on October 31, 1887. He received military training in China and Japan. At the age of 20, he joined Sun Yat-sen's revolutionary National People's Party, or Kuomintang, usually called the Nationalist Party. Chiang participated in the 1911 revolution that overthrew the 267-year-old Manchu dynasty and established the Chinese Republic. In 1924 he became head of the Whampoa Military Academy, where many of China's future military leaders were trained.

After Sun's death in 1925, there was a struggle for leadership of the party. Chiang had the support of some of Sun's friends and relatives. (In 1927 he married Mayling Soong, a sister-in-law of Sun.) Through a combination of political alliances and military victories, Chiang was able to become president of a new Nationalist government in Nanking in 1928. He was forced to resign as president in 1931, but he remained powerful. He built a modern army and led the fight against the Chinese Communists, who had established a separate military base in southeastern China. By 1935, Chiang had managed to drive the Communists into remote northwestern China.

In 1937 the second Sino-Japanese War began. The Japanese invasion of China forced Chiang to form a united front with the Communists. Under Chiang's leadership, China fought the Japanese alone until 1941, when the United States entered World War II. China then became one of the Allied nations, and Chiang was appointed supreme commander of the Allied air and land forces in China.

The struggle for power between Chiang and the Communists had been overshadowed by the war with Japan. After the Japanese surrender in 1945, negotiations between Chiang and the Communists failed, and civil war broke out. By this time the Chinese people were weary of war, and Chiang had lost much of his popular support. He tried to respond to his critics by making his government more democratic. In 1948, under a new constitution, he was chosen president by an elected national assembly. But he lost to the Communists and fled to Taiwan in 1949. There he headed the Nationalist government until his death on April 5, 1975. Under his leadership, Taiwan began a period of rapid economic growth.

Reviewed by SAMUEL C. CHU
Ohio State University

See also SUN YAT-SEN.

CHICAGO

Chicago—the Windy City—is located in northeastern Illinois along the southwestern shore of Lake Michigan. It is the third largest city in the United States (after New York and Los Angeles) and ranks among the major metropolitan centers of the world in terms of industry, commerce, transportation, education, and culture.

Approximately 2.8 million people live in the city of Chicago, which is also the seat of Cook County. The greater metropolitan area, covering nine counties, is home to more than 7.5 million.

Downtown Chicago has two well-known sections, the Lake Shore area and the Loop. The Lake Shore has many lovely parks and impressive buildings, including three of the nation's tallest buildings—the Amoco Building, the John Hancock Center, and the Sears Tower, which until 1996 was the tallest building in the world. The Loop, the commercial heart of the city, is so named because of the elevated trains that encircle the area.

▶ LAND

The city proper covers 228 square miles (591 square kilometers). The Chicago River divides the city into three sections—the North Side, South Side, and West Side. The river once emptied into Lake Michigan, but in 1900, engineers reversed its flow into Chicago's canal system to stop sewage from entering the lake. Ever since, it has been known as the River That Flows Backward.

▶ PEOPLE

The population of Chicago is ethnically and racially diverse. In the 1800's, most residents were immigrants from Germany, Poland, and Italy. But today the city's population is approximately 40 percent African American, 20 percent Hispanic, and 4 percent Asian.

Education and Libraries

Chicago has long been a leader in education. The city supports a two-year college system and is also the home of more than two dozen colleges and universities. Among the best known are the University of Chicago, the Illinois Institute of Technology, Chicago State University, and the Chicago campuses of the University of Illinois. DePaul University and Loyola University of Chicago are among several of the city's Roman Catholic and theological schools. Northwestern University is in suburban Evanston. Several of the universities have large medical schools and hospitals.

Museums and the Arts

Chicagoans have access to a great variety of cultural activities and institutions. The Chicago Symphony Orchestra is one of the finest in the world. The Art Institute of

Chicago's impressive skyline is dominated by the Sears Tower, the nation's tallest building. Lakefront parks provide a welcome escape from the bustle of city life.

Chicago, located in Grant Park, houses a world-famous collection of French paintings. Other attractions in Grant Park include the John G. Shedd Aquarium, the Adler Planetarium, and the Field Museum of Natural History. The Museum of Science and Industry, in Jackson Park, has many popular exhibits.

Parks

Chicago has more than 500 parks, covering 6,841 acres (2,736 hectares). Lincoln Park, the largest, features several beaches along the North Side lakefront and also contains the Lincoln Park Zoo. Other notable lakefront parks are Grant, Burnham, and Jackson. Forestlands are preserved in many areas along the city's west side.

Sports

Chicago supports numerous professional sports teams. The Chicago Bulls of the National Basketball Association play in the United Center, as do the Chicago Blackhawks of the National Hockey League. The Chicago Bears of the National Football League play in Soldier Field. The Chicago Cubs of baseball's National League play in Wrigley Field, while the Chicago White Sox of the American League play in Comiskey Park.

▶ ECONOMY

The Chicago metropolitan area is one of the nation's leading industrial centers. Chief products include electrical equipment and machinery, canned and frozen foods, chemicals, and printed materials. The Chicago area also has the largest capacity in the world for producing steel and fabricated metal products. Most of the iron and steel mills are in east and south Chicago and along the lakefront in nearby Indiana.

Chicago is also a world center of commerce and finance. Much of the wholesale trade of the Midwest originates there. The Chicago Board of Trade is the center of grain-trading activities. The Chicago Mercantile Exchange is the largest exchange for perishable goods, such as eggs and cattle, in the world. The Chicago Stock Exchange is the nation's second largest securities market, after the New York Stock Exchange. Chicago's large convention halls and hotels accommodate the many trade and business conventions held in the city each year.

Exhibits at Chicago's Museum of Science and Industry help people understand the basic principles of science and the uses of science in industry.

Transportation

Chicago lies at the heart of a vast transportation network. It is one of the world's largest and busiest railroad and trucking centers. A huge volume of freight passes through the area each day. Commuter railroads and bus lines carry thousands of people between the city and suburbs. Airliners from all over the world land at O'Hare International Airport, the world's busiest air terminal. Chicago Midway Airport and Meigs Field also handle air traffic.

Chicago is the only inland port city in the United States connected by water to both the Atlantic Ocean and the Gulf of Mexico. Vessels from the Atlantic pass through the St. Lawrence River and the Great Lakes into Chicago. Barges from the Gulf coast reach Chicago by way of the Mississippi River, the Illinois Waterway, and the Chicago Canal System.

Communication

Chicago's three daily newspapers, the *Chicago Tribune*, the *Chicago Sun-Times*, and the *Chicago Daily Defender*, have a com-

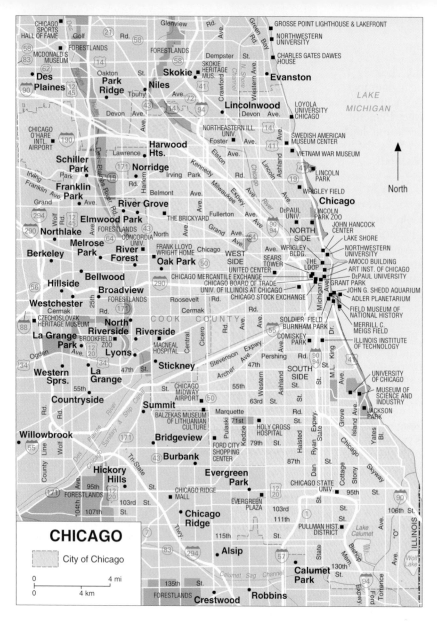

CHICAGO

City of Chicago

0   4 mi

0   4 km

down the Chicago River into Lake Michigan. They were the first Europeans to pass through the area now called Chicago.

A small French trading post was in existence at the southern end of Lake Michigan throughout the 1700's. In 1795 the Potawatomi Indians gave a tract of land near the mouth of the Chicago River to the newly formed United States. Captain John Whistler was sent by the U.S. government to take charge of the new land. He built Fort Dearborn in 1803. But in 1812 it was destroyed and the settlers were killed in an Indian uprising. Fort Dearborn was rebuilt four years later.

Chicago was incorporated as a town in 1833, with a population of a few hundred. Within four years the population had grown to over 4,000, and Chicago became a small city. Farmers in the eastern states and immigrants from Europe were flocking to the wide prairies of northern Illinois and southern Wisconsin.

In 1848 the Illinois and Michigan Canal was completed, connecting the Illinois River with the Chicago River and Lake Michigan. The first train entered Chicago the same year. Canals and railroads ensured the future growth of the city. By the 1850's, Chicago had become the railroad center of the country and the largest market for grain, cattle, and lumber in the United States.

A great fire started on the night of October 8, 1871, and burned for 27 hours. More than 17,000 buildings were destroyed, and thousands of people were left homeless. There is a legend that the fire was started when a cow owned by a Mrs. O'Leary kicked over a kerosene lantern. But the actual cause of the fire is unknown. The city was almost

bined circulation of more than 1.3 million copies. The city also has many commercial and public television and radio stations.

▶ GOVERNMENT

Chicago is governed by a mayor and a city council of fifty aldermen, all elected to 4-year terms. Other elected officials include a city treasurer and city clerk. City department heads, such as the police, school, and fire commissioners, are appointed by the mayor.

▶ HISTORY

In 1673 two French explorers, Father Jacques Marquette and Louis Jolliet, paddled

Famous People

Alphonse (Al) Capone (1899–1947), born in Brooklyn, New York, became the most infamous of American gangsters. Known as Scarface Al, he settled in Chicago and made millions during the prohibition years of the 1920's dealing in liquor and other illegal goods. Capone was said to be responsible for the notorious St. Valentine's Day Massacre of seven rival gang members in 1929. He was finally arrested in 1931 on charges of income tax evasion and imprisoned for eight years, after which he retired to Florida.

Richard J. Daley (1902–76), born in Chicago, served six terms as mayor of Chicago, from 1955 until his death. A lawyer, Daley was admitted to the bar in 1933, later serving in the state legislature (1936–46). As mayor he became one of the most powerful Democrats in the country, acting as an adviser to Presidents John Kennedy and Lyndon Johnson. Considered the last of the old-time big city political bosses, Daley virtually ruled Democratic politics in Illinois for more than twenty years. His son, **Richard M. Daley** (1942–), has served as mayor of Chicago since 1989. Another son, **William M. Daley** (1948–), became secretary of commerce in 1997 under President Bill Clinton.

Jean Baptiste Point Du Sable (1745–1818), probably born in Haiti, was an early black pioneer. About 1779, Du Sable built a cabin and trading post on the north

Lorraine Hansberry

Richard J. Daley

bank of the Chicago River, where he ran a profitable business trading with the Indians. He is the first known person to settle where Chicago now stands.

Marshall Field (1834–1906), a prominent merchant and philanthropist, was born near Conway, Massachusetts. In 1856, he went to Chicago to work as a clerk, and within eight years he had become head of his own department store, which became Marshall Field and Company in 1881. An innovator in merchandising, Field stocked goods on an enormous scale, and the store itself occupied an entire city block. Field made large gifts to the University of Chicago and founded the Field Museum of Natural History (1893). His grandson, **Marshall Field III** (1893–1956), born in Chicago, founded the *Chicago Sun* newspaper (1941), which later merged into the *Chicago Sun-Times* (1948). He also founded the Field Foundation (1940) to fund social welfare and educational programs.

Lorraine Vivian Hansberry (1930–65), an influential playwright, was born in Chicago. In 1959 she received the New York Drama Critics Circle Award for her first play, *A Raisin in the Sun*, about the struggles and dreams of a black family living in Chicago. It was the first work by an African American to be produced on Broadway. After her untimely death, Hansberry's writings were compiled in the publication *To Be Young, Gifted and Black* (1969).

Michael Jeffrey Jordan (1963–), born in Brooklyn, New York, is widely considered the greatest basketball player of all time. In the 1990's, Jordan led the Chicago Bulls to six NBA championships. He has served as spokesperson for a wide variety of commercial products, and in 1996 he starred as himself in the movie *Space Jam*. Jordan retired from basketball in 1999. For more information, see the article BASKETBALL (Great Players).

Allan Pinkerton (1819–84), born in Glasgow, Scotland, settled in Chicago, where in 1850 he founded one of the first professional detective agencies in the United States. In 1861 he escorted newly elected President Abraham Lincoln from Springfield, Illinois, to Washington, D.C., and later became chief of the first federal secret service program. His employees, known as Pinkerton Men, often were hired by large corporations to help break up labor strikes, including Chicago's famous Pullman Strike (1894).

---

entirely rebuilt within two years. By 1890, Chicago was second only to New York City as the largest manufacturing city in the United States. Two world's fairs were held in Chicago—the World's Columbian Exposition in 1893 and the Century of Progress Exposition in 1933–34.

During its history, Chicago has witnessed much controversy. In the late 1800's, the city's industrial growth made it a hotbed for labor unrest, especially with the Haymarket Riot (1886) and the Pullman Strike (1894). In the 1920's, Chicago became associated with the criminal activities of the notorious gangster Al Capone. In 1942, during World War II, the physicist Enrico Fermi produced the first nuclear chain reaction of atomic energy in a laboratory on the campus of the University

of Chicago. And in 1968, Chicago police were denounced for their brutal handling of race rioters and anti–Vietnam War demonstrators at the Democratic National Convention.

Chicago has also been the target of much criticism over its deteriorating public housing facilities and drug-plagued neighborhoods. But in recent years, many of the old high-rise buildings have been torn down and replaced with smaller family-housing units. Other urban renewal projects included the 1995 development of the Navy Pier into an attractive recreational center.

JAMES E. PATTERSON
Illinois State University

CHICKEN POX. See DISEASES (Descriptions of Some Diseases).

CHICKENS. See POULTRY.

CHILD ABUSE

Child abuse is the mistreatment of infants, children, and adolescents by their parents or other caretakers. Countless numbers of children are abused around the world every day. It is estimated that in the United States, one in every 100 children is abused or neglected, and that 2,000 of these children die each year. Children of any age can be victims of child abuse. Those below the age of 3 are at the greatest risk.

Cases of child abuse often go unreported. Sometimes abused children say nothing because they feel that they are the cause of problems in the family and deserve to be punished. Other children feel that they should suffer in silence, to get their parents' love. But child abuse is not the fault of the child, nor does the child deserve punishment. Recently enormous interest in preventing child abuse has developed, and more cases are being reported. There are many sources of help for abused children.

▶ TYPES OF CHILD ABUSE

Child abuse can be mild or severe. It may consist of any of the following types of abuse or a combination of several types.

Physical abuse is intentional injury. The child may have bruises, burns, broken bones, or injuries to the head. The term "battered child" describes a child with many such injuries in different parts of the body.

Sexual abuse is the sexual molestation of a child by an older person. There is increasing awareness of this problem. In most cases the molesters are friends, neighbors, or relatives of the child.

Nutritional deprivation occurs when food or drink is not given to children, so that they do not grow and thrive properly.

Emotional deprivation occurs when a child is constantly rejected and "picked on." The child feels threatened and does not get the love and understanding that she or he deserves.

Parental neglect refers to situations in which parents do not give their children the right food, clothing, shelter, medical care, and protection from accidents.

▶ CAUSES OF CHILD ABUSE

Adults who abuse children come from all parts of society—from different ethnic, geographic, religious, educational, and economic groups. It is difficult to understand why these adults use violence against children or why they fail to love and protect them.

Many of these adults were abused as children themselves. They are immature, unstable, lonely, and unloved. They cannot control their violent outbursts, and they repeat what was done to them in the past. They may want to give the love that they did not get as children but they are unable to do so. The child may be both loved and hated, which confuses the child.

Adults who abuse children often treat one child as a favorite and think of another as "bad." Eventually the child thought of as bad does something wrong out of frustration. The child is hoping for love instead of punishment. But the parents use this to convince themselves that they were right all along.

Certain situations increase the risk of child abuse. These situations are unemployed parents, financial difficulty, a poor relationship between the parents, parents who drink too much alcohol ŏr who use drugs, and single parents who are overwhelmed by their responsibilities. These problems cause stress and tension, which is sometimes expressed in neglect or violence toward the children.

▶ TREATMENT

Every state in the United States has laws that require doctors, nurses, and social workers to report suspected cases of child abuse. Other people may report child abuse, too. Children who are victims of child abuse, or witness another child being abused, should tell an adult they can trust—a family member, a teacher, a guidance counselor, or a neighbor.

Children's protective services and family courts are available to help abused children and their families. In cases of severe child abuse, a child may be temporarily removed from the home for safety and psychological help.

Parents who abuse children need help, too. They can get it through therapy, which can give support and teach them to be better parents. There are also self-help groups for these parents, such as Parents Anonymous.

SUBHASH C. INAMDAR, M.D.
New York University School of Medicine

SARLA INAMDAR, M.D.
New York Medical College

Children grow and develop in a sequence of changes from infancy through adolescence. Motor skills needed to reach out for objects are learned early. As children develop strength and co-ordination, they are able to climb a jungle gym. Throughout childhood, youngsters develop intellectual and social skills as they become independent and prepare for adulthood.

CHILD DEVELOPMENT

The human infant is a very special person. Most infants are born with the potential to develop through childhood and adolescence into healthy, productive adults. Every person is unique in the way he or she develops. Many special characteristics make each individual different from everyone else. But we are all members of the human race, and that makes us similar in many ways.

It is the balance of these similarities and differences that makes child development an important field of study. Parents are always interested in the processes of growing up. But specialists in many fields—doctors, nurses, psychologists, teachers—study how children change as they develop into adults.

These specialists have learned that children pass through many developmental stages. These changes usually occur at about the same age in each child. Thus 2-year-old children are much the same as one another, but they are different from 3-year-old children.

Many different factors can influence a child's development, however. While some experiences help to further development, others can delay progress. It is important to understand what some of these influencing factors are.

▶ INFLUENCES ON CHILD DEVELOPMENT

The two major factors that influence child development are **genetics** and the **environment.** Genetic factors are those traits passed on to the unborn baby by the parents. The environment is the world around us. Scientists have long argued whether genetic traits or the environment is more important in the development of people. It is now believed that both factors are important in the complex process of human growth.

Genetics

What role does genetics play in child development? Mothers and fathers give an equal amount of genetic factors (**chromosomes**) to each child. The ovum, or egg, from the mother has 23 chromosomes. The ovum is joined by the sperm from the father, which also has 23 chromosomes. Together, the ovum and sperm form the beginnings of a new baby, who has 46 chromosomes. The genetic factors determine the baby's hair, eye color, and body size and build and contribute to personality, or temperament. Because mothers and fathers both contribute an equal number of chromosomes, each is equally important in the development of the new baby. However, mothers have another valuable role. The mother's body is the unborn baby's first environment.

Environment

The unborn baby (also called a **fetus**) grows and develops in a special organ in the mother's body called the **uterus.** During the 9 months of pregnancy, the baby is protected in the environment within the mother's body. It is important that a pregnant mother keep her body safe and healthy for her unborn baby. She must eat a balanced diet and get plenty of rest and fresh air. Doctors and other health professionals have learned that many factors that affect the health of the mother also affect the health of her growing baby. Cigarette smoking and a poor diet can cause the baby to be smaller than normal. Excessive use of alcohol or drugs can change the development of the baby's brain. Even tension and worry in the mother can be transmitted to the baby. Good health during pregnancy is an important beginning for the human infant.

From birth through adulthood, a baby's genetic potential can be changed by the environment in helpful or harmful ways. The environment may be thought of as all of the people and things with which a child comes in contact. The first major environmental influence after birth is the baby's **home and family.** Mothers and fathers are usually the first important people in a young person's life. The mother, who has already had a special relationship with the baby during pregnancy, continues to be of prime importance during the early years. Fathers also have a special relationship with their children. They care for and play with infants in unique ways that are different from those of mothers. Each parent provides a balance in childcare.

Some children have mothers and fathers living in the same home, whereas many others live with only one parent. There may be brothers and sisters, grandparents, or other relatives in the family. Every child grows and learns about life through the family environment.

Another part of the environment is the **community.** A child's neighborhood, day-care center or school, parks, and stores all form the community. The people in this environment are friends and neighbors, teachers, babysitters, police officers, fire fighters, and many others. Children learn about life and their world through contact and friendships with all of these people. The most important people outside the family are usually friends and teachers at day-care and school.

A third part of the environment is the **country** in which the child lives. Each country is made up of a group of people, with their own language, culture, and customs. In countries all over the world, children are growing and learning about life and the world around them. Because life is different in each country, and even from one community to the next, the lessons the children learn are different.

Most children in the world live in poverty. Many of the lessons they learn are about how to get food and survive. Societies in which people have enough food to eat, schools to attend, and good health care are called affluent societies. Children in these societies do not have to worry about their own hunger. Their survival is taught in terms of using seat belts in the car, being very cautious of strangers, not playing with matches, and other safety lessons.

Each of the lessons learned by children all over the world helps the process of growth and development. In order to appreciate what children in different parts of the world are learning, it is necessary to understand their environment. It is also necessary to understand what normal development is.

▶ WHAT IS NORMAL DEVELOPMENT?

Scientists who study child development apply three criteria, or standards, to assess developmental changes. The first criterion is that the change seen is orderly. The second is that the change is long-lasting. The third is that the new level of ability is more advanced than the old level.

Normal child development can be thought of as occurring along set pathways, or developmental lines. There are five major kinds of development—physical development, motor development, language development, development of thought and ideas, and social development. Some children develop faster and some slower, but most grow along these lines at about the same rate.

A baby is born ready to do some amazing things. The soft skin, fuzzy hair, tiny fingers, and beautiful movements of babies make adults and children want to pick them up and cuddle them. Babies can see and hear at birth. If they are spoken to very softly and gently, they will turn and look right at the speaker. A baby's head and eyes will move to follow a slowly moving face, or even a bright, red ball.

All of these abilities help make the parents become attached to the infant. This is the start of the child's capacity to help shape the environment so that development can take place under the best possible conditions.

Physical Development

Babies have already grown a lot by the time they are born. They may have all the right body parts, but their heads are bigger in proportion to their bodies than are those of adults. This is because humans are born with big brains. As children grow, their heads grow more slowly than their bodies, so that by about 12 years of age, the proportions of children's bodies are similar to those of adults.

Children grow at different rates at different ages. There is very rapid growth in the first year of life. Growth is slow but steady throughout the rest of childhood. During these years, the child's strength, intellectual ability, and co-ordination increase.

There is another period of rapid growth in adolescence, which results in the person looking like an adult. There are important changes in a child's body beginning at about 12 years of age. At first, girls grow more rapidly than boys and begin to develop the sex characteristics of women, such as breasts and menstruation. Boys grow rapidly a little later, at about 14 years of age. They are usually bigger than girls at the end of this growth spurt, and they have the sex characteristics of men, such as deep voices and body hair.

The process of growing takes a lot of energy. Children need food to fuel growth and development. Babies eat a lot of food for their size. Young children's appetites are small but get proportionately greater with age.

Children also need a lot of sleep. Sleep is very important because it allows the child's brain to organize and remember all of the information the child has learned that day. It also allows the child to rest so that there is energy for the next day's activities.

Motor Development

Some of the most striking changes throughout childhood are those involving movement and co-ordination. At first a baby's movements are jerky and undirected. But by 3 months of age, most babies can put their hands together voluntarily. Almost all babies are sitting at 7 months of age and are walking by themselves a little after their first birthday.

Learning how to walk requires a lot of growth and energy. The baby's muscles have to be strong, and the brain has to grow so it can co-ordinate the movements. Big muscles develop before small muscles. This means that young children learn to run, jump, and climb stairs before they learn to write and do complicated puzzles.

As children get older, their co-ordination improves. Simple tasks have to be mastered before complex tasks. Thus a child can do up buttons at about 3 years of age but cannot tie shoelaces before about 5 years of age. Co-ordination between hand and eye allows school-age children to learn to write, do artwork, and enjoy complicated hobbies.

Children get stronger with increasing age, and they learn to play sports. Their increasing abilities allow them to play tennis as well as baseball and other team sports. Strength and co-ordination increase tremendously in adolescence, so that by 19 or 20 years of age, people have their full adult motor capacities.

A very complex motor function of the human body is that of producing language. Approximately 25 muscles have to be precisely co-ordinated in order for words to sound clear and intelligible.

Language Development

Learning and using language is one of the most difficult tasks human beings perform. Infants learn about language very early in life. They hear lots of different voices and produce many sounds, beginning with crying and advancing to cooing and babbling.

Children can understand language before they can express themselves. Commonly an 18-month-old child will understand a request but may not be able to respond in words. As the child grows, language increases in sophistication and in its uses. At 1 year of age, most children have a few identifiable words, usually nouns. By the third birthday, they have a vocabulary of several hundred words.

An amazing thing about children learning language is that in the first two years of life, children figure out the rules of language just by listening. At 4 or 5 years of age, they can speak very well without any formal schooling.

Once children go to school, their language is much more like that of adults. They use language as the major tool of learning as well as the main means of communicating ideas to one another. Adolescents are noted for their use of **jargon,** special words that only they understand. They also spend many hours talking on the telephone, in part to test this private language.

An important feature of language is that young children can learn to speak almost any language to which they are exposed. Preschool children are particularly good at learning foreign languages. Children reared in homes where two languages are spoken often become fluent in both languages.

Language is a vital part of any society. It is important in handing on traditions and folklore, just as it is important in helping express love, affection, and the values of the culture in which the child is developing.

Development of Thoughts and Ideas

Children learn about themselves and the world around them in many different ways. They begin to learn by seeing and touching things. As they get older they gradually learn to use language to express thoughts and ideas.

Newborn babies do not remember their mothers when they cannot see them. During the first year of life, they learn to remember them, and they learn that their mothers still exist even when they cannot see them. This early remembering is called **object permanence.**

By 2 years of age, toddlers have learned how to make a wind-up toy run. They are then ready to begin the gradual process of using language to communicate ideas and think about the world.

Thought is said to progress from the concrete to the abstract. Something that is concrete can be seen, touched, or heard. An abstract thought is one that cannot be directly related to an object. A toddler first understands what a drinking glass is and what it is used for. This is an example of a concrete thought. An older child will learn about the volume, or the internal space, of the glass. This is an example of an early abstract thought. An example of an advanced abstract thought is the concept of outer space. The first two ideas have to be understood before the last one can be understood.

The development of abstract thought allows children to think about themselves and their place in the world in more complex ways. As they go through school and into adolescence, they learn more and more about themselves, their friends, and their families. This increasingly sophisticated knowledge helps prepare them for adulthood.

Social Development

All human beings are members of a social community. As children grow up they learn different things about their social world at different ages.

The important needs of a young baby are to feel loved and cared for. If these needs are met, that child will feel much more confident about venturing out into the world in play and exploration. This is because the young child will have a good sense of self-worth.

Two-year-old children always seem to be saying no. This period of development is known as **autonomy.** It is a very important stage in which children explore their own individuality and learn how the rules of the world operate.

Most children are in day-care or preschool for the two years before they enter school. They learn how to play with one another and to share.

At the age of 5 or 6, most children enter school. This is a period of adjustment to external rules and regulations. It is also a time in which children make good friends. Those friends are often almost as important to a growing child as is the family.

Adolescence is a time of intense emotions and friendships. Peers, or friends of the same age, are very important to children at this stage of development. And for most adolescents, the most important thoughts and values are those of the peer group rather than the family.

Adolescence is the bridge between childhood and adulthood. Thoughts of future occupation become important, as do thoughts of marrying and having children. Thus the development of a child comes full circle.

MICHAEL D. MCKENZIE, M.B. CH.B.
LEE H. MCKENZIE, R.N., M.S.N.
T. BERRY BRAZELTON, M.D.
Children's Hospital and
Harvard Medical School

See also PSYCHOLOGY; LEARNING; BABY; ADOLESCENCE; FAMILY.

CHILD LABOR

In the late 1700's and early 1800's, power-driven machines replaced hand labor for the making of most manufactured items. Factories began to spring up everywhere, first in England and then in the United States. The owners of these factories found a new source of labor to run their machines—children. Operating the power-driven machines did not require adult strength, and children could be hired more cheaply than adults. By the mid-1800's, child labor was a major problem.

Children had always worked, especially in farming. But factory work was hard. A child with a factory job might work 12 to 18 hours a day, six days a week, to earn a dollar. Many children began working before the age of 7, tending machines in spinning mills or hauling heavy loads. The factories were often damp, dark, and dirty. Some children worked underground, in coal mines. The working children had no time to play or go to school, and little time to rest. They often became ill.

By 1810, about 2,000,000 school-age children were working 50- to 70-hour weeks. Most of them came from poor families. When parents could not support their children, they sometimes turned them over to a mill or factory owner. One glass factory in Massachusetts was fenced with barbed wire "to keep the young imps inside." The "young imps" were boys under 12 who carried loads of hot glass all night for a wage of 40 cents to $1.10 per night.

Church and labor groups, teachers, and many other people were outraged by such cruelty. They began to press for reforms. The English writer Charles Dickens helped publicize the evils of child labor with his novel *Oliver Twist*. Britain was the first to pass laws regulating child labor. From 1802 to 1878, a series of laws gradually shortened the working hours, improved the conditions, and raised the age at which children could work. Other European countries adopted similar laws.

In the United States it took many years to outlaw child labor. Connecticut passed a law in 1813 saying that working children must have some schooling. By 1899 a total of 28 states had passed laws regulating child labor.

Many efforts were made to pass a national child labor law. The U.S. Congress passed two laws, in 1918 and 1922, but the Supreme

In 1900 an American textile mill employed these children to work ten-hour days with little pay. Today child labor laws prohibit such practices.

Court declared both unconstitutional. In 1924, Congress proposed a constitutional amendment prohibiting child labor, but the states did not ratify it. Then, in 1938, Congress passed the Fair Labor Standards Act. It fixed minimum ages of 16 for work during school hours, 14 for certain jobs after school, and 18 for dangerous work.

Today all the states and the U.S. Government have laws regulating child labor. These laws have cured the worst evils of children's working in factories. But some kinds of work are not regulated. Children of migrant workers, for example, have no legal protection. Farmers may legally employ them outside of school hours. The children pick crops in the fields and move from place to place, so they get little schooling.

Child labor has been less of a problem in Canada because industry there did not develop until the 1900's. The Canadian provinces today have child labor laws similar to those in the United States. Most other countries have laws regulating child labor, too. But the laws are not always enforced, and child labor remains a problem.

Reviewed by MILTON FRIED
Amalgamated Clothing Workers of America

CHILDREN'S LITERATURE

Today literature for children consists of an enormous and exciting array of books written and published especially for young listeners and readers. It also includes a few choice adult books that children have taken over as their own.

In the United States alone, there are approximately 49,000 different books for children. Each year about 3,000 new titles are published. The books that make up children's literature are called **trade books** by publishers to distinguish them from school textbooks. Often children call them ''library books.''

Although many trade books are full of accurate and fascinating information, these books are published chiefly for the reader's entertainment and the general background of information everybody likes to have.

▶THE BEGINNINGS: ORAL LITERATURE

Today, literature is associated with books and reading, but there was a time when there were almost no books because there were no printing presses. And because there were so few books, few people could read.

But people heard the tales of good storytellers and later retold the same tales—with a few trimmings of their own. They sang the folk songs they had learned by ear. Mothers sang old lullabies to their babies and repeated old nursery rhymes—the same ones their mothers had taught them. At work, men and women chanted old songs that paced the rhythm of their hoeing or rowing.

These tales, rhymes, and songs made up the literature of people who had few books. Theirs was an oral literature—that is, a literature that is spoken or sung, not written down.

Children were often a part of these singing and storytelling sessions at home and in the village. They took over those segments that appealed to them—the song with a dozen stanzas and a chorus that imitated various animals, the stories of the little person who outsmarted bigger people, the nonsense rhymes and singing games, the riddles and tongue twisters. Eventually, with the invention of the printing press, these songs, tales, games, and rhymes, once a part of oral literature, were to become part of our printed books.

▶THE FIRST PRINTED LITERATURE

Until the mid-1400's, books were lettered by hand or were printed from woodcuts. Both required slow, careful work. Books were few in number and so costly that only the great monasteries and universities could have them. Most people were without books. Then, a German inventor, Johann Gutenberg, developed a printing press with movable type that revolutionized printing. It produced printed literature for thousands of people who had previously relied only on oral literature.

Years passed before books were printed especially for children. One of the first picture books for children was a textbook in Latin called *Orbis Sensualium Pictus (The Visible World in Pictures.)* It was written in 1658 by John Amos Comenius, a Czech educator and bishop. It was translated into English in 1659.

However, printed books were too expensive for most children to have, even for their lessons. A low-cost substitute, called a hornbook, was widely used in England and in the British colonies of North America.

In the same period, printers were turning out quantities of news sheets, ballads, and booklets that were unbound and often un-

The hornbook looked nothing like a modern book. It was a small wooden paddle on which was pasted a lesson sheet of paper or parchment. A thin, clear covering made from boiled animal horn protected the sheet.

This article is a historical survey of literature for children from its earliest beginnings to its present trends. It is accompanied by a list of recommended modern children's books. Information on two major American literary prizes awarded to children's book authors and artists may be found in a separate article, CALDECOTT AND NEWBERY MEDALS.

The article also includes profiles of well-known children's book writers and illustrators. Consult the Index to find biographies of many others, including those cited in this article. If you are interested in sampling some of the stories and poems mentioned here, literary excerpts accompany the biographies of the following authors of books for children: ALCOTT, LOUISA MAY (*Little Women*); ANDERSEN, HANS CHRISTIAN (selected fairy tales); CARROLL, LEWIS (*Alice's Adventures in Wonderland*); DEFOE, DANIEL (*Robinson Crusoe*); GRAHAME, KENNETH (*The Wind in the Willows*); GRIMM, JACOB AND WILHELM (selected fairy tales); MILNE, A. A. ("Missing"); POTTER, BEATRIX (*The Tale of Jemima Puddle-Duck*); STEVENSON, ROBERT LOUIS (*Kidnapped*), selections from *A Child's Garden Of Verses*); SWIFT, JONATHAN (*Gulliver's Travels*); and WHITE, E. B. (*Charlotte's Web*). A sampling of illustrated NURSERY RHYMES appears in the article of that title. Selections of the work of Charles Perrault may be found in the article FAIRY TALES. Some works of Edward Lear are included in NONSENSE RHYMES.

Illustrations accompany the biographies of the following children's book artists: CALDECOTT, RANDOLPH; GREENAWAY, KATE; SENDAK, MAURICE; and SEUSS, DR. Reproductions of the work of several other well-known illustrators of books for children may be found in the article ILLUSTRATION AND ILLUSTRATORS.

stitched. These were sold by street vendors and peddlers, called chapmen. The little booklets were commonly called chapbooks or penny histories, because they were sold for a penny each, along with a toy or trinket. Most chapbooks were published for adults, but many were adventure tales that appealed to children. Chapbooks were sold by the thousands. In many homes, they may have been the only reading matter besides the Bible.

In the 1600's, strong religious feelings were building up in England and New England. Books published for children warned of sin, death, and eternal punishment. A book for adults—*Pilgrim's Progress* (1678) by the English writer and preacher John Bunyan—grew out of this same religious atmosphere. But Bunyan, who had been a reader of the chapbooks himself, knew how to tell a good story, and many children enjoyed his book.

The New England Primer, printed about 1690 in Boston, contained the alphabet, spelling words, the catechism, and verses for religious training.

▶THE SPIRIT OF THE FAIRY TALES

The first break in this stern scene came with a collection of eight stories published in France in 1697. It included "Cinderella," "Puss in Boots," "The Sleeping Beauty," and "Little Red Riding Hood." All were told simply—even joyously—with no threat of gloom or doom and no religious teaching.

The title of the book, translated from the French, was *Stories or Tales of Long Ago with Morals.* No author was named in the first edition. But Charles Perrault, a high-ranking French civil servant and writer, is believed to be the one who retold the old stories. What is most interesting is the light touch that marks these stories and the brief moral following each one. The picture at the beginning of the book shows an old woman before an open fire telling stories to young listeners. On the door behind her is a sign: "Contes de ma mère l'oye," which means "Tales of My Mother the Goose." In 1729 this little collection of stories was brought out in English with the title *Tales of Mother Goose.*

One of the pioneers in this development was John Newbery, a London printer, publisher, writer, and merchant. Newbery was evidently a keen businessman, who saw a market in these children who had been reading the chapbooks and now the *Tales of Mother Goose.*

In 1744, Newbery published his first children's book, *A Little Pretty Pocket-Book,* in covers of gilt and flowered paper, "for the instruction and amusement" of children. The tiny book included fables, rhymed directions for games, poems, letters from Jack the Giant-Killer, and rules for children's behavior.

The book was so successful that Newbery brought out more and more books for chil-

The publication of Perrault's *Tales of Mother Goose* sparked a movement to bring beauty and delight to children through books made especially for them.

Beverly Cleary

Roald Dahl

Lloyd Alexander (1924–), born in Philadelphia, Pennsylvania, is considered a master of modern children's literature. Ancient Welsh legends inspired him to write the Prydain Chronicles, a five-novel series about an imaginary land. He won the Newbery Medal in 1969 for the fifth book in the series, *The High King.* Alexander also received the National Book Award in 1971 for *The Marvelous Misadventures of Sebastian* and the 1982 American Book Award for *Westmark.* His other works include *The Illyrian Adventure* (1986) and *The Philadelphia Adventure* (1990), two books in a series featuring the adventurous young heroine Vesper Holly; and *The Fortune-tellers* (1992).

Natalie Babbitt (1932–), an author and illustrator, was born in Dayton, Ohio. Her entertaining stories often deal with basic human emotions and conflicts. Her best-known work, *Tuck Everlasting* (1975), concerns a family that has drunk from a spring that gives them eternal life. Among other books Babbitt has written and illustrated for children are *Kneeknock Rise* (1970), *Herbert Rowbarge* (1982), *The Devil's Other Storybook* (1987), and *Bub, or The Very Best Thing* (1994).

Marcia Brown (1918–), an author and artist, was born in Rochester, New York. Her illustrated books for children are highly regarded and have won many honors. Three of her books—*Cinderella* (1954), *Once a Mouse* (1961), and *Shadow* (1983)—won Caldecott Medals.

Margaret Wise Brown (1910–52), an author and editor, was born in New York City. In the 1930's she studied at the Bureau of Educational Experiments in New York and became interested in writing for children. She wrote more than 100 children's books, many of which are considered classics. They include *The Runaway Bunny* (1941), *Little Lost Lamb* (1945), *The Little Island* (1946), and *Goodnight Moon* (1947).

Jean de Brunhoff (1899–1937) was a French author and illustrator, born in Paris. His series of books about Babar the elephant began as stories told to his young sons. They revolutionized the style of children's books and have become classics. Books in the series include *The Story of Babar, the Little Elephant* (1933) and *The Travels of Babar* (1934). Babar's adventures were continued by Jean's son Laurent.

Betsy Byars (1928–), a popular author of realistic fiction for middle school and junior high school readers, was born in Charlotte, North Carolina. She won the Newbery Medal in 1971 for *The Summer of the Swans*, a sensitively told story about a mentally handicapped boy and his sister. Her other books for young readers include *The Midnight Fox* (1968); *The Pinballs* (1977); *The Night Swimmers* (1980), which won an American Book Award; *The Burning Questions of Bingo Brown* (1988); and *McMummy* (1993).

Beverly Cleary (1916–), born in McMinnville, Oregon, worked as a children's librarian before becoming a writer. Her first book, *Henry Huggins* (1950), was a great success. Her other books include *Henry and the Clubhouse* (1962), *Runaway Ralph* (1970), and *Ramona and Her Mother*, which won an American Book Award in 1981. Cleary won the Laura Ingalls Wilder Award in 1975 for her "lasting contribution to literature for children" and the 1984 Newbery Medal for *Dear Mr. Henshaw.* Her childhood memoir, *A Girl from Yamhill*, was published in 1988.

Barbara Cooney (Barbara Cooney Porter) (1917–2000), a writer and illustrator, was born in Brooklyn, New York. The daughter of an artist, she began to draw and paint as a young girl. She retold and illustrated a story by Geoffrey Chaucer, *Chanticleer and the Fox*, for which she received the Caldecott Medal in 1959. In 1980, she received the same honor for *Ox-Cart Man*, written by Donald Hall.

Cooney won an American Book Award for her picture book *Miss Rumphius* (1982). Her other books include *King of Wreck Island* (1941), *Captain Pottle's House* (1943), *Island Boy* (1988), and *Hattie and the Wild Waves* (1990).

Roald Dahl (1916–90), a British author born in Llandaff, Wales, was noted for the fantastic, sometimes bizarre, occurrences in his tales for young readers. After serving as a fighter pilot in World War II, he began to write articles and stories for adults. Bedtime stories he told to his five children launched him on his career as a children's writer. His books include *James and the Giant Peach* (1961), *Charlie and the Chocolate Factory* (1964), *The Witches* (1983), and *Matilda* (1988). Dahl also wrote two autobiographies, *Boy* (1984) and *Going Solo* (1986).

Paula Danziger (1944–), born in Washington, D.C., is a popular author with young adults. Her humorous books, written in a light style, are mostly about family and social situations. They include *The Cat Ate My Gymsuit* (1974), her first and probably best-known novel; *Can You Sue Your Parents for Malpractice?* (1979); and *Everyone Else's Parents Said Yes* (1989).

Tomie (Thomas Anthony) de Paola (1934–), an author and illustrator born in Meriden, Connecticut, has said that even as a child, he wanted to "make books with pictures." He has won many prizes for his children's books, which he writes and illustrates with delicate but brightly colored drawings. His best-known works include *Charlie Needs a Cloak* (1974), *Strega Nona* (1975), *Helga's Dowry* (1977), *Fin M'Coul* (1981), *Country Farm* (1984), *The Legend of the Indian Paintbrush* (1991), and *The Unicorn and the Moon* (1995). De Paola has also been

Diane and Leo Dillon

Virginia Hamilton

put her thoughts and feelings on paper. Later in her life, she began to write. Her book of poetry *Honey, I Love* was named a Notable Book by the American Library Association in 1978. She has also written *Koya DeLaney and the Good Girl Blues* (1992) and *Talk About a Family* (1993).

Virginia Hamilton (1936–), a gifted and prolific author of children's books, was born in Yellow Springs, Ohio. In 1975, Hamilton won a National Book Award and the Newbery Medal for the novel *M. C. Higgins, the Great*. Her other works include *Zeely* (1967), *The Planet of Junior Brown* (1971), *Anthony Burns: The Defeat and Triumph of a Fugitive Slave* (1988), and *Plain City* (1993), as well as two acclaimed collections of African American folktales: *The People Could Fly* (1985) and *Her Stories* (1995). She was the recipient of the Laura Ingalls Wilder Award in 1995.

Steven Kellogg (1941–), an author and illustrator, was born in Norwalk, Connecticut. As a child, Kellogg made up stories for his sisters and drew pictures of them. Many of the characters in his books are based on people and animals he knows—the Pinkerton books, for example, are about his Great Dane. Books he wrote and illustrated include *Can I Keep Him?* (1971), *Ralph's Secret Weapons* (1983), and *Johnny Appleseed* (1988). Books by other authors that he illustrated include *Matilda Who Told Lies and Was Burned to Death* (1970) and *A, My Name Is Alice* (1984).

E. L. (Elaine Lobl) Konigsburg (1930–) was born in New York City but grew up in small towns in Pennsylvania. She is known for her humorous novels and stories for young readers. Her popular book *From the Mixed-Up Files of Mrs. Basil E. Frankweiler* won the Newbery Medal in 1968. Another of her books, *Jennifer, Hecate, Macbeth, William McKinley, and Me, Elizabeth*, was runner-up in the same year. In 1997, Konigsburg won the Newbery Medal for her book *The View from Saturday*. Among her other books are *About the B'Nai Bagels* (1969) and *Amy Elizabeth Explores Bloomingdale's* (1992).

an art teacher, a theatrical designer, and a painter. Many of his works of art were done for churches and monasteries in his native New England.

Leo Dillon (1933–), born in Brooklyn, New York, and **Diane Dillon** (1933–), born in Glendale, California, a husband-and-wife team of illustrators, met while students at the Parsons School of Design. They soon began collaborating. The Dillons designed adult book jackets and album covers before turning to children's book illustration. Two of the books they illustrated, *Why Mosquitoes Buzz in People's Ears* (1975), by Verna Aardema, and *Ashanti to Zulu: African Traditions* (1976), by Margaret Musgrove, won Caldecott Medals. Their later work includes illustrations for two collections of African American folktales by Virginia Hamilton: *The People Could Fly* (1985) and *Her Stories* (1995).

Mary Mapes Dodge (1831–1905), born into a prominent family in New York City, was a powerful influence on American children's books of the 1800's. Widowed as a young woman, she turned to writing to help support herself and her two sons. Her best-known work is the classic tale of Dutch children, *Hans Brinker; or the Silver Skates*. Dodge was also the first editor (1873–1905) of the acclaimed children's magazine *St. Nicholas*.

Paula Fox (1923–), born in New York City, has been praised for the honesty of her novels for young readers, which often deal with serious subjects. Her books include *How Many Miles to Babylon?* (1967); *Blowfish Live in the Sea* (1970); *The Slave Dancer*, which won the Newbery Medal in 1974; *A Place Apart* (1980), which won an American Book Award in 1983; and *Monkey Island* (1991).

Russell Freedman (1929–), an author of nonfiction books, was born in San Francisco, California. His first book was *Teenagers Who Made History* (1961), a collection of biographies. In 1988, he won the Newbery Medal for *Lincoln: A Photobiography*. Freedman has also written about human and animal behavior.

Jean Fritz (1915–), an American writer, was born in Hankow, China. The recipient of the 1986 Laura Ingalls Wilder Medal for her lasting contribution to children's literature, Fritz is considered one of the best authors of historical biographies for children. She is known for the chatty, often witty, style of her biographies, many of which focus on Revolutionary War figures. Fritz has also written young people's novels set in the same time period. Some of her books are *Why Don't You Get A Horse, Sam Adams?* (1974), *Will You Sign Here, John Hancock?* (1976), *Shh! We're Writing the Constitution* (1987), and *You Want Women to Vote, Lizzie Stanton?* (1995). Her autobiography, *Homesick: My Own Story*, was published in 1982.

Jean Craighead George (1919–) was born in Washington, D.C. She writes and illustrates entertaining stories that also teach about nature and ecology. Her novel *Julie of the Wolves* was awarded the 1973 Newbery Medal. Her other novels include *My Side of the Mountain* (1959), *Who Really Killed Cock Robin?* (1971), *The Cry of the Crow* (1980), *The Talking Earth* (1983), and *The Missing 'Gator of Gumbo Limbo* (1992). She has also written much nonfiction.

Eloise Greenfield (1929–), a writer born in Parmele, North Carolina, has said she did not like to write when she was a child because she was too shy to

dren. One of the most popular was *The History of Little Goody Two-Shoes* (1765). It is probably the first book of fiction written for children and with illustrations drawn especially for the story.

Before this, printers used any woodcuts they had on hand to illustrate the chapbooks for children. One old chapbook used the picture of a sailboat on the page facing a poem about a good child saying his prayers. Because the woodcut was too wide to show the boat sailing across the page, the printer turned it on end to sail straight up the page.

One of the first artists to become an illustrator of children's books was Thomas Bewick, an English engraver who worked in wood. The first book he designed and illustrated for children was *Tommy Trip's History of Beasts and Birds* (1779). Bewick pictured the beasts and birds in exquisite detail.

After John Newbery's death in 1767, his publishing house continued to bring out children's books that were charming and entertaining. One of these was *Mother Goose's Melody; or, Sonnets for the Cradle*. It did not include any of the stories from Perrault's *Tales of Mother Goose*. Instead, it brought together 52 old English nursery rhymes plus 16 songs from Shakespeare—all in the Newbery covers of flowers and gilt. Since 1922, John Newbery's work has been commemorated through the Newbery Medal, awarded annually for the most distinguished children's book published that year in the United States.

While Newbery and, later, his heirs were bringing out charming books for children in England, several American printers and publishers were following his lead. Frequently, they duplicated English books without giving credit to the source.

Yet these books for children's pleasure were the exception rather than the rule in both England and the United States. There were still many religious books for young readers. In the late 1700's many instructional stories began to be published as well. But children have a way of finding adventure tales, too. One way has always been to turn to books published for adults. Two adult books published in England in this period became children's classics. *Robinson Crusoe* (1719), by Daniel Defoe, was about a man who had been shipwrecked on an uninhabited island. A part of *Gulliver's Travels* (1726), by Jonathan Swift, told of adven-

For more than 100 years the illustrations by Sir John Tenniel have been inseparable from the amusing nonsense of Lewis Carroll's *Alice in Wonderland.*

tures in a land of Lilliputians (tiny people). Both stories had elements that were difficult for children to understand. Evidently, the children skipped the heavy parts and enjoyed the adventures. Since then, both books have been published in shortened form with dramatic illustrations for children to enjoy.

▶ IMAGINATION AND LAUGHTER FOR CHILDREN

The 1800's brought a number of new books that bore no trace of the preaching or teaching that had been in most children's books. One of these came from Germany—the folktales collected by Jacob and Wilhelm Grimm, two university scholars. The Grimm brothers recorded the tales just as they had heard them from storytellers in the countryside. Here were stories of talking beasts and dancing princesses, of elves and dwarfs, and even of a princess who slept for a hundred years. The tales were recorded in the rhythmic language of the storyteller and with the same buildup of suspense that had held listeners spellbound for centuries. They were first published in 1812 in Germany. In 1823 these tales were brought out in England, where they became known as *Grimm's Fairy Tales*.

Another of the new books came from Denmark, where Hans Christian Andersen, following the lead of the Grimms, also turned to folktales. But unlike the Grimms, Andersen retold the old stories in his own way. He also added new stories that he created on the old folktale pattern. Andersen's *Fairy Tales and Stories* was translated into English in 1846.

That same year humor was introduced into children's books in England. This came with the publication of Edward Lear's *Book of Non-*

sense. It is a collection of limericks (humorous five-line poems with a special rhyme and rhythm) illustrated with hilarious cartoons drawn by Lear.

It is probably the first children's book to be created for real-life children, whom Lear consulted on every limerick and drawing. Lear's humor produced ridiculous people and situations and equally funny drawings. Unlike *The New England Primer,* which begins "In Adam's fall/We sinned all," Lear's book was all nonsense and laughter.

In much the same spirit, Charles Dodgson, a distinguished mathematician and university scholar, began telling stories to three little girls, one of them named Alice. These stories were published in 1865 as *Alice's Adventures in Wonderland* under the pen name Lewis Carroll. Alice goes down a rabbit hole, where she shrinks to the height of a flower, meets the Cheshire cat, nearly drowns in her own tears, and takes part in a mad tea party. Nonsense is spoken with great seriousness, and foolish doings multiply. Alice's adventures were continued in *Through the Looking-Glass,* published in 1872. Both books were illustrated by Sir John Tenniel, a cartoonist for *Punch,* London's magazine of humor.

▶COLOR COMES TO THE PICTURE BOOKS

The illustrations of Lear and Tenniel were black-and-white line drawings. These artists used pen and ink to make sharp lines that could be easily printed. Almost all books of that day were printed in black and white only.

In the 1860's, Edmund Evans, an English printer, became interested in bringing out inexpensive children's books with fine color illustrations. Evans planned them for very young children—the nursery-school age. The first of these "toy books," as Evans called them, were nursery rhymes illustrated by Walter Crane, a fine wood engraver. Crane used flat colors and bold black lines. *The House That Jack Built* and *A Baby's Own Aesop* were the first of many nursery picture books illustrated by Crane and printed by Evans in the 1860's and 1870's.

Another artist with whom Evans worked was Kate Greenaway. In 1878 he brought out a book of verses that she had written and illustrated, *Under the Window.* Greenaway's drawings had a style of their own—sweet children in old-fashioned clothes, with birds and

Walter Crane's *A Baby's Own Aesop* (top) and Randolph Caldecott's *Hey-Diddle-Diddle* were among the first books for young children to be printed in color.

blossoms surrounding them—all in soft pastels. Many Kate Greenaway books for children followed.

At the same time, Randolph Caldecott was becoming known for his cartoons and sketches in English magazines and newspapers. Edmund Evans added Caldecott to his team of artists, and more "toy books" were under way. Caldecott spent part of his youth in the country, where he absorbed the sights and sounds of fox hunts, cattle fairs, and country-folk. All of these show up in his drawings, which are done in simple, vigorous lines full of movement and sly humor.

The best-loved Caldecott books are the nursery rhymes, such as *Hey-Diddle-Diddle, Sing a Song of Sixpence,* and *Baby Bunting.* In tribute to the artist, the Caldecott Medal is awarded annually for the most distinguished picture book for children published in the United States that year.

Jerry Pinkney

P.L. Travers

Jill Krementz (1940–), born in New York City, is known for her photography and books for children. She began her journalism career as an assistant editor, then worked as a magazine reporter and a newspaper photographer before becoming a freelance photographer. Krementz is well known for her A Very Young series, which includes *A Very Young Rider* (1977) and *A Very Young Musician* (1991). In these books, written in the first person and illustrated with Krementz' photographs, children discuss their various activities. Krementz also wrote and illustrated *How It Feels When a Parent Dies* (1981) and other How It Feels books, which discuss issues such as adoption, divorce, and physical disability.

Karla Kuskin (1932–), an author and illustrator, was born in New York City. She wrote, designed, and illustrated her first book, *Roar and More*, as a student at the Yale University School of Fine Arts. Published in 1956, it was named one of the best children's books for 1955–57 by the American Institute of Graphic Arts. Her other books include *The Philharmonic Gets Dressed* (1982), *The Dallas Titans Get Ready for Bed* (1986), *Jerusalem Shining Still* (1987), and *Soap Soup* (1992). She has used the pen name Nicholas Charles in writing some of her books.

Madeleine L'Engle (1918–), born in New York City, was an actress and teacher as well as an author. The daughter of a journalist and a pianist, she wrote her first stories at the age of 5. She is best known for her Time Fantasy series of novels: *A Wrinkle in Time*, which was awarded the Newbery Medal in 1963; *A Wind in the Door* (1973); *A Swiftly Tilting Planet*, which won the American Book Award in 1980; and *Many Waters* (1986). Her other books for young readers include *A Ring of Endless Light* (1980) and *A House Like a Lotus* (1984).

Leo Lionni (1910–), an artist and children's author, was born in Amsterdam, the Netherlands. After a career in advertising, he published his first children's book, *Little Blue and Little Yellow* (1959), which began as a story to entertain his grandchildren. His other books, all praised by critics, include *Inch by Inch* (1962), *Swimmy* (1963), *Frederick* (1966), *Alexander and the Wind-Up Mouse* (1969), *It's Mine* (1986), and *Matthew's Dream* (1991).

Arnold Lobel (1933–87), an author and illustrator, was born in Los Angeles, California. He was the illustrator of nearly 100 books for children, some of which he wrote. His works, aimed mainly at beginning readers, were praised for their engaging style. Lobel won the Caldecott Medal in 1981 for his illustrations for *Fables* and a Caldecott Honor in 1971 for *Frog and Toad Are Friends*. Its sequel, *Frog and Toad Together*, was a 1973 Newbery Honor Book. Two of his most ambitious projects were *The Random House Book of Poetry for Children* (1983) and *The Random House Book of Mother Goose* (1986), for which he painted pictures to illustrate 306 Mother Goose rhymes.

Lois Lowry (1937–) was born in Honolulu, Hawaii. She has written books featuring the character Anastasia Krupnik, a consistent favorite with young readers. She was awarded the 1990 Newbery Medal for her novel *Number the Stars*, a book about Nazi-occupied Denmark, and the 1994 Newbery Medal for *The Giver*, a science fiction novel.

David Macaulay (1946–), born in Burton-on-Trent, England, is well known as an author and illustrator. He has always been fascinated with how objects are constructed and how things work. His first book was *Cathedral: The Story of Its Construction*. His other books include *Castle* (1977) and *The Way Things Work*. Macaulay is the recipient of the 1991 Caldecott Medal for his picture book *Black and White*.

Patricia MacLachlan (1938–) was born in Cheyenne, Wyoming, and grew up in Minnesota. She is perhaps best known for the 1986 Newbery Medal book *Sarah, Plain and Tall*, which is based on MacLachlan's own background. Other books include *Through Grandpa's Eyes* (1980) and *The Facts and Fictions of Minna Pratt* (1988).

Robert McCloskey (1914–), an illustrator and author, was born in Hamilton, Ohio. He served as a sergeant in the army during World War II, drawing training pictures. Primarily an illustrator, he conceived his stories in picture form first. Words and pictures together express the beauty found in ordinary life. His *Make Way for Ducklings* (1941), a Caldecott Medal winner, has become a children's classic. His other works include *Homer Price* (1943), *Blueberries for Sal* (1948), and *Time of Wonder* (1957), for which he won a second Caldecott Medal.

David McCord (1897–1997), a poet, was born in New York City. McCord's poems are often used to teach children how to write poetry. His collections of poetry for children include *Take Sky* (1962), *For Me to Say* (1970), *Speak Up: More Rhymes for the Never Was and Always Is* (1980), and *The Star in the Pail* (1986).

Milton Meltzer (1915–), born in Worcester, Massachusetts, is known for his biographies and historical books about social issues. His books include *The Terrorists* (1983), *The American Revolutionaries: A History in Their Own Words* (1987), and *Crime in America* (1990). Among his biographies are *Betty Friedan: A Voice for Women's Rights* (1985) and *Frederick Douglass: In His Own Words* (1995).

Eve Merriam (1916–92), born in Philadelphia, Pennsylvania, worked as a copywriter and an editor while writing poetry. In 1946, she received the Yale Younger Poets Prize. She also wrote fiction and nonfiction for children and adults as well as several plays but is best known for her children's verse. Among her poetry books for children are *The*

Birthday Cow (1978), Blackberry Ink (1985), Fresh Paint: New Poems (1986), and The Singing Green (1992).

Katherine Paterson (1932–), an American author of children's books, was born in Qing Jiang, China. She taught school and served as a missionary in Japan before beginning her writing career. Paterson's The Master Puppeteer won a National Book Award in 1977. In 1979 another of her works, The Great Gilly Hopkins, won the same award. Paterson won the Newbery Medal in 1978 for Bridge to Terabithia and in 1981 for Jacob Have I Loved.

Chris Van Allsburg

Jerry Pinkney (1939–), an illustrator of children's books, was born in Philadelphia, Pennsylvania. Pinkney discovered early in life that he loved to draw. After attending the Philadelphia Museum College of Art, he opened his own studio. Two books that he illustrated, Mirandy and Brother Wind (1988) and The Talking Eggs (1989), were Caldecott Honor Books.

Jack Prelutsky (1940–) was born in Brooklyn, New York. When he was younger, Prelutsky was interested in becoming an opera singer, but he said he abandoned the idea when he heard Luciano Pavarotti sing. Prelutsky then found he could write poetry. His books include Nightmares: Poems to Trouble Your Sleep (1976) and Something Big Has Been Here (1990).

J. K. (Joanne Kathleen) Rowling (1965–) was born in Chipping Sodbury, England. She achieved instant fame in 1997 with Harry Potter and the Sorcerer's Stone, the first in a series of best-selling novels about a young boy's adventures at a school for wizards. It was followed by Harry Potter and the Chamber of Secrets (1998), Harry Potter and the Prisoner of Azkaban (1999), and Harry Potter and the Goblet of Fire (2000). Rowling's books were as popular with adults as they were with children.

Cynthia Rylant (1954–), born in Hopewell, Virginia, is a popular children's author. Rylant grew up in West Virginia. She is the author of When I Was Young in the Mountains (1982), a picture book about life in rural West Virginia, and Missing May, which earned the 1993 Newbery Medal.

Richard Scarry (1919–94), born in Boston, Massachusetts, was an author and illustrator of children's books that have sold millions of copies around the world. They are filled with colorful pictures that are detailed and full of action. The stories are often humorous and educational tales featuring animals. Some of his most popular books are Richard Scarry's Best Word Book Ever (1963), I Am a Bunny (1967), and Early Words (1976).

Shel Silverstein (1932–99) was born in Chicago, Illinois. Silverstein wrote and illustrated books of prose and poetry for children that featured clever wordplay, mischievous humor, and odd situations. His classic books include The Giving Tree (1963), Where the Sidewalk Ends (1974), A Light in the Attic (1982), and Falling Up (1996). Although he was most famous for these and his other children's books, Silverstein also wrote plays, folksongs, and musical scores for films.

Elizabeth George Speare (1908–94) was born in Melrose, Massachusetts. Her books are concerned primarily with American history. The first, Calico Captive, was followed by The Witch of Blackbird Pond, which won the Newbery Medal in 1959. She also received Newbery Medals for The Bronze Bow (1961) and The Sign of the Beaver (1983).

Mildred Taylor (1943–) was born in Jackson, Mississippi, and grew up in Toledo, Ohio, graduating from the University of Toledo. She was awarded the 1977 Newbery Medal for her book Roll of Thunder, Hear My Cry. She used childhood memories and her family's oral history to create this story of an African American family's life during the Great Depression of the 1930's. Taylor's books Song of the Trees (1975) and Let the Circle Be Unbroken (1981) chronicle the same family.

P. L. (Pamela Lyndon) Travers (1899–1996), a British author born in Queensland, Australia, was the creator of the popular character Mary Poppins. The beloved nanny with magical powers first appeared in Mary Poppins (1934). The book sold millions of copies and was translated into more than 20 languages. It was followed by several sequels and inspired a 1964 Disney movie musical.

Chris Van Allsburg (1949–), an author and illustrator, was born in Grand Rapids, Michigan. He earned a degree in fine arts from the University of Michigan and a master's degree in sculpture from the Rhode Island School of Design (RISD). His first children's book, The Garden of Abdul Gasazi (1979), won several awards, and he received a Caldecott Medal for his second effort, Jumanji (1981). His later works include The Mysteries of Harris Burdick (1984); The Polar Express (1985), for which he won a second Caldecott; and The Two Figs (1993). Van Allsburg's work has been exhibited at the Whitney Museum of American Art in New York.

Cynthia Voigt (1942–), born in Boston, Massachusetts, has written many books on serious subjects for young adults. Her first book, Homecoming (1981), began the saga of the Tillermans, four abandoned children. Dicey's Song, its sequel, won the Newbery Medal in 1983. Voigt's other books include Tell Me If the Lovers Are Losers (1982), The Wings of a Falcon (1993), and When She Hollers (1994).

Garth Williams (1912–96), an illustrator born in New York City, is best known for his illustrations of E. B. White's Stuart Little (1945) and Charlotte's Web (1952). The son of artists, he graduated from the Royal Academy of Art in London. Williams also illustrated Laura Ingalls Wilder's Little House series.

Charlotte Zolotow (1915–) was born in Norfolk, Virginia. Her books, written from her memories of watching her children grow, explore the day-by-day events and discoveries in the lives of children. Zolotow's many works include The Storm Book (1952), Mr. Rabbit and the Lovely Present (1962), and But Not Billy (1983).

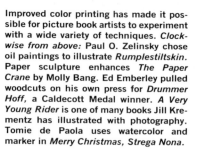

Improved color printing has made it possible for picture book artists to experiment with a wide variety of techniques. *Clockwise from above:* Paul O. Zelinsky chose oil paintings to illustrate *Rumplestiltskin.* Paper sculpture enhances *The Paper Crane* by Molly Bang. Ed Emberley pulled woodcuts on his own press for *Drummer Hoff,* a Caldecott Medal winner. *A Very Young Rider* is one of many books Jill Krementz has illustrated with photography. Tomie de Paola uses watercolor and marker in *Merry Christmas, Strega Nona.*

▶THE BEGINNINGS OF REALISM

Randolph Caldecott brought new life and movement into the drawings for children's books. His people run and dance and leap. Their faces show delight and anger. Even the animals seem as real as the dog next door.

This was the beginning of greater realism in both stories and illustration in books for children. The new authors did not write about children who were as stiff as wood and either too good to be true or too bad. Instead, they began to create flesh-and-blood characters who had their strong points and their weak points, who laughed and cried, loved and hated, as living people do.

A landmark in this development was Louisa May Alcott's *Little Women,* published in two volumes (1868 and 1869) in Boston. The story tells of the everyday ups and downs of the four teenage March sisters. This heartwarming book was based on the author's experiences in the Alcott family—whose members, in spite of their poverty, lived lives rich in imagination and individuality.

Realism in children's books went even further when Mark Twain's *Adventures of Tom Sawyer* was published in 1876. Poor folk and strange, shady characters from "across town" lived in Tom's world. Tom was from a "respectable" family, but his best friend Huck was the son of the town drunkard. The boys had some remarkable experiences. They witnessed a grave robbery and saw a murder being committed. They even attended their own funeral. These adventures were not the kind previously found in books for children. The sequel, *The Adventures of Huckleberry Finn,* was told in the rough river-town language of Huck himself. Both books give details of the rugged Mississippi River life as it was in those days. After Kate Greenaway's flower gardens and Lewis Carroll's Wonderland, the world of Tom and Huck seemed bold, harsh, and thrilling.

▶TRENDS IN EARLY POETRY

Poetry for children has gone through similar changes. The earliest poems were rhyming verses with a definite moral purpose. Then came the teaching poems—"For a Bad Boy," "For a Selfish Child," and the like—again in rhyming verse with heavy-handed lessons.

Eric Carle's layered collages and die-cut pages of *The Very Hungry Caterpillar* portray the metamorphosis of the title character (*left*) into a colorful butterfly. *Scroobious Pip* (*below*) is brought to life by Nancy Ekholm Burkert's colored pencils.

Then, in 1789, came a book of truly lyrical poetry singing the joys of childhood in a world sustained by love. This was *Songs of Innocence* by the great English poet William Blake. These poems are still widely read, usually more by adults than by children.

Almost 100 years later *A Child's Garden of Verses* (1885) by Robert Louis Stevenson appeared. The children in Stevenson's poem climb trees, play with their shadows, go up in swings, and have a joyous time. There are no morals in these poems and no frightening warnings—only the invitation to enjoy each moment to the fullest.

▶20TH-CENTURY LITERATURE FOR CHILDREN

Literature for children in the United States has expanded dramatically in the 1900's. The growth of paperback publishing means that more books are available. A good children's paperback can now have the same lovely illustrations that were used in the hardcover edition, and the price is considerably lower.

In this period, distribution of children's books has grown because of the tremendous increase of school libraries where children can easily borrow books on a regular basis. At the same time, paperback book clubs have swept the country, enabling children to buy their own low-cost paperbacks right in the classroom.

As children's literature has grown in the number of books published and the quantity distributed, certain early trends have continued to develop and grow. Among these are the popularity of the picture book, growing realism in the stories, and the appeal of imaginative literature or fantasy.

The Popularity of the Picture Book

In most of the earliest books for children, the illustrations were an afterthought. But in the Caldecott "toy books," the pictures were as important as the few lines of copy, and they occupied far more space. One can almost read the nursery rhyme from the dramatic action in the pictures.

Since that time hundreds of highly successful picture books have been published in England and the United States. In these the text and illustrations seem to go together perfectly. Often one person is both author and illustrator—for example, Robert McCloskey of *Make Way for Ducklings;* John Burningham of *Mr. Gumpy's Outing;* and Arnold Lobel of *Frog and Toad Together.* Many equally successful picture books have been produced by an author-artist team, as in *The Story About Ping,* written by Marjorie Flack and illustrated by Kurt Wiese; *The Happy Lion,* written by Louise Fatio and illustrated by Roger Duvoisin; and *Why Mosquitoes Buzz in People's Ears,* written by Verna Aardema and illustrated by Leo and Diane Dillon.

Wordless picture books have also become popular in this period. With a little help, a 3- or 4-year-old likes to follow the sequence of the pictures and tell the story they suggest. A delightful example of the wordless picture book is *Sunshine,* created by Jan Ormerod.

For many appealing picturebooks, American publishers have drawn on artists from other countries. Among them are Leo Lionni from Italy, Feodor Rojankowsky from Russia, Roger Duvoisin from Switzerland, Taro Yashima from Japan, and Ludwig Bemelmans from Southeast Europe. These artists have brought great diversity to American children's book illustration and have sharpened interest in original, imaginative work.

Growing Realism

Realism, which began to appear in children's books in the 1870's, has grown bolder and more widespread since 1950—even for the picture-book age. One vivid example is *Apt. 3,* written and illustrated by Ezra Jack Keats, who tells of two lonely boys and a blind man in an ugly tenement—in picture-book format with superb illustrations.

Equally piercing are those stories that hinge on the breakup of a family and the struggle children make to adjust. In *Homecoming* by Cynthia Voigt, four children, abandoned by their mother, make their way from Connecticut to southern Maryland to seek a home with an unknown grandmother. In *Dear Mr. Henshaw* by Beverly Cleary, a 10-year-old writes in letters and his journal of his frustrations over his parents' recent divorce.

There are some splendid books of nonfiction that also deal with such situations. Notable among these is *How It Feels When Parents Divorce* by Jill Krementz, a collection of actual reports of nineteen youngsters, ages 7 to 16. Their comments are very revealing.

Old age and death have become more frequent topics in children's books as well. In *Maxie* by Mildred Kantrowitz, apartment house neighbors gather to help the old woman upstairs who feels unloved and unneeded. Often it is a grandmother or grandfather who is seen to be failing physically. Such a book is *Annie and the Old One* by Miska Miles, the tale of a little Navajo girl who finds she cannot prevent the death of her aged grandmother.

In *Bridge to Terabithia*, Katherine Paterson writes of the beautiful companionship of two children that is shattered by death—a topic that until recently was considered inappropriate for children.

A Taste of Blackberries by Doris Buchanan Smith tells the story of a boy's death from bee stings and the grief and feeling of guilt that hang over his friend. And in *Bridge to Terabithia,* Katherine Paterson writes of the beautiful companionship of two children that is shattered by death.

For some children, parents are a problem, too, especially those parents whose plans and expectations put the child in an unhappy situation. Manolo, the son of a famous Spanish bullfighter, is in that predicament in *Shadow of a Bull* by Maia Wojciechowska. Few children are expected to become famous bullfighters, but they understand Manolo's problem and admire his revolt against adult demands.

In *Freaky Friday* by Mary Rodgers, a 13-year-old wakes up one Friday to find she is her own mother, saddled with the problems common to all mothers. Parent-child conflicts are thus seen from a new perspective.

Despite the growing realism in children's books, few have shown an accurate picture of our multiracial society in the United States. When Native Americans were part of the story, they were often pictured with war paint and tomahawks. Black Americans were almost always shown as smiling servants dependent on their white masters. In text and art, Asians and Mexican Americans were often pictured as ignorant and inferior.

However, in the 1950's and 1960's, the movement for racial equality began to gather force in the United States. Partly in response to this movement, the all-white world of children's books began to give way to a world where people of all races were pictured realistically and sympathetically.

The Snowy Day by Ezra Jack Keats, *Stevie* by John Steptoe, and *Everett Anderson's Goodbye* by Lucille Clifton are picturebook stories of black children in the inner city. *Ten, Nine, Eight* by Molly Bang is a story of a black father and his little girl. These are warmly real, lovable children with humor, curiosity, and wisdom—qualities sometimes reserved for white children in years past.

For middle-grade readers, *Sounder* by William H. Armstrong is the bittersweet story of a black sharecropper's family. *Roll of Thunder, Hear My Cry* by Mildred D. Taylor tells of a black Mississippi family's fight against economic injustice and racial violence during the Depression.

Young readers inevitably root for the slightly naughty hero of Beatrix Potter's animal fantasy *The Tale of Peter Rabbit*.

Fantasy in Children's Literature

Despite the surge of realism in literature for children in the later 1900's, fantasy has persisted. Indeed, it has flourished.

Familiar folktales have been reissued in new formats and with new illustrations. Now there are beautifully illustrated tales from Haiti, China, Russia, West Africa, and middle European Jewish folklore as well as from Canada and Western Europe.

Many modern writers and illustrators have created their own tales of "the never was." Among the most popular are the stories in which animals have human qualities.

One of the most loved of these storybook animals is the hero of *The Tale of Peter Rabbit* (1901), written and illustrated by Beatrix Potter of England. The rabbits speak perfect English and are pictured in the dress of villagers at the turn of the century.

Also from England came *The Wind in the Willows* by Kenneth Grahame, illustrated by E. H. Shepard. This tells of the adventures of four devoted friends: Rat, Mole, Toad, and Badger, who reside on the banks of the Thames River.

Probably the most popular book of American children is an animal fantasy: *Charlotte's Web*, written by E. B. White and illustrated by Garth Williams. The unlikely friends are Wilbur the pig, Templeton the rat, and Charlotte the spider, who could write messages in her web.

The characters in many popular fantasies seem as real as the reader. But then things seem to happen, unbelievable things, and fantasy takes over. *Pippi Longstocking*, by

Astrid Lindgren of Sweden, is the story of a girl who lives with her monkey and horse and walks a tightrope in a circus.

The widely popular *Harry Potter* books by British author J. K. Rowling have a similar appeal. Readers of all ages sympathize and identify with the title character as he escapes his grim home life and enters the magical world of a school for wizards.

In contrast are those characters in tales of fantasy who are gentle and understanding, the ones who are searching for meaning in all they do. In *Tuck Everlasting*, Natalie Babbitt leaves the reader wide-eyed, for young Winnie Foster meets members of the Tuck family, who once drank from the spring that gave them life everlasting.

Horror stories, such as the *Goosebumps* series by R. L. Stine, are another form of fantasy that has become very popular with older children. Not actually meant to "horrify," these books provide scary thrills with tales about ghosts and monsters.

Children's Book Awards

Many awards recognize excellence in children's books. Two of the best-known U.S. awards are the Newbery Medal, given each year to the author of the most distinguished American children's book, and the Caldecott Medal, an annual award for American illustrators. Both medals are awarded by the American Library Association (ALA). For more information on these awards and for lists of winners, see the article CALDECOTT AND NEWBERY MEDALS in this volume. The

A fable loved by both children and adults, E. B. White's *Charlotte's Web* tells of the rescue of Wilbur the pig by his friend Charlotte, a spider. This gentle essay on friendship is illustrated by Garth Williams.

The Random House Book of Poetry offers children 572 fine, funny, illuminating poems exuberantly illustrated by Arnold Lobel.

ALA also awards the Laura Ingalls Wilder Award to an author or illustrator for a body of work. The award, established in 1954, is given every three years.

Each year since 1947, the Canadian Association of Children's Librarians has bestowed the Book of the Year for Children Award on outstanding Canadian books in both English and French.

In England, the Carnegie Medal is awarded annually to the most outstanding book by a British author. It was established in 1937 by the Library Association of England. Since 1957, the association has also awarded the Kate Greenaway Medal for distinguished work in the illustration of British children's books.

The Hans Christian Andersen Medal was established in 1956 by the International Board on Books for Young People. It is presented every two years to both an author and an illustrator for a complete body of work.

▶ THE NEW BOOKS OF INFORMATION

The earliest books for children were created to give information. Facts were spelled out with a heavy hand, sometimes almost a threat.

Now 300 years later, the best informational books for children are written in a lively, appealing style and have many illustrations.

Many of these books are written simply to appeal to young readers, often covering only a small topic within a broad subject. For example, Franklyn M. Branley has written several short, easy-to-read books about the weather, such as *Flash, Crash, Rumble and Roar* about thunderstorms.

Once children have been introduced to a subject in such simple and inviting books, they are ready to hunt up more books for further exploration.

For advanced readers there are many informational books in almost every subject area. Here again, the more appealing books seem to be those that introduce only a limited segment of a total field. For example, *The Glorious Flight* by Alice and Martin Provensen presents not the history of aviation, but the picture story of one of the first flying machines.

▶ POETRY REFLECTS EVERY TREND

Since World War II, the number of poetry books for children has increased tremendously. Sometimes a single poem with illustrations becomes a one-poem picturebook, such as *Listen Rabbit* by Aileen Fisher, illustrated by Symeon Shimin. *The Random House Book of Poetry for Children*, compiled by Jack Prelutsky, includes more than 400 delightful illustrations by Arnold Lobel. Thus these new books of poetry have a very different look from those of 75 years earlier.

The realism that marks many of the outstanding books of fiction shows up in poetry as well. Now there are poems about littered streets and heavy traffic, about the broken washing machine and the city dump.

But these are only part of the whole. There are many poems about people, sometimes glad, sometimes sad. Some poems are hilarious, such as *Oh, What Nonsense!* and *Hurry, Hurry, Mary Dear;* others, like *Honey, I Love,* are love poems.

The distinguishing feature of the poems popular with children today seems to be their emotional appeal. Children are drawn into the exaggerated, sometimes wacky humor of Shel Silverstein. But they also like the poems that leave them thinking and allow them to share the poet's feelings. As one fourth grader said of the poet David McCord, "He is just like me. He feels."

▶ IDENTIFYING WITH BOOKS

Most children seem to want to become involved when they select a book, be it poetry or prose, fiction or nonfiction. They hang onto every word of *Charlotte's Web* because they identify emotionally with the characters— laughing, sighing, weeping as the story unfolds. Judy Blume's books are completely different in character, setting, and plot, but they touch young readers' emotions and pierce their inner thoughts.

When this happens, children keep reading. As Daniel Fader, American writer and educator, puts it, they are "hooked on books."

NANCY LARRICK
Author, *A Parent's Guide to Children's Reading*

Children's Books Too Good to Miss

The past 50 years, often called a golden age in children's books, produced many books that have become modern classics, ones too good to miss. Each year more treasures are added to the wealth of choices for children. The lists below contain some of the best current books, as well as classics from earlier times.

The books are grouped by age level or category and listed alphabetically by title within each group. Following the book titles, the author or editor, illustrator, publisher, date, and a brief annotation are given. To indicate the age level for which each book is likely to be most appropriate, the following code is used:

N = Nursery school and kindergarten (age 5 and under)

P = Primary (ages 6 to 8)

I = Intermediate (ages 9 to 11)

A = Advanced readers (ages 10 to 13)

FOR THE YOUNGEST

Fish Eyes: A Book You Can Count On, written and ill. by Lois Ehlert. (Harcourt Brace 1990). Dramatic collages make this counting book a visual delight. N–P

Freight Train, written and ill. by Donald Crews. (Greenwillow 1978). A black steam engine pulls brightly colored train cars and, of course, a red caboose, through cities and countryside. N–P

Goodnight Moon, by Margaret Wise Brown. Ill. by Clement Hurd. (HarperCollins 1947). This captivating bedtime story has lulled millions of children to sleep. N

Have You Seen My Duckling?, written and ill. by Nancy Tafuri. (Greenwillow 1984). An adventurous duckling keeps his mother guessing as to his whereabouts. N–P

Ira Sleeps Over, written and ill. by Bernard Waber. (Houghton 1972). Ira wants to take his teddy bear when he spends the night at Reggie's house but fears ridicule. P

In the Small, Small Pond, written and ill. by Denise Fleming. (Holt 1994). Tadpoles wriggle, frogs jiggle, dragonfly wings quiver in the small, small pond. N–P

Old Black Fly, by Jim Aylesworth. Ill. by Stephen Gammell. (Holt 1992). A fly buzzes through the alphabet toward a smashing end. N–P

Max's First Word, written and ill. by Rosemary Wells. (Dial 1979). Ruby tries to teach her brother, Max, to say the right word but Max has a mind of his own. N

My Mama Needs Me, by Mildred Pitts Walter. Ill. by Pat Cummings. (Lothrop 1983). Jason stays close to his mother in case she needs him to help with his new baby sister. P

The Napping House, by Audrey Wood. Ill. by Don Wood. (Harcourt Brace 1984). An assortment of people and things pile on top of a snoring Granny in a rhythmic cumulative tale. P

Sunshine, ill. by Jan Ormerod. (Lothrop 1981). Wordless picture book records the start of a little girl's day. N

Ten, Nine, Eight, written and ill. by Molly Bang. (Greenwillow 1983). A father and daughter play a rhyming countdown game as a bedtime ritual. N–P

In Jan Ormerod's *Sunshine,* a small girl is awakened early by the sun. Her morning routine, which culminates as the family leaves the house, is expressed so well in richly shaded pictures that there is no need for words at all.

Chris Van Allsburg won the 1982 Caldecott Medal for *Jumanji*, in which a board game springs to life. The black-and-white drawings hold an ominous light and recall many a lazy afternoon spent at home with time to imagine the improbable.

Tomie de Paola's Mother Goose, selected and ill. by Tomie de Paola. (Putnam 1985). Over 200 traditional rhymes, cheerfully illustrated. N-P

The Very Hungry Caterpillar, written and ill. by Eric Carle. (Philomel 1981). A hungry caterpillar eats his way through the week, makes a cocoon, and finally turns into a gloriously colored butterfly. N-P

Taro Yashima successfully pairs a poignant story with vivid yet sensitive pictures in *Crow Boy.*

PICTURE STORY BOOKS

Amazing Grace, by Mary Hoffman. Ill. by Caroline Binch. (Dial 1991). Grace discovers she can be anything she wants to be. P

Arthur Goes to Camp, written and ill. by Marc Brown. (Little Brown 1982). Life at summer camp is as bad as Arthur fears it will be, until he becomes a hero. P

The Art Lesson, written and ill. by Tomie de Paola. (Putnam 1989). Tommy is frustrated by demands to color within the lines, but an understanding art teacher gives him freedom to improvise. P-I

Bartholomew and the Oobleck, written and ill. by Dr. Seuss. (Random House 1949). A king, tired of rain, snow, sunshine, and fog, is more upset when green oobleck falls from the skies. P

Bedtime for Frances, by Russell Hoban. Ill. by Garth Williams. (HarperCollins 1960). A badger child named Frances manages to postpone bedtime. N-P

Chair for My Mother, written and ill. by Vera Williams. (Greenwillow 1982). A young girl helps to save money for a new chair after a fire destroys their home. P

Corduroy, written and ill. by Don Freeman. (Viking 1968). No one wants to buy the bear Corduroy because he lost a button on his shoulder straps. P

Crow Boy, written and ill. by Taro Yashima. (Viking 1955). A shy mountain boy in Japan wins respect in his school at last. P

Curious George, written and ill. by H. A. Rey. (Houghton 1952). A mischievous monkey has great adventures. N-P

Doctor DeSoto, written and ill. by William Steig. (Farrar 1982). A mouse dentist must extract a tooth from an ailing fox patient. P

Fly Away Home, by Eve Bunting. Ill. by Ronald Himler. (Clarion 1991). Homeless, Andrew and his father live at the airport, where they try not to be noticed. P-I

Frederick, written and ill. by Leo Lionni. (Knopf 1967). Frederick dreams while other field mice store food for winter, but he feeds them with his poems. P

George and Martha, written and ill. by James Marshall. (Houghton 1972). Two hippos prove the worth of true friendship. N-P

Gorilla, written and ill. by Anthony Browne. (Knopf 1985). A single father shows his daughter, Hannah, that he loves her. P

Grandfather's Journey, written and ill. by Allen Say. (Houghton 1993). Grandfather moves between Japan and the United States, always homesick for the other place. P-I

Jumanji, written and ill. by Chris Van Allsburg. (Houghton 1981). Two children find a board game that brings jungle animals to life. P

In *Doctor DeSoto,* by William Steig, a mouse dentist uses a clever ruse to treat a foxy patient—and survive!

Madeline, written and ill. by Ludwig Bemelmans. (Viking 1939). In a French boarding school, little Madeline leads all the rest. P

Make Way for Ducklings, written and ill. by Robert McCloskey. (Viking 1941). A family of mallards stops traffic in Boston as the mother marches them across the street. P

Mike Mulligan and His Steam Shovel, written and ill. by Virginia Lee Burton. (Houghton 1939). Mike and his steam shovel, Mary Anne, dig their way to new fame. P

Millions of Cats, written and ill. by Wanda Gag. (Coward/Putnam 1928). An old man looks for a cat and finds millions and billions and trillions of cats. P

Ezra Jack Keats received the Caldecott Medal for his depiction of an inner-city snowfall in *The Snowy Day.*

Mirandy and Brother Wind, by Patricia McKissack. Ill. by Jerry Pinkney. (Knopf 1988). Mirandy catches the wind in her first dance contest. P

Mirette on the High Wire, written and ill. by Emily Arnold McCully. (Putnam 1992). Mirette helps Bellini, a retired high-wire walker, to regain his courage. P-I

Miss Nelson Is Missing, by Harry Allard. Ill. by James Marshall. (Houghton 1977). One day at school, a mean substitute teacher, Miss Viola Swamp, replaces gentle, kind Miss Nelson. The class shapes up quickly. P

Miss Rumphius, written and ill. by Barbara Cooney. (Viking 1982). Great Aunt Alice travels widely before she fulfills her grandfather's request to make the world more beautiful. P-I

Mr. Gumpy's Outing, written and ill. by John Burningham. (Holt 1970). Mr. Gumpy takes children and farm animals on a boat ride but warns them "Don't flap about." P

Nana Upstairs and Nana Downstairs, written and ill. by Tomie de Paola. (Putnam 1973, 1987). Tommy visits his 94-year-old great-grandmother upstairs and his grandmother who lives downstairs. P-I

Officer Buckle and Gloria, written and ill. by Peggy Rathman. (Putnam 1995). Policeman Buckle gives boring talks about safety until Gloria, the dog, joins him. P-I

Owl Moon, by Jane Yolen. Ill. by John Schoenherr. (Philomel 1987). Poetic story about a father and daughter who search for an owl on a moonlit night. P

Ox-Cart Man, by Donald Hall. Ill. by Barbara Cooney. (Viking 1979). In the 1800's, a New England farmer takes his wares to market. P-I

Pink and Say, written and ill. by Patricia Polacco. (Philomel 1994). An African American Union soldier befriends a wounded white soldier during the Civil War. I-A

The Relatives Came, by Cynthia Rylant. Ill. by Stephen Gammell. (Bradbury 1985). Rousing warmth, humor, and turmoil during a family reunion. P

Smoky Night, by Eve Bunting. Ill. by David Diaz. (Harcourt 1994). Daniel and his mother watch riots outside their Los Angeles apartment before escaping to a shelter. Spectacular art matches the intensity of the story. I-A

The Snowy Day, written and ill. by Ezra Jack Keats. (Viking 1962). Peter explores a new snowfall and tries to take a snowball home in his pocket. N-P

Song and Dance Man, by Karen Ackerman. Ill. by Stephen Gammell. (Knopf 1988). Grandpa demonstrates his old vaudeville acts to his grandchildren. P

Stevie, written and ill. by John Steptoe. (Harper 1969). Robert resents his mother's attention to Stevie, a younger child for whom she babysits. N-P

Sunday Outing, by Gloria Pinkney. Ill. by Jerry Pinkney. (Dial 1994). Ernestine takes the train to North Carolina to visit her birthplace. P

Tale of Peter Rabbit, written and ill. by Beatrix Potter. (Warne 1901). A favorite of all generations. N-P

Tar Beach, written and ill. by Faith Ringgold. (Crown 1991). Cassie dreams of flying over the necklace of the bridge lights from her rooftop tar beach. P

Uncle Jed's Barbershop, by Margaree Mitchell. Ill. by James Ransome. (Simon & Schuster 1993). Uncle Jed uses his savings for family emergencies instead of keeping it for the barbershop he wants. P

When I Was Young in the Mountains, by Cynthia Rylant. Ill. by Diane Goode. (Dutton 1982). Poetic narrative about traditions in the author's rural mountain home. P

Where the Wild Things Are, written and ill. by Maurice Sendak. (HarperCollins 1963). Max tames the wild things on his voyage out of his bedroom one night. N-P

FOLK TALES, FAIRY TALES, AND LEGENDS

Duffy and the Devil, a Cornish Tale, retold by Harve Zemach. Ill. by Margot Zemach. (Farrar 1973). A variation of the Rumpelstiltskin folktale about spinning gold from straw and guessing names. P-I

Jump! The Adventures of Brer Rabbit by Joel Chandler Harris, adapted by Van Dyke Parks and Malcolm Jones. Ill. by Barry Moser. (Harcourt Brace 1986). The wily trickster of African American folklore remains free. I

Legend of the Bluebonnet: An Old Tale of Texas, retold and ill. by Tomie de Paola. (Putnam 1983). The Comanche Indians suffer a long drought until a child makes a great sacrifice to bring the rain. P-I

Three sisters outwit a hungry wolf in *Lon Po Po*, a Chinese folk tale retold and illustrated by Ed Young.

In Maurice Sendak's Caldecott Medal–winning *Where the Wild Things Are*, even the fiercest-looking creatures cannot frighten young Max. Young readers revel in the story of Max's bravery and his safe return home.

Alexander wakes up with gum in his hair—just the first of many things that go wrong in Judith Viorst's classic *Alexander and the Terrible, Horrible, No Good, Very Bad Day*. The illustrations are by Ray Cruz.

Little Red Riding Hood, retold from the Brothers Grimm and ill. by Trina Schart Hyman. (Holiday 1983). A faithful retelling of the little girl taking food to her grandmother. P-I

Lon Po Po: A Red-Riding Hood Story from China, translated and ill. by Ed Young. (Philomel 1989). Three sisters alone at home outwit the wolf who comes to eat them. P-I

The Mitten, retold and ill. by Jan Brett. (Putnam 1989). Numerous forest animals keep warm by squeezing into a lost mitten. P

Mufaro's Beautiful Daughters: An African Tale, written and ill. by John Steptoe. (Lothrop 1987). The king must choose between the good sister and bad sister in a tale inspired by African folklore. P-I

The People Could Fly: American Black Folktales, by Virginia Hamilton. Ill. by Leo and Diane Dillon. (Knopf 1985). Rich folklore, including tales of slavery. P-I

Dr. Seuss uses only 175 different words to tell the rollicking story of *The Cat in the Hat.*

Princess Furball, retold by Charlotte Huck. Ill. by Anita Lobel. (Greenwillow 1989). A version of the Cinderella story lovingly retold and illustrated. P-I

Rapunzel, retold from the Brothers Grimm by Barbara Rogasky. Ill. by Trina Schart Hyman. (Holiday 1982). The girl hidden in the witch's tower lets down her long braid of hair for the prince to climb up. P-I

Rough-Face Girl, retold by Rafe Martin. Ill. by David Shannon. (Putnam 1992). An Algonquin Indian version of the Cinderella story lets inner strength and beauty shine through. P-I

Rumpelstiltskin, by Jacob Grimm. Retold and ill. by Paul Zelinsky. (Dutton 1986). The miller's daughter gets help spinning straw into gold. P

The Sword and the Circle: King Arthur and the Knights of the Round Table, by Rosemary Sutcliff. (Dutton 1981). Strong, poetic retelling of the Arthurian legend. I

The Talking Eggs: A Folktale from the American South, retold by Robert San Souci. Ill. by Jerry Pinkney. (Dial 1991). A version of the good sister-bad sister story adapted from a Creole folktale. P-I

Tikki Tikki Tembo, retold by Arlene Mosel. Ill. by Blair Lent. (Holt 1967). The story of a Chinese boy whose long name interferes with his rescue from a well. P

The True Story of the Three Little Pigs, by Jon Scieszka. Ill. by Lane Smith. (Viking 1989). A fractured fairy tale told from the point of view of the wolf. P-I

Why Mosquitoes Buzz in People's Ears: A West African Tale, retold by Verna Aardena. Ill. by Leo and Diane Dillon. (Dial 1975). A cumulative tale set in motion by a buzzing mosquito. P

Yeh Shen: A Cinderella Story from China, retold by Ai-Ling Louie. Ill. by Ed Young. (Philomel 1990). A Chinese version of the Cinderella story. P-I

Zlateh the Goat and Other Stories, by Isaac Bashevis Singer. Ill. by Maurice Sendak. (Harper 1966). Seven tales from Middle-European Jewish folklore. P-I

BOOKS FOR INDEPENDENT READING, AGES 5–8

Alexander and the Terrible, Horrible, No Good, Very Bad Day, by Judith Viorst. Ill. by Ray Cruz. (Atheneum 1972). When everything goes wrong, Alexander wants to run away to Australia. P

Are You My Mother?, written and ill. by P. D. Eastman. (Random 1960). A baby bird searches for its mother in a rhythmic, lyrical story told in only 100 different words. P

Brown Bear, Brown Bear, What Do You See?, by Bill Martin, Jr. Ill. by Eric Carle. (Holt 1963). A repetitive, patterned question-and-answer story game that beginning readers master quickly. N-P

Cam Jansen and the Mystery of the Stolen Diamonds, by David Adler. Ill. by Susanni Natti. (Viking 1980). Cam's photographic memory helps make her a great detective. Series. P-I

The tender affection between two best friends is the theme of Arnold Lobel's Frog and Toad books.

Caps for Sale, written and ill. by Esphyr Slobodkina. (HarperCollins 1947). A troupe of monkeys tease a cap peddler by imitating everything he does. P

The Cat in the Hat, written and ill. by Dr. Seuss. (Random 1957). An uninvited cat marches in; a hilarious story in verse. P

Chicka Chicka Boom Boom, by Bill Martin, Jr. and John Archambault. Ill. by Lois Ehlert. (Simon & Schuster 1991). A rollicking rhyme about the alphabet and a coconut tree. N-P

Danny and the Dinosaur, written and ill. by Syd Hoff. (HarperCollins 1958). A boy and a museum dinosaur have a day on the town. P

Fox and his Friends, by Edward Marshall. Ill. by James Marshall. (Penguin 1994). Fox plans adventures with his friends but must babysit his little sister. Series. P

Frog and Toad Are Friends, written and ill. by Arnold Lobel. (HarperCollins 1970). Five short stories about the adventures of true friends. Series. P

Good Work, Amelia Bedelia, by Peggy Parish. Ill. by Lynn Sweat. (Greenwillow 1976). A literal-minded maid makes a sponge cake from sponges and a chicken dinner only a chicken would eat. Series. P

Harry's Mom, by Barbara Porte. Ill. by Yossi Abolafia. (Greenwillow 1985). Harry reads the definition of an orphan and decides he must be one. Series. P-I

Henry and Mudge and the Bedtime Thumps, by Cynthia Rylant. Ill. by Sucie Stevenson. (Bradbury/Macmillan 1991). Henry loves his dog Mudge very much. Series. P

In the Tall, Tall Grass, written and ill. by Denise Fleming. (Holt 1991). A caterpillar crawls through tall grass to observe busy animals. N-P

King Bidgood's in the Bathtub, by Audrey Wood. Ill. by Don Wood. (Harcourt 1985). The king creates a crisis because he won't get out of the bathtub. P

Little Bear, by Else Holmelund Minarik. Ill. by Maurice Sendak. (HarperCollins 1957). The adventures of a lovable little bear. P

Nate the Great and the Missing Key, by Marjorie Sharmat. Ill. by Marc Simont. (Putnam 1981). Nate the Great, a boy detective, solves any kind of mystery. Series. P

Oliver Pig at School, by Jean Van Leeuwen. Ill. by Ann Schweninger. (Dial 1990). Four short stories about Oliver's first day at school. Series. P

Rosie's Walk, written and ill. by Pat Hutchins. (Macmillan 1968). Rosie leads the fox who is chasing her on a wild goose chase. N-P

Wiley and the Hairy Man, written and ill. by Molly Garrett Bang. (Macmillan 1976). Wiley and his mother foil the hairy man; based on black American folklore. P

STORIES FOR AGES 9 TO 12

Anastasia Krupnik, by Lois Lowry. (Houghton 1979). Anastasia's list of likes and dislikes changes dramatically with the arrival of a new baby brother. I

Annie and the Old One, by Miska Miles. Ill. by Peter Parnall. (Little 1971). An Indian girl tries to forestall her grandmother's death and learns a beautiful lesson. I

Are You There, God? It's Me, Margaret, by Judy Blume. (Bradbury/Macmillan 1970; 1982). Eleven-year-old Margaret discusses all her concerns with God. I

Babe: The Gallant Pig, by Dick King-Smith. Ill. by Mary Rayner. (Crown 1983). A sheepdog adopts the piglet Babe, who learns to become a sheep pig. I

Bingo Brown and the Language of Love, by Betsy Byars. (Viking 1989). Bingo Brown is challenged by mixed-sex conversations. I

The Book of Three, by Lloyd Alexander. (Holt 1964). An assistant pig-keeper becomes a hero in a fantasy based on Welsh myths. I

The Borrowers, by Mary Norton. Ill. by Beth and Joe Krush. (Harcourt 1953). Little people live by "borrowing" from the giant world around them. I

Bridge to Terabithia, by Katherine Paterson. (Crowell 1977). A 10-year-old boy and his new friend establish a magic kingdom in the woods. I

The Cabin Faced West, by Jean Fritz. Ill. by Feodor Rojankovsky. (Coward 1958). Loneliness vanishes as 10-year-old Ann learns to cope with life in western Pennsylvania in 1784. I

Charlotte's Web, by E. B. White. Ill. by Garth Williams. (HarperCollins 1952). A gentle spider saves the life of Wilbur the pig by spinning messages in her web. P-I

The Children of Green Knowe, by L. M. Boston. Ill. by Peter Boston. (Harcourt 1955). An English boy encounters three 17th-century children in his great-grandmother's ancient house. I

Class Clown, by Johanna Hurwitz. Ill. by Sheila Hamanaka. (Morrow 1987). Third grader Lucas tries to be perfect in school. I

The Dark Is Rising, by Susan Cooper. Ill. by Alan Cober. (Atheneum 1973). When he turns 11, Will finds he is one of the Old Ones who must triumph over the evil forces of the Dark. I-A

Dear Mr. Henshaw, by Beverly Cleary. Ill. by Paul O. Zelinsky. (Morrow 1983). A 10-year-old boy pours forth his frustrations over his parents' recent divorce. I

Dragonwings, by Laurence Yep. (HarperCollins 1975). A young Chinese boy in turn-of-the-century San Francisco helps his father build a flying machine. I

Dick King-Smith's *Babe: The Gallant Pig* gained new fans when it was made into a popular film in 1995.

Laura Ingalls Wilder's Little House books have been popular with children since the 1930's.

From the Mixed-Up Files of Mrs. Basil E. Frankweiler, by E. L. Konigsburg. (Atheneum 1967). Two runaway children hide out in the Metropolitan Museum of Art. I

Harriet the Spy, written and ill. by Louise Fitzhugh. (HarperCollins 1964). A self-appointed spy, age 11, faces resentment when her notebook is seized. I

Homer Price, written and ill. by Robert McCloskey. (Viking 1943). Small-town resident Homer Price gets involved in some hilarious projects. P-I

The House of Sixty Fathers, by Meindert DeJong. Ill. by Maurice Sendak. (HarperCollins 1956). Through war-torn China, a small boy and his pet pig search valiantly for his family.

The Hundred Dresses, by Eleanor Estes. Ill. by Louis Slobodkin. (Harcourt 1944). Wanda, a Polish girl who always wears the same dress, is ridiculed by her classmates. I

James and the Giant Peach, by Roald Dahl. Ill. by Nancy Ekholm Burkert. (Knopf 1961). Magical adventures await readers who ride with James inside a giant peach. I

Jar of Dreams, by Yoshiko Uchida. (Atheneum 1981). Rinko learns strength and love growing up in her Japanese-American community. I

The Lion, the Witch and the Wardrobe, by C. S. Lewis. (Macmillan 1950). Four children enter a magical, wintry country through an old wardrobe. I

Little House in the Big Woods, by Laura Ingalls Wilder. Ill. by Garth Williams. (HarperCollins 1953). Autobiographical story of a pioneer family in Wisconsin in the 1870's. P-I

Mary Poppins, by P. L. Travers. (Harcourt 1934). An extraordinary nursemaid who blew in with the east wind and slides up the banister with ease. P-I

Mrs. Frisby and the Rats of NIMH, by Robert C. O'Brien. Ill. by Zena Bernstein. (Atheneum 1971). Rats, the subjects of a laboratory experiment, learn to read, write, and think. I

Number the Stars, by Lois Lowry. (Houghton 1989). Ten-year-old Annemarie and her family help Ellen Rosen's family escape from the Nazi soldiers. I

Pippi Longstocking, by Astrid Lindgren. (Viking 1950). Escapades of a 9-year-old Swedish girl who lives with a monkey and a horse. I

Sarah, Plain and Tall, by Patricia MacLachlan. (Harper 1985). Caleb and Anna hope Sarah, from Maine, likes their Nebraska farm and their father well enough to stay and marry. P-I

The Sign of the Beaver, by Elizabeth George Speare. (Houghton 1983). Twelve-year-old Matt is the sole guard of the family cabin in the Maine woods of 1768. I

Sounder, by William H. Armstrong. Ill. by James Barkley. (HarperCollins 1969). A black share-cropper's family struggles to survive. I-A

Tuck Everlasting, by Natalie Babbitt. (Farrar 1975). Winnie Foster's encounter with the Tuck family leads to a serious choice of accepting eternal life. I

The Wind in the Willows, by Kenneth Grahame. Ill. by E. H. Shepard. (Scribner 1908). Mole, Water Rat, Badger, and Toad take on human qualities in this poetic, humorous tale of river life. I

A Wrinkle in Time, by Madeleine L'Engle. (Farrar 1962). Three youngsters are whisked off to a remote planet by extraterrestrial beings. I

STORIES FOR AGES 12 AND UP

Across Five Aprils, by Irene Hunt. (Follett 1964). How a boy does a man's work during the five springs of the American Civil War. A

Afternoon of the Elves, by Janet Taylor Lisle. (Orchard /Watts 1989). Hillary and Sara-Kate create an elf world in the backyard. I

Dicey's Song, by Cynthia Voigt. (Atheneum 1982). Dicey takes responsibility for her younger siblings. I-A

The Giver, by Lois Lowry. (Houghton 1993). Jonas inherits the job of being the receiver of memories in the controlled world he lives in. I-A

Hatchet, by Gary Paulsen. (Bradbury 1987). Brian, 13, survives 54 days in the Canadian wilderness armed with only a hatchet. I-A

Island of the Blue Dolphins, by Scott O'Dell. (Houghton 1960). The haunting story, based on fact, of an Indian girl who is forced to spend 18 years alone on an island off the coast of California. A

Jericho: A Novel, by Janet Hickman. (Greenwillow 1994). Great-grandmother's recollection of a distant past sometimes pleases and sometimes shocks 12-year-old Angela, who has concerns of her own. I-A

Missing May, by Cynthia Rylant. (Orchard/Watts 1992). A girl helps her uncle face the grief of losing his beloved wife. I-A

My Brother Sam Is Dead, by James Lincoln Collier and Christopher Collier. (Four Winds

A 12-year-old girl seeks to learn about her family history in *Plain City*, by Virginia Hamilton.

1975). Tim's family is torn apart when his brother joins the rebels in the Revolutionary War. A

My Side of the Mountain, written and ill. by Jean George. (Dutton 1959). A runaway New York City boy tells of his year living in a hollowed-out hemlock tree in the Catskills. I-A

Plain City, by Virginia Hamilton. (Blue Sky/Scholastic 1993). A 12-year-old girl of mixed parentage tries to search for her family history. A

Prairie Songs, by Pam Conrad. (HarperCollins 1985). Louisa and her brother are entranced by the doctor's wife, who tries to adjust to life on the Nebraska prairie. A

Redwall, by Brian Jacques. (Philomel 1986). The animals who live in Redwall Abbey are forced to fight an evil rat and his band of thugs. A

Roll of Thunder, Hear My Cry, by Mildred Taylor. (Dial 1976). A close-knit black family faces the realities of life in Mississippi during the Depression. A

So Far From the Bamboo Grove, by Yoko Kawashima Watkins. (Lothrop 1986). Eight-year-old Yoko escapes from Korea during World War II in this disturbing and triumphant autobiography. I

Taking Sides, by Gary Soto. (Harcourt 1991). Lincoln Mendoza must adjust to the move from his Hispanic neighborhood to a white suburban school. A

Walk Two Moons, by Sharon Creech. (HarperCollins 1994). Sal goes with her grandparents to try to find her mother in a story within a story. A

Where the Red Fern Grows, by Wilson Rawls. (Bantam 1961; 1992). Heartache and joy await a boy in the Arkansas mountains who raises two coon dogs. I-A

The Witch of Blackbird Pond, by Elizabeth Speare. (Houghton 1958). A girl from Barbados is drawn into the witchcraft hysteria of colonial New England. A

A Wizard of Earthsea, by Ursula K. LeGuin. Ill. by Ruth Robbins. (Houghton 1968). A young wizard's pride unleashes powerful forces in this rich psychological fantasy. A

The Young Landlords, by Walter Dean Myers. (Penguin 1979). A group of teenagers try to fix up a tenement in Harlem they inadvertently buy for a dollar. A

Z for Zachariah, by Robert C. O'Brien. (Atheneum 1975). Ann believes herself to be the only survivor of nuclear war until she sees smoke from a campfire. A

REAL PEOPLE: BIOGRAPHY

Alvin Ailey, by Andrea Davis Pinkney. Ill. by Brian Pinkney. (Hyperion 1993). Alvin Ailey's dance troupe revolutionized African American dance. I

Anthony Burns: The Defeat and Triumph of a Fugitive Slave, by Virginia Hamilton. (Knopf 1988). Anthony Burns escaped to Massachusetts but was found there, tried, and returned to the South. A

Black Americans: A History in Their Own Words, 1619–1982, edited by Milton Meltzer. (Crowell 1984). Letters, speeches, and other contemporary documents relate the history of blacks in America. I-P

Cleopatra, by Diane Stanley and Peter Vennema. Ill. by Diane Stanley. (Morrow 1994). Follows the life and relationships of the famous Egyptian queen. I-A

Commodore Perry in the Land of the Shogun, by Rhoda Blumberg. Ill. with Hiroshige prints. (Lothrop 1985). Vivid account of the opening of Japan in 1853. I

Diary of a Young Girl, by Anne Frank. Translated from Dutch by B. M. Mooyaart. (Doubleday 1967). Anne Frank's record of hiding in Amsterdam during the German occupation, 1942-1944. I-A

Eleanor Roosevelt: A Life of Discovery, by Russell Freedman. (Clarion 1993). Engaging story of an outstanding woman's life. A

The Glorious Flight: Across the Channel with Louis Bleriot, July 25, 1901, written and ill. by Alice and Martin Provensen. (Viking 1983). Picture story of an early flying machine. P-I

Homesick: My Own Story, by Jean Fritz. (Putnam 1982). The noted biographer tells movingly of her childhood in China in the 1920's. I

Immigrant Kids, by Russell Freedman. (Dutton 1980). Contemporary photos illustrate turn-of-the-century immigrant children at work, at play, at school. I

Lincoln: A Photobiography, by Russell Freedman. (Clarion 1987). Lincoln's life portrayed in clear text and historical photographs. I-A

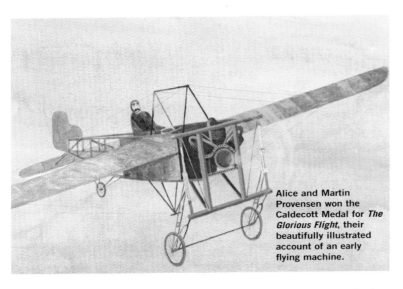

Alice and Martin Provensen won the Caldecott Medal for *The Glorious Flight*, their beautifully illustrated account of an early flying machine.

Make Way for Sam Houston, by Jean Fritz. Ill. by Elise Primavera. (Putnam 1986). Houston, an adopted Indian, officer, and lawyer, was the founding father of Texas. I-A

Michael Jordan: A Life Above the Rim, by Robert Lipsyte. (HarperCollins 1994). The story of basketball and a player that made the game great. I-A

Shaka, King of the Zulus, by Diane Stanley and Peter Vennema. Ill. by Diane Stanley. (Morrow 1988). Shaka learns to defend himself and becomes a great Zulu chief. I

Sojourner Truth: Ain't I a Woman?, by Patricia McKissack and Frederick McKissack. (Scholastic 1992). A freed slave who becomes an abolitionist and feminist. A

To Be a Slave, by Julius Lester. Ill. by Tom Feelings. (Dial 1968). Direct quotes from those who were slaves tell this tragic history of slavery. I-A

War Boy: A Country Childhood, by Michael Foreman. (Little 1990). Foreman grew up in Britain during World War II. I-A

What's the Big Idea, Ben Franklin?, by Jean Fritz. Ill. by Margot Tomas. (Coward/Putnam 1976). A light-hearted story of an inventor, philosopher, and statesman. I

INFORMATIONAL BOOKS: SOCIAL STUDIES AND SCIENCE

Boys' War: Confederate and Union Soldiers Talk about the Civil War, by Jim Murphy. (Clarion 1990). Excerpts from diaries, journals, and letters of young Confederate and Union soldiers show the heartaches of war. I-A

Castle, written and ill. by David Macaulay. (Houghton 1977). Macaulay's drawings show how a fictional 13th-century Welsh castle is built. I

The Great Migration: An American Story, Paintings by Jacob Lawrence. Poem by Walter

Dean Myers. (HarperCollins 1993). African Americans migrate from the rural South to the industrial North. I-A

The Magic School Bus Inside the Earth, by Joanna Cole. Ill. by Bruce Degen. (Scholastic 1987). Surprising, inventive, accurate, and very funny science writing. I

One Day in the Tropical Rain Forest, by Jean Craighead George. Ill. by Gary Allen. (HarperCollins 1990). Hourly increments show destruction of rain forests. I

Saturn, by Seymour Simon. (Morrow 1985). A breathtaking view of the beautiful planet Saturn. Color photos. I

Saving the Peregrine Falcon, by Caroline Arnold. (Carolrhoda 1985). Clear text and colorful photos document the falcon's near-extinction and apparent comeback. I

Volcano: The Eruption and Healing of Mount St. Helens, by Patricia Lauber. (Bradbury 1986). How plant and animal life recover from the devastation of a volcano; full-color photos. I

The Way Things Work, by David Macaulay. (Houghton 1988). Macaulay explains principles underlying technological devices and the way machines work. I-A

Weather, by Seymour Simon. (Morrow 1993). Simon explains wind belts, landforms, and air movement. I-A

POETRY FOR ALL AGES

All the Small Poems, by Valerie Worth. Ill. by Natalie Babbitt. (Farrar 1987). Delicate poems and vivid images. P-I

Been to Yesterdays: Poems of a Life, by Lee Bennett Hopkins. (Wordsong/Boyds Mills 1995). Bittersweet but hopeful autobiographical poems capture meaningful events during the author's thirteenth year. I-A

Brown Angels: An Album of Pictures and Verse, by Walter Dean Myers. (HarperCollins 1993). Poems and turn-of-the-century sepia photographs of children speak clearly of family love. P-I

Brown Honey in Broomwheat Tea: Poems, by Joyce Carol Thomas. Ill. by Floyd Cooper. (HarperCollins 1993). Pride in family heritage emanates from poems and art. P

Dogs & Dragons, Trees & Dreams, written and ill. by Karla Kuskin. (HarperCollins 1980). Sparkling poems with introduction and notes to match. P

Dream Keeper and Other Poems, by Langston Hughes. Ill. by Brian Pinkney. (Knopf 1994). Outstanding poems from the African American experience. I-A

In *The Great Migration*, paintings by noted artist Jacob Lawrence tell the story of the mass movement of African Americans, beginning during World War I, from the rural South to the industrial North.

Families: Poems Celebrating the African American Experience, selected by Dorothy S. Strickland and Michael R. Strickland. Ill. by John Ward. (Wordsong/Boyds Mills 1994). Celebrations of family love. P-I

Good Books, Good Times!, selected by Lee Bennett Hopkins. Ill. by Harvey Stevenson. (HarperCollins 1990). A poetic celebration of the joys of reading. P

Hailstones and Halibut Bones, by Mary O'Neill. Ill. by Leonard Weisgard. (Doubleday 1961). Imaginative poems about colors. I

Halloween A B C, by Eve Merriam. Ill. by Lane Smith. (Macmillan 1987). Spooky poems for each letter of the alphabet. P-I

Honey, I Love, by Eloise Greenfield. Ill. by Diane and Leo Dillon. (HarperCollins 1986). Short, loving poems in language that "seems to slide out of (the) mouth." P

If I Had a Paka: Poems in Eleven Languages, by Charlotte Pomerantz. Ill. by Nancy Tafuri. (Greenwillow 1982; 1993). A poet uses eleven languages to speak in the universal language of poetry. P

I Like You, If You Like Me: Poems of Friendship, selected by Myra Cohn Livingston. (McElderry 1987). Shows the pathos and joy of budding and lifelong friendships. I

In for Winter, Out for Spring, by Arnold Adoff. Ill. by Jerry Pinkney. (Harcourt Brace 1991). A young girl celebrates her family life through the seasons. P

A Jar of Tiny Stars, edited by Bernice E. Cullinan. Ill. by Andi MacLeod. Portraits by Marc Nadel. (Wordsong/ Boyds Mills Press, National Council of Teachers of English 1996). Children's choices of poems from the work of winners of the NCTE Award for Poetry for Children. P-I-A

Joyful Noise: Poems for Two Voices, by Paul Fleischman. Ill. by Eric Beddows. (HarperCollins 1988). Poems about insect noises written for two readers. I-A

A Light in the Attic, by Shel Silverstein. (HarperCollins 1981). Whimsy and broad humor appeal to children. I

Listen, Rabbit, by Aileen Fisher. Ill. by Symeon Shimin. (HarperCollins 1964). A narrative poem of a boy who observes a rabbit in its natural habitat. P

Meet Danitra Brown, by Nikki Grimes. Ill. by Floyd Cooper. (Lothrop 1994). Two African American girls celebrate their special friendship. P

Neighborhood Odes: Poems, by Gary Soto. Ill. by David Diaz. (Harcourt Brace 1992). A Mexican American child celebrates memories of warm tortillas and summer fun. I

New Kid on the Block, by Jack Prelutsky. Ill. by James Stevenson. (Greenwillow 1984). Surprise endings and irreverent humor permeate poems and illustrations. P

Not a Copper Penny in Me House: Poems from the Caribbean, by Monica Gunning. Ill. by Frané Lessac. (Wordsong/Boyds Mills 1993). Autobiographical poems and vibrant colors from a Caribbean child's world. P-I

One at a Time, by David McCord. Ill. by Henry B. Kane. (Little 1978). Joyous, tender, humorous, and always appealing to children. P-I

Oxford Book of Children's Verse in America, selected by Donald Hall. (Oxford University Press 1985). Comprehensive collection of high-quality poetry for children. I

Piping Down the Valleys Wild, selected by Nancy Larrick. Ill. by Ellen Raskin. (Delacorte 1968). More than 200 poems, ranging from folk literature to modern poetry. P-I

The Place My Words Are Looking For, selected by Paul Janeczko. (Bradbury 1990). Poets talk about their work. I-A

The Random House Book of Poetry for Children, compiled by Jack Prelutsky. Ill. by Arnold Lobel.

(Random 1983). More than 570 poems: fine, funny, old, and new. I

The Reason for the Pelican, by John Ciardi. Ill. by Dominic Catalano. (Wordsong/Boyds Mills 1994). Poems that "crackle with energy and overflow with word music," says X. J. Kennedy, fellow poet. I

Reflections on a Gift of Watermelon Pickle and Other Modern Verse, edited by Stephen Dunning and others. Ill. with photos. (Lothrop 1966). More than 100 poems filled with vivid words and imagery. A

Sing a Song of Popcorn, compiled by Beatrice Schenk de Regniers and others. Ill. by 9 Caldecott Medal artists. (Scholastic 1988). More than 100 poems by renowned poets—poems that are funny, spooky, touching, heartwarming, everything children love. N-P-I

Somebody Catch My Homework, by David Harrison. Ill. by Betsy Lewin. (Wordsong/Boyds Mills 1993). Humorous poems about the trials and tribulations of school. P-I

Some of the Days of Everett Anderson, by Lucille Clifton. Ill. by Evaline Ness. (Henry Holt 1970). Six-year-old Everett Anderson celebrates every day in special ways. P

Spirit Walker: Poems, by Nancy Wood. Ill. by Frank Howell. (Doubleday 1993). Taos Indian beliefs and spirits permeate haunting poems and dramatic art. A

Sunflakes: Poems for Children, selected by Lilian Moore. Ill. by Jan Ormerod. (Clarion 1992). An anthology of work chosen by a qualified poet. P-I

Thirteen Moons on Turtle's Back: A Native American Year of Moons, by Joseph Bruchac and Jonathan London. Ill. by Thomas Locker. (Philomel 1992). Poems based on Native American legends from 13 North American tribal nations. I-A

Visit to William Blake's Inn: Poems for Innocent and Experienced Travelers, by Nancy Willard. Ill. by Alice and Martin Provensen. (Harcourt Brace 1981). Poet and artists recreate life in an imaginary inn run by William Blake. I-A

Water Music: Poems for Children, by Jane Yolen. Photos by Jason Stemple. (Wordsong/Boyds Mills 1995). Evocative poems and stunning photographs of drops on a petal or in ponds, rivers, and oceans make water memorable. I-A

When We Were Very Young, by A. A. Milne. Ill. by E. H. Shepard. (Dutton 1924). Poems written for a little boy, about his fun and fantasy. N-P

Where the Sidewalk Ends, poems and drawings by Shel Silverstein. (HarperCollins 1974). Wonderfully appealing to modern youngsters. P-I-A

Words with Wrinkled Knees: Animal Poem, by Barbara Esbensen. Ill. by John Stadler. (Crowell 1986). Strong images create animals as words. P-I

You Come, Too, by Robert Frost. (Holt 1959; 1987). A sampling of Frost's poetry selected for young readers. I

CHILE

The nation of Chile lies along the southwestern coast of South America. Long and narrow in shape, it is partly isolated by geography from its neighbors. In the east, the Andes, one of the world's highest mountain chains, divides Chile from Argentina. The forbidding Atacama Desert in the north separates Chile from Peru and Bolivia. To the west, Chile is bounded by the Pacific Ocean. Southern Chile ends at Cape Horn, the southernmost point of South America.

▶ THE PEOPLE

The Chilean people are mainly of mixed Indian, Spanish, and other European descent. The faces of many Chileans reflect their Indian heritage. But the remaining true Indians number only about 500,000. Most of them are known as Araucanians or *Mapuche*. The Araucanians live on reservations in southern Chile. They survive by fishing, farming, and making handicrafts. In 1997, the oldest known site of human habitation in the Americas— dating back 12,500 years—was discovered at Monte Verde, in southern Chile.

Chilean culture is based largely on Spanish customs. Spanish is the national language, and most of the people are Roman Catholics. Immigrants from other parts of South America, Europe, and the Middle East also contribute to Chile's ethnic makeup. Although few in numbers, they contribute much to Chilean society. Many have become successful in business, agriculture, and politics.

Way of Life

In Chile today, a huge gap still separates the few rich from the many poor. Wealthy Chileans own the factories, banks, and large farms and ranches. They live mainly in the capital city of Santiago or on the great estates surrounding Santiago.

When cities began to grow in the early 1900's, a middle class developed there. The members of this group include doctors, teachers, clerks, merchants, mechanics, agricultural technicians, engineers, and soldiers.

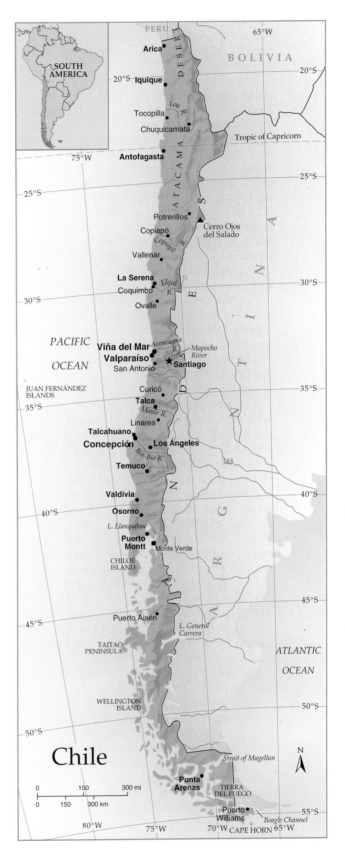

Often both husband and wife work outside the home, while a maid takes care of the house and children.

Poor Chileans are mostly mestizos, whose ancestors combined European and Indian blood. They try to earn a living as farmhands, miners, factory workers, and common laborers. But as many as one fourth of all Chileans have no jobs. Many live in shacks on the great estates or in city slums. The urban poor are called *rotos* ("broken ones"). The rural poor are known as *huasos* ("cowboys"). The rural poor toil in the fields from dawn to dusk. The *huasos* seen by tourists and at rodeos are actually wealthy landowners wearing fancy flat-topped hats, pointed silver spurs, and ponchos and sashes colored red, white, and blue to match the national flag.

Food and Drink. Many wealthy and middle-income Chileans eat four meals a day. For breakfast they usually have just a roll and coffee. Lunch is large and lengthy. Teatime at the end of the afternoon includes breads and pastry. Dinner often is not served until ten o'clock at night.

The most common national dishes are *empanadas* (meat pies filled with onions, raisins, and olives), chicken soup, fish stew, noodles, and steak with fried eggs on top. Chilean food, unlike Mexican food, is not spicy. Even children drink the local wines with their meals.

Entertainment. Chileans enjoy many sports. Whatever their income, they follow the national pastime of soccer, called *futbol.* Some Chileans play basketball, polo, golf, tennis, and cricket. Boxing and horse racing are also very popular, and livestock shows and rodeos draw big crowds outside the capital city. People enjoy swimming and fishing in the lakes and the ocean. Ski centers in the mountains attract wealthy Chileans and tourists. Almost everyone gambles on lotteries, which contribute to charitable causes.

Chileans also attend movies, plays, and operas and other musical events. The International Song Festival takes place each year in the seaside resort of Viña del Mar. Folk music and dancing are popular forms of entertainment, especially in rural areas. The *cueca,* the national dance, is a fast-moving, stomping courtship dance between a man and a woman in peasant costumes. The dancers flirt and wave handkerchiefs.

Chileans celebrate traditional Roman Catholic holidays. The July Feast of the Virgin of Carmen, the patron saint of the armed forces, attracts much attention. Christmas and New Year are also important holidays. At harvest-time many rural villages hold wine and food festivals. The biggest national holiday is Independence Day, September 18.

Education

In the 1850's only 14 percent of all Chileans could read and write, but nearly 90 percent can do so today. Some preschools now provide extra instruction, along with meals, for the poor. Schooling is required for all children from ages 6 to 14. But most Chileans do not go beyond the fifth grade because they must work. Only about one third of those who complete primary school attend secondary school. Most young people in high school take technical training—for example, in accounting, agricultural management, and mechanics— and enter the growing middle class. Only a few prepare for college.

The University of Chile, the leading public university, was founded in 1738 by the king of Spain. It was reorganized by the Venezuelan scholar Andrés Bello and reopened in 1843. Both the University of Chile and the major private university, the Catholic University of Chile, are in Santiago. These universities provide professional and cultural training. But very few Chileans—mainly the sons and daughters of the wealthy—complete a college education.

The Arts

Chilean crafts include colorful weavings, rugs, ponchos, black pottery, and copper sculptures. Many handcrafted items are sold to tourists. In rural Chile, folk songs, creative folk tales, and legends are handed down from generation to generation.

For a small country, Chile has made an important contribution to world literature. Two Chilean poets won Nobel prizes for literature —Gabriela Mistral (Lucila Godoy de Alcayaga) in 1945 and Pablo Neruda in 1971. Novelist Joaquín Edwards Bello gained fame in the 1920's for his book about the Chilean *roto*. Several Chilean authors became well known during the international boom in Latin-American novels that began in the 1960's, especially

Osorno Volcano towers over Lake Todos los Santos in the Chilean lake district, south of Temuco. Chileans and tourists come to this region to swim, sail, fish, and ski.

José Donoso. Many Chilean artists left the country after the military took control of the government in the 1970's.

Chile has also inspired writers from other countries. The British author Daniel Defoe based his story *Robinson Crusoe* on the adventures of a Scotsman stranded on one of Chile's islands in the early 1700's. The British scientist-author Charles Darwin formed some of his ideas about evolution during a visit to Chile in the 1800's.

▶THE LAND

Chile stretches more than 4,120 kilometers (2,600 miles) from north to south but averages only 160 kilometers (100 miles) in width. It is like the west coast of the United States turned upside down, with the colder, rainy zone in the south and the hot, dry part in the north.

Northern Chile

In parts of the Atacama Desert in what is called the Great North, no rainfall has ever been recorded. Although harsh, this region attracts settlers because of its rich mineral deposits. Over the centuries it has been a source of gold, silver, nitrates, iodine, iron, and copper. Peru and Bolivia controlled the Great North until a war won by Chile in the 1880's. The area has a long history of boom towns,

mining camps, violence, and bandits. Chile's highest mountain peak, Cerro Ojos del Salado, is located here. It rises to about 6,875 meters (22,550 feet) on the border with Argentina.

Below the Great North is a region called the Little North. It is a mixed zone of mining and farming. Not very many people live in either the Little North or the Great North.

Middle Chile

Until the late 1800's, the Chilean government really controlled only the middle of the country. The heart of this region is known as the Central Valley because it lies between the Andes and a range of coastal mountains. This fertile region extends from the Aconcagua River in the north to the Bío-Bío River in the south. The climate is mild, much like that of central California. Over two thirds of the people live in this region, mainly in the cities of Santiago and Valparaíso. Three fourths of Chile's industry is located in the Central Valley, as are most of the rich farms and great estates.

Southern Chile

This frontier region was held by the Araucanian Indians until they were defeated by the national army in the 1880's. The region is for-

Copper is Chile's leading export. Chuquicamata, shown above, is one of the world's largest copper mining and smelting centers. Another well-known Chilean export is wine, which comes from grapes grown in vineyards like the one pictured at the left.

ested and rainy, much like the Pacific Northwest in the United States. The manufacturing city of Concepción is situated here, but southern Chile is mainly an agricultural region. Snow-capped volcanoes and many rushing rivers and mountain lakes add to the scenic beauty of the area, which is sometimes rocked by earthquakes.

Few people live in the far south, which reaches down to the Antarctic Circle. Chile claims part of frozen Antarctica, but claims to Antarctica are not recognized internationally. The official boundaries of the nation stop at windswept Cape Horn. Before the Panama Canal was opened in 1914, ships had to use this long, southerly route to cross between the Atlantic and Pacific oceans.

Chile and Argentina have nearly gone to war over conflicting claims to three small islands in the Beagle Channel near Cape Horn. A treaty signed in 1984 ended the century-old dispute. The two countries share the island

called Tierra del Fuego ("Land of Fire"). It seems odd that such a cold, wet island should have this name. But early explorers passing by saw Indians burning fires along the coast.

Chile owns other important islands off its west coast, including the Juan Fernández Islands. The most famous of these rocky outposts in the Pacific is Easter Island, which is known for the great stone heads that people there carved long ago. The origins of these statues continue to puzzle archeologists.

▶THE ECONOMY

For centuries, more Chileans worked at agriculture than anything else. Many of them lived on the great estates, called *fundos,* where they worked the property of the wealthy landowners in exchange for low wages and small pieces of land on which to grow food for themselves. These tenant farmers were known as *inquilinos.* Other poor Chileans owned tiny plots of their own or traveled from farm to farm looking for work. Since the 1930's the government has discouraged farming while encouraging the growth of business and industry in the cities. As a result, most Chileans now live and work in urban areas. Mining does not employ large numbers of people, but it is very important to the economy.

Agriculture

Although it has declined in importance, agriculture still employs about 20 percent of the Chilean workforce. The major farming region is the fertile Central Valley, where corn, beans, wheat, fruits, and tobacco are grown. The region also has some cattle ranches and many vineyards producing excellent wines. Farms in the south are not as large as those in the Central Valley. Cereal grains and potatoes are the leading crops here, and ranchers raise sheep and cattle. Sheep are also grazed on pastures of the Little North. Fruits, wines, and vegetables are among Chile's leading exports.

Mining and Manufacturing

Under Spanish rule and into the early 1800's, silver and copper were Chile's chief mineral exports. By the late 1800's, however, they had been replaced by nitrates (used to make fertilizer and gunpowder). Today, copper is the country's major source of export income. Chileans say that "copper is the salary of Chile." Chuquicamata, high in the Andes, is one of the world's largest copper mines. This and other large mines were owned by U.S. companies until the 1970's, when Chile took them over because of their economic importance to the nation. Chile is now the world's largest producer of copper.

Iron ore, molybdenum, gold, and silver are other important metals. Iodine and boron are valuable by-products of nitrate mining. Coal, sulfur, petroleum, and some natural gas are also produced.

In the 1800's the government began to encourage the development of local industries. Manufacturing developed rapidly and is the single most important element of the economy today. Processed foods, wood and wood products (including paper), transportation equipment and machinery, wines, and textiles are some of the chief manufactured products. Chile's long coastline has also made commercial fishing a major industry.

Service Industries

Service industries now account for more than half of the country's labor force. They include such varied occupations as doctors and other health care professionals, teachers and other government employees, clerks in shops, banks, and insurance companies, and restaurant and hotel workers.

▶CITIES

Changes in living patterns have paralleled the changing economy. In the 1830's, some 75 percent of Chile's population lived in rural communities. By the 1990's, about 85 percent lived in urban areas.

Santiago, the capital and largest city, dominates all the other cities. About 30 percent of all Chileans live in this sprawling metropolis, which is spread over a wide plain along the Mapocho River. The city consists of tall skyscrapers, buildings dating from colonial times, numerous parks, modern suburbs, and old and new slums. Some of these poorer neighborhoods are created by new arrivals from the countryside. Because these squatter communities often pop up overnight, they are called "mushrooms." An article on SANTIAGO appears in Volume S.

The second largest city, Valparaíso, is Chile's major Pacific port. Built on steep hills encircling a bay, it reminds visitors of San Francisco, in California. Cable cars carry passengers up the steep hillsides. Adjoining Valparaíso is the beach resort of Viña del Mar. Another large Chilean city is Concepción, which was founded in 1550. It grew from a frontier outpost to a regional industrial center.

▶HISTORY AND GOVERNMENT

Indians lived in Chile for thousands of years before the Spanish conquest. There were small tribes at the southern tip of the country and in the northern desert. The tribes in the north, who made their living by fishing and by farming on the oases, came under the control of the Incas of Peru in the second half of the 1400's. The Incas built forts in central and southern Chile, but they were unable to defeat the Araucanians living there.

The many Araucanian groups developed different ways of life to adapt to Chile's different regions, but all of them shared a common language. They lived in family groups and in small villages. They hunted game, gathered fruits and vegetables, caught fish, and traded with other Indians. They were also involved in many tribal wars.

Colonial Times

The first Spaniards came to Chile from Peru, where Indians had told them imaginary stories about precious metals to be found in the new land. Diego de Almagro be-

Santa Lucia Hill, in Santiago, has been called one of the most attractive urban parks in the world. It is located on the south bank of the Mapocho River near the downtown business district.

lieved the Peruvian Indian tales and went to Chile in 1535. He found no riches in the Central Valley, and many of his soldiers died. Pedro de Valdivia launched an expedition to Chile in 1540. Valdivia established permanent Spanish rule over the Central Valley, but he was killed in an Araucanian rebellion led by his former Indian groom, Lautaro.

The Araucanians in southern Chile continued to struggle against the Spanish during the first two centuries of colonial occupation. Because the Araucanians had no powerful central government, the Spanish could not simply capture their top ruler, as they did with the Incas in Peru and the Aztecs in Mexico. The mobile Araucanians adopted Spanish weapons and techniques of warfare, including the use of horses in battle. Those who were captured by the Spanish were enslaved by their conquerors and forced to work in the mines or on the farms. Fighting and disease reduced the number of Araucanians by two thirds during the first 100 years of Spanish occupation.

Under Spanish rule, Chile was a frontier colony held for defense against the Indians and coastal pirates. It was governed by the Spanish king through the viceroy in Peru. Because Chile lacked the mineral wealth of Peru or Mexico, many Spaniards created great estates worked by Indians and mestizos. They exported some agricultural products and handicrafts, as well as a little copper.

Many Chileans grew increasingly dissatisfied with Spanish rule. The Spanish king's hold over Spanish America was broken by a French invasion of Spain in 1808. When the French removed the Spanish king from his throne, Chileans refused to obey the French, the Spanish, or the Peruvians. Instead, they founded their own government on September 18, 1810. Some Chileans were simply waiting for the king to return to power in Spain. But others sought full independence.

Independence and Later Times

Bernardo O'Higgins became the most important leader of the fight for independence. The Spanish drove him to Argentina, where he joined forces with José de San Martín. The two led an army back over the Andes to defeat the Spanish in 1817. After other battles, Chile declared its national independence in 1818.

Following the victory over Spain, Chileans fought one another for control of the new government. O'Higgins served as supreme director until 1823, when he was forced to resign and go into exile in Peru. (A biography of O'Higgins appears in Volume O.) Civil wars raged until 1830.

From 1830 to 1891, Chile built a stable republic with a democratic, civilian government. Diego Portales, a cabinet minister, established order and helped create the Constitution of 1833, which lasted until 1925. The landowning families, the merchants, and the Roman Catholic Church ran the country. Only 1 percent of the people voted in elections. The government obtained money from increased exports of silver, copper, and wheat. The importance of nitrates developed after Chile gained the northern nitrate fields as a result of its victory in the War of the Pacific (1879–84), fought against Bolivia and Peru.

During this period, there was a struggle between Chilean political leaders, and efforts to strengthen the office of the presidency led to a civil war. From 1891 to 1925, the legislature was supreme politically. However, under President Arturo Alessandri Palma (1920–25; 1932–38), a new constitution reasserted presidential authority.

Recent History

From the 1930's through the 1950's, political reform parties encouraged the growth of industry, education, health care, and housing. From 1964 to 1970, President Eduardo Frei Montalva led a reform government that provided for higher pay and better working conditions for workers in the cities and more land for poor peasants in the countryside.

The Allende Government. President Salvador Allende Gossens pushed reforms even further after his election in 1970. Allende was the first Marxist ever chosen by popular vote to head a government in Latin America. During his administration the government took over the banks and the copper mines and other industries. Allende at first gave to the poor much of the property that had belonged to the wealthy. But industrial and agricultural production fell, and inflation soared. In 1973 the Chilean military overthrew Allende, who died during the coup.

The Pinochet Era. A military government was established under General Augusto Pinochet Ugarte, the commander of the army, who became president in 1974. To reverse the policies of Allende, the Pinochet government restored most of the factories, farmlands, and other properties to their former owners. The government was successful in reducing inflation, but it was condemned for violating human rights.

Return to Democratic Rule. In a 1988 vote, Pinochet was rejected for a new term as president, paving the way for a democratic election. In 1990 a civilian government was installed, headed by Patricio Aylwin Azócar as president. In 1994, Aylwin was succeeded by Eduardo Frei Ruiz-Tagle, son of the former president. In 2000, Ricardo Lagos Escobar became the first Socialist candidate to succeed to the presidency since Allende was overthrown in 1973.

The government in Chile today is based on a transitional constitution that was approved in 1980. It is headed by the president, who is elected for six years and is not eligible for immediate re-election. The legislature is the National Congress. It is composed of two houses: the Senate, whose appointed and elected members serve 8-year terms; and the Chamber of Deputies, whose elected members serve 4-year terms. The judicial branch is headed by a 21-member Supreme Court.

Recent Events. In 1998, Pinochet resigned as commander of the army and was named senator for life. Soon after, a Spanish judge brought charges of human rights abuses against Pinochet, while he was hospitalized in Britain. Pinochet spent 16 months under house arrest in Britain while the courts battled the case. In 2000 he was declared mentally and physically unfit to stand trial. Nevertheless, he was stripped of his diplomatic immunity by the Chilean Supreme Court.

PAUL W. DRAKE
University of California, San Diego

CHIMPANZEES. See APES.

FACTS and figures

REPUBLIC OF CHILE (República de Chile) is the official name of the country.

LOCATION: Southwestern coast of South America.

AREA: 292,257 sq mi (756,945 km²).

POPULATION: 15,000,000 (estimate).

CAPITAL: Santiago.

MAJOR LANGUAGE: Spanish.

MAJOR RELIGIOUS GROUP: Roman Catholic.

GOVERNMENT: Republic. **Head of state and government**—president. **Legislature**—National Congress (consisting of the Senate and Chamber of Deputies).

CHIEF PRODUCTS: Agricultural—potatoes, corn, wheat, and other grains, wine grapes, fruits, livestock. **Manufactured**—processed foods, wood and wood products (including paper), metals, transportation equipment and machinery, wine, textiles. **Mineral**—copper, nitrates, silver, molybdenum, gold, iron ore, petroleum, coal.

MONETARY UNIT: Peso (1 peso = 100 centavos).

CHINA

Left: The People's Republic of China
Right: The Republic of China

More than 400 years ago, a Portuguese trader visited China and wrote a description of that country. He was overwhelmed by "the hugeness of the kingdom" and "the multitude of people." Almost everyone who has written about China since then has noted these same facts. China is the largest nation in Asia, the third largest in the world (exceeded in area only by Russia and Canada), and has more people than any other country. China's population is more than 1 billion, which means that more than one fifth of all the people on earth live in China.

If China's many people could be spread out over all parts of the country, they would not be especially crowded. But much of China is covered with high mountains, lofty plateaus, and desert, where the land is not suited to cultivation (farming), and relatively few people can live. Vast areas of China are almost empty of people, and one can travel for days without seeing signs of human life.

Most of the people in China live in the eastern part of the country, along the coast, on the plains, and in the basins drained by the great rivers. In contrast to other parts of China, the east teems with people, and almost every piece of usable land is under cultivation. The largest concentration of people is in the region that stretches north from the great Chang Jiang

The Great Wall is probably the best-known symbol of ancient China. Built over a period of many centuries, it was designed to protect China against invaders from the north.

The family was traditionally the most important institution in Chinese life. Under Communism, the government has taken over many of the traditional responsibilities of Chinese family life.

(Yangtze River) to Beijing (Peking), the capital. Here, in North China, Chinese civilization first began some 4,000 years ago.

Historical Background. For most of its long history, China was an empire, ruled by its emperors with the aid of a highly centralized government. Under the emperors there were periods of prosperity and good government, as well as times of economic want and political unrest. When the country's problems became too great, the people would revolt, and out of the civil strife would emerge a new emperor, who would found a new dynasty, or ruling house. This pattern of Chinese history is known as the dynastic cycle.

Altogether, there were 25 such dynasties. Some lasted for several centuries, while others held power for only a few decades or even less. China's first dynasty under a unified empire was the Qin (originally spelled Ch'in, from which the name "China" was derived), founded in 221 B.C. The last dynasty was the Qing (Ch'ing), also known as the Manchu, which lasted from 1644 to 1912, when it was overthrown by a revolution.

Between these eras, China underwent continuous expansion, grew into a great power, and developed a remarkable civilization. Early travelers to China from Europe discovered that the Chinese had invented gunpowder, the magnetic compass, paper, and printing long before these were known in the West.

China, however, had very little large-scale contact with Western nations until about the middle of the 1800's. This contact was not at first a happy one for China. The European nations were by now more powerful than China, in part because of their technological advancements. Seeking trade privileges and other concessions, they forcibly established themselves on Chinese territory.

The impact of the West was chiefly responsible for the weakening of the Chinese empire and the overthrow of its last dynasty. In its place the Chinese founded a republic in 1912. In 1949, following World War II and a bitter civil war, the republic was replaced by the Communist government that rules almost all of China today.

▶THE PEOPLE

The great majority of the people of China are known as the Han. The name comes from the Han dynasty, which ruled China for more than 400 years, from about 202 B.C. to A.D. 220. While the Han are the dominant group, China has 55 national minority groups of varying sizes. These include the Zhuang (Chuang), who live in the southwest and are culturally close to the Han; the Uygurs (Uighurs) in the northwest, who speak a Turkic language and are Muslims; the Hui, Han Chinese who adopted the Muslim religion; the Tibetans, who inhabit the vast Xizang (Tibetan) plateau in the west; and the Mongols, who live in Nei Mongol (Inner Mongolia).

The Family

For many hundreds of years, the Chinese taught their children that duty to the family came first. It was the chief loyalty. A Chinese family might include a man, his wife, his mother, his unmarried sisters, and aunts, his sons and their wives, his unmarried daughters, and his sons' children. In the past the father, as the head of the family, made all important decisions. All family members were supposed to obey him, although he usually talked over important matters with the other adults.

If a family owned the land or business from which it made its living, the property belonged to the entire family. There was only one family purse, and everyone shared whatever money there was. The family decided about the children's education, and it decided when and whom a young man or woman should marry.

The family in the old days was supposed to take care of its own. Family members who became ill or suffered some other misfortune counted on the family to take care of them. They knew that they would not lack necessities so long as the family had anything. They knew that if they died, brothers and cousins would take care of their children.

Changes in the Traditional Family. Families are still important in China. But the process of modernization, resulting from the impact of the West and increasing under Communism, brought many changes. Land can no longer be bought and sold, and marriages can no longer be arranged by parents. Many women now work in commerce or in industry. The government has taken over many traditional duties of the family, providing child-care centers and medical care. To keep the population at a manageable level, couples are strongly urged to have only one child. This is a strong break with the past, when large families were considered desirable.

Language—Spoken and Written

If a Chinese from Guangzhou in the south and a Chinese from Beijing in the north met, they might not understand each other. Each would speak a different form of the Chinese language. These different forms are called dialects. Dialects are regional variations in pro-

nouncing the same syllable, or speech sound. Spoken Chinese is a tonal language, in that each syllable has four or more tones and each tone may represent a different word. For example, the four tones of the syllable *ma* mean mother, jute (a plant fiber used in making sacks), horse, and scold. By far the most extensively used of the eight major dialects of Chinese is Mandarin. Mandarin Chinese is the official language of China.

The different dialects do not affect written Chinese, because Chinese writing is not based on the sounds of the spoken language. Instead, each written word has its own special sign, called an ideograph or character. This system of writing has been used throughout China for thousands of years and is understood by Chinese no matter where they live.

There are more than 40,000 different characters. Most are rarely used, but a person must still understand 3,000 to 5,000 characters in order to read a newspaper.

There are two main systems of representing Chinese words in the Roman alphabet. In this article, the newer Pinyin spelling is generally used. Names in the older Wade-Giles spelling are often noted in parentheses.

Attempts at Language Reform. The government has tried to make Chinese writing simpler. It has adopted an official system that simplifies characters by reducing the number of strokes needed to write the more complex ones. The use of an alphabet, much like that used in writing English, has also been introduced. Chinese alphabetic writing is based on the sound of the spoken official language, Mandarin. Children in school learn both the characters for a word and the alphabetic spelling of its pronunciation. However, at this time the alphabet has not replaced the characters, and it seems unlikely that it will ever do so.

CHINESE WRITING

Chinese writing is made up of numerous characters that stand for one-syllable root words. Here are some examples:

MAN	人	MOUNTAIN	山
SUN	日	TIGER	虎
MOON	月	TREE	木

These basic characters can be combined in many ways to form other words or to express ideas:

FOREST	林	[TWO TREES]
BRIGHT	明	[SUN AND MOON]
WIFE	婦	[WOMAN AND BROOM]
GOOD	好	[WOMAN AND CHILD]

Learning is highly valued in China. Under the emperors, government officials were classical scholars. Education in science and technology is emphasized today.

Problems of an Alphabetic Language. Some Chinese leaders have said that once everyone in China speaks Mandarin, the characters will no longer be used. This has both advantages and disadvantages. It would be easier for large numbers of people to learn to read and write Chinese in the new alphabetic form. But if they did not learn the characters, also, they would not be able to read the writings of the past, unless these were translated into the alphabetic system. A number of Chinese fear that this would result in the loss of China's centuries-old literary heritage.

Education

The most famous Chinese in history was a teacher, Confucius, or K'ung Fu-tzu (551–479 B.C.). This tells us an important thing about the Chinese—their great respect for education and learning. Chinese families often made great sacrifices so that an especially gifted son might become a scholar.

The Classical System. The emperors in past centuries chose their officials from among scholars who had passed examinations in history, poetry, and, above all, the writings of Confucius. A young man wishing to become an official would study for many years. He would take the first examination in his home district. If he passed this test, he could take the examination in his province. Those who passed this second test could then take national examinations in the capital. Sometimes the national examinations were supervised by the emperor himself. Those who passed the examinations received special titles or degrees. Not all the scholars who received degrees were given official positions. Yet it was an honor to pass the examinations even if one never received any other reward.

Educational Reforms. Great changes have taken place in Chinese education in modern times. In the 1890's, a group of Chinese leaders came to believe that China needed new kinds of schools. It was no longer enough to know the old classical books. They felt that the Chinese should study the mathematics and sciences brought from Europe and America. In 1905 the imperial examination system was abolished. Numerous modern schools then opened all over the country.

The Communist leaders also encouraged education after they came to power. Government-run schools are used as a means of spreading Communist ideas and showing Communism in a favorable light. But the campaign for education has taught millions of people to read. Education today is not just for children or for the privileged few. Adult factory workers, soldiers, and farmers attend "spare-time schools."

Emphasis on Science and Technology. In recent years, increasing emphasis has been placed on scientific and technical education. Special schools for the gifted have been established, and bright students no longer need to spend a period of time working in fields or factories before they are allowed to enter the universities. Millions of Chinese are learning English as a second language in classrooms and through English-language lessons on television. Since 1989, when pro-democracy demonstrations were harshly suppressed, students have had to undergo a year of political education before beginning university study, and restrictions have been imposed on study abroad.

This giant Buddha was carved from the rock of the Lung-men caves near Luoyang in Henan province. The huge sculptures date from about A.D. 500.

Religion

The Chinese have a saying: "The Way has more than one name. There is more than one wise man." This saying tells much about the Chinese view of religion. China has several religions, and the Chinese have not thought that any one of them was the only way of truth.

The ancient Chinese believed that the world contained many spirits. There were spirits of the rain, wind, thunder, trees, rivers, and mountains. There was a spirit of the kitchen and another in charge of marriage. The spirit of Heaven was usually thought of as the greatest of all. People believed that it was necessary to perform certain ceremonies in order to live on good terms with the spirits.

Ancestor Worship. Ancestor worship was the oldest and most widespread religious practice in China. One's ancestors were honored and in turn were believed to watch over and safeguard their descendants.

Confucianism. The Chinese do not regard Confucianism as a religion so much as a social and moral philosophy. Confucius was mainly concerned with teaching people how to live together in harmony. But he did stress the importance of ancestor worship and of properly performing the ancient ceremonies and rites. For more information on Confucius, see the article in Volume C.

Taoism. The Taoists, like the followers of Confucius, took over many old rituals and beliefs. Lao-tzu (604–531? B.C.), the supposed founder of Taoism ("the Way"), said very little about spirits or gods. But his followers of later times worshiped a vast number of them. Taoist priests claim magical powers for the ceremonies they perform.

Buddhism. Buddhism came to China from India, its birthplace, almost 2,000 years ago. It flourished in China and soon became one of the predominant religions of the country. For more information on Buddha and Buddhism, see the article in Volume B.

Other religions of China include Islam, the religion of the Muslims, which was introduced by Arab traders; and Christianity, which began to win Chinese converts after the arrival of Jesuit missionaries in the 1500's. Small numbers of Jews also settled in China.

Religion Under Communism. Until the late 1970's the Communist government discouraged the practice of organized religion. Chinese Christians were persecuted most severely. In recent years, however, the government has liberalized its policy on religion. Many Buddhist and Taoist temples, as well as Christian churches and Muslim mosques, which had been taken over by the government, were restored to their former owners. Religious activities, though still not encouraged, are now permitted.

For more information on the religions of China, see the article RELIGIONS OF THE WORLD in Volume Q–R.

▶THE LAND

North China—Land of the Huang He. The Huang He is the great river of North China. *Huang* is a Chinese word for "yellow" and *he* is one of the words for "river." Huang He thus means Yellow River. Its muddy yellow color comes from the yellowish soil washed down from the hills and plains.

The river's source is high on the Xizang (Tibetan) plateau. It flows for some 3,000 miles (4,800 kilometers) before emptying into the Bo Hai, a gulf that is an arm of the Huang Hai, or Yellow Sea. The soil washed down by the Huang He over many centuries has built up a great plain along its lower course. This low plain is easily flooded whenever the Huang He rises. For hundreds of years, the Chinese have built dikes along the river in an effort to hold back the flood waters. It has been necessary to build these dikes higher and higher, so that in some parts of North China the river is now higher than the surrounding countryside. However, the river still occasionally breaks through the dikes.

In spite of the threat of floods, millions of people live on this great plain, many of them farmers. Neither of the two most important cities of North China are situated directly on the Huang He itself. Beijing lies on the northern edge of the plain. Tianjin

Although it is a vast country, China has very limited areas of fertile soil to support its many people. Terraced fields (*right*) are used to cultivate rice crops on every bit of usable land in densely populated South China. By contrast, Nei Mongol, or Inner Mongolia (*below*), is a thinly populated region of desert and grassland, suitable only for raising livestock. It is the home of the Mongols, who are famed for their skill with horses.

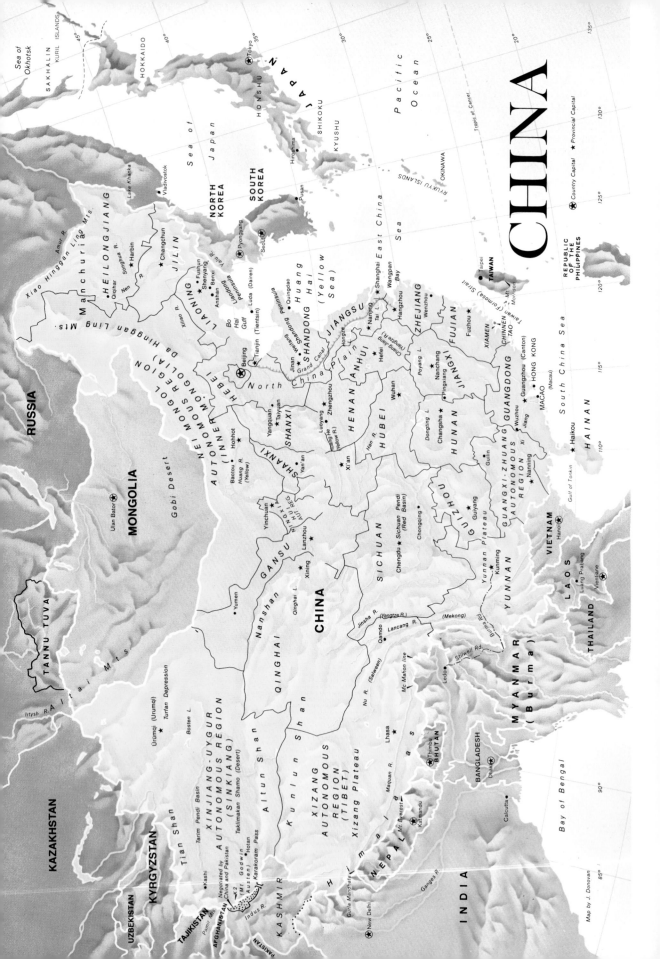

(Tientsin), the great port of North China, lies north of the Huang He.

Winters in North China are cold and dry. Winds from the deserts to the northwest blow clouds of fine yellow dust over the land. Summers are short, but the days are often hot. Rain comes chiefly in summer.

The Land Along the Chang Jiang. The Chang Jiang, also known as the Yangtze River, is China's longest river and the third longest in the world, after the Nile and the Amazon. Its name, appropriately, means "Long River," with *jiang* being another Chinese word for "river." Millions of Chinese live within the great basin of the Chang Jiang—the land drained by the river.

Rising in western Qinghai (Tsinghai) province, the river flows swiftly for great distances through deep mountain gorges and canyons, across the heartland of China. About halfway on its journey to the East China Sea, the Chang Jiang widens to form the Sichuan Pendi, or basin, also called the Red Basin, which occupies the eastern two thirds of Sichuan (Szechwan) province.

The mountains that surround the basin protect it from the worst of the cold winter

---

FACTS and figures

PEOPLE'S REPUBLIC OF CHINA is the official name of the country.

LOCATION: Eastern Asia.

AREA: 3,705,390 sq mi (9,596,961 km²).

POPULATION: 1,262,000,000 (latest estimate).

CAPITAL: Beijing.

LARGEST CITY: Shanghai.

MAJOR LANGUAGES: Chinese (Mandarin dialect official).

MAJOR RELIGIOUS GROUPS: Taoist, Buddhist, Muslim, Christian.

GOVERNMENT: Communist republic. **Head of state**—president. **Head of government**—premier (prime minister). **Legislature**—National People's Congress.

CHIEF PRODUCTS: Agricultural—rice, wheat, potatoes, sorghum, peanuts, tea, livestock (especially pigs). **Manufactured**—iron and steel, machinery, cotton textiles, petroleum products, chemicals, processed foods. **Mineral**—coal, iron ore, petroleum, antimony, tin, tungsten, bauxite, manganese, mercury, lead.

MONETARY UNIT: Yuan (1 yuan = 100 fen or 10 jiao).

FACTS and figures

REPUBLIC OF CHINA is the official name of the Nationalist government based in the province of Taiwan.

LOCATION: Islands off the southeastern coast of the Chinese mainland.

AREA: 13,885 sq mi (35,961 km²).

POPULATION: 22,200,000 (estimate).

CAPITAL AND LARGEST CITY: Taipei.

MAJOR LANGUAGES: Chinese (Mandarin dialect official), Taiwanese (Min).

MAJOR RELIGIOUS GROUPS: Buddhist, Taoist, Christian.

GOVERNMENT: Republic. **Head of state**—president. **Head of government**—premier appointed by the president to head the Executive Yuan. **Legislature**—Legislative Yuan (part of National Assembly).

CHIEF PRODUCTS: Agricultural—rice, corn, vegetables, fruit, tea, pigs, poultry, beef, milk, fish. **Manufactured**—electronics, petroleum refining, chemicals, textiles, iron and steel, machinery, cement, food processing. **Mineral**—coal, petroleum, marble, gold.

MONETARY UNIT: New Taiwan dollar (1 dollar = 100 cents).

---

winds. Temperatures do not often go below freezing, and rainfall is plentiful. The millions of farmers who live in the basin make the most of this. They not only farm the lowlands but also terrace and cultivate the hillsides.

The lower Chang Jiang becomes very wide and serves as an important source of transportation. Ocean-going ships can sail up the river as far as the tri-city of Wuhan, capital of Hubei (Hupeh) province.

The Chang Jiang, like the Huang He, has built up a flat plain near its mouth. Thousands of canals crisscross the plain. Small boats carry people and goods on the canals. People also fish in the canals, and farmers use the water to irrigate rice fields.

The climate along the lower Chang Jiang is warm and humid, although at times winter temperatures dip below freezing. Many cities are located on the river's plain. They include Shanghai, China's largest city and its most important port, and Nanjing (Nanking), which was China's capital for many years. For more information, see the article YANGTZE (CHANG) RIVER in Volume W-X-Y-Z.

Shanghai is China's largest city, chief port, and a center of industry. The city quickly grew in importance after it was first opened to foreign trade in the mid-1800's.

The South China Coast. There are no broad river plains in China south of the Chang Jiang. Much of the land is hilly and mountainous. Most of the people live along the coast in the narrow river valleys and on the deltas. The sea furnishes the people with much of their food, and many of them earn their living by fishing. Guangzhou (Canton) is the chief city of South China and one of the country's major ports.

The Xi Jiang (Si Kiang) is the largest of South China's rivers. Its delta is home to many Chinese. Hong Kong, a former British colony, is located at the mouth of the river. It returned to Chinese control on July 1, 1997. An article on Hong Kong appears in Volume H. The former Portuguese colony of Macao lies across the bay from Hong Kong. This coastal area is very densely populated. Many of its people live on boats that fill the rivers and bays. Some of the boat people earn their living by fishing or transporting goods. Others have jobs on land.

The people of South China rarely see snow or frost except on high mountains. The warm climate and plentiful rain keep this region green throughout the year.

Taiwan. Taiwan, also known as Formosa, is the largest of the many islands along the South China coast. It lies about 90 miles (145 kilometers) from the mainland. Taipei is the capital and largest city.

The Nationalist government, which lost control of the mainland of China to the Communists in 1949, established itself on Taiwan. As the Republic of China it still considers itself the true government of China. A separate article on Taiwan appears in Volume T.

The Borderlands. Manchuria, which the Chinese call simply the Northeast, includes the provinces of Heilongjiang, Jilin, and Liaoning. It consists of a rich, fertile plain. It is less crowded, however, than other agricultural regions. Deposits of iron ore and coal have led to the development of heavy industry, such as steelmaking, in this region.

Xinjiang, the northwestern borderland, is mostly desert. Most of its people are herders of livestock who move with their animals across the dry pastures. Some farmers live on oases on or near the mountain slopes. Xinjiang has deposits of minerals, including one of China's most important oil fields.

Xizang, better known as Tibet, is the "roof" of China. Streams draining off this highland are the sources of several of China's great rivers. Relatively few people live on this high, cold, largely desert region. Some animal herders keep sheep, goats, and yaks, the long-haired mountain oxen. Most of the farmland is in the sheltered valleys of the southern part of the plateau. Lhasa is the principal city. An article on Tibet appears in Volume T.

▶THE ECONOMY

Importance of Agriculture. Agriculture has been an essential part of China's way of life since earliest times. Most Chinese in the past were farmers, and most still are. Almost three out of every four Chinese workers today are engaged in agriculture. Because less than 20 percent of China's land is suitable for farming, the Chinese have learned to make good use of every available bit of land. Chinese farmers can grow two or even three crops each year on the same land. Farmers in South China grow two rice crops a year. In North China, farmers plant wheat in the fall and harvest it in early summer. They then usually plant a summer crop such as soybeans or sweet potatoes. Land must be heavily fertilized when it is used so intensively.

When the Communists first came to power, they took the land away from the landlords and gave it to those who worked it but could not afford to own it. At first each family farmed its own small plot independently.

The Commune System. The government decided that the many small farms would not increase production. The tiny plots were so small that the owners could not afford to buy new equipment or use it efficiently. It was hard to get millions of individual owners to try new methods.

In the 1950's, the government forced the farmers to merge their small plots into very large ones called communes. In the communes, thousands of farmers worked together under the management of government officials. The farmers were organized into work units somewhat like units in an army. The people in communes were expected to work collectively for the common good. Small children were cared for in nurseries so that their mothers could work. The government told the farmers what to grow and how much they were expected to produce. Prices were also set by the government.

However, the communes did not produce as much as the government expected, and China had to import large quantities of food to feed its people. By the late 1970's, the commune system had virtually been abolished. Individual farmers were again permitted to work their own plots of land and also to engage in agriculture-related activities.

Chief Crops, Livestock, and Fish. China is the world's leading producer of rice, accounting for more than one third of the world harvest. Other important crops include wheat,

Agriculture is vital to the Chinese economy, employing nearly 75 percent of the work force. China is the world's chief producer of rice, the country's most important crop.

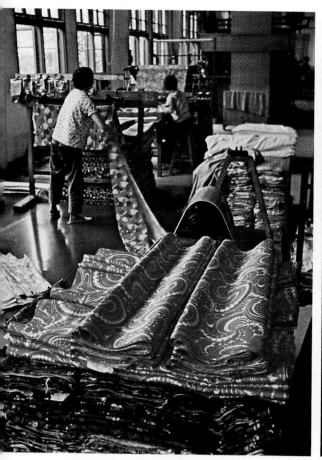

The development of industry is one of the main goals of China's leaders, who hope to make their country one of the world's leading industrial nations by the year 2000. To do so, they have signed trade agreements with a number of countries. Textiles (*left*) and steel (*right*) are among China's most important manufactured products.

corn, and other grains, potatoes, sweet potatoes, soybeans, green vegetables, fruits, sugarcane, cotton, and tea. China produces almost 40 percent of the world's pigs, its chief livestock. Fish make up an important part of the Chinese diet. They are caught in large numbers in China's rivers and seas and are also raised domestically in special ponds.

Mineral Resources. China has large deposits of minerals, including coal, iron ore, and petroleum. Its other important minerals are antimony, tin, tungsten, bauxite (aluminum ore), manganese, mercury, and lead.

Industry. The aim of China's leaders is to make their country one of the world's leading industrial nations, and they have made some progress in that direction. Among the country's important manufactures are iron and steel, cotton textiles, processed foods, petroleum products, chemicals, and machinery.

But many of China's industries are inefficient and have outdated equipment. The Chinese have signed trade agreements with many nations to help them build modern factories, make full use of mineral resources, and train technical experts.

▶**GOVERNMENT**

Under the Emperors. The Chinese were once taught that the emperor was "the father of the people." They owed the emperor the same respect and obedience that children owed their parents.

The emperor had complete power over the people but was supposed to rule them by setting a good example rather than by using force. The ruler was also supposed to enlighten them through education and to care for them by giving aid in time of flood, drought or other disaster.

The Chinese believed that if an emperor ruled badly, Heaven would show its displeasure. According to the teachings of the Confucian school, the people had the right to overthrow a bad ruler.

The Republic. The overthrow of the last emperor, in 1912, brought with it new ideas about government. Sun Yat-sen, a doctor, who was the first president of the republic, said that government belonged to the people, but that they did not actually run it.

Sun's plan for a republican China called for three stages of political development. The first was the unification of China by force of arms. The second involved a period of political guidance by the Nationalist Party. In the last stage, constitutional democracy would finally be achieved.

In 1949 the National Congress, under the Nationalists, adopted a constitution and elected Chiang Kai-shek president. (Chiang had become leader of the Nationalists in 1927). But by that time the civil war against the Communists had raged out of control.

When the Nationalists moved their government to Taiwan after the establishment of the People's Republic of China in 1949, they continued to follow the ideas of Sun Yat-sen. The people of Taiwan elect some representatives who make laws and others who elect the president. The president has great powers. Chiang Kai-shek served as president of the Nationalist government until his death in 1975. His son Chiang Ching-kuo was president from 1978 until his death in 1988.

The People's Republic. The constitution of the People's Republic of China states that China is a socialist nation, under the dictatorship of the working class. But it also says that the people must exercise their power through the Communist Party. The National People's Congress, or legislature, does not really debate and decide issues. Mainly it listens to reports from Communist Party leaders and approves what they have done. Under a new constitution adopted in 1982, a president serves as head of state.

From the founding of the People's Republic until his death in 1976, Mao Zedong (Mao Tse-tung) was chairman of the Central Committee of the Communist Party. Since 1982 the Central Committee has been headed by a general secretary. There are other important groups within the party. A politburo and its

The Summer Palace in Beijing, China's capital, was one of the many residences of the Chinese emperors. The area near the palace is now a public park.

standing committee set broad guidelines that are put into effect by a secretariat. A military affairs committee directs the army, and an advisory commission advises party leaders.

While the Communist Party of China makes all the major policy decisions, the day-to-day administration is in the hands of the government. The central government is run by the State Council, headed by a premier (prime minister). There are a number of ministries, which are similar to departments in the U.S. federal government. Below the central government in Beijing, there are 22 provinces and five autonomous regions, in addition to the three municipalities of Beijing, Shanghai, and Tianjin. The provinces and autonomous regions are further divided into many districts or counties, each of which has an administrative structure similar to the central government.

Confucius, who lived from 551 to 479 B.C., was China's greatest philosopher and teacher. To enable people to live together in harmony, Confucius stressed two main principles: love for humanity and appropriate behavior toward one's fellow human beings.

▶ HISTORY

Beginnings. People have lived in North China since long before recorded history. Not far from Beijing (formerly Peking), scientists have found the bones of people who lived here about 500,000 years ago. We do not know much about the Peking man, as this early type of human being is called. But the remains of crude stone scrapers and spear points indicate that tools and weapons were already in use.

The earliest farmers of China also lived in the north, on the delta lands of streams that flow into the Huang He. They grew grains and vegetables and kept livestock.

The Shang. About 1523 B.C. a warrior people, the Shang, won control of most of North China. The Shang ruled the region for more than five centuries.

The Shang had a highly developed culture and knew how to write. We still have some of their writings on pieces of animal bone and tortoiseshell. People of that time believed that it was possible to learn the future through certain magical ceremonies. A priest would write a question on a bone or shell about going to war, hunting, health, or even the weather. One question actually reads: "Rain or not?" Evidence shows that after writing on the bone or shell, the priest pressed a hot bronze point against it, causing it to crack. Then the priest interpreted the cracks much as fortune-tellers today claim to read the lines in the palm of a person's hand.

The Zhou Kings and Philosophers. West of North China, along the Wei River, lived the Zhou (Chou) people. In the 1000's B.C. a king of the Zhou led his people east across the Huang He and defeated the Shang armies. The Zhou went on to conquer both North China and the Chang Jiang plain.

Some of the early Zhou kings were great rulers. But the persons best remembered and honored were the teachers and philosophers, such as Confucius, who taught how the country could be peaceful and well governed. The people, they said, must begin with themselves. If each person practiced self-control, each family would be well governed. Then the whole kingdom would be well governed.

Shi Huangdi: First Emperor. One group of philosophers, known as the Legalists, taught that there could be peace in China only if the whole land was ruled by law, under a single, strong ruler. The lord of Qin (Ch'in), one of the states in the west, listened eagerly to those who said that a single warlike lord might conquer the other lords as easily as "sweeping off the dust from a kitchen stove."

The Qin ruler followed this advice. In 246 B.C. he made war against all the other Chinese states. In 221 B.C., when his armies had conquered them, he proclaimed himself Shi Huangdi (Shih Huang Ti), which means "first emperor."

Shi Huangdi made sure that no one could challenge his authority. He destroyed the walls of the cities he conquered and collected all weapons. He appointed his own followers to govern but kept a close watch on them. Those who served him well were richly rewarded, but those who did not were severely punished.

Shi Huangdi ordered that there be but one set of laws and rules throughout his empire. Everybody had to use the same weights and measures. All scholars had to write with the same script. All farmers had to put the wheels on their carts the same distance apart, so that all wheels could use the same ruts in the roads.

To protect China from invasion, Shi Huangdi, in 214 B.C., began construction of the Great Wall. Today it extends across northern China for a distance of about 1,500 miles (2,400 kilometers).

The Rise and Fall of Dynasties. Shi Huangdi believed that his empire would last for 10,000 generations. But his family did not rule for long. Within a few years after Shi Huangdi's death in 210 B.C., a revolt ousted his son, and a new emperor came to the throne.

Of the many dynasties that ruled China, the Han, Tang, Sung, and Ming are best known. The Han dynasty, which replaced the Qin in 202 B.C., lasted for more than 400 years. Under the Han, China became a great empire, expanding into Korea and Central Asia.

Many Chinese consider the nearly 300 years of Tang rule (618–906) as the most glorious period in their country's history. Even today some Chinese still refer to themselves as "the people of Tang." At the height of its power, the Tang extended Chinese influence across much of Asia, from Korea in the northeast to India in the southwest. It was also a period of great artistic achievement, especially in painting and poetry.

The Sung period (960–1279) was China's golden age of arts and sciences. The invention of movable type made possible the printing of huge encyclopedias. Literature and landscape painting flourished. Gunpowder was first used in battle, and the magnetic compass was applied to navigation. Although the Sung ruled for more than 300 years, they were not strong enough militarily to prevent the invasion and eventual conquest of China by the Mongols.

A Period of Foreign Rule. Kublai Khan, grandson of the great conqueror Genghis Khan, became the first emperor of the Yuan, or Mongol, dynasty in 1260. He completed the destruction of the last Sung in 1279, becoming the first foreigner to rule all of China.

Kublai Khan understood Chinese ways and tried to govern like a Chinese emperor. He built his capital at Beijing and supported Confucian colleges. He employed many Chinese officials, although he made use of foreigners, too. One of these, an Italian merchant named Marco Polo, lived in China during the reign of Kublai Khan and later wrote a famous account of his travels.

The Yuan ruled for about 100 years before their overthrow in 1368, when the Ming dynasty began. Under several able emperors, the Ming acquired what is now northern Vietnam and dispatched a powerful fleet to East Africa and the Persian Gulf.

The Manchus: The Last Dynasty. The invasion of the Manchus in 1644 brought an end to the three centuries of Ming rule and established the Qing, or Manchu, dynasty. Although they were foreigners who came from north of the Great Wall, from the region known as Manchuria, the Manchus respected Chinese culture and tradition. They quickly adopted Chinese ways of living. Under the early Manchu emperors, China enjoyed some 150 years of peace and prosperity. Although the Manchus continued to rule until a republic was established in 1912, their power steadily declined.

Arrival of the Europeans. A few Europeans, like Marco Polo, had made the long, difficult overland journey to China. However, the discovery by the Portuguese of a sea route to Asia around southern Africa provided easier access to the eastern part of the continent. A Portuguese ship reached the South China coast in 1514. It was the beginning of the West's long involvement in China.

The Europeans were received reluctantly by the Chinese, who limited the places where they could trade. Christian missionaries followed the traders. Probably the best known was an Italian Jesuit priest, Father Matteo

The victory of the Mongol armies over the Chinese brought Kublai Khan to the throne of China in 1260 as the first emperor of the Yuan, or Mongol, dynasty.

IMPORTANT DATES IN CHINESE HISTORY

1523–1028 B.C.	Shang dynasty: traditional beginning of Chinese history proper.
1028–256 B.C.	Zhou (Chou) dynasty: feudal period; earliest philosophers, poets, and historians; Confucius (551–479 B.C.), greatest teacher; first part of the Grand Canal built; first part of the Great Wall built; coinage; astronomy.
221–207 B.C.	Qin (Ch'in) dynasty: centralization of government; empire established.
202 B.C.–A.D. 220	Han dynasties (Western and Eastern): empire became nearly as large as Roman Empire in Europe; supremacy of Confucianism established; Buddhism introduced from India; legal code adopted; papermaking invented.
220–265	The Three Kingdoms: empire broken up into three parts, each with a separate dynasty.
479	Second division of the empire.
581–618	Sui dynasty: China reunited into a single empire; first printing of books from wooden blocks.
618–906	Tang dynasty: expansion of empire; great art and poetry.
907	Third division of the empire.
960–1279	Sung dynasties (Northern and Southern): Central and South China reunited; use of gunpowder in war; literature and painting flourished; first use of abacus.
1260–1368	Yuan (or Mongol) dynasty: China conquered by Kublai Khan; Marco Polo visits China.
1368–1644	Ming dynasty: Mongols driven from power.
1644–1912	Qing (or Manchu) dynasty: last Chinese dynasty.
1839–42	Opium War with Britain; China forced to cede Hong Kong and to open ports to foreign trade.
1894–95	China defeated in war with Japan.
1900	Boxer Rebellion.
1912	Republic established.
1937–45	War with Japan.
1945–49	Civil war.
1949	People's Republic of China proclaimed after Communists win control of mainland China; Republic of China established on Taiwan.
1950–53	People's Republic takes part in the Korean War.
1965	Tibet officially made an autonomous region of China.
1966–69	Great Proletarian Cultural Revolution.
1971	People's Republic enters the United Nations, taking the seat held by the Republic of China (Taiwan).
1975	Chiang Kai-shek dies.
1976	Mao Zedong dies.
1979	The United States and the People's Republic officially establish diplomatic relations.
1989	Student democracy movement crushed by the military.
1992	Jiang Zemin elected president.
1997	Deng Xiaoping dies; Hong Kong reverts to Chinese control.
1998	New premier Zhu Rongji institutes major economic reforms.
1999	Macao returned to China.

Ricci, who founded a mission in Beijing in 1601. Father Ricci won the respect of the Chinese because he showed respect for them and their ways. He learned the Chinese language and dressed as a Chinese scholar.

Growth of Foreign Influence. China's relations with the European nations remained fairly limited until the 19th century. By then the British had become the most active traders in China. The British disliked the restraints that the Chinese government placed on trade. They wanted to buy the silk, tea, and porcelain (which they called china) for which China was famous, and they wanted to sell the Chinese manufactured goods, such as textiles. Later, the British started exporting opium, a narcotic drug, grown in their colony of India.

The Opium War. Chinese efforts to enforce their laws against the import and sale of opium led to the Opium War (1839–42). Defeated by the British, China was forced to sign the Treaty of Nanjing (1842), which ceded Hong Kong to Britain and opened the ports of Shanghai and Canton (now Guangzhou) to foreign trade.

Other nations demanded the same privileges in China. France, Germany, and Russia also acquired control of large areas of Chinese territory as their "spheres of influence." Japan, too, won territorial concessions after defeating China in the first Sino-Japanese War of 1894–95.

The Boxer Rebellion. The resentment felt by the Chinese led to a short but savage rebellion against foreign merchants, missionaries, and diplomats. Known as the Boxer Rebellion, it was put down in 1900 by foreign troops, which included some U.S. Marines.

Founding of the Republic. Chinese intellectuals were aware of their country's political and economic backwardness under its Manchu rulers. Many of these intellectuals had been influenced by such Western ideas as democracy and nationalism. A group of these Chinese, led by Dr. Sun Yat-sen, began the revolution that overthrew the Manchus and established a republic in 1912.

The Warlords. The new republic faced many problems. To try to bring unity to the nation, Sun gave up his post as provisional president to Yuan Shikai, a military leader, who undermined the government by expanding his own power. Yuan's death in 1916 was followed by the period of warlordism. The warlords were men with their own armies who controlled large areas of China.

The Kuomintang. Sun's followers organized themselves into the Kuomintang, or Nationalist Party, and established themselves in the South. After Sun's death in 1925, leadership of the party eventually passed to Chiang Kai-shek. Chiang led an army against the warlords, defeated them, and formed a new national government with its capital in Nanking. (For more information on the life of Sun Yat-sen, see the article in Volume S.)

China Under Chiang. Under Chiang Kai-shek, China faced serious difficulties both at home and abroad. The threat at home concerned the Chinese Communists, who sought to bring about their own revolution in China. Sun had accepted them into the Nationalist Party. Chiang expelled them and in several military campaigns drove their forces into the remote northwest.

The threat from abroad came from Japan, which was determined to expand its empire by conquering China. In 1931, Japanese troops occupied Manchuria. Full-scale war with Japan broke out in 1937 and was to last for eight years. Faced with a common enemy, the Nationalists and Communists formed a United Front and co-operated in fighting against the Japanese.

The People's Republic. When World War II ended in 1945, the Communist forces had grown in strength and numbers. The Nationalists, on the other hand, found it difficult to rally popular support. In 1949, after four years of civil war, Chiang and his government were forced to flee to the island of Taiwan, which became the site of the Republic of China. The Communists under Mao Zedong (Mao Tsetung) established the government of the People's Republic of China in Beijing. (For more information on Chiang Kai-shek, see the article in this volume.)

The creation of the People's Republic did not end the struggle for power in China. Conflict continued between Communist factions. One faction, called the pragmatists (practical people), felt that the revolution was over. They wanted the Chinese to devote themselves to the economic development of the country. Another faction, called the radicals, believed that the most important thing was to keep the revolutionary spirit alive.

The Cultural Revolution. Mao Zedong supported the radicals' views. In 1966 he launched the Great Proletarian Cultural Revolution. The radicals organized thousands of young people into groups called the Red Guards and encouraged them to demonstrate against officials who had supposedly lost the revolutionary spirit. At first the Red Guards

Training with wooden rifles, Young Pioneers followed the revolutionary teachings of Mao Zedong. Many young Chinese took part in the Cultural Revolution of the late 1960's.

only insulted their opponents, but later they resorted to violence against them. Schools were closed, and industry was disrupted. Disorder was so widespread that Mao finally ordered the army to put a stop to the movement.

Death of Mao and New Leadership. The struggle between the pragmatists and the radicals continued behind the scenes. It was difficult for outsiders to know who really held power. When Mao Zedong died in 1976, many thought that the radicals would take over. Yet within a month four radical leaders, including Mao's widow, Jiang Qing, were under arrest. The "gang of four," as they were called, were charged with various crimes. The new government, led by Communist Party Chairman Hua Guofeng and First Deputy Premier Deng Xiaoping, believed that China's political revolution was over. They wanted to lead an economic revolution that would modernize the nation's economy by the end of the 20th century. Deng was a pragmatist whom the radicals had twice driven from office. In 1978, however, after Hua Guofeng was removed from his post as head of the Chinese Communist Party, Deng emerged as China's most powerful political leader. (See the article on Mao Zedong in Volume M, and the one on Deng Xiaoping in Volume D.)

Foreign Relations. The Soviet Union signed a treaty of friendship with the People's Republic soon after the Communist government came to power in 1949. But relations between them worsened during the 1950's. After years of hostility, leaders of the People's Republic and the Soviet Union resumed normal ties at a summit meeting in China in 1989.

China has long disputed some boundaries with its neighbors, including the Soviet Union and India. In 1962 the People's Republic and India fought a short border war over disputed territory. Tibet was occupied by Chinese troops in 1950. It was officially made an autonomous region of China in 1965.

The People's Republic supported North Korea with troops during the Korean War (1950–53). It also aided Communist forces in Southeast Asia during the Vietnam War.

The People's Republic was admitted to the United Nations in 1971, taking the seat that was formerly held by the Republic of China (Taiwan).

Another result of China's expanding relations with other countries was the return of the British colony of Hong Kong in 1997, followed by the Portuguese colony of Macao in 1999.

China and the United States. The United States long refused to recognize the People's Republic as the legal government of China. It supported the claims of the Nationalists on Taiwan, to whom it gave large-scale financial assistance. In 1972, Richard M. Nixon became the first U.S. president to visit the People's Republic. The United States and the People's Republic of China officially established diplomatic relations in 1979. Although formal diplomatic relations between the United States and Taiwan were ended, economic and cultural ties between the two countries continue on an unofficial level.

ADMINISTRATIVE DIVISIONS OF CHINA

Place names are given in the Pinyin spelling, with the older Wade-Giles spelling, when different, in parentheses. Provinces and other divisions are listed in order of population.

Provinces	Capital
Sichuan (Szechwan)	Chengdu (Chengtu)
Henan (Honan)	Zhengzhou (Chengchow)
Shandong (Shantung)	Jinan (Tsinan)
Jiangsu (Kiangsu)	Nanjing (Nanking)
Guangdong (Kwangtung)	Guangzhou (Canton)
Hebei (Hopei)	Shijiazhuang (Shihkiachwang)
Hunan	Changsha
Anhui (Anhwei)	Hefei (Hofei)
Hubei (Hupeh)	Wuhan
Zhejiang (Chekiang)	Hangzhou (Hangchow)
Liaoning	Shenyang
Jiangxi (Kiangsi)	Nanchang
Yunnan	Kunming
Heilongjiang (Heilungkiang)	Harbin
Shaanxi (Shensi)	Xian (Sian)
Guizhou (Kweichow)	Guiyang (Kweiyang)
Fujian (Fukien)	Fuzhou (Foochow)
Shanxi (Shansi)	Taiyuan
Jilin (Kirin)	Changchun
Gansu (Kansu)	Lanzhou (Lanchow)
Hainan	Haikou
Qinghai (Tsinghai)	Xining (Hsining)

Autonomous Regions	
Guangxi Zhuang (Kwangsi Chuang)	Nanning
Nei Mongol (Inner Mongolia)	Hohhot (Huhehot)
Xinjiang Uygur (Sinkiang Uighur)	Urumqi (Urumchi)
Ningxia Hui (Ninghsia Hui)	Yinchuan (Yinchuen)
Xizang (Tibet)	Lhasa

Municipalities	Special Regions
Beijing (Peking)	Hong Kong
Shanghai	Macao
Tianjin (Tientsin)	

Thousands of students gathered in Tiananmen Square in Beijing in 1989, calling for a more democratic government. The demonstrations were later crushed by the army.

▶ **CHINA TODAY**

For more than a century China has been in a state of turmoil and change. It has been difficult for such an ancient civilization, long governed by tradition, to adjust to the new conditions of the modern world. The Communist revolution was China's most recent effort to adjust to a changing world.

The Four Modernizations. While China under Mao Zedong had gone too far in trying to bring about change, China's new leaders followed a different road toward what they call the Four Modernizations. Their aim was to modernize agriculture, industry, national defense, and science and technology. In order to achieve this, China began encouraging foreign investment and economic cooperation with other nations, even capitalist ones.

The Democracy Movement. But many younger Chinese also were calling for political reforms. In the spring of 1989, thousands of university students, joined by some workers, demonstrated in Beijing. For more than six weeks they occupied the capital's vast Tiananmen Square, demanding democracy and an end to corruption in government.

The students received support from Zhao Ziyang, the head of the Chinese Communist Party. However, Deng Xiaoping and other government leaders saw the democracy movement as a threat to Chinese Communism. Troops and tanks were called in to crush the demonstrations, killing hundreds of students. Zhao was removed from the leadership of the Communist Party. Many protestors were later arrested and some were executed. (See the article on Zhao Ziyang in Volume W-X-Y-Z.)

The use of brutal force by the Chinese Communist leadership to suppress the democracy movement greatly damaged China's image abroad. Economic reforms continued, and the 1991 collapse of the Soviet Union left China as the world's only Communist superpower. Tensions between the mainland and Taiwan increased after a pro-independence candidate was elected president of Taiwan in 2000.

KENNETH S. COOPER
George Peabody College, Vanderbilt University

Reviewed by C. T. HU
Coauthor, *China: Its People, Its Society, Its Culture*

See also BEIJING; CHINESE ART; CHINESE LITERATURE; GUANGZHOU; HONG KONG; SHANGHAI; SHENYANG; TIENTSIN; WUHAN.

Palace Ladies Tuning the Lute, a Chinese scroll, was painted about 800 by Chou Fang, an artist of the T'ang dynasty. It shows the elegance of life at a Chinese royal court.

CHINESE ART

China has one of the oldest continuous artistic traditions in the world. The beginnings of Chinese art can be traced to 5000 B.C., when Stone Age people made decorated objects of bone, stone, and pottery.

▶PAINTING

Earliest Chinese painting was ornamental, not representational. That is, it consisted of patterns or designs, not pictures. Stone Age pottery was painted with spirals, zigzags, dots, and lines but very rarely with human figures or animals. It was only during the Warring States period (475–221 B.C.) that artists began to represent the world around them.

Figure Painting. Artists from the Han (206 B.C.–A.D. 220) to the T'ang (618–907) dynasty mainly painted the human figure.

Much of what we know of early Chinese figure painting comes from burial sites, where paintings were preserved on silk banners, lacquered objects, and the walls of tombs. Many of these early tomb paintings were meant to protect the dead or help their souls get to paradise. Others illustrated the teachings of the Chinese philosopher Confucius or showed scenes of daily life.

During the Six Dynasties period (265–581), people began to appreciate painting for its own beauty and to write about art. From this time we begin to know about individual artists, such as Ku K'ai-chih. Even when these artists illustrated Confucian moral themes—such as the proper behavior of a wife to her husband or of children to their parents—they tried to make their figures elegant and graceful.

During the T'ang dynasty, figure painting flourished at the royal court. Artists such as Chou Fang showed the splendor of court life in paintings of emperors, ceremonies, beautiful palace ladies, and imperial horses. Figure painting reached the height of elegant realism in the art of the court of the Southern T'ang (943–960).

Most of the T'ang artists outlined figures with fine black lines and used brilliant color and elaborate detail. However, one T'ang artist, the master Wu Tao-tzu, used only black ink and freely painted brushstrokes to create ink paintings that were so exciting that crowds gathered to watch him work. From his time on, ink paintings were no longer thought to be preliminary sketches or outlines to be filled in with color. Instead they were valued as finished works of art.

Figure painting continues to be an important tradition in Chinese art. However, from the Sung dynasty (960–1279) onward, artists increasingly began to paint landscapes.

Landscape. Many critics consider landscape to be the highest form of Chinese painting. The Five Dynasties and Northern Sung period (960–1127) is known as the Great Age of Chinese Landscape. In the north, artists such as Ching Hao, Fan K'uan, and Kuo Hsi painted pictures of towering mountains, using strong black lines, ink wash, and sharp, dotted brushstrokes to suggest the rough stone. In the south, Tung Yüan, Chü Jan, and other artists painted the rolling hills and rivers of their native countryside in peaceful scenes done with softer, rubbed brushwork. These two kinds of scenes and techniques became the two classical styles of Chinese landscape painting.

During the Southern Sung period (1127–1279), court painters such as Ma Yüan and Hsia Kuei used strong black brushstrokes to sketch trees and rocks and pale washes to suggest misty space.

While many artists were attempting to represent three-dimensional objects and to master the illusion of space, another group of painters pursued very different goals. At the end of the Northern Sung period, the famous poet Su Shih and the scholar-officials in his circle became serious amateur painters. They created a new kind of art in which they used their skills in calligraphy (the art of beautiful writing) to make ink paintings. From their time onward, many painters strove to freely express their feelings and to capture the inner spirit of their subject instead of describing its outward appearance.

During the Yüan dynasty (1271–1368), painters joined the arts of painting, poetry, and calligraphy by inscribing poems on their paintings. These three arts worked together to express the artist's feelings more completely than any one art could do alone.

Some painters of the Ming dynasty (1368–1644) continued the traditions of the Yüan scholar-painters. This group of painters, known as the Wu School, was led by the artist Shen Chou. Another group of painters, known as the Che School, revived and transformed the styles of the Sung court.

During the early Ch'ing dynasty (1644–1911), painters known as Individualists rebelled against many of the traditional rules of painting and found ways to express themselves more directly through free brushwork. In the 18th and 19th centuries, great commercial cities such as Yangchow and Shanghai became art centers where wealthy merchant-patrons encouraged artists to produce bold new works.

Top: Clearing Autumn Sky over Mountains and Valleys, by Northern Sung artist Kuo Hsi.
Bottom: Happy Fishermen of the River Village, by Shen Chou, an artist of the Ming dynasty.

In the late 19th and 20th centuries, Chinese painters were increasingly exposed to the art of Western cultures. Some artists who studied in Europe rejected Chinese painting; others tried to combine the best of both traditions. Perhaps the most beloved modern painter was Ch'i Pai-shih (1863–1957), who began life as a poor peasant and became a great master.

▶CALLIGRAPHY

Calligraphy, the art of beautiful writing, is considered the highest form of the visual arts in China. Unlike the Western art of oil painting, in which artists can paint over their work many times, the brushstrokes of calligraphy cannot be changed once they are placed on the paper. Thus it is a very direct form of expression, and Chinese admirers believe they can understand a calligrapher's feelings, taste, and even personal character by looking at his or her work.

The earliest Chinese writing was scratched into pottery, bone, and shell; inscribed in clay; or cut into stone. Later, people used brushes made from animal hair to write with ink on strips of bamboo, silk, or paper. Because the earliest writers used rigid instruments such as a knife, their script had smooth, even lines. But from the Han dynasty on, calligraphers took advantage of the flexible brush tip to produce thickening and thinning lines or flaring strokes. Over time, new kinds of scripts developed that gave the artist more opportunities for expressive movement.

All the different scripts that developed over the centuries remain available to writers. For example, they may use one style of calligraphy for ceremonial or decorative purposes and another to express their feelings in a flash of inspiration.

Calligraphy and painting are considered to be sister arts. The scholar-painters adapted the brushstrokes and structures of writing for painting. They also judged these paintings according to the standards of calligraphy.

▶DECORATIVE ARTS

The Chinese were masters of bronze, jade, and ceramics. Decorative objects made of these materials are among China's greatest contributions to world art.

Bronze. Bronze metalwork is the greatest art form of ancient China. The Great Bronze Age of China lasted from the Shang (16th–11th century B.C.) to the Han dynasty. During the Shang dynasty, bronzes were used for ritual purposes. Bronze shapes and designs became more and more elaborate, especially those produced at Anyang, the last Shang capital.

During the Chou dynasty (11th century–256 B.C.) bronze vessels increasingly were used as symbols of wealth and status. But during the Han dynasty, other kinds of luxury goods began to be more desirable than bronze.

Jade. Jade is a hard, beautiful stone that was highly valued by the Chinese. Jade ornaments and sculptures are found at many early burial sites. Because jade is brittle and difficult to work with, the earliest jades are very simply carved. During the Eastern Chou period (770–256 B.C.) improved tools allowed artists to produce exquisite jades with complicated

Right: A jade carving from the 19th century shows a mountainous landscape. *Below left:* An elaborately designed bronze vessel from the early Chou dynasty (11th century) was used for ceremonial purposes. *Below right:* A glazed green ceramic vase, of a kind known as celadon, was made in the 12th century during the Sung dynasty, the classical age of Chinese ceramics.

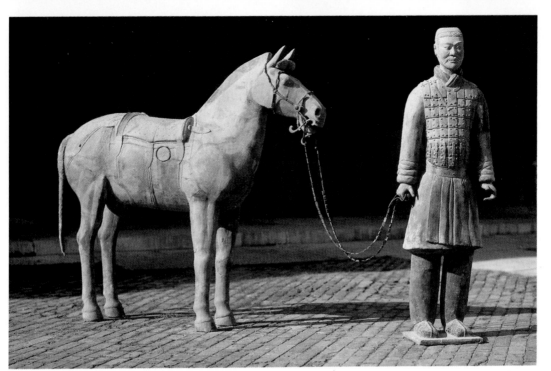

This soldier and saddle horse are part of an "army" of some 7,000 life-size clay sculptures that were unearthed near the tomb of Ch'in Shih-huang-ti, the first emperor of China.

shapes and curved, complex patterns. Jade working continues to be one of the main handicraft traditions of modern China.

Ceramics. Over many centuries, Chinese potters learned to control the temperatures of their kilns (special ovens for firing pottery), to refine clays, and to perfect glazes—the glassy coat that helps make ceramics waterproof and enhances their appearance. These techniques enabled them to produce ceramics that were admired throughout the world.

The classical age of Chinese ceramics is the Sung dynasty, when beautiful wares were produced for the royal court. Among the most valued ceramics are a group glazed in different shades of green, which are known in the West as "celadons." The blue and white wares of the Ming dynasty are also widely admired.

▶SCULPTURE

Some of the earliest known examples of Chinese sculpture are objects made to be buried with the dead. The most impressive collection of burial sculptures was found near the tomb of Ch'in Shih-huang-ti, the first emperor of China (reigned 221–206 B.C.). Pits near the tomb contained some 7,000 life-size clay sculptures of foot soldiers, charioteers, officers, and horses. The sculptures were intended to protect the emperor after death.

During the Han and T'ang dynasties sculptors made small clay models of dancers, servants, fierce guardians, farmyards, towers, dogs, and horses. All were designed to accompany the dead in the spirit world.

In addition to burial sculptures, monumental stone sculptures were placed above ground along the "Spirit Road" leading to the tombs of important people. Among the most outstanding of these sculptures are the stone lions that guard the Liang tombs near Nanking.

The great tradition of Buddhist sculpture is seen in massive figures cut into the stone of huge cave temples. The first cave temples were made in the 4th century, and as Buddhism flourished, many others were carved. Buddhist monasteries and temples were fitted with magnificent sculptures carved in wood and painted, as well as with gilt-bronze figures of the Buddha and his attendants.

Many critics believe the T'ang dynasty was the golden age of Buddhist sculpture. Later sculptors continued to follow the traditions of both Buddhist and nonreligious sculpture. During the 20th century, Western realistic styles were used in sculptures honoring important persons and events.

MAGGIE BICKFORD
Art Historian

See also ORIENTAL ART AND ARCHITECTURE.

In China, both literary ability and calligraphy—the art of beautiful writing—are highly valued. This hanging scroll combines poetry and calligraphy with painting.

CHINESE LITERATURE

With a history of nearly 3,500 years, the Chinese literary tradition is one of the oldest in the world. The earliest known examples of Chinese writing are inscriptions found on bronze vessels and other objects dating from 1765–1122 B.C.

Writing ability has long been highly valued in China. But the Chinese written language, which uses thousands of word signs (see CHINA–Chinese Languages), is very difficult to master. In the past, only people who studied for many years were considered true scholars. Often these scholars became government officials. They were expected to write government records and historical documents as skillfully as they composed poetry. This is why so many scholarly works hold an important place in Chinese literature, along with stories, poetry, and plays.

Chinese literature can be divided into two major groups. Literature written before 1911, the last year that China was ruled by an emperor, is known as classical literature. After 1911, most writers no longer used the forms, techniques, and themes of classical literature. Their works are known as modern literature.

▶CLASSICAL LITERATURE

Chinese literature of the classical period traditionally has been divided into four categories: *ching, shih, tzu,* and *chi.*

Ching refers to a collection of ancient texts known as the "13 Classics." Five of these texts have been especially treasured by the Chinese because they were thought to have been written or edited by the great Chinese philosopher Confucius (551–479 B.C.). These five texts are *The Book of Songs,* an anthology of 305 poems, mostly of folk origin; *The Book*

of Documents, a collection of historical writings; *The Book of Changes,* a book on an ancient system of predicting the future; *The Book of Rites;* and *Spring and Autumn Annals.*

The *ching* texts greatly influenced the thoughts and writings of China's scholars. They were thought to contain important truths, including highly practical teachings about morality, human relationships, and the art of governing. Later writers often referred to the *ching* texts in their own writings and also used them as a model of literary style.

Shih refers to writings of historical significance, including histories of dynasties, chronicles, biographies, calendars, and geography. The most important work in this collection is *The Historical Records,* written about 109–91 B.C. by Ssu-ma Ch'ien (145–86? B.C.). This book covers a period of more than 3,000 years in 130 chapters totaling 500,000 words. Especially noted for its vivid biographies, it also contains records of emperors, writings on Chinese government and institutions, and histories of important families. The book's format was used as a model for later historical writings. Its simple but elegant writing style also influenced later historical prose.

Tzu refers mainly to works on Confucianism, Taoism, and Buddhism. Confucianism is a belief based on the teachings of Confucius, while Taoism developed from the teachings of two great philosophers, Lao-tzu (571?–? B.C.) and Chuang-tzu (?–275? B.C.). Buddhism, a religion that began in India, reached China in the 1st century A.D. All three of these great beliefs have helped to shape and define Chinese thinking.

One of the major works in this category is *The Way and Its Virtue (Tao Te Ching),* traditionally attributed to Lao-tzu but more likely compiled in the 4th century B.C. This book describes the ideals of Taoism, which rejects artificiality and advises people to live in unity with nature.

Chi refers to collections of poetry and essays. These works are admired for their beauty rather than for their informative value.

One important volume in this category is a collection of early poetry entitled *The Songs of Ch'u*. These poems were produced in the southern region of Ch'u, in the Yangtze River valley. Many of them were written by Ch'ü Yüan (340?–278? B.C.), a loyal statesman who was slandered and finally committed suicide in exile. Lyrical in nature and romantic in spirit, the poems in *The Songs of Ch'u* are written in highly emotional language and use elaborate imagery and plant symbolism.

Later poetry in this category includes poems written as lyrics to songs or ballads. One type of song was meant to be performed in plays. The structure of these poems was determined by the tunes to which they were sung.

Some Chinese prose has a highly structured form that is similar to poetry. But a less technically demanding style has proved to be more popular. This form has a clear, simple style and derives its power from this simplicity. After the 10th century this second style was accepted for all types of prose writing.

▶ **MODERN LITERATURE**

Modern Chinese literature differs from classical works in form and technique and in content and spirit. Modern writers pattern their writing after spoken language and reject the use of references to little-known passages of ancient texts. They write for and about ordinary people rather than nobility and strive for a realistic style.

Fiction. The most important writer of modern Chinese fiction is Lu Hsün (1881–1936), the author of two outstanding novels, *The Diary of a Madman* and *The True Story of Ah Q*, along with many short stories and essays. Published in 1918, *The Diary of a Madman* attacks traditional Chinese society. It is considered by many to be the first notable story of social protest in China's new literature. *The True Story of Ah Q*, published in 1921, also has a critical purpose. Through the character of a hateful villager named Ah Q, it criticizes the flaws that Lu Hsün saw in Chinese society: self-deception, defeatism, fear of the strong, and oppression of the weak and helpless.

Lu Hsün was followed by other great authors who were equally dedicated to a realistic, socialistic new literature. The 1930's, in particular, were very productive years for contemporary Chinese literature. In his gigantic trilogy *Turbulent Currents—Family* (1931), *Spring* (1938), and *Autumn* (1940)—Pa Chin (1904–   ) depicts the decline and eventual downfall of a traditional patriarchal family. The works of Mao Tun (1896–1981), on the other hand, concern economic crises of his time. For example, rural depression is the theme of his short story "Spring Silkworms" (1932), while his novel *Midnight* (1933) treats conflicts between labor and management. *Hsiang-tzu the Camel* (1936), by Lao She (1899–1966), tells the story of a rickshaw boy who is a victim of social injustice.

After the Communist Revolution of 1949, China was divided into the People's Republic of China on the mainland and the Republic of China on the island of Taiwan. Most literature in the People's Republic is written in praise of the working class. Writers in Taiwan, on the other hand, often treat social problems that arise from rapid economic development.

Drama. It was also during the 1930's that China's greatest dramatist, Ts'ao Yü (1910–   ), produced some of his best plays. These include *Thunderstorm* (1934) and *Sunrise* (1935). Realistic in content and spirit, they portray the corrupt lives of wealthy people—both members of the old upper class and newly rich financiers and industrialists. The plays show a strong Western influence in their vivid dialogue, skillful characterization, and well-constructed plots full of conflicts and suspense. It was largely due to Ts'ao Yü that spoken drama finally succeeded in drawing audiences from opera and American movies.

Poetry. In general, modern poetry has experienced less growth than fiction and drama, despite periods of development. Modern Chinese poetry is written in a kind of Western-style free verse. Several contemporary poets, such as Hsü Chih-mo (1895–1931), Ai Ch'ing (1910–   ), and the Taiwan poet Yü Kuang-chung (1928–   ), have experimented with new themes, images, and forms.

SHARON SHIH-JIUAN HOU
Pomona College

CHISHOLM, SHIRLEY. See NEW YORK CITY (Famous People).

CHLOROPHYLL. See PHOTOSYNTHESIS.

Seeds of the cacao tree are fermented and roasted to make chocolate.

CHOCOLATE

One food more than any other seems to inspire great enthusiasm and loyalty on the part of those who eat it. This food was once regarded as a gift from the gods. The United States Army includes 4-ounce bars of it fortified with vitamins in its combat rations. Astronauts take it into space, and mountain climbers have taken it to the top of Mount Everest. Books have been devoted to its use and to its praise. This food is, of course, chocolate.

Chocolate is made from the beans of the cacao tree, which has the botanical name *Cacao theobroma*, meaning "food of the gods." The ancient Aztecs believed that the seeds of the cacao tree came from Paradise. Their Spanish conquerers, led by Hernando Cortés in 1519, apparently agreed with them. Cortés wrote his king that "chocolate is the divine drink that builds up resistance and gives strength." Along with Aztec treasure, he shipped back to Spain three chests of cacao beans. Those three chests were the first ship-

ment in a trade that today involves 1,760,000 tons of cacao beans per year.

The main use of cacao is for chocolate products. Some of the cocoa fat, or cocoa "butter," which is separated from the cocoa powder in the manufacturing process, is used for cosmetics. Most of the cocoa butter, however, remains with the cocoa powder to make chocolate used in baking. Additional cocoa butter is added when making chocolate candy. The hulls, or shells, of the beans are sometimes used in feed extenders for animals and for fertilizer.

▶CULTIVATION

The cacao tree is a tropical plant that grows best within an area that lies about 1,400 miles (2,250 kilometers) north or south of the equator. It requires daytime temperatures of about 80°F (27°C) but must be protected from sun and wind, so it is usually planted in the shade of taller banana, breadfruit, or rubber trees. The tree is kept pruned to a height of 15 to 20 feet (5 to 8 meters). A cacao tree growing wild might live for 200 years, but the cultivated variety is usually replaced after 20 to 30 years.

The three basic varieties of cacao are Criolo, which has the best and mildest flavor; Forestero, which is a hardier plant; and Trinitario, which is probably a natural hybrid of the other two and has good flavor and hardiness. More hybrids are being developed to improve the quality of the bean, increase yield, and increase resistance to disease and pests.

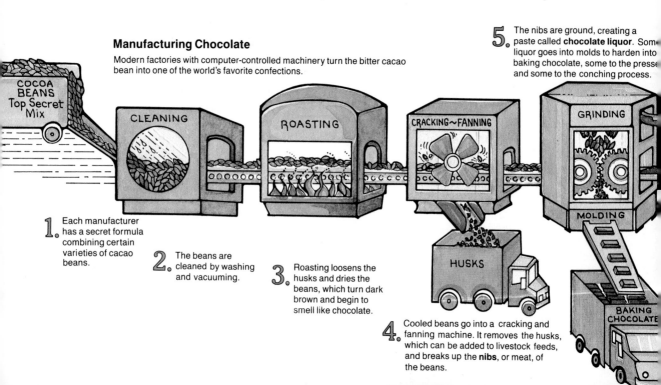

Manufacturing Chocolate

Modern factories with computer-controlled machinery turn the bitter cacao bean into one of the world's favorite confections.

COCOA BEANS Top Secret Mix

CLEANING

ROASTING

CRACKING~FANNING

GRINDING

HUSKS

MOLDING

BAKING CHOCOLATE

1. Each manufacturer has a secret formula combining certain varieties of cacao beans.

2. The beans are cleaned by washing and vacuuming.

3. Roasting loosens the husks and dries the beans, which turn dark brown and begin to smell like chocolate.

4. Cooled beans go into a cracking and fanning machine. It removes the husks, which can be added to livestock feeds, and breaks up the **nibs**, or meat, of the beans.

5. The nibs are ground, creating a paste called **chocolate liquor**. Some liquor goes into molds to harden into baking chocolate, some to the press, and some to the conching process.

In regions where rain falls throughout the year, the cacao tree will produce seed-bearing pods continually. If there is a rainy and a dry season, there may be a main crop and a small harvest between seasons.

Pickers use long-handled knives and machetes to cut the ripe pods, which grow on both the branches and the trunk of the tree. Workers gather the melon-shaped pods, cut them open, and scoop out the pulp that surrounds 20 to 40 beans. Pulp and beans are put in piles, boxes, or trays, covered with banana leaves, and left to ferment for 2 to 7 days. Fermentation creates a temperature of about 125°F (92°C), which stops the beans' growth. The beans then begin to acquire the characteristic chocolate aroma and color. After fermentation, the beans are dried in the sun or heated buildings. It takes about 400 dry beans to make a pound (900 beans to a kilogram).

At shipping centers buyers cut some beans in each batch to be sure they are brown inside. The chocolate brown color indicates the beans have been fully fermented. The good beans are shipped immediately before their flavor is damaged by tropical heat and moisture. Because cacao beans may spoil, all chocolate manufacturing is done in temperate climates.

The Ivory Coast in Africa, with 30 percent, and Brazil, with 20 percent, are the leading producers of cacao beans, followed by Ghana, Nigeria, Malaysia, Cameroon, Ecuador, and Colombia. One fifth of all manufactured chocolate products are from the United States, followed by Germany, the Netherlands, Britain, and Switzerland.

▶ **CHOCOLATE AND HEALTH**

Chocolate in the form of candy has about 145 calories an ounce (30 milliliters), or about 220 calories in the average chocolate bar. A 1½-ounce (43-gram) chocolate bar has more than 5 percent of the U.S. Recommended Daily Allowance for protein, riboflavin, and calcium. Milk chocolate is about 35 percent fat and 50 percent carbohydrate. Although chocolate contains caffeine, it would take more than a pound of chocolate to equal the caffeine in one cup of coffee.

When chocolate was first introduced in Europe, it was thought to have many health benefits that have never been proved. In recent times it was thought to cause acne and dental cavities. Studies have shown that chocolate does not cause acne and that it is less likely to cause cavities than many other candies.

Chocolate is the favorite flavor for candy, cookies, ice cream, and other sweets in the United States, where consumption (the amount eaten) averages about 10 pounds (4.5 kilograms) per person per year. But the United States is only eleventh in worldwide consumption of chocolate. The leader is Switzerland, where average consumption per person is as high as 22 pounds (9.5 kilograms) per year.

Reviewed by DR. RHONA APPLEBAUM
Director of Scientific Affairs
Chocolate Manufacturers Association

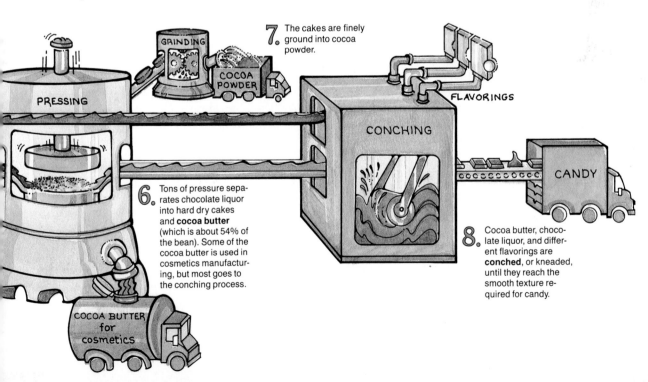

7. The cakes are finely ground into cocoa powder.

GRINDING

COCOA POWDER

PRESSING

FLAVORINGS

CONCHING

CANDY

6. Tons of pressure separates chocolate liquor into hard dry cakes and **cocoa butter** (which is about 54% of the bean). Some of the cocoa butter is used in cosmetics manufacturing, but most goes to the conching process.

8. Cocoa butter, chocolate liquor, and different flavorings are **conched**, or kneaded, until they reach the smooth texture required for candy.

COCOA BUTTER for cosmetics

An accomplished pianist at age 8, Chopin wrote most of his music for the piano. His mazurkas and polonaises were based on the folk music of his native Poland.

CHOPIN, FRÉDÉRIC (1810–1849)

Frédéric François Chopin, one of the greatest composers for the piano, was born near Warsaw, Poland, on March 1, 1810. His mother was Polish, and his father was a Frenchman who taught French to the sons of Polish nobles. Chopin grew up among his fa-

ther's pupils, and in the process became something of an aristocrat himself.

At a young age, Chopin showed an amazing talent as a pianist. He played a difficult concerto in public when he was only 8. He took lessons in composition, too, and published his first work at the age of 15.

In 1829, Chopin began a concert tour that included Vienna, Munich, and Paris. His playing won such high praise in Paris that he decided to settle there for life. He never returned to Poland. In Paris, Chopin played at concerts and also gave piano lessons. He was a capable and a very fashionable teacher. Young French and Polish aristocrats begged him to take them as pupils.

But above all, Chopin composed. Soon he was recognized as the greatest piano composer of his time. Though he wrote two concertos for piano and orchestra, his best works are short compositions for piano alone—preludes, études, nocturnes, waltzes, and, reflecting his Polish heritage, polonaises and mazurkas.

While still a young man, Chopin developed tuberculosis. In spite of this he carried on with his concerts and teaching, but finally retired. He died on October 17, 1849, when he was only 39 years old. His expressive and melodic music is considered part of the Romantic Age. It is still widely enjoyed by piano students and professionals alike.

Reviewed by BARBARA-SUE WHITE
Founder, Princeton String Quartet

CHORAL MUSIC

Choral music is music meant to be sung by a chorus or choir. Both terms are derived from the Greek word *choros* and refer to a large group of singers who combine their voices in several parts, or melody lines.

The most common type of choral group today performs music in four parts. Each part is assigned to a different voice range: soprano (high female), alto (low female), tenor (high male), and bass (low male). However, choral works can be written in more or less than four parts, from as many as several dozen to as few as one. Some choruses perform **a cappella** (without instrumental accompaniment), but many great choral works have been written for chorus and instruments.

▶ **EARLY CHORAL MUSIC**

Choral singing has had a very long history. It was heard in Sumerian temples as early as 3000 B.C. In ancient Greece, children were taught singing in school, where there were choral competitions as there are in many schools today.

Choral singing was used from a very early period in religious services in Hebrew synagogues. The chorus was often divided into groups, each of which took turns singing responses to a solo singer, or cantor. The words used were from the Bible, mostly from the book of Psalms.

The religious vocal music developed in Christian churches was called **plainsong**, or chant. At first, chants were monophonic; that is, they consisted of a single melody sung without harmony or instrumental accompaniment. But beginning in the 800's a new kind of music began to develop, in which several melodies were played or sung at the same time. This kind of music is called polyphonic music. By the late 1100's, music written by composers such as the French organist Perotin combined all the musical elements of melody, rhythm, harmony, and polyphony. The music was performed by chorus, solo singers, and a variety of instruments.

The most important choral work of the 1300's is the famous *Notre Dame* Mass, written about 1364 by the French composer and poet Guillaume de Machaut. A **mass** is a musical setting of the prayers from the main service of the Catholic Church. It became one of the chief forms of music in the 1400's and 1500's. Machaut's work is one of the earliest polyphonic settings of the mass. It was performed by voices and instruments.

▶RENAISSANCE

During the Renaissance, a period that extended from about 1450 to 1600, choral music continued to be closely associated with the church. The favorite form of church music was the **motet**, a choral work based on a biblical text and sung in Latin. Renaissance choral music was polyphonic, with most pieces written for four or five voices. Many pieces were written for two or three choirs, with a total of eight or twelve parts. A famous piece by the English composer Thomas Tallis called for eight choirs of five voice parts each.

Choral music in Renaissance style first developed in northern France in about the mid-1400's. Its first great composer was Guillaume Dufay, of Burgundy. Dufay wrote many masses and motets, as well as secular (nonreligious) songs called **chansons**. Flemish composers such as Jean d'Ockeghem and Jacob Obrecht developed a richer kind of choral music. Some of the best Renaissance choral music was written by another Flemish composer, Josquin des Prez. His music, which included motets, masses, hymns, chansons, and ballads, influenced choral music style for several generations.

After Josquin, a great many composers of fine choral music emerged in almost every country in Europe. Two outstanding figures of the later Renaissance are the Italian composer Giovanni Palestrina and the Flemish composer Roland de Lassus. Palestrina masterfully blended melody, harmony, and rhythm in more than 100 masses and some 500 motets, while De Lassus merged religious and secular influences in his madrigals, chansons, motets, and masses.

▶1600'S AND 1700'S

In the 1600's it became common practice to include instrumental parts in choral compositions. New forms of choral music were invented. Among the most important were the **church cantata** and the **oratorio**. Oratorios were musical settings of stories from the Bible. They were composed for chorus, soloists, and instruments. Almost always they were performed without action or scenery. A church cantata is like a short oratorio, but it can be performed by a smaller group of musicians. Masses and motets were now composed for soloists, chorus, and orchestra.

The Italian composer Claudio Monteverdi wrote some important choral works, such as his famous setting of the vespers, or evening service. In his *Vespers* (1610), Monteverdi combined solo, choral, and instrumental groups in many different ways. The German composer Heinrich Schütz wrote many psalms, motets, oratorios, and Passions. A **Passion** is a musical setting of the story of Christ's death. Schütz used chorus and soloists but no instruments in his Passions.

Two of the greatest of all composers of choral music were Germany's Johann Sebastian Bach and George Frederick Handel. Their many choral works have become staples of the choral music repertory. Bach's *St. Matthew Passion* (1729) and Handel's oratorio *Messiah* (1742), especially, are widely performed. In most of the great choral works of Bach and Handel, orchestra and solo instruments play a very important part. Biographies of Bach and Handel can be found in volumes B and H of this encyclopedia.

The period following Bach and Handel, known as the classical period, is best known for its instrumental music and operas. But some classical composers wrote important choral works as well. Classical composers tried to put more drama and variety into their choral music than did earlier composers, and they gave the orchestra a bigger part to play.

A chorus and orchestra perform at the Cathedral of Notre Dame, Strasbourg, France. Many of the world's greatest composers have written works of choral music, both for voices alone and for chorus with instrumental accompaniment.

Austria's Franz Joseph Haydn composed some of his most stirring music for his masses and for such oratorios as *The Creation* (1798) and *The Seasons* (1801), which match those of Handel in size and dramatic power. Another great choral work of the 1700's was the last composition of Austria's Wolfgang Amadeus Mozart, his beautiful *Requiem* (1791). A **requiem** is a mass for the dead. Left unfinished at his death, Mozart's *Requiem* has become his most frequently performed choral work. Mozart's operas also contain many fine choral passages, as do those of Germany's Christopher Willibald Gluck.

The choral music of German composer Ludwig van Beethoven is very dramatic. In his finest choral work, the *Missa Solemnis* (1823), the orchestra is as important as the chorus and soloists. Beethoven also used a chorus in the finale ("Ode to Joy") of his Ninth Symphony (1824).

Biographies of Haydn, Mozart, and Beethoven can be found in the appropriate volumes of this encyclopedia.

▶ **1800'S**

Until the end of the 1700's, choirs and choruses were usually quite small, rarely consisting of more than about 12 to 16 singers.

These singers were highly trained musicians. But during the 1800's, concert choruses of 100 or more singers became widely popular. By 1850 large amateur choral societies had been started in almost every large city in Europe and the United States.

Many composers of the 1800's wrote outstanding choral works. Those by Austria's Franz Schubert include six masses that follow the models of Haydn and Beethoven. In addition, Schubert wrote a number of short nonreligious choral pieces of great beauty. German composer Felix Mendelssohn's best-known work for chorus, soloists, and orchestra is the oratorio *Elijah* (1846).

Enormous compositions for several choruses, a huge orchestra, and soloists were written by France's Hector Berlioz. His highly original works include the *Requiem* (1837), *Te Deum* (1849), and *Damnation of Faust* (1846). One of the most popular choral works of the 1800's is the *Requiem* (1874) by Italian composer Giuseppe Verdi.

Austria's Anton Bruckner wrote three great masses and many smaller choral pieces before he started composing symphonies. Later in life he produced his most famous work for chorus, orchestra, and soloists—the *Te Deum* (1884). It is Bruckner's most deeply felt hymn of praise to God. *A German Requiem* (1868), by Germany's Johannes Brahms, is one of that composer's best-loved works. The text consists of passages from the Bible chosen by the composer.

Other important choral works from the 1800's are *A Faust Symphony* (1857), by Hungarian composer Franz Liszt, and two works by French composers—*The Beatitudes* (1879), by César Franck, and the lovely *Requiem* (1887) of Gabriel Fauré.

Biographies of Schubert, Mendelssohn, Berlioz, and Verdi, as well as of Brahms and Liszt, can be found in the appropriate volumes of this encyclopedia.

▶ **MODERN CHORAL MUSIC**

Many of the leading composers of the 1900's have written excellent choral music. Some of the most successful works of the Russian composer Igor Stravinsky are for chorus and instruments. They include the *Symphony of Psalms* (1930) and the choral composition *Threni* (1958). The *Gurre-Lieder* (1911), by Austrian composer Arnold Schoenberg, was composed for three male choruses, one mixed chorus, soloists, and a gigantic orchestra. (Biographies of Stravinsky and Schoenberg can be found in Volume S.) British composer Ralph Vaughan Williams wrote a great deal of choral music, including a fine setting of the Mass. The *Lamentations of Jeremiah* (1942) by Austrian composer Ernst Krenek is an outstanding work for unaccompanied chorus.

Important modern choral music has been composed also by Charles Ives of the United States, Hungary's Béla Bartók and Zoltán Kodály, France's Arthur Honegger, Germany's Paul Hindemith and Carl Orff, and England's Sir William Walton and Benjamin Britten.

PAUL BOEPPLE
Former Conductor, Dessoff Choirs, Inc.

CHOUTEAU (Family). See FUR TRADE IN NORTH AMERICA (Profiles).

CHRÉTIEN, JEAN (1934–   )

Jean Chrétien became Canada's 20th prime minister in 1993, after the Liberal Party defeated the incumbent Progressive Conservative government in a general election held in October of that year.

He was born Joseph Jacques Jean Chrétien on January 11, 1934, in Shawinigan, Quebec. After receiving his law degree from Laval University, he returned to Shawinigan to practice law, but his strong family background in politics soon inspired him to seek election to Parliament.

Chrétien won election to the House of Commons in 1962 and rose quickly through the ranks of the Liberal caucus. In 1977, during the long administration of Prime Minister Pierre Trudeau, Chrétien became the first French Canadian to be appointed minister of finance. Later, as minister of justice and minister responsible for constitutional negotiations, he played an important role in achieving the Canada Act of 1982 and a constitutional reform package that resulted in the creation of the Canadian Charter of Rights and Freedoms. After Trudeau resigned in 1984, Prime Minister John Turner appointed Chrétien deputy prime minister and secretary of state for external affairs. Chrétien returned to his law

practice in 1986 but returned to politics in 1990, when he was chosen to succeed Turner as Liberal Party leader. In October 1993, the Liberal Party won a crushing victory over the Progressive Conservatives in the general elections. Chrétien, whose campaign had focused on restructuring Canada's economy, relieving unemployment, and preserving national unity with Quebec, succeeded Kim Campbell as prime minister.

During Chrétien's first administration, Canada's deficit was reduced by 70 percent, Parliament ratified the North American Free Trade Agreement (NAFTA), and Quebec's 1995 referendum for independence failed. In 1997, Chrétien called another election. Although his party won, the Liberal majority was reduced.

ANDREW HEARD
Simon Fraser University

Jesus chooses Simon and Andrew as disciples, promising to make them "fishers of men." Simon, later renamed Peter, was to become the leader of the early Christians.

CHRISTIANITY, HISTORY OF

"Ye shall be witnesses unto me both in Jerusalem, and in all Judaea, and in Samaria, and unto the uttermost part of the earth." In the Acts of the Apostles (1:8) these are reported as the last words spoken by Jesus Christ before he returned to heaven. The mission that Christ entrusted to his followers would not be completed until they had carried the "good news" (or gospel) he had taught them to the ends of the world.

This enormous task was partly completed during the lifetime of the original Christians. The New Testament tells of the spread of Christianity from Jerusalem, where the disciples were instructed by Christ, through the towns of Judaea and Samaria and then out to the chief cities of the Mediterranean world.

Christianity came to Antioch, Athens, Corinth, and Ephesus and to Rome, the center and capital of the empire.

In the beginning this work was largely carried out by the disciples—notably by Saint Peter and Saint John—all of whom had been taught by Jesus Christ during his lifetime. The good news was passed on and soon won many converts. At first the converts were men and women who, like the original Apostles, had been Jews before their conversion.

The most important of the early converts was Saint Paul. Paul had been suddenly converted during a journey to Damascus by seeing Christ in a vision. He inspired people with his own missionary zeal and formed groups of Christian converts in the many cities where he preached. There is a clear picture of all this early missionary work in two books in the New Testament: the Acts of the Apostles, probably written by Saint Paul's friend Saint Luke; and Saint Paul's own letters, which are called the Epistles. The Epistles are full of interest because (like all genuine letters) they were not written as formal essays. They discussed practical day-to-day problems as they arose. In his later years St. Paul made his way to Rome. He was shipwrecked on the Mediterranean island of Malta on the way. When he finally arrived in Rome, he was welcomed by a Christian community that had already been established, according to tradition, by Saint Peter. It is more likely, however, that the community was founded by Christian missionaries whose names have been lost.

For the years after the record in Acts ends, evidence for the history of the Christian Church becomes more scanty. There began to be passing references to it in works by pagan writers. These writers make it seem likely that the Roman Emperor Nero blamed the Christians for the burning of the city of Rome in A.D. 64. It is also very likely that Saint Peter and Saint Paul were put to death in Rome at about this time. Another landmark in the history of the early Church was the destruction of Jerusalem by the Roman armies in the year 70. In the earliest years Christians would have seemed to the outsider to be a group of Jews who differed from other Jews only because they held special beliefs about Jesus Christ. But after the fall of Jerusalem the religious differences between Christians and Jews became much clearer.

In the later years of the 1st century (70–100), many of the books of the New Testament were written, including almost certainly the Gospels of Saint Matthew and Saint John and perhaps (though these may be even earlier than A.D. 70) those of Saint Mark and Saint Luke.

▶THE AGE OF PERSECUTIONS

By the end of the New Testament period the Church was firmly established. The next stage in the Church's life is from about A.D. 100 to the year 313.

This period was a time of rapid expansion of Christianity. An ever-growing number of people heard about Christianity and found in it inspiration and faith. The pagan religions they knew had lost their vitality. Even pagan priests did not seem to take their gods seriously. Many people tried to find religious help in the mystery religions. These religions came from the East (Egypt, Asia Minor, Persia, Babylonia). They promised eternal life to those people who were willing to practice elaborate religious and magical rites. But the mysteries lacked something important that Christianity had—a moral code by which people could live. Christianity from the first stressed the importance of morality. It had inherited from the

Jews a strict moral code, including the Ten Commandments. This moral teaching had been set forth and expanded by Jesus Christ in the Sermon on the Mount and elsewhere in the Gospels.

And so Christianity spread. Around A.D. 200 a Christian writer named Tertullian wrote that in his day there were Christians in almost every town. It has been estimated that 100 years later nearly half the population of Asia Minor was Christian.

The organization of the Church developed in this period. Christianity at first was a missionary religion, directed by the original Apostles. They traveled from place to place and left behind them small groups of Christians in the towns where they preached. When the original Apostles died, the leadership of the Church was taken over by local pastors, known as bishops. Under them were ministers of lower rank, known as the presbyters and deacons. The Church organized the area of the Roman Empire into provinces. The bishops at the head of the Christian communities in the large cities such as Rome, Antioch, Alexandria, and Carthage ranked highest. At first the Christians assembled for their weekly worship in private houses. However, as time went on, it became necessary to build churches in the larger cities.

During this period the Church was frequently persecuted. Because traditional pagan religion was part of the accepted way of life of the people, refusal to take part in pagan ceremonies aroused suspicion. Suspicion was strengthened by the apparent secrecy of Christian rites. Men and women, boys and girls, too, suffered imprisonment and even death for their Christian belief. The two worst persecutions of Christians took place in the 3rd century, when Christianity was gaining more and more converts. Paganism tried to make a final stand. Under the Roman Emperor Decius (249–251) an edict (proclamation) was issued in January, 250, requiring all citizens to make sacrifices in the pagan temples in honor of the emperor. Many thousands of Christians, including Pope Fabian of Rome, were put to death for refusing to take part in the pagan rituals. The worst of the persecutions, however, broke out in 303 during the reigns of the Emperor Diocletian (284–305) and his successors. A series of edicts brought to death a very large number of Christian martyrs.

In this 12th- or 13th-century Italian fresco (*above*), Constantine, the champion of Christianity, leads Pope Sylvester I (on horseback) into Rome. St. Augustine of Hippo (*below*), the great writer of the early Christian Church, at his desk (Sandro Botticelli, 1480).

▶ THE PERIOD OF THE FATHERS (313–800)

The new era in the history of Christianity began with the Roman Emperor Constantine (280–337). Constantine, who reversed the policy of earlier Roman emperors, became a supporter of Christianity. In the West this change dates from A.D. 313. After Constantine had made himself ruler of the whole civilized world in 324 at the Battle of Chrysopolis, he also established Christianity in the East. He introduced laws supporting Christian moral teachings. He also supported the observance of Sunday as a Christian holy day. The Christian bishops and other ministers, who had always been in danger of persecution, were given special privileges and honors. Constantine bestowed lavish gifts on the Church and erected fine churches at several of the leading Christian shrines. These included major churches, called basilicas, that were built over the tombs of the apostles Saint Peter and Saint Paul in Rome.

Under these new conditions pagans were converted to Christianity in large numbers. At first no one was forced to convert. Although Christians held privileged positions, their religion was still only one faith among many. But later, by the time of the emperor Theodosius the Great (346?–395), Christianity became the one official religion of the Roman Empire. Not only paganism, but also unorthodox forms of Christianity were forbidden. The new faith was taught in the universities and schools. Large numbers of books were written dealing with the relation of Christianity to the leading ideas of the day. The only emperor in the 4th century who tried to stop the spread of the new faith and keep pagan beliefs alive was Julian the Apostate (331–363). But his efforts failed.

In the 5th century the Barbarian people of northern Europe began attacking the Roman Empire. The Vandals and the Visigoths were two of the strongest of these Barbarian tribes. In 476 the Roman Empire finally came to an end. In a period when the political outlook was dark, hope and inspiration came from the Church alone. Moreover, some of the Barbarian leaders had already accepted Christianity. In the next 200 or 300 years Christianity became generally accepted throughout western Europe.

A notable development in this period was the building of monasteries. A monastery is a community of men who live and work together and devote their lives to prayer. These men are called monks. Already in the 3rd century large numbers of Christians had become monks. Some monks had even gone into the desert to get away from the world. The earliest settlements of monks were in Egypt. Later came the communities of Saint Basil (330?–379) in Cappadocia in Asia Minor and of John Cassian (360?–435?) in the south of France. At the end of the 4th century many devout and well-to-do Christians at Rome, weary of the luxury and corruption of life in the Western capital, decided to go to Palestine. There they helped the poor and the ever-growing number of Christian pilgrims who came to see the holy places of their religion. In Celtic lands and especially in Ireland the monasteries played an important role in the development of the Church from the first. In the middle of the 6th century Saint Benedict drew up a new "rule," a set of regulations for the life of a monk and the running of monasteries. The Rule of Saint Benedict and the way of life it helped to bring about were to be the inspiration of much that was best in Western Christianity for the following 1,000 years.

Another mark of the 3rd century was the rise of the great heresies. From the first,

Christianity required that all of its members believe specific things about Christ and his Church. The basic beliefs of the Church were not understood. Some men made up their own distorted versions of these beliefs. These distortions were called heresies. In some ways the most dangerous heresy was the theory of Arius, who refused to accept the full divinity (godliness) of Jesus Christ. He produced a version of Christianity that was enough like the basic Christian creed to be believed by Christians. Arianism, as the heresy of Arius is called, was able to win over some of the most noted thinkers of the day. It was this heresy that was the chief matter in dispute at the first General Council of the Church, which met in 325 at Nicaea in Asia Minor. The council was sponsored by the Emperor Constantine. Although almost all the approximately 350 bishops who met at Nicaea rejected Arianism, this heresy continued to trouble the Church. It was finally condemned at the second General Council, held at Constantinople in 381.

The Church had the support of Christian rulers in crushing heresies. Those who refused to give up their heretical ideas were banished from the empire. Their exile led indirectly to the spread of Christianity, for the heretics were still Christians even though their beliefs differed from orthodox Christian doctrine. They introduced their versions of the Christian religion wherever they went in exile. Christian missionaries also spread the religion. Some of them reached India as early as the 5th century and China by the 7th century.

It was largely to defend itself against these heresies that the Church developed her own body of teaching, known as theology. The men who wrote the accepted theology of the Church became known as the Fathers. Most wrote in Greek or Latin. Among the leading Greek Fathers were Saint Athanasius (293?–373), Saint Gregory of Nazianzus (329?–389), and Saint Gregory of Nyssa (331?–395?); among the Latins, Saint Ambrose of Milan (340?–397), Saint Jerome (340?–420) and Saint Gregory the Great (540?–604). Most important of all was Saint Augustine of Hippo, who lived in North Africa in the 5th century. Saint Augustine was the greatest Christian theologian since the New Testament times. Among his many books two are very well known—the *Confessions* and the *City of God*. In his *Confessions* he gives a vivid picture of his early life and of the struggles by which he came to accept Christianity. In the *City of God* he gives a splendid description of what man's life in heaven will be like, contrasting it with the passing pleasures of earthly life.

We do not know how or when Christianity first reached the British Isles. Three British bishops took part in a council at Arles in the south of France in 314, so it must have been well established by the beginning of the 4th century. Conversions of the people from paganism to Christianity first took place on a large scale in Ireland under Saint Patrick (389?–461?), called the Apostle of Ireland. Before long Irish missionaries made their way into Scotland and the northern and western parts of England. The conversion of the Anglo-Saxons in the southeastern part of England, however, was not begun until the last years of the 6th century. Pope Gregory the Great sent Saint Augustine of Canterbury (?–604), the Apostle of the English, to England with a small band of Benedictine monks. Nearly 100 years after that the English Church was organized, largely through the efforts of Archbishop Theodore of Tarsus (602?–690). Two well-known Christian leaders of the next generation were English. Saint Boniface (680–754), called the Apostle of Germany, was a native of Devon. He carried the Christian faith from England through Holland and the south of Germany and after a life of many hardships was killed by pagans. The Venerable Bede (673?–735), another great English Christian leader of the period, lived in the monastery of Jarrow, near Durham. He lived a life of holiness, devoting himself to the study of the Scriptures and Christian learning. Among his many writings is a history of the early English Church.

▶ **THE MIDDLE AGES**

The next stage in the history of Christianity begins on Christmas Day in the year 800. On this day Charlemagne, King of the Franks, was crowned first Holy Roman Emperor by Pope Leo III. The influence of this alliance between the pope and the greatest political leader in Europe was immense.

Charlemagne wanted to build a civilization guided by Christian principles. When he conquered the pagan tribes in Saxony and elsewhere, he forced them to be baptized as Christians. Moreover, he loved everything Roman. He used Roman law in the lands he ruled and ordered the use of the Roman form of Christian religious worship. He invited the most learned and devoted scholars of the age to his court. By encouraging the founding of new schools, especially in the monasteries, he increased the Church's support of learning and education. This enthusiastic support continued through the Middle Ages.

Christianity thus became the framework for life in Europe. Countless Gothic cathedrals and parish churches all over Europe still stand as examples of the strong faith that inspired their building. The painting, sculpture, and books of the period also show the great influence of the Church and its teaching on the people. Beautiful objects of religious art show the labor and skill that men and women used in making things to be used in their religious services. In the later Middle Ages, especially after Pope Urban IV had instituted the Feast of Corpus Christi (the Body of Christ) in 1264, Christian services centered increasingly on the Sacrament of the Eucharist (Holy Communion).

Throughout the Middle Ages the clergy and the religious orders of monks had great influence on the people and their government. Many of the most important governmental offices were filled by bishops. Monks were to be found everywhere. New orders of monks and new reforms of the older orders came into being to meet new needs. In the earlier part of the period, these reforms usually followed more or less closely the Rule of Saint Benedict; the best known of them were the Cluniacs, the Cistercians, and the Carthusians. Later in the Middle Ages came the Friars (from the Latin word *fratres,* which means brothers), whose work consisted largely, though not entirely, in preaching and helping the poor and sick in the cities. Saint Francis of Assisi (1182–1226), with his devotion to the "Lady Poverty" and his love of the simple life and of animals, was the most famous of the friars. Saint Dominic (1170–1221) was known for his defense of Christianity against heretics. Among the men inspired by Saint Dominic was Saint Thomas Aquinas (1225–74), one of the greatest of all Christian writers and philosophers.

▶ THE AGE OF REFORMATION (1517–1648)

By the 15th century the medieval system had largely lost its vigor and was showing signs of breaking up. One reason was the growth of what was called the New Learning. The Christian Church of the East—of Greece especially—had awakened an interest in the classical age of ancient Greek culture. Men began to study the Greek classic literature and learned of the freedom of ancient Greece and the glories of its art. The improvement of printing in Europe in the 15th century enabled many more men to read. Countless new books were available. And, most important of all to Christians, the Bible could be printed. As a result of reading and learning, people were not as willing to believe without question everything their religious leaders told them. A fresh view of human nature was taken by such brilliant men as the painter and inventor Leonardo da Vinci (1452–1519) and the famous scholar Desiderius Erasmus (1466?–1536). These humanists, as they were called, led men and women to question many traditional religious practices accepted in the medieval Church. Moreover, people were unhappy with the finances of the Church. There were many instances of graft and corruption in the handling of money contributed by the people to the Church. Money intended to help the poor and the sick sometimes ended up in the pockets of high church officials. Large sums of money were collected by means of indulgences. An indulgence was the way the Church had of releasing a person from the punishments of a sin. This meant that a person who had committed a sin could have his penance (punishment) shortened or removed by an indulgence. His penance might be one placed on him while he was living on earth. It could also be a penance that was to be suffered by his soul after death. Sometimes an indulgence was granted if prayers were said. At other times an indulgence might be gained by making a contribution to the Church. Indulgences were widely resented, especially as the money that was sometimes paid for them passed into the papal treasury in Rome. Above all, the grow-

Life in a monastery today is much the same as it was for monks in the Middle Ages.

ing spirit of nationalism (interest in one's own country) was present in a large part of Europe. Some countries began to want freedom from Rome. The movement in which some countries broke away from Roman religious control and formed their own churches was called the Reformation. The Reformation was largely a nationalist movement. From the beginning it took different forms under its different leaders in the various countries where it was established.

The event that brought the Reformation to Germany took place on October 31, 1517, when Martin Luther, a former Augustinian monk and Roman Catholic priest, posted on the church door at Wittenberg a set of 95 propositions attacking the system of indulgences set up by the Church. Luther tried to show that the whole medieval system of indulgences was wrong. The system rested on the belief that what the Christian faith demanded of its disciples was good works. But such a doctrine, Luther said, was contrary to the teaching of Saint Paul. According to Saint Paul, what justifies a man in the sight of God is not good works, but simply faith in Jesus Christ. Luther soon won over a number of the princes in Germany, who were glad of this opportunity to free themselves from Rome. He also gained great influence among the people through his splendid German translation of the Bible. Hitherto the Scriptures had been available only in Latin. And only a small educated group in Europe knew Latin. The medieval services, including the Mass, were abolished in favor of others that Luther believed to follow the teaching of the New Testament more closely.

In northern Switzerland another Protestant movement was led by Huldreich Zwingli, Pastor of Zurich from 1519. In France the Reformation found its leader in John Calvin (1509–64), who, though a very different man from Luther and Zwingli, also left the mark of his personality on the movement that he began. Calvin, a native of Picardy, in the north of France, was a great organizer, a great disciplinarian, a great Biblical commentator, and a great theologian. In 1536 he set out his doctrines in a book known in the English-speaking world as the *Institutes*. This work, a book about Christian life, discusses the Ten Commandments, the Apostles' Creed,

Martin Luther, still wearing his monk's habit, nails the 95 propositions to the church door in Wittenberg (pen-and-ink sketch done around 1850).

the Lord's Prayer, the Sacraments, and church government. In 1541 Calvin established his authority at Geneva, where his religious principles were strictly enforced, and from 1555 on Calvinism was supreme there. One of the chief marks of Calvinism was the importance attached to the government of the church by elders, or presbyters, who were to replace bishops. Another was the belief that God had determined the destiny of every human soul; men had no power to save themselves. Calvin's system of discipline and belief became a model for large numbers of Protestants.

In England the Reformation took an independent course. Here its beginnings were less theological. Henry VIII (who reigned from 1509 to 1547) wished to end his marriage with Catherine of Aragon in order to marry Anne Boleyn. He asked Pope Clement VII for a divorce from Catherine. The Pope refused. Henry decided that the simplest way to get what he wanted was to reject the authority of the Pope in England and put himself at the head of the Church of England. Henry got Parliament to agree to his plan. At the same time England's wealthy monasteries were dissolved. In 1532 Thomas Cranmer became the new archbishop of Canterbury, the most important position other than the king's in the independent Church of England.

Unlike the European reformers, Henry VIII wanted little change in the Church of England. In his early years he had even written a treatise against Martin Luther. And though in middle age he had shown a certain sympathy with some of the new doctrines, later he definitely rejected them. In 1539 he promoted an act (called the Whip with Six Strings) to stop further changing of the services of the Church of England. It was only after his death that Protestantism became the official policy of the Church of England.

After an attempt to carry the principles of the Reformation to extremes under the boy-king Edward VI (1547–53) and a strong return to Catholicism under Mary I (1553–58), the Reformation in England reached a compromise in the long reign of Elizabeth I. Members of the Church of England and the other Anglican or Episcopal churches throughout the world believe that their Church is at once Catholic and Protestant.

They feel that it follows a middle path between Roman Catholicism and Protestantism. This has been possible because no single theologian such as Luther or Calvin ever dominated the English Church. While retaining bishops, priests, and deacons, the Church of England rejected other elements of the medieval Church and the authority of the pope. The Church of England also encouraged the study of the Scriptures and in 1611 issued a famous new version of the Bible, known as the King James Version.

The Reformation was accepted only in the north of Europe. Most countries nearer Rome continued faithful to the papacy. In fact, the Reformation brought fresh life into the Roman Catholic Church in many lands. This renewal came to be known as the Counter-Reformation. It arose partly through a new awareness in the Roman Catholic Church of a need to reform itself, partly in reaction to the Protestant movements in the north. Abuses were corrected, and a new religious spirit swept both the clergy and the people. The Roman Catholic clergy accepted a stricter discipline in their private lives, the service books were revised, and countless other reforms were made. At the head of this reforming movement was the Society of Jesus (Jesuits) founded by the Spanish priest and former soldier Saint Ignatius of Loyola, who died in 1556. Another important step in the Counter-Reformation was the General Council of Trent (1545–63). Though it had to face many difficulties and though it failed to bring the Protestants back into the Church, the Council helped greatly to form the basis for modern Roman Catholicism.

▶ MODERN MOVEMENTS (SINCE 1648)

The Peace of Westphalia (1648), which closed the great conflict known as the Thirty Years' War, ended many struggles started by the Reformation. The peace divided Europe between Catholics and Protestants and left it almost as it is still divided today. Italy, France, Spain, Austria, South Germany, and Poland were the main countries and regions that remained Roman Catholic. Britain, North Germany, North Holland, and the Scandinavian countries were Protestant. The Orthodox Church in the East continued until recent times to stand apart from Roman Catholicism and Protestantism.

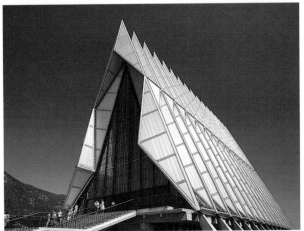

The Air Force Academy chapel in Colorado Springs, Colorado, is one example of modern church architecture.

The Growth of Toleration

The modern world may be said to date from the later 1600's. It was marked by the rapid growth of the ideal of toleration. Before this time people had thought that it was the duty of the Christian state to uphold religious truth and to punish those who refused to conform to Christian beliefs. The Reformation did not immediately change this view, which continued to be held by Catholics and Protestants alike.

But after the Thirty Years' War—under the influence of such thinkers as Voltaire, John Locke, and Wilhelm Leibniz—more liberal ideas began to take over. Religious beliefs came to be regarded as a private matter between God and each individual, not as a concern of the state. People began to question whether a nation ought to have an official state church. In many countries the ties between Christianity and the government were loosened or completely dissolved.

One of the effects of this freedom was the growth of independent Christian sects. It is true that in England the Church of England continued to have a privileged place. Its bishops continued to sit in the House of Lords, and it was the religion of the king. But toleration was granted to other Protestant bodies in 1689. The Congregationalists, the Baptists, and the Presbyterians enjoyed a new liberty and began to develop into the large bodies that they are today. The Roman Catholics were not granted this freedom until 1829. Because of English toleration for Protestant groups, the great Methodist leaders John

Wesley (1703–91) and Charles Wesley (1707–88) were able to carry their religious ideas to the people. Their preaching would have been impossible 100 years earlier.

Christianity in the New World

Until the 1600's, most Christians were Europeans. But the expansion of European peoples all over the world spread Christianity. The growth has happened in two ways. When European settlers went to countries with few or no inhabitants, they tried to set up in their new lands the church organization and forms of worship that they had known at home. When they went to lands that were already populated, they tried to convert the population to Christianity.

North America. Many of the early settlers of North America, such as the Pilgrims, came from minority groups. They sought religious freedom in the New World. In general, the churches in America were liberal, and most of the early colonies adopted a Congregational form of church government. New York was originally the seat of a Dutch Reformed Church, but Anglicanism was introduced by the British in 1664. The only colony founded by Roman Catholics was Maryland, and it became officially Anglican in 1702. The Declaration of Independence (1776) did not set up an official Christian church, although it assumes belief in God.

Since 1776 the history of Christianity in the United States has closely followed the history of the nation. The Anglican Church (officially known as the Protestant Episcopal Church) was soon established on a firm basis. The first American bishop was Samuel Seabury, who was consecrated at Aberdeen, Scotland, in 1784. In the 19th century, the large immigration from Ireland, Poland, and Italy brought many Roman Catholic settlers. The following century saw a huge influx of Hispanic peoples from Mexico, Puerto Rico, and other Latin-American countries, adding to the number of Catholics. As a result, the Roman Catholic Church is now the largest single Christian body in the United States.

In Canada, Christianity came originally with the first French settlement of 1534 and was at first almost entirely Roman Catholic. The first bishop of Quebec was appointed in 1674. English colonists did not arrive until much later, and the first Anglican bishop was appointed in 1787. As the population increased, the churches grew in number and influence, and other denominations were established. The largest of these Protestant groups were the Methodists, the Presbyterians, the Baptists, and the Congregationalists. In 1925 the Methodists, Congregationalists, and most of the Presbyterians formed the new United Church of Canada. This is now the largest single Protestant church in Canada. At the present time over 40 percent of the Canadian population is Roman Catholic.

For many years, revivals (periods of renewed religious interest) have played a part in Christianity's continuing influence in the Western World, especially in North America. A return to fundamentalism—literal interpretation of the Bible as fundamental to Christian life and teaching—has been evident in Protestant movements. Often they are led by evangelists (ministers or others who preach at special services), such as Dwight Lyman Moody (1837–99) and William Franklin (Billy) Graham (1918–). The evangelists preach a modified fundamentalism and urge all people who hear them to repent and be saved. Protestants and Catholics in the United States take part in the revival, or evangelical, movements.

Latin America. Latin America, which was colonized by the Spanish and the Portuguese, is about 90 percent Roman Catholic today. This area was a feudal, largely agricultural society until well into the 20th century. Many Latin Americans must still struggle to survive on low incomes. In the past, the Church was largely conservative and did little to help better the lot of the poor. But by the middle of the 20th century, some changes were beginning to appear. A "theology of liberation" was developed in the 1960's. In this theology, the work of Christ is seen as a mission to liberate all people from ignorance, hunger, misery, and oppression—to free them from injustice and hatred. Many priests and bishops are now behind the efforts for social justice for all people of Latin America.

The Ecumenical Movement

Throughout the history of Christianity, there have been many conflicts and divisions. But the past century has seen a trend toward unity. Missionary movements brought co-operation among Protestant churches and led to the World Missionary Conference of Edinburgh (Scotland) in 1910. This conference may be said to be the beginning of the movement toward worldwide Christian unity, later called the ecumenical movement.

In 1948 many Protestant churches joined to form the World Council of Churches. The World Council grew to include more than 200 member churches. The Orthodox Eastern churches joined in 1961. The Roman Catholic Church is not a member, but it now participates actively in this movement toward unity.

One of the most important events in the ecumenical movement was the second Vatican Council, summoned by Pope John XXIII in 1962. The council examined the relations of the Catholic Church with other churches and non-Christian groups, and a program for the promotion of worldwide Christian unity was developed. Many Christians now disregard the particular groups to which they belong and form alliances with one another. They have taken stands in major political and social concerns of the modern world, such as war, poverty, civil rights for minorities, and the ordination of women as members of the clergy. Great differences still exist among the followers of Jesus Christ, but the trend toward ecumenism continues today.

F. L. CROSS
Editor
Oxford Dictionary of the Christian Church

See also APOSTLES, THE; BIBLE; BIBLE STORIES; CRUSADES; DEAD SEA SCROLLS; EASTERN ORTHODOX CHURCHES; JESUS CHRIST; PROTESTANTISM; REFORMATION; RELIGIONS OF THE WORLD; ROMAN CATHOLIC CHURCH; and names of popes, saints, and other Christian leaders.

CHRISTIE, AGATHA. See MYSTERY AND DETECTIVE STORIES (Profiles).

CHRISTINA (1626–1689)

Christina, queen of Sweden, was born in Stockholm on December 6, 1626. As the only heir of her father, King Gustavus II Adolphus, she became queen, at the age of 6, after his death in battle in 1632. During the years that she was too young to rule, the country was governed by a regency council, headed by the powerful chancellor, Count Axel Oxenstierna. Under the regency, the aristocracy increased its power at the expense of the monarchy and the other classes of Swedish society.

When she began her own rule in 1644, at the age of 18, Christina was determined to restore the royal authority. Her efforts were weakened, however, by her extravagance and the grants of crown lands to her favorites. Intelligent and eager to acquire learning, she surrounded herself with artists and scholars, including the French philosopher René Descartes. Under the influence of Descartes and others, she was secretly won over to Roman Catholicism. Since Sweden was officially Lutheran, she could not be a Catholic and remain queen. After securing the right of succession for her cousin, who became King Charles X Gustavus, she abdicated in 1654.

Having resolved never to marry, Christina left Sweden and openly adopted the Roman Catholic faith. Thereafter she lived a restless life in exile, unable to refrain for long from political intrigue. In 1656–57, she supported a secret French plan to conquer the Kingdom of Naples from Spain and place her on its throne. But the plan failed, possibly through betrayal by her secretary, the Marquis Giovanni Monaldeschi. For this she had him put to death, creating a sensation throughout Europe. Her later years she spent in Rome as a lavish patroness of learning and the arts. She died there on April 19, 1689, and is buried in St. Peter's Basilica.

H. ARNOLD BARTON
Southern Illinois University at Carbondale

nd it came to pass in those days, that there went out a decree from Caesar Augustus, that all the world should be taxed.

(And this taxing was first made when Cyrenius was governor of Syria).

And all went to be taxed, every one into his own city.

And Joseph also went up from Galilee, out of the city of Nazareth, into Judaea, unto the city of David, which is called Bethlehem; (because he was of the house and lineage of David:)

To be taxed with Mary his espoused wife, being great with child.

And so it was, that, while they were there, the days were accomplished that she should be delivered.

And she brought forth her firstborn son, and wrapped him in swaddling clothes, and laid him in a manger; because there was no room for them in the inn.

And there were in the same country shepherds abiding in the field, keeping watch over their flocks by night.

And lo, the angel of the Lord came upon them, and the glory of the Lord shone round about them: and they were sore afraid.

And the angel said unto them, Fear not: for, behold, I bring you good tidings of great joy, which shall be to all people.

For unto you is born this day in the city of David a Saviour, which is Christ the Lord.

And this shall be a sign unto you; Ye shall find the babe wrapped in swaddling clothes, lying in a manger.

And suddenly there was with the angel a multitude of the heavenly host praising God, and saying,

Glory to God in the highest, and on earth peace, good will toward men.

And it came to pass, as the angels were gone away from them into heaven, the shepherds said one to another, Let us now go even unto Bethlehem, and see this thing which is come to pass, which the Lord hath made known unto us.

And they came with haste, and found Mary and Joseph, and the babe lying in a manger.

from The Gospel of St. Luke, Chapter 2, verses 1–16.
Holy Bible, King James Version

CHRISTMAS

Christians the world over celebrate December 25 as Christmas, the anniversary of the birth of Christ. It is a joyous holiday, marked by family gatherings, colorful decorations, traditional songs, and the exchange of gifts. Many people also take part in special religious services.

The name "Christmas" comes from the Old English *Christes Maesse,* or "Christ's Mass." The story of Christmas is told in the Bible. The Gospels of Saint Matthew and Saint Luke tell how Jesus was born in Bethlehem, how angels announced his birth to shepherds outside the town, and how a bright star led the three Wise Men to him. But the Gospels do not tell the date of Christ's birth. It is thought that December 25 was chosen because it was around the time of various pagan festivals, such as the Roman Saturnalia. These festivals marked the winter solstice, the time of year when days begin to grow longer in the Northern Hemisphere. Many Christmas customs are thought to have begun with practices associated with these pagan festivals.

The early Christian churches were divided over when to celebrate Christmas. The Western church, based in Rome, chose December 25, while the Eastern church chose January 6. Eventually the holidays merged, and Christmas was celebrated in a twelve-day festival that included both days. Today only the Armenian church observes Christmas on January 6. In other churches, this day is known as Epiphany and is said to mark either the visit of the Wise Men or (in Eastern churches) Christ's baptism. But to many people, the Christmas season extends for an even longer time—from the end of November through New Year's Day.

▶CHRISTMAS CUSTOMS

Each country that celebrates Christmas has developed its own particular customs associated with the observance of the holiday. But some customs are found in most countries where Christmas is observed.

Gift Giving. Gift giving was part of many pagan midwinter festivals and became part of Christmas as well. In some countries, gifts are exchanged on New Year's Day or on Epiphany rather than on Christmas Eve or Christmas Day.

Children's gifts are often said to be brought by a magical and mysterious figure. In the United States, this figure is Santa Claus—a jolly, fat elf in a fur-trimmed red suit. The original Santa Claus is thought to have been St. Nicholas, a 4th-century bishop in Asia Minor who was famous for his generosity. He became the patron saint of children. The children of Germany, Belgium, Luxembourg, and the Netherlands still know him as Saint Nicholas. He is called *Père Noël* in France, and Father Christmas in Britain.

Decorations. Christmas decorations are another ancient custom. In pagan times, northern Europeans brought evergreen boughs indoors in winter to serve as a reminder that life would return with spring. Some evergreen plants, such as mistletoe, were thought to have magical properties. It was said that if two enemies met under a branch of mistletoe, they would drop their weapons and embrace. This old belief may have been the origin of the modern custom of kissing under the mistletoe.

Christians adopted these decorations and gave them new meaning. Holly, for example, became associated with the crown of thorns Jesus wore to his crucifixion. The prickly leaves stood for the thorns, while the red berries stood for drops of blood. Wreaths, which symbolized the continuance of life through winter, came to stand for the eternal life promised by Christ. Fires, candles, and other lights, important to pagan festivals as reminders of the sun, came to stand for Jesus as the light of the world.

The Christmas tree also originated in northern Europe. In the Middle Ages, a tree called the Paradise Tree—an evergreen hung with apples—was a prop in a play about Adam and Eve. People began to set up similar trees in their homes on December 24, the feast day of Adam and Eve. As the trees became more associated with Christmas, people added candles and, eventually, cookies and other decorations.

The Christmas tree custom was introduced in the United States by German settlers in the 1700's. But it did not become widely popular until the mid-1800's, when a German prince, Albert of Saxe-Coburg-Gotha, married Queen Victoria of England and had a decorated Christmas tree set up in Windsor Castle. Today a Christmas tree decorated with glittering ornaments, candy canes, and electric lights is the focus of many family Christmas celebrations. Huge outdoor trees are also set up in many communities. Two of the largest in the United States are put up each year in Rockefeller Plaza, in New York City, and on the White House lawn in Washington, D.C.

New decorations have been added to traditional ones. The poinsettia, a bright tropical plant, was discovered by Joel R. Poinsett, a U.S. minister to Mexico in the 1800's. It became a popular Christmas decoration because its leaves showed the traditional Christmas colors—green, standing for the continuation of life, and red, standing for the blood shed by Christ.

Christmas Cards. The first Christmas greeting card was created in 1843 by John C. Hor-sley, a British artist. His card was designed like a postcard, lithographed in black and white and colored by hand. It showed a family having Christmas dinner. Another British artist, William Egley, designed a card at about the same time. Both these early cards bore the now-familiar message "A Merry Christmas and a Happy New Year."

By the 1860's, Christmas cards were popular throughout Britain. Louis Prang, a German emigrant printer, began to design and sell colored Christmas cards in the United States in 1874. In less than ten years, his shop was turning out 5,000,000 cards a year. Today greeting cards have become a major industry, and billions of cards are sent all over the world each year.

Family Gatherings. In medieval Europe, Christmas was a wild celebration of feasting, dancing, and merrymaking that lasted for weeks. Today it is a time for families and friends to get together, often for a special meal. Foods of the season include turkey, goose, duck, fish, roast beef, and an abun-

Christians observe many delightful customs in the celebration of their holiday season. Homes, offices, and public buildings are set aglow with colored lights. Gaily decorated Christmas trees appear outdoors as well as in. Friends and families gather for merrymaking—and exchange greetings by mail as well. And boys and girls eagerly anticipate a visit from jolly Santa Claus with his bag full of gifts.

dance of other good things to eat and drink. In some European countries, the custom of serving a roast suckling pig with an apple in its mouth is still observed.

Of all Christmas desserts, perhaps the most popular in Britain and the United States are mince pie and plum pudding. Superstition says that eating mince pie on Christmas brings good luck. In many lands, specially baked cakes and cookies are traditional. Preparation of these treats is begun weeks ahead of Christmas dinner.

▶CHRISTMAS ARTS

Since early times, Christmas has served as an inspiration for music, art, and poems and stories. Many of these works have become closely associated with the holiday.

Music. Christmas music covers a wide range, from light popular tunes to regal works such as Handel's *Messiah*. Tchaikovsky's ballet *The Nutcracker* and Gian Carlo Menotti's opera *Amahl and the Night Visitors* are often performed during the Christmas season.

Carols are the most traditional Christmas music. Early carols were based on dance tunes and refrains from ballads and folk songs. During the Protestant Reformation in England, carols were banned. This was because the Puritans, who took control of the country in the mid-1600's, felt that the music and merrymaking associated with Christmas were pagan customs. Carols returned after 1660, when the monarchy was restored.

Most of the carols we sing today were written in the 1800's. They include "Silent Night, Holy Night," "Hark the Herald Angels Sing," "Away in a Manger," and "Joy to the World." These traditional songs have been joined by modern ones, such as "White Christmas," "Here Comes Santa Claus," and even "Jingle Bell Rock."

Bells are also a traditional part of Christmas music. Every Christmas Eve, church and cathedral bells ring loud and clear to call families to church services. Bells are used as decorations on Christmas trees, wreaths, and gift wrappings.

Art. The scene of the nativity has been painted by many artists. Among them were some of the great masters of the Renaissance, including Giotto, Fra Angelico, and Sandro Botticelli. The nativity is also depicted in three-dimensional crèche scenes. (*Crèche* is the French word for "crib.") St. Francis of Assisi is given credit for setting up the first crèche, using live figures, in Greccio, Italy, in 1223. In many Catholic countries, the crèche is the center of a Christmas Eve pageant that tells the story of the three Wise Men bringing gifts to the infant Christ.

Literature. Charles Dickens' *A Christmas Carol* is one of the most popular Christmas stories ever written. Several film versions of this tale have been made. "The Gift of the Magi," by O. Henry (William Porter), is another well-known story. It tells of the efforts of a young husband and wife to find gifts for each other.

The poem "A Visit from St. Nicholas" has been part of Christmas in the United States since 1823, when it was first published. Clement C. Moore wrote it for his family, and it did much to create the present image of Santa Claus. These traditional Christmas works have been joined by some modern favorites, such as Dr. Seuss's *The Grinch Who Stole Christmas*.

▶RELIGIOUS CEREMONIES

Religious ceremonies marking the birth of Christ begin some four weeks before Christmas. The fourth Sunday before Christmas Day is the first day of Advent, the period of preparation that comes before the holiday. Many people keep track of the days in this period with Advent calendars or Advent candles. The calendars have Christmas scenes and tiny windows, one of which is opened each day to uncover a picture or verse. The candles carry the dates leading up to Christmas and are burned a set amount each day, so that on Christmas day they are used up.

Many people also have Advent wreaths in their homes. These wreaths have four candles, one for each of the Sundays of Advent. Each Sunday, the family lights candles—one candle the first Sunday, two candles the next, and so on—and prays.

In churches, children often take part in nativity pageants, in which they act out the scenes of the Christmas story. On Christmas Eve, churches are decorated with evergreens and candles, and special candlelight and carol services are held. Most churches also hold services on Christmas Day. The message at these services is the central message of Christmas: Peace and goodwill among all people.

▲ People in France celebrate Christmas with special foods such as the *buche de Noël*, or Yule log, a delicious cake served after a holiday dinner in many homes.

◄ In Sweden, the holiday season begins on December 13, Santa Lucia Day. The oldest daughter wears a white robe, red sash, and a wreath of candles on her head as she serves coffee and saffron buns.

◄ Christmas trees are central to the holiday observance in Germany. The custom was brought to North America by German settlers in the 1700's.

▼ Christians from all over the world gather in Bethlehem, the town in which Jesus was born, to celebrate the anniversary of his birth. A Christmas Eve candlelight service is customary in churches everywhere.

▶**CHRISTMAS CUSTOMS AROUND THE WORLD**

Christmas is celebrated in many ways. Here are some of the traditional customs in countries around the world.

France. Children in France welcome the visit of Père Noël at Christmastime. Instead of hanging stockings, they leave their shoes by the fireplace to be filled with gifts. On Christmas Eve, after midnight Mass, many families have a special supper called *Le réveillon*. Turkey is the favorite food on Christmas Day, followed by a special Christmas cake called *buche de Noël*.

Scandinavia. In the Scandinavian countries, Christmas gifts are brought by a jolly old man called *Jultomten* in Sweden and *Julenissen* in Norway and Denmark. His elflike helpers, who sometimes help people throughout the year, are called the *tomtar*. In Sweden the Christmas season begins on December 13, St. Lucia Day. On this day the oldest daughter of the house—dressed in white and wearing a wreath with candles on her head—serves coffee and buns in bed to the rest of the family.

Germany. For German children, Christmas festivities begin on December 6, when they leave their lists of Christmas wishes for St. Nicholas and receive candy in return. Christmas gifts are brought by the *Weihnachtsmann*. A Christmas tree, often decorated with small, spicy cookies, is the focus of many family celebrations. Fruit-filled breads called *stollen* are a seasonal treat.

Christmas in the Holy Land. In Bethlehem, which is now in Israel, Christmas Eve is marked with a colorful procession. People file through the narrow streets carrying an image of Jesus in a cradle to the Church of the Nativity, where it is placed in a special glass and marble manger. Pilgrims from all parts of the world take part.

Italy. A nativity scene called a *presepio*, rather than a Christmas tree, is the focus of celebrations in most Italian homes. The figure of the Christ child is added to the scene on Christmas Eve. Many families have a Christmas Eve supper of *capitone*, or fried eels. Other Christmas specialties include *panettone* (a bread with dried fruit) and *torrone* (a candy made with nuts and honey). Presents are brought on Epiphany by *La Befana*, a kindly witch. But Italian parents tell their children that *La Befana* will leave only ashes if they are naughty.

Britain. British children hope to receive gifts from Father Christmas, and they enjoy a Christmas dinner of roast turkey and mince pie or plum pudding. Wassail, a punch made from ale, apples, spices, and other ingredients, is served. People go from house to house singing carols, often to raise money for charity.

Japan. Because there are relatively few Christians in Japan, Christmas is not widely celebrated. But many Western Christmas customs have been adopted by Japan. People exchange gifts, and streets and stores are decorated with evergreens and bright lights.

Mexico. In Mexico and many other Latin American countries, children have a Christmas party that includes a *piñata*. This is an earthenware jug or papier-mâché figure filled with candies and small toys. It hangs by a rope from the ceiling or a tree branch, and the children take turns putting on a blindfold and hitting it with a stick until it breaks and the sweets and toys tumble out. In the days leading up to Christmas, people take part in *posada* processions that re-enact the search of Mary and Joseph for lodgings in Bethlehem.

The Netherlands. Saint Nicholas brings presents to Dutch children on the eve of December 6. He is said to arrive by boat from Spain, and he rides through the streets on a white horse. He is assisted by his helper, *Swarte Piet* (Black Pete).

ELAINE PASCOE
Writer, *The New Book of Knowledge Annual*

See also CAROLS; GREETING CARDS.

CHROMIUM. See ELEMENTS, CHEMICAL.

CHROMOSOMES. See GENETICS.

CHRYSLER, WALTER P. See KANSAS (Famous People).

▲ In England, carolers enjoy dressing in the style of their Victorian ancestors and gathering to serenade passersby. Carols may tell sacred stories or be festive songs of the season.

► Although there are few Christians in Japan, many Western Christmas customs are observed. Santa Claus is even a popular figure.

► In Mexico, children dressed as Mary and Joseph go from house to house asking for lodging. Eventually someone will invite them in for a party.

▼ Sinterklaas, in bishop's robes, and Swarte Piet bring gifts to Dutch children on the eve of December 6. The children leave hay and carrots in their shoes for Sinterklaas' horse.

Winston Churchill served twice as prime minister of Britain. He is remembered best as Britain's leader during the difficult years of World War II.

CHURCHILL, SIR WINSTON (1874–1965)

A biography of Sir Winston Churchill is almost a history of 20th-century Britain. Churchill was involved in every important event of his country from the Boer War to World War II. He served six British monarchs, from Queen Victoria to Elizabeth II. Statesman, soldier, author, journalist, and twice prime minister, Churchill's career has no parallel in modern history.

Winston Leonard Spencer Churchill was born at Blenheim Palace in Oxfordshire, England, on November 30, 1874. His father, Lord Randolph Churchill, was a brilliant politician. His American mother was the beautiful Jennie Jerome. One of his ancestors was John Churchill, Duke of Marlborough, a great military hero.

▶EARLY YEARS

Winston Churchill himself showed no early signs of greatness. He was a stubborn, red-haired boy and a poor student. He spent four years at Harrow, one of England's finest schools, at the very bottom of his class. However, he was fascinated by military subjects and did much better at Sandhurst, the Royal Military Academy. Young Churchill graduated eighth in his class and in 1895 joined the British Army. He served in Cuba, India, and the Sudan.

While in India, Churchill took part in a military expedition against the fierce Pathans. Out of this experience came his first book, *The Story of the Malakand Field Force.* In 1899 he gave up his military career to enter politics but was defeated for a seat in Parliament. He then left for South Africa to cover the Boer War as a newspaper reporter.

Although he was not there as a soldier, Churchill insisted on taking part in the fighting and was captured by the Boers. A month later he made a daring escape, crossing hundreds of miles of enemy territory to reach the British lines. When he returned to England, he was a hero. He ran again for Parliament as a Conservative and won.

▶POLITICAL CAREER

Churchill disagreed with the Conservatives in 1904 and joined the Liberal Party. In 1905 he was appointed to his first political office, undersecretary for the colonies. He received his first cabinet post, president of the Board of Trade, in 1908. That same year he married Clementine Hozier.

In 1911, Churchill became first lord of the Admiralty. Foreseeing the possibility of war with Germany, he immediately began a program to increase Britain's naval strength. Thus the Royal Navy was better prepared than any other military branch when World War I broke out in 1914.

Gallipoli. Churchill faced his greatest political disaster in 1915. With typical daring he had launched a campaign against the Turkish peninsula of Gallipoli. His idea was to force the Dardanelles, thus opening a supply line to Russia. But the plan was badly carried out. Many soldiers were killed, and Churchill was forced to resign. He rejoined the Army and left for the fighting in France.

In 1916, Churchill returned to Parliament. The following year he was appointed minister of munitions. He rejoined the Conservative Party in 1924 and was appointed chancellor of the exchequer, a post his father once held. But money matters bored him. He served for five years but was not a success.

The "Wilderness" and Prime Minister. Churchill spent the next ten years in what he described as the "wilderness." Although still a member of Parliament, he held no important office and disagreed with his own party. During the middle 1930's, Prime Minister Neville Chamberlain gave in to Nazi Germany's aggressive demands in order to avoid war. Churchill opposed this policy of appeasement. He spoke out vigorously against Hitler. But not until 1939, when Germany invaded Poland, were the people ready to listen to him. When World War II began, Churchill again became first lord of the Admiralty. Chamberlain was forced to resign in 1940, and Winston Churchill became prime minister. Six weeks later France fell, and England faced Germany alone.

Wartime Leader. Churchill was an inspiring orator, and his confidence rallied the British people during the difficult early days of the war. We will never surrender, and we will win, he told them. Every day the people saw him, grim as a bulldog, a big cigar clamped firmly between his teeth, and his hand raised in the famous V for victory sign. Nothing seemed to disturb him, not even the bombs falling in the London streets.

But no sooner was the war in Europe over than the British people felt it was time for a change. On July 26, 1945, the Labour Party won the elections, and Clement Atlee replaced Churchill as prime minister.

▶ **THE LATER YEARS**

Churchill's fighting spirit continued even out of office. He denounced the Soviet Union's policies and coined the term "Iron Curtain." He urged the unification of Europe. He also spoke warmly of an English-speaking union joining Great Britain and the United States. During these years out of office, Churchill wrote his memoirs, published under the title *The Second World War*.

In 1951 at the age of 77, Churchill again became prime minister. He finally accepted knighthood, the Order of the Garter—one of England's highest honors—in 1953. That same year he received the Nobel Prize for literature. In 1963, Churchill was made an honorary citizen of the United States. He died on January 24, 1965, at the age of 90.

Reviewed by J. M. S. CARELESS
University of Toronto

CICERO, MARCUS TULLIUS (106–43 B.C.)

Marcus Tullius Cicero was the greatest orator (public speaker) of ancient Rome. Born in Arpinum (now Arpino, Italy) in 106 B.C., he spent his boyhood in Arpinum and Rome, where he studied law, philosophy, and public speaking. When he was 25, Cicero began practicing law in Rome.

In 70 B.C., Cicero won great public acclaim by successfully prosecuting a government official named Verres for his dishonest rule over the island of Sicily. Cicero's popularity grew, and in the year 63 B.C. he reached the height of his career by winning an election for the consulship—the Roman Republic's highest office.

Cicero's chief opponent in the election was Catiline, a revolutionary with a large following among the Roman mob. Catiline denounced the election as unfair. He gathered some men and made secret plans for murdering Cicero and seizing power by force. Cicero, however, discovered the plot just in time. In the senate, before all the leading men of

Rome, he denounced Catiline in a stinging, powerful speech. Catiline, who was present, fled and was killed soon after.

When Julius Caesar rose to supreme power in Rome, Cicero opposed him. He saw in Caesar an ambitious politician bent on destroying the republican system of government that Cicero loved. Cicero applauded Caesar's assassination (44 B.C.), though he himself took no part in the plot. Then Mark Antony, Caesar's chief lieutenant, gained power. In a series of brilliant speeches Cicero spoke out against Antony's plans for dictatorship. He was killed by Antony's soldiers in 43 B.C.

Cicero was also a great master of Latin prose. Of his work more than 50 speeches, nearly 800 letters, and many essays survive.

Reviewed by GILBERT HIGHET
Author, *The Classical Tradition*

CINCINNATI. See OHIO (Cities).

CIPHERS. See CODES AND CIPHERS.

CIRCADIAN RHYTHMS. See BIOLOGICAL CLOCK.

CIRCLES. See GEOMETRY.

CIRCULATORY SYSTEM

A large, modern city needs a complicated system of streets and roads to link houses, offices, stores, factories, hospitals, and other important places. The human body is even more complicated than a city, and it, too, needs its own system of roadways over which materials can be transported.

The body's roadways are actually waterways. They are made up of a watery fluid called **blood** flowing through tubes called **blood vessels.** More than 62,000 miles (100,000 kilometers) of blood vessels branch and crisscross through a person's body, linking the cells of the brain, the heart, the lungs, the fingertips, and every other organ and body part into a connected circulatory system. The vessels range from thick, muscular arteries, the largest an inch (2.5 centimeters) in diameter, down to tiny capillaries so thin that they cannot be seen without a microscope.

▶ WHAT THE CIRCULATORY SYSTEM DOES

The blood vessels of the circulatory system are lifelines for the body's cells. The cells would starve to death without the food and oxygen brought to them by the flowing blood, and the cells could be poisoned if the blood did not carry away their waste products.

Digested food materials pass into the capillaries around the intestines and then are transported to all parts of the body. Oxygen from the air breathed into the lungs passes into the blood vessels surrounding the lung's tiny air sacs. Carbon dioxide and other waste gases pass from the blood into the air sacs and are sent out of the body with the next exhaled breath. The circulatory system also carries waste products from the body cells to the kidneys. There the wastes pass out of the blood through thin capillary walls and start their one-way trip out of the body in the urine.

Foods, oxygen, and wastes are not the only things carried in the blood. Complicated chemicals called hormones act as chemical messengers and help control and co-ordinate the activities of the body. Other substances called enzymes direct chemical reactions. Blood also contains a sort of chemical repair kit, which can form a solid **clot** to plug up a hole in a damaged blood vessel.

Special kinds of cells travel through the vessels of the circulatory system. Some, the **red blood cells,** are like barges floating along in the bloodstream. They carry loads of oxygen or carbon dioxide. Others, the **white blood cells,** are like migrant workers that travel the body's waterways to get to wherever they are needed. They are the body's defenders, which battle invading viruses and bacteria. They also clean up old, worn-out cells, and they attack body cells that have changed and might turn into cancer cells.

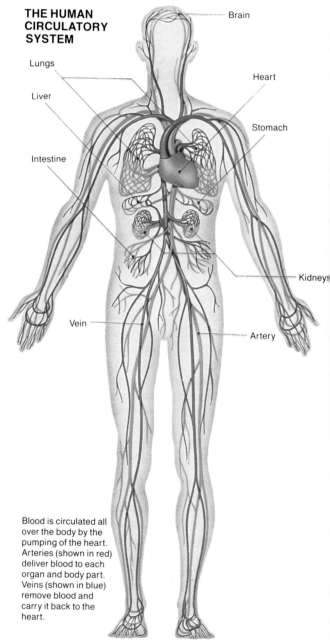

THE HUMAN CIRCULATORY SYSTEM

Brain

Lungs

Heart

Liver

Stomach

Intestine

Kidneys

Vein

Artery

Blood is circulated all over the body by the pumping of the heart. Arteries (shown in red) deliver blood to each organ and body part. Veins (shown in blue) remove blood and carry it back to the heart.

Even the fluid part of the blood is important. It provides water for the body cells and also helps absorb and carry away excess heat, keeping the body temperature even.

▶ORGANS OF THE CIRCULATORY SYSTEM

The human circulatory system is a network of tubelike blood vessels that link all parts of the body and are ultimately connected to a central pump, the **heart.** The thick, muscular walls of the heart enclose four **chambers,** which fill with blood and then empty with each heartbeat. To hear the heart at work, roll a piece of paper into a long, thin tube and place one end against a friend's chest. If you put your ear to the other end, you can hear a rhythmic lubb-dup, lubb-dup sound coming from the heart. The ''lubbs'' and the ''dups'' are the sounds of flaps in the heart called **valves** snapping shut. Valves between the compartments of the heart and valves at the outlets into the arteries close with each heartbeat to keep the blood from flowing backward. The diagram below shows how these valves work. The heart keeps on beating steadily, all through a person's lifetime. If it stopped, the blood could not flow through the circulatory system.

Blood flowing into the heart enters the two upper chambers, the **atria** (singular, **atrium**). From these receiving chambers it passes down into the **ventricles,** the pumping chambers. The blood collected from all over the body empties into the right atrium. It flows down into the right ventricle, and in the next heartbeat it goes shooting out into blood vessels leading to the lungs. There the blood picks up a fresh supply of oxygen and unloads its waste carbon dioxide. The blood is returned to the heart by blood vessels emptying into the left atrium. This oxygen-rich blood flows down into the left ventricle, and in the next heartbeat it is pumped out into a thick-walled artery called the **aorta.** This is the largest artery in the whole body. From the heart it loops up, over, and down, branching as it goes into smaller and smaller blood vessels that eventually supply all parts of the body.

The blood vessels that carry blood away from the heart are arteries. They have thick, muscular walls. The rhythm of the heartbeat can be felt in the artery walls in various parts of the body where the arteries pass close to the surface. For example, this rhythmic **pulse** can be felt at the wrists and the temples. As the arteries branch again and again, they form smaller and smaller blood vessels. The smallest are called **capillaries.** These are very narrow, thin-walled tubes, too small to be seen without a microscope and so thin that the red blood cells have to travel through them in single file. The capillaries may be tiny, but there are so many of them that they make up 99 percent of the length of all the blood vessels. They are the part of the circulatory system that services the individual body cells.

Eventually the capillaries combine into larger blood vessels, forming the **veins** that carry blood back to the heart. Veins are larger than capillaries, but their walls are not as thick and muscular as those of arteries. The veins are equipped with valves, flaps set up in a one-way arrangement that keeps the blood from flowing backward, even when it is going upward against the pull of gravity.

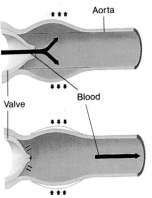

Valves in the circulatory system prevent blood from flowing the wrong way. When blood is pumped into the aorta (a muscular artery), the flaps of a valve open (top). Any backward flow forces the flaps closed (bottom). The aorta's flexible walls help produce a smooth flow of blood around the body.

Aorta

Valve

Blood

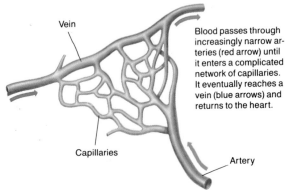

Vein

Capillaries

Artery

Blood passes through increasingly narrow arteries (red arrow) until it enters a complicated network of capillaries. It eventually reaches a vein (blue arrows) and returns to the heart.

The heart beats steadily on its own, at a rhythm set by a structure called the **pacemaker.** This is a specialized portion of the heart muscle, located in the wall of the right atrium. Hormones and nerve messages can speed up or slow down the heart and widen or narrow the arteries, adjusting the blood flow to the body's needs. When you get excited, your heart beats faster. More blood flows to your muscles, providing the extra food and oxygen they will need in case you have to fight or run away. But when you are sitting quietly after a meal, extra blood flows to your stomach and intestines, to help you digest your food. When it is very cold, the tiny blood vessels near the surface of the body narrow, conserving body heat. But when it is hot, these blood vessels widen and radiate out the excess heat. Various systems of the body co-operate in co-ordinating the work of the heart and blood vessels.

The arteries, capillaries, and veins of the circulatory system are organized into two closed loops. Each one begins and ends at the heart. The smaller loop is called the **pulmonary circulation.** The larger loop, which leads through branching networks to all parts of the body and supplies all the organs and body systems, is called **systemic circulation.** If you were to follow a drop of blood through both loops of the circulatory system, the whole trip would take less than a minute!

The body has still a third system of circulation, but it does not carry blood. It carries a fluid called **lymph** and is called the **lymphatic system.** Lymph is formed from the watery part of the blood, together with dissolved chemicals and white blood cells. The walls of the blood capillaries are so thin that fluid leaks out of them into the tissues. The fluid drains into tiny open-ended lymph capillaries, which combine to form larger vessels called **lymphatics.** The lymphatics are very similar to veins. They empty into two large lymphatic ducts, which in turn drain into large veins that return blood to the heart.

▶OPEN CIRCULATORY SYSTEMS

All vertebrates (animals with backbones, including human beings) have a **closed circulatory system,** meaning the blood is enclosed in vessels. Many invertebrates (animals without backbones, such as insects, clams, snails, and lobsters) have a different sort of circulation.

Theirs is an **open circulatory system,** because the blood flows only part of the way in blood vessels. It empties out of the aorta into large, open spaces in the animal's body, called **sinuses.** Blood moves slowly through the sinuses, past various organs, and finally empties back into the heart.

▶DISORDERS OF THE CIRCULATORY SYSTEM

Cardiovascular disease—disease of the heart and blood vessels—is the number one cause of death in the United States and other developed countries. More than half a million Americans die of heart attacks each year, and hundreds of thousands more die of other cardiovascular diseases. For millions more, such diseases bring years of pain and disability.

One common kind of cardiovascular disease is **arteriosclerosis,** often called "hardening of the arteries." This occurs when fatty deposits form along the inner walls of the arteries and narrow the channel through which the blood flows. Sometimes the artery even becomes plugged up completely. When this happens in an artery leading to the brain, brain cells starve and die, and the person suffers a **stroke.** When the coronary arteries that supply the heart become blocked, a portion of the heart muscle dies, and the person suffers a **heart attack. Hypertension,** or high blood pressure, is another condition that can lead to a heart attack or stroke. You can read more about these conditions in the DISEASES article in Volume D.

Drugs can help treat high blood pressure, clogged arteries, and even an irregular heartbeat rate. Various surgical techniques, including the implanting of artificial pacemakers and the opening or replacing of blocked or damaged arteries, can also be used to keep a damaged cardiovascular system working. These medical advances are helping to bring down the number of heart disease deaths. But medical experts believe that changes in life-style are even more helpful. Getting enough exercise and eating a balanced diet low in salt, saturated fat, and cholesterol can help to keep the arteries clear, the blood pressure low, and the heart strong and healthy.

ALVIN SILVERSTEIN
College of Staten Island, CUNY
VIRGINIA SILVERSTEIN
Co-authors, *Circulatory Systems*
and *Heart Disease: America's #1 Killer*

See also HEART; BLOOD.

CIRCUS

For more than two hundred years, the circus has been providing exciting entertainment for those whom the ringmaster calls "children of all ages." The circus is a live show that presents feats of human skill and daring performed in, above, and around a ring, alongside the zany antics of clowns.

A circus consists of seven different kinds of acts: clowns; acrobats; performing horses and riders; thrilling demonstrations by aerialists; trainers and trained wild animals; rare and exotic animals and people; and daredevils.

The circus often opens with a spectacle: Lavishly costumed performers—both human and animal—parade around the rings before the individual acts begin.

Most circus acts take place in rings. (*Circus* is a Latin word meaning "circle" or "ring.") Circuses range in size from one- and two-ring shows to the largest, which have three rings. Today most circuses are held under tents. The main tent, where the acts are held, is called the **big top**. Some of the largest circuses are held in giant arenas that can accommodate thousands of spectators.

▶ **AT THE CIRCUS**

Often the circus opens with a big parade, called a **spectacle**, or **spec**—but the spec may come anywhere in the show where the management decides it fits best. All the human and animal performers take part, dressed in colorful costumes that carry out the theme of the spec. An Arabian Nights theme may feature all the camels in the circus menagerie, while a Wild West theme will have bison and performers costumed as cowboys riding the circus horses. Some parades feature exotic animals such as giraffes or hippopotamuses.

Different acts may go on in the rings at the same time. For example, there may be a juggler in ring one, a performer doing magic tricks in ring two, and several performers in ring three presenting a dog and pony act. Often, however, one finds similar **displays**, as circus acts are called, in all three rings. Rin-gling Bros. and Barnum & Bailey Circus likes to present three rings of teeterboard acrobats, each from a different eastern European country that specializes in such acts.

Clowns are a favorite with many circus goers. Old and young alike laugh when clowns throw pies at each other, walk on tall stilts, and engage in other humorous stunts.

Other popular acts are the aerial and cannon acts. Timing is the all-important element in these difficult stunts. Aerial acts include the cloud swing (with ropes and ladders), the trapeze, and high-wire walking. Some acrobats use poles to balance, and others use only their arms.

Trained-animal acts are popular among circus goers. People have always been amazed by a trainer's ability to make an animal perform on command. Some horses are trained to canter around the ring while their riders (called **bareback riders**) perform acrobatic feats. Other trained horses, called **liberty horses**, do their tricks without riders or lead reins.

Wild-animal acts are always crowd pleasers, perhaps because of the element of danger that is present. A wild animal is trained, but never tamed. Especially popular are acts with tigers and elephants. Tiger acts usually take place in cages to protect audiences from any mishaps.

Daredevils include performers who get shot out of a cannon and land in a safety net, or get shot like arrows from giant bows, or dive, blindfolded, through a flaming wheel made of a whirling rim studded with daggers, clearing their sharp points by only a fraction of an inch.

Music is important in the circus. The bandleader knows the acts in every show. The background music is arranged according to the tempo of each act. For example, the bareback-riding act requires a tempo different from that for the aerialists, elephants, or jugglers. The bandleader combines popular and classical music, old-time circus music, and music for parades.

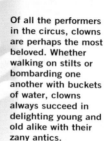

Of all the performers in the circus, clowns are perhaps the most beloved. Whether walking on stilts or bombarding one another with buckets of water, clowns always succeed in delighting young and old alike with their zany antics.

▶ CIRCUS LIFE

Circus life has always seemed romantic to outsiders. In reality, it is a hard and demanding regimen that nevertheless gets into the blood—most circus people never want to do anything else. Shows travel by truck (these are called **mud shows** because

This seven-person pyramid is one of the amazing feats performed on the high wire. Aerial acts are perennial circus favorites.

of the muddy roads that circuses once traveled on) and also by train. Performers and animals traveling with railroad circuses live on the trains. Performers in shows that travel by truck usually live in motorized house trailers. Their animals travel with them or in separate trailers, except for large or dangerous animals such as elephants and tigers, which travel by truck.

The setting up of shows is a fascinating sight. Circus trains or trucks unload at dawn, and workers called **roustabouts** set up tents for the show or equip arenas with rings, props, animal cages, and the rigging used by acrobats and aerialists. The elephants and other animals are given food and water, and performers rehearse.

Many circus people teach their own children their acts. Children from circus families often follow in their parents' footsteps and may excel in an act before they graduate from high school. Many performers marry within the circus.

In winter quarters, when the season is done, performers take one or more months to organize and print the new program. Production numbers are set, music is orchestrated

Top: Trapeze artists fly through the air, dazzling the spectators below. *Above:* Wild-animal acts, with their element of danger, are always exciting.

and rehearsed by the circus musicians, dances are choreographed, wardrobes are designed and sewn, equipment is repaired and re-painted, and performers rehearse daily. After routes are set by the producer and permits obtained for the use of facilities in the communities where the circus will appear, the circus leaves its winter home for the first engagement of the new season.

▶ **HISTORY**

The origins of the circus date back thousands of years. Pottery found in ancient ruins depicts acrobats, jugglers, and trained bears. In ancient Rome, an arena called the Circus Maximus was the scene of exciting chariot races and other feats of skill and daring. In olden times, however, these feats were not combined with clowning. Clowns developed separately, from the fools in Greek and Roman pantomimes to the court jesters of the Middle Ages to the Arlecchino (Harlequin) and Pulcinella (Pierrot) of the *commedia dell'arte* of the 1500's.

The modern circus developed in England. In 1768, a riding instructor named Philip Astley found that he could ride standing up if his horse cantered in a circle at a constant speed while both he and the horse were leaning slightly inward—centrifugal force helped Astley keep his balance. Further, he discovered

that a horse cantering in a circle of a certain size would provide just the right amount of centrifugal force for achieving the most graceful balance. This led to the invention of the circus ring. Its diameter would eventually be standardized at approximately 42 feet (13 meters).

Astley's show began as just another exhibition of horseback riding. Then one day, Astley interrupted his feats with some equestrian clowning called "Billy Buttons, or the Tailor Riding to Brentford." After seeing so much good riding, the audiences laughed at the sight of a bumbling rider trying to climb on a horse—and falling off. With that addition, the modern circus was born. The contrast between some performers showing off their skill and daring and others making fun of this sense of superiority by comically failing to do the trick became the heart of the modern circus.

On August 27, 1785, the circus reached the United States when Thomas Pool put on the first American circus in Philadelphia, Pennsylvania. In 1793, President George Washington went to the Philadelphia circus of John Bill Ricketts. Washington liked it so much he kept on attending. In 1797, he sold Ricketts his white horse, Jack, which he had ridden in the Revolutionary War (1775–83). The horse, exhibited in a special stall, was the first circus **sideshow** in history. Later sideshow attractions included unusual people such as midgets (Charles Sherwood Stratton, known as General Tom Thumb, was the most famous), giants, and sword swallowers. Sideshows are no longer a part of most modern circuses.

One of the best-known names in American circus history is that of P. T. Barnum (1810–91). In 1871, he presented a traveling circus that he called the "Greatest Show on Earth." Ten years later, Barnum teamed with James A. Bailey to create the Barnum & Bailey Circus. In 1907, the Ringling Bros. Circus purchased Barnum & Bailey, ran it separately for a dozen years, then merged it in 1919 into the Ringling Bros. and Barnum & Bailey Circus.

In the days before roads became filled with traffic, the circus would parade to the showgrounds, with a brass band blaring energetically on the band wagon. The musical instrument called a calliope trailed clouds of steam and drew fascinated crowds of small boys and girls.

One of the most famous animals in circus history was the elephant Jumbo. Standing 13 feet 4 inches (406 centimeters) and weighing 6 ½ tons, Jumbo was billed by Barnum as the biggest of all elephants. (The word "jumbo" is now used to describe anything that is an unusually large example of its kind.)

Perhaps the best-known wild-animal trainer of the 20th century was Gunther Gebel-Williams. In one of his most spectacular acts, he rode on the back of an elephant, holding a tiger on a leash and flanked by two horses with tigers on their backs.

Famous clowns in history include Dan Rice, who delighted the young Mark Twain by pretending to be a drunken man who barges into the ring and insists on riding a circus horse bareback; Frank "Slivers" Oakley, who played a two-team baseball game all by himself; Emmett Kelly and Otto Griebling, the sad-faced tramp clowns whose gardens would not grow because Emmett ate the seeds; and Frosty Little, who could cram more clowns into a single car than anyone else. Among today's clowns is David Larible, a modern pied piper who plays seven different musical instruments to bring children from the audience into the ring, then gets them singing along with his antics.

Besides the Ringling Bros. and Barnum & Bailey Circus (whose home base is Venice, Florida), other well-known circuses include the Clyde Beatty–Cole Brothers Circus of Deland, Florida; the Cirque de Soleil, which makes its home base at Walt Disney World near Orlando, Florida; the Big Apple Circus of New York City, New York; the Cirque d'Hiver ("Winter Circus") of Paris, France; and the Moscow Circus of Russia.

C. P. Fox
Ringling Bros. and Barnum & Bailey
Reviewed and revised by John Culhane
Author, *The American Circus:
An Illustrated History*

See also Barnum, Phineas Taylor; Carnivals; Clowns.

WONDER QUESTION

What was the greatest feat in the history of trapeze flying?

In 1982, performing with the Ringling Bros. and Barnum & Bailey Circus in Tucson, Arizona, Miguel Vazquez, 17, became the first human being ever to achieve the quadruple somersault (four rolls in midair) from the flying trapeze to the hands of the catcher.

The Ginza, a shopping district in Tokyo, one of the world's most modern cities.

CITIES

Cities are the largest communities where people live and work. Whenever people are living together in one place, they form a community. Communities can generally be divided into three classes—farming villages; small towns, including the suburbs of large cities; and cities.

Have you ever wondered why great numbers of people choose to live in cities? Today about half of the people of North America, somewhat more than one third of the people of South America and Europe, and one tenth of the people of Africa and Asia live in cities of at least 100,000 people. People live in cities because they find something there that they want or need.

Throughout history, cities have been centers of activity and development. Some—like ancient Jerusalem and modern Salt Lake City—have been centers for religion. People gathered there originally to build a temple or shrine. Other cities have been centers of government, as Rome and Athens were in ancient times and Washington, D.C., London, Paris, Beijing, and Moscow are today. Others are cultural, financial, and manufacturing centers—such as Rio de Janeiro, Chicago, and Toronto. Many cities have grown up around universities. Cities contain the world's greatest museums and libraries. It is not simply its size that makes a city important. It is what the city offers the people who live there.

It may seem that people who want to be at the center of cultural, intellectual, or political life would naturally live in cities. One might also imagine that those who dislike crowds and prefer open spaces and outdoor activities would choose to live in suburbs or in farming villages. But people do not always live where they want to live. Often they must live in places where they can find work. And often, work is found in cities. People select the community in which they live largely because it meets their needs.

▶ HOW CITIES DIFFER FROM OTHER COMMUNITIES

One of the most important differences between the three kinds of communities is their crowdedness, or population density. Farming communities are the least crowded; cities, the most crowded. We can find the population density of a community by dividing the total number of residents by the area.

How crowded a city is helps determine its individual character. For example, New York

Above: Paris and other French cities are noted for their quaint sidewalk cafés, where people can eat, drink, and watch the crowds stroll by. *Below:* Much of New York's Fifth Avenue is lined with shops and department stores.

City and London have about the same population. But London occupies more land area than New York. New York has about 9,700 people to each square kilometer (25,000 people to each square mile). London, on the other hand, has only about half that many people to each square kilometer. For this reason, the typical Londoner can live in a small one-family house, while the typical New Yorker lives in an apartment.

Density can vary greatly. One of the most crowded cities in the world is Calcutta, a port city on the east coast of India. Calcutta has about three times as many people to each square kilometer as New York City. One of the least crowded cities is Flagstaff, Arizona. It has about 170 people to each square kilometer (440 people per square mile).

The crowdedness of cities is both good and bad. When a city is overcrowded, there is not enough room for parks and play areas. Streets are congested, with dangerous intersections. Apartments are small, crowded, and dark, especially for families with little money. But if people are widely scattered, the result is isolation—without shops, schools, hospitals, and cultural institutions nearby.

Density alone does not define a city. Another important characteristic is diversity. This term describes the variety that is part of city life. People of many different races and nationalities mingle in cities. Diversity cannot be measured mathematically, as density can. Hospitals, theaters, clubs, shops, hotels, railroad stations, schools, and government buildings are located in cities. And cities attract people with all the skills necessary to operate these institutions.

The diversity of peoples is especially noticeable in port cities such as San Francisco, Hong Kong, and the French port of Marseilles. The different groups often start neighborhoods in cities that reflect and continue their national traditions. Chinese, Italian, Hispanic (Spanish-speaking), and other communities can be found in cities around the world. London is dotted with Pakistani and Cypriot neighborhoods. Paris has many Algerians and people from other parts of Africa.

Neighborhoods in cities offer their residents certain advantages. These include a feeling of stability and safety, a sense of belonging to a group, and the experience of

Above: High walls surround the Kremlin in the heart of Moscow, Russia's capital and largest city. Once the seat of czars and rulers of the Soviet Union, it is now the site of the government of the Russian Federation. *Below:* Jerusalem, a city sacred to three religions (Judaism, Christianity, and Islam), is the capital of Israel.

neighborliness that is said to be characteristic of small towns. But neighborhoods in cities can also have disadvantages. Sometimes they discourage new residents, who differ from the people already there in race, religion, or national origin. And they may prevent immigrants from mixing with the society of their new country.

▶ THE HISTORY OF CITIES

The development of cities has been influenced by many factors. These include social or political organization, economic conditions, advancements in technology, and the general history of the areas in which the cities are located.

Development of Cities

People could not live in cities—or help to build cities—until the surrounding area produced enough food to make city life possible. People in cities produced neither grain nor meat. They made goods such as cloth and pottery and offered services such as protection from enemy invaders. The people who lived outside the city were willing to trade some of the food they produced for these goods and services.

After people had learned to plant and harvest crops, permanent settlements began in areas where surplus food was produced. Often these settlements grew up in locations that could be easily defended. And they were usually near a source of water that could be used for transportation as well as drinking. Cities grew up where trade routes crossed and around shrines erected to gods.

Cities of the Ancient World

Archeologists have discovered traces of cities in Mesopotamia that existed as early as 5000 B.C. Other early cities were founded in Egypt and China.

Mesopotamia. Mesopotamia was the land between the Tigris and Euphrates rivers, in southwestern Asia. Some of the earliest cities—Ur, Babylon, and Nineveh—grew up there. The fertile land around these cities pro-

Athens, Greece, as it may have appeared in ancient times.

vided a good supply of food for city dwellers. After 3500 B.C., the cities of Mesopotamia became centers of trade, politics, religion, military command, and government administration. The people built houses and city walls, developed written alphabets, and founded legal systems. Often the cities became centers of science, learning, and the arts.

The years from 2000 to 1000 B.C. were marked by wars in Mesopotamia and elsewhere in the Middle East. Many of the cities fell under the rule of the Hittite, Mycenaean, or Egyptian empires. But at the end of this period, new city-states developed in the Middle East and especially in Greece.

Greek City-States. A city-state is a self-governing unit that includes the city proper and the surrounding countryside. After 1000 B.C., a number of such states developed in Greece. In these city-states, the idea of government based on a specific constitutional and legal framework took hold. Various forms of government developed. The first rulers were kings, followed later by the richest and most powerful citizens. In Athens, the most renowned of the city-states, democracy ruled for two centuries. Athens also became famous as a center of learning and art.

The Greek city-states were rivals in trade, and from time to time they fought one another. In the 4th century B.C., most of them were conquered by Macedonia, to the north. Later they were ruled by Rome.

Rome. The greatest ancient city was Rome. Advances in technology—such as good roads and aqueducts to carry water—eventually enabled the city to spread well beyond the original settlement by the Tiber River. During the reign of the emperor Augustus (27 B.C. to A.D. 14), Rome's population reached 800,000.

Roman armies conquered a vast empire, bringing political stability and a system of justice. In return, Rome took the treasures of the countries it ruled. These treasures included furs and leathers, metals, precious jewels, and art. They could be used to buy the food that Rome's large population needed.

The Roman Empire needed fortified cities other than Rome, located in strategic sites in all the countries occupied by Roman armies. Some of these cities, such as Jerusalem and Ephesus, were already famous in the ancient world. Others were founded by the Romans and have remained important in the modern world. These include Massilia (Marseilles, the great French port on the Mediterranean Sea) and a small settlement on the Seine River in northern France called Lutetia, which we now know as Paris. London, too, first became important under Roman rule.

In the 3rd century, the empire was divided. Rome ruled the western part. The eastern part was ruled from the city of Byzantium (later Constantinople) for more than 1,000 years.

Centuries Without Cities

By 500 A.D., Rome was occupied by invading Germanic tribes. They could not and did not try to keep up the elaborate military and political structure that Rome had created.

In Europe, the period known in western history as the Dark Ages followed. People who lived in later years called the period from about 500 to 1000 A.D. "dark" because so few examples of human accomplishment, such as literature and works of art and architecture, were left behind.

These years could also be described as the "centuries without cities" in the Western world. With the collapse of Roman organization and the Roman system of justice, cities faded out—perhaps not completely, but in great part. Invaders destroyed many of them. People had to find food for themselves. A few fortresses remained, as did a few monasteries and other religious communities.

In the 10th century, with the rebirth of trade, settlements of traders began to rise near fortresses and monasteries. Life began to flicker again on the sites of ancient cities. Within a few hundred years, the medieval cities of Europe had grown up. They were different from those of the ancient world, although technically they had not made much progress.

But during this same period, Asian cities in Japan and China had been flourishing. When Marco Polo traveled from Venice to China around 1275, he saw cities far greater than any in Europe. He described Asian cities of paved streets and magnificent buildings. European cities of that period had mud or cobblestone streets, and no buildings except cathedrals could be called beautiful.

This painting from the 15th century shows peasants working in the fields outside the walls of a town.

The Middle Ages

As in the ancient cities of Mesopotamia, the outstanding characteristic of the medieval city was its walls. The walls surrounded the city and provided protection from invaders. But they kept even small populations living in crowded conditions. A few cities in Europe still have walls standing very much as they did in the late Middle Ages. Carcassonne, in France, is a well-known example of a medieval walled city that has changed little over the centuries.

Usually the cathedral was the largest building in the medieval city. In front of the cathedral there was often a large marketplace. There trade was conducted, and religious fairs and celebrations were held. City streets were extremely narrow.

The walls, the cathedral, the marketplace—representing military power, religious faith, and commerce—gave the residents of the medieval city a sense of unity. They wor-

shiped in a single church. They owed their political allegiance to one ruler. And they bought and sold what they needed in a single place. These qualities of city life helped the residents to feel secure in the face of dangers like famine, war, and disease.

Life was difficult in the medieval city. The water supply came from wells, easily contaminated with germs and filth. The streets of the city were its sewer and garbage disposal system. Unsanitary conditions spread disease, and plagues killed many people.

The growth of trade turned some medieval cities into specialized workshops. From the 11th to the 15th centuries, guilds (associations of people who do the same kind of work, such as weavers or merchants) were formed. Guilds for teachers and students aided in the formation of the university system. Some highly specialized medieval cities—such as Bruges, Belgium, a center of woolen manufacture—have survived to modern times almost unchanged in their basic design.

In the 1300's, trade began to thrive. More land was farmed, manufacturing increased, and trade based on money rather than barter became the rule. New towns were founded at strategic rivers, harbors, and crossroads. London and Paris became important cities. But in many respects—water supply and roads, for example—the medieval cities were not as advanced as those built by the Romans more than a thousand years earlier.

In the 15th century, the use of gunpowder made feudal walls and castles less effective as defenses. And the printing press revolutionized communications and stimulated the growth of universities. The universities, in turn, attracted more people to cities. Gradually cities began to spread outside their high walls.

Most cities suffered during the 14th and 15th centuries from wars among European nations. Financing these wars placed a heavy strain on the cities. Merchants came to resent this. Over a period of years they helped to form a strong middle class that demanded and obtained important changes in trade regulations and political processes.

In addition, new social patterns were evolving. For example, in Germany, members of the rising class of merchants were devising modern city governments of councillors

The important seaport of Lisbon, Portugal, during the 16th century.

and mayors. As they became more powerful, the merchants wanted to govern themselves. They were able to purchase the independence of the towns from their rulers. This trend toward self-government encouraged the growth of individual freedom.

Later, merchants played a key role in the cities of eastern Asia. For example, in Japan, merchants rose from the bottom of the social scale in the 17th century to dominate the economy and the arts in the 19th century.

The Renaissance

The Renaissance in Europe, which began in the 14th century and extended into the 17th century, was a time of vigorous trade. This trade stimulated the growth of cities and of city-states. In Italy, important cities included Venice, which was the main port of the Renaissance, and Milan, which was located where important trade routes crossed. Powerful city-states also developed in Germany. Hamburg and Cologne are two such cities that remain important today. To protect their interests, the German city-states formed an association called the Hanseatic League.

Renaissance interest in the past—especially in classical Greece and Rome—brought new ideas about cities. Ideal cities were designed, with vast open spaces and spacious streets radiating from a central square. Many of these designs remained only plans. But the Renaissance was a time of great building in cities, especially in those such as Paris that were centers of royal power.

During this period, city life was flourishing in the Western Hemisphere. In 1519, the Spanish explorer Hernando Cortes was dazzled by the cities of the Aztecs in Mexico. The city of Tenochtitlán (now Mexico City) was built over a lake. It was joined to the land by long causeways that were perhaps beyond European engineering skills.

The Industrial Age

If you happened to live in the United States in 1789, when George Washington became its first president, you would probably have been living in a farming village, as did most people in the 18th century. If you had been alive when Franklin D. Roosevelt became president in 1933—144 years later—you very

A 19th-century lithograph of Pella, Iowa. Such factory towns developed during the Industrial Revolution.

likely would have been living in a city. In the early 1930's, more people of the United States lived in cities than in suburbs or on farms. Today the suburbs are more likely to be your home. More people live in the suburbs than in the cities, and many more than in farming villages.

The Industrial Revolution in the late 18th and early 19th centuries drastically changed cities. Factories developed with the invention of machines to do work that previously had been done by hand. They became the centers of industrial cities. People left rural areas to seek work in the cities.

The Industrial Revolution marked the beginning of immense growth in population, especially in cities of the English-speaking world such as London, Birmingham, Manchester, Glasgow, and New York. It has been estimated that in 1800 under 3 percent of the world's population lived in cities of 20,000 people or more. Today about 25 percent of the world's population lives in areas of 20,000 people or more.

Improvements in transportation speeded industrial development and the growth of urban areas. Improvements in oceangoing carriers encouraged migration to cities. These ships also brought raw materials to be used in the factories and took factory products to be sold all over the world.

Industrial cities expanded in all directions.

Expansion carried some built-in problems, especially in the areas of housing and traffic congestion. In the early 1800's, cities concentrated on building factories, railroads, and bridges. Often there was not enough labor or materials for housing construction. Cheaply constructed, ugly tenements or row houses were built. There were problems of water, sanitation, and congestion. City death rates were far higher than those of rural areas.

By the middle of the 1800's, a social reform movement was working to ease these problems. Frederick Olmstead (1822–1903) designed parks such as New York City's Central Park, which brought sunlight, fresh air, and green space into the center of overcrowded cities. Jacob Riis (1849–1914), a Danish immigrant to New York, wrote about New York's slums, stimulating housing reform. Ebenezer Howard (1850–1928) started a movement in England to build "garden cities" outside the big cities. Inspired by his idea, the British Government financed "new towns" in England, Scotland, and Wales.

Few people did more to help the cities than the engineers, designers, and politicians who developed and fought for sewage systems, water supply systems, and transportation systems. These systems relieved some of the problems of urban life. The advent of cheap electric power, rapid transit, new building materials, and rising incomes also helped.

▶MODERN CITIES

Today the world is dotted with giant cities. Some are growing larger, others are in a state of decline, and some are being rebuilt. Each city has its own individual characteristics, but there are some problems that are shared by cities all over the globe.

Sometimes geography influences the character of a city, as well as the problems it faces. Two examples are New York, which is built largely on islands, and Rio de Janeiro, which is hemmed in by mountains and the sea. These cities have limited land area. They have expanded upward, with skyscrapers. Los Angeles, California, has had room to spread out. But its location between the Pacific Ocean and the Santa Monica Mountains has given it other problems—the mountains frequently trap polluted air over the city, and the area is subject to earthquakes.

History has also played a part in shaping modern cities. Cities such as Rome can tell their own histories through many ancient buildings that remain. But other cities have been almost totally destroyed and then rebuilt. An example is Tokyo, which was struck by a severe earthquake in 1923 and was bombed during World War II. Today it is one of the most modern of the world's large cities. Many European cities also suffered damage from bombing during World War II.

Some cities face unusual problems—Mexico City, for example, has difficulty providing water to its growing population. But most modern cities share certain problems.

Problems Shared by Cities

In general, modern cities are suffering from the effects of too much industrialization and too rapid urbanization. Often buildings that were built hastily in response to urgent need are now decaying. Crime and drug addiction continue to be serious problems for city residents. Poverty and crowded conditions contribute to these problems.

The diversity of city populations has sometimes brought racial conflict. Since World War II, cities in North America and Europe have received large numbers of people from rural areas. Most of these migrants have had little chance in their original homes to learn the ways of an industrial urban society. It is difficult for present-day cities to provide employment and services for many of these people.

Traffic and Pollution. The automobile has been a mixed blessing for the city. It has helped relieve some of the crowdedness of cities because it allows people to live in suburban areas and commute to work. But the automobile contributes to two of the worst problems a city must face—traffic congestion and pollution. Thousands of cars clog city streets during peak travel hours.

Pollution from automobile exhaust adds to pollution caused by industry. The effects of air pollution on the health of city residents cannot be calculated.

Another serious crisis for many cities is disposal of the waste products of city life. These include garbage and sewage, as well as the many chemicals used in industry. Often the

With a population exceeding 8 million, Mexico City is the largest city in North America and one of the most densely populated areas in the world. Cities of this size tend to be overcrowded, a condition that can lead to housing shortages, inadequate public facilities, and pollution-control problems.

rivers and lakes surrounding large cities are polluted with these wastes.

Housing. Many cities lack adequate housing, particularly for low-income residents. This problem is perhaps most severe in the cities of Africa and Asia that are receiving the greatest influx of people from rural areas. But few cities are without slum areas.

Financial Problems. Many cities must charge their residents high taxes to pay for services such as police and fire protection and waste disposal. In some cases, high taxes have contributed to the cities' decline. The high costs of doing business in a city—in taxes, salaries, and the like—have caused many firms to move to rural or suburban areas. This

lems of decline. Industrial cities of Europe such as Birmingham, Liverpool, Glasgow, Turin, Milan, and the German cities on the Ruhr River have had similar problems. In the United States, decline has been most marked in the older cities of the northeastern and north central states.

Some people argue that the decline of cities cannot be prevented. They point to new inventions that threaten cities. Televisions and the telephone make it possible for people to exchange information without actually meeting. Diesel trucks and public highways now handle more freight than railroads. This means that it is no longer necessary to have factories located near the railroad yards of cities so that goods

The statue of Christ the Redeemer, crowning Brazil's Sugarloaf Mountain, overlooks the city of Rio de Janeiro, one of the largest cities in South America. Rio's location was chosen for its sheltered harbor on Guanabara Bay, leading to the Atlantic Ocean.

means that there are fewer jobs in the city. And the residents who remain must bear the full cost of providing services.

New York City, for example, must struggle to repay money it borrowed in the 1960's to build housing for middle-income families. The high taxes needed to raise the funds to repay the borrowed money have discouraged manufacturers and other businesses from moving into the city.

Urban Decline

New York is only one example of a city that, in a time of growth, made commitments that weakened its ability to adjust to later prob-

can be shipped by rail. Increased air travel and transportation reduce the importance of seaports, except for certain types of heavy freight that must travel on cargo vessels. Universities are often located in towns or small cities rather than big cities. The effect of these changes, it is argued, is that new locations —away from the older cities and their many problems—are becoming more feasible and more attractive.

Hope for Cities

In recent years, some government programs have had dramatic success in bringing the economies of cities back to life. In the United

States, for example, the Model Cities Program provided large sums of money for job training and improvement of schools. Other programs have concentrated on housing, sewage treatment, caring for the aged, helping members of minority groups, elimination of slums, and the planning of city development. European regional development programs have also had some measure of success in Britain, Scandinavia, Germany, and the Netherlands. The Spanish seaport of Barcelona contains an old section with many medieval buildings and a new section that is a fine example of city planning. And new cities in such widely scattered areas as South America, India, and Israel show the widespread concern of city planners about the future of the city.

Dallas, Texas, is an example of a city that has enjoyed renewed growth. In 1967 a program called Goals for Dallas was started. Its purpose was to reverse the loss of population and retail trade to the city's growing suburbs. With public and private funds, a new airport and several downtown retail projects were built. These projects brought new health to the city's economy.

People who believe that there is a future for cities argue that governments will provide financial aid for several reasons. One reason is that cities can be good savers of energy. Electric power can be distributed economically in cities. People save energy when they use the public transportation of cities instead of private cars. City buses and subways—and elevators, traveling from floor to floor—take the place of highways and cars that are needed outside cities to move people over greater distances to their homes.

People also say that the city must be understood in relation to the economy and culture of the entire country. The city provides a place where contact among people generates ideas. This face-to-face exchange of ideas cannot be replaced by long-distance telephone circuits. It enables the citizens of great cities to move in new directions. It has made city life interesting to novelists, playwrights, and artists throughout history.

▶ THE FUTURE OF CITIES

Each person who thinks about cities leans to one side or the other in the endless argument about their future. Some believe that cities will become more like one another as modern technology leads to rapid exchange of ideas and information. Skyscraper office buildings were built in New York because Manhattan, New York's central borough, is an island of limited area. Skyscrapers soon spread to other cities because they had become a symbol of the up-and-coming commercial city. Now they are found in such places as Sydney, Australia, and Warsaw, Poland.

Yet a contrary movement has been developing. It is based on the desire to retain traces of each city's past. Older, pre-skyscraper buildings differ from city to city. They make people remember their city's traditions. Some people demand that they be protected from demolition and decay. When old buildings are declared landmarks, they cannot be demolished or changed.

Many people believe that the city of the future will be the **megalopolis**. This is a word sometimes used to describe a "super city." It is a combination of two Greek words— *megas,* which means "large," and *polis,* which means "city." The megalopolis is a natural extension of the spread of urban areas, as cities and their surrounding suburbs expand into one another.

The densely populated area between Boston and Washington, D.C., is often called a megalopolis. It includes about 40,000,000 people. Similar areas in North America have developed along the Great Lakes and around Los Angeles and San Francisco, Houston and Dallas, and Miami. Megalopolises in Europe include the area around London and the Midlands, Paris and its surroundings, central Belgium, parts of the Netherlands, and the industrial basin around the Ruhr in northwestern Germany. In Japan, the Tokyo-Osaka area is also considered a megalopolis.

Whatever the city of the future is like, it probably will be different from the city of today. Throughout history, cities have adapted to new ways of life. Because they have done so, such cities as Rome, Paris, London, and Moscow remain living symbols of history. To a great extent, the history of cities is a record of civilization.

ROGER STARR
Editorial Board, New York *Times*

See also URBAN PLANNING; articles on individual cities.

In 1986, Chief Justice Warren Burger administered the oath of U.S. citizenship to thousands of people at a ceremony commemorating the Statue of Liberty's 100th birthday.

CITIZENSHIP

A citizen is a participatory member of a political community. Citizenship is gained by meeting the legal requirements of a national, state, or local government. A nation grants certain rights and privileges to its citizens. In return, citizens are expected to obey their country's laws and defend it against its enemies.

The value of citizenship varies from nation to nation. In some countries, citizenship can mean a citizen has the right to vote, the right to hold government offices, and the right to collect unemployment insurance payments, to name a few examples.

Living in a country does not mean that a person is necessarily a citizen of that country. Citizens of one country who live in a foreign country are known as **aliens**. Their rights and duties are determined by political treaties and by the laws of the country in which they stay. In the United States, aliens must obey the laws and pay taxes, just as U.S. citizens do. They must register with the U.S. government to obtain legal permission to stay for an extended length of time. Legal aliens are entitled to protection under the law and to use of the courts. They may also own property, carry on business, and attend public schools. But aliens cannot vote or hold government office. In some states they are not allowed to practice certain professions until they become citizens.

Under United States law, a **noncitizen national** is a person who is neither a citizen nor an alien but who owes permanent loyalty to the United States. People in this category have some but not all of the rights of citizens. For example, inhabitants of a United States territory may not have the right to vote. Noncitizen nationals of the United States include those people on the Pacific islands of American Samoa who were born after the territory was taken over by the United States in 1900.

▶BECOMING A CITIZEN

Every nation provides ways of becoming a citizen. For most people citizenship is a matter of birth. For others it may be acquired through a process known as naturalization.

Two rules are used to determine citizenship by birth: (1) *jus sanguinis* ("law of the blood"); and (2) *jus soli* ("law of the soil"). Under *jus sanguinis*, children take their parents' nationality regardless of where they are born. For example, a child born to Italian parents in Britain is a citizen of Italy. On the other hand, the rule of *jus soli* says that children are citizens of the nation in which they are born, no matter what the parents' nationalities are. Thus a child born to Italian parents in Britain is also a citizen of Britain. Since most nations apply both of these rules, a person can become a citizen of two nations. This is called dual citizenship.

Dual citizenship can result from naturalization, which is the legal way in which people change their citizenship. Internal law protects naturalized citizens as long as they live in their new country. But they may lose their new citizenship if they return to the country of their birth and remain for a long time. In wartime, a serious problem could arise if both countries demand their services in the armed forces.

Citizens in democratic countries have the privilege and responsibility to vote for their government representatives. Voting booths are enclosed to assure privacy.

CITIZENSHIP UNDER THE U.S. CONSTITUTION

The United States Constitution, drafted in 1787, did not explain citizenship, but it did mention "citizens of the States" and a "citizen of the United States." Citizens of the United States became entitled to the rights guaranteed to them by the Constitution and its later amendments. Among these rights were the right to vote, own property, seek elective office, and to be protected by the laws of the land.

Because the young United States followed British common law, it accepted the rule of *jus soli*, or place of birth. As early as 1790, Congress recognized the rule of *jus sanguinis*, or blood relationship, by passing laws giving citizenship to a child born in a foreign country if the father was a citizen of the United States.

The 14th Amendment

The first official written explanation of American citizenship was included in the 14th Amendment to the Constitution (1868). Section 1 of this amendment declares that "All persons born or naturalized in the United States, and subject to the jurisdiction thereof, are citizens of the United States and of the State wherein they reside." The wording of this amendment places national citizenship before state citizenship. In other words, an American is first a citizen of the United States and then a citizen of the state in which he or she lives. Citizens are entitled to the rights granted by both the national government and their own state's government.

The 14th Amendment was passed to guarantee citizenship to blacks who were freed from slavery after the Civil War (13th Amendment, 1865). The amendment made the rule of *jus soli* (place of birth) a law for all U.S. citizens. This means that any child born in the United States becomes a citizen at birth, even if its parents are aliens. (However, the rule does not apply to children born to foreign diplomats or United Nations officials.)

The 14th Amendment does not include *jus sanguinis*. American citizenship acquired at birth in a foreign nation is usually determined by the law that is in effect at the time the child is born. The Immigration and Nationality Act of 1952, amended in 1965, 1976, and 1978, gives the requirements.

For a child born on or after December 24, 1952, both parents must have been American citizens. In addition, one parent must have lived in the United States for ten years (and for at least five years after the age of 14) before the birth of the child.

U.S. Citizenship By Naturalization

The U.S. Constitution gives Congress the power to make naturalization laws for the United States. No state can give citizenship to aliens.

A person can become a naturalized citizen of the United States individually or as part of a group. Generally any person who has come into the United States as an immigrant may become a naturalized citizen. To do so, a person must be over 18 years old and must have lived in the United States for five years, without leaving for more than a total of 30 months (and not more than twelve consecutive months) throughout that five-year period.

People who wish to become U.S. citizens must file a petition for naturalization and take an examination that shows that they can read, speak, and write simple English and have a fair knowledge of American history, government, and the Constitution. They must be able to prove that they are of good, moral character. Two American citizens whom they know well must verify that the applicant will be a good citizen and loyal to the United States.

Once an applicant has passed the requirements and examination, he or she may become a U.S. citizen by taking an oath of allegiance. Group naturalization ceremonies often take place on September 17—Citizenship Day. Naturalized citizens are entitled to all of the rights granted to natural-born citizens, except they may not become president or vice president of the United States.

Congress has granted honorary citizenship, an extremely high honor, to only two foreigners. Sir Winston Churchill, who was prime minister of the United Kingdom, was the first to receive this honor in 1963. Raoul Wallenberg, a Swedish diplomat who rescued tens of thousands of Hungarian Jews during World War II, received the honor in 1981.

Loss of Citizenship

Most nations permit individuals to give up their citizenship. This act, known as **expatriation**, means that a person no longer wants the rights and responsibilities of citizenship in a particular country. Such a person may then become a citizen of another country or may become a stateless person (one without a country). If U.S. citizens wish to give up their citizenship, they must declare this on a form provided by the secretary of state.

A citizen of the United States loses U.S. citizenship by becoming a citizen of a foreign country unless a special exception is made by the State Department. A person can also lose U.S. citizenship for serving in the armed forces of, or holding office in, a foreign government. U.S. citizenship can also be taken away from people who have been convicted of a major federal crime, such as treason. But people cannot lose their citizenship for something they were forced to do. A person who is forced to serve in a foreign army, for example, will not lose U.S. citizenship.

Interestingly, Robert E. Lee, one of the greatest generals of all time, lost his U.S. citizenship when he took command of the Confederate forces during the American Civil War. Due to a mistake, his citizenship was not restored to him until Congress acted on the matter in July 1975.

▶ HISTORY OF CITIZENSHIP

The idea of citizenship came into being many centuries ago. In the ancient city-state of Athens, citizenship was granted to males of certain classes. Citizenship was also granted to a few foreigners and freed slaves. Citizenship meant that a man could vote, hold office, serve on committees and juries, and give military service. He was also expected to share the work of government. Women, slaves, and practically all foreigners were protected under the law but had few of the rights and privileges of Athenian citizens.

Citizenship was also important to the people of ancient Rome. Roman citizens often took part in their government. Roman citizenship was extended to foreign soldiers serving in the army and to men of conquered lands. By A.D. 212 almost all of the men in Roman provinces, except slaves, were citizens.

After the fall of the Roman Empire, in the 400's, the idea of citizenship became less important for many centuries. The feudal system spread through western Europe in the Middle Ages. This system was based on services and loyalty to a higher person in exchange for his protection. Millions of serfs worked the land for lords. The lords owed their allegiance to overlords. The overlords in turn were controlled by the king. In this system the king and nobles, rather than any government independent of these rulers, gave the people rights and privileges.

By the 1600's some kings had made many small states into nations. The common people no longer owed allegiance, or loyalty, to the nobles in their immediate region. Their first allegiance now was to the king. They began to take pride in their whole country. They also began to feel that they should have a voice in their country's government. As these changes took place, people started thinking of themselves as citizens of a nation as well as the loyal subjects of their king.

Today, most people place a high value on their citizenship. They know that when they pledge allegiance to their flag, they are willing to fulfill specific obligations to their country and will be granted many rights and privileges in return.

WARD WHIPPLE
Editor, *Civic Leader*

See also ALIENS; IMMIGRATION; NATURALIZATION; UNITED STATES, CONSTITUTION OF THE.

CITRUS FRUIT. See LEMON AND LIME; ORANGE AND GRAPEFRUIT.

CIVETS. See MONGOOSES, MEERKATS, AND THEIR RELATIVES.

The Civil Rights Memorial in Birmingham, Alabama, commemorates the victims and landmark events of the civil rights movement of the 1950's and 1960's.

CIVIL RIGHTS

Civil rights are freedoms and benefits that are guaranteed to people by law or tradition. The term "civil rights" refers to guarantees by law of fair and equal treatment for all people, regardless of race, religion, ethnic origin, age, sex, sexual orientation, disabilities, or personal beliefs.

The term "civil rights" is often used interchangeably with the terms "civil liberties" and "human rights." Together, these phrases refer to the natural desire of all people to achieve freedom, equality, and justice. They include such basic rights as freedom of speech, religion, and assembly; the right to take part in the political process; and the right to fair and equal treatment under the law. These rights are also protected against government interference. Civil rights and civil liberties are the cornerstones of a free society.

The Idea of Civil Rights

The idea of civil rights and civil liberties in Western civilization has grown out of three main schools of thought. Some philosophers in the 1600's developed the theory of natural law. They argued that because human beings are created by God or nature, people have certain natural rights. The idea of natural rights was later included in the American Declaration of Independence of 1776. It states that "all men are created equal" and are "endowed by their Creator with certain unalienable Rights."

A second school of that time took the position that rights and liberties came from the political state or society to which a person belonged. According to this group of thinkers, a person living outside organized society had no rights except that of self-defense. Therefore, it was argued, only a government with the power to enforce the law can protect the rights of an individual. In order to have rights, then, a person must accept society's rule.

The third school held that human rights were utilitarian (useful) because society benefited from the free and open exchange of ideas. One of the leaders of this school of thought was the English philosopher John Stuart Mill (1806–73), who believed that freedom was good for both society and the individual. Freedom made people think and act for themselves, and in Mill's view this made them better people.

Threats to Civil Rights

Although many people agree in principle with the ideas behind civil rights and civil liberties, governments often will try to restrict those rights. In a dictatorship (rule by one party, the army, or a single political leader), the rights of the people usually are limited. They may not be allowed to vote freely or to publish whatever they wish. Often they are not permitted to protest social conditions or government actions. Even in democracies, the government may attempt to hold onto its power by silencing its critics, a goal usually achieved through censorship of radio and television broadcasts, books, newspapers, and motion pictures.

Legal Protections

Because people's civil rights and civil liberties have been threatened throughout history, most countries recognize that laws are required to protect them. Many nations have drawn up legal documents listing the rights and liberties guaranteed to their citizens. The earliest such document in Western history was the Magna Carta (1215), which forced the king of England to grant certain rights to his barons. Many centuries later, in 1689, the English Parliament, or legislative body, passed a law that included a **bill of rights**. For the first time, the law made Parliament, which represented the people, more powerful than the king and provided that the people would have certain basic liberties.

When the first United States Congress met in 1789, a bill of rights similar to the English one was proposed. The U.S. Bill of Rights— made up of the first ten amendments to the U.S. Constitution—became a reality in 1791. It guarantees such rights as freedom of speech and the right to petition the government about grievances. It also provides for a free press, due process of law, trial by jury, and freedom of religion; it protects the citizen against cruel and unjust punishment and against unlawful searches and seizures.

The rights set forth by the nation's founders in the Bill of Rights, however, were not enough to assure equal treatment for all. Several later amendments to the Constitution were required to secure civil rights in the United States, particularly those of minority groups. For example, until slavery was abolished by the 13th Amendment in 1865, African Americans had no legal rights whatsoever. The 14th Amendment (1868) guaranteed them equal treatment under the law. The 15th Amendment (1870) guaranteed men of all races the right to vote. Voting rights were not extended to women until the ratification of the 19th Amendment in 1920.

Many nations that have been formed since the late 1800's have bills of rights in their constitutions. In 1982, Canada revised its bill of rights and named it the Charter of Rights and Freedoms. In addition to broad, traditional rights, it contains specific clauses that protect the rights of Canada's many ethnic groups and native Indian and Inuit populations.

SELECTED CIVIL RIGHTS ORGANIZATIONS

American Association for Affirmative Action Promotes affirmative action and serves as liaison to private and governmental agencies concerned with fairness in education and employment.

American Civil Liberties Union (ACLU) Defends the constitutional rights of all American citizens.

American Indian Movement (AIM) Seeks to guarantee equal rights and improve living conditions for the native populations of the United States and Canada.

Anti-Defamation League of B'Nai B'rith Fights anti-Semitism and racial bigotry.

Congress of Racial Equality (CORE) Seeks to identify racism and reverse discrimination.

Congressional Hispanic Caucus Institute Emphasizes the civil rights of Hispanics and their legal concerns.

Equal Employment Opportunity Commission (EEOC) Seeks to enforce federal laws to prevent discrimination in hiring.

Federation of Southern Cooperatives Land Assistance Fund Provides legal and technical assistance to black landowners.

Lawyers' Committee for Civil Rights Under Law Assists in providing volunteer legal services.

Mexican American Legal Defense and Educational Fund Assists in providing legal services to Mexican Americans.

National Association for the Advancement of Colored People (NAACP) Works to eliminate racial injustice and to guarantee full and equal opportunity.

National Black Caucus of State Legislators Promotes more effective leadership among black state legislators.

National Organization for Women (NOW) Fights to end legal discrimination against women in personal matters as well as in educational and professional areas.

National Senior Citizens Law Center Provides legal education and support to senior citizens and retirees.

National Urban League Seeks equal economic and political opportunity for all Americans, with emphasis on African Americans.

Native American Rights Fund Provides civil rights education and support to Native Americans.

Puerto Rican Defense Provides legal advice and assistance to Puerto Ricans in civil rights disputes.

Southern Christian Leadership Conference (SCLC) Seeks to improve civic, religious, economic, and cultural conditions through direct, nonviolent action.

Southern Poverty Law Center Provides legal advice to impoverished individuals and acts as a liaison with legal-aid groups and the American Civil Liberties Union.

Civil Rights Movements

International agreements and even bills of rights do not always guarantee that a person's civil rights will be protected. In the United States, constitutional guarantees did not stop discrimination against minorities in voting rights, property ownership, job opportunities, and other areas. In the 1960's, in an effort to secure their civil rights, African Americans and their supporters staged protests and demonstrations that sometimes grew into riots and clashes with police. Congress then passed specific laws, such as the Civil Rights Act of 1964 and the Voting Rights Act of 1965, to ensure that those rights were protected. (For more information, see the article CIVIL RIGHTS MOVEMENT following this article.)

Similarly, in the 1970's, many American women pressed for the adoption of the Equal Rights Amendment to the Constitution. The amendment, which would have prohibited discrimination on the basis of sex, was defeated when three-fourths of the states failed to ratify it by June 30, 1982. (For more information, see the article WOMEN'S RIGHTS MOVEMENT in Volume W-X-Y-Z.)

Today the United States and many other countries have government and private agencies that aim to protect civil rights and civil liberties. Where laws and international agreements fail, public opinion can help. The United Nations, the governments of democratic countries, and private organizations such as Amnesty International use their influence to try to stop the most serious cases of injustice, including slavery, which is still practiced in China and several Third World countries.

South Africa provides a specific example of how outside pressures can influence a government to act on behalf of civil and human rights. In the 1980's many countries imposed trade restrictions and other economic sanctions (penalties) on South Africa in an effort to persuade the all-white government of that country

Left: The First Amendment to the U.S. Constitution guarantees a citizen's right to petition the government "for a redress of grievances." Following the 1993 murder of a doctor outside an abortion clinic in Florida, protesters gathered to demand that the federal government guarantee safe access to abortion clinics.

Below: South Africa's first true democratic national election, in 1994, marked an astounding civil rights victory for black South Africans. Previously blacks had been denied the vote as well as representation in the national legislature.

to change its racial policies and grant equal rights to people of all races. Such efforts contributed to the end of apartheid (legal separation of the races) in the early 1990's, and by 1994, black South Africans had achieved the right to vote.

ROGER N. BALDWIN
Adviser, International Affairs
American Civil Liberties Union
Reviewed by ELAINE PASCOE
Author, *Racial Prejudice*

See also BILL OF RIGHTS; CIVIL RIGHTS MOVEMENT; HUMAN RIGHTS; WOMEN'S RIGHTS MOVEMENT.

CIVIL RIGHTS MOVEMENT

"I have a dream that my four little children will one day live in a nation where they will not be judged by the color of their skin, but by the content of their character.

". . . When we let freedom ring, when we let it ring from every village and every hamlet, from every state and every city, we will be able to speed up that day when all of God's children, black men and white men, Jews and Gentiles, Protestants and Catholics, will be able to join hands and sing in the words of the old Negro spiritual, 'Free at last! Free at last! Thank God Almighty, we are free at last!' "

Excerpts from the speech "I Have a Dream," delivered by Martin Luther King, Jr., on August 28, 1963, at the height of the civil rights movement.

There have been many movements in the United States in which various groups of citizens have fought to secure personal and property rights guaranteed them by the U.S. Constitution. The civil rights movement in the United States, however, generally refers to the campaign of African Americans, who, for reasons of prejudice, had long been denied many of the rights of citizenship enjoyed by white Americans. The racial injustices inflicted on African Americans led to a period of extreme social unrest in the 1950's and 1960's, when the black community, supported by many white sympathizers, rose up and challenged the social systems and public authorities that were depriving them of their rights as citizens.

Background to the Civil Rights Movement

After the Civil War (1861–65), three amendments to the Constitution, generally referred to as the Reconstruction Amendments, were ratified (approved). The 13th Amendment (1865) ended slavery; the 14th Amendment (1868) made citizens of ex-slaves; and the 15th Amendment (1870) guaranteed African American men the right to vote. However, prejudice against blacks was so pervasive that the new laws, and the rights that accompanied citizenship, often were ignored.

With the enactment of the Civil Rights Act of 1875, Congress took the first legislative steps to forbid government at any level to discriminate against blacks in public facilities. However, the U.S. Supreme Court later held that this law only applied to legislation passed by the federal government. Many states, particularly in the South, took advantage of this ruling and quickly passed a series of racially discriminatory laws that segregated (separated) the blacks from whites in public accommodations. These laws were strengthened by the U.S. Supreme Court in the 1896 "separate but equal" ruling *Plessy* v. *Ferguson*. For more than half a century these laws effectively gave whites legal permission to treat blacks as second-class citizens.

The Civil Rights Movement Begins

It can be said that the modern civil rights movement began on May 17, 1954. On that day, the Supreme Court overturned *Plessy* when it ruled in the case of *Brown* v. *Board of Education of Topeka* (Kansas) that the principle of "separate but equal" was unconstitutional in the public school system. It was generally understood that this principle should apply to all areas of public life.

Then in 1955, a black seamstress in Alabama named Rosa Parks refused to yield her

Daisy Bates and the Little Rock Nine receiving the NAACP's Spingarn Medal in 1958.

Coretta Scott King (1927–), born in Heiberger, Ala., became one of the civil rights movement's most dedicated activists following the 1968 assassination of her husband, Dr. Martin Luther King, Jr. As head (1969–95) of the Martin Luther King, Jr. Center for Nonviolent Social Change, in Atlanta, Ga., she worked on behalf of minorities, women, the poor, and others. Her memoir, *My Life with Martin Luther King, Jr.*, was published in 1969.

Bayard Rustin (1910–87), born in West Chester, Pa., helped found the Congress of Racial Equality (CORE) in 1942 and the Southern Christian Leadership Conference (SCLC) in 1957. In 1947, Rustin pioneered the first freedom rides into the South to test the results of court rulings against discrimination on interstate transportation. A supporter of nonviolent protest, he was a chief organizer of the 1963 March on Washington. From 1964 until his death, he headed the A. Philip Randolph Institute in New York City, promoting social and economic reforms.

Roy Wilkins (1901–81), born in St. Louis, Mo., led the NAACP from 1955 to 1977. Although a strong civil rights supporter, he believed that African Americans could achieve equality through constitutional means, and he rejected the militancy of the growing Black Power movement in

Consult the Index for more information in *The New Book of Knowledge* on the following civil rights leaders and activists: Ralph Abernathy, Mary McLeod Bethune, Frederick Douglass, W. E. B. Du Bois, Benjamin Hooks, Jesse Jackson, Martin Luther King, Jr., Thurgood Marshall, Rosa Parks, A. Philip Randolph, and Booker T. Washington.

Daisy Lee Gatson Bates (1915?–99), born in Huttig, Ark., led the effort to desegregate the schools in Arkansas. In 1957, while president of the Arkansas NAACP, Bates attempted to enroll nine black students in Little Rock's all-white Central High School. Day after day angry mobs blocked their entrance. Finally, on September 25, 1957, federal troops sent by President Dwight D. Eisenhower escorted Bates and the children safely into the school.

Medgar Wiley Evers (1926–63) was born in Decatur, Miss. As a field secretary (1954–63) for the NAACP, he organized rallies, voter registrations, marches, and boycotts of stores that would not hire blacks. In 1963, the year he was awarded the NAACP's Spingarn Medal, Evers was murdered. After two mistrials in the 1960's, his assassin, Byron De La Beckwith, was finally convicted of the crime in 1994. Medgar's brother, **James Charles Evers** (1922–), also active in the NAACP, served four terms (1969–81; 1985–89) as mayor of Fayette, Miss. Medgar's widow, **Myrlie Evers Williams** (1933–), was named head of the NAACP in 1995.

James Leonard Farmer (1920–99), born in Marshall, Tex., supported nonviolent forms of protest to achieve racial integration. In 1942 he founded, with others, the Congress of Racial Equality (CORE) at the University of Chicago and served as its national chairman (1942–44) and national director (1961–66). He was a major force behind the freedom marches and civil rights demonstrations of the 1960's. Farmer later served as assistant secretary

of the U.S. Department of Health, Education, and Welfare (1969–70).

Fannie Lou Hamer (1917–77) was born in Montgomery County, Miss. In 1962 after registering to vote, Hamer was fired from her job and threatened with violence. This led her to become a civil rights activist and in 1964 she cofounded the Mississippi Freedom Democratic Party (MFDP) to challenge the exclusion of blacks from the Democratic National Convention. Hamer's persuasive argument that an all-white delegation was not representative of Mississippi's large African American population eventually led to the inclusion of black delegates, herself among them, at the 1968 convention.

Vernon Eulion Jordan, Jr. (1935–), born in Atlanta, Ga., served as a field secretary (1962–64) for the NAACP before he became the director (1964–68) of the

Medgar Evers

Vernon E. Jordan, Jr.

Roy Wilkins

Voter Education Project of the Southern Regional Council. During his tenure the council registered nearly 2 million black voters in the South. Later, as executive director (1972–81) of the National Urban League (NUL), Jordan fought for affirmative action, full employment, and national health and housing programs. Wounded by a sniper in 1981, he resigned his post and went into private law practice. In 1992 he briefly returned to public life to head President-elect Bill Clinton's transition to the White House.

the late 1960's. Wilkins won the NAACP's Spingarn Medal in 1964.

Whitney Moore Young, Jr. (1921–71), born in Lincoln Ridge, Ky., was executive director (1961–71) of the National Urban League (NUL) during the critical years of the civil rights movement. Although criticized by black militants, Young favored cooperation rather than confrontation with whites. His goals were to achieve better education, employment, housing, and health care for African Americans.

During a 1963 civil rights rally in Birmingham, Alabama, demonstrators were attacked by police dogs, beaten with clubs, and assaulted with high-powered fire hoses.

The March on Washington

On August 28, 1963, more than 200,000 people of all races gathered at the Lincoln Memorial in Washington, D.C., to urge the government to take action against racial discrimination and segregation in the United States. It was at this gathering that Dr. King electrified the nation with his speech "I Have a Dream," one of the most stirring appeals for human justice ever delivered.

Legislation Is Passed

On July 2, 1964, President Lyndon B. Johnson signed into law the Civil Rights Act of 1964, prohibiting discrimination based on a person's race, color, national origin, religious beliefs, or sex. The bill, which was strongly opposed in the Senate, protected every citizen's right to use public facilities, to seek employment, and to vote. However, many law enforcement officers, particularly in the South, failed to protect the rights of blacks at the polls. This prompted another demonstration, in 1965, in which 30,000 blacks and whites, led by Dr. King, marched from Selma to Montgomery, Alabama. This directly resulted in the Voting Rights Act of 1965, which banned literacy tests and poll taxes (voters could no longer be tested or required to pay in order to vote). Since that time, the main thrust of civil rights activity has been directed toward preserving the integrity of these two laws and making sure they are properly enforced.

President Lyndon B. Johnson signed the Voting Rights Act of 1965 shortly after the Selma-to-Montgomery march.

seat on a bus to a white man. For this act of protest, Parks was arrested. No longer willing to "sit at the back of the bus," blacks in Alabama soon launched a boycott of the Montgomery bus system and chose a young minister, Dr. Martin Luther King, Jr., to lead them in their protest.

Peaceful Demonstrations
Are Met with Violence

The larger impact of the Montgomery boycott was that it encouraged other African Americans to press for desegregation and civil rights. Dr. King, an enormously effective spokesperson, gave voice to the protest movement and touched the moral sense of the nation. Radio and television coverage of boycotts and the so-called freedom rides and sit-ins awakened the nation to the violent and degrading nature of racism. In addition, Dr. King and literally thousands of others were repeatedly jailed for protesting racial segregation in the South, which was their constitutional right under the First Amendment.

No matter how united in their purpose, African Americans still required the force of government to achieve their goals. But resistance to their struggle was fierce. In 1957 violence against blacks compelled a reluctant Congress to enact the first modern civil rights bill to protect them. One civil rights law, however, was insufficient.

RUSSELL L. ADAMS
Chair, Department of Afro-American Studies
Howard University

See also AFRICAN AMERICANS; CIVIL RIGHTS; SEGREGATION; SPINGARN MEDAL.

CIVIL SERVICE

All of the people who work for a federal, state, or municipal government (except elected officials, judges, and members of the armed forces) are called civil servants. They deliver mail, research cures for diseases, and perform many other essential jobs.

History

Civil service employees are hired through the **merit system**. This means that they are hired according to their skills and abilities. But hiring was not always handled this way.

For a long time there was no merit system, and presidents could fire almost any government workers and fill the jobs with their own friends and political supporters. This was known as the **spoils system**. For example, President Andrew Jackson replaced 2,000 of the 11,000 people working for the government during his two terms (1829–37).

The spoils system was tolerated for many years, but as the American government grew more complex, problems with the system increased. President Lincoln complained that so much of his time was taken up with people asking for government jobs that he hardly had time to read the reports from the Civil War battlefront. Still, no effective reform was passed until President James A. Garfield was assassinated in 1881 by a man who felt that his political support made him deserving of a job with the government. When he did not get the job, he became angry and killed the president. As a result of this, Congress passed the Pendleton Act in 1883 and established the Civil Service Commission to manage the government's workforce and ensure that jobs would be awarded fairly, according to skill and ability.

In 1978, Congress passed the Civil Service Reform Act, which replaced the Civil Service Commission with the Office of Personnel Management (OPM) and the Merit Systems Protection Board (MSPB). The OPM emphasizes rewarding employees with good performance records and disciplining those with bad performance records. The OPM also continues to test people who want to work for the government and classifies the many government jobs. The MSPB helps civil service managers and employees solve disputes that they are unable to resolve themselves.

Civil Service Today

Most federal jobs are in the **competitive service**, which means that applicants must take written examinations and compete with other applicants for available jobs. The people who receive the highest test scores are offered the jobs first. (Military veterans are granted certain advantages because of their service in defending the nation.)

For certain professional occupations, such as lawyers and doctors, formal tests are not given. These jobs are called **excepted service** because the applicants are excepted from taking the competitive exams. Their qualifications are judged according to their previous work experiences and achievements.

To apply for a full-time civil service job, applicants must be 18 years of age. (High school graduates who earn their diploma at age 16 may also apply.) Though a high school diploma is not required, chances of employment are increased by at least twelve years of education.

The OPM maintains Federal Job Information centers across the United States. These centers administer tests for government jobs and carry a list of jobs available.

Today there are about 3 million federal government employees in the United States. The largest employers are the Department of Defense (35 percent—not including soldiers and other uniformed personnel); the U.S. Postal Service (27 percent); and the Veterans Administration (8 percent).

More civil servants work for U.S. state and municipal governments than for the federal government. State governments employ more than 4 million people, and municipal governments employ more than 10 million.

Other Countries

Many other countries in all parts of the world have civil service systems. The Canadian Civil Service Commission was created by the Civil Service Act of 1918. This act established a civil service commission and put most jobs under a merit system. France and England have civil service systems that employ many thousands of workers, many of whom are hired under very highly developed merit systems.

Updated by MARY ANN MALONEY
Public Information Office
Office of Personnel Management

CIVIL WAR, UNITED STATES

At 4:30 A.M. on Friday, April 12, 1861, a signal rocket rose high above the harbor of Charleston, South Carolina, and exploded in flame. Other rockets followed, lighting the sky and revealing the dark outlines of Fort Sumter on an island in the wide harbor. After the rockets came a barrage of shells from batteries of artillery ringing the shoreline. Fort Sumter was soon shrouded in the smoke of exploding missiles.

The order to fire on Fort Sumter had been given by Confederate General Pierre G. T. de Beauregard at the direction of Jefferson Davis, the Confederate president. Major Robert Anderson, who commanded Fort Sumter, surrendered after a 34-hour bombardment. The flag of the United States was lowered, and the red and blue Confederate flag was raised in its place. The United States Civil War had begun.

▶BACKGROUND OF THE WAR

What had brought the rich, powerful, and growing United States to such a pass? The reasons were many. In the early 1800's the Northern states, especially those in New England, turned from farming to manufacturing. But in the South, farming remained the most important way of making a living. Southern planters found cotton and tobacco to be their most profitable crops, and they used black slaves to work their fields.

Slavery was introduced into what is now the United States in 1619, when a Dutch merchant ship brought 20 black Africans to Jamestown, Virginia, and sold them to the colonists. For years the whole country practiced black slav-

Confederate soldiers in the Civil War had gray uniforms, while Union soldiers wore dark blue. The two armies were sometimes referred to as "the Blue and the Gray." The Confederates were not always well equipped: Shoes and uniforms were often taken from the dead.

ery, but it soon disappeared in the North. One reason was that the Africans could not stand harsh winters in the North. Another was the high price of slaves. A sturdy field hand cost up to $1,800, and small landowners, in both the North and South, could not afford to keep slaves. Finally, as the North turned toward industry, mechanics rather than farmhands were needed.

Conditions were different in the South. To meet a rising worldwide demand for cotton and tobacco, the planters farmed large areas of land. Slave labor seemed best suited for producing these crops, and the number of black slaves increased.

Slavery Becomes an Issue

As slavery spread, sentiment against it began to grow. People felt it was morally wrong for one human being to own another. In 1808 the United States Government passed a law forbidding the slave trade. This meant that captains of ships could no longer haul cargoes of black Africans to Southern ports in the United States and sell them at auction.

However, this law did not affect slaves already in the country, and slavery continued to flourish in the South. But by the 1840's a movement to abolish slavery had taken root in the North. The people who supported this movement were called abolitionists.

The Missouri Compromise

As the United States expanded westward, the slavery problem grew worse. New states were carved out of the territories west of the Mississippi and admitted to the Union. At first an uneasy balance was kept between "slave"

Union soldiers were generally better clothed and armed than their Confederate counterparts. Unlike "Johnny Reb," "Billy Yank" usually had a tent to sleep in, enough food, sturdy shoes, an official uniform, his own rifle, and plenty of ammunition.

THE NATION DIVIDED 1861-1865

Oregon

Minnesota

Wisconsin

Michigan

Maine

Vt. N.H.

Mass.

New York

R.I.

Ct.

Pennsylvania

New Jersey

Territories

Iowa

Illinois

Ohio

Indiana

Del.

Md.

W. Va.

Virginia

California

Kansas

Missouri

Kentucky

North Carolina

Tennessee

Arkansas

South
Carolina

Alabama

Mississippi

Georgia

Louisiana

Texas

Florida

During the Civil War, the nation divided into the Union (free states) and the Confederacy (slave states). The border states fought for the Union, even though they had been slave states and contained large numbers of Confederate sympathizers.

The Union

Border States

The Confederacy

Territories

and "free" states. To satisfy both North and South, a free state was brought into the Union for every slave state.

Then in 1820, Maine, which had been part of Massachusetts, applied for admission to the Union as a free state. Missouri, the next territory seeking statehood, should have come in on the slavery side. But Missourians were themselves divided on slavery. Some favored it; others opposed it. Violence broke out between the two groups.

Congress enacted the Missouri Compromise to prevent more serious trouble. This law allowed Missouri to enter as a slave state and Maine to enter as a free state. But slavery in any new state to be formed on a line north of the 36th parallel was prohibited.

Abolitionist Feeling Grows

The Missouri Compromise worked well enough until 1845, when Texas was admitted as a slave state. As a result of the Mexican War in 1846, the United States acquired all of

present-day California, Utah, and Nevada, and vast new regions were opened to slavery. The North protested vigorously at the prospect that the balance of power between free states and slave states would be broken.

In 1852, public feeling against slavery was increased by the publication of Harriet Beecher Stowe's novel *Uncle Tom's Cabin.* Picturing slavery at its worst, the book caused thousands of people to join the abolitionists.

To help slaves escape to Canada, where they would be free, the abolitionists created the Underground Railroad. This "railroad" was actually a string of hiding places for fleeing slaves. It reached from the South to the Canadian border. Homes, barns, cellars, and stables were the secret hideouts, or stations, on the railroad.

Angry Southerners demanded justice, claiming that the abolitionists were stealing their property. But nothing was done to stop the Underground Railroad, and bad feelings between North and South rose even higher.

Trouble in Kansas

Affairs came to a boil in Kansas Territory, where fighting broke out between free-state people, called jayhawkers, and proslavery people, known as bushwhackers. This situation was brought about by the Kansas-Nebraska Act, passed in 1854, which replaced the Missouri Compromise. This law required that a new state be admitted free or slave according to the will of the people who lived in it, regardless of its boundary lines.

The Kansas-Nebraska Act succeeded only in stirring savage conflict in Kansas. The jayhawkers received abolitionist backing. Rifles were shipped to them from the East in crates marked "Bibles." Because this idea had originated with the Reverend Henry Ward Beecher, brother of Harriet Beecher Stowe, the rifles were called Beecher's Bibles.

The ugly Kansas war brought attention to John Brown, an abolitionist fanatic (one who is overly enthusiastic) who believed that he had been chosen by God to free the slaves. Brown and his followers attacked proslavery settlers in Kansas and massacred a number of them at a place called Pottawatomie Creek. In January, 1861, Kansas voted to enter the Union as a free state.

The Dred Scott Case

Still more heat was added to the slavery issue by the Dred Scott case. Dred Scott was a slave who traveled with his master into free Wisconsin Territory. Scott sued for his freedom, claiming that once he had left slave territory, he was no longer a slave.

In 1857 the United States Supreme Court ruled against Scott. According to Chief Justice Roger Taney, Congress had no right under the Constitution to forbid slavery in the territories. Scott's position, therefore, had not been altered by entering Wisconsin. Angered by Taney's decision, Northern antislavery groups swore to keep slavery out of the territories at any price—even war, if necessary.

States' Rights

Not only slavery but also the question of states' rights had long caused problems within the United States. Did the federal government have the power under the Constitution to control the states in all matters?

"No!" roared the South.

Southerners wanted no interference by the federal government in their state affairs. They reserved the right to reject any federal laws they did not like.

In 1832, South Carolina had disapproved a federal tariff law and refused to obey it. When the government insisted, the fiery Carolinians prepared to secede from the Union. But it all came to nothing when President Andrew Jackson threatened to use military force against South Carolina and secession talk ended.

▶THE NATION MOVES CLOSER TO WAR

Thus, because of slavery and states' rights, a wide rift developed between North and South. The situation worsened in October, 1859, when John Brown and a devoted band of followers captured the United States Arsenal at Harpers Ferry, Virginia. Brown called

The homes of abolitionists served as "stations" on the Underground Railroad (*left*), a network of hiding places for slaves escaping to the North. John Brown (*right*) tried to stir up a slave rebellion and was hanged for attacking a federal arsenal to steal guns.

Left: Abraham Lincoln (in his famous debate with Stephen Douglas) became president in 1860. *Right:* Jefferson Davis (*at left*) was the Confederate leader.

on the slaves in the surrounding countryside "to rise up and destroy" their masters.

Brown's uprising was crushed by United States marines under Colonel Robert E. Lee. Brown was convicted of treason against Virginia and was hanged. But John Brown's cause did not die with him. Abolitionists began to sing that although "John Brown's body lies a-mold'ring in the grave," his truth "goes marching on!" They hailed Brown as a hero, while Southerners regarded him as a villain. The nation was more divided than ever.

The Election of 1860

In 1860 the Republican Party picked as its candidate for president a lanky lawyer from Illinois, Abraham Lincoln.

Although he was not an abolitionist, Lincoln had spoken against the spread of slavery into the territories. Since it was known that Lincoln opposed the spread of slavery, Southerners looked upon Lincoln as an enemy.

But slavery supporters found no comfort in the Democratic candidate, Stephen Douglas, who also objected to the extension of slavery into the territories. As a result, Southern Democrats nominated John C. Breckinridge of Kentucky for president. Leading Southerners announced that they would demand secession from the Union if Lincoln won the election. On November 6, 1860, the voters chose Abraham Lincoln to succeed James Buchanan in the White House.

Secession

Secessionists proved true to their threat. South Carolina seceded in December, 1860. Mississippi, Florida, Alabama, Georgia, Louisiana, and Texas followed South Carolina in leaving the Union. These states claimed to have a legal right to secede from the Union. They had voluntarily joined it, and the Constitution did not specifically prohibit withdrawing from the Union. They established a new nation, the Confederate States of America, with its capital at Montgomery, Alabama. (The Confederate capital was moved to Richmond, Virginia, in May, 1861.)

On February 4, 1861, delegates met in Montgomery to draw up a Confederate constitution and appoint a president and a vice president. The convention chose Jefferson Davis for president and Alexander Stephens for vice president.

The original Confederate states were later joined by Virginia, Arkansas, Tennessee, and North Carolina, while in the border states of Kentucky and Missouri, Unionists and Secessionists fought for control.

The Firing on Fort Sumter

As each state seceded, it seized all federal properties within its borders. Most United States military establishments surrendered without resistance. But in December, 1860, Major Robert Anderson, commanding Fort Moultrie at Charleston, South Carolina, refused to give in. Instead he moved his military post, which included only 68 fighting men, to nearby Fort Sumter, a more defensible position in Charleston's harbor. After long negotiations, the War Department decided that Fort Sumter must hold out as long as possible.

Anderson held grimly to his post in the face of growing Confederate forces. Lincoln was inaugurated on March 4, 1861. Five weeks later he sent ships to supply Anderson with rations since the fort's food supply was almost gone. The relief fleet was due to arrive at Charleston on April 12. Just before it reached the harbor mouth, the Confederates opened fire and forced Anderson's surrender.

The Confederates had committed an act of war that Lincoln could not ignore. The President of the United States took immediate action. He called 75,000 men into service and ordered a blockade of Southern ports. If the South wanted war, it would have it.

▶ 1861: THE WAR BEGINS

Although there were military preparations throughout the land and some clashes in Missouri and western Virginia, no major battle was fought until July, 1861. Then Federal forces under General Irvin McDowell clashed with a Confederate army commanded by General Pierre G. T. de Beauregard at Manassas, Virginia, on the banks of a stream called Bull Run.

This battle, fought by untrained armies totaling about 70,000 men, ended in an overwhelming defeat of the Northern forces. However, nothing was settled by it.

The Rise of General McClellan

After the First Battle of Bull Run (Manassas), General George B. McClellan was placed in command of all Northern forces in Virginia and Washington, D.C. He did a brilliant job of reorganizing what was now called the Army of the Potomac. McClellan built his troops into a fighting machine—but fought no battles. He wanted to make sure they were ready before he moved. The only action during this

General George McClellan (*left*) reorganized the Union Army after their defeat at Bull Run. The renamed Army of the Potomac (*below*) drilled for months before they took to the field—and lost their first battle.

The first battle ever fought between armored ships occurred during the Civil War. The Confederacy's steam-powered *Virginia*, or *Merrimack* (*above, at left*), battled the Union *Monitor* in 1862. The *Monitor*'s crew is pictured at right.

time took place in August, when Federal soldiers captured Fort Hatteras and Fort Clark on the North Carolina coast.

In October, McClellan marched at last, only to lose a bloody battle at Ball's Bluff, Virginia. The aged commander in chief of the Northern army, Lieutenant General Winfield Scott (hero of the Mexican War), resigned in November, and George B. McClellan replaced him. McClellan now commanded all the Union armies as well as his own Army of the Potomac.

▶ 1862: THE FIGHTING QUICKENS

The war that had stalled after Bull Run flared again in 1862. Battles raged in Kentucky and Tennessee. The Union won stunning victories at Mill Springs, Kentucky, and took Fort Henry and Fort Donelson, key posts guarding the approaches to Tennessee.

The capture of Fort Henry and Fort Donelson marked the rise of a short, bearded, cigar-smoking Union general, Ulysses S. Grant. It was Grant who coined the phrase "unconditional surrender" when asked for terms by Fort Donelson's commander.

The Ironclads

The year 1862 saw the first battle ever fought by ironclad warships. On March 8 the Confederate ironclad *Virginia,* also known as the *Merrimack,* sailed out of Norfolk, Virginia, and attacked the wooden ships blockading Hampton Roads, the entrance of Norfolk harbor. The *Virginia* caused a great deal of dismay throughout the North by sinking or damaging several of the big wooden frigates.

However, the *Virginia*'s career ended suddenly. When it sailed forth on March 9 to finish off the remaining Federal ships, its path was blocked by a strange-looking foe. This was the USS *Monitor,* an armored gunboat described as a "cheesebox on a raft." The two ironclads blasted each other for hours without a decision. At last the *Virginia* withdrew, never to fight again. When Union troops captured Norfolk on May 10, the retreating Confederates blew up the *Virginia.*

The battle between the ironclads made all the wooden navies of the world old-fashioned. It opened a new era in naval warfare.

Union Armies Push Toward Richmond

The pace of the conflict quickened. On April 6–7, Grant fought a costly battle at a place called Shiloh in Tennessee. The North won after a two-day battle that caused more than 23,000 to be killed and wounded in both armies.

Later during the same month a Federal flotilla (a small fleet) led by Admiral David Farragut captured New Orleans, Louisiana, at the mouth of the Mississippi River—a shocking loss for the Confederates.

Meanwhile, in Virginia, McClellan finally began his long-awaited offensive. A massive effort to capture Richmond with 100,000 splendidly trained and equipped men was begun. The campaign saw furious fighting on the Virginia peninsula. McClellan came within 5 miles (8 kilometers) of Richmond but failed to capture the enemy's capital. At the Battle of Fair Oaks (Seven Pines), Federal troops actually entered the city's outskirts but had to fall back.

During the fighting around Fair Oaks the Confederate commander, General Joseph E. Johnston, was wounded. General Robert E. Lee, whom Lincoln had once offered command of the Union Army, took over. The Confederate Army of Northern Virginia and Virginia's great military leader were at last united.

Lee Pushes Back

Lee drove McClellan back in a week of combat called the Seven Days' Battles. McClellan retreated from Richmond, and the peninsular campaign ended when the Army of the Potomac was withdrawn to its old lines around Washington.

A new commander in chief of the Union armies, General Henry W. Halleck, had replaced McClellan in March. Halleck took several regiments from McClellan and formed the Army of Virginia under General John Pope, with orders to march on Richmond. Pope fought a series of disastrous battles against Lee and Stonewall Jackson between August 28 and September 1. The worst defeat took place on the old Bull Run battlefield. Pope's army fled to Washington in disorder. Halleck disbanded the Army of Virginia and returned the men to McClellan's command.

The Battle of Antietam

McClellan proved his worth as an organizer once more. The army regained its spirit, and when Lee crossed the Potomac River to invade Northern soil for the first time in the war, McClellan was able to meet the test.

The Army of the Potomac and the Army of Northern Virginia clashed near the village of Sharpsburg, Maryland, on the banks of rambling Antietam Creek. They fought for 14 hours on September 17. After both armies had lost a total of 24,000 men, Lee retreated across the Potomac River. McClellan, relieved at beating off the attack, did not pursue.

Confederate soldiers (*top*) fought bravely and well, but they did not have the resources of the North behind them. Both sides suffered equally from the primitive medical help provided them (*below*).

After the Battle of Antietam, Lincoln (in top hat) visited General McClellan "to try to get him to move" faster. But McClellan would not, so Lincoln replaced him.

The Emancipation Proclamation

While the battle of Antietam brought no clear-cut victory to the North, Lincoln used its results as a springboard to strike a blow against slavery.

Some Northern officers had already acted. In 1861, General John Frémont freed all slaves in Missouri, only to have the order revoked by Lincoln, who did not want to lose the support of Missouri Unionists.

Slavery was abolished in the District of Columbia during April, 1862, because the government felt it was wrong for slavery to flourish on its own doorstep. By September, 1862, Lincoln felt the nation was ready for a strong step against slavery. The President announced to the nation on September 22 that effective January 1, 1863, "all persons held as slaves within any State or designated part of a State . . . in rebellion against the United States shall be then, thenceforward, and forever free."

The abolitionists were displeased by the Emancipation Proclamation. They felt it did not go far enough. On the other hand, Lincoln's words infuriated proslavery people and enraged the South.

Still, for all its shortcomings, the Emancipation Proclamation was a giant stride toward the abolition of slavery in the United States.

More Bloodshed

After the Battle of Antietam, neither army launched any major offensive. McClellan began an advance in October, but his progress was so tedious that Lincoln relieved him of command, remarking, "He has got the slows." McClellan's successor, General Ambrose Burnside, was no improvement. Burnside fought one battle at Fredericksburg, Virginia, in December, 1862. On the last day of the year, a fierce battle started at Stones River near Murfreesboro, Tennessee. It lasted until January 3, 1863, without decisive results, although both sides lost heavily.

▶THE NORTH GAINS MOMENTUM

Early in 1863, General Burnside was relieved of his command of the Army of the Potomac. He was succeeded by General Joseph "Fighting Joe" Hooker, a seasoned veteran of Antietam (Sharpsburg) and Fredericksburg, who vowed he would succeed in crushing the Confederate Army. But during his first campaign, Hooker was defeated by Lee at Chancellorsville, Virginia, May 1–6. After the battle, Hooker asked to be relieved of command. The South, although victorious, also suffered a great loss at Chancellorsville with the death of Stonewall Jackson, one of Lee's favorite generals.

THE ENEMY
IS APPROACHING!

As the Confederate Army advanced northward in June, 1863, the people of Pennsylvania were warned by bold headlines of the approach of the enemy. Fresh volunteers were called up to meet the danger.

Gettysburg

Shortly after Chancellorsville, Lee started another invasion of Northern territory. He crossed the Potomac River and marched up through Maryland toward Harrisburg, Pennsylvania. Even as Lee marched with his veteran army of 90,000 men, the Army of the Potomac had another change of commanders. Fighting Joe Hooker was replaced by stubborn General George Meade. Meade's army fought Lee at Gettysburg, Pennsylvania, from July 1 to 3, 1863. The casualties sickened the nation and shocked the world. More than 28,000 Confederates and 23,000 Union soldiers were killed, wounded, or missing.

Lee managed, somehow, to bring his shattered troops back into Virginia. Never again would the Army of Northern Virginia invade the North.

Meanwhile Vicksburg, the Confederate stronghold on the Mississippi River, had been under attack by Union forces since December, 1862. The Confederate post commanded by General John Pemberton was hopelessly trapped. Both soldiers and civilians were reduced to eating mules and grass to stay alive, but the city still held out for 47 days.

At almost the same time that Lee's gallant legions met defeat at Gettysburg, the Confederates surrendered Vicksburg, on Saturday, July 4, 1863. This triumph won control of the Mississippi River for the North, and Lincoln could write: ''The Father of Waters again goes unvexed to the sea. . . .''

Gettysburg, Pennsylvania, was as far north as the Confederates ever advanced in the war. General Lee (*left*) wanted to move the war out of Virginia. The Battle of Gettysburg (*below*) was fought in July, 1863. Lee was defeated but escaped with his army after three days of bloody fighting.

Draft Riots

But Northern victory celebrations were marred by five-day-long rioting (July 13–17) in New York City. The riots began when violent crowds protested a law to draft men for the army. The disorders were aimed at a clause in the law that permitted a man to buy his way out of the draft by paying the United States Government $300. This particularly angered the people who could not afford to pay that sum.

New York City had never known such ugly disturbances as the so-called Draft Riots. More than 1,000 persons were killed or wounded. Blacks were lynched, and houses and stores were looted and burned. Only after eleven regiments were rushed to the city from Gettysburg was the rioting finally put down.

Fighting near Chattanooga

As Meade and Lee maneuvered for position in Virginia, Confederate and Union forces fought for control of Tennessee. Despite losses at Vicksburg and Gettysburg, the Confederates fought on. They won a battle at Chickamauga, in the northwest corner of Georgia, near Union-held Chattanooga, Tennessee. General Braxton Bragg defeated Union General William Rosecrans. The Union Army was forced to flee. They would have been crushed completely before they reached the safety of Chattanooga if it had not been for the stand made by Union troops under General George Thomas. Thomas won the title "the Rock of Chickamauga."

Peachtree Street in Atlanta (*above*) was deserted when Union troops arrived on September 2, 1864, after weeks of bombardment. The Gatling gun (*right*) was an early machine gun, first used by Union troops at the long siege of Petersburg, Virginia.

The last major fighting of the year occurred outside Chattanooga. There the Union Army practically destroyed Bragg's forces. Fighting Joe Hooker made up for his Chancellorsville failure by storming Lookout Mountain and smashing the center of Bragg's lines. This Confederate defeat ended any serious Southern military threat in Tennessee.

▶1864–65: TRIUMPH AND TRAGEDY

Both sides knew great events would take place in 1864, which was the year that a presidential election would be held in the North. On March 9, President Lincoln summoned General Grant, promoted him to the rank of lieutenant general, and made him commander in chief of all the Union armies. Grant prepared an all-out offensive in Virginia and the West.

Grant in the Wilderness

On May 4 the Army of the Potomac crossed the Rapidan River in Virginia and headed for Richmond through an area known as the Wilderness. At the same time General William T. Sherman started a large army marching from Chattanooga through the heartland of the South to Atlanta, Georgia.

Grant kept moving forward despite terrible losses in the Wilderness campaign. But though he lost many men, Grant inflicted heavy casualties on Lee. The Southerners could not replace their losses. The war in Virginia settled down to a grim game of "pounding away." Out west Sherman pressed on, fighting battles almost daily against forces led by General Joseph Johnston.

So the war continued with its strings of victories and defeats. In June the Republicans renominated Lincoln and for vice president chose Andrew Johnson of Tennessee.

The North Pushes for Victory

In Virginia, Grant placed Petersburg under siege. Grant knew that Lee could no longer maneuver at will. If Lee moved out of Petersburg, Richmond had to fall, for Petersburg was the key to the Confederate capital.

Grant knew he had only to keep Lee cooped up in Petersburg and the long-sought victory would be his. But the country was impatient and demanded a quick victory. Criticism against Grant and Lincoln mounted.

Not even the capture of Alabama's Mobile Bay by Union naval forces under Admiral David Farragut satisfied the Northerners. Lincoln's supporters were worried about his re-election. On August 29 optimistic Northern Democrats nominated General George B. McClellan as their presidential candidate.

On September 1–2, Sherman captured Atlanta. Almost overnight the national mood changed. Lincoln was returned to office on November 8 by a substantial vote. One week later Sherman, after burning Atlanta, began his famous March to the Sea, cutting across Georgia to Savannah, which he took on December 21. To climax a triumphant year, General Thomas scattered a Confederate army at Nashville, Tennessee.

Continued on page 347

The end of the war came as a relief to both sides. General Grant (*right*) spent the winter of 1864–65 resting his army after their march across Georgia. In February, 1865, he headed north. In April, Union forces finally captured Petersburg and Richmond (*below*), the Confederate capital.

William T. Sherman

Edwin M. Stanton

Sarah Edmonds

Consult the Index to find more information in *The New Book of Knowledge* about the following people associated with the Union: President Abraham Lincoln; Generals Ulysses S. Grant, William T. Sherman, Ambrose Burnside, John C. Frémont, George Armstrong Custer, and Joshua Chamberlain; admiral David Farragut; abolitionists John Brown and Harriet Beecher Stowe; nurses Clara Barton and Mary Ann "Mother" Bickerdyke; photographer Mathew Brady; U.S. government officials Salmon P. Chase and William H. Seward; and the fugitive steamer pilot Robert Smalls.

Martin Robinson Delany (1812–85) was born a free black in Charles Town, Va. (now W. Va.). Delany worked with Frederick Douglass on the antislavery newspaper *North Star* and assisted fugitive slaves on the Underground Railroad. A graduate of Harvard Medical School (1852), Delany served as an army surgeon during the Civil War. In

George Gordon Meade

1865 he became the first African American to attain the rank of major in the U.S. Army.

Sarah Emma Evelyn Edmonds (1841–98), born in New Brunswick, Canada, became the most famous of the hundreds of women who fought in the Civil War. Using the name Franklin Thomp-

son, she joined the Second Michigan Volunteer Infantry, serving first as a "male" nurse and later as a spy. Her true identity was not revealed until after the war. In the early 1880's, the U.S. Congress awarded her a military pension.

George Brinton McClellan (1826–85), born in Philadelphia, Pa., was a graduate of the U.S. Military Academy (1846) and a veteran of the Mexican War (1846–48). McClellan was given command of the Army of the Potomac after the Union was defeated at the First Battle of Bull Run (or Manassas; July 21, 1861). Overly cautious, he later failed to defeat the Confederates during the Peninsular Campaign (March–July 1862) and did not pursue the enemy after his narrow victory at Antietam (or Sharpsburg; September 17, 1862). Angered by McClellan's lack of initiative, President Abraham Lincoln declared, "If McClellan is not using the army, I should like to borrow it for a while." Lincoln relieved McClellan of command in November 1862. In 1864, McClellan unsuccessfully challenged Lincoln for the presidency. He later served as governor of New Jersey (1878–81).

George Gordon Meade (1815–72) was born in Cadiz, Spain, but grew up in Philadelphia, Pa. After graduating from the U.S. Military Academy (1835), Meade fought in the Second Seminole War (1835–42) and the Mexican War (1846–48). Commissioned a brigadier general at the beginning of the Civil War, Meade was severely wounded in the Peninsular Campaign (March–July 1862). He later took part in the battles of Second Bull Run (or Manassas; August 29–30, 1862); Antietam (or Sharpsburg; September 17, 1862); Fredericksburg (December 13, 1862); and Chancellorsville (May 1–6, 1863). He succeeded General Joseph Hooker as commander of the Army of the Potomac just two days before the Battle of Gettysburg (July 1–3, 1863), where he won a stun-

ning victory. But President Abraham Lincoln later criticized him for not pursuing the ragged Confederate army, which might have ended the war. In 1864, Meade fought under General Ulysses S. Grant at the battles of the Wilderness (May 5–6); Spotsylvania (May 8–18); Cold Harbor (May 31–June 12); and Petersburg (June 15–18). On April 9, 1865, he witnessed Lee's surrender to Grant at Appomattox Court House. After the war, he commanded the Reconstruction forces in Alabama, Florida, and Georgia.

Philip Henry Sheridan (1831–88), born in Albany, N.Y., was a graduate of the U.S. Military Academy (1853). While commanding the cavalry of the Army of the Potomac in May 1864, Sheridan led a raid near Richmond that resulted in the death of the Confederate general Jeb Stuart. The following August he was given command of the Union forces in the Shenandoah Valley. In 1865 he won significant victories in Virginia, which sped the Confederate surrender on April 9. After the war, Sheridan became one of the nation's fiercest commanders of the Indian wars on the western frontier. In 1884 he was named general in chief of the U.S. Army.

Edwin McMasters Stanton (1814–69), born in Steubenville, Ohio, served as U.S. attorney general (1860–61) under President Buchanan before President Lincoln appointed him secretary of war in 1862. Despite an abrasive personality that offended military and civilian leaders, Stanton masterfully coordinated the Union's massive war effort. After the war, he fiercely opposed President Andrew Johnson on many Reconstruction issues. When Johnson fired him in 1867, the U.S. House of Representatives voted to impeach the president. Stanton died on December 24, 1869, just four days after the U.S. Senate confirmed his appointment to the U.S. Supreme Court.

Pierre G. T. Beauregard

Mary Chesnut

Joseph E. Johnston

Consult the Index to find more information in *The New Book of Knowledge* about the following people associated with the Confederacy: President Jefferson Davis; Generals Robert E. Lee, Jubal A. Early, Jeb Stuart, Thomas J. "Stonewall" Jackson, Albert Sidney Johnston, and John C. Breckinridge; cabinet officer Judah P. Benjamin; and the spy Belle Boyd.

Pierre Gustave Toutant de Beauregard (1818–93), born near New Orleans, La., directed the attack on Fort Sumter (April 12, 1861) that started the Civil War. Promoted to general after the First Battle of Bull Run (or Manassas; July 21, 1861), the Confederacy's first major victory, Beauregard took command at the Battle of Shiloh (or Pittsburg Landing; April 6–7, 1862). He later defended the south Atlantic coast against Union naval attacks and bravely held off a Union advance before the nine-month siege of Petersburg began in June 1864. After the war he served as commissioner of public works for New Orleans.

Braxton Bragg (1817–76) was born in Warrenton, N.C. A graduate of the U.S. Military Academy (1837), he fought in the Second Seminole War (1835–42) and the Mexican War (1846–48). After the Battle of Shiloh (or Pittsburg Landing; April 6–7, 1862), Bragg was promoted to the rank of general and placed in command of the Army of Mississippi. His defeat at the Battle of Perryville (October 8, 1862) forced his retreat from Kentucky. His later victory at the Battle of Chickamauga (September 19–20, 1863) was quickly overshadowed by his defeat by Union general Ulysses S. Grant at the Battle of Chattanooga (November 23–25, 1863). Replaced in the field by General Joseph E. Johnston, Bragg was then named military adviser to President Jefferson Davis. After the war, he returned to a career in civil engineering.

Mary Boykin Miller Chesnut (1823–86), born in Pleasant Hill, S.C., became famous for her personal chronicles of the Civil War. The wife of a Confederate officer, Mary accompanied her husband on several military campaigns. A keen observer of events and personalities, Chesnut's vivid commentaries and first-hand accounts of the war were published after her death first as *A Diary from Dixie* (1905) and later as *Mary Chesnut's Civil War* (1981).

Joseph Eggleston Johnston (1807–91), born in Prince Edward County, Va., graduated from the U.S. Military Academy (1829) and was a veteran of the Second Seminole War (1835–42) and the Mexican War (1846–48). As commander of the Confederate army in Virginia, Johnston successfully led his troops in the First Battle of Bull Run (or Manassas; July 21, 1861) and in the Peninsular Campaign (March–July 1862). The following year, as commander in the west, Johnston failed to hold his position in Jackson, Mississippi, which led to the 47-day siege of Vicksburg (May 18–July 4, 1863). Johnston later took command of the Army of Tennessee, defeating Union general William T. Sherman at the Battle of Kennesaw Mountain (June 27, 1864). But in July, President Davis relieved Johnston of command when he failed to stop Sherman's advance on Atlanta. He was reinstated the following February. After the war, Johnston served as a U.S. representative (1879–81) and as U.S. commissioner of railroads (1887–91).

James Longstreet (1821–1904), born in Edgefield District, S.C., was a graduate of the U.S. Military Academy (1842) and a veteran of the Mexican War (1846–48). Nicknamed Lee's Old War Horse, Longstreet fought at First Bull Run (or Manas-

sas; July 21, 1861), the Peninsular Campaign (March–July 1862), Second Bull Run (or Manassas; August 29–30, 1862), Antietam (or Sharpsburg; September 17, 1862), Fredericksburg (December 13, 1862), Gettysburg (July 1–3, 1863), Chickamauga (September 19–20, 1863), and the Wilderness (May 5–6, 1864), where he was accidentally wounded by his own men. After the war, Longstreet served as U.S. minister to Turkey (1880) and as a U.S. marshal in Georgia (1881), which angered his former Confederate comrades. Longstreet's last post was U.S. commissioner of railroads (1896).

Alexander Hamilton Stephens (1812–83), born near Crawfordville, Ga., served as vice president of the Confederate States of America (CSA) throughout the war. A former U.S. representative (1843–59), Stephens had long been a staunch supporter of states' rights but did not favor secession. After the war began he often opposed the autocratic policies of

Alexander Stephens

President Jefferson Davis, which many believed weakened the leadership of the Confederate government. After the war, Stephens was arrested by Union soldiers and imprisoned for five months. Later he served again as a U.S. representative (1873–82) and as governor of Georgia (1882–83).

A CIVIL WAR CHRONOLOGY

The Civil War began on April 12, 1861, in Charleston, South Carolina, when Confederates fired on Fort Sumter, a U.S. military base in the South.

1861

March 4: Abraham Lincoln inaugurated president of the United States.

April 12–13: Confederate guns fire on Fort Sumter.

April 15: Lincoln calls for 75,000 Union volunteers.

May 8: Richmond, Virginia, made capital of the Confederate States of America (CSA).

May 24: Northern troops occupy Alexandria, Virginia.

June 10: Battle of Big Bethel, Virginia.

July 21: First Battle of Bull Run (Manassas), Virginia.

October 21: Union troops badly defeated at Ball's Bluff, Virginia.

November 1: General Winfield Scott resigns as commander in chief of Union armies; is succeeded by General George B. McClellan.

November 8: Confederate envoys James M. Mason and John Slidell removed from British steamer *Trent*. Crisis with England.

1862

January 19: Union troops defeat the Confederates at Mill Springs, Kentucky.

February 6: Union forces under General Ulysses S. Grant capture Fort Henry, Tennessee.

March 8–9: Sea battle between *Monitor* and *Merrimac*.

April 4: McClellan launches the Peninsular Campaign.

April 6–7: Battle of Shiloh, Tennessee, a Union victory.

April 25: New Orleans captured by the U.S. Navy.

May 5: Battle of Williamsburg, Virginia.

May 31–June 1: Battle of Fair Oaks (Seven Pines) on the Virginia Peninsula.

June 26–July 2: General Robert E. Lee attacks McClellan, launching battles of the Seven Days.

July 17: Congress authorizes acceptance of blacks into United States Army and Navy.

August 28–30: Battle of Groveton followed by Union defeat at the Second Battle of Bull Run (Manassas).

September 17: Battle of Antietam (Sharpsburg).

September 22: Lincoln issues preliminary Emancipation Proclamation.

December 13: Battle of Fredericksburg, Virginia.

December 31: Lincoln signs bill admitting West Virginia to the Union.

1863

January 1: Emancipation Proclamation goes into effect.

May 1–6: Battle of Chancellorsville, Virginia.

May 22: Siege of Vicksburg begins.

June 15–26: Lee invades Pennsylvania.

July 1–3: Battle of Gettysburg.

July 4: Grant accepts surrender of Vicksburg, Mississippi.

July 13–17: Draft Riots in New York City.

September 19–20: Union defeat at Chickamauga.

November 23–25: Northern victory at Chattanooga, Tennessee.

1864

March 12: Grant made commander in chief of all Union armies.

May 5–6: Battle of the Wilderness, Virginia.

June 15–18: Grant starts siege of Petersburg, Virginia.

September 2: General William Tecumseh Sherman enters Atlanta.

September 19–22: General Phil Sheridan, Union cavalry leader, defeats General Jubal Early at Winchester and Fishers Hill, Virginia.

October 19: Sheridan beats Early at Cedar Creek, Virginia.

November 15: Sherman begins the March to the Sea.

December 15–16: Confederate forces defeated at Nashville, Tennessee.

December 21: Sherman takes Savannah, Georgia.

1865

February 1: Thirteenth Amendment to the U.S. Constitution, abolishing slavery, is proposed to Congress.

February 18: Charleston, South Carolina, is abandoned by the Confederates.

February 22: Union forces take Wilmington, North Carolina.

April 2: Petersburg, Virginia, captured by Union forces.

April 3: Richmond falls to the Union.

April 9: General Lee surrenders to General Grant at Appomattox Court House, Virginia.

The Civil War ended on April 9, 1865, in Appomattox Court House, Virginia. Confederate general Robert E. Lee surrendered to U.S. general Ulysses S. Grant.

Surrender

As 1865 began, the feel of victory was in the Northern air. At the end of January, Congress passed the 13th Amendment to the Constitution, forever prohibiting slavery in the United States.

Sherman marched out of Savannah on February 1 and headed north through the Carolinas. City after city fell to the rugged Union troops as Sherman moved northward. By mid-February, Charleston, South Carolina, was in Union hands, and the Stars and Stripes again flew over Fort Sumter.

Abraham Lincoln was sworn in for a second term on March 4. In his inaugural address he called for a peace "with malice toward none, with charity for all ...."

A month later peace seemed close indeed. On April 2, Petersburg fell. The next day Federal soldiers entered Richmond. A week later, on April 9, Lee surrendered to Grant at Appomattox Court House, Virginia.

▶ THE BITTER AFTERMATH

And so the Civil War was over. In a way it was the last of a type of war—the war of the individual fighting man. Not that men would not fight with skill and bravery in later wars. But always the individual soldier would be dwarfed by the vast machinery of warfare—the huge armies, the poison gases, the tanks, bombs, and planes.

But if the Civil War was the last of one kind of war, it was the first of another. Never before had there been so much slaughter and suffering in a war. Everywhere the story was the same—on the battlefield, where as many as 24,000 men died in a single day; in the countryside, where thousands of acres of land were ravaged; in the crude, understaffed field hospitals, where the sick and wounded suffered horribly; in the prisoner-of-war camps, where men turned into living skeletons. More American soldiers—both Union and Confederate—died in the Civil War than died in the two world wars combined.

Yet even the ending of the war did not bring real peace. On Friday, April 14, eleven days after Union troops had entered Richmond, an actor named John Wilkes Booth assassinated Lincoln as the President watched a play from his box in Ford's Theatre, Washington, D.C. The one man who might have brought about a just peace was dead.

Results

The Civil War solved many problems in the United States. Three amendments to the U.S. Constitution (13, 14, and 15) were ratified to outlaw slavery and to guarantee citizenship and voting rights to all Americans, specifically the recently freed slaves. The Union had been preserved. And many of the problems involving states' rights were also put to rest, as the federal government emerged as the supreme authority in the United States. Also, before the Civil War, the development of industry and transportation had been slow. But during the grim years of the war, American industry had learned new ways of manufacturing and had developed more efficient methods of transporting people and supplies.

Nevertheless, many new problems surfaced. First, the Southern economy, which had been almost entirely based on agriculture, had collapsed. The war had destroyed the plantations and ruined much of the farmland. Many Southern cities and towns had also been destroyed, and the people of the South were desperately poor. Many of the political decisions made during the Reconstruction Period (1865–77) were made to help rebuild the South and put its people back to work. Second, at the end of the war, the Southern states found themselves without governments. These states had to be readmitted to the Union, but they could not rejoin the United States until they had established legal state governments. Finally, 4 million former slaves had to start new lives as free people.

Few slaves had been taught to read and write or taught a useful trade. At the end of the war, the Bureau of Freedmen, Refugees, and Abandoned Lands (later known as the Freedmen's Bureau) was set up to assist them. But many Southern states later passed legislation known as Jim Crow laws to prevent blacks from joining white society. It took another hundred years before the civil rights movement gave African Americans the opportunities they should have been granted in 1865.

IRVING WERSTEIN
Author, *The Many Faces of the Civil War*

See also ABOLITION MOVEMENT; BOOTH, JOHN WILKES; COMPROMISE OF 1850; CONFEDERATE STATES OF AMERICA; DRED SCOTT DECISION; EMANCIPATION PROCLAMATION; KANSAS-NEBRASKA ACT; MISSOURI COMPROMISE; RECONSTRUCTION PERIOD; SLAVERY; and names of individual generals and other leaders.

CLARINET

The clarinet is a wind instrument usually made of wood. It has a cylinder-shaped body with a single-reed mouthpiece at one end and a bell-shaped opening at the other. One of the most popular woodwind instruments, the clarinet is also one of the most versatile. It is equally at home in the symphony orchestra, in military and dance bands, and in jazz and chamber music. It is often used as a solo instrument.

The single reed and the shape of its body give the clarinet a rich, mellow tone, which contrasts strongly with the sharp, nasal sound of its close cousin, the oboe. The reed is made of cane, a kind of coarse grass, carefully shaved until its tip is as thin as paper. This thin tip vibrates when the player blows through the mouthpiece. The vibrations make the clarinet sound. Different notes are played by opening or closing the holes along the body of the instrument. When all the holes are closed, the sound is low in pitch. As the holes are opened one at a time the pitch rises from one note to the next.

In early clarinets most of the holes were covered by the player's fingers. Only nine holes could be covered at a time. Keys were added one by one over the years to cover more holes. This made it possible to play higher and lower notes, so that today the clarinet has a range of some 40 notes or more.

The clarinet is the youngest woodwind instrument. Yet less is known about its early history than that of other instruments hundreds of years older. According to legend Johann Denner invented it around 1690. Almost nothing is known about Denner except that he was a German flute maker, and not one of his clarinets still exists.

The great composers did not begin to write music for the clarinet until many years after its invention. The first to use it often was Mozart. It was one of his favorite instruments. He liked its wide range and variety of tone quality—from lush, creamy, low notes to piercing high notes—and he wrote some of his most beautiful music for it. Nearly every great composer since Mozart has given the clarinet an important place in the orchestra. In the modern band it is more important still, playing the leading part, as do the strings in

One of the great modern masters of the clarinet was Benny Goodman, a jazz musician and bandleader who was equally skilled as a performer of classical music.

the symphony orchestra. In jazz, as well as in classical music, the clarinet is a brilliant solo instrument.

The clarinet most often used for these solo parts is the B-flat clarinet, which is about 26 inches (66 centimeters) long. But it is only one of a large family. Some clarinets are less than 20 inches (50 centimeters) long. Others are much larger. These include the alto and bass clarinets and the largest of all, the great contrabass, which is almost 50 inches (127 centimeters) long.

Most early clarinets were made of boxwood, a yellow wood that looks like ivory. But today clarinets are usually made of ebony or similar dark, heavy woods found in Asia and Africa. These woods are almost as hard as iron, and they are very rare and costly. Clarinet makers have tried making instruments of metal and hard rubber, but these materials are not as suitable. However, well-made clarinets of molded plastic are excellent musical instruments. Because they are relatively inexpensive, they are frequently used in school bands and orchestras.

BENNY GOODMAN
Clarinetist

See also WIND INSTRUMENTS.

CLARK, CHARLES JOSEPH (1939–)

Charles Joseph (Joe) Clark became Canada's youngest prime minister in 1979. The leader of the Progressive Conservative Party, he succeeded Liberal Party leader Pierre Trudeau, who had governed for eleven years.

Joe Clark was born on June 5, 1939, in High River, Alberta. He earned degrees in history and political science from the University of Alberta.

After a visit to the House of Commons in 1956 inspired him to enter politics, Clark became a Progressive Conservative Party (PCP) worker in Alberta. In 1967 he ran unsuccessfully for the Alberta legislature.

In 1972, Clark won election to Parliament as the member from Rocky Mountain, Alberta. He was re-elected in 1974. In Parliament his work focused on youth matters and the environment, and his debating skills received attention.

In 1976, Clark was elected leader of his party, defeating several older politicians. He was viewed as a candidate who could bring together different factions of the party. The party's popularity rose and fell during the next two years. In the fall of 1978 the PCP won 10 of 15 by-elections (special elections held to fill vacant seats).

The 1979 parliamentary election was fought on two main issues—the economy and national unity. Clark asserted that Trudeau's government had contributed to unemployment, inflation, and poor relations with the provincial governments. Although Clark's party did not win a majority of seats, he headed a minority government for nine months. It was defeated in December over a controversial budget calling for higher energy prices. In elections held in 1980, the Liberals regained power.

Clark lost the Progressive Conservative leadership to Brian Mulroney in 1983. He was appointed to Prime Minister Mulroney's cabinet as external affairs minister after the Progressive Conservative Party won a large majority in the 1984 election.

DON M. CREGIER
University of Prince Edward Island

CLARK, GEORGE ROGERS. See REVOLUTIONARY WAR (Profiles).

CLARK, WILLIAM. See LEWIS AND CLARK EXPEDITION.

CLARKE, ARTHUR C. See SCIENCE FICTION (Profiles).

CLASSICAL AGE IN MUSIC

In the history of music, the period from about 1760 to about 1825 is usually called the classical era. We call a work classical, or classic, if it is of the highest quality, or class. Such a work must have lasting value and be a model worthy of study. The word "classical" is also used to indicate perfection of form. Classical works of music have been created in most periods of history. But the classical age in music produced so many that it well deserves its name.

The music of the classical age includes the works of four of the world's greatest composers: Franz Joseph Haydn (1732–1809), Wolfgang Amadeus Mozart (1756–91), Ludwig van Beethoven (1770–1827), and Franz Schubert (1797–1828).

One of the characteristics of 18th-century musicians was that they liked to write treatises, or textbooks, about music. Musical dictionaries, encyclopedias, and books on music theory and instrument playing appeared in great abundance. Everything that could be known about music seemed to be explained in these scholarly books. One that is still famous today is *Essay on the True Art of Playing Keyboard Instruments,* by Johann Sebastian Bach's son Carl Philipp Emanuel (1714–88). Mozart's father, Leopold (1719–87), wrote a similar book on violin playing. Because of these scholarly works, musicians felt that all the rules of their art were clearly defined and understandable.

A great deal of the music of the classical age was understood and appreciated for itself alone. It was not dependent on dance, drama, poetry, or religious ceremonies as earlier music usually had been. Music was enjoyed for its own sake simply as pure music.

Concerts as we know them today are a result of this approach to music. Today many people go to concerts to listen to music performed by orchestras or soloists. Others listen to concerts at home on the radio or the phonograph. Music is listened to for its own sake and not because it is part of a dance, story, or picture. The new audiences of the classical era supported concerts. They played instruments in their homes and bought new music for their children to practice.

▶ **NEW INSTRUMENTAL GROUPS**

In the classical age the orchestra played on the concert stage as well as in the opera pit and the ballroom. The classical orchestra was built on a foundation of stringed instruments: first and second violins, violas, cellos, and double basses. The piano was new in the 18th century but soon replaced the harpsichord. It had a big tone and did not require the constant tuning of the older keyboard instruments. It became the leading solo instrument in concerts. The combination of piano and violin became a familiar duet team. The piano trio came to be the standard grouping of piano, violin, and cello. The string quartet—two violins, viola and cello—began its exciting development.

▶ **CLASSICAL MUSICAL FORMS**

New ideas about music and the new instrumental groupings led composers to develop new musical forms. The classical forms were closely related to the classical sonata. The word "sonata" is very old and has been used in a variety of ways. In the music of the classical age, it has a special meaning.

Sonata Form

The word "sonata" comes from the Italian *sonare,* "to play." Before the classical age any piece of instrumental music could be called a sonata.

When baroque composers began writing long instrumental works of several parts, they called them sonatas. These were the first sonatas consisting of several movements. (A movement is a section of composition that is divided into separate contrasting parts.) Many of them are still played today.

Classical composers invented new forms for the sonata. It continued to be an instrumental piece with several movements. The structure of the first movement in a classical sonata came to be called sonata form. This is the special and important meaning of the word "sonata." It is the name for the most important musical form of the classical age.

Sonata form has three main parts: exposition, development, and recapitulation. The exposition presents the themes, or subject matter, of the movement. It consists of usually two or three main themes of contrasting character. The development section works out, or develops, the themes of the exposition. It is a test for the composer's musical imagination. He tries to vary the melodies and rhythms in the most interesting way he can. The development may be short or long. It may use only one or all of the themes given in the exposition. It usually moves rapidly through several different keys. It ends with a return to the main theme, which begins the recapitulation. The recapitulation repeats the exposition, often with important changes, and concludes the movement.

In the sonata form the composer seems to be saying to us: "These are the subjects I will talk about" (exposition); "Now I discuss them" (development); "This is what I have tried to tell you" (recapitulation).

The sonata form proved so useful that composers used it in many pieces not called sonatas. It was used in opera overtures, chamber music, and symphonies. Thus, a symphony is really a sonata for orchestra. A string quartet is a sonata for four stringed instruments. Sonata form was also used for movements other than the first. Sometimes it was used two or three times in the same work. All four movements of Beethoven's great Seventh String Quartet are in sonata form.

Sonata form has been used as a model by almost every composer since the 18th century. It is the most important and characteristic heritage of the classical age in music.

Minuet-Trio, Theme and Variations, and Rondo

In addition to sonata form, other classical forms included the minuet-trio, the theme-and-variations form, and the rondo. The minuet-trio came from the ballroom, court ballet, and the opera. It is in a three-part, or A–B–A, form. The minuet is a short piece, the trio another. After they are both played, the minuet is repeated, thus completing the piece. The theme-and-variations form consists of a theme, or melody, followed by a series of variations on the theme. Each variation is a repeat of the theme but with some aspect of the music changed. In a rondo the main melody alternates with a number of contrasting sections, or episodes. The chief feature of a rondo is the constant return of the first melody.

All these forms show endless possibilities for contrast and variety. A true understanding of them is possible only through an acquaintance with the music itself. Here are easily available examples of each form:

Sonata form: Mozart, Symphony No. 40 in G minor (K. 550), first, second, and fourth movements.

Minuet-trio: Mozart, Piano Sonata No. 11 in A major (K. 331), second movement.

Rondo: Beethoven, Two rondos for piano, Opus 51.

Theme and variations: Haydn, Symphony No. 94 in G major *(Surprise)*, second movement.

▶ OPERA IN THE CLASSICAL AGE

Long before the classical age people had begun to tire of the old-style opera. It was thought to be too artificial. The stories were not lifelike and were often rather silly and complicated. The music and the action did not blend well. The dissatisfaction with this kind of opera came to a climax at the beginning of the classical age.

Christoph Willibald Gluck (1714–87) decided to reform the opera. He began his reforms with *Orpheus and Eurydice* (1762). Gluck gave the opera nobility and dramatic life. He made the music closely follow the action of the story. The music is simple and natural. The singers seem like real people with real feelings and passions. All these qualities are found in the great operas by Gluck, which include *Alceste* (1767), *Iphigenia in Aulis* (1774), and *Iphigenia in Tauris* (1779). Gluck's reforms attracted worldwide attention and strongly influenced opera composers who came after him.

The development of *opera buffa,* or comic opera, contributed to operatic reform. *Opera buffa* used contemporary stories and characters that came alive on the stage. The increasing use of native languages in opera also aided the reform. Most of the earlier operas were sung in Italian.

Hundreds of operas were written in the classical age. Those by Mozart are most characteristic of the period. *The Marriage of Figaro, Don Giovanni, Così fan tutte,* and *The Magic Flute* are Mozart's finest and most famous operas. The first three have Italian texts, and the stories contain strong comic elements. *The Magic Flute* is in German and also features broad comic scenes. All four operas made biting comments on the weaknesses and ideals of the people in the audience.

After Mozart, opera began to lose some of its classical qualities. Some of the characteristics of later Italian opera appear in the operas of Domenico Cimarosa (1749–1801) and Gioacchino Rossini (1792–1868). During the Revolutionary and Napoleonic eras, French opera was represented by the works of André Grétry (1741–1813) and Luigi Cherubini (1760–1842). Beethoven's only opera, *Fidelio* (1805), is a unique masterpiece. It has a German text with spoken dialogue.

▶ THE LIED

One of the important developments in the classical age was the appearance in Germany and Austria of the lied. A lied is a song with piano accompaniment that reflects the meaning and feeling of the poem being sung. The expressive capabilities of the piano made it well suited for this type of song. Franz Schubert was the greatest composer of this kind of song. He inspired a succession of great song composers that flourished until late in the 19th century. A great number of Schubert's songs are classical examples of the lied. However, they expressed some of the musical ideals of the period that followed.

▶ THE VIENNESE CLASSICAL COMPOSERS

Haydn, Mozart, Beethoven, and Schubert were the greatest composers of the classical era. Mozart was a pupil of Haydn's brother and a friend of Haydn himself. Beethoven went to Vienna to study with Mozart. He played for him but was then called back to Bonn by his mother's illness and death. When Beethoven returned to Vienna, Mozart was dead, so he took lessons from Haydn. Schubert spent his life in Vienna, where Beethoven lived. He served as a torchbearer at Beethoven's funeral. By Beethoven's and Schubert's time, Vienna had become the center of the musical world. Vienna was the city in which all four of these composers worked. Thus, they are often called the Viennese classical composers.

These four great men were surrounded by hundreds of active but lesser composers. The

The great classical composer Franz Joseph Haydn is shown leading a string quartet. Haydn is sometimes called the father of the string quartet, a musical form that reached its greatest development during the classical age.

orchestra at Mannheim, Germany, was a laboratory for experimenting with the symphony. The composers in Mannheim helped to lay the foundations for the works of Haydn and Mozart. At least two sons of the great Bach, Karl Philipp Emanuel and Johann Christian (1735–82), were important composers. Their music for keyboard had a strong influence on the piano music of both Haydn and Mozart.

Haydn is often called the father of the string quartet and the symphony. His 83 string quartets and at least 104 symphonies make him the great originator of all such music.

In his short life Mozart composed well over 600 works. With this great genius the classical period reached its highest perfection. Mozart's later operas, the *Requiem*, the last ten string quartets, several quintets, many of the piano concertos, and at least the last four symphonies are among the great treasures of Western music.

Beethoven began in the classical tradition. He mastered all the technical and formal elements of the music of Haydn and Mozart. But in Beethoven's hands classical music began to show some of the characteristics of a later musical style.

With Beethoven the development of the piano sonata reached its highest point. His 32 sonatas showed new possibilities for the piano. The length and difficulty of the later sonatas set a new standard for this form. Beethoven also enlarged the symphony and made it express his own personality. His 16 string quartets form the core of the chamber music repertory.

Franz Schubert was one of music's greatest melodists. Much of his music seems to have been directly inspired by poetry. Many of his songs are masterpieces of extraordinary beauty. Most of Schubert's great instrumental music received very little attention during his short lifetime. The music lovers of Vienna appreciated Beethoven, but they did not recognize the masterpieces that came from Schubert's pen: the Ninth Symphony, the string quartets, the String Quintet in C, the Piano Trio in B flat, and many others. They were composed in the classical forms. But, like Beethoven's music, they already showed some of the characteristics of the music of the romantic age, the period that followed the classical.

THEODORE M. FINNEY
University of Pittsburgh

See also ROMANTICISM (Romanticism in Music).

CLASSICAL ART. See GREECE, ART AND ARCHITECTURE OF; ROME, ART AND ARCHITECTURE OF.

CLASSIFICATION OF LIVING THINGS. See TAXONOMY.

Addressing the U.S. Senate, Henry Clay pleads for adoption of the Compromise of 1850. Clay sought to maintain the Union in the troubled years before the Civil War.

CLAY, HENRY (1777-1852)

Henry Clay was one of America's great statesmen during the troubled years before the Civil War. He served as a congressman, senator, and secretary of state and was several times a candidate for the presidency of the United States.

Early Life. Clay was born on April 12, 1777, on a frontier farm in Virginia. His father, a minister, died when Henry was 4, and the boy received only a few years of formal schooling. At the age of 15, Clay found work as a clerk in a Richmond court. He studied law in his spare time and became a lawyer in 1797. Attracted by opportunities farther west, the 20-year-old Clay moved to Kentucky. The tall, gangling young lawyer was popular and a skillful orator, and he won election to the state legislature.

National Politics. Clay first entered the U.S. Senate in 1806, to fill the unexpired term of another senator. He was to spend a total of 19 years in the Senate during his career.

In 1811, Clay was elected to the U.S. House of Representatives. He was chosen Speaker of the House and became leader of a group of young congressmen called the War Hawks. The United States and Britain were then quarreling over American naval rights. The War Hawks urged President James Madison to declare war. But the War of 1812 was not the success they had expected. Clay was one of the commissioners sent to sign the Treaty of Ghent in 1814, ending the war.

With the coming of peace, the United States began to grow. In Congress, Clay developed what he called his American System. He urged federal aid in building roads and canals to link different parts of the country. He favored a national bank. And to protect the new industries of the North, he proposed a high tariff, or tax on imports.

Lifelong Ambition. Clay's lifelong ambition was to be elected president of the United States. He ran unsuccessfully for the presidency three times—in 1824, 1832, and 1844. When told that one of his speeches had hurt his chances for the presidency, he replied: "I would rather be right than be president."

Clay was appointed secretary of state by President John Quincy Adams in 1825 and served until 1829.

The Great Compromiser. As the United States grew, sectional quarrels became more intense. The question of slavery and the problem of the tariff separated North and South. Clay, though a slaveholder himself, favored freedom for the slaves. But he was determined, above all, to preserve the Union. He said: "I know no North, no South, no East, no West. . . ." In 1820 he helped pass the Missouri Compromise, which admitted Missouri into the Union as a slave state so that Maine could enter as a free state. In 1832, South Carolina threatened to secede because of a tariff that it considered unjust. Clay, then in the Senate, proposed a compromise tariff that prevented war.

In 1850, Clay, now old and ill, was once again able to prevent the United States from splitting apart. The Compromise of 1850 was his greatest achievement. Two years later, on June 29, 1852, he died, mourned by the whole nation as the Great Compromiser.

Reviewed by RICHARD B. MORRIS
Columbia University
Editor, *Encyclopedia of American History*

See also COMPROMISE OF 1850; MISSOURI COMPROMISE; WAR OF 1812.

CLAY MODELING

There is something very satisfying about modeling with clay. Using only your fingers as tools, you are able to transform a shapeless, wet lump into a useful or decorative object.

There are many different kinds of clay and clay substitutes. Clay may be purchased from craft, toy, or hobby stores. You can even make your own "clay" by using one of the recipes in this article.

Natural clay is a hardening clay, which means that it will dry and harden when exposed to air for a period of time. If you do have natural clay in the soil in your area, it needs preparation before it can be used for modeling. The clay must be dug up and thoroughly mixed with water. Next it should be strained through a wire screen to remove twigs and pebbles, left in a pail until the clay settles to the bottom, and the excess water drained off the top. The remaining paste should be allowed to dry until it is just the right consistency to mold. Then it should be stored in an airtight container so it does not completely harden before you have a chance to model it.

Natural clay projects should be wrapped in a damp cloth until they are finished and you are ready to let them harden. They will dry to a very hard finish that can be painted with tempera or glazed to form a smooth, glossy surface.

Modeling clay, sometimes called plasticine, is not really clay, although it can be modeled like natural clay. One of the differences between natural clay and modeling clay is that modeling clay contains oil, so it will not harden and can be used over again. This can be an advantage for practicing or playing, but your finished project will not harden and cannot be painted.

Play dough is another popular modeling material that is not really clay. Its advantages are that it comes in many colors and can be found in most toy departments. It is much more pliable than modeling clay, making it popular with children.

▶ MAKE YOUR OWN CLAY

A homemade substitute for hardening clay is baker's dough. This dough is easily molded and cut with cookie cutters. The finished projects can be painted with tempera paints or permanent markers before being given a shiny finish. To make baker's dough, thoroughly mix together 1 cup of salt, 2 cups of flour, and 1 cup of water. Projects made with this dough can be dried in a slow oven (325°) or air-dried over several days.

Potter's clay is a good clay to use with larger projects such as bowls and dishes. To make it, mix ½ cup of flour and ½ cup of cornstarch together with just enough water to make a paste. Dissolve 1 cup of salt in 3¾ cups of boiling water and add it to the paste. Cook this mixture until it is clear, and let it cool overnight. Add 6 to 8 cups of flour and squeeze the mixture over and over until it forms a dough that is easy to work with. If it becomes too sticky, sprinkle it with salt.

▶ WORKING WITH CLAY

Clay can be molded into almost any form. One way to work with clay is to roll it into basic shapes—balls, squares, and so on—and then pinch these shapes together to form objects. Clay can also be worked by "pulling" or shaping objects from a single ball of clay.

Larger clay figures, particularly those with long pieces sticking out, must be built around a wire frame for support. This frame is called an **armature** and supports a clay figure in the same way your skeleton supports you. An armature can be made from stiff wire bent to any shape you wish. The base of the armature should be attached to a board for figures that will stand up. Pinch small pieces of clay around the wire to build the shape of the figure, then smooth and blend the clay together.

Small bowls are popular projects. One way to make a bowl is to press your thumbs into the middle of a ball of clay and pinch the clay to the outside of the ball so that the middle is hollowed out. Another way is to roll a lump of clay on the table to form a long coil or "snake." Wind this coil around and around in a spiral to form a flat bottom for the bowl. Then add other coils to build up the sides of the bowl.

Designs can be made in clay using sticks, pencils, or paper clips. Objects such as keys, shells, and cookie cutters can be used to press shapes into clay. Imagination can help you create your own original clay artworks.

KATHY ROSS
Director, Kenwood Nursery Schools

CLEARY, BEVERLY. See CHILDREN'S LITERATURE (Profiles).

CLEMENCEAU, GEORGES (1841–1929)

Georges Clemenceau was a French statesman who led France during its darkest days of World War I. He was born on September 28, 1841, at Mouilleron-en-Pareds, the Vendée. From his father he acquired a fierce love of democracy, and he grew up on ideas of liberty, equality, and patriotism. In 1865 he visited the United States. Although trained as a doctor, he earned a living as a journalist and French teacher. He married an American, Mary Plummer, but the marriage only lasted seven years.

Returning to France, Clemenceau was appointed mayor of the Montmartre district of Paris. In 1876 he was elected to the French Chamber of Deputies, where he served for nearly 20 years. A Radical, he won fame as a fiery speaker on behalf of the poor, the oppressed, and all victims of injustice. Clemenceau, defeated in 1893 for re-election, turned to journalism to speak out against those in power. He returned to office in 1902 as a senator. He became minister of the interior in 1906 and premier of France a few months later. But in 1909 he lost Radical support and was forced to resign.

World War I, which began in 1914, brought Clemenceau his chance for greatness. He became premier again in 1917, when the war was going badly for France. His ferocity and stubbornness were directed toward one goal—victory. French soldiers and civilians alike were inspired to greater efforts by the "Tiger," as Clemenceau was nicknamed. After the war was won in 1918, Clemenceau played a key role in the writing of the Versailles Peace Treaty. In the 1920 elections, he was passed over for the office of president, and he resigned as premier. He died on November 24, 1929.

JEAN T. JOUGHIN
The American University

CLEMENS, SAMUEL LANGHORNE. See TWAIN, MARK.

CLEOPATRA

Cleopatra was the name of seven queens of Egypt. The most famous was Cleopatra VII, who lived from 60 to 30 B.C. She was not Egyptian but the last of the Macedonian-Greek dynasty, or royal family. The dynasty had been established by Ptolemy I, one of Alexander the Great's generals, after Alexander's death in 323 B.C. The historical Cleopatra is often lost in romantic legend. She is best remembered for her relations with two Roman rulers, Julius Caesar and Mark Antony. She was not beautiful, but her intelligence, charm, vitality, and self-confidence made her attractive to powerful men.

Cleopatra became joint ruler of Egypt with her brother Ptolemy XIII in 51 B.C., but she was driven from Egypt by him in 48 B.C. Determined to rule Egypt and restore its power, she appealed to Julius Caesar. Caesar deposed Ptolemy XIII and returned Cleopatra to the throne in 47 B.C. as ruler with another brother, Ptolemy XIV. She bore a son, Caesarion, and proclaimed Caesar the father. She joined Caesar in Rome, but returned to Egypt after his assassination in 44 B.C. When Ptolemy XIV died (possibly murdered by her order), she made Caesarion her co-ruler.

Cleopatra supported Mark Antony in his struggle with Octavian for supremacy in Rome. As their relationship deepened, she bore him three children. Defeated by Octavian at the Battle of Actium in 31 B.C., they fled back to Egypt. Cleopatra committed suicide to avoid humiliation as a Roman captive. Antony had killed himself shortly before. According to legend, she used an asp—a poisonous snake and an Egyptian royal symbol—to kill herself.

Cleopatra appears in numerous works of literature. The most famous are William Shakespeare's *Antony and Cleopatra* and George Bernard Shaw's *Caesar and Cleopatra*.

ALLEN M. WARD
University of Connecticut

See also ANTONY, MARK; CAESAR, GAIUS JULIUS.

CLEVELAND

Cleveland, the second largest city in Ohio, is one of the nation's most important industrial centers. Located at the mouth of the Cuyahoga River, it is also a major port on Lake Erie. Cleveland forms the center of a metropolitan area of more than 2.7 million people. Approximately 493,000 people live within the city limits.

Cleveland ranks high in the production of heavy machinery, transportation equipment, machine tools, metal fasteners, electrical machinery and appliances, business machines, paints, chemicals, and clothing. In recent years it has also become a major center for industrial research and the production of polymers, which are used to create all kinds of synthetic materials. Cleveland Clinic, a major medical center, is the city's largest employer.

Near Public Square, at the heart of the city, a landscaped mall extends toward Lake Erie. Nearby are Cleveland Public Library and one of the nation's twelve Federal Reserve banks. Places of interest along the Lake Erie waterfront include the Rock and Roll Hall of Fame

Cleveland, Ohio, is a major industrial center and port city on Lake Erie. More than 2.7 million people live in its greater metropolitan area.

and Museum and the Great Lakes Science Center. To the east of Public Square lies University Circle, which includes Severance Hall, home of the world-renowned Cleveland Orchestra; the Cleveland Museum of Art; the Cleveland Museum of Natural History; the Cleveland Children's Museum; the Institute of Art; the Institute of Music; and the museums of the Western Reserve Historical Society. Case Western Reserve University, Cleveland State University, and Cuyahoga Community College are among the city's institutions of higher learning.

For outdoor recreation, Cleveland offers an enormous metropolitan park system known as the Emerald Necklace because it encircles the city. Lake Erie offers sailing, boating, and fishing. Local sports enthusiasts cheer for the Indians of baseball's American League, the Cavaliers of the National Basketball Association, the Rockers of the Women's National Basketball Association, and the Lumberjacks of the International Hockey League.

In 1796, Moses Cleaveland surveyed the lakeshore at the mouth of the Cuyahoga River and drew plans for a town. By 1820, Cleaveland had about 600 settlers. Eventually, the first letter *a* was dropped from the spelling of Cleveland. Location was the key to Cleveland's growth. In 1825 the city was chosen as the Great Lakes terminus of the Ohio and Erie Canal. It became a shipping headquarters and attracted many businesses. One of the world's major oil companies, the Standard Oil Company, was founded there in 1870 by John D. Rockefeller.

Industry brought many foreign immigrants as well as African Americans to work in the city. In 1967, Cleveland became the first major U.S. city to elect an African American, Carl Stokes, as mayor.

GEORGE W. KNEPPER
Author, *Ohio and Its People*

GROVER CLEVELAND (1837–1908)

22nd and 24th President of the United States

FACTS ABOUT CLEVELAND

Birthplace: Caldwell, New Jersey
Religion: Presbyterian
College Attended: None
Occupation: Lawyer
Married: Frances Folsom
Children: Ruth, Esther, Marion, Richard, Francis
Political Party: Democratic
Office Held Before Becoming President: Governor of New York
President Who Preceded Him: Chester Alan Arthur (first term); Benjamin Harrison (second term)
Age on Becoming President: 47
Years in the Presidency: 1885-1889; 1893-1897
Vice President: Thomas A. Hendricks (first term, died 1885); Adlai E. Stevenson (second term)
President Who Succeeded Him: Benjamin Harrison (first term); William McKinley (second term)
Age at Death: 71
Burial Place: Princeton, New Jersey

DURING CLEVELAND'S PRESIDENCY

Center: The Statue of Liberty was dedicated by President Cleveland (1886). The American Federation of Labor (AFL) was organized (1886). The Interstate Commerce Act was adopted by Congress (1887) to regulate the nation's growing railroads. *Left:* George Eastman introduced the Kodak hand-held, roll-film box camera (1888). The Department of Agriculture was made a cabinet-level office under a secretary of agriculture (1889). Gold was discovered in the Klondike region of Alaska (1896). *Below:* Henry Ford built his first gasoline-powered automobile in Detroit (1896). Utah became a state (1896).

CLEVELAND, STEPHEN GROVER. Grover Cleveland was one man, but he is counted as two presidents. In 1884, Cleveland was elected the 22nd president. He ran again in 1888 but lost to Benjamin Harrison, who became the 23rd president. However, in the election of 1892, Cleveland came back to defeat Harrison. A question then arose, Was Cleveland the 24th president—or was he still the 22nd? The usually accepted answer is that he was both.

▶ EARLY LIFE

Stephen Grover Cleveland was born on March 18, 1837, in Caldwell, New Jersey. He was the fifth of nine children. His father, the Reverend Richard Falley Cleveland, was minister of the Presbyterian church in Caldwell. When Grover was 4, the family moved to Fayetteville, New York. Here Cleveland lived until he was 13.

Though he was named Stephen Grover, he was always called Grover. He was chubby and round-faced, with blue eyes and sandy hair. By the time he was 13, "Grove" could out-

swim and out-wrestle most of the other boys of his age. He learned to fish, and that remained his favorite sport all his life.

In his early years, Grover attended school in a one-room, one-teacher schoolhouse. However, in 1850 the family moved to Clinton, New York, where Grover attended the Liberal Institute. He was a good student, but more because he worked hard than because he was unusually bright. Generally, his childhood was not much different from that of most American boys of his time, although as a minister's son he probably had to attend church more often than most. Like most boys, he sometimes got into mischief. There are stories about Grover's rigging up a device to ring the school bell at midnight, and helping to carry off garden gates on Halloween.

The Clevelands had a large family but not very much money. So when he was 14, Grover went to work as a clerk in a store at Fayetteville at a salary of $50 a year. Here he learned something about bookkeeping, and here, too, his true character began to

Photograph of President Grover Cleveland.

Frances Folsom Cleveland, the President's wife.

show. The clerks in the Fayetteville stores often entertained each other at ham-and-eggs suppers by filching the refreshments from the stores. Cleveland refused to attend any party unless everything was paid for. This made enemies of some of the clerks. But it was the only honest thing to do, and he was brave enough to do it.

HIS FATHER DIES

In 1853, when Grover was 16, his father died suddenly. Grover had hoped to go to college to study law, but now, with four young children for Mrs. Cleveland to take care of, there was no money for college. One of his older brothers was a teacher at a school for the blind in New York City, and Grover got a job there as an assistant instructor. But after a year in the school, he made up his mind to go someplace where a young man's chances were better. He decided on the city of Cleveland, Ohio.

On the way he stopped to visit an uncle who had a fine herd of dairy cattle near Buffalo, New York. His uncle made Grover an offer. If he would stay and help him, he would pay Grover $50 and would also try to find him a permanent job as clerk in a lawyer's office. Cleveland accepted the offer, and his real career began in Buffalo.

LAW AND POLITICS

At that time there were few regular law schools. Most young men gained their training for the bar by working as clerks for lawyers and studying law in their offices. Cleveland worked and studied hard. Less than 10 years after he came to Buffalo, he had not only been admitted to the bar but had also been made assistant district attorney for Erie County.

Cleveland's record of honesty and fairness in the district attorney's office led to his election as sheriff of Erie County. And in 1881, when the city government had become so corrupt that it disgusted many voters, the Democrats nominated Cleveland for mayor. As mayor he threw out the dishonest politicians and their friends and broke up their deals ruthlessly. This made Cleveland many enemies, but honest men liked him.

Then in 1882 the reform Democrats nominated the young mayor of Buffalo for governor of New York, and he was elected. As governor, Cleveland followed the same course of strict honesty and was hated equally by dishonest Democrats and dishonest Republicans.

Cleveland was the perfect presidential candidate for the Democrats in 1884. In that year the country was rocked by scandals in

Washington, and the Republican candidate, James G. Blaine, had been involved in some of them. The Democrats had not elected a president since James Buchanan in 1856. It was plainly good politics for them to name a man famous for his honesty. The speaker who seconded Cleveland's nomination explained, "We love him most for the enemies he has made."

The campaign was dirty. The Democrats tried to prove that Blaine was a thief, which he was not. And the Republicans, since they could not attack Cleveland's honesty, tried to prove that he was immoral and a Confederate sympathizer. But many reform Republicans, called Mugwumps, disliked Blaine. They deserted their party and supported Cleveland. Near the end of the campaign, one of Blaine's friends called the Democrats the party of "Rum, Romanism and Rebellion." This so offended the Irish Catholics in New York that many of them voted for Cleveland. By carrying New York he won a majority of the electoral votes, though he beat Blaine by only a small number of popular votes.

▶ HIS FIRST TERM

In winning the presidency Cleveland also won a great deal of trouble. The Democrats had elected a majority in the House of Representatives. But the Senate remained Republican, and was not inclined to do anything that would help a Democratic president. More than that, after 24 years out of office the Democrats naturally wanted to put their own men in every federal job. Some of

the party leaders recommended men who were useful to them but not fit for the job. Cleveland refused to appoint such men, which made the leaders furious.

One of the most difficult issues that faced Cleveland was the long-unsolved problem of the tariff (the tax on goods imported into the United States). The high tariff was causing an unhealthy surplus of money in the treasury as well as high prices on some products. Though Cleveland asked Congress to reduce the tariff, the tariff bill that resulted was a failure.

Another problem was the flood of pension bills for Union veterans of the Civil War that Congress sent to the President for his signature. Many of the pension claims were false. Although it angered the veterans, Cleveland vetoed many of the bills.

The one bit of really good fortune that came to Cleveland during this term was his marriage, on June 2, 1886, to Frances Folsom, daughter of one of his former law partners. The wedding ceremony was performed in the White House, the only time a president has been married there.

▶ HARRISON DEFEATS HIM

In the election of 1888 the Republicans nominated Benjamin Harrison, a grandson of President William Henry Harrison. Cleveland seemed likely to win. But just before the election, the British minister in Washington, D.C., made the mistake of writing a letter stating that the British government hoped to see Cleveland re-elected. This was regarded as foreign interference in American affairs. It so infuriated many anti-British people that Cleveland lost New York and with it the electoral vote, even though he got 95,000 more popular votes than Harrison.

Cleveland retired to New York, where he spent 4 years contentedly practicing law and going fishing with friends. He would have been satisfied to stay there the rest of his life, but the party needed him. Harrison got into trouble with Republican leaders. And by 1892 it was fairly plain that Cleveland, but probably no other Democrat, could beat him. So Cleveland was nominated for the presidency again. This time he received over 350,000 more votes than Harrison and won easily.

IMPORTANT DATES IN THE LIFE OF GROVER CLEVELAND

1837   Born at Caldwell, New Jersey, March 18.

1855   Arrived in Buffalo, New York.

1859   Admitted to the bar.

1863– Assistant district attorney for Erie County,
1865   New York.

1871– Sheriff of Erie County.
1873

1882   Elected mayor of Buffalo.

1883– Governor of New York.
1885

1885– 22nd president of the United States.
1889   (Defeated for re-election in 1888 by Benjamin Harrison.)

1893– 24th president of the United States.
1897

1908   Died at Princeton, New Jersey, June 24.

IN DARKEST CONGRESS.

A cartoon showing Cleveland as a missionary, trying to convert congressmen ("Indians") to his policies.

▶ HIS SECOND TERM

Cleveland had hardly taken office when the great business panic of 1893 broke and was followed by a long depression. Cleveland called a special session of Congress and asked for repeal of the Sherman Silver Purchase Act of 1890. Under this act the government was required to buy a set amount of silver each month and coin it into money. This caused a drain on the gold supply in the treasury. Cleveland favored a "hard," or gold, currency and felt that silver money would cause wild inflation. The repeal of the Silver Purchase Act antagonized many western Democrats—silver mine owners and farmers who favored silver. It caused a split in the Democratic Party that was to lead to its defeat in the election of 1896.

There were other problems, too. During the campaign Cleveland had promised to lower the tariff. However, conservative Democrats combined with the Republicans to pass a tariff bill so bad that Cleveland called it "party perfidy and party dishonor." During a railroad strike in Chicago, Cleveland sent in federal soldiers, although the governor of Illinois said they were not needed. So the President was out of favor with his own party because of the silver question, the tariff, and his use of federal troops.

Problems in Hawaii and Latin America

During President Harrison's administration American sugar planters in Hawaii had staged a revolution against the native king. A treaty to annex the islands had been sent to the Senate. But Cleveland felt that the United States had taken advantage of a weak country and withdrew the treaty.

A revolution also broke out in Cuba, which was then a Spanish colony, and some Americans tried to help the Cubans. Since this was against international law, Cleveland stopped them.

A more serious dispute arose between Venezuela and Great Britain over the boundary of British Guiana. When Great Britain extended her claims into Venezuelan territory, Cleveland told the British that this was a violation of the Monroe Doctrine. He did so in such blunt terms that there was almost a declaration of war.

In each case Cleveland did what he believed was the honest thing, but in each case he angered some powerful group in his own party. So in 1896 the Democrats turned away from Cleveland and chose as their candidate William Jennings Bryan, who was defeated by Republican William McKinley.

Cleveland retired to Princeton, New Jersey, where he lived until his death on June 24, 1908.

For a time Cleveland was ignored by politicians and almost forgotten by the public. But as the years passed, men began to realize how often his decisions, though unpopular, were wise and right. Slowly it became clear that even when he was mistaken it was an honest mistake. He asked no favors. At the height of the panic of 1893, doctors told Cleveland that he had cancer of the mouth. He went secretly on board a ship, where an operation was performed. He had recovered and was back at work before the country learned that he had been ill.

Grover Cleveland was not one of the great presidents, but for courage, honesty, and patriotism he has never been surpassed.

GERALD W. JOHNSON
Author, *The Presidency*

CLIMATE

Climate is the overall state of weather in a region over a long period of time. The weather at a specific place may be cold and rainy on a particular day. But that place may have a warm, dry, sunny climate. This is because weather and climate are not the same. Weather comes from the temporary, often changing conditions in the atmosphere. Climate is the combination of weather conditions over a period of many years. Scientists learn about the climate of a place by studying its weather patterns and the types of plants that grow there. These scientists are called **climatologists**, and the study of climate is known as **climatology**.

Temperature and precipitation (moisture that falls to the ground, such as rain or snow) are the two most important weather conditions that describe the climate of a place. Other conditions include humidity (moisture that stays in the air), cloudiness, fog, storms, sunshine, and wind.

▶ CAUSES OF DIFFERENT CLIMATES

What makes one place hot all year long while another place is cold, one place a desert and another a rain forest, one place sunny and another cloudy? The differences in climate from place to place are caused by **climatic controls**. The most important climatic control is latitude. Other major climatic controls are altitude, land and water bodies, prevailing winds, pressure centers, ocean currents, mountains, and urbanization.

Latitude

The main factor that determines the climate of any place is its distance from the equator. This distance is measured in degrees of latitude. Near the equator (0° latitude), the sun is never very far from being directly overhead at noon. Near the North Pole (90° north latitude) and the South Pole (90° south latitude), the sun is never very high in the sky. Regions close to the equator remain

This Italian coastal town enjoys a mild climate because of its latitude and the effects of the nearby sea.

warm throughout the year. At higher latitudes, farther away from the equator, there are colder climates. In the middle latitudes, the sun is high in the sky in summer and low in winter. So places like Portland, Maine (about 45° north latitude), have warm summers and cold winters.

Altitude

Temperature typically decreases as altitude increases. At high altitudes the air is less dense, and it does not absorb and hold as much heat. On the average, the temperature drops about 3.5° Fahrenheit for every 1,000 feet (2° Celsius for every 300 meters). Thus snow may fall on a cold mountaintop and stay there without melting while rain falls in the warmer valley below.

Land and Water Bodies

Land warms up rapidly when heated by the sun and cools off rapidly at night. But large bodies of water change temperature more slowly. This is mainly because water holds more heat than land can. Water is also transparent, allowing sunlight to warm the layers below. When water heats up more slowly than nearby land does, it has a cooling effect on the land. Similarly, when water cools off more slowly, it has a warming effect on the land. As a result, seacoasts usually have milder winters and cooler summers than mid-continental places with little water.

Prevailing Winds

Winds affect climate because they carry heat and moisture. Winds that blow from the same direction most of the time are called prevailing winds. For example, the prevailing westerlies (winds that blow from the west) pick up moisture in the air brought northward from the Gulf of Mexico and carry that moisture in an eastward direction. This shift leads to less rainfall and short grasses in the

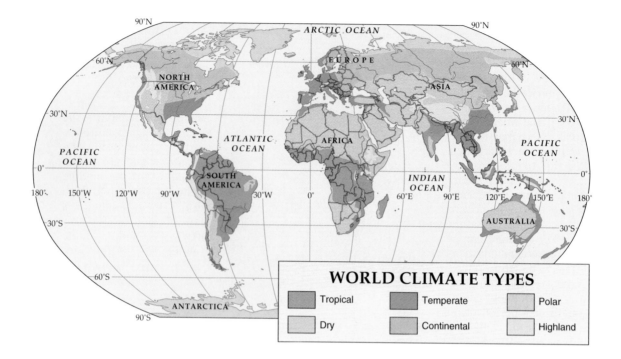

WORLD CLIMATE TYPES

- Tropical
- Dry
- Temperate
- Continental
- Polar
- Highland

Climates of the world can be classified according to their latitudes and the plants that grow there. The descriptions of climate types below are based on a system developed in the early 1900's by Wladimir Köppen, a German climatologist and amateur botanist.

Tropical Climates

Between 20° south latitude and 20° north latitude are three types of tropical climates. A **tropical wet** climate (near the equator or on windward mountainsides) is warm and rainy all year. This gives rise to dense rain forests. Places farther from the equator have a **tropical savanna** climate. Tall grasses and scattered trees grow here because the climate is too dry for forests. A region with a **monsoon** climate has both a wet and a dry season.

Dry Climates

Between 20 and 40° latitude, in both the northern and southern hemispheres, are three types of dry climates. Toward the equator are warm **subtropical deserts** where little vegetation can grow. These can be found in Northern Africa, the coast of Peru, and central Australia. Farther from the equator are cooler **mid-latitude deserts**, such as the deserts of the southwestern United States. On the leeward side of mountains are **steppe** climates, where short grasses grow. Steppes are found in the high plains of the United States from Montana to Texas, as well as western Argentina and parts of central Asia and southeastern Europe.

Temperate Climates

Between 30 and 60° latitude in both hemispheres are three types of mild, or temperate, climates. These generally occur in the mid-latitudes where prevailing westerly winds blow. Rainy **marine west coast** climates can be found on the North American west coast, north of California, as well as in much of northwestern Europe. Closer to the equator lie the **Mediterranean**

climates. Named for the southern European region, climates here have dry summers. Coastal California and New Zealand also have Mediterranean climates. **Humid sub-tropical** climates cover large mid-latitude areas in eastern parts of the continents. They are forest climates with cold winters and warm summers.

Continental Climates

These climates occur between 40 and 70° north latitude across vast areas of North America, Europe, and Asia. In contrast to temperate climates, continental climates have greater extremes in temperatures, with cold winters and warm summers. Much of the northern United States eastward from the Dakotas, southern Canada, and parts of eastern Europe have **humid continental** climates. Locations farther north are colder and have less precipitation in all seasons. Even farther north lie **sub-Arctic** climates, which have generally less forest growth.

Polar Climates

These climates occur from roughly 60° north and south latitude to the poles. The **tundra**, where the climate is too cold for trees, is home to grasses, mosses, and lichens. Greenland and Antarctica have a **polar** climate, where great ice caps exist because of year-round temperatures below freezing.

Highland Climates

Unlike the other five types of climate, which are determined largely by latitude, highland climates are due to the effects of altitude. These climates are cooler than the climates of the surrounding lowlands. Highland climates are found on the highest mountains of the world, even on the equator. In the mid-latitudes and tropics, climates can vary greatly with altitude. This gives rise to different kinds of vegetation growing in zones up the slopes of mountains.

Left: Northern Pakistan has a highland climate, with various types of vegetation at different altitudes. *Right:* Areas of Alaska have a polar climate, in which it is too cold for trees to grow.

western parts of Texas, Oklahoma, and Kansas. Rainfall is greater toward the Mississippi River, where forests and tall grasses are more common.

Pressure Centers

Pressure centers are large parts of the atmosphere where the pressure is much lower or much higher than in surrounding areas. Low-pressure centers usually cause stormy weather. High-pressure centers usually bring clear, sunny weather. If low- or high-pressure centers tend to form or move over an area at certain times of the year, this weather pattern helps determine the climate of that area. Heavy rains in warm belts of low pressure near the equator create a tropical rain forest climate. Dense tropical forests grow well in this climate. High-pressure centers are the primary cause of tropical desert climates like those of central Australia or the Sahara in northern Africa.

Ocean Currents

Ocean currents are great streams of water moving in the oceans. Some currents carry warm water to cool regions. Others carry cool water to warm regions. These currents affect climate in many parts of the world. The Gulf Stream, for example, is a warm ocean current. It carries warm water from the western tropical Atlantic toward the coasts of northwestern Europe. As a result, winters in western France are warmer than winters in the state of Maine in the United States, even though both are at about the same latitude.

Mountains

Mountains form barriers that affect the movement of prevailing winds. As winds approach mountains, air is forced to rise. The air uses energy to rise and becomes colder in the process. If the rising air contains enough water vapor, the vapor cools and condenses to form clouds and precipitation. This creates a "rain shadow" effect: More precipitation falls on the **windward** side of mountains (the side against which the wind blows) than on the **leeward** side (the side protected from the wind). A clear example of this effect is the two different climates on either side of the Sierra Nevada mountains in California. The windward slopes on the west side are covered

WONDER QUESTION

How can scientists tell what climates were like a long time ago?

People have been keeping accurate records of temperature and rainfall for only the past hundred years or so. To learn about ancient climates, scientists turn to nature's own weather records. For example, cross sections of tree trunks reveal alternating wide and narrow rings in the wood. These rings, which reflect the changing growing conditions from season to season, can provide clues about the temperatures of a place hundreds of years ago. Fossils of tiny organisms from lakebeds and ice from glaciers can provide clues about temperature and precipitation thousands of years ago.

Shifts in rainfall and vegetation growth can bring about changes in climate. Such changes can turn grasslands into deserts, similar to the one above.

with trees. The leeward slopes on the east side have scrubby vegetation.

Urbanization

Scientists have discovered that as cities and urban areas grow, local temperatures rise. This is partly caused by the greater amount of concrete and asphalt, which absorb the sun's heat. The result is the creation of "urban climates" that may be different from the surrounding climates.

▶ CHANGES IN CLIMATE

Climates have changed throughout Earth's history. Those changes have had major impacts on nature and people as well. Large populations of people and animals have migrated to new locations because of changes in rainfall patterns and vegetation growth. This occurs especially in areas called **transition zones**, which lie between one type of climate and another. During the 1970's, drought in northern Africa caused people to flee drying areas for nearby grasslands.

There are many theories that attempt to explain climatic changes. Among the possible causes are changes in the amount of energy put out by the sun, changes in Earth's orbit, or changes in the tilt of Earth's axis. Some scientists believe that dark patches on the sun, known as **sunspots**, are responsible for certain cycles of drought.

Dust in the atmosphere can lower the amount of solar energy that reaches Earth's surface, causing temperatures to drop. Volcanic eruptions can push ash high into the at-mosphere. Large clouds of dust can also be lifted into the atmosphere by meteor impacts. Ancient impacts could have caused major changes in Earth's climates, resulting in the extinction of dinosaurs and other creatures.

Climate is also influenced by the amount of certain gases in the atmosphere. The two most important gases are carbon dioxide (produced in part by volcanoes, forest fires, and other natural processes) and water vapor. Decaying organic matter produces another gas, methane. These three gases trap part of the heat generated by incoming sunlight and prevent that heat from radiating back into outer space. This is known as the **greenhouse effect** because the gases in the atmosphere act somewhat like a very large glass greenhouse. Without the greenhouse effect, Earth would be too cold to support life.

Since the early 1980's, however, scientists have gathered evidence indicating that temperatures are gradually rising around the world. Many scientists believe that this trend, known as **global warming**, may be caused by the burning of fossil fuels in homes, factories, and automobiles. These fuels (coal, oil, and gasoline) release carbon dioxide and other greenhouse gases when burned. Over the past 200 years or so, the release of these gases may have been so great that they have enhanced Earth's natural greenhouse effect.

Changes in the land and oceans are other possible causes of climatic change. Geologists have found evidence of shifts in Earth's crust. The movement of continents and the building up and wearing down of mountains would change temperature, rainfall, and wind patterns. A difference in the strength or direction of ocean currents could also be a factor in widespread changes of climate.

Several factors probably have acted together to change climates during Earth's history. Climatologists are still searching for complete answers. If they can learn more about how climates change, people may be able to plan for those changes in the future.

H. MICHAEL MOGIL
Meteorologist, How the Weatherworks

See also ATMOSPHERE; ENVIRONMENT; GLACIERS; SEASONS; WATER; WEATHER; WINDS.

CLINTON, DE WITT. See NEW YORK (Famous People).

CLINTON, GEORGE. See VICE PRESIDENCY OF THE UNITED STATES.

WILLIAM CLINTON (1946–)

42nd President of the United States

FACTS ABOUT CLINTON

Birthplace: Hope, Arkansas
Religion: Baptist
Colleges Attended: Georgetown
  University, Oxford University,
  Yale University Law School
Occupation: Lawyer, public official
Married: Hillary Rodham
Children: Chelsea
Political Party: Democratic
Office Held Before Becoming President:
  Governor of Arkansas

President Who Preceded Him:
  George Bush
Age on Becoming President: 46
Years in the Presidency: 1993–2001
Vice President: Albert Gore, Jr.

Clinton won the presidential nomination at the 1992 Democratic convention in New York City (*below*). He was renominated in Chicago in 1996.

CLINTON, WILLIAM. William (Bill) Clinton, at age 46, was the youngest person to be elected president of the United States since John F. Kennedy won election in 1960 at the age of 43. But despite his youth, Clinton entered the White House with considerable experience in executive government. By the time he was elected in 1992, he had already served nearly twelve years as governor of Arkansas. There, too, Clinton had been distinguished for his accomplishments and youth. With his rise to the presidency, he was the first of the generation born after World War II, the so-called baby boomers, to achieve the country's highest office.

▶ EARLY YEARS

Clinton was born William Jefferson Blythe in Hope, Arkansas, on August 19, 1946. He was named for his father, William Jefferson Blythe, who had been killed in an automobile accident three months before Bill's birth. At the age of 2, he was sent to live with his grandparents, who also resided in Hope,

while his mother, Virginia Blythe, studied nursing in New Orleans. When he was 4, his mother married Roger Clinton, a car salesman, and they moved together as a family to Hot Springs, Arkansas. The boy later took his stepfather's last name.

Young Bill attended school in Little Rock. He was an honors student, played the saxophone, and was popular with his classmates. But life at home was not always pleasant. The elder Clinton was an alcoholic, and when he had too much to drink, he could be abusive. One day, when Bill was about 14, he stood up to his stepfather. Although his stepfather kept drinking, the abuse stopped. As Bill grew older, he came to understand his stepfather's problem and so was able to forgive him before he died.

▶ YOUTHFUL AMBITION AND EDUCATION

Clinton thought of becoming a doctor or a reporter or even a musician. But after a fateful meeting with President John F. Kennedy, while still in high school, he made up his mind to enter politics. The meeting came about in 1963, when he was a delegate to the American Legion Boys' Nation, a youth program in which students learn about government. Clinton was part of a group that was invited to the White House to meet the president. Kennedy, who only months later was to be assassinated, shook hands with the young Clinton and made a lasting impression on him.

After graduating from Hot Springs High School in 1964, Clinton enrolled at Georgetown University in Washington, D.C. In his spare time he worked in the office of Senator J. William Fulbright of Arkansas. Upon his graduation from Georgetown with a degree in international affairs in 1968, he won a two-year Rhodes scholarship at Oxford University in England. He returned to the United States in 1970 to study law at Yale University. In 1972 he took time off to work for the presiden-

tial campaign of Democratic Senator George McGovern of South Dakota, who was defeated by Richard M. Nixon. The following year Clinton received his law degree.

▶ EARLY CAREER AND MARRIAGE

Clinton served briefly as a staff lawyer for the U.S. House of Representatives Judiciary Committee, before joining the faculty of the University of Arkansas Law School in 1974. The same year he tried, unsuccessfully, to launch his own political career, running for Congress against a popular four-term Republican. Although Clinton lost, he received more votes than any other Democratic candidate in the district had in 25 years. One reason Clinton did so well was that many voters had turned against the Republicans that year because of the Watergate scandal that forced President Nixon's resignation.

Clinton's political career was distinguished by his youth as well as his accomplishments. His election as governor of Arkansas at the age of 32 (*above*) made him the youngest governor in the nation. With his wife, Hillary, and daughter, Chelsea, at his side (*right*), Clinton won the Democratic nomination for the presidency in 1992. He was the youngest person to be elected president since John F. Kennedy in 1960. Clinton credited his meeting, while still in high school, with President Kennedy in 1963 (*above right*) for his decision to enter politics.

In 1975, Clinton married Hillary Rodham, whom he had met while attending Yale Law School. Mrs. Clinton established her own very successful law practice in Little Rock. The Clintons have one child, a daughter named Chelsea.

Clinton's second try for political office was more successful, winning him election as attorney general of Arkansas in 1976.

▶ **GOVERNOR OF ARKANSAS**

Two years later, Clinton was elected governor of Arkansas. Then 32, he was the nation's youngest governor. Arkansas voters, however, unhappy with tax increases that Clinton had imposed on gasoline to pay for improving the state's highways, rejected his bid for re-election in 1980. But in 1982, when he ran for governor again, he won easily and went on to win re-election three more times.

▶ **THE 1992 CAMPAIGN**

In announcing his intention to seek the 1992 Democratic presidential nomination, Clinton called for a jobs plan to lift the country out of its economic recession, tax cuts for the middle class, and a form of national health insurance. During the campaign, Clinton was pursued by questions about his character. He was attacked by some for evading military service and appearing to cover it up. Nevertheless, he won enough delegates to assure his swift nomination at the Democratic convention in New York City. For his vice-presidential running mate, Clinton chose Senator Albert (Al) Gore of Tennessee.

Capitalizing on the poor state of the nation's economy, Clinton won 370 electoral votes to 168 for his Republican opponent, President George Bush. H. Ross Perot, a Texas billionaire, ran as an independent and made a strong showing.

▶ **PRESIDENT: FIRST TERM**

Domestic Affairs. Soon after taking office, Clinton called for nearly $500 billion in tax increases and spending cuts. Although Republicans and some conservative Democrats opposed his plans to raise taxes, Congress finally gave the new president much of what he had asked for. Clinton also won congressional approval for the North American Free Trade Agreement (NAFTA) with Canada and Mexico.

IMPORTANT DATES IN THE LIFE OF WILLIAM CLINTON

1946	Born in Hope, Arkansas, August 19.
1968	Graduated from Georgetown University.
1968–70	Rhodes scholar, Oxford University.
1973	Graduated from Yale University Law School.
1975	Married Hillary Rodham.
1977–79	Served as attorney general of Arkansas.
1979–81	Served as governor of Arkansas.
1983–93	Again served as governor of Arkansas.
1993	Inaugurated as 42nd president of the United States.
1996	Won election to a second term as president.
1998	Impeached by the U.S. House of Representatives.
1999	Acquitted by the U.S. Senate on two articles of impeachment.

However, one of Clinton's top priorities—health reform—met with stiff opposition. Critics complained that his proposal would cost too much and lead to government interference in the health care system. Clinton had to abandon the idea.

Meanwhile, Clinton devoted considerable time to dealing with allegations of misconduct prior to his election as president. One controversy stemmed from investments that he and First Lady Hillary Rodham Clinton had made in the Whitewater Development Corporation, an Arkansas real estate development firm. The other concerned charges of sexual harassment made by a former Arkansas government employee, Paula Jones.

These issues contributed to the Democratic Party's defeat in the 1994 midterm elections and helped the Republicans gain control of Congress for the first time in 40 years. But later Republican efforts to balance the budget while cutting back spending and reducing taxes led to a shutdown of the federal government. This angered the American people, many of whom sided with President Clinton, who had opposed the Republican plan. He eventually won this struggle, and that success paved the way for his re-election in 1996.

Foreign Affairs. In international matters, Clinton helped bring about an agreement between Israel and the Palestinian Liberation Organization (PLO) concerning self-rule for Palestinians in the West Bank and Gaza Strip. And in the Balkans, he sent 20,000 American troops to serve as part of an international peacekeeping force.

In 1993, President Clinton hosted a meeting between Israeli prime minister Yitzhak Rabin (left) and Palestinian leader Yasir Arafat (right), during which the two leaders came to a historic agreement on self-rule for Palestinians living in Israeli-held territories. A second agreement was signed in 1995.

▶ SECOND TERM

Clinton easily won re-election in 1996, with 379 electoral votes. But he received only 49 percent of the popular vote running against the Republican nominee, former U.S. senator Robert (Bob) Dole of Kansas, and independent candidate H. Ross Perot.

Domestic Affairs. On the domestic front, the president's popularity benefited from sustained economic prosperity. His first major accomplishment was reaching an agreement with the Republican-controlled Congress on a plan to achieve a balanced budget. Despite tax cuts worth $95 billion, the plan also trimmed $263 billion from federal expenditures. Meanwhile, the number of people receiving welfare dropped, in part because of the welfare reform law Clinton pushed through Congress in 1996.

Seeking to ease racial tensions, Clinton in 1997 launched a year-long campaign of town hall meetings and conferences. He called for reconciliation between the races, defended affirmative action, and pointed out that by the end of the next half-century there would no longer be a majority race in America.

Allegations of misconduct continued to plague the president. In addition to the ongoing investigation into Whitewater and the Paula Jones case, his re-election brought new charges that he and Vice President Gore had engaged in questionable fund-raising activities during the 1996 election campaign. Republicans called for appointment of a special prosecutor. Clinton insisted that he and Gore had acted "within the letter of the law" and urged Congress to enact campaign finance reform laws.

But soon another scandal disrupted Clinton's presidency. This controversy stemmed from charges that he had an improper relationship with a 21-year-old former White House intern, Monica Lewinsky, and then tried to cover it up. Independent Counsel Kenneth Starr, who had been investigating the Whitewater case, launched an inquiry. His probe focused on whether Clinton had committed perjury by denying the affair with Lewinsky in a sworn deposition in the Paula Jones case, and also whether Clinton had tried to get Lewinsky to lie in her own sworn statement in the Paula Jones lawsuit. At first Clinton denied the charges, but when Lewinsky confirmed the affair in testimony before a grand jury, he was forced to admit he had not told the truth. Starr meanwhile issued a report, contending that the president's actions could be grounds for impeachment.

In the 1998 mid-term congressional elections, Democrats won more seats than expected, indicating that a majority of Americans continued to support the president. Nevertheless, on December 19, Clinton was impeached by the House of Representatives on charges of perjury and obstruction of justice. Only one other president has been impeached— Andrew Johnson in 1866. After a trial in the Senate, the president was acquitted on both the impeachment and perjury charges. However, he faced the possibility of a future indictment on criminal charges connected with the Lewinsky scandal at the end of his term. Despite these difficulties, Clinton was able to reach an agreement with Congress on a program designed to bolster the Social Security system in the long run. In 2000 the Clintons were cleared of any wrongdoing in the Whitewater matter.

Foreign Affairs. Clinton's scandals at home did not prevent him from playing an active role abroad. At a summit meeting in Helsinki, Finland, he persuaded Russian president Boris Yeltsin to accept the expansion of NATO by admitting some former Soviet Bloc countries as members. Following terrorist bombings of U.S. embassies in Nairobi,

Kenya, and Dar es Salaam, Tanzania, Clinton unleashed retaliatory strikes at terrorist sites in Afghanistan and the Sudan. The president also ordered the bombing of Iraq when that country refused to allow U.N. inspection of its weapons facilities.

In a peacekeeping role, Clinton helped negotiate a Mideast pact between Israel and Palestinian leaders. Israel agreed to withdraw its troops from land claimed by the Palestinians in return for a promise by the Palestinians to stop terrorist attacks against Israel.

Soon after the end of his impeachment trial, Clinton set in motion the biggest military operation of his presidency, joining other NATO countries in a massive bombing campaign against Yugoslavia. The aim was to force Yugoslavian president Slobodan Milošević to stop attacks on ethnic Albanians in the province of Kosovo. After ten weeks of bombing, Milošević agreed to withdraw his forces from Kosovo, and Clinton claimed victory. The United States had not lost a single soldier in combat.

In the last year of his presidency, Clinton made yet another effort to ease Mideast tensions when he held a summit meeting with Israeli prime minister Ehud Barak and Palestinian leader Yasir Arafat. The talks were intended to clear the way for establish-

On February 12, 1999, the U.S. Senate acquitted President Clinton on two articles of impeachment passed by the House the previous December.

ment of a Palestinian state, but the two leaders were unable to reach an agreement.

Seeking Continuity. As the 2000 presidential election approached, Clinton gave his support to his vice president, Al Gore, who won the Democratic nomination, and whom Clinton hoped would continue his own policies in the White House.

WILLIAM A. DeGREGORIO
Author, *The Complete Book of U.S. Presidents*
Reviewed by ROBERT SHOGAN
The *Los Angeles Times*

See also NORTH AMERICAN FREE TRADE AGREEMENT (NAFTA).

CLOCKS

Clocks are instruments that measure, record, and show the passage of time. They tell us when it is time to wake up, eat our meals, go to school, and watch our favorite television programs. Without them, people would not be able to keep the busy schedules of work and home. Public transportation would be impossible because planes, trains, and buses operate on exact time schedules.

Clocks are used in the home as timing devices for lights, ovens, video recorders, and lawn sprinklers. In industry they control machines and record employee work time. The tick or hum of the clock measures the hours, minutes, and seconds of our busy lives.

▶ KINDS OF CLOCKS

The two most common kinds of clocks used today are mechanical clocks and electric

clocks. These clocks differ from each other in the source of power that runs them and in how their timekeeping is regulated.

Mechanical Clocks. Mechanical clocks are powered by devices that are either weight-driven or spring-driven. These types of clocks need to be wound periodically.

In a weight-driven clock, a drum is connected by a cord to a heavy weight that supplies the clock's power. As the clock is wound, the cord wraps tightly around the drum, raising the weight. Gravity pulls the weight downward, turning the drum as the cord unwinds. The drum is attached to a series of gears of varying sizes called the train. (See the article GEARS in Volume G.)

The escapement and the pendulum work together to allow the weight to fall slowly and thus regulate the movement of the train.

The **pendulum** is a weight that swings steadily back and forth. The **escapement** consists of a toothed wheel (or escape wheel) and **pallets**, which are rocked back and forth by the pendulum to release the escape wheel one tooth at a time. The movement of the pallets as they catch each tooth of the escape wheel produces the ticking sound in clocks. As the escape wheel slowly turns, it moves the gears of the train, which move the clock's hands at the proper speed.

Spring-driven clocks use a coiled spring, or **mainspring**, as their source of energy. The mainspring is attached to the largest gear. The clock is wound by hand, tightening the mainspring. The mainspring slowly begins to unwind, moving the train. In some spring-driven clocks, batteries rewind the mainspring automatically.

The **balance wheel** replaces the pendulum in other spring-driven clocks. The balance wheel consists of a wheel with a coiled spring, called the **hairspring**, attached. The hairspring

Although sundials often make attractive garden ornaments, they are of very limited use as timekeepers in today's world.

coils and uncoils and makes the balance wheel swing evenly back and forth. This swinging motion moves the pallets to catch and release the escape wheel one tooth at a time so that it turns the train.

Electric Clocks. Clocks that are powered by electrical current are called **line-powered**, whereas those that use a battery are called **battery-powered**. Most digital clocks are one of these two types of clocks.

Line-powered clocks consist of an electric motor connected to a set of gears that turn the hands. The speed of the motor is determined by the 60-cycle-per-second alternating current (AC) used in most North American homes. The gears of the clock are designed to move at the proper rate to keep time. The accuracy of electric clocks depends on the stability of the alternating current.

In battery-powered clocks, the energy generated by the battery can be regulated by a balance wheel or pendulum. Or the electricity can be applied to a bar of quartz crystals. This makes the quartz vibrate. Quartz always vibrates at the same rate, so an electronic device is able to translate the number of vibrations into units of time. Quartz clocks can be accurate to within one minute per year.

Time is displayed on the clock's face by means of either dials with hands driven by gears, or digits. In digital clocks, an electronic circuit counts the changes in direction of electrical current and translates this information into numbers displayed on the clock's face. Models that light up use electronic digital displays, which include light-emitting diode display (L.E.D.) and liquid crystal display (L.C.D.). In L.E.D. time display, the digits are illuminated by light-emitting devices called diodes. An L.C.D. display uses liquid

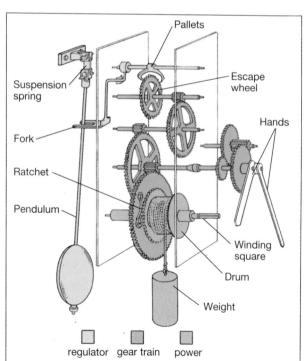

Pallets

Escape wheel

Hands

Suspension spring

Fork

Ratchet

Pendulum

Winding square

Drum

Weight

regulator   gear train   power

The weight, pulled down by gravity, turns the drum, which turns the gears. To prevent the drum from unwinding all at once, the pendulum, pallets, and escape wheel regulate the power. The pendulum rocks the pallets. The pallets catch and then release the escape wheel, one tooth at a time. This alternately stops and frees the movement of the gears. The rocking of the pallets moves the fork, which, helped by the suspension spring and gravity, propels the pendulum through its arc. A key fits on the winding square to turn the drum and rewind the cord. The ratchet frees the drum to turn in the winding direction without moving the gears.

crystal material that reflects light to form numbers on the digital clock face.

The most accurate timekeeper is the atomic clock. Atomic clocks measure time by counting the vibrations of the cesium atom, and in 1967 the standard second was established as the time it takes that atom to vibrate 9,192,631,770 (more than 9 billion) times. The most accurate atomic clock will not lose or gain a second in 20 million years.

▶ HISTORY OF CLOCKS

Primitive people recorded the passing of time by observing the length of their own shadows. As the sun moved across the sky, a longer shadow indicated that a day was beginning or ending, while a short shadow indicated midday. This observation led to the first crude shadow clock consisting of a simple vertical rod with rocks placed at specific intervals on the ground to measure the rod's shadow.

Sundials. Sundials use a pointer (called the gnomon) secured in place to cast a shadow on a flat surface or dial. Dials were first marked to show hours and later to show minutes also. The earliest existing sundials go back several thousand years to the ancient Egyptians, who were the first to divide the day into twelve periods of time. Sundials spread to Greece and Rome, where they appeared on public buildings and in gardens. Portable sundials were worn as jewelry.

Sundials continued to be used in Europe until the 1700's, when they began to be replaced by watches and clocks.

Clepsydras. The first water clocks, named *clepsydras* ("water thieves") by the Greeks, originated in Egypt about 2000 B.C. Their main advantage over sundials was that they could be used indoors and at night. Early water clocks were made simply of a vessel of water with 24 markings inside and a small hole at the base. The passing of time was measured by the number of markings visible inside the vessel as water dripped out through the hole. In 140 B.C. the Greeks and Romans improved on the water clock by placing a float joined to a toothed wheel inside the vessel. Water dripping into the vessel caused the float to rise, activating the wheel, which turned the hands on a circular dial. Clepsydras were widely used in Europe until the early 1500's.

Hourglass. The hourglass, or sandglass, measured time by the flow of sand at a steady rate from one glass to another. Its advantages over the water clock were that it was generally more portable and that sand does not freeze or evaporate. Adjoining hourglasses were built on racks with varying amounts of sand in them to measure an hour and parts of an hour.

Hourglasses first came into use in Greece in the A.D. 700's and were commonly used in Europe during the Middle Ages (500–1500), remaining popular until the 1600's. For centuries the hourglass was the only reliable timekeeper aboard ships.

Mechanical Clocks. Although the inventor of the first mechanical clock is not known, crude weight-driven clocks first appeared in the monasteries of Europe in the 1000's. They had no hands and used a bell to indicate the hour. By the Middle Ages large clocks were on cathedrals and public buildings. These first clocks were simply constructed but weighed several tons because they were made of iron and powered by heavy weights. The hour was marked by a bell tolling or being struck by a mechanical figure.

The bulky weight-driven clocks of the Middle Ages were improved on with the invention of the mainspring in 1500 by Peter Henlein (1480–1542), a clockmaker of Nuremberg, Germany. The mainspring made possible the construction of small, portable clocks, but these clocks were hardly more accurate than their predecessors because no means had been found to regulate the mainspring's force. Clocks of this time were purchased for their ornamental rather than practical value. They were often designed with

Some mechanical clocks, such as this finely crafted example (*above*), were made to be both accurate timekeepers and decorative works of art.

Because it can accurately indicate the time down to a tenth of a second, the digital clock has become the standard timekeeping device at sporting events.

mechanisms to strike a bell or play a tune each hour. People still relied on the sundial, water clock, and hourglass for telling time.

By the 1600's the balance wheel and hairspring had been invented to regulate the force of the mainspring. They greatly improved the accuracy of timepieces and led to the production of the first watches. In 1656 a Dutch scientist, Christiaan Huygens, devised a clock that used a pendulum to control the escapement and could record an exact 60-minute hour.

Gears and escapements were then perfected, and a metal hairspring replaced earlier ones made of hog bristle. The increased accuracy of pendulum clocks led to the addition of the minute hand. (Ships' clocks, or chronometers, are discussed in the article WATCHES in Volume W-X-Y-Z.)

Clocks were made by hand until the mid-1800's, when American manufacturers began to mass-produce them with precision machines. The electric clock appeared in many homes by the 1920's. Battery-operated clocks first appeared in the 1930's, and the first atomic clock was built in 1949. Digital clocks came into use in the 1970's.

AMY J. SMITH
Associate Editor, *The Bulletin*
The National Association of
Watch and Clock Collectors

See also GEARS; TIME; WATCHES.

CLOTHING

Humans have worn clothing of some sort for thousands of years. One reason for this is that humans, unlike other animals, lack a thick fur or tough skin, and clothing is needed to protect the body from the weather.

But there were other reasons for the development of clothing. One important factor is that early people, like people today, enjoyed decorating their bodies with clothing and makeup in order to improve their appearance. Later, when humans began to live in large tribal families, clothing and body decoration also came to symbolize a person's place in the tribe. Out of this development came the use of clothing to show a person's occupation. Today, for example, we can often identify soldiers, police officers, postal workers, and nurses by the uniforms they wear. Special clothing may also identify someone as a member of a certain group, such as the Girl Scouts or a basketball team.

Clothing can be a way to mark an important event. People dress up for weddings, parties, and other special occasions. In most Western cultures, black is a symbol of mourning, and people often wear black clothing to funerals. White is often a symbol of purity. A bride may wear a white dress on her wedding day. Priests and other church leaders don special robes to conduct religious ceremonies.

Clothing developed from several basic ways of placing skins or woven materials on the human body. One simple way was to wrap an animal skin around the body; another was to hang the skin from the neck like a cape. Still another was to make holes in the skin and lace it around the body with leather thongs.

After the invention of weaving, in about 5000 B.C., pieces of cloth could be sewn together, leaving openings for the arms and neck, to create a semi-fitted garment. Much later, humans attempted to improve on nature: They produced clothing that artificially changed the shape of the body.

▶ CLOTHING AROUND THE WORLD

Despite similarities in basic construction, clothing in different parts of the world developed differently. Climate usually influenced the type of clothing that developed in a region. People living in cold climates generally wore close-fitting clothes made of heavy, warm materials. In warmer climates, people wore loose, lightweight garments that provided pro-

Traditional Costumes

South Africa

India

China

Egypt

The Netherlands

Russia

Greece

Germany

Scotland

Mexico

United States
(American Indian)

United States
(cowboy)

United States
(Eskimo)

tection from the sun while allowing air to circulate around the body.

Other factors that caused differences in clothing were the types of fibers available from which to weave cloth and differing standards of beauty. The customs and traditions of a culture also influenced the way its people dressed. What a person wore for certain occasions often was governed by tradition. Many people still wear national or traditional costumes, such as the Scottish kilt or the Japanese kimono, to celebrate a special event.

In Oriental and Islamic cultures, clothing traditions that developed early in the culture's history were later established as rules to be followed. Respect for tradition thus discouraged change in styles of dress. The same is true of clothing in Africa, Polynesia, and the native cultures of Latin America.

In the West the tradition developed that change and experimentation in clothing styles were to be admired. Only in the history of Western dress, therefore, has there been great variety and change.

We can learn about the clothing of early cultures by examining paintings and sculptures from the past. *Far left:* Royal men and women of ancient Egypt wore pleated clothing of bleached linen, along with beaded collars, wigs, and fancy headdresses. *Center:* The fringed garments of the Sumerians were made from the fleece of sheep. *Near left:* The ancient Greeks wore tunics that fastened at the shoulders and draped around the body.

▶ HISTORY OF CLOTHING

Historians know a great deal about the clothing of past Western cultures, both from paintings and sculptures and from written records. The clothing styles of a period tell us much about the people who wore them: their religious and political beliefs, their feelings about themselves and the world around them, and the extent to which their technology had developed. For this reason, tracing the development of clothing styles can provide a clue to understanding the history of a culture.

The Ancient World

Egypt. The Egyptian civilization developed about 3000 B.C. in the Nile Valley. The Egyptians used the fiber from the flax plant to weave a cloth called linen. Sometimes the fabric was woven so subtly that it was transparent. The Egyptians bleached the linen white to stand out against their dark bodies, and sometimes they starched and pleated it into stiff, triangular forms.

Egyptian women wore skin-tight, often transparent skirts that came up under the breast, as well as shoulder capes and transparent tunics. Men wore starched and pleated skirts, tunics and robes. Both men and women wore beaded collars, wigs and wig covers, exaggerated makeup, and complex headdresses and jewelry.

Sumeria. At about the same time, in the delta area of the Tigris and Euphrates rivers in the Middle East, a people known as the Sumerians made skirts and shawls from the fleece of sheep. Sumerian men also wore carefully groomed beards, as hair and fleece were seen as symbols of male strength. Later, when the Babylonians, Assyrians, and Persians each conquered the area, they continued the tradition, wearing fringed tunics, fringed shawls wrapped diagonally over the body, and carefully manicured beards for men.

Crete. The island of Crete, near Greece, was inhabited by a people called the Minoans. Minoan men wore loincloths, and women wore flared, triangular skirts and tightly fitted jackets that exposed their breasts. This sophisticated culture was conquered about 1500 B.C. by Mycenaeans from the Greek mainland.

Greece. During the period known as Archaic Greek, narrow pieces of wool were sewn together to make semi-fitted tunics. With the coming of the Golden Age of Greece in the 5th century B.C., the Greeks developed wider tunics of lighter and more supple linens and woolens than had been worn in the past. They also discovered the beauty of draping and pinning these soft fabrics around the body rather than cutting and sewing them. A rectangle of material was folded in half, and half was placed to the front and half to the back of the body to make tunics called **chitons.** Decorative pins or clasps called **fibulae** were used at the shoulders (and sometimes down the arm) to hold the material on the body. Women's

Left: Like the Greeks, the ancient Romans wore simple, draped clothing. The Roman toga was a large half circle of fabric that was draped over the left shoulder and under the right arm. *Right:* While the clothing of the ancient world revealed much of the body, clothing styles of the Middle Ages concealed the body under long robes, cloaks, and leggings.

chitons usually had an overfold at the top, like a bib, while men's did not. For outer wraps the Greeks wore either a short, square garment called a **chlamys,** fastened by a fibula on the right shoulder, or the rectangular **himation,** which was wrapped over the left shoulder and over the right arm. During the Golden Age, simplicity and beauty of draping were the ideal, and decoration was limited to simple, geometric borders. During the Hellenistic Age that followed, however, Greek clothing became rich, decorative, and complex.

Rome. Roman clothing styles were mainly borrowed from the Greeks. The women in particular dressed very much like the Greeks, except for more complicated hairstyles. Men wore a T-shaped **tunica,** or tunic, with a Greek-style outer garment called the **pallium.** But they also wore another garment, the **toga,** that was distinctively Roman. The toga was a huge half circle of fabric draped over the left shoulder and under the right arm. It could only be worn by Roman citizens. The toga of a government official always had a purple border. During the Roman Empire, imperial togas and tunics were often made of embroidered silk imported from China.

The Middle Ages

In the 4th century A.D. the capital of the Roman Empire was moved to Constantinople, in the East, and the empire in the West declined rapidly. At the same time the Christian faith, centered in Rome, became the most powerful intellectual and spiritual force in Europe. Gradually, both in the East and in Western Europe, the Greek and Roman custom of revealing much of the body was replaced by the early Christian belief that the body should be completely covered.

In the East, silk fabrics embroidered with gold and silver threads became standard for the nobility. The art of mosaics also influenced clothing for the wealthy, and emperors and their wives were so covered with jewels that they looked like walking mosaics.

In the West, layers of clothing concealed the body. Tunics were worn one over the other and topped with a huge mantle, or cloak. Women wore kerchiefs that covered the head and neck. Men covered their legs with close-fitting trousers, called **bracchae,** often cross-laced to the knee. Charlemagne, who was crowned Holy Roman Emperor in A.D. 800, dressed for the occasion in silks and jewels, but most people's clothing was made of wool.

During the later Middle Ages, trade with the East brought richer fabrics and more decorative styles to Europe, and clothing became more sophisticated. In the 13th century, clothes still concealed the body, but fabrics were softer and could be draped more gracefully around the body. In the 14th century, the art of the tailor and seamstress rose to new heights of craftsmanship as garments were produced that were fitted to the shape of the body. This was achieved with the use of darts —tapering folds that were stitched into the fabric, allowing the clothing to follow the contours of the body.

Men wore a close-fitting jacket that ended at the hips, known as a **cotehardie.** The same name was given to a low-necked dress for women that fitted the upper body tightly and spread out at the hips into a full skirt. Men wore smoothly fitted hose to cover their legs. By the end of the 14th century they also wore a great gown with flowing sleeves known as the **houppelande.**

The clothing of wealthy people was fancifully decorated, inspired by the decorations of Gothic architecture. Women wore steeple headdresses, called **hennins,** that recalled the spires of Gothic cathedrals. Sleeves were scalloped, and men's jackets had padded shoulders and heavily pleated bodies. In the 15th century some of these complex shapes were replaced by plainer styles.

The Renaissance

During the 15th century in Italy an interest in classical Greece and Rome and a belief in the beauty of the human form led to clothing that was simple and youthful. By the close of the century, young men in Italy wore small caps and very short, low-cut jackets that were laced over soft, low-cut shirts. Sleeves were tied to the jacket with laces rather than sewn. Legs were encased in tight hose that reached the waist, and a piece of fabric known as a **codpiece** was tied over the opening below the waist. Women wore simple, high-waisted gowns with sleeves tied in and laced to the arm. The fancy headdresses of the past were replaced by natural, braided hair. Older people wore loose, flowing gowns. The ideal was to show off the body through the lacings of the outer garments.

In the early 16th century, the High Renaissance ideal of full, rounded forms replaced the youthful ideal. Puffed sleeves, full skirts, and a full silhouette were the result in both male and female dress. During the Reformation clothing in Europe became artificial and unnatural in shape, color, and decoration. By the later 16th century men's **doublets,** or jackets,

Clothing of the late 16th century was stiffened and richly decorated, featuring large pleated neck ruffs. Farthingales—padded hoops—extended women's skirts.

and the upper parts of women's dresses were stiffened and pointed at the waist. Shoulders were heavily padded. Stiff, pleated neck ruffs made the head appear as if it were sitting on a platter. Women's hips were extended by large, padded hoops called **farthingales** and men's by padded trunks. The whole was covered with great amounts of jewelry and braid, and outer fabric was often sliced to show the lining underneath. The ideal was to encase the body in a stiff, bejeweled box. Common people wore simpler, less stiffened versions of these styles.

The 17th Century

In the early years of the 17th century, clothing became more relaxed, losing the stiffness and excessive decoration that had characterized the Reformation. Fabric was chosen for

At the start of the 17th century, clothing styles relaxed. Men of the time wore soft shirts, high leather boots, and broad-brimmed hats. Wide lace collars replaced stiff neck ruffs. Men's hair was long and hung loose to the shoulder.

its own natural beauty. Men wore soft, natural-waisted doublets with full sleeves, unbuttoned to show a soft silk shirt. They had wide lace collars instead of ruffs; soft, knee-length pants; and loose leather boots with big cuffs. Cloaks were thrown loosely over one shoulder, and hair was worn full to the shoulder. Women's gowns had natural, uncorseted waists; full, floor-length skirts; puffed sleeves to the forearm; and low-cut necks with lace trim. Both men's and women's clothes were trimmed with bows and ribbons, and hats had larger brims than ever before.

About the middle of the century, corsets returned for women, waists became more pointed, and necklines were wide and curved. Skirts were often looped back with ribbons to show embroidered petticoats. Men wore small, short **bolero** jackets with short sleeves that fully displayed the shirt beneath. Full skirts known as **petticoat breeches,** edged in ribbon loops, were worn by men over hose or full knee pants. Men's shoes had high heels and large bows, and long hair was replaced by a full wig.

As Louis XIV of France became the most famous and powerful monarch in Europe, clothing at his court became heavier and more formal. These styles were imitated by the rest of Europe's aristocracy. Coats, inspired by a Persian design, replaced doublets. Vests reached to the knees, covering the shirt, and a scarf called a **cravat** with long lace ends replaced the collar. Female costume became heavier, with a large overskirt draped back into a train; tighter, lace-trimmed sleeves; and a square neckline trimmed with ribbon bows.

The hair was piled high and finished with a headdress of ribbons and small lace fans called a **fontange.** Common people wore less ornate versions of these same styles.

The 18th Century

For most of the 18th century, the French court continued to set fashion in Europe and the New World. After Louis XIV died in 1715, clothing styles again relaxed somewhat. Heavy clothing was gradually replaced by garments made of lighter, shiny fabric in pastel colors. Smaller, powdered wigs curled close to the head. This was the rococo age, when lightness, elegance, and charm were dominant in all the arts. Men's coats now had much fuller skirts, and vests gradually became shorter. Knee breeches fit tightly to the leg over white silk stockings, while shoes had a lower heel and buckles instead of bows. Men's three-cornered hats were called **tricornes.** Women wore undergarments stiffened with bone to create a bell-shaped skirt. Later, hoops called **panniers** expanded the skirts at the sides.

Women's hairdressing reached a period of excess about 1778, when piles of powdered hair were built up over a frame on the head. But a new taste for naturalness, simplicity, and the outdoor life began to emerge in Europe in the 1780's, inspired by the writings of Jean Jacques Rousseau. Clothing styles reflected this trend. Women discarded the pannier and corset in favor of the tunic or **chemise** dress of a thin fabric called muslin. The dress was fastened at the waist with a silk sash. Hair was natural and windblown, slippers replaced

Left: For much of the 18th century, dress was influenced by the styles of the French court. For women this meant fancy gowns trimmed with lace, ribbons, and flowers and elaborate headpieces set atop piles of powdered hair. *Right:* But by the 1780's social change led to a new simplicity. The chemise dress was inspired by the tunic of ancient Greece. Men wore riding clothes, reflecting an interest in outdoor life.

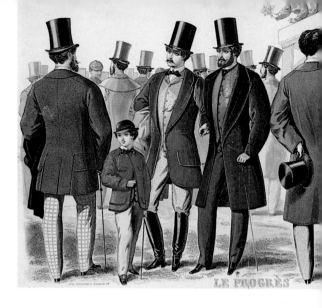

high heels, and large shawls were used as wraps. The image for women was vaguely Greek, symbolizing the new interest in democracy rather than the aristocratic individual. For men the natural look meant outdoor riding clothes; coats with tails, tight trousers that ended at the calf, boots, short vests, natural hair, and flat-brimmed hats with tall crowns.

The French Revolution brought wild exaggeration to this new "natural" look. In the years that followed the Revolution, wild hair, huge lapels, and exaggerated cravats were the rage for men. Stylish women wore huge bonnets, transparent dresses, and Greek-style shawls.

The 19th Century

The new century began with a slightly more conservative look, but symbols from Greece and Rome continued to be used. The romantic movement led to nostalgic borrowings from styles of the past. Women's high-waisted dresses were still light in color and made of muslin, but romantic accessories like turbans and ruffles added richness to dress. Men continued the outdoor, natural look. They adapted long trousers, worn by the peasant males since the Renaissance into a form-fitting pantaloon.

The technical advances of the Industrial Revolution brought many changes to clothing. For example, the jacquard loom, first used in the early 1800's, wove complex brocaded patterns into cloth. After the middle of the century the sewing machine allowed the mass production of ready-to-wear clothing, leading to the development of a clothing industry.

Male dress about 1830 consisted of coats fitted tightly at the waist, flared top hats, and trousers that fastened under the shoes. Beards and mustaches were worn again for the first time in almost 200 years. Women's dresses had low, off-the-shoulder necklines, tight waists, and very full skirts worn over many petticoats. With them were worn great flared bonnets decorated with many ribbons and flowers. The curving slim-waisted "hourglass" figure was desirable for both men and women.

By mid-century, flair and color in men's clothing had given way to the dark colors and straight lines of frock coats, tailed coats, and the new three-piece business suit. Women's figures were given an unnatural shape with the hoop skirt and later the bustle. The hoop replaced the many layers of petticoats that had been used to expand women's skirts. It became a symbol of the artificial distortions of women's figures during the Victorian age.

The rise of the first fashion house in Paris under Charles Worth in the mid-1800's launched the fashion industry, which encouraged even more rapid changes in clothing styles.

Top: In the mid-19th century, men's clothing became darker and more plain. Top hats were popular headwear, and most men sported mustaches or beards. *Right:* Women's dresses had off-the-shoulder necklines and full skirts that billowed out over layers of petticoats. Hair was smoothed over the ears or arranged in loose ringlets.

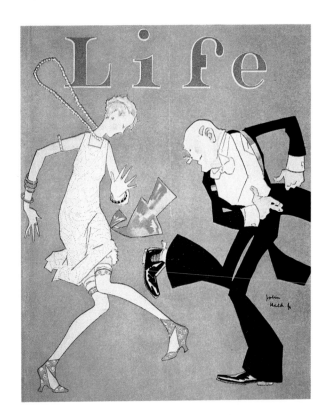

Left: At the start of the 20th century, women's clothing became more practical. The active woman adopted men's ties, shirts, jackets, and straw boaters for daily wear. *Right:* In the 1920's, the flapper's short, unfitted dresses and sleek, bobbed hair permitted complete freedom of movement and became a symbol of women's newfound independence.

The 20th Century

At the beginning of the century women's gowns, influenced by the sparkling light and bright colors of impressionist art, were made of frothy layers of tulle, chiffon, lace, and feathers. Men continued to wear somber business suits, frock coats, straight trousers, and top hats. The only change for men came in sporting clothes—blazers, oxford shoes, soft collars, and straw boater hats were adopted for casual wear. The new outdoor woman adopted full pants for bicycling and wore men's jackets, shirts, and ties for hiking.

Just before World War I came a revolution in women's dress. Under the leadership of the French fashion designer Paul Poiret, stiff corsets and complicated designs were discarded for the Japanese kimono or the tunic dress. As they fought for the right to vote, women were becoming more active and independent. They wanted practical clothing that allowed them to move freely. After the war, skirts were raised to the knee, exposing women's legs for the first time.

In the 1920's the ideal in Western society was the machine, and both men and women wanted clothing that gave the body a sleek, mechanized look. Women's and men's hair was short and sleek. Women's short, tube-like dresses did not define the bust or the waist,

and men's suits were close-fitting and trim. This general look continued into the 1930's.

Skirts rose again during World War II, and as women went to work in factories they began to wear slacks. The postwar "New Look" by the French designer Christian Dior featured a more traditionally feminine silhouette, with fuller, longer skirts. But through the 1950's and early 1960's the ideal was still a sleek, polished look for both men and women. The youth movement of the mid-1960's broke with this conventional look. Young English designers introduced the miniskirt for women, and both sexes wore the bright colors and patterns, bell-bottom pants, and exotic accesso-

The "New Look" was introduced in 1947 by French designer Christian Dior. It featured a more traditionally feminine silhouette, with snugly fitted waistlines and long, full skirts.

Left: The miniskirt, introduced by young English designers in the mid-1960's, was part of a fashion revolution that broke with conventional styles. *Right:* Today, while a wide variety of clothing choices continue to permit individual expression, both men and women often choose a conservative suit for business dress.

ries such as beads and medallions. At the same time, a trend toward more casual and comfortable clothing led to the widespread popularity of blue jeans and other work clothes. The clothing industry quickly adopted these ideas, creating styles of great variety.

After 1975, a more traditional look returned. Nostalgia for earlier styles led to revivals of the classic Chanel suit from the 1950's, padded shoulders from the 1930's, and low-waisted dresses from the 1920's. A wide selection of styles in ready-to-wear clothes allowed for more individual expression, especially in casual and sports clothes. However, both men and women favored a conservative look for business dress.

▶ THE CLOTHING INDUSTRY

Until the 19th century, most clothing was made in the home. Only wealthy people could afford to hire tailors and seamstresses to make their clothes. But by the 1820's a growing demand for ready-to-wear clothes led to the development of a clothing industry.

Early clothing factories were different from those we know today. They were really places where fabrics were cut, bundled, and handed out to workers. The sewing was done mostly by workers in their own homes.

The invention of the sewing machine revolutionized garment production. One of the earliest machines was patented by Elias Howe in 1846. Unfortunately, the machines were cumbersome to operate, and this slowed down their use in the factories. The worker had to crank the wheel with one hand to make it go.

At the same time the material had to be guided with the other hand. The invention of the foot-treadle machine by Isaac M. Singer a few years later freed both hands of the operator for sewing. Later, factory managers discovered that when each operator was given the same section to do repeatedly, even unskilled workers could sew faster.

With the rise in mass production, it was noticed that certain measurements came up over and over again. It became possible to work out a system of standard sizes and patterns for apparel. But it was many years before manufacturers could make ready-to-wear clothes that fit well.

Working conditions were very poor in many of these early clothing factories. They were called sweatshops—a name that tells us how hard this system was on the workers. It took many years, but labor laws and clothing workers' unions eventually did away with the evils of the sweatshops. You can read more about the early years of the clothing industry in the article INDUSTRIAL REVOLUTION in Volume I.

Today the manufacture of clothing is a worldwide industry that employs millions of people. Three important elements in this industry are the making of fabric, the design of clothing, and the manufacturing process.

Fabrics

For centuries all fabrics were obtained from natural fibers: silk from the silkworm, linen from flax, wool from sheep, and cotton from the cotton plant. But early in the 20th century the first **synthetic**, or man-made, fiber was created. It was called rayon. After World War II, nylon, polyester, and many other synthetic fibers were developed.

Synthetic fibers have some advantages over natural fibers. For example, they may be stronger, less expensive to produce, and less likely to wrinkle or shrink. The use of synthetics reached a peak in the early 1970's. Later an interest in natural fibers returned. Often synthetics are used together with natural fibers, producing fabric that combines the beauty and comfort of the natural with the practicality of the synthetic.

Design

It is often said that the French queen Marie Antoinette inspired the first occurrence of fashion design. The beautiful dresses made for the queen by her personal seamstress, Rose Bertin, were greatly admired. Many of the designs for her dresses were printed in fashion pamphlets so that people could copy them.

Fashion design became an industry in the mid-1800's with the founding of the House of Worth in Paris by Charles Worth and has continued to grow ever since. Today Paris is still a center of fashion, as are New York, Tokyo, Milan, and several other major cities. A new line of fashions is designed and showings are held for each season of the year. A single showing in Paris may be attended by more than 2,000 industry buyers. For more information on the fashion industry, see the article FASHION in Volume F.

Designers get ideas from styles of the past and from other cultures as well as from fabrics themselves and how they can be fitted on the body. The designing of a garment begins with a sketch. Then a plain piece of muslin is pinned and draped on a model or a dressmaker's dummy to make a sample garment. The actual fabric may also be used for the sample if its texture and pattern are important to the design. The designer then makes the last changes before the garment is made in its final form.

Manufacture

If a design is to be made in large numbers, cardboard or plywood patterns are made for each section of the sample garment. Different sizes are obtained by changing the dimensions of the original pattern. Then the fabric is cut. The pattern is placed on a pile of fabric—

Top: A clothing designer fits a garment on a dressmaker's dummy. *Above:* When a design is mass produced, machines are used to cut many pattern pieces at once.

sometimes as many as 200 layers—and a machine cuts all the pieces at once. Both the making of patterns and the cutting of fabric are often done by computer.

Then the pieces are taken to the sewing rooms, where many separate operations are carried out. Each garment may be sewn by several different machine operators. One operator may sew all the straight seams, and another may set in all the sleeves. Still another may sew on buttons or do finishing stitches such as embroidery. The machines can sew more than 5,000 stitches a minute.

The completed clothes are inspected and pressed with large steam irons. Then they are packed and shipped to stores, where they are sold to retail customers.

DOUGLAS A. RUSSELL
Author, *Costume History and Style*

CLOUDS

Have you ever watched the clouds overhead and imagined that they formed giant pictures? You may have seen a dragon or a bird, a racing car or a sailboat. But have you ever stopped to think what you were really watching?

Clouds are collections of enormous numbers of tiny water droplets or ice crystals in the air. The droplets are so small that they fall very slowly through the atmosphere and are easily kept aloft by air movements. (Air movements also change the shapes of clouds and move them across the sky.) After a period of time, the droplets grow too large to stay aloft, and they fall to earth as rain, hail, or snow.

Although clouds are usually found high in the sky, they actually have their beginning on the surface of the earth. Day and night, surface waters of oceans, lakes, and rivers evaporate. This means that the water changes from a liquid to a gas, called water vapor. Water vapor, which becomes one of the gases in the air, is the stuff necessary for cloud formation. But before clouds can form, two things must happen. The air hovering above the earth's surface must be cooled, and tiny particles of dust and other matter must mix with it.

▶ HOW THE AIR IS COOLED

The air is cooled in two ways. One is by rising. The higher you go, the colder it gets, at least for the first 7 miles (11 kilometers) or so. For every 300 feet (92 meters) of altitude, the temperature drops 1 Fahrenheit degree (1.8 Celsius degrees). So when the temperature on the ground at sea level is 80°F (27°C), it will be about 63°F (17°C) at an altitude of 5,000 feet (1,500 meters). When air near the ground is heated, it expands and becomes lighter than the colder air around it. Because it is lighter, the heavier surrounding air forces it to rise. As the warm air rises into the colder regions of the atmosphere, it cools. This type of cooling is called **adiabatic cooling.**

During the cooling process, something happens to the parcel of air—it ''loses'' some of its water vapor. This happens because cool air cannot hold as much water vapor as warm air. Let us see how this works.

Suppose that the air in a room is 70°F (21°C) and contains all the water vapor that it can at that temperature. The air is said to be **saturated.** No matter how hard we try, we cannot add more water vapor to the air so long as it remains at that temperature. This point is called the **dew point,** or **saturation temperature.**

Cloud formation begins when warm, moist air rises and cools. Cool air cannot hold as much water vapor as warm air, so the vapor condenses into water droplets that form clouds.

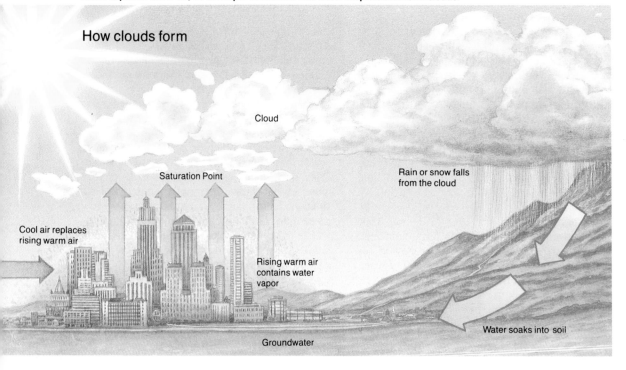

How clouds form

Cloud

Saturation Point

Rain or snow falls from the cloud

Cool air replaces rising warm air

Rising warm air contains water vapor

Water soaks into soil

Groundwater

If we lower the temperature, the air is forced to give up some of its water vapor. Your have often seen this happen. When you take a hot bath, the warm air in the bathroom becomes laden with invisible water vapor that comes from the hot water in the tub. If you open a window and suddenly let cold air in, you lower the temperature, and the bathroom air is forced to give up some of its water vapor. What happens is that the invisible water vapor turns into visible water droplets and forms fog, or a cloud, in the bathroom. Drops of water also form on the walls and plumbing fixtures.

▶ HOW VAPOR CONDENSES

Like the air outside, the air in the bathroom contains billions upon billions of tiny dust particles. As the water vapor comes into contact with these particles, it collects around them and changes back into a liquid. This process is called **condensation.** Around each dust particle a tiny water droplet forms—in the shape of a sphere. It is these droplets, billions upon billions of them, that you see as the bathroom cloud.

Exactly the same thing happens when clouds are formed outdoors. Warm air laden with water vapor rises and cools. Its water vapor comes into contact with dust and other particles in the air. As this happens, the vapor condenses, and a droplet of liquid water forms around each tiny particle.

It has been estimated that 100,000,000 droplets may be needed to form one large raindrop. If this estimate is anywhere near accurate, it means that a typical cloud is made up of an enormous number of droplets. It would take more than a million million million droplets to make up a cloud 1 mile wide, 1 mile long, and 1 mile deep. Such a cloud may have hundreds of tons of water in droplet (liquid) form and thousands of tons of water in water-vapor (gas) form.

The water vapor condenses into droplets around many kinds of particles. All such particles are called **condensation nuclei.** These nuclei (singular, nucleus) can be dust particles blown from deserts, dry topsoil or volcanoes. They can be tiny crystals of salt that have been sprayed into the air from the oceans or minute solid particles from the burning of soft coal and wood. Many kinds of tiny substances can act as condensation nuclei.

▶ SUPERCOOLED CLOUDS AND ICE CRYSTAL CLOUDS

Some of the clouds we see on a cold winter day are made of supercooled water. This is water that does not turn to ice even though the temperature is below freezing. Water droplets have been known to stay in a liquid state in temperatures as low as $-40°F$ ($-40°C$). The droplets making up supercooled clouds are formed in the same way as the droplets mentioned earlier. Exactly why these water droplets remain as water and do not freeze is not fully understood.

Thin, feathery clouds are sometimes seen very high in the atmosphere, where the temperature is well below freezing. These are made of ice crystals. Sometimes they are formed when droplets of supercooled water become so cold that they turn into ice crystals. But these feathery clouds can also be formed in another way. Instead of turning into water droplets, the water vapor sometimes changes directly from a gas into a solid—ice crystals. This process is called **sublimation.** The ice crystals may remain suspended in the cloud by wind currents, or they may fall to the ground as snow. There is still much to learn about how snowflakes and ice-crystal clouds are formed. Special kind of nuclei, called sublimation nuclei, are needed. Although the best nuclei seem to be ice crystals themselves, tiny soil particles and certain particles produced by burning are known to work.

▶ CLOUDS FORM A HEAT BLANKET

The coldest winter days occur when there are no clouds in the sky. Why should this be so? The sun is constantly emitting many different kinds of radiation. Some of it we see as light. Some of it we feel as heat. And some of it (such as X rays and ultraviolet rays) we cannot sense at all.

If there is a cloud covering overhead, short-wave radiation from the sun penetrates the clouds and strikes the earth. The soil and ocean waters receive this radiation, are heated by it, and then radiate some of the heat back into the atmosphere. But this radiation is given back to the atmosphere in the form of long waves. They cannot penetrate up through the cloud layer. So they become trapped between the clouds and the ground. In this way, clouds act as a blanket, holding in heat. When the sky is cloudless, much more heat escapes.

Left: Cumulus clouds are typically associated with fair weather.
Right: Cirrocumulus clouds are easily identified by their many ripples.

Left: Stratus clouds stretch across the sky in long, gray layers.
Right: Altostratus clouds appear in large sheets that may bring light rain or snow.

Left: Cirrus clouds, made entirely of ice crystals, are seen high in the sky.
Right: Cirrostratus, also high-altitude clouds, produce a thin, whitish veil.

Left: Stratocumulus clouds form an almost unbroken ceiling low in the sky.
Right: Nimbostratus clouds are low, thick rain clouds.

Left: Altocumulus clouds are identified by their very thin edges.
Right: Cumulonimbus clouds are storm clouds. Strong vertical winds give them great height.

Nearly all clouds are found at altitudes of ½ to 7 miles (1 to 11 kilometers) above sea level. Sometimes clouds form on or near the ground. When they do, we call them fog.

Clouds take many different shapes. To the weather forecaster, their shapes are one clue to weather-in-the-making.

Main Cloud Types

Broadly speaking, there are three main forms of clouds—cumulus, stratus, and cirrus.

Cumulus. These clouds are fluffy and cauliflower-shaped, with broad, flat bases. Cumulus clouds usually form on top of rapidly rising currents of warm air and have sharp outlines. They resemble towers of cotton wool and move majestically across the sky in groups.

Stratus. In appearance these are perhaps the least interesting clouds. They can best be described as fog that has formed high above the ground. Usually they stretch across the sky in long, horizontal layers. Sometimes the layers are thick, while at other times they are thin. Unlike cumulus clouds, stratus clouds are a sign of a slow, large-scale rising of air.

Cirrus. These clouds are the "mares' tails" seen high in the atmosphere. They are made up entirely of ice crystals and are so thin that at night you can sometimes see the stars shining through them. Cirrus clouds are often the source of sublimation nuclei for snow clouds floating in the atmosphere at lower altitudes. The great height of cirrus clouds makes them appear to be hardly moving. Sometimes, however, they are moved by strong winds at speeds of 100 to 200 miles (161 to 322 kilometers) an hour.

Subgroups of Cloud Types

The three main groups of clouds can be further divided into subgroups.

Stratocumulus. These clouds sometimes form an unbroken ceiling, or they may be more loosely packed together. Different types of stratocumulus clouds occur at different altitudes.

Altocumulus. These clouds look like stratocumulus clouds. Cauliflower-shaped, they often parade across the sky in broken groups seen at different altitudes. The very thin edges of the altocumulus clouds provide a good way of identifying them. They may be seen at altitudes from about 6,500 to 20,000 feet (2,000 to 6,000 meters).

Cirrocumulus. These clouds form high in the sky, from about 10,000 to 30,000 feet (3,000 to 9,000 meters). They are thin ice-crystal clouds that look like fine sand ripples made by waves on a beach. The expression "mackerel sky" has long been used to describe cirrocumulus clouds.

Altostratus. You can see these clouds between altitudes of about 6,500 to 20,000 feet (2,000 to 6,000 meters). They form gray or bluish sheets. Sometime they are thick enough to block out the moon or sun. At other times they are so thin that you can see the moon outlined through them.

Cirrostratus. These are high-altitude clouds that cause us to see a halo around the moon or sun. One way to tell cirrostratus clouds from altostratus clouds is by looking for shadows. The sun's light causes objects to cast shadows when it shines through the thin, white veils of cirrostratus clouds. But no shadows are cast when it shines through altostratus clouds.

Nimbostratus. These clouds bring long spring rains. Their dark bases may be only 330 feet (100 meters) above the ground and are seldom higher than 3,300 feet (1,000 meters). Nimbostratus clouds are much thicker and darker than ordinary stratus clouds. You can see them develop when altostratus clouds grow thicker and sink lower as steady rain falls from them.

Cumulonimbus. Members of the cumulus family, these clouds are storm clouds. Thunder showers, sometimes accompanied by hail, burst forth from cumulonimbus clouds. On summer afternoons you can often see them building up from large cumulus clouds. The strong vertical wind currents within them cause these clouds to reach towering heights. At the top of a cumulonimbus cloud is an anvil-shaped cloud of ice crystals. The anvil is formed by the strong winds blowing near the top of these clouds. If you see cumulonimbus clouds forming in the morning, you can expect showers in the afternoon.

ROY A. GALLANT
Author, science books for young people
Reviewed by JEROME SPAR
Author, *The Way of the Weather*

See also FOG AND SMOG; RAIN, SNOW, SLEET, AND HAIL; THUNDER AND LIGHTNING.

CLOWNS

Clowns are skilled entertainers who perform to make people laugh. Usually found at circuses, they are great favorites of children. Clowns are easily identified by their colorful costumes and exaggerated makeup. They often perform juggling, acrobatic, or magic stunts, but typically they act out skits in which they struggle to solve everyday problems by using humorously unsuitable methods.

Clowns provide the comic pauses between the daring, and sometimes dangerous, circus acts, such as swinging from a trapeze or walking on a tightrope. These breaks allow an audience to relax, laugh, and catch its breath.

Clowns usually perform in pantomime, which means they do not use words to express their humor. Rather, by using exaggerated body movements, facial expressions, behavior, and dress, clowns amuse their audiences by making fun of common human weaknesses.

Nobody knows who the first clown was, but many ancient societies had a "fool" who was proud enough to think that he could treat the gods as equals. The ancient Greeks called this kind of pride "hubris." These early clowns did not look much like today's circus clowns, but they are definitely related.

The first clowns to use full face makeup came from China. The Chinese began the tradition of face painting about 500 B.C. Actors used makeup to re-create the mask that King Lan Liu wore into battle. By the 8th century B.C. the practice of impersonating others was firmly established in China. At that time a clown character was created to impersonate Bo Bi, the Chinese prime minister of Wu. Bo Bi was considered to be an opportunist, taking advantage of everyone to gain money and power. His impersonators used a white patch over the eyes and nose to indicate Bo Bi's disregard for serious matters and his unreliability.

In the West, clowns remained village fools and court jesters with bare faces until the 1500's. At that time Italian street theater, known as the *commedia dell'arte*, became very popular. The *commedia* characters contributed to the evolution of the clown and influenced all of the Western clowns that followed: Deburau, who created the Pierrot character, was the first Western clown to wear makeup; Harlequin donated his love of pranks; Pantaloon gave his baggy clothes; and Brighella passed along his overblown sense of humor. However, the most important influences came from Pulcinella, who developed into Punch of Punch and Judy, and a minor character called Clown.

Early in the 1800's, Joseph ("Joey") Grimaldi, a British comic singer and mime, developed Clown, a white-faced, grotesquely costumed character, which he performed on stage. Circus clowns today are still called "Joeys" in Grimaldi's honor.

After Grimaldi's time, clown makeup became increasingly colorful and extravagant.

Why Don't Most Clowns Speak?

In the late 1800's, American circuses grew immensely popular and evolved into the three-ring format, where several acts would perform in different rings at the same time. The audiences became so large that the talking clown could no longer be heard. Clowns then began to rely on "sight" gags, pantomime, and slapstick comedy. The "walk-around," or moving parade of clowns doing nonverbal gags and stunts, was inspired by the addition of the race course or Hippodrome track that surrounded the three rings in many American circuses.

Clowns are professional actors whose colorful costumes, bumbling antics, and humorous skits delight audiences at parties, carnivals, and circuses.

SUGGESTED WAYS TO APPLY CLOWN MAKEUP

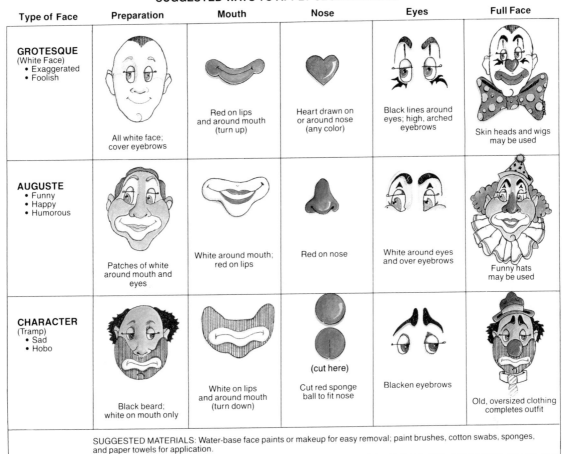

Type of Face	Preparation	Mouth	Nose	Eyes	Full Face
GROTESQUE (White Face) • Exaggerated • Foolish	All white face; cover eyebrows	Red on lips and around mouth (turn up)	Heart drawn on or around nose (any color)	Black lines around eyes; high, arched eyebrows	Skin heads and wigs may be used
AUGUSTE • Funny • Happy • Humorous	Patches of white around mouth and eyes	White around mouth; red on lips	Red on nose	White around eyes and over eyebrows	Funny hats may be used
CHARACTER (Tramp) • Sad • Hobo	Black beard; white on mouth only	White on lips and around mouth (turn down)	(cut here) Cut red sponge ball to fit nose	Blacken eyebrows	Old, oversized clothing completes outfit

SUGGESTED MATERIALS: Water-base face paints or makeup for easy removal; paint brushes, cotton swabs, sponges, and paper towels for application.

Gradually the styles of makeup evolved into three very general types that reflected the personalities of various clowns: the *Auguste* clown, who deals in slapstick humor, has a partially white face painted with many colors, especially red and blue; the *Grotesque* clown, who is pompous and foolish, has an all-white face, a large red mouth, and a bulbous nose; the *character*, or "tramp," clown, who typically acts sad, has a darkened face and dresses like a hobo.

Not all clowns use brightly colored makeup. Dan Rice, a 19th-century American clown, relied on his red, white, and blue suit and top hat to make people laugh. His striking costume inspired the first popularized drawing of "Uncle Sam," a lasting symbol of Americana.

The *commedia* clowns used makeup to make their characters appear bigger than life. Modern clowns use makeup for the same reason. Today, most clowns perform in front of large audiences. They must use heavy makeup so that the audience can see their features clearly.

A clown's makeup is as distinctive as a fingerprint. Because a clown's makeup is mask-like, any two people wearing the same face (style of makeup) will look alike. To prevent others from copying their styles, many clowns copyright, or register, their faces. This means that only they are legally entitled to wear their own designs.

Today's clowns still have a lot in common with the clowns of the past. They may differ from one another in behavior and dress, but they are all alike in that they are living, breathing cartoons of particular types of human beings. Clowns help us recognize that the mistakes we all make are really not so serious after all.

Toby Sanders
Author, *How to be a Compleat Clown*
Reviewed by John E. Mackiewicz
Bongo the Clown

COAL AND COAL MINING

Coal is a rock, usually black but sometimes brown in color. It burns easily and gives off large amounts of heat. As a fuel, coal has played an important part in the development of industry in many countries since the 1700's. People have used it in their daily lives for centuries, to cook food and heat houses.

One of the most important uses of coal today is to generate electricity. Another is in the making of steel. Chemicals that come from coal are used to make hundreds of materials that we use every day, such as plastics, nylon, drugs, dyes, and fertilizers.

▶ HOW COAL IS FORMED

Like petroleum and natural gas, coal is a **fossil fuel**—a fuel that comes from once-living things. Coal was formed from plants. It is made up largely of the element carbon, but it also contains hydrogen and small amounts of most other elements.

The coal that is mined today began to form long before people appeared on the earth. Giant ferns, reeds, and primitive trees grew in swamps. When the plants died, they fell into the swamps and began to decay. A thick layer of partially decomposed vegetation gradually was built up. As centuries passed, the plant material at the bottom was pressed tightly together by the weight of material above it. Under this pressure it turned into a brown, spongy material called peat.

How did soft, spongy peat become hard, black coal? As more time passed, the land sank, and the peat was buried under many feet of mud or sand. The weight of the mud and sand pressed some of the moisture out of the spongy mass. As the layers grew thicker and heavier, they pressed harder. This pressure, along with heat from within the earth, gradually turned the peat into a hard, black rock—coal.

Types of Coal

Coal has no set chemical formula, so coal deposits may vary greatly from place to place. These variations are caused by differences in the original plant material, the amount of time the material has been acted upon, and the kinds of processes it has undergone. One useful way of classifying coal is by **rank,** which indicates chiefly the amount of change it has

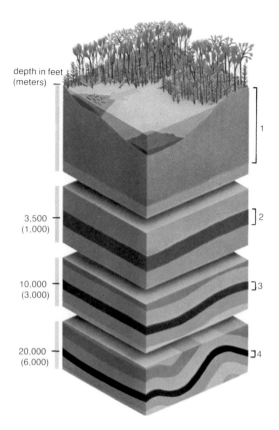

depth in feet (meters)

3,500 (1,000)

10,000 (3,000)

20,000 (6,000)

Coal is formed from plants. When they die, they form thick layers of partially decayed matter. Under the pressure of more and more layers, peat (1) forms. As the pressure builds, the peat becomes lignite (2), then bituminous coal (3), and finally anthracite (4).

undergone. Major coal ranks include peat, lignite, bituminous, and anthracite.

Peat is often found in bogs and is the lowest-ranking coal-like material. It is much like the spongy brown substance that is the beginning of the coal-making process. Often peat must be dried out before it can be used.

Lignite is sometimes called brown coal because of its color. It, too, often must be dried before use. It is soft and crumbly and produces less heat than higher-ranked coals.

There are a number of different sub-ranks of **bituminous** coal. This is the most abundant and most useful kind of coal. Usually called soft coal, it burns well and gives a good deal of heat. One of its important properties is that it can be heated to form **coke,** the nearly pure carbon used in making steel.

The coal that has undergone the most change is **anthracite,** or hard coal. It is shiny and black. It is the coal that is closest to pure carbon. It burns slowly with a clean flame and is good for heating houses.

▶COAL MINING

Coal was first discovered in places where it crops out on the surface of the earth. Later, as people learned to follow the **seams** (layers of coal) deep into the earth, various methods for mining coal were developed.

Deep Mining

Deep, or underground, mining is the method that has been used for centuries. Underground mines are of three types—**shaft, slope,** or **drift.** The type depends on the kind of opening that lets the miners in and out and permits the coal to be removed. In shaft mines, shafts are dug straight down into the earth, and elevators are installed. In slope mines, the coal is reached by way of slanting tunnels. And in drift mines, there are horizontal tunnels—into the side of a hill, for example. Some large mines have more than one kind of opening.

The earliest mining method was to chop away at the coal wall, or **face,** with pickaxes. When explosives became available, miners used them to break up the coal. The loose coal was then shoveled into carts and hauled outside. Another method that is more common today uses the **continuous mining machine.** This digs the coal from the face with hardened "teeth" mounted on a drum. Coal is thrown onto a part of the machine that rakes it up and loads it onto cars or conveyor belts.

Two methods are used in developing coal mines. The older one is called the **room-and-pillar** method. The coal is cut out in "rooms," leaving pillars standing to support the roof. Where the coal seam is uniform, mining companies use the **long-wall** method. They attack the coal face along a broad front, removing the coal as they go. The roof is propped up over the miners but is allowed to collapse behind them as they move along.

A machine called a continuous miner digs the coal out of the coal face and loads it onto a shuttle car or conveyor belt. A continuous miner can greatly increase the production of a mine.

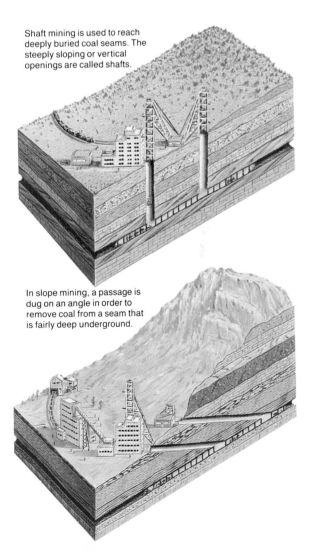

Shaft mining is used to reach deeply buried coal seams. The steeply sloping or vertical openings are called shafts.

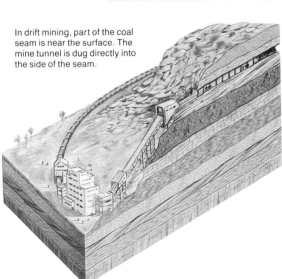

In drift mining, part of the coal seam is near the surface. The mine tunnel is dug directly into the side of the seam.

In slope mining, a passage is dug on an angle in order to remove coal from a seam that is fairly deep underground.

Strip-mining is used when the entire coal seam is near the surface. The rock layer covering it is removed, and the coal is "stripped" away with power shovels.

Strip-mining is used mainly in the western states. It is cheaper than deep mining, but "reclaiming" the stripped land after mining may result in additional costs.

Strip-mining

Strip-mining, or surface mining, is used where coal seams are close to the surface. The overlying soil and rock must first be removed to expose the coal. Giant power shovels, excavators, and explosives dig and blast away surface layers. The uncovered coal is then broken loose, dug out, and removed by truck.

Strip-mining is cheaper than deep mining. It gets out more of the coal, and it is generally less dangerous for miners. Until the 1970's, only about one third of all the coal mined in the United States was produced by stripping. Now, with increased mining in the western states, the amount is probably closer to one half.

▶COAL PROCESSING

As it comes from the mine, coal is not always fit for immediate use. The lumps may vary in size, or the coal may contain rocks and other impurities. If the lumps are too large, the coal is put through crushers, or in the case of anthracite, through preparation plants called **breakers.** To sort lumps by size, the coal is passed through screens with holes of different dimensions. Separation of impurities is sometimes done by immersing coal in water that has been made denser by the addition of chemicals. The coal floats and is skimmed off, while the impurities sink.

Gasification and Liquefaction

Coal can be converted into a gas—mostly carbon monoxide and hydrogen—by burning it in the presence of oxygen and steam. This gas, called **town gas,** was used extensively as a fuel and for lighting in the 19th century.

Other safer, more efficient processes have been developed to generate synthetic natural gas, fuel oil, and even gasoline from coal. These processes have so far been used only in special situations, but it is thought that as the world's supply of petroleum decreases, it will become necessary to use coal to produce substitutes for petroleum-derived fuels.

▶THE USES OF COAL

The Chinese mined and used coal hundreds of years before the birth of Christ. An ancient Greek writer described coal in a book on rocks. Coal mining in western Europe is described in documents from the 12th century.

During the Middle Ages much wood was burned, in part because it takes a great deal of wood to produce a useful amount of heat. Coal quickly became an economical alternative wherever it was available. By 1688, England —then the leading coal center of the world— was producing 3,000,000 tons a year. With the development of the steam engine and its increasing use in ships, locomotives, and factories, coal came into wide use.

In the United States, coal came into use more slowly because of the abundant supplies of wood. The development of the iron and steel industry and the spread of railroads increased the demand. By 1900 the United States produced more coal than Britain.

The peak years of coal use in the United States came in the late 1940's, when coal supplied 50 percent of the country's energy. But home owners turned increasingly to oil, gas, and electricity for heat because they were inexpensive and convenient. The railroads shifted to oil-burning diesel locomotives. The long decline in the use of coal was reversed only in the 1970's, when the cost of petroleum and natural gas increased.

Coal is still used to heat some homes and industrial plants. It is becoming attractive as a source of heat for some industrial manufacturers because of the relatively high cost of natural gas and petroleum products. But the main users of coal are now electric power companies and the iron and steel industry. Coal is also an important source of chemicals.

Electric Power Generation. More than half of all the electricity used in the United States is produced in coal-burning plants. In these plants, pulverized coal (coal in the form of powder, or dust) is burned in furnaces, and the resulting heat is used to convert water to steam. The pressure of the steam spins the great fanlike wheels of turbines. These, in turn, run the electric generators.

Steel Manufacture. In nature, most metals are combined with oxygen or other impurities. Coal is used to refine them—that is, to separate the impurities from the metal. Burning coal and the gases formed by the burning combine with the impurities, leaving the metal in its pure state. Much of the iron and steel produced today is made with coal, usually in the form of coke. When steel is made from iron, some of the carbon in the coke is taken up by the iron to produce a chemical mixture, or **alloy.** This alloy of iron and carbon is steel.

The leading coal-mining countries in the world today are China, the United States, Russia, and Ukraine. Some coal is also mined in Europe. In the United States, the leading coal-producing states are Kentucky, West Virginia, Wyoming, and Pennsylvania.

Chemical Production. Many important chemicals are obtained as by-products when coke is made from coal. **Ammonia,** for example, is given off. It can be used to make fertilizers. Among the other chemicals produced are **phenols** (such as carbolic acid) and **pyridine bases.** Most of these substances are used in the manufacture of dyes, plastics, drugs, paints, adhesives, and synthetic fibers.

▶**PROBLEMS IN COAL PRODUCTION AND USE**

Explosions and fires are a constant problem in mines. Many explosions once were set off by the lamps that miners carried. The safety lamp, invented in 1815, and today's electric lamps were important steps toward safer mines. Fans are used to sweep gases from mines. Coal dust is made inflammable by spraying tunnel walls with very pure powdered limestone—a process called **rock dusting.**

Cave-ins are another danger. Wooden and steel supports help prevent them, as does **roof bolting.** In this procedure, long rods are inserted through the layers of rock that make up the roof of the mine. The rods help keep the ceiling from collapsing.

Constant breathing of coal dust in the mine can lead to a serious and often fatal disease called **black lung.** Efforts to combat dust in the mines have helped prevent this disease. It is also helpful for miners to wear masks.

Environmental Disturbances

Underground mines can produce mountainous waste. Open-pit mines can scar landscape and leave vast piles of stripped surface material. When high-sulfur coal is burned, the sulfur dioxide produced causes acid rain.

There are methods for dealing with these problems. Waste piles can be spread out and landscaped. Other surface damage can be repaired by careful reclamation. **Scrubbers** or other devices remove sulfur dioxide before it gets into the atmosphere. The procedures are expensive, and they add to the cost of coal.

Despite these added costs, however, coal is frequently the most economical fuel available for many uses. As other fossil fuels become more and more expensive and as supplies decrease, the world may have to turn increasingly to coal to meet its energy needs.

DAVID M. LOCKE
University of Florida
Reviewed by GAYLE MCCOLLOCH
West Virginia Geological and Economic Survey

See also ACID RAIN; CARBON; ENERGY SUPPLY; GEOLOGY; MINES AND MINING; ROCKS.

COAST GUARD. See UNITED STATES, ARMED FORCES OF THE.
COATIS. See RACCOONS AND THEIR RELATIVES.
COBB, TYRUS RAYMOND (TY). See GEORGIA (Famous People).
COCHISE. See INDIANS, AMERICAN (Profiles).
COCOA. See CHOCOLATE.

Coconuts grow in clusters near the top of the coconut palm, a tree whose bare trunk can reach a height of 100 feet. A thick husk surrounds the nut as it ripens.

COCONUT

A grinning face seemed to be peering at the Portuguese sailors as they peeled the husk from an unfamiliar nut. These 15th-century explorers called the nut *coco*, from their word for "grimace."

The face was made by three eyes, or undeveloped buds, on one end of the husked coconut. The outer fibrous husk cushions this inner seed, or nut. The nut is about 10 inches (25 centimeters) long. Just inside the hard, dark shell is a layer of dense white meat. The central cavity is filled with a watery liquid called coconut milk.

Coconuts are an important cash crop of the tropics. A mature coconut palm flowers throughout the year and almost always has a few ripe nuts. The flower clusters develop into coconuts after blooming. It may take a year or more for the nut to mature. The average yearly production of a palm is 50 nuts.

The single bare trunk of the coconut palm shoots up as high as 100 feet (30 meters) and is crowned with a tuft of long, feathery leaves. The palm grows near the sea because its shallow roots can find moisture there. The husk is not harmed by salt water, and the nut can be carried a long distance by the sea to land and take root on a faraway beach. It is thought, however, that people spread the coconut by carrying nuts with them.

Coconuts are harvested by climbing the palms and cutting off the cluster of nuts or by gathering ripe nuts from the ground. The husk is removed by hand after splitting it on a sharp iron or wooden stake driven into the ground. Large plantations may use machines.

For centuries the coconut palm has supplied the people of the Pacific islands with food, drink, shelter, and most of their other needs. The roots furnish a dye; the trunks are used for posts in buildings; and the harder outer part is cut into boards called porcupine wood.

Coconut meat is eaten in a variety of ways. The coconut cream used in cooking is prepared by grating coconut meat into a little water and sifting out the coarse particles. The liquid inside a green coconut is a refreshing drink. The sap drained from the palm by slicing the unopened flower clusters is made into vinegar, sugar, or the alcoholic beverage called arrack.

Thatching, mats, hats, baskets, and rope are made out of the leaves, midrib, and a fiber from the husks called coir. Coir is exported to other countries to make matting.

The most important commercial product of the coconut is **copra** and the oil pressed from it. Copra is the dried meat of coconuts. One hundred nuts will produce about 50 pounds (23 kilograms) of copra, which in turn will yield up to 60 percent oil. After pressing out the edible oil, the leftover copra cake and meal make good cattle feed because of their high protein, sugar, and vitamin content.

The major uses of coconut oil are in soaps and margarines. Other uses include bakery products, candles, cosmetics, and printing ink. Dried coconut meat is used in candies, cakes, cookies, and pies.

Leading producers and exporters of copra and other coconut products are the Philippines, Indonesia, India, Oceania (the islands of the west central Pacific ocean), and the Federation of Malaysia.

HAROLD F. WINTERS
U.S. Department of Agriculture

See also NUTS.

COCOONS. See BUTTERFLIES AND MOTHS.

COD. See FISHING INDUSTRY.

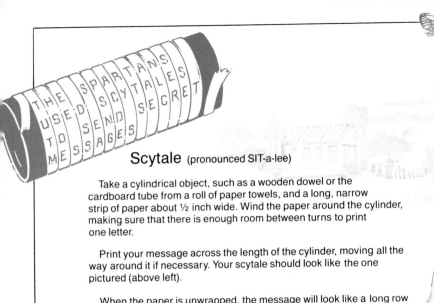

Scytale (pronounced SIT-a-lee)

Take a cylindrical object, such as a wooden dowel or the cardboard tube from a roll of paper towels, and a long, narrow strip of paper about ½ inch wide. Wind the paper around the cylinder, making sure that there is enough room between turns to print one letter.

Print your message across the length of the cylinder, moving all the way around it if necessary. Your scytale should look like the one pictured (above left).

When the paper is unwrapped, the message will look like a long row of letters.

The person who receives the message must wrap the paper around a cylinder the same thickness as yours. Then the letters will line up properly, and the message can be read.

CODES AND CIPHERS

Have you ever had an important secret to share with a friend, but you didn't want anyone else to find it out? By using codes and ciphers, you can pass along a message to a friend, and no one else will be able to read it. Codes and ciphers are ways of writing in secret. In a code each word of a message is replaced by a secret code word or number. For example, ''balloon'' could be a code word for ''camera.'' In a cipher each letter is changed. The use of codes and ciphers for secret writing is called **cryptography.**

▶CIPHERS

There are two types of ciphers: transposition and substitution. In a transposition cipher the letters of the message are jumbled. In a substitution cipher the letters of the message are replaced, either by different letters or by other symbols.

Transposition Ciphers. To construct a simple transposition cipher, first draw a square grid of boxes, as shown below. The number of boxes in the grid can vary depending on the length of your message. Write the original message, called the **plaintext,** in the grid, placing one letter in each box. Each row should contain an equal number of letters, so fill in any unused boxes at the end with

dummy letters, called **nulls.** The message MEET ME AT SIX TOMORROW might be written like this:

M	E	E	T
M	E	A	T
S	I	X	T
O	M	O	R
R	O	W	L

Next, decide on some route to follow, such as up and down the columns, and copy the letters in that order. If you start at the upper left-hand corner and go down the first column and up the next, the message will read MMSOR OMIEE EAXOW LRTTT.

The person receiving the jumbled message must know or must figure out which route was followed. Then he or she can reconstruct the message.

Substitution Ciphers. In a substitution cipher the letters of the message do not change their order. Instead, other symbols are substituted for the message letters. Every R in the message might be replaced by a T, or every B by a !, or every C by a 3, for example.

A famous substitution cipher was used by Julius Caesar about 58 B.C. To put a message into the Caesar cipher, first write out the alphabet. Then underneath it, write the alphabet again, but shift forward three places so that

Rail Fence Cipher

Write your message on two lines, putting every other letter on the bottom line. The letters should follow the zigzag path of a rail fence. The message MEET ME AT NOON would be written like this:

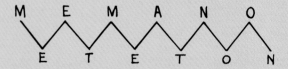

Then write out the letters in the top line, followed by the letters in the bottom line: MEMANO ETETON. If you wish, you can break the letters up into smaller groups to resemble words: ME MANO ET ETON.

To decode a message written in this cipher, divide the message in half. Place the letters back in the rail fence pattern, with the left half on top and the right half on the bottom. Then read in a zigzag pattern, taking the first letter from the top row, the second from the bottom, and so on.

Pigpen Cipher

To use the pigpen cipher, the letters of the alphabet are placed in special grids:

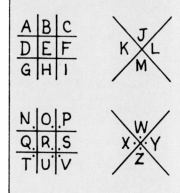

---

the A in the bottom row is under the D in the top row. Continue writing the alphabet until you reach the Z in the top row. Then go back and place the three leftover letters—X, Y, and Z—under the A, B, and C in the top row. Your two rows should look like this:

A B C D E F G H I J K L M N O P Q R S T U V W X Y Z
X Y Z A B C D E F G H I J K L M N O P Q R S T U V W

To write your secret message, substitute the letter in the bottom line for the letter in the top line wherever it appears in the message. Here is a **cryptogram,** or secret message, based on the Caesar cipher: MBQBO EXP QEB MIXKB QFZHBQP. And here is the solution: Peter has the plane tickets.

If you received this secret message but did not know the key—which letter was substituted for which—you might still be able to decipher the message. You could try different letters of the alphabet, beginning with the ones most often used. In English the letter E is used most often, so E would be tried in place of the letter that appears most frequently in the cipher. The letter T is the next most used, so it would be tried for the next most frequent letter in the cipher, and so forth.

Numbers can also be used to replace letters in a substitution cipher. If 1 is substituted for A, 2 for B, and so on, the message MEET ME AT THE LIBRARY would appear:

13-5-5-20 13-5 1-20 20-8-5
12-9-2-18-1-18-25

You may also count backwards, so that Z is 1, Y is 2, and so on.

Simple substitution ciphers play an important part in two famous stories—Edgar Allan Poe's *Gold Bug* and Arthur Conan Doyle's *Adventure of the Dancing Men.*

▶SECRET CODES

Codes are worked word by word instead of letter by letter. Because it would be very difficult to learn a code by heart, a code book must be used. When George Washington set up his spy system during the American Revolution, he had his spies use a code book that listed numbers for all the words they might need. The messages were written and decoded according to the numbers given in the book.

Of course, if a code book is lost or stolen, its code system loses its value. The finder or thief could decode any secret messages sent in that code. For example, the captain of a naval vessel during wartime must have a code book for sending and receiving messages about the enemy. If his ship is about to be captured by the enemy, he must destroy his code book.

Secret codes that are spoken rather than written are called jargon codes. They are particularly useful to people like air force pilots. In jargon codes important words are replaced by other words that seem to make sense when put together in a sentence. For instance, a list of code words may show that the jargon word LIBRARY stands for JACK'S HOUSE, MEET stands for GO, and ALWAYS stands for NOT. The sentence WE ALWAYS MEET

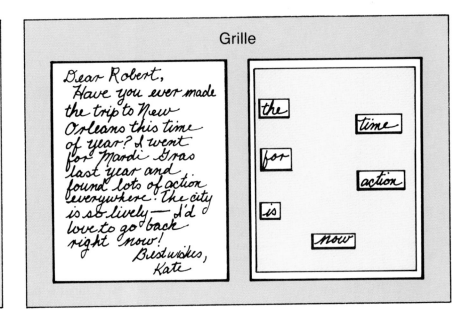

Grille

To write a message, replace the letter you want to use with the section of the grid that contains that letter. For example, ⌐ would stand for A, ⌐ for B, and ⊏ for S.

Here is a message written using the pigpen cipher:

And here is the solution: DELIVER THE PACKAGE TODAY.

AT THE LIBRARY would be decoded as DO NOT GO TO JACK'S HOUSE.

Secret languages like pig Latin are a form of jargon code. They follow one simple rule. In pig Latin the rule is to move the first letter of each word to the end of the word and add the letters AY. DOG becomes OGDAY. CATCHER becomes ATCHERCAY.

▶HIDDEN MESSAGES

Another way to send a secret message is to hide it within an innocent-looking text. One method of doing this is to use a grille. To make a grille, take two sheets of stiff paper and cut identical holes in each one. Then give one sheet to a friend and keep the other for yourself. Whenever you want to write a message, put the grille over a clean sheet of paper and write the secret message through the holes. Then remove the grille and fill up the rest of the paper with words that will make some sense. When the person who has the other grille puts it over the writing, the secret message will be revealed.

▶HISTORY

Codes and ciphers have played an important part in the history of the world. Military leaders have often used them to prevent important information from reaching enemy hands. As we have seen, Julius Caesar used a cipher to send secret messages to his generals, and George Washington's spies used a code to send him information about the enemy British during the Revolutionary War. In World War II the Americans "broke," or figured out, Japan's most important naval code and got enough information to destroy a powerful Japanese fleet.

In the 16th century, codes and ciphers were very popular among scientists. They wrote messages to one another in code so that no one else would learn their secrets. One of these scientists, Giambattista della Porta, wrote a book about codes. He is sometimes called the father of modern cryptography. Galileo Galilei, the famous Italian astronomer and physicist, recorded his discovery of the phases of the planet Venus in a kind of cipher.

Today, codes and ciphers continue to be used by military organizations and government agents to protect top-secret information. Business executives may use them to hide plans from competitors. Personal letters and diaries are sometimes written in code. In addition, many people enjoy working out codes and ciphers simply as a hobby.

The ciphers and codes used by experts are far more complicated than any described in this article, but the basic methods of construction are the same. It takes years of training and practice to become an expert at making and breaking codes, but anyone can have fun using simple ciphers and solving the mysteries of a coded message.

Reviewed by SAM AND BERYL EPSTEIN
Authors, *The First Book of Codes and Ciphers*

CODY, WILLIAM FREDERICK. See BUFFALO BILL.

COELENTERATES. See JELLYFISHES AND OTHER COELENTERATES.

The coffee plant (*left*) produces white flowers and then red berries (*center*), or "beans." The beans (*right*) are dried, roasted, ground, and packaged for sale.

COFFEE

When coffee was first introduced to Western Europe, about 1615, some people said it was intoxicating. Others thought it was poisonous. But gradually coffee was accepted. Coffee houses became centers of social, literary, and political life. Today the "coffee break" is a regular morning ritual in homes and offices in many parts of the world.

▶THE COFFEE PLANT

Coffee is a beverage made, or brewed, from the roasted bean (seed) of the coffee plant. Most of the coffee raised today comes from one kind of plant, called *Coffea arabica,* or Arabian coffee plant, although it is grown in coffee regions all over the world. Arabian coffee plants are evergreen shrubs or small trees, with dark green, waxy leaves.

Coffee grows best in tropical highlands, where lower temperatures and slow ripening produce a mild coffee. In areas having definite wet and dry seasons, coffee plants begin to flower toward the end of the dry period.

It takes 5 to 7 months for the fragrant white blossoms to turn into ripe fruit. The bright red berries are bunched in clumps between the leaves. Each berry contains two seeds. A layer of sweet, sticky pulp lies between the seeds and the outer skin. A thin, parchmentlike covering and a silvery inner skin further protect the seeds.

The plants do not come into full production for 6 to 7 years. Their productive life varies from 15 to 30 years, depending on the variety, climate, soil, and care. An annual yield of 1,000 pounds (454 kilograms) of dry coffee beans per acre is considered a good crop.

Harvesting the Berries

Because a coffee plant flowers in several "flushes," or intervals, the berries do not all ripen at once. Berries of different ages are found on the same tree at the same time. The berries are usually picked as they ripen.

Harvesting has remained a hand operation, but changing the berries into "coffee beans" is done by machine. In the **dry method** the berries are first dried. Then the pulp, the parchment shell, and the silver skin are removed to reveal the gray-green seeds, or beans. The **wet method** is thought to give coffee a better flavor. The berries are put through a machine that removes the outer skin and as much of the pulp as possible. The seeds are then fermented in tanks of water until the remaining pulp loosens and can be washed away. The clean seeds are dried for several days in the sun or in a mechanical hot-air drier before the parchment coat and silver skin are peeled off.

Coffee is shipped to market in coarse fiber bags. A bag of coffee beans weighs about 132 pounds (60 kilograms). Dry coffee, properly stored, can be kept for several years without affecting its quality.

Processing the Beans

Roasting the coffee beans brings out the characteristic coffee tang and aroma. Most coffee products are a mixture of different varieties of *Coffea arabica* beans. The only way to discover what a mixture will taste like is to select, roast, and brew a test batch. Skilled coffee tasters sample the brew and judge its quality.

After the outside shells are cracked off, the roasted beans are ground into different grades of fineness. The standard grades are drip, regular, and fine. Each grade is meant to be brewed in a different kind of pot.

In many European countries and in the American South, the root of the chicory plant is roasted with the coffee beans. Chicory gives the coffee bulk. It also makes the coffee's color darker and its taste more bitter.

One of the most important steps in coffee processing is careful and rapid packaging. Once coffee has been roasted, it loses its flavor unless it is sealed away from the air. Vacuum-sealed cans, jars, and foil packages keep the coffee fresh until it can be used.

▶BREWING A CUP OF COFFEE

To someone who has never tasted coffee before, its rich aroma may be more appealing than the first bitter sip. But to people who have acquired a taste for coffee, it is delicious.

Most experts say that the best cup of coffee is brewed by the **drip,** or filter, method. Hot water is poured onto ground coffee held in a paper filter. The brewed coffee drips down into a container. Most drip coffee makers are automatic. Water is boiled inside the electric appliance and filters through the coffee.

Coffee may also be brewed in a percolator —a pot in which boiling water repeatedly rises through a tube and drips down again through a basket containing ground coffee. **Espresso** coffee is darker and stronger than regular coffee; it is traditionally made in a special espresso machine by forcing steam through

Coffee beans are roasted in revolving metal cylinders. The beans are then cooled, sorted according to grade, ground, and vacuum-packaged for freshness.

dark-roasted and finely ground beans. **Café au lait** is made of equal quantities of freshly brewed coffee and hot milk.

Instant coffee is actually coffee made twice. The manufacturer brews a strong coffee and then dries it into powder in a vacuum. **Freeze-dried** instant coffee is made by brewing the coffee, then evaporating the water out of it. The resulting extract is frozen and then placed in a pressurized chamber where moisture in the form of ice is drawn off, leaving dried coffee crystals. Both types of coffee can be drunk once hot water is added.

Manufacturers have also developed a special kind of coffee called **decaffeinated**. The coffee bean contains from 1 to 2 percent caffeine, a stimulant that keeps some people awake or makes them nervous. Caffeine is removed by soaking the unroasted beans in a chemical solvent or by steaming them.

▶HISTORY OF COFFEE

No one knows exactly how coffee was discovered. The first coffee plants probably grew in Kaffa, a province of southwestern Ethiopia. This province may have given coffee its name. Persian armies in the 6th century probably carried coffee seeds to the Arabian Peninsula. There the Arabs brewed the bitter but stimulating seeds into a drink to make them taste better. Soon the new beverage spread to Europe. By the beginning of the 17th century, so much coffee was passing through the Arabian port of Mocha that mocha became another word for coffee.

During the 18th century, coffee culture spread to Asia and the New World. The Netherlands East Indies, now called Indonesia, dominated the world market for nearly a century. Brazil then took over the leading position and has held it for many decades.

After Brazil, the leading coffee-producing countries are Colombia, Mexico, Indonesia, Vietnam, Ethiopia, Uganda, and Guatemala. The United States is the leading consumer, followed by Germany, Japan, France, Italy, Scandinavia, and Spain.

HAROLD F. WINTERS
U.S. Department of Agriculture

See also TEA.

COFFIN, LEVI. See UNDERGROUND RAILROAD (Profiles).

COHAN, GEORGE M. See RHODE ISLAND (Famous People).

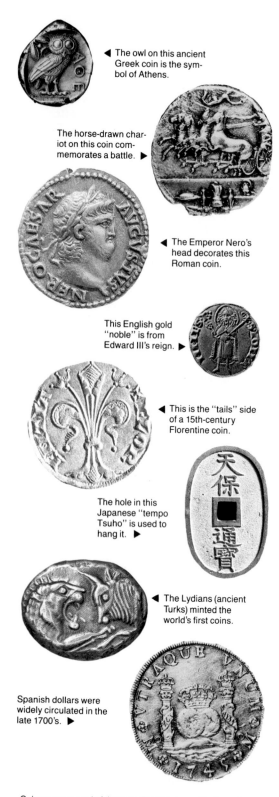

The owl on this ancient Greek coin is the symbol of Athens.

The horse-drawn chariot on this coin commemorates a battle. ▶

◀ The Emperor Nero's head decorates this Roman coin.

This English gold "noble" is from Edward III's reign. ▶

◀ This is the "tails" side of a 15th-century Florentine coin.

The hole in this Japanese "tempo Tsuho" is used to hang it. ▶

◀ The Lydians (ancient Turks) minted the world's first coins.

Spanish dollars were widely circulated in the late 1700's. ▶

Coins are a record of the past. They may provide the only portraits of some ancient rulers; they commemorate famous battles; and they can tell us something about the daily lives of the people who used them.

COINS AND COIN COLLECTING

Coin collecting—referred to as **numismatics**—is one of the oldest known hobbies. It is also a pleasant way to save money. The word "numismatics" comes from the Greek word *nomisma* and the Latin word *numisma*, meaning a coin. People who collect coins are called numismatists.

The designs on coins tell many stories. Some ancient coins tell us all we know about a country or a period of history. They bring us portraits of otherwise unknown rulers. Coins of past centuries tell us about the art, mythology, religion, and fashions of people who lived long ago.

A great variety of things were used as money before coins were invented. The article MONEY in Volume M explains the development of the money we use now.

Almost 3,000 years ago the Chinese had a form of money made from metal. But the first coin with a fixed value was not struck (made or minted) until the 7th century B.C. in Lydia (now Turkey). Ever since, coins have helped the world carry on its trade and commerce.

▶STARTING A COLLECTION

Your special interests will help you decide the kind of coin collection you would like to assemble. You may wish to collect the coins of one country or one part of the world. Or you may want your collection to contain coins from all over the world but limited to a certain period of time.

Some people choose to collect the coins of their own country, while others are interested in ancient Greek and Roman coins. Many ancient coins are quite easy to obtain. Small ancient bronze pieces in average condition can often be bought fairly cheaply. A collection of present-day coins from countries forming the United Nations is not costly and is worldwide in scope.

▶CARING FOR YOUR COLLECTION

There are many ways to arrange coin collections. Some collectors keep their coins in small square envelopes. A complete description of the coins should be written on the outside of the envelopes. These envelopes are arranged in cardboard boxes. Envelopes and boxes may be bought at any coin store. You can also use transparent envelopes.

For a worthwhile collection, numismatists advise that you choose the coin in the best condition you can find. Experts classify the condition of coins according to the amount of wear they have received. **Proof** coins are struck especially for collectors and have a very shiny surface. **Uncirculated** coins were struck for general use but were never circulated. These are the most valuable coins to collect— and the hardest to obtain. **Extremely fine, very fine,** and **fine** coins have been in circulation and show varying degrees of wear. **Very good** and **good** coins are worn, but the details of the design can be seen clearly. And coins in **fair** condition show much wear but can still be identified.

Never clean a coin unless it is caked with dirt. Remove the dirt by washing the coin gently with soap and warm water. Do not use scouring powder, metal polish, or steel wool. This will damage both the looks and value of the coin.

▶**STUDYING YOUR HOBBY**

To get the most enjoyment from your hobby of coin collecting, read as much as you can on the subject. Try to form a group of collector friends. Visit special exhibitions and have a reliable dealer through whom you can buy your coins. If you have an old or foreign coin, find out where and when it was made, its name and value, and what you could have bought with it when it was in use.

Many thousands of books and publications have been written about coins. Your public library probably has a number of them. Of interest to the collector of modern coins are: *Handbook of United States Coins,* R. S. Yeoman, Racine, Wisconsin (published annually); and *Modern World Coins: An Illustrated Catalog with Valuations,* R. S. Yeoman, Racine, Wisconsin.

Among the monthly magazines is *The Numismatist,* the official publication of the American Numismatic Association. Many notes of interest may also be found in weekly journals such as *Coin World* and *Numismatic News.*

For answers to your coin collecting problems, write the Division of Numismatics, Smithsonian Institution, Washington, D.C. 20560. The Smithsonian, however, will not advise on the money value of coins. Consult a coin dealer for this kind of information.

◀ Special mint and proof sets of U.S. coins are available to collectors. This set includes the Kennedy half-dollar.

U.S. quarters (worth ¼ dollar) issued after 1965 contain no silver. ▶

◀ The dime (¹/₁₀ of a dollar) is the smallest U.S. coin in circulation.

The Lincoln cent (¹/₁₀₀ of a dollar) was first minted in 1909. ▶

◀ A competition decided the design of the Jefferson nickel.

The "P" in this mint set indicates that it was minted in Philadelphia, the first U.S. mint (1792). ▶

Why Are Some Coins Grooved Around the Edge?
Pennies and nickels have smooth edges, but coins of higher value are milled, or grooved, around the edge. When coins were made of silver and gold, people used to trim the edges and sell the precious metal. The best way to stop this was to mill the edges of the more valuable coins so that trimming would be noticed. This practice continues, even though few coins of precious metal are circulated.

▶**COLLECTING UNITED STATES COINS**

One way to start a coin collection is to select the best examples of coins now in use. You may be able to assemble an interesting series of United States coins with different dates and mintmarks. Special mint sets and proof sets of United States coins are sometimes available. For information, write to the Office of the Director of the Mint, U.S. Treasury Department, Washington, D.C. 20220.

The first coins of the United States were authorized by the Mint Act of April 2, 1792. By 1793 the Mint in Philadelphia was issuing gold, silver, and copper coins. The gold coins were eagles with the value of ten dollars. There were also half eagles and quarter eagles. The silver coins were dollars, half-dollars, dimes, and half dimes. The copper coins were cents and half cents.

Historic U.S. coins (*left to right*): A colonial dollar, designed by Benjamin Franklin; an 1873 $20 gold piece; an Indian-head penny, made from 1859 to 1909; Delaware's commemorative quarter, featuring statesman Caesar Rodney riding to cast the state's vote for independence during the Revolutionary War.

Since then there have been many changes in coins and the laws governing coinage. Among the coins no longer made or issued are half dimes and half cents. The five-cent coin appeared in 1886. No silver dollars were coined from 1935, and none issued from 1964 until 1971, when the first silver-clad Eisenhower dollars were minted.

A coin's design may not be changed more than once in 25 years, except by an act of Congress. In 1965, Congress passed a law making the first major change in coinage in more than 100 years. Because of shortages, silver was left out of dimes and quarters. Silver in half-dollars was reduced in 1965 and stopped altogether after 1970.

The latest change came in 1999 when the first in a series of 50 new quarters commemorating each state was issued. Five quarters will be issued per year, until 2008, in the order the states joined the Union. Each quarter will have a unique design on the back.

For information on coin-collecting clubs, contact the American Numismatic Association, based in Colorado Springs, Colorado.

V. CLAIN-STEFANELLI
Curator, Division of Numismatics
Smithsonian Institution

COKE.   See FUELS.

COLD, COMMON.   See DISEASES (Descriptions of Some Diseases).

COLD WAR

The Cold War dominated political life in the second half of the 20th century. It began in 1945, as World War II was ending, and continued through several phases until it was formally declared over in 1990.

The Nature of the Cold War. The Cold War, in one sense, was a power struggle between the two nuclear military giants of the age, the United States and the Soviet Union. But on a more basic level, the Cold War was a contest between two opposing ways of life. One was democratic capitalism, whose leading representatives were the United States and the nations of Western Europe. The other was totalitarian Communism, the system of the Soviet Union and its "satellite" nations in Eastern Europe.

Between 1945 and 1990, despite constant tensions and an alarming buildup of nuclear arms on both sides, the United States and the Soviet Union officially remained at peace—hence the name the "cold" war. Yet it was hardly a peaceful era.

The Cold War Begins. The Cold War started when the Soviet Union began imposing Communist regimes on weaker countries throughout Eastern Europe. The United States and its allies feared both this sudden increase in Soviet power and further Soviet expansion. Deep mistrust of the ruthless Soviet dictator Joseph Stalin only intensified Western fears.

To contain the spread of Communism, the United States under President Harry S. Truman introduced the **Truman Doctrine** (1947) and the **Marshall Plan** (1948). The Truman Doctrine provided military and economic aid to Greece and Turkey. The Marshall Plan provided economic assistance to all the war-torn countries of Western Europe. Although these programs weakened Communist influences throughout Western Europe, by 1948 the Soviets had firmly established Communist rule in Eastern Europe.

The Soviets countered the Marshall Plan with the Berlin Blockade. They hoped to force the United States, Great Britain, and France to abandon their postwar occupation of West Berlin, which was surrounded by Soviet-controlled territory in Germany that later became the Communist state of East Germany. But the allies defeated the blockade with the Berlin Airlift (1948–49). Meanwhile, in 1949, the United States, Britain, France, Canada, and eight other nations formed the North Atlantic Treaty Organization (NATO), a common defense treaty to prevent Soviet aggression. In 1955, the Soviet Union and its Eastern European satellites formed the Warsaw Pact to counter NATO's military strength.

The Cold War intensified in 1949 when the Soviet Union tested its first atomic bomb. That same year in China, the Communists under Mao Zedong won a civil war that brought the world's most populous nation into the Communist camp.

The Cold War turned hot in Asia in 1950, when Communist North Korea, with Soviet approval, invaded non-Communist South Korea. The United States, under the banner of the United Nations, led the defense of South Korea during the Korean War (1950–53).

To the Brink of Nuclear War. Joseph Stalin's death in 1953 led to a brief improvement in Soviet-American relations. But in 1962, with John F. Kennedy in the White House and Nikita Khrushchev leading the Soviet Union, the Cold War reached its most dangerous moment. For two weeks during the Cuban Missile Crisis, the two superpowers stood at the brink of nuclear war before finally resolving their differences.

Vietnam and Détente. After the Cuban missile crisis, the United States became increasingly involved in an unsuccessful war to stop Communist expansion into South Vietnam. However, while the Vietnam War was at its height in the late 1960's and early 1970's, Soviet-American relations improved, despite the Soviets' aid to North Vietnam. This détente (relaxation of tensions) between the superpowers produced the first nuclear arms control agreement, in 1972. Another important event during this period was the deepening feud between the Soviet Union and Communist China, which divided the Communist world.

The End of the Cold War. Several crises, including a Soviet invasion of Afghanistan in 1979, ended détente. But relations improved again in 1985, when Mikhail Gorbachev, who wished to end Cold War tensions, became the Soviet leader. He found an enthusiastic partner in U.S. president Ronald Reagan, who earlier had called the Soviet Union an "evil empire." In 1987, the two leaders signed the first treaty to eliminate an entire class of nuclear weapons.

In 1989, popular discontent led to the collapse of the Soviet Union's Communist allies in Eastern Europe. The most dramatic event of that year took place when the disintegrating government of East Germany tore down the Berlin Wall, the most powerful symbol of the Cold War. By 1990, at a meeting in Paris, U.S. president George Bush was able to announce, "We have closed a chapter in history. The Cold War is over." The following year, the Soviet Union ceased to exist.

MICHAEL G. KORT
Boston University

See also BERLIN; CAPITALISM; COMMUNISM; CUBAN MISSILE CRISIS; DISARMAMENT; KOREAN WAR; SOCIALISM; UNION OF SOVIET SOCIALIST REPUBLICS (The Cold War); UNITED STATES, HISTORY OF THE (World Power); VIETNAM WAR.

COLE, THOMAS. See NEW YORK (Famous People).

COLEMAN, ORNETTE. See JAZZ (Profiles).

COLFAX, SCHUYLER. See VICE PRESIDENCY OF THE UNITED STATES.

In the 1950's and 1960's many people feared that the Cold War between the world's superpowers would end in nuclear war. As a precaution, some Americans built bomb shelters to protect their families.

COLLAGE

A collage is a picture made by pasting pieces of paper, cloth, or other materials onto a flat surface such as a piece of cardboard. *Collage* is a French word for "pasting."

The collage technique has been used in folk art for centuries. Modern artists began to use collage about 1912. Artists such as Pablo Picasso and Georges Braque added parts of newsprint, wallpaper, and other materials to their paintings and drawings.

Collages are easily made at home. All you need are ordinary materials such as old newspapers and magazines, theater or bus tickets, some rags, and perhaps colored tissue or construction paper. Contrasting textures may be added to your collage with bits of a burlap bag or sandpaper. The most important tools you need, however, are paste and your own imagination.

Your first collage may be something simple—a birthday or holiday card, for example. With a little more work, you can make pictures of children playing in a park, a barnyard with animals, or a still life with a bowl of fruit.

One of the most interesting kinds of collage you can make is an abstract design. To create such a collage, cut and tear your paper and fabric into shapes that do not resemble real objects. When you paste them on your cardboard, try to contrast the different shapes and textures.

The best collages will result from experiments. Colored tissue paper, when pasted flat with rubber cement, is transparent, and countless effects can be created by pasting tissue on top of newspaper, sandpaper, or cloth. On the other hand, it is often effective to wrinkle the tissue when pasting it down. Some of whatever is underneath then shows through, while other parts do not. Another way to achieve interesting effects is to sprinkle sand, coffee grounds, or uncooked rice over a glue-covered area. The grains stick to the glue, creating unusual and varied textures.

A collage may be made quickly, with no planning at all, or it may be made with great detail. The way you make yours depends on how you like to work, but as a beginner it is best to try both. Make one collage by quickly tearing, cutting, and pasting shapes onto a piece of cardboard. Then try planning a second collage. Cut out all the shapes you plan

Many different types of materials, including currency and playing cards, were used in making this abstract collage entitled *Future Traders #2*.

to use and lay them on the cardboard. Add more shapes, take some away, or change the form of others. Use a pencil to trace lines around each shape on the cardboard. Remove and coat the shapes with paste, then replace them within their proper guidelines.

GIUSEPPI BAGGI
Collage Artist

See also CUBISM; DESIGN; MODERN ART.

COLLECTIVE BARGAINING. See LABOR-MANAGEMENT RELATIONS.

COLLEGES AND UNIVERSITIES. See UNIVERSITIES AND COLLEGES.

COLLINS, WILKIE. See MYSTERY AND DETECTIVE STORIES (Profiles).

COLOMBIA

Colombia is the fourth largest and second most populous country in South America. Located on the northwestern part of the continent, it is bounded on the west by the Pacific Ocean and on the north by Panama and the Caribbean Sea. Its neighbors to the east are Venezuela and Brazil and to the south, Peru and Ecuador. The equator passes through the country's southernmost regions. Colombia was named for Christopher Columbus, the explorer who claimed much of the New World for Spain in the late 1400's.

The landscape features rugged mountains, high plateaus, and deep valleys as well as vast expanses of lowland tropical forests and grasslands. Varied climates, soils, vegetation, and mineral resources, together with the difficulty of travel in the mountains, have led to the development of several different ways of life. Food, dress, housing, and livelihoods vary significantly from region to region.

▶ PEOPLE

Colombia's people represent a mix of ethnic groups. About 58 percent are mestizos (people of mixed European and Indian ancestry). Another 20 percent are of European (primarily Spanish) ancestry. About 14 percent are mulatto (people of mixed European and African ancestry); 4 percent are of African ancestry; and 3 percent are a mix of African and Indian. Pure-blooded Indians survive in scattered settlements and account for only 1 percent of the population.

Language. The official language of Colombia is Spanish, the language spoken by the early colonial settlers. However, Colombia's constitution recognizes the languages of Colombia's native Indian groups.

Religion. About 95 percent of Colombians belong to the Roman Catholic Church, which exercises considerable influence and holds a privileged legal status. Small Protestant and Jewish communities exist as well.

Education and Libraries. Elementary education is free and required by law for a minimum of five years. There are some large, modern school buildings in the cities, but many schools in the countryside have only one or two classrooms. Religious instruction is required in all public schools. Illiteracy remains a national concern.

Colombians represent a variety of ethnic groups, including (*clockwise from left*) Europeans (primarily Spanish); Africans; mestizos (a mix of European and Indian); and Indians.

Colombia has numerous colleges and universities. The largest is the National University of Colombia, in Bogotá. The National Library, founded in 1777, administers town and village libraries throughout the country.

Dress. A traditional sleeveless Colombian garment is the *ruana*, or poncho. It consists of a square of material, usually wool, with a slit in the center for one's head to slip through. Handwoven fiber hats and fiber shoes, or *alpargatas*, are also typically worn.

Sports. Soccer (*futbol* in Spanish) is the favorite national sport. *Tejo* is a Chibcha Indian game similar to pitching horseshoes. Baseball, long played on the Caribbean coast, is becoming equally popular in the interior. Crowds also turn out to watch bullfights and cockfights, traditional Spanish sports, as well as long-distance bicycle races and horse races.

▶ **LAND**

Land Regions. Three great ranges of the Andes mountains divide the country into three major regions—the highlands, the east-

The eastern plains, or *llanos* (*above*), cover about two-thirds of the Colombian landscape. However, the highlands within the Andes Mountains (*far right*) and the coastal lowlands along the Caribbean Sea (*right*) are more densely populated.

ern plains, and the coastal lowlands. The highlands contain Colombia's largest cities as well as its prime agricultural areas. Grassy plains, or *llanos*, cover the vast expanse of thinly populated land that stretches eastward from the Andes toward the Orinoco and Amazon rivers. More people live on the wide coastal plain leading to the Caribbean. This region contains the country's highest point, Pico Cristóbal Colón, which rises to a height of 19,020 feet (5,797 meters). The Pacific coastal region is densely forested.

Rivers. The principal river of Colombia is the broad Magdalena. It flows northward for about 1,000 miles (1,600 kilometers) between the central and eastern Andean ranges and empties into the Caribbean. Farther west is the Cauca River, a tributary of the Magdalena. Its upper valley, around Cali, contains Colombia's richest farming area.

Climate. Like most countries close to the equator, temperatures vary little throughout the year. Differences depend on elevation, with the higher the land above sea level, the cooler the temperature year-round. In the Andes, average temperatures range from 57°F (14°C) to 73°F (23°C). The hottest climate is found in the Caribbean coastal plain, where temperatures average 82°F (28°C).

Most of Colombia experiences four seasons, two wet and two dry. The wet seasons last from March to May and from September to November; the dry seasons occur between

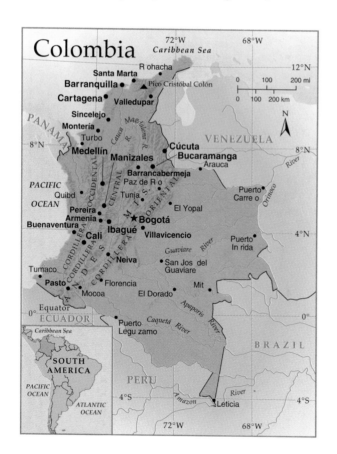

December and February and June through August. The area along the Pacific coastal lowlands is one of the rainiest in the world, with annual precipitation exceeding 300 inches (7,600 millimeters).

Natural Resources. Soils are Colombia's most important natural resources, owing to the country's dependence on agriculture. Colombia also has rich mineral deposits of coal, copper, iron ore, nickel, antimony, bauxite, silver, and gold.

The country's rivers offer great potential for the development of hydroelectric power. The upper Cauca River has been harnessed to provide electric power and control floods.

For many years rain forests in the Amazon Basin have been cleared for a variety of commercial reasons. Thus, the preservation of Colombia's forest resources has become a matter of international concern.

▶ ECONOMY

Colombia's economy, once dependent on agriculture, has become increasingly diversified. Today, agriculture accounts for 19 percent; manufacturing and mining together account for 26 percent; and services account for 55 percent. Not included in Colombia's

official statistics is the estimated $300 million brought in annually through the cultivation of coca and the illegal cocaine trade.

Services. Colombia's service industries employ more than half of Colombia's workforce. They include banking, insurance, transportation, communication, wholesale and retail sales, and personal services. Tourism, which is limited due to long-standing social and political turmoil, is centered around the country's national parks, beaches, and archaeological sites.

Manufacturing. Industry is rapidly expanding. Principal products include textiles, processed foods, oil, clothing and footwear, beverages, chemicals, and cement. Iron ore is used to make steel.

Agriculture. Agriculture employs more than 25 percent of Colombia's workforce. The most important crops are coffee, flowers, bananas, rice, and tobacco. Colombia ranks second only to Brazil in coffee production. Livestock (sheep and beef cattle), forest products, and shrimp are also significant.

Mining. Colombia is the world's leading producer of emeralds and South America's leading producer of gold. Oil, recently discovered east of Bogotá, is also mined. This, along with the country's reserves of coal and natural gas, should make Colombia self-sufficient in energy for many years to come.

Trade. Oil, coffee beans, bananas, and cut flowers are the leading exported goods, with the United States ranked as their primary destination. Colombia is also a major exporter of coal. The major imports are industrial and transportation equipment, consumer goods, chemicals, and paper products.

REPUBLIC OF COLOMBIA (República de Colombia) is the official name of the country.

LOCATION: Northwestern South America.

AREA: 439,735 sq mi (1,138,914 km²).

POPULATION: 38,500,000 (1998 estimate).

CAPITAL AND LARGEST CITY: Bogotá.

MAJOR LANGUAGE: Spanish.

MAJOR RELIGIOUS GROUP: Roman Catholic.

GOVERNMENT: Republic. **Head of state and government**—president. **Legislature**—Congress (consisting of a senate and a house of representatives).

CHIEF PRODUCTS: Agricultural—coffee, flowers, bananas, rice, tobacco, corn, sugarcane, cocoa beans, forest products, livestock, and aquaculture. **Manufactured**—textiles, food processing (particularly coffee), clothing and footwear, beverages, chemicals, cement. **Mineral**—petroleum, coal, iron, natural gas, gold, emeralds and other precious stones.

MONETARY UNIT: 1 Peso equals 100 centavos.

Transportation. The mountainous landscape has always made it difficult to build highways and railroads across Colombia. Rivers, particularly the Magdalena, have thus been the main transport system. Pack mules and horses are used to carry goods and people overland. In 1961 a railroad line was completed between the Caribbean coast and Bogotá. Four major highways link cities in the interior with Caribbean ports and with the port of Buenaventura, on the Pacific coast. Air transport is also of major importance. International airports are located in Bogotá, Medellín, and Cali.

Communication. *El Tiempo* of Bogotá is one of the most influential newspapers in the Americas. Colombia also has a very active book publishing industry, as well as commercial and state-owned radio and television broadcasters. Cable television services operate in the larger cities.

▶ **MAJOR CITIES**

Although Colombia's major cities are very different from one another, all are growing in

The red berries of the coffee plant are harvested by hand. Colombia is the world's second largest producer of coffee, after Brazil.

population. The large numbers of people moving in from the countryside in search of industrial jobs has led to an epidemic of urban poverty and lack of adequate housing.

Bogotá, the capital, is home to approximately 6 million people. It is the national center of commerce, education, and culture. For more information, see the article BOGOTÁ in Volume B.

Medellín, with a population of 2 million, is Colombia's second most populous city. It is the center of industry, coffee growing, and mining. Many large, modern textile factories are also located there.

Barranquilla, Colombia's chief port and a center of shipbuilding, is situated where the Magdalena River empties into the Caribbean Sea. It is noted for its carnival celebration.

Cali is the chief city of the Cauca Valley. Sugar is an important local crop. Textiles, paper, soap, and plastics are the city's chief manufactured goods.

▶ **CULTURAL HERITAGE**

Music. Colombian music expresses the diversity of its people. Oldest in origin is the music performed on simple wood flutes, still favored in the Andean highlands. The African

tradition is evident in dance music called *cumbia*, which combines native flutes with African-style drums, shakers, and scrapers. Also African in origin is *currulao*, or marimba, music. *Vallenata*, a type of music that originated among the mestizos, features the accordion. Salsa incorporates bits of several traditions in a modern jazz style.

Art and Architecture. Native art—gold works, stone carvings, utensils, textiles, and other objects dating from before the colonial era—are featured exhibits at the Archaeological and Gold museums in Bogotá. Modern artists are also celebrated, among them Omar Rayo and Fernando Botero. Architecture traditionally shared many features of Spanish colonial style but has been modified over time.

Literature. Colombia is sometimes called the land of poets, because it has produced so many fine writers of verse. One of the best-known Colombian writers of fiction is the novelist Jorge Isaacs (1837–95). His romantic novel *María*, published in 1867, is still widely read. Gabriel García Márquez (1927–   ), the most widely acclaimed Colombian novelist of recent times, was awarded the Nobel Prize for literature in 1982.

▶ **GOVERNMENT**

Colombia is a republic. It is headed by a president, who is elected for a 4-year term and cannot serve two terms in succession. The president appoints a cabinet to help run the national government.

The legislative body is the Congress, composed of a senate and a house of representatives. Members are elected for 4-year terms at the same time as the president. Local government is managed within 32 departments, or states, each with its own elected governor. All citizens 18 years or older may vote.

In 1991, Colombia's constitution was revised, primarily to modernize the judicial system and reduce political interference in court proceedings.

▶ **HISTORY**

Early History. Colombia's first inhabitants are believed

Traditional Colombian architecture, such as this church in Bogotá's Plaza Bolívar, followed the Spanish colonial style.

Gold jewelry and other pre-Columbian artworks exhibit the skill and artistry of Colombia's Native Indian ancestors.

to have come down from Central America. Because the first people built with wood rather than stone, little remains of their ancient cultures.

Spanish Colonial Period. When the first Spanish expeditions into Colombian territory began in 1499, three large groups of Indians lived in what is now Colombia—the Chibcha, the Quimbaya, and the Chocó. For more information, see the article INDIANS, AMERICAN in Volume I.

The first permanent European settlement in Colombia was made at Santa Marta, on the Caribbean coast, in 1525. The Spanish conquistador (conqueror) Gonzalo Jiménez de Quesada journeyed up the Magdalena River to conquer the Chibcha, and in 1538 he founded the city of Bogotá. The Indians survived the Spanish conquest. But their numbers were greatly reduced by disease and warfare.

In 1549 the former Chibcha Empire was incorporated into the new Spanish colony of New Granada, along with territories that later became the countries of Ecuador, Venezuela, and Panama. After two centuries of foreign rule, however, the people of New Granada began to demand independence.

Independence. Colombia's Independence Day, July 20, commemorates the day in 1810 when patriots set up the first free Colombian government. But it was nine years before the country was really free of Spanish rule. During that time, the battle for independence was led by a Venezuelan, Simón Bolívar. After his

In 1999, in an effort to end Colombia's long-standing civil war, President Andrés Pastrana Arango met with the leader of the guerrilla rebel group Revolutionary Armed Forces of America (FARC) to negotiate an end to the violence.

victory at Boyacá in 1819, Bolívar became president of the Republic of Gran (Greater) Colombia, which included the present nations of Ecuador, Venezuela, Panama, and Colombia. (For more information, see the article BOLÍVAR, SIMÓN in Volume B.)

In 1830, Venezuela and Ecuador broke away from Gran Colombia. Two years later, Francisco de Paula Santander became the first president of the renamed Republic of New Granada.

During the early years of the republic, two competing political parties developed—the Conservatives and the Liberals. The Conservatives favored a strong central government,

allied with the upper classes, the army, and the Catholic Church. The Liberals wanted a loose confederation of states and wished to take away the power and privileges of the church. The struggle was frequently bloody, and in 1899 the country descended into a full-scale civil war, known as the War of a Thousand Days. The war ended in 1902 when the two groups reached an agreement.

The 1900's. In 1903, Colombia negotiated the Hay-Herrán Treaty with the United States. The treaty gave the United States the right to lease a zone across Panama (then still a province of Colombia) in order to build a canal that would link the Atlantic and Pacific oceans. When the treaty was rejected by the Colombian Senate, Panamanians revolted. Then, with U.S. assistance, they proclaimed their independence.

In 1903 the Liberals won election and controlled the government for the next 16 years. Labor unions were made legal, and other social reforms were begun. Years later, in 1948, a well-known Liberal leader, Jorge Eliér Gaitán, was assassinated. Colombia was again plunged into a period of violence, known as *La Violencia*, in which approximately 300,000 Colombians lost their lives. In 1957, in an effort to end the political turmoil, the two parties formed an alliance called the National Front, which formally ended in 1974.

Recent History. Colombia's recent history has continued to be marked by violence. Kidnappings, assassinations, and even mass murders have become commonplace. The crimes have been committed mostly by guerrillas (rebels) opposed to the government or by gunmen hired to protect Colombia's notorious illegal drug trade.

Andrés Pastrana Arango, a Conservative, was elected president in 1998. The following year, Colombia was devastated by a major earthquake that killed more than one thousand people. In the same year, the government and members of the rebel group Revolutionary Armed Forces of America (FARC) held peace talks for the first time in seven years in an attempt to end the decades-long civil war.

JAMES J. PARSONS
University of California, Berkeley
Reviewed by THOMAS E. SKIDMORE
Author, *Modern Latin America*

COLONIALISM. See IMPERIALISM.

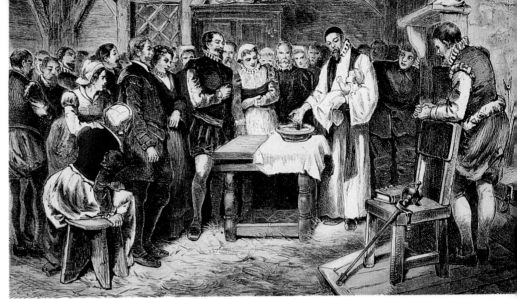

In 1587, Virginia Dare became the first English child born in what is now the United States. She and her parents were part of Roanoke Island's "lost colony." These colonists mysteriously disappeared before 1591, and they were never found.

COLONIAL LIFE IN AMERICA

The colonial period of American history (1607–1776) began with the first permanent English settlement in Jamestown, Virginia, and ended when the 13 colonies declared their independence from England. Within a 180-year span, the colonies evolved from a scattered group of small English settlements into a united country with people of many nationalities, who were capable of self-government and hungry for complete independence from what they saw as the meddling demands of the mother country—England.

In the early days of settlement, the English did not know how to live in the wilderness. George Percy, one of the Jamestown settlers, wrote, "There were never Englishmen left in a foreign country in such misery as we were in this newly discovered Virginia." Though they were occasionally threatened by the Indian natives, the settlers suffered mainly from hunger, exposure, and disease. When the food they had brought from England ran out, many died. They did not know how to hunt in the American forests even though the forests were filled with game. They might have planted gardens, but anyone strong enough to work had to help fortify the town and build houses. In addition, they wasted time looking for gold. Because the settlers did not know how to build log cabins, they quickly constructed less sturdy mud and frame houses like those built by poor farmers in England.

Throughout the 1600's people faced the same problems in almost every new settle-

This article describes the development of American colonial society from 1607 to 1776. It discusses family life, work, the home, religion, education, and amusements. For more information about the settlement of each of the 13 original colonies and the settlers' relationships with the Indians and the English, consult the THIRTEEN AMERICAN COLONIES article in Volume T.

The political revolution that led to the War for Independence from England is discussed in the REVOLUTIONARY WAR article in Volume R.

ment. In Massachusetts, the Plymouth settlers, sick and hungry, spent most of their first winter (1620–21) on board the *Mayflower*. The first Puritan settlers spent a winter (1630–31) in wigwams and sailcloth tents. Nearly one quarter of them died before a vessel from England brought fresh supplies.

In time the English learned how to live in the wilderness, learning by their own trials and errors and from some of the more friendly Indian tribes. By the 1700's, small cities and towns were well established. The fear of starving was behind them, and the colonists began planning a future for themselves, their children, and their grandchildren. They began to build permanent homes and public buildings; their farms and businesses flourished. As each new generation was brought into the world, memories of their English homeland began to fade. The colonists slowly developed their own customs and life-styles. Eventually they began to feel that this new land was now their true home.

The kitchen was often the center of colonial family life. Family members, working side by side, would complete their daily chores in the light and warmth of the fireplace.

Only the very wealthiest colonists could readily afford beautifully handcrafted silver items, such as this baby's rattle.

▶FAMILY LIFE IN COLONIAL AMERICA

Life in colonial America centered around the family. Most people worked, played, learned, and worshiped at home within the family circle. Their relatives and friends lived nearby. It was quite common for some people to live their entire lives without moving outside their circle of family and friends.

A typical example of a child growing up in the early 1700's is Benjamin Franklin, who later became one of the most highly accomplished people of the colonial period.

When Ben was a boy in Boston, he could look across the dinner table and count as many as 13 brothers and sisters. He might also see his Uncle Benjamin, his parents, and a neighborhood friend. In his home he might listen as his elders talked about local affairs or sang or played the fiddle. Sometimes the congregation of Boston's Old South Church held prayer services in the Franklin home. Franklin learned

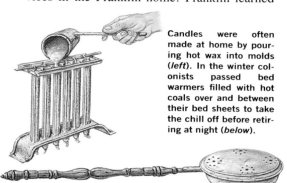

Candles were often made at home by pouring hot wax into molds (*left*). In the winter colonists passed bed warmers filled with hot coals over and between their bed sheets to take the chill off before retiring at night (*below*).

to read at home long before his parents decided to send him to school. He went to school at the age of 8 but was only allowed to stay for two years. At 10, young Ben began learning his father's trade of candle and soap making. He saw his elder brothers and sisters marry and leave home. Then, at the age of 12, he also left home to become his brother's apprentice in the printing trade.

Benjamin Franklin's family was not unusual. Most families did not have as many children as the Franklins, but the birth rate in colonial America was very high. Half the people of colonial America were less than 16 years old.

A large family was necessary in colonial days. Much work had to be done to keep a family fed, clothed, and sheltered. The more hands to do the work, the better. Men were considered the head of the household. They made all of the decisions concerning their families and earned the money to support them. Women worked in the home, raising the children, preparing the meals, sewing clothes, preserving food for the winter, scrubbing laundry, fetching water, and stoking fires.

By the time they had reached the age of 14, most children were already considered adults. Boys would soon take up their father's trade at home or leave to become an apprentice. Girls learned to manage a house and were expected to marry young, probably by the time they were 16 and surely before they were 20.

Clothing and Feeding the Family

The great majority of colonists did not dress elegantly. Most families bought long-wearing linen or flannel and made their own clothing. In rural New England and on the distant frontier, people often made their own cloth. Day after day the women sat at home sewing the dull green, brown, or mottled gray material. They also patched and altered clothing as long as there was any wear left.

Men wore coats, vests, shirts, kneebreeches (short pants), and long stockings. Laboring men often wore tough leather breeches. Women wore long, full dresses and shawls. Only the most wealthy people could afford to wear clothes of fine wool, silk, or velvet, as these fabrics were imported from England and were very expensive.

Even more time went into keeping the family fed. Where labor was scarce, a garden might have only cabbages, beans, corn, and

pumpkins. Potatoes became common some time after the 1720's. More prosperous gardeners grew carrots, beets, turnips, onions, leeks, radishes, and melons. Apples, plums, cherries, peaches and pears came from the orchards. As for meat, flocks of chickens and ducks were to be found in farmyards, and the woods were teeming with wild game. Stories have come down to us from colonial times of great herds of 200 deer and of flocks of 100 wild turkeys. Deer were so plentiful that some frontier families ate venison (deer meat) for nine months every year. A 30-pound (14kg) turkey could be bought for about a shilling (then worth about 25 cents) in Pennsylvania. Pheasant, partridge, woodcock, and quail were hunted in large numbers. There were so many pigeons that flocks would darken the sky and break the limbs of trees on which they perched. Squirrels were so numerous that they became a problem, and many towns began paying a bounty for their heads. In 1749, in Pennsylvania, more than 600,000 squirrels were killed for bounties. Perch and trout were caught in the streams, and fish, clams, lobsters, turtles, and oysters were gathered from the sea.

Although they had no refrigeration and did not know how to can foods, colonial families had ways of preserving their food. They dried beans and fruits, hung strings of onions in high, dry places, pickled cabbage in large crocks, and stored vegetables in a "root cellar." They salted, spiced, and smoked meats of all kinds. Many farmers even made their own beverages—cider, beer, and even brandy.

Bringing Up the Children

One of the hardest jobs that parents had in colonial days was keeping their newborn children alive. Shocking numbers of young children died of diphtheria, smallpox, scarlet fever, and measles. In Hingham, Massachusetts, where records were kept, one death out of five in the community was of an infant less than 2 years old. The famous Massachusetts clergyman Cotton Mather and his wife saw nine of their children die before their second birthdays. Tragedies like this were common. The few doctors in the colonies in those days had very limited medical knowledge. One remedy, for example, was to give a sick child a mixture of roots, rum, and water.

What did the colonists eat?

Brewis, crusts cut from a loaf of thick, hard bread, and stewed in milk or other fluids.

Dumbfish, codfish that has gone through a curing process called dumbing or dunning.

Jerky, beef cut into strips and dried before a fire.

Nocake, parched corn pounded into powder. In winter the parched corn was mixed with snow, and in summer it was mixed with water.

Pompion, an affectionate nickname for pumpkin.

"Rye-an' injun," a loaf of bread made with equal parts of rye flour and corn meal.

Samp, corn pounded into a coarse powder and eaten with milk and butter. Roger Williams called it "a diet exceedingly wholesome for English bodies."

Suppawn, or **hasty pudding,** corn meal boiled with milk into a thick porridge.

Men in colonial towns and cities gathered at local inns and taverns, where they drank beer, played cards, and read newspapers in "reading rooms" (*left*). Proper women were not welcome in these places. Tavern signs (*right*) were painted by artists called limners.

Like parents today, colonial parents wanted their children to grow up to be responsible adults. To many parents in colonial times, bringing up a child properly sometimes meant being strict. Colonial parents expected their children to be obedient and polite. Their children were about as well behaved as children today. Some were polite. A few were rude.

Colonial children usually learned about the adult world by doing things the way their parents did. They were expected to help with a share of the family's work. Self-reliance was emphasized. In the South it was common for a father to hand his young son a gun and send him out alone into the woods. Thomas Jefferson's father did this when his son was 10, although all young Tom managed to kill was a wild turkey that he found trapped in a pen.

Young girls too did a great deal of work. Four-year-old girls could knit stockings. One young girl in New Hampshire became so skilled that she knitted the whole alphabet and a verse of poetry into a single pair of mittens.

As for formal schooling, most children in early colonial times never saw the inside of a schoolhouse. Some well-to-do families sent their children to dancing masters or to music teachers. A few of the richer families hired private tutors, who then set up a little school for all the young people of the family. There were some neighborhood schools in New England, but a great many children learned to read at home.

Family Amusements

Colonial children played many of the same games that children play today. They cared for their pets, played with dolls, shot marbles, pitched pennies, and went fishing. They also played tag, stickball, and blindman's buff.

Adults too managed to take time out from their work to enjoy themselves. Most country people loved to dance, and at weddings the dancing and card playing often lasted all night. On militia days men would get together to practice military drilling and marching so that they would be prepared to defend themselves and their families against enemy attacks. Once they had finished their practice, they would drink beer or rum punch and tell each other tall tales.

Men and boys sometimes came from all over a rural countryside to watch a cockfight or to race their fastest horses. Women would often get together to complete laborious sewing projects, such as making quilts. These quilting, sewing, and spinning "bees" also made such long projects enjoyable.

Everyone looked forward to fairs, when countryfolk would come to town from miles around to sell produce and have a good time. There were races, prizes, dancing, puppet shows, and magicians. Prizes went to those who could catch a greased pig, climb a greased pole, or whistle a tune without laughing.

In the towns there were always things to do. Taverns had billiard tables, skittle tables, and shuffleboards. Many had bowling greens outside. A public race track ran around Beaver Pond on Long Island, and most towns south of New York had at least one track for horse racing. There were public dances in the towns and elegant parties in the ballrooms of the great mansions. In the 1600's, racing, dancing, and gaming were prohibited in New England, but during the 1700's, Boston had dancing schools, and stableboys matched pennies in the streets. By the middle of the 1700's there were theaters and musical clubs that gave concerts of violin, flute, and organ music.

▶HOW PEOPLE EARNED A LIVING

Because England did not allow the colonies to mint their own coins, colonial families used money less, and bartered more, than people do today. They made many things for themselves that we buy in stores. Even so, every family had to have some way to earn money. Most Americans were farmers, but there were artisans (skilled workers) who made such things as furniture and shoes. Others worked as miners, millers, shipbuilders, shopkeepers, or merchants. In every colony there were also teachers and preachers, lawyers, doctors, and government workers. A well-to-do man often earned his money in more than one way. He might be a farmer, a lawyer, and a government official; or a merchant, a manufacturer of rope, and a shipbuilder. But most people made their living by one kind of work that could be done at home.

Farming

Most American colonists lived in the country, and the vast majority of them were farmers. Farm families worked very hard. The women cared for vegetable gardens and the dairy. The men and their sons plowed the fields, split rails for fences, and cleared new land. Work went on throughout the year, from the spring planting of crops to the making and repairing of tools in the winter.

A farm family's work never ended, but it was busiest at harvesttime in the fall. On a Pennsylvania farm when hay was ready to be mowed, the family arose at dawn. The men sharpened sickles while the women prepared breakfast. Then neighboring farm families began to arrive to help in the fields. Farmers helped one another with major jobs, such as harvesting wheat or building barns. By six o'clock in the morning, 15 to 20 men, women, and children were in the fields, mowing hay with the sharp, curved sickles. After a stop at ten o'clock for lunch, they raked and hauled hay to the barns until late afternoon, when they stopped again for supper. Then, starting in again, they mowed until dark.

New England farms were smaller than those elsewhere. The farmers did not have any one

Farming was by far the most important industry in colonial America. Oxen (*above left*) were commonly used to pull wooden plows (*above*). The farmlands of the Middle Colonies were cultivated by religious immigrants from Central Europe, England, Scotland, and Ireland. Each group introduced its own farming methods to the New World. Bethlehem, Pennsylvania (*left*), was settled by Moravians in the mid-1700's.

413

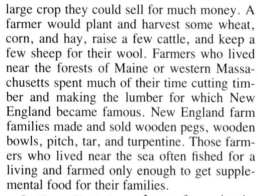

large crop they could sell for much money. A farmer would plant and harvest some wheat, corn, and hay, raise a few cattle, and keep a few sheep for their wool. Farmers who lived near the forests of Maine or western Massachusetts spent much of their time cutting timber and making the lumber for which New England became famous. New England farm families made and sold wooden pegs, wooden bowls, pitch, tar, and turpentine. Those farmers who lived near the sea often fished for a living and farmed only enough to get supplemental food for their families.

Southern Plantations. Large farms in the South were called plantations. Southern planters used slaves to do the work. Tobacco was grown in the best fields because the plant required rich soil. Within six or seven years, tobacco would exhaust the soil and the planter would have to clear new land. Clearing fields, growing tobacco, and cutting timber to make hogsheads (barrels) in which the tobacco was packed to be shipped to England kept planters and their workers very busy. But growing rice called for even more labor. The rice plantations of South Carolina could not operate without large numbers of slaves. Rice planters frequently chose to live in Charleston during the hot summer months, leaving hired supervisors in charge of inland plantations.

Above left: Skilled woodworkers were in great demand in colonial America since most farm tools were made of wood and required constant repair and replacement. *Above:* The Chandler Wedding Tapestry shows a New England wedding scene in 1765. *Left:* Boston, Philadelphia, and New York were the chief silversmithing cities in the colonies. This teapot was made by Paul Revere.

Crafts, Manufacturing, and Business

Artisans were skilled workers. Cobblers made shoes, stonemasons built chimneys, and millers ground flour. Every town had its carpenters, cabinetmakers, tailors, printers, hatmakers, potters, weavers, wigmakers, and saddlemakers. There were also bakers, tallow chandlers (candlemakers), cutlers (knife repairers), wheelwrights, coopers (barrelmakers), and apothecaries (pharmacists). The artisan's shop was often in front of the house, which made it convenient for the family to help with the work. Behind the house were the family garden and pens for the pigs and chickens.

A few Americans ran businesses. Some operated iron furnaces and forges, while others were merchants who imported supplies from Great Britain and sold goods manufactured in America overseas. Businessmen often worked in partnerships with relatives in England or

America. Very few had enough money or credit to establish a large business by themselves.

In the colonies a young man often learned a trade by serving as an apprentice. Apprentices began living in their masters' households when they were about 14 years old. They were legally bound to their masters for six or eight years. The master fed, clothed, and housed his apprentices. He taught them his craft and to read and write. Sometimes the master was paid for his trouble. The son of a prosperous family might be sent to England to learn about business from a great merchant.

Many lawyers and doctors in colonial America also learned their professions by serving as apprentices. Law was not taught in any American college until 1755, and the first medical college was not established until 1765. The only way a young man could learn the skills required in these professions was by assisting a colonial doctor or lawyer at his work.

Servants and Slaves

Most well-to-do town families had servants, often country farm girls who came into town to work. Some colonists in the North as well as the South "owned" black slaves. Farm families in New England usually hired workers who had no land of their own to help with the farming.

Some servants were called indentured servants. They were poor immigrants who bound themselves to work for masters who paid the costs of the expensive journey to America. In Pennsylvania, Maryland, and Virginia their term of service was frequently four years, and in New England, seven years. While in service, they were fed, clothed, and cared for within the family. The master had the same authority over them as he had over his own children. For example, they could not marry without his consent. When their time of indenture (service) was up, the master gave them money, clothing, and tools to start them on their way as free citizens.

Farmers in the South bought slaves to help with crops that required a great deal of labor. The farmers fed and clothed the slaves, and cared for them when they were sick. But slaves had to labor at every kind of job that needed to be done without any hope of freedom.

▶ **COLONIAL HOUSES**

The first settlers in America built very crude kinds of shelters with the most readily available materials, wanting only to get a roof over their heads as quickly as possible. In Jamestown the settlers built one-room thatch and mud huts, with a hole in the roof to let out smoke. The homes of the first Massachusetts settlers resembled the wigwams of the local Indians. In Plymouth the earliest shelters were merely man-made caves dug into hills and covered over by a bark roof supported by poles. These English settlers were as yet unfamiliar with the one-room log cabin that later became so common on the American frontier. It was the Swedes who introduced the log cabin to America in their settlements on the lower Delaware River in 1638.

Later the colonists began to build plain wooden houses, since wood was plentiful in the colonies and cheaper than stone or brick. The houses were modeled after the rural houses the colonists had lived in in England. They were sturdy but not large or elaborate. Usually the house was a box-shaped frame of heavy beams covered with rough hand-split boards or shingles. These were left unpainted to weather to a silver gray. The upstairs had three or four small, square bedrooms with low ceilings. The downstairs was divided into rooms where the family ate and did household chores.

Colonial houses in New England, such as this saltbox in Bennington, Vermont, were designed to protect the colonists from the harsh northern winters.

Northern Houses. New Englanders built houses that were one and a half stories high in the front and one story high in the rear. The roofs of these "saltbox" houses (so called because they looked like the wooden boxes in which the colonists stored salt) sloped steeply so that snow would slip off easily and not damage the roof in the wintertime. Saltbox houses had central chimneys made out of brick or stone that heated the entire house. The main hearth was located in the kitchen.

Windows were small and few had glass panes. Wooden shutters kept out the cold and rain. Floors were made out of hand-packed dirt sprinkled daily with fresh sand. Later floors were made out of wide, unpainted boards.

Southern Houses. At first, Southerners built plain, wooden houses similar to those in New England. Eventually a more popular design was adapted that was better suited to the warmer southern climate. By the late 1600's brick became the preferred building material, and the houses became larger and more open. Chimneys were placed on both ends of a house, and large windows and a central hall provided ventilation. As planters and merchants accumulated wealth, they sought to imitate the style of the large country manors of the British ruling class, particularly the Georgian style, which appeared around the 1730's. Plantation houses also had a group of service buildings behind the main house. These buildings often included a summer kitchen (where slaves would cook to keep excessive heat out of the main house), a smokehouse, and laundry. Farther away were the stables, carriage house, and slaves' cabins.

Furniture. In the 1600's most colonial furniture was plain but sturdy. Chairs, stools, beds, and tables were made out of unpainted oak, maple, or pine. Most rooms had large cupboards, since there were no built-in clothes closets. Some colonists cherished a few pieces of silver and some fine chairs of polished oak, which had been made in England.

In the 1700's more people could afford to buy imported English goods, and fine pieces of brass and pewter began to brighten the rooms of most houses. Mansion walls were paneled in wood or covered in wallpaper imported from France or England. Persian rugs, mahogany tables and chairs, damask and silk draperies, portraits, gilt mirrors, and gleaming silver urns and teapots blended to create homes as beautiful as America has ever known.

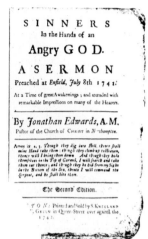

SINNERS
In the Hands of an
Angry GOD.
A SERMON
Preached at *Enfield*, *July* 8th 1741.
At a Time of great Awakenings ; and attended with
remarkable Impreſſions on many of the Hearers.

By *Jonathan Edwards*, A.M.
Paſtor of the Church of CHRIST in *Northampton*.

Amos ix. 2, 3. Though they dig into Hell, thence ſhall
mine Hand take them : though they climb up to Heaven,
thence will I bring them down. And though they hide
themſelves in the Top of Carmel, I will ſearch and take
them out thence ; and though they be hid from my Sight
in the Bottom of the Sea, thence I will command the
Serpent, and he ſhall bite them.

The Second Edition.

BOSTON : Printed and Sold by S. KNEELAND
& GREEN in Queen-Street over againſt the ,
1742.

Left: Nineteen people accused of witchcraft in Salem, Massachusetts, were hanged in 1692. *Right:* Puritan sermons promoted the belief that torment awaited sinners after death.

▶LIFE IN THE NEW ENGLAND COLONIES

In colonial America, as in all civilized places, there were schools, churches, markets, and governments. But ways of living differed from colony to colony. New England in the 18th century was a land of tidy fields and villages. Many towns were built around a common (village square). The church, the school, and sometimes a town hall were built on the common.

Religion in New England

The Puritans who came to New England in the 1600's were deeply religious Christians. Everything in the New England Puritan communities centered around the church. They believed that God had chosen them to be an example for others of the good Christian life. Therefore, their most important duty was to worship God and spread the Puritan religion.

On Saturday afternoons all activities came to a halt in the Puritan towns as the preparations for Sunday began. On Sunday everyone had to go to church services. The services began in the morning and lasted well into the afternoon, with one intermission around noon. Sermons lasted for two to three hours, and prayers from one to two hours. Psalm singing would sometimes last for half an hour. The deacon would read aloud while the congregation stood and sang after him. In winter the people had to bundle up warmly, for the churches were unheated until late into the century.

The church was also the center of the political life of the Puritan community. Town meetings were held in the church, and the Puritan ministers were respected leaders in the communities.

Justice was closely tied to the religious beliefs of the community. Anyone who disobeyed a rule of the religious society was punished, often in the public square for all others to see. It was believed that public humiliation would speedily reform an offender and serve as a warning to others. Many types of public punishments were given out for more serious crimes, such as stealing. A thief might be whipped, branded with a hot iron, or have an ear cut off. Such cruel punishments were customary in Europe and in other colonies.

The Puritans had come to America to gain religious freedom. But the religious freedom they sought was for themselves and not for others. The Puritan leaders believed that dissenters (people who disagreed with their religious ideas) would have a bad effect on Puritans. Therefore, they not only failed to practice religious toleration but thought it dangerous. Dissenters, such as Roger Williams and Anne Hutchinson, were forced to go to other colonies. Quaker missionaries who tried to make converts among the Puritans in the 1650's were imprisoned and put to death.

Superstition was also a part of life in New England. To the Puritans, as to other people of the 1600's, the world was a battleground

Left: The first edition of Benjamin Franklin's enormously popular *Poor Richard's Almanack* was published in 1733. *Above:* Education was especially important to the northern colonists. In some states, children were required by law to attend school, unless they were learning a trade or being tutored privately at home.

where good and evil forces fought. They believed that devils and witches were everywhere, causing storms, making people sick, sinking ships, and ruining crops. The Puritans believed that the devil sometimes won people over to his side and made them witches.

There were two periods of witch-hunting in New England in the 1600's. Between 1647 and 1663 hundreds of people in Massachusetts and Connecticut were accused of witchcraft, and 14 were actually executed. Later, from 1688 to 1693, there was another witch-hunt, in Salem, Massachusetts, during which 19 people were hanged. In the end the witch-hunt frenzy became so bad that even community leaders were accused of being witches. It was then that the power of the witch-hunters was broken. They had gone too far.

By the early part of the 1700's many people with less religious zeal than the early Puritan settlers were moving into the colonies. Puritan ministers in the 1700's no longer played such active roles in town affairs.

New England Schools

To the Bible-reading Puritans of New England, education was important. Puritans had to be educated so that they could read the Bible and understand their ministers' sermons. An even better education had to be provided for young men who wanted to become ministers. Schooling was so important to the Puritans that the government in Massachusetts passed laws requiring towns to have schools. New England had more schools than any other region of colonial America. The Boston Latin School, founded in 1635, carefully prepared

its boys for entrance to college. Most other schools taught little more than reading, writing, and arithmetic. A few schools were also set up to teach Indian children and to try to convert them to Christianity.

In 1636, Massachusetts set up Harvard College, the first college in the colonies. Before the end of the colonial period, New England had three more colleges—Yale, Brown, and Dartmouth.

The New England colleges tried to keep alive a spirit of learning. Latin, Greek, science, and philosophy took up most of the students' time. They also learned to debate and to write well. Graduates became the clergymen, lawyers, doctors, and leaders in their communities, even though they were not trained for any particular profession. They often got their special training by serving as apprentices.

New England Books and Newspapers

New England was the center for the printing of books and newspapers. The first American printing press began operation in 1638. By 1715, New England had six busy presses. The Boston *News Letter*, founded in 1704, was the first newspaper printed in the colonies. The printers also published copies of English books, sermons, pamphlets, and government documents. Newspapers and almanacs became popular with readers in every colony.

Public Affairs in New England

The first New England leaders believed that their government had the special approval of God. They debated among themselves to decide what God's will was. Thus a tradition of public debate and discussion began. Leading citizens debated town problems as well as religion. Everyone could join in the town-meeting debate. New England men who were landowners could vote for more public officials than most other colonists.

The New England Economy

New England colonists grew most of their own food, made much of their own clothing, and produced many of their own supplies. But they had to buy most of their cloth, tools, and luxury items from England, and the colonists had few goods of comparable value to sell overseas. So the colonists came up with a clever trade scheme that involved rum, molasses, and slaves.

Trade Routes. New England colonists preserved codfish, halibut, and mackerel in great quantities, which they could sell in Spain, Portugal, and the West Indies. What they could sell in the West Indies was traded for molasses. They brought the molasses back home and made rum, which they sold in the colonies or took to the coasts of Africa, where they would sell the rum and buy slaves. Then they sold the slaves in the West Indies or in the Southern colonies. With the money they made from selling slaves, they could buy goods that they needed from England. New England traders also made money by selling iron pots, kettles, and tools in other colonies.

▶LIFE IN THE MIDDLE COLONIES

Living side by side in New York, New Jersey, and Pennsylvania were people who spoke different languages and worshiped in different ways. In Albany and New York City, ministers preached in Dutch to their Dutch Reformed congregations for a hundred years after the Dutch had surrendered their claim to the colony in 1664 and it became an English possession. Though the most prominent English people in New York were Anglicans (members of the Church of England), many other English people, as well as Scots, were Presbyterians. There were also Baptists, Jews, and Roman Catholics in New York City.

The English who named and settled Pennsylvania were Quakers. They hoped Pennsylvania would be a place where they could worship simply and live peacefully. Several German religious groups also came to Pennsylvania. Among these were Mennonites, Moravians, Dunkers, and Schwenkfelders. Lutherans and German Reformed groups as well as Scottish and Irish Presbyterians and Anglicans became active in Pennsylvania affairs.

Philadelphia had more civic, social, and religious organizations than any other city. Unlike New England villagers, people living in Philadelphia in the middle of the 1700's expected to see separate schools run by the Quakers, Baptists, Lutherans, and Moravians, among others. There were many different clubs and societies. Some were to help the poor; others supported libraries; and one kept alive the songs and legends of Ireland. There were insurance companies, fire companies, and organizations of merchants or artisans. One group of doctors opened a hospital. Philadelphia and New York bustled with the activity of citizens meeting, planning, and doing things together.

In 1720, Philadelphia with its busy waterfront was second only to Boston as the colonies' major port and commercial center. By 1775 it was the largest city in the colonies.

The Economy of the Middle Colonies

The Middle Colonies, like the New England Colonies, produced many things. Farmers raised more than enough food for the growing population. Pennsylvania was a center for iron mining and making iron tools, nails, and pots and pans. The Philadelphia artisans were known throughout America for their fine furniture and well-designed silver, but many luxuries were still being imported from Europe.

The main products they sold abroad were wheat, flour, barley, and oats. Flour milling was a major industry, and millers of Pennsylvania and New York competed for the reputation of making the best flour in America. Merchant millers sometimes built bakehouses and made hard bread (bread that would keep for a long time) to be sold abroad. Pennsylvania butchers bought cattle from as far away as North Carolina, and sold thousands of barrels of salted beef and pork each year to other colonies and to European countries. The best markets for wheat and flour were in Spain and Portugal. The West Indies offered good markets for all types of food. Less important exports were flaxseed sent to Ireland and iron ore and ships to Great Britain. Trade was so brisk that the Middle Colonies became very prosperous.

▶ LIFE IN THE SOUTHERN COLONIES

In the 1700's it took a long time to travel by land from Savannah, Georgia, to Baltimore, Maryland. The roads were often only paths through the woods, and there were no signs to point out the way. One could easily get lost. Travelers were rare, so farmers along the route would often give them food and a place to sleep in exchange for their company and news of public events.

The South was large and its people were scattered. Southerners who lived in the western country, past the Piedmont and Blue Ridge Mountains all the way to the Appalachians, had little contact with the eastern communities. They had their own way of life.

Charleston and the Chesapeake Country

During much of the 1700's life in Charleston was similar to that in Philadelphia and New York. Most of the white people were English, but there were some Scots and a number of French Protestants called Huguenots. The Anglican Church was strong, and

Many southern homes, such as the Taylor House in Williamsburg, Virginia (*rear*), had outside service buildings (*middle and front*) where much of the work was done.

there were few congregations of other religious groups. Slaves made up a large part of the population and did most of the manual labor. More often than in New York or Boston, the Charleston merchants were agents of British firms. Charleston was famous for its social clubs and lively parties.

Most of the people in the Chesapeake country lived on farms and plantations. About half of them were slaves; most of the rest were English. There were a few Irish workers and, in the villages, some Scottish storekeepers and traders. Two towns, Norfolk and Baltimore, began to grow as trading centers just before the American Revolution. Families in the Chesapeake area lived too far apart to take part in many community activities. There were few schools and churches except in the villages. William and Mary College, founded in 1693 at Williamsburg, was the only college in the South for 25 years.

Public affairs were in the hands of the county court and the colonial government. The vestry was the governing body of the parish church. Vestrymen looked after the church and cared for orphans and the poor. The county court heard legal disputes and cases involving law violations. It also was in charge of issuing licenses to tavern keepers and building and repairing roads. Members of the county court were appointed by the colonial governor. The most important local occasion was when the county court met. Lawyers came to try cases. Merchants were there to buy crops and to collect debts. Farmers came to do business and just to see one another.

Above: Southern kitchens were often separated from the houses they serviced. Well-to-do Southerners could afford exotic fruits and vegetables imported from the West Indies. *Below:* An 18th-century newspaper advertised the arrival of 250 blacks, who were to be sold as slaves off the coast of Charleston, South Carolina.

TO BE SOLD on board the Ship *Bance-Ifland*, on tuefday the 6th of *May* next, at *Afhley-Ferry*; a choice cargo of about 250 fine healthy

NEGROES,

juft arrived from the Windward & Rice Coaft. —The utmoft care has already been taken, and fhall be continued, to keep them free from the leaft danger of being infected with the SMALL-POX, no boat having been on board, and all other communication with people from *Charles-Town* prevented.

Auftin, Laurens, & Appleby.

N. B. Full one Half of the above Negroes have had the SMALL-POX in their own Country.

The Southern Economy

The people of the Chesapeake area grew large crops of tobacco, corn, and wheat. The planters of South Carolina grew rice and indigo. The cakes of valuable blue dye made from the indigo plant were much sought after by cloth manufacturers. From the pine trees of Carolina and Virginia, farmers made pitch, tar, and turpentine. Upland farmers herded cattle and hogs. A few Virginia mines yielded iron ore.

Unlike the New Englanders the Southern colonists produced many things wanted in England. Tobacco was the most valuable colonial export to England (as yet little cotton was raised). When prices were high, Southerners could make good money from farming. As a result, they manufactured less and imported more tools and household goods then the colonists of the North. Few Southerners became merchants. English and Scottish merchants brought them most of their goods and bought their tobacco and rice.

▶ THE FRONTIER

In 1670, when the first American colonies were fairly well settled, the population was about 115,000. A hundred years later, a few years before the Revolutionary War, it was nearly 2,250,000. Since 1607 the colonial population had more than doubled every 25 years. Colonial America was no longer a number of settlements on the Atlantic coast. Now it was a great stretch of land reaching hundreds of miles inland and being pushed farther west by pioneers every day. People in the earliest settlements had their established patterns of living, but the pioneers were facing the wilderness just as the first American settlers had.

By the 1700's colonial pioneers like James Robertson and Ethan Allen lived deep in the wilderness far from the coast. New Englanders began moving westward into central Massachusetts and northward up the Connecticut River valley. By the 1760's they were settling Vermont and western New Hampshire, and pushing back the frontiers of Maine. To the south, pioneers settled western New York, Pennsylvania, western Maryland and Virginia, and the Piedmont region of North and South Carolina. Some of the pioneers came from the colonies that had already been established on the Atlantic coast. Others were new immigrants to America—mainly Germans and Scotch-Irish, Scots who had earlier migrated to Northern Ireland. Before the American Revolution, pioneers had begun crossing the Cumberland Gap into eastern Kentucky and clearing fields in the valleys of eastern Tennessee.

ROBERT POLK THOMSON
George Peabody College

See also THIRTEEN AMERICAN COLONIES; JAMESTOWN; PLYMOUTH COLONY; REVOLUTIONARY WAR.

An illustrated listing of authentic colonial sites you can visit today appears on the following two pages.

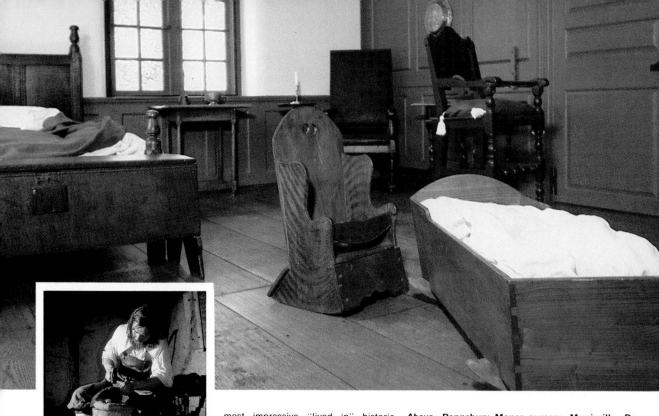

COLONIAL SITES YOU CAN VISIT TODAY

Of the hundreds of colonial sites open to the public, the following, arranged geographically, are among the most authentic and interesting:

Shelburne, Vt. The Shelburne Museum includes a number of houses and antiques dating from the late 1700's.

Portsmouth, N.H. The original settlement at the mouth of the Piscataqua River, known as Strawbery Banke, has restored historic buildings dating from 1695 to 1830.

Salem, Mass. The Essex Institute has restored one 17th- and several 18th-century houses with authentic furnishings. The House of Seven Gables is another good example of early architecture. Pioneer Village is a modern reconstruction of the original settlement at Salem.

Boston, Mass. Within the city are many 17th- and 18th-century houses. Many of the historic structures are indicated on maps of the "Freedom Trail."

Plymouth, Mass. On the outskirts of modern Plymouth is "Plimoth Plantation," a reconstruction of the Pilgrims' first village.

Deerfield, Mass. As a result of cooperation among the townspeople, the local historical society, and the privately endowed Heritage Foundation, Deerfield has become one of the most impressive "lived in" historic sites. The main street has been restored to very nearly its 18th-century appearance.

Mystic, Conn. "Mystic Seaport" is a skillful re-creation of an early 19th-century seaport village with many colonial buildings and vessels. Most of the houses have been moved to the site and restored.

Morrisville, Pa. Pennsbury Manor, the historic home of William Penn, contains a collection of 17th-century English furniture and accessories.

Philadelphia, Pa. In the Independence Hall area are many well-known public buildings that have been preserved, while the "Society Hill" section of the city is composed of privately owned town houses restored to their 18th-century exterior appearance.

Wilmington, Del. Within a small radius are three important historic institutions: The Hagley Museum, a group of restored and reconstructed mill buildings along the Brandywine River; the Eleutherian Mills, the du Pont family's first powder factory in America; and Winterthur, a museum housing the antiques collection of Henry F. du Pont.

Alexandria, Va. George Washington's estate, Mount Vernon, has been carefully preserved and gives the observer a graphic idea of an 18th-century plantation.

Williamsburg, Va. The most famous historic site in America, "Colonial Williamsburg" includes more than 80 original buildings preserved from Virginia's colonial capital and many skillful reconstructions. Guides in costume complete the authentic setting. At the nearby site of Jamestown, the first permanent English settlement in America, the Jamestown Festival Park includes replicas of 17th-century buildings.

Charleston, S.C. Many buildings from the colonial era, both public and private, have been preserved.

Above: Pennsbury Manor nursery, Morrisville, Pa. *Insert left:* Colonial craftsman (re-enactment), Jamestown, Va. *Below:* Barnard House, Deerfield, Mass. *Bottom:* Colonial gardener (re-enactment), Plimoth Plantation, Plymouth, Mass.

Above left: Mount Vernon estate, Alexandria, Va. *Left:* Apothecary shop, Colonial Williamsburg, Va. *Above:* Christ Church ("Old North" Church), Boston, Mass. *Below:* Mystic Seaport, Mystic, Conn.

The beauty and variety of colors in nature delight the eye. Our appreciation and use of color can be heightened by an understanding of its essential qualities.

COLOR

Our world is filled with color. The brilliant blue of a summer sky, the vivid yellow of a bunch of daffodils, and the soft pink tint of a seashell are examples of the many ways in which color surrounds us in nature. We also use color to add beauty and variety to our lives. When we choose our clothing, decorate our homes, or paint a picture, we select colors that please us and create a particular mood or feeling.

The great variety of color that surrounds us is usually accepted as commonplace, an everyday fact of life. Yet color is anything but commonplace. Many of its qualities remain a mystery, even to today's scientists. What we do understand about color is best explained by answering the question: What is color?

▶THE ABC'S OF COLOR

The objects commonly called "colors"— paints and crayons, for instance—may display color, but none of them actually are color.

Color has neither body nor substance; you cannot touch or feel it. A rug may be both soft and red, but the two qualities are not at all similar. Waking up at night and without turning on the light, you can still feel the softness of the rug, but you cannot see its red color. The rug appears to be black or dark gray. Colors can be seen only in the presence of light; without light there is no color. In bright light, colors are more intense. When the light fades, the colors fade along with it. All this makes sense once you realize that color is, in fact, light.

In 1665 the English scientist Sir Isaac Newton performed a simple experiment that revealed the relationship between color and light. He caused a narrow beam of sunlight to pass through a solid, three-sided piece of glass called a **prism.** As the light made its way through the prism, it was bent, or **refracted.** This forced the narrow beam to spread out and change, until it emerged on the other side of the prism as a wide band, or **spectrum,** of colors ranging from red, through yellow, green, and blue, to violet.

Newton then reversed the process by guiding that beam of colored light through another prism, which turned it back into a narrow beam of colorless light. With this experiment, he provided absolute proof that colorless or "white" light is actually made up of several bright colors.

In time, scientists determined that light is a series of waves of differing lengths. The different **wavelengths** are seen by us as different colors. An object looks colored if it is able to throw back, or **reflect,** one or more of the light waves while taking in, or **absorbing,** the rest. For example, a red ball appears red because it reflects the red light waves and absorbs the other light waves. And a green shirt looks green because it reflects the green light waves and absorbs the others. Light such as sunlight that contains all the wavelengths appears colorless or white.

Mixing the Colors of Light. White light is made up of only three basic colors—red, green, and violet—called **primaries.** Red has the longest wavelength that we can see and violet the shortest. All other colors are mix-

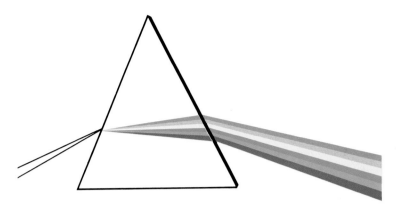

When a beam of ordinary light is passed through a prism, the light is refracted, or bent, causing it to separate into a spectrum of colors. This experiment, first performed by Isaac Newton, shows that "white" light is actually made up of several bright colors.

tures of the primaries. Yellow light is a combination of red and green light. Blue light is a combination of green and violet light. The third mixture, red and violet, is not visible in the spectrum but can be produced by combining a beam of red light with a beam of violet light. The result is a light of a deep pink hue known as magenta. (Remember that we are referring to mixtures of colored light. Mixing paint or crayon colors produces very different results and is discussed below.)

When a color created by a mixture of any two primaries is added to the third primary, white light is produced. Thus yellow (red + green) plus violet makes white light, as do blue (green + violet) plus red, and magenta (red + violet) plus green. Because they complete the number of primaries needed for white light, the mixed colors are often called **complementaries.**

In the diagram of interlocking color disks on this page, the primary colors of light are shown on the left. Mixed, or complementary, colors result wherever two primaries overlap. These mixed colors are lighter than the primaries because they contain twice as much light. In the center, where all three overlap, white light is produced, proving that the colors of light are **additive,** that is, with each added primary, more light is produced.

Mixing Pigments. Mixing different-colored **pigments**—chemical coloring substances such as paints—is not the same as mixing light of different colors. Pigment colors, shown on the right in the diagram, are **subtractive** because pigments can display color only by absorbing, or subtracting, portions of white light while reflecting the rest. Each of the pigment primaries—yellow, magenta, and blue—shown in the diagram absorbs one third of white light and reflects two thirds. For example, yellow pigment absorbs the violet light and reflects

The three primary colors of light are shown at left. Wherever any two overlap, lighter secondary colors are produced. At the center of the diagram, all three primaries combine to make white light.

Three primary pigment colors are shown at right. When any two combine, darker secondary colors are produced. In the center black results from the mixing of all three pigment primaries.

the red and green light. (As we have seen, red and green light combine to produce yellow.) Wherever two pigment primaries overlap and are mixed, darker **secondary** colors are produced because less light is reflected by the mixture. For example, adding blue pigment (which absorbs red but reflects green and violet) to yellow pigment (which absorbs violet but reflects green and red) leaves only green light to be reflected. This is why the mixture of blue and yellow pigment looks green. When all three pigment primaries are mixed, black results, rather than the white that results when the three primary colors of light are mixed.

Pigment colors are classified according to **brilliance** and **saturation.** Brilliance refers to the amount of reflected light. A color of high brilliance reflects a large portion of white light, and a color of low brilliance only a small part. Saturation is the degree of purity. A red of high saturation means it reflects most of the red light, and only red light reaches your eyes. **Shades** and **tints** are variations of a particular color. Shade usually designates the deeper qualities, while tint refers to the lighter qualities. A tint of yellow typically means a little yellow pigment mixed with a lot of white.

Understanding all these facts about color helps artists who create paintings using pigment colors. Knowledge of how colors interact is also essential for color printing, in which just three colors plus black are used to produce a full range of colors in every shade and tint from light to dark. To read more about the color printing process, see the article PRINTING in Volume P.

▶COLORS IN NATURE

Most man-made colored objects depend on chemical coloring substances such as pigments. Many of nature's colors are also produced by such chemical substances. Flower colors, for instance, are usually pigment colors. The most universal pigment in nature is **chlorophyll,** the green coloring matter of plants.

Structural Colors. Many other colors in nature, however, are not caused by pigments. Scientists call them **physical** or **structural** colors, meaning they are pure light reflected by tiny structures in organic or inorganic matter. Most white hues in nature are structural. The white of snow, for example, results from total scattered reflection of all incoming light by crystal or tissue structures. The blue of the sky is another structural color, produced by air

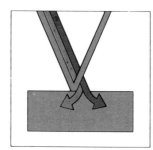

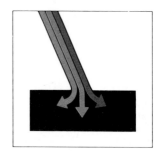

White light is made up of three primary colors, each associated with a different wavelength of light. An object appears to have color if it reflects one or more of the light waves to our eyes while absorbing the rest. *Top left:* If an object reflects all the light waves striking it, it appears white. *Middle left:* A red object looks red because it reflects mostly the red light waves to our eyes and absorbs the other light waves. *Bottom left:* Objects that absorb all light appear to us as black.

Although some of the magnificent colors found in nature seem to be purely ornamental, others serve a purpose. *Above:* The bright summer plumage of the male goldfinch helps him attract a mate during the breeding season. *Right:* The peacock's display of brilliant, iridescent feathers also serves to attract females.

molecules and tiny impurities in the atmosphere that reflect and scatter the blue/violet part of the spectrum.

Most beautiful of all structural colors in nature are the pure, incredibly brilliant **iridescent** colors displayed by many birds and insects, including hummingbirds and some butterflies. A hummingbird's throat may look yellow from one angle, orange from another, and flame red from a third angle. Being pure light, these colors seem to glow with a life of their own. All are produced by a process called **light interference.** The scales or feather branches contain huge numbers of tiny structures that bend and reflect incoming light, reinforcing some colors while weakening or eliminating others. Depending on the angle, different colors appear and re-appear rapidly, shining with a purity never found in pigment colors. You can read more about light interference in the article LIGHT in Volume L.

Uses of Color in Nature. The great variety of color in nature has led scientists to look for proof of its usefulness, in the belief that all special qualities in nature must have a purpose. Many plant and animal colors are indeed useful to their owners. The colors of flowers attract insects that fertilize them. Some animal colors serve as a disguise, allowing the animal

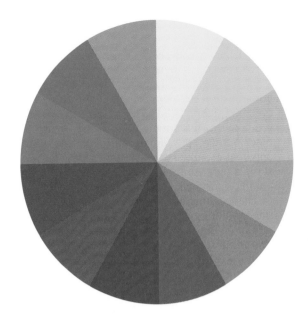

The color wheel above was made with just three pigment primaries: red, yellow, and blue. To understand how it was done, you can make your own simple color wheel using red, yellow, and blue crayons. First draw a circle on a piece of paper and write numbers on it from 1 to 12. Your drawing should look like a clock with no hands. With a ruler make three lines: one from 12 to 6, one from 2 to 8, and one from 4 to 10. Your circle should now have six sections. Color in blue all three sections to the left of the line that goes from 12 to 6. Then color in red the sections above the line from 4 to 10. The section between the numbers 10 and 12 will turn purple. Finally color in yellow the sections under the line that goes from 2 to 8. The section between numbers 6 and 8 will become green, and the section between numbers 2 and 4 will turn orange.

Left: Plant leaves get their green color from the pigment chlorophyll, which plays a vital role in photosynthesis. *Above,* another example of useful coloring: In winter the long-tailed weasel's brown coat turns white, allowing it to blend with its snowy surroundings.

to blend with its natural surroundings so well that it cannot be seen. Other animal colors serve as warning signs to discourage attackers. Among many birds, reptiles, and fish, bright colors help the males attract a mate during the breeding season. Many other colors, however, seem to be little more than ornamental. In other words, they are beautiful but have no apparent usefulness. Even those colors that do serve a purpose often are not necessary for an animal's survival.

There seems to be only a single color—or rather coloring substance—in nature that is essential not only to the plants that display it but also to most other living creatures. That color is the green pigment chlorophyll, which absorbs the red and violet parts of the spectrum while reflecting the green part. The plant gains energy from the absorbed light, and this energy is used to produce food for the plant in a process called **photosynthesis.** Because of that vital function, chlorophyll is indeed the essence and color of life itself.

Brightly colored hot air balloons liven up a summer sky, vivid examples of the many ways in which people use color to interest and please the eye.

▶COLOR VISION

The ability to see different wavelengths of light as colors is not shared equally by all animals. Many one-celled animals, such as amoebas, have no eyes and cannot see. Even ordinary vision does not automatically include color vision, and the ability to see color may differ. Honeybees, for instance, cannot see red, but they do see yellow, green, blue, and violet, as well as ultraviolet, which is invisible to humans. Most fish, amphibians, reptiles, and birds, on the other hand, seem to see the same color range as humans.

Most mammals, even though their bodies are highly complex, have little or no color vision. Many of them are active at night or during the twilight hours, when the sense of smell and hearing are of more value than even ordinary vision. The ability to see color is not important to these animals. Only monkeys and apes share with humans the ability to see the colors of the spectrum.

How We See Color. All vision in higher animals depends on certain structures in the eye that receive the image; on the optic nerve, which passes along that image in the form of impulses; and on the optic lobe, the part of the brain that translates the impulses into the picture we see. All of this happens with such speed that we see images the moment we look at them. Color vision exists in addition to ordinary vision if special color-receptive structures are present in the eye. Without these color receptors, an animal is color-blind, even though its ordinary vision may be good. A person may be color-blind if his or her brain cannot process the information from the color receptors. One in about every 30 humans is either partially or completely color-blind. Color blindness in humans is a genetic defect that is passed on from parents to their children. It rarely affects women.

Color Illusions. Because what we see is largely determined by the eyes and the brain, instances of color illusions often occur. We may see colors that are not there. For example, if we look at certain color combinations for a while and then look at a sheet of white paper, we may see an **afterimage,** a mental picture whose colors are different from those we saw in the real picture. Examples of pictures that can produce afterimages are found in the article OPTICAL ILLUSIONS in Volume O.

Another type of color illusion demonstrates that the same color can look different under different conditions. A color looks darker when seen against a light background than when viewed against a dark background. Colors can also look brighter or duller depending on the colors that surround them.

▶ COLOR IN OUR LIVES

Color is important to us in many ways. Bright, "warm" colors such as yellow and red can have a cheerful or exciting effect, while a "cool" color such as blue can produce feelings of calmness and tranquility. Colors help make our environment more interesting and attractive; we enjoy surrounding ourselves with beautiful colored objects and using color in painting and arts and crafts.

Color Association. Over the centuries, certain colors have acquired symbolic meanings because people relate them to familiar objects or ideas. This is known as color association. For example, red, the color of blood, often signifies courage as well as excitement and danger. Green, the color of ever-renewing plant life, is widely considered the symbol of hope and life. Purple stands for royalty, because purple robes were once worn by kings and queens as a sign of their high rank. In many cultures black has come to stand for death, evil, and fear of the unknown. White most often stands for purity and innocence.

Color can be used for practical reasons as well as for pleasure. Color coding of wires in telephone cables helps workers identify which wires to join.

Although some color associations are almost universal, others differ from one culture to another. In some countries white stands for sorrow. In India red is a holy color, and in China red symbolizes joy.

Other Uses of Color. Today, apart from its many uses in arts and crafts, decorating, clothing, photography, and printing, color has numerous other uses in business and industry. Our responses to and feelings about color are important considerations in designing toys and games, appliances, and packaging for foods and other products. Color is also used in technology for everything from traffic signs and signals to color coding for electronic wiring.

Color television is based on a process called **phosphorescence.** The inside of the tube is coated with tiny dots of the primary colors of light: red, green, and violet. When stimulated by electrons, these primaries are mixed to form all the colors of the spectrum.

The ability to see color is not necessary for human survival—color-blind persons, after all, lead perfectly normal lives. But this ability greatly enriches the lives of those who have received the gift of seeing as bright colors the various wavelengths of white light.

Reviewed by PETER GOODWIN
Kent School
Author, *Physics Can Be Fun*

Against different color backgrounds, colors seem to change. Both the red and the green rectangles look lighter on blue and darker when viewed against yellow.

COLORADO

Colorado—the Spanish word for "red"— is the name early explorers from Mexico gave the state's major river, with its spectacular red sandstone canyons. Colorado is not only red, but white with snow. With the highest mountain ranges in the United States, Colorado receives a great deal of snowfall that feeds four major western rivers that originate in the state—the Colorado, the Rio Grande, the Arkansas, and the Platte. For this reason, Colorado is sometimes called the Mother of Rivers. Its official nickname, the Centennial State, serves as a reminder that Colorado became a state in 1876, the year that marked the 100th anniversary of the Declaration of Independence.

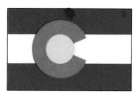
State flag

With an average elevation of about 6,800 feet (2,070 meters), Colorado has the highest altitude of any state in the nation. Coloradans joke that it would also be the largest state—if it could only be ironed out flat! Actually, Colorado is the eighth largest state. It covers nearly twice the area of all the New England states put together.

Colorado, with more than 3.6 million residents, is the most populous of the Rocky Mountain states. Yet it is sparsely settled, particularly the Western Slope, which includes the mountains and plateaus west of the Continental Divide. Three-fourths of all Coloradans live along the Front Range in the east, where the mountains meet the plains.

A gold rush in Colorado in 1858–59 brought thousands of new settlers into the land that was home to the Ute, Arapaho, and Cheyenne Indians. Miners found not only gold but silver, lead, zinc, coal, and oil. To feed the miners, farmers learned to grow wheat, potatoes, lettuce, and other crops in Colorado's cool, dry, sunny climate. Denver, Colorado's capital city, grew up as a supply depot for the miners.

Spectacular scenery and 300 days of sunshine a year make Colorado a favorite among tourists. Its mountain resorts, famous for skiing, include Vail, the largest ski area in North America. Other ski areas have given new life to the former mining towns of Aspen, Breckenridge, Crested Butte, Keystone, and Telluride. Colorado's mountains also draw summer tourists, who can still throw snowballs in August. People also bike or hike the mountains, fish the trout streams, climb the peaks, and run the white-water rivers with rafts and kayaks.

For many years, the state's dry climate attracted people with lung diseases and other respiratory ailments. Health care became an important business, along with mining, agriculture, and tourism. In recent decades, computer and cable-television industries have added to the wealth of the Centennial State.

▶ LAND

Colorado is one of the Mountain States that contain parts of the Rocky Mountains of North America. Colorado's Rockies are part of the Southern Rocky Mountains.

Land Regions

Colorado lies at the center of the western United States. Shaped like a rectangle, it has three main landforms—plains, mountains, and plateaus.

The Great Plains, in eastern Colorado, are part of an enormous region that covers much of the central part of the United States. From the base of the Rockies, the plains slope down and eastward toward the Colorado-Kansas border. Long ago the Great Plains

Opposite page, clockwise from left: The Rocky Mountains dominate much of Colorado's landscape. Denver, the state capital, is the largest regional center of trade and culture. Cowboy hats and other Western fashions are popular among Coloradans of all ages.

State flower:
*Rocky Mountain
columbine*

State tree: Colorado blue spruce

FACTS AND FIGURES

Location: Western United States; bordered on the north by Wyoming and Nebraska, on the east by Nebraska and Kansas, on the south by Oklahoma and New Mexico, and on the west by Utah.

Area: 104,091 sq mi (269,595 km²); rank, 8th.

Population: 3,662,000 (1994 census); rank, 25th.

Elevation: *Highest*—14,433 ft (4,399 m) at Mount Elbert; *lowest*—3,350 ft (1,021 m) on the Arkansas River at the Colorado-Kansas border.

Capital: Denver.

Statehood: August 1, 1876; 38th state.

State Motto: *Nil sine numine* ("Nothing without providence").

State Song: "Where the Columbines Grow."

Nickname: Centennial State.

Abbreviations: CO; Colo.

State bird: Lark bunting

Clockwise from above: Horses graze on valley pasturelands. Wildflowers bloom in the meadows of Rocky Mountain National Park. Aspens turn brilliant yellow in the fall.

were covered by an inland sea. Now they are a sea of grass. Awesome sandstone formations, such as the Garden of the Gods at Colorado Springs and Red Rocks at Morrison, are reminders of the sandy beaches left by the inland sea.

The Rocky Mountains rise up sharply from the western edge of the Great Plains. Colorado has five major mountain ranges—the Front Range, the Park Range, the Sawatch Range, the San Juan Mountains, and the Sangre de Cristo ("blood of Christ") Mountains.

Colorado has 3,232 mountains that have been named and hundreds more that are unnamed. Scattered among them are 53 peaks higher than 14,000 feet (4,300 meters) above sea level. Colorado's highest mountain is 14,433-foot (4,399-meter)-high Mount Elbert in the Sawatch Range near Leadville.

The Colorado Plateau is a western extension of the Rocky Mountains. The Colorado River and its branches have cut the plateau into high, flat-topped, and steep-sided hills called mesas (the Spanish word for "tables"). The largest of these, Grand Mesa, between the

Colorado and the Gunnison rivers, is sometimes called the world's largest flat-topped mountain. Other tablelands range from a height of 7,500 feet (2,286 meters) at Mesa Verde in the southwest to a height of 11,000 feet (3,353 meters) at Flat Tops in the northwest. The highest mesas receive enough rain and snow to support forests and lush meadows. The canyons at the bottom of the mesas often approach desert conditions.

Rivers and Lakes

More than two-thirds of all Coloradans live in northeastern Colorado in the valley of the South Platte River and its main tributaries: Plum Creek, Cherry Creek, Clear Creek, Boulder Creek, Big Thompson River, and Cache la Poudre River.

The Arkansas River begins near Leadville and flows out of the Rockies through the 1,000-foot (305-meter)-deep Royal Gorge just west of Canon City. The Arkansas River waters the farms and ranches of southeastern Colorado before flowing through Kansas and Arkansas into the Mississippi River.

The Rio Grande (Spanish for "large river") starts in the San Juan Mountains of southwestern Colorado and flows east to the San Luis Valley.

The Colorado River originates in Rocky Mountain National Park and flows westward to drain all of western Colorado. Its tributaries include the Fraser, Blue, Grand, Eagle, Roaring Fork, and Gunnison rivers. The Colorado carries almost two-thirds of Colorado's total stream flow—more water than the Arkansas, Platte, and Rio Grande combined. A system of ditches, reservoirs, and tunnels diverts some of this water from the Western Slope to the much more developed, populous cities and towns east of the Rockies.

Grand Lake, Colorado's largest natural lake, is located on the southwestern edge of Rocky Mountain National Park. Hundreds of other natural lakes lie in the mountains and on the higher plateaus. Dams have been built to create artificial lakes, or reservoirs. Blue Mesa, Granby, John Martin, and other reservoirs are larger than any of Colorado's natural lakes. They are open for swimming and boating in the summer and for ice-skating and ice-fishing in the winter.

Climate

Colorado's climate generally is dry, cool, and sunny. However, the higher the elevation, the wetter and colder it gets. The high mountains average 45 inches (1,143 millimeters) of precipitation a year, mostly as snowfall. The low-lying eastern plains and the western canyons average only about 15 inches (381 millimeters) of moisture each year.

In the Rockies, snow can fall anytime—even in July or August. Snow begins in September or October and continues to whiten the mountains into April or May. Melting snow swells mountain streams from May to September, providing water for cities and farms lying on the eastern plains and in the western canyons.

Plant and Animal Life

Wide temperature changes, little moisture, and high winds keep Colorado's natural veg-

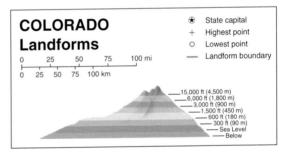

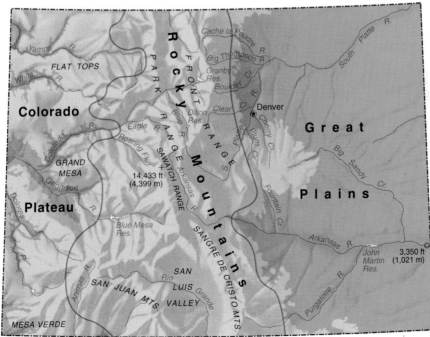

etation relatively limited. Blue grama and buffalo grass on the eastern plains are mixed with sage, tumbleweed, and sunflowers. Cottonwoods, the only common native prairie tree, line Colorado's river valleys. Mountain foothills are forested with aspens, ponderosa, and piñon pine. Higher up are Douglas firs, blue spruce, and lodgepole pines. The Englemann spruce is the only tree to survive at timberline, which is 10,000 to 11,000 feet (3,048 to 3,353 meters) above sea level. Above timberline, high winds and the very short growing season discourage tree growth, but alpine wildflowers thrive, bursting into color in June and July, before freezing weather and blizzards in August or September end the short high-country summer. Western plateaus and canyon lands also have aspen, spruce, and pines, as well as woody shrubs such as sage and rabbitbrush. Lower, drier areas have desert plants such as cactus.

Colorado's vast remote areas support many animals, especially mule deer and elk. Antelopes, bighorn sheep, black bears, and mountain goats are less common. Golden eagles are native and pheasants thrive. Bison are making a comeback on some ranches, but grizzly bears and wolves have not been seen in Colorado for decades.

Natural Resources

Minerals, fossil fuels (coal, oil, and natural gas), and forests are major sources of Colorado's natural wealth. Molybdenum, used to harden steel, accounts for almost half of Colorado's total metallic mineral production.

▶ PEOPLE

The 1858–59 gold rush brought to the area some 35,000 settlers, who began competing with the Native Americans for land and resources. By 1900, half a million people called Colorado home. The population reached a million in 1930 and has since continued to grow rapidly. Nearly 80 percent of the state's population is of European ancestry. About 16 percent is Hispanic. About 4 percent is African American and 1 percent is Asian. Some 35,000 Native Americans live in Colorado, including about 8,000 Utes, who live on the state's two Indian reservations, the Southern Ute and Ute Mountain.

Education

Coloradans set high standards for their locally supported elementary, middle, and high schools. Colorado claims to have the most highly educated residents in the country—18 percent of the state's residents have one or more college degrees.

The state owns and operates four universities, five state colleges, and sixteen community colleges. The University of Colorado (1876) is the largest, with campuses in Boulder, Denver, and Colorado Springs. Colorado State University (1870), in Fort Collins, began as the state agricultural school. The University of Northern Colorado (1889), in Greeley, began as a teachers college. Smaller and newer is the University

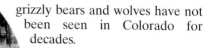

Top: Elk gather at a crossroads in Estes Park. *Left:* Wind and water sculpted the flat-topped mesas at Colorado National Monument on the Colorado Plateau.

Bottom: White-water rafting on the Arkansas and other rivers is a popular summer sport. *Right:* Many Coloradans learn to ski at an early age.

of Southern Colorado in Pueblo (1933). The Colorado School of Mines (1874), in Golden, claims to be the "World's Foremost College of Mineral Engineering." Other state colleges serve Alamosa, Durango, Grand Junction, Gunnison, and Trinidad. Community colleges offering two-year programs operate in 16 other towns, while Colorado Mountain College offers courses in a half dozen more communities.

The University of Denver (1864) is Colorado's oldest and largest private school. The Regis University (1877) is a private Catholic Institution in Denver. The Colorado College (1874), a private liberal arts institution, and the United States Air Force Academy (1954) are located in Colorado Springs.

Libraries, Museums, and the Arts

Colorado has more than 160 public libraries. The central branch of the Denver Public Library, with a fine western history department, is among the nation's largest and most comprehensive.

Colorado's biggest, best-known museum is the Denver Museum of Natural History. It has elaborate dinosaur exhibits, life-size dioramas of wild animals, a mineral hall, and a planetarium. The natural history museum shares Denver's City Park with the Denver Zoo. The zoo features exhibits, such as Bird World, Northern Shores, and Tropical Discovery, that show animals in their natural habitats. The Denver Art Museum has a strong Native American collection, while the Colorado Springs Fine Arts Museum specializes in Hispanic folk art.

The Colorado History Museum in Denver's Civic Center features a research library, the state historic preservation office, and Anasazi pottery and other artifacts from

PEOPLE

Population: 3,662,000 (1994 estimate).

Density: 35 persons per sq mi (14 per km²).

Distribution: 82% urban; 18% rural.

Largest Cities (1994 estimates):

Denver 493,559   Lakewood 126,031

Colorado Springs 316,480   Pueblo 100,471

Aurora 250,717

Persons per sq mi	Persons per km²
over 250	over 100
50-250	20-100
5-50	2-20
0-5	0-2

Denver
Lakewood · ·Aurora
Colorado
· Springs
Pueblo ·

Source: U.S. Bureau of the Census

Mesa Verde. The museum has eleven sites, including the Georgetown Loop Railroad, the Ute Museum in Montrose, and Fort Vasquez, an adobe trading post. Many communities have historical museums.

Among many music events are summer festivals, such as the Aspen Music Festival and School and the Telluride Bluegrass Festival. Denver's Center for the Performing Arts is home to the Colorado Symphony Orchestra, Opera Colorado, the Colorado Ballet, and a variety of theaters. The Central City Opera House, constructed in 1878, has been restored for summer operas.

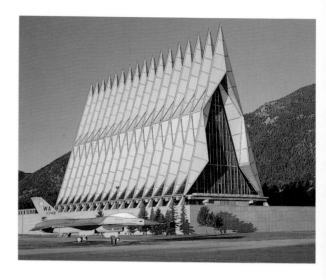

Sports

Colorado's sunny climate and challenging mountains attract millions of outdoor-sports enthusiasts. In summer and fall, hiking, running, mountain climbing, and mountain biking are popular. Snowy winter slopes attract about 11 million skiers and snowboarders a year to 30 major ski areas.

Colorado's professional sports teams are centered in Denver. Fans go to Mile High Stadium to watch the Denver Broncos of the National Football League and to Coors Field to watch the Colorado Rockies National League baseball club. The Denver Nuggets of the National Basketball Association and the Colorado Avalanche of the National Hockey League play their home games at McNichols Sports Arena.

▶ ECONOMY

Mining, Colorado's first major industry, was surpassed after 1900 by agricultural production. Since the 1930's, government, business, and service industries have been more impor-

tant. Today, cable television and computer-age businesses are the fastest-growing businesses in eastern Colorado, while skiing and tourism dominate the economy in the western part of the state.

Services

Services, which include banking, communication, government, insurance, real estate, retail trade, and utilities, have become the largest segment of Colorado's economy in recent decades.

The federal government is also a major employer in Colorado. The Denver metropolitan area employs more United States government workers than any city other than Washington, D.C.

Manufacturing

Colorado's most important manufacturing industry is the making of machinery, electronic instruments, and computer compo-

Top: The Academy Cadet Chapel at the United States Air Force Academy is an architectural landmark near Colorado Springs. *Left:* Cliff Palace at Mesa Verde National Park is one of Colorado's most popular tourist attractions. These dwellings, built right into the side of the cliff, once housed a community of Anasazi Indians. Also known as the Cliff Dwellers, they are the ancestors of today's Pueblo Indians.

PRODUCTS AND INDUSTRIES

Manufacturing: Machinery, food processing, electronic instruments, computer components, printing, publishing.

Agriculture: Cattle, corn, wheat, dairy products.

Minerals: Oil, coal, natural gas, molybdenum.

Services: Wholesale and retail trade; finance, insurance, and real estate; business, social, and personal services; transportation, communication, and utilities; government.

*Gross state product is the total value of goods and services produced in a year.

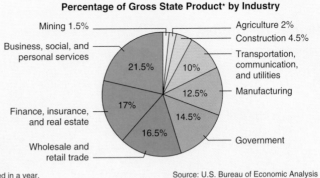

Percentage of Gross State Product* by Industry

Mining 1.5%
Agriculture 2%
Construction 4.5%
Transportation, communication, and utilities 10%
Manufacturing 12.5%
Government 14.5%
Wholesale and retail trade 16.5%
Finance, insurance, and real estate 17%
Business, social, and personal services 21.5%

Source: U.S. Bureau of Economic Analysis

nents. Food processing is also important and uses the state's many agricultural products for meatpacking and the canning and bottling of beer, fruits, and vegetables. Printing and publishing are also top industries, while the manufacture of sporting goods is on the rise. Local breweries, called microbreweries or brew pubs, have also been profitable.

Agriculture

Colorado's dry, changeable climate is hard on farmers. Even in the lowland valleys, frost can come as early as September and continue into late May. Because farmers have a short growing season, they concentrate on cool-weather crops such as hay, lettuce, onions, potatoes, peas, and wheat. Irrigated farmlands in the lower Arkansas and the South Platte river valleys produce alfalfa, sugar beets, beans, and other vegetables. Rocky Ford, on the Arkansas River, is known for its melons. The Colorado River valley, around Grand Junction, is noted for

its peaches, cherries, and apples. Land that is too dry or too cold to grow fruit, grain, or vegetables is often used to raise cattle, sheep, hogs, turkeys, and chickens. Livestock brings more income to Coloradans than crops.

Mining and Construction

In recent decades, oil, natural gas, and coal have become more valuable to the state's economy than gold and silver. Oil is produced from wells in the Rangely field, in northwestern Colorado, as well as in smaller fields scattered around the state.

Tungsten, uranium, radium, vanadium, and oil shale also have been produced in recent decades. Between the 1920's and the 1970's, the Climax mine near Leadville produced almost two-thirds of the world's supply of molybdenum.

As Colorado's population has boomed in recent decades, so has its construction industry. Cement is the basis for much new construction, such as office buildings, airport runways, and highways. The building boom

Left: Colorado farms produce a variety of crops, such as alfalfa, beans, and sugar beets.
Right: Coins are made in Denver at the United States Mint, one of four operated by the U.S. Department of the Treasury.

437

Places of Interest

Buffalo Bill's Grave, Lookout Mountain

Royal Gorge, near Canon City

Pro Rodeo Hall of Champions, in Colorado Springs

Kissing Camels, Garden of the Gods

About a fourth of Colorado's land has been set aside for national forests, grasslands, parks, monuments, and wilderness areas.

Bent's Old Fort National Historic Site, near La Junta, is a reconstructed early outpost for trappers that was later a center of the fur trade.

Black Canyon of the Gunnison National Park, on the Gunnison River northeast of Montrose, includes several miles of Colorado's deepest and narrowest river gorge.

Dinosaur National Monument, in the northwest, stretches into Utah. Reconstructed skeletons of *Apatosaurus* and *Stegosaurus* give visitors an idea of these giants that roamed Colorado when it was a tropical swamp.

Florissant Fossil Beds National Monument, near Florissant, preserves ancient fossil insects, seeds, and leaves.

Great Sand Dunes National Monument, in the San Luis Valley near Alamosa, has dunes up to 600 feet (180 meters) high. The dune field of about 50 square miles (130 square kilometers) nestles against the snowcapped Sangre de Cristo Mountains.

Hovenweep National Monument, west of Cortez on the Colorado-Utah border, includes groups of prehistoric pueblos and rock towers.

Lookout Mountain, west of Denver, includes a scenic high drive to the grave of Buffalo Bill Cody and a museum.

Mesa Verde National Park, in southwest Colorado, includes the Southwest's finest cliff dwellings. These stabilized ruins, pit houses, nature walks, camping facilities, and museums draw tourists from all over the world.

Mount Evans is reached by America's highest paved highway. It winds through terrific views and herds of mountain goats to a high-altitude laboratory on the 14,264-foot (4,348-meter) summit.

Pro Rodeo Hall of Champions, in Colorado Springs, features historical photographs and memorabilia of rodeo competitions.

Railroads. Colorado has a number of historic railroads. The **Cumbres Toltec Scenic Railroad** steam train snakes through Toltec Gorge and Cumbres Pass. This summer trip between Antonito, Colorado, and Chama, New Mexico, covers 63 miles (191 kilometers) on America's highest and longest narrow gauge rail. The **Durango and Silverton Narrow Gauge Railroad** has been operating through the awe-inspiring Animas River gorge since 1882. This steam-powered antique offers summer passenger service through the San Juan Mountains. The **Georgetown Loop Railroad** is a restored line over a narrow track that loops back over itself to make the steep climb between Georgetown and Silver Plume in scenic silver-mining country.

Rocky Mountain National Park is a scenic mountain region straddling the Continental Divide northwest of Denver. Lakes, fishing streams, trails, and Longs Peak are the main attractions.

State Recreation Areas. For information on Colorado's numerous state parks and camping grounds, write to Colorado State Parks, 1313 Sherman Street, Room 618, Denver, Colorado 80203.

has made sand, gravel, and limestone some of modern Colorado's most profitable natural resources.

Transportation

Coloradans have one of the nation's highest rates of motor vehicle ownership. Interstate highways and scenic state and local highways reach all parts of the state. Amtrak provides year-round rail passenger service.

A dozen Colorado cities offer regularly scheduled commercial flights. Denver is the hub of state and regional air travel, with one of the busiest airports in the world. Denver International Airport, opened in 1995, occupies an enormous 54-square-mile (140-square-kilometer) site with plenty of room for expansion.

Communication

Colorado has more than 20 daily newspapers and 100 weeklies. The best-known newspapers are the *Denver Post*, founded in 1892, and the *Rocky Mountain News*, Colorado's first newspaper, started in 1859. The state's first radio stations of the 1920's, KOA and KLZ in Denver and KFKA in Greeley, are still broadcasting, along with about 175 other licensed stations. Television began broadcasting in Denver in 1952. The state now has about 23 licensed television stations as well as many cable stations.

▶ CITIES

Colorado's largest cities are at the eastern base of the mountains, stretching from Fort Collins in the north to Pueblo in the south.

Denver, the capital and largest city, has a metropolitan area with more than 2 million residents. Denver began in 1858 as a mining camp and became the seat of government in 1867, when Colorado was still a territory. Denver today is the economic, transportation, and cultural center of Colorado. An article on Denver appears in Volume D.

Colorado Springs, the state's second largest city, is located near the base of Pikes Peak. William J. Palmer, president of the Denver & Rio Grande Railroad, founded Colorado Springs in 1871. He planned a park system that includes the Garden of the Gods and helped found the Colorado College.

Recent growth of the city has centered around the manufacture of electronics and precision instruments. Nearby are Pikes Peak, Fort Carson, and the U.S. Air Force Academy. Also located in Colorado Springs is the United States Olympic Training Center.

Pueblo, the major city of southern Colorado and the Arkansas Valley region, was founded at the junction of Fountain Creek and the Arkansas River as a trading fort in 1842. Destroyed by Utes in 1854, Pueblo was rebuilt in 1858 and became an important industrial center for smelting ores to extract gold and silver. Later, steel mills gave Pueblo the nickname the Pittsburgh of the West. All the smelters and most of the mills have closed in recent decades. Other industries, however, continue to process foods from the Arkansas Valley and make such products as machine parts and building materials.

Fort Collins was founded as an army post in 1863. An agricultural center, it became the site of the state's agricultural college, which later evolved into Colorado State University. High-tech industries and breweries, as well as traditional farming and ranching, have made Fort Collins a modern boomtown.

Greeley is the largest city in northeastern Colorado. Founded as Union Colony in 1870 by Horace Greeley, the founder and editor of the *New York Tribune*, the town was established as a model agricultural colony. Together the settlers built houses, farms, and irrigation ditches. They prospered by growing

Pikes Peak, Colorado's best-known mountain, rises 14,110 feet (4,301 meters) near Colorado Springs, the state's second largest city.

GOVERNMENT

State Government
Governor: 4-year term
State senators: 35; 4-year terms
State representatives: 65;
  2-year terms
Number of counties: 63

Federal Government
U.S. senators: 2
U.S. representatives: 6
Number of electoral votes: 8

For the name of the current governor, see STATE GOVERNMENTS in Volume S. For the names of current U.S. senators and representatives, see UNITED STATES, CONGRESS OF THE in Volume U-V.

INDEX TO COLORADO MAP

The 13th step of the entrance to the gold-domed state capitol building in Denver is exactly 1 mile (1.6 kilometers) above sea level, giving Denver the nickname the Mile High City.

potatoes and sugar beets and raising sheep and cattle. Today Greeley remains an agricultural center. It is home to the University of Northern Colorado.

▶ GOVERNMENT

Colorado's constitution, adopted in 1876, is still in force, although it has been amended many times. The executive branch of the state government is headed by the governor, who is assisted by the lieutenant governor, secretary of state, attorney general, and treasurer. The legislative, or lawmaking, branch consists of a senate and a house of representatives. The state judicial system is headed by the supreme court. Its seven justices are appointed by the governor. Colorado also has an intermediate court of appeals below the supreme court. The major trial courts are district courts. Lower courts include county and municipal courts.

▶ HISTORY

One thousand years ago, Indians known as the Anasazi ("ancient ones") lived in fantastic cliff houses made of stone and mud. Ute Indians occupied the mountains, where they enjoyed Colorado's many natural hot springs. Cheyenne, Arapaho, Apache, and Comanche hunted bison on the eastern plains.

Exploration and Settlement

In 1541, the Spanish explorer Francisco Coronado may have crossed the southeast

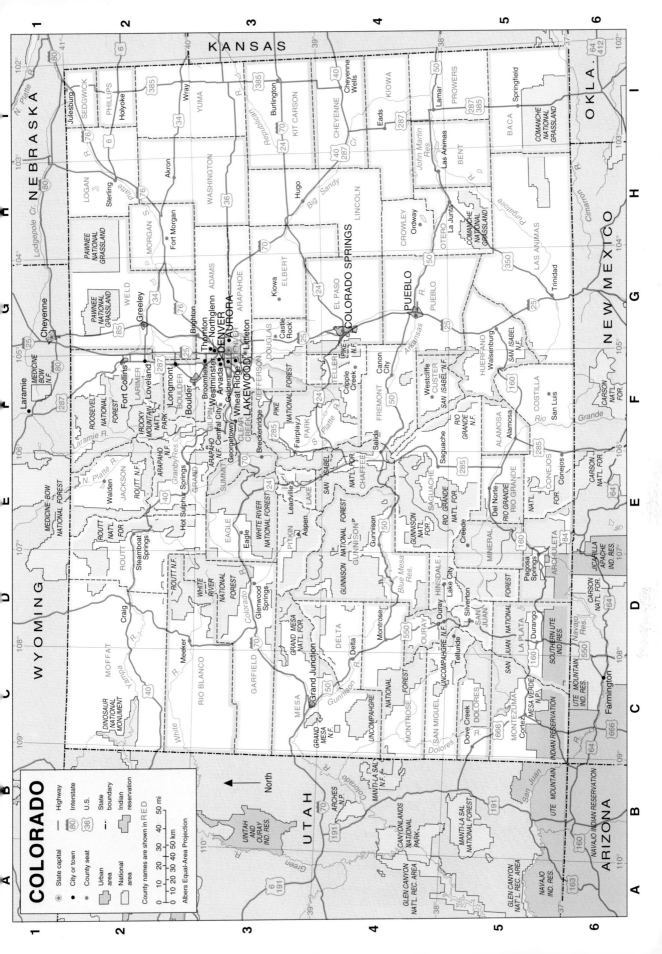

Famous People

"Aunt" Clara Brown (1802–85), born in Virginia, worked as a slave until her owners freed her in 1857. Her husband and children had been sold to other owners. She went to Colorado in 1859 and became a laundress in Central City. With earnings from washing the miners' clothing, she helped build Central City's St. James Methodist Church, which still stands. She also gave away money to help poor friends from the South start a new life in Colorado.

William Harrison "Jack" Dempsey (1895–1983), born in Manassa, was one of the world's great heavyweight boxing champions. Nicknamed the Manassa Mauler, Dempsey became famous in 1919 when he knocked out Jess Willard, who outweighed Dempsey by 57 pounds (26 kilograms). Known for his flamboyant and aggressive style, Dempsey held the

Jack Dempsey

Douglas Fairbanks, Sr.

heavyweight title for seven years until he was defeated by Gene Tunney in 1926.

John Evans (1814–97), a native of Waynesville, Ohio, moved to Chicago, where he helped found Northwestern University and the suburb of Evanston. In 1862 he accepted President Lincoln's appointment to be the second territorial governor of Colorado. Governor Evans promoted railroads and other business projects that made Denver the Queen City of Colorado. Hoping to civilize the wild

Colorado Territory, he founded the Colorado Seminary, which later became the University of Denver, and promoted the building of churches, schools, and other cultural institutions. Mount Evans, west of Denver, is named for him.

Douglas Fairbanks, Sr. (Douglas Elton Ullman) (1883–1939), born in Denver, was one of the most popular movie stars of the silent era. Trained as a Shakespearean actor, he was brought to Hollywood in 1914 by the great early film director D. W. Griffith. Fairbanks was famous for his swashbuckler roles in such early blockbusters as *The Mark of Zorro* (1920), *The Three Musketeers* (1921), and *The Thief of Bagdad* (1924). In 1919, he cofounded the United Artists studio with his wife, Mary Pickford, and his friends D. W. Griffith and Charlie Chaplin.

Emily Griffith (1880–1947), an Ohio native, became a frontier schoolteacher by the age of 14. In the Denver public

corner of Colorado while searching for gold. More than 150 years passed before Spanish explorers from Mexico claimed the Rio Grande Valley of Southern Colorado for Spain in 1706.

In 1776 two Spanish missionaries, Father Silvestre Escalante and Father Francisco Domínguez, led the first party to explore, map, and report on Colorado. Soon after, French trappers and traders explored the Platte and Cache la Poudre rivers, claiming that these tributaries of the Mississippi River belonged to French Louisiana.

In 1803, President Thomas Jefferson bought eastern Colorado as part of the

Louisiana Purchase and sent Zebulon M. Pike to explore the new territory. Pike followed the Arkansas River into the Rockies and reported on the strange new land. In 1820, Major Stephen H. Long explored the South Platte Valley of northeastern Colorado. Like Pike, he found the region dry and rugged. Long created a map and dubbed the region the Great American Desert.

Despite Major Long's advice that Colorado be left to the Native Americans, trappers and traders built Bent's Fort on the Arkansas River and other trading posts on the South Platte River during the 1830's. After the Mexican War ended in 1848, Mexico sold to the United States the rest of what is now Colorado.

In 1886 this wagon train camped for the night in Denver at the present site of Market Street between 15th and 16th streets.

Gold Strikes

Americans mostly ignored the Great American Desert and the rugged, remote Rockies until gold was found near the present site of Denver in 1858. Thousands of gold seekers soon settled in Denver and in the smaller towns. In 1861, Congress created Colorado Territory. Colorado's population more than quadrupled between 1870 and 1880. Cities such as Denver and

schools, she took an interest not only in children but in their parents. Many adults, she found, had trouble finding jobs because they lacked skills and could not speak, read, or write English well. For such adults and for "all who wish to learn," Emily set up the Public Opportunity School within the Denver public school system. After her death, it was renamed the Emily Griffith Opportunity School. The school continues to offer daytime, evening, and weekend classes to those wanting to improve their language and job skills.

Benjamin Barr Lindsey (1869–1943), born in Jackson, Tennessee, moved with his family to Denver at the age of 11. Overcoming teenage poverty and depression, he became a lawyer and a politician. A tiny man who weighed only 98 pounds, Lindsey nevertheless was a giant among

Florence Rena Sabin

Ouray

Colorado's reformers. In Denver he developed the world's first model juvenile court. He sought to reform child offenders rather than send them to adult prisons, which were often just schools for crime. Lindsey also attacked political corruption and exploitation of the poor.

Ouray (1833–80), the son of a Jicarilla Apache father and a Tabeguache Ute mother, was born near Taos, New Mexico. Following tradition, he and his father went to live with his mother's people. A

peacemaker rather than a warrior, Ouray became the spokesperson for his people in treaty making with the U.S. government. Some said he gave away too much. Others said he saved his people from extinction and enabled them to at least keep two reservations in southwestern Colorado, the Southern Ute and Ute Mountain.

Florence Rena Sabin (1871–1953), born in Central City, was a medical researcher in the field of human embryology. She was the first woman to become a full professor at Johns Hopkins University and the first woman elected to the National Academy of Sciences (1925). After distinguishing herself in the fields of public health and tuberculosis research in the East, Dr. Sabin returned to Colorado in 1938. She retired briefly and then sought to reform Colorado's public health laws.

Colorado Springs served as supply points for the miners and quickly grew prosperous.

Conflicts with the Native Americans

At first, the Native Americans had welcomed the gold seekers. But as the new settlers crowded the Native Americans off their land and killed off the bison and antelope, conflict with the natives grew. On November 29, 1864, Colorado militiamen attacked a Cheyenne and Arapaho village at Sand Creek, slaughtering more than 130 people, including women, children, and the elderly. The Native Americans sought revenge by attacking U.S. Army and government workers at Beecher Island (1868) and with the Meeker Massacre (1869). But by 1881, they had all been removed from the state, except for those living on two small Ute reservations in the southwestern corner.

From Statehood to the Present

Colorado's population swelled as a result of the mining bonanza, making statehood possible in 1876. The boom years lasted until 1893, when the silver market collapsed. Gold mining remained important until the early 1900's, when labor wars and dwindling mineral deposits caused the industry to decline.

During this time, farming and ranching thrived. Farmers learned to grow wheat, sugar beets, and other crops on Colorado's dry, high plains with the help of water ditches and dry-land farming skills. The agricultural boom ended when the Great Depression of the 1930's dried up markets for crops and livestock. Dust storms and grasshopper plagues added to the problems, leaving the eastern plains of Colorado littered with abandoned farms, ranches, and towns.

In the 1940's, President Franklin Roosevelt's New Deal policies and World War II transformed Colorado by providing many people with federal jobs. In addition, the federal government built or helped to build dams and parks, military bases and government buildings, and roads and airports. These improvements helped attract a million newcomers to the state by the 1990's.

THOMAS J. NOEL
Co-author, *Historical Atlas of Colorado*

See also DENVER.

COLUMBUS (OHIO)

Columbus, located on the Scioto River near the center of Ohio, is the state's capital and largest city. More than 635,000 people live within the city limits. About 1.4 million live in the greater metropolitan area.

The city's economy is based on business and social services, chiefly finance, insurance, real estate, medical care, education, scientific research, and federal, state, and local government. Columbus is also one of the world's leading centers for processing computer-based scientific information. Locally manufactured products include appliances and automotive parts.

Higher education further supports Columbus' economy. Ohio State University, with one of the largest enrollments of any university in the United States, has its main branch in Columbus. Capital University and Franklin University also are located within the city. Denison and Ohio Wesleyan universities are nearby.

Columbus also offers a variety of cultural and entertainment opportunities. Attractions include the Center of Science and Industry

Columbus—the capital of Ohio and the state's largest city—is an important center of government, education, and computer information services.

and its planetarium; the Columbus Museum of Art, featuring the work of a Columbus-born artist, George Bellows; the Ohio Historical Center, which includes one of the nation's finest collections of prehistoric Indian artifacts; the Wexner Center for the Arts, located on the campus of Ohio State University; and the Thurber House, a home of writer James Thurber.

Lovers of music and dance attend the performances of the Columbus Symphony Orchestra and the local ballet company. Other popular attractions include Ohio State University cultural and sports events and the Columbus Zoo, known for raising endangered species. The Ohio State Fair, held every August, maintains permanent fairgrounds in the city. Columbus also has an extensive public park system.

In 1812, when the state legislature was considering a location for the state capital near the center of Ohio, many towns sought the honor. The legislators chose a site on the high bank east of the Scioto. Named in honor of the great explorer Christopher Columbus, the city became the state capital in 1816.

Because the Scioto River cannot accommodate ships, Columbus lacked the excellent water facilities that helped Cincinnati and Cleveland become industrial and manufacturing centers. With a smaller industrial base, the city grew slowly and attracted only small numbers of foreign-born settlers, mostly German. African American migrants from the southern states found employment in many of the city's public service establishments. However, since World War II, Columbus has experienced uninterrupted growth. Its service industries, ideally suited to the Information Age, have been quick to assume leadership in computer-related segments of the economy.

Reviewed by GEORGE W. KNEPPER
Author, *Ohio and Its People*

Christopher Columbus, an Italian navigator in the service of Spain, made four pioneering voyages (1492–1504), which led to the European colonization of the Americas.

Columbus' First Impressions of the Native Americans
Friday, October 12, 1492

"*As I saw that they were very friendly to us and perceived that they could be much more easily converted to our holy faith by gentle means than by force, I presented them with some red caps, and strings of glass beads to put round their necks, and many other trifles of small value, which gave them great pleasure . . . this made them so much our friends that it was a marvel to see. Afterwards they came swimming to the boats, bringing parrots, balls of cotton thread, javelins, and many other things . . .*

"They all go as naked as when their mothers bore them, even the women, though I saw but one girl. All whom I saw were young, not above thirty years of age, well made, with fine shapes and faces. Their hair is short, and coarse like that of a horse's tail. . . . Some paint themselves black, some paint themselves white, others red, and others with such colors as they can find . . . .

"It appears to me that the people are ingenious and would be good servants, and I am of the opinion that they would very readily become Christians, as they appear to have no religion . . . . If it please our Lord, I intend at my return to carry home six of them to your Highnesses, that they may learn our language . . . ."

Excerpt from *The Log of Christopher Columbus' First Voyage to America in the Year 1492, As Copied Out in Brief by Bartholomew Las Casas.*

COLUMBUS, CHRISTOPHER
(1451–1506)

When Christopher Columbus sailed west into the unknown waters of the Atlantic Ocean in 1492, he was not trying to prove that the earth is round; scholars already were aware of this fact. Nor was he trying to discover a New World; few Europeans dreamed that such a world existed. Columbus, like many people of his time, dreamed of finding a sea route to Asia that would lead to a wealth of gold, jewels, and spices. Eventually he became possessed by the idea that he could reach Asia by sailing west.

When Columbus finally embarked on his voyage, it proved to be an unparalleled historic event with far-reaching effects, not only on the American continents, but on Europe as well. In addition, historians have recognized Columbus' navigational skills. Not only did he find the best route across the ocean to the Americas, but he found the best eastern route back to Europe as well—routes still used hundreds of years later.

▶**EARLY LIFE**

Christopher Columbus (in Italian, Cristoforo Colombo) was born in 1451 in Genoa, in present-day Italy. His father was a poor weaver, and Christopher worked for him. The boy had little schooling; few people of his day did. Genoa, however, was a thriving seaport, and Christopher learned much from sailors' tales of their voyages. As soon as he could, he went to sea. He made short fishing trips at first, then longer ones with merchants who traded their goods at various ports along the coast of the Mediterranean Sea. Between voyages he studied mapmaking and geography. In his early 20's he sailed as a common seaman with a merchant fleet to transport goods to northern Europe. They sailed through the Strait of Gibraltar off the southern coast of Spain and into the Atlantic Ocean.

In 1476, Columbus found himself living in Portugal, the greatest European seafaring center of the age. Everything about this center for explorers heated this adventurous young man's desire to find new and unknown lands. During his years in Portugal he mastered the art of navigation and absorbed all he could from the writings of such travelers as Marco Polo, who had voyaged to strange lands as far away as Asia. Polo's story of his journey to Cathay (China) in 1275 described a land rich in spices, jewels, and silks.

▶IN SEARCH OF A ROUTE TO ASIA

In Columbus' time the only known route to Asia from Europe was to sail eastward across the Mediterranean Sea and then travel by caravan across ancient routes through deserts and mountains. Europeans were eager to find an easier route for their trading ships. Already Portuguese explorers were sailing south into the Atlantic, hoping to find a way to Asia by going all the way around Africa. (Afraid to venture too far out into the unknown waters of the Atlantic, the fearful seamen took care to keep the African coast in their sight.)

From his study of geography and from the tales of other sailors, Columbus concluded that India and eastern Asia were on the other side of the Atlantic Ocean. That was the route to take.

A man of powerful will, Columbus tried for nearly ten years to interest European rulers in his plan. Some agreed that Asia lay to the west. But how far? No one knew. Columbus estimated that Japan must be about 2,500 miles (4,000 kilometers) due west of the Canary Islands. He miscalculated, however, because he estimated that the earth was smaller than it really is. Japan, in fact, is more than 10,000 miles (16,000 kilometers) away from the islands.

▶COLUMBUS' FIRST VOYAGE TO THE NEW WORLD

Finally, in 1492, King Ferdinand and Queen Isabella, the rulers of the Spanish kingdoms of Castile and Aragon, agreed to outfit three ships for Columbus. They promised to make him viceroy (governor) of any new lands he might acquire and offered him 10 percent of all the wealth that he would bring to Spain.

With his fleet of three ships—the *Niña*, the *Pinta*, and the *Santa María*—Columbus sailed west on August 3, 1492. The ships were manned by a crew of about ninety men, most of them Spanish, except for Columbus and a few others. Columbus kept a careful log of his voyage. Much of what we know about the voyage comes from this source. After the ships stopped at the Canary Islands to make repairs and take aboard fresh food, the fleet headed out into the open Atlantic—the Sea of Darkness.

As the days passed, tension mounted in the crew. None had ever been out of sight of land for so long. And with the wind blowing steadily from the northeast, they wondered whether they would be able to sail against it to return home. Seeing how nervous the men were, Columbus gave them smaller estimates of the number of miles sailed, so they wouldn't know how far they really were from their home port.

Nevertheless, rumbles of mutiny swept through the crew as Columbus pressed on. On the 17th day, (days after Columbus had already expected to reach Japan) a lookout sighted land. It was early on the morning of October 12, 1492. They landed on one of the islands of the Bahamas, which Columbus named San Salvador. The island natives came down to the shore to see Columbus' strange ships. Thinking he had reached the East Indies, Columbus called these people Indians.

Columbus had discovered what Europeans would soon call the New World of the Americas. Of course, it was not a New World to the millions of Native Americans already living there. They had been there thousands of years before the Europeans would "discover" them.

THE COLUMBIAN EXCHANGE

A major consequence of Columbus' voyages was the eventual exchange of goods between the Old World (Europe) and the New World (the Americas). Listed below are some of the goods that were shared in this "Columbian Exchange" between the continents.

From Europe to the Americas

Bananas	Lettuce
Barley	Lilacs
Cabbages	Olives
Carnations	Oranges
Chickens	Peaches
Coffee	Pears
Cows	Pigs
Crabgrass	Rice
Daffodils	Sheep
Daisies	Sugarcane
Dandelions	Tulips
Horses	Turnips
Lemons	Wheat

From the Americas to Europe

Avocados	Pineapples
Beans	Poinsettias
(kidney, navy, lima)	Potatoes
Bell peppers	Pumpkins
Black-eyed Susans	Quinine
Cacao	Rubber
(for chocolate)	Squashes
Chili peppers	Sunflowers
Corn	Sweet potatoes
Cotton	Tobacco
Marigolds	Tomatoes
Papayas	Turkeys
Peanuts	Vanilla beans
Petunias	Zinnias

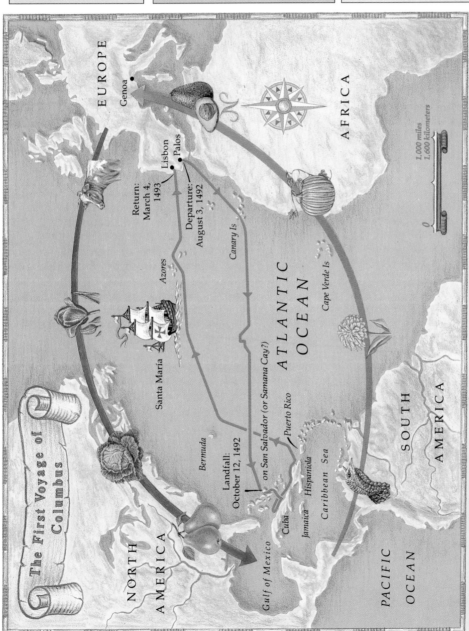

The First Voyage of Columbus

NORTH AMERICA

Genoa

EUROPE

Lisbon
Palos

Return: March 4, 1493

Departure: August 3, 1492

AFRICA

Azores

Canary Is

Santa María

Cape Verde Is

ATLANTIC OCEAN

Bermuda

Landfall: October 12, 1492 on San Salvador (or Samana Cay?)

Puerto Rico

Cuba

Jamaica   Hispaniola

Gulf of Mexico

Caribbean Sea

PACIFIC OCEAN

SOUTH AMERICA

0   1,000 miles
     1,600 kilometers

Although Christopher Columbus reached the Bahamas and the islands of the Caribbean, he never set foot on the mainland of either North or South America. However, his discovery of the region encouraged other explorers to follow, and soon they found, explored, and settled the American continents.

What were the consequences of Columbus' voyage in 1492?

Columbus' voyage and "discovery" of the Americas in 1492 introduced the modern era. His voyage opened up, particularly to the Europeans, a whole new world, rich in natural resources and filled with opportunities they could not possibly immediately recognize.

By exploiting these newly discovered resources, Western Europeans soon gained a great deal of wealth and power; so they began building permanent settlements in these new lands. Their presence, however, greatly disrupted the lives of the American Indians, who already lived there.

An unforeseen and terrible consequence of this contact between the Old and the New Worlds were the deaths of at least two thirds of the native populations, mostly from diseases brought to their land by the newcomers. In addition, the Indians were forced to endure enslavement by the Europeans, beginning with Columbus' own men. Many who would not obey were killed.

Most people agree that, ever since their first encounter with the Europeans, Native Americans have been mistreated and displaced from their rightful homes. However, others argue that Columbus deserves credit for his bold vision and brave voyage, which gave birth to a new age that enormously expanded the world's horizons.

Looking for the rich cities of Asia, Columbus spent the next ten weeks exploring the islands of the Caribbean. He landed on the heavily populated islands of Hispaniola (shared today by the Dominican Republic and Haiti) and Cuba, which he thought was the Asian mainland.

Near Hispaniola, Columbus' flagship, the *Santa María*, ran aground, and the waves smashed it to pieces. Leaving several men behind to establish a fort, Columbus set sail for Spain in the *Niña*. On the voyage home, he wrote a report of his discoveries. Believing he had reached Asia, Columbus wrote glowingly of its "gentle and peaceful" people, its fertile soil, its spices, its superb harbors, and its "great mines of gold and other metals." This last, however, was his fantasy; he had not found the quantity of riches he had sought.

Holding out the promise of greater riches, Columbus offered to give Ferdinand and Isabella "as much gold as they need…and as many slaves as they ask" if they would finance another voyage. As proof of what he could do, he brought them back a small amount of gold, parrots, plants, and some Indians he had kidnapped and enslaved.

▶ **LATER VOYAGES**

Between 1493 and 1504, Columbus made three more trips to the Americas, still searching for the great cities of Asia that Marco Polo had described. On his second voyage he found that the men he had left on Hispaniola had all been killed by the Indians. Apparently, as soon as Columbus left, the Spanish had begun to quarrel and fight among themselves and had made no common effort to build a lasting community. Bands of Spanish thieves roved the countryside, plundering native villages. They forced the Indians to hunt for gold and took women as their prisoners. The Indians, obliged to defend themselves, had killed the intruders.

Columbus never found the gold and jewels he had expected. Apart from his hunt for wealth, his mission was to convert the natives to Christianity. The idea that the Indians might have a right to determine their own way of life and to govern themselves never occurred to him. He also thought he had a right to claim the lands they inhabited for Spain. Because he saw himself as a redeemer of souls, he could justify all the harmful consequences of his great enterprise.

▶ **COLUMBUS IS RECALLED TO SPAIN**

Failure to deliver what he had promised to Ferdinand and Isabella and reports of chaotic conditions in the colonies led to the downfall of Columbus. In 1500 he was sent back to Spain in chains and was removed as governor of the Indies. In the end, he retained only empty honors. Sick, disappointed, and ignored, he died in Spain in 1506.

MILTON MELTZER
Author, *Columbus and the World Around Him*

See also EXPLORATION AND DISCOVERY; FERDINAND AND ISABELLA.

COLUMBUS DAY. See HOLIDAYS.

COMANECI, NADIA. See OLYMPIC GAMES (Profiles).

COMBUSTION. See FIRE.

COMETS, METEORITES, AND ASTEROIDS

When the planets of our solar system were formed, bits and pieces of matter were left over. Most of these pieces of matter are the size of grains of sand, but the largest pieces are hundreds of miles across. Some are rocky and metallic objects called **asteroids** that orbit the sun in the inner solar system. Others are icy objects called **comets** that usually remain at the outer fringes of the solar system. Pieces of asteroids or comets that pass through the Earth's atmosphere and fall to the ground are known as **meteorites**.

Formation of Asteroids and Comets

Astronomers think that the solar system was formed about 4.5 billion years ago from the collapse of a huge interstellar cloud of gas and dust. As the sun began to condense and shine at its center, the outer areas of this whirling, pancake-shaped cloud began to condense into countless bodies of solid matter. The planets and their moons were formed when this matter gathered together into larger and larger chunks. The matter that was left over from the formation of the planets became the asteroids and comets. Most of the asteroids in the solar system are located within the gap that exists between the orbits of Mars and Jupiter, where they are less likely to collide with a planet. Most of the comets are located in zones between the orbits of the outer planets and within an immense spherical-shaped area of space called the Oort Cloud, which lies outside the orbits of the outer planets and stretches almost to the stars that are nearest to our solar system. Occasionally, an asteroid or comet is dislodged from these regions and begins traveling in a path that brings it close to the Earth and the sun. When pieces of these asteroids or comets reach the Earth, scientists have an opportunity to study rocks that were present at the creation of the solar system.

Entering Earth's Atmosphere

Larger asteroids occasionally strike the Earth, explode, and leave craters like the large Meteor Crater near Winslow, Arizona. Fortunately, the largest asteroids are widely spaced in the solar system, and they strike the Earth only every million years or so. Many scientists think that an enormous asteroid 10 miles (16 kilometers) in diameter struck the Earth about 65 million years ago. The resulting explosion, equal to a hundred thousand billion tons of dynamite, may have destroyed most species of life on Earth, including the dinosaurs.

Asteroids that strike Earth create craters like the large Meteor Crater in Arizona (*below*). Scientists study such craters to better understand similar craters that exist on the Earth's moon and on Mars.

A meteor appears as a vertical streak of light against the stars in this time-exposure image (*above*). The streak is a glowing fragment of an asteroid or comet. This meteorite (*inset*), believed to have originated on Mars, was found in Antarctica.

from the moon, meteorites were the only samples of extraterrestrial matter (material from outside Earth) known to scientists. By studying pieces of meteorites, scientists have learned a great deal about the origin and formation of the planets.

Asteroids

Asteroids are small planets made up mostly of rocks and metal. Most asteroids orbit the sun in a region between Mars and Jupiter known as the "main belt." Two large clouds of asteroids, known as the Trojan asteroids, are actually in the same orbit as Jupiter, but they travel either in front of the planet or behind it as it orbits the sun. Earth also shares its orbit with an asteroid, which is the only natural companion to our planet other than the moon.

The orbits of most asteroids are more elliptical, or oval shaped, than the orbits of the planets. They are also often tipped somewhat to the general plane of the solar system. Because of their elliptical and tilted orbits, asteroids sometimes collide with each other. Remains of large asteroids shattered by these collisions can form "families" of smaller asteroids. These asteroids travel in similar orbits. By studying different members of an asteroid family, astronomers can sometimes discover what the once-hidden core of the original large asteroid was like.

Gravitational forces from Jupiter have produced relatively empty areas of space called Kirkwood gaps within the asteroid main belt between Mars and Jupiter. Any asteroid that strays into one of these gaps has its orbit changed by Jupiter's gravitational forces. These forces sometimes dislodge asteroids and cause them to career into the inner solar system. These so-called "Earth-approaching asteroids" are those most likely to collide with the Earth, and they are the source of most meteorites that reach the Earth's surface.

Astronomers have measured the light reflected from different asteroids and learned that, like different rocks on the Earth, the asteroids are made up of different minerals. Some black, carbon-rich asteroids look similar

The chance of such a disastrous event occurring in our lifetimes is very remote even though countless tiny pieces of asteroids and comet dust enter the Earth's atmosphere all the time. As the tiny particles fall through our atmosphere, friction causes them to burn up, leaving trails of light to mark their paths. On clear, dark nights you can see these **meteors**, also called shooting stars, flashing across the sky every few minutes. During a meteor shower, several shooting stars may appear each minute.

Sometimes a larger piece of material from an asteroid or comet does not burn up completely as it enters the Earth's atmosphere. Instead, it survives atmospheric friction and plummets all the way to the ground. As it descends, it appears as a spectacular **fireball** in the night sky, perhaps brighter than the brightest star or even as bright as the moon. The strange rocks and lumps of metal that are sometimes found in fields or meadows may be pieces of asteroids or comets that have reached the Earth's surface. They are known as meteorites. Until astronauts brought back rocks

to ancient meteorites that have never been modified since the time when the planets in the inner half of the solar system were formed. Other asteroids appear to consist of material similar to solidified volcanic rocks found on Earth. Still others seem to be composed of a greenish rock called olivine, which is found within the Earth's crust. Some asteroids are composed of solid metal. The composition of all of these types of asteroids reflects a process of intense heating and melting during their formation. This heating may have been the result of strong electromagnetic forces produced by the sun, or the decay of radioactive elements formed by exploding stars called supernovas. Scientists hope to discover more about how asteroids were formed because the same processes may have affected the formation of the planets.

By studying asteroids with telescopes, astronomers have discovered that asteroids have strange shapes; they are rarely as rounded as the planets. Powerful radar telescopes can now bounce echoes off some asteroids and map their surfaces. In 1991 the *Galileo* spacecraft took the first close-up pictures of the asteroid Gaspra, showing that asteroids look very different from comets and planetary moons.

In 1996, scientists launched the *Near Earth Asteroid Rendezvous* (NEAR), the first space probe designed to orbit an asteroid (named 433 Eros). *NEAR*'s pictures of the asteroid, and another named 253 Mathilde, revealed surfaces pitted by craters.

Meteorites

Until about the early 1800's, people were mystified by the rocks that fell from the sky. Scientists now realize that these rocks, called meteorites, are pieces of asteroids or comets. The rocks that fall through the atmosphere are called "falls," while those that are simply found on the ground are called "finds."

The most common meteorites found on Earth, called chondrites, are made of ordinary rocks and bits of metal. Although the black, carbon-rich meteorites are more common in space, most burn up in the atmosphere before reaching the ground. Metallic and stony-iron meteorites are quite rare in space, but they easily penetrate the Earth's atmosphere. Such meteorites are very interesting because of their odd shapes and the structure of their metallic crystals, which can be seen on their polished surfaces. Scientists known as cosmochemists study the chemical composition of these chondrite meteorites for clues to their origins and to the formation of the solar system.

Meteorite Craters.   Until the 1950's, there was a great deal of controversy about whether any craters on Earth were made by the impact of objects from outer space. Studies of the Meteor Crater in Arizona resolved the controversy. Not only were meteorites found strewn around the crater, but forms of common minerals were found that could only have been produced by the extraordinary explosive pressure occurring from a tremendous impact.

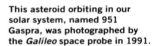

This asteroid orbiting in our solar system, named 951 Gaspra, was photographed by the *Galileo* space probe in 1991.

Since then, about 130 meteorite craters have been found on Earth. The largest is more than 110 miles (180 kilometers) in diameter and is located in the Yucatan Peninsula of Mexico. The existence of this crater provides some evidence to support the idea that an enormous global catastrophe occurred about 65 million years ago. Other evidence comes from small glassy bits of material found near Haiti. These glassy materials, known as tektites, are formed when material from Earth is thrown into space by a tremendous explosion, then re-enters the atmosphere, is heated by friction, and falls back to the ground. Many of the mass extinctions of lifeforms on Earth may be the result of such catastrophic impacts of large objects from space.

The moon, inner planets, and many planetary satellites show scars of asteroid impacts. Planets with active geology, like Earth, have few craters because older ones are destroyed by erosion and other forces. However, scientists have detected remnants of ancient meteorite craters below our planet's surface.

Halley's comet (*left*) swept past Earth in 1986. Special images of the comet (*inset*) taken by the *Giotto* space probe help scientists study its composition.

Comets

Before astronomers knew what comets were, many people feared them, thinking they were a sign of impending disaster. Today, however, we know that a comet is just a mass of ices, rocks, and dust traveling around the sun.

Comets are abundant in the distant regions of the outer solar system, where they are invisible even to the most powerful telescopes. Occasionally, a few are pulled into the inner solar system. As they approach the sun, the sun's heat causes their icy outer layers (frozen water, carbon dioxide, and other substances) to vaporize, releasing dust particles and gases. Pressure from the solar wind—electrified particles and radiation emitted from the sun—pushes the dust particles and gases away from the comet, forming a long tail.

By observing the comet tails, scientists have been able to determine the composition of a comet's nucleus, or core. Studies of Halley's comet in 1986 showed that it was rich in compounds of carbon, hydrogen, oxygen, and nitrogen. Comets appear to be weak, fluffy objects somewhat like dirty snowballs. Some split into pieces as they approach the sun. All comets within the inner solar system are in the process of disintegrating. Those with relatively small orbits rarely last more than a few thousand years before all their ices evaporate, leaving a small dim core. Comets with larger orbits may last longer because they approach the sun only once in thousands, or even millions, of years.

Brownlee Particles. The dust released by a decaying comet forms a stream of **meteoroids**, meteors that are still outside the Earth's atmosphere. Sometimes the Earth passes through such a stream, and many of the tiny dust particles enter the Earth's atmosphere, producing a meteor shower. Some dust particles from comets and from asteroids entering the Earth's atmosphere slow down enough not to be vaporized. High-flying aircraft can collect these microscopic particles, which are called Brownlee particles after Don Brownlee (1943–), an American astronomer who pioneered their study. Scientists study Brownlee particles in order to determine the properties of interplanetary materials.

Viewing Comets on Earth. Large comets can present a spectacular sight in the night sky. As the sun's heat evaporates the ices in the comet's core, a huge glowing sphere of gases called the **coma** can be seen on Earth. The coma may be as much as 1 million miles (1.6 million kilometers) in diameter. Streaming behind the coma is a glowing tail of gases and sunlit dust that may stretch 100 million miles (160 million kilometers). The solar wind causes the tail to point away from the sun.

In 1997, comet Hale-Bopp treated scientists and sky watchers to one of the most brilliant celestial displays of the century. One of the largest comets ever catalogued, Hale-Bopp was discovered while still some 650 million miles (1.05 billion kilometers) from Earth.

Perhaps the most famous comet is Halley's comet, named after the English astronomer Edmund Halley (1656–1742). He was the first to determine that this comet neared Earth about every 76 years.

Sampling Comets. In 1999, scientists launched *Stardust*—the first space probe ever sent to bring back a sample of a comet. The probe is designed to gather particles flying off comet Wild-2 and return them in a capsule that will land on Earth in 2006.

CLARK R. CHAPMAN
Planetary Science Institute

See also ASTRONOMY; SPACE PROBES.

COMIC BOOKS

Most people are familiar with comic books and comic strips. The **comic strip** is usually found in daily newspapers. It is made up of three or four picture panels telling a story with one or more characters. Some comic strips tell a different incident every day. In other comic strips the story continues from day to day until it is finished, and then a new story begins with the same main characters. The Sunday newspapers usually include sections of comic strips in which the story is told in a greater number of pictures and in color. The comic strips on Sunday often continue the weekday stories.

Comic books are extensions of comic strips into magazines. Each magazine is about one set of characters, and the pictures tell a complete story.

Generally comic books are printed in color. The words are printed in balloons over a speaker's head to indicate the person speaking. A few sentences may be used to bridge a gap in a story, but most of the plot is carried by direct conversation and by action in the pictures. Comic book covers are printed on glossy paper, and there are generally the same number of pages—usually 32—in each book in a particular series. Most books contain a single story, though some will have more than one, and most will include some advertising.

Comic books are published regularly, that is every month, every two months, or once a year. Because of the regularity of publication, they are often called comic magazines. Approximately 200 different titles are published.

This seal on the cover of a comic book shows that the magazine has been approved for publication. Look for it when buying comic books.

The exact number varies from month to month. It is estimated that about 150,000,000 copies of comic books are sold each year.

Different Kinds of Comic Books

Comic books or comic strips are not all humorous stories. The Comics Magazine Association of America lists these types of comic books: adventure, animal, biography, detective, fantasy-mystery, history, humor, military, religion, romance, satire, science-fiction, teen-age, "kiddie," and western. Some types, such as adventure and humor, sell better, so there are more of them. However, the popularity of comic books has led many kinds of groups to use them to tell a story. Sunday school papers have used comic strips, the Army has used the comic-strip technique in training soldiers, and many companies use comic books to tell the story behind a product or the history of their company.

How Comic Books Began

Comic strips began appearing in newspapers as early as the 1870's. The first comic strip to appear in newspapers on a regular basis was *The Yellow Kid,* in 1896.

Comic books similar to those published today first appeared in the 1930's and were collections of comic strips previously printed. The next step in comic book history was the writing of stories for comic book use alone, using a single set of characters in two or three plots.

The development of animated cartoon movies led to comic books about the same characters, such as Mickey Mouse. Sometimes a comic book retells a plot from a movie or a popular old book. In at least one case—Superman—the comic strip and comic book character led to television and movie versions. Television shows that are popular with young people are often made the subject of comic books because the publishers know they will quickly find buyers.

Originally developed as entertainment, the comic book is now used to educate as well. Public service messages such as the antismoking one above appeal to a wide range of readers in the comic book format.

Comic Books—Good or Bad?

Comic books increased in popularity very quickly, and soon there were many different kinds aimed at pleasing different age groups and interests. During World War II the comic book industry grew fast. Unscrupulous publishers began using themes of sadistic violence and sex. This brought the wrath of parents and organizations such as the P.T.A. against the whole comic book industry.

The improvement of comic books came about through the efforts of leading members of the comic book industry—the people who publish, print, and distribute comic books. In 1954 the Comics Magazine Association of America was organized for the purpose of setting up a code of approval for comic magazines. The code covers the story content—text and artwork—and the advertisements. Comic books published by members of the association are carefully scrutinized before publication to see that they conform to the code. When an issue of a comic magazine is cleared for publication, it may carry the code authority's seal on the upper half of the front cover.

The major comic magazine publishers belong to the group that conforms to the code. However, some publishers do not belong, and some of their comic books still carry a great deal of violence or sex. People who buy comic books should shop carefully for the better kinds.

For years many of the most popular comic books contained stories of adventure or crime prevention. These were usually built around the exploits of a leading character of super-human or exceptional powers. Other popular stories were in the realm of fantasy or science-fiction. But by the 1970's comic books were being read by a more sophisticated audience. This audience preferred heroes who coped with the real world. Thus comic books began to feature stories on such subjects as ecology, race relations, and women's rights.

The comic book form is sometimes used to teach as well as entertain. Comic books are used to help explain complicated subjects. They are also useful tools to civic organizations in public information campaigns. A reference list of free and inexpensive materials will include many comic books such as those published by electric utility companies or large manufacturing companies. Such material often contains valuable information. However, it is wise to keep in mind the source of the material. Material from a book sponsored by one company is not likely to contain information about the competitive products of another company.

Telling a story through pictures will probably continue to be a popular means of entertainment and education for some time to come. However, comic books have changed a great deal since they first began. Other changes will very likely come in the future.

CONSTANCE CARR McCUTCHEON
Author, *Substitutes for the Comics*

Reviewed by J. DUDLEY WALDNER
Comics Magazine Association of America, Inc.

COMMERCE. See TRADE AND COMMERCE.

COMMERCE, UNITED STATES DEPARTMENT OF

The U.S. Department of Commerce (DOC) is the executive agency responsible for promoting economic growth, technological advancements, and trade with foreign countries. The DOC is headed by a secretary, who is appointed by the president with the approval of the Senate. As a member of the president's cabinet, the secretary advises the president on policies and programs affecting the nation's economy. A variety of undersecretaries, assistant secretaries, and directors help administer the agencies described below.

The **International Trade Administration** (ITA) promotes the export of American-made goods, nonagricultural commodities, and services to foreign countries. It also helps defend American industry against unfair foreign trade practices.

The **Bureau of Export Administration** processes export license applications and enforces export control laws and policies to curb illegal trade activities.

The **Economic and Statistics Administration** (ESA) analyzes economic trends. Its major agencies are the Bureau of Economic Analysis (BEA) and the Bureau of the Census, which updates national population statistics every ten years and national economic statistics every five years.

The **National Oceanic and Atmospheric Association** (NOAA) collects data on the oceans, atmosphere, space, and sun. Its National Weather Service provides weather forecasts and issues storm warnings.

The **Technology Administration**, the DOC's center for science and technology policy, seeks to improve the productivity and competitiveness of American industries. Agencies include the Office of Technology Policy (OTP); the National Institute of Standards and Technology (NIST), formerly the National Bureau of Standards; and the National Technical Information Service (NTIS).

The **National Telecommunications and Information Administration** (NTIA) supports the development and growth of the nation's telephone, broadcast, and satellite communications industries.

Secretaries of Commerce and Labor		
Name	Took Office	Under President
George B. Cortelyou	1903	T. Roosevelt
Victor H. Metcalf	1904	T. Roosevelt
Oscar S. Straus	1906	T. Roosevelt
Charles Nagel	1909	Taft

Secretaries of Commerce		
Name	Took Office	Under President
William C. Redfield	1913	Wilson
Joshua W. Alexander	1919	Wilson
*Herbert C. Hoover	1921	Harding, Coolidge
William F. Whiting	1928	Coolidge
Robert P Lamont	1929	Hoover
Roy D. Chapin	1932	Hoover
Daniel C. Roper	1933	F.D. Roosevelt
Harry L. Hopkins	1938	F.D. Roosevelt
Jesse H. Jones	1940	F.D. Roosevelt
Henry A. Wallace	1945	F.D. Roosevelt, Truman
W. Averell Harriman	1946	Truman
Charles Sawyer	1948	Truman
Sinclair Weeks	1953	Eisenhower
Lewis L. Strauss	1958	Eisenhower
Frederick H. Mueller	1959	Eisenhower
Luther H. Hodges	1961	Kennedy, L.B. Johnson
John T. Connor	1965	L.B. Johnson
Alexander B. Trowbridge	1967	L.B. Johnson
Cyrus R. Smith	1968	L.B. Johnson
Maurice H. Stans	1969	Nixon
Peter G. Peterson	1972	Nixon
Frederick B. Dent	1973	Nixon, Ford
Rogers C.B. Morton	1975	Ford
Elliot L. Richardson	1976	Ford
Juanita M. Kreps	1977	Carter
Philip M. Klutznick	1980	Carter
Malcolm Baldrige, Jr.	1981	Reagan
C. William Verity	1987	Reagan
Robert A. Mosbacher	1989	Bush
Barbara H. Franklin	1992	Bush
Ronald H. Brown	1993	Clinton
William M. Daley	1997	Clinton

* Subject of a separate article in *The New Book of Knowledge*.

The **Patent and Trademark Office** (PTO) registers corporate trademarks and protects inventors by granting them exclusive rights to the results of their creative efforts.

The **United States Travel and Tourism Administration** (USTTA) promotes the nation's profitable travel and tourism industry.

The **Economic Development Administration** (EDA) provides grants to ease unemployment in economically distressed areas.

The **Minority Business Development Agency** (MBDA) offers advice to minorities on how to start or manage a business.

On March 4, 1913, the Department of Commerce and Labor was divided into two separate departments by an act of Congress. Today, the DOC employs approximately 37,000 people worldwide. Headquarters are located at 14th Street and Constitution Avenue, N.W., Washington, D.C. 20230.

Reviewed by the Office of the Secretary
United States Department of Commerce

See also CENSUS; PATENTS.

Why every kid should have an Apple after school.

COMMERCIAL ART

The term "commercial art" is usually used to mean art created for a business purpose. Unlike fine art, such as painting or sculpture, commercial art is made for reproduction. Although the general public calls this kind of art commercial art, the artists and designers who produce it usually call it graphic design or, because it is intended to communicate ideas and information, communication design.

Advertising

Perhaps the most obvious kind of commercial art is advertising. More commercial artists work in the advertising industry than in any other.

Advertising can take the form of billboards, posters, pages or parts of pages printed in magazines and newspapers, and television commercials. Advertisements, or ads, tell people about new products or remind them to buy old ones. They publicize everything from automobiles, washing machines, and perfume to plays, movies, television programs, and books. At election time even political candidates try to "sell themselves," and ads give voters information about candidates' positions on various political issues.

Some advertising is called public service advertising. Instead of trying to sell a product, it delivers a message that is beneficial to the community in which it appears. It may remind people not to litter, caution them to fasten their seatbelts, or warn them not to drink and drive or take drugs.

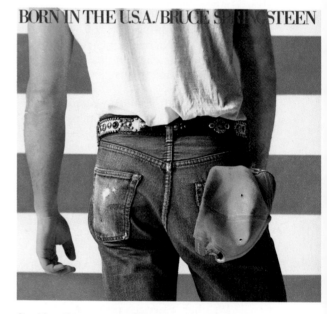

Graphic artists use many different ways to communicate commercial messages. *Above:* The designer of this compact disc cover chose an unusual photograph to command the attention of music buyers. *Top right:* The book designer placed a simple border around an illustration from the book, allowing the whimsical Paul Bunyan to attract readers. *Top left:* The computer advertisement called for strong layout skills on the part of the graphic designer, who conveyed a great deal of information about the product in a limited space.

Packaging

Also considered commercial art is the design of packages; jackets for books, compact discs, and audio and video tapes; and labels for cans and bottles. While protecting their contents, packages use advertising techniques

1903

1918

1928

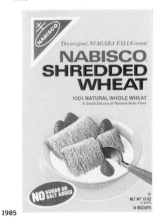

1944

1964

1985

Package design is an important commercial art. A good package design must do more than hold the product and keep it fresh. It must catch the eye of the shopper. The Shredded Wheat box has been redesigned often to keep pace with the changing taste of shoppers.

to attract the buyer's attention. In supermarkets and variety stores, products are in fierce competition with one another. The design of each package acts as a "point of sale" advertisement to make the shopper want to pick that particular product off the shelf and buy it.

Publishing

Books, magazines, and newspapers are also forms of commercial art. The designer's work usually consists of creating a layout and choosing a typeface for the text. If illustrations are to be used, the art director and designer choose an illustrator or photographer whose work expresses the ideas and feelings in the story. The designer who handles the layout decides where the illustrations will go and strives to make the pages attractive, well organized, and easy to read.

Corporate Design and Environmental Graphics

Two other kinds of commercial art are intended to convey information of a different kind. Corporate design involves work done for the business community and consists of business forms, stationery, booklets, and catalogs that companies use to carry on their daily operations. One of the most important elements in any company's corporate design program is the company's logo, symbol, or trademark. A

good symbol can give an idea of what the company's business is. It usually appears on all the printed material the company uses. The symbol may even be used on the company's cars and trucks.

Signs and symbols that give people directions in public places such as hospitals, office buildings, and airports are called environmental graphics. They are called this because they are such an important part of the environment in which we live and work. A designer who is asked to plan an environmental graphics project often works with the building's architect to decide where all the signs will go and what kind of lettering or typeface would look best. The designer has to think of details that most people take for granted, such as whether the signs can be clearly read from a distance.

Art Directors and Designers

The people who practice all these different kinds of commercial art have titles that suggest the kinds of jobs they do.

Art directors direct projects from beginning to end. First they meet with clients to discuss the assignments. If, for example, the project is the design of a book jacket for a novel, the art director discusses the story with the book's editor. Then the art director and editor discuss ways the jacket might best express the content

of the book. Later the art director decides whether to ask an illustrator to paint a picture or a photographer to take a picture for the cover. An artist may be chosen who does both illustration and lettering. Or, if the cover does not need an illustration, the art director might call upon a designer to prepare a cover that simply features the title in an appropriate typeface or hand lettering.

A designer is the person who actually plans the piece of commercial art, carrying out the art director's ideas. Many art directors were initially trained as designers.

Mechanical Artist, or Paste-up Artist

Designers may prepare artwork for printing themselves. But most of the time they give it to a mechanical artist, or paste-up artist, who pastes the type and artwork on a board, which the printer uses to reproduce the design. The finished board is called a **mechanical**. In the past even the pages of books and magazines had to be pasted up in this laborious fashion. However, now they are often laid out on computers that can put together text, photographs, and drawings and output the page in a form that is ready to be printed.

From far left: Commercial artists who specialize in corporate design create trademarks and logos such as these for McDonald's, American Airlines, and AT&T.

Right: Greeting cards—and the stamps used to mail them—are just two examples of the hundreds of kinds of commercial art surrounding us every day. Look around you!

Workplaces

Many art directors, designers, and mechanical artists work as part of the staff of a business firm or publishing company. They form the art or design department, and they are responsible for designing the printed material the company needs to run its business. Some art directors and designers set up independent design studios that work for a number of different clients. Such a studio might be asked to design a poster for a movie studio, a book jacket for a publishing house, or an annual report for a computer company.

Some designers prefer to work entirely independently. They are called **freelancers**, and many of them specialize in one particular kind of commercial art. Designers who specialize in book jackets may have several major publishing houses as clients.

Freelancers have the opportunity to accept or reject assignments as they wish, but freelancers do not always have work to keep them busy every week of the year.

CAROL STEVENS KNER
Managing Editor, *Print* magazine

See also ADVERTISING; ILLUSTRATION AND ILLUSTRATORS; POSTERS.

COMMON COLD. See DISEASES (Descriptions of Some Diseases).

COMMON MARKET. See EUROPEAN UNION.

Environmental graphics give directions and information through pictures. People need not be able to read to understand them. What is the center sign saying?

CAMPGROUND   FISHING   UTILITY OUTLET

ROW BOATING   ?   NATURE TRAIL

THEATER   MUSEUM   ACCESS for the HANDICAPPED

The Commonwealth of Independent States, made up of former republics of the Soviet Union, was proclaimed in 1991. Its founders were Boris Yeltsin (*center*), president of the Russian Federation; former Ukrainian president Leonid Kravchuk (*right*); and Stanislav Shushkevich, former president of Belarus.

COMMONWEALTH OF INDEPENDENT STATES

The Commonwealth of Independent States is a loose association of countries that were once part of the Union of Soviet Socialist Republics, or Soviet Union. The Commonwealth came into being in December 1991, in response to the breakup of the Soviet Union.

Before its collapse, the Soviet Union had been made up of 15 constituent, or union, republics, which represented the country's major nationalities. The republics varied in size and population, in language and religion, in historical and cultural background, and in their natural resources and economic development. All 15 republics are now independent nations. Twelve of these nations have chosen to become members of the Commonwealth.

Like the Soviet Union, the Commonwealth extends over a vast territory in both Europe and Asia. The total area of the countries forming the Commonwealth is nearly 8.5 million square miles (11 million square kilometers). Their total population is estimated at more than 277 million.

Background: The Soviet State. The Soviet Union was itself the successor to the Russian Empire, whose last czar, or emperor, had been overthrown by a revolution in 1917. A second revolution that year brought to power the Communist regime that officially established the Soviet Union in 1922. The Soviet system was based on the dictatorship of the Communist Party and a centrally planned economy controlled by the state. It enabled the Soviet Union to transform itself from a largely agricultural nation into a highly industrialized one.

Failure of the Soviet System. This had been accomplished at great cost, however, both in lives and in the living standard of the Soviet people, which remained far below that of Western industrialized nations. Sweeping economic and political reforms were undertaken by Mikhail Gorbachev, who became Communist Party leader in 1985 and later served briefly as the last president of the Soviet Union. But he was unable to improve the country's rapidly deteriorating economy. In the end, the Soviet Union's economic failures, the growing nationalism of its diverse peoples,

COMMONWEALTH OF INDEPENDENT STATES*	
Member	**Capital**
Armenia	Yerevan
Azerbaijan	Baku
Belarus	Minsk
Georgia	Tbilisi
Kazakhstan	Astana
Kyrgyzstan	Bishkek
Moldova	Chişinău
Russian Federation	Moscow
Tajikistan	Dushanbe
Turkmenistan	Ashkhabad
Ukraine	Kiev
Uzbekistan	Tashkent

* Articles on each member country can be found in *The New Book of Knowledge.*

and the social and political chaos that resulted proved its undoing.

Disintegration of the Union. Lithuania was the first of the Soviet republics to proclaim independence, in March 1990. By the end of the year, all of the other republics had declared their sovereignty, or right of self-determination, in one form or another. In an effort to keep the Soviet Union from breaking apart, Gorbachev tried both military force and compromise in the form of a new union treaty granting the republics greater power.

This hope was doomed when Communist Party hard-liners tried to seize control of the government in August 1991. Although the attempted coup failed, it weakened whatever chances Gorbachev had of holding the union together. The independence of Lithuania and the two other Baltic states, Estonia and Latvia, were recognized in September 1991. These three countries were to remain outside the Commonwealth. One by one the other republics also declared their independence.

The Commonwealth. On December 25, 1991, Boris Yeltsin, the elected president of the Russian republic and a popular hero for his stand against the hard-liners, and leaders of Ukraine and Belarus (formerly Belorussia) proclaimed the creation of the Commonwealth as the successor to the defunct Soviet Union. The remaining republics were invited to join. All nine eventually did so. Although Azerbai-

jan had signed the agreement creating the organization, its parliament at first voted against membership in 1992. Azerbaijan subsequently changed its mind, officially becoming a member in 1993. Georgia, after initial hesitation, also officially joined the organization, in 1994. Minsk, capital of Belarus, was chosen as the Commonwealth capital.

Prospects for the Future. Of the Commonwealth members, Russia is overwhelmingly the largest and most important. Stretching from the Polish border to the Pacific Ocean, it makes up about three quarters of the Commonwealth's total area. Since the breakup of the Soviet Union resulted in large part from the desire by other parts of the country to escape Russian domination, the role played by Russia will have a vital bearing on the Commonwealth's future. The most powerful voice for a cautious attitude has been Ukraine, second in importance to Russia.

Long-pent-up ethnic feelings within many of the states also threaten the survival of the Commonwealth. Since none of the members is self-sufficient economically, cooperation is essential. But the spirit of cooperation may fall victim to the same nationalism that helped destroy the Soviet Union.

ARTHUR CAMPBELL TURNER
University of California, Riverside

See also GORBACHEV, MIKHAIL; UNION OF SOVIET SOCIALIST REPUBLICS; YELTSIN, BORIS.

COMMONWEALTH OF NATIONS

At one time it was said that "The sun never sets on the British Empire." There was a good reason for this expression, for Britain once ruled one of the largest empires the world had ever known. That empire no longer exists. Of the many lands that once made up the old empire, most are now independent countries that belong to an organization called the Commonwealth of Nations.

The Commonwealth is a group of nations and their dependencies that try to work together for their mutual benefit. Commonwealth nations cooperate to reduce tariffs. They work together on defense and exchange ideas on industry, farming, science, and education. But each of the Commonwealth members has complete control over its own affairs. Whatever each does as part of the Commonwealth, it does voluntarily.

Some Commonwealth nations, like Canada, are monarchies. They officially recognize Queen Elizabeth II as their sovereign, even though she has no real power in their affairs.

Other nations, like India, are republics, but they recognize the Queen as head of the Commonwealth. A governor-general represents the Queen in each of the Commonwealth monarchies but, like her, has no real power.

The first step in organizing the Commonwealth as it exists today was taken at a conference in London in 1926. The **dominions** of the British Empire—the areas having the most independence—were recognized at that time as free and equal nations in the Commonwealth. Many other former British dependencies have since become independent members.

Another part of the Commonwealth is made up of the dependencies and associated states of various independent members. The amount of self-government that they have varies.

The dependencies of Australia and New Zealand are called **territories**. Each has an administrator chosen by the Australian or New Zealand government, which is responsible for defense and foreign relations. The administrator sometimes shares power with an elected assembly. Territories with complete self-government, such as the Cook Islands and Niue Island, control their internal affairs and can declare independence at any time.

Several members of the Commonwealth have withdrawn from the organization since its founding. Ireland officially withdrew in 1949. South Africa withdrew from 1961 to 1994, and Pakistan withdrew from 1972 to 1989. Fiji's membership was declared to have lapsed in 1987, and Nigeria was suspended in 1995 for its execution of dissidents.

Some British dependencies never formally belonged to the United Kingdom and are not now joined to it for citizenship purposes. They have simply made treaties permitting the British government to manage their defense and foreign relations. Other dependencies are jointly administered by two nations.

Many British dependencies are overseas territories that are officially annexed or joined to the United Kingdom. They were formerly called **colonies** or **crown colonies**. Their people are citizens of the United Kingdom. In these dependencies, the highest official is a governor appointed by the British government.

Many dependencies have increasing self-government. They may one day become independent members of the Commonwealth.

Reviewed by ROBERT BOTHWELL
University of Toronto

COMMONWEALTH MEMBERS

Independent Members of the Commonwealth: Antigua and Barbuda, Australia, Bahamas, Bangladesh, Barbados, Belize, Botswana, Brunei, Cameroon, Canada, Cyprus, Dominica, The Gambia, Ghana, Grenada, Guyana, India, Jamaica, Kenya, Kiribati, Lesotho, Malawi, Malaysia, Maldives, Malta, Mauritius, Mozambique, Namibia, Nauru*, New Zealand, Nigeria†, Pakistan, Papua New Guinea, St. Kitts–Nevis, St. Lucia, St. Vincent and the Grenadines, Seychelles, Sierra Leone, Singapore, Solomon Islands, South Africa, Sri Lanka, Swaziland, Tanzania, Tonga, Trinidad and Tobago, Tuvalu*, Uganda, United Kingdom, Vanuatu, Western Samoa, Zambia, Zimbabwe.

Dependencies and Associated States of the United Kingdom: Anguilla, Bermuda, British Antarctic Territory, British Indian Ocean Territory, British Virgin Islands, Cayman Islands, Channel Islands, Falkland Islands, Gibraltar, Isle of Man, Montserrat, Pitcairn Islands, St. Helena (including Ascension Island and the Tristan da Cunha Islands), South Georgia and South Sandwich Islands, Turks and Caicos Islands.

Dependencies of Australia: Ashmore and Cartier Islands, Australian Antarctic Territory, Christmas Island, Cocos (Keeling) Island, Coral Sea Islands, Heard and McDonald Islands, Norfolk Island.

Dependencies of New Zealand: Cook Islands, Niue Island, Ross Dependency, Tokelau.

*Special member   †Suspended 1995

COMMUNICATION

Communication means sending and receiving information. Every time you wave your hand at someone you recognize in a crowd, talk to a friend on the telephone, mail a picture you have drawn to your grandmother, or send a message to a classmate using a com-

A teacher shares his knowledge with students using both an ancient form of direct communication—speech—and a modern, computer-based form of communication—the Internet.

puter, you are communicating. Communication lets people share ideas expressed in gestures, words, images, and other forms.

The word "communicate" comes from the Latin *communicare*, which means "to share" or "to make common." Any kind of communication requires a sender, a recipient, a message (the idea one wants to communicate), and a medium (the method of carrying the message).

For most of human history, the sender and recipient were both people. People sent and received messages that could be directly sensed, or perceived, using their eyes and ears—by speech or by gesture. Such direct communication could take place only at one time and over a short distance.

When people began writing their ideas in words and pictures, messages could be seen at a later time and in a different place from when and where they were first written. As a result, knowledge was no longer limited to what a person could observe directly or find out about from others.

Today, modern communication systems can carry messages over long distances. These systems turn messages that can be directly perceived, such as spoken words, into signals that can be easily sent, such as the electrical signals of telephones. These signals are then turned back into messages that can be perceived at the receiving end.

Humans perceive information mainly through the senses of seeing and hearing. But they may use other senses, too. People who cannot see or hear can learn to communicate by the sense of touch. Sightless people read by touching raised letters with their fingertips. Deaf people communicate in sign language using their hands and fingers.

It is now often the case that the sender or recipient of communication is not a person at all. Computer systems collect weather information, for example, and can "speak" a forecast to someone who calls on a telephone. Scientists on Earth send commands to control space probes exploring distant planets.

Animals are able to communicate, too. However, animals do not use what we would call a language. They communicate by chirping, barking, and making other noises or movements. They can warn each other of danger, call their mates, or express pain and

This article surveys the wide variety of ways in which people communicate, from speaking and writing to using television and computers. The final section deals with mass communication and the rights and responsibilities of the media.

Electronic communications are covered in more depth in another survey article, TELECOMMUNICATIONS. Other topics have articles of their own. These include SPEECH, WRITING, LANGUAGES, PRINTING, PHOTOGRAPHY, SOUND RECORDING, TELEGRAPH, TELEPHONE, RADIO, TELEVISION, and COMPUTERS. Consult the Index for a complete list of the many communication-related articles in this encyclopedia.

joy. Some animals can communicate by emitting chemicals that can be smelled.

SPEECH AND SONG

We have no way of finding out how speech began. In prehistoric societies, people did not know how to write, so they could not keep records. Somehow they learned to make others understand what their vocal sounds meant, and they learned to put the sounds together into language.

Ancient tribes preserved their history in the form of spoken words and songs. People told stories over and over, so listeners would remember them and tell them to their children. The stories changed in the telling as people forgot some details and exaggerated others. After many retellings, these stories became legends and myths.

For thousands of years, only storytellers and singers preserved these legends. In Europe during the Middle Ages (A.D. 500 to 1500), minstrels did the job that books and newspapers do today. They wandered from one area to another, giving listeners stories and news in the form of songs called ballads.

PICTURES AND WRITING

Stone Age people knew how to make a picture represent an object. Cave dwellers painted pictures of animals on the walls of their caves. So thousands of years later, these people still communicate with us. Their pictures tell us what animals they hunted.

Progressing from drawing to writing as we now know it took several steps. At first, people communicated using simple **pictograms**—drawings of objects that represent the objects themselves. Gradually, the drawings no longer represented the objects but rather ideas associated with the objects. A picture of the sun, for example, might mean "day." These **ideograms**, as they are called, made it

Above: **A tribal elder from Africa uses gestures and spoken words to tell a story. In this way, traditional tales have been passed down through generations.**

possible to express more complicated messages. An example of early ideogram communication is Egyptian hieroglyphics.

The next step was to invent a written language in which each symbol stood for a single sound instead of a whole word. We call this system an **alphabet**. The word "alphabet" comes from the names of the first two letters of the Greek alphabet, *alpha* and *beta*. The Hebrews and the Phoenicians were the first to use an alphabet. Since the Phoenicians were great sea traders, they needed a simple way of writing to keep their business records. So about 3,000 years ago, they developed a system of 22 symbols, or letters, that stood for the sounds of the consonants in their language. This was much better than using a different picture to mean each word, because they could make any word they wanted from their 22 letters.

The Greeks, Etruscans, and Romans all based their writing on the Hebrew and Phoenician alphabets. The Greeks added symbols that meant vowel sounds. Over 2,000 years ago, the Romans developed the alphabet that we still use in the Western world.

Among the few people in medieval Europe who knew how to read and write were monks living in monasteries. They made copies of books by writing on parchment with pens made from quills (large feathers). These were **manuscript books**. (The word "manuscript" comes from the Latin for "written by hand.") Each book was a work of art. Only the monastery libraries and very rich people could afford these books.

Even after writing had developed, pictures still remained an important means of communication. Because many people were illiterate (unable to read or write), paintings and stained-glass windows in churches told stories from the Bible, while murals and tapestries commemorated battles and other events.

One of the reasons manuscript books were so rare was that it took so much time and skill to make them. Another reason was that there was no inexpensive, lightweight material on which people could write. As early as the A.D. 100's, the Chinese knew how to make paper from silk and from a mixture of tree bark, cloths, and rope fibers. But there was little communication between the Far East and Europe. It took another 600 years for the Arabs to begin making paper. Not until the 1100's was papermaking introduced to Europe, when the Muslims conquered Spain.

▶ PRINTING

By the 700's, the Chinese and Koreans knew how to make copies by **block printing**. Artisans carved pictures or words on blocks of wood. They carved them backward (like

A newspaper rolls off a modern printing press, some 600 years after Johann Gutenberg's invention revolutionized communication and education.

the page you see if you hold a book up to a mirror) so that they would print the right way on pages. Then they coated the surface of the wood with ink, placed sheets of paper over the block, and rubbed it. The Chinese printed entire books that way.

Between 1041 and 1048, Pi Sheng in China invented **movable type**, in which individual letters were assembled to form a page of type for printing. These letters could later be rearranged and reused. However, because the Chinese did not have a small alphabet like that of Western countries, the invention was not the huge success it would become in Europe 400 years later.

In the 1400's, Johann Gutenberg of Germany perfected a practical printing press using movable type and a technique called **letterpress**. He used a wooden handpress, similar to a winepress, to push the type against the paper. He invented molds for casting metal type, special metal alloys for type, and a new kind of oil-based ink. The famous two-volume Gutenberg Bible published in 1456 was his masterpiece. Gutenberg's press signaled the beginning of the age of printing.

Printing revolutionized communication and education. Movable type and letterpress made it possible to print books in large numbers. Many people could own copies of the same book. Ideas began to spread more rapidly. In the late 1800's and early 1900's, powered printing presses and a technique called offset printing allowed books, newspapers, and magazines to be printed faster and less expensively.

In 1938, American Chester Carlson developed another technique, called **xerography** or **photocopying**. His invention allowed anyone to make copies of printed or written documents quickly and easily using machines designed for offices. Today, it is difficult to imagine how modern offices could operate without photocopiers, which have become a handy way to copy printed pages for small groups of people.

In the 1970's, publishers began using computer-controlled **typesetting systems** to print large amounts of information for many people quickly and efficiently. These systems enabled text, and later images, to be entered into computers. Printing plates could then be produced directly without any actual type like Gutenberg's. In the 1980's and 1990's, much smaller and cheaper personal computers and printers became widely available. These systems allow individuals to print professional-looking documents that rival those printed by large publishing companies.

▶ POSTAL SERVICE

In various parts of the ancient world, relay runners carried written or spoken messages over long distances. After people learned to tame horses, post riders were used. Early Persians had developed a relay system of post riders. These riders were stationed at certain places. One would pick up the message and ride off with it to the next.

As long ago as 1000 B.C., King Solomon and the Queen of Sheba exchanged messages attached to carrier pigeons. This kind of pigeon finds its way home after being released. During the French Revolution (1789–99), pigeons carried war news to outlying districts.

Postal service in ancient times was only for very rich or important people. But in the 1500's, English rulers began to see that ordinary people needed to send messages, too. By 1683, the London penny post would deliver a letter anywhere in London for a penny.

Ships began delivering mail across oceans about this time. However, such communication was very slow. When the American colonies began to quarrel with England in the 1760's, it took weeks or months for each side to know how the other side answered the latest argument. Poor communication across the Atlantic Ocean was one of the reasons that the English and Americans could not understand each other's point of view.

After the Revolutionary War (1775–83), American leaders realized the vital importance of communication. Separate states and scattered frontier settlements had to be tied together into a single country. At first, travelers, peddlers, and circuit riders brought news from the East only occasionally to pioneers in the West. Riverboats carried letters and newspapers between towns that sprang up along rivers.

In 1860, Pony Express riders carried messages across the continent in nine to twelve days. They used a relay system not unlike that of the ancient Persians. But the Pony Express lasted only 18 months. In 1861, telegraph wires connected New York and California, enabling a message to be flashed across the country in seconds.

Horse-drawn wagons and early motorized vehicles were used 100 years ago to deliver the mail; it can now be sent around the world by airplane.

Today, government postal services and private courier companies use trucks and airplanes to carry letters and packages long distances. It is now possible to send a letter to most parts of the world in a day or two.

▶ SIGNS AND SIGNALS

Modern means of communication have not entirely replaced a very simple kind: communication by sign or signal. People often communicate without words—by a smile, a shake of the head, a wave of the hand. A driver signals for a turn. The colors of a traffic light tell drivers to slow down, stop, or go. Many signs use shape, color, or symbols rather than words. Ships use signal flags to spell out messages.

Thousands of years before the telegraph was invented, people sent messages by beating out codes on drums or hollow logs. Each beat had a particular meaning. Far away on a hilltop, the next drummer would hear the message, answer it, and pass it on.

In pioneer days, Americans on the frontier some-

Signal flags such as these are a traditional means of nautical communication. Ships use them to spell out messages.

Photography has progressed from this mid-1800's daguerreotype (the first taken in North America) to three-dimensional holograms on today's credit cards.

sender waved a blanket over a fire, making puffs of smoke go up in a certain way to form a message. Someone watching far away could read the puffs and understand the message. The ancient Chinese, Egyptians, Greeks, and Persians all signaled by smoke or fire.

Visual signals can also be sent by light beams. As early as the 400's B.C., the Greeks signaled by reflecting sunlight in a metal mirror. Until recently, ships used blinking lights to send messages to other ships or to shore.

▶ PHOTOGRAPHY

As early as the A.D. 800's, the Chinese and the Arabs had invented ways of forming an image of a scene on a screen. This enabled easier drawing of pictures. In the 1880's, several inventors experimented with ways of recording camera images chemically. The first practical photographic system was developed by a French painter, Louis Daguerre, in 1839. His pictures were called **daguerreotypes**. Early pictures were taken on metal or glass plates coated with chemicals. The photographer had to carry a huge, heavy camera, and much equipment was needed to process these pictures.

In 1889, American George Eastman produced a simple, lightweight camera. Roll film soon replaced glass plates. Photographs could be taken and reproduced in minutes. It became possible to see pictures of people and places all over the world, and eventually pictures from space showing how Earth looks. Rare old manuscripts and paintings could also be photographed so that many people could study and enjoy them.

During the 1890's, American inventor Thomas Edison and others found that by making many photographs in a rapid sequence, they could record moving images. The **motion picture camera** was born. Motion pictures quickly became a major source of entertainment and news (until the 1950's, when television news broadcasts replaced newsreels shown in theaters).

Photographs can also be taken so that each of the viewer's eyes sees a slightly different image. Such photographs create the impression of three dimensions—that is, flat two-

times used guns for signal communication. In a small town, several revolver shots meant a fire alarm. People sent messages by horn blasts, gunshots, or ringing bells.

For centuries, people have used bells to ring out important news. Bells were used to ring the curfew hour (time to be indoors, off the streets) or to announce that the town crier in the city square had something important to tell. Bells still ring in the new year and call people to church or to school. Doorbells signal that someone is at your door.

The sound of a siren tells that a fire truck or an ambulance is coming. In cities, cars stop when they hear the fire siren. During wartime, sirens signal air raids.

Sound signals are fast because sound travels at about 1,100 feet (335 meters) a second. Signals that you see rather than hear are even faster because they travel by light waves. Light moves at about 186,000 miles (300,000 kilometers) a second.

Visual signals can be sent by smoke, as Native Americans once communicated. The

dimensional pictures appear to have the added dimension of depth. In the 1960's, scientists discovered how to use lasers to make three-dimensional images called **holograms**. These are now commonly used on credit cards to make forgeries more difficult.

In the 1990's, small **digital cameras** became available, equipped with devices that convert light into electronic signals. These cameras record images not on film, but on magnetic disks and computer memory cards. Instead of using chemicals to develop film and make prints in a darkroom, a person with a digital camera can simply transfer the images to a computer and make copies of them on a printer. The computer can also be used to change the image in many ways. Colors can be brightened and special visual effects can be added.

▶ AUDIO AND VIDEO RECORDINGS

For over a century we have been able to record the spoken word and other sounds. Thomas Edison invented the first practical phonograph in 1877. The first sounds Edison recorded on a grooved cylinder were the verses of "Mary Had a Little Lamb."

In the 1920's, scientists began to record sounds magnetically on a roll of wire instead of mechanically on disks with grooves. Later they found that **audiotape**—a thin, narrow strip of magnetic tape wound on a reel—worked better. By the 1940's, the first practical tape recorders were developed.

The invention of **videotape** in the 1950's made it possible to record pictures as well as sounds. In the 1980's, the videocassette recorder (VCR) enabled people to record and play back television shows. It also let people rent or buy videocassette versions of movies and watch them at home instead of in theaters. With an added video camera, people could even make their own movies.

In the 1980's, **compact discs**, or CD's, became a popular way of recording music. Compact disc players use lasers to play back the music recorded on the plastic CD's, which are coated with a reflective metal film and protected by an outer plastic layer. In the 1990's, similar devices called **digital video discs**, or **digital versatile discs** (DVD's), were developed to play back recorded movies.

▶ TELEGRAPH

The age of electrical communication began when American inventor Samuel Morse demonstrated the first practical telegraph in 1837. In early systems, a telegraph operator would tap on a key to produce short and long buzzer signals (dots and dashes). These signals traveled as "on" and "off" electrical pulses over wires from one place to another. Messages were sent in Morse code, in which combinations of dots and dashes spell out individual letters and numbers. At the receiving end, a telegraph operator would translate the dots and dashes back into the original message.

Electrical impulses move as fast as light waves and travel as far as power and equipment permit. Thus, the telegraph enabled people to communicate over long distances almost instantly. In the 1850's and 1860's, Cyrus Field and other engineers

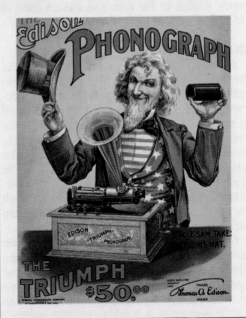

The quality of music played from a modern compact disc is much superior to the crackling sounds from an early phonograph cylinder, pictured below.

laid several underwater telegraph cables between North America and Europe. After many setbacks, they managed to connect the two continents by telegraph. Later, telegraph cables connected other parts of the world. This created a global communication system for the first time in human history.

By the 1920's, telegraph messages could be easily typed on machines with keyboards called **teletypewriters**. These teletype systems would automatically translate the message into telegraph code. The message was then sent via wire or radio to another teletypewriter, which would print out the message in typed letters.

The telegraph was the forerunner of modern **digital communications**. The word "digital" refers to any system that uses simple digits to represent information. Computers are digital because they use combinations of the digits 0 and 1 to stand for numbers, letters, and bits of data that make up pictures and sounds. In digital communications, information is converted into on-off electrical pulses, similar to the dots and dashes used in old-fashioned telegraph code.

▶ TELEPHONE

Another outgrowth of the telegraph was the telephone. In the 1870's, American inventor Alexander Graham Bell and an electrician friend, Thomas Watson, experimented to see if a telegraph wire could transmit the sound of the human voice. Bell sent the first telephone message by accident. Just as he was about to try out his transmitter, he spilled acid on his clothes. He cried out, "Mr. Watson, come here. I want you." Through the receiver in another room, Watson heard Bell's voice. The telephone worked.

Gradually, as telephones became common in most homes and businesses, telephone companies had to develop ways of handling large numbers of calls. They also had to connect calls reliably, switching automatically to a different route if a cable or other connec-tion failed to work. Such needs led to the invention of automated switching and routing devices that could do the work of human switchboard operators much more efficiently.

In 1881, Bell transmitted voice signals over a light ray. He developed a way of converting an electrical telephone signal to a variation in the brightness of a light. The signal was then converted back to sound with a special receiver. In the 1920's, a similar method was invented to convert sound to an optical signal that could be recorded at the edge of a film, adding sound to movies. Eventually, laser light was used to send large numbers of telephone calls and other kinds of information over **optical fibers**— thin glass or plastic strands that carry light long distances.

Today, many types of devices are connected to telephone lines. **Fax machines** are used to transmit images, drawings, and text from one place to another in seconds or minutes. **Answering machines** record calls and supply recorded information to callers when phones are unattended. When the messages are stored on a central system instead of a telephone, the system is called voice mail. **Videoconferencing systems** send television-like images over telephone lines, allowing people to see as well as hear one another.

Cellular phones do not require any wires and allow people to carry telephones with them all the time. Arrays of radio transmitter-receiver towers covering overlapping areas, or cells, provide a continuous connection between cellular phones and regular telephone network wires. Other devices, called **pagers**, also receive radio signals, telling someone to return a phone call. The signals are converted into audible beeps and brief text messages that appear on a small screen.

Above: Early telephones transmitted voices over electrical wires. Modern optical fibers can now carry greater numbers of conversations.

▶ RADIO

Traveling at the speed of light, radio waves can carry sounds, pictures, and digital information. Italian inventor Guglielmo Marconi first sent radio waves through the air in 1895. By 1901, Marconi was able to send his "wireless telegraph" signals, using something similar to Morse code, across the Atlantic Ocean.

Because radio needs no wires, it is of tremendous help on ships, planes, spacecraft, and other vehicles. Radios in the control towers of airfields are used to direct the airplane pilot so that the craft is landed safely. Some airplanes can now use radio signals to locate runways even in dense fog and land automatically. Police cars, delivery trucks, and taxis all use radios to find out where to go and to report their status.

Radio broadcasting began in 1920, when station KDKA in Pittsburgh, Pennsylvania, broadcast the presidential election returns: "Harding elected President." Radio then rapidly became a favorite form of entertainment and information.

Radio waves are now used for connecting many new communications devices in addition to mobile telephones and pagers. Some computer networks are now wireless. They can provide information about suspects to police officers in their cruisers, for example, or timely information such as stock quotes to traveling businesspeople.

▶ TELEVISION

By the 1920's, radio engineers had developed the first televisions, which transmitted pictures, as well as sounds, over radio waves. But technical problems and the disruptions of World War II (1939–45) slowed television's progress. TV broadcasting did not begin on a large scale until the late 1940's. Then it quickly became one of the most popular forms of communication and entertainment.

Cable television started in remote areas where over-the-air reception was difficult and required large, expensive antennas. One large receiving antenna would be connected to many homes by a cable. Gradually cable systems were installed in cities and suburbs, too, since they were convenient and provided a large number of channels. The number of channels available on cable systems gave rise to specialized programming, such as 24-hour news, sports, and weather channels.

The invention of radio in the early 1900's made wireless communication possible. It became essential for people on the move, such as soldiers on the battlefield.

In the 1990's, television began to merge with computers and computer networks. Some cable television and satellite systems allow people direct connections to such networks through their televisions. By the end of the 1990's, television broadcasting began converting to a new transmission method based on the digital language of computers. **Digital TV** provides clearer pictures, better sound, more channels, and special interactive services. These services allow viewers to shop, for example, using their TV sets and handheld remote-control units.

▶ COMMUNICATIONS SATELLITES

In the 1950's and 1960's, rockets began lifting devices with radio transmitters and receivers into space. These devices, called communications satellites, orbit high above Earth. Many of them relay radio messages across distances that are too great for signals from ground-based antennas to reach. In 1962, the first important U.S. communications satellite, *Telstar I*, was placed in orbit. For the first time, people sat at home in New York City and watched something happening in London or Paris at the moment it took place.

Many communications satellites connect just two locations. For example, satellites are used to carry video from a reporter in one place to a television station in another. But recently it has become possible for television viewers to own their own satellite receivers. Millions of viewers now receive television signals directly from satellites. Mobile phones

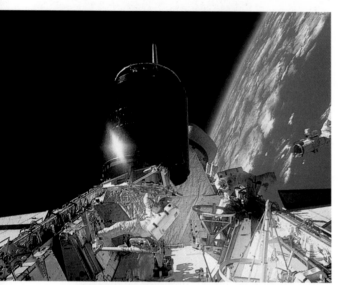

Satellites, such as this one being released from an orbiting space shuttle, now enable people virtually anywhere on Earth to communicate with one another.

can also communicate through networks of many satellites. These phones can be used to place calls from virtually anywhere on Earth, since there is almost always a satellite overhead that can connect the calls.

Satellites that generate signals rather than simply retransmitting them have become very important. Equipped with cameras or other sensors, they can collect astronomical information, help predict the weather, or gather surveillance information for military use. A group of 24 satellites called the Global Positioning System (GPS) transmits signals that people use to pinpoint their exact position. Devices called GPS receivers can be installed in vehicles as navigation aids, while some are small enough to be carried by hikers.

▶ **COMPUTERS**

Although computers were originally designed mainly to store and process data, they are now increasingly serving as communications devices. Even before computers could be connected to one another by networks, they were useful in communications in many ways. People could use a computer for entering and editing text. Or they could access information that had been stored by others in collections of records called databases.

After the first computer networks were developed in the late 1960's, computers could also exchange information among themselves. They became much more of a communications medium.

Computers can communicate with other computers through telephone wires, cables, fiber optics, satellites, or radio. In many places, computers connect to networks using a device called a **modem**, which sends digital data over regular telephone lines. Even devices other than computers can now connect to networks. Handheld devices can receive information from computers, such as music, text, and pictures. Some household appliances, such as microwave ovens, are being developed to transmit or receive information as well.

When a message is sent over a computer network, the network breaks it up into smaller amounts of information, called packets. Each packet contains the address of the computer that is to receive it. At the receiving end, the packets are reassembled into the complete message.

In the 1970's and 1980's, thousands of computers scattered across North America began connecting to a "network of networks." This eventually became what is known as the Internet. By the end of the 1990's, the Internet had grown rapidly, connecting many millions of computers around the world and becoming one of the most important methods of communication in history.

Today, the Internet and other so-called online networks connect computers in homes, schools, businesses, and governments. Internet users can exchange text, sounds, and pictures with people all over the globe through **electronic mail**, or **e-mail**. A particular method of exchanging and displaying information, called the **World Wide Web**, has become a publishing medium. Using computer programs called browsers, people can view "pages" on the Web that resemble those in print, with not only text and images but also sound and video.

The Internet has also created some concerns. It can be difficult to know whether information on the Internet is reliable, or whether a person using the Internet is trustworthy. Computer networks also make it easy to copy and distribute information. Some sources, such as online magazines, are protected by copyright laws. Copying from these sources without their permission is illegal.

In addition, computer networks make it easy to exchange and combine personal information about individual people. This means that personal information provided to one place (such as a merchant or a government agency) might end up being accessible to others. Such access deprives people of their right to privacy.

Computers have greatly expanded everyone's ability to access information and communicate with others. Some systems can even be designed to help people with disabilities communicate.

▶ MASS COMMUNICATION

The tools for mass communication are sometimes called **mass media**. Printing was the first such tool, allowing many people to share information. Over the past century or so, a great number of public libraries have grown up, letting people borrow and read more books than they could afford to buy.

Magazines reach even more people than books do. Because they appear regularly and are printed more rapidly than books, magazines can publish news and opinions on public affairs more quickly. Newspapers move even faster than magazines to print news and opinions. American and Canadian newspapers reach many millions of readers a day. Now newspapers and magazines may be read on the World Wide Web. Some of these are electronic versions of existing paper publications, and others exist only in electronic form.

The writers of the United States Constitution realized the importance of the public press. So the First Amendment to the Constitution guaranteed **freedom of the press**. That means that the government cannot decide what the news media—newspapers, magazines, radio, and television—should say. This is one of the most precious freedoms Americans have. It protects every person's right to disagree with the government or with any other authority, in public and in print.

Because of this freedom, the news media have an unwritten obligation to the public. They must print news—that is, facts—as well as opinion. The opinion part of the paper is the editorial section, where editors present various points of view. But editors are not supposed to distort or slant the news so that people are reading opinion when they think they are reading facts. Radio and television have the same obligation, too.

Mass media have a huge responsibility. They must keep people informed. They must decide which news is most important. They must be sure it is accurate. And they must make wise use of their power to influence people's thoughts and attitudes.

Only a few laws regulate mass media. It is illegal to harm people by publishing false information about them. In the United States and many other countries, laws protect the public from false or misleading statements that are considered libelous, or harmful.

The mass media of communication have enriched our lives in many ways. Television, radio, newspapers, books, magazines, and the Internet bring the world of news, ideas, and entertainment into our homes. All of this adds to the variety of our lives and to our education about the world around us.

V. Michael Bove, Jr.
Principal Research Scientist, MIT Media Laboratory
Massachusetts Institute of Technology

Left: At the height of Communist power in the Soviet Union, marchers paraded beneath giant portraits of the three major figures in the history of modern Communism: Karl Marx (left), Friedrich Engels (center), and V. I. Lenin, who established the Soviet Union as the world's first Communist state. *Below:* Like a fallen idol, a statue of Lenin lies discarded in a trash heap in 1991, after the collapse of Communism in the Soviet Union and Eastern Europe led to the breakup of the Soviet Union itself.

COMMUNISM

As a political movement, Communism was a powerful force in shaping the history of the 20th century. At one time, about one third of the world's people lived in nations governed by Communist parties. In the late 1980's and early 1990's, however, Communism suffered a blow from which it may never recover—the collapse of the Communist system in the Soviet Union (the world's first Communist state) and the Communist countries of Eastern Europe, followed by the breakup of the Soviet Union itself.

The term "communism" was first used to refer to any society in which property would be held in common (owned by everyone) rather than by individuals. This idea is very old. It was expressed, at least in part, by the Greek philosopher Plato in the 300's B.C. The modern theories of Communism, however, had their beginnings considerably later.

Beginnings. In the early 1800's the countries of Western Europe gradually began to change from an agricultural to an industrial way of life. Many people moved from the farms to the cities to work in the newly emerging factories, where they were forced to labor under very harsh conditions.

Critics of early industrial society thought that the hardships of workers would end if

there was no private ownership of property. If property was owned by all the people, they believed, the burdens and benefits of society would then be shared equally by all. They called this system socialism or communism, using the terms interchangeably.

Karl Marx. The leading theorist of Communism was Karl Marx (1818–83), a German social scientist. Marx thought that the goals of equality, freedom, and economic security would be reached through a new social order. He saw society as having developed from primitive communal life through various forms of oppression. These included slavery in ancient times; serfdom in the Middle Ages, when the workers of the land (serfs) were bound to the soil; and the harsh treatment of factory workers in his own time. Marx believed that society passed through these stages as a result of conflict between the privileged classes and the underprivileged. At each stage, the oppressed overthrew the oppressors.

In the final stage, Marx predicted, the workers in an industrial society would overthrow their oppressors, the capitalists (owners of private property), and seize power. They would then work to create Communist societies in which all the people owned the means of production, such as farms and factories, and controlled the political and social institutions. When this ideal had been reached, there would no longer be a need for the use of force by government, because there would no longer be class conflict.

The *Communist Manifesto*, written by Marx and his associate Friedrich Engels in 1848, was a call for such a revolution during a troubled period in European history.

The Soviet Model: Lenin. The Communist movement as we know it today has its origins in the policies of Vladimir I. Lenin. In 1898, Lenin founded a workers' party in Russia that became known as the Bolshevik Party. Under Lenin's leadership, the Bolsheviks came to power in the course of the 1917 Russian revolutions and established the Union of Soviet Socialist Republics, or Soviet Union. The term "soviet" referred to the councils of workers that formed the organizational basis of Lenin's party, which soon became the Communist Party. Lenin's theories on Communism are known as Marxism–Leninism.

At the time of the revolutions, Russia was mainly an agricultural country, not the industrial society in which Marx had predicted the workers would seize power. Lenin's theory that Communist rule would survive in the Soviet Union was based on his belief that the industrialized nations of Western Europe would themselves turn Communist at the end of World War I (1918). Lenin also believed that the Communist Party had to establish a one-party dictatorship to exercise total control over society during the long period before true Communism could come into being.

Stalin: Growth of Soviet Power. After Lenin died in 1924, leadership of the Soviet Union and the Communist movement passed to Joseph Stalin. By this time it was clear that

Communists were not going to come to power in any other country in the foreseeable future. Stalin was thus forced to adopt a policy of "socialism in one country." This effort to apply Communist theories to a single country that was still relatively undeveloped economically was in direct opposition to Marx's ideas.

Under Stalin the Soviet Union was transformed from an agricultural society to the beginnings of an industrialized one. It became a major world power after the defeat of Germany in World War II (1939–45), during most of which the Soviet Union was allied with the United States and other Western democracies. These achievements, however, were won at great cost. The Russian people suffered severe economic hardships, especially in the agricultural regions, where there was widespread famine. Stalin's struggle for political power resulted in large-scale purges,

WONDER QUESTION

What are the differences between Socialism and Communism?

As the use of these terms has developed, "socialism" has come to have a more general meaning. The public ownership of property advocated by socialists today can vary widely, from cooperative enterprises to complete control of the economy by national governments. Socialist governments or parties may be democratic or may favor a system of rule by a single political party. Socialist governments in democratic countries generally prefer public ownership of only selected key elements of the economy—banks, transportation, and energy industries, for example. Some Socialist parties are strongly opposed to Communism.

"Communism" usually refers to the program of the Communist parties. This program is characterized by Communist party control over all political and social activity in a country and by central planning of its economy. Communists believed that their system would spread to all countries, and they supported Communist revolutions when the opportunity arose. Communists also use the term "socialism" to describe the intermediate stage of development, before societies can achieve the long-term goal of Communism. This goal of the ideal Communist state can come about only when societies are productive enough to satisfy all human needs on a basis of equality.

A "Goddess of Liberty" was erected in Beijing, capital of China, in 1989, by students demanding democratic reforms in the world's most populous Communist nation.

in which many thousands of Soviet citizens were executed and vast numbers of them were imprisoned.

Communist Expansion. The end of European colonial rule in Asia and Africa after the war offered many new opportunities for the expansion of Communist rule. Some Communist governments were imposed by force on countries occupied by the victorious Soviet armies. This happened in Bulgaria, Czechoslovakia, East Germany, Hungary, Poland, and Romania in Europe, and in North Korea in Asia.

In other countries Communists came to power without direct intervention by the Soviet Union. These countries included Albania and Yugoslavia in Europe; Cuba in Latin America; China, Vietnam, Kampuchea (Cambodia), and Laos, among others. The Soviet Union also achieved great influence in a number of countries that were not formally under Communist rule. In addition, Communist parties existed in most of the non-Communist countries of Europe. (The small Communist party in the United States had little influence.)

To maintain their authority, Soviet leaders used force to suppress revolts in several of their Eastern European satellites: in East Germany (1953), Hungary (1956), and Czechoslovakia (1968). Soviet troops also fought a long war in Afghanistan during the 1980's to support an unpopular Communist government, which finally collapsed in 1992.

Communist expansion was strongly opposed by non-Communist nations, particularly the United States and its allies. The struggle between the two blocs for political and economic influence in the years after World War II was known as the Cold War.

Collapse of the Soviet System. In spite of some successes, the Soviet Communist model eventually proved a failure. In part this was due to conflicts among the Communist nations, who varied widely in their economic development and national interests and resented efforts by the Soviet Union to dominate them. Relations, for example, between the Soviet Union and the People's Republic of China, the world's most populous Communist country, were extremely hostile for more than thirty years.

A major cause of the collapse, however, was the very nature of the Soviet Communist system. Based on a rigid, centrally planned economy controlled by the state and the absolute rule of the Communist Party, it neither provided its people with any more than their simplest needs nor gave them a voice in their own government.

In the late 1980's, Mikhail Gorbachev, the Communist Party leader and later Soviet president, attempted far-reaching economic and political reforms. These spread quickly to the Eastern European Communist states, where, between 1989 and 1992, Communist regimes and state-controlled economies were replaced by elected governments and a free-market system. In the Soviet Union, however, the failure of economic reforms and the surge of nationalism among its many different peoples led, at the end of 1991, to the breakup of the Soviet empire.

CYRIL E. BLACK
Director, Center of International Studies
Princeton University
Author, *Communism and Revolution*

See also CAPITALISM; GORBACHEV, MIKHAIL; LENIN, VLADIMIR ILICH; MARX, KARL; SOCIALISM; STALIN, JOSEPH; UNION OF SOVIET SOCIALIST REPUBLICS.

COMOROS

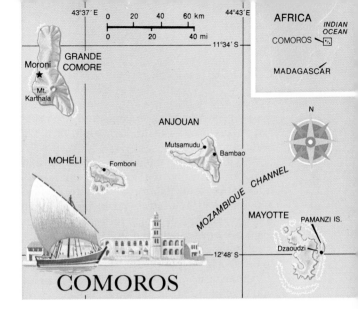

COMOROS

Comoros is a small nation made up of several islands of the Comoro archipelago. It is situated in the Indian Ocean, between the east coast of Africa and the large island nation of Madagascar. The largest and most populous island is Grande Comore (Njazidja). Moroni, the capital, is located there. Comoros' two other large islands are Anjouan (Nzwani) and Mohéli (Mwali). A fourth island, Mayotte, is ruled by France.

Comoros, a former colony of France, gained its independence in 1975. More recently, the people of Anjouan and Mohéli voted to separate from Comoros and establish their own independence.

People. The first inhabitants of the islands probably came from the African mainland. They were followed by settlers from Southeast Asia, by Arabs, and by people from nearby Madagascar. Arab influence remains strong on most of the islands. The majority of Comorans are Muslims, except for the people of Mayotte, who are largely Roman Catholic. The chief languages are Arabic, Swahili (a language of East Africa), and French.

Land. The Comoro Islands are mountainous and densely forested in many places. Most are volcanic in origin. Mount Karthala, on Grande Comore, is an active volcano. At 8,120 feet (2,475 meters), it is the highest point on the islands.

Economy. Most Comorans earn their living from agriculture and fishing. The main food crops are cassava (a starchy root), rice, sweet potatoes, and bananas, but much of the country's food must be imported. The chief exports are vanilla, cloves, and copra (dried coconut).

History and Government. The Comoros came under Arab influence in the 700's. The islands were explored by Europeans in the 1500's, but they remained largely under local rule until they fell to French control in the 1840's and 1880's. The islands became a separate overseas territory in 1946. They gained internal self-government in 1968.

In 1974 the majority of Comorans, except on the island of Mayotte, voted for independence. The mainly French-speaking people of Mayotte preferred to remain a part of France. Independence for the Comoros was achieved in 1975, but in 1976, Mayotte voted to continue its relationship with France.

Under the 1992 constitution, the country's head of state is an elected president who appoints a prime minister to lead the government. The legislature consists of an elected Federal Assembly and Senate.

Reviewed by HUGH C. BROOKS
Director, Center for African Studies
St. John's University (New York)

COMPASS. See GEOMETRY; MECHANICAL DRAWING.

COMPASS, MAGNETIC. See NAVIGATION.

COMPLEX NUMBERS. See NUMBERS AND NUMBER SYSTEMS.

FACTS and figures

FEDERAL ISLAMIC REPUBLIC OF COMOROS is the official name of the country.

LOCATION: Islands off the eastern coast of Africa.

AREA: 838 sq mi (2,171 km²).

POPULATION: 600,000 (estimate).

CAPITAL AND LARGEST CITY: Moroni.

MAJOR LANGUAGES: Arabic, Swahili, French.

MAJOR RELIGIOUS GROUP: Muslim.

GOVERNMENT: Republic. **Head of state—** president. **Head of government—**prime minister. **Legislature—**Federal Assembly and Senate.

CHIEF PRODUCTS: Vanilla, cloves, copra, perfume essence.

MONETARY UNIT: Comoran franc (1 franc = 100 centimes).

COMPOSITIONS

A composition is a written work in which the writer communicates ideas to a reader. It can be based on factual information, or it can be fictional.

A factual composition can be in the form of a report, in which the writer communicates information collected from books, magazines, and other outside sources. It can also be in the form of an essay, in which the material comes from personal experience. In a fictional composition, the writer uses his or her imagination to create events that never took place.

Although it is always important, whenever you communicate, to choose your words with care, it is especially important to do so when you write. Because you are not present to clear up misunderstandings, your composition must do all your explaining for you. It must answer questions that your readers might ask, and it must be organized in a way that allows your readers to follow your train of thought.

▶ REPORTS

Writing a factual report involves five steps: (1) choosing the reference material, (2) taking notes, (3) organizing the notes according to subject matter, (4) arranging the subjects into a logical order, and (5) translating the notes into clear, understandable prose.

Choosing the Reference Material. Let us suppose you are assigned a report on honeybees. Your best source of information on this subject will be in the library. There you will find encyclopedia articles, pamphlets, magazine articles, and nature books, all dealing with the subject of bees. Use as many of these references as possible. Eliminate only those that repeat information you have already collected.

Taking Notes. Taking notes will enable you to remember and organize your information and later to write it out in your own words.

As you read, write down every important fact, in as few words as possible, on a separate index card. Do not copy out whole sentences from the book. For example, suppose you consulted the following paragraphs from the article BEES in *The New Book of Knowledge:*

An average honeybee colony has about 30,000 bees, but there may be up to 80,000 in one hive. There are three different kinds of bees in the hive: a queen, several hundred drones, and thousands of worker bees.

The colony is headed by the queen bee. She is a big female who lays all the eggs in the colony. She starts to lay them during the first warm days of spring and continues to lay them every day till the end of the summer. At the height of the season, the queen may lay as as many as 1,000 to 2,000 eggs a day. Since she lives about 5 years, she may lay up to 1,000,000 eggs in her lifetime.

Here is what you might put down on your index cards: 30,000–80,000 in colony / Mostly workers, some drones, one queen / Queen heads colony, lays all eggs / Lays eggs in spring and summer / Up to 2,000 a day.

Organizing the Notes. Soon you will discover that the facts you collect can be grouped into separate categories according to subject matter. All your material on the queen, the workers, and the drones, for example, can be included in a category called "The Colony." Facts about how a bee develops from an egg into an adult can go under the heading "Life Cycle," and facts about the function of the stinger and the antennae can be headed "Parts of the Body." Other subject titles might be "Habitat," "The Honeycomb," "How Bees Communicate," and "How Honey is Manufactured."

The world is full of ideas for writing stories. Many ideas originate when a writer wonders, "What if *this* happened, or *that*?" The writer can build on these beginnings to create an entire story. Here are some "What if . . ." ideas that you can turn into stories of your own:

What if one day it snowed something that was not snow — like butterflies or feathers, diamonds or peas? What would the world look like? What would everybody do? What would you do?

Arranging the Subjects. Once your information is organized, you will need to arrange your subjects into an order that will make sense to your reader. It is best to put broad, general subjects first and narrow, more specific subjects later. Facts about the habitat, for example, apply to all honeybees and should come before those dealing with only the queen bee or the drones.

Remember, too, that readers must be told certain facts before they can understand others. In explaining how a bee builds a honeycomb out of wax, for instance, you should first define those parts of the bee's body that produce wax. The heading "Parts of the Body," therefore, should come before "The Honeycomb."

Translating the Notes. Your next step will be to write out all your information in paragraph form. The rules for writing and arranging paragraphs are the same as for organizing the entire report: Begin with a general or main idea and then follow with more specific details.

Before you begin to write, put all your reference books aside. Consult only your index cards, so that your report will be written in your words and not in those of some other author. The first sentence of each paragraph should state what the whole paragraph is about. Here is how you might translate your notes on bee colonies into readable prose:

"Honeybees do not live alone or in small family groups. Instead, they live in huge colonies containing anywhere from 30,000 to 80,000 bees.

"Every colony is ruled by a queen bee, who produces all the colony's eggs. She begins to lay them in the spring and keeps laying them all summer. Sometimes she lays 2,000 in one day." Following paragraphs would define the roles of the drones and the worker bees.

Vary your sentences so that they do not sound repetitious. Make some of them long, others short. Begin some with nouns, others with different parts of speech. A good report is not only informative, but pleasing to the ear.

▶**ESSAYS**

In preparing a composition based on your own experience, you will not have to depend on books or magazines for your material. Everything you need will be in your own head.

Whether you write about an event of long ago or an observation of your surroundings

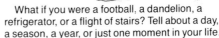

What if animals and people changed places with each other, so that monkeys and rabbits lived in houses like yours and went to work and school each day, while people lived in the jungle or underground? What would such a world be like?

What if everything big traded places with everything small, so that elephants were the size of insects and ants were 10 feet tall? What would your town look like then?

What if you discovered an old map in the cellar of your house that described the way to a hidden treasure? Tell about the adventures you might have as you search your neighborhood or town, following the clues on the map.

What if your pet suddenly began to talk? What kind of conversations might you have with your dog, cat, bird, or fish? What do you think your pet would like to tell you?

What if you were a football, a dandelion, a refrigerator, or a flight of stairs? Tell about a day, a season, a year, or just one moment in your life.

What if you were transported to another era — to prehistoric times, colonial America, or ancient Rome, for example? What would you see and do? What if someone from those days were transported to your neighborhood today? What would he or she see and do?

What if some object you owned — a marble, a glove, a ring, or a pair of skates — suddenly developed magic powers? How would you use it?

What if *you* suddenly developed magic powers? Suppose you could make people invisible or cause everything you pointed at to change color? Describe what might happen.

here and now, your task will be to describe the visions of your mind in such a way as to create similar visions in the minds of your readers.

Those visions are based on what you observe of the world around you. The more carefully you take notice of that world, the more you will be able to tell about it and about yourself as well.

Try, for example, to describe a potato without looking at one. Chances are you will say it is round and brown, hard and dusty. You might add that it has eyes. While such a description is accurate, it does not say anything new or unusual about the potato or about you as its observer.

Now pick up an actual potato and examine it for features you have never paid attention to before. Look at its tiny, smooth speckles and the web of slender lines across its skin. Think back now into your own past. What else have you seen that has speckles or lines like that? Somebody's face? An elephant's ear? Run your fingers along the potato eyes. Do they remind you of something else? Write down what you observe. Remember that no one sees your world exactly as you do, and it is this special awareness that makes your writing different from everyone else's.

Writers must take notice not only with their eyes but with their other senses as well. Close your eyes for a moment, and listen for clues that tell you where you are or what the weather is or the time of day. Now close your ears, too. What can you taste or smell or feel that reveals your surroundings?

You can apply your skills of observation to people as well as to things, and to past as well as to present experiences. Let us say you have chosen to write a composition about a visit last year to your grandmother. Try to recall special details of her behavior. Did she wrinkle her nose a lot or put her hands on her hips? What was her living room like? Some items in it were probably old, some new; some messy, some neat. Without using any of those words, describe her furnishings in exact detail. Mention things like careful stacks of magazines, worn sofa pillows, and smudges on the pages of her photograph album.

Your essay should follow some logical order, but it is not necessary to plan out that order right away. Put down your memories as they occur to you. Along the way, you may decide that your subject should really be the photograph album. In that case, your opening sentence might read, ''What I like best when I visit my grandmother is looking through her photo album.'' Go on from there to describe how you settle on the sofa next to your grandmother and turn the smudged pages of her photo album one by one.

▶**FICTION**

Composing a work of fiction is like playing a game of make-believe, except that you write down what you make up, rather than act it out.

Fiction can be either realistic or a fantasy. In realistic fiction, the events could have taken place; in a fantasy, they could not have. Tall tales, myths, fairy tales, and science fiction are examples of fantasy.

Fiction need not be long. To get started, you might simply tell a tall tale, which is an absurd exaggeration. Describe what some enormously tall—or extremely tiny—person can do. Later, try rewriting a traditional myth or fairy tale, placing all the characters in up-to-date situations and in familiar settings such as your hometown.

One kind of myth is the how-and-why tale, where a fanciful explanation is given for some occurrence in nature. Using this form, tell why leaves change their color in the fall, or why the snake sheds its skin.

Science fiction is frequently based on imaginary machines. Dream up a machine that can perform impossible tasks, or pick some everyday machine around the house and give it extraordinary powers.

When you attempt a longer story, your make-believe events should have a shape from beginning to end. This is called a plot. In most stories, the characters face some sort of problem, and the plot is formed around the development of the problem and its solution.

Do not expect the entire plot to reveal itself to you all at once. As with most compositions, stories are created little by little with an idea here and an idea there. Write them down, even if they do not seem to lead to anything at the time.

Once you have done so, you will discover that ideas are all around you. It is only when you begin to write that you will recognize them for what they are.

SYLVIA CASSEDY
Author, *In Your Own Words:*
A Beginner's Guide to Writing

COMPROMISE OF 1850

The Compromise of 1850 was an attempt to solve the problems of slavery and westward expansion in the United States in the years before the Civil War.

Victory in the Mexican War (1846–48) gave the United States a huge block of southwestern land stretching from the Texas shore of the Gulf of Mexico to the Pacific Ocean. The organization of this territory into states brought with it a serious problem. Should these new states be free or slave states?

Since 1820 southern senators had been fighting to keep the number of slave states equal to the number of free states. In 1849 California applied for admission as a state with a constitution forbidding slavery. If California were admitted as a free state, this would upset the balance between free and slave states. Southern congressmen feared slavery might also be prohibited in the Utah and New Mexico territories. Northern congressmen, on the other hand, were determined to halt the spread of slavery.

Several other problems were also involved. One was the Underground Railroad—a secret route of hiding places and back roads used by escaped slaves to reach freedom in the North or in Canada. Southerners demanded a stricter fugitive slave law. Another issue was the abolition of slavery and the slave trade in Washington, D.C., the nation's capital.

These questions threatened to split the Union. Senator Henry Clay, the Great Compromiser, tried to keep this from happening. He introduced eight resolutions into the Senate. He hoped these resolutions would persuade each side to trade something it wanted for a concession from the other side. Clay proposed that the South let California be admitted as a free state. Then the North should let the rest of the new territories decide the slavery question for themselves. Slave trade should be abolished in the District of Columbia, but slavery would be permitted there. A stricter fugitive slave law should be passed, but the future slave state Texas should give up some of its land to New Mexico.

Clay's proposals touched off a furious debate in the Senate. Northern radicals opposed even the possibility of slavery in the new land and denounced the fugitive slave law. Southerners, led by John C. Calhoun of South Carolina, also denounced Clay's proposals, saying the South could not compromise and still remain in the Union.

The brilliant orator Daniel Webster climaxed the great debate with his answer to Calhoun—the famous Seventh of March speech. Though he was a lifelong enemy of slavery, Webster said he spoke not as a Massachusetts man, but as an American. He begged the nation to accept Clay's compromise in order to save the Union. Many people, stirred by his speech, urged Congress to compromise. In September Congress passed five bills. Together these are called the Compromise of 1850.

▶ WHAT THE COMPROMISE SAID

(1) California was admitted to the Union as a free state.

(2) Texas, a slave state, gave up to New Mexico some of the land both claimed, and the federal government paid Texas $10,000,000 for it.

(3) Slave trade, but not slavery, was abolished in the District of Columbia.

(4) When the territories of New Mexico and Utah asked for statehood, they could vote whether to be slave or free.

(5) A new fugitive slave law made it a crime for anyone to help an escaped slave.

▶ THE COMPROMISE IN ACTION

The compromise did not really settle the slavery controversy. The new fugitive slave law aroused fierce anger in the North. It imposed severe penalties on those found guilty of assisting an escaped slave. The abolitionists redoubled their efforts to abolish slavery. Their cause won many new supporters through *Uncle Tom's Cabin*—a powerful antislavery novel by Harriet Beecher Stowe. The northern radicals became convinced that slavery must be outlawed everywhere in America. Southerners found it increasingly unbearable to remain in the Union under such abuse.

The Compromise of 1850 brought the United States a little more than 10 years of official peace before the Civil War broke out. But it was an uneasy peace, marked by growing hostility and violence.

Reviewed by ISADORE STARR
Queens College (New York)

Desktop computers put information at the fingertips of many people, such as these students in a geography class.

COMPUTERS

Computers help society function in many vital ways, often without our being aware of them. Computers control traffic lights and factory operations. They scan bar codes at checkout counters and track store inventories. They monitor banking, credit card, and cash machine transactions. Computer chips in our cars, home appliances, radios, televisions, and stereos help us use these and many other products every day. And computers link schools, governments, businesses, and people throughout the world.

Every time you call a friend on the telephone, you are probably using several computers. The telephone itself may have a tiny computer chip that remembers names and numbers. A computer at your local telephone company may automatically connect the call. If you are phoning long-distance, a computer on an orbiting satellite may relay your call to another part of the world. Even the operator may be a computer that answers with a human voice and recognizes your spoken commands.

▶ TYPES OF COMPUTERS

Computers are classified by how fast they compute and how much information they can store. **Supercomputers**—the most powerful computers available—perform complex tasks and handle massive amounts of information. They are used mainly by scientists and engineers for such jobs as predicting the weather or designing automobiles.

More widely used computers today include servers, workstations, desktops, laptops, and palmtops. (Older terms such as "mainframe" and "minicomputer" are rarely used anymore.) **Servers** are usually more powerful computers that perform jobs, such as storing information or connecting to a network, for groups of people using less powerful computers. **Workstations** often sit on desks, but are more powerful than average home or business computers and are used for science, engineering, or computer graphics.

Desktops, or personal computers, usually sit on a desk and are used by one person in a home, school, or business. **Laptops** usually weigh less than 10 pounds (4.5 kilograms) and fit in a briefcase. Because of their size, laptops usually cost more than desktops for the same computing power. **Palmtops**, as their name says, fit in the palm of your hand. Many palmtops have very small screens and no keyboard. You use a special pen to write directly on the screen.

▶ COMMON FEATURES OF COMPUTERS

Every computer is a system—a group of electronic components that work together to store, retrieve, and process data. The components that sit on your desk or that you hold in your hand are known as **hardware**. A computer also needs instructions that tell the hardware what to do. These instructions are called **software**. Computers can be programmed to perform different jobs, and this makes them different from simple calculators. Computers come in many shapes and sizes, and they serve many purposes.

Hardware

A computer's hardware has three types of components: processing units, input and output devices, and memory and storage.

Processing Units. The **central processing unit**, or **CPU**, carries out the instructions from the software by controlling millions of tiny electronic pulses every second.

The CPU is plugged into the **motherboard**, which holds other electronics needed to run the CPU. Support processors on the motherboard help the CPU manage all the parts. The motherboard also has slots that allow other boards called daughtercards to be attached. Daughtercards can also contain support processors for such jobs as controlling the disk drives or connecting the computer to the network.

Input and Output Devices. The processing units must be given information to process—the **input**. The results of the processing are called **output**. Output can be displayed on the screen of a monitor (similar to a television), printed on paper, saved on a disk, or sent to another computer over a network. Many devices, often called **peripherals**, are used to input and output information. A single computer system may have several input and output devices. Input devices usually include a keyboard for typing text and a mouse for controlling a pointer on a computer monitor. Input devices may also include a joystick for playing games, a scanner for inputting images, and a graphics tablet for drawing pictures. Output devices usually include a monitor and a printer. Some devices are used for both input and output, including communication devices called modems and storage devices called disk drives.

Memory and Storage. The CPU performs its calculations using **digital** data, which is information in the form of 1's and 0's. During calculations, the CPU must both save some data for later and find and use previously saved data. For storing and finding data, a computer has memory and disks. Memory is fast, usually temporary, and inside the computer on small electronic components called chips, which are plugged into the motherboard. Disks are slower but can hold much more information for a much longer time.

The smallest unit of memory is the **bit**, which is short for *bi*nary dig*it*. A bit can be 0 or 1. As a rule, 8 bits make a **byte**. One **kilobyte** is 1,024 bytes. A computer's internal memory is usually measured in **megabytes**, each of which is 1,024 kilobytes or about 1 million bytes. A computer's

These girls are using laptop computers, which can be easily carried from place to place and operate on battery power.

hard disk space is often measured in **gigabytes**. A gigabyte is about 1 billion bytes—enough to store the full text of 30 complete sets of *The New Book of Knowledge* encyclopedia. Large computer facilities often have disks or tapes for storing **terabytes** (1 trillion bytes) and are even planning to store a **petabyte**—1 quadrillion bytes.

Computers have two types of memory on chips. **Random-access memory (RAM)** holds temporary data. It is called random-access because the CPU uses it to store and retrieve data quickly. Since the late 1990's, personal computers have had at least 32 megabytes of RAM. The other type of memory is **read-only memory (ROM)**. ROM holds small amounts of data permanently, including the instructions needed to start, or boot, the computer.

Computers often need to store larger amounts of data and store it for a longer time. Computer disks are devices to hold data, and **disk drives** let the computer read data from and write data to disks. Most disks are covered with a magnetic coating, and bits are stored by arranging the microscopic magnetic particles in the coating. **Hard disks**, which are housed in devices called hard drives, stay inside the computer or in separate boxes

Palmtop computers feature touch-sensitive screens that allow a user to write on them using special pens.

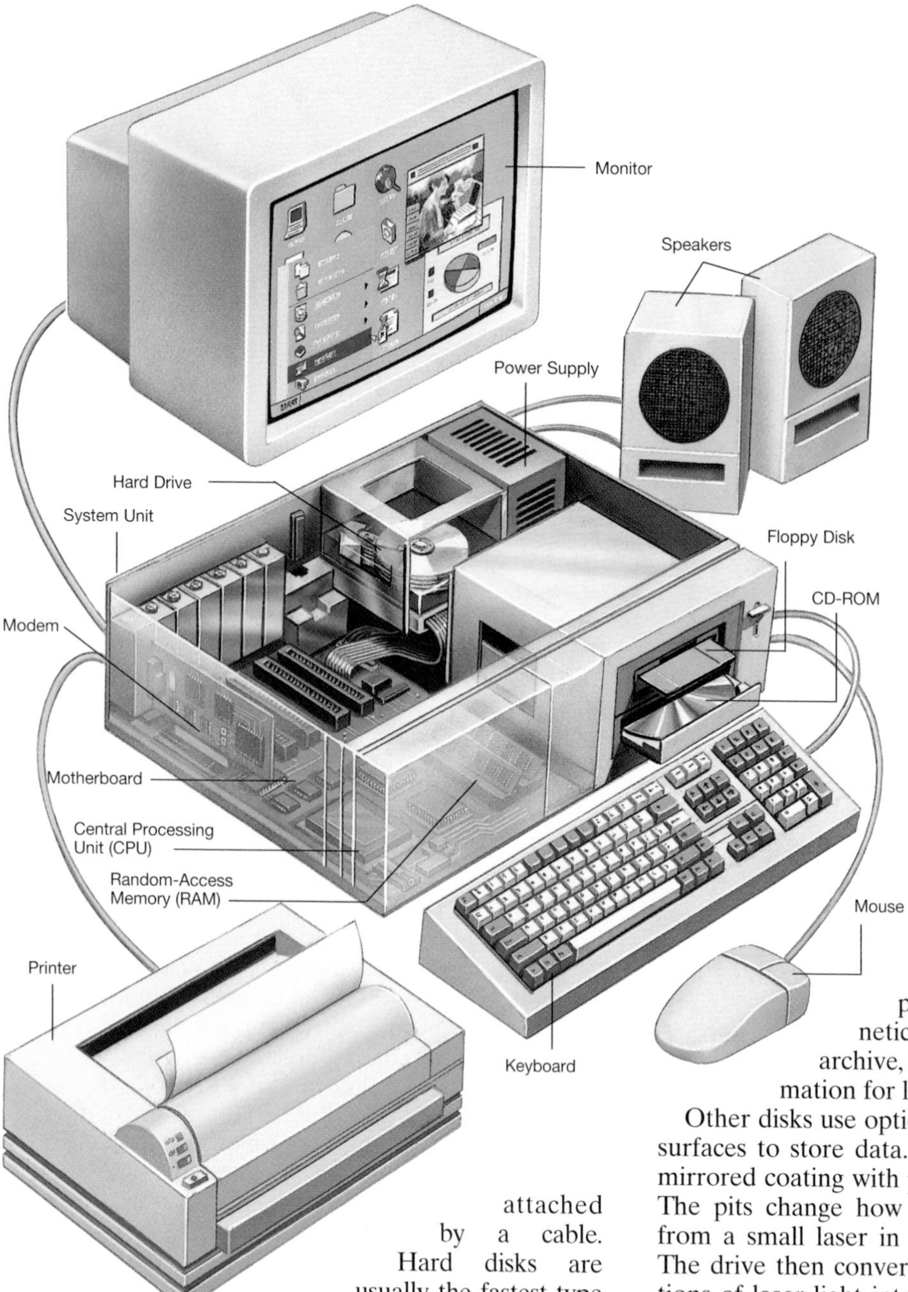

Monitor

Speakers

Power Supply

Hard Drive

System Unit

Floppy Disk

CD-ROM

Modem

Motherboard

Central Processing
Unit (CPU)

Random-Access
Memory (RAM)

Printer

Keyboard

Mouse

INSIDE A PERSONAL COMPUTER

A typical personal computer includes a system unit, which houses the central processing unit, hard drive, and other important components. Commands and data are entered using input devices, such as the keyboard and mouse. Information in the form of text and graphics is displayed on output devices, such as the monitor and printer. Sound from CD-ROM's and other sources can be heard over the speakers.

attached by a cable. Hard disks are usually the fastest type of disk and can store 1 or more gigabytes of data. Removable disks can be put into a disk drive and removed when they are filled or not needed. **Floppy disks** are 3½-inch (8.9-centimeter) removable disks, protected in hard plastic cases, and can hold about 1 or 2 megabytes of data. (They are called "floppy" because the disks used to come in soft, flexible cases.) Newer removable disks can hold hundreds of megabytes or even gigabytes of data.

Many large computer systems use magnetic tape to store, or archive, huge amounts of information for long periods of time.

Other disks use optical instead of magnetic surfaces to store data. An optical disk has a mirrored coating with pits that represent bits. The pits change how the disk reflects light from a small laser in the optical disk drive. The drive then converts the flickering reflections of laser light into electronic pulses that the computer can process. The most common disk of this type is the **CD-ROM** (compact disc read-only memory). CD-ROM's are thin disks about 4¾ inches (12 centimeters) in diameter. A single disk holds about half a gigabyte of information—the same as several shelves of books. Newer optical disks, called **digital video discs** or **digital versatile discs (DVD's)**, can store even larger amounts of data, including entire movies, on disks that are the same size as CD-ROM's.

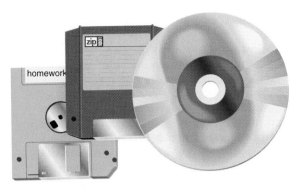

A floppy disk (*left*) can store 1 to 2 megabytes of data; a newer removable disk (*center*) can store 100 megabytes or more; a CD-ROM (*right*) can store about half a gigabyte.

Software

For the computer hardware to do useful work, it needs software—instructions that tell the computer what to do and how to do it. A single set of instructions is called a **program**. One program, the **operating system**, has instructions for running all of the hardware components and for managing the actions of other programs. The operating system directs data and instructions to and from the hardware components.

Algorithms. A clearly specified set of simple steps for solving a problem is called an **algorithm**. Each step in an algorithm might become many detailed instructions for the computer. A single program may use many algorithms to do its job. For example, a program might have algorithms for sorting a list of numbers or for checking the spelling of all the words in a document. The flowchart at the bottom of this page shows one way to describe an algorithm for outputting a message to wish someone a happy birthday. The rectangles represent instructions and the diamond represents a decision. Each of these symbols represents a step that can be written in any programming language.

Programming Languages. The language of computers is **machine language**—a series of 1's and 0's that are converted into "on" and "off" electrical pulses. The electrical pulses tell the computer what to do. Machine language is easy for the computer to understand, but it is difficult for programmers to read and write. **Assembly language** includes labels and other text in a program, and each instruction in an assembly-language program translates to a single machine-language instruction. Machine language and assembly language are called low-level languages because programmers must include every detail of what the computer must do.

Most programs are written in special languages called high-level programming languages, which use words and symbols that look more like English and make it unnecessary for the programmer to be aware of every tiny detail of instruction. Most high-level languages use special programs called **compilers** that translate an entire program into the computer's machine language. Some high-level languages use programs called **interpreters** that translate one instruction at a time into machine language and run it before translating the next instruction.

Higher-level languages, called authoring languages, make it even easier to write common programming tasks. For example, a pull-down menu—a list that appears on the screen to give users a choice of many options—can be created with a simple command, while the programming to do this requires several pages of machine-language code.

▶ COMPUTER APPLICATIONS

A computer application can be either a job accomplished with the help of a computer or the software written for that job. Computers can accomplish many different tasks because many applications have been written for each purpose.

Managing Information

Businesses rely on computers to handle important data, including employee records, payrolls, inventories, customer records, invoices, and receipts. Most of this work is done by programs that manage large collections of information called **databases**. Libraries use databases to catalog, manage, and share their

Computer programs are based on algorithms, with steps that can be represented as symbols. This algorithm tells a computer when to wish you a happy birthday.

books and reference materials. Teachers and schools use databases to keep track of student grades. Government agencies, such as the Internal Revenue Service and the Social Security Administration, use huge databases to keep track of information about millions of individuals. Databases are used by just about every type of organization.

Writing and Creative Applications

One of the most common computer applications is word processing. Many kinds of programs process text, from simple children's programs to complex desktop-publishing programs. Many of these programs combine text processing with the ability to include designs and illustrations. Some programs can convert speech into text and even translate text into different languages.

Computers also have many applications in art and music. Some programs enable artists to create their own drawings or to duplicate certain styles of painting. Others imitate or alter the sounds of musical instruments and human voices, producing entirely new sounds.

Computer Graphics

Computers are also used to create graphics, or images, that can illustrate information in books, newspapers, magazines, and television. Computer graphics can become animated characters and special effects on television, in movies, and in video games. Computer graphics also have many scientific, industrial, and educational uses.

Business Uses. Many businesses hire graphic artists who use computers to create charts, graphs, maps, and illustrations for public relations, sales, marketing, and training presentations. These graphics are used in printed materials, on slides and overhead transparencies, and even in videos to present information in a pleasing and easy-to-read format.

Science and Industry. In universities and research centers, scientists use computer graphics to make complex information—such as the movement of air in a hurricane—easier to visualize and understand. In government and industry, scientists and engineers use computer graphics to design many products, from spacecraft and submarines to everyday products. Computer graphics are also used in interpreting satellite photographs of Earth and in guiding fighter jets and missiles.

Entertainment. Computer graphics have become a basic tool in creating animation as well as two- and three-dimensional visual effects in television shows, films, and video games. While many special effects now done with computers could be done in the past using traditional methods, some have been possible only through computer technology. One example of this is called **morphing**—from the word "metamorphosis," which means a change in form. In morphing, the size, shape, and characteristics of an object change until it resembles something else. A picture of a car, for example, can be morphed into a picture of a tiger.

Education. Computer graphics are now being widely used in textbooks and on instructional CD-ROM's, videodiscs, and other computer technologies. In addition, many interactive and multimedia instructional programs in schools rely heavily on graphics that designers and artists create on computers.

Robotics and Mechanical Control

Often computers are used to control complex mechanical devices. For example, computer-controlled robots perform tedious or dangerous jobs in industry and science. Robots move

These frames from a television ad show how computer graphics technology can be used to make a car "morph," or change its form, until it resembles a tiger.

CD-ROM's can combine text, images, sound, and animation, as shown in this screen view of the *Grolier Multimedia Encyclopedia.*

large automobile parts on assembly lines and put some of the pieces together. Some police departments use robots to remove suspected bombs from buildings. Robots are also used in space exploration. In 1997, the *Mars Pathfinder* probe landed on Mars. Scientists on Earth used computers to control the probe's robotic vehicle *Sojourner* as it moved from rock to rock and performed its scientific studies.

Helping People with Disabilities

Computers can also provide assistance to people with disabilities. TDD (telecommunications device for the deaf) phones let hearing-impaired people use the telephone by typing on a keyboard and reading messages on a screen. Visually impaired people use computers with software that magnifies screen text or reads text aloud. People who have difficulty speaking or moving may also use computers. Physicist Stephen Hawking, paralyzed from amyotrophic lateral sclerosis (ALS, or Lou Gehrig's disease), has delivered many lectures using a computer to speak for him.

Research and Simulation

Scientists and engineers use computers to conduct experiments that are easier, less expensive, and safer than real-world experiments. Such an experiment starts with a model of something in the real world—for

example, a molecule, a car, or a galaxy. The model is built from mathematical equations, which are programmed in a computer to create a simulation of the real thing. Researchers experiment with the model to see how changing the model affects the outcome of a simulation. This tells the researcher how similar changes would affect the real-world object. Using computer models, government planners study traffic flow, economic development, and population growth; engineers test designs for buildings, bridges, and cars; astronomers study planets, stars, and galaxies.

Medical Uses. Computers help scientists design new drugs, scan patients' bodies for signs of disease, study how the brain works, and practice complicated operations. To design new drugs, for example, researchers view molecules as computer graphics. Then they can see how to build drugs that prevent harmful molecules from interfering with helpful ones. In the operating room, robotic

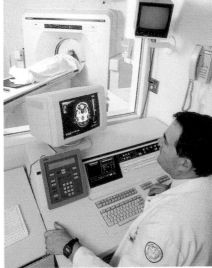

Left: A robot named Dante 2 explores Alaska's Mount Spurr, an active volcano. *Right:* Computerized axial tomography, or CAT, scanning lets doctors see inside the body.

arms handle surgical tools in some delicate operations. Computers helped American neurosurgeon Benjamin Carson rehearse the complicated surgery to separate conjoined (Siamese) twins before performing the operation in 1997. More commonly, doctors use computer-controlled devices ranging from digital thermometers and blood pressure monitors to CAT (computerized axial tomography) and MRI (magnetic resonance imaging) scanners. These devices help doctors better diagnose illnesses.

Weather Prediction. Television news programs use computers to display weather patterns around the world. Those predictions come from supercomputers that run daily weather simulations to forecast weather a few days into the future. More complex simulations try to predict the weather much further into the future. In 1997, scientists used supercomputers to predict the arrival of El Niño, a warming of water in the Pacific Ocean that changes weather around the world. This successful prediction allowed countries and cities to better prepare for heavy rains and flooding.

Flight Simulation. Computers help train pilots and astronauts without leaving the ground. In a flight simulator, a pilot sits inside a copy of an airplane's cockpit. Computers control how the

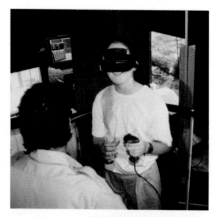

A young woman (*right*) wears special goggles with video screens that give her the impression of being inside an imaginary three-dimensional zoo, inhabited by computer-generated gorillas (*below*). Using a handheld device, she can control her views and perceived movements inside the virtual-reality zoo.

plane moves and what the pilot sees on a large video screen during a simulated flight. Airline pilots can learn how to handle emergencies before they happen in the air. Astronauts can practice complicated missions, such as docking a space shuttle with a space station or releasing a satellite. The military can test fighter pilots' performances without going into battle.

Virtual Reality. Computers can also create virtual reality—three-dimensional (3-D) models of real or imaginary worlds that you can explore with the help of special equipment. Goggles, fitted with a small video screen for each eye, let you view lifelike scenes in 3-D. Other devices, such as position sensors mounted in a headset, change your viewing angle as you move your head and body. The equipment gives you the impression of being "inside" a computer-generated, or virtual, world. Virtual worlds can be entire cities in which a psychiatrist "walks" with a person who is afraid of open spaces or heights. Biologists can create a world from the structure of a molecule and then explore this microscopic world up close. Imaginary worlds can be created for use in games. In some virtual worlds, many people can meet together even though they might be far away from each other in the real world.

▶ COMPUTERS AND THE INTERNET

For much of their history, computers have operated as independent machines. Each computer did its work alone. Starting in the 1960's, computers separated by many miles could be connected to networks and work together. Today, millions of computers are connected to one another in a worldwide network called the Internet. Education, business, entertainment, and

BOOLEAN LOGIC

The CPU and other chips are the most vital components of a computer. These chips are made up mostly of transistors called **logic gates** that enable them to carry out the instructions of a program. The logic used by the chips is the same sort of logic that World Wide Web search engines use to find information.

Chips and search engines both use what is called Boolean logic. Boolean logic is a type of math that calculates the answers to true-or-false questions. Instead of numbers, Boolean logic uses the values "true" and "false," which equal 1 and 0 for a computer. Instead of addition, subtraction, and other math operations, Boolean logic uses three basic logical operations—AND, OR, and NOT. Each transistor in an integrated circuit is a logic gate that performs one of these operations.

You can think of the logical operations as very specific ways to combine true-or-false questions. The AND, OR, and NOT operations work very much like the words *and*, *or*, and *not* in spoken English.

The AND operation takes two inputs and produces one output. The output is true (or 1) only if the first input is true and the second input is true. If either or both of the inputs are false (or 0), then the answer is false. If you are using a search engine, searching for "computer" AND "virtual reality" will return only pages that have both terms in them.

The OR operation also takes two inputs and produces one output. The output is true if either one of the inputs is true. With an OR operation, the search engine will return any page that has either one of the search terms. Many search engines rank the matching pages. Pages that match the first search term AND the second search term rank higher than pages that match only the first term OR the second term.

The NOT operation takes only one input and returns one output, the opposite of the input. If the input is true, the output is false. If the input is false, the output is true.

For example, say you wanted to use a search engine to find weather-related Web sites about thunder or lightning, but not sites about the Tampa Bay Lightning hockey team. You could use the following Boolean phrase: weather AND (thunder OR lightning) NOT hockey.

---

government are changing as the Internet connects more and more people to one another and to more information.

Networks

A network is a group of computers connected by cables, optical fibers, or telephone lines so that the computers can share information. A network often has one or more servers that hold shared data and programs. A local-area network (LAN) connects computers located near one another, in the same room or building, for example. A wide-area network (WAN) connects computers that are farther apart.

The Internet

The Internet is the worldwide network of networks. Small local-area networks are connected to other local-area networks, and these groups of networks are then connected to other, larger networks. Every computer connected to the Internet, the largest network, is called a **host**. Host computers communicate with one another by sharing a common **networking protocol**, or methodical way of exchanging information.

Internet Technology. All computers on the Internet speak the same networking protocol, called **TCP/IP** (transmission control protocol/Internet protocol), which makes sure that information sent by one host arrives at the proper destination. Every computer on the Internet has a unique Internet protocol, or IP, address—the computer version of a post office box and zip code. Because IP addresses are numbers, people usually prefer to give computers names, which are easier to remember. Some computers on the Internet called domain name servers have the job of matching computer names to IP addresses that computers understand.

When a computer sends data to another computer, special software breaks up the data and bundles it into a sequence of **packets**—envelopes stuffed with data and labeled with the receiver's and sender's addresses. A packet may make many "hops" from computer to computer to get from sender to receiver, and each packet can take a different route. The receiving computer collects the packets and reassembles the message.

Internet Services. The Internet allows many forms of communication between computer users. The oldest, and still very popular, method is electronic mail, or **e-mail**. E-mail lets people send messages back and forth, just as the postal service delivers letters. E-mail led to the creation of **newsgroups**, which let many people with similar interests take part in discussions.

People can also use the Internet to "chat," or exchange messages during live sessions. Internet chats are unlike e-mail or discussion groups, where the messages are saved and may be read later. In chats, what you type appears immediately on the screens of the other participants. Groups of people can meet in chat "rooms"—screens of messages devoted to particular topics of discussion.

The **World Wide Web** is another popular way of sharing information on the Internet. The Web provides information in a standardized way that can be understood by almost any computer, as long as that computer has a Web **browser**. A Web browser is a program that can understand documents containing instructions written in **hypertext markup language (HTML)**. Web documents can include hypertext links, also called hyperlinks or links, to other documents on the same computer or to documents on another computer on the Internet. The Web lets people share many types of information—text, images, sound, animations, programs, and databases.

Each of the millions of documents on the Web has a unique address, called a **uniform resource locator (URL)**. The most common URL format looks like this:

http://www.example.edu/file.html

The "http://" indicates that the request uses the hypertext transfer protocol, the network language of the World Wide Web. The "www.example.edu" is the name of the computer where the information can be found. And "/file.html" points to a specific file on that computer.

Internet Uses. The Internet and the Web are playing important roles in many aspects of daily life. Business, shopping, news media, education, and science are taking advantage of these new communication technologies.

Businesses provide their customers and investors with the latest information about new products, financial successes, and company changes. Companies that have traditionally sold products through retail stores or through mail order are letting customers buy products on the Web. Hyperlinks can connect advertisements directly to an advertiser's Web site. Software companies let customers download some programs directly from Web sites to their own computers.

A browser is a computer program that lets users see documents with text, photos, sounds, and other elements on Web sites, such as *The New Book of Knowledge Online.*

The news media use the Web to bring breaking news stories to a worldwide audience. The Web allows news organizations to provide up-to-date stories, photographs, and video around the clock. The Web also lets the audience view many past stories.

Schools and universities use the Web to distribute class notes and submit homework assignments. The Internet also has made what is known as distance learning much more common. Students far away from one another can listen to and see class lectures broadcast on the Internet and can communicate with teachers and other students by e-mail and chat sessions.

Scientists use the Internet to run simulations on distant computers, share information with their colleagues and their students, and meet with other scientists using e-mail and discussion groups. The Internet is even making it possible to operate complex scientific instruments, including electron microscopes and telescopes, by remote control.

Searching for Information

The Internet and the Web have put a world of information at everyone's fingertips, and more information is becoming available every day. But information on the Web can only help solve a problem if the person with the problem can find it. Finding information on the Internet would be nearly impossible without **search engines** and other services that let users find what they want to know. These search engines often use programs called **spiders** to visit as many Web sites as possible and compile an index of them. Most Web browsers include a search button that will help start a search.

Internet users need to pay careful attention to the sources of information. There is so much information that even the largest search engines may have visited only one-third of all Web sites. The Web has made it easy for just about anyone to post information on the Internet. Depending on the source, information might be very accurate or it might be completely wrong. News from an established media source on the Web is probably more accurate than the news provided by an unhappy customer or someone promoting a hoax. Businesses or activist organizations may offer biased points of view. The Internet is a community of institutions and individuals—some may be fair and honest, others might be holding a grudge, and others might not know what they are talking about.

▶ COMPUTER CAREERS

About half the jobs in the United States today involve processing data—gathering, analyzing, and storing information. It is not surprising, then, that working with computers is an important part of many careers, including some you might not think would be related to computers.

Computer programmers design software for homes, schools, and businesses. Programmers also "debug," or fix, faulty programs and create new ones tailored to a company's needs. There are exciting possibilities for creating programs that recognize handwriting and human speech and that sense nearby objects. Programming computers that are built

A computer artist at Industrial Light and Magic works on the animation of *Tyrannosaurus rex*, one of the special effects for the movie *Jurassic Park*.

into electronic devices such as telephones, televisions, and appliances provide still other challenges.

Graphic artists design magazines, Web sites, newsletters, product packaging, and advertising. Artists and animators also create computer games and multimedia software, television animations, and special effects in films.

Nearly every company, school, and organization that uses computers relies on **technicians** and **system administrators** to fix hardware and software problems.

As the Web becomes more important, many organizations are hiring employees to maintain their Web sites. **Webmasters** operate many types of software, write programs, and experiment with new technologies.

Many non-computer jobs require employees to use a computer to get their work done. Secretaries, journalists, nurses, telemarketers, air traffic controllers, assembly line workers, travel agents, real estate brokers, mechanics, bank tellers, and stock brokers—to name just a few—all use computers in more and more parts of their jobs.

▶ HISTORY OF COMPUTERS

For thousands of years, people have needed to count and calculate. In ancient times, the Egyptians, Greeks, and Chinese began using the **abacus**, a calculating device with rows of beads on wires. The first true calculating machine, an adding machine, was

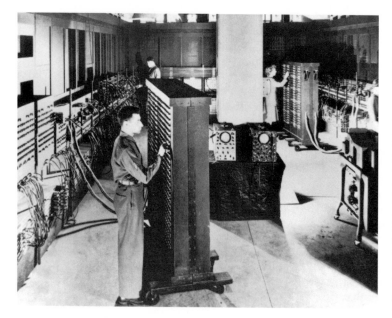

ENIAC, the first high-speed electronic computer, could not store its own programs. Instead, it had to be rewired for each new set of calculations.

built in 1642 by the French mathematician Blaise Pascal. It consisted of interlocking gears and wheels mounted on axles, and it added numbers that were dialed on its wheels. In the late 1600's, the German philosopher and mathematician Gottfried Wilhelm von Leibniz devised a system of gears that could multiply as well as add.

The First Computers

The next major advance occurred in the early 1800's, when the English mathematician Charles Babbage built what many people consider to be the first true computer. Babbage created a model of what he called an **analytical engine**, a device that could perform any set of instructions fed to it by cards with holes punched in them. Ada Byron, Countess of Lovelace, wrote instructions for Babbage's machine, which probably makes her the first computer programmer. But Babbage never produced a working machine. (In 1991, the National Museum of Science and Technology in London built a working analytical engine using Babbage's plans. Weighing hundreds of pounds and operated with a hand crank, it has never calculated a wrong answer.)

Punched cards, like those used by Babbage, turned out to be important to the development of computers. The first computer that used punched cards was created to win a contest. Because it took years to tabulate the results of the 1880 census by hand, the U.S. government sponsored a competition to de-

vise a faster method for the 1890 census. The contest was won by Herman Hollerith, a statistician. Hollerith built a mechanical coding and decoding process based on the positions of holes punched in cards. A hole in a certain place on a card represented a piece of information, such as a person's age or occupation. Hollerith also developed machines that could "read" this data by sensing the positions of holes electrically. By the end of the 1800's, people were collecting so much information that computing machinery became a necessity.

Electricity was the next key development in computing. For forty years after the 1890 census, computers used slow mechanical parts that often broke down. During the 1900's, electrical components increased the power and efficiency of computers while reducing their size.

In the 1930's, Howard Aiken and others developed a way to use vacuum tubes instead of mechanical parts to perform many computer functions. Then, during World War II (1939–45), fast computers were needed to control sophisticated weapons systems and calculate, for example, the flight paths of missiles. John Eckert and John Mauchly built ENIAC, short for Enhanced Numerical Integrator and Calculator, to calculate these missile flight paths. ENIAC needed 18,000 vacuum tubes, 1,800 square feet (167 square meters) of floor space, and 180,000 watts of electrical power. (Today, ENIAC's functions can be performed much faster using a programmable pocket calculator.)

ENIAC and other early computers were wired for specific tasks, and to reprogram the computer, engineers had to change the wiring. According to computer lore, an insect once blocked an electrical connection in a computer's wiring, causing the computer to malfunction. That is why we call an error in a program a "bug." In the mid-1940's, mathematician John von Neumann came up with the idea of storing programs inside comput-

GLOSSARY OF COMPUTER TERMS

ANALOG DEVICE: A mechanism that represents data in the form of continuous physical quantities, such as the hands on a clock.

ARTIFICIAL INTELLIGENCE: Software that can simulate certain aspects of human intelligence.

BIT: From *bi*nary dig*it*; the smallest unit of memory in a computer, represented by a 0 or a 1.

BYTE: A basic unit of computer memory, usually 8 bits.

CD-ROM: Compact disc read-only memory; a storage medium consisting of a small disk that can contain half a gigabyte or more of information.

CPU: Central processing unit; the part of a computer that carries out a program's instructions.

DATABASE: A collection of information in a form computers can use.

DIGITAL DEVICE: A mechanism, such as a computer, that uses 1's and 0's to represent information.

DISK DRIVE: The hardware that places information on or retrieves information from computer disks.

E-MAIL: Electronic mail, a way of sending messages on the Internet.

GIGABYTE: An amount of memory storage equal to 1,024 megabytes; abbreviated GB.

HACKER: A person who uses a computer to break the law—for example, by gaining unauthorized access to another computer.

HARD DISK: A magnetic disk, housed in a device called a hard drive, usually inside the computer or in an external box connected by a cable.

HARDWARE: The electrical and mechanical parts of a computer system, such as the CPU, disk drives, keyboard, and printer.

HTML: Hypertext markup language; the instructions that tell a Web browser how to display information.

INPUT DEVICE: Any hardware, such as a mouse or keyboard, used to enter information into a computer.

INTEGRATED CIRCUIT: A set of interconnected logic gates and other electronic circuits on a single semiconductor chip.

IP ADDRESS: The address of a computer on the Internet.

KEYBOARD: An input device consisting of rows of keys representing numbers, letters, symbols, and functions.

KILOBYTE: An amount of memory storage equal to 1,024 bytes; abbreviated as KB.

MEGABYTE: An amount of memory storage equal to 1,024 kilobytes; abbreviated as MB.

MODEM: Short for *mo*dulator-*dem*odulator. A device that converts digital computer signals to analog telephone signals, and vice versa.

MOUSE: An input device consisting of a palm-sized box with buttons. Moving the mouse across a surface controls a cursor, or movable pointer, on a computer screen.

NETWORK: A group of computers connected by cables, optical fibers, or telephone lines that can share information and programs.

OUTPUT DEVICE: Any hardware, such as a printer or video screen, used by a computer to give out information.

PERIPHERALS: Hardware devices that are controlled by the CPU, such as printers, modems, and disk drives.

PROGRAM: A list of instructions, written in a programming language, to be followed by a computer.

RAM: Random-access memory; a temporary type of memory in which data can be added or removed in random order.

REMOVABLE DISK: A disk, such as a floppy disk, that can be taken out of its disk drive and stored separately.

ROM: Read-only memory; a permanent type of memory containing unchanging data or instructions.

SERVER: A computer for storing data or programs that are shared by other computers on a network.

SIMULATION: A type of program that represents some event, object, or process and allows the user to experiment with aspects of it.

SOFTWARE: Instructions or programs that describe tasks to be carried out by a computer.

SUPERCOMPUTER: The fastest, most powerful type of computer.

TCP/IP: Transmission control protocol/Internet protocol; a methodical way in which computers on the Internet exchange data.

TRANSISTOR: A small electronic switch.

URL: Uniform resource locator; the address of a file on the World Wide Web.

VIRUS: A small program that can attach itself to files and destroy data or damage a computer's operating system.

WEB BROWSER: A program that lets you view HTML documents and other information on the World Wide Web.

WORD PROCESSOR: A program designed for writing and editing text.

WORKSTATION: A powerful desktop computer, usually used for science, engineering, or computer graphics.

WORLD WIDE WEB: A way to share text, images, and other information on the Internet using documents connected to other documents by HTML, or hypertext, links.

Will computers ever outsmart humans?

Chess champion Garry Kasparov contemplates a move against IBM's Deep Blue. The computer's moves were shown on a monitor and carried out by a human assistant.

In 1997, the world's best chess player, Garry Kasparov, lost a six-game match, winning only two games against his opponent. The loss made headlines because his opponent was a computer, IBM's Deep Blue. This was the first time that a computer had defeated the World Champion chess player.

However, this does not mean that computers are now smarter than humans—just faster. Kasparov examines and evaluates up to three chess positions per second. Deep Blue has 32 CPU's and examines up to 200 million chess positions per second.

The truly amazing "computer" is the human brain that can analyze a handful of moves per second and still win two games against Deep Blue. What the brain lacks in raw computing speed, it makes up for in its superior ability to think and create. Consider that Kasparov has written three books, speaks several languages, and gives talks at conferences. Deep Blue only plays chess.

Artificial intelligence (AI) researchers try to make computers think like humans, which has turned out to be very difficult. Some computer programs, called **neural networks**, are built from simple computing units connected to one other, like neurons in the brain. But like Deep Blue, a neural network is good at only one task, usually some type of pattern matching. Neural networks "learn" from examples to recognize handwriting, forecast demands for airline flights, and test tires, computer chips, and other products.

On the surface, some computers may seem smarter than humans. Computers can recognize voices and translate from one language to another. But in fact, computers must work very hard to perform tasks that are simple for humans. Other human abilities, such as consciousness and intuition, are beyond the power of computers, no matter how fast they compute.

ers and avoiding the need to rewire them for every new task. The first programs were written in low-level machine language or assembly language.

The Information Age
The 1950's witnessed the beginning of what is called the Information Age with the arrival of several advances in hardware and software. **Transistors**, small electronic switches, were developed that were much smaller and cheaper than vacuum tubes. Transistors also lasted longer, worked faster, and used less power, and they soon replaced vacuum tubes in computers. What had once taken up an entire room could now fit into a box the size of a small refrigerator. Programmers developed high-level languages, such as Fortran, to make programming easier. Fortran was created for scientific calculations. Stacks of punched cards were still used to load a program into a computer's memory.

Tiny computer chips with millions of transistors are made on wafers of silicon, which must be handled in dust-free conditions inside a manufacturing plant.

Integrated Circuits

The next major advance occurred in the late 1960's with the development of **integrated circuits**, also known as IC's or chips. The first IC's contained only a few transistors. IC's made computers much cheaper, smaller, and faster. Faster computers allowed scientists and engineers to present more complex information with clear and precise computer graphics. At about the same time, computer graphics were being used to design and manufacture many everyday products. Smaller and cheaper computers meant that there were many more computers in more places. In 1969, the Advanced Research Projects Agency (ARPA) of the U.S. Department of Defense connected two universities in an experimental network called ARPANET, the forerunner to the Internet.

Computer chips continued to become smaller and more powerful. Before IC's were invented, most early computers were room-sized devices operated by special technicians and shared by many people. By the late 1970's, computer hardware was small enough for building personal computers.

Personal Computers

By the 1980's, tiny chips containing hundreds of thousands of transistors were being produced, resulting in even more powerful, faster, and smaller computers. In 1981, the International Business Machines Corporation (IBM) introduced its own personal computer, which it dubbed the PC. In 1984, the Apple Computer Corporation unveiled its revolutionary Macintosh computer. The Macintosh showed that computers had advanced far enough to use graphics to control their operations. Instead of listing computer files in lines of text on a screen, for example, the Macintosh represented files as small images, called icons, that could be moved on a screen by a person using a mouse. Later, PC's also adopted graphical operating systems, such as Windows. As personal computers became cheaper and easier to use, people began using them more in homes and schools.

The Internet remained limited mainly to universities and large computer-related businesses throughout the 1980's. In the late 1980's, many personal computer owners got their first taste of networking by using modems to dial in to on-line services such as CompuServe or by dialing in to home-grown bulletin-board systems (BBS's).

Recent Developments

By 1990, the Internet had 600,000 computers connected to 5,000 smaller networks. In 1991, researchers at CERN, a physics laboratory in Switzerland, created what became the World Wide Web. In 1992, the Web browser Mosaic, which led to Netscape Navigator, was developed at the University of Illinois.

Computer chips containing tens of millions of transistors made inexpensive computers even more powerful. The Web led to an explosion of Internet usage by small businesses, schools, and home users. By 1998, there were nearly 30 million computers connected to the Internet and more than 2.2 million Web hosts in nearly 200 countries around the world.

Every year, computer components become smaller, memory capacity becomes larger, and computer speed becomes faster. This trend will no doubt result in even more dramatic changes in the near future. Computers today generally use one CPU, so only one operation can proceed at a time. The latest supercomputers, however, can run many programs at once by using multiple CPU's. This will allow computers to perform in-

E-mail

Trash

Word processing

Icons represent computer files and programs, which can be accessed by using a mouse. These icons stand for e-mail, trash (for deleting files), and word processing.

credibly complicated tasks, such as simulating the birth of the universe.

▶ COMPUTERS AND SOCIETY

Computers have changed society in many ways. Vast amounts of information are available to anyone who has a computer and a modem. New tasks can be accomplished, and people can communicate in ways never thought possible. Along with the benefits, however, come some new problems.

Problems

Many databases contain private information about individuals, such as health or financial records. If companies or government agencies share this information without the individuals' permission, such practices can pose a threat to people's privacy.

Hackers are people who use computers for activities that are generally considered illegal. Some create **viruses**—programs that can destroy data or damage operating systems. Others break into computers over networks and then steal or destroy data.

Another problem, illegal copying of copyrighted software, deprives programmers of income. Computers can also be used to deceive by manipulating voices and images in ways that change their original content. And in recent decades, many people have lost jobs to newer computers and robots.

Older computers can pose problems, too. For example, some systems store just the last two numbers of a year. Organizations have spent many millions of dollars fixing this so-called **Y2K bug**. The term refers to the year 2000, which some computers interpret as 1900. Such confusion can cause computers to "crash," or stop functioning.

Trends

Media. Televisions, stereos, and video cameras are now routinely connected to one another, as are computers and telephone lines. Cable modems provide Internet connections across the same wires through which cable television signals are sent. Computers and the Internet are also bringing print and broadcast media closer together. Newspapers are publishing Web sites that include video and sound, and television networks have Web sites with text-based stories. Radio stations are broadcasting to listeners across the Web.

Distributed Computing. Computers connected by networks can perform computations that previously only supercomputers had been able to perform. In a distributed computing project, one central computer manages a large problem by assigning small parts of it to thousands of computers. In one such effort, a 19-year-old college student's computer discovered the largest known prime number, a number that is evenly divisible only by itself and 1. The new prime number was 909,526 digits long. Distributed computing takes advantage of the time when the computer is not being used by its owner.

Artificial Intelligence (AI). Since computers were first built, people have wondered whether computers could "think" the way people do. This has turned out to be much more difficult than expected, but computer programs are getting better at imitating some aspects of human intelligence. (For more information on AI, see the Wonder Question in this article.)

Home Environments. Computers may change how you interact with your home. The home may soon have a central computer that controls electronic appliances throughout the house. Voice commands, even over the telephone, could turn appliances on or off. More people will also work from home, telecommuting to their office across the Internet.

Future Computers. Today's computer chips use electronic circuits to perform their computations. In the future, computers may not use electricity at all. Optical computers store data and perform computations with light. Biological computers use molecules such as DNA, the same molecule that encodes the genes of living things. Quantum computers use individual atoms and the laws of physics to perform calculations.

DAVID L. HART
Senior Technical Editor
San Diego Supercomputer Center

See also AUTOMATION; ELECTRONICS; OFFICE MACHINES; ROBOTS; TELECOMMUNICATIONS; TRANSISTORS, DIODES, AND INTEGRATED CIRCUITS.

General Robert E. Lee (*center*) meets with Confederate president Jefferson Davis (*seated, at Lee's right*) and the members of his Cabinet in Richmond, Virginia, in 1861.

CONFEDERATE STATES OF AMERICA

The Confederacy was born on December 20, 1860, when the state of South Carolina formally seceded—withdrew—from the Federal Union of the United States. A South Carolina newspaper brazenly proclaimed, "The Union is Dissolved!" Five other southern states—Georgia, Florida, Alabama, Louisiana, and Mississippi—quickly followed South Carolina's lead. The secession of these states came shortly after the election of Abraham Lincoln as President of the United States.

Delegates from the six seceding states met in Montgomery, Alabama, the Confederacy's first capital, on February 4, 1861. They drafted a constitution creating a new republic called the Confederate States of America, which was dedicated to the principles of states' rights and the preservation of the institution of slavery. Kentucky-born Jefferson Davis, a former U.S. Senator and secretary of war who was then living in Mississippi, was chosen to be president of the Confederacy. Alexander H. Stephens, a Georgian, was designated vice president. (The capital of the Confederacy was later moved to Richmond, Virginia.)

Five other southern states subsequently joined the Confederacy. These were Texas, Virginia, Tennessee, Arkansas, and North Carolina. Several southern "border states"— Missouri, Kentucky, and Maryland—did not secede. They gave troops to both sides during the Civil War.

The Confederacy lasted only from 1861 to 1865. During most of that period, the Confederacy (South) fought the Union (North) in the American Civil War. When the war ended in a Union victory, the Confederacy was dissolved. Its member states were gradually readmitted to the Union during the Reconstruction Period.

President Jefferson Davis was in many ways an able leader. But he lacked the warm personal appeal of Abraham Lincoln. Davis was an aloof, austere man. He presided over a lost cause and suffered the humiliation of imprisonment after the war. Many Confederates blamed Davis for the failure of the Southern cause, and by the end of the war, he was resented throughout the South.

But Davis performed better than most of his contemporaries thought. A graduate of West Point and a man of military experience, he appointed able commanders to head the Confederate armies and chose a group of capable people to serve in his Cabinet.

Davis also adopted a flexible military strategy of offensive defense, which made the best use of Confederate strength while minimizing its many weaknesses. Although some historians might disagree, Davis showed strong character and grew in stature as a leader during the course of the war. His tough political, social, and military measures were disliked by many southerners but were necessary to keep the Confederacy alive.

▶ SOUTHERN RESOURCES

War between the North and South began on April 12, 1861, when Confederate troops bombarded the Federal garrison at Fort Sumter, in Charleston harbor. In almost every respect the South was at a disadvantage in resources when compared to the North. The South had a white population of about 6,000,000, as compared to the North's 21,000,000. However, the South also had 3,500,000 black slaves. While they were not used as soldiers until the very end of the war, they were a valuable military resource. They built fortifications, served as teamsters and farm workers, and performed other useful services. However, the full potential of black manpower was never used.

Financial resources were almost nonexistent. In all of the South there was only $27,000,000 in currency. Few factories, iron foundries, or other industrial plants existed. Southern railroads were inferior to those of the North. Cotton, land, and courage were the South's major assets.

The myth of "King Cotton" blinded the Confederacy to the realities of financing a modern war. Southerners believed that cotton was so vital to the textile-producing nations of Europe that these nations would become their allies. They thought that their abundant farmland would enable them to feed their armies and that the fighting ability of their soldiers would offset Northern superiority in weapons and manpower.

The South was proved wrong on all counts. European countries dependent on southern cotton found other sources. Much of the South's rich farmland fell to invading Union armies. Northern technology also proved decisive. The South could never match the North's ability to produce cannon, rifles, ships, and other war matériel.

▶ SOUTHERN DIPLOMACY

Failing to win peaceful secession through negotiation, southern diplomats tried to gain foreign recognition and support. Both the French and British governments favored the Confederate cause. But the people of these countries opposed war with the United States. Many English working people sympathized with the North, because they saw southern slavery as an evil institution. After Lincoln signed the Emancipation Proclamation, in 1863, the North won vastly increased international support. Even so, Great Britain came close to recognizing the Confederacy. But as southern military fortunes declined, hope for foreign intervention faded.

Faced with these problems, the Confederacy had to rely on other measures. Most southern war supplies had to be brought in from overseas, past the Union naval blockade. Fleets of fast blockade runners shuttled between southern ports and Nassau, Jamaica, Bermuda, and Cuba. The blockade runners carried cotton, which was exchanged for European shipments of rifles, cannon, and such items as coffee, lead, textiles, and medicines.

Lack of money was the Confederacy's greatest problem. The Confederacy was able to exist because loyal Southerners accepted promissory notes. But when the war seemed lost, Confederate money became worthless. Nevertheless, Jefferson Davis kept hopes alive by such stern measures as military conscription of all able-bodied white males and impressment—the seizure of goods without payment. Impressment was a desperate measure and a serious invasion of private rights. But without it southern armies could not have been fed, clothed, and sheltered.

▶ ON THE BATTLEFIELD

The Confederacy's survival for 4 years was mainly a tribute to the courage of its soldiers and the skill of its leading generals—men like Robert E. Lee, Thomas "Stonewall" Jackson, "Jeb" Stuart, and Nathan Bedford Forrest. In the early years of the war, Confederate armies won a string of victories—including First and Second Bull Run, the Seven Days' Battles, and Fredericksburg.

But as the war progressed, a new breed of Union general emerged. Among these generals were Ulysses S. Grant, William T. Sherman,

"Little Phil" Sheridan, and George H. Thomas. Helped by superior numbers and weakening southern morale, they began to turn the tide. In July, 1863, Lee's Army of Northern Virginia was beaten at the Battle of Gettysburg, and General Grant captured the Confederate citadel at Vicksburg, Mississippi. This victory gave the North complete control of the Mississippi River.

From then on, Confederate armies had to endure the pain of defeat. In 1864, Grant hammered away at Lee in Virginia, while Sherman captured Atlanta and began his "March to the Sea." At the same time, Sheridan defeated the Confederates in the Shenandoah Valley. The Union forces destroyed the crops growing on the rich farmlands of the valley—"the granary of the Confederacy."

The end came in April, 1865. After a long siege, Grant captured Petersburg, Virginia. Lee's army was forced to retreat, abandoning Richmond, the Confederate capital, to the Union forces. On April 9, 1865, cut off and surrounded, Lee surrendered his army to Grant at Appomattox Courthouse. A few weeks later, General Joseph E. Johnston surrendered his army to Sherman.

Military defeat meant the end of the Confederacy. The South was devastated and drained of able-bodied workers and resources. But in death, the Confederacy left an enduring legend of gallantry and heroism in defense of the "Lost Cause."

FRANK E. VANDIVER
Rice University

See also CIVIL WAR, UNITED STATES.

CONFUCIUS (551–479 B.C.)

Confucius was the greatest wise man of China. Because of his wisdom, Confucius has followers even today. Confucianism is not a religion. It does not teach about God, heaven, and life after death. It is a philosophy that teaches people a way to live life on earth wisely.

"Confucius" is the European form of the Chinese name K'ung Fu-tzu, or Master K'ung. The Chinese called him master because he was a great teacher. Many legends grew up about him. It was said that dragons guarded his mother when he was born.

K'ung was born in the state of Lu (now in Shantung). His father died when K'ung was very young. And as soon as he could the boy went to work to help his mother. Still he had time to study and to practice archery and music, which he loved. He desired order and grace in behavior, like the order and harmony of music.

When he was 22, K'ung became a teacher. Pupils came to his home to learn history, poetry, and manners. He taught by talking with them and making them think. He believed that "A person's character is formed by the Odes [poetry], developed by the Rites [ancient rules of courtesy and ceremony], and perfected by music."

K'ung's way to an orderly world was this: A man must start by being honest and brave, and learn how to behave courteously and truthfully. If he could do that, he could manage his family wisely. If every family were well managed, orderly, and moral, the government would be well ordered, too. So wisdom and good government begin at home.

K'ung did not believe thinking and teaching were enough. He wanted most of all to put his ideas to use. He held several offices. But when the ruler of Lu neglected his counsel, K'ung resigned. He went into exile with his disciples and wandered for 13 years.

K'ung spent his last years writing and teaching. He left behind him the Five Classics, which he edited and compiled, plus the *Analects* (conversations) put together by his pupils. Typical of Confucius' wisdom is his version of the Golden Rule: "Do not do to others what you would not have them do to you." But he did not believe in returning good for evil. He reasoned in this way: If you reward with kindness the person who hurts you, what do you have left to give to the person who is kind to you?

Reviewed by KENNETH S. COOPER
George Peabody College

CONGLOMERATE. See ROCKS (Sedimentary Rock).

CONGO

The Republic of Congo is a nation of west central Africa. A country with a small population and limited resources, it owes much of its importance to its location on the Congo River, one of the great river systems of Africa. The Congo was formerly a colony of France, part of French Equatorial Africa, before gaining its independence in 1960.

▶ THE PEOPLE

Pygmies. The earliest known people in the Congo were the Pygmies, who originally lived throughout the region. Today they are found only in scattered areas in the northeastern part of the country. A shy people, small in size, the Pygmies live by hunting and fishing and by collecting food from the forests. They sometimes supplement their diet by trading meat and fish for agricultural products from their Bantu neighbors.

Bantu Groups. Except for the relatively few Pygmies, the people of the Congo are of Bantu stock. They are divided into 15 main groups. The largest is the Bakongo (or Kongo). Other important Bantu groups are the Batéké (or Téké), the Vili, the M'Bochi (Mbochi), and the Sangha (Sanga). The people traditionally are farmers. Many of the M'Bochi, however, have moved to the cities, where they work in industry and hold many of the civil service positions.

Where the People Live. As a whole, the Congo is sparsely settled, averaging fewer than 14 persons per square mile (about four per square kilometer). The great majority of the people live in the southern third of the country. Population density is heaviest in the area around Brazzaville, the capital.

Language and Religion. French is the official language of the country, but several Bantu languages are widely spoken. The people are

The Congo River forms part of the southern boundary of the nation of the Congo. The river, with its tributaries, is a major source of transportation in the region.

about equally divided between Christians (mainly Roman Catholics) and followers of traditional African religions. A few Congolese, mostly in the north, are Muslims.

Education. A considerable part of the Congo's budget is spent on education, which is free and compulsory for children between the ages of 6 and 16. Almost all Congolese children finish primary school. This is rare in many African countries. However, the Congo still has serious educational problems. Not enough young Congolese go on to secondary school, and too few of them graduate. In addition, about 50 percent of the population, mainly adults, is illiterate (unable to read or write). The Congo's main institution of higher education is Marien Ngouabi University in Brazzaville.

▶ THE LAND

The Congo straddles the equator and extends about 800 miles (1,300 kilometers) inland from the Atlantic Ocean. The southern border of the country follows the Congo River and its tributary the Ubangi. Most of the country consists of a low plateau, with flat, swampy valleys divided by low hills. About half the land is covered by forest.

The country's highest region is the Batéké plateau north of Brazzaville, which rises about 2,700 feet (820 meters) above sea level. Another high area, the Mayombé Escarpment, runs parallel to the Atlantic coast. These two highland areas stand as barriers between the Atlantic coastal plain and the Congo River Basin. Several rivers have cut deep valleys across the Mayombé Escarpment on their route to the Atlantic Ocean. Along the banks of one of these rivers, the Niari, lies the country's richest agricultural region.

Climate. The Congo's climate is hot and humid, with little seasonal change in temperatures. The average daily high temperature in the Brazzaville region is 86°F (30°C). Rainfall increases from the coast to areas in the interior. In the northeast, about 70 inches (1,750 millimeters) of rainfall a year is common.

Natural Resources. Except for petroleum and potash (used in making chemical fertilizer), the Congo has few large-scale deposits of minerals. However, these two, particularly petroleum, are vital to the country's economy. The Congo's large areas of forest also provide an important source of timber.

▶ MAJOR CITIES

Brazzaville, the capital and largest city, is situated on the west bank of the Congo River. It has a population of about 600,000. A major Congo River port and manufacturing center, Brazzaville is named for the Italian-born French explorer Pierre Savorgnan de Brazza, who founded the first settlement here in 1880.

Pointe-Noire, the Congo's second largest city and its seaport, lies on the Atlantic coast. It is connected to Brazzaville by a 320-mile (515-kilometer)-long railroad.

▶ THE ECONOMY

Agriculture. Most Congolese grow food just for their own use. Cassava (a starchy root) is the main crop, followed by sugar, rice, corn, and peanuts. Crop yields are low, and food must be imported to meet the people's needs. In the Niari River valley, the country's most developed farming region, sugarcane plantations produce sugar for export. Other export crops include coffee and cocoa beans.

Mining and Forestry. Mining is the most important sector of the Congo's economy. Potash was the country's chief mineral until the

---

FACTS and figures

REPUBLIC OF THE CONGO (République du Congo) is the official name of the country.

LOCATION: West Central Africa.

AREA: 132,047 sq mi (342,000 km²).

POPULATION: 2,700,000 (estimate).

CAPITAL AND LARGEST CITY: Brazzaville.

MAJOR LANGUAGES: French (official), Bantu languages.

MAJOR RELIGIOUS GROUPS: Christian, traditional African religions.

GOVERNMENT: Republic. **Head of state**—president. **Head of government**—prime minister. **Legislature** —parliament, consisting of the Senate and the National Assembly.

CHIEF PRODUCTS: Agricultural—cassava, sugar, rice, corn, peanuts. **Manufactured**—processed agricultural and forest products, refined petroleum, textiles, beverages, soap, cement. **Mineral**—petroleum, potash.

MONETARY UNIT: CFA franc (1 CFA franc = 100 centimes).

Brazzaville is the capital and largest city of the Congo. Founded in 1880 by the explorer Pierre Savorgnan de Brazza, it is an important port on the Congo River.

discovery of petroleum, which now accounts for about 70 percent of the Congo's exports. Timber, including limba wood used in making furniture, is also an important export.

Manufacturing. The Congo has a relatively well developed manufacturing base. The processing of agricultural and forest products and petroleum refining are especially important.

▶ HISTORY AND GOVERNMENT

Early History. In the late 15th century the Portuguese explorer Diogo Cão discovered the mouth of the Congo River and visited the powerful Kongo people living on its banks. The area was a source of slaves until the slave trade was outlawed in 1815.

The explorer Pierre Savorgnan de Brazza traveled up the Ogooué (Ogowe) River in 1875 and crossed into the Congo Basin. During a second expedition in 1880, he established the settlement that has since become the city of Brazzaville. The treaties he made with local rulers allowed the French to gain control over the entire area. In 1903, France gave territorial status and the name "Middle Congo" to the region. Middle Congo—along with what are today the nations of Chad, Gabon, and the Central African Republic—became part of French Equatorial Africa in 1910.

French Equatorial Africa was dissolved in 1958, and the Congo became a self-governing member of the French Community. It won complete independence on August 15, 1960.

Recent History. The Congo's brief history has been stormy. Its first president, Fulbert Youlou, was forced to resign in 1963. The next president, Alphonse Massamba-Débat, established a Marxist Socialist government. Massamba-Débat was ousted in 1968 by the military and was succeeded in 1969 by Captain Marien Ngouabi, who led the country until his assassination in 1977. Colonel Denis Sassou-Nguesso became president in 1979. He was re-elected in 1984 and 1989.

In 1992, under a new constitution, the Congo was declared a multiparty democracy with a directly elected president and legislature. Pascal Lissouba was elected president, defeating Sassou-Nguesso. But in 1997, after a four-month civil war, Sassou-Nguesso, with the help of Angolan forces, retook control of the country without being elected.

HUGH C. BROOKS
Director, Center for African Studies
St. John's University (New York)

See also CONGO RIVER.

CONGO, DEMOCRATIC REPUBLIC OF. See ZAÏRE (DEMOCRATIC REPUBLIC OF CONGO).

Twisting and turning, the Congo River flows for more than 2,700 miles (4,347 kilometers) across central Africa. The Congo is the second largest river in Africa and the most important waterway of central Africa.

CONGO RIVER

The Congo is one of the great rivers of the world. It is the second largest river in Africa, after the Nile. In volume of water flow, the Congo is second in the world only to the Amazon River of South America. The Congo is the vital waterway of central Africa.

The Congo originates near the border between the Democratic Republic of Congo and Zambia and flows, twisting and turning, for about 2,700 miles (4,347 kilometers) across central Africa before reaching the Atlantic Ocean. The Congo Basin drains an area of 1,425,000 square miles (3,690,750 square kilometers), which includes all of the Democratic Republic of Congo and parts of Angola, Zambia, Gabon, the Central African Republic, the Republic of Congo, and Cameroon.

The river varies greatly in its width, from about 7 miles (11 kilometers) to less than 1 mile (1.6 kilometers). In some places the river is shallow and sluggish. In others it flows swift and deep.

Exploration. The Portuguese explorer Diogo Cão sighted the mouth of the Congo in 1482, while sailing down the west coast of Africa. In the years that followed, many explorers, including the Scottish missionary David Livingstone, sought to penetrate the river's mysteries. But it was not until 1877 that Henry Morton Stanley succeeded in leading an expedition down the entire length of the Congo, from its headwaters to its mouth. The difficult journey took more than two years.

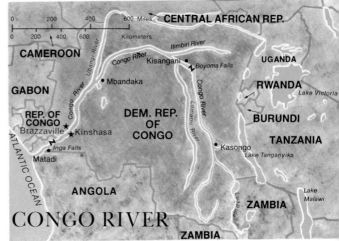

CONGO RIVER

Importance of the Congo. The Congo, along with its more than 5,000 miles (8,050 kilometers) of tributaries, plays an important part in the economy of central Africa. The river is an important avenue of transportation. At Inga Falls the river drops 800 feet (244 meters). Some 1.2 million gallons (4.5 million liters) of water a second pour past this spot. When fully utilized, it will provide hydroelectric power that will help in the mining and processing of mineral resources and also in creating new industries.

HUGH C. BROOKS
Director, Center for African Studies
St. John's University (New York)

CONGRESS OF THE UNITED STATES. See UNITED STATES, CONGRESS OF THE.

CONGRESS OF VIENNA. See NAPOLEON I.

CONIC SECTIONS. See GEOMETRY.

CONNECTICUT

Connecticut's name comes from Quin-netuckut, *an Algonkian Indian term meaning "long tidal river." It refers to the great river that divides the state almost in half from north to south. Puritans from Massachusetts first settled on the fertile floodplain of the Connecticut River near Hartford in 1636.*

The state's official nickname, the Constitution State, refers to the Fundamental Orders of 1639, the compact that bound the three original river settlements together as an independent commonwealth. It was one of the first written constitutions to be adopted by any government. One of Connecticut's unofficial nicknames, the Land of Steady Habits, emphasizes the careful and thrifty approach to problems traditionally favored by state citizens. Another, the Nutmeg State, refers to the Yankee peddlers of early days, who traveled from house to house selling Connecticut wares. These shrewd salesmen were said to occasionally trick their customers by selling them wooden nutmegs instead of real ones.

State flag

Connecticut, one of the original 13 colonies, is located in southern New England. It is bordered by New York State on the west, Massachusetts on the north, and Rhode Island on the east. Long Island Sound, a sheltered arm of the Atlantic Ocean, forms its southern boundary.

With little more than 5,000 square miles (12,950 square kilometers) of land, Connecticut is the third smallest state in the nation. One can drive diagonally across the state from one corner to another in less than three hours. Though it lacks spectacular physical features, Connecticut boasts a surprisingly varied landscape: jagged coastline, rolling hills laced with stone walls, river valleys, rural villages, mill towns, bustling cities, and sprawling suburban tracts.

Throughout its history, Connecticut has made important contributions to America's development. Connecticut delegates to the 1787 Constitutional Convention engineered a key compromise that resolved a serious dispute over state representation. During the 1800's, the pioneering mass-production techniques of inventors such as Eli Whitney and Samuel Colt put Connecticut in the forefront of the industrial age. In times of war, Con-necticut factories have been vital to the national defense, supplying the military with arms, airplane engines, submarines, and other essential products. Connecticut natives such as showman P. T. Barnum, writer Harriet Beecher Stowe, composer Charles Ives, and consumer advocate Ralph Nader have had lasting influence on American culture.

Modern Connecticut is a densely populated state. Only three other states are inhabited by more people per square mile. From the mid-1800's to the mid-1900's, most of the population lived in small- to medium-sized cities. Today, however, more people in Connecticut live, work, and shop in the suburbs than they do in urban areas.

▶ LAND

Connecticut is the most southwesterly of the six New England states. It is rectangular in shape, with a spur at its southwestern tip. The natural terrain includes low, wooded hills, broad river valleys, and 618 miles (994 kilometers) of coastline.

Land Regions

A small part of the Taconic Range occupies the northwestern corner of Connecticut. All the rest of the state lies within a region

Opposite page, clockwise from left: White-steepled churches such as this one in Litchfield are fixtures of many small Connecticut towns. Mystic Seaport recreates coastal life of the 1800's. The Hartford skyline rises behind the city's ornate state capitol.

State flower:
Mountain laurel

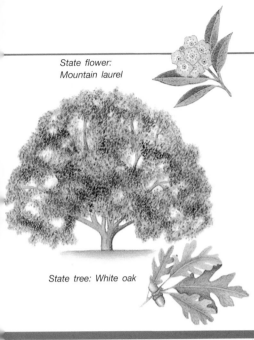

State tree: White oak

FACTS AND FIGURES

Location: Northeastern United States; bordered on the north by Massachusetts, on the east by Rhode Island, on the south by Long Island Sound, and on the west by New York State.

Area: 5,018 sq mi (12,997 km^2); rank, 48th.

Population: 3,275,000 (1994 estimate); rank, 27th.

Elevation: *Highest*—2,380 ft (725 m) on Mount Frissell, in Salisbury; *lowest*—sea level, on Long Island Sound.

Capital: Hartford.

Statehood: January 9, 1788; 5th state.

State Motto: *Qui transtulit sustinet* ("He who transplanted still sustains").

State Song: "Yankee Doodle."

Nickname: Constitution State (official); Land of Steady Habits; Nutmeg State.

Abbreviations: CT; Conn.

State bird: American robin

known as the New England Upland. It is divided into several parts: the Eastern and Western uplands, the Seaboard Lowland, and the Connecticut Valley Lowland.

The Taconic Range extends from New York and Massachusetts into northwestern Connecticut as far as the Housatonic River. The state's highest point is on the southern slope of Mount Frissell, part of the Taconics.

The Eastern Upland is an area of gentle hills cut by swift streams that have eroded the land for millions of years. There are peaks higher than 1,000 feet (300 meters) in the north, but the hills are lower to the south.

The Western Upland is a hilly region like its twin in the eastern part of the state. However, the elevation is higher in the west.

The Seaboard Lowland, also called the Coastal Lowland, is a sloping extension of the uplands. Along Long Island Sound it becomes a low, almost level plain. The mouths of the rivers in this coastal strip form harbors.

The Connecticut Valley Lowland is a narrow belt of land that extends from the Sound north through the center of the state. The terrain is relatively flat, and the soil is fertile.

Rivers, Lakes, and Coastal Waters

There are three major river systems in Connecticut. All of them flow south and empty into Long Island Sound. The Connecticut River, the longest in New England, is navigable between the coast and the city of

Hartford. Rivers of the Eastern Upland, including the Willimantic, the Shetucket, the Quinebaug, and the Yantic, join at various points to form the Thames, which drains into Long Island Sound between New London and Groton. The Housatonic and Naugatuck are the major rivers that drain the Western Upland. These two rivers merge at Derby and continue southward as the Housatonic River. They ultimately flow into Long Island Sound at Stratford.

Like the rest of New England, Connecticut is dotted with small lakes and ponds. Lake Candlewood, north of Danbury, is the largest body of water in

the state. Created artificially to supply water for power plants on the Housatonic River, it is also used for recreation.

Much of the Connecticut coastline is heavily populated. Interspersed with the numerous cities are residential communities, state parks with inviting beaches, and small harbors that are bases for commercial fishing and recreational boating.

Climate

The location of Connecticut, at the edge of the North American continent bordering the Atlantic Ocean, in the middle latitudes, determines its climate. High-pressure Arctic air sweeps across the state from the northwest in the winter, producing cold temperatures and moderate snowfall. In the summer the direction of the airflow is reversed, as moist, tropical air from the Gulf of Mexico brings warm temperatures and high humidity to the state.

The average January temperature in Hartford, located near the center of the state, is 27°F (–3°C), while the average July temperature is 73°F (23°C). The average annual precipitation in Connecticut is 46 inches (1,168 millimeters) with no extended wet or dry periods. The growing season, which begins in mid-April and continues until late October, averages 180 days.

Plant and Animal Life

Some 60 percent of Connecticut's land is wooded. The largest forests are in the northwestern corner of the state. However, most Connecticut woodlands are smaller tracts scattered throughout the state. Hardwoods such as sugar maple, beech, yellow birch, oak, and hickory are the dominant species. Mountain laurel and dogwood are abundant.

The widely dispersed wooded areas in Connecticut shelter small animals such as

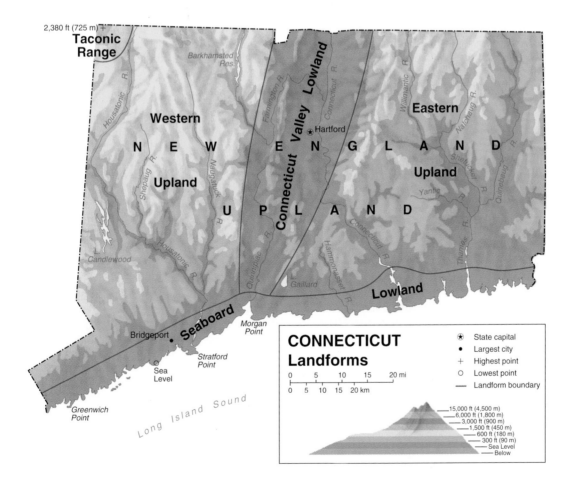

Wooded areas are scattered throughout the Connecticut countryside, covering more than 60 percent of the total land area and providing an ideal habitat for white-tailed deer and a multitude of smaller animals.

woodchuck, fox, rabbit, and squirrel. They also provide an ideal habitat for white-tailed deer, whose numbers have increased even in populous suburban areas. Pheasant, quail, wild turkey, and duck abound in the state, as do many varieties of songbirds.

Natural Resources

Connecticut's forests, soils, and minerals do not play a large role in the state economy, although the natural landscape of the state is valuable for recreation and tourism.

Connecticut's soils were deposited mainly by glaciers, and most of the land is rocky. It is only in the large river valleys that richer water-deposited soils are found in abundance. The best agricultural soils are the sandy loams in the northern portion of the Connecticut River Valley. The state's leading minerals are stone, used for road building, and sand and gravel, used mainly in construction.

Connecticut has taken steps to protect the natural environment. In 1971 the state established a department of environmental protection to administer its strict laws regulating waste disposal and reducing water and air pollution. In 1983 a mandatory motor vehicle emission inspection system was set up to improve air quality. The legislature also began a program to protect agricultural land from commercial and residential development.

▶ PEOPLE

More than 3 million people now live in tiny Connecticut, making it the fourth most densely populated state in the nation. Only about 20 percent of the people live in rural areas. Most of the population growth since the mid-1950's has been in the suburbs; Connecticut cities lost residents during the same period. The main population corridor extends from Greenwich eastward along Long Island Sound to New Haven and then north to Hartford.

The Connecticut population is a mosaic of many ethnic groups. The earliest European settlers came from England. Beginning in the 1800's, large numbers of immigrants from other European countries came to Connecticut. Today the state's largest population groups—Italian, Irish, English, German, and Polish—reflect these historic immigration patterns. African Americans make up about 8 percent of the state's population. About 300 descendants of the original Native Americans still live on reservations in eastern Connecticut. The Mashantucket Pequot tribe operates a lucrative gambling casino on their land in Ledyard.

Education

More than 100 years before the Revolutionary War, the laws of Connecticut stated that parents had to educate their children. Communities of more than 50 families were required to hire a schoolmaster. Through the years the state has maintained its tradition of respect for education.

The state supports a variety of institutions of higher education. The University of Connecticut is located in Storrs. The university also operates two-year branches in different parts of the state. The Connecticut State University system is made up of campuses in Danbury, New Britain, New Haven, and Willimantic. The state also has a regional network of technical and community colleges.

Connecticut has long been known for its private schools and colleges. Famous preparatory schools include Choate in Wallingford, the Gunnery in Washington, Hotchkiss in Lakeville, Taft in Watertown, Hopkins in New Haven, and Miss Porter's in Farmington. Yale University in New Haven, chartered in 1701, is the third oldest institution of higher learning in the United States. Two other well-

Above: The highly ranked University of Connecticut women's basketball team attracts a wide following both inside and outside the state. *Right:* The campus of Yale University, one of the oldest institutions of higher learning in the nation, is a New Haven landmark.

known Connecticut colleges are more than 150 years old. They are Trinity College in Hartford, founded in 1823, and Wesleyan University in Middletown, founded in 1831. All together, Connecticut has more than 15 private universities and colleges. The United States Coast Guard Academy is located in New London.

Libraries, Museums, and the Arts

Connecticut's first library was established in Durham in 1733. Today most of Connecticut's 169 towns and cities have public library service. The Connecticut Historical Society, in Hartford, maintains a library devoted to state history, as does the Connecticut State Library, also in Hartford. Yale University's library collections are among the largest and best in the nation. They total more than 4 million volumes.

Connecticut has many museums, both public and private. Important art museums include the Wadsworth Atheneum in Hartford, the Museum of American Art in New Britain,

the Yale University Art Gallery and the Yale Center for British Art in New Haven, a branch of the Whitney Museum of American Art in Stamford, and the Aldrich Museum of Contemporary Art in Ridgefield. Yale's Peabody Museum has a respected natural history collection. The Connecticut Historical Society Museum in Hartford contains exhibits pertaining to the history of the state. Historical societies in many of the towns and cities have fine local history museums. Some of these are located in historic homes furnished as they were in early days.

Connecticut cities offer rich opportunities to enjoy the performing arts. In Hartford the Bushnell Memorial Hall has been the site of concerts, ballet, and opera for more than fifty

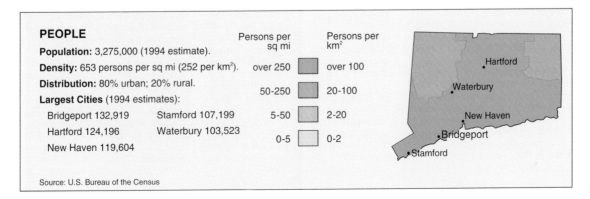

PEOPLE

Population: 3,275,000 (1994 estimate).

Density: 653 persons per sq mi (252 per km²).

Distribution: 80% urban; 20% rural.

Largest Cities (1994 estimates):

Bridgeport 132,919	Stamford 107,199
Hartford 124,196	Waterbury 103,523
New Haven 119,604	

Persons per sq mi		Persons per km²
over 250		over 100
50-250		20-100
5-50		2-20
0-5		0-2

Source: U.S. Bureau of the Census

Places of Interest

Goodspeed Opera House, East Haddam

Mark Twain House, Nook Farm, Hartford

Mystic Marinelife Aquarium, Mystic

Cornwall Bridge, West Cornwall

Cornwall Bridge, one of Connecticut's few remaining covered bridges, spans the Housatonic River at West Cornwall.

Gillette Castle, on the Connecticut River in Hadlyme, is an unusual 24-room stone castle in a beautiful woodland setting. Completed in 1919, it was the residence of William Gillette, an actor and playwright best known for his portrayal of Sherlock Holmes.

Goodspeed Opera House, in East Haddam, is a restored Victorian structure dating from 1876. Today the opera house presents a variety of productions, mainly revivals of classic American musicals.

Hill-Stead Museum, in Farmington, is an elegant mansion designed by Theodate Pope Riddle, one of the nation's first women architects, for her father, industrialist Alfred Pope. The home contains the owners' collection of impressionist paintings and decorative objects.

Historic Houses are found throughout Connecticut. Among the most interesting are the **Nathan Hale Homestead**, in South Coventry, the family home of the Revolutionary War patriot; **Tapping Reeve House and Law School**, in Litchfield, the site of the first law school in America (1784); **Webb-Deane-Stevens Museum**, in Wethersfield, which showcases three restored 1700's homes; and **Whitfield House**, in Guilford, built in 1639 and said to be the oldest stone house in New England.

Maritime Aquarium at Norwalk is devoted to the sea life and maritime history of Long Island Sound. Features include an aquarium, a museum of classic small boats, and an IMAX theater with a screen six stories tall.

Mystic Seaport, in Mystic, is a museum that re-creates life in a New England seaport of the 1800's. Among the ships on display at the seaport is the *Charles W. Morgan*, the last surviving wooden whaling ship. The nearby **Mystic Marinelife Aquarium** is another popular tourist attraction. It features more than 6,000 living sea creatures, including outdoor exhibits of seals and penguins and dolphin, whale, and sea lion shows.

Nook Farm, in Hartford, contains the homes of prominent writers and artists who lived in the area in the 1870's. The two most notable are a Victorian Gothic mansion that was the home of writer Mark Twain from 1874 to 1891 and the Harriet Beecher Stowe House, home of the author of *Uncle Tom's Cabin*.

USS *Nautilus* Memorial, in Groton, offers tours of the world's first nuclear-powered submarine. Nearby is the **Submarine Force Library and Museum**, a dramatic steel and glass building that contains exhibits tracing the history and development of the submarine.

The Valley Railroad, in Essex, offers a sight-seeing excursion through the Connecticut River valley on a vintage steam train. The trip includes an optional riverboat cruise on the Connecticut River. Also in Essex is the **Connecticut River Museum**, which features nautical displays, including a full-sized model of the *Turtle*, a submarine built before the Revolutionary War.

State Areas. Connecticut operates more than 90 state parks. For more information, contact the Department of Environmental Protection, State Office Building, Hartford, Connecticut 06106.

years. The Hartford Stage Company specializes in contemporary drama. Yale University's Woolsey Hall presents a full schedule of musical productions. The Long Wharf Theater and the Yale Repertory Theater, both in New Haven, have theater companies in residence. Also in New Haven, the historic Shubert Theater hosts touring dramas and musicals. The Stamford Center for the Arts presents nationally known musicians and dancers.

▶ ECONOMY

Connecticut residents enjoy the highest per capita income in the nation. The state's prosperity has long rested on a strong industrial base. As late as 1950, approximately half the jobs in the state were in manufacturing. Today the economy is more diverse. Four sectors—finance, insurance, and real estate; business, social, and personal services; wholesale and retail trade; and manufacturing—account for about 80 percent of Connecticut's employment and output. Beginning in the 1960's and 1970's, many large corporations moved their headquarters to Connecticut, especially to Fairfield County, which abuts New York State.

Services

The fastest-growing area of the state's economy is in service industries. Combined, they total some 75 percent of the state's economic output.

Finance, insurance, and real estate is the leading service industry. The city of Hartford has long been known as the insurance capital of the United States. Today, despite the loss of some companies through relocation and mergers, more than 100 insurance firms have their headquarters in Connecticut. Aetna Life and Casualty, based in Hartford, is the state's oldest and largest insurance company.

Next in importance are business, social, and personal services. These include such activities as health care, legal services, and advertising. Wholesale and retail trade is a third important service industry in the state. Government, including public schools and military installations, and transportation, communication, and utilities make up the remainder of the service sector.

Manufacturing

Although it has declined in importance over the past forty years, manufacturing is still a vital part of the Connecticut economy. No longer do Connecticut factories turn out large quantities of brass, silver, heavy machinery, rubber products, or textiles. Instead, a highly skilled workforce fabricates technologically sophisticated instruments such as electronic devices, telecommunications products,

Jet engine parts are produced in a Windsor factory. The manufacture of transportation equipment is a leading economic activity in the state.

PRODUCTS AND INDUSTRIES

Manufacturing: Transportation equipment, industrial machinery, fabricated metal products, scientific instruments, chemicals, electrical equipment.

Agriculture: Nursery products, flowers, fruit, vegetables, honey, wine, maple syrup.

Minerals: Sand and gravel.

Services: Wholesale and retail trade; finance, insurance, and real estate; business, social, and personal services; transportation, communication, and utilities; government.

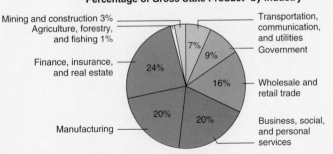

Percentage of Gross State Product* by Industry

Mining and construction 3%
Agriculture, forestry, and fishing 1%
Finance, insurance, and real estate 24%
Manufacturing 20%
20%
16%
9%
7%
Transportation, communication, and utilities
Government
Wholesale and retail trade
Business, social, and personal services

*Gross state product is the total value of goods and services produced in a year.

Source: U.S. Bureau of Economic Analysis **509**

Foxwoods Casino, run by the Mashantucket Pequot Indians on their reservation in Ledyard, is one of the world's largest casinos and a major employer.

transportation equipment, and aerospace components.

Military production in the form of jet aircraft engines, helicopters, and nuclear submarines represents an unstable segment of the Connecticut economy that has faltered since the end of the Cold War. The largest industrial employer in the state is United Technologies. However, most of the recent growth in employment has been generated by small firms with less than fifty employees.

Agriculture

Most of Connecticut's landscape is not well suited to commercial agriculture. The number of farms in the state has been shrinking since the early 1800's. Expansion of the suburbs in the years following World War II gobbled up farmland at an accelerated pace. Since 1970, thanks in part to state legislation designed to preserve the rural environment, the number of farms has stabilized at about 3,500. Most are small, averaging about 100 acres in size, and produce nursery stock, flowers, fruit, vegetables, honey, wine, and maple syrup for local markets. Shade-grown tobacco, once a profitable crop in the Connecticut River valley, is now much less significant.

Mining and Construction

At one time the mining of iron ore and copper and the quarrying of building stones were important industries. Today crushed stone, sand, and gravel used in highway construction are the state's most valuable minerals. The construction industry was spurred by a residential housing boom in the 1980's that has since declined sharply.

Transportation and Communication

Connecticut is a compact state with a well-developed transportation system. Amtrak offers regular passenger train service east to Boston, south to New York, and north to Montreal. Active commuter rail lines fan out from New York City into Connecticut as far north as Waterbury. The state has an elaborate system of multilane divided access highways without tolls.

There are 5 commercial airports and more than 50 private airports in Connecticut. The most important is Bradley International Airport, located north of Hartford. Bridgeport, New Haven, and New London have deepwater seaports.

The people of Connecticut have access to a wide variety of information sources. More than 100 daily and weekly newspapers are published in the state. The *Hartford Courant*, established in 1764 as the *Connecticut Courant*, is the oldest continuously published newspaper in the country. The state has about 70 radio stations and 11 local television stations. ESPN, the national sports television channel, is located in New Britain. In addition, New York City newspapers and radio and television stations reach a substantial audience in Connecticut.

▶ CITIES

Connecticut cities are not large; none has a population that reaches 200,000. Rather, the state has many cities of moderate size. Bridgeport, Hartford, New Haven, Waterbury, and Stamford have populations of more than 100,000. Another eleven urban centers contain between 50,000 and 100,000 people.

Hartford, the state capital, is centrally located on the Connecticut River. It was established in the 1630's by settlers from Massachusetts. For more than 150 years, Hartford was one of the two capitals of Connecticut; the other was New Haven. It became the single state capital in 1875.

The city's ornate Gothic state capitol building, opened in 1879 and completely refurbished for its centennial, anchors a complex of attractive government buildings near the downtown area. Hartford is the headquarters for many insurance companies and defense-related industries. A cluster of high-rise office buildings, including the tallest building between Boston and New York, gives the city a dramatic skyline.

Bridgeport is located on Long Island Sound at the mouth of the Pequonnock River. The arrival of the railroad in the 1830's transformed the city from a tiny maritime community into a diversified manufacturing center. Among the products shipped to all parts of the world by local factories were sewing machines, typewriters, and small appliances. However, the city lost most of its industry after the mid-1960's and thereafter faced severe financial problems, narrowly avoiding bankruptcy in 1991.

New Haven began as an independent colony in 1637 and was absorbed into the Colony of Connecticut in 1665. It was one of the few planned settlements in America, laid out in eight squares with a public square, or green, in the center. The green is still the focal point of downtown New Haven.

The city's location—on Long Island Sound at the mouth of the Quinnipiac River—and its fine harbor made it a flourishing port until the mid-1800's. New Haven later became a center for the manufacture of carriages, guns, boots, clocks, and hardware. Today the largest employer in the city is Yale University; its presence contributes to New Haven's distinctive character.

Stamford, located on Long Island Sound near New York City, was settled by Puritans in 1641. It was a center for the manufacture of hardware and a magnet for immigrant labor in the 1800's. With the decline of manufacturing in the state in the mid-1900's, Stamford became a service industry hub. Many multinational corporations relocated their headquarters from New York City to the sleek glass office towers that sprang up in central Stamford. Luxury hotels, elegant restaurants, a performing arts center, and an indoor shopping mall have replaced small businesses in the downtown area.

Waterbury, situated in a valley formed by the Mad and Mattatuck rivers, remained a poor farming community for more than 150 years after its founding in 1674. But in the early 1800's, the first brass mill began operation, and Waterbury began a period of rapid growth. Waterbury firms led the nation in brass output, and the city became known as the brass center of the world. Waterbury's brass production declined greatly after World War II. The city is the site of Teikyo Post University and Naugatuck Valley Technical-Community College.

▶ GOVERNMENT

Colonial Connecticut was governed by the Fundamental Orders, adopted in 1639. In 1662, Connecticut received a charter from the English king. It remained in effect until 1818, when a revised constitution was adopted. The state's present constitution dates from 1965.

The executive branch of the state government includes the governor and five other executive officers, all elected for 4-year terms.

Below left: Fairfield commuters wait for their train. Many residents of southwestern Connecticut commute to jobs in New York City. *Below right:* Onlookers enjoy a parade in New Britain, a moderate-sized city in the central part of the state.

Stamford, on the coast near the New York border, is one of Connecticut's largest cities. Its sleek office towers house the headquarters of many large corporations.

The legislative branch is called the General Assembly. It is made up of a senate and a house of representatives. The members of both bodies are elected for 2-year terms. Under the 1965 constitution, the state's legislature was **reapportioned**, or redivided, in response to a U.S. Supreme Court requirement that legislative districts be roughly equal in population. The judicial branch is made up of a series of courts. The state supreme court is the highest tribunal, followed by the appellate court, then the superior courts, where all legal action begins.

Local government is important in Connecticut. The state has 169 towns, each with its own government. In addition, there are 23 separate city governments. Most towns and cities have their own legislative bodies, although some retain the traditional town meeting form of government. Although the

INDEX TO CONNECTICUT MAP

● Former County Seat   Counties in parentheses   ★ State Capital

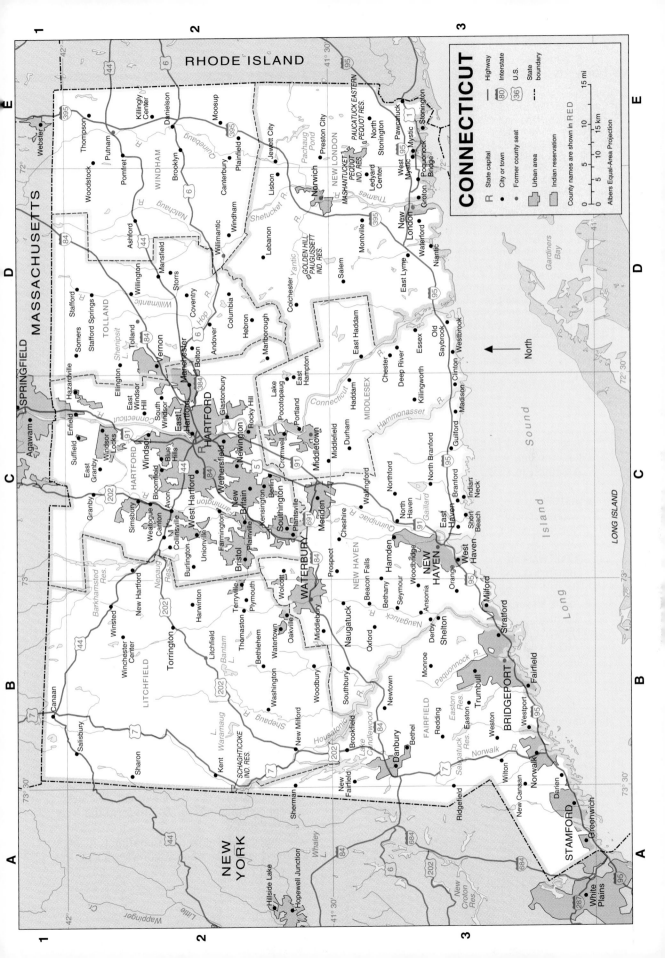

Famous People

Connecticut has a long roll call of famous citizens. Among the most noted are Revolutionary War figures Nathan Hale (South Coventry) and Benedict Arnold (Norwich), dictionary author Noah Webster (West Hartford), inventor Charles Goodyear (New Haven), abolitionist John Brown (Torrington), showman P. T. Barnum (Bethel), writer Harriet Beecher Stowe (Litchfield), composer Charles Ives (Danbury), and geneticist Barbara McClintock (Hartford). Inventor Eli Whitney and writer Mark Twain, although not born in the state, did much of their work there. Biographies of all these notables can be found in this encyclopedia.

Roger Sherman

Walter Chauncey Camp (1859–1925), born in New Britain, is known as the father of American football.

While attending Yale University and Yale Medical School, he played halfback on the football team. As a player and later as a coach at Yale (1888–92) and Stanford University (1894–95), he originated many of the present-day rules and tactics of the game. In 1889, Camp selected the first All-America team.

Prudence Crandall (1803–90), an educator and reformer, was born in Hopkinton, Rhode Island. She moved to Connecticut and in 1831 established a private school for girls in Canterbury. In 1833 she admitted a black student. When parents objected, Crandall closed the school, reopening it two months later as an academy for black girls. She was arrested, jailed, and convicted under a new state law forbidding the establishment of schools for nonresident blacks. Although her conviction was reversed, Crandall was forced to close her school for good.

Ella T. Grasso (1919–81), born in Windsor Locks, was elected governor of Connecticut in 1974, becoming the nation's first woman state governor who did not succeed her husband in office. This accomplishment capped a career in politics that included twelve years as Connecticut's secretary of state and three terms as a member of the U.S. House of Representatives. Grasso, a Democrat, was re-elected in 1978 but resigned from office in 1980 because of ill health.

Thomas Hooker (1586?–1647), a Puritan minister, was a founder of Connecticut. Born in Leicester, England, he left the country along with other Puritans in 1630 because he could not practice his religion freely. He eventually settled in New England, becoming a pastor in 1634. In 1636, Hooker led his congregation from Massachusetts to the Connecticut River

---

state is divided into eight counties, county government was abolished by the General Assembly in 1959.

▶ **HISTORY**

Connecticut's first inhabitants came to North America from Asia more than 10,000 years ago. When Europeans arrived in the 1600's, the area was home to between 7,000 and 10,000 descendants of these original people. The Native Americans were members of about 16 separate Algonkian-speaking tribes, the most powerful of which was the Pequot. They lived by hunting, fishing, and farming.

The first Europeans to reach Connecticut were Dutch traders from New Amsterdam.

In 1614 a ship commanded by Dutch explorer Adriaen Block explored Long Island Sound and sailed up the Connecticut River. Almost 20 years later, the Dutch returned and built a fort near present-day Hartford.

Colonial Period

In the early 1630's, Puritans from nearby Massachusetts began to migrate into Connecticut, attracted by the fertile soil of the Connecticut River valley. By 1636 they had established settlements at Windsor, Wethersfield, and Hartford, which together formed the Connecticut Colony. In 1639, representatives of these three river towns, led by the Reverend Thomas Hooker, drew up the Fundamental Orders, by which the colony was to be governed. This document affirmed the concept, unusual for the time, that government rests on the consent of the people.

At the same time, other settlements were being made along the coast of Long Island Sound. The most important was at New Haven, where a band of English Puritans set up a colony in 1638. It joined with five other coastal communities in 1643 to form the New Haven Colony.

Connecticut enjoyed a remarkable degree of freedom from English control during the

---

GOVERNMENT

State Government
Governor: 4-year term
State senators: 36; 2-year terms
State representatives: 151; 2-year terms
Number of counties: 8

Federal Government
U.S. senators: 2
U.S. representatives: 6
Number of electoral votes: 8

For the name of the current governor, see STATE GOVERNMENTS in Volume S. For the names of current U.S. senators and representatives, see UNITED STATES, CONGRESS OF THE in Volume U-V.

valley, and they settled near present-day Hartford. Hooker helped frame the Fundamental Orders of Connecticut.

Ralph Nader (1934–   ), a leader of the U.S. consumer protection movement, was born in Winsted, the son of Lebanese immigrants. In 1965, two years after graduating from Harvard Law School, Nader published *Unsafe at Any Speed*, which maintained that defective automobile design was a major cause of accidents and injuries. The book, and Nader's testimony before Congress, led to the passage of the National Traffic and Motor Vehicle Safety Act in 1966. Nader founded the consumer lobbying group Public Citizen in 1971 and has since focused his public-advocacy efforts on many other issues.

Roger Sherman (1721–93), a political leader, was born in Newton, Massachu-

Ella T. Grasso

Ralph Nader

setts, and moved to Connecticut in 1743. He served on the committee that drafted the Declaration of Independence and was the only American to sign four historic documents: the Articles of Association, the Declaration of Independence, the Articles of Confederation, and the U.S. Constitution. A delegate to the Constitutional Convention of 1787, he helped frame the famous Connecticut Compromise. Sherman also served in Congress, first as a representative and then as a senator.

Benjamin Spock (1903–98), born in New Haven, was a pediatrician and world-famous child care expert. After graduating from Yale University, he earned a medical degree. His *Common Sense Book of Baby and Child Care* was first published in 1946. The child-rearing methods outlined in this and other Dr. Spock books influenced a generation of parents. During the 1960's, Spock was an outspoken opponent of the Vietnam War.

Jonathan Trumbull (1710–85), born in Lebanon, was governor of Connecticut from 1769 to 1784. A supporter of the American Revolution, he supplied the Continental army with arms and provisions. His son **John Trumbull** (1756–1843) was a noted painter who specialized in scenes of the Revolutionary War and the nation's founding.

---

colonial era. In 1662 the governor of Connecticut, John Winthrop, Jr., obtained a charter, or legal title, for the colony from King Charles II of England. It gave the people of Connecticut the right to elect their own governor and pass their own laws. The charter also placed the New Haven Colony under the authority of the Connecticut Colony.

Connecticut's political independence was soon challenged by the next king of England, James II. He merged all the northern colonies into a unit called the Dominion of New England under the governorship of Edmund Andros of New York. However, Connecticut refused to give up the right to govern itself. When Andros came to Hartford in 1687 to seize the charter, legend has it that local citizens hid it in the hollow of a tree—the celebrated Charter Oak. The threat to local self-government ended quickly when James II was overthrown in 1689.

Connecticut in the Revolution

Because of its long tradition of self-government, Connecticut enthusiastically supported the Revolutionary War. Although no major battles were fought within its boundaries, the colony, under the leadership of Governor John Trumbull, Jr., supplied Washington's

army with large quantities of men, munitions, and supplies. Several individuals from Connecticut played key roles in the conflict. Nathan Hale was executed by the British as a patriot spy. General Israel Putnam was one of the heroes of the Battle of Bunker Hill. Benedict Arnold, in contrast, is remembered as a traitor. He abandoned the revolutionary cause and led English troops in a brutal attack on New London in 1781.

Connecticut delegates to the 1787 Constitutional Convention in Philadelphia, led by Roger Sherman, played a key role in resolving a dispute over the form of the new government. Delegates from large states wanted representation in Congress to be based on population, and those from small states wanted all states to have equal representation. The **Connecticut Compromise** (also called the Great Compromise) created a two-house legislature, one with representation based on population and one with equal representation for each state. Connecticut approved the Constitution on January 9, 1788, becoming the fifth state to join the Union.

Connecticut in the New Nation

In the early years of the republic, Connecticut was a politically conservative place dominated by the Federalist Party and the Congregational Church.

In contrast to this political conservatism, Connecticut's economy in the 1800's was vibrant and innovative. When the traditional agricultural base of the state declined, as young men abandoned New England's stony soil for rich land in the Midwest, industry became Connecticut's salvation. Inventors developed new products. Eli Whitney, who invented the cotton gin and pioneered in methods of mass production, is perhaps the most famous. But there were many others. Eli Terry began the mass production of clocks in 1808. Samuel Colt manufactured hundreds of his "Six-Shooter" repeating revolvers each day in his Hartford armory. Charles Goodyear developed a way to process raw rubber to turn it into useful products. By the time of the Civil War, Connecticut had gained a national reputation for the variety and quality of its industrial output.

The strong abolitionist movement in the state guaranteed that Connecticut would be a loyal supporter of the Union cause in the Civil War. More than 55,000 Connecticut soldiers served in the conflict. Governor William Buckingham harnessed the state's industrial might to produce guns, boots, uniforms, wagons, and many other items for the Northern armies. Gideon Welles, a Hartford newspaper editor, served as President Abraham Lincoln's secretary of the navy.

An Industrial State

Connecticut completed its transformation into an urban industrial state in the years after the Civil War. The New York, New Haven, and Hartford Railroad connected the state with distant markets and sources of raw materials. A thriving textile industry emerged in the eastern corner of the state. Many smaller Connecticut cities specialized in manufacturing one particular item, such as hats in Danbury and hardware in New Britain. Major urban centers turned out a variety of goods as diverse as machine tools and typewriters. Waves of southern and eastern European immigrants, attracted by jobs in the booming factories, poured into Connecticut cities between 1870 and 1920, joining the earlier Irish and German settlers. Connecticut industry played a vital role in World War I. Remington Arms in Bridgeport, Winchester Repeating Arms in New Haven, and Colt Firearms in Hartford supplied more than half the munitions used by the American soldiers in the conflict.

Such dramatic growth was accompanied by severe social tensions. Workers joined labor unions in an effort to raise wages and improve working conditions. Frequent strikes broke out.

Because of its dependence on manufacturing, Connecticut was hard hit by the Great Depression of the 1930's. Private charities and local government could not take care of the large number of unemployed. In desperation, the state voters turned to the Democratic Party, electing an elderly former Yale professor, Wilbur Cross, to three terms as governor. A rejuvenated Democratic Party dominated Connecticut politics for the next fifty years. During the depression decade, dozens of New Deal relief programs operated in Connecticut.

Modern Connecticut

It was World War II that pulled the state out of the Great Depression. Once again, Connecticut munitions factories were booming. The airplane industry, a newcomer to the state in the 1920's, was responsible for more than half of the $8 billion in war contracts placed in Connecticut. Electric Boat in Groton was so busy building submarines that they were forced to recruit new employees from as far away as Puerto Rico. Defense production continued through the 1950's and 1960's, fueling a healthy, if erratic, economy.

Two contrasting population shifts altered Connecticut life in the postwar decades. Between 1950 and 1970, the population of the state soared. During this period, many people abandoned the cities for the suburbs, following the route of the interstate highway system. Industries, corporations, and retail stores soon followed.

This mass migration took a toll on Connecticut cities, leaving many of the state's poorest residents trapped in substandard housing in deteriorating urban cores. Today Connecticut seeks ways to revive its urban centers and close the gap between these two physically separate and economically unequal societies.

HERBERT F. JANICK
Western Connecticut State University

CONRAD, JOSEPH (1857–1924)

Józef Teodor Konrad Nalecz Korzeniowski, who spoke only Polish and French until he was 21 years old, grew up to become Joseph Conrad, one of the world's greatest writers in English. His adventurous life was the basis of many of his most powerful novels.

Conrad was born on December 3, 1857, near Kiev, Russia, of Polish parents. His father, a poet and translator, was the leader of a Polish revolutionary group, and in 1862 he was sent into exile in northern Russia. Joseph's mother died there in 1865, and his father in 1869. An uncle in Cracow, Poland, became his guardian.

A lonely youth, Joseph read a great many books, and his reading made him dream of a life of adventure. In 1874 he left Poland and sailed from Marseilles to the West Indies. After several voyages, he arrived in England in 1878. He knew hardly a word of English. But eight years later, he became a British subject and adopted the name Joseph Conrad. He passed difficult exams to become a ship's master in the British Merchant Navy.

Conrad was injured in 1887 on a voyage to Southeast Asia and was hospitalized in Singapore. To fill the empty hours, he began to write about the people he had met. During the next years, he wrote whenever he could while sailing ships between England and Australia. A trip to the Congo resulted in his short-story masterpiece, *Heart of Darkness* (1902).

Conrad left the sea in 1894 and settled in England. After finishing the book he had been working on for four years—*Almayer's Folly*, based on a man he had known in Borneo—he started *An Outcast of the Islands*. These two books and his later *Lord Jim* (1900) have the same setting, the Dutch East Indies.

After his marriage in 1896 and the birth of two sons, Conrad wrote desperately to support his family. He became a writer of wide fame with *Typhoon and Other Stories* (1903), *Nostromo* (1904), *The Secret Agent* (1907), *Under Western Eyes* (1911), and *Victory* (1915). By 1923 he was one of the most revered of English authors. He died at his home in Kent, England, on August 3, 1924.

Reviewed by FREDERICK R. KARL
Author, *Joseph Conrad: The Three Lives*

CONSCRIPTION. See DRAFT, OR CONSCRIPTION.

CONSERVATION

Have you ever saved aluminum cans, bottles, or old newspapers and taken them to a collection point? Have you carpooled to a football game because it would save gasoline? If so, you have practiced conservation.

The word conservation comes from a Latin word meaning "to keep" or "to guard." It once meant careful preservation and protection chiefly of forests and wildlife. Now we know that we must apply conservation to everything in our environment. We must include all the natural resources that our planet provides—air, water, soil, forests and grasslands, wildlife, and minerals, as well as the many products that are made from these resources.

The challenge of conservation may be the greatest challenge humanity has ever faced. The world's population is growing faster than the supplies of food, drinking water, housing, and other necessities of life. We must plan now so that people of our generation and those of future generations will have the resources they need.

Individual citizens and governments must set up methods and systems that do not use up the earth's resources, but rather replace and recycle them. Such systems would include recycling programs, obtaining energy from non-polluting sources such as solar cells, and agricultural and forestry programs that build up soil and woodlands for future use.

Some conservation decisions are made by individuals—what to buy, when to drive, what to eat. Other decisions are made by governments. These public policy decisions concern matters such as how much of our national forests to devote to logging, what kinds of public transportation systems to have, and how industry must control pollution.

> This article is an overview of the subject of conservation. It describes the areas in which conservation is necessary and some ways in which individuals and governments are practicing it. More specific information on conservation practices can be found in the articles ACID RAIN, AIR POLLUTION, ENDANGERED SPECIES, ENERGY, ENVIRONMENT, EROSION, NATURAL RESOURCES, and WATER POLLUTION.
>
> Other related articles are ECOLOGY and LIFE, which tell more about the relationship of living things to each other and to their environments.

METHODS OF CONSERVATION

All methods of conservation are related because all the earth's resources—all the living and nonliving things—are linked together. For this reason the conservation or waste of one resource directly affects others.

Water. Clean water is essential to life, but we often use lakes and rivers—and especially the oceans—as sewers and dumping places for wastes, some of them poisonous. Most bodies of water can dilute and recycle some wastes. But many have been overloaded, or polluted. Sewage treatment plants have helped, as have measures taken by industries to clean up their wastes. Accidental pollution from oil spills at sea is an increasing problem. Informed and concerned citizens must take the lead in seeing that the waters of the world are protected by laws and that the laws are obeyed.

There are many simple things that individuals can do to conserve water. We can turn off the tap while brushing our teeth. We can water lawns and gardens in the evening, when less moisture will evaporate. And we can fix leaky faucets. Large quantities of water could be saved each year in these ways.

Soil. One of our most important resources is soil. Topsoil, the uppermost layer of fertile soil, is the only type of soil that will produce high yields of food crops. As many as 100 years of careful management are needed to make 1 inch (2.5 centimeters) of good topsoil. Yet it can be lost quickly—eroded by wind, rain, or flood. During the 1930's, overgrazing, poor farming practices, and years of drought stripped the grass from vast areas of the Great Plains in the United States. With no grass to hold it in place, precious topsoil was blown away. The area was known as the Dust Bowl until grass and trees were planted and reservoirs were built to hold water for irrigating the land.

Contour plowing—plowing horizontally across slopes—helps prevent erosion by water. Planting trees or bushes between fields prevents erosion by wind. Crop rotation (planting different kinds of crops each year) slows the loss of nutrients from soil.

Forests and Grasslands. Forests provide timber for building houses and making furniture, as well as wood for paper, chemicals, and many other products. As the population grows and demand for these things increases, forests are in danger of being overused.

Perhaps the most important forest conservation method is selective cutting. Only mature trees are cut down and younger ones are left to grow, so that the forest can provide a continuous supply of timber. Individual large trees are left as homes for wildlife.

Grasslands provide food for livestock that are an important part of the world's food supply. When too many animals graze in one area, the grass is devoured or trampled and never gets a chance to grow back. In the United States, federal agencies control the number of animals that are allowed to graze on public lands. In other parts of the world—particularly in Africa near the Sahara—the combination of overgrazing and drought has led to severe erosion and famine. The United Nations is helping African nations with conservation methods.

Wildlife. More than 1.5 million kinds, or species, of plants and animals inhabit the earth. Part of the wildlife kingdom has already been lost, and a great many species are threatened. The Endangered Species List, started by the United States government in 1969, contains more than 1,000 plant and animal species that are in danger of becoming extinct, or dying off. Once an animal or plant species is gone, it cannot be recreated. And we may not know until it is too late what value it might have had in the web of life.

The recycling of newspapers, glass bottles, and aluminum cans is one way in which individual citizens can contribute to the conservation effort.

ORANGUTAN

BLACK-FOOTED FERRET

ARABIAN ORYX

More than 700 animal species are in danger of extinction. Many have been killed for sport and others for their fur, ivory tusks, or meat. International treaties and laws of many nations have been made to protect endangered species, but enforcement is difficult.

BALD EAGLE

Today laws regulate hunting and fishing in many countries, although enforcement remains a major problem in many areas. Dangers to wildlife exist. As more forests are cleared, wildlife habitats are lost. New dams may threaten the existence of certain kinds of fish. A highway may cut some animals off from sources of food.

We can help conserve wildlife by obeying hunting and fishing laws, planting bushes and shrubs to provide food and shelter for wildlife, and putting out birdseed in winter.

Clean Air. Clean air is a limited resource, too. Polluted air damages crops, buildings, and the health of humans and other animals. The pollutants also come down to earth dissolved in rainwater. This is called **acid rain**. Acid rain kills certain plants and can make lakes and ponds unfit for most water life. It slowly destroys stone, brick, and metal and is damaging to human health.

The upper atmosphere's layer of ozone, which protects the earth's surface from ultraviolet radiation, has been damaged by chemicals called chlorofluorocarbons that are used in refrigeration and aerosols. Manufacturers in the United States and some other countries are now attempting to avoid these chemicals.

Concern continues to grow about the effects of poorly controlled toxic air pollutants on human health. Concerned citizens in the United States want a revision of the Clean Air Act (1977) to deal with these problems.

Minerals. Many of the things we use—cars, bicycles, appliances—are made from metals. These metallic minerals are limited in supply.

In some cases, substitutes, like certain plastics, have been found for some uses of metals. Scientists are seeking ways to reduce waste in the processing of ores. Recycling also conserves minerals. For example, when the metal in aluminum cans is used again, less new ore will be mined.

The chief mineral fuels are coal, oil, and gas burned to heat our homes, run cars and factories, and provide electricity. Fuel supplies are limited, but as the population grows, the demand for energy increases.

To conserve energy, we can insulate homes and set thermostats to use less fuel. We can walk or bicycle rather than ride in an automobile, and we can use trains and buses for longer trips. We can use fewer electric lights and electrical gadgets. Such measures save energy without harming the quality of life.

A number of states have passed laws requiring deposits on beverage containers to encourage the reuse of containers and the recycling of glass and metal.

▶ **CONSERVATION IN THE PAST**

Conservation is not a new concern of society. The farmers of China and Southeast Asia have used methods such as terrace farming for thousands of years to prevent soil erosion. The Romans realized that their coastal fisheries would be endangered if they drained the nearby wetlands where young fish were bred.

In North America, the first conservationists were the Indians. They killed only the animals that they needed, and they wasted nothing. When European settlers came to North America, they found a continent of seemingly endless resources. The new population grew, and many resources were overused and wasted.

Uncontrolled killing wiped out the Carolina parakeet, the passenger pigeon, and the Atlantic gray whale. By 1889, only a few hundred bison were left. As cities and industries grew in the late 1800's, rivers were dammed for water power or polluted by wastes.

By the early 1900's, many people in the United States were concerned about the waste of resources and the destruction of forests and places of scenic beauty or scientific or historic interest. Conservationists promoted the establishment of national parks, forests, and wildlife refuges. Eventually many other countries established national parks.

Conservation efforts of many kinds continued quietly until the 1960's and 1970's, when the growing population strained resources all over the world. The publicity given to such pollution incidents as massive oil spills and to reports of the diminishing numbers of animals helped increase interest in conservation.

▶ **CONSERVATION TODAY**

In spite of public concern, waste and pollution have continued. Population growth is only partly to blame. Technology has enabled manufacturers to turn out an almost endless stream of products requiring more wood, minerals, and energy. As a result, many countries have passed laws to conserve natural resources and protect the environment.

In the United States. The National Environmental Policy Act of 1969 requires the United States government to prepare a study, called an environmental impact statement, before it begins any project. If the government wants to build a highway, for example, it must first study the effect that the highway will have on wildlife, soil, water, and other resources. Many state and local governments have passed similar laws.

Both the nation and the states have special departments or agencies dealing with conser-vation. They have established environmental protection agencies to end or control pollution in the areas of air, water, solid wastes, noise, radiation, and poisonous substances.

There are many private organizations that work to save threatened areas, conserve natural resources, and create effective systems of conservation. One of the largest and most politically active organizations is the Sierra Club. Other private groups include the National Audubon Society, the National Wildlife Federation, and the Wilderness Society.

Around the World. A number of United Nations agencies coordinate conservation programs on a worldwide basis, and private conservation groups are active in many countries. The International Union for Conservation of Nature and Natural Resources is the oldest and largest such private organization. Its scientists research environmental problems in more than a hundred countries.

The U.S. Agency for International Development and the World Bank fund development projects such as dams and highways. Environmental organizations have helped ensure that conservation is considered whenever land is newly developed.

In some cases, land is preserved in its undeveloped state to protect natural resources and animal or plant habitats or to prevent extinction of a species. Costa Rica has gained an international reputation for its widespread and successful efforts in land preservation.

Canada has a wide range of programs and laws dealing with environmental protection. Many areas of special beauty or interest are preserved in national and provincial parks.

Palo Alto, California, developed a successful conservation program. The city makes a profit from a well-run program involving the curbside pickup and recycling of glass, metal, newspapers, cardboard, and used oil.

Conservation treaties have been signed by many European countries. Nations that border the Mediterranean Sea have agreed to work together to clean up the water and prevent oil spills. Members of the European Economic Community (Common Market) have pollution guidelines, and many countries have wildlife refuges. The countries of southern Europe, where many resources have been overused, are beginning conservation programs.

In southern Africa, several countries have developed programs to protect natural resources and endangered species. South Africa and Kenya have systems of national parks, and Kenya has banned big-game hunting.

In Asia, overgrazing, the cutting down of entire forests, and the killing of wildlife have left many countries with serious environmental problems. Some countries, such as Japan and India, have established national parks and wildlife refuges. Less has been done in nations where war or unstable governments have overshadowed conservation problems.

▶ **CAREERS IN CONSERVATION**

There are many careers in conservation in addition to the traditional ones of forest, park, and wildlife management. There is a great need for specialists in the conservation of all forms of energy. Engineers can develop new methods of recycling manufactured goods and using wastes. Soil conservationists study how soils can be made more productive. Lawyers help with the growing number of conservation regulations. Urban planners and landscape architects also contribute to conservation efforts.

For a career in conservation, courses in basic science, mathematics, and ecology are especially useful. A broad education is necessary because many conservation problems are very complex and do not fall under a single field of study.

GERARD A. BERTRAND
Chief, International Affairs
U.S. Fish and Wildlife Service

Reviewed and updated by GENE COAN
Assistant Conservation Director, Sierra Club

CONSTANTINE THE GREAT (280?–337)

Constantine I, known as Constantine the Great, was one of the most important of the Roman emperors. Through his efforts, Christianity became the official religion of the Roman state. He also founded Constantinople (now Istanbul), the capital and leading city of the later Roman and Byzantine empires.

Constantine was born about A.D. 280 in what is now Yugoslavia. It was a troubled time. The Roman Empire had been battered by barbarian invasions and soon was to be divided into western and eastern halves. Constantine's father, Constantius, eventually became emperor in the west. On his father's death in 306, Constantine was proclaimed western emperor by the Roman army in Britain and Gaul (modern France). In 312, following the outbreak of a struggle for control of the western empire, Constantine invaded Italy. He defeated Maxentius, a rival for the western throne, at the Milvian Bridge near Rome. Before the battle, Constantine claimed to have seen a sign in the sky from the Christian God indicating that he would be victorious. He placed this sign, the Greek abbreviation of the name Christ, on the shields of his troops.

Constantine and the eastern emperor, Licinius, issued an edict calling for the toleration of all religions, including Christianity. Constantine, now a convert to Christianity, began a vast program of church building. He also took an active part in church matters, among them the historic Council of Nicaea in 325.

Constantine became ruler of the entire Roman Empire after defeating Licinius in 324, the first Roman emperor to achieve sole rule in over 40 years. Constantine carried out a series of reforms to modernize the army and the administration of the empire. He also began to build a new capital to replace Rome. The site of the new capital was the ancient Greek city of Byzantium. It was strategically located at a point where Asia and Europe meet, in what is now Turkey. The city was called Constantinople, or "city of Constantine."

Constantine died in 337, and the empire was divided among his sons Constantine II, Constantius II, and Constans.

R. BRUCE HITCHNER
University of Virginia

See also BYZANTINE EMPIRE.

CONSTANTINOPLE. See ISTANBUL.

CONSTELLATIONS

Long before the invention of the telescope, people studied the stars. One of the things they observed was that stars rose in the east, moved across the sky, and then set in the west. They also noticed that as the stars moved across the sky, their positions in relation to one another never seemed to change. Instead, groups of stars seemed to form patterns in the night sky that did not change. These groups of stars came to be called **constellations**, a name that comes from a Latin word meaning "clusters of stars."

People in ancient times believed that gods and spirits lived in the sky, so they named the constellations after mythological gods and heroes, revered animals, and familiar objects that the patterns of stars resembled. Many constellations we know today were named thousands of years ago, and the naming of constellations is one of the oldest traditions still recognized in modern times.

Today, astronomers know that bright groups of stars are not gods or spirits. They know that stars appear to move from east to west because of how the Earth rotates on its axis. They also know that the stars in constellations are not connected and that their positions change over long periods of time. Nonetheless, astronomers today still locate many objects in the sky by using the constellations as a guide.

The Zodiac

One group of constellations was especially important to people. What made these constellations special was that the sun, moon, and planets appeared to move through them. These twelve constellations became known as the **zodiac**, meaning "circle of animals," because most of them were named for animals. Today, we know these constellations as Aries, the Ram; Taurus, the Bull; Gemini, the Twins; Cancer, the Crab; Leo, the Lion; Virgo, the Virgin; Libra, Pair of Scales; Scorpius, the Scorpion; Sagittarius, the Archer; Capricornus, the Goat; Aquarius, the Water Carrier; and Pisces, the Fishes.

Because of the mysterious movements of the sun, moon, and planets within these constellations, people began to use them to predict the future. This practice is called **astrology**, which is considered to be a type of fortune-telling. Astrology has no scientific basis but its practice has continued for more than 2,000 years.

Ancient and Modern Constellations

In addition to the 12 constellations of the zodiac, 36 other constellations were familiar to people of ancient times. These 48 constellations—the ancient constellations—include objects, animals, and characters from ancient Greek and Roman myths and legends.

When Europeans began exploring the world in the 1500's and 1600's, they sailed to the Southern Hemisphere and observed thousands of stars that never rose above the horizon in the Northern Hemisphere and were therefore unknown to people in Europe. Astronomers in the 1700's and 1800's grouped these stars, as well as many fainter stars in the Northern sky, into new constellations. In 1931 astronomers formally recognized a total of 88 constellations—48 ancient and 40 modern ones. The

Twelve of the 88 constellations in our sky are known as the zodiac. They are (*top, from left*) Aries, the Ram; Taurus, the Bull; Pisces, the Fishes; Leo, the Lion; Sagittarius, the Archer; and Libra, Pair of Scales; (*bottom, from left*) Gemini, the Twins; Aquarius, the Water Carrier; Capricornus, the Goat; Cancer, the Crab; Virgo, the Virgin; and Scorpius, the Scorpion.

names of the modern constellations have more commonplace origins than the ancient ones. Horologium, the Clock, and Antlia, the Air Pump, are hardly as mysterious as mythological animals, heroes, and gods.

In addition to the 88 constellations, there are many unofficial groupings of stars. Most of these are part of larger constellations and are known as **asterisms**. The best-known asterism is the Big Dipper, a group of seven stars resembling a pot with a handle. The Big Dipper is part of a larger constellation called Ursa Major, the Great Bear.

Circumpolar Constellations

Several constellations appear to circle the North and South poles throughout the year, never setting below the horizon. These are known as circumpolar constellations. The three main circumpolar constellations in the Northern Hemisphere are Ursa Major, the Great Bear; Ursa Minor, the Little Bear; and

CIRCUMPOLAR CONSTELLATIONS

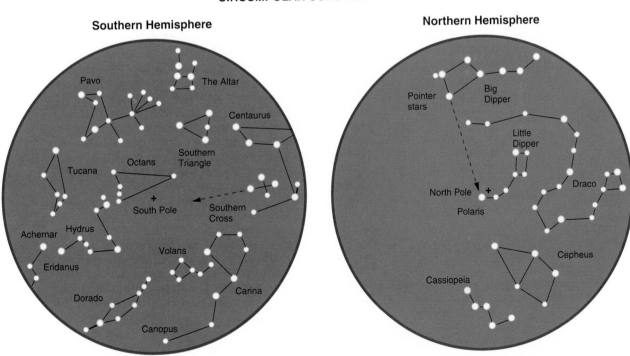

Southern Hemisphere

Northern Hemisphere

Cassiopeia (wife of Cepheus, mythological king of Ethiopia).

The Big Dipper in Ursa Major is the best-known group of stars in the Northern Hemisphere. People often use it to find Polaris, which is known as the North Star in the constellation Ursa Minor. An imaginary line followed upward through the pointer stars (the two end stars in the bowl of the Big Dipper) will end at Polaris. Polaris is the only star that does not appear to move in the sky. This is because it is almost directly in line with the Earth's axis. If the imaginary line from the pointer stars is continued past Polaris, it leads to Cassiopeia, which looks like the letter W.

People in the Southern Hemisphere see a different group of circumpolar constellations circling the South Pole. The best known of these is Crux Australis, the Southern Cross.

Seasonal Constellations

While circumpolar constellations are clearly visible throughout the year, most constella-

THE SPRING CONSTELLATIONS

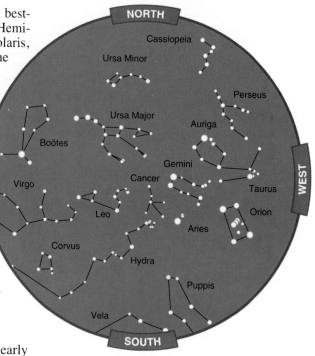

THE WINTER CONSTELLATIONS

tions are associated with a particular season. These are known as seasonal constellations. It is possible to see the stars of more than one season, however, on any night of the year. In spring, for example, the spring constellations rise overhead first. Later in the evening, these constellations set below the horizon in the west and the summer constellations rise in the east. By dawn the fall constellations will be rising in the east. Since the summer and fall constellations appear late at night and early in the morning, most people see only the spring constellations that appear in the early evening.

Winter Constellations. The best-known winter constellations are Orion, the Hunter; Taurus, the Bull; and Canis Major, Big Dog (one of Orion's hunting dogs). Orion is one of the most easily recognized constellations in the sky. Three bright stars form Orion's belt, and around these stars is a large rectangle of four bright stars that form his body. Dim stars form an upraised arm on one side of Orion and a shield on the other side. To the west of Orion—on the side with the shield—is Taurus, the Bull. A bright star called Aldebaran forms the bull's eye, and other stars mark his face and long horns. To the east of Orion is a bright star named Sirius, the Dog Star. Sirius is the brightest star in the sky and it forms the eye of Canis Major.

Spring Constellations. Four important spring constellations are Gemini, the Twins; Leo, the Lion; Boötes, the Herdsman; and Ursa Major, the Great Bear. Gemini is easy to find because of its two bright stars, Castor and Pollux, which are the heads of the twins. The twins' bodies are formed by two parallel lines of stars.

In spring, Ursa Major is high overhead, and the Big Dipper in Ursa Major can be used to find Leo. If you follow an imaginary line through the Big Dipper's pointer stars in the opposite direction from Polaris, it will point to Regulus, a bright star marking Leo's heart. Following

THE SUMMER CONSTELLATIONS

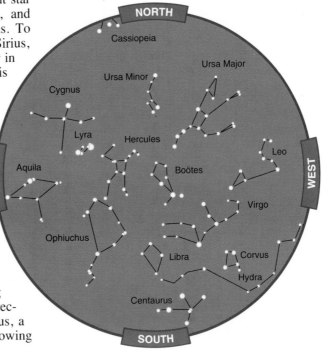

THE FALL CONSTELLATIONS

Ursa Major around the sky is Boötes, whose brightest star is Arcturus, a Latin word that means "Bear Follower." Arcturus can be found by following an imaginary arc that continues the curve of the Big Dipper's handle.

Summer Constellations. Among the important summer constellations are Lyra, the Harp; Cygnus, the Swan; and Aquila, the Eagle. Lyra is a small constellation that reminded people of ancient times of a hand-held harp called a lyre. The pattern of stars in the constellation Cygnus resembles a cross. Aquila is located below and a little to one side of Cygnus. Vega, Deneb, and Altair, which are the brightest stars in these three constellations, form an enormous triangle called the Summer Triangle.

Fall Constellations. The fall constellations are not as bright as those of other seasons. Among the best-known fall constellations are those named for characters in ancient Greek legends, including Cassiopeia, Andromeda (Cassiopeia's daughter), Perseus

THE CONSTELLATIONS

Latin Name	English Name	Latin Name	English Name	Latin Name	English Name
Andromeda	Andromeda (Cassiopeia's daughter)	Crater	Cup	Orion	Orion (the Hunter)
		Crux Australis	Southern Cross	Pavo	Peacock
Antlia	Air Pump	Cygnus	Swan	Pegasus	Pegasus (the Winged Horse)
Apus	Bird of Paradise	Delphinus	Dolphin		
Aquarius	Water Carrier	Dorado	Swordfish	Perseus	Perseus (the Hero)
Aquila	Eagle	Draco	Dragon	Phoenix	Phoenix (a mythical bird)
Ara	Altar	Equuleus	Colt		
Aries	Ram	Eridanus	Eridanus (a river)	Pictor	Painter's Easel
Auriga	Charioteer	Fornax	Furnace	Pisces	Fishes
Boötes	Herdsman	Gemini	Twins	Piscis Austrinus	Southern Fish
Caelum	Chisel	Grus	Crane (a bird)	Puppis	Ship's Stern
Camelopardalis	Giraffe	Hercules	Hercules	Pyxis	Mariner's Compass
Cancer	Crab	Horologium	Clock	Reticulum	Net
Canes Venatici	Hunting Dogs	Hydra	Sea Serpent	Sagitta	Arrow
Canis Major	Big Dog	Hydrus	Water Snake	Sagittarius	Archer
Canis Minor	Little Dog	Indus	Indian	Scorpius	Scorpion
Capricornus	Goat	Lacerta	Lizard	Sculptor	Sculptor
Carina	Ship's Keel	Leo	Lion	Scutum	Shield
Cassiopeia	Cassiopeia (wife of Cepheus)	Leo Minor	Little Lion	Serpens	Serpent
		Lepus	Hare	Sextans	Sextant
Centaurus	Centaur	Libra	Pair of Scales	Taurus	Bull
Cepheus	Cepheus (mythological king)	Lupus	Wolf	Telescopium	Telescope
		Lynx	Lynx	Triangulum	Triangle
Cetus	Whale	Lyra	Lyre (harp)	Triangulum Australe	Southern Triangle
Chamaeleon	Chameleon	Mensa	Table	Tucana	Toucan (a bird)
Circinus	Pair of Compasses	Microscopium	Microscope	Ursa Major	Great Bear
Columba	Noah's Dove	Monoceros	Unicorn	Ursa Minor	Little Bear
Coma Berenices	Bernice's Hair	Musca	Fly	Vela	Ship's Sails
Corona Australis	Southern Crown	Norma	Rule	Virgo	Virgin
Corona Borealis	Northern Crown	Octans	Octant	Volans	Flying Fish
Corvus	Crow	Ophiuchus	Serpent Bearer	Vulpecula	Little Fox

CREATING NEW CONSTELLATIONS

Use Your Imagination!

Copy the stars of one of your favorite constellations onto a large sheet of paper. You might use one of the constellations shown in the illustrations for this article. These stars form the skeleton, or framework, of an object, animal, or person as imagined by people of ancient times. Imagine that you are a shepherd lying on a hillside in ancient Greece. Draw the object, animal, or person that you see in these stars.

Now imagine that you are living 2,000 years in the future in a galaxy far from the Earth, where you can see stars that form different patterns in the sky. Make up a pattern of stars and draw it on a large sheet of paper. Look at this pattern. What would you see in these stars if you were a person living in this faraway galaxy? Draw what your imagination suggests. Then have a friend try to determine what your new constellation represents.

(Andromeda's hero), and Pegasus, the Winged Horse. Pegasus is easy to find because of an asterism in it called the Great Square, which lies beyond Cassiopeia in line with the Big Dipper's pointer stars (in Ursa Major). Once Pegasus has been located, it is easy to find Andromeda because this constellation contains two lines of stars extending outward from one corner of the Great Square. Perseus is located between Cassiopeia and Taurus.

Looking at Constellations

Many constellations are best seen on clear, dark nights. Since bright lights interfere with viewing stars, it is also easier to see constellations in areas that are far from large towns or cities. It takes patience to identify and locate constellations, but doing so can be fun and rewarding.

RICHARD BERRY
Author, *Discover the Stars*

See also GREEK MYTHOLOGY; MILKY WAY; STARS.

CONSTITUTION, UNITED STATES. See UNITED STATES, CONSTITUTION OF THE.

CONSTRUCTION. See BUILDING CONSTRUCTION.

Consumerism has resulted in laws making businesses and manufacturers responsible for safe, honestly described, fairly priced products and services.

CONSUMERISM

In 1912, angry Chicago women sold eggs on street corners for 24 cents a dozen. They were protesting the price of 34 cents in city markets. Twenty years later, Detroit housewives refused to buy meat for six weeks in order to bring down high prices. These women were part of a new social movement that did not yet have a name. In the 1960's the term **consumerism** was created to describe the efforts of buyers to obtain a fair product for a fair price. The word derives from **consumer,** a person who uses or buys a product.

Everyone is a consumer, but until the 1900's there was little help for the buyer in the marketplace. The rule of business was caveat emptor (a Latin phrase meaning "let the buyer beware"). There was no advertising, few brand names, and a limited choice of goods. People relied on their own knowledge or a shopkeeper's honesty to select food, medicine, or a plow. Then the growth of business and technology at the end of the 1800's brought a flood of new and unfamiliar products into the marketplace. How was a person to decide which automobile, packaged cereal, gasoline, radio, or medication to buy? With no laws to control them, manufacturers could market anything. For instance, some over-the-counter drugs contained opium, a strong addictive narcotic.

Many Americans began to feel that the government had a duty to protect buyers from unsafe or inferior goods. But then as now, whenever consumer protection laws were proposed, strong business interests fought hard to defeat them. In the United States, all three major periods of consumer protection legislation occurred only after frightening scandals had aroused the public. In 1906, Upton Sinclair's book *The Jungle* told the shocking true story of the unsanitary conditions in the Chicago meat-packing industry. The resulting public outrage brought about the first important consumer protection law, the Pure Food and Drug Act. This law attempted to protect Americans from unsafe foods and medicine. In 1937 a poorly tested sulfa drug killed 100 Americans. New consumer laws followed. In 1962 the country was horrified by the thalidomide drug tragedy that deformed many babies. That same year, John F. Kennedy became the first president to urge Congress to protect consumer interests. He felt that the average person needed government's help in a highly technological marketplace. To buy intelligently, a person needed to be "an amateur electrician, mechanic, chemist, toxicologist, dietician and mathematician," he said.

From 1962 to 1975, Presidents Kennedy, Nixon, and Ford outlined six basic consumer rights: (1) the right to safety—to be protected from goods harmful to life or health; (2) the right to be informed—to be protected from misleading product information and advertising; (3) the right to choose—to have a variety of goods at competitive prices; (4) the right to be heard—to have government listen and respond to consumer concerns; (5) the right to complain if dissatisfied; and (6) the right to consumer education.

More than 50 federal bureaus and agencies have some responsibility to promote or enforce these consumer rights. The Food and Drug Administration (the FDA, established in 1927) oversees the safety of foods, drugs, and cosmetics. The Federal Trade Commission (the FTC, established in 1914) monitors product labeling and advertising practices. The National Highway Traffic Safety Administration (the NHTSA, established in 1970) is concerned with automobile recalls and safety. The

Consumer Product Safety Commission (CPSC, established in 1972) works to prevent product-related injuries. The Office of Consumer Affairs (established in 1971) is the federal agency watching over the general interests of consumers. Most states have consumer-fraud divisions as well, often operating under the state attorney general. Many county agencies also look out for consumer interests.

Government agencies, although important, are not the only sources of power and information. Since the founding in 1898 of the National Consumers' League, hundreds of citizens' consumer organizations have been formed. Many of these action groups are members of the Consumer Federation of America, founded in 1967. The CFA uses its considerable influence to lobby (try to sway lawmakers) in Washington for strong consumer laws. It is in turn a member of the International Organization of Consumers Unions (IOCU), a worldwide consumer action organization headquartered in The Hague.

The individual who has had the most impact on the American consumer movement is probably Ralph Nader. Nader first attracted public attention with his book *Unsafe at Any Speed.* His congressional testimony on dangerous automobile designs and the automobile manufacturers' attempt to discredit him made front page news in 1966. Since then the controversial lawyer and his investigating teams called "Nader's Raiders" have founded a number of consumer action organizations, including the Center for Auto Safety and Public Citizen.

Pressure from Nader and others has proved necessary in order to force reluctant legislators to enact consumer protection laws. Examples of hard-won federal and state regulations include: truth-in-lending laws requiring banks and other lenders to reveal the real costs of a loan; truth-in-advertising regulations holding advertisers responsible for the claims made about a product; truth-in-packaging rules requiring accurate labeling of ingredients, size, and weight; unit-pricing regulations requiring stores to list per-ounce or -pound prices for easier product comparisons; and open-dating rules requiring food manufacturers to stamp last-date-of-purchase information on perishable goods. Because these and other consumer protection laws may vary from state to state, some American consumers are better protected from abuses than others.

But consumerism goes beyond protective laws. It is what stimulates a man to write a complaint letter to the Better Business Bureau about a fraudulent mail-order company. It prompts a woman to sue a dishonest plumber in small-claims court. It convinces a child to stop shopping at a store that will not take back defective toys. Consumerism is in action whenever a person stands up for his or her right to a fair deal at a fair price. Today's consumers have many more sources of information on their side than in the past.

Any magazine stand stocks a number of publications dedicated to helping consumers. The best known is *Consumer Reports* magazine. Since 1937, *Consumer Reports* has been testing products and reporting on health and financial matters. Its children's version, *Zillions* magazine, helps younger consumers, aged 8 to 13. Two other useful magazines are *Consumers Research Magazine* and *Kiplinger's Personal Finance Magazine.* Newspaper columns, Internet Web sites, and television reports also highlight consumer interests. The popular television program *60 Minutes* often focuses on consumer problems.

Although Americans support strong laws on unsafe food and drugs, not all consumer protection laws are popular. Business argues that consumer protection is not without cost. Some rules may raise product prices or cut down on consumer choice. The controversy over requiring air bags on all cars is a case in point. These safety devices inflate automatically in front of passengers to cushion them from the impact of an accident. They would surely save many lives. But many car owners wonder why everyone should be forced to pay for expensive air bags just because some people refuse to wear their seat belts. Others want the government to concentrate on giving more product information to the consumer, rather than directly control a manufacturer's product.

The consumer movement has made life safer. It has also made it easier to choose products and to get satisfaction (a refund, for example) if a product fails. And one of its most important accomplishments has been to show that ordinary citizens can work together to make improvements in the lives of everyone.

JEANNE KIEFER
Associate Editor
Penny Power (now *Zillions*) magazine

CONTACT LENSES. See LENSES (Contact Lenses).

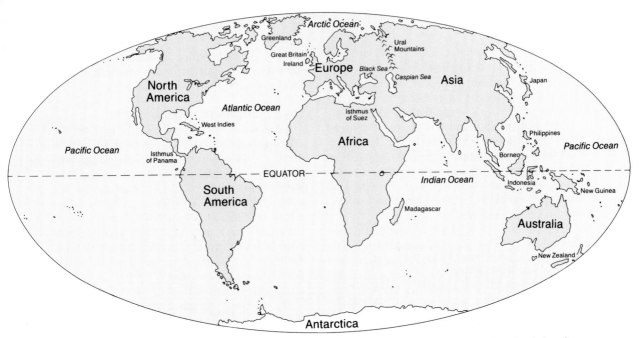

The traditionally recognized continents are Asia, Africa, North America, South America, Antarctica, Europe, and Australia. Europe and Asia are sometimes considered as a single landmass called Eurasia. Each continent's landmass includes its adjacent islands.

CONTINENTS

A continent is a large, continuous landmass located on the surface of the earth. Seven continents are generally recognized. They are Asia, Africa, North America, South America, Antarctica, Europe, and Australia. In some cases, Europe and Asia are viewed as a single continent—Eurasia. The continents of Asia, Europe, and Africa form what is known as the Old World. North America and South America make up the New World. Two continents —Australia and Antarctica—are islands.

The strict definition that every continent is a single landmass bounded at sea level is rarely used. In practice, every continent not only includes its own landmass, but nearby islands as well. For example, Greenland is usually thought of as part of North America.

Altogether, the earth's seven continents cover 29 percent of the surface area of the globe. Oceans and other bodies of water cover the remaining 71 percent.

▶SIZE AND SHAPE

The continents vary considerably in size. Asia, the largest continent, has almost 30 percent of the world's total land surface. After Asia, the continents in order of area are Africa, North America, South America, Antarctica, Europe, and Australia. Australia, the smallest continent, is less than one fifth the size of Asia, and has less than 6 percent of the world's land surface.

The continents also vary significantly in shape. Africa is the most compact continent and has the most regular coastline. Its ratio of length of coastline to total area is the lowest of any continent. Europe has the longest coastline of any continent and the highest ratio of coastline to total land area.

Five of the seven continents are connected to another landmass. North America and South America are connected at the Isthmus of Panama. (An isthmus is a narrow strip of land that connects two larger bodies of land.) Africa is joined to Asia at the Isthmus of Suez. Europe is actually a peninsula of Asia.

Boundary Between Europe and Asia. When Europe and Asia are treated as separate continents, the boundary between them lies mainly within Russia (the largest part of the former Soviet Union), which occupies land in both continents. This boundary is generally agreed to run along the eastern edge of the Ural Mountains, southwest to the shore of the Caspian Sea, westward along the Caspian's northern coast to the Caucasus Mountains, and along the crest of the Caucasus to the northern coast of the Black Sea.

POPULATION

Asia, the largest continent in area, also has the greatest number of people. Including the Asian part of Russia, it is home to about 60 percent of the world's population. Europe, although only sixth in area, is the most densely populated continent. Counting the European part of Russia, it ranks second in population with more than 14 percent of the world total. Thus, when the populations of Europe and Asia are combined, Eurasia has almost three quarters of humanity.

The inhabited continents, in order of population after Asia and Europe, are Africa, North America, South America, and Australia. Antarctica has no inhabitants, except for the scientists who come to study this desolate, ice-covered continent.

DISTRIBUTION

North and South. The continents are irregularly, but not randomly, distributed on the surface of the earth. With the exception of Antarctica, all the continents are broader in the north than in the south. They taper toward the south. Partly as a result of this, approximately two thirds of the world's land surface lies in the Northern Hemisphere—that part of the globe north of the equator (0° latitude). By contrast, on the opposite side of the world (the antipode) the Pacific Ocean covers an area larger than the world's total land surface.

Land and Water Hemispheres. Because of this uneven distribution of landmasses, geographers sometimes divide the world into land and water hemispheres. The land hemisphere is that half of the earth with the most land. The water hemisphere is that half of the world with the most water. The geographic center of the land hemisphere lies in northwestern Europe near the city of London in the United Kingdom. The geographic center of the water hemisphere is located in the southern Pacific Ocean, southeast of New Zealand.

SOME CONTINENTAL COMPARISONS

Land Surfaces. The land surfaces of the continents have some degree of similarity. In general, interior plateaus and plains are bordered by mountains on one or more sides. The Rocky Mountains of North America and the Andes of South America rim the western edges of these continents. The Pyrenees mountains and the Alps form the southern boundary of Europe. The Ural Mountains and the Himalayas mark Asia's western and southern borders. Antarctica is ringed with high mountains of ice.

By contrast, the continents of Africa and Australia tend to have central plateaus that cover their land areas and extend from coast to coast.

Lowest and Highest Continents. Australia is the lowest as well as the flattest continent. Its average elevation is only 800 feet (244 meters) above sea level. Africa, North America, and South America have average elevations that are very close to the world average of 2,100 feet (640 meters). Asia, due largely to the great peaks of the Himalayas, has an average elevation of 3,200 feet (975 meters). Antarctica has the highest average elevation—6,500 feet (2,000) meters, or twice that of any other continental landmass.

PAUL W. ENGLISH
Chairman, Department of Geography
The University of Texas at Austin
Author, *World Regional Geography:
A Question of Place*

See also individual articles on the continents. For information on how the continents were formed, see the articles EARTH; EARTH, HISTORY OF.

CONTINENTS IN ORDER OF POPULATION

	POPULATION ESTIMATE
Asia[1]	3,501,000,000
Africa	732,000,000
Europe[2]	728,000,000
North America	458,000,000
South America	323,000,000
Australia[3]	29,000,000
Antarctica	no permanent inhabitants

[1] Includes Turkey in Europe.
[2] Includes Russia in Asia.
[3] Includes New Zealand and Oceania.

CONTINENTS IN ORDER OF AREA

	TOTAL AREA	
	sq mi	(km²)
Asia[1]	17,297,000	(44,780,000)
Africa	11,708,000	(30,324,000)
North America	9,406,000	(24,362,000)
South America	6,883,000	(17,827,000)
Antarctica	5,405,000	(14,000,000)
Europe[2]	4,066,000	(10,531,000)
Australia[3]	3,287,000	(8,513,000)

[1] Includes Russia in Asia.
[2] Includes Russia in Europe and European Turkey.
[3] Includes New Zealand and Oceania.

CONTRACEPTIVES. See BIRTH CONTROL.

COOK, JAMES (1728–1779)

On the morning of January 18, 1778, Captain James Cook, commander of the British ship *Resolution,* suddenly spotted land. The two islands were Oahu and Kauai—part of the chain we now know as Hawaii. Captain Cook and his British sailors were the first Europeans known to have set foot there.

James Cook won fame and honor for his explorations and for his work as a navigator who used the latest scientific methods. Many consider him the greatest British explorer. Cook was born in Yorkshire, England, on October 27, 1728. His family was poor, and James had to go to work when he was only 12 years old. After serving as an apprentice for a shipping company, he joined the Royal Navy. An intelligent and ambitious young man, Cook was promoted quickly. By 1759, he was the master of his own ship.

Cook studied mathematics, astronomy, and geography in his spare time. Because of his scientific knowledge, he was chosen to lead an expedition to the Pacific. His mission was to observe the planet Venus passing between the earth and the sun, a rare occurrence. But Cook also carried secret orders to look for new lands in the South Pacific that could be settled as British colonies.

Cook's ship, H.M.S. *Endeavour,* left England in the summer of 1768, sailed around Cape Horn, and reached the island of Tahiti, in the Society Islands, a year later. Cook and the scientists who were with him observed the passage of Venus. Cook then went on to map and explore the coasts of New Zealand.

Early in 1770, Cook reached the previously uncharted east coast of Australia. He claimed the territory for Britain and named it New South Wales. When he returned to England, he won praise for his achievements and was promoted to captain.

Besides finding new lands, Cook helped to improve the lot of sailors. Their living quarters were often dirty and infested with rats. Cook required his men to bathe regularly and keep the ship clean. He had them eat fresh vegetables and fruit to prevent scurvy, a disease caused by lack of vitamin C.

In 1772, Cook once again put out to sea. His two ships, the *Resolution* and the *Ad-*

Captain James Cook was a British naval officer and one of the world's greatest explorers. He is best known for his voyages to the Pacific Ocean and North America.

venture, headed for the southern oceans where some scientists predicted a new continent would be discovered. There was no southern continent, as Cook proved by sailing into the frigid waters below the Antarctic Circle. But he discovered New Caledonia and Norfolk Island, south of New Hebrides. And his ships were the first to cross the Antarctic Circle.

Cook sailed on his third and final voyage in 1776. It was during this voyage that he came upon the Hawaiian Islands, which he named the Sandwich Islands in honor of his patron, the Earl of Sandwich. Cook claimed the islands for George III of England, although Polynesians had discovered them centuries earlier.

From Hawaii, Cook moved up the west coast of North America as far as the Bering Strait and the Arctic Ocean. Only when his way was blocked by solid ice did he turn back. Late in 1778, he returned to Hawaii. There, on February 14, 1779, he was killed during an argument with some islanders who he believed had stolen one of his small boats. It was a tragic ending to the life of one of the greatest seagoing explorers of all time.

HENRY I. KURTZ
Author, *John and Sebastian Cabot*

COOKING

In its strictest sense, the word "cooking" means using heat to prepare food. Many people use the word to refer to any method of preparing and serving food—even fixing a cold salad. Whether heat is used or not, the goal of cooking is generally to make food more appetizing and, often, easier to digest.

No one knows how long ago people began to cook. There is evidence that Stone Age people cooked food over open fires. Cooking advanced as people learned to grow grain and make clay (and later metal) pots. The ancient Egyptians are thought to have been the first to make leavened (raised) bread, which they baked in clay ovens heated by fire. The ancient Romans were fond of huge banquets, at which elaborately prepared dishes were served.

Fire was the basic source of heat for cooking right into the 1800's, when coal stoves were invented. Today most home kitchens in developed countries have electric or gas ranges and other modern conveniences, such as microwave ovens. Cooking is easier and faster. But many of the basic steps in preparing and cooking food have not changed for centuries.

▶GETTING STARTED

The basics of cooking are not difficult, but until you learn them, you should follow recipes precisely. Some basic recipes are given in the article RECIPES in Volume Q-R, and you will find many more in cookbooks. There are cookbooks that outline the most basic kinds of cooking and specialized ones that cover cooking of a particular food, foods of a certain region, or a special cooking method.

Choose a cookbook by reading several recipes to see whether they are well outlined and detailed. Ingredients should be listed in the order they are used, and instructions should be precise. For example, a recipe should not specify a vague amount, such as "one heaping tablespoon of sugar." It should give exact amounts, such as "1½ tablespoons."

Measuring Ingredients. It is best to use glass measuring cups for measuring liquids such as water, milk, or broth. This is because the cup may be held at eye level to make certain the measurement is accurate.

It is best to use metal measuring cups or spoons for measuring solids such as flour or sugar. This is because when any given cup or spoon is filled, you may level off the top with a flat knife or spatula to get an exact measurement.

There are eight tablespoons of butter in one stick. One stick of butter when melted equals one half cup. Two sticks of melted butter equal one cup. Four sticks of butter equal one pound.

Three precisely measured teaspoons of anything, liquid or solid, equal one tablespoon. Four tablespoons of any ingredient, liquid or solid, equal one fourth of a cup, and eight tablespoons of any ingredient, liquid or solid, equal one half cup. Two cups of any ingredient equal one pint. And logically, one cup of any ingredient equals one half pint. Two pints or four cups of anything equal one quart. Four quarts equal one gallon. Eight quarts equal one peck, a measurement used for things such as peaches, apples, and pears.

Following a Recipe. Cooking begins before you put on an apron or light your stove. The

---

This article is an introduction to cooking for the beginner. It includes information on how to follow a recipe and how to accomplish basic cooking techniques. Methods for preparing different types of food are discussed, and a glossary of kitchen terms is included.

For specific recipes appropriate for beginner cooks, consult the article RECIPES in Volume Q-R. Additional recipes can be found in OUTDOOR COOKING AND PICNICS. More advanced cooks may want to consult the herb usage chart in the article HERBS, SPICES, AND CONDIMENTS.

The New Book of Knowledge contains a number of related articles concerning food, among them FOOD AROUND THE WORLD, which describes the specialties of many nations. Other related articles include FOOD SHOPPING, FOOD PRESERVATION, NUTRITION, and VITAMINS.

first step is to study the recipe, taking note of the ingredients and instructions. Then, before you start, you should assemble all the ingredients and equipment you will need.

For example, suppose that you want to bake a cake and that the recipe calls for a cup of sifted flour, two well-beaten eggs, one fourth cup of cocoa powder, a half cup of milk, and one fourth cup of sugar. Sift your flour, measure it accurately, and set it aside. Break the eggs into a small bowl, beat them well, and set them aside. In the same way, measure and set aside each of the other ingredients. Get out the bowls and beaters you will need to mix your batter and the cake pan you will use to bake it. If the recipe calls for a greased cake pan, grease the pan and put it aside. And remember to set the oven to the temperature called for in the recipe and turn it on before you begin mixing your ingredients—it will probably need to be preheated for about 15 minutes before you put the cake in.

Then you can begin to mix your ingredients, following the steps outlined in the recipe. When you are preparing food, it is important to keep your hands clean. Wash them before you begin and again any time you blend food with your fingers. You should also keep your hair combed back, to keep stray hairs from falling into the food. Professional chefs wear hats or caps to keep this from happening. An apron will keep food from splattering onto your clothes. The best apron is a practical, tailored one that is large enough to give some protection.

As you gain experience, you will find ways to save labor in preparing food. For example, if you want to peel vegetables or fruits, lay a strip of waxed paper or newspaper on your work surface. Then, when you are finished peeling, you can gather up the peelings in the paper and throw them out.

▶METHODS OF COOKING

The same basic methods of cooking are used to prepare many different foods. Some of the most common methods are explained here. You will find more cooking terms in the box on page 535.

Baking. Baked foods are cooked in the dry heat of an oven. Although the term can be used for any food cooked this way, it usually refers to breads, pastries, and desserts like cakes and puddings.

Roasting. This term refers to cooking foods such as meat and poultry uncovered in an oven. Often the foods are basted with a liquid such as melted butter or broth to keep them from drying out. Sometimes this term refers to foods that are cooked on a spit or embedded in hot coals, such as roast chestnuts.

Broiling. This term generally refers to cooking foods under open heat, one side at a time.

Grilling. Grilling is the opposite of broiling. The food is placed on an open grill, with the source of heat—usually gas, electric, or charcoal—below. Some foods cooked on a flat metal pan are also said to be grilled; a grilled cheese sandwich is an example.

Frying. Fried foods are cooked in fat or oil. There are two basic methods. Shallow frying involves cooking the food in a small amount of fat, usually in a skillet. In deep-fat frying, the fat is deep enough to cover the food. Deep-fat frying can be done in a deep skillet, a kettle or casserole, or a special fryer.

Simmering. Foods are simmered when they are cooked in a liquid, such as water or broth, that is barely bubbling. The temperature of the liquid is generally from 140 to 180°F (60 to 82°C).

Boiling. In boiling, the liquid reaches a temperature of about 212°F (100°C) and bubbles vigorously. Sometimes foods are first

Baking   Roasting   Broiling   Grilling

Deep frying/ Frying

Simmering/Boiling

Steaming

Microwaving

brought to a boil and then simmered until they are cooked.

Steaming. Foods are generally steamed by putting them on a rack or a perforated pan (one with small holes in it) that is placed over simmering or boiling water. Steaming is an excellent way to prepare fish and many other foods. Pressure cookers are special pots that cook food in steam under pressure.

Microwave Cooking. A microwave oven uses short radio waves to heat food more quickly than conventional ovens. Only nonmetal pans and utensils can be used in microwave ovens. One of the finest uses of these ovens is to reheat cooked food.

▶ **COOKING TYPES OF FOOD**

Unless you are an experienced cook, it is best to follow a recipe as carefully as possible. Here are some of the common ways of preparing different kinds of food and a few general rules for cooking them.

Knowing how to prepare a meal from the vast array of foods available to us is an important skill. A good cook should be able to enhance the taste and eye appeal of raw foods while retaining their basic nutrients.

Vegetables. Vegetables may be steamed, simmered, boiled, or baked. They should generally be cooked for as short a time as possible. Some, such as corn on the cob, asparagus, and new peas, should be cooked only until they are barely tender. Boiled potatoes should be tender but not mushy. Potatoes may also be baked in the oven in their skins.

Fruits and Berries. Many fruits and berries are best when they are eaten raw. If they are to be eaten with their skins on, they should first be rinsed well under cold water and patted dry. Fruits and berries may also be cooked in pies and other pastries and in cobblers and other deep-dish desserts. Follow the recipes for these dishes with care.

Milk. We think of milk mostly as a chilled beverage, but its uses in cooking are beyond count. It is used in the preparation of breads and pastries, soups, and ice creams and sherbets. One of its most common uses is in the preparation of a cream or white sauce. This sauce is made by blending melted butter with flour and adding milk while stirring briskly over moderate heat. Dishes containing milk are usually cooked over low to moderate heat to prevent curdling.

Besides sweet milk, other forms of milk are used in the kitchen. They include buttermilk, which is made from naturally fermented (soured) milk; and condensed milk, which is generally sold in cans. Cream is used to add a smooth texture to many dishes. Heavy cream can be whipped to make a topping for desserts; this is best done when the cream, bowl, and beaters are thoroughly chilled. Sour cream, another fermented milk product, also has many uses. It may be blended with mayonnaise and herbs to make a sauce, used as a topping for soups and other dishes, and used in making cakes and cookies.

Cooking Terms

Baste: To spoon or brush a liquid such as broth or melted fat over a food as it cooks.

Batter: A liquid mixture based on eggs and flour. Fritter batters are blended to stick to foods that are dipped into them and then fried. Pancake batters usually contain baking powder. The blended ingredients for a cake are also called batter.

Beat: To stir ingredients briskly.

Blanch: To cook or steam food briefly in water (from the French word *blanche,* which means "white").

Blend: To mix ingredients so that their flavors and textures are thoroughly combined.

Braise: To cook food in liquid, covered, until it is tender.

Bread: To coat with bread crumbs. The classic method is to dip the food—a veal chop, for example—first in flour, then in beaten egg, and finally in the bread crumbs.

Broth: A liquid, generally clear, made by cooking meats or vegetables and seasonings in water.

Chop: To cut food into pieces.

Coddle: To cook a food, such as an egg, in water just below boiling. It is one of the gentlest ways to cook food.

Cream: To blend ingredients to a smooth consistency. Also, to mix foods with cream sauce, as in creamed chicken or creamed spinach.

Dice: To cut foods into small cubes.

Fold in: To mix one ingredient into another by stirring up, over, and down.

Glaze: To coat a food with a liquid preparation, such as a sauce or syrup.

Grate: To shred or powder an ingredient by rubbing it over a rough surface.

Grease: To coat a surface with oil or fat to keep food from sticking as it cooks.

Julienne: To cut food into thin, matchlike strips.

Marinate: To cover food with a tasty liquid called a marinade.

Mash: To crush an ingredient such as a clove of garlic with a mallet or the side of a heavy knife. Also, to put food through a food mill or a strainer to produce a puree.

Whipping

Grating

Mince: To cut food into very small pieces.

Parboil: To partially cook food in water or another liquid.

Pare: To cut away the outer skin of an vegetable or fruit, such as an apple.

Peel: To remove the skin or rind of fruits such as lemons and bananas.

Puree: To give foods such as cooked potatoes or carrots a fine, smooth texture by putting them through a food mill or strainer.

Roux: A paste made by melting fat such as butter and stirring in flour until well blended. A roux is used to thicken many sauces.

Sauce: A thickened, well-seasoned liquid that is served with food.

Sauté: A French term meaning to fry food in a small amount of fat, usually butter.

Scald: To heat liquid until it almost boils.

Sift: To put a fine-textured ingredient such as flour or cornmeal through a sieve, to lighten its texture.

Skim: To remove floating material from the top of a liquid. The main reason for skimming foods such as soup is to remove fat and scum that may rise to the top.

Soufflé: An elegant dish made from thickened white sauce, beaten egg yolks, flavoring, and beaten egg whites. As the soufflé bakes, the egg whites expand and cause it to rise.

Steep: To soak a food in a liquid.

Stew: To cook a food by letting it simmer over a period of time.

Stir: To move or mix ingredients, generally with a circular motion.

Stir-fry: To fry quickly over high heat in a lightly oiled pan, stirring constantly. Stir-frying is used in many Asian dishes.

Stock: A liquid in which meats, vegetables, and seasonings have been cooked. Stocks are the basis for many stews, soups, and the like.

Toast: To heat and brown food, such as bread, under a broiler or in an electric toaster.

Whip: To beat or stir briskly. Common utensils for whipping food are wire whisks, electric beaters, and wooden spoons.

Folding

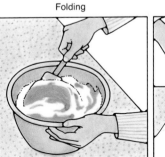

Sifting

Eggs. Eggs may be boiled in the shell, scrambled or turned into omelets, and cooked in countless other ways. But eggs should nearly always be cooked gently. In fact, a more accurate term for a "hard-boiled" egg is "hard-cooked"—the egg is cooked in the shell until yolk and white are firm, but this should be done over gentle heat.

One of the few exceptions to the rule of cooking eggs over gentle heat is in making omelets. The eggs are broken into a bowl and beaten thoroughly. Butter is heated in a skillet over fairly high heat, and when it is quite hot, the eggs are added. They are stirred and, the moment they are "set" on the bottom, rolled into a cylinder and turned onto a plate. Scrambled eggs are cooked in much the same way but over low heat. They are stirred constantly so that they cook evenly.

Shirred eggs are broken into small, buttered baking dishes. The dishes are placed in water in a skillet, and the water is brought to a simmer. The eggs are then placed in a preheated oven and baked until the whites are slightly firm and the yolk is still soft. They are served in the baking dishes.

Cheese. Cheese has many uses in the kitchen and on the dining table. It may be served as an appetizer, snack, or breakfast food, and it has many uses in cooking. It may be melted and served hot, as in a rarebit or cheese fondue. It may be the principal ingredient in a loaf, in soufflés and fritters, and even in cheese soup. Hard cheeses such as Parmesan are often grated and sprinkled on certain foods, such as spaghetti. Like milk, cheese is usually cooked with low or moderate heat.

Meat, Poultry, and Fish. The term "meat" most often refers to beef, pork, lamb, and veal, as distinguished from poultry and fish. Besides being roasted, broiled, and grilled, meat and poultry are often cut into pieces and cooked with liquid in stews, which are covered and simmered for a long time. The longer the ingredient simmers, the more tender it becomes. Fish is often fried, baked, broiled, or steamed. It is important not to overcook fish, because it will dry out. The fish should flake easily with a fork when it is done.

Cereals. Ground into flour, cereals (or grains) form the basis for bread, cakes, and many other foods, including noodles and macaroni. Cereals are also served cooked in many dishes, among them rice, oatmeal, hominy grits (made from ground corn), and bulgur (made from wheat). Generally these grains are boiled or steamed, so that they absorb moisture and become tender.

▶ **USING SEASONINGS**

The commonest seasonings used in cooking are salt and pepper. Many recipes tell you to add salt "to taste" rather than specify an exact amount. Be cautious and add salt in small amounts—remember that more may always be added but that salt cannot be subtracted if the flavor is too strong. Remember, too, that the flavor of salt will become more concentrated as the dish cooks.

Herbs and spices are more sophisticated seasonings. Both come from plants, and the precise differences between them are sometimes difficult to pin down. Generally, herbs are more delicate than spices. Many herbs are the tender leaves of plants, and they can be used freshly picked or dried. Some of the most common herbs include basil, chervil, chives, dill, garlic, cloves, marjoram, mint, onions and shallots, parsley, rosemary, sage, sorrel, tarragon, thyme, and watercress.

Spices are generally the most fragrant part of a plant. Common spices include allspice, anise and star anise, cardamom, cayenne, coriander and cumin seeds, curry powder, juniper berries, mustard, nutmeg and mace (the outer husk of the nutmeg seed), paprika, pepper, saffron, sesame seeds, turmeric, and vanilla.

The quantity of an herb or spice to use in any recipe is largely a question of individual taste. In the beginning, use herbs and spices sparingly. As with salt, you can always add more, but you cannot subtract. As you gain experience, you may learn to substitute one herb or spice for another. Perhaps a recipe calls for rosemary, but you prefer the flavor of tarragon. Go ahead and make the substitution, but do so cautiously.

Herbs may be far stronger when they are dried than when they are fresh. As a rule, if a recipe calls for a certain amount of a fresh herb, use about half that amount dried. But be guided by your own taste and good judgment.

CRAIG CLAIBORNE
Food Editor
The New York Times

See also HERBS, SPICES, AND CONDIMENTS; OUTDOOR COOKING AND PICNICS; RECIPES.

CALVIN COOLIDGE (1872–1933)

30th President of the United States

FACTS ABOUT COOLIDGE

Birthplace: Plymouth Notch, Vermont
Religion: Congregationalist
College Attended: Amherst College,
  Amherst, Massachusetts
Occupation: Lawyer
Married: Grace Goodhue
Children: John, Calvin
Political Party: Republican
Nickname: "Silent Cal"
Office Held Before Becoming President:
  Vice President
President Who Preceded Him:
  Warren G. Harding
Age on Becoming
  President: 51
Years in the Presidency:
  1923-1929
Vice President: Charles
  G. Dawes (1925-29)
President Who
  Succeeded Him:
  Herbert Hoover
Age at Death: 60
Burial Place: Plymouth
  Notch, Vermont

DURING COOLIDGE'S PRESIDENCY

Below: The first diesel electric locomotive was placed in service (1924). The first airplane flight over the North Pole was claimed (1926) by Richard E. Byrd and Floyd Bennett. U.S. Marines were sent to Nicaragua (1926) during a crisis to help stabilize its government. *Left:* The first feature-length "talking" movie, *The Jazz Singer,* was produced (1927). *Above:* Charles A. Lindbergh made the first solo nonstop airplane flight across the Atlantic Ocean, from New York to Paris, in the *Spirit of St. Louis* (1927). The Kellogg-Briand Pact, a U.S. and French plan to prevent war, was signed (1928) by 15 nations.

COOLIDGE, CALVIN. For Americans, July 4 marks Independence Day. For John and Victoria Coolidge of Plymouth Notch, Vermont, July 4, 1872, also marked the birth of a son. Their son, whom they named John Calvin Coolidge, was to become the 30th president of the United States.

▶ THE COOLIDGES OF PLYMOUTH NOTCH

Calvin Coolidge's ancestors came to America from England in about 1630. The first Coolidge to live in Plymouth Notch was John Coolidge of Massachusetts, a soldier in the Revolutionary War, who settled there in the 1780's. The Coolidges were hardworking farmers and storekeepers. Some of Calvin's ancestors had been deacons in the community church and served in local political offices. Calvin's father had been elected to the Vermont legislature. The Coolidges' ideals of honesty, thrift, and hard work were passed down from generation to generation. And young Calvin Coolidge was brought up to believe in these ideals.

▶ "SILENT CAL"

Young Calvin helped with the chores on the farm and went to the one-room village school. When he was 13, he entered Black River Academy at Ludlow, Vermont. In 1891 he was admitted to Amherst College in Massachusetts.

Coolidge was not a brilliant student at Amherst, but he studied hard and in 1895 he was graduated with honors. He did well as a debater and public speaker and was chosen as one of the speakers at his graduation. In private conversation, however, he was a man of few words. His nickname of "Silent Cal" was well earned. There is a story that is frequently told about him. A man once bet a friend that he could make Cal say at least *three* words in a conversation. When the man met Coolidge, he told him of the bet. All Coolidge said was, "You lose."

After graduation Coolidge decided to become a lawyer. He went to work in a law office in Northampton, Massachusetts, and studied for the bar examination. Although 3 years of study were required, he passed the examination after less than 2 years.

In 1898, at the age of 25, Coolidge opened his own law office in Northampton. He kept a careful account of his earnings and noted that in his first year of practice he earned $500.

Coolidge's upbringing made him place great emphasis on thrift. He never owned an automobile and, until he retired from the presidency, he never owned his own home. In later years he liked to remark that there were two ways to be self-respecting: "To spend less than you make, and to make more than you spend." Coolidge always spent less than he made.

▶ EARLY POLITICAL CAREER

Coolidge had shown some interest in politics at college, and he soon began to take an active part in Northampton politics. He worked hard for the Republican Party, and in 1898 he was elected to his first office—city councilman.

In 1906 Coolidge was elected to the Massachusetts House of Representatives. He was a conservative in politics and did not trust reformers. But he did vote for two reform resolutions that later became amendments to the United States Constitution. One resolution called for the direct election of United States senators by the people (senators were then elected by the state legislatures). The other gave women the right to vote.

After two terms in the legislature, Coolidge returned to Northampton. In 1909 he was elected mayor. With his goal of thrifty government, Coolidge lowered taxes and reduced the city debt. At the same time he was able to raise the pay of many city employees.

While in Northampton, Coolidge met Grace Goodhue, a teacher at a school for the deaf. They were married in 1905 and had two sons. Mrs. Coolidge was gay and full of fun—just the opposite of her quiet, careful husband.

▶ GOVERNOR OF MASSACHUSETTS

In 1911 Coolidge returned to the legislature as a state senator. His re-election to a second and third term in the Senate made him an important figure in state politics. In 1915 he was elected lieutenant governor, and 3 years later he became governor of Massachusetts.

The Boston Police Strike. In 1919 an event occurred that made Governor Coolidge a national figure. On September 9, 1919, most of the Boston police force went on strike for higher pay. For 2 days there was rioting and robbery in the city of Boston. Finally, in response to the mayor's call for help, Coolidge called out the National Guard, and order was restored. In reply to a plea for sympathy for the striking policemen, Coolidge issued his

Left, Calvin Coolidge as a student at Amherst College in 1895. Right, as governor of Massachusetts, with Mrs. Coolidge and their sons, Calvin (*left*), and John (*right*).

President and Mrs. Coolidge on the way to his inauguration in 1925. Senator Charles Curtis is at right.

Above, President Coolidge opens the baseball season by throwing out the first ball. Below, the President celebrating a western-style Fourth of July at Rapid City, S.D.

famous statement: "There is no right to strike against the public safety by anybody, anywhere, any time." He became a national hero and a symbol of law and order.

In the 1920 Republican Party convention, Senator Warren G. Harding won the nomination as candidate for president. When one of the delegates suggested Coolidge's name for vice-president, the cry of "We want Coolidge" rang out through the convention hall. Coolidge became the vice-presidential candidate, and in the election of 1920 Harding and Coolidge won an overwhelming victory.

▶ **PRESIDENT**

On the morning of August 3, 1923, Vice-President Coolidge was in Plymouth, visiting his father, when the news of Harding's death reached him. Coolidge was now president of the United States. His father, a notary public, administered the oath of office to him.

Soon after Coolidge entered the White House, the scandals of Harding's administration came to public attention. The worst was the Teapot Dome oil scandal, which involved members of Harding's cabinet. Secretary of the Interior Albert B. Fall went to jail for his part in the affair, and Secretary of the Navy Edwin Denby was forced to resign. Attorney General Harry M. Daugherty was involved in another scandal and almost went to jail. Coolidge was never connected with the scandals, and his reputation helped to save the Republican Party from disgrace.

Coolidge was so popular that he had no trouble winning the election of 1924. His campaign slogan was "Keep Cool with Coolidge," and he received almost twice as many popular votes as his Democratic opponent, John W. Davis.

The Roaring 20's

Calvin Coolidge was president during one of the most colorful periods in American history. The 1920's are often called the Roaring 20's and the Jazz Age. It was the era of Prohibition. The Volstead Act, the 18th amendment to the Constitution, had made the sale of alcoholic beverages illegal. But many people ignored this highly unpopular law and purchased liquor from "bootleggers" or in "speakeasies." The most notorious of the bootleggers was a man who helped make the word "gangster" a part of the language—Al Capone.

The 1920's were exciting years. The population of the United States grew from less than 106 million to almost 123 million. And for the first time in American history, more people lived in cities and towns than in rural areas. The 19th amendment to the Constitution gave women throughout the United States the right to vote. Charles A. Lindbergh became the first person to fly nonstop and alone across the Atlantic Ocean. The first feature-length "talking" movie, *The Jazz Singer*, starring Al Jolson, was produced. Babe Ruth was hitting home runs. And Gene Tunney defeated Jack Dempsey for the heavyweight boxing championship of the world.

Coolidge's Popularity

Coolidge was popular because the people saw him as a symbol of the prosperous times. They also admired his old-fashioned virtues of thrift and common sense. As president he was conservative in his views on economics. He did not believe in government interference in private business. However, his support of a high protective tariff, or tax on goods imported into the United States, aided American business. With his respect for thrift,

Coolidge worked to limit government spending, to reduce the national debt, and to lower taxes. But, though there was prosperity, not everybody shared in it. Many industrial workers were paid low wages, and farmers were hard hit by declining prices on their crops.

Foreign Affairs

Coolidge took little interest in foreign affairs. He opposed the United States's joining the League of Nations, although he did favor U.S. membership in the World Court. But Congress' insistence on certain membership conditions kept the United States out of the Court. The Kellogg-Briand Pact, a U.S. and French plan to outlaw war, met with more success. It was signed by the United States and 14 other nations in 1928.

Coolidge showed more concern about Latin American matters. Revolutions in Nicaragua prompted him to send 5,000 marines to that country to protect American interests. When relations between Mexico and the United States became strained in a dispute over oil lands, the president named a new ambassador, who improved relations.

▶ COOLIDGE LEAVES THE WHITE HOUSE

Many people thought that Coolidge would run again for president. He surprised the nation when he said: "I do not choose to run for president in 1928." In the election of 1928, Herbert Hoover became president.

Some historians and economists have criticized Coolidge for a lack of forcefulness and political leadership. They argue that his administration was partly responsible for the Great Depression that began in 1929, soon after President Hoover took office. However, during the 1920's most Americans supported Coolidge's policies.

After Coolidge left the White House, he retired to Northampton. He wrote articles for a newspaper, giving his opinion on current events and politics, and also published his autobiography. On January 5, 1933, he died suddenly of a heart attack.

DAVID M. REIMERS
New York University

COONEY, BARBARA. See CHILDREN'S LITERATURE (Profiles).

COOPER, GARY. See MONTANA (Famous People).

COOPER, GORDON. See SPACE EXPLORATION AND TRAVEL (Profiles).

IMPORTANT DATES IN THE LIFE OF CALVIN COOLIDGE

1872	Born in Plymouth Notch, Vermont, July 4.
1895	Graduated from Amherst College.
1897	Became a lawyer in Northampton, Massachusetts.
1898	Elected city councilman in Northampton.
1905	Married Grace Goodhue.
1907–08	Served in the Massachusetts legislature.
1910–11	Mayor of Northampton.
1912–15	Massachusetts state senator.
1916–18	Lieutenant governor of Massachusetts.
1919–20	Governor of Massachusetts.
1920	Elected vice-president of the United States.
1923	Became 30th president of the United States upon the death of President Warren G. Harding, August 3.
1924	Elected to a full term as president.
1929	Retired from the presidency.
1933	Died in Northampton, Massachusetts, January 5.

COOPER, JAMES FENIMORE (1789–1851)

James Fenimore Cooper was the first internationally acclaimed American novelist. He is best known for his Leatherstocking Tales, a series of novels about the American frontier.

Cooper was born in Burlington, New Jersey, on September 15, 1789. His father, William, was a wealthy community leader who twice served in Congress. When James was about a year old, he moved with his family to Cooperstown, their settlement on the New York frontier.

There James spent much time exploring the nearby woods. He attended school in the village, and after private tutoring he entered Yale in 1803. Dismissed from the college for misbehavior in his third year, he went to sea in preparation for a naval career. He was commissioned as a midshipman in 1808 and stationed with the U.S. forces on Lake Ontario. But he resigned from the Navy shortly after his marriage in 1811.

Cooper had inherited money and property from his father, but by 1820 the family's wealth was almost gone. With a wife and several children to support, Cooper turned to writing as a way of making money. His first novel, *Precaution* (1820), was unpopular. But his second book, *The Spy* (1821), a story of the American Revolutionary War, was an immediate success.

Cooper attained greater fame with his third novel, *The Pioneers* (1823), a frontier romance based on his family's experiences in Cooperstown. In it he introduced the skilled woodsman Natty Bumppo, also called Hawkeye and Leatherstocking, and his Mohican companion Chingachgook. Natty's life and adventures were the basis for four later novels. *The Last of the Mohicans* (1826) is among the most famous books in American literature. It takes place during the French and Indian War. In *The Prairie* (1827), Natty is an old man living on the Great Plains. In *The Pathfinder* (1840), also set during the French and Indian War, he is middle-aged. *The Deerslayer* (1841) describes Natty's early adventures. Together the novels are known as the Leatherstocking Tales.

Cooper's fourth novel, *The Pilot* (1824), is a tale of the sea. It reflects the knowledge and love of ships that he had acquired as a sailor. *The Pilot* was followed by other popular sea stories such as *The Red Rover* (1827) and *The Water-Witch* (1830).

In 1826, Cooper went to Europe, where he wrote a series of three novels with European settings. These works were not popular with his American audience, and on his return to the United States in 1834, Cooper angrily declared that he would not write any more fiction.

Instead he wrote a political satire, *The Monikins* (1835), and an essay, *The American Democrat* (1838). Both were critical of American society. He also wrote five European travel books and a history of the U.S. Navy. He also produced two novels, *Homeward Bound* (1838) and *Home as Found* (1838), in which he expressed his bitter disappointment with America. These works were so severely attacked by the press that Cooper brought a series of libel suits against his critics. He argued some of his own cases in court and won most of them. Despite his victories, these legal battles wasted Cooper's energy and harmed his image with the public.

Cooper wrote his two final Leatherstocking Tales in 1840 and 1841 and with these works again charmed his American readers. The last decade of his life was his most productive as a writer. He produced 16 novels, including three works known as the Littlepage Series (1845–46), about a New York frontier estate; *Wyandotte* (1843), a grim Revolutionary War tale; and eight more sea novels, including *The Sea Lions* (1849), a brooding tale of the South Atlantic. He died at the family mansion in Cooperstown on September 14, 1851, the day before his 62nd birthday.

WAYNE FRANKLIN
Author, *The New World of James Fenimore Cooper*

▶THE LAST OF THE MOHICANS

The Last of the Mohicans takes place during the French and Indian War, in which the French, aided by their American Indian allies, fought the British for possession of the American colonies. The woodsman Natty Bumppo, called Hawkeye; his friend Chingachgook, a Delaware Mohican Indian; and Chingachgook's son Uncas help a small British group led by the soldier Duncan Heywood. In this scene, Hawkeye and his friends have overcome a party of hostile Indians led by Magua, a Huron, who had captured the British group.

The woodsman Natty Bumppo and the Mohican Indians Chingachgook and Uncas share a canoe in James Fenimore Cooper's *The Last of the Mohicans*. The scene was painted by the noted American illustrator N. C. Wyeth.

Chingachgook and Magua, both famed for their skills in battle, continue in a desperate fight as the Mohican's friends look on, unable to help him.

The battle was now entirely terminated, with the exception of the protracted struggle between Le Renard Subtil and Le Gros Serpent. Well did these barbarous warriors prove that they deserved those significant names which had been bestowed for deeds in former wars. When they engaged, some little time was lost in eluding the quick and vigorous thrusts which had been aimed at their lives. Suddenly darting on each other, they closed, and came to the earth, twisted together like twining serpents, in pliant and subtle folds. At the moment when the victors found themselves unoccupied, the spot where these experienced and desperate combatants lay, could only be distinguished by a cloud of dust and leaves which moved from the centre of the little plain towards its boundary, as if raised by the passage of a whirlwind. Urged by the different motives of filial affection, friendship, and gratitude, Heyward and his companions rushed with one accord to the place, encircling the little canopy of dust which hung above the warriors. In vain did Uncas dart around the cloud, with a wish to strike his knife into the heart of his father's foe; the threatening rifle of Hawkeye was raised and suspended in vain, while Duncan endeavored to seize the limbs of the Huron with hands that appeared to have lost their power. Covered, as they were, with dust and blood, the swift evolutions of the combatants seemed to incorporate their bodies into one. The death-like looking figure of the Mohican, and the dark form of the Huron, gleamed before their eyes in such quick and confused succession, that the friends of the former knew not where nor when to plant the succoring blow. It is true there were short and fleeting moments, when the fiery eyes of Magua were seen glittering, like the fabled organs of the basilisk, through the dusty wreath by which he was enveloped, and he read by those short and deadly glances the fate of the combat in the presence of his enemies; ere, however, any hostile hand could descend on his devoted head, its place was filled by the scowling visage of Chingachgook. In this manner the scene of the combat was removed from the centre of the little plain to its verge. The Mohican now found an opportunity to make a powerful thrust with his knife; Magua suddenly relinquished his grasp, and fell backward without motion, and seemingly without life. His adversary leaped on his feet, making the arches of the forest ring with the sounds of triumph.

"Well done for the Delawares! Victory to the Mohican!" cried Hawkeye, once more elevating the butt of the long and fatal rifle. "A finishing blow from a man without a cross will never tell against his honor, nor rob him of his right to the scalp."

But, at the very moment when the dangerous weapon was in the act of descending, the subtle Huron rolled swiftly from beneath the danger, over the edge of the precipice, and falling on his feet, was seen leaping, with a single bound, into the centre of a thicket of low bushes, which clung along its sides. The Delawares, who had believed their enemy dead, uttered their exclamation of surprise, and were following with speed and clamor, like hounds in open view of the deer, when a shrill and peculiar cry from the scout instantly changed their purpose, and recalled them to the summit of the hill.

COOPER, PETER (1791–1883)

Peter Cooper was an American inventor and manufacturer. His interest in and use of the technological advances of his time helped develop industry in the United States. Today, Cooper is remembered not only as a successful industrialist but as a philanthropist—one who uses personal wealth to help other people.

Cooper was born in New York City on February 12, 1791. By the time he was 16, he had worked as a hatter, a brewer, a store clerk, and a brickmaker. His only mechanical training came from working for a carriage maker.

When Cooper was in his 20's, he bought a glue factory. Soon his factory was supplying most of the glue used in the United States. Later he became the owner of a number of iron and steel mills. The first iron for fireproofing buildings was rolled in Cooper's ironworks.

Cooper worked out the design of the first steam locomotive built in the United States. It was so small that it was called the "Tom Thumb." In 1830 the "Tom Thumb" was entered in a race against a horse. At first the machine puffed along in the lead. But mechanical trouble stopped the engine, and the horse won. Still, "Tom Thumb" had traveled at the then surprisingly fast speed of 15 miles (25 kilometers) an hour. It helped prove that steam locomotives were practical.

Cooper became a very wealthy man. He used his wealth to work for reforms in which he believed strongly. One of these concerned education. Cooper felt that education should be available to everyone, not just the rich. In 1859 he founded Cooper Union in New York City. This institution still provides a free college education in the arts and sciences.

In 1876, Cooper was nominated for president of the United States by the Greenbacks, a reform political party. But he won only a small number of votes. Cooper died in New York City on April 4, 1883.

Reviewed by DAVID C. COOKE
Author, *Inventions That Made History*

COPENHAGEN

Copenhagen is the capital and largest city of Denmark. Its name in Danish is København, meaning "merchants' harbor." It is the country's chief port and the center of its political, economic, and cultural life. Copenhagen forms a separate administrative district with a population of about 1,500,000. The city proper has a population of about 680,000.

Location. Copenhagen is situated on the island of Zealand (Sjælland) and partly on the small island of Amager. The city faces the Øresund (The Sound), a narrow waterway that separates Denmark from Sweden. Copenhagen owes its importance largely to its location. It lies between the Baltic and North seas and links Scandinavia (Denmark, Norway, Sweden) with central Europe.

Attractions of the City. Probably Copenhagen's best-known attraction is Tivoli, an amusement park located in the center of the city. It offers roller coasters and other rides, a pantomime theater, and a concert hall, as well as tree-lined paths and gardens and a variety of restaurants.

The city's main shopping area is Strøget, a pedestrian walkway, which connects Town

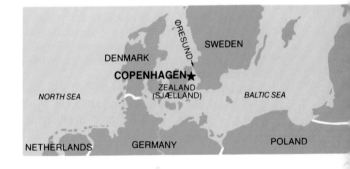

Hall Square and its imposing Town Hall with Kongens Nytorv (The King's New Market). Facing Kongens Nytorv is the Royal Dramatic Theater. Nearby is the Amalienborg Palace, home of Denmark's kings and queens since the end of the 18th century. The Danish parliament is housed in Christiansborg Palace, which adjoins the National Library.

Other buildings of great interest are the Cathedral; the Round Tower, which dates from 1642; and the 17th-century building housing the Stock Exchange, the spire of which is formed in the shape of intertwining dragons' tails. The many museums include the National Museum; the Thorvaldsen Museum, containing the works of Denmark's greatest sculptor,

Town Hall Square (Raadhuspladsen, in Danish) is at the center of Copenhagen's busy life. The city's most famous shopping street, Strøget, leads into the square.

Bertel Thorvaldsen; the Ny Carlsberg Glyptotek, with its renowned collection of international sculptures; and the Rosenborg Palace, known for its silver, porcelain, and paintings.

Copenhagen is the home of Denmark's oldest university, the University of Copenhagen, which was founded in 1479.

Facing toward the Øresund is the statue of the Little Mermaid, inspired by the tale by the 19th-century Danish author Hans Christian Andersen. The statue has become the symbol of Copenhagen.

History. The earliest mention of the city, then called Havn, dates from 1043. In 1167, Bishop Absalon, regarded as Copenhagen's founder, built a great fortress there. Copenhagen became the capital of Denmark in 1416 and has had an eventful history. It was besieged by the Swedish king Gustav X in 1658. In 1801, during the Napoleonic Wars, a British fleet under Admiral Lord Nelson destroyed the Danish fleet in Copenhagen harbor; six years later the city itself was bombarded by the British. During World War II, Copenhagen and the rest of Denmark were occupied by the Germans. Copenhagen's liberation in 1945 began a period of growth that has seen it become a leading city of northern Europe.

ERIK J. FRIIS
Co-author, *Scandinavian Studies*

COPERNICUS, NICOLAUS (1473–1543)

Nicolaus Copernicus is thought of as the founder of modern astronomy. He was born in Torun, Poland, on February 19, 1473. Little is known about his early life except that his father died when Nicolaus was 10 and he was adopted by an uncle, who was a bishop.

Copernicus went to the university in Cracow. There he studied such subjects as Latin, mathematics, and astronomy. It was probably at this time that he changed his Polish name, Niklas Koppernigk, to the Latin form of Nicolaus Copernicus. In 1496, Copernicus went to Italy, where he spent the next ten years at

Nicolaus Copernicus, the founder of modern astronomy, proved that the earth and other planets orbit the sun.

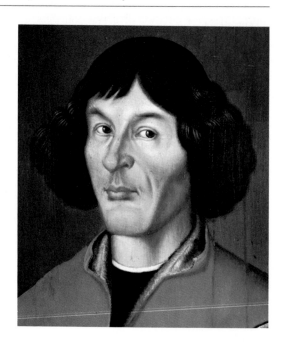

various universities. He studied medicine, obtained a degree in canon (church) law, and pursued his interest in astronomy.

Copernicus questioned the system of astronomy that had been put forth 1,400 years earlier by Ptolemy of Alexandria and was still upheld not only by scholars but also by the church. This system viewed the earth as the center of the universe, and all things—the sun, the stars, and the planets—were thought to be moving around the earth.

Copernicus' System. Using mathematics and logic, Copernicus concluded that Ptolemy's system was wrong. For one thing it could not account for the motion of the planets as they seemed to go back and forth across the sky. So Copernicus worked out a different system that accounted for their movements. It was his view that all of the planets, including the earth, move through space in orbits around the sun. He also concluded that while the earth is traveling through space, it is revolving on an axis once every 24 hours. This rotation accounts for the apparent movement of the sun and stars rising and setting each day.

Copernicus did not announce his findings because he did not want to quarrel with the official position of the church. In fact, he was a staff member of the Cathedral of Frauenburg (now Frombork), a post he held until his death. Instead, he submitted his ideas in unsigned form to other scholars. Finally he allowed his work to be published. His great book, *On the Revolutions of the Heavenly Bodies,* appeared at the very end of his life. Legend says that Copernicus saw the first copy on the day he died, May 24, 1543.

Copernicus had expected his book to cause an uproar. But it caused none. Because the book was highly technical, almost no one could understand it. Still, some scholars did read the book, among them Galileo and Kepler. Its influence on them was great. They realized that Copernicus' view of the universe was the correct one, and they carried on his work. The theories Copernicus developed became the basis for modern astronomy.

JOHN S. BOWMAN
Author and science editor

See also ASTRONOMY; SOLAR SYSTEM.

COPLAND, AARON (1900–1990)

The American composer Aaron Copland was a leading figure in 20th-century music. He wrote successfully in many different styles and helped to make American music known and respected abroad. He was also a pianist, teacher, conductor, and author of many articles and books about music.

Copland was born in Brooklyn, New York, on November 14, 1900, the son of Jewish immigrants. He learned to play the piano from an older sister. While in high school he began to study harmony, counterpoint, and composition. At the age of 20, he went to Paris, for more advanced study of music.

Copland returned to New York in 1924. His first compositions reflected his European training. But he soon introduced American jazz elements into works such as *Music for the Theater* (1925). In the 1930's he became concerned about composing music that would appeal to a large public. He began to simplify his music and to adapt popular folk rhythms. *El Salón México* (1936), based on Mexican popular tunes, was an immediate success. His ballet

scores—*Billy the Kid* (1938), *Rodeo* (1942), and *Appalachian Spring* (1944)—were even more popular. One of his best-known works on an American theme is *A Lincoln Portrait* (1942). Another popular work is *Fanfare for the Common Man* (1942).

Copland reached a somewhat different audience with *The Second Hurricane* (1936), an opera for children, "with a chorus of parents." In the 1940's he wrote the scores for several films, including *The Heiress* (1949), for which he received an Academy Award. He later made use of the twelve-tone method of composition developed by Arnold Schoenberg. But his major works of this period, *Connotations* (1962) and *Inscape* (1967), were not so popular as his earlier works.

Copland taught composition at the Berkshire Music Center (Tanglewood) in Massachusetts. In 1964 he received the Presidential Medal of Freedom. He died in North Tarrytown, New York, on December 2, 1990.

DIKA NEWLIN
Author, *Bruckner-Mahler-Schoenberg*

COPPER

Copper is one of our most plentiful metals and is used often in our daily lives. Copper wiring carries electricity for lights, radios, television sets, and air conditioners. Copper wire is also an important part of electric motors and generators. Copper tubing and pipe is used in plumbing, gas and oil lines, and solar energy collectors. Many parts of airplanes, missiles, automobiles, and satellites are made of copper. Copper sulfate is used in plant sprays and to keep algae from growing in swimming pools. It is used in electroplating and in some batteries.

Copper can be combined with other metals to form alloys. The most common copper alloys are bronze (copper and tin) and brass (copper and zinc). Copper is also used in art.

Special qualities of copper make it a useful metal. It conducts heat and electricity better than any other metal except silver. It is very malleable (easy to shape) and ductile (easy to draw into wire). Copper is also durable and resistant to corrosion. A piece of copper pipe used by the ancient Egyptians more than 5,000 years ago is still in good condition.

Copper is found in nature in two forms—as "native copper" (the metal itself) and in mineral ores (combined with other elements). More than 160 known ores contain copper. About half of the world's copper supply is found in a bright yellow mineral called chalcopyrite. This ore, which is often called copper pyrite or fool's gold, is a compound of copper, iron, and sulfur. It contains 34.5 percent copper. One of the richest copper ores is dark gray chalcocite, sometimes known as copper glance, which contains almost 80 percent copper. Other important and colorful copper ores are cuprite, malachite, and azurite.

Copper is used in greater amounts than any metal except iron and aluminum. Close to 3 million tons of copper are used by U.S. industries every year. About half of this copper is used by the electrical industry.

Copper was given its name by the ancient Romans, who called it *aes Cyprium* ("metal of Cyprus"), and later *cuprum.* The island of Cyprus was the chief source of copper for the Romans.

The first Europeans who went to the New World found native people using copper for jewelry and decoration. Native Americans got much of their copper from the region around Lake Superior.

The industry of copper mining and processing began early in the United States. A copper mine was established in Lynn, Massachusetts, in 1664. Many new deposits of copper were discovered in Michigan during the mid-1800's. Later, prospectors in search of gold in the West uncovered some of the richest veins of copper in the United States. These formed the basis of today's copper mining.

Small deposits of copper are scattered all over the world, but most of the world's copper comes from five main areas. These are the Rocky Mountain and Great Basin regions of the United States, particularly Utah, Montana, Nevada, and New Mexico; the Andes mountains, in Peru and northern Chile; Zambia and the Democratic Republic of Congo, in Africa; central Canada and northern Michigan; and the Ural Mountains, in the Russian Federation.

About two-thirds of the copper that is used each year in the United States comes from the mines. The rest is obtained by importing copper from other countries and also by melting down scrap copper. Discarded copper objects and copper parts from buildings and worn-out machinery are sources for this "secondary" copper.

ROBERT C. CARMODY
Copper and Brass Research Association

See also ALLOYS; BRONZE AND BRASS; METALS AND METALLURGY; TOOLS.

COPRA. See COCONUT.

COPYRIGHT

Copyrights protect the rights of creative people. Writers, artists, filmmakers, composers of music, and developers of computer programs all hold copyrights on their works. This gives them the legal right to decide how and when their works should be published or performed. No one can reproduce the copyrighted works without their permission.

The United States has had copyright laws since 1790. In 1978 a new copyright law went into effect. Under it, the creator of a work can obtain a copyright without waiting for the work to be published. In most cases the copyright continues for 50 years after the creator's death. If the work was commissioned by an employer, the employer may hold the copyright. Such a copyright lasts for 75 years from the date of publication or for 100 years from the date of creation, whichever is shorter.

Permission to use a copyrighted work is usually granted on payment of a fee. Every time a disc jockey plays a song on the radio, the authors of the words and music must be paid. When a play is performed, the producer must pay the playwright. Authors of books receive payments for all copies of books that are sold. These payments are called royalties.

Using copyrighted material without permission is a form of stealing. The owner of the copyright can sue someone who does this. But there are exceptions to the law. Films and plays may be presented for educational purposes if tickets are not sold. Teachers may make a few copies of a work for class use, but whole books may not be copied in this way.

Many countries have copyright laws. But the laws of one country do not protect authors if their work is used in other countries. Two treaties provide such protection. They are the Bern Convention of 1886 and the Universal Copyright Convention of 1952.

The symbol © or the word "copyright" appears on all copies of a copyrighted work. In a book this notice is usually on the back of the title page. Look for it in this volume.

JESSICA DAVIDSON
Attorney

See also PATENTS; PUBLISHING; TRADEMARKS.

CORALS

A chunk of coral is made of the skeletons of tiny marine animals called coral polyps. The polyp's skeleton grows outside its body. Cup-shaped, it both protects and supports the polyp's body and grows as the animal grows. When the polyp dies, the skeleton is left. Coral reefs and islands are formed of billions upon billions of these tiny skeletons.

▶CORAL POLYPS

Coral polyps belong to a group of animals called coelenterates. The two main kinds of coelenterates are jellyfish and polyps. Jellyfish float freely; polyps live attached to the sea bottom, to rocks or to one another.

The coral polyp has a soft, hollow, tube-shaped body with an opening at the top. Around the opening are fingerlike tentacles, which can be drawn inside the cup or extended into the water. With its waving tentacles, the coral polyp captures small sea animals that drift within its reach. Each tentacle has poison stingers that paralyze the

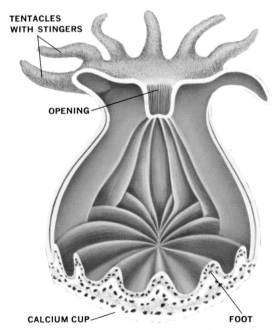

A coral animal, or polyp. A coral reef is made up of the skeletons (calcium cups) of billions of polyps.

prey as the tentacles push it into the opening. The waving tentacles look like flower blossoms. That is one reason why people long thought that corals were plants, not animals.

At the other end of the polyp's body is a round foot. It is anchored to the cup, or skeleton, into which the polyp can withdraw. The cup consists mainly of calcium, given off by the polyp's body, and is covered by living tissue. Food eaten by the polyp may cause the skeleton to be tinted pink or red.

Polyps hatch from eggs. They swim about briefly and then settle down, usually in a coral colony. When they join the colony, they start making their skeletons. Each is attached to a solid base, such as a rock or the skeletons of earlier generations.

▶ CORAL REEFS

Coral colonies are found in all the earth's seas. But reef-building coral polyps are found only in warm, shallow waters. Yet in some parts of the world, coral reefs rise from great ocean depths. How could those coral reefs have formed? The person who solved the riddle was Charles Darwin, the famous naturalist.

Darwin knew that the earth's surface changes. Mountains are forced up in one place; in another the earth's crust sinks.

Studying coral reefs, he noted three kinds: fringing reefs, barrier reefs, and atolls (rings of coral). Putting all this information together, he worked out the following theory.

A volcanic island forms where an undersea volcano rises above the water. In the shallow waters of the island shores, corals build a fringing reef. As time passes, the volcano sinks back into the sea. The fringing reef is now separated from the island, and it goes on growing to become a barrier reef. If the volcano vanishes into the sea, only the coral reef is left; it has become an atoll, a ring of coral surrounding a lagoon.

Scientists now know that island shores may rise or sink and ocean levels may rise or fall. All these changes help explain the building of atolls, barrier reefs, and fringing reefs.

Today, many coral reefs are threatened by pollution and other human activities. At the same time, people are working to preserve reefs, which provide habitats for many marine species. Corals are also important because they produce substances that show promise as new medicines for humans.

BARBARA LAND
Columbia Graduate School of Journalism
Reviewed N. J. BERRILL
McGILL UNIVERSITY

See also JELLYFISH AND OTHER COELENTERATES.

Formation of coral reefs: A ring of coral grows around the top of an undersea volcano, to form a fringing reef. Later, the volcano sinks as the coral grows, leaving a barrier reef. Still later, the volcano sinks below the ocean's surface, leaving an atoll.

FRINGING REEF

BARRIER REEF

ATOLL

CORK

Cork has been used for many things, from shoe soles to hat linings. This useful material is the outer layer of bark of a tree called the cork oak.

The bark of the cork oak tree is made up of tiny cells with tough, elastic walls. In one cubic inch of cork there are about 200 million cork cells. The many tough cell walls make the cork springy and durable. The cell walls are lined with a waxlike material that keeps water and air from passing through. The hollow air spaces inside the cells make the cork light and spongy. In fact, over half the volume of cork is air.

The cork oak tree grows mainly in Portugal, Spain, and North Africa. Portugal is the world's leading producer. Attempts have been made to establish cork groves in the United States in the Far West and the Southwest. The tree will grow quite well there. But so far these attempts have not been successful economically. The tree grows to a height of 30 to 40 feet (9 to 12 meters), with a trunk 3 to 4 feet (about 1 meter) thick. The tree can produce cork for about 150 years if properly cared for. The cork is usually thick enough to be stripped off for the first time when the tree is 20 to 25 years old.

When the cork is stripped, two cuts are made around the tree trunk, one near the ground and one just under the main branches. Cuts are then made up and down the tree trunk, and the cork is peeled off in sections. The cutting and stripping must be done very carefully. If the inner layer of bark, called the cork cambium, is damaged too much, the tree will die.

After the first stripping, cork can be taken from the tree every eight to ten years. The first cork cut from a tree, called virgin cork, is rough and of poor quality. After the third or fourth cutting, the cork is of much better quality and is called reproduction cork.

When the cork has been cut, it is dried and boiled. The boiling makes the cork more flexible so that it can be flattened and baled for shipment to the processing plant.

Uses for Cork

More than 2,000 years ago the ancient Romans used cork to keep their fishing nets and marker buoys afloat. The Romans made shoe

Cork is the outer layer of bark from the cork oak tree. Every eight to ten years a new layer of bark matures and is cut away from the trunk.

soles of cork. It has also long been used as bottle stoppers, which we even call "corks."

Floats, shoe soles, and bottle stoppers were the chief uses of cork until the early 1900's, when many new uses for ground cork were discovered. Ground cork can be mixed with adhesive binders and pressed into various shapes or sliced into sheets or blocks. It can be used to make such products as automobile engine gaskets, inner soles for shoes, insulation, and a variety of useful products.

Cork is still used in buoys and in life preservers because it floats well. Because it is tough and durable, it is a good material for floor and wall coverings. Cork conducts heat poorly, and it is not easily penetrated by air or water. This makes it a useful material for insulation and cap liners for food and beverage containers.

During World War II (1939–45), the supply of cork was greatly reduced. Attempts were made to develop cork substitutes by using synthetic materials or the bark of other kinds of trees, and even peanut shells. Synthetic materials are often cheaper than cork, and they can be made in large quantities. Most of them are made of glass or various types of plastics. These have replaced cork for many uses. But cork is still used for many products because of its distinctive qualities.

Reviewed by ARTHUR L. FAUBEL
President, Cork Institute of America

CORN

Corn is the most important cereal (grain grown for food) in the Western Hemisphere and the second most important in the world, after wheat. For a long time, corn was known only in the Americas. Then in 1492, Columbus found Indians growing corn in Cuba. The Indians called it maize, which is still its name in most countries.

The Corn Plant. The corn plant has large, coarse stalks and leaves and belongs to the grass family. A full-grown plant may be 3 to 15 feet (1 meter to 4.5 meters) tall. The main stalk, which has a tassel full of pollen at the top, usually bears one to three ears, each encased in a leafy husk. A ripe ear is 3 to 18 inches (7 to 45 centimeters) long.

An ear of corn consists of rows of seeds, or kernels, on a cob. The immature kernels, or pistils, send out long threads called silks. The corn silks form a clump at the top of the husk. Wind carries pollen from the tassel at the top of the plant to the silks.

Growing Corn. Most corn grown today is **hybrid** corn, developed by combining different varieties of corn to produce a new corn with desirable characteristics. Some new varieties are **genetically engineered**, containing biological instructions, or genes, from other organisms, such as bacteria. Both types of corn can be developed to produce high yields and to resist disease.

There are six main types of corn. **Dent corn**, named for the dent in the top of the kernel, is the most widely grown type in the United States. **Flint corn** has a hard, undented kernel and withstands cold and disease. Dent and flint corn are used as livestock feed, in processed foods, and in industrial products. **Sweet corn**, which is high in sugar, is eaten as corn on the cob. South American Indians grind the starchy **flour corn** into flour. The small, hard kernels of **popcorn** explode or "pop" when heated. **Waxy corn** has a waxlike appearance and is used as a thickener in puddings.

Corn grows best in rich, well-drained soil, and in a climate with regular rainfall and warm summer temperatures averaging 70° to 80°F (21° to 27°C). These conditions occur in the Corn Belt of the United States. Stretching from Ohio to Nebraska and from Minnesota to Missouri, the Corn Belt produces three-fourths of the country's corn. The United States produces

Corn is one of the world's most important human and animal food crops. There are several thousand varieties. The yellow sweet corn shown above is a popular American food.

about two-fifths of the world's corn crop, with the rest coming from Asia, Europe, South America, Africa, and Canada.

Corn is harvested four to five months after sowing. Machines pick the ears, husk them, and remove the kernels from the cob. Several weeds (Johnson grass, pigweed), diseases (corn smut, corn stunt), and insects (corn borers, corn earworm) are pests of corn.

Uses of Corn. In the United States about 90 percent of the corn crop is used to feed livestock, which can eat the entire plant. The rest is used as human food and in hundreds of other products including soaps, plastics, paper, alcohol, adhesives, explosives, and corncob pipes. Food products made from corn include breakfast cereals, margarine, corn bread, pudding, popcorn, and grits. Corn oil, cornstarch, corn sugar, and corn syrup are used in many foods. Corn is also used in making **gasohol**, a cleaner-burning gasoline that contains ethanol fermented from corn.

Outside North America, most corn is used for human food. The grain is often ground into meal and made into foods such as corn bread, porridge, and thin cakes called **tortillas**, which are used in place of bread.

REVIEWED BY DAVID R. HERSHEY
Department of Horticulture
University of Maryland

See also GENETICS; GRAIN AND GRAIN PRODUCTS; PLANT PESTS.

CORNET. See Wind Instruments.

CORNWALLIS, CHARLES, MARQUESS. See Revolutionary War (Profiles).

CORONADO, FRANCISCO (1510?–1554)

Francisco Vásquez de Coronado was a Spanish explorer of the American Southwest. For two years he led an army over thousands of miles of uncharted territory in search of the fabled Seven Cities of Cíbola and the riches of Gran Quivira.

Coronado was born in Salamanca, Spain, around 1510. In 1535 he traveled to New Spain (Mexico) with Viceroy Antonio de Mendoza and in 1538 was appointed governor of the Spanish province of New Galicia.

In February 1540, Coronado organized a huge expedition of Spanish soldiers and Indian allies to explore the area north of the Rio Grande. Starting out from Compostela, they traveled northward through present-day Arizona and into New Mexico. By July, Coronado had captured what they thought were the Seven Cities of Cíbola (which were almost certainly the multi-storied pueblos of the Zuñi Indians), but they found no treasure.

By April 1541, Coronado had passed through the open prairie lands of the Texas

Spanish explorer Francisco Coronado searched the American Southwest in vain for the fabled riches of Gran Quivira and the Seven Cities of Cíbola.

and Oklahoma panhandles, traveling as far as the Arkansas River in Kansas. There he found Wichita Indian villages, but nothing more.

In the spring of 1542, Coronado led what remained of his forces back to New Spain. He retained the governorship of New Galicia until he fell from favor in 1544. He died on September 22, 1554, and was buried in the Church of Santo Domingo in Mexico City.

Cass Sandak
Author, *Explorers and Discovery*

CORSICA (FRANCE). See Islands.

CORTÉS, HERNANDO (1485–1547)

One of the boldest and most infamous of the Spanish conquistadors was Hernando Cortés, who conquered the Aztec Empire of Mexico.

Hernando (also known as Fernando or Hernán) Cortés was born in 1485 in Medellín, Spain. In 1504, eager to gain fame and fortune, he sailed for the West Indies, where he became a planter on the island of Hispaniola.

In 1519, Diego Velázquez, the new governor of Cuba, appointed Cortés to verify reports of great riches in Mexico. Velázquez later canceled the expedition, but Cortés disregarded his orders and took off for Mexico with eleven ships and a small army.

News of Cortés reached Montezuma (or Motecuhzoma) II, the Aztec emperor. Hoping to avoid a bloody confrontation, Montezuma ceremoniously welcomed Cortés to Tenochtitlán (now Mexico City). Nevertheless, Cortés captured Montezuma and his city.

Velázquez sent forces to arrest Cortés for his disobedience, and Cortés was forced to leave Tenochtitlán to defend himself. While away, his lieutenant killed many Aztec nobles. Cortés rushed back to Tenochtitlán, but the Aztecs were already in rebellion. By the time Cortés fled the city, half his men had been killed, as was Montezuma.

In 1521, Cortés returned to Tenochtitlán with a new army. For ten weeks the combined forces of Spaniards and rival Indians attacked the Aztecs. Finally, near starvation and with their capital in ruins, the Aztecs surrendered. Cortés cleared himself of the charges of misconduct and then set out to rebuild Tenochtitlán. In 1539 he returned to Spain, where he died on December 2, 1547.

Reviewed by Daniel Roselle
Author, *Our Western Heritage*

See also Montezuma.

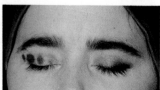

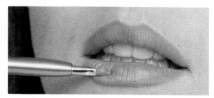

The most popular types of cosmetics include (*clockwise from far left*) foundation, which gives the skin a smooth, even-colored look, and rouge, which is applied to bring a healthy glow to the cheeks. Lipstick can add a dash of dramatic color to the face, while shadow and liner draw attention to the eyes.

COSMETICS

Styles in cosmetics are continually changing. Men have often used more perfume, powder, and oils than women. Women painted their cheeks so brightly in the 18th century that the British Parliament passed a law about makeup. The law forbade using cosmetics to catch a husband. In the Victorian period all makeup was frowned upon.

Cosmetics today are used from head to toe and by people of all ages. There are three kinds of cosmetics. One kind can be seen, like lipstick, eye makeup, and nail polish. Another kind is rubbed in or hidden, like hand lotion, perfume, hair dressing, and antiperspirant. A third kind of cosmetic is used during the course of a treatment and is then wiped, rinsed, or rubbed off. Examples are shaving cream, shampoo, mouthwash, and bathing preparations. Soap is not usually considered to be a cosmetic.

Manufacture of Cosmetics

Three types of ingredients, singly or in combination, are the basis of most cosmetics. Fats or oils form a base. Water or alcohol acts as the liquid. Vegetable gums and emulsifiers hold the mixture together. Colors, perfumes, and preservatives are added to make a cosmetic attractive and long lasting.

Face powder is made by blending several different dry materials. Talc, a very soft mineral, is an important ingredient. Others include zinc oxide, chalk, and metallic stearates to make the face powder spread evenly and stay on the skin longer. Mild perfumes may be added to make the powder more pleasant to use. Hypoallergenic cosmetics, however, generally contain no perfume, because some people's skins are sensitive to perfume.

Cake rouge is made in much the same way as powder. Gum or some other binder is added to hold the cake more tightly together. Liquid, cream, powder, and gel rouges are also sold.

Lipsticks are made of a combination of castor oil and waxes, which are melted together. Dye or colored powder is added to the mixture for color. Exact shading is a delicate job. Once the colors are mixed, the mass is reheated and poured into molds. The final step is placing the cooled lipsticks in metal or plastic holders.

Eye makeup usually has a base of beeswax or some other kind of wax. A fat such as lanolin or cocoa butter makes eye cosmetics creamier and easier to apply. Special preservatives are added to help prevent eye infection.

Hand lotions and face creams are often called skin foods. They help put back into the skin materials that have dried up or have been rubbed off by everyday exposure to air, wind, clothing, and the sun. Mixed in with the chemical ingredients in these creams are some surprising natural ingredients. Avocado oil, turtle oil, and cod-liver oil are some of the natural oils that help soften the skin.

Regulation of Beauty Products

It was common in the ancient world to use mineral products in making cosmetics. But often the minerals damaged the skin and caused blemishes. The lead used as a whitener in Elizabethan times was especially harmful.

Today, cosmetic chemists work with physicians and dermatologists (skin doctors) to make products that will not harm skin or eyes, will not cause allergic reactions, and are not poisonous. In many cases drugs are added to cosmetics to give them a double action. Antiperspirants, hormone creams, and acne preparations are products that contain drugs.

In the United States the Food, Drug, and Cosmetic Act of 1938 brought government control to the manufacture and sale of cosmetics. New regulations are passed frequently to keep the act up-to-date. For example, manufacturers are now required to list all ingredients on the packages of most cosmetics, so that customers will know what is in them. Poisonous substances, habit-forming drugs, and dirt cannot be put into cosmetics. Government inspectors visit cosmetic factories regularly to see that conditions are sanitary and that only proper materials are used.

History of Cosmetics

The earliest cosmetics had religious uses. Bright colors were painted on the body to please the gods. Incense and oils were used to anoint the living and the dead in religious ceremonies.

The Egyptian queen Cleopatra bathed in milk to make her skin more beautiful and used strange perfumes. She is said to have painted her eyebrows and eyelashes black, the upper part of her eyelids blue-black, and her lower lids green.

In Rome the great public baths and the many barbershops supplied perfumes, oils, bleaches, dyes, and lotions. A fashionable

To see how the proper use of cosmetics can make a dramatic difference in one's appearance, look at the woman at left. Her complexion looks faded and her eyes and lips seem to disappear against her face.

This is the same woman wearing cosmetics. An ivory foundation was applied to her pale skin, and then her face was "warmed up" with blush and lipstick appropriate for her coloring. Eye makeup dramatizes her eyes.

man fresh from the barbershop would wear his dyed curls perfumed with cinnamon. A fashionable woman would be made up with a mixture of chalk and white lead on her face and arms and ashes to darken her eyebrows.

In Europe cosmetics were once a luxury that only a few people knew about and even fewer could afford, but when the Crusaders returned from the religious wars in the East, they brought back cosmetics and exotic perfumes. By the 16th century, commoners and royalty alike were experimenting with cosmetics.

In the 17th and 18th centuries, the ideal was to have a smooth, white skin. This was achieved by avoiding the sun and using white powder or paint to hide blemishes. Rouge was used heavily, but eye makeup was not used at all. Black cloth patches, at first used to hide blemishes, became a fashion.

In the United States and Canada, the early pioneers found the materials for their cosmetics in the woods and fields near their homes. They scrubbed their faces with buttermilk to remove freckles. Flour was used as face powder. To color their lips and cheeks, they used the juice from red berries.

In the early 19th century, a few peddlers tried mixing their own cosmetics and branding them with trade names. Soon people were buying the peddlers' brands instead of making their own cosmetics at home.

Just before the beginning of the 20th century, the United States firm of Daggett and Ramsdell began using mineral oil in its cold creams. The mineral oil replaced vegetable oils, which rapidly became rancid. For the first time, long-lasting cosmetics could be made. One company after another introduced products that eventually became so successful as to be known around the world.

Today cosmetics are an important part of careful grooming for men and women alike. Bottles, boxes, and jars of cosmetics crowd dressers and dressing tables in many homes. More bottles, jars, and sprays fill family medicine cabinets. This amazing collection can clean the skin and change a person's appearance in many ways. Many people today follow the latest trends in cosmetics as closely as they watch fashions in clothing.

RICHARD K. LEHNE
Contributor, *Cosmetics: Science and Technology*

Reviewed by JOAN G. KIERNAN
Beauty Editor, *Redbook*

COSMIC RAYS

At every moment of every day, billions of tiny particles come streaming out of the sky. These particles—fragments of atoms traveling close to the speed of light—are known as cosmic rays. So small that they cannot be seen or felt, cosmic rays pass through almost every type of material, including the human body. Some even travel thousands of feet into the Earth before stopping.

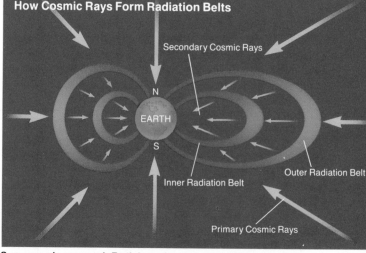

How Cosmic Rays Form Radiation Belts

Secondary Cosmic Rays

N
EARTH
S

Inner Radiation Belt

Outer Radiation Belt

Primary Cosmic Rays

Some cosmic rays reach Earth but others are trapped by its magnetic field and form invisible radiation belts around our planet.

▶DISCOVERY OF COSMIC RAYS

Early in the 1900's scientists had detected a form of radiation that was always present in their laboratories no matter how well they shielded their instruments from radioactive sources. Victor F. Hess (1883–1964), an Austrian physicist working in America, decided to try to detect this radiation from a balloon. In 1912 he took his instruments aloft and discovered that the amount of radiation increased with altitude. This indicated to him that it was coming from somewhere in space. Scientists now know that this radiation comes from cosmic rays.

Scientists have found radiation far down in mines and deep beneath the sea, although it is weakest in these places. By putting observation equipment on mountains, they have found that the radiation there is much stronger than at lower elevations. The strongest radiation is recorded by instruments sent high into space in balloons, rockets, and satellites.

▶TYPES OF COSMIC RAYS

Most cosmic rays that reach Earth come from objects and events in deep space. The cosmic rays that reach us from space are called **primary cosmic rays**. However, when particles in the primary rays strike molecules of gas in the Earth's atmosphere, both may be shattered. Particles resulting from the collision make up **secondary cosmic rays**.

Primary Cosmic Rays. The sun may be a source of primary cosmic rays within our own solar system. Deep in the core of the sun, powerful reactions take place. As hydrogen is burned, some of it is converted into helium. A small bit of the matter in this reaction is converted into pure energy, producing the light and heat that we get from the sun. This process is called a **nuclear reaction**. Sometimes, during what is called a solar storm, some of this energy can be trapped beneath the surface of the sun. This energy is absorbed there by protons (particles of matter that carry positive charges of electricity) and neutrons (particles of matter that have no electric charge)—the major components of the nucleus (center) of an atom. When these particles escape from the sun, they do so with great speed. This is one possible source of primary cosmic rays.

WONDER QUESTION

Why are cosmic rays important?

Though tiny and invisible, cosmic rays are very important to our understanding of the universe. These messengers from deep space can help us unravel the mysteries of events occurring in our own sun and even far beyond our solar system.

Secondary cosmic rays include fragments of molecules from the atmosphere. Scientists study the secondary rays to help determine what gases are found in the upper atmosphere. These studies can help monitor changes occurring more than 50 miles (80 kilometers) above our heads. Some secondary cosmic ray particles are pieces of material that come from far out in space. As fragments of events happening there, cosmic rays are the only direct specimens we have of mysteries like supernovas and galactic cores. They can help us understand these distant events and the huge amounts of energy they release and perhaps even how the universe may have begun.

Primary rays from outside our solar system also reach the Earth. One of the most powerful sources of cosmic rays is at the center of the Milky Way galaxy. Many stars are relatively close to one another there, and violent collisions between stars could produce cosmic rays.

Another possible source of primary rays is an exploding star, called a **supernova**. When large stars get old, their centers, or cores, collapse and powerful reactions result. Eventually these stars become unstable and destroy themselves in gigantic explosions. Large numbers of cosmic rays could be released by such explosions. If a nearby star were to explode in this way, the Earth would be flooded with cosmic rays, possibly enough to endanger life.

Hot, young supergiant stars, usually blue-white in color, may also produce large numbers of cosmic rays. They may even come from the hot gas surrounding these stars.

Cosmic rays with the highest energy may come from yet another source: **quasars**. Located at the edge of the universe, quasars are among the brightest objects in space.

Primary cosmic rays consist mostly of the nuclei of various atoms like hydrogen. Very few of these actually reach the surface of our planet. The Earth's magnetic field traps many cosmic rays in radiation belts thousands of miles above its surface. Over time these particles escape and move toward the Earth.

Secondary Cosmic Rays. When primary rays escape from the radiation belts, they encounter the Earth's atmosphere. These primary rays collide with molecules of gas, and both the cosmic rays and the molecules can be shattered. When this happens, electrons (negatively charged particles that are lighter than protons or neutrons) may be stripped from the molecules of gas, and protons may break free from the atomic nuclei in the molecules.

Other unusual particles called positrons (positively charged particles with the same mass as electrons) and mesons also appear as a result of these collisions. A meson is like a proton or neutron that is missing a piece. Mesons are unstable by themselves and will not last long before breaking up into electrons and positrons. In fact, at most, mesons only last a few hundred millionths of a second. However, because of their great speed many of them do reach the surface of the Earth.

Some of the secondary particles that have been formed may also collide with other mol-

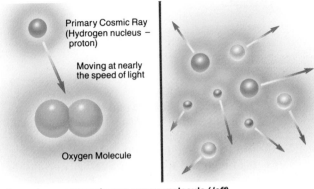

Cosmic Rays

Primary Cosmic Ray
(Hydrogen nucleus –
proton)

Moving at nearly
the speed of light

Oxygen Molecule

A cosmic ray approaches an oxygen molecule (*left*). After impact (*right*), a shower of particles—protons (red), mesons (blue), and electrons (brown)—is produced.

ecules in the atmosphere, producing even more secondary cosmic rays. In this way, a single primary cosmic ray particle can produce a large shower of smaller secondary particles.

▶ **DETECTING COSMIC RAYS**

Because cosmic rays have an electric charge, there are several ways to detect them. Some detection devices, such as mass spectrometers and Cherenkov counters, simply react to the electric charge of a cosmic ray when the ray strikes the device.

Cosmic rays can also show up on film. Although invisible to the human eye, they leave a trail in stacked photographic film plates carried into the upper atmosphere by balloons.

Another detection device, called a spark chamber, is a container filled with an inert gas, usually helium or neon. Metal plates in the chamber are charged with pulses of electricity. When a cosmic ray enters the chamber, its electric charge reacts with the charged metal plates to produce a spark along its path.

A bubble chamber, on the other hand, uses compressed liquid hydrogen, at a temperature of $-371°F$ ($-222°C$). Under these conditions it takes only a tiny amount of energy to cause the liquid hydrogen to boil. A cosmic ray entering the chamber supplies the necessary energy, and bubbles of hydrogen gas form along the path of the cosmic ray.

JOSEPH KELCH
Davis Planetarium, Maryland Science Center

See also ATOMS; RADIATION; RADIATION BELTS.

COSMOLOGY. See UNIVERSE.
COSMONAUTS. See ASTRONAUTS.
COSMOS. See UNIVERSE.

COSTA RICA

COSTA RICA

Costa Rica is the second smallest of the nations of Central America. (Belize is the smallest.) Its neighbors are Nicaragua to the north and Panama to the southeast. Costa Rica borders both the Caribbean Sea and the Pacific Ocean.

Historical Background. Christopher Columbus landed on the shores of this tropical region in 1502, on his fourth voyage to the Americas. He named it Costa Rica (''rich coast'' in Spanish), perhaps because of the gold jewelry worn by many of the native Indians. Neither Columbus nor the Spanish colonists that followed him ever discovered much gold. But the settlers did find a land with a mild climate and fertile soil, where they built large plantations and small, prosperous farms.

Costa Rica was ruled by Spain for some 300 years, until 1821. For a time it was part of a union of Central American states, before becoming an independent republic in 1838.

▶ THE PEOPLE

Ethnic Groups. Most Costa Ricans (or ''Ticos,'' as they like to call themselves) are descended from the early Spanish settlers. The Spaniards settled largely in the fertile Meseta Central, or Central Plateau, where most of the people live today. Some of the Indian inhabitants were killed in warfare with the colonists. Others saved themselves by hiding in the forests along the Caribbean coast, where their descendants still live as farmers and hunters.

The first blacks to arrive in Costa Rica were runaway slaves, escaping from British-ruled Caribbean islands. More blacks came in the 1880's to help build Costa Rica's railroads. Others arrived in the 20th century to work on plantations. Blacks today make up about 3 percent of the population. Most live in the Caribbean province of Limón.

Language and Religion. Spanish is the language of Costa Rica. Both the Indians and blacks, however, are likely to speak English as well.

The people are predominantly Roman Catholic in religion. A special religious festival takes place every year on August 2 in the city of Cartago. Pilgrims from all over Central America come to worship at the shrine of Our Lady of the Angels, whose tiny black stone statue was found here by a country girl in the 17th century. On the festival day the statue is carried in procession to the various churches of Cartago.

Way of Life. Old Spanish customs still survive in Costa Rica, but they are weakening. Once it was usual for young men and women to meet each evening in the plaza of their town or village for a band concert, or *retreta*. During the *retreta* the young women would circle the plaza in one direction, and the young men in another. As they passed, the men would call out compliments to the women and perhaps arrange to see one of them later.

But this tradition is dying out, especially in the larger towns. Today, young people are more likely to meet at fast food shops or go to the movies together. Coffee shops are still popular with adults, who meet there to talk and do business together.

Decorative Arts. Probably because of its small Indian and black populations, Costa Rica has less variety in its arts and crafts than some of the other Central American nations. But the Costa Ricans love brilliant color and use much of it in their homes. Houses are painted in bright pinks, greens, and blues, and are decorated with colorful flowers that bloom all year round.

The main symbol used in Costa Rican art is the oxcart, once the chief form of transportation in the countryside. Oxcarts traditionally were decorated in dazzling designs, with owners trying to compete with each other in brilliance of color. Today the oxcart is losing out to the jeep and the pickup truck as a source of transportation. But small oxcart replicas are still made and are popular, especially with tourists.

Education. Costa Ricans are proud of their modern school system. About 93 percent of the people are literate (able to read and write), one of the highest rates in the world. A minimum of six years of school attendance is required. Of the several institutions of higher education, the largest is the University of Costa Rica in San José, the capital.

Sports. By far the most popular sport is *futbol* (soccer). It is a national passion, and every town has at least one team. Basketball is probably the next most popular game but has none of the following that *futbol* enjoys. Baseball is popular near Limón. Bullfighting is often treated as a form of comedy, and the bull is never killed.

▶ **THE LAND**

Geographical Regions. The heartland of Costa Rica is the Meseta Central, on which the capital and several of the country's other large cities are located. This Central Plateau is surrounded by rugged mountains, including several volcanoes, two of which are still active. The action of the volcanoes has created the fertile soil of the plateau. The Pacific and Caribbean coastal lowlands make up the other geographical regions.

Climate. The Meseta Central has a pleasant, moderate climate, while the coastal lowlands are hotter, with heavier rainfall. There are two distinct seasons—rainy and dry. The rainy season lasts from May to November; the dry season usually lasts from December until April.

Cities. San José is the capital and largest city. Alajuela and Cartago are the next largest towns on the Meseta. The chief seaports are Limón on the Caribbean and Puntarenas on the Pacific coast.

San José, with a population of about 330,000, almost completely dominates the nation politically and economically. Large numbers of people commute daily from nearby

Costa Rican decorative artists use bright colors and dazzling designs. Small models of oxcarts, once a common form of transportation, are a favorite subject.

FACTS and figures

REPUBLIC OF COSTA RICA (República de Costa Rica) is the official name of the country.

LOCATION: Central America.

AREA: 19,575 sq mi (50,700 km²).

POPULATION: 3,400,000 (estimate).

CAPITAL AND LARGEST CITY: San José.

MAJOR LANGUAGE: Spanish.

MAJOR RELIGIOUS GROUP: Christian (Roman Catholic).

GOVERNMENT: Republic. **Head of state and government**—president. **Legislature**—Legislative Assembly.

CHIEF PRODUCTS: Agricultural—coffee, bananas, rice, beans, sugarcane, tobacco, cotton, cacao, coconuts, fruit, abaca fiber, livestock. **Manufactured**—processed foods, textiles, drugs, wood products, chemicals. **Mineral**—gold, bauxite, sulfur, limestone.

MONETARY UNIT: Colón (1 colón = 100 céntimos).

Coffee has traditionally been Costa Rica's most important crop. Most of the coffee is grown on large plantations on the Meseta Central, or Central Plateau, which is the fertile heartland of the country.

villages to work in the capital each day. The city, which dates from the early 18th century, has a mixture of Spanish colonial and modern architecture. Perhaps its most attractive building is the National Theater, built in the late 19th century as an opera house.

▶THE ECONOMY

Agriculture and Fishing. Although the number of farms is declining, Costa Rica is still basically an agricultural country. Coffee has been the most important product since early in the 19th century. Coffee *fincas* (plantations) are located on the Meseta Central. Bananas, grown in the hot coastal regions, are the next most important crop, and in some years their value has exceeded that of coffee. Other commercial crops are sugarcane, tobacco, cotton, cacao (from which chocolate is made), coconuts, fruit, and abaca fiber, used in making rope. The raising of cattle has become increasingly valuable as a source of export income.

Fishing is especially important in waters off the Pacific coast, where tuna, herring, and shrimp are harvested.

Industry and Mining. In the 1980's, construction and trade have increased considerably more in value than has agriculture. Processed foods, textiles, drugs, wood products, and chemicals are the chief manufactured goods.

Costa Rica has limited mineral resources. The most important minerals are gold, bauxite (aluminum ore), sulfur, and limestone.

▶GOVERNMENT

Costa Rica is a republic whose most recent constitution went into effect in 1949. The nation is famous for its democratic government and for its peaceful political tradition. Even when elections are very close, the government in power does not interfere, and all Costa Ricans accept the results. The head of state and government is the president, who is elected for a single 4-year term and is assisted by two vice presidents and a cabinet of 16 ministers. The legislature is made up of a single chamber, called the Legislative Assembly, which is also elected for four years. The constitution prohibits the formation of an army, a matter of great pride to Costa Ricans.

▶HISTORY

Spanish Colonial Period. When Christopher Columbus arrived on the Caribbean coast of what is now Costa Rica in 1502, he repaired his ships, accepted gifts from the Indians, and sailed on. For the next 60 years the Spanish did little to develop the interior of the region but kept their settlements close to the coast.

In 1564, Cartago was founded as the capital of the province of Costa Rica. The Indians fled from the colonists, refusing to labor for them in the manner common elsewhere in Latin America. Without slaves, the Spaniards were forced to cultivate the soil by themselves. Costa Rica thus became largely a land of small farmers, who were cut off from the outside world by high mountains.

Attempted Union and Independence. Under Spain, Costa Rica was governed from Guatemala City by a captain-general, who was under the authority of a viceroy in Mexico City. The viceroy represented the king of Spain.

Life changed little for the Costa Ricans until 1821, when Mexico rebelled against Spain. Most of Central America joined the new Mexican Empire established by Augustín Iturbide. When he was overthrown in 1823, the five Central American states—Costa Rica, El Salvador, Guatemala, Honduras, and Nicaragua—formed a union, called the United Provinces of Central America. This union lasted from 1824 until 1838, when it officially dissolved and the states all became separate republics.

Period of Trial. Costa Rica grew very slowly. It badly needed roads and schools. Its main income was from coffee, which had to be transported to ships on the Pacific coast, because the heavily laden oxcarts could not manage the impassable forests and mountains on the Caribbean side. At a time when the Panama Canal did not exist, this meant that the coffee had to be shipped all the way around the southern tip of South America to reach its chief markets in Europe.

In 1855–56 an American adventurer, William Walker, invaded Central America. Costa Ricans joined other Central Americans to defeat Walker's forces and his aim of creating his own empire in the region. A Costa Rican drummer boy, Juan Santamaría, became a national hero when he lost his life blowing up Walker's ammunition dump at the Battle of Rivas. There is a statue of Juan in Cartago, and the anniversary of the battle, April 11, is a national holiday.

Democracy was not yet well established in Costa Rica. However, the rule of Colonel Tomás Guardia, a dictator who held power from 1870 to 1882, caused Costa Ricans to make changes in their government.

A Tradition of Democracy. In the 1880's a group of young Costa Ricans organized themselves to prevent another dictatorship. Through their efforts the election of 1889 was the first free and honest election in the nation's history. It was also one of the first free elections in all of Central America.

With only two exceptions, free elections have been held in Costa Rica ever since. In 1917, Federico Tinoco Granados and his

San José is the capital and largest city of Costa Rica. Founded in the early 18th century, the city has a mixture of old Spanish colonial and modern architecture.

brother, Joaquín, overthrew the elected government and ruled for about 30 months until they were forced to resign. In 1948 a coalition (alliance) of Communists and conservatives tried to prevent President-elect Otilio Ulate Blanco from taking office, and a brief, but bitter, civil war resulted. Ulate was supported by José Figueres Ferrer, who organized an army and defeated the coalition. After 18 months as president of a temporary government, Figueres turned the presidency over to Ulate. Figueres himself was later elected president of Costa Rica twice—in 1953 and 1970.

Costa Rica Today. In the years since, Costa Rica has maintained its traditions of democracy and stable government, in spite of economic difficulties at home and political unrest in much of Central America. Oscar Arias Sánchez, who was president of Costa Rica from 1986 to 1990, introduced a Central American peace plan that helped bring a negotiated end to the civil wars in other countries of the region. For this, he was awarded the Nobel Peace Prize in 1987. José Maria Figueres Olsen, son of former president José Figueres Ferrer, succeeded Rafael Calderón Fournier as president in 1994. Costa Rica's 1998 presidential elections were won by Miguel Angel Rodriguez.

THOMAS L. KARNES
Author, *The Failure of Union: Central America 1824–1975*

COSTUME. See CLOTHING.

COTTON

Cotton is the single most important and abundant natural textile fiber. It is grown in more than 80 countries throughout the world. Each year a total of about 80 million bales, each weighing nearly 500 pounds (227 kilograms), is produced.

▶ PRODUCTS FROM COTTON

The many weaves and varieties of fabric made from the fibers of the cotton plant are popular around the world for their easy care, ease of dyeing, and durability. The cotton seed is important as well. Oil pressed from the seed is used in salad oil, margarine, and shortening and in the manufacture of cosmetics, soaps, and paints.

After the oil is extracted from the seed, what remains is the meal and the hull. The meal is an excellent animal feed and can be used as an organic fertilizer. The seed hulls are also used for livestock feed and for the manufacture of plastics. The fuzzy hairs on the seeds, known as **linters**, are used in making microcircuit boards, photographic film, phonograph records, lacquer, and explosives.

▶ THE COTTON PLANT

Cotton is a warm-weather plant that grows in the wild as a perennial, a plant that lives many years. However, the varieties cultivated in the United States must be planted every year. The cotton plant grows to heights of from 1½ to 6½ feet (0.5 meter to 2 meters).

Its roots may grow as deep as 4 feet (1.2 meters) under the ground.

The plant has cream-colored flowers that turn purple the day after they open. When the flower falls off the plant, a seed pod about the size of a ping-pong ball, called the **cotton boll**, remains. Inside the boll are the seeds and white fibers. Those fibers are as strong as a steel wire of the same thickness.

Different kinds of cotton are classified according to the **staple**, or length of their fiber. Most of the cotton grown in the United States and elsewhere in the world is **American Upland cotton**, which has a fiber length of about 1 inch (2.5 centimeters). This is a short-staple cotton. **Egyptian cotton**, which actually originated in Peru, has fibers about 1¼ inches (3.2 centimeters) long and is known as long-staple cotton. **Pima cotton** is a popular long-staple cotton grown in the United States and is a crossbreed of Egyptian and American plants.

▶ GROWING COTTON

Cotton grows in a temperate to hot climate. In the United States it is found south of a line running from central California to northern North Carolina. The chief growing areas in the United States are Texas and California, followed by the Mississippi River valley, North Carolina, and southern Arizona.

Cotton requires fertile, well-drained soil and moisture during the growing season. Irrigation is often used during summer droughts. Cotton is usually planted and cultivated by machine. Weeds are kept down with herbicides (weed-killing chemicals). After the stem of the plant has grown a heavy bark, flame applied in quick bursts by flamethrowers can kill weeds without harming the cotton plant.

Cotton's main enemy is an insect called the boll weevil, the larvae of which eat

Boll weevils are tiny (less than half an inch) but do millions of dollars worth of damage to cotton every year. Chemicals and good cultivation methods help control this pest.

cotton boll fiber. Since entering the United States from Mexico in 1892, the pest has caused some $12 billion in crop damages. In recent years, boll weevils have been trapped and killed with pesticides. As a result, the insect has been wiped out in many areas.

To help the cotton grow, fertilizers are applied before planting and again when the plants are young. Later, chemicals are applied to the mature plant to make the leaves fall off. Then the cotton bolls are exposed to the sun and air to speed up ripening and prevent the fiber from rotting. Sometimes chemicals are used just before harvest to hasten ripening.

When the ripe bolls open, about 130 to 180 days after planting, the cotton is ready to harvest. Mechanical cotton-picking machines are able to pick the cotton fiber with the seeds from the boll. Then the cotton is trucked to the **cotton gin** (short for "engine").

Modern cotton gins work on the same principles as the original one invented by Eli Whitney in 1793. The cotton fiber is pulled by rotating teeth through a steel grate that separates fiber from seed. Then the fiber is cleaned and pressed into bales. Today, gins process one bale of cotton, about 500 pounds (227 kilograms), in 6 to 8 minutes.

▶ **FROM FIBER TO FABRIC**

At the textile mill, the ginned cotton is cleaned and formed into large rolls, called

A two-row picker harvests a row of cotton between each pair of yellow dividers. The fully loaded bin is then tilted to dump the cotton into a waiting wagon.

laps. The laps are fed into **carding machines**, which straighten and smooth the tangled fibers and remove any impurities. If the cotton is to be woven into fine fabric, it will be combed. **Combing** straightens out the fibers and removes the shorter fibers. This produces a smoother, more even yarn.

Carding and combing produce ropelike strands of cotton called **slivers** (pronounced "slyvers"), which are about ½ inch (1.3 centimeters) thick. These strands must then be pulled and twisted to form a tight, thin thread. This pulling, or **drawing**, is done on a drawing frame. It is repeated several times, drawing the fibers out into finer and tighter strands. A **spinning frame** twists the fibers together into a yarn that can be woven or knitted into a fabric. You can learn more about these processes in the article TEXTILES in Volume T.

▶ **NEW DEVELOPMENTS**

Since the 1930's, synthetic materials such as rayon, nylon, and fiberglass have challenged cotton's position as the leading textile fiber. Between 1966 and 1976 cotton's share of the total U.S. fiber market fell from about one-half to less than one-third. Cotton manufacturers, looking for ways to improve the product, have produced stretch fabrics and fabrics resistant to wrinkles, mildew, water, and fire. As a result of these new products and renewed demand for all-cotton fabrics and blends of cotton and synthetics, cotton gained new popularity beginning in the 1980's.

Other uses for the cotton plant are also being invented. Recent research has resulted in products from the meal of cotton seeds that humans can eat and that have a content of 95 percent protein, a vital part of human nutrition.

New genetically engineered, or transgenic, varieties of cotton have been developed to resist herbicides and insects. These varieties contain molecules called genes from other organisms such as bacteria. By the late 1990's, about half the U.S. cotton crop was transgenic.

▶ **COTTON PRODUCTION**

China is the world's leading producer of cotton, with an annual output of approximately 20 million bales. The United States holds second place with an output of roughly 18 million bales. Other leading cotton-producing countries include India, Pakistan, Uzbekistan, Turkey, and Australia.

A modern cotton gin processes 500 pounds of cotton every 6 to 8 minutes. The first cotton gin, which was operated by hand, processed about 10 pounds a day.

▶ HISTORY OF COTTON

Cotton was cultivated in Mexico 7,000 years ago and in India 5,000 years ago. Arab merchants probably brought cotton into the Mediterranean world from India. They gave us the English name for it, which comes from the Arabic word *qutun*.

During the Middle Ages, the use of cotton spread throughout Europe, arriving in England sometime before the 1200's. Cotton was used mainly for candlewicks, embroidery yarn, and clothing.

In the 1700's and 1800's, inventions of spinning and weaving machines made England the leader in production of cotton cloth.

Cotton in the New World. When the Spanish came to the New World, they found the Indians growing cotton in many places. The Incas in Peru, the Aztecs in Mexico, and some of the farming tribes in what is now the southwestern United States made excellent cloth from this native cotton.

During the American Revolution, the supply of cotton cloth from England was cut off. This speeded up the development of the cotton textile industry in America. In 1793 the first large cotton mill was built at Pawtucket, Rhode Island.

The Cotton Gin. The first American cotton was the short-staple variety in which the seeds and fibers cling more tightly than the other varieties. Picking the seeds out of the fibers had to be done by hand. The long-staple variety grown in Egypt and India and used in England could be separated easily by simply squeezing the cotton between two rollers and forcing the seeds out. The American cotton picker could only clean about 1 pound (0.5 kilograms) of cotton a day. If an inexpensive, fast way to pull out the seeds could be found, American cotton could be sold in enormous quantities to English textile mills.

Eli Whitney found the way. He invented the cotton gin in 1793. The cotton gin had a revolving cylinder with stiff wire hooks and a metal plate with slots. When the cylinder was turned, the wire hooks went through the slots, snagged the cotton fiber, and pulled it down through the slots. The seeds caught on the metal plate. Turned by a hand crank, the gin produced almost 10 pounds (5 kilograms) of cotton a day. Using horse or waterpower to turn the crank increased production by at least five times. Whitney's invention was so simple and efficient that the basic idea of the original cotton gin has never been changed.

The number of textile mills increased rapidly in the northeastern United States. Within ten years the value of raw cotton increased fifty times. To meet the great demand, some growers formed huge cotton plantations in the South requiring many workers. Many slaves were imported to do this work, a factor that became a major cause of the Civil War.

Because wages were low in the South after the Civil War, many textile mills were built there. This also saved transportation costs between the grower and the mills. Today, the U.S. cotton textile industry is located almost entirely in the South.

Cotton Moves West. Until the 1920's, all cotton was grown in the South. Then the boll weevil arrived from Mexico and caused many changes. The boll weevil was first seen in Texas in 1892 and in 30 years had overrun the entire southeastern United States, severely damaging cotton production. Because the boll weevil does not thrive in a dry climate, cotton growers began to raise their crops in the high plains of western Texas, then in New Mexico, Arizona, and southern California. Irrigation projects in these areas increased the western movement of cotton cultivation. It was also encouraged by erosion and decreased fertility of the soils in the South.

Reviewed by Jack R. Mauney
U.S.D.A., Agricultural Research Service
University of Arizona

See also Fibers; Textiles; Whitney, Eli.

COUNTING NUMBERS. See Numbers and Number Systems.

Nearly every major country performer has appeared at the Grand Ole Opry, site of a popular stage and radio show that helped make Nashville, Tennessee, the center of country music.

COUNTRY MUSIC

Country music, also called "country and western," is a native American music. Its origins lie in the folk songs of the English, Scottish, and Irish people who settled the southeastern United States. By the early 1800's, the sentiments and rhythms of their songs had changed to suit the rugged, challenging country in which they lived.

In its early stages, this music was called hillbilly music—a reference to the "hill country" of the Appalachian Mountains. Songs were passed from family to family and friend to friend. But for the most part, the music remained within its own community. In small towns and among close-knit families, it was one of the main sources of entertainment.

From the beginning, country music was a music of struggle and determination. The songs celebrated hard work and good fun. They told tales of the joys and sorrows of love, the hardships of poverty, and the strength to be found in religion.

▶ INSTRUMENTS AND STYLE

In the beginning, most country music was played with the fiddle, the five-string banjo, and the guitar. Often small bands made up of two fiddlers and two guitarists played very

fast, complex, and delicate melodies for lyrics that were sung in high, close harmonies. In the 1940's, Bill Monroe and other country musicians adapted this traditional style, adding mandolin and string bass, to create bluegrass music.

Other country musicians were influenced by jazz and the popular "big band" sound of the 1930's. They added piano, drums, and electric guitar to their bands. One of the most notable of these so-called Western swing bands was the Texas Playboys, led by Bob Wills.

Over the years, country music continued to change and grow, blending with other styles such as blues, sentimental ballads of the Southwest, gospel music, and rock music.

▶ THE SPREAD OF COUNTRY MUSIC

Country music originally was performed in the home and at local events like church suppers or county fairs, and for many years its audience remained small. Country music began to increase in popularity in the 1930's, as it became part of the thriving entertainment industry. Radio and records gave country performers such as the Carter family, Jimmie Rodgers, Roy Acuff, and Ernest Tubb their first exposure to audiences throughout the United States. The most important country radio show was broadcast from the Grand Ole

Opry, a huge, barn-shaped music hall in Nashville, Tennessee. The Grand Ole Opry presented country music shows every Saturday night, and it made Nashville the center of country music. Many country performers of the time made their homes there, and recording studios were built in the area.

Western movies also contributed to the rise of country music. Singing cowboys such as Gene Autry, Roy Rogers, and Tex Ritter displayed their musical talents in these movies and became popular heroes.

By the late 1940's, country music had a large, devoted audience, and many popular singers recorded hit records. Country music became a recognized musical form, as had rhythm and blues before it. Country stars and their bands crisscrossed the country in buses, playing hundreds of one-night shows.

One of the first major stars of country music was Hank Williams. He was an important figure not only because he was an exciting performer but also because he wrote many of his songs. Before Williams, most country singers either adapted traditional folk and country songs or used songs written by professional songwriters. Williams wrote songs about loneliness and isolation as well as about good times. Most of his songs were either slow, mournful ballads or fast-paced tunes accompanied by piano that came to be known as honky-tonk music. Other performers who specialized in honky-tonk were Lefty Frizzell, Webb Pierce, and Ray Price.

As country music grew in popularity throughout the 1950's, some radio stations began to specialize in broadcasting only this kind of music. Country music of this period offered songs, by performers such as Johnny Cash and Marty Robbins, that told exciting stories about heroes and common people. The 1950's also saw the rise of women as important country performers. Kitty Wells and Wanda Jackson were leading singers of the time.

The Country Music Association, founded in 1958, began to present annual awards to top country performers and songs. It later established the Country Music Hall of Fame and Museum, in Nashville.

▶LATER TRENDS

During the 1960's, country musicians took full advantage of the newest technology of the recording industry. They used orchestral string sections and brass instruments such as trumpets, saxophones, and even French horns. Oddly enough, it was a guitarist who pi-

Left to right: The heartfelt songs of Johnny Cash concern ordinary people. Dolly Parton's songs appeal to pop audiences. Hank Williams was one of the first stars of country music.

Left: Willie Nelson, a veteran songwriter, gained fame as a singer. *Right:* Ricky Skaggs and his band adapted the instrumental and vocal styles of traditional country music.

oneered these changes. Chet Atkins, whose skillful guitar playing had accompanied nearly every country performer, became Nashville's most acclaimed record producer. His elaborately orchestrated records sold in the millions. This new style was called the Nashville sound. The key to its success was smoothness and polish. Many traditional performers thought this new sound was an undignified attempt to appeal to the large pop music audience. But other artists like Eddy Arnold, Charlie Pride—country music's first black star —and Buck Owens recorded strings of hit songs using the new methods.

The Nashville sound remained important throughout the 1970's. Singers such as Tanya Tucker and Bill Anderson recorded popular story-songs by writers such as Tom T. Hall. But many country performers, including the singer-songwriters Loretta Lynn, Merle Haggard, and Johnny Cash, continued to work within the traditions of country music. Others, like Dolly Parton and Kenny Rogers, produced pop- and rock-influenced songs that appealed to both country music fans and wider audiences.

As happens with any vital, growing musical form, there were those who disagreed with the main trends. Some younger performers believed that much of country's original strength had been in its rough energy and lack of restraint. They felt that the calm, polished Nashville sound denied the music this sort of energy. These performers also enjoyed rock music, and rock's loud volume and beat began to find its way into the new country music.

These dissenting artists were referred to as "outlaws" because they made their music outside the usual Nashville studios. Austin, Texas, in particular, became a center for this new country sound. The most prominent outlaws were Waylon Jennings and Willie Nelson, a veteran Nashville songwriter who became a singer.

Other younger artists, such as Ricky Skaggs, returned to the traditional arrangements and pure vocal harmonies that characterized the earliest days of country music.

Country music in all its various forms— from traditional styles such as bluegrass to the outlaw's country rock—continues to evolve and flourish. And the number of people who enjoy it is increasing all the time.

KEN TUCKER
Music Critic
Los Angeles *Herald Examiner*

COURTS

A court is a forum, or meeting place, established by a government, in which people gather to fairly and peaceably enforce laws and settle disputes. Courts decide whether a person or organization accused of a crime is guilty or innocent and determine the punishment for those who are found guilty. Courts also settle disputes between two or more people.

There are two types of courts in the United States: state courts and federal courts. Each state has its own court system and handles cases according to its own laws. Federal courts are limited by the Constitution to hear only cases that are based on federal laws and to settle disputes between people from different states.

▶ CIVIL AND CRIMINAL SUITS

Courts handle two kinds of disputes: civil and criminal. In general, a civil case is a dispute between two citizens. The term "civil" can also describe the legal system in most European and Latin American countries. In the United States, judicial decisions are often made based on "precedent," or past decisions in similar cases. In civil law countries, judges must decide cases according to written codes established by the government. Juries are rarely used in civil law countries.

In a civil suit, the court must decide which person is right. For example, if one person signs a written promise to pay money to another, the second person has a right to expect payment. If the first person fails to pay, the second person may sue the first in civil court.

Other civil suits arise from accidents. Often, the people involved in an accident disagree about whose fault it was. The civil court must decide. The **plaintiff** (the accuser) usually asks for money in compensation for damages caused by the **defendant** (the accused).

Criminal law, on the other hand, is a public matter. Here, the injury is thought to harm the community as a whole. For example, if a thief breaks into a shop and steals money, the crime affects the shopkeeper and all of the people in the community because everyone's sense of peace and security is threatened. Therefore, it is a case for the criminal courts. People are sent to jail fairly often when convicted in criminal cases, but only rarely in civil cases.

The Supreme Court in Washington, D.C., is the highest federal court of appeals in the United States.

▶ HOW COURTS WORK TO SETTLE DISPUTES

In a civil case, one person sues another. The plaintiff complains that the other party has injured him or her. A lawyer writes out a **complaint** and files it with the court. This piece of paper tells what the argument is about. The filing of the complaint by the plaintiff's lawyer starts the case.

Next, the defendant's lawyer prepares an **answer** to the complaint and files it with the court. The complaint, the answer, and similar papers are called **pleadings** because they are requests, or pleas, to the court. The lawyers may make various motions, or claims, concerning the pleadings until the dispute is clearly stated. Then "**the issue is joined**." That means the case is ready to be decided by the court. (Most civil cases, however, are settled before reaching the courts. Usually a plaintiff will try to reach a compromise with a defendant to avoid the cost, inconvenience, and possibility of losing a court trial.)

A criminal case, on the other hand, starts when a police officer arrests someone (who becomes the defendant) for breaking the law.

The arrested person is told the reason for the arrest and what his or her legal rights are. For some crimes, a police officer must actually see a person breaking the law in order to make an arrest. For others, a police officer may make an arrest upon the word of a witness to the crime. The police officer arranges for the arrested person to appear in court.

In court, a **complaint** is drawn up. In a criminal complaint the police officer or the victim accuses the defendant of doing certain things that are considered criminal. The complaint (accusation) is read to the defendant who is not yet required to answer it. The defendant has a right to have a lawyer's advice and is given time to prepare a defense. In the meantime, if the defendant can put up a specified amount of money, he or she will probably not have to stay in jail. This money is called **bail** and assures the court that the defendant will return to answer the charges.

The next step in a criminal case is for the **prosecutor** (usually called a district attorney) to prepare formal written charges against the defendant. In many cases, the prosecutor must call witnesses before a group of citizens known as a **grand jury.** The jury decides whether or not to make an accusation. If they vote to accuse the defendant of a crime, their charge, or accusation, is called an **indictment.** If they feel there is not enough evidence, they may dismiss the charge, and the defendant is free to go.

Sometimes witnesses are called and evidence is presented to a grand jury before an arrest is made. In such a case, the defendant is arrested after being indicted. Where there is no grand jury or the crime committed is not serious, the formal accusation is made by the district attorney. This is sometimes called an **information.**

The defendant may be charged with a serious crime (a **felony**) or a less serious crime (a **misdemeanor**). After the accusation is filed with the court, the defendant and the defense attorney are called in to answer it. This is called an **arraignment.** The defendant then is asked, "How do you plead?" The defendant may admit to the charge by pleading guilty or may deny the accusation or refuse to admit guilt by pleading not guilty. If the defendant pleads not guilty, the case is ready for the court. The court trial will decide whether or not the defendant is guilty.

▶**THE TRIAL**

A trial is frequently called a search for truth, and that is what it should be. It is not supposed to be a battle of wits or an appeal to sympathy. It is meant to be an effort by two opposing sides to arrive at the truth by reason, logic, and good sense. Sometimes the decision is in the hands of one fact finder, a **judge.** More often, in serious cases, a **jury** of 12 citizens decides. Either way it is the job of the fact finders to decide who is telling the truth and what really happened. For example, did the accused break into a store with the intention of stealing from the safe?

The lawyer for the defense and the lawyer for the prosecution each presents evidence to prove each is right. That evidence may be the testimony of **witnesses,** people who know something about the case from their own observation. A witness may be a taxi driver who saw the defendant running away from the store, the expert who found the defendant's fingerprints on the safe, or a friend who heard the defendant talk about how much he needed the money. A witness for the defense might say that the defendant was having dinner with him at the time and could not have stolen the money.

In addition to firsthand accounts by witnesses, evidence may include physical objects —the stolen money found in the defendant's pocket at the time of the arrest, for example, or the tool that was used to force open the store window. These items are called **exhibits.**

What can be used as evidence and how it is to be considered by the jury are legal questions. The law governing evidence is based on fairness, or **materiality** (which means helpfulness in deciding the issue). When the lawyer for one side or the other thinks certain testimony should not be considered by the jury, he or she objects. The lawyer may think that the evidence has nothing to do with the questions or may think it would create unfair prejudice. Then the judge must decide the legal question of whether or not to admit that evidence.

Witnesses at the trial give testimony **under oath.** That means they swear (promise) to tell the truth. Sometimes they may fail to keep their promise, or they may be honestly mistaken, or they may have forgotten what happened and be mixed up. So one of the most important and difficult jobs for the fact finders is to determine whether a witness is accurate and telling the truth. The law has set down certain guidelines to help the jury decide these questions. For one thing, they are allowed to consider the witness's **demeanor** (behavior on the witness stand, tone of voice, or attitude). If the witness gave a different story in the past, the jury may be told of it. They may also consider the interest the witness may have in the outcome of the case or any other prejudice that might affect the witness's testimony. They may take into account bad character shown by previous criminal or immoral acts.

But the best way of testing the truthfulness and reliability of a witness is by **cross-examination.** When a lawyer asks questions of a witness whose answers will help the defense's case, that is called direct examination. When the lawyer on the other side questions the same witness, it is called cross-examination. If there is anything wrong with the witness's story, the lawyer hopes to find it out.

▶REACHING A VERDICT

After the jury has heard all the evidence, the judge instructs the jury by explaining the law that applies in the case. This is called the court's **charge** to the jury. In a jury trial these 12 citizens become judges for that case. They are the ones who must decide what happened. But they must also know some law in order to hand down a decision, or **verdict**—either guilty or not guilty in a criminal case, or an award of money as **damages** in a civil case. The judge tells them all the law necessary for that particular case.

After the charge, the jury leaves the courtroom. Alone in the jury room, they talk over the case, make up their minds, and try to reach a verdict. They must remember that in the United States a person is considered innocent until proven guilty. As long as a juror has a "reasonable doubt" about a defendant's guilt, a verdict of not guilty must be returned.

In a criminal case everybody on the jury has to agree. In a civil case a strong majority is enough. Sometimes jurors reach a verdict in minutes. Sometimes it takes days. If the jurors never can agree, the jury is said to be **hung,** or deadlocked. Then the case must be tried over again, before a different jury.

When the verdict is returned, the court— that is, the judge—makes it final by giving a judgement based on the verdict and the judge's interpretation of the law. This is usu-ally done at a later date. If the verdict is guilty in a criminal case, the judge sentences the defendant—says what the punishment shall be. The more serious the crime, the longer the jail sentence that the judge may impose. To a large extent it is up to the judge to do justice in the case. Usually a judge will do one of three things: send the defendant to jail for a specified time, impose a fine, or release the defendant on **probation**—that is, on condition of good behavior in the future.

To help decide what is fair, the judge usually has a complete report on the defendant. What kind of person is this? What sort of life has he or she led? What were the circumstances of the crime? Justice may depend on special circumstances. A sentence that would be fair in one case might be too easy or too harsh in another.

▶APPEALS

After judgment is pronounced, the trial court's work is over. But frequently the case is not. The trial may have been unfair. Perhaps the judge made mistakes in the ruling. So there are higher courts that may review the judgment of the trial court. This review is called an **appeal** and is sent to an **appellate** court. In a civil case either side or both may appeal. In a criminal case usually only the convicted defendant can appeal.

There are no juries, witnesses, or evidence in the appeal case. Instead of one judge, as in the trial court, the higher, appellate court has three, five, seven, or even nine judges. They hear the appeal—the arguments of lawyers on both sides. Then they decide whether the trial court's verdict was right or wrong. If they decide it was right, they **affirm** it. If they think it was wrong, they **reverse** it. The case is then either "dismissed" (ended) or sent back to a lower court for a new trial. Sometimes these judges write opinions to accompany their decision. These opinions express the judges' interpretations of the law and may themselves become law for future cases.

After a review by an appellate court, lawyers may appeal the case further, to a still higher court. In rare instances there is a final review by the Supreme Court of the United States, the highest court of the land.

H. Richard Uviller
Assistant District Attorney in Charge of
Appeals Bureau (New York City)

COWBOYS

The cowboy is one of the most familiar figures of the Old West. The cowboys we see in films, on television, and in novels seem to be leading exciting lives filled with adventure. Real cowboys, however, spent most of their time doing work that was difficult, dirty, and often boring. Most cowboys never fought Indians or engaged in gunfights with **rustlers** (cattle thieves), but they did play an important part in a great western business—cattle ranching.

Although people had been raising cattle for centuries, many skills of the modern American cowboy developed in southern Texas before the American Civil War (1861–65). These techniques were a mixture of those practiced by Mexican herders (vaqueros) and those who tended cattle in the Gulf states to the east.

Early Texas cowboys learned to use horses to tend the tall, lanky cattle of that region, called **longhorns.** They also developed much of the equipment that later cowboys were to make famous. **Chaps** protected a man's legs as he rode through the thick, thorny brush. A large, broad-brimmed hat, called a **stetson** after a well-known manufacturer, shielded his face from the hot sun. Special spurs and a riding whip, or **quirt,** were needed to control his horse, and a strong rope, or **lariat,** caught and held the powerful cattle. Though the air was often full of dust kicked up from pounding hooves, a cowboy could cover his mouth with a colorful kerchief, called a **bandana.**

▶THE GOLDEN AGE (1860's–1880's)

When the Civil War ended, Americans in the northern and eastern states looked to Texas to supply meat for their dinner tables. Many farms had been neglected during the war, and much of the food had been used to feed the armies. A booming cattle industry developed, first in Texas and later in the western territories of west Texas, New Mexico, Colorado, Wyoming, Nebraska, Montana, and the Dakotas.

Ranchers needed rugged men to do the hard work in this rapidly expanding business. Many cowboys were ex-soldiers; about one third were freed black slaves and Mexicans. The average cowboy was 16 to 30 years old. He was paid very little money (about $1.00 a day) and the work was often tedious.

Cowboys symbolize the adventurous spirit of the Old West. In this painting by Charles Russell, "The Bolter," a cowboy ropes a runaway steer with his lariat.

Much of the country where the cowboys worked was unfenced "open range" that all of the ranchers used to graze their cattle. Cowboys spent long hours keeping track of the cattle, caring for the sick ones, and tending to the orphaned calves, or **dogies.**

The cowboy's most useful tool was his horse, and he might wear out three or four of them in one day, riding up and down the cattle trails and over a ranch's great spaces. Some ranchers had their cowboys capture wild horses, called **mustangs,** but most raised their own or bought the ones that they needed. A **bronco** was a horse being broken or trained. A **wrangler** had the job of caring for the horses and broncos. Many wranglers were young boys who were learning how to be cowboys.

Roundup Time. Every spring, cowboys from neighboring ranches herded in all the cattle from the range to a central location. Ranchers could tell which cattle belonged to them by the **brand,** or unique mark, burned into the cattle's hides. Ranchers would claim new calves and brand them. Once the sick cattle had been removed from the herds, the ranchers would decide which ones would be taken north to market.

Before returning to their ranches at the end of the roundup, the cowboys would amuse themselves by holding **rodeos** in which they could compete and show off their skills. (You can read more about this in the article RODEOS in Volume R.)

Trail Drives. In the days before railroads provided direct links between Texas and the North and East, cowboys performed the important task of driving the herds northward to Kansas, Nebraska, and Wyoming, where the cattle could be loaded onto freight cars and sent to slaughterhouses in Chicago and other big cities.

Beginning in March or April, the cowboys began to move the cattle, usually 1,500 to 3,000 head to a herd, along the great cattle trails to Kansas "cow towns." The Chisholm Trail started at the Mexican border and went to Abilene; the Great Western Trail led to Dodge City; and the Shawnee Trail led to Kansas City and St. Louis.

The cowboy herders traveled about 15 to 20 miles (24 to 32 kilometers) a day. They had to make sure that the cattle had plenty of grass to eat and water to drink, and that none strayed from the herd. They often carried pistols or rifles, but these were used mainly to hunt for food, kill wild animals that threatened the herd, or to control a **stampede** (when the cattle would be frightened and all run away at great speed). Only occasionally did cowboys have to worry about rustlers or **desperadoes** (bandits).

In the evenings, the cowboys would settle around a camp fire to eat "prairie strawberries" (beans) and bacon that their **cookie** had prepared in the **chuck wagon.** They would then lay out their bedrolls to sleep under the open sky and "keep an ear to the ground" to listen for restless or roaming cattle.

End of an Era. As the railroads pushed further into the cattle country in the late 1800's, the ranching business and the cowboy's job changed dramatically. There was no longer a need to drive the cattle long distances to market, and cattle drives became a thing of the past. At the same time, ranchers began buying and leasing open range land for their own private use, and cowboys soon began spending more of their time building and repairing the barbed-wire fences that divided property lines.

The demise of the trail drives and the open range system put an end to many of the cowboys' traditional duties. But, even today, though they ride in pickup trucks as well as ride horses, cowboys still protect and care for cattle and do much of the difficult work on a ranch. (You can read more about the lives of modern cowboys in the article RANCH LIFE in Volume R.)

▶**FOLKLORE**

In the late 1800's the public became fascinated with these men on horseback. Cowboy heroes began to appear in short books called "dime novels" and in traveling "wild west shows" that grew immensely popular in the United States and Europe. The most famous of these shows featured William F. "Buffalo Bill" Cody.

In 1902, Owen Wister's famous novel, *The Virginian,* was published. Since then, writers, such as Zane Gray and Louis L'Amour, have written thousands of action-packed books with cowboys as heroes—and villains.

The movie industry also has contributed greatly to cowboy folklore. The white-hatted "good guys" battle the black-hatted "bad guys," who are forever slinging six-shooters and brawling their way through cow-town saloons. Some of Hollywood's most popular actors, such as Roy Rogers and John Wayne, spent much of their careers playing cowboy heroes.

Television too helped celebrate the life of the cowboy, especially in the early 1950's through such shows as *Hopalong Cassidy, The Lone Ranger,* and *The Gene Autry Show.*

The qualities of a cowboy—however real or fictitious they might be—are important to Americans because they have come to symbolize what many believe are the traits of the true American spirit—strength, independence, and self-reliance. Though the days of the Old West are long gone, the pioneer spirit lives on through the legend of the cowboy—the great American hero.

ELLIOTT WEST
University of Arkansas, Fayetteville

See also ROPING.

COWS. See CATTLE; DAIRYING AND DAIRY PRODUCTS; HOOFED MAMMALS.

CRABS

Take a walk along the sandy shore of almost any body of salt water, and you will probably see one of the fast-moving animals known as crabs. Crabs are **crustaceans**, animals whose bodies are covered with hard shells. They belong to the same scientific class as lobsters, shrimps, and crayfish. Like other crustaceans, most of the 4,500 kinds of crabs live in or near the ocean, although some live in fresh water or on land. Crabs breathe through gills and reproduce by laying many jelly-covered eggs. The smallest crabs are the pea crabs, less than ¼ inch (about .5 centimeter) in diameter. The largest are the giant spider crabs with 12-foot (3.7-meter) leg spans.

A crab's long legs, large claws, and eyes mounted on stalks give it a most unusual appearance. It even walks and runs in an unusual direction—sideways!

The Body Plan

A crab has three main body parts, which are covered by a large, shieldlike shell called a **carapace**. Attached to the head section are two movable stalks that support the animal's compound eyes. The middle and largest section is the thorax. The abdomen is the third body section. In most crabs it is very small and is folded back under the thorax.

Appendages. A crab's appendages are the jointed limbs connected to both sides of the body. Some of the appendages on the head are **antennae** used for feeling and smelling. Others function as mouthparts, tearing food into pieces and putting it into the crab's mouth.

Five pairs of large appendages are attached to the thorax. The last four pairs are the animal's legs. When moving along the shore or ocean bottom, crabs walk or run sideways rather than straight forward.

Each of the two front appendages on the thorax is equipped with a strong **chela**, or claw, that enables the crab to seize and hold objects with a powerful grip. Crabs use their claws to capture fish and other food to hold it up to their mouths. The large claws are also used in self-defense.

A Crab's Shell. The hard shell that covers most of a crab's body is called an **exoskeleton**. It serves the same purpose as the bony skeleton of the human body. The crab's muscles are attached to the shell, and the animal's internal organs are protected by this tough covering.

One kind of crab is not completely covered by a hard shell. The hermit crab, unlike its relatives, has a long, soft abdomen that sticks out at the back of its body. To protect itself, the hermit crab borrows a shell that once belonged to a marine snail and pushes its abdomen into the shell. When the hermit crab grows too big for one shell, it searches for a larger one and quickly moves from the old dwelling to the new.

Eating and Being Eaten

Crabs spend a large part of their time looking for food. They are not picky eaters and will feed on almost anything they can get their claws on. Small fish and shellfish are favorite foods, but some crabs live on seaweed or algae that they scrape off rocks with their claws. Shore crabs, such as ghost crabs and fiddler crabs, are often scavengers, eating the remains of dead animals and plants that they find.

Crabs also make meals for other animals, including humans. Shore birds eat crabs, and some fish enjoy crab legs as much as people do. Young, immature crabs (called larvae) swimming in the sea are devoured in large numbers by all kinds of sea creatures.

Humans have a large appetite for crabs, and crab fishing is an important industry along the shores of many of the world's oceans. On the Atlantic coast of North America, thousands of blue crabs are caught in nets each year. On the Pacific coast, the large Dungeness crab is a favorite catch.

SYLVIA A. JOHNSON
Author, *Crabs*

CRANE, STEPHEN
(1871–1900)

The American writer Stephen Crane was born in Newark, New Jersey, on November 1, 1871, the son of a Methodist minister. He briefly attended Lafayette College and Syracuse University but left to pursue a career as a writer. To support himself while he wrote fiction, he worked as a reporter for the *New York Tribune* and other newspapers.

Crane's first novel, *Maggie: A Girl of the Streets* (1893), was a shocking story of life among the poor in New York's slums. The novel is an example of literary naturalism: Its characters are doomed to unhappiness and violence by the circumstances of their lives. Concepts like justice and morality have no real meaning in their grim world. The book was not a commercial success, but it made a strong impression on some writers and critics.

The Red Badge of Courage (1895) was Crane's second book and his greatest success. This famous novel describes the bloody experiences of the Civil War from the point of view of ordinary soldiers. A classic study of terror and isolation, the novel had a great impact on later writers, including Ernest Hemingway.

Crane's other works include *The Little Regiment* (1896), a collection of Civil War stories, and *The Black Riders* (1895), a volume of poems that show the influence of Emily Dickinson. Crane's poems offer striking glimpses into the fearful randomness and chaos that he believed lie at the heart of existence.

By the time he was 25, Crane was suffering from the tuberculosis that would take his life. He traveled widely as a war correspondent, visiting Mexico, Cuba, and Greece. On the trip to Cuba, he was shipwrecked and spent three days in an open boat at sea. This experience became the basis for his famous story "The Open Boat." Crane died on June 5, 1900, in Badenweiler, Germany, where he had gone to seek a cure for his illness.

PETER CONN
Author, *Literature in America:
An Illustrated History*

CRAZY HORSE. See INDIANS, AMERICAN (Profiles).

CREDIT CARDS

A credit card is a special card that enables a person to buy goods or services and pay for them at a later date—a convenience that eliminates the need to carry much cash.

Some department stores, chain stores, and oil companies issue "charge cards" that can be used only in their own stores and service stations. But the most popular cards are all-purpose charge cards such as MasterCard, VISA, and American Express that are issued by banks or corporations. These cards can be used to buy almost any good or service in most stores, hotels, restaurants, and businesses.

People who apply for a credit card must provide information about their income, employment, debts, and savings. The bank or corporation issuing the card uses this information to decide if the applicant is a good credit risk and to determine the maximum credit limit. If approved, the person is issued a card.

The credit card company sends the cardholder a monthly bill for purchases. Some credit card accounts, such as American Express, must be paid in full each month. Others, such as VISA and MasterCard, offer the option of paying all or only a portion of the bill. The cardholder is charged interest on any unpaid balance. Credit card companies make money from service charges to merchants, interest on unpaid balances, and annual fees charged to cardholders.

Many merchants use the credit card service instead of requiring cash because they feel people will buy more if they do not have to pay immediately. Customers need to remember, however, that the unpaid credit card bill is a loan and that interest charges make the real cost of their purchases higher. Also, people need to be careful not to build up a large debt they can never repay.

DONALD BADDERS, President
National Foundation for Consumer Credit, Inc.
See also BANKS AND BANKING; MONEY.

CREDIT UNIONS. See BANKS AND BANKING.
CREEK INDIANS. See INDIANS, AMERICAN.
CRETE. See ANCIENT CIVILIZATIONS.

Rival cricket teams in traditional white "flannels" face each other across the pitch. The batsman has just swung at the ball, which can be seen next to the wicket behind him.

CRICKET

Cricket is one of the most popular games in England, Australia, India, and Pakistan. It is played in all English-speaking nations, including Canada and the United States.

Cricket is played with a ball and bat on a grassy field by two teams of eleven players each. The ball is about the size of a baseball. The bat may be no longer than 38 inches (96.5 centimeters) and has a flat striking surface.

The object of the game is for a team to score more runs during an **innings**, or turn at bat, than the opposing team. A run may be scored in several different ways, and as many as 300 or 400 runs may be scored in a single match.

Cricket is played on a large oval or circular grass field, or **ground**. The center of the field, where most of the action takes place, is called the **pitch**. On the pitch are two **wickets**, 22 yards (20 meters) apart. A wicket consists of three stumps, or stakes, set in the ground closely enough together so that a ball may not pass between them. Two small **bails**, or sticks, fit into grooves in the tops of the stumps.

Play begins with one player from the batting team, called a **batsman**, at each wicket, and the fielding team in various positions around the ground. A player of the fielding team, called the **bowler**, throws the ball to try to knock the bails off the wicket at the opposite end of the pitch.

The batsman must prevent this by hitting the ball in any direction with the bat. If the bowler succeeds in knocking off the bails, the batsman is said to be "bowled out." The bats-man may also be put out if any part of his body except the hand obstructs a bowled ball; if he knocks a bail off the wicket with his bat or body; if he crosses the popping crease (a line in front of the wicket); or if he hits the ball and a fielder catches it before it hits the ground.

If the batsman hits the ball, he may choose to run to the opposite wicket, exchanging places with the batsman there, who then runs to the wicket opposite him. The two batsmen need not run at all, but if they do, they may score as many runs as they can safely—that is, without a fielder intercepting the ball and hitting the wicket with it while the batsman is between the two wickets.

Runs may be scored in other ways. For example, if the batsman hits the ball and it crosses the boundary of the field, six runs (for a ball in the air) or four runs (for a ground ball) are automatically scored. There is no "foul ball" in cricket.

A bowler delivers six balls for an **over**, after which another bowler at the other end of the pitch bowls an over. The two bowlers alternate bowling until ten batsmen have been put out, ending the innings.

Each team has one or two innings, as agreed on in advance. Games of a single innings are usually played in one day. Games of two innings, such as international (test) matches, usually last several days. If the side that bats second is behind when the time allotted for the match has run out, neither team is the winner.

DONALD KING
Canadian Cricket Association

CRIME AND CRIMINOLOGY

A crime is an act that is considered harmful to society and is forbidden by law. Criminology is the scientific study of crime, criminals, and the criminal justice system. Criminologists are professionals who try to discover why people become criminals, when and where various types of crimes occur, and how crime can be prevented.

Crime has been a part of society ever since people began to live together in groups. However, at different times and in a wide variety of societies, people have had different ideas about crime. Thus an act that is considered a crime in one society or country may be legal in another. For example, in the United States people are free to practice any religion they choose, whereas in some other countries it may be a crime to practice certain religions.

Some laws prohibit behavior that endangers people or property, while others outlaw behavior that is viewed as morally wrong. Values and morals change over time, and so do beliefs about what behaviors should be considered crimes. Despite such differences, however, certain acts are considered crimes in most modern societies.

▶ TYPES OF CRIME

Crimes are classified in several ways. One of the most common ways is according to how serious they are, or how much harm they cause. Crimes are also classified according to their object, or target. And they are classified according to who commits them and why.

Felonies and Misdemeanors. Serious crimes are called felonies. Felonies include crimes such as murder, rape, robbery, kidnapping, theft, and assault. Because these crimes may cause serious harm, in the United States felonies are punishable by at least one year in prison. Some felonies may even carry a sentence of death. Most people who are convicted of felonies are sent to a state prison to serve their sentences. A person who commits a felony is called a **felon**.

Less serious crimes are called misdemeanors. These include crimes such as illegal gambling, vandalism, and being drunk in pub-

lic. Misdemeanor offenses are punishable by imprisonment for up to one year, and the sentence is usually served in a county jail. A person who commits a misdemeanor is called a **misdemeanant**.

Each state in the United States has its own laws. These laws generally agree on which acts are felonies and which are misdemeanors. However, it is possible for a crime to be a felony in one state and a misdemeanor in another.

Crimes against Persons or Property. Crimes against persons include violent acts such as murder, assault, rape, and kidnapping. These crimes are generally punished severely because the victim may be hurt or killed. Crimes against property include theft, burglary, vandalism, and automobile theft. The punishment for these crimes may be less severe because they usually do not involve injury to the victim. Robbery is difficult to classify because it involves taking property from a person through the use of force. Legally, robbery is classified as a crime against a person.

"Victimless" Crimes. Some crimes do not seem to have a victim at all. Crimes such as drunkenness, illegal drug use, and certain acts of vice may not seem to harm persons or property because the "victims" willingly take part. However, these acts may threaten the social order or violate the moral beliefs of society. So-called victimless crimes generally receive less severe punishments than other types of crime. Sometimes people disagree as

Two uniformed police officers handcuff three crime suspects. Crime is a major social concern in societies all around the world.

to whether these behaviors should be considered crimes.

Organized Crime. Sometimes people form an organized group for the purpose of committing crime. Organized crime generally focuses on activities such as illegal gambling, importing and selling illegal drugs, and lending money at illegally high interest rates. The group may use bribery and intimidation to keep these crimes from being discovered.

White-Collar Crime. Crimes conducted in the course of business activities are often called white-collar crimes, for the white shirts associated with office workers. These crimes generally are not violent. They may include cheating on income taxes, embezzling money from an employer, or charging customers for services that were not actually performed.

Terrorism. Terrorist crimes are committed in the name of a political cause. These crimes are often directed against governments, although individuals may be the victims. Terrorist acts include bombing, assassination, and hostage-taking. Governments around the world are working to develop security measures to guard against such crimes.

▶ **CAUSES OF CRIME**

Criminologists spend a lot of time trying to understand why criminals commit crimes. Still, no one knows exactly what causes crime, probably because different people commit crimes for different reasons. One person may steal things he or she cannot afford to buy, while another may simply find a thrill in the wrongdoing. Some offenders commit violent crimes out of anger, while others may use violence to obtain money. The criminal who murders someone during an argument is not likely to be motivated by the same factors that lead a car mechanic to charge for repairs that were never performed.

There are three main schools of thought about the causes of crime. **Biological** explanations look for physical differences between criminals and non-criminals. This idea was extremely popular in the 1700's and 1800's. Today most criminologists do not believe that people are born to be criminals. But they do believe that physical and hereditary factors may influence some criminal behavior.

Psychological explanations see crime as caused by personality differences, emotional processes, or early childhood experiences. For example, some adult criminals were neglected or abused as children. Others suffer from various forms of mental illness. Most criminologists believe that psychological factors may contribute to, but not fully explain, criminal behavior.

Social explanations focus on the society in which criminals live, rather than on individual criminals. These theories consider how factors such as poverty, unemployment, poor housing, lack of education, and racism may contribute to crime. They assume that behavior is affected by the society in which people live.

No single theory explains all criminal behavior. Today, some criminologists are combining biological, psychological, and social theories to produce more complete explanations of crime.

▶ **THE CRIMINAL JUSTICE SYSTEM**

The criminal justice system is a network of specialized agencies set up to deal with crime and criminals. The three main areas of the U.S. criminal justice system are the police, the courts, and corrections.

Police. The police are the first line of defense against

Police investigate the shooting of a homeless man near the White House in Washington, D.C. Whenever a crime occurs, the police are the first to be called to the scene.

crime. They are responsible for enforcing the law and preventing crime. When a crime is committed, they attempt to solve it and to arrest a suspect.

Courts. The courts decide whether a suspect who has been accused of violating the law is guilty or innocent. They also determine what punishment is given to those who are found guilty. The penalty, or **sentence**, is influenced by the seriousness of the crime and the offender's background. Offenders who have committed other crimes in the past may be given harsher sentences than offenders who have not. Laws also help determine the penalty, by stating what types of punishments may be imposed for what types of crimes.

The least serious punishment the court may impose is **probation**. An offender put on probation remains free but must meet certain conditions. These conditions may include meeting weekly with a probation officer appointed by the court or participating in drug-abuse counseling. Offenders who violate the conditions of probation may be sent to prison.

The court may also order the offender to pay a fine, a fixed sum of money, to the court. For more serious crimes, the court may sentence an offender to a term of imprisonment. The amount of time spent in prison (or jail) is longer for felonies than for misdemeanors. In some states, the most serious crimes, such as murder, may be punished by death (capital punishment).

Corrections. After the court imposes a sentence, the correctional system sees that it is carried out. This branch of the criminal justice system is responsible for running prisons and jails and for supervising offenders who are on probation or undergoing any type of court-ordered punishment.

There are several goals of punishment. One is **retribution**, to penalize an offender for

DNA analysis is a reliable crime-fighting tool. Detectives use it to identify a suspect's unique genetic material.

what he or she has done wrong. Another goal is **incapacitation**, to isolate criminals from society so that they are unable to commit further crimes. A third goal is **rehabilitation**, to help offenders become law-abiding citizens who will no longer want to commit crimes. The fourth goal is **deterrence**, to discourage people from committing crimes. **Specific deterrence** uses punishment to persuade an offender not to commit any more crimes. **General deterrence** makes an example of one offender in an attempt to persuade others not to engage in similar behavior.

▶ **CAREERS IN CRIMINAL JUSTICE AND CRIMINOLOGY**

Criminal justice and criminology offer many possible career choices. Law enforcement and security jobs are available at local, state, and federal levels, with police and sheriff's departments, the Federal Bureau of Investigation (FBI), the Secret Service, and many other agencies. Attorneys, judges, bailiffs, court reporters, and paralegals work in the courts. Correctional officers, parole and probation officers, rehabilitation counselors, substance-abuse counselors, and child-care workers are among those who work in corrections.

Criminologists study the nature of crime, criminals, and the criminal justice system. Their research may help prevent crime and help society develop better ways to treat offenders, so that they will not commit future crimes. Criminologists work for police departments and various government agencies. Teaching and research positions are available at universities, community colleges, and many criminal justice agencies.

ELLEN G. COHN, PH.D.
Florida International University

See also COURTS; FEDERAL BUREAU OF INVESTIGATION; JURY; JUVENILE CRIME; LAW AND LAW ENFORCEMENT; POLICE; PRISONS; TERRORISM.

The charge of the British light cavalry brigade at the Battle of Balaklava (1854) was the most dramatic event of the Crimean War. Obeying a mistaken order, the 673 cavalrymen made a heroic but hopeless attack against Russian artillery, suffering more than one-third casualties. Their bravery was immortalized in Tennyson's famous poem, *The Charge of the Light Brigade.*

CRIMEAN WAR

In the Crimean War (1853–56), Russia fought against Britain, France, the Turkish Ottoman Empire, and Sardinia (now in Italy). The war took its name from the Crimea, a Russian peninsula in the Black Sea, where most of the fighting occurred.

The immediate cause of the war was a dispute between France and Russia over the right to protect Christian pilgrims and holy places in Palestine, then part of the Ottoman Empire. When in 1852 the French appeared to win in this dispute, the Russian emperor, Nicholas I, demanded the right of protection over the Orthodox Church's holy places and all 12 million Orthodox subjects of the Turkish sultan.

Outbreak of War. When the sultan rejected this demand, Russian troops crossed into Turkish territory in July 1853. Diplomatic efforts by Britain and France to avoid war were not successful, and in October 1853, Turkey declared war against Russia. Britain and France came to the aid of Turkey by also declaring war against Russia, in March 1854. Their reason for doing so was to prevent Russia from becoming too powerful in the Balkans, a region of southeastern Europe still claimed by a weakening Ottoman Empire.

The Campaign. In September 1854, British, French, and Turkish troops were landed in the Crimea. Their goal was the capture of the Russian fortress of Sevastopol, located on the southwestern tip of the peninsula. The siege of Sevastopol, which began in September 1854 and went on for a year, was the most costly campaign of the war.

Sevastopol and such noted battles as the Alma River, Balaklava, and Inkerman produced many examples of self-sacrifice and heroism. Perhaps the most famous incident of the war took place at Balaklava, where the British light cavalry brigade made a heroic but hopeless charge against Russian artillery. Their exploit was immortalized in a poem by Alfred Lord Tennyson, *The Charge of the Light Brigade.* The total loss of life from military action and disease was thought to be as high as 600,000.

Another kind of heroism involved the work of Florence Nightingale, the English founder of modern nursing. She organized the care of British war wounded and improved sanitation in military hospitals, saving thousands of lives. See the article on Florence Nightingale in Volume N.

The Treaty of Paris. When the battered fortress of Sevastopol surrendered in September 1855, the military campaign moved toward its end. But only after the death of Nicholas I in March 1856 did diplomatic efforts to end the war make progress. In the Treaty of Paris, signed on March 30, 1856, Russia agreed to restore all Turkish territories seized during the war. Russia also gave up its claim of protector of Orthodox Christians in the Turkish empire. In return the Ottoman sultan proclaimed religious equality for all Turkish subjects, including Christians. The treaty also assured that the Black Sea would be closed to warships while remaining open for the merchant ships of all nations.

PETER CZAP, JR.
Amherst College

CROATIA

Croatia is one of the six republics that formerly made up the nation of Yugoslavia. In area and population it was second only to Serbia, the largest of the republics. In 1991, Croatia declared its independence, one of four republics to break away from Yugoslavia. Croatia is bounded by Slovenia and Hungary on the north, Serbia on the east, Bosnia and Herzegovina on the south, and the Adriatic Sea on the west.

The People. The Croats, like most of the other peoples of Yugoslavia, are South Slavs. At independence, Croats made up about three quarters of Croatia's population. Serbs were the largest minority, and there were smaller numbers of Magyars (Hungarians), Slovaks, Slovenes, Czechs, and Italians.

Language, Religion, Culture. Croats speak the same Serbo-Croatian language as the Serbs. However, in writing, the Croats use the Latin alphabet, while Serbs use the Cyrillic script, based on Greek. The two also differ in religion. The Croats are mainly Roman Catholic, the Serbs chiefly Eastern orthodox.

These differences symbolize the sharply different cultural background of the two peoples. Once part of the Austro-Hungarian Empire, the Croats became urban (city-dwelling) and Westernized, shaped by Central European

and Mediterranean civilization. The Serbs, who were influenced by the eastern Byzantine Empire and long ruled by the Ottoman Turks, remained a more isolated and traditional people. Their cultural differences often created suspicion and hostility between the two largest South Slavic peoples.

The Land and Climate. Croatia is situated in the northwestern part of the Balkan Peninsula in southeastern Europe. It includes the historic provinces of Dalmatia, part of Istria (both on the Adriatic Sea coast), Croatia (in the middle of the country), and Slavonia (in the east). The Dinaric Alps stretch like a spine down the center of Croatia. The Pannonian plain lies in the east. The major rivers are the Drava and Sava,

An open-air food market attracts shoppers in Zagreb, the capital and largest city of Croatia. Formerly a part of Yugoslavia, Croatia proclaimed its independence in 1991.

which flow into the Danube. Forests cover about one third of the land.

The Adriatic coast has a Mediterranean climate, marked by short, cool winters and long, hot summers. Inland areas, by contrast, generally have a continental type of climate, with greater extremes of temperature.

Major Cities. Zagreb is the capital and largest city, with a population of about 770,000. Located near the Drava River, it is the center of Croatian culture. The city's site is an ancient one, dating to Roman times. Split and Rijeka are the next largest cities. The walled city of Dubrovnik, situated on the Dalmatian coast, was a popular tourist attraction. It suffered damage during the fighting that followed independence.

The Economy. Croatia is a prosperous industrial and agricultural country. Its mineral resources include abundant supplies of bauxite (aluminum ore), brown coal, iron ore, copper, and petroleum. Its chief manufactures are aluminum, machine tools, petroleum products, chemicals, cement, lumber, paper, and textiles. Shipbuilding is also important.

Agriculture, particularly in the Pannonian plain, focuses on such crops as corn, wheat, and other grains, sugar beets, potatoes, and fruits. Olives and wine come from Dalmatia. Livestock production is also important. The mild climate of the Adriatic coast and its picturesque cities and towns have made tourism a leading economic activity.

History and Government. The ancestors of the Croats probably migrated to the region in the A.D. 600's and were converted to Christianity in the 800's. The first Croatian king, Tomislav, was crowned by the pope in 925. In 1102, Croatia accepted a political union with Hungary. When the Habsburg dynasty of Austria gained control of Hungary in 1526, it acquired Croatia as well. In 1867, Croatia became a part of the newly formed Austro-Hungarian Empire. Many Croats, however, supported the idea of union with other South Slavic peoples in an independent state of their own.

With the breakup of the Austro-Hungarian Empire in 1918, at the end of World War I, Croatia became part of the new Kingdom of Serbs, Croats, and Slovenes. The country was renamed Kingdom of Yugoslavia in 1929. Serbian attempts to dominate the other nationalities and Croatia's resistance to this weakened the new country. In 1941, during World War II, Nazi Germany invaded and occupied Yugoslavia. A separate Croatian state was created under German control.

The Communists came to power in 1945 under Tito (Josip Broz), who established a federal system based on ethnic republics. After Tito's death in 1980, the complex arrangement of federal and republic governments and Communist parties proved increasingly unworkable. The years after 1989 saw the fall of Communist regimes in Eastern Europe and the Soviet Union. Yugoslavia was also caught up in the rising tide of nationalism. But when Croatia declared its independence in 1991, Serbia sent in Yugoslav federal military forces. In 1992, after many thousands had been killed and wounded, Croatian independence was recognized by Serbia. Croatia was admitted to the United Nations the same year.

The Croatian government consists of an elected parliament, called the Sabor; a prime minister who heads the government; and a president who is head of state. Franjo Tudjman served as president from independence until his death in 1999. Stipe Mesic was elected to succeed him in 2000.

JOSEPH F. ZACEK
State University of New York at Albany

FACTS and figures

REPUBLIC OF CROATIA is the official name of the country.

LOCATION: Southeastern Europe.

AREA: 21,829 sq mi (56,537 km²).

POPULATION: 4,300,000 (estimate).

CAPITAL AND LARGEST CITY: Zagreb.

MAJOR LANGUAGE: Serbo-Croatian.

MAJOR RELIGIOUS GROUP: Roman Catholic.

GOVERNMENT: Republic. **Head of state**—president. **Head of government**—prime minister. **Legislature**—parliament (Sabor), made up of the House of Counties and the House of Representatives.

CHIEF PRODUCTS: Agricultural—corn, wheat, and other grains, sugar beets, potatoes, fruits. **Manufactured**—aluminum, machine tools, petroleum products, chemicals, cement, lumber, paper, textiles. **Mineral**—bauxite (aluminum ore), brown coal, iron ore, copper, petroleum.

MONETARY UNIT: Kuna (1 kuna = 100 para).

CROCHETING

Crocheting is a form of needlework that is done with a hooked needle. It produces a fabric of interlocked looped stitches. Its name comes from the French word *crochet,* meaning "hook." All crochet patterns are based on three stitches—chain, single crochet, and double crochet. Crocheting instructions are available wherever yarn is sold. This article shows you how to do the basic stitches and how to increase and decrease so that you can shape your crochet work according to instructions in a pattern.

To Begin

1. Make a slip loop. Notice that the short end of the yarn is in the left hand and the ball end in the right (Diagram 1a).
2. Slip the hook through the loop and pull the yarn until the loop fits snugly around the hook (Diagram 1b).
3. Weave the ball end of the yarn between the fingers of the left hand, passing it over the back of the forefinger (Diagram 1c).
4. Adjust until the fingers of the left hand just reach the hook with no slack in the yarn. The hook is held in the right hand as you would hold a pencil (Diagram 1d). Yarn for each new loop is always picked up from where it lies over the forefinger of the left hand.

1a

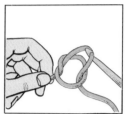

1b

1c

1d

Chain Stitch

1. Hold the starting tail between the thumb and forefinger of the left hand. Pass the hook under the yarn (Diagram 2a).
2. With a scooping motion, draw the yarn through the loop on the hook (Diagram 2b).

Make loops just loose enough so that the hook can be inserted through them later in making new stitches. For your practice piece, make 21 chain stitches.

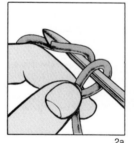

2a

2b

Single Crochet Stitch

In England this is the double crochet stitch.
1. Insert the hook from the front under the chain (Diagram 3a).
2. Scoop up a loop and draw it through the chain, making 2 loops on the hook (Diagram 3b).
3. Scoop up another loop and draw it through both loops, completing a single crochet.
4. Finish the row in the same way. You now have 20 single crochets.
5. Chain 1 and turn the work around so that the other side is facing you. Insert the hook in

3a

3b

the opening after the first stitch of the previous row, and make a single crochet. Continue across the row.

Double Crochet Stitch

In England this is called the treble stitch.

Make 3 extra chain stitches at the end of your sampler to allow room for turning. This is called making stitches to turn, or making the turning chain.

4a   4b

4c   4d

1. *First row:* Loop yarn on the hook. Then insert it under the two top threads in the opening after the first stitch in the last row. This is 4 stitches behind the needle (Diagram 4a).

2. Loop the yarn around the needle again, and draw it back through the stitch—3 loops on hook (Diagram 4b).

3. Loop the yarn over the hook and draw it through the first 2 loops, yarn over again, and through the last 2 loops (Diagram 4c), completing the double crochet—1 loop left on hook (Diagram 4d).

Repeat across the row, making 20 stitches, including the turning chain, which counts as the first stitch.

All Following Rows: Chain 3 stitches, but skip the first double crochet in the previous row and double crochet across, making the last stitch into the top of the turning chain of the previous row.

5a   5b

Decreasing

With any of the above stitches, decreasing consists of combining 2 stitches by completing them as if they were one stitch. Bring any stitch, whether it is single, double, or treble, to the point where there are just two loops on the hook. Then make the next stitch and bring it to the same point (Diagram 5a). Next, pull a loop through all loops at once (Diagram 5b). More than two stitches can be combined into one in the same way to make cluster stitches.

Increasing

To increase, simply make another stitch in the same opening in which you have just made the previous stitch.

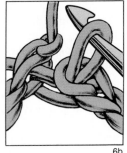

6a   6b

Slip Stitch. (In England this is called the single crochet stitch.) This is a joining stitch, and it is never used alone. Insert the hook where the join is to be made and draw up a loop, pulling it through the stitch and the loop on the hook in one continuous motion (Diagrams 6a and 6b).

Almost any yarn or thread can be crocheted. Fine cotton thread is used for delicate lace; heavier yarns are used for sweaters or for blankets.

ROXA WRIGHT
Contributing Editor
Woman's Day Magazine

American politician and adventurer Davy Crockett is best known for his tall tales of frontier life and for his heroic death at the Alamo in 1836.

CROCKETT, DAVID (DAVY) (1786–1836)

Davy Crockett was one of the United States' most famous frontiersmen and folk heroes. The story of his life is so mixed with legend that it is difficult to know where fact begins and fiction ends. But his life symbolizes the hardy American pioneer's fight for the rights of all people to liberty and opportunity.

Crockett was born in the backwoods of Tennessee on August 17, 1786. He had only five years of schooling before he ran away from home at the age of 13. After a few years of roaming, Davy returned home and went to work. With some extra money he earned, he bought a rifle. His skill as a hunter soon became legendary.

In 1806, Davy married Polly Finley (or Findlay), borrowed $15, and settled down as a farmer. Although he was a good hunter, he was a bad farmer. During the next nine years, he often depended on his rifle to keep his family well fed.

In 1815, Polly died. Davy married again. He was appointed a judge, elected to the Tennessee legislature, and eventually elected to Congress three times. Crockett delighted voters with fanciful accounts of his hunting skill. One story was about a raccoon in a tree. The animal, recognizing the great Crockett, cried, ''You needn't take no further trouble, for I may as well come down without another word.'' Crockett was easy to recognize in Washington, D.C., for he often wore frontier clothing.

Crockett eventually was defeated for re-election because of his opposition to President Andrew Jackson. Disappointed, Crockett decided to move west, so he and four companions set out to explore Texas. In February, 1836, he arrived in San Antonio. Texas was then in revolt against Mexican rule, and Crockett joined the fight. The Texans were barricaded in the Alamo, an old Catholic mission church. On March 6, 1836, more than 5,000 Mexican soldiers stormed the Alamo. Crockett—who used his rifle as a club when he ran out of ammunition—and the other Americans in the Alamo were killed.

MARY LEE SPENCE
University of Illinois at Urbana-Champaign

CROCODILES AND ALLIGATORS

Crocodiles and alligators are reptiles, a major class of animals that also includes the snakes, lizards, and turtles. All the living reptiles are descended from animals that roamed the earth about 250,000,000 years ago. Today some 25 species of reptiles belong to a group called the crocodilians. It includes the caymans and gavials, as well as the more familiar crocodiles and alligators.

All crocodilians look much alike. They have long tails and large jaws. Their skin, or hide, consists of many small bony plates and scales that are like hard leather. Despite their similarities, however, there are ways of telling one kind of crocodilian from another. The snout of the true crocodile is long and tapering, and the head has an almost triangular shape. In addition, the teeth of this animal meet in such a way that it appears to be grinning. The snout of the alligator is broad and rounded, as is that of the cayman. The gavial's snout is extremely long and thin.

Crocodilians spend their lives in or close to water. Most of them frequent freshwater lakes, rivers, or swamps, but some are found in coastal waters. They are all good swimmers. They swim with twisting strokes of their powerful tail. The legs are held close to the body. On land they run only for short stretches. Sometimes they travel overland to get from one waterway to another. They also leave the water to sun, to rest, and to wait for prey.

Most crocodilians are found in the tropics. But some inhabit the warm, moist regions of the temperate zones. Various species of the true crocodiles live in parts of North and South America, Australia, Africa, and Asia. Except for one alligator native to a small area of eastern China, the alligators are restricted to the Americas. They frequent the coastal areas of the southern United States, the West Indies, Central America, Colombia, and Ecuador. Caymans are found in South America, mostly in the rivers of eastern Brazil. The gavials live only in India and parts of southeastern Asia.

The crocodilians are egg-laying animals. The number of eggs in one clutch varies from 20 to 90, depending on the species and the crocodilian's size. The eggs of most crocodilians are long, white, and shiny and have a hard, thick shell. Some crocodilians lay their clutch of eggs in a hole scooped out of a stream or riverbank. Others make a nest of plant materials in which they deposit their eggs.

On hatching, the young feed on fishes, water insects, and shellfish. The mother alligator is one of the few reptiles that guard their offspring. But the young soon leave the nest and go off on their own.

Adult crocodilians feed on fishes, birds, or almost any other animal they can catch—including their own relatives. Sometimes a crocodilian waits just below the surface to snap up a duck, muskrat, or other water animal. At other times a crocodilian uses its powerful tail to knock its prey from a stream bank into the water. The crocodilian also waits near a watering hole to seize an animal that comes to drink. It has been known to attack pet dogs and cats, and with its strong jaws a crocodilian can even grip animals as large as deer and cattle. Once the prey is in the water, the crocodilian—twisting and turning—drags it beneath the surface to drown. Some crocodilians attack people, and all are dangerous when cornered or wounded.

The crocodilian is well adapted for swimming or floating at the water's surface. Eyes, ears, and nostrils are on the top of the head and snout; they remain above the waterline while the crocodilian floats, with the eyes acting as periscopes. Although its jaws are not watertight, its throat can be blocked off by a valve of flesh. This keeps water from flowing down the throat when the crocodilian is submerged. An air passage goes from the nostrils to an opening behind the throat valve. The nostrils also have valves that close when the

Strong jaws and a mouthful of sharp teeth make these Nile crocodiles one of the fiercest animals in their habitat. They will eat fish, turtles, birds, and even large mammals such as deer and cattle.

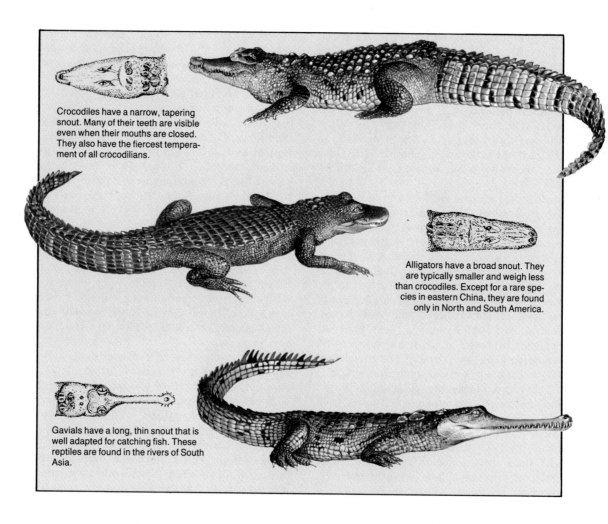

Crocodiles have a narrow, tapering snout. Many of their teeth are visible even when their mouths are closed. They also have the fiercest temperament of all crocodilians.

Alligators have a broad snout. They are typically smaller and weigh less than crocodiles. Except for a rare species in eastern China, they are found only in North and South America.

Gavials have a long, thin snout that is well adapted for catching fish. These reptiles are found in the rivers of South Asia.

crocodilian dives. It is reported that crocodilians can stay underwater for at least two hours and perhaps as long as five hours. Their bodies automatically direct the supply of oxygen to the important organs and tissues.

As a group, crocodilians are fairly long-lived. Ages of 20 or 30 years for those in captivity are not uncommon. Alligators are less active than their crocodile cousins and tend to live longer. The oldest alligators on record have lived more than 50 years.

The crocodilians are also among the heaviest reptiles. An adult American alligator weighs about 500 pounds (227 kilograms). An American crocodile was reported to weigh about 1,350 pounds (612 kilograms).

Crocodilians make all kinds of booming, barking, croaking, and grunting noises. But there are times when they remain silent. If there is a long period of hot, dry weather, the crocodilian buries itself deep in the mud. There the animal goes into a state of estivation (deep summer sleep). If the weather becomes too cold, the crocodilian goes into hibernation (deep winter sleep). During such periods its bodily processes slow down until the animal is barely alive.

The crocodilians have some value for people and even other animals. The American alligator clears plants out of waterways, making a better habitat for fish and waterfowl. In many regions crocodilian flesh is eaten. The hides are used to make shoes and other leather articles. This practice has brought these reptiles close to extinction in some places. As a result, some governments have passed laws to protect the crocodilians.

WILL BARKER
Author, *Familiar Reptiles
and Amphibians of America*

CROMWELL, OLIVER (1599–1658)

For one short period in history, England had no king or queen. After the English Civil War (1642–49), the nation was governed by a commoner. He was Oliver Cromwell, who was given the title Lord Protector.

Cromwell was born in Huntingdon, England, on April 25, 1599. He attended Cambridge University and was deeply influenced by the Puritans, who sought to purify or reform the Church of England.

In 1628 and again in 1640, Cromwell was elected to Parliament, where he joined with members who opposed the political and religious policies of King Charles I. The King wished to rule without interference and quarreled bitterly with Parliament. In 1642, civil war broke out between the followers of the King and those who supported Parliament. The war ended with Charles's defeat and his execution in 1649.

Although he had no training as a soldier, Cromwell had proved himself a brilliant general during the civil war. He played a prominent role in the trial that led to the execution of the King on a charge of treason. After Charles's death, Cromwell became a leader of the Commonwealth, as the English republic was called. In 1653 he was named Lord Protector and ruled with the power of a king, though he refused a crown. He built a strong army and navy and made England an important power. Cromwell, too, had difficulties with Parliament. After one dispute he stormed into the chamber with his soldiers and had the members of Parliament forcibly removed.

Cromwell was often harsh in carrying out what he believed was God's work. When rebellions broke out in Scotland and Ireland, he suppressed them cruelly. But, for his time, Cromwell allowed considerable religious freedom. He permitted the Jews, who had been expelled centuries before, to return to England. He was a simple and direct man. To the artist who painted his portrait he said: ". . . paint my picture truly like me . . . pimples, warts, and everything. . . ."

Cromwell died on September 3, 1658. His son, Richard, succeeded him as Lord Protector. But Richard was a weak ruler. In 1660 the son of Charles I was recalled from exile and crowned King Charles II. The monarchy was restored, but never again would it be as strong as it was before Oliver Cromwell.

Reviewed by ANTONIA FRASER
Author, *Cromwell: The Lord Protector*

See also ENGLAND, HISTORY OF.

CRONKITE, WALTER.   See JOURNALISM (Profiles).
CROOKES, SIR WILLIAM.   See ELECTRONICS.

CROQUET

Croquet is a lawn game that everyone, young and old, can play. It can be played by up to six opponents or by teams of two or three players each. The players use mallets to knock balls through a series of wickets on a grass court.

The name "croquet" is thought to have come from an old French word, *croche*, meaning "shepherd's crook," or from the Irish word *cluiche*, meaning "play." Versions of the game were played in both France and Ireland before reaching England (and soon after, America) around 1850.

In the United States the game of croquet is most often played on lawns or any level, grassy plot. The court can be of any size up to 50 by 100 feet (15 by 30 meters). Nine 5-inch (13-centimeter)- wide bent-wire wickets and two stakes are set into the grass in the shape of a squared-off figure eight. The equipment includes six colored wooden or plastic balls and mallets striped to match.

The object of the game is to hit a ball through the nine wickets in correct order. When individuals play, the first player to hit the home stake wins the game. When teams play, all members of a team must touch the home stake in order for the team to win.

Croquet is also played as a sport, and tournaments are often held. The sport of croquet uses only six wickets, which are narrower than those used for the game. The balls are larger and only one finishing stake is used.

Reviewed by JACK R. OSBORN
President, U.S. Croquet Association

Rules for a popular backyard version of croquet follow.

The game pictured here is a popular backyard version of American croquet. British croquet and tournament croquet have different rules.

A croquet court can be adapted to almost any backyard. An average court might be 88 feet long by 38 feet wide. On such a court there would be 88 feet between the posts, and about 6 feet between the posts and wicket 1 and another 6 feet between wickets 1 and 2. Wicket 3 should be 16 feet forward and 19 feet to the right of number 2, and there should be 32 feet between wickets 2 and 4. Wickets 5 through 9 are placed in symmetry with 1 through 4, as shown. All of these measurements can be adjusted proportionally to any length court.

Up to six players can play. The order of play is determined by the order of colors on the starting post, the top color going first. To begin play, the ball must be placed one third of the distance from the starting post to the first wicket. The ball must be struck with the mallet, not pushed. Player Yellow is shown taking his first turn.

The ball must first move through wickets 1–7; hit the turning post; then move through wickets 7, 6, 8, 4, 9, 2, and 1; and finally, hit the finishing post, or home stake. The first player to accomplish this wins the game. Player Blue and Player Red have already hit the turning post and have passed through wicket 8 on their return play toward the finishing post.

A player receives an extra shot for passing through a wicket. Player Black is measuring whether or not her ball passed through wicket 3 by laying her mallet against the side of the wicket from which the ball was struck. If the handle of the mallet does not touch the ball, then she has cleared the wicket and can take her second shot. A player who passes through two wickets at once receives two extra shots.

If Player Yellow passes through wickets 1 and 2 with his opening shot, he will have two turns to move toward and pass through wicket 3. If he then passes through wicket 3, he will have one shot to move toward wicket 4.

A player who strikes (roquets) another ball receives two extra shots. There are three choices for playing the shots: (1) placing one's ball against the other ball, holding a foot down on one's own ball to hold it in place, and driving the other ball away (Player Red has just done this to Player Blue); (2) hitting only one's own ball; or (3) hitting both balls together. Once a player roquets a ball, that player is "dead" on that ball and cannot hit it again until after making another wicket or hitting a stake.

If a player fails to pass through a wicket or hit another ball, that player's turn is over.

After going through the last wicket, but before hitting the home stake, a player may become a rover. If teams play, the rover can assist a partner and keep the players of the opposing team from getting to the home stake.

CROSSWORD PUZZLES

Word games known as crossword puzzles are among the most popular indoor pastimes in the United States. They appear in almost every newspaper and in many magazines. Different kinds of crossword puzzles are also popular in European countries such as England, France, Spain, Italy, Russia, and the other republics that made up the Soviet Union.

A crossword puzzle consists of a diagram of squares, along with a list of definitions or clues. The solver must guess the words that the clues define and fill them in on the diagram. Words run both across and down on the diagram. Here is an example of a very small crossword puzzle:

ACROSS
1. Garfield of comics
4. Ancient language
6. Opposite of out
7. Exist
8. Made a lion less ferocious
10. Allow or permit

DOWN
1. The Erie or the Panama
2. "Casey ___ the Bat"
3. World's highest land
4. Ignited
5. A boy in *Little Men*
9. "Take ___ Out to the Ball Game"

Game." If you are familiar with this song, you know that the missing word is "Me." Write the letters "M" and "E" in the correct squares. Now you have a start on 10 Across. The definition is "Allow or permit." Since you already have the middle letter, "E," you can probably guess that the answer is "Let."

The hardest word in this puzzle is 3 Down, which is defined as "World's highest land." Even if you do not know that it is Tibet, the answer might come to you when you fill in the crossing words. That is why many people feel that crossword puzzles are educational.

Usually, the answers to a puzzle are printed in the back of the newspaper or magazine or are published on a later day. This is how the answer to the above puzzle would look:

The people who construct, or make up, crossword puzzles must obey many rules. For example, the black squares in the diagram must be diagonally symmetrical. In other words, if a black square is placed in the upper left corner, another one must appear in the bottom right corner.

The constructor of the puzzle then thinks of the words that will go into the diagram. All of them must make sense, and every letter in an Across word must also be part of a Down word. Finally, the constructor of the puzzle creates the clue for each word. Numbers are placed in the diagram that correspond to each numbered clue. In the above puzzle, for example, the clue for 1 Across is "Garfield of comics." The answer will begin in the square numbered 1 and continue across for three squares, with each square containing one letter. The clue for 1 Down is "The Erie or the Panama." This answer will also begin in the square numbered 1 but will continue down the diagram for five squares.

The best way to solve a crossword puzzle is to look at all the clues before you start. Then begin by answering one that you are sure you know. For instance, the clue for 9 Down in the above puzzle is "Take __ Out to the Ball

▶HISTORY

Throughout history many people, including the ancient Egyptians and Greeks, created word games using blank diagrams. But the first modern crossword puzzle was invented by Arthur Wynne in 1913. He was an editor of the New York *World* Sunday magazine and created the puzzle to include on a page called "Fun."

Many readers liked Wynne's puzzle so much that they begged for more. Others sent their own crossword puzzles to him. Crossword puzzles became so popular that an organization, the Amateur Crossword Puzzle League of America, was founded. In 1924 the league and Margaret Petherbridge (later Farrar), who had worked with Wynne, created all the rules for construction of the puzzles. The first crossword puzzle book was published the same year.

In the years since their creation, crossword puzzles have changed and expanded. Entries of two or more words are now allowed. Puns and anagrams, diagramless puzzles, and crosswords containing quotations have appeared. Clues have become more original and challenging. For example, "nest" would no longer be defined simply as "Bird's home."

Instead, the clue might be "Nutcracker's suite" or "Raven's haven."

One problem with crossword puzzles will always remain. In order to make the puzzles work out, constructors sometimes use unusual little words, such as "esne" (feudal serf), "anoa" (wild ox), or "erne" (sea eagle). Such words are called "crosswordese." Experienced puzzle solvers recognize them and fill them in easily, but newcomers are often stumped. However, the rewards of solving the puzzles far outweigh this difficulty. That is why so many people continue to take pencils in hand and try to solve crossword puzzles.

EUGENE T. MALESKA
Puzzle Editor, *The New York Times*
Author, *Across and Down: Inside the Crossword Puzzle World*

CROUP. See DISEASES (Descriptions of Some Diseases).

CRUSADES

One November day in the year 1095 a large crowd gathered on an open field outside the French town of Clermont. Nobles, knights, and many common people stood listening to the words of Pope Urban II, who spoke to them from a platform high above the gathering. Pope Urban urged the crowd to arm and drive out the "wicked race" of Turks, who occupied the Christian lands of the East. Moved by the Pope's words, the crowd vowed that they would march to the East and battle the Muslims.

Thus began the first of a long series of expeditions known as the **Crusades**—wars in the name of Christianity. The "True Cross," made of wood from the cross on which Christ was crucified, was the symbol of the Crusades. In the following years many groups of Western Christians from France, Germany, Italy, and England set out for the East. The lands for which the Crusaders fought are now the countries of Israel, Turkey, Syria, Lebanon, Jordan, and Egypt.

At one time Christians had ruled all the Holy Land. Then the Muslims began their conquest of the East. By 1095 the Muslims held everything except the Christian Byzantine Empire, ruled by Emperor Alexius at Constantinople. Alexius was at war with the Muslim Turks and needed more troops. He appealed to Pope Urban to urge Christians in western Europe to serve in his army.

Europeans were interested in the Holy Land because they wished to visit the places where Jesus had walked the earth. Journeys to such holy sites are called **pilgrimages.** For years the Muslims had permitted Christian pilgrims to come and go freely, but recently returning pilgrims had told of being mistreated by the Turks.

Religion was not the only reason to go on the Crusades. Many people, having heard of the East's great wealth, hoped to make their fortunes there. And some, no doubt, went for the adventure.

▶**THE FIRST CRUSADE**

The First Crusade, begun in 1096, was a pilgrimage as well as a military expedition. The first to set out were a large group of common people, led by the popular preacher Peter the Hermit. These people were of all sorts—unarmed men, priests, and even women. Few had horses, so they went on foot. They had scarcely any supplies or money, so they had to depend on whatever they could get as they went along.

By the time they reached the outskirts of Constantinople, they were a ragged, sorry-looking crowd. Emperor Alexius was disappointed. He had asked for fighting men and instead had gotten a crowd of ragged, hungry pilgrims. The Byzantine Emperor gave them supplies and transported them across the water to Asia Minor. Then this strange crowd of pilgrims foolishly attacked the Turks, and the Turks destroyed almost all of them.

Bands of knights also began to arrive at Constantinople in the summer of 1096. They too created a problem for Alexius. He had wanted men from Europe to come and fight under him. Instead armies came with their own leaders. The Byzantines suspected that some of the Western nobles had their eyes on the great wealth of Constantinople and even on the Emperor's throne. Alexius, therefore, did not allow the armies from the West to stay within the walled city. Yet in spite of such mistrust, Alexius gave the Crusaders supplies and guides to help them on their way.

This 15th-century Flemish painting shows the fall of Jerusalem to the Crusaders in 1099. Jerusalem represented the most important goal of the European Crusaders—to recapture the Holy Land from the "wicked race" of non-Christian Turks who occupied it.

The Crusaders faced many hardships as they marched into Asia. They crossed deserts and mountains. Many of their horses died, and they loaded their baggage on goats, dogs, and even hogs. Tents rotted and wore out, and food and water ran short. The Westerners tried eating all sorts of fruits and plants that they found along the way. This was how they discovered sugarcane, a plant not known in Europe.

In spite of the hardships and even though the Muslims outnumbered them, the Crusaders won victories because the Muslims were badly divided among themselves. In 1099 the Crusaders finally took Jerusalem. The Europeans displayed great courage and skill in the bloody battle for Jerusalem. They also showed a fierce and greedy spirit once they had won the city, killing many of the people and looting.

The Crusaders' States in the East

The Crusade leaders divided the conquered lands into states for themselves, one of the most important being the Kingdom of Jerusalem. Since the Crusaders were so few in number, they wanted other Christians to come and settle these newly won lands.

The rulers of the Crusader states collected tribute from the conquered peoples, and they sometimes used brutal means to make them pay. Baldwin, the first to take the title of king of Jerusalem, learned one day that a rich tribe of Arab Bedouins—wandering herders—was camped across the Jordan River. The king took a band of his men, attacked the camp at night, killed most of the Bedouins, and carried away their treasure. After this, the nearby tribes and villages began sending "gifts" as tribute to Jerusalem. As long as the people paid tribute and did not revolt, the Crusade rulers did not greatly disturb them. They even allowed the Muslims to keep their own laws and religion.

Many of the Crusaders who stayed in the East adopted the customs and habits of the people they ruled, and some learned to speak Arabic. They furnished their houses in the Eastern fashion, sitting on carpets and cushions rather than chairs. They ate the food of the East. They found the loose-fitting clothing of the East more comfortable in the hot climate than the tight-fitting garments they had brought from Europe. Pilgrims newly arrived from the West were sometimes shocked at the sight of Christian settlers living so like their Muslim neighbors.

The Crusades began in France and later drew Christians from all over Europe. This illustration from a medieval manuscript shows French knights setting off on a Crusade.

▶LATER CRUSADES

The Crusaders ruled only a narrow strip of land, mostly along the Mediterranean coast. Muslim rulers made war from time to time, trying to win back some of this territory, and the strip grew still narrower. In 1187 a great and powerful Muslim leader, Saladin, recaptured Jerusalem.

News of these losses made people in Europe realize the seriousness of the Crusaders' plight. They launched the Second Crusade in 1145 and the Third Crusade in 1189. Kings and emperors took part in these Crusades.

One of the kings was Richard I of England, or Richard the Lion-Hearted. Richard was a fine figure of a crusading knight in armor, but his Third Crusade failed to recover the Holy City of Jerusalem. Richard took Cyprus and had Acre surrounded, but he never reached Jerusalem. He did keep Saladin from driving the Westerners out entirely, however, and they still held a few port cities.

The Capture of Constantinople

The West continued to send Crusades to the East, but one of these, the Fourth Crusade (1202–1204), never reached the Holy Land. Instead it conquered Constantinople. It seems strange that Crusaders should have conquered the Byzantine capital, since the First Crusade had come to help the Byzantines. But there had been trouble between the Western and Eastern Christians from the very beginning. Neither group really trusted the other, and the distrust grew. By the time of the Fourth Cru-

sade, the quarrel had grown so bitter that in 1204 the leaders of the Crusade decided to take Constantinople before going on to fight the Muslims. The city's great riches tempted them to try to get some of this wealth for themselves. Perhaps this is why the Fourth Crusade never reached the Holy Land.

The Children's Crusade

The Crusades stirred strange waves of excitement in the West. In 1212, bands of children and young people gathered in Germany and France and called for the reconquest of Jerusalem. They marched from town to town, and those in Germany followed a boy named Nicholas across the Alps into Italy. According to one old tale the children expected the sea to open up so that they could walk to the Holy Land. Since this did not happen, the bands broke up. Some returned home; some were sold as slaves. It is not known whether any of them reached the Holy Land.

There were a number of later Crusades. One of them had some success. Frederick II, Holy Roman Emperor, King of Sicily, and leader of the Sixth Crusade, managed to get the Muslims to recognize him as the ruler of Jerusalem in 1229. But the Muslims regained control of the city within 15 years. By 1291, Muslims had conquered the last small Crusader state. The movement begun by Pope Urban II in 1095 was ended.

KENNETH S. COOPER
George Peabody College

CRUSOE, ROBINSON. See DEFOE, DANIEL.

CRUSTACEANS

What do a shrimp on your dinner plate, a tiny water flea in a pond, a barnacle on the hull of a fishing boat, and a sow bug hiding under a log have in common? They are all crustaceans, a type of **invertebrate,** or animal without a backbone. Crustaceans are for the most part aquatic animals. They have an **exoskeleton** (hard outer covering), jointed legs, and a body made up of several segments.

About 25,000 different kinds, or species, of crustaceans are known. They range in size from the water flea, which is difficult to see without a magnifying glass, to the giant spider crab, which may grow to be 12 feet (3.7 meters) from the tip of one outstretched claw to the other.

Crustaceans can be found in all the oceans of the world. Many live along ocean shorelines. Some species are found in freshwater rivers, lakes, or ponds. A few kinds live on land.

Many kinds of environments can support at least one kind of crustacean. Krill, small shrimplike animals, can survive in the icy waters of the Antarctic Ocean. Other crustaceans live in the hot tropics—sometimes a crab can be found on top of a palm tree! Hot springs deep in the ocean are home to large white crabs with no eyes. Even a very salty environment, such as the Great Salt Lake in Utah where few animals can survive, is home to a crustacean called a brine shrimp.

▶KINDS OF CRUSTACEANS

The crustaceans best known to most people are those that are often used for food. These are the **decapods,** crustaceans with ten legs. They include the familiar shrimps, lobsters, crabs, and crayfish. Decapods can be recognized by their relatively large size, by one or more pairs of claws, by their large eyes, and by their antennae used for sensing their surroundings. Specific information on three kinds of decapods can be found in the separate articles SHRIMPS, LOBSTERS, and CRABS in this encyclopedia.

Less well known but very important to marine life are the many kinds of smaller crustaceans known as **copepods.** These animals are just barely visible to the eye—about ⅛ of an inch (0.25 centimeter) in length. They are found in very large numbers—as many as

Crustaceans have no internal skeleton as people do. Instead, they are protected and supported by a hard outer covering, called an exoskeleton. Three of the many kinds of crustaceans are goose barnacles (*above*), a Japanese spider crab (*top right*), and a krill, a tiny shrimp-like animal (*right*).

100,000 tiny animals in 10 square feet (about 1 square meter) of water. Copepods make up much of the **plankton** in the sea, the drifting and floating plants and animals that provide food for larger marine life.

If you turn over a rock or a log in your backyard, you may see flat, shiny **isopods** running about. Many of the animals in this crustacean group live on land.

▶PHYSICAL DESCRIPTION

The most noticeable characteristic of crustaceans is their exoskeleton, which is also called a **cuticle.** The exoskeleton is made of a hard material called **chitin** (pronounced KI-tin). It cannot stretch the way our own skin does when we grow, so a growing crustacean must shed its exoskeleton in a process called **molting.** Underneath is a new body covering that soon hardens into a stiff exoskeleton. A crustacean that has just molted is quite soft for a day or two and is likely to be injured or eaten by other animals.

Body Parts of a Crustacean

A crustacean's three main body parts are the head, thorax, and abdomen. Each of these parts is made up of several segments, and each includes at least one pair of jointed limbs, or **appendages.** The appendages can be used for sensing the environment, catching or chewing food, breathing, walking, swimming, or carrying eggs—depending on where they are located on the body.

If a crustacean loses one of its walking legs or claws, it can grow a new one. This process is called **regeneration.** The new limb starts to grow within a few days, and after several weeks a tiny, complete new leg or claw is formed. After two or three molts, the regenerated limb catches up to normal size.

▶**DIET**

Many crustaceans, both large and small, eat particles of plants, bacteria, or other animals. They scrape the particles off the ocean floor or trap them from the water. Crustaceans that spend most of their lives swimming use their appendages to filter water and extract food. This is called **filter feeding.** Barnacles are filter feeders. They extend their many legs to form a net that traps food.

Some crustaceans are predators—that is, they catch and eat other animals. Many lobsters and crabs are equipped with strong claws for cutting and crushing their prey. Their diet includes smaller crustaceans, worms, snails, and clams. Even some of the tiny copepods are predators. They have mouthparts that can be extended to grab onto smaller animals such as young fish or shrimps.

▶**LIFE CYCLE**

Crustaceans reproduce by laying eggs. The eggs may be shed directly into the water or carried by the female, either in a special sac called a **brood pouch** or attached to her swimming legs. The number and size of the eggs produced by the female depend on her size, her food supply, the temperature, and many other factors. A large crab or lobster may carry several thousand eggs on her swimming legs until they hatch several weeks or up to a year later, depending on the species.

Some kinds of young crustaceans, such as crayfish, hatch from their eggs looking very much like their parents. Most crustaceans, especially those in the ocean, hatch as a tiny larva, called a **nauplius.** It has just three pairs of appendages that beat the water to help it swim and a single eye in the center of its head. A nauplius does not resemble its parents; it will molt several times and change its appearance before it finally looks like the adults.

The life spans of crustaceans are varied. A fairy shrimp may live for only a few months in a seasonal pond. A giant lobster may live deep in the ocean for more than 40 years. The life span of most crustaceans is between one and three years if they can avoid being captured by predators.

▶**CRUSTACEANS AND PEOPLE**

Commercial fishing for crustaceans is an important industry. Shrimps, lobsters, crabs, and crayfish are the main types harvested for food. Scientists are also experimenting with ways to raise these animals in special ponds on aquatic farms.

Crustaceans can be harmful as well. Too many barnacles attached to the bottom of a boat can slow it down in the water. Some land-dwelling crabs and crayfish may burrow into the soil and prevent crops from taking root. They may also feed on the plant's tender young shoots. Some isopods bore, or dig holes, in wooden docks causing them to decay sooner than usual.

LINDA H. MANTEL
City College of New York
Co-editor, *The Biology of Crustacea*

See also CRABS; LOBSTERS; SHRIMPS; PLANKTON.

CRYSTALS

Crystals are solids whose atoms are arranged in a repeating, orderly pattern. Crystals can be found in computers and television sets, in jewelry, in the food we eat, and even in our own bodies. Some crystals, such as gems like diamonds and rubies, are large enough to be seen with the naked eye. Crystals of normal table salt can be seen under a magnifying glass. Most crystals, however, are so small that they can only be observed under a high-powered microscope.

▶ WHAT ARE CRYSTALS MADE OF?

Atoms, ions, and molecules are the basic building blocks of crystals. These building blocks fit together in an orderly way to form crystals with definite shapes.

A crystal can be made up of atoms of just one type—with each atom having the same size and shape. For example, a diamond crystal is made up entirely of carbon atoms.

Some crystals are made up of certain kinds of atoms, called **ions.** Ions are atoms or groups of atoms that carry a positive or negative electrical charge. At least two different kinds of ions, one positively charged and one negatively charged, are needed to form an ionic crystal. The attractive forces between the charged atoms hold the crystal together.

One of the simplest ionic crystals is common table salt, known chemically as sodium chloride. It is made up of negatively charged chloride ions and positively charged sodium ions. The ions are arranged in the orderly pattern shown on the following page. (Although spheres are used to represent the ions, atoms are not solid spheres. It is better to think of atoms as clouds of electrons. They are more like cotton balls than marbles.) The diagram is greatly magnified and shows just a small section of a single salt crystal. An average-size crystal in a kitchen salt shaker contains at least 5,000,000,000,000,000,000 (quintillion) ions. The individual ions are much too small to be seen through a microscope.

Crystals can also be made up of groups of atoms that are bonded together to form molecules. Each molecule acts as a building block in the crystal. For example, one kind of sugar (known chemically as glucose) is made up of glucose molecules. Each molecule contains atoms of carbon, hydrogen, and oxygen.

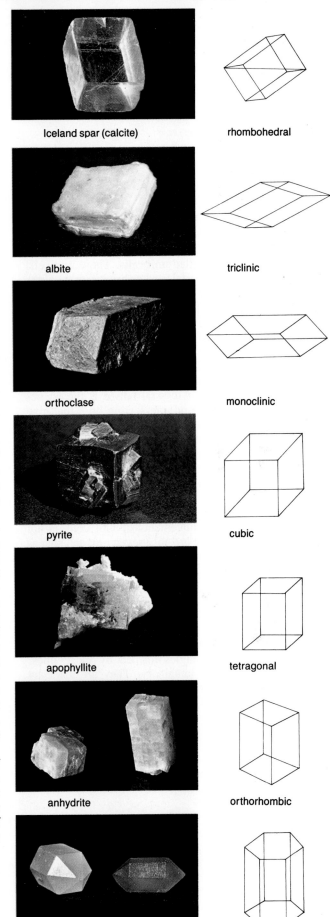

Iceland spar (calcite) — rhombohedral

albite — triclinic

orthoclase — monoclinic

pyrite — cubic

apophyllite — tetragonal

anhydrite — orthorhombic

quartz — hexagonal

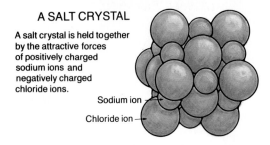

A SALT CRYSTAL

A salt crystal is held together by the attractive forces of positively charged sodium ions and negatively charged chloride ions.

Sodium ion
Chloride ion

Unit Cells

The individual atoms or molecules that make up a crystal are not packed together in a random way. They are arranged in small, orderly groups called **unit cells.** These unit cells make up the crystal, just as bricks are the units that make up a brick wall.

A unit cell in a sugar (glucose) crystal, for example, is made up of four glucose molecules. These four molecules fit together in a very specific way, such that all glucose unit cells are exactly the same. When unit cells are stacked together, they form what is called a **crystal lattice.** A crystal lattice is the framework of points and intersecting lines that give the crystal its shape. The crystal lattice is similar to the steel girders that make up the skeleton of a tall building.

The shape of the unit cell determines the **crystal system** to which the crystal belongs. To understand a crystal system, it is important to understand that the number of possible shapes and arrangements of unit cells is not limitless. There are only seven unit cell shapes that can be stacked together in an orderly and efficient way. These seven arrangements define the seven possible crystal systems.

▶TYPES OF CRYSTALS

In general, the unit cell is characterized by six features—the lengths of three lines and the size of three angles formed by these lines. (The lines are imaginary. They are made by connecting certain points within the unit cell.)

These six features are used to define the seven crystal systems. Their names are triclinic, monoclinic, orthorhombic, tetragonal, rhombohedral, hexagonal, and cubic. In the most general system, triclinic, the line lengths and angle sizes can be almost any number. The crystal systems become more and more orderly until they reach the cubic system, in which all three line lengths are equal and all three angles are right angles—exactly 90°.

Liquid Crystals

A few kinds of matter are more orderly than liquids and gases but are less orderly than true crystals. They flow like liquids, but, like crystals, their atoms and molecules are arranged in an orderly way. They are called liquid crystals.

Liquid crystals are transparent, allowing light to pass through as it would through a clear window. However, when an electric current is applied to the liquid crystals, the crystals are temporarily rearranged. Light cannot pass through them, and the areas receiving the current become visible to the eye.

*L*iquid *c*rystal *d*isplay (L.C.D.) watches and calculators make use of this property. The numerals in the L.C.D. contain liquid crystals. Electronic circuits in the watch or calculator send electric currents into some numerals but not into others, making it possible to read the time or numbers on display.

Some liquid crystals also respond to heat. They show different colors at different temperatures. They are used in some thermometers and can also be used to detect certain diseases. The crystals are spread out to coat a large screen, which is placed next to a patient's body. The crystals are affected by the body's heat, so the screen becomes a kind of "map" of body temperatures. Areas that show as hot spots may indicate the presence of infections or tumors.

A GLUCOSE CRYSTAL

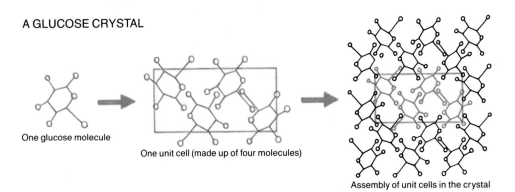

One glucose molecule

One unit cell (made up of four molecules)

Assembly of unit cells in the crystal

▶X-RAY DIFFRACTION

One of the most powerful techniques used in crystallographic studies is X-ray diffraction. Shortly after X rays were discovered in 1895 by Wilhelm Roentgen, scientists found that when a crystal is placed in an X-ray beam, the crystal bends the radiation. If the beam is directed at a radiation-sensitive screen, a pattern of spots will appear. This process of bending X rays is called diffraction.

The distance between the spots on the detector screen (or suitable X-ray film) can be used to determine the crystal lattice type and exact unit cell dimensions of a sample substance. Some of the spots on the screen will be very weak (low intensity), while others will be very strong (high intensity). The difference in intensity of the spots is caused by the arrangement of atoms and molecules in the crystal lattice.

A simple sugar crystal will produce a complex pattern of more than 2,000 spots, each spot having its own position and intensity. By measuring the spacings and intensities of all these spots, scientists can determine exactly what the atoms or molecules in the crystal look like and how they are arranged in the crystal.

Each crystalline substance has its own unique pattern. That pattern is like a set of fingerprints and can be used to identify the substance. This is especially useful in police work. For example, the identity of a suspected drug or poison can be determined when the exact unit cell dimensions and crystal lattice type are known. X-ray diffraction makes this possible.

GROWING YOUR OWN CRYSTALS

1. Add ¼ cup of Epsom salts to ¼ cup of boiling water. (Children should request help from an adult in handling the hot water.)

EPSOM SALTS

2. Stir well. Put the solution in a quiet place so it will not be disturbed. Allow it to sit overnight.

3. You will find one or more crystals floating on the water's surface. Carefully lift them out and display on colored paper.

▶HOW CRYSTALS GROW

In nature, crystals are formed, or grow, when materials and conditions are just right. This can happen in one of several ways. When a gas or liquid gets cold enough, it can crystallize. Ice crystals are formed when liquid water freezes. Snow crystals are formed from water vapor (a gas) in the air. Quartz and other minerals are formed when hot, molten volcanic rock cools and crystallizes.

Crystals can also grow from solutions. This happens when substances dissolved in a solution start connecting together in the orderly arrangement of a crystal. For example, seawater is a solution. Salt and other minerals washed from the land are dissolved in it. When salty seawater evaporates, crystals of salt are left behind.

To be perfect, crystals must grow slowly while the conditions remain just right. This does not always happen in nature. But in the controlled conditions of a laboratory, scientists can grow crystals that are much more perfect than most crystals found in nature. Some crystals are difficult to grow, but others are easy, as in the activity described above.

WILLIAM L. DUAX
President
American Crystallographic Association

See also DIAMONDS; GEMSTONES; MINERALS; ORES; QUARTZ; ROCKS.

X-RAY DIFFRACTION

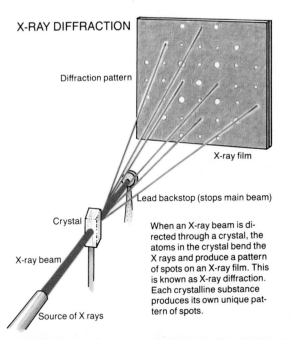

Diffraction pattern

X-ray film

Lead backstop (stops main beam)

Crystal

X-ray beam

Source of X rays

When an X-ray beam is directed through a crystal, the atoms in the crystal bend the X rays and produce a pattern of spots on an X-ray film. This is known as X-ray diffraction. Each crystalline substance produces its own unique pattern of spots.

CUBA

Cuba is an island nation in the Caribbean Sea and the largest and most populous of the many islands of the Caribbean. It is a close neighbor of the United States, lying just about 90 miles (145 kilometers) from the southern tip of Florida. The republic of Cuba is, in fact, made up of one main large island surrounded by more than 1,600 small islands, islets, and keys.

Cuba was claimed for Spain by Christopher Columbus on his first voyage of discovery to America in 1492. He described the island as "the most beautiful land human eyes have ever seen."

Cuba remained a Spanish colony for some 400 years. Conquered and colonized in the 1500's, the island was important to Spanish trade and shipping for almost two hundred years. Cuba's struggle for independence spanned the years between 1868 and 1898 and ended in a joint Cuban-U.S. victory over Spain in 1898. Cuba became a republic in 1902 but remained partly dependent on the United States.

In the years following independence, both dictators and democrats came to power in Cuba. The country's political problems were made worse by corruption and violence. In 1959, revolutionaries led by Fidel Castro overthrew the government. The Castro government seized private land and property and began new programs to help the poor. Many members of the middle class fled the country, most settling in the United States. Under Castro, Cuba became the first Communist nation in the Americas. It developed close ties with the Soviet Union, an association that lasted until the Soviet Union fell apart in 1991.

▶ **PEOPLE**

Most of the original Indian population died within one hundred years of the Spanish conquest of the island. The majority of Cubans today are of Spanish and African ancestry. Cuba also has a smaller population of people made up of Chinese descent.

Language and Religion. The language of the country is Spanish. An estimated 40 percent of Cubans are Roman Catholic. In addition, many Cubans belong to one of the many Protestant denominations, including Baptists, Methodists, Presbyterians, and Quakers. A small Jewish community is located mainly in Havana. Many Cubans are devoted to *Santería*, a set of religious practices that combine Catholic religious beliefs and saints with African beliefs and deities.

Education, Libraries, and Museums. State-controlled education is free. Children attend kindergarten for one year, followed by six years of elementary school. They then have three years of

Left: Havana is Cuba's capital, largest city, and chief port. *Above left:* A schoolgirl from Havana. Most Cubans today are of Spanish and African ancestry.

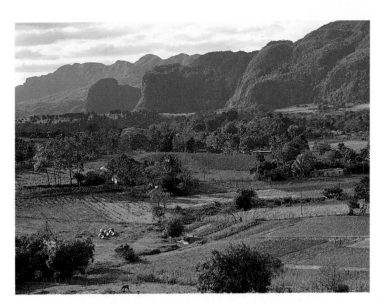

Fertile soil and rolling hills are ideal for growing crops in Pinar del Río, a province in western Cuba.

basic secondary school, which includes broad general education as well as pre-vocational or technical courses.

Afterward, students may elect three years of upper secondary education at one of Cuba's commercial, fine arts, agricultural, industrial, technical, and teacher-training institutes. Finally, students may choose to attend one of the many national universities. The largest of these, the University of Havana, was founded in 1728.

A large number of libraries and museums are distributed across the land. The two largest libraries are the José Martí National Library and the Literature and Linguistic Library, both in Havana. Among the most important museums in Havana are the National Fine Arts Museum, the National Museum of Music, the Museum of the Revolution, and the Ernest Hemingway House, former home of the famous American writer.

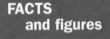

FACTS and figures

REPUBLIC OF CUBA (República de Cuba) is the official name of the country.

LOCATION: Caribbean Sea.

AREA: 44,218 sq mi (114,524 km²).

POPULATION: 11,300,000 (estimate).

CAPITAL AND LARGEST CITY: Havana.

MAJOR LANGUAGE: Spanish.

MAJOR RELIGIOUS GROUP: Christian (Roman Catholic).

GOVERNMENT: Communist republic. **Head of state and government**—president of the Council of State and the Council of Ministers. **Legislature**—National Assembly of People's Power.

CHIEF PRODUCTS: Agricultural—sugar, tobacco, coffee, rice, citrus fruits, potatoes, sweet potatoes, bananas, livestock. **Manufactured**—sugar and sugar by-products, tobacco products, refined petroleum, textiles, processed foods (including seafood), shoes, chemicals, paper and wood products, cement. **Mineral**—nickel, iron, chromium, manganese, copper, asphalt.

MONETARY UNIT: Cuban peso (1 peso = 100 centavos).

Food and Recreation. Traditional Cuban foods include pork dishes, rice with beans, and fried plantain (a kind of banana). Rum, beer, and coffee are popular beverages.

Baseball is a favorite pastime in Cuba. Other popular sports include basketball, boxing, swimming, and track.

▶ LAND

About 40 percent of Cuba's land is mountainous. The chief mountain ranges are the Sierra de los Órganos, in the western part of the country; the Sierra de Trinidad, in central Cuba; and the Sierra Maestra, in the east. The highest point in Cuba, Pico Turquino, rises to 6,542 feet (1,994 meters) above sea level and is located in the Sierra Maestra mountains. The rest of Cuba consists of plateaus, valleys, and gently rolling hills.

Cuba's most important river is the Cauto, which flows about 150 miles (240 kilometers) in southeastern Cuba but is navigable for only about 40 miles (65 kilometers). The long coastline is deeply indented and possesses many natural harbors.

Climate. Cuba has a semitropical climate with two distinct seasons—dry and rainy. During the dry season, which lasts from November until the end of April, temperatures average about 70°F (21°C). The rainy season lasts from May to October, during which the temperature averages about 81°F (27°C). Rainfall averages 54 inches (1,370 millimeters) a year. Cuba's climate is moderated by the cooling breezes of the trade winds.

Right: Workers harvest sugarcane in a field in Cienfuegos. Sugar has been Cuba's most important crop since Spanish colonial times. Cuba is one of the leading producers and exporters of sugar, which provides most of the country's income.

Below: Working entirely by hand, workers fill and roll cigars in a factory in Havana. Cuba is known the world over for its cigars, and their manufacture is an important source of foreign revenue.

Natural Resources. The most important mineral resources include nickel, iron, chromium, manganese, copper, and asphalt. Small amounts of petroleum have been discovered on the island.

▶ **ECONOMY**

Cuba is largely a producer of raw products, mostly in the form of agricultural and mineral goods. The economy in all its major aspects, including production and distribution, is state-operated. Cuba depends on sugar, minerals, and, most recently, tourism to provide needed revenue. Efforts to diversify Cuba's economy to avoid dependence on sugar have generally been difficult. Cuba's most pressing problems, however, are due to the collapse of the Soviet Union, its main trading partner and provider of economic aid, and continued hostility from the United States in the form of a trading ban on all goods.

Agriculture. Cuba's climate and fertile soils have made agriculture a mainstay of the economy. Sugar has been the island's most important crop since Spanish colonial times.

Cuba ranks among the world's leading producers and exporters of sugar, which provides most of the country's income.

Other important crops are tobacco, coffee, citrus fruits, rice, bananas, potatoes, and sweet potatoes.

Mining and Manufacturing. Cuba has one of the world's largest known deposits of nickel and is the fourth leading producer of this metal. It is one of the country's most important money earners.

In addition to sugar, other agricultural products, and minerals, Cuba produces manufactured items such as textiles, shoes, chemicals, and cement. The manufacture of cigars is an important source of foreign revenue. Other important industrial activities include oil refining and the production of fertilizers, paper and wood products, processed food, pharmaceuticals, and leather goods.

Tourism. With the collapse of the Soviet Union, Cuba sought to diversify its economy and find alternative sources of national income. For this, it turned to the tourist industry. In cooperation with foreign investors, mostly from Spain, Italy, Canada, and Mexico, Cuba expanded its tourist facilities and developed its beaches, mountain resorts, and nightlife.

▶ **MAJOR CITIES**

Havana is Cuba's capital, chief port, and largest city. One of the oldest cities in the New World, it was founded at its present site on the north coast of Cuba in 1519. Modern Havana, with a metropolitan population of more than 2 million, is the largest city in the Caribbean.

Cuba's second largest city, Santiago de Cuba, is an important manufacturing center. Other important cities include Camagüey, Holguín, Santa Clara, Cienfuegos, Matanzas, and Pinar del Río.

▶ **CULTURAL HERITAGE**

A number of Cubans have made contributions to the arts and to science. José Enrique Varona is considered Cuba's foremost philosopher. José Martí, a hero of Cuban independence, was both a poet and a political leader. Other well-known poets include Gertrudis Gómez de Avellaneda, José María de Heredia y Heredia, and Julián del Casal. Among the best-known writers of the 1900's are novelists Alejo Carpentier, Carlos Loveira, and Virgilio Piñera. Prominent Cuban painters include Amelia Peláez, Carlos Enríquez, and Wilfredo Lam. Notable musicians include Moisés Simón and Ernesto Lecuona. Alicia Alonso, a world-renowned ballerina, was the founder and long-time director of the National Ballet of Cuba.

▶ HISTORY AND GOVERNMENT

Cuba's first inhabitants included the Ciboney Indians, who settled in the coastal regions and the offshore islets and keys. The Arawak lived in the fertile uplands and high ground away from the coast, mostly in the central regions of the island.

Spanish Colonial Period. The conquest and colonization of Cuba was carried out by Spain during the early 1500's. Because Cuba had little gold, the Spanish went on to conquer and colonize other parts of the New World. Cuba served as a port of transit for troops, ships, and arms destined for the mainland and New World wealth destined for Spain.

The Spanish *flota*, or treasure fleet, stopped at Cuba twice a year to obtain supplies for its journey to and from Spain. The cultivation of sugar and tobacco began during the 1600's.

Coffee became important in the 1800's. As sugar and coffee production expanded, the demand for cheap labor increased. Between the 1700's and 1800's, many hundreds of thousands of black slaves were brought from Africa to work on the plantations.

Struggle for Independence. Efforts to gain independence from Spain began in 1868–78 (the Ten Years' War) and resumed in 1895–98 (the War for Independence). The principal leaders of the Cuban independence struggle were Carlos Manuel de Céspedes, Máximo Gómez, Antonio Maceo, and José Martí. Martí led the final struggle, which began in 1895 and involved the United States and Spain in a short war (the Spanish-American War) in 1898. After a four-year military occupation by the United States, Cuba obtained independence. However, an amendment to the Cuban Constitution of 1901 (the Platt Amendment), imposed by the United States, gave the U.S. government the right to intervene in Cuban internal affairs and establish a naval station in Guantánamo Bay. The Platt Amendment was abolished in 1934, but the United States retained permanent exclusive use of a naval base at Guantánamo.

The Cuban Republic. Cuba's sugar plantations made some Cubans rich but many more poor. United States corporations also profited from their investments in Cuba's agriculture, banking, manufacturing, and transportation. Many Cubans suffered from low wages, unemployment, and lack of

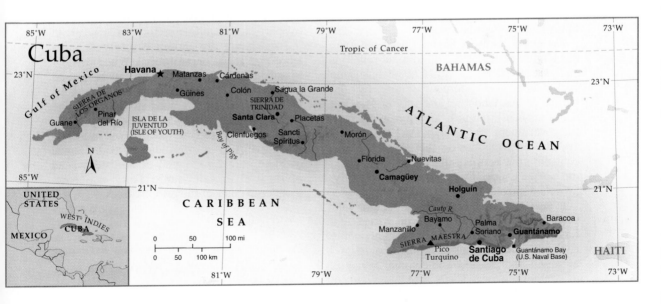

Pope John Paul II's visit to Cuba in 1998 did much to improve relations between the Catholic Church and the Cuban government.

schools, housing, and medical care.

Some of Cuba's leaders were self-seeking and tyrannical. Two became dictators—Gerardo Machado, who governed from 1925 to 1933; and Fulgencio Batista, who was in and out of power between 1933 and 1959. Yet Cuba had democratic governments between 1940 and 1952.

Cuba was in urgent need of reforms. Farmers and peasants needed land to work. Large numbers of workers needed full-time employment. Cubans demanded better schools, adequate housing, and minimum health care.

Castro Comes to Power. Batista was overthrown in 1959 by Fidel Castro, a young revolutionary who promised reforms. The new revolutionary government redistributed land among farmworkers. Housing projects were built and education and health care services were provided for the poor. The government nationalized industry and all foreign businesses. Land passed under state ownership, and the economy was regulated by the government. Under Castro, Cuba became a Communist country. It received economic and military assistance from the Soviet Union. Many Cubans fled the country.

Bay of Pigs and the Missile Crisis. In 1961 the United States broke diplomatic relations and cut off all trade with Cuba. That same year Cuban exile forces, trained by the United States, landed at the Bay of Pigs but failed in their attempt to overthrow the Castro government. In October 1962 the discovery of Soviet missiles on the island led to a confrontation between the United States and the Soviet Union. The crisis ended when the Soviets removed the missiles.

A Revolutionary Foreign Policy. Cuba supported revolutionary groups in Africa and Latin America. Cuban troops fought in the civil war in Angola, aided the Ethiopian government, and assisted anti-colonial struggles in southern Africa. These activities were an obstacle to better relations with the United States. The passage of the Torricelli Law (1992) and the Helms-Burton Law (1996) added new U.S. pressures against the government of Fidel Castro by making foreign investment and foreign trade with Cuba more difficult. The visit of Pope John Paul II in 1998 contributed to improvement of relations between the Catholic Church and the Cuban government. As a result of the Pope's visit, political prisoners were released. In 1999, the United States eased some restrictions, although the trading ban remained in place.

Cuba Today. Life for Cuba's poor improved after Castro came to power. Free education, modern medical care, and other social services became available. But food and consumer goods were often rationed or unavailable. Despite official restrictions on emigration, there have been periodic waves of departures. Tens of thousands of Cubans tried to reach the United States in small boats in 1994. The 1994 exodus was caused partly by the loss of Soviet aid, which greatly increased Cuba's economic difficulties.

Cuba's government is based on the constitution of 1976, which was amended in 1992 to allow direct, secret elections for the legislature. The Communist Party is the only political party, and candidates for 5-year terms in the legislature are chosen by party-affiliated labor and social organizations. When the legislature is not in session, laws can be passed by the Council of State, which is chosen by the legislature from among its members. The president of the Council of State appoints a Council of Ministers to run the government.

Fidel Castro is president of the Council of State and the Council of Ministers, head of the Cuban Communist Party, and commander in chief of the armed forces.

HUMBERTO PIÑERA
New York University
Revised and updated by LOUIS A. PÉREZ, JR.
Author, *Cuba: Between Reform and Revolution*

See also CASTRO, FIDEL; CUBAN MISSILE CRISIS; SPANISH-AMERICAN WAR.

CUBAN MISSILE CRISIS

The Cuban missile crisis of October 1962 was the most dangerous episode of the Cold War, a political struggle between the world's two great superpowers, the United States and the Soviet Union. The Cold War lasted from the end of World War II until the early 1990's. No battles were actually fought. But the Cuban missile crisis for the first time raised the possibility of nuclear war between the United States and the Soviet Union.

In the spring of 1962, Soviet leader Nikita S. Khrushchev—with the permission of the Cuban leader Fidel Castro—ordered nuclear missiles to be installed on the Caribbean island of Cuba, a mere 90 miles (145 kilometers) from the United States. The military buildup took place during the summer and autumn of 1962.

The Cuban missile crisis started on October 16, 1962, when U.S. president John F. Kennedy was informed that American intelligence had detected the presence of Soviet missiles in Cuba. The crisis, which lasted 13 days, consisted of two periods.

During the first period, from October 16 to 22, President Kennedy and his advisers discussed how to react to the presence of Soviet missiles in Cuba without informing the American public or other nations of the situation. The president's advisers made a number of recommendations, including a military attack on the missile sites. But Kennedy chose instead to establish a naval blockade around Cuba in order to halt any further deliveries of Soviet missiles to the island. On October 22 in a televised speech, the president informed the American public about the missiles and his decision.

During the second phase of the crisis, from October 22 to 28, millions of people throughout the world feared that a nuclear war between the two superpowers was inescapable. On October 24 the American blockade went into effect. Soviet ships approached the line of blockade, and for a time a U.S.-Soviet

clash on the seas seemed likely. Much to Kennedy's relief, however, the Soviet ships stopped before crossing the line of blockade and headed back toward the Soviet Union.

Ultimately, Kennedy and Khrushchev used diplomacy to end the crisis. Through an exchange of letters between the two men, a settlement was reached. The Soviet leader agreed to remove the nuclear weapons from Cuba, while Kennedy publicly pledged that the United States would not invade the island. Privately, Kennedy also pledged in due course to remove American missiles stationed in Turkey

Aerial photos taken over Cuba in 1962 showed evidence of Soviet missile erectors and launch stands. After the Cuban missile crisis ended, all the Soviet missile bases in Cuba were dismantled.

near the Soviet border. But this fact was not made known to the public.

The Cuban missile crisis changed Soviet-American relations. Both Kennedy and Khrushchev, sobered by the events of October 1962, moved to reduce tensions between the superpowers and to minimize the possibility of another dangerous confrontation. In 1963, Kennedy called for a more tolerant attitude toward the Soviet Union. Shortly afterward, the United States, the Soviet Union, and Great Britain signed the Limited Test Ban Treaty, designed to limit further nuclear testing.

MARK J. WHITE
Author, *The Cuban Missile Crisis*

CUBISM

Cubism was one of the most important art movements of the 1900's. Cubist artists transformed the way that typical subjects—people, places, and things—are presented in art by breaking them up into basic geometric shapes and patterns. Cubists also departed from traditional painting methods by depicting figures and objects from several different viewpoints at once. For example, a woman might be painted with three eyes in order to show her face from the front and the side at the same time. (This style of painting, in which subjects are distorted and difficult to recognize, is known as **abstract** art.)

Spanish artist Pablo Picasso and French artist Georges Braque invented many of cubism's characteristics. Between 1908 and 1914, these two artists worked closely together in France to create a new style of painting that went beyond realism. For centuries, artists had used perspective, a technique that gives a painting the appearance of depth, to render subjects as they appear in the real, three-dimensional world. Picasso and Braque, however, wanted to emphasize the flat, two-dimensional surface of the canvas. So they began dividing their subjects into flat surfaces, or planes. Their collaboration led to two phases of cubism: analytic and synthetic.

Analytic cubism began about 1910. During this phase, Picasso and Braque made paintings that were more about thought than emotion, using neutral colors such as black, brown, gray, and white rather than their usual vivid colors. They obscured their subjects in a puzzle of broken planes that seem to shift before one's eyes. In a typical analytic cubist work, such as Picasso's *Ma Jolie* (*Woman with a Zither or Guitar*, 1911–12), it is a challenge to find the subjects themselves. It takes a keen eye to piece together the musician's tri-

Pablo Picasso's *Woman with a Mandolin* (1914) has the flat shapes that are characteristic of cubism.

angular head at the top of the painting with her bent arm strumming just a fragment of the instrument at the painting's center.

Synthetic cubism emerged in 1912. Now Picasso and Braque's subjects are easier to identify because they appear as flatter, more colorful shapes. In Picasso's *Woman with a Mandolin* (1914), which has the same subject matter as *Ma Jolie*, the woman and instrument are more visible—even though she has two overlapping faces. During this phase, Picasso and Braque also glued cloth, newspaper, and other materials directly onto their canvases. This technique became known as **collage**, derived from the French verb *coller*, meaning "to glue."

By 1913, many cubist innovations were being tested by other artists. In Paris, French painters Fernand Léger and Robert Delaunay, Spanish-born artist Juan Gris, and Russian-born sculptor Alexander Archipenko made significant contributions to cubism. In Italy, a group of artists calling themselves futurists borrowed the shifting, broken shapes of analytic cubism to suggest the motion of machinery in their art. In Russia, an art movement led by Kazimir Malevich took cubism's abstraction of forms even further. These artists, who were known as suprematists, chose to paint only basic geometric shapes such as squares and circles.

Picasso and Braque's collaboration ended when Braque was called to fight in World War I (1914–18). But they and numerous other artists continued to devise new styles based on cubism into the second half of the 1900's. In fact, many cubist techniques are still used today, especially collage.

CHERI L. COFFIN
Family Programs, Department of Education
The Museum of Modern Art

CUB SCOUTS. See BOY SCOUTS.

CURIE, MARIE (1867-1934) AND PIERRE (1859-1906)

Until the end of the 1800's, chemistry and physics were treated almost as separate sciences. Gradually the barriers between these fields came down, through the work of scientists like Marie and Pierre Curie.

Marie Curie was born Marja Sklodowska in Warsaw, Poland, on November 7, 1867. At 15 she was graduated from high school with a medal for excellence. Because the family was far from rich, Marja went to work at 17 as a governess. By 1891 she had saved enough money to go to Paris. When she registered at the Sorbonne (part of the University of Paris), Marja changed her name to its French form, Marie.

Within two years Marie took the master's examination in physics and scored highest in the class. In 1894, she met the physicist who became her husband.

Pierre Curie, born on May 15, 1859, in Paris, France, showed an early talent for science. While in his 20's he discovered that an electric current could be produced by exerting pressure on quartz crystals. This was the beginning of a new field of research, piezoelectricity. Curie's Law is named after his later discovery about the relationship between magnetism and temperature.

In a year's time Pierre and Marie were married. They settled in a small apartment in Paris near the School of Physics and Chemistry, where they shared a laboratory. In the second year of their marriage their first daughter, Irène, was born. Though money was scarce, they hired a nursemaid to take care of the baby while Marie was at the laboratory. A second daughter, Eve, was born several years later.

Both Curies had become interested in the work of another French scientist, Antoine Henri Becquerel. In 1896 he had discovered that uranium gave off invisible radiations, and Marie wanted to find out what these radiations were.

Using a device invented by her husband, Madame Curie measured the radiations coming from pitchblende—an ore containing uranium. She discovered that there was far more radioactivity in the pitchblende than uranium alone could produce.

During the next few years the Curies made several important discoveries. They were first to prove that the atoms of some elements are continually breaking down, all by themselves. In breaking down, such elements give off radiations that can pass through many other materials. The Curies called these elements radioactive.

In their search for the hidden element in pitchblende, the Curies discovered not one but two new elements. The first was named polonium, in honor of Marie's native country. The second, a glowing element, was named radium.

In 1903 the Curies and Becquerel won the Nobel prize in physics for their discovery of radioactive elements. Madame Curie was the first woman ever to receive that honor. On April 19, 1906, the Curie research team came to a sudden end. Pierre was run over by a heavy cart and killed.

Marie continued with her research and in 1911 was awarded a second Nobel prize—this time in chemistry—for her discovery of radium and polonium. She was the first person to receive two Nobel awards in science.

Madame Curie was at work on the isolation of a new element when she died on July 4, 1934. After her death it was discovered that her body tissue had been poisoned by exposure to too much radioactivity.

The Curie daughters achieved their own honors. In 1935, Irène and her husband, Frédéric Joliot-Curie, were awarded the Nobel prize for their work with synthetic radioactive elements. Eve became a musician and author whose best-known book is the story of her famous mother.

BARBARA LAND
Formerly, Columbia University

Marie and Pierre Curie in their laboratory in 1896. Together they discovered the chemical element radium.

CURLING

Button, hog line, and bonspiel are some of the colorful terms used in the game of curling. Players slide heavy stones along a strip of ice toward a target called the **house**.

Curling is played by two **rinks** (teams) of four players each. The players alternate **delivering**, or sliding, the stones along a 138-foot (42-meter) course called the **sheet**. The object of the game is to get as many as possible of the team's eight stones closer to the **button**, the center of the house, than any of the opposing team's stones. When all 16 stones have been delivered, an **end** is complete. Eight or ten ends usually make a game.

Curling has been called the "roaring game" because of the sound the stones make sliding across the ice, which has been roughened by being sprinkled with water. Players known as **sweepers** use brooms to smooth the ice ahead of the stone to extend and guide its course. If a broom touches the stone itself, the stone is fouled and is removed from play.

The team captain, or **skip**, stands in the target area pointing with his broom to where the stone should be aimed and signaling the type of shot to be used. The skip decides if the stone should block an opponent's stone or knock one away from the button. Or he may want it to push another of his own team's stones closer to the button. The skip also directs the sweepers when to start and stop sweeping.

Curling is a game in which players slide stones down a strip of ice toward a target. Curlers use brooms to sweep a path ahead of a moving stone.

The stones are about 1 foot (30 centimeters) in diameter and have a maximum weight of 44 pounds (20 kilograms). The bottom curves inward so only a tiny outer rim touches the ice. Using its metal handles, the players put one of two turns on the stone when delivering it—an **inturn**, which is clockwise, or an **outturn**, which is counterclockwise. This gives the stone's path its "curl." Curling is known for good etiquette; opponents shake hands before and after a game and praise good shots made by one another.

Invented in Scotland more than 400 years ago, curling is a major winter sport in Canada and is popular in sections of the northern United States and in Europe. Teams play in tournaments called **bonspiels** held in many countries. The most important Canadian bonspiels are the Labatt Brier for men and the Scott Tournament of Hearts for women. The first world championship was held in 1959, and curling became an official Olympic sport at the 1998 Winter Games.

Reviewed by JAN BIERSACH
U.S. Women's Curling Association

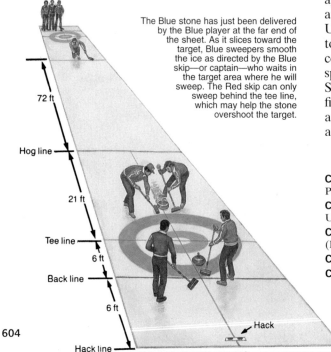

The Blue stone has just been delivered by the Blue player at the far end of the sheet. As it slices toward the target, Blue sweepers smooth the ice as directed by the Blue skip—or captain—who waits in the target area where he will sweep. The Red skip can only sweep behind the tee line, which may help the stone overshoot the target.

72 ft

Hog line

21 ft

Tee line

6 ft

Back line

6 ft

Hack

Hack line

14 ft

CYPRUS

The island nation of Cyprus is located in the northeastern corner of the Mediterranean Sea. It is so beautiful that the ancient Greeks believed that Aphrodite, their goddess of love and beauty, was born there.

▶THE PEOPLE

Cyprus has had close associations with Greece for most of its recorded history. But many Turks settled on Cyprus during the 300 years the island was ruled by Turkey. Strife between the island's Greek- and Turkish-speaking inhabitants led to the division of Cyprus into separate Greek and Turkish areas in 1974.

About 80 percent of all Cypriots speak Greek; most of the remainder speak Turkish. Greek Cypriots generally are Christians who belong to the Greek Orthodox Church in Cyprus. Turkish Cypriots are predominantly Muslims.

According to legend the first Greeks arrived several hundred years before the Trojan War —about the 12th century B.C. The Turks came in the 16th century A.D. Although the island's inhabitants differ in their languages and religions, they are much alike in appearance and customs. The houses, clothes, and food of Greek-speaking Cypriots are much the same as those of their Turkish-speaking neighbors.

Before Turkish troops invaded Cyprus in 1974, Greek and Turkish Cypriots lived throughout the island. After the invasion about 200,000 Greek Cypriots fled the northeastern, Turkish-occupied part of the island. Smaller numbers of Turkish Cypriots resettled in the northeast, where Turks from Turkey also settled.

▶THE LAND

The island of Cyprus is about 65 kilometers (40 miles) south of Turkey. Mountains border

Marathasa Valley, famous for its fruit orchards and vegetable farms, is in the Troodos Mountains of southwestern Cyprus, not far from Mount Olympus.

both the northern and southern coasts of the island. The Troodos Mountains in the south reach elevations of over 1,800 meters (6,000 feet). But they are less rugged than the lower Kyrenia Mountains in the north. The mountains receive plenty of rain and snow. For this reason their higher slopes are covered with forests of pine and cedar. Most of the island's people live on the plain between the mountains. Because the plain is dry except after heavy rains, settlements generally are located where irrigation water is available from mountain streams or underground wells.

The climate of Cyprus, like that of other Mediterranean areas, is mild, with rainy winters and hot, dry summers. In the mountains much of the precipitation falls in the form of snow.

▶THE ECONOMY

Most Cypriots are farmers. Crops such as wheat, vegetables, and fruit (including oranges and olives) ripen early due to the mild winters. As a result, Cyprus can sell much of its produce to northern European countries before the crops of these countries are ready for harvest. Cyprus also has numerous vineyards, and wine is a major export.

The island was once a copper mining center, and it still has deposits of iron pyrites,

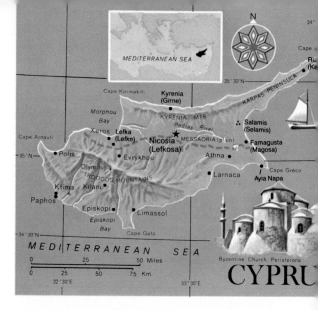

CYPRUS

gypsum, and asbestos. But mining is no longer important to the economy. Tourism has become the leading industry in both parts of Cyprus. Textile manufacturing and other light industries have been developed in the Greek part of Cyprus, where incomes are higher than in the Turkish part of the island. Many international and Middle Eastern companies have been attracted to the Greek part of Cyprus in recent times. It offers them excellent telecommunications and banking facilities, tax advantages, and a convenient location for trade by sea.

▶CITIES

The city of Nicosia (Lefkosa in Turkish) is the capital of both the Greek and Turkish parts of Cyprus. A wall divides the city into Greek and Turkish sectors, and there is only one crossing point between the two parts. The Turkish sector includes most of the old city and the northern suburbs. Larnaca and Limmasol are other important cities in Greek Cyprus. Kyrenia (Girne in Turkish) is the chief port in Turkish Cyprus.

▶HISTORY AND GOVERNMENT

Following its settlement by Greeks, Cyprus fell under the successive domination of the Assyrian, Egyptian, Persian, Roman, and Byzantine empires. The Greek-speaking Byzantines ruled the island for about 800 years. Between the late 1100's and the 1400's, it was a French kingdom. In 1489 it came under the control of the Venetians. The Turks conquered Cyprus in 1571 and ruled it for the next 300 years. In 1878 they gave over the island to Britain, which formally annexed it in 1914.

FACTS AND FIGURES

REPUBLIC OF CYPRUS is the official name of the country. The northeastern region declared itself the **TURKISH REPUBLIC OF NORTHERN CYPRUS** in 1983. But only Turkey recognized its independence.

THE PEOPLE are known as Cypriots.

LOCATION: Island in the eastern Mediterranean Sea.

AREA: 3,572 sq mi (9,251 km²).

POPULATION: 670,000 (estimate).

CAPITAL AND LARGEST CITY: Nicosia (Lefkosa).

MAJOR LANGUAGES: Greek, Turkish.

MAJOR RELIGIONS: Greek Orthodox, Muslim.

GOVERNMENT: Republic. **Head of state and government—** president. **Legislature—**House of Representatives.

CHIEF PRODUCTS: Agricultural—wheat and other grains, vegetables, fruits. **Manufactured—**processed agricultural products, textiles, wine, shoes. **Mineral—**copper.

MONETARY UNIT: Cyprus pound (1 pound = 100 cents); Turkish lira (1 lira = 100 kurus).

Most Greek Cypriots had long desired union with Greece. The movement for union, called *enosis,* grew in the 1950's into a guerrilla war against British rule. Turkish Cypriots feared domination by the Greek majority, and they sought partition (division) of the island. In 1960, Cyprus was given independence under terms that forbade either *enosis* or partition. Britain kept control of two military bases along the southern coast.

The constitution provided for a Greek Cypriot president and a Turkish Cypriot vice president. Seats in the legislature, the House of Representatives, were allotted by population. Archbishop Makarios III, the head of the Orthodox Church in Cyprus, became the first president of the country.

But mistrust between Greek and Turkish Cypriots remained. In 1963, when President Makarios attempted to change the constitution, fighting erupted between the two communities. United Nations peacekeeping forces were sent to Cyprus in 1964. Fighting broke out again in 1967, threatening to involve Greece and Turkey in war. In 1974, Greek Cypriots who favored *enosis,* led by Greek Army officers, briefly took control of the government. Turkey, citing the terms of the independence agreement forbidding *enosis,* sent troops who occupied the northeastern part of the island.

Divided Cyprus. Makarios died in 1977 and was succeeded by Spyros Kyprianou as president. George Vassiliou was elected president in 1988 and Glafcos Clerides in 1993. Meanwhile, Turkish Cypriots had established a separate government administration in the part of the island they controlled and in 1983 had proclaimed an independent Turkish Republic of Northern Cyprus, with Rauf Denktash as president. However, only Turkey has recognized its independence.

Several attempts have been made to resolve the dispute, including meetings between Greek and Turkish Cypriot leaders. But thus far, all efforts to restore harmony between the two communities have proved unsuccessful. The long-standing dispute has also strained relations between Greece and Turkey.

ALEXANDER MELAMID
New York University

CYRUS THE GREAT. See PERSIA, ANCIENT.

CYSTIC FIBROSIS. See DISEASES (Descriptions of Some Diseases).

Above: Kyrenia (Girne in Turkish) is the chief port city in the Turkish part of Cyprus. It lies at the foot of the Kyrenia Mountains. Below: The Church of St. Sophia in Nicosia, the capital, was built in the 13th century. The building is now a mosque. Nicosia is divided into Turkish and Greek Cypriot sectors.

CZECH REPUBLIC

Czechoslovakia, which was first founded as a nation in 1918, came to the end of its existence on January 1, 1993, when it was divided into two independent countries—the Czech Republic and Slovakia. The breakup of the country followed the surge of ethnic rivalries and national passions that spread across much of Central and Eastern Europe after the collapse of Communist regimes in the region. It became unavoidable when leaders of the Czech and Slovak republics making up Czechoslovakia were unable to agree on what political and economic form the country should take following the end of Communist rule. The division of the country was accomplished peacefully, and the two nations were expected to maintain close cooperation. For more information, see the article on Slovakia in Volume S.

▶ THE PEOPLE

Ethnic Groups, Language, Religion. The Czechs make up about 95 percent of the country's population and, like the Slovaks, are a West Slavic people. The ethnic minorities, all of them quite small, include Slovaks, Gypsies, Poles, and some Germans. Czech, along with Slovak and Polish, belongs to the West Slavic language group. The Czech and Slovak languages are closely related and both peoples can easily understand each other. In religion, most Czechs are traditionally Roman Catholics. There are also several Protestant denominations and a small Jewish community. As many as 40 percent of the country's people, however, consider themselves nonreligious.

Way of Life. For a thousand years the Czechs had been in close contact with, and under the influence of, the Germans of neighboring Austria and Bavaria. For nearly 400 years of that period, the Czech lands were ruled by the Austrian Habsburgs.

The result was that Czech habits, customs, and much of their way of life today are, to a great extent, like those found in Austria and Bavaria. This similarity shows in their food and drink (including the enjoyment of beer and

Left: Floodlights illuminate historic Hradčany Castle in Prague, the capital and largest city of the Czech Republic. Situated on a height overlooking the Vltava River, which flows through the city, the castle was once the home of Czech kings and is now the official residence of the president of the republic. *Opposite page:* The spring sun makes an outdoor café a popular meeting place in Prague's Old Town, in the heart of the city, where some of the buildings date from the Middle Ages.

coffee), the sports they like (such as soccer, ice hockey, skiing, gymnastics, and tennis), and in most of the holidays they celebrate. It can also be seen in the Czech's love for music and dancing, visiting favorite cafés and taverns, and in escaping the cities, where most of the people live, to spend weekends at cottages in the countryside.

Effects of Communism. The period of Communist rule of Czechoslovakia, from 1948 to 1989, also left its mark on the people. Having long been accustomed to doing as they were told by authoritarian governments, they had difficulty adjusting to the new conditions of political freedom. They have tended to abuse this newly regained freedom by being unwilling to compromise and by splitting into many political factions and parties.

At the same time, under the Communist regime all aspects of the economy were controlled by the state. Economic mismanagement by the Communists and their emphasis on the development of heavy industry at the expense of consumer goods led to a lowering of the people's living standards, including an acute shortage of housing.

Nevertheless, the Czechs have reason to be hopeful for the future. Their experience with Communism has only strengthened their affection for Western ways as well as their commitment to democracy, which was a part of their pre-Communist past.

▶**THE LAND**

Situated in the heart of Europe, the Czech Republic is bounded by Germany in the north, west, and southwest, by Poland in the northeast, by Austria in the southeast, and by Slovakia in the east. The country consists of the historic lands of Bohemia and Moravia and a slice of southern Silesia.

Landforms. Bohemia is a region of rolling hills, plains, and river valleys, surrounded by mountains. It is drained by the Labe (Elbe) River and its main tributary, or branch, the Vltava (Moldau), which provide an important water route to the North Sea. Silesia and northern Moravia are mostly hilly and mountainous, while southern Moravia is a lowland, linked, geographically, to the plains of northern Austria. The chief rivers of Moravia are the Morava, a tributary of the Danube, and the Odra (Oder), which flows north to the Baltic Sea.

Climate. The climate is a mixture of the relatively moderate oceanic type found in Western Europe and the harsher continental type characteristic of Eastern Europe. Summers are warm, with only occasional periods of very hot weather. Winters are cold. Below-freezing temperatures are frequent, and snowfall is usually heavy in the mountains. Rainfall averages about 20 inches (508 millimeters) a year.

Natural Resources. Coal is the most important of the Czech Republic's mineral resources. But most of it is the brown coal variety (lignite), which is the main industrial pollutant. Other minerals are produced but not in quantities sufficient for large-scale industrial use. Iron ore, crude oil, and natural gas must all be imported. There are, however, numerous mineral springs, including such world-renowned spas as Karlovy Vary (Karlsbad) and Mariánské Lázně (Marienbad).

The Czechs are more fortunate in having much good farm land, especially in the fertile river valleys, including those of the Labe River and the Haná region of southern Moravia. More than one quarter of the country is covered by forests, but many were badly damaged by polluting factory emissions.

▶ THE ECONOMY

Industry and Agriculture. A highly industrialized country, the Czech Republic derives as much as 64 percent of its income from the production of manufactured goods. Its output includes textiles, shoes, glass and chinaware, machinery, wood products, iron and steel, armaments, chemicals, and processed foods. Agriculture and forestry contribute about 14 percent of the country's national income. The main farm crops are wheat, rye, barley, sugar beets, and potatoes. Hay and other forage crops are grown as feed for livestock, including cattle, horses, hogs, and poultry. High-quality hops, used in brewing beer, are produced in western Bohemia.

Foreign Trade. During the 1920's and 1930's, most of Czechoslovakia's trade had been with Germany and the countries of Western Europe. After the Communists took power in 1948, more than 70 percent of the country's trade was redirected toward the Soviet Union and the Eastern European Communist states. As a result, Czechoslovakia was unable to earn enough hard currency (such as U.S. dollars) with which to buy the advanced technology from Western industrialized countries that it badly needed to modernize its industry.

Toward a Free-Market System. The restructuring of the ailing economy has been the government's top priority. Laws enacted in 1990 and 1991 began to transform the state-controlled economy into a more efficient free-market (or free-enterprise) system. During

1991 and 1992, smaller publicly held businesses, such as restaurants, hotels, and retail stores, were auctioned off to the highest bidders. Most of the largest state enterprises, such as factories and assembly plants, were converted to joint-stock companies. Some were sold to private developers, but most of the stock shares were purchased by individual citizens.

Problems of Economic Reform. However, the changeover to a free-market economy turned out to be more difficult than had been anticipated. A great many of the state-run enterprises had been operating at a loss and are threatened with bankruptcy as their government subsidies are eliminated. Many are inefficient and produce goods whose quality is often below international standards. This has made it hard for the country to earn income by exports to Western markets and to compensate for the sharp decrease in its foreign trade with the economically ravaged former Communist countries of Eastern Europe.

▶**MAJOR CITIES**

Prague (Praha in Czech) is the capital of the Czech Republic and its largest city. It is also the country's commercial, industrial, and cultural center. Situated amid hills on both banks of the Vltava River, it is one of the most beautiful capitals in Europe. An ancient city, it has buildings dating from the Middle Ages, with fine examples of Gothic, baroque, and Renaissance architecture. See the article on Prague in Volume P.

Other major cities include Brno, the capital of Moravia and an important textile center; Ostrava, a center of iron and steel production; and Plzeň (formerly Pilsen), home of the giant Škoda manufacturing works and the brewery making the famed pilsner beer.

▶**CULTURAL HERITAGE**

The Czechs have a long and rich cultural heritage. It has been particularly noteworthy in such fields as music and literature.

Music. The first Czech composers to gain international stature, Bedřich Smetana (1824–84) and Antonin Dvořák (1841–1904), captured the spirit of the people in their music, which can be both joyful and sad. Smetana is best known for his symphonic poem *My Country* and the comic opera *The Bartered Bride*; Dvořák for his symphonies, *Slavonic Dances*, and chamber music. Leoš Janáček (1854–1928), born in Moravia, wrote symphonic and choral works, as well as operas, including *The*

The Czech cultural heritage includes composers (*top row, from left*) Bedřich Smetana (1824–84), Antonin Dvořák (1841–1904), and Leoš Janáček (1854–1928). Major Czech literary figures (*bottom row*) include dramatist and novelist Karel Čapek (1890–1938); poet Jaroslav Seifert (1901–86), winner of the Nobel Prize for literature (1984); and Václav Havel (1936–), playwright and first president of the Czech Republic.

Cunning Little Vixen, which is performed regularly today.

Literature.   One of the earliest Czech literary figures was the religious reformer Jan Hus (1372–1415), whose sermons were written in the ordinary language of the people. The writings of Jan Amos Komenský (known as Comenius) (1592–1670), an educator and theologian, included one of the first illustrated schoolbooks for children. Komenský, like many Czechs, was forced to leave his oppressed homeland to seek freedom in exile.

Some of the best-known works of Czech literature were written after the creation of Czechoslovakia. The play *R.U.R.*, a satire on technology by Karel Čapek (1890–1938), gave the world the term "robot," from the Czech word for "worker" or "drudge." *The Good Soldier Schweik*, a series of novels by Jaroslav Hašek (1883–1923), pokes fun at the military and authority. Jaroslav Seifert (1901–86), a poet, was the first Czech to win the Nobel Prize for literature (1984). Important present-day writers include the novelist Milan Kundera (1929–   ) and the playwright and political leader Václav Havel (1936–   ).

▶**GOVERNMENT**

The government is based on the constitution adopted in December 1992. Legislative power is vested in a parliament consisting of the Chamber of Deputies and the Senate. Executive power rests with the president, who is elected by parliament to a 5-year term, and the Council of Ministers, headed by a chairman. The chairman and members of the Council are appointed by the president and must have the confidence of the Chamber of Deputies. Václav Havel was elected the Czech Republic's first president in 1993. He was re-elected in 1998.

The Constitutional Court, appointed by the president, guarantees that no laws are adopted that violate the constitution.

▶**HISTORY**

Early History.   The Czechs are believed to have settled in what is today the Czech Republic in the A.D. 500's and 600's. Their first major state, named Great Moravia, emerged here in the 800's. However, after Great Moravia was overpowered by the Magyars (Hungarians) in 904–905, the political center of the Czech state shifted to Bohemia and its

---

FACTS and figures

CZECH REPUBLIC is the official name of the country.

LOCATION: East central Europe.

AREA: 30,469 sq mi (78,916 km^2).

POPULATION: 10,300,000 (estimate).

CAPITAL AND LARGEST CITY: Prague (Praha).

MAJOR LANGUAGE: Czech.

MAJOR RELIGIOUS GROUPS: Roman Catholic, Protestant.

GOVERNMENT: Republic. **Head of state**—president. **Head of government**—chairman of the Council of Ministers (appointed by the president). **Legislature**—parliament (consisting of the Chamber of Deputies and the Senate).

CHIEF PRODUCTS: Agricultural—wheat, rye, barley, sugar beets, potatoes, livestock, hay, hops. **Manufactured**—textiles, shoes, glass and chinaware, machinery, wood products, iron and steel, armaments, chemicals, processed foods. **Mineral**—coal (mainly brown coal, or lignite), small amounts of other minerals.

MONETARY UNIT: Koruna (1 koruna = 100 haléřů).

---

capital, Prague. One of the most important events of this early period of Czech-Moravian history was the introduction of Christianity.

The Czech Kingdom.   From the early 900's to 1306, the country was ruled by the dukes and (from 1158) kings of the Přemyslide dynasty, or family. The most revered of these rulers was Václav (reigned 921–29), who became the patron saint of Bohemia and is best known as the Good King Wenceslaus of the Christmas carol.

After the throne became vacant in 1306, the crown was offered to John of Luxembourg. Under his son and successor, Charles I, Bohemia reached the height of its power. His long reign (1346–78) was marked by peace and prosperity and a flowering of culture, including the founding of Charles University (1348), the first university in Central Europe. As Charles IV, he was crowned emperor of the Holy Roman Empire (1355), which made Prague the imperial capital.

The Hussites.   In the early 1400's the Czechs became deeply involved in the movement for reform of the Roman Catholic Church. The leader of the movement, Jan Hus, was a popular preacher and president of Charles University. Accused by the church of teaching heresy, Hus refused to recant, or give up, his beliefs and was burned at the stake in 1415. His death provoked a revolt by his followers, called Hussites, and years of war with Catholic forces.

Habsburg Rule. When the Bohemian throne again became vacant in 1526, the Czechs elected the Habsburg Ferdinand of Austria as their king. It was a fateful mistake. The nearly 400 years of Habsburg rule were the most somber chapter of Czech history. The rights of the people were denied, and their language and culture were suppressed in favor of German. The refusal of Czech nobles, in 1618, to accept a new Habsburg ruler, and their election of a Protestant king, led to the outbreak of the Thirty Years' War, which devastated Bohemia. See the article on the Thirty Years' War in Volume T.

A cultural revival, begun in the late 1700's, succeeded in reawakening Czech nationalism during the 1800's. But political independence for the Czechs and the Slovaks, who had been under Hungarian rule since the 1000's, was to come only after a world war.

Creation of Czechoslovakia. When World War I broke out in 1914, a Czechoslovak national council, established in exile by the philosopher-statesman Tomáš Masaryk and Eduard (or Edvard) Beneš, won the support of Britain, France, and the United States for an independent Czechoslovak state. This was achieved with Austria-Hungary's defeat in the war (along with Germany) and the breakup of its empire. Czechoslovakia was officially proclaimed on October 28, 1918. Masaryk was elected its first president. He was succeeded, after his retirement in 1935, by Beneš.

Dismemberment. The independence of the young democracy was to last for only 21 years. In 1938 the Nazi dictator Adolf Hitler threatened to invade Czechoslovakia unless its western border regions (known as the Sudetenland), whose population was largely German, was handed over to Germany.

The Czechoslovak government at first refused to do so. But when it saw that no help would be forthcoming from its allies, France and the Soviet Union, it bowed to French and British pressure to avert war and ceded the Sudetenland to Germany. Less than six months later, on March 15, 1939, Hitler completed the destruction of Czechoslovakia by occupying the Czech lands and annexing them as the "Protectorate of Bohemia-Moravia." Slovakia was converted into a puppet state. In September 1939, Hitler invaded Poland, setting off World War II.

See the article on World War II (The Munich Pact) in Volume W-X-Y-Z. An article on Tomáš Masaryk appears in Volume M.

Communist Rule. When Soviet troops helped liberate Czechoslovakia from the Germans in 1945, they made sure that key posts

Left: **Tomáš Masaryk, Czechoslovakia's first president, signed his country's declaration of independence in Independence Hall, Philadelphia, in 1918.** *Below:* **In 1938 a triumphant Adolf Hitler entered the Sudetenland, which Czechoslovakia had been forced to cede to Nazi Germany. The rest of the country was dismembered by the Germans in 1939, just before the outbreak of World War II.**

of the government went to top members of the Communist Party. The Communization of the country was therefore already well under way even before President Beneš and his government-in-exile returned to Czechoslovak soil. In February 1948 the Communists staged a coup and took over all agencies of the government. Four months later, Beneš resigned and was succeeded as president by Communist Party head Klement Gottwald.

The Communists, who ruled Czechoslovakia for 40 years, turned the country into an obedient ally of the Soviet Union and refashioned its political, cultural, and social system after the Soviet image. But they failed in their main endeavor, which was to convert the people into true believers in Communism. Even high Communist Party functionaries eventually became disillusioned with Soviet-style Communism.

The "Prague Spring." In January 1968 a group of reform-minded Communist leaders elected a moderate, Alexander Dubček, to head the party. Dubček immediately set about giving the people the reforms they wanted. Within a few months that came to be known as the "Prague Spring," Czechoslovakia was

Czechoslovaks celebrated the fall of their country's Communist regime in 1989. But political and economic disagreemtns between Czech and Slovak leaders led, on January 1, 1993, to the division of Czechoslovakia into two independent nations, the Czech Republic and Slovakia.

transformed into the most liberal of the Communist countries. But in August 1968, armies of the Soviet Union and four of its allies occupied the country, arrested its leaders, and canceled the reforms. The Czechoslovaks had to wait 21 years for a second chance to rid themselves of Communist rule.

The "Velvet Revolution." This came in the late 1980's, when the Soviet Union, under the new leadership of Mikhail Gorbachev, launched its campaign for democratic reform of the Soviet system. Taking advantage of the new political climate, in November 1989, Czechs and Slovaks launched massive demonstrations against their Communist regime, which quickly collapsed and was replaced by a government formed by democratic forces. Since the takeover had occurred without violence, it was called the "velvet revolution."

In elections for a new Federal Assembly in 1990, the first free elections since 1946, the people gave an overwhelming majority to the Czech Civic Forum and the Slovak Public Against Violence, the two groups that had spearheaded the revolution. The leader of Civic Forum, Václav Havel, was elected president of the country, and the leader of Public Against Violence, Alexander Dubček, was elected chairman of the Federal Assembly.

Separation. But the jubilant unity of the first months after the liberation was soon disrupted by growing disagreements between the Czechs and Slovaks over how to solve the problems the Communists left behind. The greatest conflicts were over how to reform Czechoslovakia's economic system. The political differences between the two sides, and the unwillingness of either to compromise, made the breakup of the country inevitable.

World Affairs. On January 1, 1993, the Czech Republic became an independent nation. That same year it became a member of the United Nations. In 1997, the country was invited to join the North Atlantic Treaty Organization (NATO), an alliance of western nations. Despite limited popular support, the Czech Republic became one of the first former Soviet satellites, along with Poland and Hungary, to join NATO, in 1999. By that time, talks were also under way for the Czech Republic to join the European Union (EU).

EDWARD TABORSKY
University of Texas at Austin
Author, *Communism in Czechoslovakia*

Index

CAD/CAM (cont.)
picture(s)
automobile design **A:**553, 556
Caddis flies (insects) **I:**247
Caddo (Indians of North America) **I:**178, 180; **L:**326
Cadeau, Le (The Gift) (dadaist sculpture by Ray) **M:**393
picture(s) **M:**394
Cadence (in music) **M:**540
Cadency, mark of (in heraldry) **H:**112
Cadets (students at United States Military Academy) **U:**111
picture(s) **U:**108
Cadette Girl Scouts **G:**215–16
picture(s) **G:**214, 217
Cadillac (automobile)
picture(s) **A:**544
Cadillac, Sieur Antoine de la Mothe (French soldier) **F:**522
profile
Cadillac Mountain (Maine) **M:**38
Cádiz (Spain) **S:**375
Cadmium (element) **E:**171; **N:**371
Caduceus (symbol of the doctor)
picture(s) **M:**208c
Cady Stanton, Elizabeth (American reformer) *see* Stanton, Elizabeth Cady
Caecilians (land-water animals) **A:**214b–216
picture(s) **A:**216
Caedmon (English poet) **E:**268
Caernavon Castle (Wales) **U:**62
Caesar, Gaius Julius (Roman general and statesman) **C:**6, 303; **R:**315–16
Antony, Mark **A:**317
Augustus **A:**494
ciphers used in secret messages **C:**393–94, 395
Cleopatra **C:**355
England invaded by **E:**235
Julius Caesar (play by Shakespeare) **S:**134–35
pirates, captured by **P:**262
place in Latin literature **L:**75
quoted **B:**134; **Q:**20
Roman calendar **C:**15
Caesar Augustus *see* Augustus
Caesarea (ancient city in Israel) **I:**374; **U:**20
Caesura (in music) **M:**540
Café au lait (mixture of coffee and milk) **C:**397
Cafés (restaurants)
picture(s) **C:**312
Cafeterias (restaurants) **R:**186
Caffeine (substance in coffee and tea) **C:**397
chocolate **C:**281
drugs as stimulants **D:**329, 331
tea **T:**34
Cagayan River (Philippines) **P:**185
Cage, John (American composer) **M:**399, 548; **U:**210
picture(s)
score for *Atlas Eclipticalis* **M:**548
Cagney, James (American film actor) **M:**486 *profile,* 491
picture(s) **M:**491
Cagniard de la Tour, Charles (French doctor) **F:**90
Caguas (Puerto Rico) **P:**531
Cahaba lilies (flowers)
picture(s) **A:**133
Cahokia (capital of Mississippian Indian kingdom) **I:**171
Cahokia Mounds State Historic Site (Illinois) **I:**70
Cahuilla (Indians of North America) **I:**187
Caiaphas (in the New Testament) **B:**167
Caicos Islands *see* Turks and Caicos Islands
Caimans *see* Caymans
Cain and Abel (in the Old Testament) **B:**167
Cairngorm *see* Smoky quartz
Cairn terrier (dog) **D:**250
Cairo (capital of Egypt) **C:**7–8; **E:**107, 108; **M:**302
rainfall pattern **D:**328
picture(s) **A:**47, 343; **C:**8; **E:**105
Cairo (Illinois) **I:**65
Caisson disease *see* Bends, the

Caissons (watertight chambers used in construction work) **B:**400, 435
"Caisson Song" (by Gruber) **N:**25
Caius, Saint (pope) **R:**290
Cajuns (in Louisiana and Texas) **L:**318, 327; **N:**196
music **L:**320
Cakes (for parties) **P:**91
Cakewalk (dance) **U:**208
Calah (city in ancient Assyria) *see* Nimrud
Calamity Jane (American frontier personality) **M:**440 *profile*
picture(s) **M:**440
Calcite (form of calcium carbonate) **M:**315, 317; **R:**266
Calcium (element) **E:**171
bones contain calcium compounds **S:**184a
calcium ions help muscle contraction **M:**519
coral polyp content **C:**548
functions performed in body **N:**426; **V:**370b
lime needed for plant growth **F:**96
minerals needed by the body **V:**371
table(s)
food sources and RDA's **V:**372
Calcium hypochlorite (disinfectant) **D:**214
Calculators (machines for solving mathematical problems) **O:**58
abacus **A:**2–3
arithmetic **A:**400–401
automation **A:**529
electronics **E:**160
solar batteries **B:**103c
picture(s)
"Napier's bones" **M:**165
Calculus (branch of mathematics) **M:**157–58
Bernoulli family **B:**153
Leibniz, Gottfried Wilhelm von **L:**138
mathematics, history of **M:**167–68, 169
Newton, Isaac **N:**206
Calcutta (India) **C:**9, 312; **I:**122–23
picture(s) **C:**9
Caldecott, Randolph (English artist) **C:**10
children's literature, history of **C:**233, 236, 237
picture(s)
illustration for "Hey-Diddle-Diddle" **C:**233
illustration for the ballad "The Diverting History of John Gilpin" **C:**10
Caldecott Medal (book award) **C:**10, **11–12,** 233
Calder, Alexander (American sculptor) **U:**135
modern art **M:**396b
sculpture of forms in motion **S:**104–5
picture(s)
mobile **N:**40
Red Petals (mobile) **D:**136
stabile **S:**103
Caldera Rodríguez, Rafael (Venezuelan president) **V:**299
Calderas (caved-in summits of volcanoes) **V:**380
Crater Lake (Oregon) **L:**29
Calderón de la Barca, Pedro (Spanish dramatist) **D:**299; **S:**389, 392b
Calderón Fournier, Rafael (Costa Rican president) **C:**559
Calderón Sol, Armando (Salvadoran president) **E:**199
Calendar (for keeping track of time) **C:**13–17
Advent calendars **C:**299
ancient Egyptian **A:**222
Aztec year divided into 18 months **A:**577
Caesar, Julius **C:**6
Easter: how the date falls **E:**43
electronic calendar systems **O:**54
Incas **I:**109
international date line **I:**266
map of the year **T:**201
Maya **M:**186
New Year's Day around the world **N:**208
religious holidays by different calendars **R:**153
study schedules **S:**471–72
Why are abbreviations "B.C." and "A.D." used with dates? **C:**16

Calender (machine with heavy rollers)   P:56; R:348a
Čalfa, Marian (Slovak political leader)   S:202
Calfskin leather   L:107
Calgary (Alberta)   A:170
  Olympic Games (1988)   O:118
Calgary Exhibition and Stampede (Canadian rodeo)   A:170
Calhoun, John C. (American statesman)   C:17
  Compromise of 1850 opposed by   C:479
  Jackson opposes his states' rights theories   J:6–7
  South Carolina   S:309
  Texas, annexation of   T:367–68
  vice presidency   V:325 *profile*
  picture(s)   S:310
    as vice president   V:326
Cali (Colombia)   C:406
Calibers (diameters of gun bores)   G:415, 419–20; R:231
Calico scallop (mollusk)
  picture(s)   S:147
California   C:18–33
  California Trail   O:279–81
  Compromise of 1850   C:479
  Declaration of Rights   B:184
  goat production   L:272
  gold discoveries   G:250–51
  Indians, American   I:186–87
  lemon growing   L:139
  Los Angeles   L:303–8
  Mexican War   M:239b; P:376–77
  olive trees   O:101
  orange industry   O:187
  Salton Sea   L:28
  San Diego   S:29–30
  San Francisco   S:31–32
  San Francisco earthquake (1906)   E:40
  San Jose   S:34
  Santa Clara Valley   G:104
  wine   W:190
  Yosemite National Park   Y:362–63
  map(s)   C:31
  picture(s)
    agriculture   C:26
    Big Sur   C:20
    coastal erosion   O:19
    Cypress Point   C:19
    Death Valley   C:21; D:131
    Disneyland   C:28
    elephant seals   C:21
    gun-control demonstration   D:105
    Hearst Castle   C:28
    Hollywood   C:25
    landslide   A:558
    Los Angeles   C:27; G:104; L:303, 306, 307
    Mount Palomar Observatory   O:6
    Napa Valley vineyards   C:20
    Oakland expressway   N:283
    Sacramento   C:29
    San Andreas fault   E:14, 34
    San Carlos de Borromeo Mission   C:28
    sand castles on Pacific Beach   C:24
    San Diego   S:29
    San Francisco   C:19; S:31, 32; U:95
    San Francisco earthquake (1906)   C:32
    San Francisco earthquake (1989)   E:36
    San Jose   S:34
    Shasta Dam   D:17
    skiing at Lake Tahoe   C:28
    students at Berkeley   C:24
    Yosemite National Park   C:22; Y:252
California, University of   C:23; U:222
  Los Angeles   L:304
  UCLA basketball team   B:98
  UCLA's traditional cheer   C:194
  picture(s)
    campus at Los Angeles   U:222
    students at Berkeley campus   C:24

California gold rush   C:18, 30; G:250–51; M:324
  overland trails   O:280–81
  San Francisco   S:32
  picture(s)   U:185; W:144
California laurel (tree)
  picture(s)   T:304
California Raisins (cartoon characters)
  picture(s)   A:289
California sea lions   S:106
California State University   C:23; L:304–5; U:222
California Test of Basic Skills   T:118
California Trail   O:279–81; P:383
  map(s)   O:273
Californium (element)   E:171
Caligula (Roman emperor)   R:316
Caliper (instrument)   T:230
Caliph (Islamic leader)   A:345; I:347–48
Calisthenics (exercises) *see* Floor exercises
Calixtus III (antipope)   R:291
Calixtus I, Saint (pope)   R:290
Calixtus II (pope)   R:290
Calixtus III (pope)   R:291
Call and response (type of singing)   A:79; J:58, 60
Callao (Peru)   P:164
Callas, Maria (American opera singer)   O:140 *profile*
Callaway Gardens (Pine Mountain, Georgia)
  picture(s)   G:140
Callbacks (second auditions)   P:337
Callers (for square dancing)   F:299, 303
Calles, Plutarco Elías (Mexican president)   M:251
Calligraphy (art of fine handwriting)   H:25
  art as a record   A:438c
  Chinese art   C:275, 276; O:225
  folk art   F:294
  illuminated manuscripts of Islam   I:78
  Islamic art   I:351, 355
  Japan   J:30, 49
  picture(s)
    Chinese literature   C:278
    Islamic art   I:354
    samples of different styles   H:25
Callimachus (Greek scholar and librarian)   G:359
Calling (giving directions to theater crews)   P:336
Calling of St. Matthew, The (painting by Caravaggio)   B:64
  picture(s)   B:64
Calliope (in Greek mythology)   G:367 *see also* Muses
Calliope (musical instrument)   C:310
Callisto (moon of Jupiter)   J:161; P:279
  picture(s)   J:159
Call letters (of radio stations)   R:57
Call number (of books)   L:183
Call of the Wild, The (book by London)
  excerpt from   L:299–300
Callot, Jacques (French artist)   F:426
  picture(s)
    Two Clowns (etching)   G:304
Calonne, Charles de (French statesman)   F:468
Caloric theory (of heat)   H:88–89
Calories (heat units)   E:214; H:87–88; W:117
  food energy measured in   H:74
  nutrition   N:423
Calorimeter (instrument for measuring heat)   H:87–88, 89
  diagram(s)   H:87, 88
Caloris Basin (on Mercury)   M:229
  picture(s)   M:231
Calotype (photographic process)   P:213
Calumet (peace pipe)   I:196
Calumet region (Indiana)   I:150
Calusas (Indians native to Florida)   F:271
Calvary (place of Jesus Christ's crucifixion)   J:88
Calvert, Cecil (2nd Lord Baltimore)   M:132, 133; T:177
Calvert, George (1st Lord Baltimore)   M:132; T:177
Calvert, Leonard (first governor of Maryland colony)   M:132; T:177
Calverton National Cemetery (New York)   N:31

Capitalism   C:103;   E:59; S:224 *see also* Free enterprise
     system
     Cold War   C:400–401
     Marx's analysis of   M:117
Capitalization   P:543–44
Capital loan (in economics)   B:472
Capital punishment   C:104, 574, 576
     ethics and society   E:329
     juvenile crime   J:170
Capitals (letters of the alphabet)   A:194a; P:543–44
Capitals (of columns)   G:351
Capitol, United States   C:104–5;   U:128; W:29
     picture(s)   C:104; U:161
Capitol Reef National Park (Utah)   U:250
     picture(s)   U:244
Capone, Al (American gangster)   C:221 *profile,* 540; I:76;
     P:485
Caporetto, Battle of (1917)   W:289
Capote, Truman (American writer)   L:326 *profile*
Capra, Frank (American film director)   M:493 *profile*
Capri (island at entrance to Bay of Naples)   I:363
Capricorn (constellation)   C:522
     picture(s)   C:522
Caprification (pollination of fig tree flowers)   F:121
Capri figs   F:121
Caps (of bottles)   B:347
Capsids (protein coats of viruses)   V:363, 364
Capsomeres (building blocks making up viruses' coats)
     V:363, 364
Capsule (section of spacecraft)   S:340d
     Apollo 11   S:340g, 340h–340j
     picture(s)   S:340j
Captain (chief officer of a ship)   O:32
Capture theory (of the moon's origin)   M:454
Capuchins (monkeys)
     picture(s)   M:420
Capulin Volcano National Monument (New Mexico)   N:188
Capybara (rodent of South America)   R:272, 276; S:283
     livestock   L:273
Carabiner (snap link used in mountain climbing)   M:500
Caracals (lynxlike wild cats)   C:146, 148
Caracas (capital of Venezuela)   L:65; V:295, 298
Caramanlis, Constantine (Greek political leader) *see* Karamanlis
     (Caramanlis), Constantine
Caramels (candy)   C:98
Carapace (shell on the back of some animals)
     crabs   C:571
     shrimps   S:167
     turtles   T:355
Caraquet (New Brunswick)   N:138d, 138e
Carats (units for measuring gemstones)   J:94, 95 *see also*
     Karats
Caravaggio, Michelangelo Merisi da (Italian painter)
          C:105;   I:401
     art of the artist   A:438d
     baroque art   B:64
     nature copied faithfully   P:23
     Rembrandt influenced by   R:155
     picture(s)
          Calling of St. Matthew, The (painting)   B:64
          Death of the Virgin (painting)   I:401
          Entombment (painting)   C:105
Caravans (companies of travelers)
     picture(s)   F:331
Caravans (houses on wheels)   H:175, 177
Caravel (sailing vessel)
     picture(s)   S:152
Caraway, Hattie Wyatt (American senator)   A:428 *profile*
Caraway seed   H:114
Carbines (guns)   G:420
     picture(s)   G:420
Carbohydrates
     body chemistry   B:269, 291–92; L:199
     bread is an important source   B:385

digestion of   D:161, 162–63
     nutrition   N:424
     starch   S:425
     sugar   S:483
Carbolic acid (used to stop infection)   S:513
Carbon (element)   C:106;   E:166, 171
     alloys   A:190
     archery equipment, materials used for   A:365
     atomic number   A:486
     atomic structure   A:486
     batteries   B:103a
     chimney fires   F:147
     coal, chief ingredient of   C:388
     diamonds   D:144
     fuels   F:488
     lamp filaments   L:234
     matter   M:177
     steel is an alloy of iron and carbon   I:329, 332
     structural formulas   C:201
     diagram(s)
          carbon-12 atom   A:486
Carbon-14 (radioactive variety of carbon)   A:360; R:65–66
Carbon arc lamps   L:235
Carbon black   R:348a
Carbon dioxide   C:106 *see also* Dry ice
     acid rain   A:10
     apple storage   A:333
     atmosphere   A:479, 482
     atomic structure   A:488
     blood carries   B:256, 280
     climate, possible effects on   A:295; I:16
     deep-sea collection plan   U:27
     dissolved in most natural water   W:49
     Earth, history of the   E:23
     fermentation   F:90
     fires, dangers of   F:148
     greenhouse effect   C:364; F:144
     human body's waste product   B:278, 279, 281
     Lake Nyos (Cameroon) disaster   C:41
     lungs exchange gases   L:343, 344
     Mars   M:108
     oceans are natural disposal sites for   O:36
     ocean water, dissolved in   O:17
     photosynthesis   L:118; P:220
     Venus's atmosphere   P:276; V:303, 303a, 303b
     diagram(s)
          molecule   A:486, 488
Carbon disulfide   C:199
Carboniferous periods (in geology)   E:25, 28
     table(s)   F:384
Carbonization (fossilizing process)   F:381
Carbon monoxide (poisonous gas)
     acid rain   A:10
     air pollution   A:123
     atmosphere   A:479
     fires, dangers of   F:148
     hyperbaric chambers used in cases of poisoning   M:210
     low-pollution automobiles being developed   E:304
     poisoning   P:356
Carbon steels   I:329
Carbon tetrachloride   P:355
Carbon tissue (for gravure printing)   P:477
Carborundum (abrasive)   G:391, 392
Carburetors (of internal-combustion engines)   I:264
     automobiles   A:547
     venturi tube   A:38
Carcassonne (France)   C:316
Carcinogens (cancer-causing agents)   C:93
Carcinomas (cancers)   C:92
Cardamom seed (spice)   H:114
     picture(s)   H:115
Cardano, Geronimo (Italian mathematician)   M:165
Cardboard   P:57
Card catalogs (in libraries)   L:183–84, 186
Cárdenas, García López de (Spanish explorer)   G:290

Cárdenas, Lázaro (Mexican political leader)   I:194; M:251
Card games   C:107–11;   G:16
 video games   V:332c
 What is the origin of the suits in a deck of playing cards?
  C:107
 picture(s)
  early playing card factory   G:10
Cardiac arrest (stoppage of the heart)   H:83
Cardiac muscle   B:276; M:517
 picture(s)   B:275
Cardiac orifice (entrance to the stomach)   S:460, 461
Cardiac physiology   B:197
Cardiff (capital of Wales)   U:68; W:3
Cardiff giant (famous hoax)   G:203
Cardinal Albert of Brandenburg as Saint Jerome in His Study
  (painting by Cranach)
 picture(s)   G:170
Cardinals (birds)
 picture(s)   A:269
  state bird of Illinois   I:63
  state bird of Indiana   I:145
  state bird of Kentucky   K:213
  state bird of North Carolina   N:307
  state bird of Ohio   O:61
  state bird of Virginia   V:347
  state bird of West Virginia   W:127
Cardinals, Sacred College of
 forms of address   A:22
Carding (of fibers)
 cotton   C:561
 wool   W:235
Cardiomyopathy (heart disorder)   H:83
Cardiopulmonary resuscitation (first aid technique)   F:158
 picture(s)   F:158
Cardiovascular disease (of the heart and blood vessels)
  C:306; H:82–85
Cardiovascular drugs   D:333
Cardoso, Fernando Henrique (president of Brazil)   B:384
 picture(s)   B:383
Carducci, Giosuè (Italian poet)   I:408
Careers *see* Vocations
Caretaker, The (play by Pinter)
 picture(s)   D:303
Carew, Rod (American baseball player)   B:88 *profile*
 picture(s)   B:88
Cargo bay (of a space shuttle)   S:364–65
Cargo (Trade) cults (of the Pacific Islands)
 picture(s)
  face markings   P:10
Cargo ships   O:30
 Roman cargo ships   S:154
 picture(s)   D:95
  Baltimore harbor   M:126
Carib (Indians of South America)   I:197
 Caribbean islands   C:112
 Dominica   D:279
 Grenada   G:379
 Saint Lucia   S:17, 18
 Saint Vincent and the Grenadines   S:20
 Suriname   S:516
 Trinidad and Tobago   T:315
Caribbean Community and Common Market (CARICOM)   I:271
   see also Organization of Eastern Caribbean States
Caribbean Sea and islands   C:112–15
 Antigua and Barbuda   A:314
 Barbados   B:60
 cities   N:299–300
 Cuba   C:596–600
 dances   D:30
 dolls are popular tourist souvenirs   D:272
 Dominica   D:279
 Dominican Republic   D:280–83
 emigration to the United States   I:93
 Grenada   G:378–79

Haiti   H:9–12
 Indian tribes   I:197–98
 Jamaica   J:15–19
 Latin America   L:47–59
 outlying areas of the United States   U:93
 pirates   P:264
 population   N:295, 298
 Puerto Rico   P:526–32
 Saint Kitts and Nevis   S:13
 Saint Lucia   S:17–18
 Saint Vincent and the Grenadines   S:19–20
 Trinidad and Tobago   T:314–15
 Turks and Caicos Islands   T:353
 water supply   N:293
 picture(s)
  flags of the countries   F:239–40
Cariboo Road (British Columbia)   B:405
Caribou (hoofed mammals) *see* Reindeer and caribou
Caricatures (drawings)   C:127
 Daumier, Honoré   D:42
Caries *see* Dental caries
Carillons (sets of bells for ringing tunes)   B:142; K:240
 picture(s)   B:141
Cariocas (people of Rio de Janeiro)   B:375; R:234
Carissimi, Giacomo (Italian composer)   B:70
Carle, Eric (American author)
 picture(s)
  illustration from *The Very Hungry Caterpillar*   C:237
Carleton, Sir Guy (British army officer and colonial governor)
  C:82; Q:13
Carleton, Mount (New Brunswick)   N:138
Carleton Martello Tower National Historic Site (New Brunswick)
  N:138e
Carleton University (Ottawa)   O:253
Carl XVI Gustaf (king of Sweden) *see* Charles XVI
Carlist Wars (in Spanish history)   S:378
Carlota (empress of Mexico)   M:250
Carl Sandburg Home National Historic Site (North Carolina)
  N:314
Carlsbad Caverns (New Mexico)   C:155–56, 158
Carlsbad Caverns National Park (New Mexico)   N:188
Carlson, Chester (American inventor)   C:464
Carlton, Steve (American baseball player)   B:88 *profile*
 picture(s)   B:88
Carlyle, Thomas (Scottish historian, critic, and philosopher)
  E:284; F:145; I:222
Carmack, George Washington (Canadian prospector)   Y:374
Carman, Bliss (Canadian poet and journalist)   C:86
Carmel (California)   C:28
Carmen (opera by Bizet)   O:152
Carmona, António Óscar de Fragoso (president of Portugal)
  P:395
Carnatic music (of India) *see* Karnatak music
Carnation (flower)
 Mother's Day observances   H:159
 picture(s)
  state flower of Ohio   O:61
Carnauba (wax palm tree of Brazil)   B:377; W:78
Carnegie, Andrew (Scottish-born American industrialist and
  philanthropist)   C:115; P:139
 libraries   L:175
 peace movements   P:105
 Pittsburgh   P:266
 picture(s)   P:140
Carnegie, Dale (American author and lecturer)   M:379 *profile*
Carnegie Company
 Homestead strike   L:14
Carnegie Corporation   F:391
Carnegie Hall (New York City)   N:231
Carnegie Institute (Pittsburgh, Pennsylvania)   C:115
Carnegie Medal (book award)   C:240
Carnegie Museum of Natural History (Pittsburgh, Pennsylvania)
 picture(s)   P:134
Carnegie Peace Palace (The Hague, Netherlands)   P:105
Carnelian (chalcedony quartz)   Q:6

Carnera, Primo (Italian boxer)   B:353
Carnic Alps   A:194b
Carnival of the Animals, The (instrumental suite by Saint-Saëns)
    F:446
Carnivals   C:116–17
    Brazil's Carnival   B:374–75; R:234
    holidays   H:157–58
    Latin-American celebrations   L:55
    pre-Lenten celebrations   E:44
    Quebec's Winter Carnival   Q:17
    picture(s)   C:117
        Brazil's Carnival   B:374; F:332; S:284
        Caribbean carnival dress   N:282
        Venezuela's Feast of Corpus Christi   S:285
Carnivora (order of mammals)
    picture(s)
        brown bear as example   M:66
Carnivores (meat-eating animals)   A:279–81
    bears   B:104
    cats, wild   C:141–50
    dinosaurs   D:168–69
    fish   F:199
    mammals   M:72
    sea lions   S:106
    seals   S:108
    snakes   S:216
    teeth   A:277
    walruses   W:6–7
Carnivorous plants   L:118; P:314; W:147
Caro, Anthony (English sculptor)   E:264
Carol I (king of Romania)   R:300
Carol II (king of Romania)   R:300
Carolina (American colony)   T:178; U:174
Carolina Bays   N:308
Carolina jessamine (flower) *see* Yellow jasmine
Carolina wren (bird)
    picture(s)
        state bird of South Carolina   S:297
Caroline Islands (Pacific Ocean)   P:8; T:115
    Micronesia, Federated States of   M:280
    Palau   P:40b
Carolingian kings (France)   F:413
    France, art and architecture of   F:421–22
    Louis I–Louis V   L:309
Carols (songs)   C:118, 299
    picture(s)
        English carolers   C:301
Caroní River (Venezuela)   S:277
Carotene (substance convertible to vitamin A)   M:307; T:308
Carotenoid (plant pigment)   L:115
Carothers, Wallace Hume (American scientist)   D:100
    profile;   F:110; N:440
Carousel (amusement park ride)
    picture(s)   W:196
Carousel (musical by Rodgers and Hammerstein)   M:558
Carowinds (amusement park, Charlotte, North Carolina)   P:79
Carp (fish)   F:199
    goldfish   P:179
    Japanese symbol of courage   J:31
Carpals (bones of the wrist)   S:183
Carpathian Mountains (Europe)   B:22; E:344; P:358; R:297;
    S:200
    picture(s)   R:296
Carpenter, Karen (American singer)
    picture(s)   N:426
Carpenter ants
    picture(s)   I:248
Carpenter bees   B:121
    picture(s)
        bee and nest   B:121
Carpenters' Hall (Philadelphia, Pennsylvania)   P:180
Carpentier, Alejo (Cuban novelist)   C:599
Carpentry   W:230
    building construction   B:432–33
    carpenter's pencil   P:144

Carpetbaggers (Northerners in the South after the Civil War)
    R:120
Carpetbag rule *see* Reconstruction Period
Carpet beetles (insects)   H:263
Carpets *see* Rugs and carpets
Carpi, Ugo da (Italian artist)   G:304
Carpini, Giovanni de Piano (Italian explorer)   E:401
Carpooling (sharing rides)   T:269, 270
Carr, Emily (Canadian artist)   B:406d
Carra, Carlo (Italian painter)   I:403
Carracci, Annibale (Italian painter)   B:64; I:400–401; P:23
    picture(s)
        Farnese Palace frescoes   I:401
Carrantuohill (mountain in Ireland)   I:318
Carranza, Venustiano (Mexican statesman)   M:251
Carreño, Maria Terese (Venezuelan pianist)   R:123
Carrera, Rafael (Guatemalan political leader)   G:398
Car retarders (in railroad classification yards)   R:85
Carrhae, Battle of (53 B.C.)   P:156
Carriage (of a typewriter)   T:372
Carriages *see* Wagons, carts, carriages, and coaches
Carrier, Roch (Canadian writer)   C:87
Carrier, Willis Haviland (American inventor)   A:102
Carriers of disease *see* Vectors
Carrier transmission (in electronic communication)
    radio   R:53, 54, 58
    telephone   T:47
Carrier wave (high-frequency electromagnetic wave)   T:63
Carrion beetle
    picture(s)   B:127
Carroll, Charles (American Revolutionary War leader)   M:132
    profile
Carroll, Lewis (pen name of Charles Lutwidge Dodgson, English
    mathematics professor and writer)   C:119–20, 233;
    E:286
    "Jabberwocky" (poem)   N:273
    number puzzles   N:391
    words, invention of   L:40
Carrots   F:333; V:290
    picture(s)
        flowers   F:282
        roots   P:303
"Carrying coals to Newcastle" (expression)   U:67
Cars (of railroad trains)   R:82
Cars, electric *see* Electric automobiles
Cars, motor *see* Automobiles
Carson, Benjamin (American neurosurgeon)   C:485
Carson, Johnny (American comedian)   N:94 *profile*
Carson, Kit (American frontiersman)   C:121; N:131, 192
    profile, 193
    picture(s)   O:279
Carson, Rachel (American writer and biologist)
    C:121; E:306; N:70; S:75
    picture(s)   N:70
Carson City (capital of Nevada)   N:129, 131
    picture(s)   N:132
Carson National Forest (New Mexico)   N:194
Carstens, Asmus Jacob (German artist)   G:171
Carstensz, Mount (New Guinea) *see* Puncak Jaya
Cartagena (Spain)   S:375
Cartago (Costa Rica)   C:556, 557, 558
Carte, Richard D'Oyly *see* D'Oyly Carte, Richard
Carter, Amy (daughter of President Carter)
    picture(s)   C:124
Carter, James Earl, Jr. (39th president of the United States)
    C:122–25; U:202
    Egyptian-Israeli peace talks   I:376
    human rights   H:286
    presidential library   G:137
    picture(s)   F:368; P:453; U:202
Carter, Lillian Gordy (mother of James E. Carter)   C:122
    picture(s)   C:123
Carter, Rosalynn Smith (wife of James E. Carter)   C:123;
    F:180a
    picture(s)   C:124; F:180

Caudillos (South American military chieftains)   A:394; L:59
Cauliflower (vegetable)   V:290
Caulkins, Tracy (American swimmer)   S:537 *profile*
    picture(s)   S:537
Cauterization (in surgery)   S:513, 515
Cauto (major river in Cuba)   C:597
Cauvery Falls (India)   W:63
Cauvery River (India)   I:125
Cavalier of the Rose, The (opera by Strauss) *see Rosenkavalier, Der*
Cavalier poets (in English literature)   E:274
Cavalleria Rusticana (opera by Mascagni)   O:152
Cave, Edward (Sylvanus Urban) (English printer and publisher)   M:19
Caveat emptor ("let the buyer beware")   C:527
Cave dwellers
    art *see* Rock art
    fire, use of   F:141
Cavelier, Robert *see* La Salle, Robert Cavelier, Sieur de
Cavell, Edith Louisa (English nurse)   W:282 *profile*
    picture(s)   W:282
Cavemen *see* Cave dwellers
Cavendish (Prince Edward Island)
    picture(s)   P:463
Cavendish, Henry (British chemist)   F:365; H:316; L:83
Cave of the Mounds (Wisconsin)   W:200
Cave paintings *see* Rock art
Cave pearls (cave formations)   C:156
Caverns (kind of cave) *see* Sea caves
Caves and caverns   C:155–58
    art *see* Rock art
    bats   B:101
    Blanchard Spring Caverns (Arkansas)   A:424
    Buddhist cave-halls in India   I:136, 138–39
    Cave of the Mounds (Wisconsin)   W:200
    Hindu cave temples   B:310b
    homes of the past   H:177
    Kiev's cave monastery   K:245
    spelunking   S:400–401
    Wyandotte Cave (Indiana)   I:152
Caviar (roe of sturgeon)   A:574; R:359; U:37
Cavill, Richard (Australian swimmer)   S:536
Cavill, Sydney (Australian-American swimmer)   S:536
Caving (method used to remove ore deposits)   M:322
Cavities (tooth decay)   D:114; T:44
    bacteria   B:11
    chocolate does not cause   C:281
Cavour, Camillo di (Italian leader)   I:389
Caxton, William (English printer)   A:34, 442
Cayenne (capital of French Guiana)   F:466
Cayley, Sir George (English inventor)   A:560–61
Cayman Islands (West Indies)   C:114
Caymans (reptiles)   C:582, 583; R:180
Cayuga (Indians of North America)   I:175
Cayuse Indians (of North America)   I:205
CBC *see* Canadian Broadcasting Corporation
CBI *see* Cumulative Book Index
CB radio *see* Citizens band radio
CCC *see* Civilian Conservation Corps
C clef (in musical notation)   M:538
CD-ROMs (compact discs that can be read by computers)   C:482, 491
    encyclopedias   E:207
    journalism   J:141
    reference materials   R:129
    video games   V:332b
    picture(s)   C:482, 483
CD's *see* Certificates of deposit; Compact discs
Ceaușescu, Nicolae (Romanian political leader)   B:421; R:299, 301
Cebu City (Philippines)   P:186, 187
Cecil, William (English statesman)   E:191
Cecilia, Saint   S:18d *profile*

Cecropia moth
    picture(s)   I:234
        cocoon   I:233
        moth and larva   B:483
Cedar Breaks National Monument (Utah)   U:250
Cedar City (Utah)   U:247, 251
Cedar Point (amusement park near Sandusky, Ohio)   P:78
Cedar Rapids (Iowa)   I:299
Cedar trees (conifers)
    of Lebanon   L:120
    uses of the wood and its grain   W:227
    picture(s)
        red cedar   T:304
        uses of the wood and its grain   W:223
Cédras, Raoul (Haitian military leader)   H:12
Ceiba (Silk cotton tree) (yields kapok fibers)   K:192
Céilis (Irish musical entertainments)   I:322
Cel (in animation art) *see* Cels
Cela, Camilo José (Spanish author)   S:392
    picture(s)   S:392
Celadon (kind of porcelain)   C:277; K:298–99
    picture(s)   C:276; K:300
Celebes (Sulawesi) (island in Indonesia)   I:208, 209
"Celebrated Jumping Frog of Calaveras County, The" (story by Twain)   T:360
    excerpt from   T:362
Celery (vegetable)   F:333; V:290
Celery seed (spice)   H:114
    picture(s)   H:115
Celesta (keyboard instrument)   K:240; O:196; P:149
Celestial navigation   N:74–76
Celestial poles (of the celestial sphere)   S:110
Celestial sphere   S:110
Celestina, La (novel by Fernando de Rojas)   S:387
Celestine II (antipope)   R:290
Celestine I, Saint (pope)   R:290
Celestine II (pope)   R:290
Celestine III (pope)   R:291
Celestine IV (pope)   R:291
Celestine V, Saint (pope)   R:291
Cell, voltaic *see* Voltaic cell
Cella (inner chamber of Greek temple)   A:373
Cell biology   S:66
Cell bodies (Somas) (of neurons)   B:362
Cellini, Benvenuto (Italian sculptor)   D:76; F:424
    picture(s)
        saltcellar   D:76
Cello (musical instrument)   M:552; O:196
    picture(s)   M:551; S:468
Cell phones *see* Cellular telephones
Cells (basic units of life)   C:159–62; L:200 *see also* Eggs; Embryos
    aging   A:83–84, 86
    algae   A:180–81
    animal kingdom   K:254
    blood cells   B:255–56
    body, human   B:269–70
    body chemistry   B:291–99
    cancer   C:92–95
    cell membrane in body chemistry   B:295
    cell theory in biology   B:200
    cork cells   C:549
    degenerative diseases   D:185
    egg cell division to become an embryo   E:101–2
    fungi   F:496
    gene splicing of bacteria   G:83
    genetics   G:78–79, 80
    Hooke, Robert   H:221
    how antibiotics work   A:308
    lytic viruses kill cells   V:364–65
    microscope, how to look at body cells through a   M:283
    nerve cells of the brain   B:362–63
    nutrition   N:423, 425
    one-celled organisms   M:274

organisms are made of cells   **B:**193, 194
  osmosis   **O:**242–43
  plants   **P:**302
  protozoans   **P:**495–97
  reproduction   **R:**175
  science, milestones in   **S:**71, 72
  tumors   **D:**185
  diagram(s)
    mitosis   **C:**162
  picture(s)   **B:**197
    cancer cells   **C:**92
Cells (that produce electricity) *see* Batteries; Fuel cells;
    Photoelectric cells; Solar cells
Cellular respiration (in plants)   **L:**116
Cellular telephones   **C:**468; **E:**162; **O:**56; **T:**47, 56
  picture(s)   **A:**454; **T:**55
Celluloid (plastic material)   **P:**328
Cellulose
  algae cells   **A:**181
  fibers   **F:**108–9, 110, 111; **N:**436, 439
  fungi can digest   **F:**500
  fungi's cell walls   **K:**257
  made up of glucose units   **L:**199
  naturally occurring polymer   **P:**323, 327
  paper making   **P:**53
  plant cells   **C:**161; **P:**294
Cellulose nitrate (guncotton explosive)   **E:**420
Cell walls (of bacteria)   **B:**10; **K:**259
Cell walls (of fungi)   **K:**257
Cell walls (of plants)   **K:**256
Cels (in animation art)   **A:**289
Celsius, Anders (Swedish scientist)   **H:**87
Celsius scale (of temperature)   **H:**86, 87; **T:**163; **W:**116
  diagram(s)
    compared to Fahrenheit scale   **H:**86
Celsus (Roman writer)   **M:**204
Celtic art and architecture   **C:**163, 164; **E:**256, 257
  picture(s)
    Ardagh chalice   **C:**163
    carving of horse   **C:**164
Celtic languages   **C:**163; **E:**352; **I:**325
Celtic literature   **C:**163
Celtic mythology
  picture(s)
    Cernunnos   **M:**566
Celts (people)   **C:**163–64
  Arthur, King   **A:**442–43
  England, history of   **E:**235
  France   **F:**403
  handball, origin of   **H:**17
  Iceland   **I:**33
  Ireland   **I:**317, 322–23
  Scotland   **S:**85
  Spain   **S:**369–70
  Wales   **W:**3, 4
Cement   **C:**165–66
  adhesives   **G:**242
  How is cement made?   **C:**165
  masonry   **B:**392–94
Cement trucks   **T:**321
  picture(s)   **T:**320
Cementum (bonelike material of teeth)   **T:**43
Cemeteries *see also* Funeral customs; Tombs
  gravestone rubbings   **R:**348b
  national cemeteries of the United States   **N:**29–31, 54
  United Nations cemetery   **P:**552
Cenerentola, La (opera by Rossini)   **O:**152
Cenozoic era (in geology)   **E:**29; **F:**388; **P:**433–34
  table(s)   **E:**25; **F:**384
Censorship (restriction of the freedoms of speech and the
    press)
  civil liberties, violations of   **C:**325
  English drama   **E:**277
  First Amendment freedoms   **F:**163
  motion pictures   **M:**491

Census (official count of people and property)   **C:**167
  automation used for data   **A:**529
  Domesday Book   **W:**174
  Hollerith cards and machines used in the census of 1890
    C:490
  House of Representatives apportionment   **U:**168
  How is the U.S. population census taken?   **C:**167
  human geography   **G:**102
  statistics   **S:**439
Census, Bureau of the *see* United States Bureau of the Census
Centaurs (in Greek mythology)   **G:**363
  picture(s)   **G:**363
Centaurus A (galaxy)
  picture(s)   **R:**72
Centennial State (nickname for Colorado)   **C:**430, 431
Centerboard (on a sailboat)   **S:**11
Center-fire cartridges (for guns)   **G:**419
Center for Research Libraries (Chicago, Illinois)   **L:**178
Center of gravity   **G:**324
Center pass (in field hockey)   **F:**119
Centers (in basketball)   **B:**95b
Centers for Disease Control (Atlanta, Georgia)   **D:**213; **H:**79;
    P:514
  picture(s)   **P:**513
Centigrade scale *see* Celsius scale
Centimeter (measure of length)   **W:**111–12
Centipede (game)
  picture(s)
    box   **G:**22
Centipedes (many-legged animals)   **C:**168–69
Central African Republic   **C:**170–71
  picture(s)
    flag   **F:**226
Central air conditioning   **A:**102
Central America   **C:**172–75 *see also* the names of individual
    countries
  agriculture   **N:**300
  Caribbean Sea and islands   **C:**112–15
  cities   **N:**299
  immigration to the United States   **H:**132, 137
  Indians, American   **I:**166–67, 169, 194–95
  lakes of the world   **L:**29
  Latin America   **L:**47–59
  Maya   **M:**184–87
  Monroe Doctrine and Roosevelt Corollary   **R:**331
  Organization of American States   **O:**220
  Panama Canal   **P:**49–51
  population   **N:**295, 298
  pyramids   **P:**556
  refugees   **R:**137
  picture(s)
    flags   **F:**241
Central American Common Market (CACM)   **C:**175; **I:**271; **L:**59
  El Salvador   **E:**197
Central American Cordillera   **H:**196
Central Arizona Project (CAP) (water use)   **A:**406, 415; **P:**193
Central Asia (Inner Asia)   **A:**446, 453; **U:**34, 39, 40, 41
  Kazakhstan   **K:**200–201
  Kyrgyzstan   **K:**311–12
  Tajikistan   **T:**10–11
  Turkmenistan   **T:**351–52
  Uzbekistan   **U:**257–58
Central banks   **M:**415
Central heating   **H:**95–97
Central Intelligence Agency (CIA)   **C:**176; **S:**407
Central Lowland (North America)   **U:**80–81
Central nervous system   **B:**364; **N:**116, 118
Central Park (New York City)   **N:**231; **P:**77
  Cleopatra's Needle   **O:**5
  picture(s)   **N:**231
    ice skating   **I:**38; **P:**77
Central plan (in church architecture)   **I:**392
Central Powers   **W:**283, 285, 289, 290
Central processing unit (of a computer) *see* CPU
Central University of Venezuela (Caracas)   **V:**295

Central Valley (California) **C:**18, 20, 23, 25
Centrifugal casting (of metals) **M:**234
Centrifugal force (of the Earth) **E:**10; **G:**323
  picture(s)
    amusement-park ride **G:**323
Centrifugal pumps **P:**541
  dredging machines **D:**320
Centrifuge
  uranium 235 separated from uranium 238 **U:**230
Centrioles (of cell) **C:**161, 162
Century 21 Exposition (Seattle, 1962) **F:**17
Century Dictionary and Cyclopedia, The **D:**155
Century of Progress (world's fair, Chicago, 1933–1934) **F:**17
Century plant
  picture(s) **N:**286
Century year **C:**14, 15
Cephalopods (mollusks) **M:**407; **O:**292–93
Cephalothorax (head-chest section of crustacea and arachnids)
  S:402
Ceramics **C:**176–78
  Chinese art **C:**277
  Islamic art **I:**359
  Japanese art and architecture **J:**51
  pottery (ceramic vessels) **P:**407–13
  superconductivity **H:**92
  tile as a building material **A:**371, 373
  picture(s)
    Chinese art **C:**276
    Islamic art **I:**358
Ceratopsia (dinosaurs) **D:**174
Ceratosaurus (dinosaur) **D:**169
Cerberus (watchdog in Greek mythology) **G:**362, 367
Cerci (feelers of some insects) **I:**231
Cereal grains *see* Grain and grain products
Cereal grasses (those with seed that can be eaten) **G:**317–18
Cereals, breakfast **G:**284
  Battle Creek (Michigan) **M:**269, 273
  food shopping **F:**349
Cerebellum (part of the brain) **B:**366, 367; **N:**116
  nervous system **B:**284, 285
Cerebral cortex (of the brain) **B:**364–65, 367, 368, 369
Cerebral hemispheres (halves of the cerebrum) **B:**364
Cerebral palsy (disorder of the nervous system) **D:**190
  occupational therapy **O:**14
Cerebrospinal fluid (in the brain) **B:**364
Cerebrum (part of the brain) **B:**364–65, 367; **N:**116
  nervous system **B:**284–85
Ceremonies *see* Rites and ceremonies
Ceres (asteroid) **A:**473; **P:**278
  compared to Pluto **P:**341
  Gauss, Carl Friedrich **G:**64
  solar system **S:**244
Ceres (Roman goddess) *see* Demeter
Cereus (night-blooming cactus) **C:**5
Cerium (element) **E:**172
Cermets (materials that combine the qualities of ceramics with
  the tensile strength of metals) **C:**178
CERN *see* European Organization for Nuclear Research
Cernan, Eugene (American astronaut) **S:**342
Cernunnos (Celtic god)
  picture(s) **M:**566
Cerro (geographic term) *see* individual mountains by name, as
  Punta, Cerro de
Certificates of deposit (CD's) (in banking) **B:**56
Certified mail **P:**399
Certified Public Accountant (C.P.A.) **B:**313
Certosina (ivory inlay) **D:**77
Cervantes Saavedra, Miguel de (Spanish writer)
  C:178; **N:**358; **S:**388
  Don Quixote, quotation from **Q:**20
  fiction **F:**115
  satire **H:**290
Cervera y Topete, Pascual (Spanish admiral) **S:**392d
Cervical cap (birth control device) **B:**248
Cervical vertebrae (of the spine) **S:**183

Césaire, Aimé (West Indian poet) **A:**76c–76d
Cesium (element) **C:**371; **E:**172; **T:**201
Cespedes, Carlos Manuel de (Cuban revolutionary) **C:**599
Cesta (basket used in jai alai) **J:**12, 13
Cestus (leather covering for Greek and Roman boxers' hands)
  B:353
Cetaceans (marine mammals)
  dolphins **D:**273–78
  whales **W:**149–53
  picture(s)
    gray whale as example **M:**70
Ceuta (Spanish enclave in Morocco) **S:**375
Ceylon *see* Sri Lanka
Cézanne, Paul (French painter) **C:**179
  French art **F:**431
  modern art **M:**388
  Picasso and Cézanne **P:**243
  postimpressionism **I:**106
  style of his still-life painting **P:**29
  watercolor painting **W:**60
  picture(s)
    Apples and Oranges (painting) **F:**430
    Kitchen Table (painting) **P:**28
    Mont Sainte-Victoire (painting) **I:**106
    Mount Sainte-Victoire with Tall Pine (painting) **C:**179
    Rocky Landscape (painting) **M:**389
CFCs *see* Chlorofluorocarbons
Chaco (region of South America) **S:**277, 282
  Paraguay **P:**62, 63, 64, 66
Chaco Culture National Historical Park (New Mexico) **N:**188
Chaconne (musical form) **M:**544
Chaco War (1932–1935) **S:**295
Chad **C:**180–81
  Libya, relations with **L:**190
  picture(s)
    flag **F:**226
Chad, Lake (north central Africa) **A:**48; **C:**180, 181; **L:**33–34
Chador (veil)
  picture(s) **I:**305, 349
Chadwick, Edwin (English reformer) **M:**208
Chadwick, Florence (American swimmer) **S:**537 *profile*
  picture(s) **S:**537
Chadwick, Sir James (English physicist) **P:**239
Chaeronea, Battle of (338 B.C.) **G:**344
Chaetae (hairs of an earthworm) **E:**42
Chaffee, Roger (American astronaut) **S:**352
Chagall, Marc (Russian painter) **C:**182; **R:**375
  picture(s)
    I and the Village (painting) **C:**182
    painting showing Moses receiving the Ten
      Commandments **M:**469
Chagres River (Panama) **P:**49
Chaillot, Palais de (Paris) **P:**70
Chain dance **D:**28
Chain dredge *see* Ladder bucket dredge
Chained books (in early libraries)
  picture(s) **L:**178
Chain lightning **T:**187
Chain mail armor **A:**433
  picture(s) **A:**434
Chain newspapers **N:**205
Chain of command (of the United States armed forces)
  picture(s) **U:**106
Chain reactions (of atoms) **F:**223; **N:**369, 373
  nuclear weapons **N:**374
Chains (of mountains) **M:**501
Chain stitch (in crocheting) **C:**580
Chain stitch (in embroidery) **N:**98
  picture(s) **N:**99
Chain stores **S:**21
  retail stores **R:**188
  supermarkets **S:**498
Chair lifts (for transporting skiers) **S:**185

Chairs
> upholstery **U:**228
> *picture(s)*
>> Aalto's molded plywood chair **F:**515
>> caning **W:**130
>> Chinese chairs **F:**507
>> Chippendale chair **F:**512
>> Eames dining chair **I:**214
>> Egyptian folding stool **F:**507
>> Hepplewhite chair **F:**512
>> Mies van der Rohe chairs **F:**515
>> Robert Adam chair **D:**69
>> Saarinen's tulip chair **F:**515
>> sandpaper used to finish wooden chair **G:**392

Chaka (Zulu chief) **S:**272
Chakri dynasty (Thailand) **B:**47; **T:**152
Chalcedony (quartz) **G:**74, 97; **Q:**6
Chalcocite (Copper glance) (copper ore) **C:**546
Chalcopyrite (mineral) **C:**546; **G:**249; **M:**315
> *picture(s)* **M:**314
> *table(s)* **M:**315
Chaldean (Neo-Babylonian) Empire (of Mesopotamia)
> **A:**241–42
> *picture(s)* **A:**243
Chalets (houses) **H:**169
Chaleur Bay (New Brunswick) **N:**138, 138c
Chaliapin, Feodor (Russian operatic bass) **O:**140 *profile*
> *picture(s)*
>> as Boris Godunov **O:**147
Chalice (cup used at a Communion service)
> *picture(s)* **D:**74; **G:**230
Chalk (form of limestone) **R:**266
> white cliffs of Dover (England) **E:**233
> *picture(s)*
>> cliffs of Normandy **F:**407
>> Kansas' chalk country **K:**178
Chalk River (Ontario) **O:**130
Challenger (United States space shuttle) **S:**340j, 348, 352, 365
> Feynman, Richard P. **P:**236
> first untethered space walk **S:**348
> submersibles searched for remains **E:**416
> *picture(s)*
>> display at Space Center in Iowa **P:**274
>> explosion **S:**352
Challenger Center for Space Science Education **S:**340a
Challenger Deep (greatest known ocean depth) **O:**21; **P:**2
Challenger **expedition** (oceanographic expedition) **O:**41
Châlons, Battle of (451) **A:**490; **B:**103e
Chamber (rear section of a gun's barrel) **G:**415
Chambered nautilus *see* Pearly nautilus
Chambered Nautilus (painting by Andrew Wyeth)
> *picture(s)* **W:**333
"Chambered Nautilus, The" (poem by Holmes) **H:**159b
Chamberlain, Sir Austen (British statesman) **C:**183
Chamberlain, Joseph (British statesman) **C:**182–83
Chamberlain, Joshua (American Civil War hero) **M:**48 *profile*
> *picture(s)* **M:**48
Chamberlain, Neville **C:**183, 303; **E:**253; **W:**286
Chamberlain, Wilt (American basketball player) **B:**95i *profile*
> *picture(s)* **B:**95i
Chamberlain family **C:**182–83
Chamberlain's Men (an acting company) **S:**131–32
Chamber music **C:**183–84
> basic record library **R:**125
> chamber orchestras **O:**182
> festivals **M:**559, 560
> musical instruments **M:**552
Chamber orchestra **C:**183–84; **O:**192
Chambers, Whittaker Jay David (American secret agent for the
> Soviet Union) **S:**408 *profile*
Chambord (château, France)
> *picture(s)* **F:**424

Chameleons (lizards) **L:**277
> Why do chameleons change color? **L:**275
> *picture(s)* **A:**280; **L:**275, 276
Chamizal National Memorial (Texas) **T:**132
Chamois (animal)
> *picture(s)* **H:**219
Chamomile tea **F:**281
Chamonix (France)
> Olympic Games (1924) **O:**109
Chamorro, Violeta Barrios de (Nicaraguan political leader)
> **N:**248
> *picture(s)* **N:**247
Champagne **W:**190a
> Why are ships christened with champagne? **S:**156
Champaign (Illinois) **I:**72
Champion (title earned by prize-winning dogs) **D:**248
Champion, William (English manufacturer) **Z:**389
Champlain, Lake (New York–Vermont) **L:**28; **N:**213; **V:**306,
> 309, 310, 313, 318
> War of 1812 **W:**11
> *picture(s)* **V:**309
Champlain, Samuel de (French explorer) **C:**185
> Canada **C:**80
> exploration of the New World **E:**408
> Great Lakes **G:**327–28
> Maine, history of **M:**49
> Nova Scotia **N:**356
> Quebec **Q:**14, 15
> Saint Lawrence River, settlements near **S:**14
> *map(s)*
>> expeditions **C:**185
Champlain Valley (Vermont) **V:**309
Champlevé (enameling technique) **D:**74; **E:**205
Champollion, Jean François (French archaeologist) **L:**331
Champs-Elysées, Avenue des (Paris)
> *picture(s)* **P:**71
Chams (a people of Southeast Asia) **C:**35; **V:**334
Chance, science of *see* Probability
Chancellorsville, Battle of (1863, Civil War) **C:**340; **J:**9
Chance music **F:**448; **G:**189; **M:**548
Chancery cursive script
> *picture(s)* **H:**25
Chan Chan (ancient city of Peru) **I:**109
Chandigarh (India) **I:**139; **L:**124
Chandler, Dorothy Buffum (American patron of the arts) **L:**308
> *profile*
Chandler, Norman (American newspaper publisher) **L:**308
> *profile*
Chandler, Otis (American newspaper publisher) **L:**308 *profile*
Chandler, Raymond (American author) **M:**562 *profile*
> *picture(s)* **M:**562
Chandler Wedding Tapestry
> *picture(s)* **C:**414
Chandni Chowk (Street of Silver) (Delhi, India) **D:**103–4
> *picture(s)* **D:**104
Chandragupta II (king of northern India) **I:**130
Chandragupta Maurya (king of Magadha (modern Bihar), India)
> **I:**130
Chandrasekhar, Subrahmanyan (Indian astrophysicist) **S:**368
Chandra X-Ray Observatory **O:**10; **S:**367, 368; **T:**60
Chaney, James (American civil rights volunteer) **M:**363
Changelings (fairy children substituted for humans) **F:**11–12
Chang Heng (Chinese scientist) **G:**108
Chang Jiang (Long River) (China) *see* Yangtze River
Chang Myon (Korean statesman) **K:**301
Changpai (volcano, Korea–Manchuria) *see* Paektu-san
Chang River (China) *see* Yangtze River
Chang Tang (region of Tibet) **T:**190
Channeling (in quarrying) **Q:**4b
Channel Islands (Great Britain) **I:**363; **U:**60, 69
Channels (in sound recording) **S:**267
Channels (television) **T:**63

Channel Tunnel (between England and France)   **E:**233; **T:**340; **U:**66, 69
  London transportation   **L:**297
  picture(s)   **F:**420; **W:**220
Chansons (French songs)   **C:**283; **F:**445; **M:**543
Chantilly lace   **L:**19
Chants (in church music) *see* Gregorian chants; Plainsong
Chanukah *see* Hanukkah
Chanute, Octave (American engineer)   **G:**240
Chao Phraya River (Thailand)   **T:**149
Chaos (in Greek mythology)   **G:**361
Chaos theory (in mathematics)   **M:**159, 170
  weather prediction   **W:**93
Chapala, Lake (Mexico)   **L:**29; **N:**287
Chaparral (thick vegetation)   **B:**205–6; **P:**319
  picture(s)   **P:**321
Chaparral birds *see* Roadrunners
Chapbooks (early paperbacks)   **P:**58a
  ballads   **B:**24
  children's literature   **C:**229, 232
Chaplin, Charlie (English actor)   **C:**185–86; **M:**489
Chapman, John (American folk hero) *see* Appleseed, Johnny
Chappe, Claude (French engineer)   **T:**51
Chaps (worn by cowboys)   **C:**569
Chapultepec, Battle of (1847)   **M:**239b
  picture(s)   **P:**377
Chapultepec Park (Mexico City)   **M:**253
Char, René (French poet)   **F:**442
Character clown   **C:**387
Character count (in book design)   **B:**327
Characters, literary
  book reports concentrating on   **B:**316
  fiction   **F:**114, 115, 116
  in novels   **N:**358
  realism in children's literature   **C:**236
  short stories   **S:**162
Characters of Chinese words *see* Chinese writing
Charades (game)   **C:**186–87
Charbonneau, Toussaint (interpreter for Lewis and Clark expedition)   **I:**59; **L:**164
Charcoal   **C:**106
  drawing material   **D:**309
  outdoor cooking uses   **O:**263
  picture(s)
    drawing material   **D:**308
Charcot, Jean Martin (French physician)   **F:**474
Chardin, Jean Baptiste Simeon (French painter)   **F:**428; **P:**24
  picture(s)
    still life with a pipe   **F:**428
Chardonnet, Hilaire, Count de (French inventor)   **N:**439–40
  rayon   **F:**110
  textiles   **T:**141
Chares of Lindos (Greek craftsman)   **W:**219
Charge accounts
  department stores   **D:**120
  interest   **I:**255
  mail order   **M:**35
Charge carriers (in conducting electricity)   **T:**274–75
Charge-coupled devices (in cameras)   **E:**160
  television cameras   **T:**62
  tools used in observatories   **O:**11; **T:**57
"Charge of the Light Brigade" (poem by Tennyson)   **C:**577
Charges, electric *see* Electric charges
Charging (of batteries)   **B:**103a, 103b–103c; **E:**143
Chariot (sculpture by Giacometti)
  picture(s)   **M:**395
Charioteer (statue)   **G:**350
Chariots (ancient wheeled vehicles)   **W:**159, 160
Chari River *see* Shari River
Charities (for distribution of aid)
  foundations   **F:**391
  income tax deduction   **I:**111
  Muslim almsgiving   **I:**353
  Red Cross   **R:**126–27

  Salvation Army   **S:**25
  UNICEF   **U:**28
Charlemagne (Charles I; Charles the Great) (ruler of the Franks)   **C:**188
  architecture   **A:**375–76; **F:**421–22
  Christianity, history of   **C:**290
  education furthered by   **E:**77–78
  founded Germany's First Reich   **G:**158
  France, history of   **F:**413
  Holy Roman Empire   **H:**160
  jury system   **J:**163
  legends based on actual deeds   **L:**130
  Middle Ages   **M:**290
  mother, Bertha, thought to be original Mother Goose   **N:**415
  religious reform by force   **R:**285
  signature reproduced   **A:**527
  picture(s)   **G:**160
    flag   **F:**248
    tomb at Aachen   **F:**421
Charles (Prince of Wales)   **E:**192, 255
  picture(s)   **E:**254; **S:**88
Charles, Ezzard (American boxer)   **B:**353
Charles, Jacques (French scientist)   **A:**560; **B:**35; **G:**57
Charles I (emperor of Austria)   **A:**525
Charles I (king of England)   **C:**189, 585; **E:**245–46, 259
  gave Maryland to George Calvert   **T:**177
  Prado contains treasures from his estate   **P:**423
  Puritans engaged in civil war against   **P:**550
  South Carolina   **S:**296, 308
  picture(s)
    Van Dyck portrait   **E:**259
Charles II (king of England)   **C:**189; **E:**246, 259
  beginning of English political parties   **P:**369
  brought ice skating from Netherlands   **I:**38
  gave Pennsylvania to William Penn   **T:**176
  South Carolina   **S:**308
Charles II (the Bald) (king of France) *see* Charles II (Holy Roman Emperor)
Charles III (the Simple) (king of France)   **C:**189; **V:**342
Charles IV (the Fair) (king of France)   **C:**189
Charles V (the Wise) (king of France)   **C:**189
Charles VI (the Mad or Well-Beloved) (king of France)   **C:**189
Charles VII (the Well-Served) (king of France)   **C:**189; **F:**414; **J:**112
Charles VIII (king of France)   **C:**189–90; **F:**414
Charles IX (king of France)   **C:**190; **L:**332
Charles X (king of France)   **C:**190; **F:**417
  Huguenots   **H:**279
  Louis Philippe   **L:**312
Charles II (Holy Roman Emperor) (Charles II, king of France, called Charles the Bald)   **C:**189, 190; **F:**99, 413
Charles III (Holy Roman Emperor)   **C:**190
Charles IV (Holy Roman Emperor)   **C:**190, 612; **P:**425
Charles V (Holy Roman Emperor) (Charles I, king of Spain)   **H:**2, 3 *profile*, 163; **S:**376–77
  Austria   **A:**523
  Luther, Martin   **R:**130, 131
  picture(s)   **H:**3
Charles VI (Holy Roman Emperor)   **A:**524; **C:**190; **H:**2–3
Charles VII (Holy Roman Emperor)   **C:**190
Charles III (prince of Monaco)   **M:**409
Charles II (king of Spain)   **H:**2; **S:**377
Charles VIII (king of Sweden)   **C:**190
Charles IX (king of Sweden)   **C:**190
Charles X (king of Sweden)   **C:**190
Charles XI (king of Sweden)   **C:**190
Charles XII (king of Sweden)   **C:**190; **S:**529
Charles XIII (king of Sweden)   **C:**190
Charles XIV (king of Sweden)   **C:**190
Charles XV (king of Sweden)   **C:**190
Charles XVI (king of Sweden)   **C:**190
Charles Bridge (Prague, Czech Republic)   **P:**425
  picture(s)   **P:**425
Charles XVI Gustav (king of Sweden)   **S:**528

Cherry (fruit)   P:108, 109
Japanese cherry blossom viewing   J:31
picture(s)   M:259; P:109
Cherry barb (fish)   F:204
Cherry County (Nebraska)   N:86
Cherry Orchard, The (play by Chekhov)   C:196
picture(s)   R:379
Chert (sedimentary rock)   R:267
Cherubini, Luigi (Italian composer)   F:446
Chesapeake (American warship)   W:9, 10
Chesapeake and Delaware Canal (Maryland–Delaware)   D:98, 102; M:123
Chesapeake and Ohio Canal (Maryland)   M:128
Chesapeake Bay (eastern United States)
colonial life   C:420–21
conservation laws   M:123
Maryland   M:120, 122, 127
Virginia   V:346, 348, 350, 353
Chesapeake Bay Bridge-Tunnel   B:401; M:122; V:353
Chesapeake Bay Maritime Museum Lighthouse (Saint Michael's, Maryland)
picture(s)   M:128
Chesapeake Bay retriever (dog)   D:249
Che School (in Chinese art)   C:275
Cheshire (England)
picture(s)
Little Moreton Hall   E:258
Chesnut, Mary Boykin Miller (American Civil War diarist)   C:345 *profile*
picture(s)   C:345
Chesnutt, Charles Waddell (American author)   A:209
Chess (game)   C:212–17; G:13
Kasparov's loss to computer   C:492
Union of Soviet Socialist Republics   U:36
picture(s)   I:66
chess pieces   G:12
Kasparov's loss to computer   C:492
Little Havana (Miami, Florida)   F:265
Union of Soviet Socialist Republics   U:34
Chester Dale Collection (of art)   N:39
Chesterton, Gilbert Keith (English author)   E:289
Chestnut blight (bark disease)   N:433; P:287
Chestnuts   N:433; P:287
Chests (furniture for storage)   F:509
picture(s)   F:508
Chetniks (Yugoslav faction)   S:125; Y:368
Chevrolet (automobile)
picture(s)
Blazer   A:545
scale model   A:534
Chevrotains (mouse deer)   H:212
picture(s)   H:213
Chewa (a people of Zambia)   Z:381
Chewing gum   R:185
stain removal   L:82
Chewing pests   P:288
Cheyenne (capital of Wyoming)   W:339, 340, 341, 346
picture(s)   W:343
Cheyenne Indians (of North America)   C:443; I:180, 205
picture(s)   I:200
Chi (collections of Chinese poetry and essays)   C:279
Chia, Sandro (Italian painter)   I:403
Chiang Ching *see* Jiang Qing
Chiang Ching-kuo (Chinese political leader of the Nationalist government on Taiwan)   C:267; T:9
Chiang Kai-shek (Chinese general and president of Nationalist China)   C:217, 267, 271; T:9
Mao Tse-tung and Chiang Kai-shek   M:90
Chiapas (province in Mexico)   N:304
Chiaroscuro (painting technique)   I:397; L:153; R:156
Chibchas (Indians of South America)   C:407–8; I:195
Chicago (Illinois)   C:218–21; I:62, 65, 67, 68, 75, 76
aquarium   A:337
Century of Progress (1933–1934)   F:17

fire (1871)   F:146
Palmer House   H:259
World's Columbian Exposition (1893)   F:16
writers group   A:210
picture(s)   A:369; I:63
Art Institute of Chicago   I:67
baseball game in Grant Park   P:77
Field Museum   M:523
Lake Shore Drive Apartments   M:306
Marshall Field & Co. department store   D:118
Museum of Science and Industry   C:219; M:524
Sears Tower   C:218; W:220
Chicago, University of (Illinois)   C:221
Laboratory School   K:250
Chicago Board of Trade   I:68
Chicago Bulls (basketball team)   B:99
Chicago Cubs (baseball team)   B:91
Chicago Fire (1871)   C:220; I:76
Chicago Mercantile Exchange   I:68
Chicago River (Illinois)   C:218
Chicago Tribune (newspaper)
picture(s)
on-line service   N:205
Chicago White Sox (baseball team)   B:91
Chicago Working Woman's Union (labor organization)   H:136
Chicanos (term for Mexican Americans)   H:136
Chichén Itzá (Mexico)   I:172; M:187
picture(s)
Maya temple   M:248
ruins   N:283
Chichewa (language)   M:52
Chickadees (birds)
picture(s)
blackcapped chickadee is provincial bird of New Brunswick   N:138
feet   B:216
state bird of Maine   M:37
state bird of Massachusetts   M:137
Chickamauga (Georgia)   C:342
Chickamauga and Chattanooga National Military Park   T:82
Chickasaw (Indians of North America)   A:134, 139; I:178, 179; M:359, 362
Chicken pox (virus disease)   D:190; V:361, 367
Chickens (poultry)   P:414–16
Arkansas poultry industry   A:422
Delaware's Sussex County   D:88, 95, 102
eggs and embryos   E:99
important agricultural products   A:95
pets   B:247; P:178
picture(s)
blue hen chicken is state bird of Delaware   D:89
"chicken factory"   A:95
chicks hatching in incubator   I:70
embryo   E:374; K:254
Rhode Island Red is state bird of Rhode Island   R:213
Chickering, Jonas (American piano builder)   P:242
Chickweed   W:104
picture(s)   W:105
Chicle (juice of sapodilla trees)   G:396; R:185
Chicory (plant)   C:397
Chicot, Lake (Arkansas)   A:418
Chicoutimi (Quebec)   Q:12
Chief cells (in the stomach)   S:461
Chief justices (of Canada)
list of   S:506
Chief justices (of the United States)   S:509, 510; U:170
forms of address   A:22
impeachment   I:99
Chignecto, Isthmus of (Canada)   N:138, 350
Chihuahua (dog)   D:250, 253
Chihuahuan Desert (Mexico)
picture(s)   D:125
Chikamatsu Monzaemon (Japanese dramatist)   D:294; J:53
Chilam Balam (book describing ancient Mayan religious beliefs)   M:187

Chilcotin (Indians of North America)   I:188

Child, Francis James (American philologist and collector of ballads)   B:24; F:309

Child abuse (mistreatment of children)   **C:222;**   J:168; V:344

Childbirth   H:247; N:417; R:179

Child development   **C:223–26** *see also* Adolescence
baby   B:3–4
brain   B:368
family group   F:37–43
intellectual abilities   I:253
love, theories of   P:510
play   P:333–34
progressive education   K:249–50
reading skills, development of   R:108–11
spell, starting to   S:398
teachers as models of behavior   T:38
teeth   T:42
television programs   T:70–71
toys for all ages   T:248–50

Childe Harold's Pilgrimage (poem by Byron)   E:282
excerpt from   B:486

Child labor   **C:227**
early factories of the Industrial Revolution   I:221
government regulation   L:6
human rights violations   H:286
picture(s)
coal mining   L:13
English Industrial Revolution   E:250

Child Labor Act (United States, 1916)   W:181

Child psychology *see* Child development

Children *see also* Child development; Child labor; Child welfare
abuse   C:222
adoption   A:26–27
automobile seat restraints   A:552
baby   B:2–4
camps, organized   C:49
Christmas figures who bring gifts to children   C:297, 300–301
colonial America   C:411–12
day care   D:45
development *see* Child development
disabled people   D:176, 177
divorce, problems involving   D:230–31
educating the blind   B:254
family group   F:37–43
fashion modeling   M:385
fires caused by   F:147
first aid   F:156–62
folk music   F:325–26
how to be an entrepreneur   B:472
human rights   H:286
juvenile crime   J:167–70
kindergarten and nursery schools   K:246–50
lead-poisoning hazards   L:94
libraries   L:177
literature for children   C:228–48
museums for   M:527–29
nature organizations have special programs for   N:70
percentage in populations   P:385–86
pioneer life   P:256–57
playgrounds   P:80
public assistance   W:119–20
public health   P:515
Red Cross child memberships   R:127
reform schools   P:482
retardation, mental   R:190–91
Rome, ancient   R:311–12
safety   S:3–5
speech disorders   S:397–98
sports *see* Children's sports
storytelling   S:463–65
television programs for children   T:70–71
toys   T:247–51
UNICEF   U:28

vaccination schedule   V:261
picture(s)
pioneer life   P:256
playing   P:333

Children's Crusade   C:590

Children's Day   H:159a
Japan   H:159a; K:267–68

Children's dictionaries   D:155

Children's Encyclopedia, The   E:207

Children's Games (painting by Bruegel)
picture(s)   D:356

Children's literature   **C:228–48** *see also* Fables; Fairy tales; Folklore; Nursery rhymes; Storytelling; the names of authors
Caldecott, Randolph   C:10
Caldecott and Newbery Medals   C:11–12
children's services in libraries   L:177
figures of speech   F:123–24
folk music   F:325–26
illustration of children's books   I:82–83, 84
Laura Ingalls Wilder Award   W:170
magazines   M:17–18
modern books   B:322
Newbery, John   N:137
nursery rhymes   N:414–16
poetry   P:349–54

Children's sports   C:225
ice hockey   I:31
Little League Baseball   L:264–67
playground activities   P:80
track and field   T:261–62
youth soccer   S:222–23

Children's zoos   Z:392

Child's Garden of Verses, A (by Robert Louis Stevenson)
children's literature, history of   C:237
poems from   S:450–51

Child welfare   W:119–20
adoption   A:26–27
child abuse   C:222
child labor laws   C:227
foster care   F:390
social work with child welfare agencies   S:229
teachers' obligations   T:37–38

Child with a Dove (painting by Picasso)
picture(s)   P:243

Chile   **C:249–55**
earthquake (1960)   E:41
Easter Island   I:364
Latin America   L:47, 49, 50, 55, 56
O'Higgins, Bernardo   O:59
San Martín, José de   S:36
Santiago   S:37
wine   W:190
map(s)   C:249
picture(s)
Atacama Desert   S:277; W:95
flag   F:238
Indian circular-pit grave   A:352–53
Monte Verde   L:57
special stamp   S:421
vineyard   S:275
wine industry   S:290

Chile, University of (Santiago)   C:250; S:37

Chilean pudus (deer) *see* Pudus

Chili, Manuel (Ecuadorian sculptor) *see* Capiscara

Chili powder (blend of spices)   H:114

Chilkat (Indians of North America)
picture(s)
ceremonial dancing blanket   T:141

Chillers (in air conditioning systems)   A:103

Chiluba, Frederick (president of Zambia)   Z:382

Chilung (Taiwan) *see* Keelung

Chimborazo (inactive volcano, Ecuador)   E:66

Chimera (monster in Greek mythology)   G:364

Choctaw (Indians of North America)   A:134, 139; I:178, 179
   Mississippi   M:354, 359, 362
   Oklahoma's name   O:80
Choi Kyu Hah (Korean political leader)   K:301
Choirs (music) *see also* Choral music
   ancient Hebrew   A:246
   hymns sung by professional choirs   H:320
   training in Flemish and French schools   D:365
   picture(s)
      Icelandic choir   I:37
      medieval church choir   M:543
Choiseul (one of the Solomon Islands)   S:252
Choke (valve on a carburetor)   I:264
Choking on foreign bodies   S:4
   Heimlich maneuver (first aid)   F:157–58
Chola period (in Indian history)   I:136
Cholera (disease)   K:291
Cholesterol (chemical in animal tissues)
   body chemistry, lipids in   B:295
   butter   B:474
   hardening of the arteries   D:189
   heart disease, danger of   H:75, 84; N:429–30
   liver produces   L:268
Cholla (cactus)   A:406
   picture(s)   N:286
Cholon (Vietnam)   H:145
Cholula (early Mexican Indian kingdom)   I:173
Choluteca River (Honduras)   H:196
Chomedey, Paul de *see* Maisonneuve, Paul de Chomedey
Chomolungma (Tibetan name for Mount Everest)   E:370
Chondokyo (native Korean religion)   K:294
Chondrites (meteorites)   C:451
Chong Son (Korean painter)   K:299
Chopi (a people of Africa)   A:78
Chopin, Frédéric (Polish pianist and composer)   C:282
   France, music of   F:446–47
   romanticism in music   M:546; R:304
   picture(s)   M:546
      portrait by Delacroix   R:302
Chopin, Kate (American writer)   A:207
Chops (meat)   O:263
Chop suey (food)   F:334
Chorale (musical form)   B:70; M:542–43
Chorales (German hymns)   G:184; H:322
Choral music   C:282–85
   African American spirituals   H:324–25
   ancient Hebrew   A:246
   basic record library   R:125
   English   E:291, 293
   Estonia   E:324
   festivals   M:559, 560
   German   G:183, 184
   hymns   H:320–26
   Latvia   L:80
   Lithuania   L:262
   Mass as musical form   D:365
   Mormon Tabernacle Choir   U:247
   picture(s)
      Estonia   E:324
Choral Symphony (by Beethoven) *see* Ninth Symphony
Chords (in music)   M:537, 540
   jazz   J:57
   rock music   R:262a
Choreography (arrangement of dances)   D:22
   avant-garde dancers   D:34
   ballet   B:25–33
   dance music development   D:36
   Dunham, Katherine   I:74
   Joffrey, Robert   W:27
Choreomanias (dance manias of Middle Ages)   D:24
Chores (for pioneer children)
   picture(s)   P:256
Choroid layer (of the eye)   E:429–30
Chorti (descendants of the Maya)   H:195
Choruses (in ancient Greece)   A:247

Chorus Line, A (musical)   M:558
Chosen people (in Judaism)   J:143
Choson ("Land of Morning Calm") (Koreans' name for their
   country)   K:294
Chosroes I (Persian king)   P:157
Chotts *see* Shotts
Chouart, Médart *see* Groseilliers, Médart Chouart, Sieur des
Chou (Zhou) Dynasty   C:268
   Chinese art   C:276–77
   transportation advances   T:282
Chou Fang (Chinese artist)   C:274
   picture(s)
      Palace Ladies Tuning the Lute (painting)   C:274
Chouteau, René Auguste (American fur trader)   F:522
   profile;   S:16
Chouteau family (fur dynasty)   F:521, 522 *profile*
Chow chow (dog)   D:244, 251
   picture(s)   D:250
Chow mein (food)   F:334
Chowringhee Road (street in Calcutta, India)   C:9
Chrétien, Jean (Canadian prime minister)   C:85, **285**
   picture(s)   C:78, 285
Chrétien de Troyes (French poet)   F:114, 436
   Arthurian legends   A:443
Christ *see* Jesus Christ
Christchurch (New Zealand)   N:240, 241
Christ Church (Philadelphia, Pennsylvania)   P:180
Christian, Fletcher (British sailor)   B:251
Christian art *see also* Church architecture
   Angelico, Fra   A:259
   art as a record   A:438a–438b
   baroque period   B:64, 66
   Byzantine art and architecture   B:487–94
   Caravaggio   C:105
   Christmas art   C:299
   communication, history of   C:463
   decorative arts   D:74
   drawing, history of   D:313
   Dutch and Flemish painting   D:351–60
   English art and architecture   E:257
   Ethiopia   A:75
   Francesca, Piero della   F:449
   illuminated manuscripts   I:77–78
   Italy   I:391–92, 393, 399–400
   Raphael   R:106
   Renaissance   R:162, 166
   Romanesque sculpture   S:97–98
   sculpture   S:96–97
   Spain   S:382–83, 384
Christian Church (Disciples of Christ)   P:492
Christiania (Norway) *see* Oslo
Christianity   C:286–95 *see also* the names of saints, popes,
   Christian leaders
   Abraham honored by   A:9
   Africa   A:57
   African Americans   A:79c
   Anglo-Saxon England becomes Christian   E:237
   Apostles, The   A:328–29
   art *see* Christian art
   Asian religions   A:458
   Augustine, Saint   A:494
   Beowulf written by Christian poet   B:144b
   Bible   B:156–66
   Byzantine church   B:496
   chivalry partly a Christian code   K:275
   Christmas   C:296–301
   church calendar   C:17
   clothing, history of   C:375
   codex form used by early Christians   L:173
   Constantine the Great and the church   C:521
   Crusades   C:588–90; E:401
   dance a part of worship in the early church   D:24
   divorce   D:230
   Easter   E:43–44

Chuquicamata (copper mine, Chile)   **C:**253
  picture(s)   **C:**252
Church and state
  battle for the common school   **E:**83
  Christianity in modern times   **C:**293
  divorce   **D:**230
  England, Church of   **E:**242–43
  England, history of   **E:**240
  freedom of religion   **F:**163
  Jefferson's reforms in Virginia   **J:**67
  Latin America   **L:**58
Church architecture
  art as a record   **A:**438b
  basilica   **A:**374; **I:**392
  Byzantine churches   **A:**375; **B:**487–94
  cathedrals   **A:**376–77; **C:**133–35
  English architecture   **A:**379; **E:**257
  France, development in   **F:**421–23
  Gothic architecture   **G:**264–71; **S:**98
  Italian architecture   **I:**392, 393
  Latin America in 16th century   **L:**60–62
  mosaics used in   **M:**464
  Renaissance architecture   **A:**378; **R:**167
  Romanesque architecture   **A:**376; **R:**295; **S:**97–98
  Russia, architecture of   **R:**370–72
  Spain, architecture of   **S:**382–83
  stained-glass windows   **S:**417–18
  picture(s)
    Air Force Academy chapel   **C:**293, 436
    Italian architecture   **I:**391–93
    modern Swedish church   **R:**149
    Saint Andrew's (Kiev, Ukraine)   **K:**245
Church calendar   **C:**17
Church councils
  Arles (314)   **C:**290
  Constantinople (381)   **C:**289
  Nicaea (325)   **C:**289
  Trent, Council of   **C:**293; **G:**377
  Vatican Council II   **C:**295; **R:**292–93
Churchill (Manitoba)   **M:**83
Churchill, John *see* Marlborough, Duke of
Churchill, Sir Winston (British statesman)   **C:**302–3; **E:**253, 288
  called George Marshall "true organizer of victory"   **M:**110
  coined the phrase "Iron Curtain"   **M:**372–73
  honorary citizen of the United States   **C:**324
  Marlborough, Duke of, was his ancestor   **M:**104
  oratory   **O:**191
  World War I   **W:**284
  picture(s)   **P:**459
    with Roosevelt and Stalin   **R:**326; **U:**50
    Teheran Conference (1943)   **W:**298
Churchill Downs (race track in Louisville, Kentucky)   **H:**232–33; **K:**212
  picture(s)   **K:**220
Churchill Falls (formerly **Grand Falls**) (Newfoundland)   **N:**142
Churchill River (formerly **Hamilton River**) (Labrador)   **C:**56, 62
Churchill River (western Canada)   **S:**43
Church music
  baroque period   **B:**70, 71
  choral music   **C:**282–85
  Dutch and Flemish music   **D:**365
  early use of plainsong in Italy   **I:**410
  France, music of   **F:**444, 446
  hymns   **H:**320–26
  Middle Ages   **M:**296–97
  musical forms   **M:**542
  Palestrina, Giovanni Pierluigi da   **P:**43
Church of Christ, Scientist (Christian Scientists)   **P:**492
Church of England *see* England, Church of
Church of Jesus Christ of Latter-day Saints *see* Mormons
Church of Saint Séverin, The (painting by Utrillo)
  picture(s)   **U:**256
Churn (vessel for making butter)   **B:**474

Churriguera, José (Spanish architect)   **D:**77
Churrigueresque (baroque style of art and architecture)   **D:**77; **S:**384
Churrúas (Indians of South America)   **U:**237
Churun River (Venezuela)   **S:**274
Chutes and Ladders (game)   **G:**14–15
Chuuk (Pacific island)   **M:**280; **P:**8
  picture(s)
    Micronesian man   **P:**9
Ch'ü Yüan (Chinese statesman and poet)   **C:**279
Chyme (partially digested food)   **D:**162; **S:**461
CIA *see* Central Intelligence Agency
Ciardi, John (American poet and author)
  "The Reason for the Pelican" (nonsense rhyme)   **N:**275
Cíbola, Seven Cities of   **C:**551
Ciboney Indians (of Cuba)   **C:**599
Cicadas (insects)   **I:**236
  picture(s)   **I:**248
    mouthparts   **I:**238
Cicero, Marcus Tullius (Roman orator and statesman)   **C:**303
  Antony, Mark   **A:**317
  disapproved of dancing   **D:**23
  oratory   **O:**190–91
  place in Latin literature   **L:**75
Cichlids (fish)   **F:**182, 197, 198
Cid, Le (play by Pierre Corneille)   **D:**299
Cid, The (El Cid) (Spanish national hero)   **L:**130
  beginnings of Spanish literature   **S:**386–87
  bullfighting   **B:**448
Cider (apple beverage)   **A:**329
Cierpinski, Waldemar (German athlete)   **O:**115
Cierva, Juan de la (Spanish aeronautical engineer)   **H:**103
Cigarette lighters   **F:**147
Cigarettes
  arteriosclerosis   **D:**189
  avoiding health hazards   **H:**76
  bronchitis and emphysema   **D:**190, 192
  cancer   **C:**95
  smoking and health problems   **S:**207
  tobacco   **T:**213
  warning labels   **S:**207
Cigars   **T:**213
  picture(s)   **C:**598
Cilia (hairlike threads on some cells)
  animal movement in fluid   **A:**278; **L:**196
  lungs   **L:**345
  paramecia   **M:**276
  protozoans   **P:**496–97
Ciliary body and muscle (of the eye)   **E:**430
Ciliates (protozoans)   **P:**496–97
Ciller, Tansu (Turkish prime minister)   **T:**349
Cimabue, Giovanni (Florentine painter)   **P:**18
Cimarosa, Domenico (Italian composer)   **I:**412
Cimarron Cutoff (part of Santa Fe Trail)   **O:**272
  map(s)   **O:**273
Cimarron National Grasslands (Kansas)   **K:**184
Cimarron River (United States)   **O:**274
Cimbalom (musical instrument)   **S:**469
Cimmerians (a people of Europe)   **R:**364
Cimon of Cleonae (Greek painter)   **G:**348
Cinchona (tree)   **P:**297; **R:**100
Cincinnati (Ohio)   **O:**65, 66, 69–70
  civic fountain   **F:**394
  picture(s)   **O:**70
Cincinnati Reds (baseball team)   **B:**93
Cinco de Mayo (Mexican holiday)   **H:**134
  picture(s)   **H:**132
Cinder cones (of volcanoes)   **V:**380
Cinderella (folktale)
  Disney's animated cartoon   **M:**493
  Korean version   **F:**308–11
  La Cenerentola (opera by Rossini)   **O:**152
Cinema *see* Motion pictures
Cinemascope (motion picture projection system)   **M:**494
Cinerama (motion picture projection system)   **M:**494

City-states   **C:**315
  Greece, ancient   **G:**340–41
  Italy, history of   **I:**388; **R:**157
  Maya   **M:**184
City University of New York (CUNY) System   **N:**217, 229
Ciudad Bolívar (Venezuela)   **V:**298
Ciudad Guayana (Venezuela)   **V:**298
Ciudad Juárez (Mexico)   **E:**194; **M:**247
Civets (catlike animals)   **M:**419
Civics (study of government and laws)   **S:**228
Civil Aeronautics Board (CAB) (former U.S. agency)   **A:**568
Civil code (French law) *see* Napoleonic Code
Civil disobedience
  Gandhi leads India's movement for self-rule   **G:**23
  Indian national movement   **I:**133
  Martin Luther King's philosophy   **K:**251
Civil Disobedience (essay by Thoreau)   **T:**181
Civil engineering   **E:**225
  canals   **C:**88–90
  dams   **D:**16–21
  road building   **R:**249–50
  tunnels   **T:**337–40
Civilian Conservation Corps (CCC)   **N:**138h; **R:**324
Civilian Distinguished Service Medal (American award)
  picture(s)   **D:**66
Civilian Radioactive Waste Management, Office of   **E:**218
Civilians (people not in the military)
  Geneva Conventions   **G:**93
Civilizations, ancient *see* Ancient civilizations
Civil law (based on ancient Roman law)   **L:**85
Civil law (of the United States) *see* Private law
Civil liberties *see* Civil rights
Civil rights   **C:**325–27 *see also* Civil rights movement;
    Freedom of assembly; Freedom of petition; Freedom
    of religion; Freedom of speech; Freedom of the press
  African American history   **A:**79b, 79m–79p
  Alabama   **A:**130, 138, 143
  Baldwin, James   **B:**21
  Bill of Rights, American   **B:**181–84
  Canada   **C:**75
  censorship in wartime *see* Censorship
  Civil Rights Acts (1964, 1968)   **A:**79o
  civil rights movement   **C:**328–30
  compensatory education   **E:**90
  courts   **C:**566–68
  Declaration of Independence   **D:**61–62
  democratic privileges   **D:**106
  Douglas, William O.   **D:**288
  First Amendment freedoms   **F:**163
  Fourteenth Amendment   **J:**118
  genetic testing   **G:**90
  Hispanic Americans   **H:**136, 137
  Hooks, Benjamin L.   **H:**221
  human rights   **H:**284–86
  Human Rights, Universal Declaration of   **U:**75, 77
  international law   **I:**267
  Jackson, Jesse   **J:**8
  Johnson, Andrew, and Reconstruction   **J:**118–19
  jury, trial by   **J:**163–64
  juvenile offenders   **J:**170
  King, Martin Luther, Jr.   **K:**251
  law and law enforcement   **L:**86
  Magna Carta   **M:**26
  Malcolm X   **M:**59
  National Association for the Advancement of Colored
    People (NAACP)   **N:**27–28
  New York, history of   **N:**224
  Nixon administration   **N:**262e
  Northern Ireland   **N:**337
  Reconstruction in the South   **R:**118
  segregation in the United States   **S:**114–15
  Supreme Court of Canada   **S:**505
  Supreme Court rulings   **S:**509
  Tennessee   **T:**87

  United States, history of the   **U:**199–200
  women's rights movement   **W:**212–15
  Yasui, Minoru   **O:**215
Civil Rights, United States Commission on *see* United States
    Commission on Civil Rights
Civil Rights Act (United States, 1875)   **A:**79h; **C:**328
Civil Rights Act (United States, 1964)   **A:**79n, 79o; **C:**327,
    330; **U:**200, 202
  segregation   **S:**113, 115
  women's rights movement   **W:**213
Civil Rights Act (United States, 1968)   **U:**200
Civil Rights Memorial (Birmingham, Alabama)
  picture(s)   **C:**325
Civil rights movement   **C:**327, **328–30**
  Abernathy, Ralph David   **A:**142
  Cannady, Beatrice   **O:**214
  folk music used to protest injustice   **F:**328
  Kennedy administration   **K:**209
  Mississippi   **M:**363
  Parks, Rosa   **A:**143
  South Dakota   **S:**327
  Tureaud, Alexander Pierre   **L:**327
Civil service   **C:**331 *see also* Spoils system
  Arthur's administration   **A:**438f
  Pendleton Act (1883)   **A:**439
  police appointments   **P:**368
Civil Service Commission   **C:**331
Civil Service Reform Act (United States, 1978)   **C:**331
Civil suits (in courts)   **C:**566–68
Civil war (in China)   **C:**271
Civil War, English (1642–1649)   **E:**246
  Cromwell, Oliver   **C:**585
  English literature, effect on   **E:**275
  Milton given post in Cromwell's government   **M:**312
  Puritans   **P:**550
Civil War, Spanish (1936–1939) *see* Spanish Civil War
Civil War, United States (1861–1865)   **C:**332–47; **U:**186 *see*
    also Reconstruction Period; Slavery; the names of
    individual leaders
  abolition movement   **A:**6, 6b
  Adams, Charles Francis   **A:**11
  African American history   **A:**79b, 79g
  Alabama location of formation of Confederate States of
    America   **A:**142
  American literature   **A:**205
  Andersonville National Cemetery   **N:**30
  Arkansas   **A:**426, 428
  Barton, Clara   **B:**75
  Bickerdyke, Mary Ann Ball   **O:**74
  Boyd, Belle, was a spy   **S:**408
  Brady, Mathew B.   **N:**224
  Brown, John   **B:**411
  Buchanan was unable to prevent it   **B:**420
  Compromise of 1850   **C:**479
  Confederate States of America   **C:**495–97
  Davis, Jefferson   **D:**43, 44
  Delaware   **D:**88, 102
  draft laws   **D:**292
  Dred Scott decision   **D:**321
  Early, Jubal Anderson   **V:**358
  Emancipation Proclamation   **E:**200–201
  Farragut, David   **F:**62
  first blood spilled in Baltimore (Maryland)   **M:**134
  Gettysburg Address   **G:**191
  Gettysburg National Cemetery   **N:**30
  Grant, Ulysses S.   **G:**294–95
  guerrilla warfare   **G:**399
  guns and ammunition   **G:**419, 420, 422, 425
  Illinois   **I:**75
  Jackson, "Stonewall," was Confederate general   **J:**9
  Kansas-Nebraska Act   **K:**191
  Kentucky   **K:**226
  Lee's campaigns   **L:**125–26
  Lincoln, Abraham   **L:**244–46

Civil War, United States (cont.)

Louisiana   **L:**328
Maine   **M:**50
Medal of Honor established   **D:**65
Michigan   **M:**272
Mississippi   **M:**358, 362
Mississippi River   **M:**365
Missouri   **M:**366, 380
Missouri Compromise   **M:**381
New Hampshire soldiers   **N:**162
New Mexico   **N:**193
New York   **N:**224
nullification doctrine   **K:**227
Ohio   **O:**74
Pennsylvania   **P:**139
Reconstruction Period   **R:**117–20
Sherman, William Tecumseh, was Union general   **S:**150
slavery   **S:**196–97
songs   **N:**24–25
South Carolina   **S:**296, 310
Stuart, Jeb   **S:**470
submarine made first successful attack   **S:**473–74
Tennessee   **T:**86
underwater archaeology   **U:**20
unidentified dead buried in Arlington National Cemetery   **N:**29
Vermont   **V:**319
Virginia   **V:**360
Virginia historical sites   **V:**354
West Virginia   **W:**138–39
picture(s)
African American soldiers   **A:**79g
Army of the Potomac   **C:**337
Atlanta (Georgia)   **C:**342
cannon   **G:**424
Confederate soldiers and flag   **C:**332, 339
Fort Sumter bombing   **C:**346
Gettysburg, Battle of   **C:**341
Lee's surrender to Grant   **C:**346
Lincoln and McClellan   **C:**340
Monitor and *Merrimack*   **C:**338
railroads   **R:**86
Richmond, capture of   **C:**343
Union soldiers and flag   **C:**333
United States Marine Corps uniform   **U:**123
Civil wars
Africa   **A:**69
Central America, history of   **C:**175
Rwanda   **R:**385
Cladding (coating on optical fibers)   **F:**106
Claiborne, William Charles Coles (American public official)   **L:**326 *profile*
Claims adjusters (in insurance companies)   **I:**252
Clairvoyance (kind of extrasensory perception)   **E:**428
Clamps, surgical   **S:**513
Clams (mollusks)   **M:**406, 408; **O:**290–91
fishing industry   **F:**217
Rhode Island shellfish   **R:**215
shells   **S:**148
picture(s)
clam digging in Massachusetts   **M:**137
clam dredger in Chesapeake Bay   **M:**126
fossil clams   **F:**387
shells   **S:**149
table(s)
United States aquaculture production   **F:**208
Clans and clan system   **A:**303; **F:**39 *see also* Family
Albania   **A:**159–60
Australian Aborigines   **A:**7
Japan   **J:**41
Clapboard houses   **H:**169
Clapperton, Hugh (Scottish explorer of Africa)   **S:**7
Clapton, Eric (English rock guitarist)   **R:**262b *profile*
Clare of Assisi, Saint   **S:**18d *profile*
Clarín (Leopoldo Alas) (Spanish writer)   **S:**390

Clarinet (musical instrument)   **C:**348; **M:**554; **W:**184
ancient instrument   **A:**245
orchestra seating plan   **O:**196
picture(s)   **M:**553; **W:**184
Clark, Charles Joseph (prime minister of Canada)   **C:**349
Clark, George Rogers (American Revolutionary War leader and explorer)   **I:**156; **R:**204–5, 208 *profile*
Clark, M. Lewis, Jr. (American founder of Kentucky Derby)   **K:**227
Clark, Mark Wayne (United States Army general)   **W:**297
Clark, Ron (American balloonist)   **B:**36
Clark, William (American explorer) *see* Lewis and Clark expedition
Clark, William A. (American financier)   **M:**428
Clark County (Nevada)   **N:**128
Clarke, Arthur C. (English author)   **S:**81 *profile*
Clarksburg (West Virginia)   **W:**132
Clarkson, Thomas (English abolitionist)
picture(s)   **S:**194
Clarksville (Missouri)
picture(s)
flood (1993)   **F:**256
Clash (English rock group)   **R:**262d
Class action (lawsuit in which a few people represent a larger group)   **L:**88
Class distinction
Aztec society   **A:**575–76
France   **F:**406, 467
Marx's analysis of   **M:**117
Maya   **M:**185
Rome, ancient   **R:**311
suits in playing cards based on social classes in Middle Ages   **C:**107
Turkmenistan   **T:**351
Classes (divisions of biological classification)   **A:**264; **L:**209; **T:**27, 28
Classical Age (Golden Age) (of Greek civilization)   **A:**438a; **G:**343, 350–51; **H:**283
Classical age in music   **C:**349–52 *see also* Romanticism
German composers   **G:**185–86
history of Western musical forms   **M:**544–46
orchestra   **O:**194
Classical art *see* Greece, art and architecture of; Rome, art of
Classical literature *see* Greece, literature of; Latin literature
Classical music *see* Art music
Classical mythology *see* Greek mythology
Classical period (in Chinese literature)   **C:**278–79
Classic detective story (type of fiction)   **M:**565
Classicism (in French literature)   **F:**437–39
Classification (in biology)   **B:**200 *see also* Taxonomy
bacteria   **B:**12
kingdoms of living things   **K:**253–59; **L:**207–9
Linnaeus, Carolus   **L:**250
plants   **P:**301–2
races, human   **R:**28–31
picture(s)
insects, orders of   **I:**248
Classification (of stars)   **A:**474–75
Classification yards (of railroads)   **R:**84–85
Classified ads (in newspapers)   **N:**203
Class numbers (of books in libraries)   **L:**182, 184
Classrooms (of schools)   **K:**247–48; **S:**61
Class struggle (theory of history)   **C:**473; **M:**117
Claudel, Paul (French poet and dramatist)   **D:**302; **F:**442
Claude Lorrain (Claude Gellée) (French painter)   **B:**66; **F:**426, 427
picture(s)
Harbor at Sunset (painting)   **F:**426
Claudius I (Roman emperor)   **E:**235; **N:**114; **R:**316
Claudius Caecus, Appius (Roman official)   **E:**227
Clavichord (keyboard instrument)   **K:**237–38; **M:**552–53; **S:**469
picture(s)   **S:**468
Clavicle (collar bone)   **S:**183

Clavius (lunar crater)   M:451
   picture(s)   M:450
Claw hammer (tool)   T:227, 234
Claws (of animals)
   bats   B:100
   cats   A:276–77; C:143
   crabs   C:571
   lobsters   L:279, 280
   picture(s)
      cats   C:143
Clay   S:235
   aluminum   A:194c
   ancient cities built with clay   A:220
   archaeological dating   A:361–62
   bricks   B:390–92, 430
   buoyancy experiment   F:253
   ceramics   C:176–77
   clay modeling   C:354
   Japanese sculpture   J:48
   pottery clay   F:142; P:407–8
   sculptors' material   S:91, 92
   tablets for writing   A:220–21, 224
Clay, Cassius M. (American abolitionist)   K:226
Clay, Cassius Marcellus, Jr. (American boxer) see Ali,
      Muhammad
Clay, Henry (American orator and statesman)   C:353
   Adams, John Quincy, and Clay   A:18; J:5
   Compromise of 1850   C:479
   Missouri Compromise   M:381
   nullification crisis   J:7
   opposes statehood for Texas   P:375, 376
   personal and political feud with Tyler   T:365, 366, 367
   picture(s)   C:353
Clay, Laura (American women's rights advocate)   K:225
      profile
Clay modeling   C:354 see also Ceramics; Pottery
Clay tablets   A:220, 224; B:318; L:171
Clayton Antitrust Act (United States, 1914)   U:191; W:181
Clayton-Bulwer Treaty (1850)   T:33
Clean Air Act (Great Britain, 1956)   L:292
Clean Air Acts (United States laws)   A:125; C:519
   amendments (1990)   A:10
   automobile emission standards   A:544
Cleaner shrimps (crustaceans)   A:281; S:167
Cleanliness
   food preparation   C:533
   hair   H:7
   hand washing helps prevent spread of diseases   D:191,
      194
   health   H:76
   hospitals   H:250, 252
   teeth in braces, care of   O:237
   time management   T:206
Clean room (for manufacturing integrated circuits)   T:278
Clean Water Act (United States, 1977)   W:71
Clear and present danger test (in United States law)   F:163
Clear-cutting (of timber)   L:340
Clearing Autumn Sky over Mountains and Valleys (painting by
      Kuo Hsi)
   picture(s)   C:275
Clearinghouse (for checks in banking)
   diagram(s)   B:56
Clearing of land
   farm machinery   F:53–54
   pioneers   P:251–52
Clear Lake (California)   C:21
Clearstory see Clerestory
Cleary, Beverly (American children's author)   C:230 profile,
      238
   picture(s)   C:230
Cleavage (cell division)   E:101
Cleavage (of minerals)   M:315
Cleaveland, Moses (American pioneer)   C:356
Clefs (in musical notation)   M:538, 539, 540
Cleghorn, Sarah (American reformer and writer)   V:318 profile

Clemenceau, Georges (French statesman)   C:355;   F:418;
      W:282, 290
   picture(s)   P:459; W:290
Clemence Irons House (Johnston, Rhode Island)   R:220
Clemens, Roger (American baseball player)
   picture(s)   B:93
Clemens, Samuel Langhorne see Twain, Mark
Clement, Amanda E. (Mandy) (American baseball umpire)
      S:326 profile
Clement III (antipope)   R:290
Clement VII (antipope)   R:291
Clement I, Saint (Clement of Rome) (pope)   R:290
Clement II (pope)   R:290
Clement III (pope)   R:291
Clement IV (pope)   R:291
Clement V (pope)   P:182; R:287, 291
Clement VI (pope)   R:291
Clement VII (Giulio de' Medici) (pope)   C:292; M:202; R:291
Clement VIII (pope)   R:291
Clement IX (pope)   R:291
Clement X (pope)   R:291
Clement XI (pope)   R:291
Clement XII (pope)   R:291
Clement XIII (pope)   R:291
Clement XIV (pope)   R:291
Clemente, Francesco (Italian painter)   I:403
Clemente, Roberto (American baseball player)   P:527
   picture(s)   B:94
Clementi, Muzio (Italian-English composer)   E:293; I:411
Cleopatra (queen of Egypt)   C:355
   Antony, Mark   A:317
   Caesar, Julius   C:6
   cosmetics and perfumes   C:553; P:150
   Ptolemaic rulers of Egypt   E:108
   picture(s)
      relief carvings in her temple   E:117
Cleopatra's Needle (Egyptian obelisk)   O:5
Clepsydras see Water clocks
Clerestory (part of a church)   A:374
Clerides, Glafcos (president of Cyprus)   C:607
Clermont (first steamboat)   F:491
   picture(s)   I:282
Cletus, Saint (pope)   R:290
Cleveland (Ohio)   C:356;   O:65, 66, 67, 68, 69
   Stokes, Carl   O:75
   picture(s)   C:356; O:61, 64
      Museum of Art   O:65
      riverfront   W:71
      Rock and Roll Hall of Fame   O:68
Cleveland, Frances Folsom (wife of Grover Cleveland)   C:359;
      F:173–74
   picture(s)   C:358; F:173
Cleveland, Grover (22nd and 24th president of the United
      States)   C:357–60; M:427; N:225
   picture(s)   P:450
Cleveland, Mount (highest peak in Glacier National Park,
      Montana)   G:220
Cleveland, Rose (acting first lady in Cleveland's first
      administration)   F:173
Cleveland Indians (baseball team)
   picture(s)   O:66
Click beetle
   picture(s)   B:126
Click languages (of Africa)   A:56
Client (in Roman society)   R:311
Cliff dwellers (Indians in the American Southwest)   I:172
   Arizona   A:410, 412
   Colorado   C:440
   New Mexico   N:190
   Utah   U:252
   picture(s)
      Arizona   A:410
      Colorado   C:436; I:172
      textile making   T:145

Cliff Dwellers (painting by Bellows)
  picture(s) U:132
Clifton, Lucille (American writer) C:238
Climate C:361–64 *see also* Weather; individual continent,
    country, province, and state articles
  affects the food supply F:350–51
  Antarctica's ice sheet and world climate A:295
  Arctic region A:386c
  atmosphere A:479–82
  biomes B:204–10
  climatology (study of world climate) G:101–2
  clothing and climate C:372–73
  dinosaurs' extinction is possibly the result of changes in
    D:174
  Does sunspot activity affect the Earth's climate? S:494
  equator areas E:308
  extinction E:425, 426
  fruitgrowing F:481–82
  gardening to suit climates G:30, 51
  global precipitation patterns R:97
  homes adapted to H:168–70
  How can scientists tell what climates were like a long time
    ago? C:363
  ice ages I:8–16
  leaves help determine global climate patterns L:118
  mountains influence climate M:507
  nuclear war's projected effects N:377
  ocean currents E:19; O:18, 34
  oceans and climate O:36, 42
  ocean water stores the sun's heat E:20
  physical geography G:99
  prairies P:426
  prehistoric people's environment P:438
  rain forests affect Earth's climate R:100
  seasons S:109–11
  soils, effect on S:237
  trade winds T:268
  vegetables, seasonal crops of V:287–88
  winds W:186–89
  map(s)
    world climate C:362
Climatologists (scientists who study climate) C:361
Climatology (study of climate) C:361; G:101–2
Climax community (plants and animals of a biome) B:204
Climax vegetation (dominant vegetation of a biome) B:204
Climbing (of animals)
  climbing perch A:268
  snakes S:215
Climbing cranes (machines) H:146
Clingmans Dome (Tennessee) T:75
Clingstone peaches P:107
Clinical psychology P:504
Clinical trials (medical experiments) S:67
Clinkers (in cement making) C:165
Clinker style (of ship building) V:339
Clinton, Chelsea (daughter of William Clinton) C:367
Clinton, De Witt (American statesman) E:313; N:224 *profile*
Clinton, George (vice president, United States) N:222, 224
    profile; V:325 *profile*
Clinton, Sir Henry (English military commander) R:204, 206,
    207; W:41
Clinton, Hillary Rodham (wife of William Clinton) C:367;
    F:180b; U:205
  picture(s) C:366; F:180b
Clinton, William (42d president of the United States)
        C:365–69; U:205
  impeachment I:99
  picture(s) A:428; C:365; N:200; P:453; U:170, 205
    with Fernando Cardoso B:383
    with Rabin and Arafat C:368
    with Richard Nixon N:262f
Clipper ships (Yankee clippers) (sailing ships) S:155–56
  importance to transportation T:284
  picture(s) S:152
Clips (as jewelry) J:99

Clips (containers for cartridges) G:422
Clitellum (section of a worm) E:42; W:319
Clive, Robert (Baron Clive of Plassey) (British soldier and
    colonial administrator) E:47; I:132
Cloaca (body organ in amphibians) A:216
Cloaca Maxima (sewer of Rome) M:204
Clock bells B:142
Clocks C:369–72 *see also* Watches
  antiques and antique collecting A:317
  atomic clocks L:46d; T:201
  Big Ben (London) L:293
  chronometers in navigation N:77
  early clocks I:285; T:200–201
  Huygens invented pendulum clock H:310
  standards of time changes T:199–200
  time locks L:283–84
  water clocks T:201; W:73
Clocks, biological *see* Biological clock
Clog dancing F:302
Cloisonné (enameling technique) D:74; E:205
Cloister (part of a monastery) A:377
Cloisters (museum, New York City) M:239a
Cloning G:91; S:73
  Is cloning a way to create new life? L:210
  livestock L:273
  picture(s)
    cloned mice S:65
Clontarf, Battle of (1014) I:323
Closed captioned television programs D:50; T:67
Closed-circuit television systems T:65
Closed primary elections E:128
Closed shop *see* Open and closed shop
Closed universe (in astronomy) U:218
Close-hauling (in sailing) S:11
  diagram(s) S:10
Closets, organization of I:260–61
Close-up lenses (for cameras) P:202, 203
Closure *see* Filibuster
Closure properties (of numbers) N:398
Cloth *see* Textiles
Clothes moths (insects) H:261
  picture(s) B:483
Clothing C:372–81 *see also* Fans; Uniforms; the people
    section of continent and country articles
  academic dress U:223
  ancient invention I:286
  buttons B:484
  camping C:45
  colonial American C:411
  cowboys' clothing designed for protection R:103
  dry cleaning process D:339
  dyes and dyeing D:368–74
  Easter symbols E:44
  fashion F:65–70
  fibers F:108–12
  folk dance F:302
  fur F:501–5
  gloves G:240–41
  hats H:45–47
  hiking and backpacking H:124
  home economics training H:165
  ice-skating I:39
  Inuit I:191, 275
  laundry L:82
  Metropolitan Museum of Art Costume Institute M:239
  modeling, fashion M:384–85
  pioneer life P:255
  poverty means inadequate clothing P:418, 419
  quilting for warmth and protection N:101
  rubberizing process R:343
  sewing S:128a–128b
  shoes S:158–59
  textiles T:141–46
  weight lifting W:107

Coast Ranges (mountain belt extending from Alaska into
            Mexico)   C:20, 21; U:82
      Oregon   O:202, 206, 207
Coated abrasives   G:392
Coated steels   I:337
Coatings, chemical
      silicones   S:173
Coatis (animals related to raccoons)   R:26–27
Coat of many colors (given to Joseph)   J:133
Coats of arms   H:110–12; K:272–73
      picture(s)
            guilds   G:404
Coatsworth, Elizabeth (American author)
      "No Shop Does the Bird Use" (poem)   F:124
Coaxial cables
      telecommunications   T:47
      telephones   T:54
      television   T:48, 63, 65
Cobalamin see Vitamin B₁₂
Cobalt (element)   E:172
      Congo, Democratic Republic of, is world's major producer
            A:49; Z:378
      table(s)   M:235
Cobalt (Ontario)   O:138
Cobb, Lee J. (American actor)
      picture(s)   D:304
Cobb, Ty (American baseball player)   B:88 profile;   G:144
            profile
      picture(s)   B:88
COBE (space satellite) see Cosmic Background Explorer
Cobia, USS (submarine)   W:200
      picture(s)   W:200
Coblenz (Germany)
      picture(s)
            Church of Saint Astor   R:295
Cobras (snakes)   M:419; S:211–12, 218
      picture(s)   M:419; S:210
Cobs (male swans)   D:344
Coca (shrub whose leaves yield cocaine)   B:307; P:160
Coca-Cola Company
      picture(s)
            building   G:138
Cocaine (drug)   C:405; D:331
Coccus (ball-shaped bacterium)   B:12; D:182; M:275
Coccyx (bones in the spine)   S:184
Cochineal (dye made from insects' bodies)   D:371
      picture(s)
            cochineal insect   D:369
Cochise (Chiricahua Apache chief)   A:414 profile;   I:184
            profile
Cochiti (Indians of North America)   I:183
Cochlea (inner ear)   E:4
      picture(s)   E:5
Cochlear implants (to aid deaf people)   D:50
Cochlear nerve (of the inner ear)   E:4, 5
Cochran, Barbara (American skier)   O:114
Cochran, Elizabeth (American newspaper reporter) see Bly,
      Nellie
Cockatoo (bird)
      picture(s)   P:85
Cockerill, William and John (English industrialists)   I:224
Cocker spaniel (dog)   D:249
Cockle (mollusk)
      picture(s)   S:147
Cocklebur (plant)   P:313
Cockneys (Londoners)   L:295
Cockpit Country (area of Jamaica)   J:16
Cockroaches (insects)   H:263
Cocks (kind of valve)   V:269
Cocks (male chickens)   P:414
Cocoa   C:280 see also Cacao
Cocoa butter   C:280, 552; O:76
Coconut (fruit of the coconut palm)   C:392
      copra   P:5

seed dispersal   P:313
Which plant has the biggest seed?   P:307
      picture(s)
            copra   M:113
Coconut oil   D:140; O:76
Coconut palm trees   C:392
      picture(s)   T:302
Cocoons (of insects)   I:232–33, 249
      ants   A:321
      bees   B:119
      butterflies and moths   B:476
      silkworm cocoons   S:175
Cocopa (Indians of North America)   I:183
Cocos Island (off the coast of Costa Rica)   P:264
Cocteau, Jean (French writer and artist)   F:442
Cod (fish)   F:217, 218, 219, 221
      egg laying of   E:100; F:196
      Grand Banks   C:79
C.O.D. (Collect on Delivery) (mail service)   P:400
Coda (Final section) (in a sonata cycle)   M:540
Code Civil see Napoleonic Code
Code emphasis reading programs   R:109
Codeine (narcotic drug)   N:15; P:297
Code Napoléon see Napoleonic Code
Code of Chivalry (of knights)   K:274–75, 277
Code of Terpsichore (by Carlo Blasis)   D:25
Codes (in communications)
      International Code of Signals for use at sea   F:247
      International Morse Code   R:63
      ZIP codes   P:401–2
Codes (of law)   L:84–85
      canon law   L:85
      Hammurabi   A:221; L:84
      Louisiana's legal system based partly on the Napoleonic
            Code   L:314
      Napoleonic Code   N:11
      picture(s)
            Hammurabi   A:220
Codes (secret writing)   C:393, 394–95
      Navajo language used in World War II   I:185
Codex (early Roman book)   B:319; I:79; L:173
Codicils (additions to wills)   W:177
Codling moths   A:332
Codpiece (in fashion)   C:376
Cod wars (conflict between Iceland and Great Britain over
            coastal fishing limits)   I:37
Cody (Wyoming)   W:343
Cody, William Frederick see Buffalo Bill
Coe, Sebastian (British runner)   O:115, 116; T:259 profile
      picture(s)   O:116; T:259
Co-education (in universities and colleges)   U:220, 223
Coelacanths (lobe-finned fish)   F:184, 185
      picture(s)   F:386
Coelenterates (soft-bodied water animals)   A:267; J:72–77
      coral polyps   C:547–48
      What is a reef community?   J:75
Coelophysis (genus of dinosaurs)   D:168–69
Coenzyme (in body chemistry)   B:296; V:370a
Coeur d'Alene (Indians of North America)   I:188
Coeur d'Alene mining district (Idaho)   I:46
Cofan (Indians of South America)
      picture(s)   I:194
Coffee   C:396–97
      Brazil, important crop in   B:374; S:39
      Central American export crop   C:173, 175
      Colombia   C:405
      El Salvador is a leading producer   E:196, 198
      Guatemala   G:397
      named for Kaffa (region in Ethiopia)   E:332
      north African crop carried to Brazil and Indonesia   A:99
      Vienna's coffee   V:333
      picture(s)   A:93; C:406; E:197
            beans being roasted   C:397
            beans being sifted in Brazil   S:275

Costa Rican crop **C:**173
Costa Rican plantation **C:**558
Guatemala **G:**396
Mexico **M:**247
Puerto Rican plantation **P:**528
Coffeehouses
Austria **A:**520
established in England **R:**186
picture(s)
Austria **A:**519
Coffeepots (for brewing coffee) **C:**397
picture(s)
antique **A:**316a
Chemex coffee maker **I:**214
Cofferdams (temporary structures) **D:**18
Coffin, Levi (American abolitionist) **U:**16 *profile,* 17
Coffin, Stewart (American puzzle maker) **P:**553–54
Coghlan, Eamonn (Irish runner) **T:**263
Cognitive psychology (field of psychology) **P:**504
Cognitivism (school of psychology) **P:**507, 509
Cog railroads **L:**288; **R:**80
picture(s) **L:**288
Cohan, George M. (American actor and songwriter) **M:**557; **N:**25; **R:**225 *profile;* **U:**209
picture(s) **R:**224
Cohansey Aquifer (New Jersey) **N:**167
Cohen, Ben (American entrepreneur) **V:**318 *profile*
Cohen, Stanley (American scientist) **G:**91
Coherent light **L:**46b
Cohesion (in physics) **L:**254, 255
picture(s) **L:**254, 255
Coils, induction **E:**134
Coil springs (of suspension systems) **A:**551
Coimbra (Portugal) **P:**392, 393
Coinage Act (United States, 1792) **D:**257
Coin laundries **L:**82
Coins and coin collecting **C:**398–400
dollar **D:**257, 259
history of coins **M:**413
mint is place where money is coined **M:**340
nickel **N:**250
probability and tossing coins **N:**382–83
silver **S:**177–78
stamped out by coining dies **D:**157
Susan B. Anthony dollar **A:**299
United States Mint **T:**294
Why do people throw coins into fountains? **F:**394
picture(s)
ancient Roman **A:**232
historic U.S. coins **C:**400
United States Mint **C:**437; **T:**295
Coir (fiber of coconut husk) **C:**392; **F:**109
Coke (carbon fuel) **C:**106, 388, 391; **F:**489
Industrial Revolution **I:**220
use in processing of iron and steel **I:**331
Coke (drug) *see* Cocaine
Colbert, Jean Baptiste (French statesman) **L:**313
Gobelins rug and tapestry workshops **R:**353; **T:**22
Colchis (part of republic of Georgia) **G:**147, 148
Cold (meaning "having little heat") **H:**86
climate **C:**361–64
flowering requirements of plants **F:**287
refrigeration **R:**133–35
Cold, common *see* Common cold
Cold-blooded animals **A:**266–67; **L:**202
dinosaurs **D:**165
fish, temperature of **F:**182
frogs and toads **F:**476
hibernation **H:**119
insects **I:**239
lizards **L:**275–77
reptiles **R:**179–80
snakes **S:**208–18
Cold box *see* Liquefaction fractional distiller
Cold cream (cosmetics) **C:**553

Cold front (in meteorology) **W:**85, 92–93
picture(s) **W:**86
Cold light *see* Bioluminescence
Cold rolling (of metals) **B:**410; **I:**336
Cold sores (blisters caused by a herpes virus) **D:**194; **V:**369
Cold storage (of food) **F:**340
apples require **A:**333
refrigeration **R:**135
Cold type (in typesetting) **T:**370
Cold War (in international relations) **C:**400–401, 474; **R:**369
Cuban missile crisis **C:**601
disagreements over division of Germany **G:**165
Geneva Accords **G:**93
Kennedy, John F. **K:**208–9
Stalin's seizure of lands in Eastern Europe **S:**419
Union of Soviet Socialist Republics **U:**51
United States, history of **U:**196–97
Cold-water suits (for skin diving) **S:**187
boardsailing **B:**261
Cole, Thomas (American painter) **N:**224 *profile*
picture(s)
Oxbow (painting) **U:**129
Coleman, Ann (fiancée of James Buchanan)
picture(s) **B:**418
Coleman, Ornette (American jazz musician) **J:**63 *profile,* 64
picture(s) **J:**63
Coleridge, Samuel Taylor (English poet) **E:**281
figures of speech **F:**122
odes **O:**50
quotation from *The Rime of the Ancient Mariner* **Q:**20
Wordsworth, William **W:**242
Colette (French author) **F:**442
Colfax, Schuyler (American politician) **V:**327 *profile*
picture(s)
as vice president **V:**327
Coligny, Gaspard de (French Huguenot leader) **H:**279
Colladon, Daniel (Swiss physicist) **F:**106
Collage (in art) **C:**402
Braque, Georges **B:**371
cubism **C:**602
modern art **M:**390–91, 393
Picasso **P:**243
used by some 20th century painters **P:**30
picture(s)
Grandmother (by Dove) **D:**137
Collagen (protein) **V:**370d
Collar cells (of sponges) **S:**412
Collared anteater (mammal) *see* Tamandua
Collators (office machines) **O:**57
Collections (of dresses) **F:**69–70
Collective bargaining (by labor unions) **L:**5
labor's position **L:**12
management's position **L:**5, 6, 7–9
Collective farms
Albania **A:**160
Bulgaria **B:**440–41
Cambodia **C:**38
Israel **I:**372
Romania **R:**298
Russia, history of **R:**363, 368
Union of Soviet Socialist Republics **U:**41, 50
Vietnam **V:**334b
Collective security (in international relations) **L:**95
Collectors and collecting
antiques **A:**315–17
autographs **A:**526–27
automobile models **A:**534–35
buttons **B:**484
coin collecting **C:**398–400
dollhouses **D:**265
dolls **D:**271
leaves **L:**115
nature, study of **N:**68
paper money **D:**259

human beings' skin and hair   **H:**281
lobsters   **L:**280
mammals   **M:**73
octopus   **O:**292, 293
parrots   **P:**85
turtles   **T:**355–56
Why do chameleons change color?   **L:**275
Colorado   **C:**430–43
Denver   **D:**116–17
gold discoveries   **G:**251
Rocky Mountain peaks   **R:**271
map(s)   **C:**441
picture(s)
aspens   **C:**432
Buffalo Bill's grave   **C:**438
Cliff Palace   **C:**436; **I:**172
Colorado National Monument   **C:**434
Denver   **C:**431, 440; **D:**117
elk   **C:**434
farm   **C:**437
Garden of the Gods   **C:**438
Glacier Gorge   **I:**13
harvesting sugar beets   **S:**486
horses grazing in pasture   **C:**432
national forests   **N:**32
Pikes Peak   **C:**439
Pro Rodeo Hall of Champions   **C:**438
Rocky Mountain National Park   **C:**432
Rocky Mountains   **C:**431
Royal Gorge   **C:**438
United States Air Force Academy   **C:**293, 436
United States Mint   **C:**437
wagon train in Denver (1886)   **C:**442
white-water rafting   **C:**435
Colorado, University of (Boulder, Colorado)   **C:**434
Colorado blue spruce trees
picture(s)
state tree of Colorado   **C:**431
Colorado College (Colorado Springs, Colorado)   **C:**435
Colorado Desert (California)   **C:**18
Colorado National Monument (Colorado)
picture(s)   **C:**434
Colorado Plateau   **C:**432; **N:**182; **U:**82
Colorado River (Texas)   **T:**127
Colorado River (United States)   **R:**240
Arizona   **A:**402, 404, 405, 415
California   **C:**20, 23
Colorado   **C:**430, 433
Grand Canyon   **G:**290–92; **W:**51
Hoover Dam   **D:**20
lakes, formation of   **L:**28
Los Angeles (California) water source   **L:**303
Nevada   **N:**124, 125
Utah   **U:**244, 245
picture(s)   **N:**283; **R:**241
Grand Canyon   **G:**292; **W:**50
Hoover Dam   **D:**17
Parker Dam   **D:**19
Colorado School of Mines (Golden, Colorado)   **C:**435
Colorado Springs (Colorado)   **C:**439
picture(s)
United States Air Force Academy   **C:**293
Colorado State University (Fort Collins, Colorado)   **C:**434
Color balance (of photographic film)   **P:**205
Color blindness (inherited disease)   **C:**428; **E:**431–32
Daltonism   **D:**15
Colored Farmers' Alliance (African American protest organization)   **A:**79i
Coloreds (people of mixed races in Africa) *see* Coloureds
Colorimeters (optical instruments)   **O:**185
Coloring (of hair)   **H:**8
Color negative film (in photography)   **P:**204
Color photography   **P:**205, 216
film   **P:**204, 205
video production at home   **V:**332h–332i

Color Purple, The (novel by Alice Walker)   **A:**214a
Color reversal film (in photography)   **P:**204
Color separation (in printing)   **P:**472–73
Color television   **C:**429; **T:**62, 65
Color wheel
picture(s)   **C:**427
Colosio, Luis Donaldo (Mexican political leader)   **M:**252
Colosseum (Roman arena)   **A:**232; **R:**306, 318
picture(s)   **I:**387; **R:**308
Colossians (book of the Bible)   **B:**165
Colossi of Memnon (statues)
picture(s)   **E:**115
Colossus of Rhodes   **W:**219
Coloureds (people of mixed races in South Africa)   **S:**268, 269
Colt, Samuel (American inventor)   **C:**516; **G:**421–22
Colter, John (American explorer)   **N:**44; **W:**343, 346 *profile*
Yellowstone National Park   **Y:**355
Coltrane, John (American jazz musician)   **J:**63–64; **N:**320 *profile*
picture(s)   **J:**63
Colt revolvers   **G:**421–22
picture(s)   **G:**422
Colts (young horses)   **H:**243
Colubrids (family of snakes)   **S:**208, 211
Columba, Saint (Irish missionary)   **L:**281
Columbanus, Saint (Irish monk)   **R:**284
Columbia (capital of South Carolina)   **S:**301, 305, 310
places of interest   **S:**304
picture(s)
State House   **S:**308
Columbia (Maryland)   **M:**129
Columbia (United States space shuttle)   **S:**340j, 348, 355, 364; **T:**292
first space shuttle mission   **S:**347
space stations   **S:**366
picture(s)
STS-50 mission   **S:**343, 344, 345
Columbia, Cape (northernmost tip of Canada)   **C:**56
Columbia, Mount (Alberta)   **J:**54
Columbia Basin Project (Washington)   **W:**20
Columbia Fur Company (fur traders)   **F:**523
Columbia Glacier (Alaska)   **G:**223
picture(s)   **I:**5, 17
Columbia Icefield (Alberta)   **J:**54
Columbia Plateau (region of the United States)   **U:**82
Idaho   **I:**46, 48
Nevada   **N:**124
Oregon   **O:**204, 209
Washington   **W:**16
Columbia River (North America)   **R:**240
Canada   **B:**402; **C:**64
dams   **D:**19–20
discovered by Captain Robert Gray   **O:**202
Indians, American   **I:**188
Lewis and Clark expedition   **L:**164
Montana   **M:**430
Oregon   **O:**204–5, 206, 207, 211, 215, 216
Washington   **W:**14, 17, 21, 26
picture(s)   **R:**237
gorge   **O:**205
Grand Coulee Dam   **G:**99; **W:**22
windsurfers   **O:**203
"Columbia, the Gem of the Ocean" (song)   **N:**24
Columbia University (New York City)   **N:**217, 229
Pulitzer Prizes   **P:**533
Columbines (flowers)
picture(s)
state flower of Colorado   **C:**431
Columbium *see* Niobium
Columbus (Georgia)   **G:**141
Columbus (Ohio)   **C:**444; **O:**65, 69
picture(s)   **C:**444; **O:**69
capitol building   **O:**72
Ohio State University   **O:**65

Columbus, Christopher (discoverer of the New World)
        C:445–48
    Atlantic Ocean, historical background of   **A:**479
    Caribbean Sea and islands   **C:**114
    Costa Rica   **C:**556, 558
    Cuba   **C:**596
    Dominican Republic, history of   **D:**282
    exploration of the New World   **E:**404, 407, 409
    Expo '92 commemoration   **F:**17
    Ferdinand and Isabella   **F:**88
    Haiti, history of   **H:**11
    holiday honoring   **H:**153
    Honduras   **H:**198
    New World discovered instead of the spice lands   **H:**113
    Nicaragua, discovery of   **N:**246
    South America   **S:**292
    Spain, history of   **S:**376
    spice trade between the New and Old World   **F:**332
    What were the consequences of Columbus' voyage in
        1492?   **C:**448
    Where did Columbus really land on his first voyage to the
        New World?   **C:**446
    picture(s)   **C:**445; **E:**405; **S:**376
        flag   **F:**248
        statue in Barcelona (Spain)   **S:**374
Columbus Day   **H:**153
Columnists (newspaper writers)   **N:**198
Columns (in architecture)
    Greek orders   **A:**373; **G:**351
    Rome, architecture of   **R:**319
    picture(s)
        optical illusions used in building Greek columns
            O:177
Coma (cloudlike head of the comet)   **A:**473; **C:**452; **S:**248
Comanche (Indians of North America)   **I:**180
Comaneci, Nadia (Romanian gymnast)   **O:**115
    picture(s)   **O:**115
Combat, trial by *see* Battle, trial by
Combat arms (of the United States Army)   **U:**107
Combative sports (in the Olympics)   **O:**107
Combat service support (in the United States Army)   **U:**108
Combat support arms (of the United States Army)   **U:**107
Combat units (of the United States Army)   **U:**108, 109
Combat video games   **V:**332c
Combination locks   **L:**283
    diagram(s)   **L:**283
Combination pliers (tools)   **T:**230
Combination square (measuring tool)   **T:**230
Combinatorial chemistry   **S:**72
Combine paintings (of Robert Rauschenberg)   **M:**396b
Combines (farm machinery)   **F:**57–58; **W:**157
    picture(s)   **A:**88; **F:**60; **S:**45
Combing (of cotton fibers)   **C:**561
Combustion (burning)   **F:**141 *see also* Fuels
    chemical terms   **C:**204
    explosives   **E:**419
    internal-combustion engines   **I:**262–65
    Lavoisier's explanation   **L:**83
    phlogiston theory   **C:**208
    provides energy for missiles   **M:**344
    rapid oxidation   **O:**286–87
Combustion chamber (in jet engines)   **A:**116
Comédie-Française (national theater of France)   **P:**70; **T:**160
Comedy (form of drama)   **D:**294
    English   **E:**277, 289–90
    Greek   **G:**357
    motion pictures   **M:**489, 492
    musical comedy   **M:**557–58
    origin of the word   **D:**296
    slapstick and farce   **H:**289
Comedy of Errors, The (play by Shakespeare)   **S:**133
Comedy of manners (in English drama)   **E:**277, 289–90
Comenius, John Amos (Czech educator and theologian)   **C:**228,
        612; **E:**80
Comet Falls (Washington)   **W:**63

Comets   **C:**449, 452;   **S:**241, 248
    astronomy, history of   **A:**473
    dinosaur extinction theory   **D:**175; **G:**112
    Jupiter bombarded by   **J:**162
    nucleus formed of ice and dust   **I:**4
    radar astronomy studies   **R:**76
    picture(s)
        Halley's comet   **C:**452
Comic books   **C:**453–54
Comic opera *see* Opéra bouffe; Opéra comique
Comics Magazine Association of America   **C:**454
Comic strips   **C:**127, 128–29, 453
    German forerunners   **G:**178
    Schulz, Charles M.   **M:**339
Coming about (in sailing)   **S:**11
Coming and Going of the Pony Express (painting by Remington)
    picture(s)   **P:**383
Comino (island, Malta)   **M:**63
Command (Air Force unit)   **U:**112
Command economies   **E:**59
Commander in chief (title of the United States president)
        P:449, 452–53; **U:**170
Command module (CM) (section of spacecraft) *see* Capsule
Command ships   **U:**119
Commas (punctuation marks)   **P:**542
Commedia dell'arte (Italian company of character actors)
        C:309, 386; **D:**298
Commemorative stamps   **P:**399
Commensalism (a way some different organisms live together)
        L:206
Commerce *see* International trade; Trade and commerce
Commerce, United States Department of   **C:**455;   **P:**447
    Merchant Marine Academy   **U:**126
    Patent and Trademark Office   **P:**99
Commercial art   **C:**456–58 *see also* Advertising; Posters
    industrial design   **I:**213–15
Commercial banks   **B:**53, 54–55
Commercial property   **R:**112d, 113
Commercials (in advertising)   **A:**30, 32; **T:**68
Commissioned officers (United States Army)   **U:**110
Commission form (of city government)   **M:**514
Commissions (on sales)
    percents, use of   **P:**146
    real estate sales   **R:**113
Committee for Industrial Organization (CIO)   **A:**79k; **L:**16
Committee for Original Peoples Entitlement (political group)
        I:276
Committee of Public Safety (French Revolution)   **F:**471
Committees (in organizations)   **P:**82
Committees (of the United States Congress)   **U:**142–43, 166
Committees of correspondence   **A:**20; **R:**196–97
Commodus (Roman emperor)   **R:**317
Common bond (in masonry)
    picture(s)   **B:**391
Common carriers (in the trucking industry)   **T:**321
Common cold (virus disease)   **B:**300; **D:**190–91; **H:**76
    picture(s)
        rhinoviruses   **V:**361
Common dolphins   **D:**274
Common fractions   **F:**397
Common law   **L:**85
    Canada   **S:**506
    origin in medieval England   **E:**239
Common Market *see* European Economic Community
Common Market, Central American *see* Central American
        Common Market
Common Market, Southern *see* Mercosur
Common nouns   **P:**92
Common (Harbor) porpoises   **D:**274
    picture(s)   **D:**275
Commons *see* Village greens
Commons, House of (British Parliament)   **E:**240, 245; **U:**68
    Astor, Lady   **V:**358
    parliamentary system   **P:**83
    picture(s)   **U:**69

Commons, House of (Canada)   **C:**75
Common schools   **E:**82–83
Common Sense (pamphlet by Thomas Paine)   **A:**199; **D:**59; **P:**13
Common stocks (shares in a company)   **S:**454
Common time (in music)   **M:**540
Commonwealth (term)   **U:**92
   four states of the United States   **K:**212; **P:**136; **V:**355
   Puerto Rico's status   **P:**530
Commonwealth, English   **C:**585
Commonwealth of Independent States   **C:**459–60; **G:**263;
      U:52 *see also* the names of individual countries
Commonwealth of Nations   **C:**461; **E:**254 *see also* United
      Kingdom; the names of individual member nations
   Commonwealth Day   **H:**154
   United Kingdom   **U:**55, 66
Communal farms (in Mexico)   **M:**246
Commune (form of government in Florence, Italy)   **F:**259
Commune of Paris (1871)   **F:**417
Communes (China's government-run farms)   **C:**265
Communes (local political units in France)   **F:**412
Communicable diseases *see* Infectious diseases
Communication   **C:**462–71 *see also* Languages; individual
      country, province, and state articles
   advertising   **A:**28–35
   alphabet   **A:**192–94a
   animals *see* Animal communication
   blindness, coping with   **B:**253–54
   cables   **T:**51
   commercial art   **C:**456–58
   communications satellites   **C:**469–70; **S:**54; **T:**66
   deaf, communication with the   **D:**49
   flags are a form of   **F:**225
   glass fibers   **M:**154
   handwriting   **H:**22–25
   Internet   **C:**486–89
   inventions advance   **I:**284–85
   journalism   **J:**135–41
   language arts   **L:**36
   letter writing   **L:**158–61
   magazines   **M:**16–20
   mail order   **M:**34–35
   microwaves   **M:**288
   musical notation   **M:**537–43
   newspapers   **N:**197–205
   orchestra conducting technique   **O:**201
   organization of scientific societies   **S:**71
   paper   **P:**53
   postal service   **P:**396–402
   printing   **P:**468–79
   product marketing   **S:**21
   propaganda   **P:**488–89
   public relations   **P:**517–18
   public speaking   **P:**518–20
   publishing   **P:**523–25
   radio   **R:**50–61
   scientific discoveries   **S:**67–68
   sound recording   **S:**266–67b
   speech   **S:**395–96
   telecommunications   **T:**46–50
   telegraph   **T:**51–52
   telephone   **T:**53–56
   television   **T:**61–71
   underwater laboratory   **U:**25
   writing   **W:**329–32
Communication design *see* Commercial art
Communications Act (United States, 1934)   **T:**68
Communications satellites   **C:**469–70; **S:**54; **T:**48, 66
   electronics   **E:**161
   journalism   **J:**141
   microwave communications   **T:**55
   radio signals, transmission of   **R:**40
   telegraph messages   **T:**52
   television   **T:**63

diagram(s)
   how satellite works   **T:**64
Communion *see* Eucharist
Communism   **C:**472–74;   **S:**224
   Balkans   **B:**23
   civil war in China   **C:**271
   Cold War   **C:**400–401
   communes (government-run farms in China)   **C:**265
   communist (people's) republics   **G:**274
   Czechoslovakia   **C:**609, 613–14
   economic system   **E:**59
   education in China   **C:**259
   Fascism and Communism in Italy   **F:**63
   Geneva Accords   **G:**93
   Hungary   **H:**296, 298
   Jews in the Soviet Union   **J:**109
   Khrushchev, Nikita   **K:**240–41
   Korean War   **K:**302–4
   Lenin, Vladimir Ilich   **L:**140
   Marx, Karl   **M:**116–17
   Minnesota   **M:**339
   Nazism   **N:**80
   one-party system   **P:**373
   religion in China   **C:**260
   Russia, history of   **R:**362, 364, 368
   Southeast Asia   **S:**335–36
   Stalin, Joseph   **S:**419
   Un-American Activities Committee, House   **U:**13
   Union of Soviet Socialist Republics   **U:**33–34, 36,
      40–41, 44, 49, 50
   What are the differences between Socialism and
      Communism?   **C:**473
Communist China *see* China, People's Republic of
Communistic societies
   Amana colonies (Iowa)   **I:**298
   New Harmony (Indiana)   **I:**157
Communist Manifesto   **C:**473; **M:**117
Communist Party, Cambodian *see* Khmer Rouge
Communist Party, Chinese   **C:**267; **M:**90
Communist Party, Cuban   **C:**600
Communist Party, Ethiopian *see* Workers' Party of Ethiopia
Communist Party, Polish *see* Polish United Workers' Party
Communist Party, Romanian   **R:**299, 301
Communist Party, Vietnamese   **V:**334c
Communist Party, Yugoslav   **T:**211
Communist (People's) republics (form of government)   **G:**274
Communities (of kingdoms of living things)   **B:**196;
      L:204–6; **P:**318
Community antenna television (CATV) *see* Cable television
Community centers
   nurses and nursing   **N:**419
   senior citizens' centers   **O:**100
Community college   **U:**220
Community ecology   **E:**53–54, 55
Community foundations   **F:**391
Community life
   child development, influences on   **C:**224
   cities   **C:**311–21
   colonial America   **C:**409–23
   disease prevention   **D:**211–12
   fighting mental illness   **M:**228
   4-H clubs   **F:**395–96
   hospitals   **H:**253
   parent-teacher associations   **P:**66–67
   pioneers   **P:**257, 258
   police relations with communities   **P:**365
   social work   **S:**229–30
   sociology, the study of   **S:**231
Community Planning and Development, Office for   **H:**270
Community theaters   **T:**159
Commutative properties (of numbers)   **N:**398
Commutators, electric   **E:**134, 153
Commuter trains (of railroads)   **R:**81, 82
Como, Lake (Italy)
   picture(s)   **L:**32

Comoros (Indian Ocean)   **C:**475
　　picture(s)
　　　　flag   **F:**226
　　　　Moroni mosque   **I:**350
Compact 35 cameras   **P:**202
Compact bone (in the body)   **S:**184
Compact discs (CD's) and players   **H:**121, 122; **P:**195;
　　　　S:267a, 267b *see also* CD-ROMs
　　communication, advances in   **C:**467
　　lasers, uses of   **L:**46c
　　outstanding jazz recordings   **J:**57
　　plastics   **P:**322
　　records and record collecting   **R:**125
　　picture(s)   **C:**467
　　　　compact disc player   **S:**267b
　　　　pits on surface   **P:**322; **S:**267a
Compacting machinery   **E:**32
Company (infantry troop unit)   **U:**109
Compaoré, Blaise (president of Burkina Faso)   **B:**452
Comparative anatomy *see* Anatomy, comparative
Comparative planetology   **A:**476d
Comparative religion *see* Religions
Comparators (Contour projectors) (optical instruments)   **O:**184
Compass (tool for drawing geometric figures)   **M:**200
Compass, magnetic (navigation instrument)   **N:**73
　　airplane navigation   **A:**118
　　electricity and magnetism   **E:**140
　　gyrocompass   **G:**437
　　magnets and magnetism   **M:**28, 29
　　points of compass named for Norse dwarf gods   **N:**279
　　south-pointing chariot   **G:**66
　　transportation, history of   **T:**283
　　picture(s)   **E:**403; **M:**29; **N:**75
　　　　south-pointing chariot   **G:**66
Compass rose (on maps)   **M:**94
Compatible numbers   **A:**401
Compensation *see* Workers' compensation
Compensatory education   **E:**90
Competency tests   **T:**38, 119
Competition (in biological communities)   **L:**206
Competition (in economics)
　　business in a free enterprise system   **B:**473
　　feature of capitalism   **C:**103
　　how to be an entrepreneur   **B:**472
　　How will goods and services be produced?   **E:**58
　　pricing policy   **S:**21
　　responsibilities of labor and management   **L:**4
　　tariff   **T:**23
Competitive service (in civil service)   **C:**331
Compiler (computer program)   **C:**483
Complaint (in law)   **C:**566, 567
Complementary colors (in light)   **C:**425
Complete flowers   **F:**282
Complete proteins   **N:**423
Complex carbohydrates   **N:**424
Complexes (personality problems)   **J:**156
Complex numbers   **N:**402
Complex viruses   **V:**362
Composite flowers   **F:**283
Composite materials   **F:**105
Composite numbers   **N:**385
Composite volcanoes *see* Stratovolcanoes
Composition (in music)   **M:**535–49
　　baroque period   **B:**71–72
　　electronic music   **E:**155–56
　　jazz   **J:**62
Composition (in photography)   **P:**209
　　picture(s)
　　　　effects of changing camera lenses   **P:**204
Composition (in printing)   **B:**330
Composition (paintings by Mondrian)
　　picture(s)   **D:**132, 364
Composition III (painting by Kandinsky)
　　picture(s)   **M:**391
Composition boards (wood products)   **W:**227

Compositions (in writing and speaking)   **C:**476–78
　　essays   **E:**321–22
　　outlines   **O:**265–67
　　proofreading   **P:**487
　　researching reports   **R:**182–83
Compositor (person who sets type)   **B:**329; **T:**370
Compost (decayed organic material)   **G:**30
　　fertilizers   **F:**96
　　solid-waste disposal   **S:**33
Compound bow (in archery)   **A:**364–65
　　picture(s)   **A:**364
Compound fractures (broken bones) *see* Open fractures
Compound interest   **I:**255
Compound leaves   **L:**112; **P:**306
　　picture(s)   **L:**113
Compound microscopes   **M:**281–82, 286
　　lenses   **L:**146–47
Compound ore (metal found joined with other substances)
　　O:217
Compounds, chemical   **C:**198, 204; **L:**199
　　atomic combinations   **A:**483, 485
　　body, human   **B:**269
　　body's cells, composition of   **B:**291
　　structure of matter   **M:**176–77
Comprehensive schools   **E:**84, 85
Comprehensive Test Ban Treaty (1996)   **D:**180; **F:**36; **N:**379
Compressed air   **G:**59
　　pneumatic systems   **H:**314
　　scuba diving   **U:**22
　　shock waves produced by airplanes   **S:**501
Compression (in physics)   **B:**430
Compression-ignition engines *see* Diesel engines
Compression ratio (of engines)   **D:**160; **I:**263
Compression refrigerating system   **R:**133, 135
Compression waves (of earthquakes) *see* P-waves
Compression waves (of sound)   **S:**256–57
　　picture(s)   **S:**258
Compressors (for gases)
　　air conditioning   **A:**102
　　engines   **E:**230–31
　　gas turbines   **T:**343
　　jet engines   **A:**116; **J:**90, 91
　　refrigeration systems   **R:**133
Compromise of 1850   **C:**479; **U:**184
　　achievement of Fillmore's administration   **F:**129
　　Calhoun's protest   **C:**17
　　Clay, Henry   **C:**353
　　Fugitive Slave Law   **U:**17
　　Zachary Taylor's opposition   **T:**32–33
Compton, Arthur (American physicist)   **S:**368
Compton, John G. M. (prime minister of Saint Lucia)   **S:**18
Compton Gamma-Ray Observatory   **O:**10; **S:**367, 368; **T:**60
Comptroller of the Currency, Office of the   **T:**294
Compulsory education   **E:**83
Compulsory figures (in ice skating)   **I:**41
Compurgation (in law)   **J:**163
Computational fluid dynamics (aeronautics)
　　picture(s)   **S:**501
Computed tomography (CAT scan) (X-ray technique)   **I:**85;
　　　　M:208c, 208h; **X:**351
　　brain disorders   **B:**369
　　cancer detection   **C:**94
　　diagnosis of disease   **D:**208
　　electronics   **E:**161
　　picture(s)   **C:**485; **I:**86
Computer-aided design and manufacturing *see* CAD/CAM
Computer chips (electronic components)   **C:**481, 487, 493;
　　　　T:277, 278
　　electronic watches   **W:**45
　　video games   **V:**332b
　　picture(s)   **C:**493; **E:**160; **T:**277
　　　　inspection of   **A:**408; **C:**25
Computer graphics   **C:**484, 489, 493
　　animation   **A:**290

Conches (mollusks)   **O:**294; **S:**148
  oil lamps   **L:**231
Conchobar (legendary king of Ulster)   **I:**325
Conchology see Shells (of mollusks)
Conciergerie, La (Paris)   **P:**73
Concise Oxford Dictionary of Music, The   **R:**129
Conclusions (in logic)   **L:**289, 290
Conclusions (in scientific experiments)   **S:**78
Concord (capital of New Hampshire)   **N:**153, 157, 162
  picture(s)
      Christa McAuliffe Planetarium   **N:**158
      State House   **N:**159
Concord (Massachusetts)   **M:**144
  Alcott's home   **A:**174
  Emerson's home   **E:**202
  Revolutionary War begins   **R:**198
Concordat (kind of treaty)
  Concordat of 1801   **N:**10–11
  Concordat of Worms (1122)   **R:**285
Concorde (supersonic passenger plane)   **A:**117, 567; **S:**500;
      T:287
  picture(s)   **A:**568
      water tunnel test   **A:**37
      wind tunnel test   **A:**112
Concorde, Place de la (Paris)   **P:**69–70
  obelisk brought from Egypt   **O:**5
Concord grapes   **G:**297
"Concord Hymn, The" (poem by Emerson)   **E:**202
Concordia University (Montreal, Quebec)   **Q:**10a
Concrete   **C:**165–66
  architectural possibilities   **A:**382, 384–85, 386
  building construction   **B:**436, 438
  building material   **B:**430
  climate, urbanization's effect on   **C:**364
  dams   **D:**16–21
  highway surfaces   **R:**250
  homes   **H:**175
  masonry   **B:**394
  railroad ties   **R:**78
  Rome, architecture of   **R:**318
  picture(s)
      building material   **B:**433
Concrete arch dams   **D:**16
  picture(s)   **D:**20
Concrete nouns   **P:**92
Concrete thought   **C:**226
Concurrent powers (shared by state and national governments)
      U:162
Condensation   **H:**91–92
  action of geysers   **G:**193
  cloud formation   **C:**383
  dew   **F:**291
  distillation process   **D:**218–19
  fog   **F:**290–91
  hurricane formation   **H:**303
  rain   **R:**93
  water, forms of   **W:**48
  water cycle on Earth   **W:**49
  water desalting   **W:**56
  weather, creation of   **W:**84
Condensation nuclei (tiny airborne particles of matter)   **R:**93
Condensation theory (of the origin of the solar system) see Solar
      system—theories of formation
Condensed milk   **C:**98, 534; **D:**10
Condensers, gas and vapor
  air conditioning   **A:**102
  distilling equipment   **D:**218
  refrigeration systems   **R:**133
  Watt's invention   **S:**444
Condiments see Spices and condiments
Conditioned reflexes (Responses) (in psychology)
  impulses to take drugs   **N:**16
  learning   **L:**98–99
  Pavlov, Ivan   **P:**103
Conditioning (of the body) see Exercise

Condom (birth control device)   **B:**248
Condominium (joint ownership of property)   **H:**183
Condorcanqui, José Gabriel (Peruvian Indian leader) see Tupac
      Amaru II
Condors (birds)   **C:**22
  Andean region   **A:**253; **S:**283
  picture(s)   **E:**209
Conducting (of music)   **O:**198–201
  ancient music   **A:**245
Conduction (movement of heat through matter)   **H:**93–94, 95
  metals, property of   **M:**233
  diagram(s)   **H:**93
Conductivity, electrical
  seawater   **O:**38
Conductors (on trains)   **R:**86
Conductors, electric see Electric conductors
Cone-bearing trees see Conifers
Cones (in geometry)   **G:**124
Cones (of retina of the eye)   **E:**430
Cone shell
  picture(s)   **S:**147
Conestoga wagon (freight carrier)   **P:**138; **T:**283
  pioneer life   **P:**252
  Santa Fe Trail   **O:**272
  picture(s)   **P:**250; **W:**142
Coney Island (amusement park, New York City)   **P:**78
Coneys see Pikas
Confectioners' sugar   **S:**483
Confectionery see Candy and candy making
Confederated Unions of America   **L:**17
Confederate Memorial Day   **H:**154
Confederate States of America   **C:**495–97
  Benjamin, Judah Philip   **L:**326
  Civil War   **C:**336
  Davis, Jefferson   **D:**43, 44
  Jackson, Thomas Jonathan ("Stonewall")   **J:**9
  Lee, Robert E.   **L:**125–26
  Lincoln, Abraham   **L:**244–46
  Tyler was a representative of Confederate Provisional
      Congress   **T:**368
  picture(s)
      flags   **F:**243
      soldiers   **C:**339
      uniforms and flag   **C:**332
Confederation see also Articles of Confederation
  early government of United States   **U:**177
Confederation, Congress of the (United States, 1781–1789)
      W:140
Confederation Bridge (Canada)   **C:**66; **P:**462
Confederation Centre of the Arts (Charlottetown, Prince Edward
      Island)   **P:**465
Confederation of Canada   **C:**83; **P:**465, 467; **Q:**14
Confederation of the Rhine   **N:**12
Conference calls see Teleconferencing
Confession (form of prayer)   **P:**430–31
Confessional poets   **A:**214
Confessions (branches of Christianity)   **E:**45
Confessions of Saint Augustine   **A:**494
Confirmation (in Reform Judaism)   **J:**145, 147
Confirmation (sacrament of the Roman Catholic Church)
      R:294
Confucianism   **C:**260, 497; **R:**147–48
  Chinese literature   **C:**278
  Chinese tomb paintings   **C:**274
  compared with religions of Asia   **A:**458
  Korea   **K:**294, 300
  saints   **S:**18c
Confucius (Chinese philosopher)   **A:**459; **C:**259,
      497; R:147–48
  birthday is a holiday in Taiwan   **H:**153
  ideas on government   **C:**267, 268
  national sage of China   **C:**260
  Thirteen Classics   **C:**278
  picture(s)   **A:**463
Conga (Cuban dance)   **L:**72

Conga drum   D:338
Congaree River (South Carolina)   S:298, 300, 305
Congaree Swamp National Monument (South Carolina)   S:304
Congeners (impurities in distilled beverages)   W:161
Congenital disabilities and diseases (birth defects)   D:177, 181, 184
 blindness   B:252
 cerebral palsy   D:190
 deafness   D:48
 Down syndrome   D:289
 frog deformities may be caused by holes in ozone layer   F:478
 German measles during pregnancy can cause   D:192
 heart diseases   H:85
 mental retardation, causes of   R:190–91
 Siamese twins   T:364
Congestive heart failure   D:193; H:83
Conglomerate (rock)   R:267
 picture(s)   R:266
Congo (People's Republic of the Congo)   C:498–500
 picture(s)
  Brazzaville   C:500
  flag   F:226
Congo, Democratic Republic of see Zaïre
Congo-Kinshasa see Zaïre
Congo River (central Africa)   A:48; C:501; L:33; Z:378
 map(s)   C:501
 picture(s)   C:498, 501; Z:378
Congregate system see Auburn system
Congregational Church   C:293, 294; P:492
Congress Hall (Philadelphia, Pennsylvania)   P:180
Congressional Budget Office (United States)   U:165
Congressional districts   E:129; U:168
Congressional Hispanic Caucus Institute   C:326
Congressional Medal of Honor see Medal of Honor
Congressional Record, The   U:143
Congress of Industrial Organizations (CIO)   L:16, 162; U:13
Congress of People's Deputies (Soviet government)   U:44, 52
Congress of Racial Equality (CORE)   A:79L; C:326; J:8
Congress of the United States see United States, Congress of the
Congress of Vienna see Vienna, Congress of
Congress Party (of India)   I:133, 134
Congreve, William (English designer of rockets)   M:343
Congreve, William (English dramatist)   D:299
Congrid eels   E:98
Congruence (in geometry)   G:125
Conibo (Native American language)   I:197
Conic projection (of maps)   M:97
Conic sections (geometric figures)   G:122–23
 diagram(s)   G:122
Conifers (trees)   P:301; T:310
 biomes   B:208; P:319
 forests   F:373
 forests, animals in   A:274
 history of plants on land   E:27
 picture(s)
  animal life in forest   A:274
  cone   P:307
  forests   P:321
  sexual reproduction   P:309
Conjoined twins see Siamese twins
Conjunction (in astronomy)   S:246
Conjunctions (words that join words, phrases, or clauses)   G:289; P:94
Conjunctivitis (eye infection)   E:431
Conkling, Roscoe (American politician)   A:438g; H:71
Connally, John B. (American public official)   K:210
Conneaut, Lake (Pennsylvania)   P:129
Connecticut   C:502–16
 colonial life in America   C:418
 Mystic Seaport   C:422
 Puritans   P:551
 thirteen American colonies   T:174

 witches, persecution of   W:209
 map(s)   C:513
 picture(s)
  Connecticut River   C:504
  dairy farm   C:504
  Foxwoods Casino   C:510
  Hartford   C:503
  jet-engine factory   C:509
  Litchfield church   C:503
  Mystic Seaport   C:423, 503
  New Haven   C:507
  Stamford   C:512
  Thimble Islands   C:504
Connecticut, University of   C:506
 picture(s)
  women's basketball team   C:507
Connecticut Compromise (Great Compromise) (for the Constitution)   C:515; U:137, 147
Connecticut Lakes (New Hampshire)   N:152
Connecticut River   C:502, 504
 Massachusetts   M:138
 New Hampshire   N:152
 Vermont   V:308, 309
 picture(s)   C:504
  covered bridge   N:152
  valley   M:138
Connecticut (Hartford) Wits (American authors)   A:201
Connecticut Yankee, A (musical by Rodgers and Hart)   M:558
Connective tissue (of the body)   B:271
Connolly, James (American athlete)   O:108
Connolly, James (Irish patriot)   I:324
Connolly, Maureen (Little Mo) (American tennis player)   T:96 profile
 picture(s)   T:96
Connor, Ralph (Canadian writer)   C:86
Connors, Jimmy (American tennis player)   T:96 profile
 picture(s)   T:96
Connotation (of a word)   S:117
Conon (pope)   R:290
Conquistadors (Spanish soldiers)   C:551; L:48, 50; S:292–93
Conrad, Frank (American engineer)   R:55
Conrad, Joseph (Polish-born English writer)   C:517; E:288; N:361
 spy novels   M:563
 picture(s)   E:289
Conrail (railroad company)   R:90
Conscientious objector (one who is opposed to participation in military service)   P:106
Conscription see Draft (conscription)
Conservation   C:517–21 see also Environment; Natural resources; individual country, province, and state articles
 agricultural land management   A:95–96
 air conditioning and energy conservation   A:103
 beavers' role in   B:112
 biogeography   G:100–101
 caves and caverns   C:158
 dams, benefits of   D:18–19
 drought prevention   D:329
 endangered species   E:208–11
 energy   C:519; E:223
 energy conservation influences architecture   A:386a
 erosion, practices to halt   E:319
 fishing industry   F:202, 221–22
 forests, protection of   F:374–76
 heating systems   H:97
 homebuilding   H:184
 hunting, rules of sportsmanship in   H:299–300
 Interior, United States Department of the   I:256
 irrigation   I:339–41
 mammals, protection of   M:76
 mountains and human activities   M:507
 Muir, John   M:511
 National Forest System   N:32–36

Cook, James (cont.)
    Hawaii   H:54, 61
    New Zealand   N:235, 241
    oceanography, beginnings of   O:41
    Pacific Ocean and islands   P:5
    Vancouver, George   V:276
    Washington   W:26
    picture(s)   H:61; P:7
Cook, Mount (New Zealand)   N:237
Cookbooks   C:532
Cooke, Ebenezer (American writer)   A:197
Cooke, Rose Terry (American writer)   A:207
Cooke, William Fothergill (English inventor)   I:285; T:51
Cookies (food)   B:388b
    recipes   R:115, 116
    safety of refrigerated foods   F:343
Cooking   C:532–36 *see also* Food shopping
    bread and baking   B:385–88b
    camp meals   C:45–46, 47
    candy and candy making   C:97–99
    cooking terms, list of   C:535
    fire in the home   F:143
    fires, cooking-related   F:146, 154
    flour, kinds of   F:276–77
    French   F:406
    herbs, spices, and condiments   H:113–15
    kindergarten activities   K:247
    mathematics in everyday life   M:160
    mealtime around the world   F:333–38
    microwave ovens   M:288
    outdoor cooking and picnics   O:263–64
    party refreshments   P:91
    pressure cooker   H:91
    recipes   R:114–16
    recipes originated from limited food supply   F:330
    restaurant specialties   R:187
    terms   R:114
    Why do foods cook faster in a microwave oven?   M:288
    table(s)
        metric conversions for the kitchen   W:113
Cook Inlet (Alaska)   A:149
Cook Islands (Pacific Ocean)   P:8
    picture(s)
        children   P:8
Cookworthy, William (English porcelain maker)   P:412
Cool (style of jazz)   J:62–63
Coolant *see* Cooling
Cooley, Charles H. (American sociologist)   S:231
Coolgardie (Australia)   A:513
Coolidge, Calvin (30th president of the United States)
        C:537–40
    vice presidency   V:329 *profile*
    picture(s)   C:537; H:32; P:451; V:318
Coolidge, Grace Goodhue (wife of Calvin Coolidge)   F:176–77
    picture(s)   C:538, 539; F:177
Coolidge, William David (American physicist)   I:278
Cooling
    air conditioning principle   A:101–3
    automobiles' cooling systems   A:546, 548
    cooling system of an internal-combustion engine   I:265
    fog resulting from   F:290
    helium used as coolant   H:106
    liquid gases   L:253
    matter, changes in volume of   M:174
    nuclear reactor coolants   N:371
    refrigeration   R:133–35
Cool storage (of food) *see* Cold storage
Cooney, Barbara (American writer and illustrator)   C:230
        profile
Cooper, Charlotte (British tennis player)   O:108
Cooper, Gary (American film actor)   M:440 *profile*
    picture(s)   M:440
Cooper, James Fenimore (American novelist)   A:202;
        C:541–42; N:360
    The Last of the Mohicans, excerpt from   C:541–42

Cooper, Kenneth (American physician)   J:113
Cooper, L. Gordon, Jr. (American astronaut)   S:346 *profile*
Cooper, Peter (American industrialist and philanthropist)
        C:543; R:88
Co-operation, international *see* International co-operation
Co-operative apartments   H:183
Co-operative education programs   U:221
Cooperative Extension System   F:396
Co-operatives
    Danish farms   D:111
    European farms   E:355
    Germany   G:154
    Israel's moshavim   I:372
    Korea   K:297
    mutual savings banks   B:55
    Romania   R:298
    rural electrification   F:58
    Saskatchewan Wheat Pool   S:48
    Shakespeare's acting company   S:131
    Tanzanian farms   T:18
Cooper's hawks (birds)   H:64
    picture(s)   H:64
Cooperstown (New York)   B:88; N:214, 217
Cooper Union (New York City, New York)   C:543
    Lincoln's speech in 1860   L:244
Coordinate (Analytic) geometry   A:183–84; M:157, 166
    Huygens, Christiaan   H:310
Coosa River (Alabama)   A:132, 133
Coots (birds)   B:225
Copacabana Beach (Rio de Janeiro, Brazil)
    picture(s)   R:234
Copán (Honduras)   H:198; M:184
    picture(s)   H:198; I:169
Copenhagen (capital of Denmark)   C:543–44; D:108, 109,
        112
    amusement parks   P:78
    picture(s)   D:113
Copepods (very small crustaceans)   C:591, 592
    ocean life   O:24
    vectors   V:283
    zooplankton   P:284
Copernican system (of astronomy)   A:471–72; P:233; S:70,
        241
    Galileo developed   G:6
    picture(s)   A:472
Copernicus, Nicolaus (Polish astronomer)   A:471–72;
        C:544–45; R:160–61
    physics, history of   P:233
Coping saws (tools)   T:228
Copland, Aaron (American composer)   C:545; D:36
Copley, John Singleton (American painter)   U:127
    picture(s)
        Paul Revere (painting)   U:127
Copper   C:546; E:172
    alchemy   C:207
    alloys   A:190, 191
    antiques   A:316b
    Arizona   A:414
    beginnings of the history of chemistry   C:206
    bronze and brass   B:409–10
    Chile is world's largest producer   C:253
    coins and coin collecting   C:399
    Congo, Democratic Republic of   Z:378
    copper-producing regions   M:318; N:293
    metallurgy, history of   M:236
    Montana   M:428, 435, 440, 441
    prehistoric people discovered how to use metal   P:442
    silver found in copper ores   S:177
    Utah has largest open-pit mine in North America   S:24;
        U:248
    water purification   W:57
    wire   W:191
    picture(s)
        Bingham Canyon mine   U:249
        open-pit mines   C:252, 292; M:317, 318; N:63,

Corn earworm (larva of moth)   C:550
Corneille, Pierre (French dramatist)   D:299; F:437–38
Cornelia (first wife of Julius Caesar)   C:6
Cornelius, Saint (pope)   R:290
Cornell, Joseph (American sculptor)   S:105
Corner Brook (Newfoundland)   N:141, 146
Cornering the market (stock-market term)   S:458
Cornet (musical instrument)
    picture(s)   W:185
Cornhusker State (name for Nebraska)   N:82, 83
Corning Glass Center (Corning, New York)   N:214
    picture(s)
        Museum of Glass   M:523
Corning Glass Works (Corning, New York)
    fiber optics   F:107
Cornish (New Hampshire)
    picture(s)
        covered bridge   N:152
Corn Maidens (in Native American mythology)   M:574–75
Corn oil   O:76
Corn Palace (Mitchell, South Dakota)   S:320
    picture(s)   S:318, 320
Corn plant (houseplant)
    picture(s)   H:268
Corn rootworm (plant pest)   P:288
Corns (thickening of skin)   B:273
Corn silks   C:550
Corn smut (plant disease)
    picture(s)   P:289
Cornstalk (Shawnee chief)   W:138
Corn State (nickname for Illinois)   I:62, 63
Corn syrup   C:97, 98
Cornwall (county, England)   U:61
Cornwallis, Charles, 1st Marquess (British general)   R:202,
        207, 208–9, 208–9 profile;   W:41
    picture(s)   R:209
Cornwallis, Edward (English founder of Halifax)   N:357
Cornwell, David (English writer) see Le Carré, John
Cornwell, Dean (American illustrator and painter)ˉ   I:82
Coroebus of Elis (Greek athlete)   O:103
Corolla (part of a flower)   F:282, 285–86
Corona (luminous halo around the sun)   E:51, 52; R:74;
        S:495–96
    picture(s)   E:50; R:76; S:488
Coronado, Francisco (Spanish explorer)   A:412;
        C:551; E:407; I:202; N:192 profile
    Oklahoma   O:92
    picture(s)   C:551; U:174
Coronary arteries (of the circulatory system)   H:81
Coronary artery disease   H:82–83
Coronary care units (in hospitals)   H:248
Coronary circulation of blood (in the heart)   D:193
Coronation of Napoleon, The (painting by David)
    picture(s)   N:11
Coronation of the Virgin (painting by Fra Angelico)   P:20
Corot, Jean Baptiste (French painter)   F:429; P:29
Corporal punishment   P:481
Corporation for Public Broadcasting (CPB)   T:68
Corporations (in business and industry)
    accounting   B:313
    business organization, types of   B:471
    corporate and industrial video careers   T:69
    corporate design is a kind of commercial art   C:457
    Delaware is nation's corporate capital   D:95, 100
    foundations   F:391
    labor and management represented   L:3
    stocks and bonds   S:454–59
Corps (army combat unit)   U:109
Corpus callosum (band of nerve fibers in the brain)   B:364
Corpus Christi (Body of Christ), Feast of   C:290; R:154, 284
    picture(s)   S:285
Corpuscles see Platelets; Red blood cells; White blood cells
Corpuscular theory of light (of Isaac Newton) see Particle theory
        of light
Correctional facilities see Prisons

Correctional system (in law)   C:576
Corrective Optics Space Telescope Axial Replacement (COSTAR)
    S:368
Corrector plate (lens of a Schmidt telescope)   T:59
Correggio, Antonio Allegri da (Italian artist)   I:398
Corregidor (Philippines)   W:293
Correlational study (in psychological research)   P:503
Correspondence see Letter writing
Corridos (Latin-American folk music)   F:309, 324; L:72
Corries see Cirques
Corrosion see also Rust
    aluminum resists   A:194d
    anticorrosive paints   P:33
Corrugated paper   P:57
Corruption, political
    Clinton administration   C:367, 368; U:205
    Iran-Contra Affair   I:310
    railroads, history of   R:90
    Watergate   W:64–65
Corsairs, Barbary (pirates)   O:262; P:263
Corsica (island south of Genoa)   I:363; N:10
Cortés, Hernando (Spanish conqueror of Mexico)   A:578;
        C:551;   I:173
    cacao beans (chocolate) introduced to Spain   C:280
    exploration of the New World   E:407
    factors important in helping Cortés conquer Mexico
        M:248
    Honduras   H:198
    Montezuma II   M:443
    picture(s)   M:249, 443
        conquest of Aztecs   I:173
Cortex (of the brain)   B:364–65, 367
Cortex (of the kidney)   K:242
Corticosteroids (drugs)   D:188
Cortina d'Ampezzo (Italy)
    Olympic Games (1956)   O:111
Cortona, Pietro da (Italian artist)   B:64–65
    picture(s)
        Triumph of Divine Providence, The (fresco)   B:63
Corundum (gem mineral)   G:71, 391
    picture(s)   M:316
Corvinus, Matthias see Matthias Corvinus
Cory, Peter (Canadian Supreme Court justice)
    picture(s)   S:505
Corydon (Indiana)   I:157
Cos (Greek island, home of Hippocrates)   M:203
Cosa Nostra see Organized crime
Cosby, Bill (American comedian and actor)
    picture(s)
        in a commercial   A:29
Cosby, William (American colonial governor)   Z:384
Coscoroba swan (bird)   D:344
Cosecant (ratio in trigonometry)   T:312, 313
Così fan tutte (opera by Mozart)   O:153
Cosine (ratio in trigonometry)   T:312, 313
Cosmetics   C:552–53 see also Perfumes
    apples, uses of   A:330
    Federal Food, Drug, and Cosmetic Act (1938)   F:345
    makeup, theatrical   P:337; T:158
    picture(s)
        makeup, theatrical   T:158
Cosmic Background Explorer (COBE) (space satellite)   S:340b
    picture(s)
        Big Bang plus 300,000 years   U:218
        microwave map of the sky   U:211
Cosmic background radiation   U:217
Cosmic rays   C:554–55
    radiation belts   R:48
    radioactive dating   R:65
    Why are cosmic rays important?   C:554
Cosmochemists (scientists)   C:451
Cosmology (branch of metaphysics)   P:192, 232, 239
    Aristotle's contributions to astronomy   A:471
    Hawking, Stephen William   H:63
    relativity   R:139–44

Counting-out rhymes N:276
Count of Monte Cristo, The (novel by Alexandre Dumas *père*)
  D:347
Countries *see* Nations
Country dances D:29
Country music C:563–65; R:261, 262
  Branson (Missouri) M:366
  Nashville N:18; T:74, 80
  United States, music of the U:210
  picture(s)
      Branson M:370
      Tennessee T:75, 80
Country Music Association C:564
Country School, The (painting by Homer)
  picture(s) S:60
County agent (adviser on agriculture) A:96
Coup d'etat (overthrow of government) L:58
Coup d'État of 18 Brumaire (in French history) N:10
Couperin, François (French composer) F:445–46
Couple dances F:301
Couple on Horseback (painting by Kandinsky)
  picture(s) R:375
Couplet (in poetry) E:276; P:353
Coupons (for discounts on products) F:347
Courbet, Gustave (French painter) F:429; M:386–87; P:29
Coureurs de bois (French-Canadian fur traders) F:520
Court, Margaret Smith (Australian tennis player) T:96 *profile*
  picture(s) T:96
Courtly love (in French literature) F:436
Court martial (military court) L:88
Court of Justice (European Union) E:369
Courts (of law) C:566–68 *see also* Law and law enforcement;
    Lawyers; Prisons
  adoption laws A:27
  Canada C:78
  common law's origin in England E:239
  Delaware's Court of Chancery D:100
  divorce D:230
  how laws are enforced L:87
  how laws are made L:86
  International Court of Justice I:267, 269–70; U:73
  journalism, issues in J:137
  jury J:163–64
  juvenile courts J:167, 169–70
  lie detector's use L:193
  penalties for crimes C:576
  president's judicial powers P:451
  probate proceedings for wills W:177
  state courts (the judiciary) S:438
  Supreme Court of Canada S:505–6
  Supreme Court of the United States S:507–10
  United States, government of the U:170–71
  picture(s)
      court officer swearing in a witness L:88
Courtship (of animals)
  cats, wild C:145
  fish F:195
  monarch butterflies B:476
  snakes S:217–18
  spiders S:405–6
Court tennis R:34b *see also* Tennis
Couscous (African dish) F:333; L:188; M:459; T:335
Cousin, Jean, the Elder (French artist) F:424
Cousins (family members) F:42
Cousins, Robin (British figure skater) O:116
Cousteau, Jacques-Yves (French inventor of the Aqualung)
    S:187
  underwater archaeology U:18
  underwater exploration E:416; U:27
  picture(s) E:416; I:281
Cousy, Bob (American basketball player) B:95i *profile*
  picture(s) B:95i
Couturiers (designers of high fashion) F:70
Covalent bond (in chemistry) A:487; C:204; M:152
  diagram(s) A:488

Covenant (in Judaism) J:143
Covenant on Civil and Political Rights (United Nations)
  H:285
Covenant on Economic, Social, and Cultural Rights (United
    Nations) H:285
Covent Garden (London, England) L:294
Coventry Cathedral (England) C:135
Cover (false identity of a spy) S:409
Cover crops (for soil conservation) S:236
Coverdale, Miles (English ecclesiastic and reformer) B:157;
  R:132
Covered bridges B:401
  Cornwall Bridge (Connecticut) C:508
  Vermont V:314
  world's longest (Hartland, New Brunswick) N:138e
  picture(s)
      Cornwall Bridge (Connecticut) C:508
      Hartland (New Brunswick) N:138e
      Indiana I:146
      New Hampshire N:152
      Vermont V:307, 314
Covered wagons *see* Conestoga wagon
Coveys (of quail) *see* Quail
Covilhã, Pedro de (Portuguese explorer) E:404
Covington (Kentucky) K:222
Coward, Noël (English actor and playwright) D:302; E:290
Cow beef C:152
Cowbirds B:228
Cowboys C:569–70
  Argentina's gauchos A:390
  Chile C:250
  llaneros of Venezuela V:296
  National Cowboy Hall of Fame and Western Heritage Center
    O:86, 88
  overland trails O:281–82
  ranch life R:102–3
  rodeos R:277–78
  roping R:335
  Spanish words in American English H:133
  Wyoming, history of W:346
  picture(s)
      Arizona A:406
      costume, traditional C:373
      National Cowboy Hall of Fame O:85
      overland trails O:282
      ranch life R:103, 104
      South Dakota S:313
      Utah U:244
      Wyoming W:344
Cowboy State (nickname for Wyoming) W:335
Cowcatcher (device to remove animals from railroad tracks)
  picture(s) T:285
Cowens, Dave (American basketball player) B:95i *profile*
  picture(s) B:95i
Cowhands *see* Cowboys
Cowley, Abraham (English poet) O:50
Cowling (engine cover) A:115
Cowpens, Battle of (1781) R:208
Cowper, William (English poet) E:278
Cowpox (virus disease) I:98; J:78; M:207
Cowries (mollusks) O:294
Cows C:151, 153
  dairy cattle D:3–8
  milk M:307
  picture(s)
      embryo development E:374
      Jersey cow H:216
      sacred to Hinduism H:130
      Vermont dairy cows V:308
Cow's Skull: Red, White and Blue (painting by O'Keeffe)
  picture(s) O:79
Cow towns (Kansas) C:570; K:176, 189
Cox, Archibald (American lawyer) N:262f; W:64
Coxey's Army (demonstrators for public works) O:74

Coxswain (steersman of racing boat)   R:340
Coxwell, Henry (English balloonist)   B:36
Coyote (Native American god)   M:569–70
Coyote Gulch (Utah)
  picture(s)   P:216
Coyotes   A:275
  scientific name   L:207
  picture(s)   A:269, 284; B:207; D:240; L:207
    fur   F:502
Coyote State (nickname for South Dakota)   S:312
Coypus see Nutrias
Coysevox, Antoine (French sculptor)   F:427
  picture(s)
    relief at Versailles   F:426
C.P.A. see Certified Public Accountant
CPB see Corporation for Public Broadcasting
CPR see Cardiopulmonary resuscitation
CPU (central processing unit) (of a computer)   C:480–81,
    491, 493
  picture(s)   C:482
Crab (constellation) see Cancer
Crab apples   A:330
  picture(s)
    seedling   G:40
Crabeater seals (animals)
  picture(s)   S:107
Crab-eating raccoon   R:25
Crabgrass
  picture(s)   W:105
Crab Nebula (supernova)   A:476; N:96
  pulsars   P:539
  radio astronomy observations   R:75
  X-ray ring   S:368
  picture(s)   A:476a; P:539
Crabs (crustaceans)   C:571, 591, 592
  horseshoe crab is related to crabs   H:245
  picture(s)   A:265
    Maryland crabs are a delicacy   M:121
    red crab   A:267
    snow crab fishing in Nova Scotia   N:353
Crack (form of cocaine)   D:331
Crackers (food)   B:388b
Cracking (extracting gasoline from petroleum)   G:62
Cracow (Poland)   P:360
  picture(s)   P:360
Cradle (device for washing gold from sand)   G:251
Cradle of Liberty (nickname for Boston, Massachusetts)
    M:136
Craft guilds   G:403–4
Crafts see Handicrafts; Hobbies
Crafts (trades) see Vocations
Craftsman style (of furniture)   F:516
  picture(s)   F:514
Craft unions   L:12, 14
Craig, James (Scottish architect)   U:236
Craigie House (Longfellow's home in Cambridge,
    Massachusetts)   L:301
Cramer, John Baptist (English composer)   E:293
Crampons (for mountain climbing)   M:500
Cramps (painful muscle spasms)   M:519
  menstruation   M:222
Cranach (Kranach; Kronach), Lucas (German artist)   G:170
  picture(s)
    Cardinal Albert of Brandenburg as St. Jerome in His
      Study (painting)   G:170
    Luther, Martin, portrait of   L:346
Cranberries   G:301; M:142
  picture(s)   G:300; P:296
Cranbrook (educational and cultural center, Bloomfield Hills,
    Michigan)   M:265
Crandall, Prudence (American educator and reformer)   C:514
  profile
Crane, Ichabod (character in The Legend of Sleepy Hollow)
    A:202
Crane, Stephen (American novelist)   A:207; C:572; F:115

Crane, Walter (English illustrator)   C:233
  picture(s)
    "Fox and the Crane, The"   C:233
Crane fly
  picture(s)   I:240
Cranes (birds) see also Whooping cranes
  crowned crane   U:6
  sandhill cranes   N:86
  picture(s)
    crowned crane   B:230
    sandhill cranes   N:85
Cranes (machines)   H:146–47
  picture(s)
    railroad freight yard   R:85
    shipbuilding   S:157
Cranial nerves   N:116
Cranium (bones of the skull)   S:183
Crankcase (of an automobile)   A:548; I:265
Crankshaft (of the internal-combustion engine)   A:547; I:262
Cranmer, Thomas (archbishop of Canterbury)   C:292; E:243;
    H:108
Crannogs (island refuges in lakes) see Lake dwellers
Cranston (Rhode Island)   R:221
Crappie (fish)   F:213
Crassus, Marcus Licinius (Roman statesman)   C:6; R:315
Crater Lake (Oregon)   L:29; O:205, 210; U:82
  picture(s)   L:27; O:210
Crater Lake National Park (Oregon)   O:210
Craters (cup-shaped holes)
  geology in the solar system   G:118
  Mars   M:106; P:278
  Mercury   M:229–30; P:275
  meteorites   C:451; G:112
  Mimas   S:58
  moon   M:450–51, 452, 455
  Venus   P:277; V:303b
  volcanoes   V:380
  picture(s)
    Mercury   M:231
    moon   M:447, 450, 451
Craters of the Moon National Monument (Idaho)   I:54
Cravat (scarf)   C:377
Crawfish (crustaceans) see Crayfish
Crawl (swimming stroke)   S:533
  picture(s)   S:534
Crawler cranes (machines)   H:147
Crawler tractor (farm machine)   F:53–54
Crayfish (crustaceans)   C:591, 592
  picture(s)
    boiled with corn and potatoes   L:315
  table(s)
    United States aquaculture production   F:208
Crazy Eights (card game)   C:110
Crazy Horse (chief of Oglala Sioux Indians)   I:180 profile
Crazy Horse Memorial (South Dakota)   S:320
  picture(s)   S:320
Crazy quilt (form of needlecraft)   N:101
Cream (fat content of milk)   B:474; C:534; M:307
Cream cheese   D:13
Creams (cosmetics)   C:552, 553
Creationism (belief that the Bible's account of creation is
    literally true)   E:379; L:209; S:84
Creation myths   M:568–70, 571–73
  Greek mythology   G:361, 363–64
  Native American folklore   F:113
  Norse mythology   N:279–80
Creation of Adam (painting by Michelangelo)
  picture(s)   E:363; M:255
Creative writing see Writing (authorship)
Crèche (French word for crib, Christmas Nativity)   C:299
Crèche (group of penguin chicks)   P:122
Crécy, Battle of (1346)   H:291–92; K:274
  picture(s)   E:240

Credit
in bookkeeping **B:**311
credit cards **C:**572
department store charge accounts **D:**120
Credit cards (used to charge purchases that will be paid for at a later date) **B:**58; **C:**467, **572; M:**415
picture(s) **C:**466; **M:**415
Crédit Mobilier of America (company involved in bribe scandal) **G:**53–54; **U:**187
Credit union **B:**55
Cree (Indians of North America) **I:**177, 190
legends illustrated in paintings **C:**71
Creek (Indians of North America) **I:**178, 179
Alabama **A:**134, 139, 140
Florida **F:**272
Horseshoe Bend, Battle of (1814) **J:**4
Creep (of ice) *see* Flow
Cremation (of the dead) **F:**493
Cremona (Italy) **B:**71; **I:**388
Crenshaw melons **M:**216
Creole (language) **L:**50
Dominican Republic **D:**280
Haiti **H:**9
Mauritius **M:**181
Seychelles **S:**129
Creoles (people)
Belize **B:**137
French Guiana **F:**466
Louisiana **L:**318; **N:**196
Mauritius **M:**181
Sierra Leone **S:**171
Suriname **S:**516–17
Creole State (nickname for Louisiana) **L:**315
Creosote **F:**147
Creosote bush (plant) **N:**122
Crepe rubber **R:**347
Crescendo (musical term) **M:**540, 542
Crescent moon **M:**447, 448
picture(s) **M:**448, 449
Crest masks **A:**74
Crests (in heraldry) **H:**112
Cretaceous period (in geology) **E:**25, 28–29
birds **B:**243
dinosaurs **D:**164, 169, 171, 172–73, 173–74
mass extinction **E:**425, 426
plants **F:**387
picture(s)
dinosaurs **D:**165
drifting continents **G:**113
table(s) **F:**384
Crete (island southeast of Greece) **I:**363
ancient civilization **A:**228–29
bull dancing in ancient Crete **B:**448
clothing, history of **C:**374
Greece, landforms of **G:**333
Minoan art and architecture **A:**236–38
Minoan palaces **A:**372
painting at Knossos **P:**15–16
water and drainage system **P:**340
World War II **W:**290
picture(s)
Greek man **E:**351
ruins at Knossos **A:**355
Crevasses (in glaciers) **G:**222; **I:**5
Crèvecoeur, Saint John de (French-born American writer) **A:**201
Crewelwork (form of embroidery) **N:**98, 100
Crias (baby llamas) **L:**278
Crick, Francis H. C. (English biochemist) **B:**201; **G:**86–87; **S:**74
picture(s) **B:**201; **G:**86
Cricket (game) **C:**573; **L:**296; **U:**60
picture(s) **U:**59

Crickets (insects)
picture(s)
cave cricket **C:**157
Crime and criminology **C:**574–76
arson **F:**147
biotechnology **G:**85–86
capital punishment **C:**104
child abuse **C:**222
computer crimes **C:**494
courts **C:**566–68
Federal Bureau of Investigation **F:**76–77
fingerprinting **F:**133
forensic science **F:**371–72
guns **G:**426
Holocaust **H:**159c–159d
jury **J:**163–64
juvenile crime **J:**167–70
law and law enforcement **L:**84–92
lie detection **L:**193
mentally ill, problem of the **M:**228
narcotics addicts **N:**17
police **P:**363–68
prisons **P:**480–82
terrorism **T:**116–17
violence and society **V:**344
Crime and Punishment (novel by Dostoevski) **D:**287
Crimean War **C:**577; **O:**262
France **F:**417
Nicholas I **N:**248
Nightingale, Florence **N:**259
Russia **U:**47
Crimes against humanity **C:**181; **G:**96; **H:**284
Crimes against persons **C:**574
Crimes against property **C:**574
Crime stories (in literature) **M:**562
Criminal law **L:**87, 90
courts **C:**566–68
jury **J:**163–64
juvenile crime **J:**167–68
lawyers' work on criminal cases **L:**91
Criminals *see* Crime and criminology
Criminology *see* Crime and criminology
Crinoids (Sea lilies) (marine invertebrates) **F:**386, 387
Criollos (Latin Americans of European descent) **L:**48–49, 58
Mexico **M:**248
South American independence movements **S:**293–94
Crioulo (language of Guinea-Bissau) **G:**407
Crippen, Robert L. (American astronaut) **A:**469; **S:**347 *profile*
picture(s) **S:**347
Crisis (African American journal) **A:**79h
Crisis, The (pamphlets by Paine) **R:**202
Cristero revolt (in Mexican history) **M:**251
Cristiani, Alfredo (Salvadoran president) **E:**199
Cristóbal Colón, Pico (highest point in Colombia) **C:**404
Cristofori, Bartolommeo (Italian inventor of the piano) **I:**411; **K:**239; **P:**241
Critical assembly (in nuclear fission) **N:**369
Critical mass (in nuclear fission) **N:**369, 374
Criticism, literary *see* Literary criticism
Croatia **B:**22; **C:**578–79; **Y:**364, 368, 369
picture(s)
flag **F:**235
Croatoan Island (North Carolina) **T:**166
Croats (a people of Europe) **B:**338; **C:**578; **S:**124–25; **Y:**364, 367
racism **R:**34a
Crocheting **C:**580–81; **T:**142
Crocidolite (mineral) **A:**443
Crockett, Davy (American frontiersman) **C:**582
Crocodiles **C:**582–84; **R:**179–80
related to dinosaurs **D:**168
Crocodilians (reptiles) **C:**582–84
Crocoite (mineral)
picture(s) **M:**316

Crustaceans (cont.)
  fishing industry **F:**217
  lobsters **L:**279–80
  shrimps **S:**167–68
  zooplankton **P:**284
Crustal plates *see* Plates (of the Earth's crust)
Crux Australis *see* Southern Cross
Cruz, Juana Inés de la (Mexican poet) **L:**67
Cruz, Juan de la *see* John of the Cross
Cruz, Ray (American illustrator)
  picture(s)
    illustration from Viorst's *Alexander and the Terrible,*
      Horrible, No Good, Very Bad Day **C:**244
Cryogenic gases **R:**134
Cryogenics (science of low temperatures) **L:**253
Cryolite (mineral)
  aluminum refining **A:**194c
  Greenland is major source **G:**374a
Cryptography (secret writing using codes and ciphers)
  C:393–95
Crystal City (Missouri)
  picture(s)
    flood (1993) **F:**256
Crystal glass **G:**233
Crystal lattice (arrangement of atoms) **M:**151
Crystalline lens (of the eye) **L:**149
Crystallites (atomic planes) **M:**152
Crystallography (study of crystal shapes) **S:**250
  materials science **M:**154–55
Crystal Palace (International Exposition, 1851) **F:**16
  picture(s) **F:**17
Crystals **C:**593–95
  alloys **A:**190, 191
  atomic arrangements **M:**151
  defects **M:**152–53
  definition of the term **C:**204
  diamond **D:**144
  gemstones **G:**69
  geodes **G:**97
  ice crystal clouds **C:**383, 385
  minerals **M:**314
  piezoelectricity is a characteristic of quartz **Q:**5
  polarizing microscopes used to study **M:**282
  quartz **Q:**5–6
  rocks **R:**264
  semiconductors **T:**274–75
  snowflakes **R:**95
  solids **S:**250
  diagram(s)
    shapes of ice crystals **R:**94–95
C-Span (cable TV) **J:**141
CT (X-ray technique) *see* Computed tomography
CTD (instrument for measuring seawater's conductivity,
      temperature, and depth) **O:**38–39
  picture(s) **O:**38
Ctesibius (Greek inventor) **G:**66
Ctesiphon, Arch of (palace south of Baghdad, Iraq) **I:**315
Ctesiphon II (painting by Stella)
  picture(s) **M:**396a
Cuba **C:**596–600
  Caribbean Sea and islands **C:**113, 114, 115
  Castro, Fidel **C:**133
  Columbus' discovery **C:**448
  Cuban missile crisis **C:**601
  folk music **F:**323
  guerrilla warfare **G:**400
  human rights violations **H:**285
  immigration to the United States **H:**132, 137
  issue of imperialism for McKinley **M:**192–93
  Kennedy administration policies **K:**209
  Latin America **L:**49, 50
  Ostend Manifesto and the United States attempt to buy
    Cuba **B:**419; **P:**247
  refugees **I:**92; **R:**137

  Spanish-American War **S:**392c–392d
  territorial expansion of the United States **T:**112–13
  picture(s)
    cigar manufacture **C:**598
    farmland **C:**597
    flag **F:**240
    Havana **C:**596
    schoolgirls **C:**596
    sugarcane crop **C:**114
    sugarcane harvest **C:**598
Cuban Americans **H:**132, 137
  picture(s)
    men playing dominoes **H:**133
Cuban bee hummingbird **H:**287
Cuban missile crisis **C:**401, 600, **601**; **K:**209
Cubas Grau, Raúl (Paraguayan president) **P:**66
Cube (six-faced geometric figure) **G:**123
Cubed numbers (in algebra) **A:**183
Cube statue (in ancient Egyptian sculpture) **E:**113
Cubi IX (steel sculpture by David Smith)
  picture(s) **S:**103
Cubic crystal system (in chemistry) **C:**594
  picture(s) **C:**593
Cubic measure (of volume) **M:**172; **W:**113
Cubism (modern art movement) **C:602**; **F:**432; **M:**390
  art of the artist **A:**438e
  Braque, Georges **B:**371
  Cézanne's influence **C:**179; **I:**106
  Léger, Fernand **L:**136
  Mondrian, Piet **M:**410
  painting in the 20th century **P:**30
  Picasso, Pablo **P:**243
  planes (flat surfaces in design) **D:**136
  sculpture of the 20th century **S:**104
  Spain, art of **S:**385
Cubits (measures of length) **W:**109
Cubozoans (coelenterates) **J:**77
Cub Scouts **B:**356–57
  Wolf Cubs of Canada **B:**360
Cuchulain (Irish hero) **I:**325
Cuckoo (bird) **B:**229
Cucumbers **V:**291
Cucurbit family (of plants) **M:**216
Cud (partially digested food chewed by cattle) **C:**151
  llamas **L:**278
Cud-chewers *see* Ruminants
Cueca (national dance of Chile) **C:**250
Cues (in billiards) **B:**179
Cues (in theater) **P:**338
Cugnot, Nicholas (French engineer) **A:**539; **T:**286
  picture(s)
    steam car trials **A:**540
Culebra Island (Puerto Rico)
  picture(s) **P:**528
Cullen, Michael (American supermarket owner) **S:**498
Culliford, Pierrot (Belgian cartoonist) *see* Peyo
Cullinan (diamond)
  picture(s)
    Star of Africa cut from **D:**146
Cultivation (of the soil) **F:**49, 54–55; **V:**288
Cultural anthropology **A:**300–303, 305
  artifacts from past cultures compared **A:**360
  Mead, Margaret **M:**195
  psychology compared to **P:**499–500
Cultural geography **G:**102
Cultural maps **M:**96
Cultural realms (in human geography) **G:**102
Cultural Revolution (1966–1969, China) **C:**271–72; **M:**90
Culture (human beings' way of life) **H:**281–82
  emotions influenced by **E:**204
Cultured milk products **D:**10
Cultured pearls **P:**115–16
Culture heroes **M:**570
Cultures (of bacteria) **D:**207; **M:**209, 278
Culverts (drainpipes) **R:**250

Cumberland (Maryland)   M:129
Cumberland, Lake (Kentucky)   K:214
Cumberland Compact (in Tennessee history)   T:84
Cumberland Falls (Kentucky)
    picture(s)   K:215
Cumberland Gap (eastern United States)   K:219, 220, 225
    Wilderness Road   O:270–71
    picture(s)   K:214
Cumberland House (fur-trading post)   F:520
Cumberland Island National Seashore (Georgia)   G:140
    picture(s)   G:135
Cumberland Plateau (in North America)   A:132; K:212; T:74,
        81; V:348
Cumberland River (Kentucky–Tennessee)   K:214, 221; T:76,
        81
Cumberland Road (National Road)   O:270; P:260
    Maryland   M:120
    Ohio   O:73
    map(s)   O:273
    picture(s)   O:270
        Indiana   I:158
Cumbres Toltec Scenic Railroad (Colorado)   C:438
Cumin (spice)   H:114
Cumulative Book Index   I:115
Cumulonimbus clouds   C:385; W:87
    picture(s)   C:384
Cumulus clouds   C:385; W:87
    glider pilots use to locate lift   G:239
    picture(s)   C:384
Cuna Indians see Kuna Indians
Cuneiform (ancient wedge-shaped writing system)
    alphabet   A:192
    ancient civilizations   A:220, 226–27
    books   B:318
    Eblaite civilization   A:224
    how numbers were written   N:405
    picture(s)   A:220
Cunha, Euclides da (Brazilian writer)   B:382
Cunningham, Merce (American dancer and choreographer)
        D:34
Cup (measure of volume)   C:532
Cup and Ball (puzzle)   P:554
Cupid (Roman god) see Eros
Cupronickel (copper and nickel alloy)   A:191
Cups and Balls (magic trick)   M:22
Curaçao (island of the Netherlands Antilles)   C:114, 115;
        L:50
    folk dancing   D:30
    picture(s)
        Willemstad   C:113
Curators (in museums)   M:532
Curds (of milk)   C:195; D:12; M:307
Curfew   J:170
Curie, Eve (French musician and author)   C:603
Curie, Irène Joliot see Joliot-Curie, Jean-Frédéric and Irène
Curie, Marie (Polish-born French physicist)   C:603
    chemistry, history of   C:210–11
    physics, history of   P:236
    radium, discovery of   L:222; U:230
    science, milestones in   S:73
    picture(s)   S:73
Curie, Pierre (French physicist)   C:603
    radium, discovery of   L:222; U:230
    science, milestones in   S:73
Curie's Law   C:603
Curing (preservative process)
    cheese   D:12–13
    leather   L:108
    meat   M:198
    tobacco   T:213
Curitiba (Brazil)   B:381
Curium (element)   E:172
Curlews (birds)
    picture(s)   B:236

Curling (game)   C:604;   O:107
    picture(s)   C:604
Currants (berries)   G:51
Currency (coins and paper money)   M:412, 414
    coins and coin collecting   C:398–400
    dollar   D:257–59
    euro   E:368, 369
    How can you tell if a bill is counterfeit?   D:258
    monetary units of countries see individual country articles
Current electricity   E:138
Currents, ocean see Ocean currents
Curriculum (course of study)   E:88, 91
Curry, John (British figure skater)   O:115
Curry, John Steuart (American painter)   K:188 profile;   U:132
    picture(s)   K:188
Curry powder (blend of spices)   F:330; H:114
Cursive writing   H:23–25
Curtain walls (of buildings)   B:436
    castles   C:131
    picture(s)
        castles   C:132
Curtis, Charles (American statesman)   V:329 profile
    picture(s)   C:539
Curtis Cup (golf)   G:260
Curtiss, Glenn Hammond (American inventor and aviator)
        A:562
Curtiss, Lawrence (American scientist)   F:106
Curtiss JN4 (airplane)
    picture(s)   A:564
Curtiss NC-4 (flying boat)   A:563
Curved mirrors   L:214
Cuscatlán (Pipil Indian center, Central America)   E:198
Cushions   U:228
Cushites (in the Old Testament)   E:117
Cushitic languages   L:39
Cuspids (teeth)   T:43
Custer, George Armstrong (American army officer)   I:205;
        M:440 profile;   S:325
    picture(s)   M:441
Custer, Thomas (American army officer)   N:30–31
Custer Battlefield National Monument (Montana) see Little
        Bighorn Battlefield National Monument
Custer National Forest (South Dakota)   S:316
Custer's Last Stand (1876) see Little Bighorn, Battle of
Custer State Park (South Dakota)   S:320
    picture(s)   S:315
Custis-Lee Mansion (Virginia) see Arlington House, The Robert
        E. Lee Memorial
Custody (of children in divorce)   D:230; F:38
Custom, international   I:267
Customary system (of measurement) see English system
Custom-made goods   M:88
Customs see Tariff
Customs, social see the people section of continent, country,
        province, and state articles
Customs-free zones see Free ports
Customs Service, United States   P:366; T:294–95
Cut-and-cover construction (of tunnels)   T:338
Cut and paste (editorial process)   W:331
Cut glass   G:233, 234
Cuthbert, Betty (Australian athlete)   O:110–11
Cuticle (Cutin) (waxy substance of leaves)   L:113; P:306
Cuticle (of invertebrates) see Exoskeleton
Cutlery (knives, scissors, and shears)   K:283–85
Cut-pile fabric   R:354
Cuts (injuries)   F:160; S:3
Cutter (sailboat)   S:8
Cutting (of gemstones)   G:71
Cuttings (from plants)   H:267
Cuttlefishes (mollusks)   M:405, 406; O:293
Cuvier, Georges (French naturalist)   G:110
Cuyahoga Valley (Ohio)   O:68
    picture(s)   O:63, 68
Cuza, Alexandru Ion (prince of Romania)   R:299–300

PHOTO CREDITS

The following list credits the sources of photos used in THE NEW BOOK OF KNOWLEDGE. Credits are listed, by page, photo by photo—left to right, top to bottom. Wherever appropriate, the name of the photographer has been listed with the source, the two being separated by a dash. When two or more photos by different photographers appear on one page, their credits are separated by semicolons.

from *Charlotte's Web* by E. B. White, Illustrated by Garth Williams. © 1952, E. B. White, Illustrations © renewed 1980 by Garth Williams.

240 From *The Random House Book of Poetry For Children* selected by Jack Prelutsky, illustrated by Arnold Lobel © 1983 by Random House, Inc. Reprinted by permission of the publishers.

241 Illustration by Clement Hurd from *Goodnight Moon* by Margaret Wise Brown, illustrated by Clement Hurd. © 1947, by Harper & Row, Publishers, Incorporated. Renewed © 1975 by Roberta Brown Rauch and Clement Hurd; Illustration from *In the Small, Small Pond* by Denise Fleming. Illustration by Denise Fleming. © 1993 by Denise Fleming. Reprinted by permission of Henry Holt & Co., Inc.; Illustration from *Sunshine* by Jan Ormerod. © 1982 by permission of Lothrop, Lee & Shepard Books (A Division of William Morrow and Company, Inc.).

242 From *Jumanji* by Chris Van Allsburg. © 1981 by Chris Van Allsburg. Reprinted by permission of Houghton Mifflin Company; Illustration from *Doctor de Soto* by William Steig. © 1982. Reprinted by permission of Farrar, Strauss & Giroux, Inc.; Illustration from *Crow Boy* by Mitsu and Taro Yashima. © 1955 by Mitsu and Taro Yashima. Copyright renewed © 1983 by Taro Yashima. All Rights Reserved. Reprinted by permission of Viking Penguin Inc.

243 Illustration from *The Snowy Day* by Ezra Jack Keats. © 1962 by Ezra Jack Keats. All Rights Reserved. Reprinted by permission of Viking Penguin Inc.; Illustration by Ed Young reprinted by permission of Philomel Books from *Lon Po Po* by Ed Young, copyright © 1989 by Ed Young; Illustration by Maurice Sendak from *Where The Wild Things Are*, story and pictures by Maurice Sendak. © 1963 by Maurice Sendak.

244 Used by permission of Atheneum Publishers from *Alexander and the Terrible, Horrible, No Good, Very Bad Day* by Judith Viorst, illustrated by Ray Cruz. Copyright © 1976 by Judith Viorst. Illustrations copyright © 1976 by Ray Cruz; Illustration by Arnold Lobel from *Frog and Toad Together* by Arnold Lobel. Copyright © 1972 by Arnold Lobel; From *The Cat in the Hat* by Dr. Seuss. © 1957 by Dr. Seuss. Reprinted by permission of Random House, Inc.

245 Illustration by Garth Williams from *Little House in the Big Woods* by Laura Ingalls Wilder. Pictures copyright © 1953 by Garth Williams. Illustration copyright renewed © 1981 by Garth Williams, Harper & Row Publishers, Incorporated; Photofest.

246 Illustration by Floyd Cooper from *Plain City* by Virginia Hamilton. Illustration copyright © 1993 by Scholastic Inc. Reprinted by permission.

247 Illustration from *The Glorious Flight* by Alice and Martin Provensen. © 1983 by Alice and Martin Provensen. All Rights Reserved. Reprinted by permission of Viking Penguin Inc.; Copyright © 1993 by The Museum of Modern Art, New York, and The Phillips Collection.

248 Copyright © 1993 by Walter Dean Myers. Jacket copyright © 1993 by HarperCollins Publishers; Illustration by Shel Silverstein from the poem "Jumping Rope" from *Where The Sidewalk Ends* by Shel Silverstein. © 1974 by Evil Eye Music, Inc.

251 © Stockpile
252 © Jerry Frank; © Jacques Jangoux.
254 © Jonathan T. Wright—Bruce Coleman Inc
256 © Van Phillips—Leo de Wys
257 © Hays—Monkmeyer
259 © Paul Conklin—Monkmeyer
260 © Delta Willis—Bruce Coleman Inc
261 © Georg Gerster—Photo Researchers; © Marc Bernheim—Woodfin Camp & Associates.
264 © Marc Bernheim—Woodfin Camp & Associates
265 © Richard Quataert—Taurus
266 © Bruno Barbey—Magnum Photos; © Steven Burr Williams—The Image Bank.
267 © Magnus Bartlett—Woodfin Camp & Associates
268 The Granger Collection
269 © Mandel—Ziolo
271 © Marc Riboud—Magnum Photos
273 © Peter Turnley—Black Star
274 The Nelson-Atkins Museum of Art (Nelson Fund), Kansas City, Missouri

275 Courtesy of the Freer Gallery of Art, Smithsonian Institution, Washington, D.C.; Courtesy of the Freer Gallery of Art, Smithsonian Institution, Washington, D.C.
276 Sotheby-Parke-Bernet—Agent: Art Resource; Courtesy of Freer Gallery of Art.
277 The Peoples Republic of China
278 C. C. Wang Collection
280 Courtesy of Chocosuisse Union of Swiss Chocolate Manufacturers
282 Giraudon/Art Resource
284 © Guy Marche—FPG International
285 © P. Quittemelle—Publiphoto
286 National Gallery of Art, Washington, D.C., Samuel H. Kress Collection
288 Art Reference Bureau
291 Joe Barnell—SuperStock
292 The Bettmann Archive
293 © Frederica Georgia—Photo Researchers
295 Corbis-Bettmann
296 © Lee Boltin
298 © Hugh K. Koester—Tom Stack & Associates; © William Hubbell—Woodfin Camp & Associates; © Clifford Hausner—Leo de Wys.
300 © Joe Viesti; © John Louis Anderson—Black Star; © Dennis J. Cipnic—Photo Researchers; © Shlomo Arad—Woodfin Camp & Associates.
301 © Susan McCartney—Photo Researchers; © Cameramann International Ltd.; © Chip and Rosa Peterson; © Kryn Taconis—Magnum Photos.
302 The Bridgeman Art Library from Art Resource
307 Courtesy of Ringling Bros. and Barnum & Bailey Combined Shows Inc
308 © SuperStock; Courtesy of Ringling Bros. and Barnum & Bailey Combined Shows Inc.; Courtesy of Ringling Bros. and Barnum & Bailey Combined Shows Inc.; Courtesy of Ringling Bros. and Barnum & Bailey Combined Shows Inc.
309 Courtesy of Ringling Bros. and Barnum & Bailey Combined Shows Inc. (all photos on page).
311 © Amano—Ziolo
312 © George Haling—Photo Researchers; © Kunio Owaki—The Stock Market.
313 © Wally McNamee—Woodfin Camp & Associates; © Harvey Lloyd—The Stock Market.
314 Culver Pictures, Inc.
316 The Bettmann Archive
317 Library of the Hydrographic Service of the Navy, Paris—Giraudon
318 The Bettmann Archive
319 © Viviane Moos—The Stock Market
320 © Richard Steedman—The Stock Market
322 © Wally McNamee—Woodfin Camp & Associates
323 © Jim Anderson—Woodfin Camp & Associates
325 © Richard Howard
327 © Jeffrey Markowitz—Corbis-Sygma; © Juhan Kuus—Sipa Press.
328 © AP/Wide World Photos
329 © UPI/Bettmann Newsphotos; © AP/Wide World Photos; © AP/Wide World Photos; © AP/Wide World Photos.
330 © Charles Moore—Black Star; UPI/Bettmann Newsphotos.
332–333 Chicago Historical Society
335 The Bettmann Archive; The Metropolitan Museum of Art, Gift of Mr. and Mrs. Carl Stoeckel, 1897.
336 The Granger Collection
337 Philadelphia Museum of Art, The Edgar & Bernice Chrysler Garbisch Collection; The Granger Collection.
338 Gift of Anton T. and Phillip J. McCook, 1954, Collection of Chrysler Museum at Norfolk, Virginia; Library of Congress.
339 The Granger Collection; Library of Congress.
340 U.S. Signal Corps (Brady Collection)
341 The Granger Collection; Lane Studio, Gettysburg National Military Park.
342 The Bettmann Archive
343 The Granger Collection; The Bettmann Archive.
344 National Archives; Corbis-Bettmann; State Archives of Michigan; UPI/Corbis-Bettmann.
345 National Archives; Katherine Wetzel—Museum of the Confederacy; Library of Congress; Corbis-Bettmann.
346 The Mansell Collection; Appomattox Court House National Historical Park, Virginia.
348 © Theo Westenberger—Corbis-Sygma
352 The Bettmann Archive
353 The Granger Collection

355 The Granger Collection
356 © J. Quinn Photography
357 The White House Collection, © copyright White House Historical Association; The Granger Collection.
358 The Bettmann Archive (all photos on page).
360 The Bettmann Archive
361 © Jose Fusta Raga—Leo de Wys
363 © Jonathan Blair—Woodfin Camp & Associates; © H. Steenmans—Leo de Wys.
364 © Victor Englebert—Photo Researchers
365 © Geoffrey W. Hartman—Liaison Agency; © Porter Gifford—Liaison Agency.
366 UPI/Bettmann Newsphotos; © W. Hitt—Black Star; © Les Stone—Corbis-Sygma.
368 © The White House
369 © Elaine Thompson—AP/Wide World Photos
370 © Mary Steinbacher—PhotoEdit
371 © Bernard Boutrit—Woodfin Camp & Associates
372 © Cindy Charles—PhotoEdit
374 © Lee Boltin; Scala/Art Resource; © Lee Boltin.
375 The Granger Collection
376 The Granger Collection
377 The Granger Collection
378 Giraudon/Art Resource
379 The Metropolitan Museum of Art, Bequest of Edith Minturn Phelps Stokes (Mrs. I.N.), 1938; The Granger Collection; Courtesy of VOGUE © Condé Nast Publications Inc.
380 © David Hurn—Magnum Photos; © Comstock, Inc.
381 © Joseph Nettis—Photo Researchers; © John G. Ross—Photo Researchers.
384 Anthony Sas, University of South Carolina; © John Shelton.
386 © Tony Mihok—The Stock Market, Toronto
389 Courtesy of Consolidation Coal Company
390 Courtesy of Consolidation Coal Company
392 © Russ Kinne—Photo Researchers
397 © Ron Sherman—Bruce Coleman Inc.
398 American Numismatic Society; American Numismatic Society; Chase Manhattan Bank Money Museum; Chase Manhattan Bank Money Museum.
399 U.S. Mint (all photos on page).
400 Courtesy of the Museum of the American Numismatic Association; © Robert P. Carr—Bruce Coleman Inc.; © Norman Owen Tomalin—Bruce Coleman Inc.; © Norman Owen Tomalin—Bruce Coleman Inc.
401 Corbis
402 © Phoebe Beasley
403 © Carlos Angel—Liaison Agency; © Robert Frerck—Woodfin Camp & Associates; © Robert Frerck—Woodfin Camp & Associates; © Carlos Angel—Liaison Agency.
404 © Jeremy Horner—Corbis
405 © Robert Frerck—Woodfin Camp & Associates; © Kevin Schafer—Allstock.
406 © Loren McIntyre—Woodfin Camp & Associates
407 © The Purcell Team—Corbis; © Gianni Dagli Orti—Corbis.
408 © Miguel Angel Solano, Ancol—AP/Wide World Photos
409 The Bettmann Archive
410 The Granger Collection; © Lee Boltin.
412 The Granger Collection; The Connecticut Historical Society.
413 Courtesy of Plimoth Plantation, Plymouth, Mass.; Print Collection, Miriam and Ira D. Wallach Division of Arts, Prints, and Photographs, The New York Public Library, Astor, Lenox and Tilden Foundations.
414 Courtesy of Plimoth Plantation, Plymouth, Mass.; © Lee Boltin; American Antiquarian Society.
415 © Lee Snider—Photo Images
416 © Lee Snider—Photo Images; © Don Rutledge—Taurus; Courtesy of the Rhode Island Historical Society.
417 The Granger Collection
418 The Granger Collection (all photos on page).
419 Library Company of Philadelphia
420 Colonial Williamsburg
421 © Angelo Hornak; Shirley Plantation; The Granger Collection.
422 Pennsbury Manor, Pennsylvania Historical and Museum Commission; Jamestown-Yorktown Foundation, Commonwealth of Virginia; © Craig Aurness—Woodfin Camp & Associates; Courtesy of Plimoth Plantation, Plymouth, Massachusetts.
423 © Gordon Johnson—Photo Researchers; Colonial Williamsburg; © Joan Menschenfreund—

The Stock Market, Toronto; © Michel Serailler—Photo Researchers.
424 © E. R. Degginger—Animals Animals
426 © Richard Kolar—Animals Animals; © Tom Edwards—Animals Animals.
427 © R. F. Head—Animals Animals
428 © Joe McDonald—Animals Animals
429 © William Hubbell
431 © SuperStock; © Kevin Alexander—ProFiles West/Index Stock; © William C. Matthews.
432 © Wilson Goodrich—MGA/Photri; © Chad Ehlers—Photo Network; © Kent and Donna Dannen—Photo Researchers.
434 © Diane Liggett—Photo Network; © Rich Buzzelli—Tom Stack & Associates.
435 © Ricke/Hults—Photo Researchers; © Spence Swanger—Tom Stack & Associates.
436 © Rich Buzzelli—Tom Stack & Associates; © SuperStock.
437 © SuperStock; © Tom Stack—Tom Stack & Associates.
438 © Photri; © P. Buddle—H. Armstrong Roberts; © Andre Jenny—New England Stock Photo; © Rich Buzzelli—Tom Stack & Associates.
439 © Rich Buzzelli—Tom Stack & Associates
440 © SuperStock
442 UPI/Bettmann; Archive Photos; Denver Public Library Western Collection.
443 Reuters/Corbis-Bettmann; UPI/Corbis-Bettmann.
444 © William A. Holmes—The Image Finders
445 © Charles M. Pallardy
449 © John Sanford—Science Photo Library—Photo Researchers; © Roger Ressmeyer—Starlight.
450 © Pearson/Milon/Science Photo Library—Photo Researchers; NASA.
451 JPL
452 © Frank Rossoto—Stocktrek; © Max Planck Institute for Astronomy/David Parker/Science Photo Library—Photo Researchers.
453 © DC Comics Inc.; © Archie Comic Publications, Inc.; Harvey Publications, Inc.; © Hanna-Barbera Productions, Inc. Published by Charlton Publications, Inc.; © 1985 Marvel Comics Group.
454 © 1985 Marvel Comics Group
455 U.S. Department of Commerce
456 Courtesy of Apple Computer, Inc.; Courtesy of William Morrow; Courtesy of CBS Records.
457 Photos from National Biscuit Co., through Kenyon-Eckardt Advertising Agency, Courtesy of Nabisco Brands, Inc.
458 Courtesy of McDonald's Corp; Courtesy of American Airlines; Courtesy of AT&T Communications; United States Postal Service 1985; © Peter Good Graphic Design.
459 © Eva Grochowiak—Corbis-Sygma
462 © Tim Wright—Corbis
463 © Anthony Bannister—ABPL/Corbis
464 © 1990 Bob Schatz—Liaison Agency
465 © Archive Photos; © Richard Cummins—Corbis.
466 © Hulton Getty—Liaison Agency; © David Young-Wolff—PhotoEdit.
467 Photosynthesis/International Stock—Photo Network; Bettmann/Corbis.

468 © Hirz—Archive Photos
469 © Tim Page—Corbis
470 © World Perspectives/Stone
471 © James Wilson—Woodfin Camp & Associates
472 © Ken Hawkins—Stock South; © Press Studio/Lehtikuva Oy/SABA.
474 © Erica Lansner—Black Star
480 © Richard T. Nowitz—Corbis-Bettmann
481 © Porter Gifford—Liaison Agency; Courtesy, Palm Pilot III.
484 © Courtesy of Exxon Inc. and Pacific Data Images
485 © Remi Benali—Liaison Agency; © Larry Mulvehill—Rainbow.
486 © Courtesy, Zoo Atlanta
489 © ILM-Universal. All Rights Reserved.
490 Courtesy, Unisys Corporation
492 © Adam Nadel—AP/Wide World Photos
493 © Laurent Zylberman—Corbis-Sygma
495 The Granger Collection
498 © Naud—Leo de Wys
500 © Naud—Leo de Wys
501 © Abbas—Magnum Photos
503 © James Marshall; © Jim Schwabel—New England Stock Photo; © Jack McConnell.
504 © Jack McConnell (all photos on page).
506 © Leslie M. Newman; © Jack McConnell.
507 © Focus on Sports; © Michael Giannaccio—New England Stock Photo.
508 © Jack McConnell; © Jack McConnell; © Grant LeDuc—Stock, Boston; © James Marshall.
509 © James McConnell
510 © David Kampfner—Liaison Agency
511 © James Marshall; © William Hubbell.
512 © William Hubbell
514 The National Portrait Gallery, Smithsonian Institution—Art Resource
515 AP/Wide World Photos; © Bruce S. deLis—Liaison Agency.
518 © David Weintraub—Photo Researchers
520 City of Palo Alto, Public Works, operations
527 © Don and Pat Valenti—Tom Stack & Associates
531 National Maritime Museum, Greenwich Hospital Collection
532 © Janeart Ltd.—The Image Bank
534 © C. Kuhn—The Image Bank
537 The White House Collection, © copyright White House Historical Association
538 AP/Wide World Photos; Brown Brothers.
539 The Bettmann Archive; Brown Brothers; AP/Wide World Photos.
542 Photograph courtesy of the Brandywine River Museum
544 © Steve Vidler—Leo de Wys; © Hubert Josse—Musee de l'Observatoire, Paris.
546 © A.W. Ambler—Photo Researchers
549 © C. C. Lockwood—Bruce Coleman Inc.
550 © Alpha
551 The Bettmann Archive
552 Reprinted by permission of *Redbook* magazine, © 1986 by the Hearst Corporation. All Rights Reserved. Mark Babushkin; Reprinted by permission of *Redbook* magazine, © 1986 by the Hearst Corporation. All Rights Reserved. Mark Babushkin; Reprinted by per-

mission of *Redbook* magazine, © 1987 by the Hearst Corporation. All Rights Reserved. Bruno Gaget; Reprinted by permission of *Redbook* magazine, © 1986 by the Hearst Corporation. All Rights Reserved. Mark Babushkin.
553 Reprinted by permission of *Redbook* magazine, © 1987 by the Hearst Corporation. All Rights Reserved. Bernard Leroux; Reprinted by permission of *Redbook* magazine, © 1987 by the Hearst Corporation. All Rights Reserved. Bernard Leroux.
557 © Joe Viesti—Viesti Associates
558 © Jordan Coonrad
559 © Robert Fried
560 © Alan Pitcairn—Grant Heilman Photography; © Grant Heilman Photography.
561 © Alan Pitcairn—Grant Heilman Photography
562 © Alan Pitcairn—Grant Heilman Photography
563 Tennessee Tourist Development
564 © Ken Regan—Camera Five; © Owen Franken—Corbis-Sygma; AP/Wide World.
565 © Neil Leifer—Camera Five; © CBS Records, Nashville.
566 © Rick Buettner—Bruce Coleman Inc.
569 Courtesy of Woolaroc Museum, Bartlesville, Oklahoma
571 © Mickey Gibson—Animals Animals
572 The Bettmann Archive
573 © Eric Carle—Bruce Coleman Inc.
574 © David Young-Wolff/Photo Edit/PNI
575 © Jerome Friar—Impact Visuals/PNI
576 © Peter Menzel—Stock, Boston/PNI
577 Robert Harding Picture Library
578 © Filip Horvat—SABA
582 The Bettmann Archive
583 © Zig Leszczynski—Animals Animals
589 Scala/Art Resource
590 The Granger Collection
591 © Oxford Scientific Films—Animals Animals; © Tom McHugh—Photo Researchers; William Curtsinger—Photo Researchers.
593 © Walter Dawn
596 © Mark Lewis—Liaison Agency; © Mark Harris—Stone.
597 © Tibor Bognar—The Stock Market
598 © Andrea Brizzi—The Stock Market; © Saola Arne Hodalic—Liaison Agency.
600 © Liaison Agency
601 UPI/Corbis-Bettmann
602 1998 The Museum of Modern Art, New York
603 The Granger Collection
604 © Warren Gordon—Miller Services
605 © Dave Houser
607 © Van Phillips—Leo de Wys; © SuperStock.
608 © Paula Bronstein—Black Star
609 © Jeffrey Aaronson—Network Aspen
610 © Hans Kramarz—Root Resources; © Chris Niedenthal—Black Star.
611 Culver Pictures, Inc.; The Granger Collection; The Bettmann Archive; Courtesy of the Center for Contemporary Opera; The Bettmann Archive; © Edwin Walter—SABA.
613 Brown Brothers; ACME/Bettmann Newsphotos.
614 © Chip Hires—Liaison Agency